east

                even as i view
           frantic for something new
                cherry blossoms!

cherry, i confess   cherry blossoms
though i view, i do not try   though i view, i'd see far
     hard enough   more than i do!

                cherry blossoms
         i view knowing there must be
                something more

（Orig.: 見ながらもみようの足らぬ桜かな　多代女　晴霞句集　*minagara mo miyô no taranu sakura kana* = seeing-while-even see-way/try's suffices-not cherry[blossoms]!）Uncertain whether the phonetically written *miyô* in the middle of the original *ku* by the long-lived poet Tayojo (♀1775-1865) was "見よう = see-would/try," "見様 = seeing-style/method," 妙= oddness/wonder," or "冥=spirit-in-pitch-dark," I posted a question at my haiku Q&A site and received a splendid explanation from 宙虫, "space-bug:" Soramushi felt that the blossom-viewing Tayojo was disappointed because all that came to her mind was old haiku, for there were so damn many of them out there. *"The truth be told, Japanese having viewed cherry blossoms from all sides and then some, from above & below, right & left, front & back, present, past & future, no matter how much/hard you view them, someone has already seen what you have not [what you would see]. At times like that, how many people , unable to come up with anything new, have lamented in the same way!* I like Tayojo's blunt style. There are nine more of her *ku* (hokku/haiku/etc.) in this book.

west

To see the *sakura*
in flower for the first time
is to experience a new sensation.

Percival Lowell
The Soul of the Far East (1888)

◎ While I love Lafcadio Hearn and encourage you to read not only his essays on Japan but his earlier writing (eg. *Creole Sketches*), Lowell (above) and Eliza Scidmore (1891) beat him to the cherry blossoms. *I write this because there is a tendency to credit Hearn at the expense of others, whose contributions also deserve acknowledgment.* ◎

all translations
unless otherwise indicated
are by the author

Robin D. Gill. (1951~) A native Floridian (Key Biscayne). Working in Japan as an acquisitions editor and translation-checker of top nonfiction literature for Kousakusha and editions Papyrus, he introduced scores of books including Eiseley: *The Star Thrower*, Levi: *Periodic Table*, Lovelock: *Gaia*, Lopez: *Winter Count*, Prishvin: *Nature's Diary*, Thoreau: *Cape Cod*, etc., while writing seven non-fiction books in Japanese (publishers include the prestigious traditional publisher Chikuma-bunko, academic Hakusuisha and avant-garde Kousakusha) in the 1980's. Most of these books deconstructed stereotypes of difference. One concentrates on the reduction of culture to climate, one on antithetical stereotypes of the mutually exotic tongues of English and Japanese, one on the relationship of mistranslation to prejudice. More information about the books and reviews may be found at http://www.paraverse.org. Note that Gill wrote as "Robin Gill" (ロビン・ギル) in Japan/ese, but now uses his middle initial "D." religiously, because there is a theologian connected with Oxford University Press also named Robin Gill, who is a prolific writer.

Screw the third-person! My first book in English, **Rise, Ye Sea Slugs!** (Paraverse Press: 2003), a translation and essay of almost 1,000 holothurian haiku, was highly acclaimed as "a classic" from the start. The sea cucumber poems, many of which are hundreds of years old, are arranged by metaphor and dressed with natural and unnatural history. Because haiku are not precious and the book is full of ideas (not to mention what one reviewer calls "quirky facts"), even readers who *hate* most poetry may be surprised to find they enjoy it. According to a review in the Spring 2005 issue of *Metamorphoses: the journal of the five college faculty seminar on literary translation*, "For all the eccentricities one might expect (and does find) in a [480 pg] book devoted entirely to haiku on the sea slug, the author is an accomplished haiku writer, a very talented and engaging critic capable of reading with an astute understanding of culture and cultural differences. Haiku enthusiasts, scholars of Japanese literature and marine biology, and professional and amateur translators alike will certainly welcome this interesting book." (Thomas H. Rohlich, Professor of Japanese at Smith College). And, the first doyen of haiku in English, William J. Higginson, writing in the prestigious quarterly *Modern Haiku*, noted that "he has raised the bar very high in terms of a translator's responsibility" and finishes his five page review with this: "If you have read Yasuda, Blyth, Henderson, Ueda, and Shirane, then read Gill. He will expand your mind. If you have not read these guys yet, then read Gill first. He's more fun."

My *second* in English, **Orientalism & Occidentalism** *– is the mistranslation of culture inevitable?* should appeal to serious students of Japan, comparative culture and language, nationalism and translation, or any literate polyglot. It reworks some of the ground covered in his Japanese work with the non-Japanese reader in mind. *O & O* is especially recommended to readers as balance (penance?) for the differences played up and enjoyed in *Topsy-turvy 1585* (below).

My *third*, **Fly-ku*!*** breaks new ground concerning anthropomorphism and thematic development in poetry. According to Jane Reichhold in her on-line journal LYNX: "The way Gill translates is not only marvelous, it is absolutely revolutionary. Instead of giving the reader the idea that there is only one way to translate a haiku, he offers a word-for-word translation and then goes into great detail explaining the ambiguities of the Japanese language along with the secrets of Japanese behavior . . . The book is full of humor and information given in Gill's distinctive way. His mind makes huge leaps so all the information about flies or Japanese and everything else in between feels as if it has been stirred in a great cosmic blender and poured out, in a decorative manner, suggesting a teahouse snack." (First issue of 2005). Carlos Amantea, author of *The Blob that Ate Oaxaca*, marvels: "Gill strikes us as no less than amazing. Why isn't he teaching at Yale, or the University of California, or Tokyo University? His references include no end of obscure Japanese lore, plus quotes and notes from such artists as Clare, Lovelace, Steinbeck, Dumont, Verdi, Satie, Blythe, Shakespeare, Emily Dickinson." (in R.A.L.P.H., Review of Art, Literature, Philosophy & History).

My fourth, the **LONG** version of **TOPSY-TURVY 1585** (2004) translates 611 distiches contrasting Europeans and Japanese by Luis Frois, S.J. and explicates at length (740 pgs). The fifth, the **SHORT Version** of the same (2005) keeps it down to 500 pgs. Lacking publicity, neither have sold more than a dozen copies to date!

Shortly after this sixth book, number seven, **The Fifth Season,** will treat a neglected part of Japanese poetry, the New Year. It will be vol. I of *In Praise of Olde Haiku*, (IPOOH) a poetic almanac of the five traditional haiku seasons.

敬愚   robin d. gill
(*aka* keigu)

THE POETRY AND PHILOSOPHY *OF*
A FLOWERING TREE

Cherry-blossom

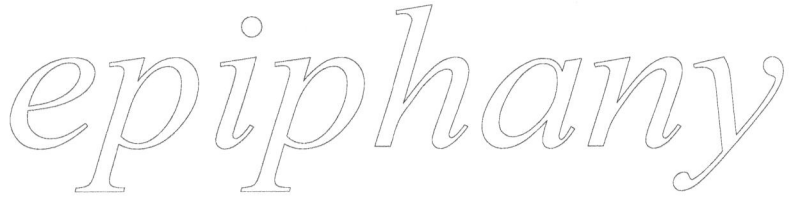

a theme from IN PRAISE OF OLDE HAIKU,
with many more poems and fine elaboration

by

robin d. gill

道可道
非常道

paraverse press

This is the sixth book published by paraverse press,
home of truly creative nonfiction, which is to say,
nonfiction that is neither journalism, nor history,
nor how-I-overcame-this-or-that. We are afraid
our books will not help you get rich, healthy
or up-to-date. Whatever their subject,
they offer one thing, always the same
yet different; and that is ideas,
*"food for thought,
all you can eat!"*

©
**2007
paraverse press
all rights reserved**

but, please quote freely, so long as you
cite this book and take care to check the *Errata*
at **our web site: http://www.paraverse.org**

we hope the Library of Congress will help us catalog
someday for, as you can see below, we need help! Meanwhile
enjoy our Publisher's Cataloging-in-Publication:

Cherry Blossom Epiphany
– the poetry and philosophy of a flowering tree –
a selection, translation and lengthy explication of
3000 *haiku, waka, senryû* and kyôka about
a major theme from I.P.O.O.H.
(In Praise Of Olde Haiku)

by robin d. gill

ISBN # 0-9742618-6-6 **(pbk)**
13-digit: 978-0-9742618-6-7

1. Haiku –Translation from Japanese to English
2. Japanese poetry – 8c-20c – waka, haiku and senryû
3. Natural History – flowering cherries
4. Japan – Culture – Edo Era
5. Nonfiction – Literature
6. Translation – applied
7. You tell me!

1st edition, 2007, make it *spring*, when the cherries bloom!
the reading copy (winter 2006) may or may not be identical
◎
printed by Lightning Source
in the United States and United Kingdom.
distributed by Ingram, Baker & Taylor, etc.
available from Amazon , B&N, etc.
◎

For more information, visit our home page, www.paraverse.org.
If you have further questions or good reason to write us, please try
info@paraverse.org, or whatever web address is provided at the site.
Forget snail-mail. The robber-barons own the land; we are homeless.

☆
dedicated
to all who have
sat in the bloomshade
of the *sakura* under a blue sky
and shivered, though not from the cold.

Table of contents

◎ Book I *The Cherry Blossom Epiphany* ◎

1 – **Waiting** for the bloom *23*
2 – **Dog** cherry, defend thy bark! *33*
3 – Cherry **hunting**, or, finding your tree *39*
4 – **First** blossoms of the tree or the spring *55*
5 – **Cold** cherries and blossom-chill *79*
6 – **Rain,** the wet-nurse *84*
7 – Old lady cherry: i call her ***babushka*** *97*
8 – In/**equality** in the bloomshade *106*
9 – Cherry blossom **intoxication** *127*
10– The **full-bloom**, or cherries in heat! *142*
11 – **Infant/boy** cherries *154*
12 – **Late** cherry, despised or admired? *159*
13 – While **bells** b(l)oom *186*
14 – **Dusk**, or cherry as time-machine *195*
15 – **Night** cherries come in two varieties *202*
16 – Cherry **zoo**, from horse to horse-fly *219*
17 – How to tell the **clouds** from the blossoms *241*
18 – Cherry-time **overcast** *260*
19 – What do **other trees** do? *264*
20 – **Miscellany** *268*. ***Sakura*** etymology *269*

◎ Book II *Drinking in the Bloomshade* ◎

21 – **Medicine** for the soul *281*
22 – **Blossom-viewing** in general *286*
23 – Companions, or **blossom buddies** *297*
24 – **People-viewing** *305*
25 – **House-sitting** while others view *320*
26 – **Drinking** up a storm *324*
27 – The Cherry **Bash** *334*
28 – **Song** and Poetry *346*
29 – **Thread** cherries (upside-down trees) *359*
30 – Life laundry, or cherry **catharsis** *367*
31 – **Fighting**, or the Edoite *hanami* *376*
32 – Eating, or **food** for the mouth, too *382*
33 – **Vendors** *393*
34 – Blossom **guards** *399*
35 – **Single** trees *404*
36 – **Dying** in the bloomshade *409*
37 – **Ise**, or, divine native cherries *427*
38 – **Buddhism** and blossoms *430*
39 – Sacred white **elephant** cherries *443*
40 – **Breaking one off,** or stealing blossoms *446*
41 – **Equinox** Cherry Trees *467*
42 – **Mountain** means wild cherries *470*
43 – **Country** cherries *489*
44 – Cherry **snapper**, the fish *491*
45 – **Scent** as glow and smell *497*
46 – **Soul/mind/heart** and cherry blossoms *502*

◎ Book III *Scattering Petals & People* ◎

47 – **Falling** blossoms, scattering petals *525*
48 – **Wind**, the perennial bad guy *550*
49 – **Cataracts** of blossoms *571*
50 – Whither go the **petals** and for what *574*
51 – Snow of petals, **blizzard** and drift *588*
52 – Petal **rafts** *593*
53 – **Women-as-**blossoms *596*
54 – Woman as blossom **or** vice versa *602*
55 – **Blossoms-as-women** *607*
56 – **House** cherry *617*
57 – **Children** at the *hanami* *625*
58 – **Yoshino**, a place beyond words *632*
59 – **Sexual** blossoms *641*
60 – **Old** people at the *hanami* *650*
61 – **Patriotism** and *sakura* *660*
62 – Eightfold: the **double-blossom** debate *671*
63 – **Conserving** cherry *682*
64 – **Return** from the viewing *700*
65 – **Sundry** cherries *708*. ***Postscript*** *713*
Bibliotica *717*. **Poet** index *725*, **Poem** index *731*.

目次　Table of contents

㊤　桜エピファニー　㊤

- 1 – 花を待つこころ
- 2 – 犬桜 よ、手折る人め噛みなさい！
- 3 – 桜狩、罪のない狩りを楽しむ
- 4 – 初花は、春初物か、その木の初物か
- 5 – 寒さの中の花と花冷え
- 6 – 蒼を太らす雨、花を叩く雨
- 7 – 姥桜、老いと美の交差点
- 8 – 木下の平等・不平等
- 9 – 花の酔いが雲の足まで？
- 10 – 花盛りは、うかれ猫の顔負けか
- 11 – 兒桜桜、乳のみ兒と恋の対象の子
- 12 – 遅櫻がエライか、つまらないか
- 13 – 鐘が鳴る考
- 14 – 暮れの桜ないし花時の時間旅
- 15 – 夜桜、本物とアレと。
- 16 – 花見の動物尽くし
- 17 – 花と雲の見分けも困るぞ
- 18 – 花曇と霞と饅頭日和
- 19 – さて、花時の他の木達は？
- 20 – 雑話求め ＋ 桜語源十三

㊥　花の陰は酒飲み　㊥

- 21 – 花の木は気の薬
- 22 – 花見一般
- 23 – 花見の連れを、連れと
- 24 – 花見ながら、人見中心主義
- 25 – 花の留守
- 26 – サケ！サケ！とは花か酒か。
- 27 – 花見よりもドンチャン騒ぎぜ！
- 28 – 歌、舞、そして、句咲くも
- 29 – 絲桜の比喩オンパレード
- 30 – 花の山は、命の洗濯場
- 31 – 喧嘩を売る江戸桜
- 32 – 花見食、なますから奈良漬まで
- 33 – 物売り色々
- 34 – 花守り＋棒突き
- 35 – 只一本の桜
- 36 – 花の陰で死を歓迎、恐怖
- 37 – 伊勢桜と神風のコネ
- 38 – 仏教の花見肯定、否定
- 39 – 普賢像の桜
- 40 – 手折り も盗みも英訳は困る
- 41 – 彼岸桜と二季咲きのお願い
- 42 – 山桜は尊きか惨めか
- 43 – 田舎の道、田舎の花
- 44 – 桜鯛、俳諧も木登りの魚
- 45 – 匂ふとは、意外に難しい概念
- 46 – 心、ココロだらけの花句、桜句

㊦　散る花、散る人　㊦

- 47 – 花も人の散るとき
- 48 – 風という悪漢を訴えて
- 49 – 花の瀧
- 50 – 花びらは何処へ、何に？
- 51 – 花の雪と吹雪
- 52 – 水に流れて
- 53 – 花となる女
- 54 – 女が花か花が女か、さっぱり
- 55 – 女となる花
- 56 – 家桜はやはり恋し
- 57 – 花見のちびっ子
- 58 – これはこれはとばかり
- 59 – セクシーな桜句
- 60 – 花見の老人と老木
- 61 – 愛国主義の桜とその反応
- 62 – 八重桜を馬鹿にするな！
- 63 – 花の苦界、桜風邪、花見虱
- 64 – 花の戻り
- 65 – 見逃した桜種　◎後書等, 和文の参考書説明, 俳人名素引, 全句の ABC（ローマ字）順素引.

WHAT IS A HAIKU?

As a rule, haiku are poems touching upon recognized seasonal phenomena, natural or human, about 7 beats (the equivalent of 5+7+5=17 *syllabets*,[1] as the sounds of the Japanese syllabary might best be called) in length, generally written in one line in Japanese (which looks fine because the vertical line has an object-like appearance)[2] or three in English. Like all poems, they should be interesting. While "haiku" came to be applied to the genre within the past hundred years or so, the poems themselves go back at least as far as the 15c [3] and I use the term retroactively, as Shiki (-1902) did when he compiled the 12 volume *Bunrui-betsu Haiku Zenshû*, or Categorized *Haiku* Anthology, which I refer to in this book as *Shiki's Categorical*. Most of the 3000 haiku in this book are pre-20c and translated here for the first time. Like Japanese, I usually refer to individual haiku (or *hokku* or *senryû*) as *ku*.

A sampling of other poems will be included. There are scores of 5+7+5+7+7=31 syllabet *waka* (lit. *gentle=Japanese[as opposed to Chinese]-song*). *Waka* are not only the prototype for modern *tanka* (lit. *short-song*), but the mother lode for pre-modern haiku. Though nature in *waka* tends to play second fiddle, serving in an allusive or metaphorical capacity to homage, grieving, longing and other human concerns, *waka* are far more attentive to seasonal themes than Occidental poetry and some themes, such as cherry blossoms pass down such an embarrassment of riches that many *ku* cannot help but copy them. Then, we have a handful of bundles of puns called *kyôka*, or "crazy-song," and scores of the haiku-sized *senryû* which play with various (stereo)types of people, professions and places. Like black-humor in the Occident, anything famous is fair game for *senryû*, and that includes *haiku* and *haijin* (*haikai* poets).

HOW I TRANSLATE

My translations are an open book. I dislike transparent – i.e., invisible – translation that allows readers to believe all that matters has been Englished *when it just ain't so*. Here, you will not only learn what I know but what I do *not* know, and what I know yet still cannot fit into the translation. In some cases, this otherwise lost information or wit may be re-created with a device rarely seen in haiku, a title, and a more unfamiliar device yet, one I recommend to all translators who work with exotic tongues, multiple translation.[4] You will find I sometimes play with poems. Interesting results are all the justification a translator needs, but let me add that it is precisely because I provide word-for-word translation (an ugly tool, not to be taken for the language itself!) and ample explanation, that I feel free to take the liberties I do.

---

1. Syllabets The Greek term *mora* is sometimes used by linguists for relatively short and uniform syllables, but it is too opaque for us to readily remember and fails to capture the alphabet-like nature of the letters making up the Japanese syllabary. The specialized Japanese term *onji* is used by some haiku enthusiasts but it shares the opacity of *mora*. So, I recommend *syllabet*.

2. Single-line Haiku – But *ku* written on rectangular art paper, often combined with a picture, are usually divided into two to five lines placed artistically here and there. See *The Fifth Season* or *Haiku In Context* for more.

3. At *least* as far Back as the 15c, a huge body of poems that can be considered haiku were composed by Sôgi and other *rengashi* (linked-verse-teachers). Most modern *saijiki* ignore them as pre-*haikai*, but Shiki includes *thousands* in his *Categorical*. He takes most of these from collections nominally *hokku* (first verses for linked-verse sequences) but, by content, haiku. One can, however, go back further. As Blyth points out in *A History of Haiku* Volume 1, a poem such as *The storm / Goes pursuing / The scattering blossoms* (see poem #48-70) by Fujiwara no Teika (1162-1241!) is clearly a haiku.

4. Multiple Translation Douglas Hofstadter explores creative multiple-translation (what I call *paraversing*) in *Le Ton Beau De Marot* (1997). In *Rise Ye Sea Slugs!* (2003), I demonstrated how such translation is not just fun but proper when exotic tongues are involved and much information would otherwise be lost or the poetry destroyed by long, explanatory translations. In order to make the practice *attractive*, at least for haiku, I invented a method of presenting multiple translation, *the cluster*. These composites help us *feel* the readings are alternative and/or complementary to one another and, in my opinion, please the eye far more than serial presentation.

Epiphany

From the Greek, *Epiphanie*, or "apparition."

骸骨の上を粧ふて花見かな　鬼貫
gaikotsu no ue o yosoute hanami kana   onitsura
(skeleton-upon[obj] dress/adorned/ing, blossom-viewing!/'tis)

dressing up
my old bones
the *hanami*

our skeletons
well dressed, off we go
blossom-viewing

all those bones
decked in robes of silk
blossom-viewing

our skeletons
dressed to a "T"
the *hanami*

This is one of the best-known *hanami,* i.e. (cherry) *blossom-viewing* haiku. It boasts countless translations (we shall see some later). The Japanese can be read in the first-person, or any other person, as per the other three readings. Such ambiguity is not unknown to English, for the pronoun "you" can be singular, plural, the other or any person including the poet; but Japanese, due to an accident of language (as explained in my book *Orientalism & Occidentalism*), generally does not use pronouns and, having no conjugations for number, has more of this sort of person-unspecified poetry than English. As we are not concerned about what a particular "you" refers to, Japanese are not aware of that ambiguity until they see it in translation and wonder at the aptness of this or that choice. In a longer narrative, such *apparent* ambiguity rarely offers choices of interpretation, for context decides. With short poems that lack a determining context, there is no way to tell for sure the person of the subject. As a rule of thumb, haiku is first-person and *senryû* third-person, but I have read too many haiku with no subject that fit other persons to follow such a "rule" closely. Moreover, the ambiguity that permits multiple readings is precisely what allows the Japanese haiku to be so full of meaning. This poses an interesting problem for philosophical linguistics as it is generally argued that the more possibilities ruled out the more something means; yet, here, we find that the opposite is also true. Style-wise, ambiguity permits a *ku* to be at once a simple personal observation and a generality (for which some Japanese critics detest this poem, as we shall see in chapter 36).

phantom/s of the *hanami*

my old bones
dressed up enjoying
the blossoms

blossom-viewing
a million skeletons
dressed to kill

This use of the turn-of-the-century Usanian slang "to kill" (meaning *gorgeously* here) is obviously not suited for the translation of any haiku that does not itself use slang (some do, but this one did not), but I will leave it and other such fun for I think more readers will enjoy it than not.

◎ *Number* in *Japanese* & the *Nature* of *Trees* 木＋林＝森

Japanese has no "s" to pluralize a noun with ease as English can. Neither has it verb endings that indicate number, nor even the internal method (mouse/mice, goose/geese) common in languages lacking an "s" type of device. It is one of many tongues where singular/plural is generally paid no heed. Of course, it has ways to show singularity or plurality when the distinction is unclear in context yet absolutely necessary; but, when there is no pressing need for knowing, we (who speak Japanese) decide for ourselves. In this respect, Japanese is what a media expert once called "hot," for, like radio (unlike TV), we need to supply the image. Reading *hana* (花), we imagine one blossom or many of them. In that sense, we do not really "decide," at least not in the conscious sense of the word. Our imagination does that for us.

The individuals of the vegetable world may be considered as inferior or less perfect animals; a tree is a congeries of many living buds, and in this respect resembles the branches of coralline, which are a congeries of a multitude of animals. Each of these buds of a tree has its proper leaves or petals for lungs, produces its viviparous or its oviparous offspring in buds or seeds; has its own roots, which extending down the stem of the tree are interwoven with the roots of the other buds, and form the bark, which is the only living part of the stem, is annually renewed, and is superinduced upon the former bark, which then dies, and with its stagnated juices gradually hardening into wood forms the concentric circles, which we see in blocks of timber. (Erasmus Darwin: *Zoomania* 1794)

Japanese also makes no distinction between the *flowers* and the *tree*, the cherry and its blossoms. If this seems odd, think again. In English, can we tell if a sunflower, a pansy, a rose or magnolia means the plant out in the yard or a particular flower? We, too, must do a bit of unconscious work before recognizing one or the other. However, the combination of this lack of distinction and lack of number means that there is *more* ambiguity, or play, as I would prefer to call it, in Japanese. One often cannot tell if *sakura* means the cherry tree, many cherry trees, all cherry trees, one of its blossoms, many blossoms, all cherry blossoms, one cherry blossom petal, *&cetera*. Indeed, the poet often intends that we take it in more than one way.

The following circumstances evince the individuality of the buds of trees. First, there are many trees, whose whole internal wood is perished, and yet the branches are vegete and healthy. Secondly, the fibres of the barks of trees are chiefly longitudinal, resembling roots, as is beautifully seen in those prepared barks, that were lately brought from Otaheita. Thirdly, in horizontal wounds of the bark of trees, the fibres of the upper lip are always elongated downwards like roots, but those of the lower lip do not approach to meet them. Fourthly, if you wrap wet moss round any joint of a vine, or cover it with moist earth, roots will shoot out from it. Fifthly, by the inoculation or engrafting of trees many fruits are produced from one stem. Sixthly, a new tree is produced from a branch plucked from an old one, and set in the ground. Whence it appears that the buds of deciduous trees are so many annual plants, that the bark is a contexture of the roots of each individual bud; and that the internal wood is of no other use but to support them in the air, and that thus they resemble the animal world in their individuality. (Erasmus Darwin: *Zoomania* 1794)

When a poem has anthropomorphic, or, rather, zoomorphic tendencies – *i.e.* it gives the tree/s/blossom/s/petal/s volition and emotion – the larger scope of play that Japanese allows becomes important for an unspecified subject seems less ridiculous than one that is. I am not sure why this should be true. Is it because something must be clear to be wrong? Or, does the kernel of truth in the metaphor take root while we ponder whether the blossoms or the tree are *rushing to bloom* or *eager to blow?*

V. 1. For the numerous circumstances in which vegetable buds are analogous to animals, the reader is referred to the additional notes at the end of the Botanic Garden, Part I. It is there shewn, that the roots of vegetables resemble the lacteal system of animals; the sap-vessels in the early spring, before their leaves expand, are analogous to the placental vessels of the foetus; that the leaves of land-plants resemble lungs, and those of aquatic plants the gills of fish; that there are other systems of vessels resembling the vena portarum of quadrupeds, or the aorta of fish; that the digestive power of vegetables is similar to that of animals converting the fluids, which they absorb, into sugar; that their seeds resemble the eggs of animals, and their buds and bulbs their viviparous offspring. And, lastly, that the anthers and stigmas are real animals, attached indeed to their parent tree like polypi or coral insects, but capable of spontaneous motion; that they are affected with the passion of love, and furnished with powers of reproducing their species, and are fed with honey like the moths and butterflies, which plunder their nectaries. (Erasmus Darwin: *Zoomania* 1794 (& Blessed be to * The Gutenberg Project * for making books such as these available to the poor and others who stay home!))

Pre*over*face*all*
about IPOOH & this *spin-off*

In Praise of Olde Haiku (IPOOH) is a 10 volume, 20 book, 200 theme *saijiki,* or haiku almanac. Most of the *ku* – a term suitable for indicating individual haiku or *hokku* (early haiku) date from 1500-1900 and are translated for the first time. The traditional haiku almanac had not four but *five* seasons, of which the first was the New Year. IPOOH is a large undertaking and only Volume I, with half of the New Year themes (*The Fifth Season*) has been published – or will be, very soon. With a score of pages per theme, IPOOH offers the first broad yet in-depth treatment of the actual subject matter of haiku. Themes too large or too interesting (admittedly, a subjective choice) to be left as chapters, are expanded into separate books. Two such IPOOH spin-offs have already been published: *Rise, Ye Sea Slugs!* a metaphor-based survey of 1000 haiku about *namako,* or, the sea cucumber (a winter-theme) and *Fly-ku!* a smaller sampling of *hae, hae-uchi,* or, flies, fly-swatting (a summer theme) haiku, focusing on the effect of translation on the nature of the supposedly anthropomorphic in poetry.

Because the botany and natural history of the Japanese cherry, or *sakura,* is already available in a single accessible book in English (Wybe Kuitert's *Flowering Cherries:* 1999), *Cherry-blossom Epiphany* does not include nearly as much natural history as *Rise, Ye Sea Slugs!* And, unlike *Fly-ku!,* there are no significant discoveries to reveal. Nevertheless, this book – or, rather, 3 books in 1, for someday, I hope to add any good poems overlooked, expand it with glosses from readers and illustrations and republish it as an attractive trilogy – may be more ambitious than either, for it explores an entire new world, a culture of the *bloomshade* (my neologism for *hana-no-kage,* the shade of the (cherry) blossom, within which not only poets but Japanese from all walks of life sat, and sit still). Some readers may have glimpsed under the flowery boughs already, but the breadth and depth of what might be called the *hanami* (blossom-viewing) paraverse within should hold surprises for all.

♪ Japanese software is more visual than English. Type *sento* and you can select a cent sign ¢ from your 27 choices, *manji* (the *man* letter) and you get 卍, mark of a Buddhist temple, *hoshi,* or "star," and you get the choice of ★ and ☆, *ue,* or "above," and among other choices, we get ↑ (an obvious and useful indicator, as are ↓ → ←) and ㊤ for the first, or upper part of a series, where the middle is ㊥ and the last, or bottom is ㊦. Unfortunately, whoever decided on the signs for Microsoft Word failed to include the cherry petal, which, I had hoped to scatter liberally throughout the book. In Japan, cherry petal decals are used to cover holes in paper doors. Cartoons show them filling the air above people making love 凸+凹 out of sight but al fresco. ω

Cherry, you say?

The red, sweet fruit of the cherry symbolizes the sweetness of character which is derived from good works. It is often called the Fruit of Paradise. A cherry, held in the hand of the Christ Child, suggests the delights of the blessed.

– George Ferguson: *Signs & Symbols in Christian Art* (Oxford University Press: 1954)

Forget the fruit!

This book is about the flower.

preface
BOOK I
Cherry Blossom Epiphany

人に花大からくりのうき世哉 一茶 文政一
hito ni hana ôkarakuri no ukiyo kana   issa 1762-1827
(people-and/with blossoms: big automaton'sfloating-world!/?/'tis)

hanami epiphany

all those men
and blossoms: the world's
an automaton

A "mountain" – often meaning only a large park – of cherry blossoms in full bloom is a sensory experience as grand as Niagara. We are thrilled, more alive than ever; yet, sitting with hearts thumping below the pink cataract, glimpsing the blue sky beyond, we also feel the chilly breath of eternity (death) and shiver. For this reason, as well as the blossoms' ephemeral beauty, there are more philosophical haiku about these tree flowers [1] than about any other subject except the fall moon, whose Buddhist baggage encourages a different sort of metaphysical musing.

If, as not a few have claimed, a haiku *must* be an "objective" description of "what is" and avoid "intellectualizing," no haiku theme is so corrupt as the cherry-blossom. But, if we do not choose to banish philosophy from poetry, the opposite might be claimed: cherry-blossom haiku are proof that haiku may be many things and still be haiku. Issa's *ku*, one of about 800 (!) he wrote about cherry blossoms, is a prime example of this. It does not simply observe what is out there but records a subjective experience of the type one might call an epiphany. Please note: Issa's metaphor is not so outlandish as one might think. *Automata* were popular in Japan and common in *senryû*. [2] *Experiencing* the world as an automaton, i.e., a sort of mechanized *maya,* is another matter. Only a mountain of cherry blossoms swarming with revelers could have evoked it.

~~~~~~

1. ***Tree Flowers*** Learning that the peony was known as the King of Flowers (*hana no ô*) despite being low down compared to the plum and cherry, a Usanian reader objected that the peony was not low for the plum and cherry were not, generally considered flowers. In Japanese "flower" and "blossom" are the same *hana* and someone asked to draw a *hana* is as likely to draw a blossoming tree as a wee plant. The lack of number may also have something to do with it, for *hana* might be one or a multitude of flowers/blossoms. Botany backs the Japanese sensitivity, for the cherry is called a *"flowering* tree." But Japanese were aware of a difference. Saigyô (-1190) "Its flower / on limbs is beyond / comparison: / no tree compares / to the cherry" たぐひなき花をし枝に咲かすれば　桜にならぶ木ぞなかりける　西行 (italics mine) *taguinaki hana o shi eda ni sakasureba sakura ni . . .*)

2. ***Automata*** There was a long tradition of automata (*karakuri*), devices that appear to operate on their own power in Japan. I found a half dozen *karakuri senryû* written a hundred years earlier (mostly in *Mutamagawa*). One even suggests our dreams were such a *karakuri*, or mechanical puppetry operated by the body's inner organs.

<u>or</u>
Cherry Blossom Bash?

花咲くやそこらは野糞の小便　一茶 文政六
hana saku ya sokora wa noguso noshôben   issa 1762-1827
(flowers bloom: there [plural] field/outdoor-shit/ting, field-piss/ing)

b-side

cherries bloom	cherries bloom
all about the fields	no end to alfresco shit
pissing! shitting!	alfresco piss

The dirty realism of this B-side *ku* is every bit as representative of cherry-blossom viewings and cherry-blossom haiku as the more elegant "Epiphany." Locations with many cherry trees close to large urban areas drew enormous *hanami* (blossom-viewing) crowds and that meant cloacal problems. The ancient Games were said to stink up all Olympia. With but one inn for the dignitaries, the camping spectators had to use pine forests (Not the Sacred Grove, I hope!) and dry river beds to relieve themselves (says Perrottet, according to Google). In Japan, where night-soil was *bought* for fertilizer [1] – excrement was not allowed to go to waste – it is doubtful that things ever got that bad. It is hard to tell from the original if we are talking about the behavior or the product and whether Issa observes what happens along a route through the countryside leading to a blossom-viewing area, on the fringes of that area, or nearby full public restrooms (curtains hung from trees made makeshift facilities) within such an area. Yet, despite the vague detail, the mere mention of shit and piss brings the picture right before our eyes.

In one sense, however, this dirty realism is not representative. [2] Far more "blossom bash" *ku* [3] concern *drunken* behavior than excremental. And, it is a fact still evident today that people out cherry-blossom viewing did and still do far more drinking than thinking and leave more refuse than poetry on the grounds. This is not meant to contradict the Western image of cherry blossom viewing as an aesthetic experience enjoyed by delicate sensibilities. The clean and elegant side of *hanami* is as real as the dirty and rude. *Ku* reflecting that proper "tea-party" side will not be neglected. My aim in this book is to present the entire spectrum of experience, from start to finish, as far as possible relying on haiku alone.

1. Night-soil in Japan   In the 16c, a Portuguese Jesuit in Japan, Luis Frois, wrote: *"We pay someone to carry our night-soil away; In Japan, they buy it and give rice and money for it."* (For a five page explanation, see TOPSY-TURVY 1585)

2. Issa's Realism   Issa may well have written more haiku on body functions than any *haijin* (when it comes to horse-shit, Shiki is the winner). But since it is almost impossible to find the entire works of most poets, and selections tell us more about the (presumed) taste of the audience the poet or editor sought to satisfy than anything else, I hesitate to call Issa unique in this earthiness, which we only know because we have so many of his poems.

3. *Ku* – Get used it!   I realize it is unusual to hit the reader with a new word and immediately use it over and over, but I believe *ku* will naturalize quickly. For my part, I have grown weary of seeing "haiku," a *genre* of poetry, used for the poem. (And, most of these *ku* are not *hokku*.)

foreword
BOOK I

The Paradoxical Benefits of a Hackneyed Theme

There is an enormous volume of (cherry) blossom-viewing haiku. In Shiki's *Categorical* (*bunrui-haiku zenshû*) there are about 8,000 cherry-blossom-related *ku*. Considering the fact that Shiki includes only a dozen or so of Issa's 800 (representing almost 5% of Issa's total output), and there are many poets far less well-known than Issa, who, themselves, must have written hundreds such *ku*, there must be hundreds of thousands if not *millions* of haiku on this subject! Yet, large contemporary Japanese *saijiki* (haiku almanac) generally include only a couple hundred, of which most are modern or contemporary. And small *saijiki*, equalizing themes for the sake of space or misguided naturalism, usually introduce a small sampling (a dozen or half-dozen *ku*), perhaps no more than that for "camellia," "peony," or "chrysanthemum.[1] In English, Blyth's *Haiku*, "Spring," has the most pre-modern cherry-blossom poems of any single book I know of: *about 70*. The Peter Pauper Press haiku collection misleadingly titled *Cherry Blossoms* has only a handful of poems about the same. In this book, we will see *thousands*.

One might wonder how a single theme can be so heavily haiku'ed without being totally covered, *used up*. Such worry is unfounded for several reasons.

First, as the Table of Content suggests, *sakura/hana* has many large sub-themes. The viewing experience, cache of allusion, and room for word-play varies broadly depending on the location of the cherry blossoms (the region of Japan, private garden, city park, up a mountain, or in a field), the type of the tree/blossoms (single-petal, double-blossomed, fast or slow, young or old), the species or name of the tree (equinox cherry, dog cherry, elephant cherry) and socio-economic position and/or poetic strategy of the poet. Whereas most flowers are noted for a *moment*, for a sweet scent, a loud bloom, or an odd shape, the flowering cherry does more than simply catch our attention. They, or rather, *we*, enjoy a long-term relationship which bears a multitude of haiku themes. We have *ku* on waiting (*hana o matsu*) for the first-bloom (*hatsuzakura*) because people so love their yearly blossom-viewings (*hanami*) that we have what amounts to a countdown; we have *ku* on "cherry-hunting (*sakuragari*) because people sought their blossoms as eagerly as we once pursued game, rain-blossoms (*hana no ame*), for viewers sat under trees for hours and sometimes spent the night, staying home (*hana no rusu*), i.e., the sadness of being the one left to guard the home while others are out blossom-viewing . . . and so forth. In most *old* haiku almanacs, these riches are reflected by the large number of example *ku* (about 1,200 *ku* or 10% of the Spring *ku* in Kaizôsha's large haikai *saijiki*).

---

1. *Exception to the Rule of Short-changing the Cherry* The tenth *Kidaibetsu Gendai Haiku Senshû* (contemporary haiku anthology by seasonal theme) published by the Haijin Kyokai (the largest association of haiku poets in Japan (1997) includes 800 cherry blossom haiku, about 2.5% of the 32,000 haiku. I believe the fact that they are selected from poems contributed by members of the association, rather than culled from magazines or books, explains this rare reflection of haiku reality. However, I cannot understand why there are only 8 mosquitoes yet 21 ant-lions in the same anthology! Are most haiku composers relatively well-off and use air-conditioning so they are unacquainted with mosquitoes while someone the previous year made the ant-lion (*arijigoku*, or "ant-hell" in Japanese) a theme for a *kukai* (haiku meet)? I have written more *ku* on 'squitoes than anything else!

Second, haiku do not only exhaust themes; they build upon and enlarge them. That is, they interact with generations of poets as well as the blossoms and fellow blossom-viewers. Purists, who prefer "fresh" themes, might say *that* is the problem with cherry-blossom haiku: *poets writing about poetry rather than nature, itself.* The charge is not completely false. But, the existence of an abundant body of poems allows one to say more about the genuinely observed subject in shorter scope than would otherwise be possible. With a few well-chosen words, we may allude to another *ku* in its entirety, and that *ku*, may, in turn, draw in further allusions and associations. Moreover, because the intended reader (contemporaries interested in *haikai*) would be familiar with many of the ideas – old saws, if you wish – they would not need to be spelled out, so the poets are, conversely, free to be sketchier, more playful, and pleasingly ambiguous with these poems than those about less-hackneyed subjects. There is a strong parallel here with improvisation in music (we find more in music with limited progressions).

Third, the fact that a theme has become a hackneyed institution reflects the ease with which it may be approached and shared. I find it hard to enjoy haiku about flowers I am unfamiliar with. But, who in Japan does not know cherry blossoms? Or, to put it differently, even if you don't have much personal experience with them, the body of poetry will have made you familiar with the *idea* of cherry blossoms. If you write about them you know you will be read with at least a modicum of understanding. And, finally, a novice poet may compare his or her poems with those already written.

On the minus side, redundancy is unavoidable when writing tiny poems on heavily written themes. But, it need not be feared. There is nothing intrinsically wrong about people writing similar or identical *ku* twice, or even dozens of times. In the case of similar *ku* in haiku, there is – or should be – a presumption of innocence on the part of the poet. Still, you might prefer to remain unfamiliar with old *ku* in order to preserve the possibility of making the same insight by yourself, unless you, like me, are blessed with a memory so poor you may read old *ku* and – *You will, Oscar, you will!* (a reply to Wilde's "I wish I had written that") – later invent them anew.

The Name Problem, or When does Flower mean Cherry?

花の春誰ソや桜の春と呼　蕪村
hana no haru ta so ya sakura no haru to yobu buson (-1783)
(blossom's/floral/celebratory/merry spring: who "cherry's spring" as call)

blossom spring:
who would call it
"cherry spring!"

flowery spring
who would call it
"cherry spring!"

who dares call it
the spring of the cherry?
hana's spring

Buson asks rhetorically "Who in the world would play upon the equivalence of the generic blossom (*hana*) and the cherry-blossom(*sakura*) to come up with *sakura-no-haru* (cherry spring) for the New Year!" Since *hana-no-haru*, i.e., *haru* (spring) modified by *hana* (blossom) usually means *The New Year* in a celebratory sense, i.e. "Happy Spring!" (see IPOOH ny 2-1) – it *might* make sense to use "cherry spring" for the later date when the cherries actually bloom, but, even then, *sakura-no-haru* sounds awkward (too many syllabets) and is rarely used. I cite the *ku* because it shows that even the Japanese are amused/confused by the ambiguous *hana*.

The order of the sub-themes in this book is mine. Many are also found in old *saijiki*, some in contemporary *saijiki*, others here alone. I will try to point this out in the respective chapters. *My categories are more for the purpose of creating manageable chapters for the reader than for the* convenience of the poet, as is usually the case for *saijiki*. But the largest difference between my categories and conventional ones is that I do not allow the existence or non-existence of a *word* to trump an idea. It is standard to separate poems with the word *hana,* meaning "flower/blossom" from those with *sakura,* or "cherry." While it is true that *hana* often does not mean "cherry" and may allude to the plum, which tended to bloom at that time, or more generally to the flowery, i.e., *festive,* spring, i.e., the New Year, in a context when the New Year or early spring makes no sense, it usually means "cherry-blossom" or even "cherry-tree." We have seen two *ku* chuckling about the polysemy (various connotations) of *hana,* but the problem is a serious one for haiku. In the huge Kodansha *saijiki,* Yamamoto Kenkichi quotes an old source to the effect that since *hana* may *also* refer to the rest of the flowers of Spring, it deserves a separate thematic listing.[1] Though Yamamoto is my favorite modern *saijiki* editor and annotator of Bashô, I beg to disagree in part.

Granted those *hana* (blossom/flower) poems that clearly allude to more or other than the cherry deserve a separate theme – neither the cherry nor the plum monopolize Spring – but *surely* the majority of *hana* haiku, whose context suggests cherry-blossoms alone, should be included with the rest of the *sakura!* Sometimes the context is not clear and it is a hard call for the editor, who, unlike other readers, cannot overlook the ambiguity unless he or she is willing to place the same poem into more than one theme. Translators can often avoid making the call in English by choosing the word "blossom," suggesting *hana* may be a *tree* flower without committing on it (in Japanese, where there is no *flower/blossom* distinction, this means nothing), though this still leaves other tree possibilities. Regardless, this is one case (unlike that of the *person* or *number* of the subject), where ambiguity is not a plus, for we – or I, at least – want to know what type of plant to imagine. A last chuckle:

木ひとつに花と桜の咲にけり 来山 夢の名残
ki hitotsu ni hana to sakura no sakinikeri   raizan   (-1716)
(tree-one-as flower/blossom and cherry's blossom/blossomed(+finality))

hana & sakura	*hana & sakura*
blooming away on one	have bloomed for good
and the same tree	on a single tree

The irony of this categorical problem is that the same haiku establishment that puts down the logocentric approach of the Teitoku school (*Teimon*), or for that matter, almost all early *haikai,* continues to group their collections in a nominal manner, with *sakura* (cherry [blossom]) here and *hana* (flower) there, while I, who unabashedly *enjoy* much of the play on the names of things, do not!

---

1. Hana/Sakura Mix Though these terms are separated in the large *Kodansha* saijiki, they are combined in the case of *hatsu-hana* (first bloom) and *hatsu-zakura* (first cherry [bloom]) in the same saijiki. The subject is more complex than my above summary might suggest.

↓ **2. Names Galore** Taigi's *ku* on the next page recalls an earlier complaint about the demands of botany on poetry: "A pain in the ass / so manifold these names / of *spring grass!*" (*iroiro no na mo muzukashi ya haru no kusa*   shadô (-1737?) いろ／＼の名 . . . 酒堂. The two *ku* share the first six syllabets. "Grass" means "plants." Shadô's idea came at a time when *saijiki* were introducing more and more themes many of which were the names of plants. Taigi's *ku* seems more a statement of his poetic philosophy, which on this count agrees with Bashô, whose work mentioned few types of cherry, and these mostly when he was young. Indeed, Bashô went further, for he favored "blossom" (*hana*) over *sakura.*

↓ **3. B-side** The *sakura* is a rank of high-class harlot. Many old *ku* contain risqué allusion, often, because they were composed in a sequence where the allusion makes the association with a previous *ku*. This does not mean the haiku is *only* an allusion, nor, does it automatically devalue the A-side reading. I note this because some people seem to think that even *considering* a B-side reading ruins the poem and denigrates the poet. I should add that my approach is rare but not unique. Japanese readers should see a book of *ku* by Buson's teacher Hajin, (『巴人の全句を読む』 1999) with round-table explanations averaging a page in length, under the direction of the recently deceased Maruyama Kazuhiko, a well-known *haikai* specialist and a very kind man.

A Role for Nominal Wit and How Cherries Encouraged It

いろ／＼の名は我言はずさくらかな 太祇
iroiro no na wa ware iwazu sakura kana   taigi (1709-72)
(manifold names [2] -as-for i say/call-not: cherry [b-side [3] = harlot?] 'tis/!)

only "*sakura*"

<table>
<tr><td>names galore
but to me a cherry
is a cherry!</td><td>not on my lips
its manifold names
the cherry!</td></tr>
</table>

Despite Bashô putting in a word for levity (*karumi*) in his last years, most of the truly light verse so prevalent in olde haiku is not included in modern *saijiki*. I think that is a mistake, for even if such *ku* are rarely good, much less great, they serve a purpose. Masterpieces in haiku (*shûku*) are often demanding, and "good" haiku (*kaku*), taken one after another can become tedious and even when encountered in linked verse, most of their allusions are missed by outsiders, while collections of haiku arranged by the calendar or author lack sufficient narrative to pull the reader along. In my opinion, witty *ku* are needed to keep the reader on his or her toes and help set up the more serious ones. In this book, I not only include all the wit I manage to translate (and some, I fear, I do not) or (re)create, but try to make every other chapter a minor theme that is intrinsically funny precisely because it encourages nominal witticism. I refer to the "names galore" about which Taigi complains, varieties of flowering cherry that went by odd names such as dog, elephant, equinox, thread, and the endearing names of cherries in various parts of their life cycle or circumstances such as boy, aunty and house cherry. Names by themselves are hardly funny, but treated as if they were metaphor and used to build trains of allegory the absurdity of the fiction makes us chuckle (as, perhaps, all translation rightly understood should, for the lack of perfect equivalence means that *all* translation is an exercise in metaphor). Be that as it may, such *ku* are seldom encountered today and some of the varieties of cherry mentioned are obsolete, nominally at least. I had at first planned to gather this treasury of nominal wit into one huge chapter, but later thought it might be appreciated more in small doses. Unfortunately, there are not enough well-haiku'ed and/or easily translated varieties of cherry to continue the every-other-chapter scheme in Book II and Book III, but these books have a larger proportion of provocative themes than Book I, so the balance of light and heavy poems – and, I trust, your interest – should remain constant throughout the *Cherry Blossom Epiphany*.

Please take care to glance at the gloss now and then, for the translations reflect my own *karumi*. Eg.:

櫻から出入る人や坂の口   吟江 夢占
sakura kara dehairu hito ya saka no kuchi   ginkô (1780)
(cherry[blossoms]-from, leave-enter people:/! slope's-mouth/entrance)

<table>
<tr><td>cherry blossoms
people going in and out
the pink tunnel</td><td>a mouth on the hill
men going in and out
of cherry blossoms</td></tr>
</table>

people going in
and out of the sakura
mons veneris

Non-Japanese-readers
¡*take note!*

KANA almost always comes at the end of a *ku* and means
"oh" "ah" "alas" "!" "?" "the ~ " "how~ !" "what~!" "'tis" "that's "

YA is written with the same Chinese character as **KANA**, and is more or less the same word;
but, because it usually comes in mid-poem, it is more likely to mean *":" or " – ."*
Confusing as it might sound, it can simultaneously mean the same as *kana*.
So, we have an emphatic that can both break *and/or* link a sentence.
Or, like *kana*, it can always mean nothing in particular: Ø

Kana is all-too-often defined as a *kireji*, or "cutting word,"
indicating a pause or division of a *ku*, with no explanation as to why it is
usually found at the end of the same, where there is no need to cut and a pause is only natural.
The reason for such nonsense is that proto-haiku was generally part of a chain of link-verse,
and the cutting word kept the *ku* apart from the next *ku*, whether another 5-7-5, or
a 7-7 cap. Its emphatic nuance is one reason it still works at the end.

.
Perhaps this is why old *ku,* such as most found in this book,
tend to have more *kana* than new ones do, though other factors also play
a role. In Japanese, the subject tends to come last, or, right before the *kana,* if there
is a *kana*. So, if the word used for the subject is three syllabets-long, there will be many *kana.*
Or, if the subject has a tiny name, like say, a "mosquito," which, in Japanese, is *"ka,"*
the *kana* serves to fill space (and, I suppose, adds alliteration, to boot).
English, with its needless *"it"* that rains or blows or simply *is,*
is also full of nonsense, so the curious reader should
have no trouble figuring out *"kana,"* or
other things for him- or herself
using my odd glosses
though it is not
necessary

CHERRY
KEY

When Humpty Dumpty told Alice that the words he used meant whatever he chose them to mean, Alice demurred: "The question is whether you *can* make words mean so many different things." Humpty Dumpty replied to this reasonable doubt with a flippant, "The question is which is to be master – that's all." The truth is that *it depends*. Words used out of context can only mean what they conventionally mean; but used repetitively, they may indeed be made to mean different things, yet still be perfectly understandable to all.

Translated haiku often lose their snap when words lacking equivalent words become explanatory phrases. One escape from this is Humpty-Dumptyism, i.e. the repetition of old words used in new ways. Another is neologism, either inventing new words or introducing foreign ones as is. Books of haiku with only a few *ku* per theme – ie. almost all books of translated haiku – cannot do this, for the reader has no time to become familiar with the novelty. By pursuing themes at length, IPOOH and its spin-offs can. Here is a list of some of the words, Japanese, new, or used in a novel manner, in this book and one odd *plum:*

Pronounce Japanese vowels as with any Latin tongue, soften the "r" with "l," and "f" with "h."

BLOOMPEAK (*hana-zakari*). The time when the cherry is literally *flourishing, i.e.*, in full bloom or full-blossom. The original occasionally has an erotic edge: *blossom-rut* or *heat of the bloom*.
BLOOMSHADE (*hana-no-kage*). "The shade of the blossoms," i.e., the area under a flowering cherry tree. A shorter, less descriptive word was needed for translation.
BLOSSOM (*hana*) "Cherry-blossoms" or "cherries in bloom." In Japanese, a "blossom" in the absence of other information generally means *cherry* blossoms. Unless we do the same, the translation is handicapped with extra syllables. Sometimes they fit and sometimes they do not.
BLOSSOM BASH (*hanami*) A boisterous "blossom-viewing." The word "viewing" (*mi*) suggests a quiet *haute culture* event, when the *hanami* is often more of a carnival.
BLOOM CLOUDS or BLOSSOM CLOUDS (*hana-no-kumo*) "Clouds of cherry blossom/flowers" is too lengthy an expression for a common Japanese trope.
BREAKING ONE OFF or BREAKING A BRANCH (*ta-ori* or *shi-ori*). Also "stealing, " etc.. Breaking off a branch of a budding or blossoming tree (here cherry, but also plum) to keep it for decoration, give it to someone or, more rarely, plant or graft it. The Japanese term is, literally "hand-break" or "branch-break."
CHERRY (*sakura*) "A cherry tree (or trees) in bloom." In English, the cherry is identified with its *fruit*, while, in Japanese, "cherry" alone means the *flower/s*, the tree in blossom, or, in the right context, the petals. In this book, the Humpty-Dumpty translator often adopts the broad Japanese connotation. *Beware!*
CHERRY BASH   Same as BLOSSOM BASH.
CHERRY MOUNTAIN (*hana-no-yama*)   A park with a grove of cherries where people view blossoms.
CHERRY RAIN or BLOSSOM RAIN (*hana-no-ame*). Rain that falls while the cherry is in bloom.
CHERRY-TIME (*hana-doki*). The time period when the cherry is in blossom and people are out blossom-viewing. The Japanese expression is relatively rare. I find it useful for Englishing vague expressions such as *sakura kana* (the cherries!) or *hanami kana* (blossom-viewing!), when the poet's concern seemed to be this magical period.
EIGHTFOLD CHERRY (*yaezakura*)   Double-flowered blossoms with 25-50 petals/flower.
HANAMI (*hanami*) Blossom-viewing. In this book, following Japanese convention: *cherry* blossom viewing.
MOUNTAIN CHERRIES (*yamazakura*)   Mountain means "wild" (uncultivated) as well as a high place.
PLUM   The botanically-minded like to call the *ume*, also *mume*, a "Japanese apricot," but I stick with poetic convention and call it a "plum," which usually means it is blooming, as is the case with the cherry.
SAKURA (*sakura*) Cherry-tree/cherry-blossom/cherry-petals. I like this Japanese word and sometimes use it as is. Some readers may be familiar with it, thanks to the song *Sakura, Sakura*. The verb *saku* means "bloom" (homophonic with splitting open) and "ra" is a plural suffix. So it seems to *mean* "bloomlings," but that oversimplifies a much-debated complex etymology, given as an appendix to Book I.

Why *Blossom* means *Cherry* and *Cherry* means *Blossom* in Japanese

> Ours is the country of *sakura* [cherry trees/blossom]. As the peony is synonymous with flower [*hana*] in Loyang, and the aronia [1] in Sichuan, we [in Japan] do not even speak of *sakura*, but simply "flowers" (*hana*).
> Ôsen (横川 1429-93)

This brief passage (a single sentence in the original) does not so much propose as confirm the triumph of the cherry, as a flowering tree, in Japan.[2] The oldest anthology of Japanese poetry, the *Manyôshû* (8c), written when the prestige of a Chinese import, the flowering plum (*ume*) was at a peak, has 110 plum poems versus only 43 cherry poems, and "blossom/s" (*hana*) by itself usually indicated the former.[3] The second major anthology the *Kokinshû* (10c), compiled after cherry-blossom-viewing had become popular, reverses the numbers with 70 poems for cherry and 18 for plum – out of 133 total spring poems! – but plums still hung on to 8 of 12 plain "blossom/s." The third major anthology, the *Shin-Kokinshû* (13c) likewise gives approximately half of the Spring to cherry blossoms and far less to plums – though I suspect Yamada, whose statistics I use may have neglected New Year plums – but more than 50 plain "blossom/s" (*hana*), presumably the lion's share, indicate the cherry. Today, the greater world of flowers, including the Western plant that was once synonymous with bloom, the rose, has weakened the cherry's monopoly in Japan. Yet in the world of Japanese traditional poetry, at least, cherry is still *the* blossom, the *hana* of *hana*.

Most English speakers are surprised to learn that the blossom, or flower, of the cherry tree, is called simply "cherry" (*sakura*). Yet, they think it perfectly normal to conflate the same tree with its fruit, something that seems odd to the Japanese, who must specify the fruit as a *sakuranbo* (cherry-bob) or *cheri* (from English!). Linguistically speaking, this is arbitrary. Historically speaking it may be significant. According to a book on the cultural history of flowers and trees by Nakao Sasuke (中尾佐助「花と木の文化史」岩波新書), the *Manyôshû* includes 166 different plants, while the Western canon of literature, the *Bible* mentions only 10, *all edible.*[4] When the Jesuits came to Japan in the 16c, they were astounded to find blossoms rather than fruit were the measure of so many trees and bewailed the paucity of plums and cherries they could sink their teeth into.[5] This complaint became a convention over the centuries and was only rarely qualified with an a word of praise for the extraordinarily diverse and delicious Japanese persimmon (*kaki*), that for me, at least, more than makes up for any shortage in the cherry and plum department. It is worth noting that this *kaki* by itself refers to the fruit rather than the flower, as is the case for the English cherry.

Although this book is in English, it is about the Japanese cherry, and will, as far as poetic license will permit, follow the Japanese connotation of cherry as blossom and of blossom as cherry. There are practical reasons for doing so. A "cherry-blossom-viewing" or "cherry-blossom petals" will not fit in the first or last line of a haiku, whereas "blossom-viewing" or "cherry petals" will.

1. **What is an Aronia?** Kuitert, in his *Flowering Cherries* (1999) – *the* source for botanical information on our plants – translates *kaido* as "crab apple" (and gives the scientific name *Malus halliana* Koehne). I could not do it, for this is a tree=blossom named after a Chinese beauty, reputed to look especially voluptuous with a face wet with rain. True, not one reader in a thousand – much less this writer – has ever heard of an *Aronia* (given by my dictionary, which sciences the *kaido* as *Malus micromalus*, doubtless the Japanese variety), but the connotations of crab apple betray the beauty, right?

2. **A Symbol of Japan?** I did a loose translation of the pseudo-Chinese (*kanbun*) changing the "precious" applied to the two Chinese flowers into "synonymous with." I did so because the only other English translation I have seen has serious problems I wanted to offset. For example, the "however" in "However, most people speak simply of "the flowers" . . .) completely misses the intent of the author to show the cherry was so closely identified with what we might call flowerhood in Japan that it was called simply "flower." Needless to say, the original has no such conjunction.

3. ***Manyôshû* Cherries** The cherry's cultural importance may be deeper than the numbers show. According to Yamada (IBID), the fact that the smaller number of cherry poems are spread out over more sections of the anthology (15 of 20 sections) than the plum (*ume*) poems (9 of 20 sections) shows that the cherry is more pervasively rooted throughout the culture, where the plum blossom is concentrated in the Sinofied parties of the aristocrats. A contemporary cherry researcher, Ogawa Kazusuke (*Sakura-shi*: 1998) points out that the cherry poems in the *Manyôshû* tend to express emotion and fall under the *waka*, or Japanese-song poetry, rubric, while the plum poems explored the (more sophisticated in both meanings of the word) sensibilities of Chinese poetry.

4. **Bible Plants** I have my doubts about Nakao's claim. What about the lily – is *it* edible? And, are the palms for palm Sunday only date palms? But quibbling aside, Judeo-Christian poetry may well have neglected blossoms that did not have issue, especially on trees.

5. **Jesuit Cherries** The 31st and 44th items in chapter 14 of Frois's 1585 treatise, respectively:

> We take care to plant in our gardens trees that bear fruit; The Japanese prize most in their *niwa* (gardens) those that bear only flowers.

> Our cherry trees bear very delicious and beautiful cherries; Those of Japan bear many small, bitter cherries and many beautiful flowers which the Japanese appreciate. (TOPSY-TURVY 1585)

1

Waiting for the Bloom
待つ桜
matsu-zakura

春になる桜の枝はなにとなく　花なけれども　むつまじきかな　西行
haru ni naru sakura no eda wa nani to naku hana nakeredomo mutsumajiki kana   saigyô (1118-90)
(spring-into become cherry's/ies' limbs-as-for vaguely/some-how blossom not-but dear/close 'tis/how!)

something about
the limbs of a cherry
in early spring

though blossomless
i hold them dear

To date, not a single pre-haiku (pre-*haikai*) poem about the subject of my first IPOOH spin-off, sea cucumbers (*namako*), has been found. The only pre-Edo era (pre-17c) sources are mythological – the *namako's* mouth is lacerated for refusing to speak up when addressed by a god -- and tribute/trade-related – the *namako* was eaten (see: *Rise, Ye Sea Slugs!*). With the cherry, there are *innumerable* old poems. While I do not wish to dilute the haiku too much, the usual haiku anthologist's occasional citation of classic 31 syllabet poems (*waka*) alluded to by, or condensed into, equally famous haiku, will not suffice. We need to see a larger sampling of *waka* to understand where certain seasonal themes and their wit, generally traced back to 17c *haikai* and sometimes to 15c *hokku* but rarely any further, comes from. Saigyô's chapter-head *waka* is a haiku in all but length. The last line in the original has no person or verb (it could be "we" hold them dear, or "how dear they are!") and the *mutsumajiki* is a hard word to English. It is most commonly used to describe a patently affectionate relationship. I am afraid my translation fails to do justice to that warmth.

おしまぬは花まつ春の日かすかな　宗祇
oshimanu wa hana matsu haru no hikazu kana   sôgi (1420-1502)
(regret-not-as-for, blossom/flower waiting spring-day-number 'tis/!/?)

waiting for the cherry blossoms

what we don't
regret are the spring days
spent waiting!

The *falling* blossoms and the *departure* of Spring was a proverbial matter of regret, but not *waiting*.

はるはみな花まちおしむ日かす哉　無記名 大発句帳
haru wa mina hana machioshimu hikazu kana   anon (p1630)
(spring-as-for all blossoms/flowers wait-regret day-number 'tis)

waiting for the cherry blossoms

in the spring
we all regret the days
lost waiting

And, like proverbs, haiku may contradict. Theoretically, *hana* might be any flower, but "waiting" suggests the longed-for cherry blossoms. Aside from the hyperbolic "all," the *ku* are equally true.

待つ程は心やさかり春の花 宗祇   待をしむ程や心の花盛 宗祇
matsu hodo wa kokoro ya sakari haru no hana sôgi   machioshimu hodo ya kokoro no hanazakari sôgi
(wait-extent-as-for, heart/mind! blooms/excites spring-blossoms) (wait-regret/bear extent: heart/mind's bloompeak)

the longer we wait   the longer the wait
the higher we get when   the more our minds bloom
spring blossoms!   spring blossoms!

Sakari means the acme of the bloom. It also means being *in heat* or *rut*. Were Sôgi not a poet of high-style, one might be tempted to write "hornier" rather than "higher." It is usually associated with the cherry and seldom used to describe the less explosive bloom and sober viewing of the plum blossom.

宗祇二百年忌　花を待心深さも昔哉　昌察 三籟
hana o matsu kokoro fukasa mo mukashi kana   shôsatsu (1734)
(blossom/flower wait/ing heart/mind's deepness too old/ancient 'tis/!/?)

sôgi's 200 year anniversary

the depth of mind
to wait for cherry blossoms
a thing of the past

This *ku* was in the same book as the anonymous one contradicting Sôgi's claim that time spent waiting is not regretted. Because of that, I believe Shôsatsu's eulogy of Sôgi is a critical reflection upon his own era's lack of patience, though *kana's* lack of specific meaning would also permit a reading to the effect that the folk of old, Sôgi, at least, shared our feelings for the budding cherry. It is also possible this has to do with the proliferation of nursery practices that sped up the bloom of potted plants (plum as well as cherry) to ensure they met cultural deadlines, i.e. holiday dates. (専門家の御意見は？.)

またるとて思ひしる世の花もなし 宗碩
mataru tote omoishiru yo no hana mo nashi   sôseki (-1533)
(waited on that perceive world's blossom even not)

faultless

no blossom
has ever realized
how we wait!

This old *ku* is trite as a statement about blossoms, but fine as a statement of the relationship between the sexes. An even sillier *ku*: "Oh, for a spring / where blossoms are informed / how long we wait!" (待つ程を花にしらする春も哉　元就　春霞 *matsu hodo o hana ni shirasuru haru mo gana*　genshû)). I can't tell how long this poet waited but another suggests that the countdown might have begun from the beginning of the year: *"The cherries, asked / replied on the sixty eighth / or ninth day"* (花をとはゝ（濁り点）答ふ六十八九日　雄山　花桜帖 *hana o towaba kotau rokujûhachi ku nichi*　yûzan -1706.)

春雨や花待つ人の心しり　貞室 句鑑
harusame ya hana matsu hito no kokoro shiri　teishitsu -1673
(spring rain: blossom-waiting person's heart/mind knows)

soul-mates

the spring rain
it shares the heart of all
who await the bloom

the spring rain
it knows the mind of men
awaiting blossoms

This is not too silly, for it brings out a fine parallel of interest between men and the elements (see chapters on the *rain* and the *late cherry*) commonly associated with prompting the bloom. There is also a poem suggesting that the waiting was mutual:

人は花はなや人まつひがし山 失名 ちり塚？
hito wa hana hana ya hito matsu higashiyama　lost name 1671?
(people-as-for blossom blossom-as-for people wait/ing east-mountain)

where men wait
for blossoms and blossoms men
East Mountain

men, blossoms　　　　　　　　　　　　men await trees
blossoms, men await　　　　　　　　　trees men: cherry blossoms
on east mountain　　　　　　　　　　 on mount east

the east mountains
where man and blossom
await the other

To me "East Mountain" suggests the place where the sun comes first, the fount of flowery Spring, proper stage for natural resurrection. To the poet, it was probably the mountains famous for their natural beauty on the East, or "upper" side of Kyôto.

ねぶき眼をひらけば花の浮世哉　成美
nemuki me o hirakeba hana no ukiyo kana　seibi -1816
(tired eyes[obj] open-when/if, blossoms' floating-world!/'tis)

my drowsy eyes
open to behold a floating
blossom world

If Seibi has come to after drinking below the bloom, this is blah, so let's assume he has awakened from a long sleep to discover the blossoms open and the surreal *time of the cherry* underway. While Spring drowsiness (caused by the lengthening days) is an old saw in Japan, this cuts well. If I am not mistaken, Seibi's cherry tree was in his own garden. Most poets were not so lucky.

花を待つ日数によこす衣哉　去来 去来句集
hana o matsu hikazu ni yogosu koromo kana   kyorai (-1704)
(blossom[obj] [i?/we?] wait day-number-by defile clothing 'tis)

> the more days
> we wait for the blossoms
> the dirtier our dress

A century later, Issa would joke *"Blossom-viewing / in soiled clothing / call me Kyorai!"* (花衣よごれ去来と見ゆる也　一茶 真蹟 *hanagoromo yogore kyorai to miyuru nari*). I *first* imagined a place for blossom-viewing staked out under a tree with ripe buds watched by men thinking "they gotta bloom today!" who sadly retreat or camp out at night after waiting in vain all day, coming out again at dawn. Ridiculous, perhaps, but look at the way people line up for previews of movies that may be had for free a year or two later. *In retrospect*, Kyorai probably meant the time that passed since people donned their new clothing for the Year, i.e. Spring, but it is more interesting to imagine a vigil.

待花や寝苦しき夜の明る程　雅因 新選
matsu hana ya negurushiki yoru no akuru hodo   gain (1773)
(wait/ing blossom! /: sleep-difficult/trying night-dawns-extent)

> the closer to dawn
> the harder it is to sleep
> waiting the bloom

Again, the blossom is definitely cherry. The question is whether a salacious "b" side reading, *i.e.,* the day the poet first sleeps with a particular woman, is called for.   There is some real call for anxiety:

世の中は三日見ぬ間に櫻かな　蓼太
yononaka wa mikka minu ma ni sakura kana ryôta (1707-87)
(world-among/in-as-for, three days see-not-space/time-in cherry[blossoms]!)

> ***cherry blossoms***
>
> that's life:
> forget her three days
> and *bloom!*

> in this world
> three days and it's over
> for the cherry
>
> ***waits for no man***

I first thought this meant that blossoming is completely underway within three days, so if you intended to catch the cherries or your house cherry break into blossom, too bad. But, I found none to agree with me in Japanese or English. Blyth waffles: *"The world, / Unseen for three days, – / And cherry blossoms!"* The grammar of the lead-off (the *wa* in *yononaka wa*) makes the *ku* a general statement about the nature of the world, but what did "world" mean to the poet? At the time of Ryota, Japanese were self-conscious of the quick pace of change – the ephemeral fads – that passed like influenza through the major cities and felt one had to be fast just to keep up. Borrowing a bit from Blyth and a bit from Peter Pauper's outrageous FIE! THIS FICKLE WORLD! / THREE DAYS, NEGLECTED / CHERRY BRANCH . . . / AND YOU ARE BARE (*Japanese Haiku*. Peter Pauper Press 1955-6).), we get:

> Things are like that –
> You stay home three days
> and the cherries . . .

> The world is cruel –
> Neglect them for three days
> and the cherries . . .

Did you note that the original has no verb indicating *what* exactly the cherries do? The noun *sakura*, or "cherry," includes *saku,* a homophone for the verb "bloom." Poets have long taken advantage of this *saku* in the *sakura,* to save words by letting the cherry bloom implicitly, which is to say by virtue of the name alone. Almost as often, they have let that bloom include the last part, the boom where the petals explode. Without an explicit verb, however, can be hard to tell what is going on. Here, chances are that the poet refers to the peak of the bloom. Why? Because it was typically said to last three-days. Have I wasted too much time on a verse that is, in Blyth's words, "almost devoid of poetry"?

油断して花に成りたる桜かな 樗良 樗良発句集
yûdan shite hana ni naritaru sakura kana chora (-1780?)
(guard-break-do blossoms-as become/became cherry[trees]!)

the *sakura* are *hana* now

drop your guard
for a wink and the cherries
become blossoms

just doze off
and they are flowers
cherry trees!

Chora is playing with the various nuances of *hana* and *sakura* which we discuss elsewhere.

散たとの状は届きつ櫻狩 園女 玉藻
chitta to no jô wa todokitsu sakuragari sonojo (-1723)
([the blossoms] fell/scattered note/message came, cherry-hunting)

an announcement
came and said "they blew!"
cherry hunting

Here, it would seem that someone was waiting, not for the the first-bloom but the bloompeak. I include it here to show the unsettled nature of the game. We will enjoy more "hunting" in chapter 3.

阿蘭陀も花に来にけり馬に鞍 芭蕉
oranda mo hana ni kinikeri uma ni kura bashô (-1694)
(hollanders-too/even blossoms-to come[emph.+finality] horse-on saddle)

hollanders too
have come for the blossoms –
saddle a horse!

even the dutch
are here for the blossoms
saddle my nag!

I hope Makoto Ueda will forgive me for centering and decapping his translation (the first, above). The *ku* plays on a *waka* from a Nô play where someone says "saddle my horse" when a gillie brings tidings of the new bloom. Even if the rhetoric is nationalistic – *you wouldn't want them foreigners to beat you to it, would you?* – I am charmed at the idea of a world which competes to *be with it* in so aesthetic a way. On the other hand, as a critic cited by Ueda notes, the blossoms may be "fictional and probably stand for the nation's prosperity," in which case, the magic is diminished. Be that as it may, before we feel too exhausted for the poor poets rushing to catch the blossoms in their prime, it bears mentioning that even if a particular tree might have required careful attention, there was much more variety before the Somei-yoshino clones became ubiquitous. Two hundred years ago, Somaru (1712-95) could still observe, *"Even as we / view the falling petals / cherries bloom!"* (散るさくら見て居ながらよ咲桜 素丸 *chiru sakura mite-inagara yo saku sakura*). The urban blossom-viewing season lasted an entire month and the mountains, as we shall see, held even more promise.

ひやつくかいなや寝て見ん初桜　素檗
hiya tsuku ka inaya netemin hatsuzakura　sobaku (-1821)
(cold/chill comes/stays or-not sleeping-see, first-cherry[blossoms])

i'll sleep-over
just have to see if it freezes
the first-blossoms

first blossoms
will it freeze over or not
let's sleep on it

うたゝねをよび起されて櫻かな　虚子
utatane o yobiokosarete sakura kana　kyoshi (1895)
(fitful/light/dreaming-sleep-from called-awake cherry[blossoms]!/?)

from fitful sleep
woken to another dream
cherry blossoms

I assume this is about the start of cherry blossom-viewing and added "another dream."

花咲て（華ざかり）七日鶴見る麓哉　芭蕉 (-1694)
hana saite (hanazakari) nanuka tsuru miru fumoto kana　bashô
(blossom blooming seven-days crane/s see/n mountain-foot/base 'tis)

how enchanting
a mountain foot: seven days
of blossoms and cranes

in full bloom
i see cranes for a week
by this mountain

I had two smoother translations ending "in the foothills," but "foothills" is not quite right and the original is more emphatic about the location, so I ditched them. A cherry was proverbially held to blossom seven days from first bloom to last petal. Most trees in Bashô's day actually blossomed longer and an alternative version of the *ku* specifies the period in question as the bloompeak (*hanazakari*). Cranes were also said to remain for seven days wherever they descended. *The cherry blossom was renowned for non-attachment to this life while the crane was a symbol of longevity.* My added word, *enchanting*, is meant to bring this out. Doubtless, the season is right, too. Another poet wrote: *"A crane's nest! / The sun finishes setting / and blossoms fall"* (鶴の巣や日は入りはてゝ散る櫻 汶村 匂塞 *tsuru no su ya hi wa irihatete chiru sakura*　bunson -1713?).

三日程花見ありけはちりにけり　成美
mikka hodo hanami arige wa chirinikeri　seibi (-1816)
(three-days period blossom-viewing appearance-as-for fall/scatter [+finality])

about three days
and blossom-viewing parties
just fall apart

in three days
the blossoms and viewers
have scattered

Because the first few blossoms and the last will not do for a proper party, and bad weather usually closes part of the window of opportunity, there are generally only a few days of ideal cherry-viewing at any particular tree. Sôi (1767?) put the idea more philosophically: *"As a rule, cherries / have a yesterday, today / and tomorrow"* (おしなへて櫻に明日きのふけふ　宗居　我庵集 *oshinabete sakura ni ashita kinô kyô*). For once, these three days can be taken literally as well as figuratively. Unless one has wings, one *does* have to be on one's toes. Proper moon-viewing is also three days.

花咲て目白の旅や廿日ほど　浪花
hana saite mejiro no tabi ya hatsuka hodo   rôka (-1703)
(blossoms blooming, white-eye's [a bird] travel: twenty-days about)

                    the cherry blooms
                    and white eyes travel
                        for twenty days

the cherry blooms   the cherries bloom
white-eye has twenty-days   white-eyes have twenty
of travel ahead   days of travel

                    the cherry blooms
                 a twenty-day long trip
                   for the white-eyes

Had men wings, they might follow the blossoms around Japan like the *meijiro,* a wee bird with white circles around the eyes. That meant about twenty days, rather than seven. Today, we can see farther than birds; the cherry-front (*sakura-zensen*) is literally forecast and the mapped coordinates shown on television and in the newspapers, as a cold-front might be in the West.

梅ちれば桃々ちれば櫻哉　京馬　新選
ume chireba momo momo chireba sakura kana   kyôma (1773)
(plum[blossoms] fall-if/when, peach, peach fall-if/when cherry!/'tis/!)

blooming progression

plum blossoms
fall and it's peach, peach falls
and it's cherry

The peach, like the cherry, means the blossom of the same. This suggests a relay or progression: *"Plum, cherry / moving from one blossom / to another"* (梅櫻花より花にうつる哉　宗砌 *ume sakura hana yori hana ni utsuru kana*   sôzei (-1455)), as one olde haiku, possibly alluding to different objects of sexual desire put it. This poem may have picked up on *Manyôshû* song #829, which follows the risque song #828. I'll give both for perspective, though the cherry doesn't figure in the first:

人毎に祈り挿頭（かざ）しつつ遊べどもいや愛づらしき梅の花かも 万葉集#828
hito goto ni orikazashitsutsu asobedomo iya mezurashiki ume no hana kamo   manyôshû (8c)

                    broken-off and worn
                    on every man's head
                    the common bloom
                   of the plum still dear

What is common (worn by all) cannot be rare, but it can be beautiful. The Japanese *mezurashiki* means both. The "dear" is not quite right but I trust a bit of the wit in the *waka* (properly translated in five lines) translates. We will look at *blossoms-as-women* and vice versa in Book III. The next *Manyôshû waka* takes us back to the cherry: *"After the plum / blossoms and falls / the cherry trees / have a ball, so / why worry at all?"* (梅の花咲きて散りなば桜花継ぎて咲くべくなりにてあらずや　万葉集 829 *ume no hana sakite chirinaba sakurabana tsugite sakubekunari nite arazuya*). The original does not really pose the rhetorical question as clearly as I did; it just says, *Doesn't the cherry bloom?* Indeed it does, and over a broad territory, one blossom follows the other, as per this *waka* and the *ku* given above; but, locally speaking, blooms might overlap – especially, peach and cherry – or conversely, fail to meet. While plum and cherry trees are widespread in Japan, the peach is generally only found in orchards. After the plum blossoms fell, there is a gap in the floral parade; one expects the next float.[1] *"Blooming flowers / the first wait: for plum / the second, cherry"* (咲く花や待一に梅二は櫻　重方　毛吹草 *saku hana ya matsu ichi ni ume ni wa sakura* shigekata (1645)), as one plain poem put it. This is better:

さかぬ間の春は櫻のはなし哉　貞徳

sakanu ma no haru wa sakura no hanashi [ha-nashi] kana　teitoku (1570-1653)

(bloom-not space/while's spring-as-for, cherry's talk=leaveless 'tis)

the part of spring when nothing blooms: the talk is about cherry	the part of spring no bloom comes and cherry boasts no leaves

The second reading is a pun (*hanashi* = talk: leafless = *ha-nashi*) subsumed in the first. Sôgi (1420-1502) wrote *"How i wish / for a blossom of solace [2] / while they bloom not"* (さかぬまをなくさめ草の花も哉　宗祇*sakanu ma o nagusamegusa no hana mo gana*) Sprucing this up a bit, we get:

The Blossom-lover's Wish

between the plum
and the cherry, a flower
to make us merry

Teitoku has provided just what Sôgi wished for with the blossom of humanity: *words*. The *hanashi/ha-nashi* pun brings out the words because words in Japanese are etymologically and graphically connected to leaves. Here the leafless=wordless cherries are the subject of conversation as we supply the words/leaves.

けふもまたさくら／＼の噂かな　一茶

kyô mo mata sakura sakura no uwasa kana　issa (-1827)

(today again/too cherry cherry's rumor/gossip/news!/?/'tis)

today, again: *sa ku ra, sa ku ra* more rumors!	today again cherry blossoms are on all of our lips

today, again
talk of the cherries
is in the air

~~~~~~

1. Filling In The Blank In my neighborhood near Tokyo, a white dogwood took the baton from the slowest branches of the slowest plum and, after its large flowers changed from bright candle flames to badminton birds and, finally, tissue-paper, the first cherry buds would open. When the dogwood was cut down to improve a garden plot and gain it a tax-exempt "green-space" designation, Keigu wrote: *"The old dogwood / now only a gap between / plum and cherry"* (梅櫻木蓮の穴うまぬ春 敬愚 *ume sakura mokuren no ana umanu haru*).

2. Blossom of Solace The Japanese is "solace-grass' blossom." I thought it derived from *tobacco*, but Sôgi predates it by a century in the East. As grass/plant (*kusa*) includes the connotation of "diversion," it might come from the joy of wandering. Or could it reflect the way a frustrated cat may take it out on plants?

Issa plays on a folk-song phrase *Sakura Sakura,* but the repetition also suggests the manner in which the condition of the cherry is on everyone's lips. I think the rumors probably concern cherries soon to bloom, so I include it with the waiting poems, of which it is by far the best. *Why* is it best? Because it is light on the ear and cool. I mean, really, do men await the bloom of a tree with bated breath as most of the other olde haiku might have us believe? Issa conveys the interest in a believable manner.

風ふかぬ世になまたれそ春の花　宗祇
kaze fukanu yo ni na matare so haru no hana　sôgi (-1502)
(wind blows-not world-in don't-wait! spring blossoms)

don't you wait for a world without wind spring flowers	please don't wait for a world without wind blossom of spring

More wind in Book III. I think Sôgi has the cherry in mind because it blooms so late that delay would take it into the calendrical summer, but a general reading, an aphorism about blossoms is possible.

花さきし（て）のち（こそ）は人こそまたれけれ　素阿
hana sakishi nochi wa hito koso matarekere(ri?)　soa (1356) つくは
(blossom bloomed after-as-for, people especially waiting-kept [+emph?])

waiting for friends the cherry blooms then it is humans that we must wait for!	**now, who's waiting!** the cherries bloom then it's the people who keep *them* waiting

after the cherry
blooms is when the real
waiting begins

There may be a problem with the transcription, but the gist of the *ku* is unmistakeable. I cannot say whether all three of my readings are close enough to be translations rather than paraverses.

たのまれてさくら見に行男かな　蕪村
tanomarete sakura mi ni yuku otoko kana　buson (-1783)
(requested, cherry look-at-for goes/going man!/?/'tis)

asked to check the cherries, off he goes a good man!	a man's duty asked to check cherries i am off!

That is to say, to check the extent of the bloom for the others. This *ku* is a simple reality check.

長じけや地神花待つ大あくび　言水 江戸ヘンケイ
nagajike ya jigami hana matsu ôakubi　gonsui (1646-1719)
([a]long-rain!/: earth-god blossoms [obj.]waiting[for] big-yawn)

a long rain-spell the earthgod yawns while waiting for blossoms	a rainy spell our homegod yawns awaiting the bloom

English's failure to keep basic words such as that for a tutelary deity or a spell of rain (as opposed to a dry-spell) from marginalized and lost when the ruling class came to favor the polysyllabic vocabulary of the Romance languages sometimes makes me wish I spoke German instead. A *jigami* is 1) the god of the element earth, 2) the god who is associated with the North-western corner of a house and is feted once a year in a tiny shrine erected for the occasion which, from the above *ku,* may have been when the cherries bloomed, and 3) the men who beat drums in the Yoshiwara Pleasure quarters. 1) is unlikely. Chances are that 2) is allegory for 3), but who knows!

宵からも寝られぬ翌の花見哉　荻人
yoi kara mo nerarenu yoku no hanami kana   tekijin (18c)
(evening-from-even sleep-not tomorrow's blossom-viewing!/?/'tis)

<blockquote>

from evening   at dawn we're off
no sleep, tomorrow   to the blossoms! tonight
blossom-viewing   not a wink of sleep

</blockquote>

Theoretically, we are talking emotion, but we may be talking preparation of food and finery. If the former, there is a solution:

朝を見んと夜を行か花の旅寝哉　淡々
asa o min to yo o yuku ga hana no tabine kana   tantan (1673-1761)
(morning[+obj] as night go [is/the] blossoms' travel-sleep!/'tis/?)

<blockquote>

wanting to see them   a real blossom trip
in the morning, i sleep   leaving at night to see them
with the blossoms   in the morning

</blockquote>

Without the Japanese term *tabine,* literally "trip-sleep," meaning sleeping away while traveling, English cannot squeeze the entire idea into a *ku*. My first reading catches the sleep but misses the trip. My second catches the trip, but misses the sleep. The second is also better for despite the reversal of the parts of the sentence, the idea, that *this* is the real blossom-lover's way to do things, is what the article *ga* (the/is) and the *kana* (together, a rhetoric different from anything in English) drive at. And, finally, a *ku* that needs no explanation:

おくれると聞くもうれしき櫻哉　士朗　アルス
okureru to kiku mo ureshiki sakura kana   shirô (-1813)
(late-being hear-even/too delighted cherry!/'tis)

<blockquote>

also a delight
to hear they're late:
cherry blossoms

</blockquote>

2
the Tail of the Dog Cherry
犬桜
inu-zakura

風吹けば尾細うなるや犬櫻　芭蕉
kaze fukeba obosônaru ya inuzakura   bashô (1654-94)
(wind blow/n when tail[branch-ends]-thin-become/s!/?/: dog-cherry)

facing the wind
it cowers thin of tail
a dog cherry

after the gale
what a scraggly tailed
dog cherry!

when it blows
i feel weak and thin of tail
dog cherry me

The Japanese prefix "*inu*=dog~" combines aspects of our denigrating "horse~" or "crab~" (chestnut, apple) and the more neutral modifier "wild." This *sakura* or "cherry" is not a cherry proper [1] but either a "bird cherry" (*P. grayana*) or "cherry laurel" (*P. spinulosa*).[2] It has small flowers little resembling cherry, strung out on thin stems (panicles) liable to break in a strong wind. The flowers diminish in size and have shorter stems at the end. An early *waka* features what might be a one-day flower arrangement or thin tail of a poor cur of a dog-cherry "out in the country" so emaciated it draws no viewers (山かげにやせさらぼへるいぬ桜おひはなたれてひく人もなく　無名　散木寄歌集*yamakage ni yasesaraboeru inuzakura ohibana tarete hiku hito mo naku* anon.(1128). Draw (*hiku*) also suggests the leash it does not have, and the *boeru* part of *yasesara-boeru* ("wasting away of thinness") puns as "howl." Bashô's "Tail-thin-become" is idiom for fleeing with one's tail between one's legs and petering-out in a pitiful manner. His *ku* pretends to be zoomorphic by extending the metaphorical name into an allegory while remaining perfectly natural, unlike my translation. Note that it is *stereo*: the image of a maltreated dog with a piteously thin tail, hanging down between its legs [2] *and* an objective description. Young Bashô writes in the nominal Teimon style (playing with the tree for its canine name), but the caesura (*ya*) before the dog-cherry allows for the third reading, too. A generation earlier, Teitoku wrote:

1. Dog Cherry in the Dog House. Dog cherry were common in olde *ku*: "Not a county / fails to raise blossoms: / dog cherries" (花ありて犬のそだたぬ里もなし　常矩　類題 *hana arite inu no sodatanu sato mo nashi* jôku (1774)), where blossom *hana* is a homophonic pun for "nose." Because the dog cherry is not strictly speaking a *cherry* at all it is not included with the cherry blossoms today. I include it in this book to affirm my focus (intended focus, for I am easily distracted) is on olde haiku, i.e., *ku* written before they were called "haiku."
2. Dog Cherry Identification. My dictionary says it is *Prunus buergeriana*. The above are from Kuitert. Check if you wish: my interest is in the metaphorical species.
3. Pitiful Dog Tail A universal symbol, for who has not seen a dog with tail between legs? A *senryû*: "The underdog / makes a loin-cloth of his tail / and flees!" (よわい犬尾ふんどしに〆てにげ　柳多留 *yowai inu ô fundoshi ni shimetenige* Y 101-22). The equation of thin and afraid may come from the fact that ownerless "cowardly curs" tend to have thin tails. Or it could be the fact that some dogs literally "narrow" (constrict) their tail rather than fatten it by bristling Regardless, "thinness" is metaphorically associated with fear and cowardice in Japanese, whereas thickness is identified with being bold.

犬櫻風をばおどす聲も哉　重頼　犬子
inuzakura kaze o ba odosu koe mo gana　shigeyori 1633
(dog-cherry wind [emphatic] threaten/scare-off voice [desired/oh, for~])

> the dog cherry
> if its bark could only
> scare the wind!

The "bark" pun only works in English. For once, the translation clearly beats the original! If the bark was effective, watch-dog-cherries could be planted around a grove of blossoming cherry. Another early poem rhetorically questions: *"Haven't you leaves=teeth? / Bite the wind, bite it! / Dog cherry!"* (葉はないか風をかめ／＼犬桜　紹一鷹筑波 *ha wa nai ka kaze o kame kame inuzakura* shôichi (1642)). Here, the translator must put his tail between his legs, for Englishing the leaf=tooth (*ha*) homophone is hopeless. The dog-cherry, unlike the most valued types of cherry, had leaves mixed with its bloom, hence, pun provided it teeth. One haiku notes this *and* uses it to mongrelize the tree: *"Blossoms mixed / with leaves, what a mottle [=spotted/mutt] / dog cherry!"* (花に葉のまじるやぶちの犬桜　宗仁 犬子 *hana ni ha no majiru ya buchi no inuzakura* sôjin 1633). While English speakers do tend to call mutts with irregular markings "Spot," they are not equivalent, so the wit fails to translate. This allegory works:

折る人の手にくらひつけ犬櫻　無名記 嵐山集
oru hito no te ni kuraitsuke inuzakura　anon. (1651)
(break[steal]-person's hand-to bite-hold dog-cherry)

> bite the hand
> of anyone who'd break you
> dog cherry!

People broke off branches of cherry early to stick in vases which, placed in warm sunlit places could blossom before the tree itself, or to give to someone unable to attend the tree, or simply for decoration (one of which was for garlands worn on the head). We will dedicate an entire chapter to the practice, for it is interesting that the Japanese who were not so avid pickers of *ground* flowers (the bouquet being an Occidental item) broke-off blossoming limbs. A similar poem suggests that the *shin* of the culprit breaking the branch ought to be *bitten and clamped* (a smooth compound verb in the original) between the jaws of the canine plant (折人のすねにかみつけ犬櫻　無名記 犬筑波 *oru hito no sune ni kamitsuke inuzakura* anon. (c1536)). Coincidentally, the name of the poetry collection in which this last *ku* is found includes "dog."

折らは我門ではほえよ犬ざくら　宗辰
oraba waga kado de wa hoeyo inuzakura!　sôshin (1651)
(broken[to steal]-if, my gate-at bark/howl, dog-cherry!)

bloom guard

> if someone rips
> a branch off, bark
> my dog-cherry!

my gate tree

> if a branch
> is broken, howl
> dog cherry!

I assume the tree is asked to help defend itself by calling out its master to save it. But – reading-two – I cannot help wondering about the off-chance the trees were planted by the gate of a garden to metaphysically defend more valuable cherry trees and their blossoms within.

2- 5~10

小便やおのが枝折の犬桜 西和 坂東太郎
shôben ya onoga shiori no inuzakura seiwa 1679
(urination! own limb-breaking=bending dog-cherry)

> call it "pissing!"
> when a dog-cherry breaks
> its own limb

"Its own" means by natural elements, as opposed to a human. In normal Japanese, one can say that a dog "*oru*" his leg when he pisses, but in English, "breaks" only makes sense as a hyperbolic metaphor. The broad connotation of *oru* – break/fold/bend – fails to translate and the poem as a poem is dead.

是をみよ人もとがめぬ犬桜 長正 続?境海草
kore o miyo hito mo togamenu inuzakura chôsei 1660? 1670?
(this[obj] look-let's, people/strangers too chastize-not dog-cherry/ies)

> what's this!
> a dog that lets me be:
> a dog-cherry

The tree does not bark at the passerby. The original is better for its brevity. "Dog" needs no repetition.

見にゆくはあぶなし山の犬桜 失名 ちり塚?
mi ni yuku wa abunashi yama no inuzakura lost name 1671?
(see-for go-as-for dangerous mountain='s dog=wolf cherry)

> ***wolf not whoof!***
>
> it's dangerous
> to go view mountain
> dog cherries

The original is witty for "mountain dog" was the taboo word (one used so as not to anger something) for *wolf*. Japanese feared wolves beyond reason, even when they were practically extinct.[1]

火ともさば狐とやいはん犬ざくら 重友 嵐山集
hi tomosaba kitsune to ya iwan inuzakura shigetomo 1651
(fire kindle-if/when fox [it is] say-let's, dog-cherry)

> kindle a fire
> and call it a fox!
> dog-cherry

The will-o'-the-wisp (*ignis fatuus*) in Japanese is always a "fox-fire." Light a fire next to a dog-cherry and it turns into a fox. The dog can also turn into a hound: *"If its bloom=nose is good / a dog-cherry may be kept / in a hunter's garden"* (はなのよくば狩人や庭の犬桜 諸重 嵐山集 *hana no yokuba kariudo ya niwa no inuzakura* moroshige 1651). Without the *blossom/nose* homophone, translation is impossible.

---

1. Dog and Wolf in Japan Issa's journal mentions several human deaths attributed to wolves and includes a particularly gory description of the clothes left behind of one victim, whose death serves to prove the Buddhist truth of here-today-gone-tomorrow. He also has *ku* about shivering at the mere name *ôkami* (wolf) or seeing scat. Scientists today believe most of these wolves were probably dogs-gone-wild.

朝鮮人来朝之春 高麗人よ覚えて帰れ犬桜 哲亜？
kôraibito yo oboete kaere inuzakura   tetsua? 1798?
(koreans, hey! remembering, return! dog-cherries)

a spring (new year) with a korean court visit

hey, koreans!
go home and remember
our dog-cherries

While Japanese men used to eat dog meat for greater stamina in the winter, it was always more common in Korea where it was also eaten for dog-day heat. I am not certain exactly what the *ku* means, but let me add that *horse*-meat eaten as *sashimi* in Japan today is called . . . *sakura-niku*, "cherry-meat" (A modern term because the bright red color of this silky meat resembles the fruit of the cherry?)!

人くひか誰も木陰に犬桜　貞徳 犬子
hitogui ka dare mo kokage ni inuzakura   teitoku 1633
(man-eating? everyone tree-shade-for/in dog=absent-cherry)

a man-eater?	a man-eater?
no one is in the shade	the shade of the dog-cherry
of the dog-cherry	is empty again

An elephant joke in my home-state of Florida: Q – *"Why do elephants paint their toe-nails orange?"* A – *"To hide in orange trees"* After disdain is expressed for so stupid a "joke," the chaser: *"Have you ever seen an elephant in an orange tree?"* This forces a groaning *"No,"* after which, *finally*, the punch-line: *"See, it must work!"* Teitoku's logic is identical. "No one is in the shade of the dog-cherry," hence they must have been eaten up. While the logic translates, much of the original wit is in the manner of its expression through a homophonic pun *dog=not there* (both *inu*). The problem with translating Teimon – Teitoku school – poems into English is that so much depends on accident and coincidence seldom found in both languages.[1] Indeed, the sweetest poem about the dog-cherry in the *Enoko-shû* (lit. "puppy-anthology") calls a dog-cherry a "puppy-(*enokoro*)-cherry" with its "bud/s= eye/s" (*me*) still unopened (めの出ぬはまだゑのころか犬桜 親重 犬子集*me no denu wa mada enokoro ka inuzakura* chikashige 1633). Without the equivalence of *bud* and *eye*, it falls flat in English.

四足の門に植ばやいぬざくら 重頼 犬子
yotsuashi no kado ni ueba ya inuzakura   shigeyori 1633
(four-legged's gate-at plant-if/hey/let's: dog-cherries)

plants that fit	***devalued blossom***
four-leg houses	if planted
the perfect place to plant	by a four-legged gate:
our dog cherries	dog cherries

---

1. Accident *vs.* Coincidence That "dog" (*inu*) sounds identical to the negative form of "to be" in Japanese is purely *accidental*. On the other hand, the fact that "leaf" and "tooth," "bud" and "eye,", and "flower" and "nose" are homophones (*ha, me* and *hana*, respectively) is, probably, *not* mere accident, so I call it a *coincidence*. I feel more regret about not being able to translate the latter, because it is significant. Is it not possible that the similarity of the parts of our faces and plants is one reason for the obvious respect with which Japanese have treated their blossoming trees? If only a very close cognitive language may – but usually won't – share an accident, coincidences such as those noted should be found in a number of unrelated tongues.

"Four-legs" was a euphemism (!) for what was close to an untouchable caste whose hereditary calling included butchering, tanning, and handling the dead. They were generally called *eta,* or "filth-many," a word which is as taboo today as "nigger" in Usania.[1]   Because, among other onerous sartorial regulations, *eta* were not permitted to wear any footwear, they were reduced to symbolic beasthood (four-leggedness) and it was enough to raise four-fingers to indicate one. Yet, Japanese society was not cast in cement: the greatest garden masters and the founder of noh were "four-legged" by birth.

家桜まぼれやそばにいぬ桜　俊屋
iezakura mabore ya soba ni inu-zakura shunya /shunoku
(house/home-cherry guard [it]!/: next-to is=dog-cherry)

dog cherry,
by our house cherry
protect it!

a home cherry,
and by its side a guard
the dog cherry

ぬる蝶の目の煩悩か犬桜　重弘　嵐山集
nuru chô no me no bonnô ka inuzakura shigehiro 1651
(sleeping butterfly's/ies' eye's/s' desires? dog-cherry/ies)

are these desires
dreamed by butterflies?
dog-cherries

The first *ku* is domestic, the second, fantastic. In the Buddhism of the Sinosphere, dangerous human desire was given the metaphysical form of "the five dogs of passion." The butterfly and blossoms are a standard pair, with the *"am-I-a-dreaming-butterfly-or-is-the-butterfly . ."* of Chuang-Tzu (4c BC), was a common allusion in Japanese poetry. Are dog-cherries only the dream of butterflies?

見る人をけつく繋くや犬桜　文性 犬子
miru hito o ketsukutsunagu ya inuzakura   bunsei 1633
(looking people[+obj] ass-bind: dog-cherry)

so they tie
the viewers to them?
dog cherries

A vulgar explanation of why these rather paltry blossoms still held viewers. *Ketsukutsunagu* means literally "ass-tie," dogs locked in coitus.

犬桜みてやおどろく猿まなこ　良徳 犬子　　　猿も木へいかでのぼらん犬ざくら　種政
inuzakura mite ya odoroku saru manako ryôtoku 1633   *saru mo ki e ika de noboran inuzakura* shusei 1651
(dog-cherry see [it]! surprized/frightened monkey's/ies' eyes)   (monkey/ies, too, tree-to how-ever climb? dog-cherry)

a dog cherry:
monkey eyes turn round
with surprize!

even monkeys
might not climb this:
a dog cherry!

In the Sinosphere, *monkey* and *dog* [2] are what *cat* and *dog* are to English speakers. While this is a purely nominal witticism, the Japanese monkey, a macaque, is one of the most apparently nervous monkeys in the world. One can imagine its excitable eyes staring at the blossoming tree.

1. No Censorship Needed I use the term *eta* rather than the modern euphemism (*burakumin,* or "hamlet-folk"), for history is history and descendents of the so-called *eta* should in no way feel demeaned for the bad name proves other Japanese behaved shamefully, not they. After all, Japanese today no longer feel the traditional occupations of the Eta are dirty, as, of course, they never were.

2. Dogs and Macaque in Japan In the Sinosphere, monkeys were symbolically identified with what we now call super-ego, horses with the ego or hard-to-control id and dogs with the more disgusting appetites we might call instinct. The horse was depicted as controllable by the monkey, while the dog was generally (there are exceptions) not. Perhaps that explains the antagonism between the two. As a matter of fact, however, it is not uncommon for monkeys to become friends with dogs in Japan. I saw a number of home-videos about macaque-dog sweet-hearts on TV shows in Japan. But, more commonly, macaque steal puppies, so dogs have a right to hate them; and dogs try to guard human produce from the macaque who have every right to hate them.

香をかけば人や逸物犬ざくら　不案 犬子
ka o kageba hito ya ichimotsu inuzakura　fuan (1633)
(scent[obj] smell-if/when human-/!/? exceptional-thing[?]trouble[?] *inu-zakura*)

~~dog cherries~~
~~if they can smell us~~
~~what are we?~~

~~sniffing is what~~
~~humans do to a fine~~
~~dog cherry~~

~~sniffing them?~~
~~do men think to mate with~~
~~bitch cherries!~~

~~anyone who~~
~~can smell them is a prize:~~
~~dog cherries~~

I have no idea how to connect the first and second half of the *ku* and have yet to find anyone confident of reading it. Maybe one of my readings=guesses works but, as you can see, I am far from confident.

Readers, what do you think? The two or three *ku* where the tree was advised to defend itself may have had some heart (*ûshin*) or sincere feeling, but it is obvious that Bashô's lead *ku* was the only one to contain an ounce of information about the actual dog-cherry. So, should we banish the nominal *ku* completely from anthologies of haiku? I prefer to include some of them, but you are free to disagree.

First, however, consider this: what if we think of the word-centered Teimon *haikai* as suggestions for adding charm to our surroundings? Is there not joy in planting a dog-cherry by the front gate as a guard and benefit to children who grow up in such a magically protected house? Will you not be more likely to notice a cat scratching a dogwood, now that you have read about the monkey/macaque and the dog-cherry?

3

Hunting the Cherry
桜狩り
kari-zakura

討物は筆はかり也櫻狩　柳几 鹿嶋立
utsu mono wa fude bakari nari sakuragari ryûki ()
(shoot/jot thing-as-for brush-only-become cherry/blossom-hunt)

cherry hunting
our only weapon
a brush

The brush, of course, is for writing haiku. The verb *utsu,* which I had to translate around, usually refers to shooting or striking with a weapon, but can be used to mean "jot down." Today it is used for typing! *Sakuragari*, or "cherry-hunt/ing," is as innocuous as "our" Easter-egg *hunt.* Because it took place way out in the woods and *also* referred to hunting parties held at this time, the parallel with hunting proper is stronger. When Issa (-1827) writes: *"Cherry hunting: / it must be against / buddha's will"* (桜狩り仏の気にはそむくべし 一茶 *sakura-gari hotoke no ki ni wa somuku beshi*), it is unclear whether he is making a nominal poke at an innocent pastime or a real one at hunting nobility.

山祭桜の神もいはふべし　一茶
yamamatsuri sakura no kami mo iwaubeshi   issa -1827
(mountain-festival/fete/service cherrr/ies' god/s, too, celebrate-should)

hunting is hunting

we should fete
the cherry's god, too
up the mountain

mountain fete

we pray to gods
for boar and deer, why not
for cherry hunts?

A "mountain-fete" is a ceremony performed for the gods of game. Issa's *ku* does not actually mention the cherry hunt, but "cherry god/s *too*" makes it clear that a contrast is implied.

櫻狩よき寺見出す都哉　蘭更
sakuragari yoki tera midasu miyako kana   rankô -1799
(cherry-hunting [?] good temple spy-out capital 'tis/!)

~~from kyôto~~
~~you spy temples good for~~
~~cherry-hunting~~

cherry-hunting
we find the good temples
that's kyôto

3- 1~4

Kyôto is surrounded by mountains, each largely occupied by temples and linked to the capital city and each other by scores of trails. Since almost any cherry spied on those mountains would be on or near the grounds of one temple or another, any "hunt" itinerary would involve temples. My second reading has the hunt uncovering the best temples which would be checked out up-close. There is soft irony here, for "hunting" is associated with temples only conversely, by virtue of its being a sin.

四方山の桜にほしや遠めがね　長頭丸　嵐山集 1651
yomoyama no sakura nioshi ya tômegane teitoku 1570-1653
(four=all-directions-mountains' cherries beautiful/scented)

      for the cherries   blossomy hills
on hills all around, i want   such beauty on all sides:
       a telescope   a telescope

The Japanese were quick to take advantage of 16c technology introduced by missionaries and traders.

歌念佛申さん嵯峨の櫻狩　不角　蘆分船
utanenbutsu môsan saga no sakuragari fukaku 1694
(song-sutras say/sing-let's: saga's cherry-hunting/partying)

  singing prayers   let's sing out
as we hunt down blossoms   our prayers in saga
  in kyôto's saga   cherry-hunting
                i'd sing out
        on a saga cherry-hunt:
               song-sutras

Saga was the Northwest quadrant of Kyôto – North, the direction of death, suitable for burial services, graveyards and the religion that served the same; West the direction of the Pureland, as Buddhist heaven was called. Many famous temples were there and the Sagadainenbutsu, one of Kyôto's three greatest Sutra-chanting events took place each year about the time the cherries bloomed. Between 1688-1736, the singing of the sutras by mendicant bonzes was in vogue. Why not, the poet muses, sing them while cherry-hunting?

花に遂て親達よはん都哉　其角　五元
hana ni togete oyatachi yoban miyako kana kikaku -1707
(blossoms-to arrived parents call! capital 'tis/!)

miyako yori oriru hito ni kototsuteshite
giving a message to someone from the capital

   said to people   ***kyôtô life***

  "tell my parents   upon reaching
we've reached the blossoms"   the blossoms you call
   that's kyôtô!   your parents

Apparently, the party reached whatever tree they have decided to stake out for a blossom-viewing and are sending back directions with a messenger, but the preface (not. From the following poem written almost a hundred years later, I like to imagine so many people out that written messages can passed hand to hand, or shouted mouth-ear-mouth-ear-mouth-ear, from mountain to city and back:

京迄は一筋道ぞ花見笠　一茶　文政五
kyô made wa hitosujimichi zo hanamigasa　issa -1827
(kyoto=capital-until one-line/stripe/way road! blossom-viewing hats)

a solid line
of blossom-viewing hats!
here to kyoto

here to kyôtô
the roads are solid
hanami hats

Imagine a bird's-eye view of lines of hats extending between the mountain tires and the capital axle. Kyôto is a special situation, but temples located as they are on wooded Japanese mountains figure heavily in blossom-viewing haiku everywhere.

花見にといはぬ人なき山路哉　宗祇
hanami ni to iwanu hito naki yamaji kana　sôgi -1502
(blossom-viewing say-not person-not mountain trail 'tis/!)

mountain trail greetings

not a soul
who doesn't say we go
blossom-viewing

everyone replies
"to a blossom-viewing"
the mountain trail

a mountain trail
everyone says the same:
"blossom-viewing!"

This is one of many Sôgi *ku* that impress me as modern – or, at least *haikai* – in its use of colloquial phrasing (the *hanami ni* with no verb is very informal). I feel the last translation is closest to the original despite the trail being on the opposite end of the poem and abandoning the double negative.

知しらす山路ハ花のゆきゝかな　宗祇
shiru shirazu yamaji wa hana no yukiki kana　sôgi -1502
(know know-not mountain-road/trail-as-for blossoms going-coming 'tis/!)

on mountain paths
known or unknown, a flow
of blossom-viewers

know it or not
mountain trails are for
blossom traffic

One respondent, not reading the *shirasu* (しらす) as *shirazu* (しらず) – that is, not filling in the little dots that can make an "s" sound a "z" sound (today, the sound is specified, but until modern times, writers let readers make the call) – imagined people meeting and exchanging information. I like that reading, for I imagine ants stopping to question one another whenever they pass, but the grammar of it escaped me.

道々や道にひろけて花櫻　無名記 うやむや
michi michi ya michi ni hirogete hanazakura　anon ( )
(road-road: road-on/by/to broadens/opens blossoming-cherry)

street after street
the bloom spills out
cherry blossoms

roam about
and all roads take you
to the bloom

walking along
the road, blossoms spilling
into the street

this way and that
broaden into the way
blooming cherries

禁札の名はかり寺の櫻哉　かしく　アルス
kinsatsu no na bakari tera no sakura kana　kashiku (18c)
(forbid-sign[regulations] name only temple's/s' cherry/ies!/?/ 'tis)

prohibition signs
ignored: cherry hunting
in temple grounds

so prohibitions
at the temple are ignored
in cherry-time?

I confess to having no idea what the first *ku* means and will let my readings be my guesses. The signs in the second probably forbid trespassing into some areas, alcohol, fire, killing things, etc.

寺々を通りぬけけり花ざかり　白雄
tera-dera o tôrinukekeri hanazakari　shirao (-1792)
(temple-demple passing-slipping-through[emphatic+finality] blossom-peak)

slipping through
one temple after another:
the bloom-peak!

bloom-peak:
slipping through temple
after temple!

Do you too recall the loves of cats, who likewise ignore religion?　Or, is it that we all love blossoms more than buddhas? Or, is it *possible* not people, but blossoms "in heat" are what slips through?

山路　道ありと下れば庭そ寺の花　淡ゝ　アルス
michi ari to orireba niwa zo tera no hana　tantan (1673-1761)
(road/path is so, descend-if garden! temple's blossoms)

mountain trails

seeing a path
we take it: a garden!
temple cherries

分け入れば人の背戸なり山櫻　希因　アルス
wakeireba hito no seto nari yamazakura　kiin (-1748)
(separate-enter [the woods] people's back-door becomes/is mountain cherry)

mountain cherries
pushing through the woods:
someone's backdoor!

parting branches
i found someone's back-door
mountain cherries

One never knows where cherry-hunting takes us. The prying apart and entering in the second *ku* is associated with travel through brush. Because Japanese clothing did not cling to the body, I imagine that squeezing through tight spots was hard. The poet was probably not *that* shocked, for most Japanese mountains where men chased cherry blossoms had more cottages than, say, caves with bears.

片陰も春は道ある櫻哉　前舟 つつきの原
katakage mo haru wa michi aru sakura kana   zenshû 1688
(half/piece-shade-even spring-road is/has cherry 'tis/!)

> the smallest shade
> has a path in springtime:
> to the cherries!

Shade means two things. First, places bathed in sunlight are thick with weeds and hard to walk through. Second, even before the stifling heat of summer cuts down on daytime travel, temperature and humidity can rise high enough that people dressed in blossom-viewing finery would have tried to keep out of the sun as much as possible as they traveled. Those who travel by foot are infinitely more aware of shade than those who travel on four legs or wheels.

よきほどに花のかげある山路かな　士朗
yoki hodo ni hana no kage aru yamaji kana   shirô -1813
(goodly amount blossom's shade/ image is/has mountain road!/'tis)

> a mountain road   a mountain road
> just the right amount of   decorated by shadows
> blossom shade   of the blossoms
>
>   just enough
>   cherry blossoms for me
>   this mountain trail

The ambiguous phonetic syllabary does not let us know whether *kage* is 陰 = "shade," or 影 = "shadow"(silhouette) or image" (the thing itself). I suspect *shade* is intended, but have myself been impressed by the dappled beauty of blossom shadow; hence, the second reading. The last reading assumes Shirô finds cherry blossoms seen in the wild, interspersed with pine and other trees, more attractive than a great number of trees gathered together for the purpose of viewing.

不許葷酒入山門・叱らるゝ所迄行け華の庭　素洗 北の山
shikararuru tokoro made ike hana no niwa   sosen (1692)
(scolded place up to go! blossom/s' garden)

after you enter the "leek and liquor forbidden" mountain gate

> keep walking
> until you get scolded!
> the cherry garden

Sake and stinky (mostly meat, but represented by "leeks") food was forbidden at many temples. The idea here would be to get as close as possible to a good cherry tree where one could still misbehave.

桜狩酒を持たねば連もなし　蝶夢
sakuragari sake o motaneba tsure mo nashi   chômu -1795
(cherry-hunt/ing *sake* bring-not-if, companion-too/also-not)

> cherry hunting   cherry-hunting
> if you don't have *sake*   i bring along no *sake*
> you go alone   and no friends

3- 16~19

The first reading is only barely possible. It would seem the poet, whose name translates as "butterfly-dream," took his cherry-hunting so seriously he insisted on doing it sober and solo?

花にゑひてしどろもどろの山路哉　立圃　空礫・花見記
hana ni yeite shidoromodoro no yamaji kana　ryûho -1669
(blossoms-to/by drunken wandering/incoherent mountain-roads!/'tis/?)

blossom-drunk:
how the mountain roads
do reel around!

do mountain trails
wind about because they're
blossom-drunk?

"Blossom-drunk" can mean either high on the scent/eros of the event or drunken while hunting and/or viewing blossoms. The poet would have liked Chesterton's *The Rolling English Road* [1] though they were made without the help of steep necessity and, perhaps, appreciated Rabelais's Island of Ode, "where the ways go up and down" (in *Pantagruel and Gargantua,* of course) because they are animal.

分入て櫻に迷ふ山路哉　魯丁（町？）翁反故
wakeirite sakura ni mayou sanji kana　rochô (-1727)
(split-entering cherry[blossoms]-among/by stray/wander mountain-road 'tis/!)

a mountain path:
through the woods, then lost
among the blossoms

after entering
the cherry blossoms, i lose it:
the mountain trail

Again, we come to the un-Englishable *wake-irite,* the parting of dense brush or tall grasses to proceed through and/or enter what lies beyond. One would normally become disoriented while doing this, not *after* coming out of the thickets. But, who is this "one" – the poet or the trail? Regardless, the poem is a hymn to the head-reeling attraction of blossoms.

coming to the cherry blossoms
the mountain trail
strays

within the cherry blossoms
the mountain trail
wanders

一人つゝ花見て来るや辷り道　成美
hitori zutsu hana mitekuru ya suberimichi　seibi -1816
(one[person] each blossom/s see-come: slippery road)

mud and flowers

one by one
coming to see the bloom
a slippery trail

the slippery trail
one by one we come
to see the bloom

---

1. <u>**Wandering Roads (a sample)**</u>

Before the Roman came to Rye or out to Severn strode,
The rolling English drunkard made the rolling English road.
A reeling road, a rolling road, that rambles round the shire,
And after him the parson ran, the sexton and the squire;
A merry road, a mazy road, and such as we did tread
The night we went to Birmingham by way of Beachy Head.

I knew no harm of Bonaparte and plenty of the Squire,
And for to fight the Frenchman I did not much desire;
But I did bash their baggonets because they came arrayed
To straighten out the crooked road an English drunkard made,
Where you and I went down the lane with ale-mugs in our hands,
The night we went to Glastonbury by way of Goodwin Sands.

Imagine a mountain trail generally broad enough for two people to walk abreast. People must go singly over slippery sections noticed like an old friend on the way back.

しなれきぬきるや遠山櫻かり　宗牧　壁草
shinareginu kiru ya tôyama sakuragari sôboku -1545)
(worn-silk/clothing wear: far-mountain cherry-hunting)

裾ぐろに山ふみ分つさくらがり　助然
susoguro ni yama fumiwakitsu sakuragari jônen c1700
(hem-soiled/black-with mountain-tread-parting cherry-hunt)

wear your rags
if you would hunt cherry
out in the hills

tramping apart
mountains with soiled hem
cherry-hunting

Cherry-blossom-viewing was a fine event. The nobility wore formal clothing and doubtless some kimono designs competed with the bloom – as our opera viewers sometimes upstaged the stage.

花なくば来る人あらし七曲　竹翁　糸巻
hana nakuba kuru hito araji nanamagari chikuô ()
(blossoms-not-if coming-people are-not seven-folds)

上へ方も道下手はなし桜狩　梅軒　蘆別舟
uekata mo michibeta wa nashi sakuragari baikan (1694)
(lords/bigshots too road-poor-as-for not cherry-hunting)

lacking blossoms
who would take this
tortuous path!

even the lords
use their own two feet
cherry hunting

Few, aside from the proverbial adepts and highwaymen, lumbermen, charcoal-makers, hunters, herbalists and others with good reason, left the well-traveled roads. Climbing for the sake of climbing, i.e. "hiking," was not found in this land where people had mixed feelings about any aimless walking.[1] A translation of the second *ku*, closer to the original syntax: *"[Among] big-shots, too / none are poor hikers / cherry-hunting"* doesn't work as well as my more creative effort. The cherry bloom or prospect of it may have inspired some sedentary men to walk, but they did not *always* walk:

花見駕籠がくて重衡桜狩　友清　太夫櫻
hanamikago gakute shôtotsu sakuragari yûsei 1680
(blossom-viewing sedans suchly? collide cherry-hunt/ing)

collisions of
blossom-viewing sedans:
cherry hunting

Most men of means rode in a sedan, a box-like compartment carried by two men. These carriers prided themselves at maintaining a quick trot for miles. They must have competed to get their charges to the best cherry bloom. I imagine sharp turns on mountain paths as the location for most mishaps.

一はなをかけよ山路の桜狩　重頼　犬子
ichihana o kake yo yamaji no sakuragari shigeyori 1633
(one/first blossom[obj] bet[?]/run-let's! mountain-road cherry-hunting)

who will bag
the first mountain bloom!
cherry-hunting

let us bet on
who bags the very first
mountain cherry

"One-ridge-run/race" means *to compete to get somewhere or something first.* That fails in English, so I play with the "hunting" aspect. At any rate, with this attitude, accidents are to be expected!

1. Hiking History   The Japanese poet toured the country functioning as a newsmonger, pilgrims went from shrine to shrine and also took in famous natural scenes, but the idea of walking *for exercise or just for the sake of walking* was not much seen in Japan until the late 19c. In the 16c Frois wrote: "We hold walking to be great fun, healthy and refreshing; Japanese have no use for it whatsoever, are puzzled by our doing so, and think we do it for some business or penance." More details (pages of it) in TOPSY-TURVY 1585 # 1-27+).

~~~~~~

さくらがり夜鷹の口をのがれたり 行露 蕉尾琴
sakuragari yodaka no kuchi o nogaretari   gyôro (1701)
(cherry-hunting, night-hawks[streetwalkers]' mouth[obj] escapes/ing)

the cherry hunt
escaping the talons
of night-hawks

This poem is by an honest-to-goodness *daimyô*, a Lord, governor of a fief who invited Kikaku (the fun-loving bonze-poet who was and was not a student of Bashô – he really was his own man) and some of his students/friends to a blossom-viewing poem-fest. A daimyô, unless *incognito*, was unlikely to be approached by a "night-hawk," a sorry-looking prostitute who chose to show herself at hours when she could catch drunken men. Since a daimyô engaged in real cherry hunts, hawking at the time the cherry was in bloom, the *ku* is probably a chuckle at the dangers faced by the only hunting commoners knew. And, as Japanese annotators write, either Kikaku and gang described the far side of the tracks to the Lord, or he knew it and is indirectly boasting *See! I know the low life, too! I am cool.* (参考 『其角と芭蕉と』今泉準一).Unfortunately, *in English*, a hawk cannot have a mouth and a woman cannot have a beak, so I switched to talons, wrong because night-hawks caught men with their tongues but right for adding a touch of danger to the cherry hunt, the point of the original.

うか／\と麦ふみ崩す桜がり　紫道
ukauka to mugi fumikuzusu sakuragari shidô (17c)
(carelessly wheat treading-crumbling cherry-hunting)

wheat trampled
by our carelessness
cherry-hunting

立どまり花見や過の畠づら　卓袋
tachidomari hanami ya sugi no hatakezura takutai (17c)
(stand-stopped blossom-viewing[emph] past's field-face)

stopped in his tracks
after the blossom-viewing:
the field's face

Wheat (mostly buckwheat) was grown in the winter, unlike rice which was soon to be planted. I think the second *ku* describes a farmer shocked at the damage to his field/plot/farm.

麓にやすらひて・足よりも目こそ先行け花のもと　立圃 空礫
fumoto ni yasuraite// ashi yori mo me koso saki yuke hana no moto   ryûho (-1669)
(foot[of mountain]-on resting[peacefully]// legs-rather-than eyes ahead go! blossom's base/place)

resting in the foothills

legs stay here!
eyes, you go on ahead
to the cherries!

This poet was surely poor (he couldn't afford to be carried by man or horse) and possibly weak, old and/or sick. "Cherries," of course, means cherry trees in bloom. The orignal says *blossoms*.

3- 29~32

弓ならぬ春や駒さへ櫻狩　宗長 大発句帳
yumi naranu haru ya koma sae sakuragari　sôchô (-1532)
(bow beome-not spring:/!/? pony even cherry-hunting)

昔哉らん都老馬引寄て櫻狩　元重 太夫櫻
mukashi yaran oiba hikiyote sakuragari　genchô (-1680)
(old-times![+?] old horse pull together cherry-hunting)

       bowless spring
when even hunting ponies
         hunt cherries

       like olden time
old ponies pull abreast
     cherry-hunting

The *koma* in the first *ku* means a frisky young horse, used for hunting, war and other manly activities. As Japanese horses for riding were small, they are usually Englished as *ponies*. Imagine a party of old men on old horses, which they once rode after real game, at the start of a cherry hunt. Another pony *ku* by the well-known Rankô (-1799): *"A court woman / on horseback arrives late / cherry hunting"* (馬にのる命婦遅れて桜狩　蘭更 *uma ni noru meifu okurete sakuragari*). Could we say she missed the kill?

似あはしや豆の粉めしにさくら狩　芭蕉
niawashi ya mamenokomeshi ni sakuragari　bashô (-1694)
(suitable tis bean-powder-rice-with/to cherry-hunting)

and keep your powder dry

bean-flour rice
the perfect food for
cherry hunting

The "bean flour" is *kinako,* roasted soybean flour with a slightly malty taste. Balls of rice (common picnic fare) may be dusted with it and some salty or sweet condiment. While rice is, by definition, fine food, this is a rustic way to eat it – compared to the fancy box lunches of the wealthy – suitable to the country Bashô was visiting and the sandy gold color of the flour would look good with pinkish petals.

三味線や茶握て借行く桜狩　如行 小弓俳諧集
shamisen ya chaya de kariyuku sakuragari　jokô (1699)
(samisen: tea-house-at borrowing-go cherry-hunting)

     at a tea shop
i borrow a *shamisen*
    cherry-hunting

    with a shamisen
borrowed from a tea-shop
    cherry-hunting

Reading about someone borrowing a musical instrument hundreds of years ago is strangely appealing. The shamisen (a three-string banjo) makes it clear that the hunting can include the party/picnic part.

うつくしきつれほしう思ふ桜狩　狐桐 新選
utsukushiki tsure hoshu omou sakuragari　kotô 1773
(beautiful companion desire think cherry-hunt/ing)

how i'd like
a beautiful companion!
cherry hunting

Is this beauty a *wakashu,* a pretty teenage boy (see Book III)? Men in Japan might have been embarrassed to be seen walking with a woman. This did not reflect their low status. It was Europe (or much of it) where women needed their husband's permission to go out and male accompaniment for protection. In Japan, they were free to come and go as they wished. (See *Topsy-turvy 1585* contrasts 2-34 & 2-35.) "We" did not catch up to Japanese until the 19c. Be that as it may, it was still safest to have company when traveling, for even if Japan was safer than Europe, robbery, rape and kidnapping was not unheard of. The closest thing to a feminist *haijin,* Rinjo (1673-1757), came up with a way to be independent yet seem protected: *"With the man / in front as my husband / blossom-viewing"* (先にゆく人を亭主にはな見哉　りん女 *saki ni yuku hito o teishu ni hanami kana*). But, if women were not seen as the ideal companion by men, they were still *desired.* One *ku* was crude enough to say so: *"I've got　/ two minds: girl hunting / cherry hunting"* or *"Sure, i'll hunt / cherries! in the neighborhood / of my girlfriend"* (気は二ついづれ妹がり櫻狩　扇角 蘆分船 *ki wa futatsu izure imogari sakuragari* senkaku 1694). The puns on *ki,* meaning "tree" or "feelings" and "-*gari,*" meaning both "hunting" and "neighborhood" (of a girlfriend), cannot be duplicated in English.

夜嵐や太閤様の櫻狩　その（女）其袋
yoarashi ya taikôsama[1] *no sakuragari*　sonojo -1723
(night-storm: father-of-imperial-advisor's cherry-hunting)

a gale tonight
the old king is about
cherry-hunting

Sonojo imagines the ghost of Toyotomi Hideyoshi (-1598), the man who unified Japan and tried to conquer Korea and China. Beloved for being a commoner by birth, he (mis)behaved like a typical *nouveau riche* hosting enormous tea parties and cherry-blossom-viewings. Sonojo's poem alludes to his *waka "I can bear / all my years and months / on Mount Yoshino, / gazing upon the cherries / in full bloom today!"* (とし月をこころにかけてよし野山　はなのさかりをけふみつるかな　秀吉*toshi zuki o kokoro ni kakete yoshino yama hana no sakari o kyô mitsuru kana*). Like most dictators, Hideyoshi took what he coveted. He found pretext to kill men who opposed his access to their wives or daughters. Hence, Sonojo's poem may be allegorical. It makes me wonder if Bashô's death poem,[2] where he says his dreams roam the withered moor, was meant to challenge the blossom-infatuated.

花鳥も色なるかなや櫻狩　宗砌
hana tori mo iro naru kana ya sakuragari　sôzei (-1455)
(flowers-birds[=poetry]-too, color=eros become!/'tis/: cherry-hunting)

even the life   so there is passion
of a poet can be erotic   in the way of the aesthete!
cherry-hunting   blossom hunting

The original says that "even flowers and birds are/become color." Flowers and birds mean the life, or world of poetry and "color" means beauty, eros and passion.

~~~~~~

↑**1. Taikô** The Shogun (warlord) Hideyoshi conquered other warlords and ruled Japan as the *taikun,* or "big-prince," while the Emperor remained (?) titular head of state. Old Hideyoshi handed over the reins to one of his sons, but his remaining rival, Tokugawa Ieyasu beat the son and made a dynasty of Japan. The Jesuits first called Japan's regional leaders "kings," which, in a sense they were, but, after the country was unified for good by Tokugawa, called the others daimyô (big-names). The Japanese, themselves, only use the word "king" (ô) for old rulers and foreign rulers. Years after Sonojo's *ku:* a possible mimic: *"Whose soul / plays among the blossoms / of the night?* anon. (たが魂のあそぶか夜の花の中＝俳諧袋 *taga tama no asobu ka yoru no hana no naka* anon (1801))

2. Bashô's Death Poem. The *ku* in question was the last the ailing Bashô composed, but some think it was not, strictly speaking, a death poem, even taking umbrage at its not reflecting the equanimity toward death a man as wise as Bashô should have. I follow convention here.

さくら狩美人の腹や減却す 蕪村
老社之句　一片花飛減却春　*sakuragari bijin no hara ya genkyaku su*　buson (-1783)
(one-petal-flower-fly-reduce/dissappear-spring // cherry-hunting beauty's belly: reduce/hunger-does)

spring wastes away one petal at a time -- rôsha

    cherry hunting　　　　　　　　　　　　　cherry hunting
the belly of a beauty　　　　　　　　　　a beauty's navel nears
    grows thinner　　　　　　　　　　　　　　her backbone

Buson plays with a line from a Chinese poem. In Japanese, to be hungry is to have one's belly "reduce." Spring is personified by a Goddess and a beauty allegorized as a flower. The *ku,* as is, bores in English, so I introduced humorous idiom in the second reading.

分登る雲の峯あり桜狩　和長　月影塚
wakenoboru kumo no mine ari sakuragari　kazunaga? ()
(parting-climb cloud-peak/s are cherry-hunting)

and there are
cloud banks we part to climb
cherry hunting

The old blossom-as-cloud, real clouds or both? "Cloud *peaks*" is the Japanese equivalent of the English idiom "cloud *banks.*" The latter expression strays from the original heights, but improves the translation by being natural. The "part" is standard for walking through the woods.

峠まで道はあるなり山桜　失名失典
tôge made michi aru nari yamazakura　lost name
(peak/pass-until road is/has is/becomes mountain cherry)

it turns out
a trail reaches the pass
mountain cherry

Evidently, enough people crossing the mountain, like the poet, visited the cherry on their way up that a trail was made up to the main trail at the pass.

人の行く兎の道や山桜　樗堂
hito no yuku usagi no michi ya yamazakura　chodô (-1814)
(people's going rabbit/hare's road/path!/?/: mountain cherry)

the hare paths　　　　　　　　　　　　　　in pursuit
traveled by humans?　　　　　　　of wild cherry, men
mountain cherries　　　　　　　　　　　on hare paths!

Such natural trails are usually called *kedamonomichi,* "beast-trails." I am familiar with those made by *tanuki,* foxes that look like raccoons. Every so far they have a rest-stop, a mound where they all do their business. But to return to *our* business, the hare path *ku* is prefixed: "Asking my clod-chopping old dad where to find the cherry blossoms, his reply "I too will end up white clouds soon,"" i.e., *The closest I'll come to a blossom-viewing is as a spirit-cloud after I die,* "inspired me to write this" (土く

れうつ老父を呼かけ花は／＼と尋れは是もいさ白雲と答へけるそをかしき). I take that to mean, the poet wrote of blossom- viewing from an old-fashioned farmer's viewpoint, as opposed to the dreaminess of these:

けふは世の外に暮しつ櫻狩　宗春　三籟
kyô wa yo no hoka ni kurashitsu sakuragari sôshun 1734
(today-as-for world's outside-of living: cherry-hunting)

cherry hunting
today, we live outside
of the world

思ひつゝ夢かいたるし桜狩　宗貞　家土産
omohitsutsu yume ga itaru shi sakuragari sôtei/munesada 1682
(think/yearn/long-while(even-as) reach/fulfill-even, cherry-hunting)

on cherry-hunts	when we can
a dream can come true	reach what we dream of:
while we dream	a cherry hunt

匂ひこそ花咲山の案内者　口遊　独活＝談林
nioi koso hanasakuyama no annaisha kôyû 17-18c
(smell/scent/eros especially blossom-blooming-mountain/s' guide)

cherry mountain
with blossom scent for
our baedeker

This is a real mountain, a "blossom-blooming-mountain" as opposed to the "blossom-mountain" which means a park made for blossom-viewing. I use the term "Baedeker" because a single word sharpens a metaphor where a descriptive phrase dulls it. The *guide* may suggest hunting – follow the scent to the game, but sightseeing was common in Japan.[1] Besides eyes and scent, we have word of mouth: *Those hollars / lacking liars are passed by / mountain cherry* (嘘つかぬ里も過たり山櫻　蕉（点＝ヨヨ）國　蕉庵再興 *uso tsukanu sato mo sugitari yamazakura* shôkoku (17-18c). The innocent country? If I read this right, slick local-yokels are competing to draw cherry-blossom viewers.

櫻狩やきのふの夢と二度の懸　永峰
sakuragari ya kinô no yume to nido no kake eihô ()
(cherry-hunting: yesterday's dream-with second-time run/attempt?)

cherry-hunting	cherry-hunting
i have a second go with	i end up at the same tree:
yesterday's dream	yesterday's dream

The final word *kake* has so many meanings that my readings are pure conjecture (研究家諸君、句意を！).

---

1. Sightseeing? Baedekker? I realize the concept of sight-seeing and a guidebook might *seem* out of place even as a metaphor, but Japan was actually the original home of tourism, where even fans were turned into maps and advertisements and tables evaluating the services at various inns, etc.. Kaempfer observed this in the late-17c, long before this before the life of Karl Baedeker 1801-59)! There were guidebooks particularly for the enjoyment of nature. Some with the various spots and dates to see various flowers and some specifically for the cherry blossoms. These included the dates and places to see the best of various species, including individual trees of note and had names such as *Blossom Tidings* (*kashinfû* = blossom-message-wind) and *Year of the Ram Bough Breaking News* (*hitsujidoshi hana no shiori* = ram-year blossom's bough-breaking [=news]). These examples come from the late-18 and early-19c are described in *Edo no Hanami* by Ono Sawako.

~~~~~~

翌の分に一山残す桜哉　一茶
asu no bun ni hito yama nokosu sakura kana   issa -1827
(tomorrow's portion-as one-mountain leave cherry[blossoms]'tis)

花花花花花
花 山 花

```
       for tomorrow                              cherry blossoms
    i leave one hill of                       i leave one mountain
       cherry bloom                              for tomorrow
```

Here, it would seem that Issa, rather than staking out a place under a certain cherry tree, preferred wandering about stopping to drink and poeticize with others.

見ぬものを見るより嬉しさくら花　千代 句集
minu mono o miru yori ureshi sakura hana   chiyo 1701-75
(see-not thing [obj] see-more-than, delighted cherry-blossom)

loving the hunt

```
      things unseen                            cherry blossoms!
  delight more than the seen               the unseen delights me
     cherry blossoms!                          more than the seen
```

Could this be an affirmation of the joy of womanhood, of the within, as opposed to the male without? That is unlikely. Feminism, for the most part, is a modern invention. I think Chiyo simply enjoys the hunt, itself, *the blossom imagined over the next hill*, more than the actual encounter.

気に入た桜の陰もなかりけり 一茶 文化十一
ki ni itta sakura no kage mo nakarikeri   issa (-1827)
(feeling-in-entered[to my taste] cherry's-shade-even not[emphatic])

```
              not one cherry
            had a blossom shade
               to my liking
```

Issa wrote in a short preface that he perambulated a mountain "around here," and my reading assumes he probably saw the best one early on and not finding anything better just kept walking and walking, ending up without a place suiting his taste.

(blyth trans)

```
           the cherry-blossoms
           that pleased me so much
           have vanished from the earth
```

As you can see, Blyth's take on the same poem (I do not feel so bad about decapping and centering him, for the poem on page 627 of *Haiku* vol. 2 "Spring" had the first "the" misprinted as "That.") is very different from mine. His comment, *that not a trace remained of the flowers that caught Issa's fancy*, suggests either blossoms seen on a mountain-side that had blown by the time Issa got there or the absence of a tree.

(blyth+me)

the cherry tree
i liked so much
had vanished

This is Blyth's reading, minus the overly dramatic language. Since the poem in Issa's *Journal* was not in a year when he complained of the fate of cherry trees that were dug up (ch 63), this reading did not seem very likely. After all, how often do trees to go missing? But, after reading Blyth's translation, I felt I had to search for the original context. In a collection of works by Issa and his friends, I found a *renga* sequence with the *ku*. The 7-7 link only two *ku* ahead was: *"Is this year its deadline? / the old cherry"* (*kotoshi girigiri to ya furuzakura*). So, Blyth's translation is probably the only one reflecting the intent of Issa's original *ku*, though his explanation (including Wordsworth's "Full many a flower is born to blush unseen, / And waste its sweetness on the desert air") makes me wonder if he understood it!

おちつきは魚屋まかせや櫻狩　利牛 アルス
ochitsuki wa sakanaya makase ya sakuragari　rigyû 17-18c
(relaxation-as-for, fish-store allow [let-do]:/! cherry-hunting)

for peace of mind	let the fish-shop	put your trust
you rely on the fish-shop	choose your fish and a gillie	in one who deals in fish
cherry-hunting	hunt your cherry	cherry-hunting

The second reading: If you don't want to poison yourself, leave the preparation of a blowfish to a professional; *ergo*, hire a pro (if such exists!) if you want a good tree. The first and third guess that all who deal in fish are good at getting up early. But, it may also be an allusion to cherry snapper (ch 44).

出頭？・花に行く我をわすれなこの柱　樗堂 再現
hana ni yuku ware o wasure na kono hashira　chodô (-1814)
(summons// blossom/s-to go me forget-not this pillar)

summons

my dear pillar,
do not forget i who am
off to the bloom!

Today, a summons in Japanese is what it is in English, but here I imagine a provincial or national lord's private blossom-viewing. The "pillar" is the main pillar of the house. In Japanese traditional architecture it is not in the wall but right in the middle, or front of the living room, where the poet, stationary when not traveling – both ideal melancholy behavior – spends so much time that said pillar glistens from being rubbed by his back. It may also allude to the poet's wife, for this main pillar and a supportive spouse – good wage earner or exemplary house-wife – were both called a *daikoku-bashira* (God of grain [=prosperity] pillar). The *kono* (literally "this") before the pillar is commonly used for direct address. While generally rude, here it seems familiar or endearing, hence my "dear" translation.

花咲ば坊主は民の道具かな　巴人
hana sakeba bôzu wa tami no dôgu kana   hajin (-1742)
(blossom/s bloom-when, bonzes-as-for, folk's tool 'tis/!/?)

cherries

when they bloom
monks become tools for
common folk

Four Japanese, in a round-table discussion of Hajin's *ku*, respectively read it as follows: A-san, citing a poem by Kikaku on a wild cherry bash, guessed the monks serve to keep people in line; B-san, thought it was because of the sporadic "cherry-rain," raincoats called *bôzu-gappa* (monk-cape), *bôzu* (monk) for short, were much in use at this time; C-san reasoned that people got drowsy, for this was the season when the days were rapidly lengthening and took naps using their cool barley-husk and tea-leaf stuffed *bôzu-makura* (monk-pillows), *bôzu* (monk) for short; D-san noted that when common people went blossom-viewing, the biggest inconvenience was carrying provisions, mats, sake, rain-gear, etc., so most parties turned it into a game called *bôzu-mochi* (monk-carries), where they carried not only their own but other's packs, *changing turns each time a monk passed by*. (『巴人の全句を読む』:1999) The last and, doubtless, correct reading, was by the head of the round-table, Maruyama Kazuhiko. No one noted it; but besides the obvious humor of indirectly turning monks into tools, the poem is witty for two reasons: *first*, because monks served within Lord's castles as tea-room supervisors and hosts for visiting dignitaries, but were not thought to be servants of the folk; and, *second*, because the "m" and "b" sound was once blurred – spelling mistakes similar to that made when Spanish confuse "b" and "v" are so common that we know this was the case – so the *tami* (folk) is a pun for *tabi* (travel). I am, in retrospect, grateful for Hajin's *ku* because there turned out to be a surprising lack of *ku* with detail about the trip to the blossoms. Moreover, it is a good example of the problem with thematic arrangement of *ku*. You will not find it with cherry-hunting *ku* because it lacks the *word* "hunting" (*kari*). Speaking of problems, it is not strictly correct to speak of people attending the nearest *urban* blossom-viewing ground as "cherry-hunting," though cherry-hunting can mean no more than going blossom-viewing, and I wonder if that could be one reason for the paucity of *ku* about the trip to the blossoms.[1] The return trip, as we will see, is better reported (see Bk III).

馬下りて高根のさくら見付たり　蕪村
uma orite takane no sakura mitsuketari   buson (1783)
(horse-descending/ed high-ridge's cherry/cherries see/saw)

after dismounting	dismounting i see
i catch sight of the cherry	a stand of wild cherries
blooming on high	up the mountain

This *ku* reminds me of one by Bashô where he has notices a tiny flower when he comes to a mountain path. We feel him breathing in the sweet air relaxing and regaining his senses. This is a type of enlightenment we all can share. I imagine Buson seated on an unstable platform, for most travel by horseback was not solo (read the 19c travelogues of Bird and Scidmore!), but he may have been riding. Either way, he would be concentrating on the path rather than looking up. And, for all we know, he may not even have been cherry-hunting. A Japanese annotator imagines him taking a walk to stretch his legs when he happened to spot the cherry/ies blooming on the top of a ridge. Note that such blossoms were idiomatic for unreachable lovers or unrealizable ideals, but the well-read Buson, may have had grander thoughts, for Japan itself (or part called nippon) was identified with high peaks (平家六「さしも日本（ニッホン　高根本ルビ）一州に名をあげ」。諸君、このために蕪村が、わざわざ「根」？).

1. Going Blossom-viewing Haiku Why is *returning* from cherry-blossom-viewing (*hana-gaeri* = blossom-returning) a traditional sub-theme, while *going there* is not? Perhaps, because people tend to go separately while they leave the blossoms together (both because they are gathered in a place and because they tend to leave within a shorter time period) and because people are still in their cherry-time trance when they return, but not so much when they go. Had I been aware of the gap at an early stage in my research, I might have combined *ku* on the blossom-viewing *hat* (*hanami-gasa*) put on when people leave, leaving people behind to guard the house (*hana-rusu*), and so forth, to create a *going-to* theme separate from the hunt.

~~~~~~

◎

道艸

さくら見に行道艸も桜かな　南昌　ももちどり
sakura mi ni yuku michi-gusa mo sakura kana namshô (1793)
(cherry[blossoms] see-to go/ing road-grass=diversions too cherry 'tis)

<table>
<tr><td>

fun on the way
to view the cherry blossoms
is also cherry

</td><td>

the diversions
found on the way are also it:
blossom-viewing

</td></tr>
</table>

The same *road/path-grass* cleverly expressed because the traveling-road (*yuku michi*) first means only that, the path the poet is on, *then* pivots with the grass (*kusa→gusa*) to become the idiomatic road-grass, meaning "diversions." I am happy the poet (or someone) used the grass written 艸 rather than the usual 草 which has the idea of grass above 早 or "early/fast." This 艸 character has a more leisurely feeling. Indeed, its hand-like appearance seems appropriately beckoning.

花に来てしばらく遣ふ扇かな　乙二
hana ni kite shibaraku tsukau uchiwa kana otsuni (-1823)
(blossom-to coming/came, a-while using fan 'tis/!)

reaching the blossoms
for a while we use
our fans

When speaking of *cherry-hunting*, we imagine a mountain where most trees are not cherries, for otherwise, it would not seem like much of a hunt. However, there were "hunts" of the best trees among thousands, in rural localities such as the renowned hills of Yoshino (ch 58), and I would not be surprised if some called even the competition to occupy the better trees at the major urban parks, of which Ueno is the prime example, a *hunt* (as some now call children rushing to grab thousands of plastic eggs in plain view at the park an Easter Egg *Hunt*), though *race* would be far more accurate. In such a case, a fan might not be the first thing reached for. A *senryû* provides the color: *"Being the first / to drive stakes into the place / of most bloom"* (いつちよく咲た所へ幕を打　柳多留 1-32 *icchi yoku saita tokoro e maku o utsu* yanagidaru 1765) . I follow Shirahata's commentary (『花見と桜』) about literally *staking out* the ground – much like gold prospectors, which releases a treasure trove of metaphor – though the verb *utsu*, "hit/drive" also has the more general nuance of vigorously setting about something, which means erecting, or pitching (?) the curtains (*maku*). We will return to those curtains, surely an odd concept to Occidental picnickers who only spread blankets *below,* at the end of the chapter on *Dis/Equality*. Here, suffice it to say that, instead of hanging the game on the wall, you hang about *it.*

4

First Blossoms
初花　初桜
hatsu-hana　　hatsu-zakura

日の神のうつ火こぼれて初桜　大江丸？俳諧袋
hi no kami no utsuh/bi koborete hatsuzakura ôemaru? 1801
(sun god's strike fire/spark overflowed/ing, first-cherry[blossom])

spring blossoms

sparks struck
by the sun god spilling
first-cherry

Hatsu-hana = "first-flower" and *hatsu-zakura* = "first-cherry" mean the first bud/s to blossom for all cherries that year, for a certain tree that year or of a young tree blooming for the very first time. The above *ku* is not much, but it is a *just-so story* and we can never have enough of them. The spring sun is building up heat and it is spilling over. The sun god probably refers to Amaterasu-Ômikami, a goddess. Japanese has a word for "goddess" (*megami*), but it is rarely used for anything but foreign deities. Plain old *kami* does fine for any/all fe/male god/s. If you cannot remove the male from "god," feel free to "goddess" my translation. When she was born she burnt the hell out of her mother (maybe even killed her – I wish I had a better memory!). Still, a male image is not impossible here, for the striking of sparks suggests a god of fire, who tends to be male and is also a *hi-no-kami*. Someone other than the poet could have used the character for "sun." The Fire God, identified with mountains, would be a perfect cherry blossom Prometheus.

一花や一木の中の初櫻　玄仍
hitohana ya hitoki no naka no hatsuzakura genyô/jô? -1607
(one-blossom!/: one-tree-among's first-cherry[blossom])

a single blossom
the first of the *sakura*
in a single tree

灸すへてみる山ちかし初櫻　吾仲 再現
kyû suete miru yama chikashi hatsuzakura gochû -1733
(moxa placing see mountain/s close first-cherry[blossom/s])

burning moxa					burning moxa
i see the mountain near:			the hills loom close
first-blossoms!				first cherries

Tiny mounds of grated mugwort (also *wormwood*) are burnt directly on the skin to stimulate points believed to affect other parts of the body – eg. there is a place on your arm that helps tooth-ache! – and, as an annual practice, to increase resistance. It is hot enough to scar, and hurts enough to open your pupils wide and concentrate attention. Did that help the poet notice the newly blooming cherry blossoms, which themselves might be thought of as moxa treating the mountain? Should I add that volcanic mountains were themselves occasionally haiku'ed as *moxa* for the land?

去年にことし昨日にけふや初桜　紹巴 発句帳
kozo ni kotoshi kinô ni kyo ya hatsuzakura   jôha 1523-1602
(last-year-to this-year yesterday-to today:/! first-cherry[blossoms])

B.C.A.C.
(before and after cherry)

as last year to this   as last year to this
yesterday is to today   and yesterday to today:
the first blossoms   the first blossoms

The most hyperlogical of the linkverse poets who pioneered *haikai*, Jôha, first wrote: *"The plum's last / and this year's blossom is / the first cherry"* (梅はこそことしや花のはつさくら　紹巴　同 *mume wa koso kotoshi ya hana no hatsuzakura*). But, making the plum (blossom) last year simply because a few may jump the gun, is not quite right, so he came up with the indirect metaphorical comparison you see above, a thought-tickler that expresses the idea everything is different before and after the first blossom/s, just as if a curtain were dropped between, such as that separating the years or the days. Here is a very different, even older *ku*.

初花に散るをな見せそ春の雪　心敬
hatsuhana ni chiru o na mise so haru no yuki shinkei -1475
(first blossom-to fall/scatter do-not show! spring-snow)

first blossoms   oh, spring snow,
oh, teach them not to fall,   don't show the first blossoms
spring snow!   how to fall!

This plaintive appeal using classical (Heian era) grammar was the first *first-blossom* (*hatsu-hana*) poem in Shiki's *Categorical*. A modern editor might find Shinkei's *ku* too artificial, or, worse, *affected*, to print, but doesn't a rhetorical expression of desire to keep the bloom on the tree for a while deserve to be read, if nothing else, as haiku *juvenilia*? The poem could concern plum blossoms or flowers in general, but cherry is most likely because of precedents such as *Kokinshû* poem #49:

ことしより春しりそむるさくら花ちるといふ事はならはざらなむ　つらゆき　古今集
kotoshi yori haru shirisomuru sakurabana chiru to iu koto wa narawazaranamu   kokinshû 905
(this-year-from spring know-begin cherry-blossom/s fall/scatter-called thing-as-for learn-not-would)

on seeing a cherry tree planted at a house blooming for the first time

*sweet cherry
knowing spring this year
for the first time*

*must you also learn to fall
from the other blossoms?*

Rodd and Henkenius boldly translate: *"oh young cherry tree / this year you have learned to dress / in spring's fresh array / but may you never learn to / let your soft petals scatter."* *Kokinshû* poem #92 follows up with a reversal: the tree is a bad influence to us! *"I won't plant / another cherry tree / for come spring / people will learn / all the wrong things (changing/fading/falling =aging+unfaithful behavior)!"* (*hana no ki mo ima wa horiueji haru tateba utsurou iro ni hito naraikeri*そせい法し). The second reason Shinkei's "spring snow / don't teach" poem fits the *cherry* rather than plum is that *falling/scattering* is a cherry thing. Because plum bloom coincided with the New Year, or coming of spring, it is all about blossoms *opening* and providing the first light from the dark tunnel of winter. As *Manyôshû* (8c) song # 833, put it, *"Every year / when spring doth call / just like this / let's deck out heads with plum [sprays] / and enjoy a good drink!"* (*toshi no ha ni kitaraba . .*). When plum blossoms fall, who notices? (unless they fall in a cup of *sake*.[1]) The cherry's bloom, however, represents *the body of the spring*. When its petals finish falling, this beautiful season is over. Back to *first bloom*:

きのふから草は踏れて初桜　李門 恒誠
kinô kara kusa wa fumarete hatsuzakura　rimon ()
(yesterday-from, grass-as-for trampled, first-cherry[blossom/s])

<blockquote>

from yesterday
grass is trampled down:
first blossoms!

first blossoms
yesterday marks the start
of treading grass

</blockquote>

After the initial greening of Spring, cherry-viewing put the entire nation on the road – or rather *made* the roads by tramping through hill and dale – at the same time.

初花にうかるゝ足や土ほこり　一草　皮草片／龍摺
hatsuhana ni ukaruru ashi ya tsuchibokori　issô 1732-1829?30?
(first-blossom/s-to/by floating[carried away/high] feet! dirt-dust)

<blockquote>

the feet of folk
high on the first blossoms!
a cloud of dust

</blockquote>

When grass was stamped down, dust rose up when it didn't turn to mud, but "dirt-dust?" Is it dust created in the country rather than the city? I hope trading in this "dirt" for a hyperbolic cloud was okay.

莟からまねきよせてや初櫻　りん女　再現
tsubomi kara manekiyosete ya hatsuzakura　rinjo 1673-1757
([blossom]bud-from invite/draw-gather/approach: first-cherry[blossom/s])

<blockquote>

even in bud
she draws men to her
first-blossom

drawing men
from the bud: cherry's
first blossom

</blockquote>

---

1. *Plum Blossoms in Sake* *Manyôshû* #840 describes the cool life: *"Spring willows / broken off to deck / our heads / and plum blossoms / floating in sake cups"* (*haruyanagi kazura ni orishi umenohana tare ka ukabeshi sakazuki no ue ni*). And MYS #852: *"A plum blossom / with real class told me / in a dream / that it really had to / float in my sake!"* (*ume no hana ime ni kataraku miyabitaru hana to are mou* [我思] *sake ni ukabe koso*). An accompanying explanation adds *"That is, 'don't let me fall in vain! i want to float on sake!'"* Floating plum blossoms in *sake* was a Chinese practice adopted by the *haute culture* of Japan, but there is an earlier mention of floating cherry petals in the *Nihonshiki* (720 AD vs. 759 AD for the *Manyôshû*) which will be discussed in "Boy Cherry" (ch.11)

Because the poet is a woman, I almost used a "we," but with the original not specifying the drawer or the drawn – felt that would be too much. In ancient Japan, pretty girls were courted from childhood. They might be adopted and groomed (Murasaki in the *Tale of Genji* being the best known example) or fought over (songs #1809, 4211,etc. of the *Manyôshû*) from a tender age.[1]

空にしるや初花櫻風もなし 肖柏 大発句帳
sora ni shiru ya hatsuhanazakura kaze mo nashi shôhaku -1527
(sky-in know:/!/? first-flower/ing-cherry wind even not)

the cosmic hush

first blossoms	a windless sky
you know it from	lets you know it's time
the quiet sky	first blossoms

Another *ku* puts it like this, *"First blossoms / something about them / feels secretive"* (初桜ひそかに咲ける風情哉　野菊　花桜帖 *hatsuzakura hisoka ni sakeru fujô kana* nogiku (1784)). And, then:

初花やおもひ遂たる一安堵　多代女
hatsuhana ya omoitogetaru hito anto tayojo (1775-1865)
(first blossom/s! think/long/desire-reach one-relief/comfort)

the first blossoms!
with our desire satisfied
a breath of relief

To most men, first sex is a triumph, to women, a watershed. If the poet identifies herself with the blossoms, she expresses the longing to transform and transforming know what it is to bloom. But it is more likely she writes as a protagonist or spectator whose longing to see the bloom has finally been satisfied. A minimalist translation:

first blossoms

they bloom!
longing satisfied
. . . respite

Either way, people and plant are in synch: the newly opened blossoms enjoy a spell of windless peace. Male poets don't usually express relief until the blossoms have blown and the whole delicate affair is over. When cherries are blamed for disturbing our peace of mind I can't help wondering if the poet is only thinking of plants. Japanese Buddhism didn't speak of an original sin *per se*, but it did blame women for creating life, desire and the sins arising there-of .

~~~~~~

1. **Tender Years** Grown men courting tiny girls, or their parents, was common in many societies. The *Manyôshû* poems concern a pretty 8 year-old who kills herself to prevent the magnificent warriors from fighting any more over her! The best description I know of the practice of marrying children to adults is in Sylvia Ardyn Boone: *Radiance from The Waters*, which is not about ancient Japan but about the 20c Mende of Sierra Leon. An attractive girl was a ticket up the social ladder for her parents, who were not above dressing up pretty *boys* as girls when they were very young to try to gain some patronage/presents! In Japan, nobles sometimes adopted these girls. Literature suggests that the sudden shift of affection required when a girl who had only known the life of a student and daughter came of age and had to become a wife, and her "father" insisted on being her husband though she might naturally favor young men could be shocking, yet it often worked out well.

first bloom

是迄の関所越てや初桜　紫白女
kore made no sekisho koete ya hatsuzakura　shihakujo (-1719)
(this/now-until's [border-]passes passing/ed! first-cherry/ies)

all the hurdles
so far are overcome
first blossoms

overcoming
all the hurdles so far
its first bloom

having passed
barrier after barrier
her first bloom

Is this *ku* by a woman about a year with plenty of storms and snowfall? A young cherry tree blossoming for the first time? About her having survived many difficulties to finally bloom as a poet (and enjoy a blossom-viewing)? About the difficulty of growing up female? Or all of these?

すなをなる空になりてやはつ櫻　紫白女
sunao naru sora/kû ni narite ya hatsuzakura　shihakujo (-1719)
(gentle/straightforward/honest/open-is-sky-become! first cherry/blossom)

be as simple
and open as the sky!
first blossoms

ready for cherry

be sincere
and empty of self!
first-blossoms

cherry spring

when the sky
becomes plain blue:
first blossoms

be without wile
a clear sky for today's
first blossoms

Sunao describes the mindset Japanese are supposed to hold before their superiors. It is the opposite of conniving or cynical. The original "sky/empty" is ambiguous. The latter, *kû,* is a Buddhist concept of nothingness that is beyond good and evil. My last reading assumes a *sunao* sky would be one without much action (few if any clouds, and those relatively still), for Chinese and Japanese poems about devious, conniving clouds may have been known to the poet.

初花や人看板のわたし舟　朝隻 蕉尾琴
hatsuhana ya hito kanban no watashibune　chôseki 1701
(first-blossom: person bulletin-board/advertizement's ferry-boat)

"the first-blossom!"
the ferry-boat man wears
an advertizement

For all the poetic hyperbole of cherry petals choking up streams and bothering fishermen, the ferry-boats must have made a killing at this time of the year.

あへば先ず皆いふ事や初櫻　宗因　三籟
aeba mazu mina iu koto ya hatsuzakura sôin (1604-82)
(meet-if/when first everyone says thing: first-cherry)

meeting, the thing
on the tip of every tongue
first-cherries

meeting all
men first mention
the first cherry blossoms

あはただし今日花咲くと人はいふ　成美
awatadashi kyô hana saku to hito wa iu seibi (-1816)
(busy today blossom blooms [conjunction] people-as-for say)

talk about busy
today someone had to tell me
they have bloomed

so busy today
people say our blossoms
bloom away

小僧来り上野は谷中の初桜　素堂
kozô kitari ueno wa yanaka no hatsuzakura sodô (1641-1716)
(small-bonze coming/came ueno-as-for valley-within first-cherry [bloom])

a servant boy
news of the first bloom
in ueno's dale

Little boys served as pages. As they love running about proclaiming things, the job is a natural. Here, the relatively new Ueno park (Edo=Tokyo's prime cherry-viewing ground) is played against the mountains from which such announcements traditionally – and in ballad – came, by horseback. While a deep valley would be too dark for first bloom, Ueno's Yanaka is actually the area between two wee hill-top lookouts, just deep enough to hold warmth without blocking sunlight.

一筆令啓上候と招れて　初花天狗のかいた文みせん　其角
hatsuhana tengu no kaita fumi misen kikaku (-1707)
(first-blossom tengu's written letter show!)

invited to write something proper

first blossoms?
just show me what
the tengu wrote

first blossom
show me the proof from
a tengu's pen

The *tengu* is a mountain goblin or an ascetic warrior-priest-doctor-wizard (also called a *yamabushi*) of esoteric arts. I think the *ku* says, "Wow, so early! I find it hard to believe! Give me confirmation from an insider!" The preface (which my translation fails to pin down) comes from a line in a popular play of the time: "The Tengu of Kurama (Saddlehorse) Mountain"). That would be Sojobo of what is one of the three most famous mountains boasting tengu masters of martial arts said to have trained legendary heroes. These mountains were home to the Way of Ascetic Practices (*shugendô*) and, sorry, but that is as far as my explanation will go (see William Scott Wilson: *The Demon's Sermon on the Martial Arts:* 2006). To catch the first blossoms, it helps to be proficient, too: *"Do they start! / A tengu grabs an arrow: / first sakura!"* (出立や天狗の矢取初ざくら　千川 *idetachi ya tengu no yatori hatsuzakura* chisen 17-18c). The tengu grabs them in-flight. Is the point *fast bloom?*

first bloom

沓足袋や鐙にのこる初ざくら 其角
kutsutabi ya abumi ni nokoru hatsuzakura kikaku -1707
(shoe-sock [foot-sheath?]!/: stirrups-in remaining first-cherry)

foot-sheaths
left in the stirrups
first blossom

The sole of the Japanese stirrup, like the pedal of the Japanese stilt (called a "bamboo-horse") runs parallel to the foot (front-back) rather than across it like "ours." It usually curls up in front. With full support, a solid boot with a heel is not needed and sock-like slippers called *tabi* may be worn. The *kutsu-tabi* is a low-rise variety. In the rush to get to those first cherries, the samurai has galloped up without his footman (who would carry spare straw horse-shoes and help keep track of his master's footwear). These next *ku* explain what happens when you take your good time getting there:

初ざくら田舎の人が見て仕廻ひ 大江丸 俳懺悔
hatsuzakura inaka no hito ga miteshimai ôemaru? 1790
(first-cherry: country people see [+undesired finality] [it])

the first blossoms
caught by those damn
country bumpkins

missed cherry   **a fast year**

what a shame!   only bumpkins
the first blossoms viewed   caught the cherries'
by bumpkins   first blossom

The helper-verb "finish" (*shimai*) implies something not desired but over and done that nothing can be done about. Putting it into words such as "a shame," "a waste" or "damn" makes the subjectivity – or, rather prejudice – implicit in the original too obvious, but what else can be done?

油断して二番ざくらのはなみ哉 大江丸 俳懺悔
yudanshite nibanzakura no hanami kana ôemaru? 1790
(careless being/was, second-batch/rate cherry's blossom-viewing!/'tis)

i dozed off   we blew it and must
a second-batch cherry   make do with a second-batch
blossom-viewing   blossom-viewing

The wit comes from using a term generally applied to steeping tea or producing *sake*. The second reading is rare for I used all but one of the standard (wrong) seventeen syllables.

油断して花に成りたる櫻かな 樗良
yudan shite hana ni naritaru sakura kana chora (-1781)
(careless being/was, blossom-into became/becomes cherry!/'tis)

ah, doze off   ah! the cherry
and the cherry turns   became a blossom
to a blossom   when i nodded

Gotta stick close to those cherries! Since *hatsu-zakura* (first-cherry) also meant an eighteen or nineteen year-old woman, there is an off-chance the poem allegorizes another guy getting the girl first. The wit in this *ku* comes from the strict denotation of *sakura* and *hana,* where most cherry blossom haiku used them in a loose (interchangeable) manner.

一日は主のみ見て初桜　蘭更
ichi nichi wa aruji nomi mite hatsuzakura rankô (1726-99)
(one/first day-as-for master only sees/ing first-cherry[blossom])

droit du seigneur

on day one
only its owner views
the cherry blossoms

on that day
only the master sees
her first bloom

This may be a tree in a field occupied by a noble party, or it may be a "house-cherry," (*ie-zakura*) with its samurai, merchant or poet owner. I hope the poet would have chuckled at my title, though Japanese lords did not have such a right.

よしの山たが初花のぬしならん　千代　吉野紀行
餞別・初花は誰ぬしなるぞよし野山　千代　松の声
yoshino yama ta ga hatsuhana no nushi naran chiyoni (1701-75)
[*senbetsu*] *hatsuhana wa dare nushi naru zo yoshino yama* chiyoni
(yoshino-mountain who first-blossom's/s' master/lord/owner/host become/is-will)
(first-blossom's/s' as-for, who master/lord/owner/host become/is [+emph] yoshino-mount.)

sending off someone braving the snow to view the yoshino sakura

mount yoshino
who will play host to
the first blossom?

who will own
the very first blossom?
mount yoshino

The original has an introductory comment I shortened into the caption. Because of my tendency to juggle the syntax in translation, I am delighted to find two versions of the poem with the mountain respectively fore and aft! *Nushi* can mean a master/lord/owner/host. Because of this, a *ku* such as that by Chiyo (the *ni* means "nun") can be read in many ways. Back to the world:

又人の立ふさがるや初桜　一茶
mata hito no tachifusagaru ya hatsuzakura issa
(again people stand-clog/crowd/choke! first-cherry)

again, we stand
shoulder to shoulder
first blossom

Imagine. Someone shouts: "the first blossom!" Suddenly an enormous crowd packs in under the cherry tree. "Let me see!" "Let me!" Another *ku*: *"The first blossom! / standing in place until your / hems are tread"* (初花や裾を踏迄立尽し尽くし焼台 *hatsuhana ya suso o fumu made tachitsukushi* – gyôdai (1732-93)). The title is: *"Wordless love/longing"* (*fugondekoi* 不言出恋). It is hard to imagine such a title for a flowering tree. But, with the idiomatic meaning of *hatsuzakura* meaning what it means, I blush to imagine the alternative.

first bloom

初花に誰か傘そ [+よ?] いま／＼し　長虹 あらの
hatsuhana ni dare ga kasa zo [+yo?]imaimashi chôkô (mid-17th c., met bashô)
(first-flower-to/in whose parasol/sombrero! [is] annoying/detestable/blasted)

first blossoms
who *dares* to raise
his parasol!

first blossoms
who *dares* to leave
his hat on!

I am not certain if the parasol means the person is not looking up with bated breath as he or she should, is disrespecting the bloom, physically endangering it, or a gambler (known for their flashy parasols). The second reading would not be because Japanese removed their hats to show respect because this they did not do – they removed their shoes for that – but because such hats could be deep enough to cover one's face. Were this a senryû, I might translate *"Who is the prick?"* for the *kasa* was (and still is) common parlance for the *glans* penis.

初花や覆面したる女子の眼　朱拙　今の昔
hatsu hana ya fukumen shitaru onago no me　shusetsu (1655-1733)
(first-blossom/s! mask-doing[wearing] woman-child [young-woman]'s eyes)

the first blossom
the eyes of a maiden
wearing a mask!

the first blossoms
as delicate as the eyes of
the masked maidens

At first, I had visions of something strange going on in the pleasure quarter (or *misery quarter*, from the other point of view), but, checking *fukumen* in the dictionary, discovered that Japanese used to wear masks when approaching precious religious objects lest their breath soil them! (So the practice of mask-wearing to protect others from one's cold, which is common in Japan but not in the West has old roots). The maiden is being as polite to the new blossoms in this *ku* as the jerk with the parasol in the last *ku* was not. The beauty of her eyes compliments that of the blossoms, while their partial revelation parallels that of the tree with its mostly yet-to-open buds. There is also the possibility, the maiden doesn't want to pass her *cold* (homophonic with the *wind*, rather than *chill* in Japanese) to others, including the delicate blossoms (Okay, this is tongue in cheek). While I first imagined the girl outside, I now see her *indoors* observing the first bud to open on a bough in a vase with a fever-flushed face. A century and half later there was a several decades-long fashion for demi-masks (*mekatsura* = eye-mask) worn, among other places, to blossom-viewings; but, as far as I know, that was not the practice in the 18c and witnessing the bloom of the "first-blossom" would not be the time to don it.

はえかゝる歯よ初花の笑ひ顔　素達　拍擧十句
haekakaru ha yo hatsuhana no waraigao　sotachi/sotatsu ()
(growing-in teeth! first-blossom's smiling/laughing face)

first blossoms
the cherry's face smiles
all milk-teeth!

baby's teething
her sweetly smiling face
a first-blossom

The smile/laugh is a standard feature of the spring landscape most often applied to mountains. It describes what we might call nature turning on all her charm. Somaru (1712-95) has a *ku* relating the mountain to the tree: *"The mountain's smile / sprinkled on the trees: / cherry blossoms* (山の笑ひ木に鏤てさくらかな 素丸 *yama no warai ki ni chiribamete sakura kana*). Sotachi's *ku* is more interesting if we do not read it as mere allegory but allegory+description of a baby under the blossoms. Cherry petals have a small depression that might have reminded the poet of "baby lace."

#4-32~35

咲く前に何か言いそうな桜の芽　R・ライト　敬愚訳
saku mae ni nanika ii souna sakura no me[hana-tsubomi?]　richard wright (20c)
(bloom-before something say-as-if cherry's bud)

before blossoming
a cherry bud looks eager
as if about to speak

(centering+decap. mine)

Buds as nipples are a dime a dozen; but *lips?* Richard Wright's haiku background was pure Blyth, i.e., old Japanese haiku, and his *ku* could have been written by a Japanese poet.

顔に似ぬ発句も出よ初桜　芭蕉　続猿蓑
kao ni ninu hokku mo ideyo hatsuzakura　bashô (1644-94)
(face-to match-not *hokku* [initial-*ku*] even come-out! first-cherry)

hunting for words
unlike my face, as fresh
as new blossoms

first blossoms
wishing to make a poem
unlike my face!

i'd make a poem
belie my old face!
first blossoms

i'd make a poem
unlike any i've made
first blossoms

A *hokku* was a *ku* suitable to start a series of verses and was supposed to be splendid in many ways. Bashô contrasts his wrinkled face (he seems to have looked old for his age) with the delicate new blossoms. I am reminded of the Renaissance paintings, where a *foil,* i.e. the epitome of ugliness – a black servant – was often placed near a pale beauty. *The last reading is best.*

散などと見へぬ若さや初櫻　太祇
chiru nado to mienu wakasa ya hatsuzakura　taigi 1709-72
(fall/scatter/die etcera [it] looks-not youngness! first-cherry [bloom])

such youthfulness
how could it ever die!
the first blossoms

a tree so young
how can its cherry
blossoms fall!

first cherry

so young a tree
who'd think your blossoms
will ever fall!

Bashô's last *ku* would work either for delicate new blossoms or for a cherry tree blooming for its very first time, but this one only works for the latter, so that must be our reading. Earlier, Chigetsu (-1703/6?8) wrote: *"It's blossoming! / Though only a tree / of five feet!"* (花さくや五尺にたらぬ木なれども　智月尼 *hana saku ya goshaku ni taranu ki naredomo* chigetsuni). Later, Issa wrote: *"Three feet high / yet this cherry is full / of blossoms"* (三尺に足らぬも花の桜哉　一茶 *san shaku ni taranu mo hana no sakura kana* (-1827)) or, more poetically:

first bloom

袖たけの初花ざくら咲にけり　一茶
sodetake no hatsu hanazakura sakinikeri issa (1763-1827)
(sleeve-height's first-blossom/celebratory/ornate -cherry blooms [finality])

elbow-high
cherry blooms away:
first blossoms!

The "finality" of the ~*nikeri* makes the poem. This little tree has *done* bloomed and there is no turning back. Issa did raise a cherry tree, but recalling all the space his journal gave to an 8 year-old *mother*, I can't help wondering whether the poem is *also* allegorical.

初桜八重の一重の好みなし　和久　古選・類題
hatsuzakura yae no hitoe no konomi nashi wakyû -1692
(first-cherry[blossom] eight-fold's one-fold's preference-none)

first cherry bloom	eightfold petal
who cares if its single or	or single: a first cherry
double-flowered	is a cherry!

"Eightfold," the profuse blossom we less accurately call "double-petal." In Japan, these were not highly regarded for reasons discussed in Book III. "Virginity," or rather its *floration,* was appreciated irrespective of face-value. How much so? See the next poem:

初花に命七十五年ほど　芭蕉
hatsuhana ni inochi nanajûgo nen hôdo bashô -1694
(first-[cherry]blossom-by life seventy-five year's extent/worth)

cherry value

first blossom
worth seventy-five years
to my life

Annotators dwell on the obvious, that young Bashô stretched the seventy-five *days* (until the cherry began to blossom measured from the New Year) into *years* and there is a saying "if you eat a first thing (*hatsumono*), your life will stretch seventy-five days." What they fail to mention is the vulgar idea that coitus with a virgin would gain the same, at the cost of seventy-five days of her life (*senryû* are full of this stuff!). I do not mean to imply that Bashô, who seems to have been the fuddy-duddy of all fuddyduddies actually did anything like that, but blossoms were closer to women than to food so he must have known his poem had a risqué aspect.

いくよ見ん今年植ての初桜　周桂　大発句帳
iku yo min kotoshi uete no hatsuzakura shûkei -1554
(going/coming! see! this-year planted first cherry[bloom])

(*sez the cherry*)	**(*sez me*)**
"i'm coming, see!"	i'm off to see
the first blossoms of my tree	the first flower of the tree
planted this year	planted this year

4- 41~44

"Going" (*iku*) is what a person might say when it is their turn to do something or when they "come" (orgasm). The innocent reading reminds me of Richard Wright: *"the first blossom / the little apple tree brags / look, look! me too!"* (Richard Wright: *Haiku*). It is possible I think too much. Hence, the second *sez me* reading.

常に似ぬ心みじかし初桜　橘平　月影塚
tsune ni ninu kokoro mijikashi hatsuzakura　kitsu/kichihei ()
(ordinarily match-not heart [is] short/jumpy: first-cherry[blossoms])

the cherry's first time

this jumpiness
is not normal for me
first blossom

today alone
my heart's on short tether
first blossoms

年／＼の花の罪ぞよ人の皺　一茶
toshidoshi no hana no tsumi zo yo hito no shiwa　issa -1827
(year-year's blossom's sin! [other?]people's wrinkles)

sinful blossoms!
year after year they give
men wrinkles

year after year
blossoms, damn them
give us wrinkles!

Why is Issa's poem in this chapter? First, because an annual occurrence is usually marked upon its first-instance. Second, because Bashô claimed the "first-*shigure* (cold-rain)" was what aged a man. Third, because the pre-haiku concept of *the cherry blossom as the cause of worry* suggests concern for catching the first-bloom as well as for the subsequent scattering. This worried conceit achieves comical heights in *waka* suggesting that life might be better were cherry trees to stop blooming altogether (We will see more on this later. I think half the worrying is metaphor for male concern for "their" females and the other half about the difficulty of coordinating successful cherry viewings and doubt if much if any was for the blossoms, themselves.) By using the word "sin" (*tsumi*), Issa brings out the woman=blossom idea because Buddhism tended to blame them for sin=desire.

七夕に契りおきてし初ざくら　鬼貫　俳諧七車
tanabata ni chigiri okiteshi hatsuzakura　onitsura 1660-1738
(seventh-evening [star lovers festival]-on troth/mate first-[cherry]blossom/s)

星合の子？

the loving stars
mated on the seventh eve
first-blossoms

first blossoms
the children of the stars?
count the months

first blossoms
as fresh as the annual
trysts of the stars

My first translation was "The Stars met / vows were exchanged / first blossoms." Blossoms bloom but once per year and in this resemble the Star lovers, hence my last reading which was really my second. Then I thought, "vows" (*chigiri*) smows! They are *screwing*. Do cherry blossom buds, then, start to form in early fall when the Herder and Weaver cross the Milky Way for their annual tryst? The blossoms are a bit premature by human standards, but do you have a better reading?

first bloom

しのび路に似たあしあとや初さくら　千代
shinobiji ni nita ashiato ya hatsuzakura　chiyo-ni (1701-75)
(sneak-path[of lovers]-to resembling footprints: first cherry [blossom])

clandestine cherry?

foot-prints
like on a lover's path
first-blossom

first blossoms
foot-prints like those
on a lover's path

This *ku*, for reasons beyond me, ended up in the "delete" list of this first lady of haiku, but I like it. Men in Japan had to sneak to their lover by moonlight and sneak out of her home and neighborhood before it was light enough to be recognized. Chiyo-ni went early to see the blossoms but someone else was up even earlier, and his foot-prints reminded her of a lover's.

何ひとつへだてぬ枝やはつざくら　素檗
nani hitotsu hedatenu eda ya hatsuzakura　sobaku -1821
(even-one separate-not branch! first-cherry [blossom])

private-viewing

not one thing
between the limb and me
first blossom

Issa's contemporary (then, better known than he was) has a ring-side seat to what seems to be a cross between a natural phenomenon and a strip-tease! Perhaps the idea is simply that it is a young tree which is not high so that all the tree can be gazed at from up close. But I get the feeling the poet wishes to titillate the reader, so I have obliged with the title and translation.

咲乱す（最中の）桃の中より初櫻　芭蕉
sakimidasu (saichû-no) momo no naka yori hatsuzakura　bashô -1694
(bloom-disarrayed (or, acme [of the bloom]) peaches-among-from first-cherry)

among peaches
in full bloom, the first
cherry blossoms

the first cherry
right in the middle of
the peach rut!

A contrast of peach blossom pink and cherry white writes one commentator. I see an observation on the progression of blossoms – first-cherry in mid-peach – and the idea of this beloved object of "viewing" framed by its strangely ignored relative.[1] The peach *momo* is also a homophone for "thigh" and for a "multitude". The latter homophone seems to work well here: lots of peaches, just one cherry.

薄色の花にこかるゝ心かな　了毛
usuiro no hana ni kogaruru kokoro kana　ryômô ()
(pale colored blossom/s by [is] scorched heart!/ 'tis)

rare attraction

it's the pale
blossoms that scorch
our hearts

4- 49~52

↑ **1. Ignored Peach Blossoms** Though the stereotypical worthlessness of the peach blossoms has been belied time and time again, they have been ignored by most poets. Sei Shonagon has good words for them in her *PillowBook*.

This haiku, or senryû – I lost my source – reveals one reason the cherry blossom was loved more than the peach. The delicacy of its color was found attractive. These aesthetics are related to the attraction of white skin, and the fact that the flower parts of women tend to darken with age. (Of course, the same could be said for men, but for men in Japan dark parts were, and still are, associated with virility.)[1]

青樓に遊ひて・きのふ見しあれか禿か初桜　蓼太 三傑
kinô mishi are ga kamuro ka hatsuzakura   ryôta (1707-87)
(yesterday saw that [thing], [a] *kamuro*? first-cherry)

playing in the blue tower

then, was that cherry
i saw yesterday a *kamuro*?
the first blossoming

I had to look up "blue tower." What fun! Among other things, it is a well-curb style turret (imagine pound-signs that are not italic piled up floor after floor) constructed to spy on the enemy *and* a brothel. The *kamuro* was a girl attending and apprenticing to be a courtesan. The "first-cherry" was argot for the first time a courtesan slept with a man. Ryôta's *ku* is good compared to such as: "Now a flower / until *yes*terday but / a bud-viewing" (けふは花さくじつ迄はつぼみ哉　成安　再現 *kyô wa hana sakujitsu made wa tsubomi kana*   seian (-1664)). ("Yesterday" (*sakujitsu*) has the verb for "blossom" (*saku*) in it, the "viewing" is my improvement). Or, *"First cherry / a treat not granted / to many"* (初桜あまたにやらぬ色香哉　昌休 *hatsuzakura amata ni yaranu iro ka kana*   shôkyû (-1552)), where the "treat" is "color-scent" (*iro-ka*), an erotic term. This is a bit better: *"Your happiness / is that, too, a surprise, / first cherry?"* (うれしさも驚くものか初桜　心祇　句鑑 *ureshisa mo odoroku mono ka hatsuzakura*   shingi (fl.1760)). We will have three whole chapters about cherry and women in Book III!

我庭や木ふり見直す初桜　沾荷　続猿蓑
waga niwa ya kiburi minaosu hatsuzakura   senka (1698)
(my garden! tree-shape/appearance take-a-second-look: first cherry)

young cherry limbs	*coming of age*
suddenly the tree in my garden looks better first blossoms	at first bloom the cherry in my garden seems another tree

The poet is not so much saying the tree looks great in bloom as the bloom makes him look at the form of the tree he had taken for granted. Terms such as *eda-buri* and *ki-buri,* respectively, "limb-shape" and "tree-shape" do not exist in the West with our purely human aesthetics. Think of a father looking with fresh eyes at his daughter (*Uh-oh, she might attract men!*) after she has her first period or her first night-crawler (as boyfriends were called). Both might be called "first flower" (*hatsuhana*) in Japanese. Such thought enhances the *ku* which really is about a tree; we feel the poet's attentiveness.

1. *Flower Colors!?* The Japanese have long (at least in the Edo era (17-mid-19c)) graded the primary sexual organs by shape and color. The significance of the color of the *nipples* is also commonplace. Soap-opera mothers in Japan discover their daughters are pregnant by spying their darkened nipples in the bath.

first bloom

雨風のあらきひまより初桜　樗良 花七日
ame kaze no araki hima yori hatsuzakura　chora (-1781)
(rain-wind's rough idleness/play-from, [=spring's]first cherry[blossom])

room to blossom

within a space contested by rain and wind the first cherry	the first cherry in a gap between violent rain and wind

Imagine the buds timidly testing the elements, hoping for enough play to pop out. The untranslatable "rough space/time/idleness/play" is a great description of the weather that makes both blooming and viewing a challenge. The *hatsu,* or "first" suggests the homophone meaning "launch" or "explode" in the original

初花は散らで匂へる嵐哉　元就　春霞
hatsuhana wa chira de nioeru arashi kana　genshû ()
(first blossom/s-as-for scatter-not-by/with/so smell/glow[with beauty] storm!/'tis)

first blossoms on the tree, beautiful during the storm	first blossoms stay on the tree, what beauty in a storm!	first blossoms not scattering, glow through the gale

This a fine observation enlivened by being contrary to the classic stereotype. Storms were hated for knocking blossoms off trees and ruining the whole affair, but buds just beginning to blossom usually could hang on. The original suggests the storm spreads, or absorbs, the blossom's eros, represented by the verb *nioeru* which means to smell fragrant and glow with beauty and splendor.

残なく一木に咲ぬはつざくら　素檗
nokorinaku hitoki ni sakinu hatsuzakura　sobaku (-1821)
(remnant-not, one-tree[=period]-in/as bloom first-cherry[blossom])

they all bloom as a single cherry tree first blossoms	cherry blooms my tree is solid blossom its first time!

At first, I thought my first reading was correct because it utilizes the homophone of "one-tree" as "one-period" (*hitoki*) better than the second; but on second thought, there is no emotion, that is, *meaning*, in it. Reading over, I had to go with the second, because Sobaku could have been honestly impressed with a tiny tree covered with blossoms.

あすはたゝ花の木となる初桜　樗堂
asu wa tata hana no ki to naru hatsuzakura　chodô (-1814)
(tomorrow-as-for just blossom's/s' tree becomes first-cherry/ies [bloom])

by tomorrow
just another blooming tree
the first blossom

This is the only poem I know where a beautiful blooming cherry tree is "just another." It is a clever way to play up the first blossoms. His next poem is even more outrageous:

初桜花の世の中よかれけり　楞堂
hatsuzakura hana no yononaka yogarikeri　chodô (-1814)
(first-cherry/ies[blossom] flowery[haute culture?]-world love-cries[+emph.])

orgasmic spring

cherry blossoms:
the whole blooming world
makes a love-cry

cherry blossoms:
the whole blooming world
moans with joy

Even Shakespeare failed to provide English with a proper word for the exciting cries peculiar to love-making. We must make do with general words like *pant, groan, moan, cry* and *yelp*. Japanese has such a verb: *yogaru*. Maybe I exaggerate a little. Call it a word for *cries of delight*.

おぼつかな花は心の春にのみいづれの年かうかれ初めけん　西行
obotsukana hana wa kokoro no haru ni nomi izure no toshi ka ukare someken　saigyô (-1190)

fuzzy recollection

loving blossoms
takes a spring mind
but who recalls

their age when first
swept off their feet?

our true love
for flowers flows from
a spring heart:

how old was i when
i first fell for them?

何歳から花に泣かせた花見哉　西愚
nani sai kara hana ni nakaseta hanami kana　saigyô+keigu
(what year-from blossoms-by cry-made, blossom-viewing 'tis/?)

bloomshade reflection

from what age
did blossoms give me
moist eyes

Saigyô's *waka* concerns yet another type of first-blossom, our first experience of cherry blossoms as an adult. True, a child enjoys flowers in a purely sensual way as much or more than an adult. But only the adult experiences the insanity expressed by the verb *ukare* (floating), idiomatic for a love-crazed person or a cat in heat (see *hana-zakari*, ch.10). Only the adult – granted, with some help from alcohol – is moved to tears. (If you are an adult and have never been moved to tears by natural beauty, try exchanging your evening or night-time drink for one in the daylight, sitting in the bloomshade.) The fuzzy recollection suggested by *obotsukanai* is a well known Saigyôism. It is appropriate for Spring with its haze, the hazy moon and sleepiness due to the shortening nights.

初花の散る時人に見られける　道彦　アルス
hatsuhana no chiru toki hito ni mirarekeru(?)　michihiko -1815
(first-blossom's falling/scattering people/others-by seen [+finality])

these first blossoms
when they scatter others
will be watching

first blossoms
are always seen when
they are blown

It is a fact, more people are around to see the blossoms fall than to see them open, not only because one has clear visual warning, but because it is more interesting to watch. Yet note, the subject of the poem *is* those first blossoms, not their falling. The original, as is often the case, permits either a particularistic or a general reading. I thought the "~ru" *must* be a mistake for *ri,* but my respondent . . .

開帳の日も早めけりはつ櫻　也有
kaichô no hi mo hayamekeri hatsuzakura　yayû 1701-83
(open-ledger[opening Buddhist temples] day, too, sped-up: first-cherry)

the shill

the opening
is moved up, too,
first cherry!

A good *ku*. The cherry's bloom might not determine the calendar, but it does determine some dates. Both temples and gambling outfits – *kaichô* is idiomatic for starting a gambling operation – took advantage of the cherry-blossoms' *draw* (indeed, today, a *sakura* is fake customer who draws others) with the former setting up under trees and the latter, as we shall examine later, opening the temple treasures to view (unlike a Christian church, Buddhist temples usually hide their interiors) and, of course, the collection box for donations. The *ku* may refer to either or both, but the gentlemanly character of Yayû and the implication that a date is set favors a temple, or temples over gamblers.

だまされて来て誠なり初櫻　千代女
damasarete kite makoto nari hatsuzakura　chiyojo 1701-75
(fooled/tricked/taken-advantage-of came, genuine [it] was: first-cherry [blossom])

fooled, i came　　　　　　　　　　　　　　　fooled, i went
and found it was true　　　　　　　　　　and then it came true
the first-blossoms　　　　　　　　　　　　first *sakura*

Did Chiyo-ni see moon-light or snow on cherry trees in the distance and *think* they were in bloom, which they were not, but, after making the trip and looking closely discover the first blossoms? Chiyo-ni had to know the *ku* would cause some men to chuckle as it seems like it might allude to her first experience, but she was strongly drawn to the theme of first cherry blossoms and may well be the most prolific *hatsu-zakura* poet. The pre-war Kaizôsha* *saijiki* carries 7 of her first-cherry poems beginning with the above. Three male poets (Bashô, Kikaku and Baishitsu) share second place, with 3 each. (* This *saijiki* is remarkable for picking up *ku* by poets who exhaust themes. It is the only *saijiki* I know which does justice to Chiyo on first-cherry and Issa's numerous *ku* about dew, etc..)

見る人も鹿（マが上に）相ななりやはつざくら 千代女
miru hito mo sosôna nari ya hatsuzakura　chiyojo 1701-75
(viewing people, too, audacious /lusty-appearance: first-cherry [blossom])

the people look　　　　　　the onlookers　　　　　　why flushed faces
bold as the first blossoms　as careless as the first　on we who witness
that they watch　　　　　　cherry blossoms　　　　　the first blossoms?

Only an extremely attentive reader of all of Chiyo's work would have any chance of guessing what exactly she means by *sosô na*. Continuing in the order in the Kaizôsha *saijiki*:

明ぬれどいよ／＼白しはつざくら　千代女
akenuredo iyoiyo shiroshi hatsuzakura　chiyojo 1701-75
(dawns/brightens but/and ever white first-cherry[blossom])

the dawn comes
but it grows whiter yet
first blossoms!

I imagine blossoms on many trees opening overnight. Chiyo's logic is lost in translation ; English lacks the concept of dawning as *whitening* and do not know most cherry blossoms lighten as they open.

見て戻る人には逢ず初櫻　千代女
mitemodoru hito ni wa awazu hatsuzakura　chiyojo
(seen-return, person/human-to-as-for meet-not first-cherry[blossom])

back home	i met no one	first blossoms
after meeting no man	who saw the first blossoms	i return home without
first blossoms	coming back	meeting a soul

Heading out at the crack of dawn to see the first cherry, seeing no one and returning is enough. But, the use of *hito-ni-wa* (person-to-as-for) rather than a simpler *dare-ni-mo* (not anyone) adds mystery. What, then, *did* she see: dogs? cats? birds? The middle reading, where "return" (*modoru*) modifies whoever sees the first blossoms seems less likely to me but more likely to my Japanese respondent.

唯かへる（只戻る）心で出た（来た）にはつざくら　千代女
tada kaeru [tada-modoru] kokoro de deta (kita) ni hatsuzakura　chiyojo
(just return [false-return] heart-from went-out-though, first-cherry[blossom])

expecting to	first blossoms
return empty-handed	here i thought i would
first blossoms!	find nothing!

Going out without great expectations itself seems odd, but we do have a happy ending.

けふ来ずば人のあとにか初ざくら　千代女
kyô kozuba hito no ato ni ka hatsuzakura　chiyojo
(today came-not [other] people's after? first-cherry [blossom])

if i skip today	first blossoms:	if i don't go
will mine be second hand?	not going today, I wonder	until tomorrow will mine be
first blossoms	about tomorrow	first blossoms?

あしあとは男なりけりはつ櫻　千代女
ashiato wa otoko narikeri hatsuzakura　chiyojo 1701-75
(footprints-as-for man [male] are/were[emphat.] first cherry[blossom])

up and adam

the footprints
are those of a man
first-blossoms

This is not the generic man, but the male. It is only a fact, but when you consider that many haiku specify this and that about women, whereas the male poet takes *his* gender for granted, it is more than a fact. *It is a fact only a female poet would record.* That is what makes the *ku* better than the "lover's path" (*shinobiji*) version or the neutral version: *"First-blossoms / these footprints mean someone / saw them first"* (足あとは誰が先に見て初さくら　千代　*ashiato wa da ga saki ni mite hatsuzakura*). A contemporary *ku* by a man:

初桜我足跡をもどりけり　巨井 文くるま
hatsuzakura waga ashiato o modorikeri　kyosei 1772
(first-cherry my footsteps[obj] return[+emphatic]!)

adam?

first blossoms
i return following
my own footprints

I wish I knew which *ku,* this or Chiyo's came first but, unlike Chiyo, this poet is not famous enough to make the poet directory I have. But, reading the above, I would like to know more about him or her.

たづね入る人には見せじ山桜　われ疾う花にあはんと思へば　西行
tazuneiru hito ni wa miseji yamazakura ware tou hana ni awan to omoeba　saigyô (-1190)

mountain cherries: *no way i'll show them* *to those who call!* *not when i'd be first* *to see the blossoms*	*mountain cherries:* *no way i'll show them* *to those who call!* *not when the blossoms* *would be mine to meet*

山桜咲きぬと聞きて見に行かん人をあらそふ心とどめて　西行
yamazakura sakinu to kikite mi ni ikan hito o arasou kokoro todomete　saigyô

let us call on
mountain cherries after
hearing they bloom!

a heart that would compete
with others should stay put

Saigyô's original does not say he wanted to be "first," but his own riposte (the above verses come one after the other) and the fact he is asked to point out the blossoms suggests they are not visible from a distance and therefore just starting to bloom. I think it possible that Chiyo-ni's haiku was written as an envoi to this *waka,* imagining footprints – she might well have actually seen – to be his.

誰が居りて石あたゝかに初桜　常牧 糸まき・芋環
da ga irite ishi atataka ni hatsuzakura　jôboku (?)
(someone sitting/lying, stone warm-as first-cherry[blossom])

someone was here and warming this stone saw the first blossoms	i sit on a rock warmed by somebody: first blossoms

Is the someone the ghost of the famous poet and beauty Ono Komachi? We shall eventually get back to that, but first let us return to Chiyo:

わき道の夜半や明くる初桜　千代女
wakimichi no yohan ya akuru hatsuzakura　chiyo (1701-75)
(side-road/alleys' night-half[early-dawn]:/! brightens first-cherry)

cherry hunting

a side-road
in dawn's first light
the first blossoms

The *yohan* (early morning hours) suggest Chiyo was walking – or camped out – on the side roads rather than waiting for dawn before going. The absence of intellectualizing may explain why this *ku* and not the "footprints of a man" (found in the older Kaizôsha *saijiki*) is included in the modern Kodansha *saijiki*.

人の為に所問はばやはつさくら　千代
hito no tame ni tokoro towaba ya hatsuzakura　chiyo
([other] people-for place-inquire:/! first-cherry [blossom])

for others　　　　　　　　　　　　　　i happen upon
i ask where to find　　　　　　　　first blossoms seeking
the first blossom　　　　　　　　　the way for others

here i am asking
for others the whereabouts
of first blossoms

Chiyo is quite the cherry hound. She would not dream of spoiling the fun by asking anyone the best place for the local cherries. But, for the sake of other people, she can be practical. Or, is the second reading correct? This poem is not in any *saijiki* I know of. *Is it too simple?* I find it *fascinating*. One wonders what went through her mind.

初花に女鐘つく御寺哉　一茶
hatsuhana ni onna kane tsuku midera kana　issa (-1827)
(first-flower-to/at/for woman bell strikes [honorific+]temple 'tis)

a temple where　　　　　　　　　　　the woman strikes
women strike the bells　　　　　　the august temple's bell
at the first bloom　　　　　　　　for the first bloom

Did Issa, knowing Chiyo's penchant for first-blossom poems, imagine her doing this, observe a simple coincidence, or record a unique practice at a particular temple? If the last, was it invented as a humorous parallel to a domestic "first-flower" observance? *Hatsu-hana* was a common euphemism for a girl's first period (It was also called "fire" (lighting a fire, fire-time), which may help explain the first *ku* in this chapter), when rice with tiny red beans would be served to the puzzlement of younger children. We will return to allegorical cherry blossoms elsewhere; I hesitate to dwell further upon such matters now, for some readers might find the mere consideration of "B-side" readings suffices to pollute otherwise pleasant streams of poetry.

first bloom

ふところを風の明けるか初ざくら　りん女　再現
futokoro o kaze no akeru ka[ga] hatsuzakura　rinjo 1673-1757
(pocket[robe's breast opening](obj) wind's open?/is first-cherry[blossom])

the breeze opens
the breast of my kimono
first blossoms

is the wind
revealing our breasts?
first blossoms

懐は山にも有て初櫻　乙由　麦林
futokoro wa yama ni mo arite hatsuzakura　otsuyû -1739
(pocket[robe's breast opening] as-for, mountain/s-in even has/have: first-cherry)

first blossoms
i found mountains, too
have pockets

so mountains, too
have warm bossoms
first cherries

A fresh breeze opening a *blouse* would be sensual. Not so for a *pocket*. But one pocket of a kimono is the entire front part which opens from the breast, and *breast* is a sensual word, so . . . Rinjo is talking about buds opened by a moist, warm breeze, but can we resist imagining her nipples? *I cannot.* I would love to translate *"Is the wind / opening your blouses? / first-blossoms"* if only Japanese had blouses. . . With Otsuyû's *ku,* an explanatory "breast of kimono" would not work.

鼻紙に蜂追ふ空や初桜　長父　伊丹句合
hanakami ni hachi ou sora ya hatsuzakura　chôfu 1714
(nose-paper-for/after wasp/bee chases sky! first-cherry [blossom])

ah, this sky where
a wasp chases tissue paper!
first cherry blossoms

I think this one of the top 100 cherry blossom haiku. As we shall see in the next chapter, this was a time noted for *colds*, and Japanese did not keep their tissues, so it is a realistic setting for the play to begin. The season is beautifully expressed. The warming earth and breeze (seeking out the bloom) are responsible for keeping the tissue aloft. There may be more to it. Besides drawing our eyes to the terrifying blue void (my experience, anyway), the tissue may indicate something I encountered in a 7-7 verse from one of Issa's last *kasen* (song-fests): *"Setting off in the direction / the tissue paper flies"* (*hanagami no tobu hô e tabidatsu*). Was the tissue encountered by the wasp thrown up to let the wind settle the path of the cherry-hunters? The wind, after all, knows where the cherries are blooming! (This delightful wind is anatomized in Book III).

いつとなく花になりけり峯の雲　梅室
itsu to naku hana ni narikeri mine no kumo　baishitsu 1768-1852
(when-not [no time in particular] blossoms became [emph.] peak's cloud)

mountain clouds
one day, they are all
cherry blossoms

Baishitsu's *ku* does not only work as an old saw = "clouds of blossoms" noticed on mountain sides = but describes the way the blossoms *suddenly pop into view*, which parallels the quickness of clouds passing or forming over peaks. An honest poem, it provides good balance for the desperate "waiting" of chapter I and the fervid quest for the "first-blossom" found in this one.

思ひ寝の夢よりそ咲く初桜　宗春
omoine no yume yori zo saku hatsuzakura　sôshun 1734?
(thinking/longing/love-sleep's dream-from! blooms first-cherry)

       from the dream
     of a sleeping lover
      the first blossom

This brings to mind old *waka* about the mist of spring – the dawn of the New Year – arising if it were from a dream about the same. It is about awakening to find a dream come true.

もろ人や見る日／＼を初桜　泰里　翁反故
morobito ya miru hi miru hi o hatsuzakura　tairi 1783
(various-people:/! watch/view day x2[+contradict?] first-cherry)

different folk	coming into bloom	first blossoms
day after day see their	oogled by a million eyes	viewed by different folk
first blossoms	day in day out	day after day

The fourteenth syllabet, the postposition "o," implies that what precedes it is emotionally significant if not traumatic or contradictory. *Morobito* is problematic in translation for it means "everyone" but implies a great variety, occassionally, *riffraff*. I favor my outside readings, where the surprise is that "first-bloom" may be viewed day after day. My respondent had no favorite.

咲花に迹の祭の木陰哉　一茶　化五
hatsuhana ni atonomatsuri no kokage kana　issa -1827
(first-blossom/s-to aftermath-festival/party[too late]'s tree-shade!/'tis)

     sitting in the shade

     the first blossoms
    have bloomed and *now*
     the party begins?

The yiddish rhetoric suggested by italics saves a translation otherwise lost for lack of an idiom equivalent to *ato-no-matsuri* ("late(afterward) celebration"). "The day after the fair," "the doctor after death," "shutting the stable door after the horse has been stolen," etc. – none work here. Another reading: *"In the bloom-shade / a party: after we miss / the first blossoms."* Of course, the real cherry bash always lags the first blossoms despite their supposed importance.

酒ぶりはぼうに見せてや初ざくら　りん女
sakeburi wa bô ni misete ya hatsuzakura　rinjo 1673-1757
(drinking-way/style-as-for, for ~~pole nothing~~/monk?boy?-showing (?): first-blossoms)

~~all that drinking~~	showing the bonzes	~~all that drinking~~
~~yet we're still uptight~~	how a woman drinks	~~yet they're still uptight~~
~~the first blossoms~~	first cherry blossoms	~~the first blossoms~~

first bloom

とめて見る色も出さでや初桜　りん女
tometemiru iro mo dasade ya hatsuzakura　rinjo (-1757)
(stop-try color/sign too show-not-with, first-cherry)

they show no sign
of stopping, none at all
the first blossoms

Both of these by the poetess Rinjo. The *bô* in the first has me stumped. ~~If a pole, I suspect a variation on an idiom I have yet to find, while~~ My respondent favors a boy or monk/s, as per the middle reading. The other *ku* suggests the start of a career of total abandon which is not necessarily autobiographical. Another Rinjo poem notes that *"They draw us / together from the bud: / first cherry blossoms"* (つぼみからまねきよせてや初ざくら　りん女*tsubomi kara maneki yosete ya hatsuzakura*). Draw, as *invite*.

無理こきも菩薩がほなり初ざくら　梢風尼
muri koki/goki/kogi? mo bôsatsugao nari hatsuzakura　shôfû-ni (1668-1758)
(unreasonable/forced pretence even /pluck bodhisattva-face becomes/is first-cherry)

so sweet a face   first blossoms
even if only pretence   the little cherry an angel
first cherry   despite herself

the little tree
puts on the face of a saint
first blossoms

The first reading takes *koki* for *goki* (虚偽), or pretence, the second for *kogimo* (小肝), or pluck. A pun on "small tree" may be intended. Bodhisattva are saints with angelic faces. The poet is a nun.

初花やかさね／＼に鹿の角　高翔　千鳥かけ
hatsuhana ya kasanegasane ni shika no tsuno　kôshô 1712
(first blossom/s: layer-layer-in deers' antlers)

first blossoms
and antlers pile up one
upon another

I can't help recalling lyrics by Loretta Lynn about hanging her angel wings upon the devil's horns; but deer shedding their antlers are a *bona fide* spring theme (IPOOH: Spring bk 1). We will see more *ku* on the coincidence of shedding horn and blossom later (30-14~17).

初花に心はちれる野山哉　宗春　三籟
hatsuhana ni kokoro wa chireru noyama kana　sôshun (1734)
(first-bloom-at/to heart/mind falls/scatters field-mountain!/'tis)

the first blossom   the first blossom
our hearts are free to fall   our minds scatter over
where they will   hill and dale!

This is clever. Usually, the heart is described as *leaving* the body with the first-bloom and returning after the petals fall. The "free" in the first reading interprets an idiom only alluded to: the world may

4- 89~93

turn to field and mountain for all we care. The bloom-seeking libido explodes, sowing wild oats (or, less prettily, goes to seed?) a portent of petals soon to blow. Issa has an untranslatable *"First blossoms" ku* where the middle 7 syllabets first suggests they *"already fall on"* us, but after last 5 *"people's faces,"* means faces=expressions fall/scatter (初桜はやちりかゝる人の顔 一茶 *hatsuzakura haya chirikakaru hito no kao*).[1] I think it *means "First blossoms / the end already seen / in our faces!"* because Issa also wrote *"People's faces / have begun to wane / first blossoms"* (人顔は下り闇也はつ桜 *hitogao wa kudariyami nari hatsuzakura*); but there is a possibility his other *ku* meant *"First blossoms / their dust already settles / on our faces."* Something actually did fall . . . pollen:

朝々にむせびながらや初桜　秋の坊? 卯七?
asa asa ni musebinagara ya hatsuzakura akinobo -1718? ushichi? -1727?
(morning morning-during choking:/! first-cherries[blossoms])

all choked up
morning after morning
first blossoms

Love doesn't so much choke me up as stuff my lungs, but this would be cedar pollen allergy.

灸居てみる山近しはつ桜　吾仲
kyû suete miru yama chikashi hatsuzakura gochû -1733
(moxa placing see/ing mountain close [is] first-cherry[blossom/s]))

burning moxa   first blossoms
i see the mountain up close   burning moxa the mountain
first blossoms   comes closer

Moxibustion or moxa cautery sounds awful, but the pain of burning tiny clumps of mugwort at various strategic points on the body is bearable yet painful enough to enough to open one's pupils.

暮行やあしたの人の初桜　羅人 古選
kureyuku ya ashita no hito no hatsuzakura rajin -1752
(darken[nightfalling]-go!/: tomorrow/morning's person/s' first-cherry)

it grows darks!   dusk falls on them
the first-cherry blossoms   the first cherries for people
for tomorrow's men   coming tomorrow

ひやつくかいなや寝て見ん初桜　素檗
hiya tsuku ka inaya nete min hatsuzakura sobaku -1821
(chill-comes? or not: sleep-see first cherry[blossom/s]))

the annabelle lee hypothesis

let's sleep and see
if it gets chilly
first cherry
bloss
om
z

5

Cold Cherries
残寒の花
zankan-no-hana

花さかぬ先は埋火ざくらかな　本包　崑山集
hana sakanu saki wa uzumibi-zakura kana   honpô 1651
(blossom/s bloom-not future-as-for buried-fire-cherry 'tis)

spring in winter	**winter in spring**
before they bloom my firepot embers spark: cherry blossoms!	until they bloom i am content to view cherry charcoal

The *uzumibi,* literally a *buried-fire*, or embers, is a pot full of ashes with a piece of burning charcoal to keep ones hands warm. This is one of those totally untranslatable poems too much fun to let go of. The original may play on a nonsense ditty on chopping New Year's greens in a smart – i.e. very noisy – manner on the cutting boards (See *The Fifth Season*). I imagine an equally crisp snapping sound coming from the charcoal, which was probably not really cherry; wild cherry was sometimes used for charcoal, but *Quercus acutissma,* an oak was used for a famous charcoal, *Sakura-*(a proper name with the same sound, different characters!) *zumi*. The second reading assumes the poet is what Japanese call a *samugariya,* someone who feels cold all the time and craves warmth like a cat.[1] There is a term for it getting cold *after* the plum or cherry blossoms bloom, *hanabie* (花冷え), and snow falling on the blossoms, *hana-no-yuki* (花の雪). *Zankan-no-hana*, or "left-over-cold blossoms" is my invention. It is often surprisingly cold when the cherries bloom in Japan.

さくらさく哉と巨燵で花見哉　一茶
sakura saku kana to kotatsu de hanami kana   issa
(cherries bloom !/: & kotatsu[skirted heater table]-at blm-vwg!/'tis)

all the comforts	***my blossom-viewing***
so, cherry blooms! i'll do my blossom-viewing from the *kotatsu*	cherries are out? well, i'll be! right here in the *kotatsu*

---

1. Cold Issa The champion *samugariya*, Issa, harped on his hate for cold – even calling snow, so dear to snow-viewing poets, "bad stuff." Issa was triply cold. First, he claimed, because his mother and grandmother died leaving him in the care of an uncaring stepmother. Second, his native country was cold and snowy. Third, he seemed physically troubled by it and claimed to have no neck to speak of for hunching up to stave off the cold!

The *kotatsu* is a table with skirts to hold in the heat housing a heater. Some farm houses have pits so legs can be let down below the *tatami* mat floor upon which one sits. The two *kana* punctuating Issa's *ku* are very rare. He had either a bough of cherry or a tree in garden.

小畳の炬燵ぬけてや花の下　丈草
kotatami no kotatsu nukete ya hana no shita　jôsô -1704
(small *tatami* [rice-straw mat-flooring units]'s *kotatsu* slip-out !/and blossom-below)

slipping out from under the *kotatsu* into the bloomshade	breaking free from my heater, i sit below a cherry tree!

The original mentions "small tatami." I think that means the *kotatsu* was only the size of half a mat. Since the table with skirts covers half of one's body, the hermit crab of a poet has moved from below, or within one thing to another. He has left the cramped house of winter to the open and more pleasant house of spring. Here, the change happens too fast for the poet to catch:

炉をふさぐ思案さ中や初桜　吾仲
ro o fusagu shian sanaka ya hatsuzakura　gochû -1733
(hearth[obj] fill-in ponder-while:/! first-cherry(blossoms))

while i ponder
filling in the hearth:
first cherry!

Snow sometimes falls in the cherry-spring – and when it does, can be very heavy – so it is only natural to want to keep one's heating options open. The poet is not, however, justifying himself, but contrasting his indecision with the blossoms' sudden appearance. While the theme is clearly *first-cherry*, it also fits my tentative theme of cold and the cherry blossom.

爐塞いで見れは櫻は咲にけり　東瓦 花櫻榴帖?
ro fusaide mireba sakura wa sakinikeri　tôga ()
(hearth filling-tried/looked-when cherry-as-for bloomed[+fin])

closing up the hearth, i see the cherry has blossomed!	hearth snuffed sure 'nouf, the cherry's done bloomed!

A chain of events? Or does closing the hearth open the mind's eye for the blossoms? In the original, *mireba* suggests causality without actually establishing it.

温石のあかるゝ夜半や初桜　露沾　続猿蓑
onshaku no akaruru yahan ya hatsuzakura　rosen 1654-1733
(warmstone's exhaust/tire-of night-half[midnight-dawn hours]: first-blossom)

cherry spring the night when i tire of hot stones: first blossoms!	***cherry spring*** as dawn gloams o'er my heater stones first blossoms!

Rather than warm whole houses, Japanese enjoyed heat on the spot. Today, they even have pocket-sized throw-away chemical heaters (懐炉) that are shaken to start. I thought the second reading right if *akaruru* (ambiguous in phonetic syllabary) meant "brightening," but KS says *no way*.

温石の肌の別れや初桜　野刀 桃百途
onshaku no hada no wakare ya hatsuzakura   yatô 1728
(warm-stone/s' skin's parting:/!/? first-cherry[blossoms])

<table>
<tr><td>

time for hot stone
and my skin to take leave
the cherry blooms

</td><td>

high time for skin
and heater stones to part
first cherry blossoms!

</td></tr>
</table>

"Skin's parting" may *also* suggest the new skin of spring, the soft petals of the cherry blossom.

旅人の鼻また寒し初櫻　蕪村
tabibito no hana mada samushi hatsuzakura   buson -1783
(traveler/s' nose still cold first-cherry[blossom/s])

the nose of
the traveler still cold:
first cherry!

山寺や花より上はまだ寒し 士朗
yamadera ya hana yori ue wa mada samushi   shirô -1813
(mountain temple/s!/: blossoms-from-above-as-for, still cold)

<table>
<tr><td>

mountain temple
above the cherry blossoms
it is still cold

</td><td>

a mountain temple:
here, above the blossoms
it is still cold!

</td></tr>
</table>

Imagine the warmth of spring like a pool of water filling the valleys and rising up and up the mountain toward the temples.

石仏風よけにして桜哉　一茶　文政三
ishibotoke kazeyoke ni shite sakura kana   issa -1827
(stone buddha[~ist figure]) wind-block-as-make/using cherry!/'tis)

<table>
<tr><td>

cherry blossoms
i use a stone buddha
for a wind-block

</td><td>

i borrow a stone
buddha for a wind-block
blossom-viewing

</td></tr>
</table>

Temperature, not wind per se is the problem. Here a cold stone sculpture is keeping a man warm.

春もまた寒さに花や苦笑ひ 政公 毛吹草
haru mo mata samusa ni hana ya nigawarai   seikô 1645
(spring, too, again coolness-at blossom, bitter/grim/wry smile/laugh)

the spring, too
is cold and her blossoms
force a smile

Blossoms are said to smile/laugh (same verb) in Japanese. The forced smiles, or painful grins – I can think of no perfect translation – in the *ku* express the fact that exceptional cold stunts blossoms. I used the pronoun "her" rather than "the" because the "too" (*mo*) seems to personify the spring as it implies a comparison: "like me/us."

小寒きはさすがに花の盛り哉　乙二
kosamuki wa sasuga ni hana no sakari kana　otsuni -1823
(small-coldness-as-for as-might-be-expected blossom's heat/flourish/peak!/'tis)

cool cherry

this cold spell,
you might expect it for
the bloom-peak!

the full bloom:
what is more fitting than
a touch of cold?

Why? Because the bloompeak is hot for sharing the vocabulary of the cat's heat or the deer's rut, so that the cold provides balance? Or, is there an allusion to humans at the peak of their beauty chilly in the face of their numerous admirers. Spring playing the coquette.

三月につめたきものはさくらかな　大江丸 俳諧袋
sangatsu ni tsumetaki mono wa sakura kana　ôemaru 1801
(third-month-in chilly/cold thing-as-for cherry[~blossoms?]!/'tis)

in month-three
the thing that's cold
is the cherry

Could the petals actually feel cold? Is beauty cold because it tends to refuse the love of the poet? Does he shiver to see the petals and, with them, the spring vanishing? There is one *ku* like that:

ちる花に向へは寒き気持哉　蘭杜 花七日
chiru hana ni mukaeba samuki kimochi kana　ransha? 1777
(falling/scattering blossoms-toward face-if cold feeling!/?/'tis)

in the face of
falling cherry blossoms
i feel cold!

this coldness
facing blossoms falling
comes from inside

This is too pat. The cold in the previous, more interesting *ku* reflects a paradox – or, I found one that the poet may or may not have intended! – the cherry blossoms which bloom in the third and warmest month of Spring *are coldest by nature* for they have resisted the urging of the elements and the wishes of the poet the longest before giving in, *i.e.*, blooming. We will have a large chapter on late bloomers for they seem to arouse the philosophical vein of the poets.

ちる風は雪より寒し山櫻　諷竹 淡路嶋
chiru kaze wa yuki yori samushi yamazakura　fûchiku 1698
(scattering wind-as-for, snow-more-than cold mountain-cherry/ies)

the wind that blows
the petals is colder than snow
mountain cherries

A mountain cherry can simply mean a wild cherry but it is certain that the trees high up the mountains tended to bloom later than the others because of the lingering chill. Sometimes, viewers could be caught in real snow (as opposed to the petal blizzard, theme of a later chapter):

残雪・いかにせん花をいそけは峯の雪 宗祇 老葉
ika ni sen hana o isogeba mine no yuki   sôgi (1420-1502)
(how-as do-would? blossoms[obj] accelerated-if/when peak/'s' snow)

remaining snow

i guess that's life
we rush out for the blossoms
to find snowy peaks

what can be done?
snowfall on peaks above trees
pushed to bloom

snowy peaks:
how can we melt the blossoms
cold, cold heart!

The question is who is rushing or rushed and what are the agents? Is it all mental or are we talking about rain or a warm spell? Were it a *senryû* rather than Sôgi, I might suspect a pun on *yuki=snow=go=coming*, but, as is, that is extremely unlikely.

花にきて雪にわするゝ家路哉 十佛 つくは
hana ni kite yuki no wasururu ieji kana   jûbutsu (1356)
(blossoms-to-coming, snow-in/by lose home-path!/'tis)

i went to them and
my way back from the blossoms
lies below the snow

This plays with older poems (waka) where petal blizzards make the blossom viewer lose his way home. I wish English had a shorter phrase, or a word for "the way back home" equivalent to the Japanese *ieji*, or "house-trail." I used an overly concrete translation to restore life to the poem.

置火燵後や花折ルふまへ物　庭女
okikotatsu nochi ya hana oru fumaemono   sonojo -1723
(portable-heater afterword!/: blossom-breaking step-on-thing)

the portable stove
after it cools, a stepstool
to steal the bloom

a carry-kotatsu
later, you step on it
to cop blossoms

This poetess who captivated the greatest poets and novelists of her day (Bashô and Saikaku for a start), claimed she wouldn't mind going to heaven but would be happy to get into hell as well, tore strips of silk from her kimono's armpits to repair sandals, broke teapots for flower arrangement vessels, threw dirty dishes into a huge tub of water and only washed them once in while (something I do!), and, best of all, left a cross-shaped strip of hair on her shaved head when she became a nun. The above *ku* is not one of her better ones, but it sure reflects her character. She has a stranger *ku* about gathering (?) various blossoms: *"Hands outstretched / plucking as i go / the plants of spring"* and/or *"Hands outstretched / as Spring leaves I pluck / of all plants"* (手を延て折行春の草木哉). We will spend a whole chapter on "blossom-breaking" (for the limbs were literally *broken off*) in Book II.

Cherry Rain, Kind & Cruel
育つ雨・散らす雨
sodatsu-ame   chirasu-ame

花をいそく心の友や夜の雨　宗因　三籟
hana o isogu kokoro no tomo ya yoru no ame　sôin 1604-82
(blossoms[obj] speed/hurry heart's friend! night's rain)

<table>
<tr><td>it speeds
the bloom: my soul-mate
night-rain</td><td>my friend
speeds the bloom
night rain</td></tr>
</table>

待つ頃の櫻にうれし夜の雨　吟江　夢占
matsu koro no sakura ni ureshi yoru no ame　ginkô 1780
(waiting time/period's cherry-to/on delighted night's rain)

<table>
<tr><td>night rain
a happy thing when
cherries wait</td><td>this night rain
how happy for waiting
men and cherries!</td></tr>
</table>

The growing cherry buds and the waiting poets rejoice in this rain. In the first *ku* the poet is one with the rain, in the second, with the trees.

花さけと催促するや雨の声　祐博　毛吹草
hana sake to saisoku suru ya ame no koe　yûhaku 1645
("blossoms bloom!" pressing/urging-does! rain's voice)

bloom, cherries!
bloom! **urges the voice**
of the rain

Hundreds of years later, Issa had wasps buzzing around melon bloom as if to say "become melons!"

雨も（ぞ）花ふれは開くる日初桜　失名　白髪集
ame mo [zo] hana fureba akuru hi hatsuzakura　lost name ()
(rain-even [!] blossom touch-if open [day] first-cherry)

when the time comes

<table>
<tr><td>first blossoms
the touch of a raindrop
and they open</td><td>even the touch
of a raindrop opens
the first cherry</td></tr>
</table>

6- 1~4

I can't help recalling a later *senryû* about a young woman ripe (?) enough to disrobe for a single ant! But the rain was not always sexy. Wind was, but the rain was generally nurturing:

子をまふけたる興行・ねふらせて養ひ立よ花のあめ　貞徳
neburasete yashinai tate yo hana no ame　teitoku 1570-1653
(sleep/lick-let nurture stand/assist! blossom's rain=candy)

for someone blessed with a child

Let him lick it,	let her sleep
And look after him well, –	she'll grow and bloom
Rain on the flowers.	blossom rain

trans. Blyth

The sex of the child is not given, but if the sex is not specified a boy is most likely. The puns don't translate. Rain becomes candy (both *ame* in Japanese). To be licked means "be a total sucker for him (= spoil him with love)." There are countless poems in Chinese and Japanese where the elements parent blossoms. Rain as wet-nurse or rather, breast: *"Bloom! bloom! / a breast for the blossoms / spring rain"* (咲々と花に乳房や春の雨　如翠　春遊 *sake sake to hana ni chibusa ya haru no ame* josotsu? (1767?)). Puns give us breasts against noses (also *hana*.). *Neburasete* can be read "letting sleep" as well as "letting lick." Children, according to a saying, grow up while they sleep (*ko wa nete sodatsu*). Another saying is "sleep if you'd be rewarded." (*kahô wa nete matte*).

寝て花の果報待けり春の雨　孝水 月影塚
nete hana no kahô machikeri haru no ame　kôsui ()
(sleeping blossom's/s' reward wait[+emph.] spring's rain)

sleeping, we wait	sleeping, the cherry
for the cherry's reward	awaits its award
the spring rain	spring rain

I guess the poem means that the cherry will blossom without making any effort itself. Perhaps the homophonic double-meaning of spring, "swelling" is in play here. I assume "we" are also sleeping and share the rewarding bloom but failed to squeeze that into a single *ku*.

雨はをや雪は祖父か春の花　重頼　犬子
ame wa oya yuki wa ôji ka haru no hana　shigeyori 1601-1680
(rain-as-for parent snow-as for grampa? spring's blossoms/flowers)

geneology of bloom

if rain is parent,
is snow grandparent?
spring flowers

The "spring" modifying the *hana* in Shigeyori's poem suggests flowers in general and not just cherry blossoms. As there are earlier poems about rain parents, I confined the question to the grandparent. Another old *ku* quips: *"Stands to reason / that rain turns into snow / it's the bloom's parent"* (雨に雪の成も道理ぞ花の親　失名　(嵐山集?) *ame ni yuki no naru mo dôri zo hana no oya* lost name (17c?)). Late snow white like the hair of the aging parent? Or a blossom blizzard?

とき遅き花にや雨の片ひいき　永治　毛吹草
toki osoki hana ni ya ame no kata hiiki   eiji 1645
(early-late, blossom-with-respect-to rain's side-favoring)

early and late
bloom: has the rain, then,
played favorites?

early and late
blossoms: favoritism
by the rain?

The *early* and *late* suggests the cherry, for the term is not generally used for other flowers. And, I assume favoritism implies parents.

花さけと打ぬる雨や親の杖　休安　俳諧古選
hana sake to [or, do] uchinuru ame ya oya no tsue   kyûan 1763
(blossom/tree bloom! [or, bloomed *but*] striking rain! parent's cane)

bloom, buds!
the rain lays it on hard:
a parent's cane

though they bloom
the rain keeps on striking:
a parent's cane

The different readings derive from the lack of "muddy-dots" (*nigori(ten)*) differentiating the *to* = と and *do* = ど syllabets. I believe the second more likely, but must admit to being puzzled, because the Jesuits in the 16c were surprised to find that Japanese, unlike Europeans, did *not* strike their children, and, they still don't. Item 3-7 in *Topsy-turvy* 1585 has a 4-page discussion of this. Jesuits disapproved of corporal punishment and were pleased to see the proof of their position in the good nature of Japanese children. (Recently, I have found a defense of caning by Johnson in *Boswell's Hebrides* (1785) based on the argument that children would get over the indiscriminate use of the cane, while the alternative of persuasion would create favoritism and lifelong sibling rivalries!)

花を雨たゝき落すや後の親　望一　犬子
hana o ame tatakiotosu ya nochi no oya   môichi 1633
(blossom/s[obj] rain strikes/beats-down! later[step]parent)

the same rain
beats down the blossom?
a step-parent

rain beats down
the blossoms: it must be
a step-parent

The two faces of the rain date back to the *Manyôshû*. In song #1869 (#12-2 in this bk), it makes the blossoms bloom, where in the very next song #1870, it threatens to make them fall. This *ku* makes *haikai* sense of this contradictory rain that nourishes and destroys at the expense of the of the bad step-parent, a stereotype challenged by Murasaki Shikibu in her novel *Tale of Genji* a thousand years before. Bad rain haiku tend to be ridiculous: *"Rain on blossoms / a parent-child quarrel: / tear-drops?"* (花に雨は親子いさかひ雫かな　一葉子　鷹つくは *hana ni ame wa oyako isakai shizuku kana* ichiyôshi (1642)). "Drops" (*shizuka*) alone would not have worked in the last line, so I over-translated the hint of teardrops. *"For slow cherries: / rain makes a good whip: / an ôtsu pony"* (遅き花に雨を鞭とや大津馬　一松　洗濯物 *osoki hana ni ame o muchi to ya ôtsu uma* isshô (1666)). The *ame* as a sweet puns into our "carrot," but it cannot be translated. *"For what sin / does the rain kick the hell / out of the blossoms?"* (科は何花をけちらす雨の足　正直　犬子 *toga wa nani hana o kechirasu ame no ashi* seichoku (1633)).　The rain "kicks" because a strand of rain such as one can see hanging down from a squall cloud is called "rain-foot/leg" (*ame-no-ashi*). I would have titled it *Dog-cherry*. If you speak Japanese, there is a lot of action going on out there!

雨に咲かぬ花や親にし不孝者　無記名　犬子
ame ni sakanu hana ya oya ni shi fukômono anon. 1633
(rain-to/by bloom-not blossom/flower: parent-to-is unfilial-one)

blossoms that
won't bloom for the rain
are unfilial

they won't bloom:
from the rain's point of view
unfilial blossoms!

If rain-as-parent nourished the buds, failure to bloom is unfilial behavior. I don't know if this refers to a late cherry – one too late for the poet at least – or to individual buds on the tree.

雨に花見れはこもらぬ枝もなし　宗長　壁草
ame ni hana mireba komoranu eda mo nashi sôchô 1447-1532
(rain-in blossom/s view/ed-when, gravid/bloated-not limb-even not)

viewing blossoms
in the rain, every branch
a gravid woman

cherry blossoms
in the rain not a branch
is not bloated

I have seen branches broken from the weight of rain-soaked blossoms as women once died in childbirth (once it was the leading cause of death for women). English can not match the Japanese *verb* for being gravid. Bloated is a bit too airy.

雨にかつつほめる花は水子哉　作者不知　ささめ事
ame ni katsu tsubomeru hana wa mizuko kana anon. (1461?)
(rain-in even pucker-up blossom-as-for water-child [still-birth])

water-babies!
blossoms that pucker up
when it rains

are blossoms
that pucker up in the rain
water-babies?

Compassionate or ridiculous? In Japanese, late-term miscarriages and still-births are "water-babies." There are temples specializing (?) in them and traveling nuns once sold women supernatural protection for themselves and their ill-fated children. Not all old *ku* were so anthropomorphic as the pluvial family relations we have seen:

昨日の雨やけふある花のえだ　出典損失
sakujitsu no ame ya kyô aru hana no eda   lost name ()
(yesterday's rain: today is blossoms'/gorgeous branch)

yesterday's rain?
this blossoming branch
we meet today

雨はれて櫻に曇るあした哉　完元法師　新筑波
ame harete sakura ni kumoru ashita kana kangen-hôshi (1495?1667?)
(rain clears, cherry[blossoms]-by/with cloud/overcast tomorrow/morning 'tis)

the rain clears
tomorrow will cloud over
with blossoms

the rain clears
and morning is overcast:
cherry blossoms

6- 16~20

Two different takes on cause and effect. The second *ku* plays on blossoms-as-cloud trope. A similar rain+cloud without causality: *"On this mountain trail / where i tread upon clouds / cherries in the rain!"* (雨中多武峰　雲を踏山路に雨の櫻哉　几菫 *kumo o fumu yamaji ni ame no sakura kana* kitô (-1789)).

吾庭に雨気催せ櫻山　龍水
waga niwa ni ameki [ûki?] moyôse sakura yama　ryûsui (?)
(my garden-to/in rain-spirit urge/incite/arouse! cherry-mountain)

bring my garden
a pluvial urge! long reign
cherry mountain!

make my garden
want to go: bring rain o
cherry mountain!

The Japanese traditionally installed free restrooms by the street to encourage people to leave their fertilizer there, rather than saving it for home. *Ki-o moyôsu* still describes what might be called *sympathetic arousal of the urge to micturate*. Here, the idea is expanded to include rain! Still, how can a garden be primed to draw rain? And why should a poet named "dragon-water" need the help of a cloud of cherry blossoms? (Dragons embody the spirit of water – not fire – in the Sinosphere.)

喜の涙そ待し花の雨　定時 毛吹草
yorokobi no namida zo machishi hana no ame　teiji (1645)
(delight/joyfulness's tears! awaited blossom/s' rain)

this long-awaited
blossom rain: call it
tears of joy!

Is this the joy of rain the parent, seeing its child blossom so beautifully, or the tears of a woman coming for the first time? Either way, it is more interesting than, say: *"Petals falling / in the rain: a beauty's / make-up runs"* (落花雨美人の化粧流し也　一束　虚栗 *rakkasame bijin no keshô nagashi nari* issoku (1683)). Another poem of ambiguous intent:

降雨もしすまし顔や花の陰　一茶 文化四
furuame mo shisumashi kao ya hana no kage issa (-1827)
(fallen-rain-too/even did-finish/triumphant face:/!/? blossom's shade)

even with rain
a shit-eating face
in the bloomshade

below the bloom
faces looking triumphant
even in the rain

both the bloom
and men below triumphant
even in the rain

even the rain
says "we did it!" under
the cherry bloom

If only Issa were older, I would have guessed this was his pride at having survived another year. Perhaps he describes another. Or, is it pride at having sat out a heavy rainfall, rather than leaving? Or, is it the pride of people who got all dressed up, prepared great lunches and made it to the blossom-viewing. Note that the *kage* or "shade" can pun for the "face" of the blossoms. Hence the third reading. Or, is Issa talking for the rain, proud parent of the blossoms? Yet another reading, call it *Erocosmos*, is possible, *barely*: "*Bloomshade thought: / rain only adds luster / to love fulfilled.*"

散る人はちらして雨の櫻哉　雅郊 句鑑
chiru hito wa chirashite ame no sakura kana　gakô 1777
(fall/scatter people-as-for scattered rain's cherry 'tis)

acid test

<table>
<tr><td>

the scatterable
have scattered: a rainy
blossom viewing

</td><td>

ah, cherry rain
scatter all who'd scatter
we'll remain!

</td></tr>
</table>

cherry blossoms
in the rain: let those who
would leave, leave!

If true beer-lovers relish warm beer, a real friend of the cherry bloom, not only puts up with rain, but even claims to like it. Another from the man *I* consider the first father of haiku:

花を見ば人なき雨の夕哉　宗祇 老葉
hana o mireba? hitonaki ame no yûbe kana　sôgi -1502
(blossoms[obj] see-if people-not rain's evening)

if you'd really
view blossoms: a rainy dusk
with no people

I can well understand the value of some clouds to improve moon-viewing, but this is a bit too *shibui* for me! As Blyth wrote, Sôgi was "almost too poetical and artistic to be human." (*History of Haiku* I)

見るうちに咲く花もあり春の雨　さかふ 新選
miru uchi ni saku hana mo ari haru no ame　sakô (1773)
(see-within/while bloom/s blossom/s-even is/are: spring's rain)

<table>
<tr><td>

some open even
as you watch: blossoms
in the spring rain

</td><td>

some blossoms
open while you watch:
the spring rain

</td></tr>
</table>

spring rain
some blossoms
open before your eyes

So *that* is what you get viewing blossoms in the rain! Does this poet have slow motion cameras for eyes? His close observation is as suspect as it is wonderful.

つく／＼と雨に昼寝の櫻哉　此藩 藤首途
tsukuzuku to ame ni hirune no sakura kana　hihan? (1731)
(keenly[sense] rain-in, afternoon-nap's cherry[blossom-viewing]!/'tis)

<table>
<tr><td>

how intense
this blossom-viewing
nap in the rain!

</td><td>

how intense
napping in the rain below
a cherry tree

</td></tr>
</table>

6- 26~29

Sometimes we are more aware when half-asleep. This *ku* strikes me as exceptionally fine. The psychological mimesis *tsuku-zuku* is more commonly identified with sight, intensely gazing outward, than with listening, with its inward vector.

身にしみて音聞く花の雨夜哉　蓼太
mi ni shimite oto kiku hana no ame yo kana　ryôta 1707-87
(body-into soak/pierce/sink sound hear/listen blossoms' rain-night 'tis/!)

<table>
<tr><td>this rainy night
of blossoms, the sounds
sinking into me</td><td>soaked to the quick
by the sound of the blossom
rain in the night</td><td>how sounds do
sink in this blossomy
night of rain</td></tr>
</table>

I tried. The original is an untranslatable train of modification for the subject: "blossom-rain-night."

寝てしらぬ夕べの雨を花の顔　吟江　心花
nete shiranu yûbe no ame o hana no kao　ginkô 1776
(sleep-know-not evening's rain[emotional "o"]: blossom's' face/s)

<table>
<tr><td>the evening rain
i would just sleep through
but for blossoms</td><td>sleeping i missed
the rain at night, but how good
the blossoms look!</td><td>i slept through
the rain but seeing the faces
of the blossoms</td></tr>
</table>

Does Ginkô mean he only notices the rain at night from concern for the blossoms, or that he knew of it because the blossoms reflected it in the morning? My respondent favors the latter.

雨露も落さで乾く櫻哉　梅室
ametsuyu mo otosa de kawaku sakura kana　baishitsu 1768-1852
(rain-dew-too, falling-not dry cherry[blossoms] 'tis)

<table>
<tr><td>cherry blossoms
dry out without spilling
the rain and dew</td><td>rain and dew
dry without dropping
from the petals</td></tr>
</table>

A fine observation. I wonder how much the blossoms absorb iand how much evaporates and whether anyone studies such things. The first reading is closest to the original, despite the reverse syntax.

雨はれて花に色そふ夕日哉　宗祇
ame harete hana ni iro sou yûhi kana　sôgi 1420-1502
(rain clears, blossoms-to/on color/beauty adds evening-sun [subj.] 'tis/!)

<table>
<tr><td>the rain clears
and evening sun adds
beauty to bloom</td><td>how the sunset
colors the blossoms
after the rain!</td></tr>
</table>

I imagine a Yôkihi-zakura, the thickly petalled blushing cherry named for the Chinese beauty Yang Kuei-fei (719-756 AD). It bears some resemblance to the Kaidô (*aronia*) a flower compared to a beauty who looked particularly stunning when sleepy and wet. Sunset is not right, but English has no short word like *yûhi* for the evening (the last hour or so before sunset) sun.

rain

ほか／＼と雨のあかりや山櫻　器水 けふの昔
hoka hoka to ameagari ya yamazakura　kisui (1699)
(warmly/steaming/fresh rain-lift-up[ends]: mountain cherry)

blossoms steam
at the end of the shower:
mountain cherries

Mountain cherries bloom late. The sun's warmth and high altitude create what looks like piping hot blossoms: a steamy effect. The mimesis *hoka hoka* suggests a pleasant glow.

一雫天窓なでけり桜から 一茶 文政三
hito shizuku atama nadekeri sakura kara　issa -1827
(one drop head caresses[+emph.] cherry[blossoms]-from)

a single drop from the blossoms carresses my head!	my white head stroked by one drop of cherry dew

This is some time after a rain; I have experienced it. Through hair or through a scarf (*tenugui*) on a shaved head, large drops of water are gently felt. Pardon my filler: Issa had white hair at the time.

よしや花の雨此杯を笠にせん 一笑 古選
yoshi ya hana no ame kono sakazuki o kasa ni sen　isshô 1763
(all right! blossoms' rain: this sake cup[obj] hat/umbrella-into make-let's/i'll)

not to worry

blossom rain?
let this sake cup be
my umbrella!

The entries for 1 of 5 *yoshi* in my dictionary include "All right!" "There, there!" "Sold!" and (to a baby) "Wooglie, dear!" Exclamations do not translate for even if they have words that seem to mean something, they have no literal value. Since our attention is gained by the use of slang, any live translation is bound to be criticized as dated, or likely to be dated. Be that as it may, I feel a hint of nonchalance in the *yoshi ya,* hence, the title. My "umbrella" is a hat as large as those called "sunbrellas" in the USA. The tiny size of the *sake* cup makes a hilarious picture. A later poem: *"Blossom rain / not one person not / wearing a fan!"* (花の雨扇かざゝぬ人もなし 一茶 *hana no ame sensu kazasanu hito mo nashi*   issa (-1827)) We cannot tell if these poems refer to a rain of petals or light rain during a blossom-viewing.

鶯も笠きて出よ花の雨　利休 古選
uguisu mo kasa kite ideyo hana no ame　rikyû 1763
(warblers/nightingales [singing-women], too, hat/s put-on come-out! blossom-rain)

warblers, too don your hats and enjoy the blossom rain	the blossom rain warblers don your hats: come out and play!

The same *kasa* I turned into an umbrella in the last poem remains a hat here. The bush warbler is usually translated as "nightingale" because it was loved for its song and caged for it. The request makes sense on the metaphorical level, too, because *uguisu* also means "singing women."

雨の日や花に色めく鳥の声　可石　花七日
ame no hi ya hana ni iromeku tori no koe　kaseki (1777)
(rainy day! blossom-to color-tint [erotically excited/charge] bird's/s' voice)

this rainy day
the blossoms come alive
with bird song

花の雨四方の上戸をうるほせり　長和
hana no ame yomo no jôgo o uruhoseri　chôwa ()
(blossom's rain four/all-sides door-ups(big-drinkers)[obj] moisten/enrich)

blossom rain
all around drinkers
drinking more

blossom rain:
it moistens the gullet
of real drinkers

blossom viewing
when rain falls, the drunks
all come alive!

The verb *uruhoseri* (*uruosu*) means making something moister, richer and more full of life. If some drinkers have fires (not always allowed), so the *sake* could be warmed, that too would encourage drinking. Far from throwing a wet blanket on the party, the rain here is oil thrown on the fire.

花の雨人を酔すに我の酔ふ　涼斗
hana no ame hito o yowasu ni ware no you　ryôto (-1717 if 涼菟)
(blossom-rain [other] person[+obj] drunk-make-with/by i/my [get]drunk)

blossom rain
pushing drink on a friend
i end up drunk

Tsuji Momoko, haiku poet herself, explains: 'This is the chilly rain of blossom-viewing time. Thinking that today, for once, maybe he [or she?] may be enticed to drink until drunk, a friend is invited over for *sake* [remember, it is warm], but before the poet knows it, he himself is drunk. We can feel the charm (艶なかんじ) of the blossom rain." (『「酔」秀句350選』1989)

膝もとへ流れ来にけり雨の花　蘭更
hizamoto e nagarekinikeri ame no hana　rankô -1798
(lap-base-to flow-come[+finality] rain's blossom)

petals flowed
in the rain all ending
up in my lap

into my lap
flowing with the rain
cherry petals

That sounds like one soaked poet. Let's hope he was full of warm *sake* and didn't catch cold! Rankô's rain apparently took place in the mountains, for he also wrote:

雨そぽ／＼花の枝に猿の尻　蘭更
ame soposopo hana no kozue no saru no shiri　rankô (1726-99)
(rain drip-drop/split-splat blossoms'/cherries' tree/limb-end/s' monkey's/s' butt/s)

monkey butts
in the blooming tree-top
dripping rain

the rain soaked
butt of a monkey way up
a blooming branch

This is a typical old-style grammatical arrangement with the whole *ku* a modification of the butt. *Kozue,* written simply "branch" (枝) here, means the tips of all the branches. Despite the hard "k" and raspy "z," it sounds euphonious, and is a common female name. We cannot tell if the poet describes an actual scene or merely invents a picture of a mountain cherry-viewing made depressing by drippy butt, or rather, the depressing mimesis, *soposopo.*

花にこそ忍ぶ物あり雨の朝　りん女
hana ni koso shinobu mono ari ame no asa　rinjo (1673-1757)
(blossoms-in especially endure/suffer[for love] thing is, rainy morning)

patient suffering
is part of loving blossoms
a rainy morning

Shinobu means "to put up with all sorts of physical or mental difficulty for the sake of seeing or not seeing a lover." I used the first half of the poem to try to communicate that. Because rain was hell for fancy clothing that had to be unstitched to be washed and the picnic-lunches were made the night before, women, in particular, spent the blossom-viewing season in terror of wet-stuff in the morning. Here, Rinjo waits anxiously to see if it stops.

雨の日をよりも撰たり花の山　一茶　文化一
ame no hi o yori mo yoritari hana no yama　issa -1827
(rainy day select even selected: blossom's mountain)

cherry mountain

of all days
i chose a rainy one
for blossom viewing

If this were a real mountain, the slippery trails might be dangerous. If, as is more likely, it is what we might call *a cherry park* (perhaps Ueno), even a small amount of rain might turn to mud. While I have already used the words "cherry mountain" for several *ku* about cherries blooming in the hills, the term *hana no yama* or "blossom mountain," which I will more often than not translate as "cherry mountain" means any place where there is a grove of cherry trees that attract crowds to view their blossoms, *even if the location is more or less flat.* Even Japanese evidently found the convention curious. *Senryû* makes black humor of it. *"Blossom mountain? / Is it someone's grave? / asks the moron"* (花の山どなたの墓とくそだわけ　柳多留 69-1 *hana no yama donata no haka to kusodawake* yanagidaru 19c). Be that as it may, the great number of people on the "mountain" assured a muddy mess when it rained. One could even get stuck. Issa wrote a number of *rained-in* poems: *"A downpour / i stay over, under / the blossoms"* (大降りや桜の陰に居過して *ôburi ya sakura no kage ni i-sugoshite*), *"Falling rain / in the bloomshade i / remain alone"* (ふる雨に一人残りし花の陰　*furu ame ni hitori nokorishi hana no kage*). A quick shower was another matter:

花びらの埃流にふる雨か 一茶 化1
hanabira no hokori nagashi ni furu ame ka issa -1827
(blossom-petals' dust flow/clean-off-for fall rain?)

    is this rain
perhaps for washing dust
      off the petals?

Another poet, playing on older poems about clouds giving respite to eyes strained from moon-viewing, wrote: *"The spring rain / gives sleepy eyes a rest / from the flowers"* (春雨は花に寝ぬ目を休めけり 草也 三崎志 *harusame wa hana ni inu me o yasumekeri* sôya?). Shikô (-1731) put the blossoms with that moon: *"If you'd rest / your eyes from moon* and *bloom: / the spring rain!"* (月花の目をやすめはや春の雨 支考 類題 *tsukihana no me o yasumebaya haru no ame*). My *italics*. This is better:

人並に帰りもせでや雨の花 一茶 文化一
hitonami ni kaeri mo se de ya ame no hana issa
(people-like-as return-even do-not: rain's blossoms)

    not returning
like other folk, i know
    rainy blossoms

Were it raining blossoms (*hana-no-ame*) rather than raining on blossoms (*ame-no-hana*), the poem would be worthless. Think about it. Like the petals that flowed onto Rankô's lap (*hizamoto e*), these are real and deserve my added word: *know*.

我のみとおもふに雨の花見かな 多代女
ware nomi to omou ni ame no hanami kana tayojo (1775-1865)
([it is] i/me only/alone think-but rain's blossom-viewing!/'tis)

  i thought myself   and i thought
alone, but now this rainy   only i viewed blossoms
  blossom viewing   in the rain

Tayojo had a preface to her poem saying she visited an old man called Ûkô. Since his name literally means "rain-thought," it stands to reason that he would join her in the rain. Since she was the daughter of a very wealthy *sake* maker, and doubtless had a retinue of servants, I do not imagine that she, like Issa, actually got wet! But the idea – that we feel alone in the rain – and, by extension, that all who view blossoms in the rain are probably surprised to discover kindred souls – is mint.

かしこくも花見に来たり翌は雨 几董
kashikokumo hanami ni kitari yoku wa ame kitô -1789
(smartly/cunningly-even blossom-viewing-to come/went next-day-as-for rain)

cherry boastful

  rain the next day!   rain! clever me
boy how smart of me to go   coming to view blossoms
  blossom-viewing!   the day before

In hindsight, he had foresight. Boasting poets are always fun to read. Reality is usually more like this:

十人の目利はづれて花の雨　一茶 文政七
jûnin no mekiki hazurete hana no ame   issa (-1827)
(ten-people-judges/cogniscenti miss blossom's rain)

>   ten experts
>   ten wrong predictions
>   blossom rain

An older *ku* is refreshingly straight forward: *"I hate my friend! / "Go tomorrow" you said but – / blossom rain!"* (友憎や翌といふたか花の雨　小女　みね 古撰 *tomo nikui ya yoku to iuta ga hana no ame*　mine (1763)). The gloss tells us Mine was a girl. Old anthologies often included a sprinkling of *ku* by children. Today, unfortunately, they are segregated into books of children's haiku.

山寺の寳物見るや花の雨　虚子 明治三十五
yamadera no hômotsu miru ya hana no ame kyoshi (1902)
(mountain-temple's treasure/s see: blossoms' rain)

>   the time to see
>   mountain temple treasures
>   blossom rain

Cherry blossom viewing in the mountains brought people to temples they rarely visited. If rain made it hard to sit outside, it was perfect for bringing people inside of the temples. This poem reflects the positive attitude, or healthy spirit, that endears Kyoshi to so many.

春雨の庭にきのふの花も哉　宗祇
harusame no niwa ni kinô no hana mo gana　sôgi 1420-1502
(spring-rain's garden/patio-in yesterday's blossoms [desired]!)

spring rain, o for yesterday's blossoms in today's garden!	spring rain falls in the garden: how i miss yesterday's bloom!

>   how i wish for
>   yesterday's blossoms in my
>   garden of rain

Sôgi is the premiere poet of blossom rain. He enjoys it so much, he wishes to have seen it at the peak of the bloom rather than later, when most might prefer it.

つらやつらやあもたいなやの花の雨　兀峰 再現
tsura ya tsura ya a motainaya no hana no ame　koppô (-1694)
(painful/wretched!/face-face: painful/wretched! ah/oh what-a-shame! blossom-rain)

oh, misery! it's a crying shame! cherry-rain	all our faces a picture of misery cherry-rain

A downpour after the blossoms open is a bummer, no metaphor can fix. *Motainaya* is an exclamation used *when something bad happens which seems such a waste compared to what might have been.* Call it "a crying shame." *Tsura,* or painful, is homophonically identical with "face;" hence, reading two.

花の雨寝ずに塗ったをくやしがり 川柳年中行事
hana no ame nezu ni nutta o kuyashigari senryû (pre-1928)
(blossom-rain sleep-not-painted[+obj] regret/chagrin[verb])

blossom rain
chagrin for losing sleep
to make up

blossom rain
chagrin for the sacrifice
of sleep for beauty

空をねめねめ弁当を内でくい 川柳年中行事
sora o neme neme bentô o uchi de kui senryû (pre-1928)
(sky[+obj] stare stare box-lunch[+obj] inside-of eat)

staring daggers
at the sky, the box lunch
eaten inside

Reading Ono Sawako's *Edo no Hanami* (Edo's blossom-viewing), I realized that my attitude toward the rain in this chapter was, despite Koppô's *ku*, strongly biased in favor of the cherry trees and the aesthetic poets. To most people, especially women who prepared most of the food and clothing and spent more time on make-up, rain was an unmitigated disaster. The above *senryû* found in said book and attributed to a 1928 collection (both may be older) give the real story. More from the same:

そりや出たよいかぬ事だと花の宵
sorya deta yo ikanu koto da to hana no yoi
(there! appeared! go-not thing is: blossom-eve)

花の宵処々に坊主の首くゝり
hana no yoi shosho ni bôzu no kubi-kukuri
(blossom-eve: place-place-in bonzes' hanging)

it's come out
i guess we aren't going
blossom eve

blossom eve
here and there you see
hanging bonzes

The little puppet called a *teratera-bôzu* (also *otenki bôzu*), or "good-weather-bonze" was dangled from the eaves and used both to predict and, hopefully, influence the weather. Here, the first *senryû* indicates that the doll was indicating bad weather. Other *senryû* mention crumpled paper and dolls and the paraphernalia of other magical undertakings.

#

Babushka, or Old Dame Cherry
姥 桜
ubazakura

杖つきの長閑に匂へ姥櫻　紹二　鷹筑波
tsuetsuki no nodoka ni nioe ubazakura   shôji 1642
(crutch-user's balmy scenting[exuding beauty] auntie cherry)

> balmy weather
> on crutches, sweetly blooming
> babushka cherry

English's closest translations for *uba*, "granny" and "auntie," sound bad with "cherry" because of the identically pronounced tail. Aunt or Grandma would be too formal. So, I will use many words, including *babushka*, a Russian word I felt familiar with the day I learned it, *uba* as is, "witch," for *uba* can be magical in a fairy-tale-like way, and other terms as the translation demands or permits. For example, this *ku* pretty much demands a witch: *"What is viewed / when wandering about: mountain / witch cherries"* (めぐり／＼見るは山姥櫻哉　俊可　鷹筑波 *meguri meguri miru wa yamaubazakura kana*   shunka (1642)). That is because the "*uba* of the mountain" was a supernatural old woman said to call upon mountain huts, incognito (testing their hospitality). The *ku* deliberately conflates her wandering with that of the cherry-hunters. On the other hand, the following *ku* would be overwhelmed by a "witch": *"Is that white hair? / Or a padded hat? / Auntie Cherry."* (しらがゝや綿帽子かや姥桜　貞順　鷹筑波 *shiraga ka ya watabôshi ka ya ubazakura*   teijun (1642)); *"Her limbs (on) crutches / her blossoms, white hair / Granny Cherry"* (枝は杖花は白髪そ姥桜　長吉　犬子 *eda wa tsue hana wa shiraga zo ubazakura*   chôkichi (1633)), whereas Shôji's *ku* smiles, for the *ubazakura* is a variety of Higan cherry, which, being long-lived, is often found propped up by numerous supports.

> with her cane   with her crutches
> quietly beautiful   quietly beautiful
> baba cherry   auntie cherry

Thanks to unspecific number in Japanese, the tree could simultaneously be an auntie with a singular cane and a tree with many supports. In English, the plural only works with "crutches."[1]

---

1. Trees on Crutches Because the Japanese greatly appreciate both the patina of age and low branches – about door-way height – on blossom or fruit-bearing trees, braces are so omnipresent they are taken for granted. Large old trees can have dozens of supports. In *The Chrysanthemum and the Robot*, Arthur Koestler expressed *horror* at discovering parks of crippled trees which reminded him of a hospital ward. There is a touch of irony here that Koestler missed. For whatever reason, modern Japanese seem uneasy before crippled *humans* (who, themselves realize it, and tend to stay home and out of sight), . . . Note that some of the trees Koestler saw needed braces because of how they were shaped ("maimed") but others were just old.

出家衆落すな寺の姥ざくら　長頭丸　崑山集
shukkeshû otosuna tera no ubazakura　teitoku　(1651)
(leave-house-crowd debase/ruin/entice-not! temple's/s' auntie/witch-cherry)

blossoms at a temple

don't you dare ruin
men who've left the world,
old dame cherry

I was hoping to find an English translation for *ubazakura* in my Kenkyusha's and I did: "a faded beauty; an elderly woman of beauty; <slang> a has-been." In the examples, we see she has "seen her best days," is "past her prime" and has "lost the bloom of youth." The last *ku* with its old tree on crutches certainly gives one such an impression, but, generally, the word was used, and I believe, still is used in a positive manner: though over-the-hill, she is still voluptuous, still a charmer, as in the above *ku*. If you can think of a *witch* as attractive, you can drop the "dame" I thought hints of remaining looks. Men (and women) who retired from the world – or were exiled from it – becoming wandering monks or sedentary hermits , were supposed to be above carnal desire, but . . . .

小町像賛・おことこそ風狂乱の姥桜　宗因　虚栗
komachizo-san // okoto koso fûkyôran no ubazakura　soin　-1682
(komachi sculpture eulogy // zither especially refinement-crazed auntie-cherry)

in praise of a komachi doll

how *goût!*
old dame cherry
with a zither

in praise of the diva poet

a wild zither
is the coolest thing
for old cherry

The caption suggests the haiku concerns Ono Komachi as a still attractive *ubazakura*. I like this *ku*, for Buddhist writers prefer to picture her as an old hag, or worse yet, with a shoot of grass associated with the low life sticking through an orbit of her skull! Still, she is old here. The *koto,* or zither, is the traditional instrument for ladies. The younger crowd would have gone for the banjo-like *shamisen* instead.   At the same time, the words used for someone mad about refinement (*fukyôran*) literally evokes *gusts of wind*, the tree as natural zither of the Taoist sage (only topped by Thoreau's beloved Aurelian harp (telegraph lines)). Another *ku*, playing on the idiomatic meaning of Komachi, *a pretty young woman*, has the sexiness transferring from generation to generation, from babushka cherry to a Komachi, also the *bona fide* name for a type of cherry: (花の色のうつるや小町姥ざくら　無記名　崑山集 *hana no iro no utsuru ya komachi ubazakura*　anon. 1651)

酒よりもせんじ茶でみよ姥桜　重頼　犬子
sake yori mo senjicha de miyo ubazakura　shigeyori 1633
(sake more-than, parched-tea-with see-let's/should auntie-cherry)

at her viewing
parched tea beats *sake*
babu cherry

Parched tea is a particularly mild tea enjoyed by the elderly. Babushka cherry would not be thrilled with a drunken cherry bash. This is an early example of blossom-viewing etiquette *ku,* found for late-cherries, plums, peony, etc..

花ぞ一重腰は二重の姥ざくら　無記名　崑山集
hana zo hitoe koshi wa futae no ubazakura　anon. (1651)
(blossoms/petals one-layer [single-petal], hips-as-for two-layer auntie cherry)

portrait of old dame cherry

single-petaled
double-hipped bounty
ubazakura

The single-layer of petals alludes to the less effusive beauty of the older woman and the double hips to the plentiful cluster of bloom. A similar descriptive poem is a translator's nightmare: *"Waves=wrinkles of bloom / break on her brow! / babushka cherry"* (花の浪額によるや姥ざくら 玉（革＋央）夢見草 *hana no nami hitai ni yoru ya ubazakura* gyokuô? (1656)). Actually, they "approach" her brow, but any translation fails. English does not think of wrinkles as waves nor waves as blossoms, so the metaphor is dead in the water.

我顔のしはをや笑ふ姥桜　無名　犬子
waga kao no shiwa o ya warau ubazakura　anon (1633)
(my/[her]own face's wrinkles[+obj]! laugh granny-cherry)

laughing away
the wrinkles on her face
babushka cherry

"Laugh/smile" is common metaphor in Japanese for a plant or a mountain showing off its shiny new leaves and bright blossoms. In this case, there are no leaves for the varieties of cherry called *ubazakura* according to the first definition in the OJD were marked by leafless bloom and this originated because leaf was homophonic with tooth, and toothlessness a mark of old age . . . The wrinkles in the *ku* suggest the bark of an old tree. While these cherries (the *higan* being the best known) tend to be long-lived – two or three hundred years, rarely up to a thousand – the individual trees are not necessarily old, but no one would call a young tree an *uba* unless it were planted on the grave of a a noble's favorite wet-nurse, this practice being another popular origin for the name as "wet-nurse" is also called *uba,* though the Chinese character/s 乳母 used is/are different. *Haikai* poets loved the toothless analogy. One even brings in the *twig = gum* homophone (*ha-k[g]uki*): *"After blooming / only her gum=leaf-stems: / babushka cherry"* (盛すぎはぐき計ぞ姥桜　正友　夢見草 *sakarisugi haguki bakari zo ubazakura* seiyû 1656). Kuitert, in *Japanese Flowering Cherries*, who calls this conventional etymology "one explanation," and offers "an ancient folk practice" he claims is "the real explanation of the name:"

> . . . in poor regions of agricultural northern Japan, old, weak and 'worthless' women were carried to remote mountains in times of bad harvests and famine, leaving their fate to the gods, and saving a mouth to fill in the village. *Prunus pendula* f. *ascendens* lives to an old age . . . It is not surprising that the trees with their black and heavy limbs holding up an umbrella-shaped crown of flowers inspired legends and lore. The phantasmal trees reminded people of the female ancestors who were left behind and were called *ubazakura*.

While infanticide was common in Japan, as it was among many if not most relatively peaceful people, I would doubt that abandoning old women was ever common. It seems more a thing of legend, as with many things Japanese, deriving from China. At any rate, I found no *ku* linking the practice with the name *ubazakura*. Issa came close with: *"The Dumped-aunty / remote mountain cherry/ies / has/have bloomed"* (姥捨し片山桜咲にけり　一茶　文化三 *ubasuteshi katayama-z(s?)akura sakinikeri* (-1827). Re-reading it as, *"Up in the hills / where auntie was left / a cherry blooms,"* we can see the *ubazakura* itself as a just-so story: *It sprung up where she died . . .* But the *sakura* in Issa's poem is not specified as an *ubazakura,* and, as it happens, Issa wrote many *uba*-abandonment *ku* without respect to cherry blossoms, for the best-known legendary location for the heinous act was in his own Shinano province. If I had to guess, I would not choose any of the etymologies as "the real explanation," but enjoy all of them. If I must favor one, it would be my witch, for she is always an *uba,* while the abandoned old woman is as often as not called an *oba.* which implies a beauty who retains her appeal in old age.

遅く咲く花はほれたか姥桜　重頼 犬子
osoku saku hana wa horeta ka ubazakura shigeyori (1633)
(late/slow blooms blossom-as-for, senile[as a verb past-tense]? granny-cherry)

blooming late
because of her senility?
babushka cherry

Today, *"horeru"* means being head-over-heels in love, or enamoured. It once meant to be senile. There is a parallel with our "dote on" and "dotage."

いまさらに春を忘るる花もあらじやすく待ちつつ今日も暮らさん　西行
imasara ni haru o wasururu hana mo araji yasuku machitsutsu kyo mo kurasan saigyô -1190

*what flower
ever forgets about
the spring*

*so wait calmly and
just let life go on*

(or, as a couplet)

*Every day, I tell myself there's nothing to fear:
The blossoms remember the spring, every year.*

I think Shigeyori may have been inspired by Saigyô's *waka* when he depicted an *uba-zakura* so forgetful in her dotage that she forgot to bloom when she should have. As a rule, the *uba-zakura* is "one of the earliest cherries to flower" (Kuitert), but individual older trees do have a tendency to slow down a bit, so Shigeyori's name-play may have a grain of the truth to it!

花袋数珠ぶくろかや姥ざくら [玄+木偏に需にしんにゅう?]嵐山集
hanabukuro juzubukuro ka ya ubazakura genju? (1651)
(blossom-bag=bud? [are they] prayer-beads?! granny-cherry)

the blossom buds
do they hold prayer beads?
babushka cherry

Buddhism has its own rosaries, *juzu,* literally, "number-pearls/beads."[1] They are fingered faster than Catholic beads and create a noise somewhat like that of an abacus, but more constant. I have mistaken them for cicada. Are the *ubazakura*'s bud clusters beadier than with most, or is it in the poet's head?

1. Rosary and Prayer Beads The similarity of Buddhist and Catholic trappings is such that the Jesuits were liable to think of it as a perverse trick of Satan (see *Topsy-turvy 1585*). The problem for a translator is that a description is often not as poetic as a name. "Rosaries" beats "prayer beads." But *rosaries* cannot be used for Buddhist prayer beads. This is doubly regrettable when we consider the fact that the cherry is in the rose family.

~~~~~~

見るうちや物忘れする姥桜　安悦　夢見草
miru uchi ya monowasure suru ubazakura　anetsu 1656
(view-while! thing-forgetting do, auntie-cherry)

while viewing
granny cherry we all
forget things

you forget things
viewing her blossoms
granny cherry

I prefer this subtle magical association to the blatant metaphors of the previous two *ku*. Other similar *ku* such as *"Those watching / the old cherry tree also / lose their marbles"* (みる人もほるゝ老木の桜哉　長頭丸　崑山集 *miru hito mo horuru oiki no sakura kana*　teitoku 1651) and *"Those watching / also in blooming-senility / gramma-cherry"* (みる人も花にほれけり姥桜　之友 or 無記名　崑山集 *miru hito mo hana ni horekeri ubazakura*　shiyû 1651) do not fully translate, for they play on the second meaning of *horeru*, being in love in the giddy manner of a teenage *crush*.

三途川越えても見はや姥桜　貞徳　犬子
santôgawa koete mo mibaya ubazakura　teitoku 1633
(santo-river [equivalent of styx] cross-even see-would: auntie-cherry)

though it meant
crossing the styx, i'd see
the *uba-zakura*

i would cross
the river styx to see
my babu cherry

Old Teitoku would not miss a cherry-blossom party, though it was still chilly and windy and might be the death of him. Or does he, knowing the tree will outlive him, mean that he will keep loving "her" after death? Or is this allegory; i.e., do we have an uxorious poet?

姥桜咲くや老後の思ひ出　芭蕉
ubazakura saku ya rôgo no omoiide　bashô 1664
(auntie-cherry blooms: old-age-after memories-come-out)

blossoms on an old tree

ubazakura
the flower of her youth
remembered

blossoms of the past

ubazakura
young memories bloom
in her dotage

Some call this one of Bashô's worst poems, written when still under the influence of the Teimon, i.e. Teitoku's "school" of poetry. Yet the wit (or is it *warmth*?) of 24 year-old Bashô's poem is best appreciated in combination with plodding *ku* such as: *"Reward: A fine bloom: / for deserving old age! / ubazakura"* (咲花は（花咲や）老の果報ぞ姥ざくら　無記名 崑山集　*hana saku ya oi no kahô zo ubazakura* anon. (1651)); *"Blossom remnants / the last of her grand-children?/ uba-zakura"* (余花は是孫子の末か姥桜　広寧　夢見草 *yoka wa kore mago ko no sue ka ubazakura*　kônei 1656) and *"Who says / the elderly don't bloom! / uba-zakura!"* (年寄に花もあるもの姥櫻　遊糸　鞭随筆 *toshiyori ni hana mo aru mono ubazakura*　yûkei 1759). My above readings of Bashô's *ku* may beat the original. For it, according to Eibara Taizô and Yamazaki Kiyoshi (日本古典全集＝芭蕉句集), Kon Eizô (芭蕉句集), Makoto Ueda (*Bashô and His Interpreters*) and others, the *ku* plays upon a nô drama about the 12c samurai Sanemori who opines that dying in battle will beat anything he can accomplish in old age (定めて討死仕るべし。老後の思ひ出これに過ぎじ。) In that case, I really should have translated, say:

auntie-cherry
she blooms and old age
is memorable

auntie cherry
blooms: old age does
have something

The problem for us is that "no event in my old age will be more memorable than that" (Ueda trans.) makes little sense, for we value the enjoyment of our lives, whereas Sanemori is thinking of *what he leaves to history.* Ueda translates: *"the old lady cherry / is blossoming – in her old age / an event to remember."* His double "old" sticks in the craw, but the content is faithful to Sanemori (or, the Kôseki interpretation he cites). We are talking of *what the world will remember* and we can see that Bashô is using the *ubazakura* to retort: *Who says the elderly can't do truly splendid things!* As noted by Ueda, Sokotsu (an early modern critic whose name translates as Rat-bones) calls this "extremely childish;" but isn't it pleasant to see a young poet celebrating age?

余花あるや老のくりごと姥桜　休安 夢見草
yoka aru ya rô no kurigoto ubazakura　kyûan (1656)
(excess-blossom/s have! old-age's harping [repeating words]: aunt-cherry)

extra bloom
granny cherry chasing
her own tale

extra blossoms
senility repeats itself
granny cherry

Yoka in *waka* generally meant cherry trees blooming late, i.e. in the summer. Here, we are talking about something else, what I translated already as "blossom remnants." Old cherries have a long bloom, with some limbs noticeably lagging others. These laggards are the *yoka* (excess/extra/ remaining blossom/s). *Yoka,* written with different characters (余暇) would mean "time to spare," or *leisure,* and taken with the colloquial *aru ya,* with a nuance of "sure has it," punfully suggests that one reason the elderly repeat themselves is because they have time to fill.

姥桜花のさかりやゆきおんな　氏重 犬子 嵐山集
ubazakura hana no sakari ya yuki-onna　shijû 1633
(auntie-cherry, blossom's acme/heat! snow-woman)

babushka cherry
in full bloom she becomes
a snow-woman!

snow-woman!
when the witch-cherry's
blossoms fly

auntie-cherry
when her bloom explodes:
snow woman!

A heavy snowfall that great beauty to the landscape and could kill an unwary person was called "snow-woman," *yuki-onna.* This was not uncommon in cherry time, so a visit from the real snow-woman was a possibility, but grammar and I favor transformation. In ch 51, we shall see scattering petals as "blossom-blizzards" (*hanafubuki*), which, like snow, are white and can bury people (even the *babushka's* pink-tinged bloom whitens by the time the petals scatter). The third reading imagines such a scene, but *sakari* suggests most of the bloom is still heavy on the limbs.

化けたるか白姥桜雪のいろ　俊次 嵐山集
baketaru ka shiro ubazakura yuki no iro   shunji 1651
(metamorphicizing? white aunt-cherry snow's color)

pale blossoms

a ghostly trick?
white babushka cherries
the color of snow!

At a glance, one might think this alludes to the snow-woman; but, as already noted, white skin was a mark of beauty associated with youth. "Snow white" does not belong to Europe alone. The poet hypothesizes that nominally old cherry – and, here, we must mean her bloom, for the bark was on the dark side – should bear the stain of age, and since it doesn't, she must be supernatural, a "changeling," so to speak. So, the *ku* would seem to celebrate a tree with particularly white blossoms, for the *ubazakura* as a rule has relatively small blossoms pinker, which is to say darker, than most cherries.

花咲て気は十八やうばざくら　一敬 嵐山集
hana sakite ki wa jûhachi ya ubazakura   ikkei (1651)
(blossoms blooming spirit-as-for eighteen! granny-cherry)

when she blooms
her spirit is eighteen:
grandma cherry

A Japanese nursery-man whose name I failed to copy wrote on an internet blog that the really old *ubazakura* (200-300 years old) have less blossoms but that this only served to raise their appeal from the merely *sexy* (*iroke* = color-spirit) to the deeply *erotic* (*iroka* = color-scent). I assume the cherry in question is a young 81, for Japanese enjoy reversing numbers.   Similar *ku:*

をさな顔花にはありや姥桜　一武 夢見草
osanagao hana ni wa ari ya ubazakura   ichibu (1656)
(juvenile-face/appearance blossom/flower-as-for is/are! auntie-cherry)

the neotonous plant

so baby faces   there are beauties
are found in flowers!   that always look young!
granny cherry   babushka cherry

花さかぬ若木も有るを姥桜 無記名 嵐山集
hana sakanu wakaki mo aru o ubazakura   anon. (1651)
(blossoms bloom-not young-tree-even are (+regret/contradiction) auntie-cherry)

though we know
young trees without bloom
babushka cherry

Flowers are typically described as short-lived but young? They may be *identified* with youth, the birth of Spring; but that is not the same. My first reading, with its baby-faced flowers follows the wording of the original closely but is a bit disingenuous because, in Japanese, *hana* means the plant itself and "a beauty," as well as flower/blossom/s. My second reading reflects that fact at the cost of the wit.

枝は百としはいくつぞ姥ざくら　勝重　嵐山集
eda wa momo toshi wa ikutsu zo ubazakura　katsushige 1651
(limb-as-for hundred years-as-for how many?! auntie cherry)

a hundred limbs
and how many years?
uba-zakura

I once counted the joints on a large number of bamboo (sure enough, there were fifty of a goodly length and a couple dozen spindly ones down to the tip, resembling our human years), but I have never tried to count the forks or limbs on a tree (might be fun to assign such a task to children, huh?). This poet probably didn't either. A hundred, especially when pronounced *momo* idiomatically means "many/plenty of/ a luxuriance of."

養老の瀧かは花の姥桜　弘永　毛吹草
yôrô no taki ka-wa[gawa] hana no ubazakura　kôei 1645
(care[for]elderly's waterfall?[river?] blossoms/gorgeous [-?]granny cherry)

fountain of relief　　　　　　　　　　　this cataract
for the aged, a gorgeous　　　　　　　for the aged, a riverside
babushka cherry　　　　　　　　　　　*ubazakura*

old dame cherry
your bloom a veritable
fountain of youth

Unlike so many supernatural legends, which hark back to China, this beneficent waterfall has a Japanese pedigree.[1] Seeing beautiful blossoms on an obviously old tree is, I think, medicine for the soul of the aged. So long as their poetry is not too self-centered, poets tend to live long, for their minds remain in the blossom of their youth. To me, the flowering old cherry represents *that*.

一たびは世ゝの昔や姥桜　和風　太夫桜
hitotabi wa yoyo no mukashi ya ubazakura　wafû 1680
(one time-as-for world/era-world/era's long-ago!/: granny cherry)

ubazakura

once the past　　　　　once it was　　　　　just once a year
of many generations　long ago for the living　many pasts are present:
granny cherry　　　　　and the dead　　　　　babushka cherry

When we see old trees, we imagine others who touched them centuries before; and when they bloom, our temporal ties are strengthened in the same way the magic of a full moon unites people separated in space.

---

1. Pedigree for a Supernatural Waterfall Two pedigrees, in fact. In one, a spring discovered on a mountain by a man with the name "filial child" [?] in Minokuni (Gifu Prefecture) spewed *sake*. For this reason, *Yôrô-no-Taki,* or "care[for the]aged waterfall," is the name for what may well be Japan's biggest chain of bars! The other, more documented pedigree, refers to a waterfall that suddenly sprang out of the side of a *Yôrô* range mountain (Southwest Gifu) in the Nara Age (710-94) and was reputed to cure many diseases. The Emperor of the time was so impressed by its efficacy that he changed the Era Name (resetting the date to year 1 of Yôrô). Both Shinto and Buddhism embraced the fall, for the Yôrô-no Taki shrine and temple remain to this day.

孫や子に手をひかれ見ん姥桜　春可 犬子
mago ya ko ni te o hikare min ubazakura   shunka 1633
(grand-child and child-by/to[?] hand[obj] pulled-see! granny cherry)

with children and
grand-children in tow, let's go
see aunt cherry

take your children
and grand-children to visit
grandma cherry

The name of the cherry gives the poet a good excuse to advocate a blossom-viewing which includes the children, who in Japan, as elsewhere, adore all their older relatives. Sure, the poem is artificial, but it is also warm.

たのもしき子を置ちるや姥桜　牧子 卯辰
tanomoshiki ko o okichiru(?) ya ubazakura   bokushi 1691
(trust-worthy child[obj] place/set/leave: babushka-cherry)

the tree that baby-sits

you can leave
a child with her and trust
granny cherry

a tree we can trust

a child abandoned
in a safe place, the lap of
wet-nurse cherry

I recall thinking that it was too bad the poet did not use phonetic syllabets for the *uba* so a "wet-nurse" reading would be possible (not that it stopped me from doing one such reading). *Later,* I found a preface to the *ku*.

<秋之坊老母追悼>

a monody for akinobô's elderly mother

trusting the promise
of her child, her petals fly
the old cherry tree

In other words, that the *ku* is allegorical. Akinobo's beautiful old mother died happily secure in the promise of her fine son, the poet Akinobô. The *ku,* ostensibly about a tree, compliments the mother and the son. It may also mean that a cherry was planted on the mother's grave or that there was a cherry planted at his mother's birth.*

---

1. *Tree-planting practices in Japan* While I know of cherry trees presented to others by nobles and the planting of cherries on graves, I have not yet grasped the entire picture of the practice of planting trees for people dead or alive in Japan. Perhaps, I will by the next edition. *Today,* the practice of planting trees for one's children is not uncommon for those who own land. In her recent book about the power of season words 季語の底力, Kai Michiko wrote of how her father, shortly before he passed away, planted a mountain ash (in Japanese, *nanakamado* = seven-stoves, for it was said not to burn unless put in the furnace seven times) for her older sister (I imagine her birthday was in the summer when this plant blossoms) and a cherry tree for her and her younger sister (Spring birthdays?). All the trees were named for the girls. Kai finds it pleasant to think of how they "still standing in the place I was born, blossom and scatter there every year, always well (元気=original-spirit)." Then, she finishes her section on the cherry blossoms with this beautiful thought: *"Every one of us has, within our heart, a cherry tree that is ours alone."* (人は皆、心の中に自分だけの桜を持っています). I think that would be true for all Japanese whether or not they had a cherry bearing their name. Could we say the same?

Cherry-Time In/Equality
花時平等
hana-doki-byôdô

君か代の日傘に成し櫻哉　辰下 玉藻
kimigayo no higasa ni nashi sakura kana   shinka 1774
([peaceful]reign's parasol-as/into becomes/is cherry[tree/blossom]!/'tis)

and they are now
the parasol of the reign
cherry blossoms!

Cherries do not bloom at the same time everywhere in Japan, but to blossom-viewers it seems so. Sitting in the pink shade, it is hard to imagine the entire world is not doing likewise.

千里をも一木に見るやはるの花　昌叱 発句帳
senri o mo hitoki ni miru ya haru no hana   shôshitsu -1603
(thousand-miles[+obj]-even one-tree-as see!/: spring blossoms

spring blossoms in just one tree i can see a thousand miles	in one cherry tree we can see a thousand miles the bloom of spring

山はみなこゝろの花のひと木かな　宗祇 老葉
yama wa mina kokoro no hana no hitoki kana   sôgi -1502
(mountain/s-as-for all heart/s' blossom/s one-tree!/'tis/?)

the mountain
a mighty tree blooms
with one mind

the mountains as one tree blooming with our spirit	the whole hill blossoming with soul as one tree

every hill now
a single tree abloom
with our hearts

"*Different? No way!*" starts one *ku* (かはらめや種は千里も花の春　昌休 *kawarame ya tane wa chisato mo hana no haru* shôkyû -1552) Another *ku* qualifies: "**Spring** /// Blooming or not / a thousand hometowns boast / flowering cherries!" (咲き咲かず千里や春の花櫻　肖柏 発句帳 *saki sakazu senri ya haru no hanazakura*   shôhaku 1442-1527). *Blooming or not.* Most of the meeting, drinking, singing, eating, fighting and even viewing under the bloom is reserved for Book II. Here, we will set the mood.

I may jump the gun on some details, but the idea is to describe the broad picture.

花の陰赤の他人はなかりけり　一茶
hananokage aka no tanin wa nakarikeri issa (-1827)
(blossom's shade red/utter-stranger-as-for not[sort of][emph.])

a touch of nature

nobody
in the bloomshade is
a stranger

<table>
<tr><td>and there are
no utter strangers
under the bloom!</td><td>under the bloom
all of mankind shares
a common womb</td></tr>
</table>

A sublime experience creates a "we are all in it together" *feeling* similar to that felt in a disaster. Unrelated people relate and, conversely, the related unrelate: *"Here are neither / friends nor masters: / blossom-viewing!"*(友となく旦那ともなく花見哉　嗜之 (in 加藤郁乎 市井風流) *tomo naku danna mo naku hanami kana* shishi 18c?). I call this "cherry-time equality." Issa's *ku* is one of the most translated cherry *ku*: *"Under cherry-flowers / [all are friends], / none utter strangers"* = Miyamori; *"Under the cherry blossoms / None are / utter strangers"* = Blyth. Miyamori, and Blyth after him, quoted the Bard: *a touch of nature makes all men kin* (note: nature=birth, kin=kind). Miyamori also sighed:

> The present Ueno at flower-time is overcrowded, the "flower-viewers" often jostling against one another. But in my student days, when the Tokyo population was much smaller, the visitors were comparatively few and they strolled leisurely under the cherry-flowers by twos and threes. Some of them carried small kegs or gourds of sake, and as they drank, kindly greeted fellow flower-lovers, "How do you do, friends?" and offered them cups of sake. I long for those good old days.

Miyamori doubtless knew Shakespeare's "kin" was associated with "kind" in the mind of his audience. He may not have known his "old days" were exceptional, perhaps the product of modernization, over-work, wars and emigration. Ueno packed them in for hundreds of years.

人ことの身の何なれやはるのはな　宗祇
hito goto no mi no nan nare ya haru no hana sôgi -1502
(people-each's body/self's what is! spring's blossoms)

what the hell
is this thing called a self
among flowers

<table>
<tr><td>what the hell
is a self or a body!
spring blossoms</td><td>what the hell
are separate bodies
in cherry time!</td></tr>
</table>

spring blossoms
have we our own bodies?
have we selves?

How odd this *ku* is not well known. It seems to express something similar to Issa's *none-are-strangers ku* on a more esoteric level though "spring's blossoms/flowers" suggests that it is not about cherry blossoms alone. Forgive my "hell." English has no grammar to make "what is" as emphatic as it is in the original. English also lacks an equivalent to *mi,* meaning both "body" *and* "self."

見しらるゝ人の盛や花の山　幸徳　再現　雪月花
mishiraruru hito no sakari ya hana no yama　kôtoku (1736)
(see-known[acquainted] people's bustling/bloompeak: blossom-mountain)

flourishing in public

a blooming bash
where all know all:
cherry mountain!

cherry mountain
where people go wild
before our eyes

One reason none were strangers was the open nature of the event. True, some parties curtained off their trees but most bloomshade was not behind closed doors. In a society with few public parties (there were no grassy plazas or town squares as in Europe), this was extraordinary.

世の中を木の下にする櫻かな　日人
yononaka o kinoshita ni suru sakura kana　watsujin 1758-1836
(world-among/society/life[+obj] tree-below-in do cherry[subj]!/'tis)

. . .
they put us
all under trees
cherry blossoms

The cherry blossoms
put the whole world
Under the trees

trans. Blyth

The *shita ni suru* – Blyth's "put . . . under" – is doubly apt: when the cherry blooms, the whole world becomes subject to it; and, that, too, is a form of equality. The simple "under the trees" is what differentiates this *ku* from the earlier one that began the chapter. The parasol was pretty but less effective. I like to think that had Blyth not translated this first, his translation might have been mine.

下々はあくらかきての櫻哉　野泉　小弓
shimojimo wa agura kakite no sakura kana　yasen 1699
(low-low(poorfolk)-as-for, crosslegged-make [+genitive] cherry!/'tis)

the lowest of the low
sit cross-legged and free
the cherries bloom!

To sit cross-legged in the meditative style seems formal to us – and I first imagined the poor behaving like monks while the wealthy danced and got drunk – but, in Japan, it meant to sit in a relaxed manner, care-free and staying put, i.e., not bothering to respond to the demands of the world. Indeed, the idiomatic meaning that probably applies here is *brazen behavior demonstrating no regard for others*.

花見には老若男女きせるとひ　宗因　滑稽伝
hanami ni wa rôjaku danjo kiseru toi　sôin (-1682)
(blossom-viewing-as-for, old-young-male-female pipe-passing)

blossom-viewing
men, women, young and old
share their pipes!

blossom-viewing
pipes are passed between
m & f, y & o

The *kiseru* is a pipe with a small bowl and long handle. The Portuguese introduced tobacco to the Far East together with Christianity. The social aspects of smoking – the peace-pipe – arose immediately.

8- 9~12

in/equality

今の世や猫も杓子も花見笠　一茶 文政九
ima no yo ya neko mo shakushi mo hanami kasa issa -1827
(now's world: cat and ladle[every one]-even blossom-viewing hat)

the latest fad

blossom-viewing
hats on everyone
and his mother

Idioms beg for idiomatic translation. "Everyone and his mother" is the best I can do for "cats and ladles." [1] We could translate "~hats on every wench / and prostitute." *Shakushi* (ladle) can also mean a *meshimori*, an inn wench who cooked, sewed and slept with guests, and "cat," courtesans; but "mother" is more fun. Hats were probably not always *de rigor*. (A 1759 *ku* indirectly tells us this: *"Though overcast / don't you dare wear a hat / hunting cherries!"* (曇とも笠着て行な桜かり 人左 桜勧進 *kumori to mo kasa kite ikuna sakuragari* jinsa). Blossom-haze=overcast, unlike other cloudiness, does not mean rain. My first inclination was to translate the *ku* to the contrary, for one can get sunburnt on a hazy day.) If they were, Issa would not have remarked upon their ubiquity.

花の山友ならぬ木はなかりけり　葛三 アルス
hana no yama tomo naranu ki wa nakarikeri   katsusan 1751-1818
(blossoms' mountain friend be/come-not-tree [is]not[sort of] [finality])

cherry mountain	not a tree there	cherry mountain
not a tree that is not	we could not befriend	not a single tree there
a friend to me	cherry mountain	played hard to get

This is one of those not-so-great *ku* a translator cannot help playing with. Katsusan died a year or two before Issa wrote "no utter strangers." Could Issa's famous *ku* be read as a take-off on his *ku*, or the next that seems more like John Muir writing warmly about his friends the boulders?

知る知らず花にもの云て通りけり 習先 新選
shiru shirazu hana ni mono iute tôrikeri   shûsen 1773
(know know-not blossoms-to something saying pass by)

something said	i find myself	known or not
in passing to the blossoms	talking to each blooming	a word for each blossom
known or not	cherry i pass	party in passim

To the blossoms/trees? To women (see Issa's depiction of verbal exchanges between strangers near the end of ch. 24)? To the viewing parties? If it is blossoms, then no cherry tree is a stranger, too.

~~~~~~

1. Cat and Ladle   Senryû are full of the idiom: *"Prosperity / means cats and ladles / turn to gold"* (*hanjô wa neko mo shakushi mo kane=kin ni naru* – Shodai Senryû); *"A cat can / get with child, but it's / hard for a ladle"* (*neko wa haramu ga shakushi wa kitsui muri* Shodai Senryu), *"Cats and ladles / come to bother / Yoshiwara"* (*neko mo shakushi mo yoshiwara no jama o suru* Y 18). etc.. The first and third are obvious, the second refers to the pleasure quarter prostitute and the inn-wench. It goes back at least as far as this 13c poem by Ikkyû: *"To be born / is to die, so / it is for all: / for the buddha, saints / cats and ladles!"* 生れては死るなりけりおしなべて しゃかもだるまもねこも杓子も 一休. Ikkyû's poem follows one by 蜷川 which reminds me of Emily Dickinson: *"All in the world / is but pretence / and lies: / this thing called death / had better be real!* 何事もみな偽の世なりけり しぬるといふも誠ならねば. Though Issa's *ku* seems completely cheerful, I imagine most of his readers would have been aware of Ikkyû's poem (道歌). For all this, I have not completely figured out the cat and ladle business.

散らぬ野辺咲かぬ山なき櫻哉　宗祇
chiranu nobe sakanu yama naki sakura kana　sôgi 1420-1502
(fall/scatter/ing-not-fields, bloom-not-mountain not cherry!/?/ 'tis)

cherry spring

not a mountain
they don't bloom, field
they don't fall!

falling on all fields
blooming on all mountains
cherry blossoms

on every field
they fall, on every hill
they bloom: cherries!

petals in the fields
blossoms in the hills
cherry everywhere

The original of this panoramic *ku* is double negative all the way: "*Not* a field [where petals are] *not* falling, *not* a mountain [where blossoms are] *not* blooming / What cherry blossoms!."

京は九万九千くんじゆ（群集）の花見哉　宗房
kyô wa kyû man kyû sen kunju no hanami kana　sôbô -1694
(capital-as-for, 99,000=rich-poor-swarm-gather's blossom-viewing 'tis/!)

here in kyôto
all ninety-nine-thousand
out for the blossoms

This young poet who would later be called Bashô (Note how his early haigô takes the 宗 of Sôgi) increased the proverbial *population* of the old capital, 98,000, by a thousand to pun an idiom for a promiscuous mix of people, *kisen-kunju* 貴賎群集 = rich-poor-swarm-gather. (Yes, *kusen* and *kisen* are not homophones. This sort of slightly off pun called a *kasuri* was common.) Sometimes, the same 98,000 was used to describe the *age* of the capital, usually pronounced *miyako*, but here pronounced "kyô." I borrowed the first and last line (only changing "to see" to "for") from Ueda (*Bashô and His Interpreters*).

櫻色にそめぬ袖なき都哉　宗祇　大発句帳
sakurairo ni somenu sode mo naki miyako kana　sôgi 1420-1502
(cherry-color-in dyed-not sleeve-even-not capital!/'tis)

not a sleeve
not dyed in cherry-pink:
the capital

While young Bashô clearly recycled an old idea, the reality remained, so his thrill may have been genuine. With his "rich-poor" idiom, Bashô may have meant that blossom-viewing in Kyôto was *more* class-blind than in most other parts. More hyperbole by double negative: "*In the spring / not a mountain isn't / a flower garden*" (春はたゝ花園ならぬ山もなし　宗祇　大発句帳 *haru wa tada hanaen naranu yama mo nashi*　sôgi). "*Wind blows / and not an inn is not / a flower garden*" (風ふけば花園ならぬ宿もなし　宗養　大発句帳 *kaze fukeba hanazono naranu yado mo nashi*　sôyô -1563)."*When morning / mists-over, no country / lacks blossoms*" (朝霞こめば花なき里もなし　宗長　壁草 *asagasumi komeba hananaki sato mo nashi*　sôcho 1447-1532). "*In full bloom / not a mountain not / in the clouds*" (花さかり雲ゐに見えぬ山もなし　宗祇　大発句帳 *hanazakari kumoi ni mienu yama mo nashi*　sôgi). The clouds in this last *ku* are "cloud-well" (雲ゐ＝井), an elegant term for "the sky" or the Imperial Court, figuratively situated on the Ninth Cloud, so if we subtract the double negative we can also translate as follows: *"In full bloom / every mountain a magic / palace in the sky!"*

花盛匂ひはちらぬ袖もなし 宗祇 大発句帳
hanazakari nioi wa chiranu sode mo nashi   sôgi 1420-1502
(blossom-peak/heat scent-as-for scatter/fall-not sleeve-even not)

the bloomheat:
every sleeve in town
scatters scent

This *ku* probably belongs with the *hanazakari* (*"full bloom"* or *"cherries in heat"*) chapter. It is boringly conventional but still faintly erotic for one steeped in classical poetry, where lovers prowl about leaving their scent like tom-cats marking territory.[1] I killed the double-negative in translation. Sôgi's previous poem, too, might read better as *"Every sleeve / is dyed in cherry pink . . ."* . Jôha (1523-1602) has yet another double-negative blossom sleeve: *"Not a sleeve / not stuffed and wrung / today, blossoms"* (花をけふつみてしほれぬ袖もなし 紹巴 *hana o kyô tsumite shiborenu sode mo nashi*). Now *that* is a full sleeve, for wringing (*shiborenu*) means it is full of tears, happy tears of emotion which the petals stuffed within hold like a sponge. *Yes, I know.* Classic in Japan sometimes means corny.

うか／＼と田の中行けば櫻哉 鬼守 未来記
uka uka to ta no naka ikeba sakura kana   kishû 1765
(carelessly field-inside go-if cherry[blossoms]!)

田田桜田田

out in the fields
i happen to run into
cherry blossoms

just carelessly
walking through a field:
cherry blossoms!

Can you see a person 人 go 行 through 中 a paddy 田 to the cherry 桜? Does *sakura* mean petals that have blown or flowed down from the mountains with water for the paddies, or a lone blooming tree?

花さけば我庵ならぬ山もなし 昌察 大発句帳
hana sakeba waga io naranu yama mo nashi   shôsatsu (1734?/1481?)
(blossoms bloom-if/when my hut becomes-not mountain-even not)

cherries bloom
and every mountain
becomes my hut

cherries bloom
and i would dwell
anywhere pink

I do not know if this means the poet feels all the mountains look *that* familiar viewed from a distance or if he means he would be happy to dwell on any of them. At any rate, he is no stranger to them. Again, I ditched the serial negatives. The second is obviously a paraverse.

---

1. Perfumed Japanese   The Heian era (794-1185) nobility that developed the culture we still think of as Japan were big on scent. They held scent-sniffing parties where not only individual scents, but complex mixes were guessed at.   The men literally perfumed (i.e. smoked) their sleeves and tossed in bags of scent before going calling on their wives, or wooing wives-to-be. As a result, in the clean houses of the nobility, the scent could linger for many hours and a good nose might even identify a visitor the eyes missed.

花の陰にしびりきらさぬ人もなし 吉政　毛吹草
hana no kage ni shibiri kirasanu hito mo nashi kissei 1645
(blossoms' shade-in benumbed-not person-even not)

under the bloom
everyone knows about
pins & needles

This is the tenth double-negative *ku* introduced in this chapter! Obviously, "no . . . no" means more than just "yes" in Japanese. It emphasizes inclusiveness. But what a delight to find an idiom with enough snap to improve the original! Yes, even Japanese cannot sit for hours with crossed legs and not experience some numbness. Roots, rocks and, for the upper classes, formal clothing exacerbate the problem.

花見には足軽ならぬ人もなし　正章　毛吹草
hanami ni wa ashigaru naranu hito mo nashi masaakira (1645)
(blossom-viewing-as-for, leg-light[foot-soldier] become-not person-not)

blossom-viewing
not a man there not
a foot-soldier

Since everyone at a blossom-viewing feels giddy whether they drink or not, I suspect a pun on foot-soldier, written with the characters "leg+light," indicating a spirit unafraid to bloom and blow, *i.e.*, die.

上野・大名を馬からおろす桜哉　一茶
daimyô o uma kara orosu sakura kana issa -1827
(big-name(fief-chief[obj]) horse-from get-off cherry!/'tis)

ueno

they force lords
off their high-horses:
cherry blossoms

The beauty of a cherry, like that of a woman, can draw a great man down to its level. It is also most attractive seen from below. Riding, one cannot enter the bloomshade and obtain the best perspective. Be that as it may, Ueno was crowded and there was an official dismount at the entrance.

人心まつしきはなし花盛　素玉　拍挙千句?
hitogokoro mazushiki wa nashi hanazakari sogyoku ()
(people-heart/mind/s impoverished/small-as-for not: blossom-peak)

in full bloom　　　　　　　　　　　　　　　　not a mind
not a single person　　　　　　　　　　　wallows in poverty
of small mind　　　　　　　　　　　　　　　cherry-time!

bloom-peak
no one feels sorry
for himself

Not stingy, nor intolerant, nor conscious of their own poverty, everybody is rich of heart. This idea has many seconds: *"No poverty / in all who make it / to Mount Cherry"* (出る人に貧しきはなし花の山　尾谷　雪月花 *deru hito ni mazushiki wa nashi hana no yama*　bikoku (1736)); *"All people / leave their troubles at home / blossom-viewing"* (皆人の苦は留守させて花見哉　淇竹　四季発句版? *minabito no ku wa rusu sasete hanami kana*　kichiku? ()). Trying to make this poetry: *"Blossom-viewing! / When the whole world leaves / its troubles home."* This same sort of *Aren't-we-all-equally-rich-in-spirit! ku* are very common in New Year *ku* (see *The Fifth Season*).

世の中の昨日は古し花の陰　成美
yononaka no kinô wa furushi hana no kage　seibi -1816
(world-among's yesterday-as-for old: blossom's shade)

within the bloom
the world of yesterday
seems ancient

so where has
yesterday's world gone?
bloomshade

within the bloom
yesterday's world
is long ago

An indirect take on the *all-together free-from-pain* mentality: *today*, not yesterday, *all my troubles seem so far away* . . . A blunter version: *Yesterday, today / in the bloom-shade forgotten / a world of woe"* (昨日今日花に忘るゝ浮世哉　亀友　花七日) *kinô kyô hana ni wasururu ukiyo kana*　kiyû (1777).

何となく座頭ましわる花見哉　五潮　花七日
nantonaku zatô majiwaru hanami kana　gochô (1777)
(anything-not (vaguely) troupe-head (blind-boss) mixes blossom-viewing tis)

in his own way
the blind pimp mixes
blossom-viewing

the blind pimp
somehow fits in
blossom-viewing

Pimp is not a pleasant word, but what can English call blind men who ran troupes of blind singing women who were harlots? (The blind had not one but two nationwide unions with many ranks and were among the most prosperous money-lenders in Japan for hundreds of years.) Should I use the Japanese euphemism "troupe-head" instead of "blind pimp"? Or, how about "blind boss"?

手車に座頭うかるゝ花見哉　嘯山　葎亭
taguruma ni zatô ukaruru hanami kana　shôzan 1717-1801
(hand-cart-in troupe-head floats (feeling high) blossom-viewing 'tis/!)

a blind pimp
high on a hand-cart
blossom-viewing

Even blind, the *zatô* catches the excitement. Hand-carts, or any wheeled modes of transport other than large ox carts, were rare. Japanese who did not walk or ride horses sat in sedans hanging from poles shouldered by a pair of runners. The cart was not so much for transport as to keep the blind-boss and his belongings together while guarding him from walking into tree limbs or getting lost in the crowd. Still, I find it hard to believe all the blind were waited on hand and foot. A mid-19c *senryû* suggests most were beggars: *"Over a thousand / blind all swarming / the cherry trees"* (盲目千人余も桜の木へたかり　柳多留 61-1 *mekura sennin amari mo sakura no ki e takari*　yanagidaru). Wealth *never* swarms.

乞食とおなじ筵や花の陰　吾仲 類題発句帳
kôjiki to onaji mushiro ya hana no kage gochû -1733
(beggar/s-with same mat:/! blossomshade)

the bloomshade:
sharing a rush mat
with a beggar!

Where else, where else other than Japan, could this be true? What is truly remarkable, however, is that not only the mat *but the aesthetic appreciation* may have been shared:

> Czars and Kaisers may well envy this Oriental Ruler, whose subjects gather by the thousands, not to throw bombs and riot for bread or division of property, but to fall in love with cherry-trees, and write poems in their praise. At the cherry-blossom season especially his inborn passion for flowers and landscapes shows itself in prince, poet, peasant, merchant, and coolie. Tattered beggars gaze entranced at the fairy trees, and princes and ministers of state go to visit the famous groves. Bulletins announce, quite as a matter of course, that Prince Sanjo or Count Ito has done to Nara or Kioto, a three day's journey, to see the blossoming trees; which is as if Bismarck or Gladstone should interrupt his cares of state to undertake a pilgrimage to a distant rose show. (Eliza Scidmore: *Jinrikisha Days in Japan:* 1891)

While some trees – parts of famous groves, or private gardens – may have been monopolized by the upper classes,[1] the rest of the space was perhaps the most promiscuous of any in Japan.

似た顔の折々まじる花見哉　句空 再現
nita kao no oriori majiru hanami kana kûkû -1714
(similar face/s' occasionally mix blossom-viewing!/ 'tis)

similar faces meet up now and then blossom-viewing	similar faces gather from year to year blossom-viewing

The problem here is with the *oriori,* or, time to time. If we take it to mean now and then *within* the blossom-viewing, we see occasional coagulations of similar types within the far-reaching chaos. If we think of it as annual, we get the second reading. I prefer the first reading, but KS favors the second. Scidmore, again: *"one procession of jinrickshas will land a group with heads tied up in gaily-figured towels all alike;"* but apparel and *faces* – though the Japanese "face" also means "expression" – are not the same thing. Did anyone observe what percentage of viewers/partiers came alone or in groups? I suspect groups dominated, but who knows? What types gathered? Samurai? Bonzes? Young-crowd (male-prostitutes)? Dancing girls? Old Poets? Maids? Blossom guards (ch.34)? Could the features of people who make a practice of viewing blossoms together year after year come to look alike?

---

1 Blossom-viewing and Classes Eliza Scidmore, who cut her teeth on *Alaska – the Southern Coast and the Sitkan Archipelago* (1885) – was quite the anthropologist. She did something *haikai* poets generally fail to do. She carefully observed the class breakdown at different blossom-viewing sites. A cherry-blossom Sunday (she visited not long after Japan adopted the Western week) in Uyeno (Ueno), which haiku suggests was a real cherry bash, was "a holiday of the upper middle class," whereas the Mukojima festival along the river bank is the one she calls a saturnalia – or was it a bacchanalia. Still, the above quote, including the coolie and the beggars, was about Ueno, so the difference was apparently a matter of degree. Ah, one *ku* does admit class difference in the abstract: *"Middle and low [folk] too / have their blossom-viewings / suitable for them"* (中下もそれ相応の花見かな 素覧 *nakashimo mo sore sôô no hanami kana* soran (-1712?)).

櫻見て行きあたりたるこじき哉　梅舌
sakura mite ikiataritaru kojiki kana　baizetsu ()
(cherry/ies seeing going dead-end beggar/s 'tis/!/?)

looking at the bloom
one beggar walks
into another

different attention　　　　　　　　　　　　　　**two aesthetes**

cherry-blossom-viewing,　　　　　　　　　oogling bloom
i run into a man　　　　　　　　　beggar and poet run into
busy begging!　　　　　　　　　　　　one another

looking at blossoms
i fall right into a trap
of beggars

I cannot help thinking of the paradox of ambiguity – how the lack of specific subject and number tells us less with the result that we cannot help making more, in this case, *four poems in one.*

乞食も一曲あるか花の陰　　一茶 文化五
kojiki mo ikkyoku aru ka hana no kage　issa -1827
(beggar/s-even one song has? blossom-shade)

the bloom-shade　　　　　　　　　　　do beggars, too
does the beggar, also　　　　　　　　have their songs to offer
have a song for us?　　　　　　　　　　under the bloom

Everyone in the party around the cherry tree performs in turn – yes, it was done long before *karaoke* – and even the beggar is asked to join in. The *even* shows beggars are indeed marginal, but they were there from the start. As Kyoshi wrote a century later in one of his erased *ku*: *"The beggars / are already here / first blossoms"* (乞食のはや来て居るよ初桜（消）虚子 *kojiki no haya kitteiru hatsuzakura*).

花さくや旅人のいふ乞食雨　一茶 文化十四
hana saku ya tabibito no iu kojiki-ame　issa -1827
(blossom/s bloom/s:/! travelers' call [it] beggar-rain)

when cherries bloom
we see what travelers call
"beggar squalls"

Or should I say "shower?" Anyone who has spent time in a poor nation needs no explanation.

花さくや下手念仏も銭が降る　一茶 文化十二
hana saku ya heta nenbutsu mo zeni ga furu　issa -1827
(blossom/s bloom/s:/! / poor sutras/chanting-even coins fall)

the cherries bloom!
coins rain down on even
the sorriest sutras

When the world is drunken on blossoms and rice beer, the poets' "~ *no* . . . *no* ~" equality proves itself in reality as hearts open and people *behave* in a more egalitarian manner, sharing resources.

芥子之介・銭降れとおがむ手元へ桜哉　一茶
keshi-no-suke // zeni fure to ogamu temoto e sakura kana　issa
([poppy-child] coins fall! praying hand/s-to, cherry[blossoms/petals]!/!/?)

into wee hands
praying *fall! coins, fall!*
cherry petals

a poppy's hand
praying for money fills
with cherry petals

ちる花に鉢をさし出す羅漢哉　一茶
chiru hana ni hachi o sashidasu rakan kana　issa
(falling blossoms/petals-to/for/in bowl extended arhat 'tis/!/?)

it reaches out
a bowl for the blossoms,
the stone arhat!

If people and stone figures were equal, well then so were cherry petals and coins. The first *ku* had a preface suggesting the beggar was a child who lived in a monastery, called a *keshi-no-tsuke*, after the poppy flower that dropped its petals so quickly it was synonymous with a tenuous existence. Such children tended to catch colds and die.

貧乏が追ても来ぬぞ花の陰　成美
binbô ga ôte mo konu zo hana no kage　seibi -1816
(poverty chasing-even come-not! blossoms' shade)

though poverty
chases, it can't reach into
the bloom-shade

The bloomshade as a sort of refuge from poverty. A clever way to restate the standard rich-of-heart poems we have already seen. Still, it seems a bit odd coming from this wealthy poet who once employed Issa, who really was poor and left us a dozen or so *ku* about his good traveling companion, the god Poverty (In Lightning Slim's words: *I didn't have bad luck, I wouldn't have any luck at all.*)

米袋空しくなれど桜哉　一茶　文化二
komebukuro munashiku naredo sakura kana issa (-1827)
(rice-sack empty-became-but cherry/blossoms 'tis/!/?)

two types of food

my rice sack
is in bad, bad shape
but, hey, cherries!

right when our
rice sacks reach "empty"
cherries bloom

This *ku* may be the first to make an important seasonal linkage: the period of greatest want, when grain stores – at least rice – drop is not in mid-winter, but Spring before the new crop is ready, right when the cherry blooms. Issa's rhetoric makes this a transcendent experience rather than complaint.

銭なしが音骨高き桜哉　一茶　正一
zeninashi ga otobone-takaki sakura kana issa
(small-change-not[people] sound-bone high cherry 'tis)

the penniless
have the highest voices
under the bloom

While Issa, as we have seen, dismounted Daimyô and otherwise played up equality under the bloom, he was too poor himself to fall for the delusion of classlessness for more than an inebriated moment.

花さくや足の乗物手の奴　一茶　文化五
hana saku ya ashi no norimono te no yakko issa -1827
(cherries bloom: legs' riding-thing (vehicle), hands' servant/slave)

to the bloom!	the bloom waits!	cherries bloom
riding my legs, my hands	i saddle my legs and	we ride our legs served
my footmen	call for my hands	by our hands

Norimono includes horses and the more common sedans shouldered by men. Lacking a poetic noun in English, I switched to verbs (ride/saddle).

骸骨の上を粧ふといへるに・銭もたぬ心の鬼も花見哉　梅室
zeni motanu kokoro no oni mo hanami kana　baishitsu 1768-1852
(coins have-not, heart's/s' demon/s-too, blossom-viewing 'tis/!/?)

speaking of robes on bones

the mind-demons	blossom-viewing
of the penniless also out	mind-demons also roam
blossom viewing	about penniless

We discuss the *ku* alluded to in the preface/title twice elsewhere. Did Issa's contemporary find the metaphor of dressed bones suggestive of poverty as well as mortality? I am not sure I get the *ku*.

ない袖を振て見せ／＼花見哉　一茶　文政一
nai sode o futte mise mise hanami kana issa -1827
(not-sleeves swinging/shaking show show: blossom-viewing tis)

poor dancer	***need a miracle***
blossom-viewing	see me multiply
i flap my sleeves my	the money i don't have
empty sleeves!	blossom-viewing

The sleeve is waved when dancing or mugging around, making what might be called dance-poses. Waving a *no/t-sleeve* means *trying to do something impossible*. Issa elsewhere complains of never learning to dance. As a step-child he was not taught, naturally clumsy, he could not learn and, as a poor man, who had to remain single until he was fifty . . . Since sleeves served as pockets, "no-sleeves" suggests a lack of money, more specifically, someone getting by juggling pennies.[1] Plainly put, Issa is trying to enjoy his *hanami* with insufficient change to buy stuff from venders, etc..

何桜かざくら銭の世也けり 一茶
nani sakura ka zakurazeni no yo narikeri issa 1805
(what-cherries? small-change's world becomes[emph.])

cherry blossoms?
what blossoms? small-change
runs the world!

Issa's crazy-verse version spells out the money entirely in onomatopoeia: *nani sakura ka <u>zakura-zakura chirijiri</u> ni hanabanashiku mo . . . .* Blossom-viewing ate up small change. For one, there were *bridge tolls* (又しても橋銭かする花見哉 一茶 文化五 *mata shite mo hashizeni ga suru hanami kana*) – something *samurai* generally were exempt from paying. Years later, he wrote: *"Just to see / the blossoms takes change / in the capital"* (花見るも銭をとらるゝ都哉 一茶 文政七 *hana miru mo zeni o toraruru miyako kana* 1824). A book published the year of Issa's death (1827) purportedly all Bashô (1644-1694) *ku* but suspected to be partly or mostly made up by the editor Nanimaru, includes detail: "One *ri* one *sen*" or *"One mile one pence: / Now I'm ready to view / the blossoms of Edo"* (一理一銭江戸の花見る用意哉 存疑芭蕉 句解参考 *ichiri ichizen edo no hana miru yôi kana* ?bashô?). A preface said he had to borrow road-money to see blossoms 130 *ri* to the East.

人足につられてまはる花見哉 吟江 夢占
hitoashi ni tsurarete mawaru hanami kana ginkô 1780
(people-legs[money/transport]-by taken circle blossom-viewing!/'tis)

on the skirt-tails   riding the money
of others i make the rounds   of other men, i get around
blossom-viewing   blossom-viewing

Poet as poor man? Or, parasite? *Ashi* means both transportation – or "wheels" in Usanian slang – and money, which, after all, gets around. *Hito-ashi*, or, "people-legs," means those provided by others.

華のもと是非来て掃除勤ばや 一茶 知友録 寛政三
留別 渭浜庵// *hananomoto zehi kite sôji tsutomebaya* issa 1791
(blossom-base/below by-all-means come cleaning/chores work-wish!)

~~blossom-viewing~~   ~~by all means~~
~~"do come, we need someone~~   ~~come to the blossoms~~
~~to help clean!"~~   ~~help clean up~~

under your tree / let me sweep the blossoms again / when i come back – trans. ueda

I thought this *ku* I titled ***a poor man's invitation*** was sarcastic and written from the perspective of a menial. On the former count, I could not have been further from the truth. Reading Ueda (*Dew on the Grass*), I found this *ku* brings up the tail of a letter from Issa to his employer Somaru, thanking him for granting a leave of absence! It *is* from a menial perspective, *but* the tone is "extremely reverent."

---

1. "no/t-sleeve/s" At first, I thought it a unique coinage, such as the "chicken-*was*" a man could not give to a woman at a toe-selling party in Zora Neale Hurston's *Of Mules and Men*. But, "not-sleeves" was both a *bona fide* idiom and used in *haikai* prior to Issa. Eg.: "The *susuki* / goes on waving / its no-sleeve" (ない袖を振て見せたる芒花かな 許六 *nai sode o futte misetaru suzuki kana* kyôroku (-1715)). The *Susuki* (*Micanthus sinensis*), sometimes translated as "pampas grass," was identified with classy moon-viewing on the one hand, *and* the low-land occupied by the poor and criminal elements of society. Its humble plume appears when it withers and dies.

in/equality

片脇に息をころして花見哉　一茶 享和句帖 享和三
katawaki ni iki o koroshite hanami kana　issa (1803)
(half-side-on/at breath killing blossom-viewing 'tis/!/?)

<table>
<tr><td>off to one side
barely breathing
my *hanami*</td><td>off to one side
afraid to wag my tongue
blossom-viewing</td></tr>
</table>

This might be an observation of someone at the social margin, such as an untouchable, but it is far more likely to refer to Issa himself, still poor and unknown in middle-age, tending a party of wealthy poets.

よき人にそつとつき行く花見哉　千代
yoki hito ni sotto tsuki yuku hanami kana　chiyo (-1775)
(good/rich/pretty-person/s-with quietly stick[with] blossom-viewing 'tis/!)

i quietly go
with the beautiful people
blossom-viewing

<table>
<tr><td>blossom-viewing:
i pretend to belong with
a wealthy party</td><td>blossom viewing
i quietly tag along with
a man of parts</td></tr>
</table>

It is hard to tell if she is crashing a party or attempting to observe what it is like to be wealthy (we know she was beautiful). Either way, this bit of fun is a far cry from Issa's class consciousness.

花見んと致せば下に／＼哉　一茶
hana min to itaseba shita ni shita ni kana　issa -1827
(blossom-viewing doing[polite]-if/when down! down! tis)

you go view
blossoms and it's
"down! down!"

The use of a polite *itaseba* for "doing" a blossom-view sets up the rude awakening later in the *ku*: Issa probably did not enjoy being ordered to hit the earth for a passing personage. Two more such Issa *ku*: "Remove your hat / even in the bloom-shade / it's 'down!' 'down!'" (花陰も笠ぬげしたに／＼哉 *hanakage mo kasa nuge shita ni shita ni kana*); "What big-shot's / blossom viewing? "get to / the side! the side!" (何者の花見や脇よれ／＼と *nani mono no hanami ya waki yore yore to*).

寝て待や切手をもたぬ花見衆　一茶 文化五
netematsu ya kirite o motanu hanami shû　issa -1827
(sleeping-wait: ticket having/carrying-not blossom-viewing-crowd)

blossom-viewing

the masses
without tickets wait
sleeping out

Is Issa describing a phenomenon more common in Japan than the USA of camping out in line to get into a popular event? To think they had been doing it for centuries! In a haiku written decades later, Issa wrote: *"My ticket pass / tied around my finger / garden sakura"* (出切手を指にむすぶや庭桜 一茶 文政八 *degitte o yubi ni musubu ya niwazakura*). The Japanese "leaving-ticket" (so one can come and go freely) has no English equivalent I know of. The *ku* is not about poverty, but it is the type of thing only a poor poet living without privilege would find worthy of notice.

花さくや日がな一日立仏　一茶 文政五
hana saku ya higana ichinichi tachibotoke   issa -1827
(blossoms bloom: day-one[all]-day standing-buddhist-statue/corpse)

cherries bloom
the whole day long
standing up

My OJD describes the *tachibotoke* as a "standing Buddhist statue." There is no figurative use given. But, I think this is a complaint about standing in lines all day, not easy for old and lame Issa, or, perhaps, a clever way to describe a pretty tree. Imagine, *it just stands there blooming away in place!*

何くれと浮世をぬすむ花の陰　鬼貫
nani kure to ukiyo o nusumu hana no kage   onitsura 1660-1738
(what['s this] "please"! floating-world[+obj] steal blossom-shade)

you don't ask,   what's this *"please!"*
you *take* your share   under the blossoms you *steal*
of bloom-shade!   the floating world

Is this advice to someone too shy to barge his way into a lightly populated bloomshade? The wealthy have retainers go early and obtain space which is guarded until they appear. For others, it is not so easy. The poor could not get away with "stealing" space. I am afraid the next *ku* is the reality:

花の陰誰隙くれしうす草履　一茶 文政七
hana no kage da ga hima kureshi usuzôri   issa
(blossom-shade who space give? thin[soled] zori)

the bloom-shade
who will give some room
to thin-sandals

Thin *zôri*. Issa has come on foot and, as a poor man, is too slow buying the replacements hawked by the road-side.

若い衆に先越れしよ花の陰　一茶 文政三
wakaishu ni saki kosareshi yo hana no kage   issa -1827
(young crowd-by ahead-passed! blossom-shade)

the young crowd
beat me to the shade
of the blossoms

This "young crowd" (*wakai shu*) is not *the* young-crowd (*wakashu*) we will encounter later. Without enough money to hire someone to find and to save one a space, an old man – especially one with palsy, like Issa – does not always get what he wants. No, even if he had money and health, competition for the ideal bloomshade would only rise a level. A contemporary of Issa's summed up as follows:

花に来てはや欲ぼるや居所　梅室
hana ni kite haya yokobaru ya iridokoro baishitsu 1768-1852
(blossoms-to coming already desire/covet/want! be/sit/stay-place)

as soon as you
see blossoms, you desire
a place to stay

soon as you reach
the bloom you grow greedy
for your own spot

as soon as you
get there you want a place
in the bloomshade

咲くからに罪作らする桜哉　一茶 文化七
saku kara ni tsumi tsukurasuru sakura kana issa -1827
(blooms-because sin/s making cherry[blossoms] 'tis/!/?)

by blooming
a cherry can turn us
into sinners

ah, the cherry
this tree creates sin
by blooming

The most impossible Commandment says thou shall not covet this and that. Buddhism says thou shall not desire, *period.* Because Issa wrote another *ku* about causing sin by feeding birds resulting in a bird fight, I think he alludes to the desire and struggle for the bloomshade occasioned by the beauty of the cherry blossom, rather than an allegory about female beauty or a vague cause-and-effect sin, namely, that of loving this world rather than *that*.

下々に生れて夜もさくら哉　一茶 文化八
shimojimo ni umarete yoru mo sakura kana issa -1827
(bottom/low x2-in born night-too cherry[blossom-viewing?] 'tis/!)

born at the bottom
of the bottom: night, too
cherry blossoms

Night blossoms can mean courtesans in the pleasure quarters beyond the means of poor men. Here I think Issa plays with that by observing that the poor man who cannot afford an inn, which is to say Issa himself, sees the blossoms all night, for he must sleep under them. But, he may be reporting on *eta* (untouchables, see *etadera* . . .) enjoying blossom-viewing at night. Or, he may allude to Etsujin (1661-1739), a drifter from the North country who ran off with a cherry-blossom, which is to say Yoshiwara courtesan and wrote: *"Called the lowest / of the low-down guests: / the blossom inn"* (下々の下の客といはれん花の宿　越人*gege no ge no* [1] *kyaku to iwaren hana no yado*). I.e., an inn for blossom-viewing *or* a cat-house.

---

1. Lowest of Lowism *Shimo* and *ge* are both pronunciations of the same Chinese character, but *ge* sounds baser. Etsujin's 3 *ge*'s beat Issa's 2 *shimo*'s, but Issa ends up winning the "low" competition, for he has a *suzumi*, or "summer-cool," *ku* with no less than 7 (!) *ge* in it: *"Oh, how cool / the low low low low low low / low country!* (*ge ge mo ge ge ge ge-no ge-koku-no suzushisa yo*). The poor Eta live on the riverside, which was liable to flood, but cooler than the higher ground where the homes of the wealthy were. Issa lived seven years by a river in Edo.

入相を惜しむは鐘のない花見 摂州 初代川柳
iriai o oshimu wa kane no nai hanami senryû (1782)
(vespers[obj] regret-as-for, moneyless blossom-viewing)

入相を待ッハうは氣な花見也 石斧 同3
iriai o matsu wa uwaki na hanami nari senryû (1783)
(vespers[obj] wait-as-for cheating blossom-viewing is)

<blockquote>
the vesper bell
is bad news for moneyless
blossom-viewing
</blockquote>

<blockquote>
blossom-viewing
cheaters eagerly await
the vesper bell
</blockquote>

The first *senryû* describes a poor man's situation, the second, written a year later, a middle-class philanderer. If you think "cheaters" too harsh, make it "swivers." My reading of the first *ku* preserves the order of the words, the second, their relationship. As we shall see later, for the wealthy, sunset was time for an express ride to a fine inn, or the pleasure quarters, with its night-cherries, plant and human.

夕桜蟻も寝所は持ちにけり 一茶
yûzakura ari mo nedoko wa mochinikeri issa -1827
(evening-cherry: ants-even sleep-place have[+finality])

<blockquote>
dusk blossoms
even ants have a place
to go to sleep
</blockquote>

There is a saying I have misplaced about ants having holes and bird's nests, etc. Issa is a man and he had no place to go. Perhaps, the rangers did not even allow him to remain under the tree. Some places were like that:

東叡山・寝とすれば棒突きまはる花見哉 其角
neyo to sureba bôtsuki mawaru hananoyama kikaku (-1707)
(sleep-try do-if stick/club-poker/s[police] circles blossom-mountain)

<blockquote>
when you'd sleep
the stick-pokers come round
on cherry mountain
</blockquote>

The "pole-stickers," *i.e.,* police/rangers, did not permit all night stays on some "blossom-mountains." I would have assumed only sleeping was forbidden, but Kikaku specifies the location, East Mt. Hiei, which is Ueno park in Edo, and a poet born the year he died specified the same in this masterpiece:

人去って櫻群集の月夜かな 蓼太
hito satte sakura gunshu no tsuki yo kana ryôta (1707-87)
(people leaving, cherry(tree/blossom) crowd/multitude's moon-night!/'tis)

<blockquote>
humans leave
and cherry trees throng
under the moon
</blockquote>

So, it would seem, that the "mountain" was cleared at night (like the state park here on Key Biscayne). The idea of the blossoming trees *alive* enjoying the moonshine is beautifully expressed. We almost feel they enjoy a spell without man. Yet, I feel for the poor who cannot enjoy even nature as the rich with their own gardens can. But, other places let even the poor stay: *"Flopped down / a blossom-viewing mat / for a wind-screen"* (寝ころんで風のおさへや花筵 沾永 雪月花 *nekoronde kaze no osae ya hanamushiro* senei (1736)).

in/equality

夜の花いやしきは灯のひかり哉　伴山 再現 花七日
yoru no hana iyashiki wa hi no hikari kana　banzan (1777)
(night-blossom base/despicable/impoverished-as-for lamp's light 'tis/!)

night-blossoms
an ignoble viewing
is by lamp-light

Would nobility or samurai have pine torches in the wild or candles in the garden?

鎌倉の穴に花さき誰が家　巴人 全句を読む
kamakura no ana ni hana saki dare ga ie　hajin -1742
(kamakura's hole/s-in blossom blooms/ing whose home/s)

a cherry blooms
in a kamakura pit
someone's home

The "hole" in the original refers to *yagura,* caves partly or entirely artificially cut into the stony sides of hills, of which there are many in Kamakura, once used for storage and for crypts, but by the Edo era occasionally used as hovels by the poor. This is ostensibly an observation of a cherry tree growing at the entrance of such a place. The original can also be read, "Whose home is it?" Maruyama, citing Bashô's *"Who's that / wearing a rush mat / in blossom[pretty/dressed-up] spring?"(komo o kite dare-bito imasu hana no haru* [1]), a New Year *ku,* writes that the someone might actually *be* someone, i.e. a hermit incognito. (「巴人の全句を読む」)

初桜花ともいはぬ伏家哉　一茶 文化四
hatsuzakura hana to mo iwanu fuseya kana　issa
(first cherry blossom/posh/fancy-even say-not hovel!/'tis)

the first cherry   the first bloom
in front of a far from   by my hovel so far from
flowery hovel   a rose garden!

This sort of contrast is always *interesting* but never *very* interesting. In translation, it is not at all interesting because "flowery" doesn't make it. The second reading *does*, but it is beyond the pale.

にくい程桜咲たる小家哉　一茶 文化六
nikui hôdo sakura sakitaru ko ie kana　issa -1827
(spiteful amount cherry blossoms small-house 'tis/!)

cherry blossoms   a small house:
spitefully abundant for   what hateful abundance
a small house   of cherry bloom!

The original is a line of modification coming to a head in the subject, the small house. Why does Issa say "small" house, rather than "poor" house (eg. *shizu-ga-ie*)? I think it is because he had come across a *senryû* (which I have read twice (and lost)) about how spiteful a large member was on a small (short) man. The word order was, if I recall correctly, very close. I include the *ku* for the way it harmonizes with the next two and because I enjoy some *spite* in verse.

↑ **1. Bashō's *dare-bito* (who's that)** Bashô wrote "five hundred years ago, there were many [sage] beggars in Saigyô's *Senjûshô*. [I wrote this *ku*] to show my sadness at feeling drawn toward good [*yoki-bito* = wealthy/ attractive/ noble, etc] people, and my desire to return to Saigyô's example." As an annotator of Bashô says a beggar on the New Year, a time when auspicious omens were sought, was a bold innovation, but we might also note that there was a folk tradition of incognito wandering gods in the guise of beggars.

誰とても見それぬものや花の顔　重方　毛吹草
dare tote mo misorenu mono ya hana no kao　shigekata (1645)
(who [emphatic] look-aside-not thing!/: blossom/s-face)

cherry power

blossom faces
is there anyone who can
not look at them?

Presumably, this is about cherry trees, but are there not people so good looking you cannot help gazing at them though everything they do or say suggests they are bereft of beauty in the heart?

えた寺の桜まじ／＼咲にけり　一茶　文化七
etadera no sakura majimaji sakinikeri　issa (-1827)
(eta[untouchables]-temple's cherry/ies boldly[staring] bloom/s[+fin.])

bold blossoms

the eta temple   the cherry trees
cherry trees: unblinking   at the untouchable temple
in their bloom   are in your face

For the untouchable class, even *looking at* someone was considered a crime, as once was the case with blacks using a white water fountain in the USA. In Max Bickerton's mistranslation (1932), and many others since, the "cherries at the Eta Temple *coweringly* blossom," (my italics) but the psychological mimesis *majimaji* in Issa's day generally meant just the opposite.[1] Cherry trees, no matter where they are, bloom boldly. Nature does not kowtow to human convention.

金の糞しそうな犬ぞ花の陰　一茶
kin no hako shisôna inu zo hananokage　issa
(golden/money shit does-seems-like dog! blossoms shade)

the bloomshade   look at that dog
a dog that looks like   i'll bet it poops gold
it would poop gold   the bloomshade

This has to be one of the strangest blossom-viewing *ku* ever written. Imagine the pampered lap-dog of a wealthy woman, treated, perhaps, to *sashimi* and resting on a silk brocade pillow worth a month or year of Issa's paltry earnings . . . Issa also wrote of *"Princes and princesses / conversing with reserve / blossom-viewing"* (宮人は歯に絹きせる花見哉　*miyabito wa ha ni kinu kiseru hanami kana*). The original suggests their beautiful clothing with the idiomatic "silk on their teeth," which means the polite language of the Kyoto Court as opposed to the openly argumentative of the Edo townsmen. Be that as it may, my point is that the reverse side of observing the poor is observing the rich. It is hard to be aware of only one of them.

1. Mistranslation MB's mistranslation is most recently reprinted in Grove's haiku anthology (Bower:1996) and remains uncorrected at an Issa website at this time because not all Japanese today are aware of the "unblinking/bold" meaning of this mimetic expression (i.e. my suggestion was overruled for a "native-speaker"). Later note: After I explained further it was re-re-corrected. The problem is that *majimaji* is that rare mimesis that can signify two very different psychological states within one and the same language. This makes a dictionary useless. One must read by context, namely, that Issa has many poems about the Eta and all are bold, none cowering. Note that some *burakumin* (the pc term for Eta, it means *hamlet-folk*) activists in Japan read Issa's *ku* correctly and one I googled upon even said it was what first made him want to become an activist!

貧乏人花見ぬ春はなかりけり　　一茶 文化四
binbônin hana minu haru wa nakarikeri   issa (age 45)
(poor-man/men blossoms see/see-not spring-as-for not (+emph.))

    not a spring   every spring
when the poor do not   the poor man has his
   see the bloom   blossoms to see

– sed tangere . . .

a poor man
can't help seeing blossoms
every spring

The only readings I have found are lyrical: *nature, free for all!* But, is *that* Issa? Issa who writes elsewhere about the cost of blossom-viewing? *Access* to blossoms, plant or human, was not always free. A man with a strong libido (after marrying, he noted the frequency of his coitus), Issa must have slobbered over the latter variety of blossom. Every spring, a poor man sees, *must see* all that beauty, beauty he cannot have! As a 1667 *ku* notes: *"In the spring / not a man but lusts / for the flowers"* (*haru wa hana ni kôshoku naranu hito mo nashi* seichû 春は花に好色ならぬ人もなし 正忠 続山の井) In Issa's time, most men in Edo, the largest city, remained unmarried for life. They had to in order to survive or to pursue their chosen (or unchosen) work. In recent decades, sympathy for the circumstances of women has become widespread in the English language world. This is good; women have long been oppressed by law, and literally beaten up by men. BUT, we forget that poor men fare no better. Unlike their sisters, they endure little or no sex and cannot even experience the joy of parenthood (i.e. children). They are completely shut out from what we think of as "a life." They, not women, are the expendable ones, mere canon fodder. They are why polygamy (by marriage or mistress) is unfair. Issa was single when he wrote the above *ku* and I am single as I write this. Had he married without money, he would have had to give up *haikai*. Likewise for me, today.

極つぶし桜の下にくらしけり　　一茶 文化三
goku tsubushi sakura no shita ni kurashikeri issa (age 44)
(extreme/grain-smashing cherry/ies' below living(+emph.))

a free-loader
i live! i live below
the cherries

Though a critic of mammon, Issa was all too aware that poet=parasite, or, in his case, "poet=*grain-cruncher*." Drunks are quick to share food and drink, and people who walk home often leave it behind. Poor young scribe-poet Issa probably made out like a bandit in the bloomshade. And, we may be sure he had poetry and stories enough to contribute so those who treated him did not feel cheated.

MONOPOLIZING BLOOM

野を仕切空もやぶれて花見哉　寂芝 失典
no o shikiri sora mo yaburete hanami kana jakushi (17-18c)
(field[obj] cordon-off sky-even breaking, blossom-viewing!/?/'tis)

    fields are divided　　　　　　　　　　blossom viewing?
and even the air broken up　　　　when fields are split and even
    blossom viewing　　　　　　　　　　　　the sky's torn up

Old artwork shows cherries in fields close to cities surrounded on two or more sides by hanging cloth which hid the bottom (3-8 feet) of the tree. Large trees might even be partitioned. I imagine highbrows blocking ugly sights to frame perfect spaces; nobles trying to keep apart from commoners; bourgeoisie intent on controlling space; lowbrows seeking privacy to behave lewdly and, perhaps, even "owners'" charging to enter or peek. Whatever, many Japanese came to feel it wrong to monopolize natural beauty. Perhaps, there was a time when most people meekly accepted being shut out as the natural order of things, but after the long Warring Period (14-16c), a Shôgun who was a commoner (Hideyoshi -1598), the rise of a middle class in the following Tokugawa Period (or Edo era), the high literacy rate, etc., Japan came to be blessed with an abundance of uppity souls. In 1660, Kinpira, lit., "gold-equal," presumably for his egalitarian philosophy, hero of a Jôruri play (a drama accompanied by ballads sung accompanied by the still relatively new, banjo-like folk instrument = the *shamisen*) decried the way the largest cherry tree at the Kiyomizu Temple was curtained off for a select few, with the result others could not see it.

    To raise a curtain to encircle and block from view a tree where rich and poor alike would mass! It's as bad as clouds blocking the moon! (貴賤こぞって群集する木のもとに幕うち回しふさぐ事、月を隠す雲とや云わん。)

This criticism has particular relevance for a temple setting because the moon stands for the light of the Buddhist Law, provided for all beings alike, and the clouds for obstacles to seeing the light if it were. The following *senryû* depict the situation a hundred years later. The first focuses our hate; the second shows what poor people put up with; the third how curtains became increasingly permeable with each day; and the last suggests that, in some locations, trees may have remained hidden until the end.

定紋であたりを囲ふいゝ花見 柳多留 24-26
jômon de atari o kakou ii hanami yanagidaru 1791
(coat-of-arms-with area[acc] surround good bl.vwg)

    the whole area
surrounded by coat of arms
    blossom-viewing

紫のそとへ花降り琴聞え 江戸の花見
murasaki no soto e hana furi koto kikoe (no date)
(purple-outside-to blsms falling koto hearing)

    outside the purple
cherry petals fall and you
    hear the zithers

ほころびを覗いて歩く花の山 柳多留 2-29
hokorobi o nozoite aruku hana no yama yanagi. 1767
(worndown[acc] peeking walk blossom-mountain)

    peeking into
the dishabille, we stroll
    cherry mountain

花の山幕のふくれるたびに散リ 柳多留 7-39
hananoyama maku no fukureru tabi ni chiri yana. 1772
(blm-mountain screen's distending time-when fall)

    mount cherry
when the curtains distend
    the petals fall

9

Intoxicating Cherries
花乃醉
hana-no-yoi

花の山誠の下戸は松許り　桂坊 古今句鑑
hana no yama makoto no geko wa matsu bakari　keibô 1777
([cherry]blossoms' mountain: genuine teetotaler-as-for pine[tree] only)

<blockquote>
cherry mountain:
the only real teetotalers
are pine trees
</blockquote>

How can we explain the *equality* found under the bloom? The proverbial equality of poets in the bloomshade may help set the stage, but the deeper spring bubbles up from something else. Call it *inebriation*. In Japanese, the connotations of drunkenness are not so unfavorable as in English. The cover of a contemporary collection of haiku titled 酔 (辻桃子編 1989), a character generally Englished as "drunk," is glossed by one English word: "ecstasy." The whole world is giddy when the cherries bloom. Even *"Men not drinking / blossom-viewing sake / [had] drunken hearts!"* (花見酒のまて人にや酔心　信直 *hanamizake noma de hito niya yoigokoro*　shinjiki ()). Above the sober pines, we behold *"The sky, drunk – / today, Yoshino's in it: / full bloom!"* (酔た天けふみよしのゝ盛哉　萬翁 *youta sora kyô miyoshino no sakari kana*　manô). Yoshino, *the* classic viewing site.

大空も花に酔りや芳野山　琴詩 花七日
ôzora mo hana ni eiri ya yoshino yama　kinshi 1777
(big-sky-even blossoms-by intoxicated! yoshino mountain)

<blockquote>
mount yoshino
the whole sky is high
on blossoms!
</blockquote>

<blockquote>
the whole sky
is high on blossoms!
mount yoshino
</blockquote>

空を酔せ人を酔せてさくらかな　素丸
sora o yowase hito o yowasete sakura kana　somaru 1712-95
(sky[+obj] drunken-making/made cherry[blosoms]!/'tis)

<blockquote>
making the sky
and making men drunk,
cherry blossoms!
</blockquote>

<blockquote>
cherry blossoms,
you have made the sky
and man drunk!
</blockquote>

<blockquote>
making heaven
and humans tipsy
cherry blossoms
</blockquote>

Reading just these *ku*, it would be impossible to guess exactly what defines *a tipsy sky*. Many, perhaps half of all Japanese flush at their first sip of *sake*. Are the cherry blossoms being credited for a colorful sunset, then? Actually, the drunken sky is a Chinese conceit developed by earlier *ku*:

天も花にゑゝるか（りや）雲のみだれあし 親重 犬子立圃 空礫 無記名 嵐山集
ten mo hana ni eeru [yoeru]ka (eeri ya) kumo no midareashi   shigeyori 1633, ryûho -1669
(heaven/sky, too/even blossoms-by inebriated ?/! clouds' wild/disarrayed legs)

is heaven, too
drunken with the bloom?
clouds in disarray

Both versions of the original feature "cloud *legs*," a common idiom for the brush-stroke-like downfall of rain from clouds viewed at a distance. While the poet (diff. in each source) may have seen more than one cloud showing "legs" slanted in different directions (it happens in the hills), he probably is only using the idiom to turn the old Chinese poetic conceit of a blossom-drunk heaven=sky into *haikai*. Those *rain-legs* provide both wit and justification, i.e. a concrete basis, for the abstract Chinese idea. The modern Japanese critic might put down the *ku* as artificial, but, despite chance being dead against it, I prefer to imagine the poet (but, poets?) took it from life. Each reader may make his or her choice. Pardon the obsolete ways of writing "drunk" that messy the Romanization of the original.

花に酔ふ天にも口は有ものか 如濁 蘆分船
hana ni you ten ni mo kuchi wa aru mono ka   jodaku 1694
(blossoms-by [get]drunk-heaven-even-to mouth-as-for have thing?/!)

blossom-drunk
so the sky really *does*
have a mouth?

drunk on blossoms
so, heaven has a mouth?
give me a break!

Unless you think the poet witnessed a wild sky – which I like to think – this is, as per the second reading, a meta-*ku* (a poem *about* a poem) of the sort that would later be called a *senryû*.

鶯の竹にさますや花の酔   潜柳 三千化
uguisu no take ni samasu ya hana no yoi   senryû 1725
(warbler/nightingale's bamboo-in cools/sobers! blossom-drunk)

the nightingale
sobers up in the bamboo!
blossom drunk

(**Note:** This Senryû is not the founder of *senryû* 川柳). Like the pine, the bamboo is straight and steadfast (little change of *color* [1]), i.e. *sober*. Art pairs the warbler, usually translated as "nightingale" because it is *the* classic song bird in Japanese literature, with the flowering plum, but no one gets drunk *plum*-blossom viewing (It is too cold and people usually keep standing). Japanese bamboo groves are open and breezy (*cool,* another association with "sober" in Japanese) because most of the shoots are eaten before they can grow. They usually belong to the sparrow, but "nightingales" evidently could visit. Does the poet mean to include birds among the blossom-intoxicated, or are these *uguisu* really female singers taking a break. I like to imagine listen to a *shakuhachi*, a wind-instrument made of bamboo.

---

1. Red-faced Japanese Drinkers Scidmore attributed it to a property of *sake*: "The Japanese drink it from a shallow porcelain or lacquer cups that hold barely a tablespoonful, but by repetition they imbibe pints. Its first effect is to loosen the tongue and limber the joints; its second to turn the whole body a flaming red." (JDIJ) The flushing is really due to the lack of an enzyme needed to break-down alcohol. Most Caucasians have it but almost half of the Asian population do not. People who redden with *sake* do so when they drink any alcohol.

東西花にも尻をからげけり 蘭更
nishi higashi hana ni mo shiri o karagekeri   rankô (-1799)
(west-east blossoms-to-even butt[+obj.] wrap-up[+emph.])

    east and westward
    we run with skirts uptucked:
    blossoms and asses

    east and west
    we even bare our buttocks
    to the blossoms

Japanese men tucked the tails of their robes into their belts when they traveled rapidly, letting their legs move more freely and their crotches stay as crotches should stay, cool. The common idiom *shiri-karage* reflects the fact that asses are what stood out. I suppose this *ku* might have fit better in the cherry-hunting chapter, but mass movements of butt-naked men is a good reflection of the drunken clouds and brings out the intoxicated spirit of cherry-time.

盃も降て来さうな櫻哉 松琵 続錦
sakazuki mo oritekisôna sakura kana   shôbi (1671-1750)
(sake cups-even falling/raining-come-seem/like cherry[blossoms/tree/s]!)

inebriating bloom

    cherry blossoms
    we feel like *sake* cups
    might rain down

The blossoms of the bell-cherry actually resemble *sake* cups, but I think this is figurative.

大勢の目に呑まれたる櫻哉 白支 千鳥掛
ôzei no me ni nomaretaru sakura kana   hakushi (1712)
(crowd's eyes-by drunken[verb] cherry[blossom]!/'tis)

blossom wine

    cherry blossoms
    drunken by a multitude
    of human eyes

    drunken up
    by a multitude of eyes
    the cherries

No Messiah needed. In Japan, blossoms turn to wine. This intoxication is catching. Here is testimony enough:

下戸の身も人に酔へし花の暮 松琴 蘆分船
geko no mi mo hito ni yoeshi hananokure   Shôkin (1694)
(teetotaler's body/self-even drunk/en blossom dusk)

    the bloom-dusk
    even teetotaler me
    drunk on people

    even teetotalers
    are drunk on people
    blossoms at dusk

The idea of psychological tipsiness is found in countless *ku*. Specification of the dusk sets this *ku* apart. It is effective because it makes us think of the effect of the dazzling pink and blue afternoon.

下戸はそも人に酔ふなり山櫻　吐月 靭随筆
geko wa somo hito ni you nari yamazakura　togetsu (1759)
(teetotaler-as-for at-last/eventually people-by drunk become mountain-cherry)

the non-drinkers	a teetotaler	the teetotalers
soon enough people-high	high on people	get pissed on people
mountain cherry	mountain cherries	wild cherries

A mountain blossom-viewing is less raucous than one in an urban park, but still . . .

一杯に下戸の酔ひたる桜哉　子規
ippai ni geko no yoitaru sakura kana　shiki (1895)
(one-cup-by teetotaler's drunken cherry[blossoms]!/'tis)

a teetotaler
drunk on one drink
blossom-viewing

Shiki's exacting realism, his *one* drink beats absolute abstention. A drink is about a tablespoon of *sake*, for that is all most *sake* cups hold. The Japanese teetotaler generally did not abstain for philosophical or religious reasons. Many Japanese are *allergic* to alcohol. It rarely makes them *mean* (a problem in the West related to our child-rearing practices and, possibly, genes), but often makes them turn beet-red, warm, dizzy, and sleepy. Such drink-handicapped are called "down-doors" (*geko*) as opposed to the highly admired heavy drinker called an "up-door" (*jôgo*). I do not know where alcoholism comes into this. It would seem to be a modern idea. At any rate, the "down-door," caught up in a festive atmosphere, against his better judgment, took a drink.

堂守が人に酔たる桜哉　一茶	交番やこゝにも一人花の酔　子規
tômori ga hito ni yoitaru sakura kana　issa	*kôban ya koko ni mo hitori hananoyoi*　shiki
(temple-hall-guard people-by drunk cherry!/'tis)	(policeman/booth!/: here-too one blossom-drunk)
the shrine guard	a policeman:
gets drunk on people	here, too, is a man
blossom-viewing	drunk on blossoms

Shiki's *Categorical* does not have as many Issa *ku* as it should. Since Shiki often comes up with *ku* resembling Issa's, I feel that Shiki did not see most of Issa's work (his unpublished journals, now available) for if he had, he would have been amazed at the similar ways they attacked various themes. His *ku* is more old-fashioned than Issa's, for it clearly plays with a famous *ku* "Upon the crag! / Here, too, is a man / moon-viewing" (*iwabana ya koko ni mo hitori tsuki no kyaku*　kyorai (-1704).) Let me re-translate to better show that resemblance:

it's in the air

upon the crag	the police booth
here, too, we find	here, too, we find
a moon-guest	a bloom-drunk

Though moon-viewing (*tsukimi*) is cooler than blossom-viewing (*hanami*) – there are no drunks – there are many parallels.

intoxicating

風尽て皆花に酔真昼かな　多代女

kaze tsukite mina hana ni you mahiru kana　tayojo 1775-1865
(wind exhausting all blossoms-by drunk/en real-day/noon!/?/'tis)

the wind dies and all are blossom drunk it's high-noon	it is high-noon the wind dies down leaving us bloom-drunk

This is the best *ku* of this chapter. It beats the evening, the single drink, the mountains, and the police box. Even without the blossoms, wind can do that to you when it stops.

見る人も気狂乱酒の花見哉　直年 or 桔梗? (LR)

miru hito mo kikyôranshû no hanami kana　chokunen or naotoshi 17c
(viewing-people even spirit-crazy blossom-viewing!/?/'tis)

even the people watching blossom-viewers: as high as kites	even people actually viewing blossoms high as kites

The "seeing/viewing people" (people who see/view) at the start is ambiguous. I think it means people not actually sitting under the trees in the viewing parties but others who serve them or just pass by and see the viewers. The second reading is unlikely because the same idea could be put much more clearly using other language. In 1888 Lowell called this high "a chronic state of flower-fever." (*The Soul of the Far East*). Sometimes, it showed symptoms of disease:

花に酔ふて頭痛すといふ女哉　子規

hana ni yôte zûtsu su to iu onna kana　shiki (1898)
(blossoms-by drunken, headache-does[has] says woman!/'tis)

blossom drunk
a woman says she has
a headache

Should we call her a "cherry blossom down-door?" We feel sorry for her allergy, but at least she has proved she is sensitive to the world. *"There are men / who never get drunk on / birds and blossoms"* (花鳥の首尾を酔はずにいる人あり　巴静　再現 *hana tori no shubi o yowazu ni iru hito ari*　hajô (1680-1744)). Birds and blossoms are short-hand for poetic interest. Such sobriety is a shame.

示僧古鏡・分別に花の鏡もくもりけり　李由 風俗文選

shi-sô-ko-kyo // funbetsu ni hana no kagami mo kumorikeri　riyû (-1705)
(show-monk-old-mirror // discretely/judiciously-with blossoms' mirror too clouds[+emph.])

monk looks in an old mirror

discretion
clouds over the mirror
of blossoms

Monks shouldn't peer into mirrors. An old mirror clouds easily. Judiciousness at a cherry-blossom-viewing is not only out of place but troublesome to the high majority.

あま酒や花にはうとき下戸の種　朧意
amazake ya hana ni wa utoki geko no shû　rôi 1680 江戸弁慶
(sweet[non-alco.] *sake*: blossoms-with-as-for estranged teetotaler ilk)

near-*sake*
estranged from the bloom
teetotalers

Sweet *sake* was non-alcoholic stuff for children and nuns. I borrowed the "near-" from "near-beer" but would prefer to use an older term if anyone knows one. The *ku* is very good.

寝ることも下戸は下手なり花の陰　蒼狐 古今句鑑
nerukoto mo geko wa hetanari hananokage　sôko 1777
(sleep-thing-even teetotaler-as-for poor-is: blossoms' shade)

a teetotaler's
even poor at sleeping
under the bloom

下戸衆はさもいんき也花の陰　一茶
gekoshû wa sa mo inki nari hananokage　issa 1763-1827
(teetotaler-crowd-as-for, how depressing-is/becomes blossom's shade)

with teetotalers　　　　teetotalers, yes　　　　the teetotalers
it's a depressing place　how gloomy they make　become depressed here
the bloomshade　　　　the bloomshade　　　　the bloomshade

浮世とは下戸の嘘也花に酒　子規
ukiyo to wa geko no uso nari hana ni sake　shiki 1896
(floating-world[troubles]-as-for teetotaler's lie is/becomes blossoms and *sake*)

the world of woe
it's a teetotaler's lie!
blossoms and wine

Shiki's take is philosophical; the rest of the *ku* seem mean-spirited (except for my third reading of Issa, almost surely wrong). But, the poets do have a point. Maintaining one's sobriety bucks the spirit of springtime and is unnatural in the face of lush blossoms. The teetotalers (supposed) grumbling and failure to let go was thought so aggravating one poet even prescribed a proper punishment:

下戸花に腹を切へし芳野越　言水 五子橋
geko hana ni hara o kirubeshi yoshinokoshi　gonsui (-1719)
(teetaler/s blossoms-to/by/at belly[obj] cut-ought yoshino-crossing)

at yoshino overlook　　　　　　　　　　　*before the blossoms*

facing this bloom　　　　　　　　　　　　i should commit
all teetotalers should　　　　　　　　　　*harakiri* – a teetotaler
cut their bellies　　　　　　　　　　　　crossing yoshino

A neutral, though unfortunately lame, translation would be "*a* teetotaler should / cut *his* belly." A later poet recorded a more reasonable approach, reminding one of the sign over Plato's Academy:

庭の花下戸な入そと書れけり 嘯山 葎亭
niwa no hana geko na iri so to kakarekeri   shôzan -1801
(garden's blossom teetotaler enter-not [it is] written[+emph.])

garden blossoms
"teetotalers keep out!"
says the sign

A *senryû* invents a novel way of assuring that a teetotaler won't get in the way of the fun:

二度とはつれぬと桜へ下戸くくし 柳多留二十
nido to wa tsurenu to sakura e geko kukushi   yanagidaru 1785
(twice-as-for bring-not [saying]-as cherry-to teetotaler/s bound)

"we won't bring you again!"
the teetotaler is bound
to a cherry tree

A translation into English by Professor U (who's usually right) has it bassackwards: "the non-drinkers tie him up." Loose grammar allows for that reading as well as mine, but anyone cognizant of the traditional disparagement of sobriety in cherry-time and the black humor of *senryû* could not imagine it any way other than the way I have it. So saying, I have found *one* neutral mention of a *geko*:

下戸ながら花に今宵の主哉 南化 太夫桜
geko nagara hana ni koyoi no aruji kana   namka 1680
(teetotaler being-while, blossoms to this evening's host!/'tis)

dry though i am   unable to drink
tonight the cherry blossoms   this evening i still host
find me the man   the blossoms

The poet is the host in charge of a party of blossom-viewers. Since most events are best run by sober people, there is humor in the qualification here. The blossoms may also refer to women. I have found only *one* old *ku* totally on the side of the teetotaler:

餅て見る人は櫻の味方かな 沾涼 猿つくは
mochi de miru hito wa sakura no mikata kana   tenryô (-1747)
(mochi (sweet-rice-cake)-with see person-as-for cherry's/ies' ally!/'tis)

those who view
with sweet-cake are friends
of the cherry trees

The non-drinker was also called a *mochi*-eater. Does the poet allude to the way drunks tear off branches, piss on roots and otherwise damage the trees they carouse under. While it is said that *"The heavy drinkers / of this world to a man / love the blossoms"* (花ぎらひ浮世の上戸なかりせは 陳次

hana-girai ukiyo no jôgo nakariseba   chinji) – Japanese folk wisdom has it that men who can hold their liquor are great womanizers – that depends on your definition of "love." *Damage* to cherry trees is discussed in chapters in Book II (*breaking-off sprays*) and Book III (*conserving cherries*). One thing is certain, in Japan, drinkers did more harm to themselves than to anyone or anything else:

井戸端のさくらあぶなし酒の酔　秋色
idobata no sakura abunashi sake no yoi   shûshiki -1725
(well-side's cherry[blossoms/tree] dangerous sake's drunkeness)

    the cherry tree   beware the cherry
  by the well is dangerous   by the well, you people
      drunken men   drunk on sake

This *ku*, holding its punch for the last 5 syllabets, may be a bit too cleverly crafted to have been made up by the poetess at age thirteen, as legend has it. A less interesting but equally true poem: *"To the tipsy / danger lurks in the low / cherry branch"* 生酔にあぶなし花のさがり枝 何来拍挙千句 *namayoi ni abunashi hana no sagari-eda*   karai 1782). Bonked heads and poked eyes were no doubt common blossom-viewing injuries. Of course, cherry blossoms could be dangerous even without drink involved. *"The raftman / looking at Saga cherries: / life and death"* (筏士の嵯峨に花見る命哉　几董　井華 *ikadashi no saga ni hana miru inochi kana*   kitô 1740-89). He sees cherry blossoms while making a living, but if he is not careful on the rapids, one look too many could cost his life. Another: *"When eyes fall / blossoms are dangerous: / a log bridge"* (*hana ni me no chirite abunashi maruki bashi* baishitsu 1768-1852). The *fall=diverted* and *hana*= nose=blossom puns fail to cross the bridge.

散かゝる櫻抱けり酒の酔　蘭更
chirikakaru sakura dakikeri sake no yoi   rankô 1726-99
([petal]falling-is[as process] cherry[tree] hug[+emph.] *sake* drunk)

hugging a tree
while its blossoms fall
a drunk man

The emphatic *keri* in the original suggests to me a holding on for dear life, followed by a slow slide downwards as the drinker passes out. Somehow, we have completely crossed over from non-alcoholic to alcoholic inebriation. Part of me says, save it for the *cherry bash* in Book II, but another part of me says to leave it here, for drunkenness is drunkenness is part of the total cherry-blossom experience as it was and still is in Japan. It is also a subject where haiku and *senryû* saw eye to eye.

花の枝もつて風雅なたおれもの　柳多留 8-40
hana no eda motte fûga na taoremono   yanagidaru (1773)
(blossom-branch holding, classy fallen-one[passed-out-drunk])

  Still holding a flowering branch,   ***the drunk***
    the fallen drunkard
    is a man of taste.   there, still clutching
                                a spray of cherry blossoms
      trans. blyth   tastefully passed out

Note, first, that tearing off branches to carry around or take home was not simply a side-effect of drunkenness. We shall have a whole chapter about it. About the poem, one might add only that because *senryû* dealt with types and this type was a *taore-mono,* which is to say a "fallen=passed-out=person," *that* should be the subject of the poem. It is not really about a particular person, or *individual,* as we would assume in the case of a haiku. Still, I am delighted by what Blyth does with the adjective *fûga* (elegant/refined) in his last line. Here are four less well known *Yanagidaru senryû*:

生酔の突当るたび花がちり y26
namayoi no tsuki-ataru tabi hana ga chiri 1796
(drunk's bump-time-each blossoms fall)

桜からさくらへこける面白さ y25
sakura kara sakura e kokeru omoshirosa 1794
(cherry-from cherry-to pass-out diverting)

hit and run

every time
a drunk bumps into one
petals fall

tree hopping

passing out
at each cherry in turn
what fun!

梅にうくひすさくらに生酔なり
ume ni uguisu sakura ni namayoi nari y18
(plum-in nightingale, cherry-in drunk is 1783)

いふことをきかぬ生酔木から落
iu koto o kikanu namayoi ki kara ochi y15
(advice listen-not drunk tree-from falls 1780)

plum blossoms
have nightingales, cherries
plastered men

a plastered man
who will not listen
falls from a tree

The slang *kokeru* in the second *senryû* does not necessarily mean passing out. We may also imagine someone plopping heavily down but remaining (barely) awake. We can easily guess what tree the drunk falls from in the last. Since a Japanese drunk's face, like a Japanese monkey's (strictly speaking a macaque) is presumably bright red, the well-known Japanese saying *"even a monkey may fall from a tree"* comes to mind. Two centuries after that *senryû* was penned, Western visitors to Japan observed:

> One wonders what the old leaders of the imperial army would have thought. In the middle of Yoyogi Koen, Tokyo's biggest swathe of parkland, and once the drilling ground for tens of thousands of the emperor's soldiers, a young man was climbing a cherry tree. He was naked, and many of the hundreds of picnickers looking on either cheered or threw insults. The sozzled tree-climber perched shakily on a limb, raised his arms aloft and then clambered down. This could only be *hanami,* or cherry blossom viewing time. . . . .
>
> A 30-year-old office worker told the newspaper *Asahi Shimbun* that her firm's *hanami* always ended the same way.
>
> "Someone gets naked and climbs a cherry tree. Last year a male worker who usually behaves like a gentleman did it. It's inevitable the same thing will happen again this year."
>
> ("The annual festival that blossoms into a binge-drinking orgy" By Michael Millett, *Herald* (what *Herald* I know not) Correspondent in Tokyo (googled))

I was in Japan twenty years and climbed a few trees to rescue cats but never had the luck to see a drunkard up one. There is, however, at least one *ku* suggesting the practice is nothing new:

だきついて梢をのぞく櫻哉 魚兒 続虚栗
dakitsuite kozue o nozoku sakura kana uoji (1687)
(hug/cling-stick *kozue* (tree-top/branch-tips) peek/gaze cherry 'tis)

      clinging fast
   i peek from the treetop
      cherry blossoms

Were this *ku* not Bashô school, I may have thought it referred to a harlot making love in the place identified with recreational sex, the second floor of a tea-shop. But, again, to the present:

> The Japanese take their cherry blossom viewing as seriously as they take their drinking, and they especially like to take them seriously at the same time. In Maruyama Park [Kyoto], near a huge cherry tree, supposedly the finest in the country, drunken young blossom viewers were stripping to their undies and diving into a shallow pond (men only – and it was cold). A man in his fifties offered us some beer, and his more sober wife looked quite pleased when we said "no, thank you." (To: newsletter / From: "Peter M. Rivard" / Subject: Traveling (googled))

With the ease of googling the internet, one could gather hundreds of reports like this and assemble a book of drunken cherry blossoms in a day! But let us get back to the past.

上下の酔倒あり花の陰 一茶 文政七
kamishimo no yoidaore ari hananokage issa (-1827)
(above-below(formal dress') drunken-collapse is/are blossoms' shade)

bloom-shade	here you may see
men in formal dress	formal tails passed out:
lie passed out	the bloomshade

Reading this poem for the first time, I did not know that "above-below" (*kami-shimo*) meant traditional formal dress – so called because informal male clothing had only a top, while formal clothing included a pair of culotte-like trousers – and, instead, imagined people *"Passed out / in the bloom-shade, drunk / upon drunk!"* I think Issa may have intended that, *too*; but cannot translate the pun. Pardon *our* "tails" in the second reading!

引組てこけたり花に酒の醉 樗良
hikikunde koketari hana ni sake no yoi chora (1729-81)
(pull/joining falling/collapsing [and-stuff] blossoms-with/at sake drunk)

pulling together	together we stand
we collapse in a heap	together we fall, drunk
cherry-bash drunks	with the blossoms

The "we" may be "they." This fine finale to a group performance is endearing to all but a Puritan. If it was nightfall and a long way back to town, drink prevented insomnia: *"Night cherry: / when a drunken sleep / feels great!"* (夜桜に酒心よしとろ／＼寝 文十カ 蘆分船 *yozakura ni kokoro yoshi torotoro-ne* monjûriki? 1694). The word for a drunken sleep, *torotoro-ne* has a mushy feeling, for the mimesis *torotoro* often describes well-stirred up, slimy half-liquefied food. Needless to say, many caught colds, but we shall get to that later (ch.64).

9 #41b-44

intoxicating

あれ程に酔てゆすらぬ櫻哉　梅霞
arehodo ni yotte yuzuranu sakura kana　baika ()
(that much drunken relinquish-not cherry!/'tis)

too drunk
to give up his cherry
bloom-shade

I imagine someone unwilling to depart with his friends but, who knows, it could be a policeman!

人を見ん桜は酒の肴なり　子規
hito o min sakura wa sake no sakana nari　shiki (1896)
(people-at look! cherry[blossoms]-as-for sake's hors d'oeuvers become)

sake rules!

look at the people!	look around!
cherry blossoms have become	blossoms have become
nibblies for *sake*	hors d'oeuvres

We began with blossoms intoxicating men; here they are mere snacks for drunks. Forgive the *nibblies*. It is Australian. Otherwise it would be French. If you prefer the Hawaiian, *pupu*, use it. It will alliterate well with *people*. The year Shiki wrote this, his friend Kyoshi wrote "*Sake* my wife / the wife my *sake*: / spring craziness" (酒を妻妻を酒にして春くるゝ　虚子 *sake o tsuma tsuma o sake ni shite haru kururu*). *Tsuma* (wife/mate/ husband) is a homophone for nibblies. How wonderful that Kyoshi could be drunk on his own wife! Two years earlier Shiki wrote:

有りやうは酒のみに来て花盛　子規
ari yô wa sakenomi ni kite hanazakari　shiki (1894)
(has-appearance-as-for sake-drinking-for come/came blossom-peak)

from the looks of it	you would think
people come here to drink	we came here to drink
the bloom-peak	cherries blooming

Observations of vulgar blossom-viewings go back centuries. But is such an observation a celebration or a complaint? Perhaps in the decades since the Opening of Japan, the carnival excess had been dampened for the sake of nation-building – indeed, many cherries trees were cut-down and replaced by trees more suitable for boat-building – so that these two fathers of modern haiku may have felt they were witnessing something new when it was actually only a return to the old way!

花ざかりいはば都の酒屋かな　守武
hanazakari iwaba miyako no sakaya kana　moritake (1452-1549)
(blossom-peak/heat so-called capital's drinking-shop!/?/'tis)

in full bloom	the bloom-peak
cherry mountain's like a bar	so this is the so-called
for the capital	bar of the capital?

Moritake was a Shinto priest (who became the head priest at the head shrine in Ise). This is the oldest *ku* that seems like it *might* be meant as a complaint about cherry-bash excess. He may, however, only be marveling. At any rate, it is an important poem, for the blossom-viewing as we know it today, the vulgar cherry bash, is usually thought to have begun with Hideyoshi's extravaganzas in the late 16c where Moritake shows us that just wasn't so!

まづ宿を酔て出でたる花見哉　白雪 蘆分船
mazu yado o yotte-idetaru hanami kana   hakusetsu 1694
(first, inn drunken depart/ing blossom-viewing!/'tis)

cherry advice

blossom-viewing
first, you leave the inn
inebriated

blossom-viewing!
you have an eye-opener
then leave the inn

first, you leave
your inn tipsy: that's
blossom-viewing

This is clearly drink-positive, If you are going to get tipsy in nature, you might as well get a head-start. The original has no person. I made it "you" because you includes "I."

酔て遊ふ木陰を花の都哉　　玄駛 藤首途
yotte-asobu kokage o hana no miyako kana   genshi 1731
(drunken-play tree-shade[obj] blossom's/posh/capital!/'tis/?)

this bloom-shade
where we drunken play?
it's our capital!

Without the Japanese connotations for *hana* and the suggestions of Kyoto in the "capital" the poem barely makes it. Indeed my favorite drinking *ku* of all is untranslatable: "*Sake*=bloom! *sake*=bloom!"/ request the bacchants / blossom-viewing (さけ／＼とねがふ上戸の花見哉　信安 鷹筑波 *sake sake to negau jôgo no hanami kana*   shinan (1642)[のぶやす=1737 没もある]). *Sake* is a homophone for the imperative of "to bloom." The poem is a beautifully simple fusion of the blossoming and drinking experience that would only work in English if *beer* and *bloom* or *wine* and *bloom* were homophones. If punch were alcoholic and generally served at ringside, I suppose we could have a similar boxing *ku*.

誰かいつし乱酒の本は花のかげ 之数 洗濯物
dare ga itsu shi ranshû no moto wa hananokage   shisû (1666)
(someone/who sometime wild-drinking origin-as-for blossom's shade)

someone said it
wild drinking was born
in the bloomshade

once someone said
the place drinking lost control
was the bloomshade

The capital? Hell, the bloomshade is the very origin of uninhibited drinking! Indeed, even today, it is where we see college students and young workers chugalug from large bottles of sake under the cherry trees. Another old *ku* explains matter-of-factly "That people / get drunk on *sake* becomes / the cherry's fault" (人酒に酔は櫻の科になし　包抄 蘆分船 *hito sake ni yoi wa sakura no toga ni nashi* hôsa 1694). I suspect an allusion to the fair sex.

intoxicating 139

酔事は天下晴れたり花の山　鳥酔 アルス
yoi koto wa tenka haretari hananoyama　chôsui (-1813)
(drunk-thing-as-for, heaven-below[whole world] clear[sky]: blossom-mountain)

blossom-viewing

nothing beats getting drunk with cherries on a clear day	*this* is drunk cherry mountain with a blue sky

While not sure how to translate the poem, I can *attest* to it. What a shame most people waste their high after-dark, in smoke-filled rooms! This *ku* is splendid for bringing out the homophonic relationship of drunk (*yoi*) and "good" (*yoi*). The above *ku* may paraverse a slightly older one that depends entirely on that pun: *"In full bloom / under a clear blue sky / it's a yoi day!"* (はな盛り天下晴れての酔日かな　素丸 *hanazakari tenka harete no yoi hi kana*　somaru (1712-95)).

何にても十六七杯花の陰　玉柳
nani nite mo juroku, nana hai hananokage　gyôkuryu ()
(anything about-even sixteen, seventeen cups[of sake]: blossom's shade)

for anything at all sixteen or seventeen cups under the bloom	the bloomshade sixteen or seventeen cups for anything at all

I think the number is supposed to suggest the bloom of youth, but who knows. Maybe that's how many cups are in jug. Remember that *sake* cups are only slightly larger than thimbles (*our* thimbles, for Japanese thimbles are rings). The *anything at all* is interesting. One would like a list of things that were toasted! At first, I titled it "cherry time toasts," but the *anything* includes drinking away troubles or drinking to come up with a good poem, etc.. and "toasts" might limit it. It is also best to save the location for last, as with the original and the first reading.

散櫻我醉顔につめたけれ　蘭更　新五子
chiru sakura waga yoikao ni tsumetakare　ranko (1726-99)
(falling/scattering-cherry[petals] my drunken face-to cold-is)

falling petals touch my drunken face they are cold	cherry blossoms falling, feel cold against my drunken face

I imagine this poet was one of the 30 or 40% [?] of Japanese who turn red when they drink, for their skin also grows warm. That would make the petals feel far colder than they actually are. The *ku seems* very factual, but I must admit to doubt. Petals sometimes catch on one's hair, but on the whole they are remarkably good at avoiding us. Reach out your hand and you will find most slip by.

徳利狂人いたはしや花ゆへにこそ　其角
tokkuri-kyôjin itawashi ya hana yue ni koso　kikaku -1707
(bottle-crazy-man [are] pitied (treated kindly) blossoms because especially)

a jug-lugging wild man's adorable thanks to the bloom	cherries bloom and the whole world loves a nut with a flask

9 #55-59

140 *intoxicating*

A farming and fishing people did not think much of the poet or sage who carried his drinking supply with him to indulge at will. They tended to drink up whatever they had at the right time for it and drank nothing other days.   Cherry-time made aesthete (?) behavior acceptable.

いさともに酔て夢見ん花の山　蘭秀
iza tomo ni yotte yume min hananoyama   ranshû ()
(well, together drunken dream-see-let's blossom's mountain)

let's get drunk
and dream together
blossom mountain

let's get drunk
and live out a dream
cherry mountain

Nice picture. Too bad we dream *less* when we drink! How about this waking dream: *"White mice / from the sake cellars! / Ueno blossoms"* (酒蔵の白鼠なり上野の花　不卜 江戸広小路 *sakagura no shironezumi nari ueno no hana*   fubaku (d 1691))? White rodents were simile for foamy white waves and associated with the god of grain and drink. Was there so much drinking at Ueno (Edo's main blossom-viewing park) that the blossoms, viewed in the moon light, were viewed as so many mice reflecting the profits of the *sake* merchants? Another drunken *ku* by the well-known poet whose name translates as "storm-snow" is, likewise, white: *"Let us spew / our white swan sake! / Cherry Mountain:"* (白鳥の酒を吐らんはなのやま　　嵐雪　*hakuchô no sake o hakuran hana no yama* ransetsu (-1707)) – the type of flask, *white-bird=swan* allows the pretense that the vomited *sake* is likewise downy white like the blossoms.

つく／＼と花にめて樽の枕哉　亀文 拍挙千句
tsukuzuku to hana ni mede+taru no makura kana   kibun (1782)
(intensely blossoms-with/by keg=joyous/doltish/celebratory's pillow!/'tis)

you really feel it
with a keg for a pillow
under the bloom

The translation is a paraverse. The written version of the *ku* combines the Chinese character for "keg=樽" (*taru*) with the syllabic start of the verb (*medetaru*), which, fusing innocent holiday joy with the careless life, is itself hard to translate. *Mede* by itself also suggests "love."

桜もる月にやうやく酔がさめ　柳多留 41-25
sakura moru tsuki ni yôyaku yoi ga same   yanagidaru ()
(cherry[blossoms] leaks moon-by gradually drunks/eness sobers)

moonshine leaking
through the cherry blossoms
i finally come to

moonshine leaking
through the cherry blossoms
the poets come to

moonshine leaks
through the blossoms, at last
the drunks come to

The last reading is probably correct, for *senryû* favor drunks and the third-person. Sometimes a things ended less pleasantly: *"I come to / as I am scolded: / blossom-viewing"* (叱られて酔のさめたる花見かな　明治廿九 *shikararete yoi no sametaru hanami kana* shiki 1896). By a policeman? Or a wife?

9 #60-65

intoxicating

お内儀に叱られて居よ花に樽　亀毛 焦尾
onaigi ni shikararete iyo hana ni taru　kimo 1701
(wife-by scolded be! blossom-with/and keg)

let the wife scold under the blossoms stick by your keg	take your wife's tongue-lashing: bring a keg to the blossoms

let the wife
scold away! blossoms
need a keg!

The "blossoms-with-*keg*" might pun as "blossoms-with *suffice*." Both sound like *taru*.

花にけふ面目もなし二日酔　黄吻 江戸広小路?
hana ni kyo menboku mo nashi futsuka yoi　kôfun 1678?
(blossoms-to today face-eyes-not(ashamed) second-day-drunk(hung-over))

hung over!
today i cannot face
the blossoms

Evidently, some things are less forgiving than police or wives. The only way around that is to take the hair of the tail of the dog before you let it bite you. I think that is what Bashô suggests:

二日酔ひものかは花のあるあひだ　芭蕉
futsuka-ei mono ka wa hana no aru aida　bashô 1644-94
(second-day-drunk(hangover) thing/what-as-for! blossoms are while)

a hangover? no way! i drink while there are blossoms	a hangover? no way! not while they bloom

This light poem, done in the Osaka *Danrin* style that appealed to young Bashô, is said to borrow the expression of astonishment of ever thinking about such a thing expression from the *Tales of Heike* (「待つ宵のふけゆく鐘の声聞けば帰るあしたの鳥はものかは」をかすめて), but is best considered a logical game – you cannot get a hang-over if you keep awake drinking. But Bashô doesn't actually say he drinks in the *ku*. My first reading fills out the poem which says no more than what is in the second reading. We will return to drinking in a more philosophical vein in the cherry-viewing of Book II.

花最中花見ぬ人の無分別　楳江 肥前諫
hana saichû hana minu hito no mubunbetsu　baie ()
(blossoms-middle blossoms see-not person's none-discrimination)

the bloom peak men not blossom viewing lack discrimination	people who miss the height of the bloom lack judgment

Did you catch it? This is a *crazy if you do, crazy if you don't* paradox. Caught up in the blossoms, you lose your mind as one who has fallen in love does. But anyone who can ignore such beauty lacks all taste, i.e., discrimination, . . .and is, logically speaking, *crazy*.

10

Blossoms In Heat
花盛り
hana-zakari

花も世もさかりは人の心哉　宗祇 大発句帳
hana mo yo mo sakari wa hito no kokoro kana　sôgi 1421-1502
(blossoms too world too frenzy-as-for peoples' heart/mind!/'tis)

this full bloom
of cherries and the world?
the mind of man

cherry blossoms　　　　　　　　　　　　　it is our mind
and the world blooming　　　　　　　this frenzy of flowers
from our hearts!　　　　　　　　　　　this rutting world

With plants, *sakari* suggests rampant growth or gorgeous masses of blossoms in full bloom; with animals, cats in heat or bucks rutting; with humans, one might expect it to refer to horny men and women running amuck, but such is not the case. It usually indicates what English might refer to as being "in the flower of his/her wo/manhood." For towns, businesses and other abiological matters, it means "flourishing/thriving/prospering. In haiku about cherry blossoms and blossom viewing, it can signify nothing more than full-bloom or a wild state of affairs with petals and spittle flying, a *frenzy*.

花さかり誰かおほゆる日かずかな 宗長 大発句帳
hanazakari dare ga oboyuru hikazu kana　sôchô 1447-1532
(blossom-full/frenzy who remember-can day-number!/?/'tis)

in the bloom-heat
who could remember
to count the days!

There was an idea that cherries blossom for so many days – usually seven – and the poet marvels that anyone can remain cool enough to actually count. *Bloom-heat* is my neologism. In the later Edo era, seven days was identified with the menses, but it is unlikely this renga poet was making that allusion.

転んでも起ても花のさかり哉　吾仲
koronde mo okite mo hana no sakari kana　gochû -1733
(falling or getting up, blossom-full-bloom/frenzy!/?/'tis)

falling down　　　　　　　　　　　　　　on your back
or getting up, the bloom　　　　or on your feet, blossoms
peak of cherry　　　　　　　　　　　　in full bloom!

Usually, it would be "standing or lying" or "awake or asleep." *Koronde* means falling by tripping. I think it expresses the mindset: *"Fall on your face, / then get up and race, cherries / in full bloom!"*

脇差はけふもささぬか花盛　花賛女
wakizashi wa kyo mo sasanu ka hanazakari kasanjo 1807-1830
(dagger-as-for today-too stab-not? blossom-frenzy)

~~my hidden dirk~~   why not wear   ~~this full bloom~~
~~today, too, i'd use it!~~   a sword on this day, too: ~~today, too, i feel like~~
~~the bloom-heat~~   the full bloom   ~~stabbing myself~~

I first thought the poet was in a-stab-herself level of excitement, but *sasu* means "wear" as well as "stab" and is perfect for the sword in question. The "too" is puzzling. Has she has been out for several days running? Or, does she mean, in addition to New Year's Day or some other festival?

痩こける身をうき立う花盛　舎蘿
yasekokeru mi o ukitatou hanazakari shara (late-17c)
(skinny/emaciated body/self[+obj] float-stand/rise blossom-frenzy)

skin and bones   the full bloom
my body still floats high   even this skeleton
bloom-frenzy   floats upward

Does the poet know from experience that thin men tend to sink? In Japanese, "floating" means "giddy" or "high." The original "float-stand" is transitive: the bloom raises/floats the bean-pole.

来年はなきものゝやうに桜哉　一茶 文化1
rainen wa naki mono no yô ni sakura kana issa (-1827)
(coming-year-as-for not thing-as cherry[blossoms]!/'tis)

as if the year   cherry blooms   we party like
to come will not come   like there is no such thing there is no next year
cherry trees   as next year   cherry blossoms

hanazakari kami mo hotoke mo achira muke ippyô (-1840)

blossoms in full bloom –   the full bloom
Buddha and Shinto gods, please   you gods and buddhas
look the other way   – ueda transl.   look away!

Issa's *sakura* can mean the tree/s, blossoms or both. Ippyô, a Buddhist priest and friend of Issa's seems to say, today there is no next *world*, either. Paradise, be damned! It's *here*. (Note: the "please" is Ueda's!)

この比や猫しづまりて花に人　大江丸 俳諧袋
konogoro ya neko shizumarite hana ni hito ôemaru 1719-1805
(this time [of year]: cats quiet up, blossoms and people)

now's the season
when cats quiet down for
men and flowers!

The blossom (*hana*) is a cherry because the *koi-zakari*, (love/sex-peak/heat) of cats comes at the start of spring, coinciding with the flowering plum, and that is supplanted by the *sakari* of humans and cherry blossoms. The plum bloomed alone in the first-month; cherries *"When the trees / bearing flowers are busy: / the second month"* (花のさく木はいそがしき二月哉　支考 *hana no saku ki wa isogashiki nigatsu kana* shikô -1731).

のどかさは夜にこそあれ花さかり 蓼太
nodokasa wa yoru ni koso are hanazakari　ryôta 1707-87
(quiet-as-for, night-in especially be! blossom-acme)

blossom-heat:
let tranquility at least
reign at night!

I like to think that a contrast with cat's in heat is implied, but the more likely reading is that the tranquility that stereotypically marked the morning in early spring could not be hoped for in cherry-time, so the night was this poet's only refuge.

何事に人走るらん花盛 由之 続虚栗
nanigoto ni hito hashiruran hanazakari　yûshi 1687
(what thing-for people run[+emphatic] blossom-acme/frenzy)

people run about   　　　　　why the hell
for practically anything!   　　do people run about?
a flower-frenzy   　　　　　　it's full bloom

A perfect picture of excitement. Who doesn't tend to run or skip after being treated kindly by a beautiful member of their favored sex? Beautiful blossoms have the same effect on us. I repeat myself, but English has no single word for this *sakari*, this *explosion of eros* that applies across the plant and animal kingdom.[1] "Full bloom" is close – Japanese has a word for "full bloom" (*mankai*), too – but the expression lacks the raw power of the original. Hence my "frenzy." Readers who dislike my new-English may substitute their own expression or use the Japanese as is, here: "*hana-zakari!*" The second reading, implying we should be content to rest below the bloom, is the more likely one.

くるゝ色は音なき花の嵐哉　昌叱
kururu iro wa oto naki hana no arashi kana　shôshitsu (-1603)
(crazing color/s-as-for, sound-not blossom-storm!/'tis)

swirling color:
the silent blossom storm!

The storm metaphor will be discussed in the chapter on the wind in Book III but the *ku* fits this chapter, too, for movement is at the heart of the frenzy. I wish I could jump into a time-machine and take a slow-motion photograph of people in kimono moving among the cherry trees.

1. *A Shell in Heat!* To give you an idea of how crazy this *sakari* thing can go, here is an old haiku: "the cherry shell / when it's mouth is open / it's in heat" (桜貝は口の ひらくをさかり哉　直知 崑山集　*sakuragai wa kuchi no hiraku o sakari kana* naotomo (1651)). This scallop-like shell is one of a few considered the closest mimics of a woman's vulva. The dictionary calls it a "carpenter's tellin" *Nitidotellina nitidula*). Since this was in a haiku, not senryû, collection, "it's in heat" presumably refers to the shellfish itself being in season, but still . . .

>   swirling color
>   it is the blossoms'
>   silent storm

The sequence of possessive connecting *no* (の) in Japanese makes it impossible to determine whether the blossoms or the storm are silent; but, in the original Japanese the problem does not arise, for, in a sense, it is both. More movement:

花の頃誰にもつくやありき神　宗貞 夢見草
hana no koro tare ni mo tsuku ya arikigami　sôtei 1656
(blossom-time who-to/with-even attaches!/: walking-god)

when they bloom	in cherry time
everyone is saddled by	we all get bitten by
the walking god	the walking bug

Wandering about is associated with the condition of *sakari*. Cats in heat do it, Japanese "night-crawling" lovers did it and so do people turned on by Spring in general and our flowering tree in particular. I borrowed the *saddle* from Zora Neale Hurston's *Tell It To My Horse* (spirit-possession in Haiti was described as being ridden by a horse). An 1830's *senryû* put it like this "*You can see / people fluttering about / on cherry hill*" (ひらり／\と舞遊ぶ花の山　柳多留 *hirari hirari to mai-asobu hana-no yama* Y 62-3). The mimesis *hirari* should apply to petals or butterflies, and "people" are not mentioned, but we know the subject of *senryû*. To bad "fluttering" is not synonymous with "giddy."

はな盛ふくべ踏わる人も有　其角 焦尾琴
hanazakari fukube fumiwaru hito mo ari　kikaku -1707
(blossom-peak/frenzy gourd tread-break people even are)

the bloom rages	the bloompeak
there are men stepping	i step on my gourd
upon their gourds	and break it

If only English could make compound verbs such as "step-break" ... Let us hope the content of the gourd was already drunken.

人心瓢箪なれや花の波　正章 毛吹草
hitogokoro hyôtan nare ya hana no nami　masaakira 1645
(person-heart gourd become!/?/: blossom-wave/s)

ye hearts of men	the human heart
become gourds upon	a gourd bobbing on waves
the blossom sea!	of cherry blossom

I translated the same *kokoro* as "mind" in the case of Sôgi's poem at the head of the chapter, but a *mind* seems less suitable than *heart* for this poem. The gourd in the Sinosphere holds wine and has connotations of sage worlds (and god knows what else), but the wave/s suggest/s that here it is, first of all, a float (In olde English poetry, the bladder of Hudibras, right?). *Floating* is part of the *sakari*. Indeed, a person in love or a cat in heat is said to be "floating" (*ukarete-iru*). But that is only part of it. The connotations of *floating* in Japanese spans the gamut from the joyfully bouyant *uki-uki* to helpless and hopeless un-anchored drifting symbolized by floating-weeds (*ukigusa*). The "floating world" is both that of the senses, where nothing is permanent and all is, in that sense, an illusion, i.e., the Buddhist *maya*, and what the water trades such as gambling, prostitution and acting were called.

花盛我も浮世のひとり哉　趙平　新選
hanazakari ware mo ukiyo no hitori kana shôhei 1773
(blossom-acme/frenzy i-too floating-world's one[man]!/'tis)

pink *anomie*

the full bloom
today, i, too, feel part of
the floating world

in bloom-peak
i find that i belong to
the floating world

flower frenzy
i join others, alone
in this world

Who can say for certain how this poet feels when he says "floating world", but I think he means he feels a sweet sorrow for the world of woe (including that of people who live the low, even criminal, life) to which he suddenly feels both more attached and at the same time suffers from feeling alone. This is the adult equivalent to the fear of death intensely felt by the child. The latter feeling did not translate in the first two readings because the Japanese expression "I too am *one[one person] of* the floating world" in English wants to become "part of" which emphasizes *belonging*, something which is soothing, whereas the original's "one of" has a lonelier nuance. Hence the title and last reading.

花咲て本ンのうき世と成にけり　一茶
hana saite hon no ukiyo to narinikeri issa -1827
(blossoms blooming real floating-world becomes [+fin.])

cherries bloom
and the floating world
becomes real!

cherries bloom
and it becomes reality:
the floating world

Camping out under the bloom, the poet shares the experience of many in the so-called water trade, and feels what is for most of the year merely catechism: that this world is *maya*, illusion. In other words, Issa's *ku* is identical to the last one, but written in a more sophisticated style not bringing the self into it in an obvious way. Being of the blunt persuasion, I prefer the older poem with its "I, too" (*ware mo*), though I think Issa's more clever for making the reality of the *maya* real and a better window on the earthy blossom-viewing, the muddy Woodstock we shall return to in a later chapter.

我年のよるともしらす花さかり　智月
waga toshi no yoru to mo shirazu hanazakari chigetsu-ni (1622/32-1703/8)
(my years age even know-not blossom-acme/frenzy)

bloompeak
i feel not
my age

If women were identified with cherry trees (see Book III) how do they view the bloom-heat? Chigetsu would seem to get carried away by it. Biographers differ on her age.

in heat

付まとふ内義の沙汰や花ざかり　大祇
tsuki matou naigi no sata ya hanazakari taigi (1709-72)
(stick-close wife-difficulties/happenings: blossom-acme/frenzy)

the bloom heat!
i just cannot escape
from my wife

never-ending
wife problems, she is
in full-bloom

the full bloom
by this time we all have
wife problems

Suddenly, down to earth! If a poet goes blossom-viewing day after day, his wife would get upset. She might even follow him to the *hanami*. Blyth introduces a relevant *senryû*: *"The cherry-flowers blooming, / The moon shining, – / These are the wife's agony."* (女房の苦は花が咲き月がさし *nyôbo no ku wa hana ga saki tsuki ga sashi* Y10-19, 1775). His comment: "The most poetical things of the spring and autumn seasons are the cause of all her woes, for this is the excuse for her husband to go out and enjoy himself with other women." I think the drinking and consequent heavy expenditures are as much a problem as philandering, but a problem it was. Blyth's books on *senryû* are still, after 50 years, the best we have. My allegorical second reading is unlikely unless Taigi had a sexy young wife.

小倅はちに泣花（の）盛りかな 一茶 文政二
kosegare wa chi ni naku hana[no] sakari kana issa (-1827)
(small-son-as-for, milk-for cries blossom-acme!/'tis)

blossoms, blossoms, everywhere

my little son
crying for milk while
cherries bloom

Issa gave his boy to a wet-nurse when his wife fell mortally sick. As it turned out, she was dry. By the time Issa discovered the fraud, his son was too weak to be nursed back to health. The title, besides bringing more heat/frenzy to the bloom, reflects the fact that, in Japanese, the dark pink bud of the cherry blossom symbolizes the nipple of a woman with child or nursing a child. The contrast between the powerful life-force of the bloom-peak and the crying of the baby thirsty for life is horrific.

さきこめて花に枝なきさかりかな　無名 失典
sakikomete hana ni eda naki sakari kana anon. (?)
(blooming-filling blossoms-on branches-not acme!/'tis)

filled by blossoms
all the cherries lack limbs
in the bloom-peak

I started the chapter with psychological takes on the bloompeak rather than description. This old *ku* provides the latter. We see trees gorged with petals; we see bones fully fleshed in pink. The *ku* antedates the creation of the Somei-yoshino cherry that became synonymous with solid bloom: it may be hyperbolic. Should we note that typically beautiful women in East Asia though not necessarily curvaceous by Occidental standards, tend to be full-fleshed and do not show collarbones, or, should we stress the metaphor of clothing, which the Sinosphere favored over muscle-oriented beauty?

ふけ嵐花はちるこそさかりなれ 心敬 発句帳
fuke arashi hana wa chiru koso sakari nare shinkei (-1475)
()

        blow ye, storm!
     what's a real *sakari* but
       scattering bloom!

すこしちれ色なきほとの花盛 宗祇 宇良葉
sukoshi chire iro naki hodo no hanazakari   sôgi (1420-)
(a bit fall! color-not amount of blossom-acme/peak)

  spill a few petals!   drop some petals
  the bloom is so full   passion has no play
    it lacks passion   in bloom so full!

すこしちれいろわくほとのはな盛 宗祇 発句帳
sukoshi chire iro waku hodo no hanazakari   sôgi (-1502)
(a bit fall! color boils amount of blossom-acme/peak)

the ideal bloompeak

             fall a little!
        let the blossom's pink
             bubble over

    let eros boil!   let petals spill
  a bloom heat that spills   i'll take a bloompeak
     over a little   that's passionate

             spill some!
        the heat of the bloom:
             passionate

The bloom feels most alive when full to the brim *and* spilling a little. A few marginal blossoms are caught by the breeze, others bumped by the birds and the bees. I have experienced this and can vouch for Sôgi's sense. He held back a bit from the more radical description of *sakari* as a tumultuous swirl of blossoms (what I call "bloom-heat") as inferred by the *ku* of his teacher, Shinkei.

やまざくら盛りに山はなかりけり 素丸   見物に山みえぬ花のさかり哉 正朝 嵐山集
yamazakura sakari ni yama wa nakarikeri somaru   *kenbutsu ni yama mienu hana no sakari kana*   shôchô
(mountain cherry acme-in mountain-as-for not[+emph.])   (sight-seeing-by mountai see-not blossom's acme!/'tis 1651)

   mountain cherries   the bloom-peak!
 in full bloom there is   cherry hill is buried by
   no mountain here   the sightseers

The first *ku* seems to mean the *blossoms* are all that can be seen. The second, older *ku, humans*. As we will discuss later, one can never tell when a mountain is a real one or a synonym for a park with cherry trees. The second *ku* may concern the latter, which has also been described critically: *"A drunk mountain / blossoms empty the dregs / of the capital"* (山酔ひ花に都の底たゝく　一味　雑中 *yama eiri hana ni miyako no sokotataki*   ichimi (pre-19c?)).

in heat

近道や木のまた通る花盛　洞木
chikamichi ya ko no mata tôru hanazakari dôboku (18c)
(shortcut:/! tree-fork/crotch pass/ing blossom-acme/frenzy)

it's a shortcut! right through tree-crotches: blossom frenzy	the bloom-peak: shortcuts right through cherry crotches

Branches are low in many viewing spots and sag further in the bloom-peak, so making a beeline for a certain tree, one might find climbing through tree crotches (the lowest forks of the trunk) easier than ducking under the limbs. Still, the eros is not unintended, for we have *ku* like this:

花の山どちら向てもよかりけり 是計 新選
hananoyama dochira muite mo yogarikeri zekei (1773)
(blossom-mountain whichever-way facing-even groans/cries/yelps[+emph.])

an orgy of blossoms

on cherry hill no matter where you face moans of pleasure	on cherry hill no matter where i look i cry aloud

My Japanese-English dictionary defines *yogaru* as "to be pleased with," "to express one's pleasure," "to be elated." What it fails to write is that by far the most common usage is *for sex*, i.e., the cries made by women (*yogari-goe*). While the *ku* probably plays on a famous *ku* where the poet could only say *"This! Oh, this!"* (i.e., *My, oh, my!*) about the cherry blossoms of Yoshino (*ku* # 58-1), what makes it good to me is that I imagine not only the excitement of the poet and other spectators but the cherry trees in a love-frenzy crying *I'm coming! I'm coming!* (or, *Ooh, aaahh! I'm dying! I'm dying!* etc.)

かねて見ぬさはりもうれし花盛 宗祇 大発句帳
kanete minu sawari mo ureshi hanazakari sôgi (1421-1502)
(previously see touch OR obstacle/problem too delightful blossom-acme)

before, i saw now touching touches me the full bloom	this full bloom we view, of course, but what a joy to touch!

cherries in full bloom

a fine sight
but their touch is also
my delight!

once viewed bad weather is good enough for me	once i've seen it even rain delights me the full bloom

The last two readings are *completely different* from the first two because *sawari*, unless written in Chinese characters (which it is not, here) can mean two completely different things. While I like the idea of touch, the existence of a *ku* by Sôgi which says even the waiting time is a joy (*ku* #1-4) suggests the *sawari*-as-obstacle, *i.e.*, rain, business (or, even a woman's period) is also possible.

散る物と思わぬ人の花盛り　柳多留 67-28
chiru mono to omowanu hito no hanazakari 19c yanagidaru
(fall/scatter thing as think-not person's/peoples' blossom-acme)

                    fall? not even
                  in their dreams: men
                     in full flower

people blooming   they can't see
below the trees think not   they'll blow away: a flower
they too will go   frenzy of people

                   you'd think they
              will never scatter: men
                   in the bloompeak

This *senryû* plays upon the old conceit: *who can imagine flourishing flowers (male or female) will ever fall! be gone?* When you think about it, almost all Western poetry is *senryû*, in the sense that the blossoms always stand for us rather than vice-versa. At the same time, the *senryû* may be considered an observation of people blossom-viewing like there is no tomorrow. The fall/scatter (*chiru*) can allude to falling from grace, dropping dead, or simply scattering and going home.

かつさくを花ハ見る人のさかり哉　宗碩 大発句帳
katsu saku o hana wa miru hito no sakari kana   sôseki (-1533)
(before blooming[contrad.] blossom-as-for see people's/s'acme/frenzy!/'tis)

    the blossoms seen,   once men viewed
behold, the viewers themselves   blossoms but now it's about
    in rampant bloom!   how *we* bloom

                    once the cherries
                  were *it:* now the viewers
                    are in full bloom

This is contemporaneous with Moritake's *ku* of the blossom mountains around Kyoto as bars. In the 15c, it would seem that both haiku as we know it and the cherry *bash* were already on.

生酔もさかり桜もさかりなり　李牛 初代川柳
nama yoi mo sakari sakura mo sakari nari   senryû (17-8c)
(drunk[person] too acme/frenzy, cherries too acme/frenzy is)

                   the drunken louts
             in full bloom and the cherries
                   in full bloom, too

桜木や同じ盛も御膝元　一茶
sakuragi ya onaji sakari mo ohizamoto   issa
(cherry-tree/s:/!/and same acme/frenzy-too laps-origin)

    the cherry trees   the cherry trees
the same heat, the same flush   and the place we sit the same
    down here with us   acme of bloom

Issa's "lap" meant the vicinity of the mats upon which the blossom-viewers sat. Issa does not make the *sakari* move from blossom to man, but describes a simultaneous excitement above and below. The older *senryû* seems negative whereas Issa's *ku* seems positive about the bash.

枝々に笑ふ声あり花盛　秀暁　靫随筆
eda eda ni warau koe ari hanazakari　shûgyô 1759
(branch branch-on/in laughing voice/s is/are blossom-acme)

every limb
has a laughing voice
full-bloom

As we have already seen, people did literally climb the trees, but chances are this refers to the din of merriment coming from all directions. The party is in full-bloom.

人は咲て浮るあふら山桜　淡々
hito wa saite?ukururu? abura yamazakura tantan 1673-1761
(people-as-for blooming, float-up fat/oil mountain-cherry)

people blooming,
the cream comes to the top:
mountain cherries!

The "cream" in the original is *oil/grease*. In Japan, tasty animal protein is described as "fat/oil-ridden" (*abura-ga notte*) and considered "sweet," i.e., *delicious*. Hence, I turned it into cream, which is full of fat and sweet and soft, which is to say synonymous with beauty, comfort and all we sought before becoming infatuated with muscles. Why *mountain* cherry? Because it is literally high, hiking into the mountains is the highest form of blossom-viewing, and people "floating/ rising" are *high* in the slang sense that spread during Usania's all-too-brief bout of sanity, the late 1960's and early 70's..

真黒に花見る人のさかりかな　子規
makkuro ni hana miru hito no sakari kana　shiki 1895
(pure-black-as blossom viewing peoples' acme/frenzy!/'tis)

solid black	how black
what a swarm of men	blossom-viewing men
blossom-viewing	in full rut

Makkuro ni, "pure blackly," has the idiomatic meaning of ardent pursuit of a single aim. At first, I fused that with a tan obtained from days in the bloomshade. *"Burned black / men who never lost sight / of the blossoms?"* But I was off-track. Y-san reminded me of older literature describing crowds of men as *black* for, viewed at a distance from above, Japanese hair makes a sea of heads a black one.

大佛うしろに花の盛り哉　路通　花つみ
daibutsu ushiro ni hana no sakari kana rotsû (1690)
(great buddha [colossal statue] behind-at blossoms' acme/frenzy!/'tis)

behind the back	blossoms rutting
of the colossal, blossoms	behind the back of the
in full bloom	great buddha!

Nothing so calm, nothing so cool as the colossal seated Buddha. My "rutting" may be a bit too much, but I vaguely recall seeing other *ku* with cats in heat near the Buddha and could not resist.

あそべとの浮世の民にさくらかな 素丸
asobe to no ukiyo no min ni sakura kana   somaru 1712-95
(play! say floating-world's people/folk-to/for, cherry[blossoms!/?])

cherry blossoms	to all us folk	they say "play!"
for all in the floating world	in the world of woe, cherries	by proving life is short
who say "play!"	tell us "play!"	cherry blossoms

The significance of life-advice depends upon whether you identify with the blossoms or the tree. I vaguely recall a Piet Hein *grook*: *"We ought to live / each day as though / it were our last one / here below. / The years have passed / and now I know / it would have killed me / long ago."* Amen.

花盛散るより外はなかりけり 樗堂
hanazakari chiru yori hoka wa nakarikeri   chodô (-1814)
(blosom-acme falling rather-different-as-for not[+finality])

bloom-peak:
what is left to do
but fall!

Chodô also wrote, *"This bloom-peak! / Today can only happen / once a year"* (けふの日の年に二度なし花盛 樗堂 *kyô no hi no toshi ni nido nashi hanazakari*). Ah, but one can look further ahead:

猶幾代盛りにかへる春の花 宗祇
nao iku yo sakari ni kaeru harunohana   sôgi 1420-1502
(still how-many eras flourish/frenzy-to return spring's blossoms)

spring blossoms:	ah, but count
just how long will they keep	the years they bloom afresh
coming into heat?	spring blossoms

We cannot come back to life and the blossom cannot return to the branch, but cherries can not only blossom time and time again, but *peak* each time.   My first reading crudely conveys that fine point.

見る人を返さぬ花のさかり哉 信照 鷹？筑波
miru hito o kaesanu hana no sakari kana   shinshô (1356?1642?)
(viewing-person[+obj] return-not blossoms' acme/rut/frenzy!/'tis)

pink power

blooming cherries!	they just won't
they just won't release	let their viewers go:
those who watch!	rutting blossoms

In a popular country song by Loretta Lynn and Conray Twitty, spouses are begged to release the cheaters for the sake of the ultimate value of *true love* (as opposed to that run cold); here we see the reverse: the blossomy mistress refusing to allow her lovers, the blossom viewers to go home. Some Japanese deny there is even a hint of rutting in the full-bloom. This *ku* says differently.

若武者の今そ軍法花盛　勝之 太夫桜
waka busha no ima zo gunpô hanazakari   shôshi 1680
(young warrior's now[+emph.] strategy blossom-peak/frenzy)

the full bloom this is when young *busha* can play war	young samurai, here's your martial art bloom! bloom!	young fighters now's your chance to fight the full bloom

We will return to this martial metaphor elsewhere. The poet knows his readers are familiar with the term *hana-ikusa,* or "blossom-battle/uprising." Here, alone, I translate the *s/zakari* as an "explosion."

満開のさくらにお城がゆれている　木崎守夫 福島県 高田小6
mankai no sakura ni oshiro ga yureteiru   kisaki morio 6th grade こども俳句歳時記
(full-open/bloom's cherry/cherries-to/with/by/at castle-the shaking/quivering-is)

cherry blossoms in full bloom are making the castle shake!	the castle trembles at the cherry blossoms in full bloom

This is not a *sakari* poem per se, but what a fine description of the power of a cherry tree in full bloom! I would not hesitate to include *ku* such as this one by a child in *saijiki*, but Japanese only do so for juvenilia by famous old poets. My first reading preserves the word order but the second is closer to the original's spirit which is subtle because *ni* can mean many things: "at/to/with/by."

大桜只一もとのさかり哉　子規 明治廿七
ôzakura tada hito moto no sakari kana   shiki 1894
(big-cherry/cherries just one base/origin's acme/heat!/'tis)

a large cherry
this heat, this rut, around
a single trunk

This is a simple yet complete masterpiece. It is good to feel not only the beauty but the draw, the power to attract of a mighty tree. Or, at least, I feel that *sakari* includes that implication. Now, for the last *ku* of the chapter, one that manages to be both natural and pedagogical, I only wish English had a way to exclaim in phonemes rather than marks without being specific.

かう居るも大せつな日ぞ花ざかり　惟然
kô iru mo taisetsuna hi zo hanazakari   izen (-1710)
(like-this be/sit-even, important day [+emph.] blossom-acme)

just to be here so momentous a day! the full bloom	an important day just to be and be *here* in the bloompeak

桜ばないのち一ぱいに咲くからに生命（いのち）をかけてわが眺めたり　岡本かの子（浴身）

11

Infant Cherry
稚児桜
chigo-zakura

天神か父母なき庭の児桜　安当　夢見草
tenjin ka/ga fubonaki niwa no chigozakura antô 1656
(heaven-person? father-mother-not garden's infant/boy-cherry)

the gods come
parentless: in my yard
a baby cherry

is it a godling?　　　　　　　　　　　　　　　　is it a sapling
in the garden parentless　　　　　　　　　　or godling, this boy cherry
an infant cherry　　　　　　　　　　　　　　　　in my garden?

little cherry
in my garden: a sapling
or a godling?

A *chigo* is 1) *an infant,* 2) *a young boy,* 3) *a boy servant at noble or samurai residences or temples, often serving or sought as a catamite,* 4) *boys all dressed up for parade or dancing at Shinto shrine or Buddhist temple events.* One does not find *chigo-matsu* or *chigo-ume,* "infant pine" and "infant plum," respectively. They are always *waka,* or "young." Why only cherry saplings are *infants*, I do not know. Perhaps because they are the tree most likely to be personified, or vice-versa, for in pre-19c Japan, a *chigo-zakura* was a beautiful infant, most commonly a sought-after pretty boy, of type 3, above. Because of the anomaly, my first thought was that *chigo-zakura* was a *variety* of cherry, but found no mention of such anywhere. All I could find was Japanese-style confectionary shaped like cherry blossoms going by that name and one local legend of a seven-headed dragon who ate sixteen children, after which a cherry tree popped up on a hill (suggestive of a burial mound), blossomed and was named "the children/infant cherry." I encountered one *ku* vaguely suggestive of that legend:

悼亡兒・土に埋て子の咲花もある事よ　鬼貫
tsuchi ni umete ko no saku hana mo aru koto yo onitsura (1660-1738)
(funeral dead infant: earth-in burying child blooms plant/s/blossoms also are thing[+emph.])

an infant's funeral

you know, there is　　　　　　　　　　　　you know, there's
a plant that blossoms with　　　　　　a plant where buried babes
the babes we bury　　　　　　　　　　　　blossom again

The style is that of a parent speaking to a child, or a child speaking to anyone. This made me feel it might be the first line of a kind just-so story about recycled lives. I imagined actual trees planted on graves and paradisiacal flowers in the underworld. That is my superficial reading of the *ku*. *Blossoming* also had the figurative meaning of finding true happiness, i.e., enlightenment, either in the Godhead, or reincarnated. As was the case with 16c and 17c Catholicism, some Buddhist priests prayed to expedite the fortune of the dead person's soul, and were paid handsomely for it: *"Believe me! / Some children blossom / after burial."* As Onitsura was not a Buddhist priest, he may have meant *"You never know / a buried child may plant / blossoms in your heart!"* and/or that a new baby might soon be conceived by the grieving parents. Be that as it may, let us see a real *chigo-zakura ku*:

おふて見よ後の山のおちこ櫻　珍舟 三重 太夫桜
ôte miyo ushiro no yama no ochigozakura　chinshû 1680
(piggy-back-try: rear's mountain's [honorific "o"]infant cherry)

i'll piggy-back
you down, infant cherry
from the hills!

Is the idea to take a cherry tree from a hill out back and bring it home? The original is so vague I can also see the poet having a friend pose hunched over as if carrying the sapling on a hill behind him.

おりくるや山から里へ兒櫻　常久 毛吹草
ori-kuru ya yama kara sato e chigozakura　jôkyû (1645)
(breaking[off a branch]=descend-coming: mountain-from home-town-to infant-cherry)

they come to take   coming home
infant cherries from the hills   with an infant cherry
down to the towns   from the hills

Because *ori* is written in phonetic syllabary, we cannot tell which reading is intended. Most boys were sent to mountain temples for an education, others (orphans, bright youth from poor families, children who threaten the rulers by birthright) because they could not remain with their families. Some became acolyte priests – monk apprentices, if you will – and stayed but most eventually returned home: *"Blossoms return / to their root: infant cherry / has a homecoming"* (花は根にお里がへりや兒櫻　重和 *hana wa ne ni osatogaeri ya chigozakura* jûwa/shigekazu).

枝伐て坊主になすな兒櫻　一徳 鷹つくは
eda kitte bôzu ni nasuna chigozakura　ichitoku (1642)
(branch cut/ting, monk=bald-into make-not! infant-cherry)

don't cut the limbs
and make a monk out of our
lovely boy cherry!

No, not the tender morsel! Actually, castration was not so common in Japan as in China, the Near-East and Europe. The *ku* equates pruning a young tree for transplantation with the *pate* of a monk. The humor is natural in Japanese where "monk-head" (*bôzu-atama*) means a shaven pate. Unlike the *ku* in the above paragraph, the tree (not boy) is indeed the subject and the practice of shaving peoples heads and putting them in monasteries is used as an allegory for the tree our poet would prefer to leave in its natural state. *Or so I would like to think* though the *ku* is probably no more than a play on the phrase "infant cherry." My "lovely boy" comes from Ueda's translation of a *ku* by Bashô: *"the moon is clear – / I escort a lovely boy / frightened by a fox."* His gloss called the *chigo* a "boy-lover."

御僧の心の花や兒櫻　可雪 洗濯物
ozô no kokoro no hana ya chigozakura kasetsu (1666)
([honorific/snide "o"] monk's/s' heart/mind's blossom: infant cherry)

<blockquote>
the blossom
that monks so love
boy cherry
</blockquote>

Monks were forbidden to fall for women who produced children and long-term attachment. But *boys* were winked at. They would get hairy, smelly and, in most cases, want girls. With time, they were bound to disappoint. This made the temple schools something like the proverbial British boarding school, but for the teachers participation. The usual allegory for boy-novices was the fragile, *poppy* (whose name *keshi-no-hana* conveniently puns as flower of *oblivion*), for the poor food, cold climate, hard work and natural weakness of boys (as opposed to girls) resulted in a high death-rate.

学問も兒桜にやすて坊主　長頭丸 崑山集
gakumon mo chigozakura ni ya sutebôzu teitoku 1651
(scholarship/learning-even boy-cherry-to/for!/: abandoning-monk)

<blockquote>
for time to study   leaving his learning
and those boy cherries, leaving   and boy cherries behind
home to be a monk   a begging monk
</blockquote>

A "sute-bôzu" is literally an "abandoning-monk," someone who leaves home=family to become a monk, or becomes a monk to abandon a home. My first reading is most likely, but I would like the second one, describing the birth of an ascetic who has abandoned a wealthy temple, to be true.

年の比衆道盛や兒櫻　梅舟 太夫桜
toshi no hishi shûdôzakari ya chigozakura baishû 1680
(year ratio/compare crowd-way[homosexual]-acme-:/! infant-cherry/ies)

<blockquote>
the full flower   age-wise, they
of their boy-love way, still   are in their gay prime
infant cherries   boy cherries
</blockquote>

A good bloom on a sapling is described by playing with two types of "male color." The term "crowd-way" (*shûdô*) is short for "young-crowd-way" (*waka-shûdô*), adolescents who generally sold their sexual favors to older men, as opposed to the innocent little *chigo* loved by bonzes. Once you start reading about risqué monks and their lovely boy cherries, you start finding them everywhere. Take a *ku* I first translated *"In Kuma valley / they hide their rears / infant cherries."* Checking the OJD for the monastery I assumed I'd find there, instead I found a reference to Kumagai Naosane, a 12c scholar warlord who reluctantly fought and killed the *infant* (actually sixteen year-old) Taira Atsumori, who came back to pick up a dropped flute rather than fleeing when the battle was lost. The *ku* was innocent and meant: *"To Kumagai / it shows not its rear / the boy cherry."* (熊谷に後や見せぬ兒櫻　一祐 太夫櫻 *kumagai ni ushiro ya misenu chigozakura* ichiu 1680). Call it an early example of a brave dying samurai cherry. As there is a variety of cherry called a *kumagai*, the *ku* may also mean that an infant cherry is blooming in the face of mature kumagai trees. Pardon all this complexity involved in reading *ku* so simple it is hard to call them poems, but please note that the added confusion coming from the lack of a single word in English for "infant" and "boy" is not found in Japanese and would be no problem whatsoever for Portuguese where *meninos* covers both.

infant / boy

親木なひか須磨の御寺の兒櫻　可通 太夫桜
oya ki nai ka suma no midera no chigozakura   katsû 1680
(parent tree not? suma's [+honorific] temple's infant cherry/ies)

    don't you have
a parent tree? infant cherry
      at suma's *midera*

Midera is a polite way to say *tera*, a Buddhist temple. Since the battle where the fine youth died for his flute was in the greater Suma area, most Suma boy cherries are *him*. But this may be different, perhaps a reference to the orphaned girl the Shining Prince Genji adopted (or did he end up marrying her?). As to whether there really were cherry saplings blooming at the Suma temple which were seen by the poet – I doubt it. The *Dayûzakura* anthology the *ku* came in covers too much ground to be real.

雨にそふ風は継母か兒櫻　友勝 鷹つくは
ame ni sou kaze wa keibo ka chigozakura   yûshô 1642
(rain-with accompany wind-as-for step-mother? infant-cherry)

     infant cherry
is that wind with the rain
    your stepmother?

Rain stands for mother's milk and other sustenance provided by parents while wind that damages or blows off the tender blossoms is an enemy (a category including lovers as we shall see later). Here, the poet comes up with the idea that the combination of rain and wind can only be the stereotypical meanie, the step-mother.

五百年や老て二度兒櫻　面白 太夫櫻
gohyakunen ya oite ni-do chigozakura   menbaku 1680
(five-hundred-years[old]:/! aging, two times infant-cherry)

second childhood

     five-hundred
years old! once again
   an infant cherry

Fifty years was once considered a man's lifetime. If a dog year is seven of ours, this poet makes ours ten of the cherry's. After finishing one lifetime, human or tree, is free to *return to start*. Such *foolish old age = foolish babyhood* – "upside downtown" as one American author put it – *ku* were quite common on poet's fiftieth, fifty-first, sixtieth (five complete Chinese zodiac animal cycles) and sixty-first birthdays (see IPOOH ny: *The Fifth Season*). But this is the only such I have found for a tree.

招く扇風もつらしや兒櫻　水吟 1680
maneku ogi kaze mo tsurashi ya chigozakura   suigin
(invite-fan-breeze, too/even painful?/: infant-cherry)

   even the breeze
from a fan is too rough
  for infant cherry

招く扇風にや散た兒櫻　宗純 1680
maneku ogi kaze nya chita chigozakura   sôjun
(invite-fan-breeze:/?/by [blossoms]fell infant-cherry)

    breeze invited
by fan scattered its petals
   an infant cherry

158   infant / boy

In both *ku,* the fan *invites* breeze. It seems to be playfully used to stir the blossoms, but the reference would be to the fan in the hands of the host of the blossom-viewing.

児桜付たる鈴やひも守り　長頭丸 崑山集
chigozakura tsuketaru suzu ya himomamori   teitoku (1651)
(infant-cherry attached bell!/?/: string-charm)

that bell attached
to the infant cherry: is it
a charm bracelet?

Charms were usually tied on (or *were*) the sashes around an infant's robe, but a boy might have a charm necklace. A bracelet is less likely but it sounded better. Japanese had and still have noise-making devices (clappers, etc.) attached between trees to frighten away deer, but, as far as I know, no charms on young trees (only Janine does that). While the *ku* is a purely nominal invention, I say, *why not!*

とく咲くはおとな恥かし兒櫻　頼実 毛吹草
toku saku wa otona hazukashi chigozakura   yorisane (1645)
(early bloom-as-for grown-up embarassed/ashamed infant-cherry)

blooming so young   blooming so fast
we feel ashamed for you   a grown-up would blush
my boy cherry!   little boy cherry

The cherry in the first reading is a precocious tree, flowering at a tender age. The second imagines it blooming early in the season. The significance of *that* will become clear in the next chapter.

散す風の手車にのるや兒櫻　親信 洗濯物
chisu kaze no taguruma ni noru ya chigozakura   shinjin 1666
(blow/scatter/ing wind's hand-cart-on ride/climb infant-cherry)

they readily climb
into the wind's wheelbarrow
boy cherry blossoms

In Japanese, "to fall for someone's clever words" is "to climb aboard a mouth-cart" (*kuchi-guruma ni noru*). That turns into a "hand-cart" (*ta-guruma*) because what Englishes as a "pin-wheel" is a "wind-cart" in Japanese. Moreover, a hand-cart, or wheel-barrow, was a proper way to transport a noble child. Even if English could match these accidents of vocabulary, the need to specify blossom, petal or tree the cherry prevents a meaningful translation. The first *ku*, below, refers to *the young flautist* –

敵味方目を驚かす兒桜　直治 1680   名をよばゝ只花若よ兒櫻　弘永 1645
teki-mikata me o odorokasu chigozakura   naoharu   *na o yobeba tada hanawaka yo chigozakura*   kôei
(enemy-friend eye/s surprise boy-cherry[subj])   (name[obj] call-fi/when just blossom-young! boych)

friend and foe   if you announce
cannot believe their eyes   make it just *blossom young*
this boy cherry   my boy cherry

– the second plays on *the custom of announcing before battle* while saluting the cherry as *the* blossom.

11 #16~20

12
Late Cherry, Beloved & Despised
遅桜
oso-zakura

    しりかたき花の心や遅櫻　樗堂 アルス
shirigataki hana no kokoro ya osozakura chodo -1814
(know-hard blossom's heart/mind/feelings!/: late/slow-cherry)

a blossom's mind
is not easy to know:
this late cherry!

The cherry (blossom and/or tree) developed a personality that may be called either *split* or *multiple* long before the short verse form later called haiku came into being. It's basic male *persona* boldly blooms and quickly blows, giving up the ghost without reserve, something long admired as the mark of true greatness – whether coming from the courage of a warrior or unattachment of a priest. In so far that the male cherry was respected, the late cherry was despised. On the other hand, as a female persona, struggling with hormonal (?) rain and the pushy male wind, the late cherry earned the poet's begrudged admiration. Yet, in contradiction to the above, male perseverance – hanging in there – is sometimes admired in late=slow=sluggish (all *oso* in Japanese) cherries, while female reticence to bloom may be criticized as un-filial when the rain is viewed as a parent (or the milk of heaven).

    春雨に争いかねて（相争不勝）。。。　万葉集 #1869
harusame ni arasoi-kanete waga yado no sakura no hana wa sakisomenikeri manyôshû (8c)

unable to	my cherry tree
beat the spring rain	couldn't hold out against
the cherry	the spring rain
blossoms at my home	i am afraid to say
have started opening	she's broken into bloom

Arasoi-kanete, "compete/fight-cannot." This *waka* from Japan's oldest anthology, the *Manyôshû*, opened my eyes to *contest* as a metaphor of natural progression (as opposed to the *parade* or *hand-off* or *transfer*, or *leaving the stage* or *birth and death*, etc.). It appears in many *waka* dealing with other plants and elements, too.[1] *Haikai* poets played with the conceit. Shigeyori (1601-1680) wrote: *"Failing to make / the pears bloom, the rain / loses face"* (*saki yara de ame ya menboku nashinohana* (*pear* is a homophone for the "loss" (*nashi*="not")).[2] Even clover, allegorically, an older woman, blooms upon losing its struggle with the dew. Sôin (1604-82) parodied such rhetoric: *"Losing their fight / against the cold drizzle / my straw sandals"* (*shigure no ame arasoikane no waraji kana*). My second reading of the *Manyôshû waka* assumes it addresses another party who had hoped to see the first bloom.

1. Forcing Rhetoric This *arasoi-kanete* also found in Manyôshû song #2116, when the clover blooms upon losing its struggle with the dew (百露に争いかねて) and the leaves turn to fall colors after losing out (あらそいかねて色づき) to the cold showers (時雨). It was a favorite term for the *haikai no renga* or *jamfest* as I call the activities that gave birth to what developed into haiku. In a Danrin=talkwoods jamfest, a *ku* linking with a waterfront situation depicts a Japanese Billy Bud: "*Losing out / in the fight for a whore / he starts dicing*" (*keisei o arasoi-kanete makurigiri*) – that is, chops up the successful John. The annotation simply cites a *Shinkokinshû* poem #577: "Unable / to fight off / the cold rain / the black pine needles / have changed color" (*shigure no ame ma nakushi fureba maki no ha mo arasoi-kanete irozukinikeri* hitomaro). If it really was by Hitomaro (so famous many poems were attributed to him), it goes back to *Manyôshû* times. With so many *arasoi-kanete* poems out there to choose from, does that mean the *irozuki* meaning "color-got" was punned into "color=sex-loving" and the leaf (*ha*) was thought to pun the identically pronounced *blade* used in the fight?

◎When I first paraversed Manyôshû poem # 1869, I reduced the *arasoi-kanete*, or failing in the struggle, to "*iyada iya da!*" (*No! No!*) Years later, I was surprised to find a funeral *ku* by Shiki: "*This* blossom / said "*No! No!*" *and* / *died for good*" (この花がいやじゃ／\と死なれけん 子規*kono hana ga iya ja iya ja to shinareken* (1894)). I cannot tell if he or she didn't want to bloom and choose to die or didn't want to die but did. (Sorry for the irregular margins: Bill Gates is to blame.)

2. Forcing Bloom If good translation of poems on this subject is stymied by English's lack of a transitive verb for bloom/blossom ("make blossom" is not quite the same), the forcing concept is itself problematic for suggesting a practice, called *wakan* 和姦 which Englishes as "peaceful-rape,". Legally, it means "rape by mutual consent," an oxymoron for the Japanese equivalent of our "legal rape" (consenting relations between adults and teens or the sane with the insane), but in common vernacular it means something altogether different: *real rape that is accepted by the victim post-facto*. By "accepted," I mean that the victim/woman ends up liking the act into which she was forced and/or falling in love with the man! I often came across this sort of thing in Japanese comics and in TV movies in the 1980's and 90's. It would seem to be based upon one or both of the following assumptions: 1) If a woman is physically pleasured, she will forgive anything and love a man, so the best way to break an impasse in a one-sided love affair is to force her into sex & orgasm; 2) That women may really want it though they claim they do not. I find the concept unpleasant to say the least, but have encountered something like it in folk practice around the world in marriage customs where "brides" were forcefully carried off (or a pretence made to satisfy old custom). This was called "rape" in English, too.

~~~~~~

子規初音そ花のおそさくら 摂津守? 毛吹草か
hototogisu hatsune zo hana no osozakura setsutsu 1645
(cuckoo[bird=its call]! first-sound! blossom/precious late-cherry)

<table>
<tr><td>

cuckoo calls
its very first! pretty
late cherry!

</td><td>

can't you hear
the cuckoo's first call
late cherries

</td></tr>
</table>

The cuckoo that marked the arrival of summer when England boasted only two seasons was also the first sound of summer in Japan. An early cuckoo and a late late-cherry would cross paths.

奥になほ人見ぬ花の散らぬあれや　たづねを入らん山ほととぎす　西行
oku ni nao hito minu hana no chiranu are ya tazune o iran yama hototogisu saigyo -1190
(depths/recesses-in still, people see-not blossom's/s' fall-not be! visit enter/make-let's mountain-cuckoo)

Ah, for cherries
blooming in the hills
unseen by man!

Let's pay them a visit
you and i, wild cuckoo!

The mountain cuckoo was quite the playboy, flying from wife to wife – like the stereotypical ruling class Japanese male – so this *waka* has a romantic ring to it. The season says the subject is late-cherries whether specified or not.

花にこきませしとや遅櫻　宗因 三籟
hana ni kokimazeshi to ya osozakura　sôin 1604-82
(blossom/ing/trees-in jumble-mixed late-cherry/ies)

mixed up
with blossoming trees
a late cherry

Here and in the next *ku* we see the late-cherry still in bud before her season has come. That is a rare perspective for a flower. We assume the other trees blossoming are normal (?) cherry trees.

散る花の中や一本遅櫻　煙霞郎 新句俳?
chiru hana no naka ya ippon osozakura　enkarô ()
(fall blossoms-among/middle! one-tree late-cherry)

standing alone
in a blizzard of blossoms
one late-cherry

The ability of Japanese to accept one word *hana* as both the scattering petals and the trees losing them, brings out the contrast with the lone exception better than my translation would have without that dramatic "blizzard," a Japanese cherry term I am afraid was *not* used in the original of this *ku*.

遅櫻梨に交りてさきにけり　布舟 明からす
osozakura nashi ni majirite sakinikeri　fushû (1685?1773?)
(late cherry/s pear[trees]-with mix/mingling bloom[+finality])

a late cherry　　　　　　　　　　the late cherries
mixed in with the pears　　　　　mingling with the pears
blooms away!　　　　　　　　　　have bloomed

Pears blossom later than the average cherry. I have read accounts by foreign visitors to Japan claiming the blossom was more profuse in many areas than the cherry and it was a shame that people paid so little heed to them as blossoms. Since late-cherries, as we shall see, tend to be profusely petaled, they would, nevertheless, stand out among the pear blossoms.

ひるの月三輪の木の間の遅ざくら　大江丸 俳諧袋
hiru no tsuki miwa no konoma no osozakura　ôemaru 1719-1805
(daytime/noon-moon, miwa's trees-between/gaps' late-cherry/ies)

daytime moon
among the trees in miwa
a late cherry

The daytime moon is more noticeable as the temperature warms and people relax and look about more. It matches the season and the late-cherry in many ways. Phase-wise, it is on the wane. So is Spring. Time-wise, it comes out late at night and remains in the daylight. The tree blooms late in the Spring and may creep into the summer. Unlike the full moon, the waning moon is seldom noticed. The cherry misses the blossom-viewing rush and is hard to find in the thick foliage. Miwa is high, in greater Nara, and has too many poetical associations to explain. This time, I won't.

万日の人のちりはや遅櫻　其角　五元集
mannichi no hito no chiri haya osozakura　kikaku -1707
(ten-thousand days' peoples' trash already late-cherry/ies)

at black valley

trash left from
the day of days already
late cherries

The *mannichi* I translated as "the day of days" is literally 10,000 days, and means the day some Buddhist sects claim is worth ten-thousand (one-*man*) days as far as prayers or temple visits were concerned. This tended to coincide with the time most cherries bloomed. The major temple at Kurodani (to the West-North-West of Kyôto) belongs to the Jôdo (*shû*), or *Pureland* (sect), whose followers were big on this celebration. Could Kikaku have found irony in a trashy "pureland"?

紙屑の所々におそさくら　柴雫　類題集
kamikuzu no[or ya] tokorodokoro ni osozakura　shida 1774
(paper-trash/scraps'/! place-place-at late-cherry)

bits of trash
here . . . and . . . there
late cherries

Trash left by blossom-viewers. The late cherry is late to the party. We will return to the seasonal significance of the late cherry soon enough, but first, let I would like to jump to what interests me most about her: the strong opinions, even ranting she evokes:

早くさけ何をしてかは遲櫻　心計　洗濯物
hayaku sake nani o shite ka wa osozakura　shinkei 1666
(quickly bloom! what [are you] doing!? late/slow/sluggish-cherry)

quickly bloom!　　　　　　　　　　　　　　hey, late cherry:
what's keeping you,　　　　　　　　　　what's keeping you? hurry-up
late cherry?　　　　　　　　　　　　　　　with the *sake!*

I enjoy the animistic imperative. Since, "bloom = *sake*!" is written in phonetic syllabary, it may pun on drink: hence the second reading. A less endearing *ku* by soldier Chûkô (岩和田弥三兵衛): *"Quick, bloom! / history has never seen such / a slow cherry!"* (はやくさけ前代みもんの遅桜　中好 *hayaku sake zendai mimon no osozakura*). Luckily, he wrote another *ku* with a first-rank hyperbole:

とてもならば師走に咲よ遲桜　中好
totemo naraba shiwasu ni sake yo osozakura　chûkô or nakayoshi ()
(too-much/prefer-if, end-of-year[period of final accounts]-until/on bloom! late-cherry)

why not be *really* late?

if that's the case　　　　　　　　　　　　then, why not
why not wait to december,　　　　　　bloom on new year's eve
slow-poke cherries!　　　　　　　　　　　late cherry!

Any later would be early again. *Shiwasu* is the period at the year's end when people settle accounts.

冬咲の椿にはちよ遅櫻　徳元
fuyuzaki no tsubaki ni hajiyo osozakura tokugen 1558-1647
(winter blooming camelia-to[compared with] ashamed-be! late-cherry)

for shame! shame!	*the last to bloom*
look at camelia	swallow your pride
she blooms in the winter,	slow cherry, the camelia
"late" cherries!	holds on to winter!

The camelia, usually *saijiki*'ed as a spring bloomer (the radicals forming its name comprise "tree+ spring"), beats out even the official spring blossom, the plum, by blooming in the winter, as Tokugen notes. The first reading is most likely the poet's intention, but I prefer the second. Such joking is charming, but some *ku* hint at more serious anti-late-cherry behavior. For example, *"Pray show not / the late cherry to men / without patience!"* (木おりなる人になみせそ遅櫻　正平 鷹筑波 *kiori naru hito ni na mise so osozakura*　shôhei (1642). This *ku* combines archaic grammar with an idiom for the single-minded, short-tempered, which is sometimes, as in this *ku*, literally written "tree-breaking." My first reading caught the archaism; now for some *English* idiom: *"Keep them away / from men with short fuses! / our late cherries."* Or, how about this next *ku*, which, I am afraid, is undated? *"Where drunks / take out their spleen: / late cherries"* 生酔の無念はらしぬ遅櫻　福富　雑中 *namayoi no munen harashinu osozakura*　fukufû) The first *ku* reminded me of the Shôgun Nobunaga, who was said to shoot the nightingale that failed to sing for him; but only a drunk could get mad at a tree.

遅いとて人も笑す遅櫻　宇中 類題
osoi tote hito mo warawasu osozakura uchû -1725
([aren't you] late [saying], people-too, laughed [at] late/slow cherry)

aren't you late!	*laughed at*
the late cherry is kidded	for being so slow
when she blooms	late cherries

隣から気（の）毒がるや遅ざくら　一茶 遺稿
tonari kara kinodokugaru ya osozakura　issa -1827
(neighbor-from feeling-sorry:/! late-cherry)

my neighbors	*my neighbor*
think it such a pity	offers commiseration
my late cherry	our late cherry

The subject of Issa's *ku* is probably his late marriage, his wife's age, or the fact they bore a child who (it was thought) would outlive them. As pure allegory, Issa's *ku* is as bad as his contempory Gekkyo's odd *ku*: *"The late cherry / feels sorry for its own / first blossom"* (遅櫻おのか初花哀なり　月居　アルス *osozakura onoga hatsuhana aware nari* -1824). What saves Issa's *ku* is that it can be read realistically as well as allegorically. We can imagine the neighbor comparing Issa's cherry tree – we know he had one – to other trees and finding it bloomed too late. Since Issa has New Year's *ku* suggesting he was short of sunlight in the morning, it wouldn't be surprising if his cherry bloomed late even for the famously late cherries of snowy Shinano. Still, I think the next, far older *ku*, a far better fusion of cherry and person.

らうさいの種をや植る遅桜 利勝 鷹つくは
rôsai no tane o ya ueru osozakura rishô 1642
(old-wife's seed[acc. + emph.] plant late-cherry)

        is my old wife
    out planting seeds now?
         late cherries

At first, I had an old man "planting" seeds in his old wife or an old wife planting the seeds of late-cherry, but OM pointed out an alternative, which I had to go with, though it makes the *ku* almost too good for its time!. The elderly are slow to come out of hibernation and their late planting or sowing coincides with said bloom rather than earlier trees. Now, back to more typical *haikai* metaphysics!

こらへ袋きれてや開く遅櫻 信相 鷹つくは
koraebukuro kirete ya hiraku osozakura   shinsô (1642)
(endure/repress-bag [patience/forbearance] cuts!/: opens/blooms late cherry)

   she can no longer   the late cherry
 contain herself! the late   finally loses control
     cherry blossoms   and blossoms

This is a nice turn on the struggle metaphor of older *waka*, where the buds fight off the warm rain, for it turns it into *an internal fight*, where the cherry, against her better judgment, *wants* to bloom. It is in her nature. I have found a paraverse identical to the above *ku* until the last five syllabets which are *fuyu no ume,* or "winter plum"(こらへ袋きれてや開冬の梅 京房 崑山集 *koraebukuro kirete ya hiraku fuyu no ume* kyôbo (1651)). Here, for the contrasting perspective, is the typical *male* blossom:

我も／＼まけじと咲くや花軍 義的 鷹つくは
ware mo ware makeji to saku ya hana ikusa giteki 1642
(me, too, me! lose-not-in-order blooms! blossom-war/uprising)

    me! me! me!   *me, first! me!*
hating to lose, they bloom   what haste to bloom!
   cherry warriors   a cherry uprising

The *hana ikusa,* or, "blossom war" is not the invention of this poet but a standard cherry-time term. But it is rare for having warriors contesting to *bloom* first rather than to *blow* first (the quickness or slowness of blossoms in bloom *to fall* is a different theme discussed in Book III.).   Quick to bloom or slow to bloom, there is clearly a psychological angle. As Jôha (1523-1602), who evidently favored late bloomers, put it: *"Exceptional / depth of character here! / a slow cherry"* (なみならぬ心深さや遅櫻 紹巴 *naminaranu kokoro fukasa ya osozakura.*).   Later *ku* would make that character concrete:

あれこれをさきへさかせて桜かな 左次
are kore o saki e sakasete sakura kana saji (lost source)
(that [and] this [obj] previous-to bloom-letting, cherry!/'tis)

    cherry blossoms!
letting this and that bloom
     ahead of them

When you really think about it, the very idea of cherry blossoms rushing to bloom is mistaken. *Cherries,* generally speaking, are late, not early bloomers. Viewed in that light, the late blooming *osozakura* may well be on the cutting edge of cherryness! Onitsura (1660-1738), one of Bashô's best known contemporaries, put a different angle on the time difference. Remember the idea of the plum as big brother for blooming first? He gives us *"Now it blooms / making the late cherry / a junior bloomer"* (咲花や年の下手なる遅櫻　鬼貫 *saku hana ya toshi no heta naru osozakura*). The next *ku,* by one of Issa's employer/ teachers, shares more with Saji's *ku* and specifies the late-cherry:

うかれ立人遣り過し遅ざくら　素丸
ukaretatsu hito yarisugoshi osozakura somaru (1712-95)
(floating/excited-leave/ing person/people let-pass[by], late-cherry)

the excitable
crowd is motioned by:
slow cherries

letting all with
ants in their pants go by,
the late cherry

Somaru's *ku* has two double-verbs: *ukare-tatsu* = rushing out of the house in an excited frame of mind, exhilarated from being in love or whatever; and, *yari-sugoshi* = letting others pass one by and go ahead. The original *ku* allows the link between human behavior and plant nature remain vague.

騒しき世をおし祓て遅桜　一茶
sawagashiki yo o oshiharatte osozakura issa (-1827)
(tumultous/agitated/excited world[obj] push-banish/sweep-away late-cherry)

pushing aside
the tumultous world
a late cherry

While D. Lanoue's *"the cure for / this raucous world . . . / late cherry blossoms"* is a fine paraverse, I am too stuck on the active verb in the original to let it go. Makoto Ueda is yet more active, bringing out the exorcistic nuance of *haratte* as Issa wrote it = 祓: *"pacifying / this clamorous world / late cherry blossoms"* (*Dew On the Grass*). His Issa humorously makes the tree "into a god that has pacified all the clamor." To me, the late cherry is a miracle, a stone holding solid in the rapids. Issa's rhetorical question to faster (i.e. normal) blossoms (*"What is wanting that you rush to fall?"* (*ku* # 47-48) suggests he favored a way of life slower than that of fast-paced Edo. Indeed, the trees in the "deep mountains" of his Shinano – a place-name he punned as "do-nothing" – bloomed as late as the "Trees-do-nothing" Fifth-month, i.e., mid-summer! (深山木のしなの五月も桜哉　一茶 *miyama ki no shinano satsuki mo sakura kana*). Another Issa *ku* gives what *may be* the late-cherries active attributes:

信濃・短夜をさっさと開く桜かな　一茶 希杖本
shinano // mijikayo o sassa to hiraku sakura kana issa -1827
(short-night/s [+obj] quickly[mimesis] open/bloom cherry/ies!/'tis/are)

shinano

short nights
cherry buds opening
lickety-split

our cherry trees
make short work of bloom
summer nights

the night short
cherry blossoms make haste
one by one

> rushing to bloom
> in the short night
> *shinano sakura!*

I borrowed the "rushing to bloom" (which I wished I had written first) from DL. Note that Issa also had grasses blossoming one after another, dewdrops hastening to cover leaves, and amazingly complexly crafted wild-flowers created in the short night. The brief time to do the work (for Issa saw a *world of work*) is part of it and the contrast with the slow pace of the hot days the other half. Were Issa's *ku* not titled "Shinano," I might have thought it a Spring *ku* and played it something like this: *"Shortening nights: / Who can get any shut-eye / they bloom so fast!"* An older *ku* makes it clear that, for some, this retardation was a plus:

遠山のおく頼もしや遅ざくら 無記名 崑山集
tôyama no oku tanomosha ya osozakura   anon. (1651)
(far-mountain recesses dependable/desireable!/: late-cherries)

> there is promise   something you can
> in the mountain depths: count on back up the hollars:
> late cherries!   late cherries

尋ね見ば初花よりや遅櫻 宗牧 大発句帳
tazunemiba hatsuhana yori ya osozakura   sôboku -1545
(asked-if first-blossoms-more-than:/! late-cherry)

> when i asked
> my "first blossoms" turned out
> to be late ones

The second *ku,* as translated, needs no explanation. The word of approval, *tanomosha,* in the first *ku* does. It seems that of an old person. If you are aged, or a slow poke to begin with, late blossoms have their benefits. Another pre-Issa poet Kankan cooed: *"That old Shinano / has its own charm: / slow cherries"* (去しなの愛想なりけり遅櫻 閑々 吉選 *saru shinano aiso narikeri osozakura* 1763). One of Issa's early teachers, Somaru quipped: *"Spring, come back! / Come back!* call the deep-mountain / cherry blossoms" (春かへれ／＼と深山ざくらかな 素丸？俳懺悔 *haru kaere kaere to miyama zakura kana* 1790). *Spring, come back!* Indeed. This was an opinion shared by many elderly. But, I prefer Issa's *ku* about cherries that dared to do things at their own pace and this *ku*:

とふ人にけふの為とや遅櫻 宗因 三籟
tou hito ni kyo no tame to ya osozakura   sôin 1604-82
(ask-person-to, "today-for" [it/i say/says]! late cherry)

> asked, i reply   if someone asks
> "it's for today's sake"   "she waited for *you*!"
> the late cherry   the late cherry
>
>   doubter, i say,
>   what's wrong with today?
>   the late cherry

A good comeback to someone who asks "Isn't that cherry blossoming rather late?" as in the first two readings (the second a dubious twist), or, to someone wondering why a man is out late-blossom-viewing. The cherry "blooming *for today*" probably comes from *Manyôshû* (8c) poem #4151 (今日のためと。。。桜かく咲きにけり 大伴家持 *kyô no tame to . . .*).

けふといふけふ咲にけり遅櫻 作者不知 毛吹草
kyo to iu kyo sakenikeri osozakura   anon. (1645)
(today-say-today[every day] bloom/s[+fin.] late-cherry)

they bloom today
they bloom everyday
our late cherries

all's well that ends well   **now is never late**

today! today!
it blooms for good today!
the slow cherry

the slow cherry:
when it blooms, like others,
blooms *today!*

today

my late cherry
always promising to bloom
today: blooms!

I have no idea which if any of the readings best reflects the nuance of the original. I like the third.

色に香に手まを取てや遅桜 清親 犬子
iro ni ka ni tema o torite ya osozakura   seishin? 1633
(color/make-up/beauty] & scent-for time/trouble take/s! late-cherry/ies)

色よ香よかゝれはこそは遅櫻 宗因 三籟
iro yo ka yo kakareba koso wa osozakura   sôin (1604-82)
(color[+emph.] scent[+emph.] strive[take trouble] especially late-cherry/ies)

because she labors
to make herself beautiful:
the late cherry

all that make-up
no wonder she is what she
is: *late* cherry

taking her time
with make-up and perfume
a late cherry

遅桜遅きを花の上手かな 子規
osozakura osoki o hana no jôzu kana   shiki (1894)
(late/slow cherry lateness[+obj?] blossom's[tree's] skillful!/'tis)

late cherries
slow because their blossoms
are well-crafted

a late cherry
slow because she's good
at blossoming?

There are conceptual precedents for these and all *ku* favoring late-cherry. In contradiction to the fast-is-manly concept, slow development was a mark of greatness (as the Chinese proverb put it, 大器晩成 "big-vessel-late-becomes") and love-making was, classically speaking, a contest between man and woman to see who could come – or, as they put it "go" – last. But, forgetting such concepts, let us just say: *Hurrah for the late cherry!* "Sweet neglect" is fine and dandy for the young beauty, but others may benefit from some of the "adulteries of thine art." I kid, for age has nothing to do with it.

It is more a matter of there being different varieties: *"A young tree / that seems to pause and think? / a late cherry"* (若木にも一思案ありおそさくら　丸夕　類題発句集 *waka ki ni mo hito shian ari osozakura* ganseki 1774). Yet, there is truth in Seishin, Sôin and Shiki's claim, for the cherry with the heaviest bloom, the *yae-zakura* (ch.62) blooms late. The profuse bloom of the camelia and its relatives over the course of the winter throws a wrench into this pleasant argument, but I think all can agree that, "Among late things / *this* may be forgiven: / late blooming cherries" (遅きものゝ中に許しつ遅櫻 山川　綿繡殿雑談 *osoki mono no naka ni yurushitsu osozakura* sansen).

待とをに思ひしことよおそ櫻　宗動 新つくは
machidô ni omoishi kotoyo osozakura　sôdô 1778?
(wait-endure-by longing thing[+emph.] late-cherry)

the long wait
makes them dear to us
late cherries

forced to wait
i know how they feel
late cherries

making me wait
my love are you
a late cherry?

having to wait
is part of true love:
my late cherry

forced to wait
how longing grows
late cherries!

咲かねてつを引せけり遅櫻　長虹 小弓
sakikanetetsu o hikasekeri osozakura　chôkô (1699)
(bloom-cannot familiar/aesthete[+obj.] attract[+emph] late-cherry)

to make us druel
they play hard to bloom
late cherries

i gulp saliva
when *will* she bloom?
my late cherry

Translator's choice. In Japanese, the same verb suggests the effect on the mouth of seeing something sour, drooling as a result of anticipation and swallowing the saliva for the same reason.

楊貴妃も四十を盛遅ざくら　紫道
yôkihi mo yonjû o sakari osozakura　shidô 17c
(yôki-princess also forty acme/flourishing late-cherry)

princess yôki
in full flower at forty
a late cherry

One of the most famous beauties in the Sinosphere Yôki-hi, or Yang Kuei-fei (719-756) excelled in the arts, became a Taoist adept and, eventually an Imperial concubine of a status equivalent to a princess. I don't know about that "forty." As far as I know, she was only 37 at the time of the uprising in which she lost her life to jealous competitors (In 1748, an Empress "beloved by the Emperor for her propriety, intelligence and thrift" = 『文字の祝祭』, died at that same age, 37. Had she lived and carried out the reforms only a beloved ruler can, China's modern history might have been completely different. Doubtless, one could write an entire book about exceptional women who died at age 37!) The *ku* is not merely allegorical. There is an eight-fold cherry (a late bloomer) named after Yôki-hi (see ch 55). (オマケ：＜楊貴妃桜＞「花も春のやうき日かけて桜哉」知之　崑山集 1651。いい語呂でしょうが、生憎なこと、不可翻訳。)

恪気する男恨みん遅櫻　川柳 家つと
rinki suru otoko uramin osozakura　senryû 1682
(jealous man/men begrudge-would late cherry/ies)

jealous men make their bloom bitter late cherries	begrudging men of whom they are jealous late-cherries	green-eyed men left her a burning heart the late cherry

This *senryû*esque *haikai* is *not* by the man whose name became associated with a genre of poetry, Karai Senryû (yet to be born). It is puzzling. The word-flow favors a jealous *man*, or men, over a jealous late-cherry; but, as OM puts it, "a man jealous of an older woman doesn't make sense." My first and third readings try to make sense of the intuitive first-choice based on the syntax. To explain further, I hypothesize that 1) a wife who kept her beauty or even improved in her thirties or forties, might have been threatening for, and thereby invite jealousy from men whose libido flagged yet could not afford a mistress, or, 2), a just-so story, namely, these blossoms/women bloom late because they dislike the jealousies attending young love. My middle-reading, far more cohesive than the original, reflects the intuitively correct interpretation based on common male/female stereotype (men, playing with girls ignore older women). For all the readings, include the unstated act of blooming and how it may associate with jealous grudges or jealousy begrudged. Sorry to make you, reader, work so hard! (I'll bet you wish I had an editor: so do I!) Let us leave this paragraph with an easy *ku,* for a change. "Blossoms slow / though you wait for them? / must be pouting" (待に遅き花はすね木の心かな 末昆狗子? *matsu ni osoki hana wa sune ki no kokoro kana* makkon). *Pouting is something beauties get away with.* That's *my* wit. That of the original lies in an untranslatable pun. Pouting is a homophone for a *twisted old tree*. The mood (*suneki*) is written すね気 while the tree is written すね木.

腐っても鯛遅ふてもさくらかな 嘯山 葎亭句集
kusatte mo tai osoute mo sakura kana　shôzan 1717-1801
(rotten-though snapper slow/late though cherry!/'tis)

though rotten
snapper is snapper, though late
cherry is cherry

A back-handed compliment if I ever heard one! It seems to me that the 18c was the turning point. After that, most Japanese picked up the snappy Edo mindset and ceased to admire late-cherries.

たんき・遅櫻禅のならひに切くへん 琴風 其袋
tanki // osozakura zen no narai ni kiri-kuben　kinpû 1690
(impatience // late/slow-cherry zen-teaching-as/for cut-feed[a fire]-let's)

following zen let's chop up and burn the late cherry	late cherry, shall i chop you up and chuck you into the fire *ala* zen?

The original is titled short-*chi*, or "Impatience." At first, I thought *kiri-kuben* was a mistranscription of *kiri-kuban,* meaning "cut & distribute" (if originally hand-written in *katakana,* the *be* and *ba* would be similar: 切クベン<v.s.> 切リクバン): "Late-cherries: / Chop them up hand them out / their Zen." Like the relics of a saint, they were an inspiration. After all, isn't *not pushing it* a central tenet of Zen practice? The notion of *storming Heaven* (to borrow the title of a great book on the psychedelic movement) is repulsive. But, as it turns out, *kiri-kuben* was just as common a compound-verb as *kiri-kuban,* and cherries were often burnt in both reality and poetry. So, I accepted it and retranslated. The new question would be whether the allusion is to apocryphal practices like dividing cats or, more subtly, to an obscure Zen phrase, *zen no sune-dori,* which, I believe, means the taking away of a sulky attitude toward meditation (Do you recall the *suneki* pun mentioned in the last paragraph?) Regardless, it is clear the *ku* that I first took as a *compliment* for late-cherries, now seems to be a threat: *If you don't bloom fast . . .* That is too bad. This paragraph was to have ended on a positive note! Most 16c *ku* had nice things to say about this plant: *"The wisdom / to bloom later, alone: / late cherries"* (独跡に咲ぬる知恵ぞ遅桜　長頭丸 嵐山集　1651　*hitori ato ni sakinuru chie zo osozakura* teitoku (1570-1653). The same has been said about the *plum* blooming early, ahead of the crowd by Mao Tse Tung, among others. Most *waka* also praised the late-cherry unless the poet was trying to make her.

見る人もなき山ざとのさくら花ほかのちりなむのちぞさかまし伊勢(880) 古今集六八にて
miru hito mo naki yamazato no sakurabana hoka no chirinamu nochi zo sakamashi ise/kokinshû (905)
(seeing-person-even not mountain-town/home's cherry-blossom, other's fall after, hey, bloom-better/want)

<table>
<tr><td>

sweet cherry tree
back in the hollars where none
comes a callin'

i'd have you bloom late,
after the rest have fallen!

</td><td>

cherry trees, high
in mountain reaches beyond
blossom-viewing eyes

wait until the rest have blown
then, bloom away, surprise!

</td></tr>
</table>

Ise (or the hero of *The Tales' of* ~) was a lady's man, but the "sweet" is my addition (a number of the *waka* found in the AD 880 tale were included in the *Kokinshû*). Be that as it may, I love to see *coaching of nature* in poems, even if it is allegory. The late-cherry itself is not mentioned but, obviously, such advice could serve as an *apologia* for them. Centuries later, the man I consider the *pater inter allis* of what came to be called "haiku," Sôgi, came up with a more practical justification for delay:

花に風よはるやまちし遅櫻　宗祇　老葉
hana ni kaze yowaru ya machishi osozakura sôgi (1420-1502)
(blossoms-to wind weaken[emphatic] awaits late-cherry)

they just wait
for the wind to weaken
late cherries

These are blossoms with brains. Why burst into bloom right when the Wind is aroused by the sight of the other blossoms? (We'll have a whole chapter for *that* Wind, later). Of course, it *is possible* that there is an allegory about waiting to commit adultery until years pass and jealousy weakens. Were these lines in *The Tales of Ise*, I would think that the case. But Sôgi, if I am not mistaken, is already in a nature-centric mindset. He is actually thinking about the plants and their blossoms. He also joked:

風も見よこの一本のおそ櫻　宗祇　大発句帳
kaze mo miyo kono ippon no osozakura sôgi (1420-1502)
(wind, too, look! this one-tree-of late-cherry)

red flag
(pink cape?)

<table>
<tr><td>

Hey, wind!
see this tree, here?
a late cherry

</td><td>

you, too, wind
look at this: one tree of
late cherry

</td></tr>
</table>

I *love* this. Imagine a day in late Spring. You are in the vicinity of a late cherry and feeling discomfort from heat for the first time in the year. Some breeze – or even the thought of breeze – would be welcome.[1] A poem like this is why I cannot agree with Blyth – and what I have read elsewhere in English or Japanese – that Sôgi's poems are all "high-toned and elegant," and that he "lacks the human warmth that Bashô had." Judging from his late cherry poems *alone*, Sôgi got down. He dared to mix proper grammar and vernacular in the style later known as *haikai*. His wit, which relies less on nominal wordplay than the Teimon school and is less particular, i.e. more universal, than the Danrin school, is often remarkably modern: "Hey, wind!" (*kaze mo miyo*) *could well have been written by Issa*. It is *absurd* that so few of Sôgi's *ku* are well-known today (*And, I mean by Japanese!*).

また風のにくみ残りや遅櫻　也有
mada kaze no nikumi nokori ya osozakura yayû (1701-83)
(still, wind's/s' hate/spite-remainder!/?/: late-cherry/ies)

<table>
<tr><td>our dislike
for the wind remains:
a slow cherry</td><td>so the wind
still has girls to tilt:
late-cherries</td></tr>
</table>

Yayu's turning of a cherry tree into both reason for and symbol of the blossom viewers' hatred for the beauty-stealing wind is witty, but not so endearing as Sôgi's light-hearted and more personal banter. Another *ku* puts Sôgi on the side of the tree: *"You and I, / let's avoid the wind=colds, / late-cherry"* (たかいへは風はよきけんおそ櫻　宗祇 *tagai e wa kaze wa yokiken osozakura*). Translation *as a poem* is impossible because, in English, "wind" and "cold" (the type we catch) are not the same.

遠里に嵐聞えて遅櫻　梅室 アルス
tôsato ni arashi kikoete osozakura　baishitsu 1768-1852
([?] far-countries[boondocks]-in storm/s heard: late-cherry/ies)

<table>
<tr><td>hear storms
out in the hills?
the late cherries bloom.</td><td>my holler home
i hear the wind howl
it's late cherry!</td></tr>
</table>

Where there is wind, there is bloom. The *ku* suggests the first reading, but allows the second, which is more likely. The riddle in the original is less obvious than in my translations, which bring out the conceptual backbone: *the late cherry tends to be way out there.* "Holler" is Appalachian dialect.

山深し鐘もとゝかず遅櫻　雨水 馬光集
yamafukashi kane mo todokazu osozakura　usui 1768
(mountain/s-deep bell/s-even reach/es-not: late-cherry)

deep in the hills
beyond reach of bells
late cherries

~~~~~~

1. Inviting Breeze. Sôgi played the wind-likes-blossom conceit in many ways. I guess the "Hey, wind!" *ku* is not just baiting the wind because of another Sôgi *ku* on "cooling down" 納涼, translated by Stephen D. Carter: *"Oh, for some blossoms – / to bid storm winds to visit / this summer garden!"* (花もかなあらしやとへんなつの庭 *hana mogana arashi ya towan natsu no niwa*) and some other *ku* we shall see in the *Wind* chapter. This *ku* is of a type I like which might be called *wistful thinking.* It is, however, written in a more classical style (So, Carter's translation is not affected, but properly conveys this) and lacks the fresh *haikai* quality of the "Hey, wind" *ku*.

Not that marking time sped the bloom, but . . . damn, that is a good *ku*. A less successful one: *"Doesn't the sound / of the nightingale reach you? / Late cherries"* (鶯の音はとゝかぬか遅櫻　鷹仙 類題 *uguisu no ne wa todokanuka osozakura* yôsen? 1774). This poet apparently thought the nightingale (bush-warbler), a bird whose singing was thought to speed bloom, kept close to town. Unfortunately, the *uguisu* rightfully belongs with the plum blossom.

不達者な（怠りし）人も待けり遅桜　由平
buttasha na (namarishi)hito mo machikeri osozakura　yûhei -1704
(un-well/hearty(vers.2 =lazy) people too wait [+emphatic] late cherry/ies)

    and they wait   and they wait
for decrepit folk, too   for lazy folk, too
     late cherries   late cherries

The weather is warm and the crowds less formidable. The only problem is that the major urban parks for blossom-viewing did not have many such late-cherries.

足弱の宿とるためか遅櫻　蕪村
ashiyowa no yado toru tame ka osozakura　buson 1715-83
(leg-weak[women and children]'s inn take sake late cherry)

   would they help   a good excuse
the leg-weak find an inn?   for weak-legs to travel?
    late cherries   late cherries

late cherries
for women who would
take a trip?

Not long ago, European men flexed their calf muscles rather than their biceps or pectorals. They would have understood. "Weak-legs" may seem an insulting term, but it covered both women and children. English lacks such a word. Perhaps women preferred to wait for the late cherries and avoid crowded inns and the dangers that represented for travelers with children. Moreover, drinking was not *de rigor*: *"Shinano Trail / no grief for teetotalers! / Late-cherries."* (信濃路や下戸はとがめじ遅桜 調栄　東る風 *shinanoji ya geko wa togameji osozakura* chôei). Indeed, *"The first day / check out a tea shop! / Late-cherries"* (一日は茶屋も見に行け遅櫻　談水　蘆分船 *ichinichi wa chaya mo mi ni ike osozakura* dansui (1694)) One *ku* even moralizes: *"Hey, someone / let's keep the drinking down! / Late-cherries"* (花見酒たれかおさへて遅櫻　遊流 *hanamizake tare ka osaete osozakura* yûryû).

花車牛のひけばや遅桜　徳元 崑山集
hanaguruma ushi no hikeba ya osozakura　tokugen 1651
(blossom[-viewing]/fancy cart/sedan ox/en-pulled-if! late-cherry/ies)

flower-carriages

pulled by oxen
we know where they go
the late cherries

Ox-carts, some of which put fancy European horse-drawn carriages to shame, were the stereotypical transport mode for noble women out blossom-viewing. Work-cart versions may also have been used by the common folk for groups of crippled and elderly people. *"Babushka, too, / drawn by oxen enjoy / blossom-viewing"* (婆ゝどのも牛に引かれて桜かな 一茶正5 *babadono mo ushi ni hikarete sakura kana* issa 1822). We know these are not early cherries.

花さかば牛に鞍をけ遅ざくら 正重 嵐山集
hana sakaba ushi ni kura oke osozakura seichô? (1651)
(blossom/tree bloom-if ox/en-to/on saddle put: late-cherry)

when they bloom
saddle up the oxen!
late cherries

Saddling up an ox? Usually, a horse is saddled for the samurai to rush off to catch the first cherry blossoms. This is a good example of what Bashô was later to call *karumi,* a light touch.

見ぬ人のためとて咲か遅櫻 秀魚 翁反故
minu hito no tame tote saku ka osozakura shûgyo 1783
(see-not [[?] see?] people's sake [as if to say] bloom? late-cherry)

do they bloom   are you finally
for people who missed out?   blooming for our sake?
late cherries   late cherries

Age and gender are not the only possibilities here. One can miss the prime-time blossom-viewing because of catching a cold. My respondent favors the first reading.

縁遠き美人也けり遅櫻 器水 春遊
endôki bijin narikeri osozakura kisui (1699)
(connections/luck-far-off beauty is [+emph]: late-ch)

a beauty with
no luck getting hitched
the late cherry

How nice to read a *ku* from the tree's perspective. At first, I misread the first word as "standoffish" and translated: *"A beauty who / keeps putting you off / the late cherry."* I'm sure there *is* such a *ku* out there for another complains: *"My heart / is an abalone, / late cherry!"* (我が心鮑の貝ぞ遅さくら 重貞 *waga kokoro awabi no kai zo osozakura* shigesada? (17c?)). The abalone, a one-sided shell, is the classic image of unrequited love.

花／\の木守り（まもり）なるかをそ櫻 徳元? 毛吹草
hanabana no ki[ko?]mamori naruka osozakura tokugen? (1645)
(blossoms' tree's[=chastity's] guardian/charm becomes/is? late cherry)

charming chastity

is she guardian
for trees of all blossoms?
the late cherry

The Japanese did not make a *fetish* of chastity in the manner of the Christian West. But chastity was respected as an indicator of something greatly valued in Japan, *self-control*, and appreciated for its connection with the heart of love in Japanese poetry, *longing*. Love (*koi*) was sometimes written with the Chinese characters meaning "alone" and "sad!" (孤悲); and, some *waka* speak of meeting in-order to "stop [the] love" (*koi-dome*). Viewed in this way, the late-cherry was an eros-building force.

さくら一木春に背けるけはい哉 蕪村
sakura hitoki haru ni somukeru kehai kana   buson 1715-83
(cherry one-tree spring-to turn-back/betray feeling-'tis/!/?)

one cherry tree
seems to turn her back
on the spring

only the cherry
seems to turn her back
on springtime

My first reaction upon reading the original was "a late bloomer, of course." Then, I thought Buson might mean the cherry, as a flowering tree, was late. But the annotators of Buson's *Zenshû* (collection of all *ku*) say it is indeed about a late-cherry unmoved by other cherries in full-blossom. Whatever the reading – the first is probably correct – one thing is certain, Buson's *ku* concerns the relationship of the cherry tree and the spring. The late-cherry provides the poet a good chance to examine just that.

遅櫻名をえてさける一木哉 宗砌
osozakura na o ete sakeru hitoki kana   sôzei -1455
(late cherry name gained blooms one-tree!/?/'tis)

one late-cherry
blooms *after* gaining
itself a name

"late cherry"
she gains that name
upon flowering

"late cherry"
earning the name one
tree blooms

There is a chance this is allegorical and refers to a woman who has a baby or gains a reputation as a poet in middle age. But, I prefer to think it is about a real tree. One cherry tree in a garden that was noticed for *not* blooming with the others, has finally let go.

遅く疾き花は見残す人もなし 宗祇 大発句帳
osoku toki hana wa minokosu hito mo nashi   sôgi 1420-1502
(late-early blossom/ing/tree-as-for see-leave-over person/people-even not)

cherry lovers

early or late
a blossom is never
passed over

men never
overlook blossoms,
early or late

蕪村文台 開の日・遅櫻人に待れて咲にけり 嘯山
osozakura hito ni matarete sakinikeri   shôzan 1717-1801
(late cherry people-by waited [on] bloom [+finality])

encore for buson

the late cherry
has people begging
for it to bloom

Sôgi's *ku* is probably allegorical, as is Shôzan's commemorating the "opening" of the desk of his friend, Buson. Did the event took longer to organize than expected or was a fine work by the late poet found within the desk? "Begging" is an over-translation, but how else to express the idea that the blossom is not saying "Look at me!" but responding after a strong demand has been generated?

残花を尋ねて・二木はかり千木にましつ遅櫻　宗春　三籟
zanka o tazunete // ni ki bakari sen ki ni mashitsu osozakura sôshun (1734)
(remaining-bloom seeking // two trees only thousand-trees-over excell/ing late-cherry)

seeking out left-over bloom

just two trees
they beat a thousand
late-cherries

一本にかたまる人やおそ櫻　也有
ippon ni katamaru hito ya osozakura yayû 1701-83
(one tree-to harden/clump people: late-cherry)

everybody
clumps around one tree
a late-cherry

木樵より外に人なし遅桜　多代女
kikori yori hoka ni hito nashi osozakura tayojo 1775-1865
(lumberjack-than other people not, late-cherry)

a lumberjack	no humans
the only man around:	but the lumberjack:
late cherries	a late-cherry

In city parks or mountain-sides visible from cities late cherries might be feted for their scarcity value, but up in the mountains, a cherry that bloomed late would be unlikely to have visitors. Wild cherries are usually alone. Tayojo also observed: *"In this thicket / where bamboo might sprout! / a late cherry"* (筍も出さうな藪や遅さくら　多代女 *takenoko mo desô na yabu ya osozakura*). One wonders whether Tayojo, who lived to be 90, was her own late-cherry.

遅桜見に来る人はなかりけり　子規
osozakura mi ni kuru hito wa nakarikeri   shiki (1896)
(late-cherry view-for come people-as-for not [+vague-emph.])

a late-cherry	a late-cherry
nobody comes	nobody comes
to view it	to see her

late cherries
not a soul comes
to view them

I thought Shiki lived somewhere people would notice the late-cherry, but apparently people who considered the blossom viewings over had their mind's eyes closed when the late-cherry bloomed.

春をおもふ花やはつをそさくら 宗祇 大発句帳
haru o omou hana ya hatsuhana osozakura sôgi (1420-1502)
(spring[+obj] think/feel[for] blossom!/: first-blossom, late-blossom)

blossoms that count

when we feel
for the spring: the first
and last cherries

blossoms that
make us think of spring
the first and last

when we first
miss spring: first bloom
of the late cherry

The last reading is different from the first two. There is a marvelous haiku term *hatsu-owarimono,* or "first of the last" for just this sort of thing. The "think/feel" here probably means feel a sweet regret for the spring's passing, a theme in *haikai* called *haru-oshimi,* "regret for the (passing of) the spring."

行春の跡にぎはしか遅ざくら 貞継 犬子
yuku haru no atonigiwashi ka osozakura   teikei 1633
(departing spring's after-bustling[party for those remaining behind]? late-ch)

spring departs:
our consolation party?
late cherries!

spring departs
we who stay stay drunk
on late cherries

You cannot stop Spring. Though you blindfold her, it is like cow pee (useless), as one awful *ku* (行はるの目にさへぎるやうしの尿 俳諧袋) put it, but those left behind can have a consolation party. Japanese have (or had, for *atonigiwashi* is obs.) – a term for a party held *after* a bride or traveler departed.

春は猶ありとやこゝに遅櫻 宗因 三籟
haru wa nao ari to ya koko ni osozakura   sôin 1604-82
(spring-as-for still is [saying+emphatic]! here-in late-cherry)

hey, spring's
still around! right here:
a late cherry

hold your horses!
spring is still here
a late cherry

as if to say
right here! spring's here!
a late cherry

花に/も春行くか帰るか遅櫻 行助 新新？増犬？つくは
hana ni/mo haru yuku ka kaeru ka osozakura   gyôjo? 1643
(flower-to/too/and spring leave? [or] return? late-cherry/ies)

this bloom: spring
is leaving? or returning?
late cherries

is the spring
off or back in bloom
a late cherry

late cherries
are you spring's blush
or her tush?

late

山姥の遊びのこして遅櫻　蕪村
yamanba no asobi nokoshite osozakura buson (1715-83)
(mountain-aunt/hag/witch's play/freedom leaving/remaining late-cherry)

    the mountain hag   the mountain hag
left them for her last dance   did her dance and left us
    these late cherries   these late cherries

late cherries
the mountain witch still
plays around

    the mountain hag   the old witches
has some play left in her   still have a place to go
     a late cherry   late-cherries

The mountain hag (today, usually pronounced *yama-uba* rather than *yamanba*) is a Sinosphere construct, a demon woman, or witch, who wanders about begging (with the usual rewards/curses doled out to those she meets: standard folklore stuff). Buson plays with a popular song that had her migrating from cherry to cherry but I suppose the *ku* may also be read to mean the late cherry is not only her handiwork but but her personification. She was old but could be sexy (like the *ubazakura*, ch 7). Buson also depicts the late-cherry as a a *kimi* (imperial wife, or concubine) with a sensual husky wind=cold [i.e., the illness] voice returning to her home country (風声の下り居の君や遅櫻 *kazagoe no ori i no kimi ya osozakura*). Again, the wind=cold homophone cannot be translated. To me, a cold voice suggests the sultry appearance of a rain-drenched late eight-fold cherry.

行春の逡巡として遅櫻　蕪村
yuku haru no shunjun to shite osozakura buson
(departing-spring's hesitantly being/acting, late-cherry)

(my trans)

      she hesitates   the spring
while leaving: the spring's   hesitates while leaving
     a late cherry   late cherry

(blyth trans)

departing spring
hesitates
in the late cherry blossoms

     (hass trans)   (behn trans)

  the end of spring   spring is almost gone
      lingers   so now this silly old tree
in the cherry blossoms   decides to bloom!

(combined)

departing
spring lingers
late cherry

Blyth chose "in" where I chose the equivalent of "as." The original specifies neither. Hass's version seems a beautified Blyth, with the "late" dropped (a typical modern approach, sacrificing information for a seamless product). Only Behn wanders so far from the original it is hard to tell if it is about this "hesitation" *ku* or the "mountain hag" we met above!

ゆく春もやとれ太山は遅櫻　紹巴 17c
yuku haru mo yadore daizan wa osozakura jôha
(departing spring too stay! thick-mt. as-for: late-chy/ies)

ゆく春のとゝまる所遅ざくら　召波 18c
yuku haru no todomaru tokoro osozakura shôha
(departing spring's stop/staying place: late-cherry/ies)

mount thick

leaving spring
you, too, stay! mt. thick's
late-cherries

saddle-horse

this rest stop
for the departing spring:
a late-cherry

Jôha's "thick" mountain is one massive enough to own its own weather. Shôha may recall the slippers left in the stirrup when someone rushed for the *first* bloom in Kikaku's older *ku* (#4-23), but he probably refers to a specific tree or trees at Saddle Horse Temple, abbreviated as simply Saddle Horse.

行春の宿のものとやおそ櫻　無名 壁草
yuku haru no yado no mono to ya osozakura anon. ()
(leaving-spring's inn's thing/person/belonging/s!/: late-cherry/ies

call her an inn
for the departing spring
a late cherry

they are inns
for the departing spring
late cherries

you'll find her
at the lodge of leaving spring
osozakura

Buson's *ku* is always almanacked with the "departing spring" rather than "late-cherry." Shôha's could go either way; but the last, anon. *ku* and the following one by Sôgi are clearly focused on the latter:

花も幾世春をくらさん遅櫻　宗祇
hana mo iku yo haru okurasan osozakura　sôgi 1420-1502
(blossom/s, too, how-many[countless]-ages/reigns spring delay-would/try late-cherry)

floral alchemy

late cherries, too
how many generations tried
to slow the spring

would blossoms, too
forever keep their spring,
my late cherries?

so flowers, too
have e'er tried to hold spring?
late cherries!

over generations

how much spring
have you flowers saved,
my late cherries?

The "too" alludes to our, human desire to stay youthful. The first reading is a beat too long in the middle, yet, even with a title, cannot quite translate the entire original. It misses the general blossoms, of which the late-cherry is the example. The second reading catches them, but turns the generations into a vague extension of spring. The third needs no comment. The last recalls Steffansson, who once added up the "years of happy belief in Santa" saved by importing reindeer to fool children.

春しはし抱て居たり遅櫻　一黛　堅並
haru shibashi idakite itari osozakura   ichiyo ()
(spring a-while embraces/sleeps[with] stays late-cherry)

i'd just keep
embracing spring a while
a late cherry

late cherries	the late cherry
they would embrace spring	would stay a spell longer
a while longer	in spring's bed.

not yet ready
to let go of her spring
the late cherry

Daku means "hug" and "embrace." Since people in Japan have never embraced each other as a greeting, it has far more erotic connotations than an English translation could. Hence, my "bed." I am not sure how to pronoun the poet. He, she, we, they, . . . The last translation sidesteps the problem.

底たゝく春の隅よりより遅櫻　几董
soko tataku haru no sumi yori osozakura   kitô -1789
(bottom-hit/rap spring's corner/nook-from late-spring)

spring has hit	the last presents
the bottom of her box	from spring's storehouse
the late cherry	late cherry bloom

In Japanese, an internal "corner" and external one are called different things. Specifying the former in English would have meant adding, say, "sweep out;" so, I replaced it with "box" and "storehouse."

山姫のわたくし物かをそざくら　盛澄　犬子
yamahime no watakushi mono ka osozakura   seichô 1633
(mountain-princess's personal thing/person/s? late-cherry/ies)

the personal effects
of a mountain princess?
these late cherries!

咲く藤に春なまかせそ遅櫻　肖柏
saku fuji ni haru na makase so osozakura   shôhaku 1442-1527
(blooming wisteria-to spring don't-entrust! late-cherry)

late cherry	ah, late cherries
don't hand-over the spring	don't let those wisteria
to wisteria!	take our spring!

The first *ku* is a sort of explanatory myth, or just-so story: it stands to reason Spring would be reluctant to give up her personal treasures, hence they remain until last. The wisteria in the next *ku* is summer's first flower. When it blooms the change of seasons is already a *fait accompli* but, the poet's archaic grammar shows where *his* heart lies. A matter-of-fact *ku* by a later poet: *"Sweet Cherry, / falling, she hands spring / to Wisteria"* (散て春を藤にゆつれる櫻哉　宗春 *chitte hiru o fuji ni yuzureru sakura kana* sôshun ().). Of course, it is the blossoms that fall/scatter and the "sweet" is all mine.

三春の役や忘るゝ遅ざくら　重頼 犬子
sanshun no yaku ya wasururu osozakura　shigeyori 1601-1680
(third-spring's role!/? forgotten: late-cherry)

spring's last act
someone forgets her role
a slow cherry

Oops! The late-cherry blows Spring's play. Tardiness in Japanese, too, connotes stupidity.

いや／\ん芝居やふりの遅桜　末祐 犬子
iya iyan shibaiyaburi no osozakura　matsuyû (1633)
(no, no-ooh! play [drama] breaking [ending] late-cherry)

boo-hoo, spring's over!

our play-house
is finally emptied by
the late cherry

auld lang syne **that ends well**

oh no, noooo!　　　　　　　　　　　the curtain closer
blossom-viewing's over:　　　　　we applaud with wet eyes:
the late cherry　　　　　　　　　　　the late cherry

Shibai-yaburi, literally "play-buster," was either an act put on to get the customers to *leave* the playhouse or the last act, usually the best, which may be called that because after it finishes people leave. In Japan it was important for Japanese plays could go on all day – different play acts leapfrogging one another – some in the audience may have dozed off. A grand finale was needed. The ambiguous *iya iyan* is a translator's nightmare.　A shout of approbation used the noisy Japanese play-goer, *Iya iya* is literally "No! No!" and also happens to be both a coy put-off and something yelped by women approaching orgasm. The "n" gives a plaintive tail to the begrudging *hurrahs* and suggests a largely female audience, as was the case for late cherry-viewing! Neither *Bravo's!* nor even *The last hurrah: / The late cherry brings / down the curtain!"* will do, for they are too buoyant.　"My first translation was a fine mistranslation: "Late cherry / no more of that *"No!" / "No-ooh!"* act!"

ゆくはるのしころは切れて遅ざくら　大江丸 俳懺悔
yuku haru no shikoro wa kirete osozakura　ôemaru (1790)
(leaving/ending spring's neck-plates[armor] is cut: late cherry)

spring's neck-plate　　　　　　　　spring's neck-plate
pops open as she departs　　　　is finally sliced open
late cherry bloom　　　　　　　　　the late cherries

Since most of Spring's buds burst long before the late-cherry bloomed, I could not bring in a "maidenhead," though I was tempted because the head was cut off after the neck-plate was cracked open or removed. This *ku* plays with the *korae-bukuro ku* #12-22. This would be a good juncture, or rather, disjuncture to decisively end the chapter; but I am afraid I have left out a small but significant sub-theme: poems relating the late-cherry to *words*:

思案せし詞の花や遅櫻　永治 毛吹草
shian seshi kotoba no hana ya osozakura eiji (1645)
(thought-pondering word/language's blossom/flower: late cherry)

time to think, for words to blossom a late cherry	call it the *flor* of words well pondered: *osozakura*

The first reading could refer to a late-blooming poet or the opinion that the late cherry evokes good *ku*. Though it turns the poem into an aphorism, the second reading seems likely, for it may be read with this cruel *senryû*esque haiku: *"The late cherry: / it's the blossom of . . . / stuttering"* (どもり言こと葉の花や遅桜　政辰　ゆめみ草？ *domori iu kotoba no hana ya osozakura* seishin 1656?).

遅桜静かに詠められにけり　子規
osozakura shizuka ni yomerarenikeri shiki 1893
(late-cherry/ies quietly/serenely read/written-are [+finality])

late cherries they can be haiku'ed with composure	how serenely we can compose late cherries

English use "read" to mean "study" or "attend a university." Japanese speak of "reading" rather "writing" poetry. And, I am afraid I have *more* late-cherry *ku*. They just keep blooming on and on:

比巴園 ぼつ／＼と咲しつまりぬ遅櫻　暁台
botsubotsu to sakishizumarinu osozakura gyôtai -1792
(biwa park // bit-by-bit [or, leisurely/cheerfully?]

the late cherries gradually bloom and things settle down	the late cherries taking their good time, bloom and settle down

<biwa park>

one after another blooming settles down: late cherries	one by one they bloom and settle late cherries

At first, I thought the *botsubotsu* was in error and the late-cherries should bloom *hotsuhotsu,* a mood mimesis of cheerful, leisurely behavior; but, on longer consideration, the quieting down that follows and the caption suggesting that the *ku,* featuring late-cherries, *also* depicts a park told me that we have the lively but anxious days of spring turning into the quietude of the thickly verdant summer. While sad to lose my *hotsuhotsu* image of the late-cherries – I kept it partially alive in the rather allegorical second reading – the depiction of the park makes for a better *ku* as it wraps up a larger timescape.

京へ来て息もつきあへず遅櫻　太祇 再現
kyô e kite iki mo tsukiaezu osozakura　taigi (-1772)
(kyoto/capital-to come, breath-even match [keep pace]-not late-cherry/ies)

here in kyôto
i find i'm out of synch
late-cherries

coming to kyôto
i find we're out of synch
late cherries

It so happens that in Kyôto, the old – compared to Edo, not the even older Nara – capital, people talk in a sweet singsong drawl and move in slow motion compared to the explosive Edoites. The cherries here are not so much allegorical as parallel to, or representative of the culture. It is enough to see a picture of Taigi (an energetic bulldog of a man) to realize how out of place he would have been.

京中の未見ぬ寺や遅櫻　太祇
kyôjû no imada minu tera ya osozakura　taigi (-1772)
(kyoto/capital-inside/everywhere still see/n-not temples!/: late-cherries)

all the temples
in kyôto i've yet to see!
late-cherries

I think this means that the poet, visiting Kyôto, let cherry blossoms dictate his schedule. He first saw the temples with earlier bloom, and waited to visit those with the late-cherries when their time came. These temples and all their treasures – which would have been opened to public view only at the time the blossoms drew crowds – are also, for him, late blossoms he can enjoy visiting in the warm days of late spring and early summer.

山深し木の芽の匂ひ遅櫻　史明 恒誠
yamabukashi konome no nioi osozakura　shimei ()
(mountain-deep/depths tree bud's smell/scent late-cherry)

high in the hills
the scent of budding trees
late cherry time

The "buds" here are for leaves, not blossoms. While early cherries hardly bloom in a scent vacuum – there is the bare earth, early grass and other herbs – the late cherries bloom in woods thick with sap. Since the blossoms have little scent, this becomes their smell, too.

遅桜蟻の飯引く深山かな　信徳
osozakura ari no han hiku fukuyama kana　shintoku -1698
(late-cherry/ies ant/s-food pull deep-mountain/s!/:/?)

late cherries
high in the hills where
ants drag food

I have been surprised to see how quickly gondola-like daddy-longlegs walked down tree trunks to carry off potato chips on one Japanese mountain, but this ant thing puzzles me, for for I thought ants did this everywhere. Does it mean that there is more wild-life, including ants, up in the mountains where there are many late cherries and people eat outside, or that the ants are noticed because of the poetic frame of mind that makes such observation likely?

此頃の森のくろみや遅櫻　吟江
konogoro no mori no kuromi ya osozakura ginkô 1780
(this (approximate) time's forest's darkness! late-cherry)

about this time
the forest grows dark
late cherries!

As the sun arches higher, trees retake the sky and cover the earth. Does the late-cherry wait for the theater to darken so her bloom will show better? The *ku* itself has no such anthropomorphizing. A *ku* less susceptible to dramatization: *"Way back / in the cedar grove: is that / late cherry?"* (杉むらの奥に見るや遅櫻　斗醉　花七日 *sugimura no oku ni mieru ya osozakura* tosui (1777). Cedar branches start relatively high up the tree, so the cherry bloom illuminates the inner recesses of the hallowed forest.[1]

長き日の背中に暑し遅櫻　几董
nagaki hi no senaka ni atsushi osozakura kitô -1789
(long day's/sun's back-on hot, late cherry)

a long day
the sun hot on my back
late cherries

Here, the trees are not in the woods. The brevity of the original suffers in translation because day and sun won't fuse in a single English word. A long day and a late cherry associate well. I imagine eight-fold petals (double or quadruple blossoms) making the tree itself look overdressed for the heat.

池の端に書画の会あり遅桜　子規
ikenoha?ni shoga no kai ari osozakura shiki 1899
(pond's edge-at write-picture's meeting is: late-cherry)

a painting club
meets by pond-side
late cherries

This is balmy as a Victorian picnic. The word used for painting in the *ku* (*shôga*) includes the probability of writing, but Shiki did not use the *haikai* term for such a miss, *haiga*. A group of people setting up easels together is Western. Shiki wanted to keep a modern-sounding term in that poem. I did it differently, with the word "club." The water cools the scene, which blends well with Kitô's hot-on-the-back *ku*.

---

1. Hallowed Forest. I write "hallowed" not to turn the woods into a temple a la John Muir, but because most large Shinto shrines and Buddhist temples in Japan are located on mountains, surrounded by *sugi* (cryptomeria, enormous cedar) and *maki* (black pine). These mountains are generally considered sacred space. Occasionally, this is noticed abroad, when a ruckus is raised about one of the small number of such mountains which is off-limits to women. I wonder if "our" (?) Gilgamesh's decimation of the foreign forest was not really an act of cultural genocide against such a tree-respecting (or, fearing) culture, a precedent for later forest-destroying excesses by Christians in North Europe after they helped deforest North Africa!

心ある庭や初花遅櫻　宗因 三籟
kokoro aru niwa ya hatsuhana osozakura sôin 1604-82
(heart is/has garden! first-blossom late-cherry)

    this garden　　　　　　　　　　　　　when do gardens
has a heart: the first　　　　　　　　move us? at first bloom, and
    late cherry　　　　　　　　　　　　　with late cherries

By "first late cherry," I mean the first *bloom* of the same. There are gardens in Japan with "heart = 心" -shaped wet or dry (gravel) ponds, but, here, the heart is both the blooming late cherry's and our's. At first I thought it may show an appreciation for the kind heart of late-bloomers, who gain appreciation for the suffering of others by enduring years of deprivation themselves, but it makes more sense yet as praise for the owner of the garden who kept a late-blooming cherry rather than replacing it with a more faddish early bloomer. The second translation puts the heart-felt interest of the visitor on both ends of the cherry blossom season. The second reading is "a bit of a stretch." (MO)

春よきてちる櫻あれは遅櫻　宗祇 老葉
haru yogite chiru sakura areba osozakura sôgi 1420-1502
(spring crossing falls cherry is-if late-cherry)

defining osozakura

if there's a cherry
that falls not in the spring
it's a late cherry

   she's the cherry　　　　　　　　　　　this one won't fall
who avoids falling in spring　　　　the late cherry wants spring
   the *osozakura*　　　　　　　　　　　　to be all bloom

It is hard to tell exactly what Sôgi intends to say. Chances are that it is a defining *ku;* but I like to imagine he meant what I clarify in the third reading, or to be even blunter:

no time to fall!

there's a blossom
who'd keep spring for blooming
the late cherry

Other late-cherry *ku* by Sôgi, most of which we have seen, make me think he is expressing something positive. I am not so sure about Ginkô, below:

行春やいまだ櫻もちりあへず　吟江 古き姿
yuku haru ya imada sakura mo chiri-aezu ginkô 1775
(leaving-spring: still cherry-even fall-meets-not)

spring leaves us
and the damn cherry still
hasn't blown

Please forgive me for a translation that, stylistically speaking, bears little resemblance to the original.

I couldn't help myself. I was also thinking about an untranslatable *ku* with a corny pun about a late cherry that misses its proper season. *You are a so-called "spring-blossom," but bloom not in it. Hence, you are no* o*so-zakura (slow/late cherry) but an* u*so-zakura (lying cherry)!* (春の花といって咲かぬやうそざくら 正式 再現*haru no hana to iite sakanu ya uso-zakura* seishiki () lost source). Perhaps that poet needed to be shown this *ku*:

遅櫻つく／＼見れば遅うなし 樗堂 アルス
osozakura tsukuzuku mireba osou nashi chodô -1814
(late-cherry/ies intently[mimesis] see-if/when, late-not)

late cherries
if you look closely
none are late

This is so simple I first thought *nashi* might mean "become" and the bloom delayed from bashfulness, but my respondent assures me that the above is correct. Cherry blooms when she and we are ready.

はるも見ぬひかりや谷のをそさくら 無記名 発句帳
haru mo minu hikari ya tani no osozakura anon. 1624~44
(spring-even see-not light/shine! / valley's late-cherry)

in the valley   light not seen
brighter than spring bloom   even in spring, this slow
a slow cherry   valley cherry

This was in a theme called 余花, or "left-over blossoms," within the *Summer* in the *Hokkuchô* (発句帳) With increased foliage, the summer woods are darker and the light of the white blossoms of the isolated late cherry stand out. Here is one last by the late-cherry lover, Sôgi:

まつ人に一春まけよ遅櫻 宗祇
matsu hito ni isshun [hitoharu?] makeyo osozakura sôgi 1421-1502
(wait/ing/ed people-to one-spring lose[knock-down, give for free]! late-cherry)

so how about
an extra spring for all who
wait, late cherry?

With the luni-solar calendar, it was not uncommon for the Spring to have an extra month and chances are that was the case in the year Sôgi's *ku* was made. As one later *ku* titled *Intercalary* put it: *"Late cherries / blooming in the third month / without dolls"* (閏月・雛の来ぬ閏にさくや遅櫻 如元 韻塞 *jungetsu// hina no konu urô ni saku ya osozakura* nyogen 1697). Doll Day was on the third day of the *first* third month. Since Spring was also equivalent to "year" – in a sense similar to the Winters or Summers typically used by Amerindians (if the English translations do not reflect an English bias) – Sôgi's *ku* pretends the late cherry is presenting us with an extra year of life. Late bloomers can use it, too.

~~~~~~

☆日本語だけの   ◎   オマケ 二句☆

すこすこと山やくれけん遅櫻 一郎友
閑古鳥なくや終日遅櫻 道彦

13

Cherry Bells
花の鐘
hana-no-kane

☆☆☆☆☆☆☆☆
いさましく晴て夜明の花に鐘　仙里
☆☆☆☆☆☆☆☆☆☆☆☆☆☆☆☆

朝飯を過すや花の鐘がなる　成美
asahan o sugosu ya hana no kane ga naru　seibi
(morning meal[+obj] pass:/! blossom's/s' bell-the rings)

after we finish
with breakfast, the peal of
the blossom bell

The "blossom bell" is the usual matins that sound at the moment the sun rises, or would, if not for the clouds or a tall mountain. I won't just say that in cherry time, the bell would sound different. I would instead guess that this bell would usually wake Seibi, for poets, especially wealthy men (he was) were generally night-owls. Anticipating blossom-viewing, Seibi woke up and ate earlier than usual.

鐘かけてしかも盛りのさくら哉　其角
kane kakete shikamo sakari no sakura kana　kikaku -1707
(bell/s hung/hanging[?] moreover full-bloom/frenzy's cherry!/'tis)

上野清水堂にて
at ueno's shimizu pavilion

the bell hung	the huge bell
and the cherries, too	and cherries to boot
in full bloom!	in full bloom

Kikaku's most famous bell *ku* is: *"Edo spring, / not a day a bell / is not sold"* (鐘ひとつ売れぬ日はなし江戸の春 *kane hitotsu urenu hi wa nashi edo no haru*). In that *ku*, spring means the New Year season, the time to note the portentous and celebrate prosperity. With one huge bell per temple, it suggests a new temple built every day. *Think of the peeling of those bells as the urban equivalent to the squealing of mice multiplied by a bountiful harvest.* It also reflects the fact that Edo, unlike the other cities, allowed more than one temple to use large bells (see *Topsy-turvy 1585*). Japanese *kane* were shaped somewhat like ours but, lacking clappers, were pounded from without. I first forced an unlikely reading of *kakete* to come up with *Booming bells / as if cherries in full bloom / need priming!* But, hung from the roof of a platform only ten feet or so above the ground, as will be explained later, the bell would be visible against the blossoms, unlike the case with those high up in belfries. Is that *enough*? Be that as it may, some poets did address the noise:

そも我は鐘に用なき櫻哉　秋色
somo ware wa kane ni yônaki sakura kana shûshoku (-1725)
(in the end, i-as-for, bell/s-for use-not cherry/ies!/'tis)

      yes, for me　　　　　　　　　　　　　　if you ask me
   bells are of no use　　　　　　　　　　　bells have no place here
     in cherry-time　　　　　　　　　　　　　with the blossoms
                 no, not for us!
           we cherries have no need
             for temple bells

The bold tone of the *ku* is superb. But, does the poet mean regular time-keeping is not needed in magical cherry-time? Or, does she find sensation enough without the addition of bells, or desire silence? Shûshoku may be glossing Kikaku's *ku,* for she was his student (and became the head of his school upon his death). Or, is there a moral angle? The bells sound from temples and, as we will see, bells in Buddhism (as with Catholicism) could carry catechism. Cherry blossoms, ready to pass away as soon as they bloom hardly needed it, and people partying in the evernow of the bloomshade needed it even less. And, finally, could she have intended a *woman=blossom identity* posited in my last reading?

曙の鐘に咲たか此櫻　申桃　千鳥かけ
akebono no kane ni saita ka kono sakura shintô? (1712)
(daybreak's bell-to/by/at/with bloomed? this cherry)

     did you bloom　　　　　　　　　　　　hoh, look at you,
 with the bell at daybreak　　　　　　　　cherry, did you bloom
    my cherry tree?　　　　　　　　　　　for the matins?

I am charmed. This obscure *ku* may be something rare, a conceptual one-of-a-kind. One can imagine a lotus opening to some sacred music, but cherry blossoms to the matins? The *kono sakura,* or, "this cherry" suggests that the poet checked out a grove of cherries the day before and saw none in bloom and just now discovered one in bloom. That makes this a fine *hatsuzakura,* or first-cherry *ku*, though the lack of said word would keep it from the proper place in most *saijiki*.

花の間やほのかに響く鈴の音　錦水　花供養
hana no ma ya honoka ni hibiku suzu no oto kinsui 1795
(blossoms among softly echo/oes bell/bells/chimes sound)

  among the blossoms　　　　　　　　　within the blossoms
   a delicate echo　　　　　　　　　　　　the soft ringing
     of chimes　　　　　　　　　　　　　　　of a bell

In Japanese, a small bell is called a *suzu,* while larger bells or gongs were called *kane.* The *fûrin,* small glass bells used to translate delicate breezes into cool tinkles – psychological air-conditioning for the summer – are *suzu,* as are the jingly trinkets carried by begging priests, or, if you prefer, *cats* (Issa, who had a *ku* in the same book, was later to *haiku* a cat bell among peonies) at the blossom-viewing. Regardless, the above *ku* does not really belong in this chapter among the real bells. Then again, it may not belong in this *book,* for the blossoms *may* adorn the Blossom-pavilion where Buddha's Birthday was celebrated/memorialized on 4/8 of the luni-solar calendar (mid-late-June). The name of the anthology the *ku* was in, *Blossom Memorial Service,* suggests that; but most *ku* in it were *definitely* about cherry blossoms, so I think the name is parody and the above *ku* could be about them.

花の雲鐘は上野か浅草か　芭蕉
hana no kumo kane wa ueno ka asakusa ka　bashô
(blossom-cloud/s bell/s-as-for ueno? asakusa?)

    bloomclouds
is that bell from ueno
    or asakusa?

The only other bell *ku* as famous as this one (we will return to in the *Cloud* chapter) is Shiki's about hearing a certain bell peal as he bit into a persimmon. Bashô wrote it from the vantage place of his "grass-hut," gazing upon distant clouds (groves) of cherry blossom. Perhaps, bells from more than one temple could be heard. Blyth translates *"A cloud of cherry-blossoms; / The temple bell, – / Is it Ueno, is it Asakusa?"* He is kind to add the "temple" and probably made the "cloud" singular to avoid another silibant ending, but it may mislead some readers to imagine petals floating in the air.

花の浪ちらす鯨やかねのこゑ　清之　嵐山集
hana no nami chirasu kujira ya kane no koe　seishi (1651)
(blossom-wave scatter/drop/blow whale/s!/?/: bell's/s' voice)

a whale scatters	is it a whale
cherry-petaled waves:	scattering blossom waves?
the bell peals!	the bell's peal

At first, I imagined a wounded whale thrashing about in a sea stained with its blood! But, then, I realized the whale extends the metaphor of "waves of blossoms" to a situation where blossoms fall as a bell peals. Is our metaphorical whale spanking the water surface with his fin or tail – or spouting?

吹降や花にあびせるかねの声　一茶
fukiburi ya hana ni abiseru kane no koe　issa -1827
(blow-fall/shower blossom-on pour/wash/drench bell's voice)

windblown rain	a driving rain!	windblown rain?
with the voice of the bell	the bell's toll drenches	how else to describe the bell
spray the bloom	the blossoms	hitting the bloom

How much do blossoms ripe for falling react to powerful waves of sound? I have clapped and knocked off petals at a distance I thought beyond any breeze made by my hands. Has anyone carefully investigated the effect of noise on blossoms? Could the raucous cherry bashes speed the fall of the blossoms? (真面目の質問ぞ— I know of experiments with music on *growing* plants going back to Charles Darwin, but this is different.). While I am drawn to my third reading, the others are sounder takes.

大寺も桜の中や鐘の声　文士　花供養
ôdera mo sakura no naka ya kane no koe　bunshi (p1795)
(big-temple-too/even, cherries-within:/! bell's-voice)

even large temples
hide within the blossoms!
the sound of bells

Issa's last poem was from the perspective of one sitting in the bloomshade or standing close to cherry trees. This *ku* is more like that of Bashô in his famous: *Is it Asakusa or Ueno?* The view is distant. The temple/s is/are buried in the enormous clouds of cherry blossom. Since Japanese bells were not in steeples but only achieved their height from the location of temples high up slopes, the bells, too, would be buried under blossoms and invisible to the outside eye. This *ku* and the one with the begging priest's bells may associate (which first, I know not). One can almost imagine the "voice" of the *kane* as alarm bells, with even the mightiest temples sinking under the waves of pink.

花咲くや廿の比の鐘もなる 一茶 化三
hana saku ya hatachi no koro no kane mo naru issa
(blossoms bloom: twenty age/about's bell too peals/booms)

後戻りして鐘きくや花の中 梅室
atomodorishite kane kiku ya hana no naka baishitsu
(behind-return-doing : bell listen!/ – blossoms-within/among)

how they bloom!
and it's the same bell
i heard at twenty

i turned and went
back to hear the bell
inside the bloom

Today, twenty means coming of age in Japan. It *meant* the flower of one's youth. Does Issa (a white-haired 44) mean that not only is the same tree still blooming as before but the bell, too, seems not to have aged? Or, does he more simply mean only that hearing the bell brought back memories? This is a concrete example of time travel within the bloom. His contemporary, Baishitsu, would seem to be a connoisseur of bells. Call it too precious if you wish, but I like what he did.

鐘消えて花の香は撞夕哉 芭蕉
kane kiete hana no ka wa tsuku yuube kana bashô (1644-94)
(bell fade/vanishing/ed blossoms' scent-as-for, strike [=arrive] evening!/"tis/?)

as the sound dies
the scent of the bloom strikes:
the evening bell

the evening bell
fades away leaving only
the bloom scent

the peal fades
and the scent strikes us:
it is the dusk!

The idea of putting the sound in the first line and the bell at the end comes from Hass's translation. It is good to keep the evening for last, though I did not do it in the creative second reading. I might add that Bashô's expression "striking the scent" is a bold pun. My last reading brings out the dusk that, after all, takes an emphatic *kana.* . Because cherry blossoms have little scent, I thought the *ku* might concern all spring flowers, but annotators feel it is a retake on the *Shinkokinshû* (1205) *waka:* "Hiking up / to see spring dusk / in the hills / there were the blossoms / falling with the vespers" (*yamazato no haru no yugure kitemireba iriai no kane ni hana zo chirikeru* 山里の春の夕暮来てみれば入相の鐘に花ぞ散りける 能因法師 新古今#116). Bashô has a late-spring *ku* wondering how villagers can bear to *live* out of the range of bells (*kane tsukanu . . .*), but the practice of situating temples on wooded hills or mountains meant that wild cherries and bells were not mutually exclusive.

ついこけて寝るとの鐘や花の陰 沾徳
tsui kokete neru to no kane ya hananokage sentoku -1726
(finally collapsing-sleep-and[+possessive] bell:/!/? blossom-shade)

the passing-out
and-falling-asleep bell?
the bloomshade

that's the bell
for finally passing-out
in the bloomshade

that bell is
the passing-out bell
bloomshade

This is an odd *ku*. Does Sentoku mean the matins for men who drank all night or the vespers for those who drank all day? Does the bell say it's time to stagger home to bed, time to pass-out, what's heard as you pass-out/fall asleep, or, less likely, the first thing you hear when you come to?

やあしばらく花に対して鐘撞く事　重頼 佐夜中山集
yaa shibaraku hana ni taishite kane tsuku koto　shigeyori 1601-80
(hey, awhile blossom-with/at/to-respecting, bell strike thing)

Hey there, wait a moment,
Before you strike the temple bell
At the cherry blossoms

trans. Donald Keene

mitsui temple scene

hold it, lady!
strike not that bell for
the blossoms!

This moderately well-known *ku* is too vague in the original to be fully appreciated without additional information. It alludes to a crazy woman (a standard character in drama) who is restrained by a monk from striking a bell over and over, as per an older song (謡曲), "Mitsui Temple," which even includes the *yaa*, or, rather, *"yaa, yaa!"* This borrowing does not make the *ku* less creative if you think of it as an expression of the poet's enthusiasm for cherry-time. Where Keene adds the "temple," as Blyth often did, I *thought of* changing "the" to *our*. Englishing the attitude is a serious problem here. Had Keene not beat me to the punch, I would have done an "at" translation as well as a "for" one. If the woman expresses her simple enthusiasm, "at" seems overly aggressive, as if she wants to make the petals jump off the trees! Or, is the woman, full of dumb sympathy, pounding out what we might call a dirge *for* the falling blossoms, perhaps reflecting a memory she cannot put to rest (which made her insane)? Either way, we cannot have someone troubling other blossom-viewers and the repose of the monks. A later unknown *ku*: *"Blossom-crazed / how long the dusking voice / of that bell"* (花にうかれ暮行鐘の声長し 奇哉 花供養 *hana ni ukare kureyuku kane no koe nagashi* kiya 1795). I cannot tell if the person striking the bell or the person listening to it creates the effect.

入相の黒みを染ぬさくら哉　言水
iriai no kuromi o somenu sakura kana　gonsui 1646-1719
(vespers' darkness[obj] dye/s cherry/ies!/'tis)

cherry blossoms
dyed by the darkness
of the vespers

cherry blossoms
dye the belfry's boom
with darkness

花の夕鐘の黒さよ大きさよ　子規
hana no yube kane no kurosa yo ôkisa yo　shiki -1902
(blossoms' evening, bell's/bells' darkness! largeness!)

the dusk bell
of the blossoms: how dark!
how grand!

Gonsui's dyeing *ku* is ambiguous. It is easiest to imagine a wave of darkness washing over the blossoms, washing over our heads, with each peal of the bell as per the first reading, but do not the bright white blossoms also bring out the dark? Shiki's *ku* is simple. The "grand" in the original means large, i.e. loud. If I am not mistaken, the *hanami* crowd would quiet down a bit at dusk and that, together with the nervous energy of the poet, would amplify the sound of the bell. *Magnificent*.

晩鐘を空におさゆる櫻かな　千代
iriai o sora ni osayuru sakura kana   chiyoni (1701-75)
(vespers[+obj] sky-in, represses/held-back cherry/ies!/'tis)

evening temple bell
stopped in the sky
by cherry blossoms

trans. donegan & ishibashi

the vesper toll
kept off the ground
by the blossoms

cherry bloom
holding the dark vesper
bell at bay!

Unlike Bashô's Ueno or Akasaka *ku*, the perspective is from below. The verb *osayuru*, "pushed [back]/kept" suggests a thick ceiling of bloom prevent the peals from settling to the earth. Or, assuming Chiyo knew Gonsui's *ku*, could the brilliant color seen just before and during sunset momentarily hold-off that dark? An earlier *ku* notes: *"They turn vespers / into a thing of broad day: / cherry blossoms"* （入相を昼にして居るさくら哉　三光　燈花三吟 *iriai o hiru ni shite-iru sakura kana* sankô? (1736)). Could the gong shock your pupils open so it looks lighter, too? Donegan and Ishibashi provide a deep reading: "from a Buddhist perspective, this haiku depicts a moment of nonduality when the mind is stopped." Perhaps, but it is also possible that the deep meaning of the *ku* might be completely different. The vesper included vulgar (?) Buddhist undertones, with each peal warding off this or that sin (as with some Catholic vespers!). As such, could the blossoms be obstructing the transit of the catechism? Or, are both speculations off target? For people in love, there are moments that last forever and so with the cherry blossom experience. Chiyo loved the blossoms. Could the peal of the bell freeze time for Chiyo, in the throes of a cherry-blossom high? Regardless, I love D & I's bold translation that conveys the magic of the frozen moment better than mine.

かねの声ハ花のほかなるゆふへ哉 宗養 発句帳
kane no koe wa hana no hokanaru yûbe kana sôyô -1563
(bell's/s' voice-as-for blsms' other/outside sounds/is dusk!)

入相の鐘きゝつけぬ花も哉 正友 綾錦
iriai no kane kikitsukenu hana mo gana seiyû -1676
(vespers' bell hear-reach-not blossoms wish-for)

the bell's voice
is outside of the bloom
this evening

oh, for blossoms
that would keep away
the vesper's toll

Could Chiyo's *ku* be a kinetic version of the first *ku* above? To the second, she replies: there *are*.

花を踏んでたたらうらめし暮の声 幽山
hana o funde tatara urameshi kure no koe yûzan -1706
(blossoms/petals[obj] treading bellows hateful dusk voice)

入相をにくみはじめや初ざくら 田女海山
iriai o nikumihajime ya hatsuzakura tajo? 1789
(vespers[obj.] hating-start!/?/'tis/: first-cherry[bloom])

treading petals
i begrudge the bellows
nightfall voice

it's the start
of hating the vespers
first-blossoms

The first *ku* is a riddle. The bellows were used when casting the giant bell that metaphorically speaking joins the poet in treading on the blossoms → petals. Unless the poet was a blacksmith, the seeming poetry is hurt by the unlikelihood of the association. The second *ku*, by a female poet without note, simply contradicts a stereotype. If people had mixed feelings about the *matins*, the vespers signaling the end of the workday, were generally welcome. But, this was not true for blossom-viewing. Wealthy men could proceed to "night cherries" (the pleasure quarters), but to poor men and women, the vespers meant one thing: *fun over.* The vesper's Buddhist associations with exorcizing desire gives the *ku* a touch of irony. It could be a *senryû*. Indeed, there *is* one:

花も人も散れとはにくし暮の鐘　柳多留 117-31
hana mo hito mo chire to wa nikushi kure no kane　yanagidaru (19c?)
(blossoms and people too, scatter![imper.]-as-for hateful, evening-bell)

<table>
<tr><td>how spiteful
the vesper scattering
blossoms and men</td><td>beat it, blossoms!
beat it, people! – we hate
the evening bells</td></tr>
</table>

In thousands of old poems (*ku* or *waka*), the *rooster* is hated for ruining the fun of lovers (the matin rarely figures, for lovers must depart *in the dark,* and it is already light by sunrise). With blossom viewing, especially in a location where overnight stays were not permitted, the vesper became the rooster in reverse. As to the *relationship* of the bells and the falling blossoms, please wait for the chapters on *Death Below the Bloom* and *Buddhist Blossoms*.

花の陰鐘もひびかぬ天気哉　沙明　花供養 1795
hana no kage kane mo hibikanu tenki kana shamyô 1795
(blossom-shade bell/s even echo/vibrate-not, [good]weather!/?/'tis)

<table>
<tr><td>the bloomshade
even bells can't be heard
in this weather</td><td>what a fine day
the belfry has no boom
under the blossoms</td></tr>
</table>

Weather by itself in Japanese means *good* weather. At first I thought this *ku* a rehash of Chiyo's *ku*. I translated: *"The bloomshade / clear skies yet the bells / are silent."* And, I explained: *In clear weather, the bells ordinarily heard far away would be dampened by the blossoms. In an area full of cherry trees, naked branches would resound much louder than branches of bloom would. Full bloom would not only block direct sound from the sky but that reflecting below* (I am very aware of natural acoustics for I constantly whistle or sing as I walk). But, on second thought, the fact the original is not "*yet* bells," but "*even* bells" means something. Are not the crowds huge because the weather is fine, and *this* maximizes the noise they make playing shamisens and singing and shouting and carousing and shouting to their friends and whatnot? The last line may be clarified, i.e.: *"What fine weather!"* I borrowed the belfry and boom from Harold Stewart's translation of what might be the same *ku*, though the different name of the poet, Fuhaku (-1803) and lack of a gloss make this hard to know.

ATMOSPHERE

How still it is! The belfry's vibrant boom
Does not so much as stir the cherry-bloom.

trans. harold stewart (*net of*)

"Boom" is splendid but the Japanese belfry is little more than a roofed platform. Because the temples were on mountain sides, this was fine for the cities below, but with some bells, the sound could also be felt in the earth. The size of Japanese bells equaled Europe's largest (see *Topsy-turvy 1585*). I am a fan of Stewart's translation not so much for his use of rhymed couplets as for his bold interpretations. *If* it is the same *ku* I think he might be wrong, but his inadvertent paraverse would still be good as is.

入相に霞のわたる桜かな 梅枝 僧 花供養
iriai ni kasumi no wataru sakura kana   baishi 1795
(vespers-to/with/by mist's spread cherry!/'tis)

. . .
. . . at vespers . .
. . . mist spreads over . . . .
  .   .   . . . the cherry blossoms . . .   .   .

So much for the aesthete's vespers. And, we have seen the complaints. Here is a unique *ku*:

入相や桜は人を散ると見ん 午飲 発句題業
iriai ya sakura wa hito o chiru to min   goin? (1820)
(vespers!/: cherries-as-for, people[obj.] scatter/drop/blow-as see/appears)

the vespers
it looks like the cherries
shed us men
ah, the vespers
to cherries it seems men
fly like petals

The lack of good verb for dropping blossoms/petals hurts here, but the creativity still translates.

心のこる花のもどりや暮の鐘 梅枝 花供養
kokoro nokoru hana no modori ya kure no kane baishi 1795
(heart remain blossoms' return!/: evening-bell)

a memorable trip
back from blossom-viewing
the evening bell
our hearts still
with the blossoms, return
with the vespers

A simple masterpiece. The bell peals and the scene viewed at that instant is etched into the copper plate of our heart. Remember, also, that this is sunset. The "heart-remains" (*kokoro nokoru*) can mean the heart is left with the blossoms as well as meaning a memory is impressed in the mind.

鐘撞の道ちりかくすさくらかな 馬光
kane tsuki no michi chirikakusu sakura kana   bakô (1768)
(bell-striking road falling/scattering-hides cherry[subj.]!/'tis)

cherry blossoms
covering the pathway
to the belfry
the path to where
the temple bell is struck
blossom-hidden

the blossoms
hide the path leading
to the bell

The active verb in the original (「江戸俳諧にしひがし」より), as per the first and last reading, hints at intent where there is none, and the subject cherry=blossoms is at the end, as per the second reading. The *ku* is good as an objective depiction of a fact, yet evokes thought about the relationship of the bell to the blossoms. The gong of the bell did, after all, shake some of those petals off the limbs prematurely.

鐘か崎・花に撞く鐘沈めしか海の底　蘭更
hana ni tsuku kane shizumeshi ka umi no soko   rankô -1799
(blossoms-to strike bell sunken? ocean-bottom)

kanegasaki

the bell once struck
for the blossoms sunken
to the sea bottom?

where's the bell
i'd strike for the blossoms?
the bottom of the sea?

The name Kanegasaki translates as Cape Bell. The poet expects to find a big bell there but does not. Bells were famous for ending up on the sea-floor; shipping them angered dragons. Such superstitions were found around the world. But, the danger was probably real. With Japanese bells among the heaviest in the world, they would have been hard to keep from shifting or tipping in a heavy sea; and, it goes without saying, that they would attract boat-splitting bolts of lightning. Be that as it may, we find bits of the bell metamorphized as a sort of plebian dragon, the sea cucumber – similar bumps are found on many Japanese bells – in haiku (#314 & 315 in *Rise, Ye Sea Slugs!*). Evidently, not all such bells ended up at the bottom of the sea.

THE LEGEND OF DÔJÔ-JI

A dusk of flowers: the dragon's rage was rolled
Around this temple-bell that still is tolled.

Harold Stewart, who translated the above, by Tsunenori (-1685) in *A Chime of Windbells*, has a page-long note I condense: In the early 10c, a young monk rejected the advances of maiden who stole into his room because he was on a pilgrimage and had to guard his ritual purity, promising to return, which he did not, infuriating her so much she turned into a dragon and pursued him to Dôjô temple where the monks hid him within a great bronze bell yet to be hung. She coiled around it several times and struck it with her tail until sparks flew and the metal grew red hot. When the bell was lifted "only the charred bones of the unfortunate Anchin" remained. A longer version ("Red Heat") translated by Royall Tyler in his *Japanese Tales*, gives us a young widow who dies before "a foul snake immensely long, suddenly issued from her room . . ." *Snake* is the standard word used in dictionary descriptions of the creature as recreated by a Noh play, if nothing else because the snake was identified with powerful envy in Japan, but one can find dragonesque snakes and serpentine dragons in the visual literature, so I would only fault Stewart for not providing the romanization of the original so I could find it.

千金につりがね惜しむくれの春　惟中
senkin ni tsurigane oshimu kure no haru   ichû -1711
(thousand-gold[pieces]-as/worth dangle-bell/s regret dusk-of-spring)

regret worth
a pot of gold: bells ringing
out the spring

The *ne* in the hanging bell's bell (~*gane*) puns as value/worth. Japanese traditionally expressed strong emotion in quantitative ways. Here, it is "thousand-gold[coins]" in the original. Confusing gold and bells (both *kane*) is common in Japanese drama; I recall one moronic servant (a favorite among play-goers) sent out to investigate the price (値 *ne*) of gold, returning to report on the sound (音 *ne*) quality of the bells at each temple!   No blossoms are mentioned in the above *ku*, but I can see their petals in the air. (オマケ:「ぞちるらん上を下へと花に鐘」 西鶴)

14

Dusk on Cherry Mountain
夕桜・花の暮
yû-zakura + *hana-no-kure*

夕ざくらけふも昔に成にけり 一茶
yûzakura kyo mo mukashi ni narinikeri issa -1827
(evening-cherry today, too, past/ancient-time-into become[+fin.])

twilight blossoms
today is already once
upon a time

blossom dusk
today too is long ago
and far away

dusk blossoms
suddenly everything
is long ago

For a beautiful depiction (". . . lanterns glimmering here and there, the trees no longer trees but blossoms suspended in the air above us and around us . . .") and gushy metaphysical commentary (". . . this feeling of time is intensified . . ."), see Blyth (*Haiku* Spring vol: pgs 617-618) who translated Issa's *ku* as *"Evening cherry-blossoms: / Today also now belongs / to the past."* His "belongs to" is a fine creative translation. The voices of others seem to come from a distant place, not this one. After a long day drinking under the blossoms without sunglasses, something changes. Keigu has his own memory of a magical evening where, as Buson put it, *"Days lengthen / until we are way back / in the past"* (See IPOOH: Spring I).

桜ほど昔の見ゆる物もなし 綺石 発句題業
sakura hodo mukashi no miyuru mono mo nashi kiseki? 1820
(cherry-as-much-as ancientimes' see-can thing even not)

time machines

for seeing the past
nothing beats
the cherry

and nothing can
take us back as well as
cherry blossoms

cherry trees
nothing makes the past
so visible!

This bold *ku* may be an aphoristic reading of Issa's *ku,* or both it *and* Issa's ku may reference Bashô's *ku* (#22~26) about recalling many things when viewing blossoms. Or, it might have been inspired by another *ku* by Issa's employer, Seibi:

世の中のきのふは古し花の陰　成美
yo no naka no kinô wa furushi hananokage   seibi -1816
(world-among's yesterday-as-for, old/stale bloomshade)

<table>
<tr><td>

all the world
of yesterday is ancient
in the bloomshade

</td><td>

in the bloomshade
a world of yesterdays
seems ancient

</td></tr>
</table>

What makes Issa's *ku* particularly charming is the expression "today, too/even has become ancient-times!" (*kyo mo mukashi ni narikeri*) because it mimics the standard opening for tales of old and what makes it the most evocative of the three *ku* is the time. Some of us may occasionally fall into the past while sitting in the bloomshade in broad daylight, but twilight is the witching hour. Who hasn't been transported by it? I do not know if Issa's *ku* pre- or post-dated Seibi's.

昔とはどこより昔　桜より遠くは見せぬ春の曇りは　築地正子　鷺の書
mukashi to wa doko yori mukashi sakura yori tôku wa misenu haru no kumori wa   chikuchi masako
(ancientimes-as-for anywhere morethan ancientimes, cherry more than far-as-for show-not spring-overcast-as-for)

Ancient Times
how far away are they?
This overcast

won't let me see further
than the blooming cherries

Does this contemporary *tanka* play with haiku *hanami* lyricism (odd, for usually *tanka* are more lyrical) by marrying it to ancient poetry where clarity was equivalent to agelessness and murkiness, the loss of the past? The conflation of time and distance, the *when* and the *where,* intrigues me, but we have both lost the dusk *and* wandered off the road of haiku as far as I wish to.

花の陰寝ても起きても夕日さす　成美
hana no kage nete mo okite mo yûhi sasu   seibi -1816
(bloom-shade: asleep-too awake-too evening-sun beams/stabs)

<table>
<tr><td>

the bloomshade
asleep or awake, the sun
shines as it sets

</td><td>

the bloomshade
the setting sun strikes you
asleep or awake

</td></tr>
</table>

暮る日の花にまばゆき光哉　春水　花七日
kururu hi no hana ni mabayuki hikari kana   shunsui 1795
setting-sun/dusking-day's blossom/s-on dazzling shine!/'tis)

the brilliant light
of the setting sun dazzling
on the blossoms

The rays of the setting sun not only illuminate the bloom but, shooting under the branches, illuminate the brilliant blossom-viewing clothing and bright faces of the viewers. Some may sleep through it, but beauty is beauty. The rising sun strikes many sleeping faces, but no one is asleep at sunset, unless they have spent the day drinking. That makes the Seibi's description particularly cherry.

花々にうつる日影や丸つくし　安明 嵐山集
hanabana ni utsuru hikage ya maruzukushi anmei (1651)
(blossom/tree-X2 -on shine/move sun-shadow/shine: complete-exhaust/cover)

from tree to tree
the sunshine is touching
all the blossoms

This may well be a video of an entire day on cherry mountain. But, I imagine the sun providing its finishing touch, so I put it in this chapter.

我影の櫻にのほる夕日哉　其袋 鷹筑波
waga kage no sakura ni noboru yûhi kana anon 1642
(my shadow's cherry/blossoms climb evening-sun!/'tis)

as the sun sets my shadow climbs up the blossoms	my shadow mounts the blossoms in the evening sun

Like the *ku* before it, this is objective for a pre-Bashô *ku*. Shadows are usually noticed on flat surfaces, not complex ones like blossoms. Because there is a cataract called Yûhi, rightly or wrongly, I cannot help but see a salmon in this.

花の香に泣きたくなりし夕哉　乙二
hana no ka ni nakitaku narishi yûbe kana otsuni (-1823)
(blossom's scent-to/at/by cry-want-become evening!/'tis)

this evening the bloom-scent made me want to cry	bloom-scent you feel like crying at nightfall

Is this maudlin? I would say, no. Most *seemingly* maudlin poems – haiku, at any rate – are *not*. Describing one's feelings, no matter how maudlin they might be, is not maudlin. It is objective, if, that is, you really were maudlin. Then, again, crying when affected by a scent is, itself, an automatic reaction rather than the result of dwelling on a loss – the little casket of a dead baby, being the country music example – so who can call it anything but a fact?

夕桜鬼の涙のかゝるべし　一茶
yûzakura oni no namida no kakarubeshi issa -1827
(evening-cherry/blossoms demon/devil's tears place/upon ought)

cherry blossoms
at dusk: enough to draw
a demon's tears

these dusk-blossoms should indeed be covered with demon tears	dusk-blossoms will wet the eyes of a demon

Dew does quickly come to cooling bloom. Issa elsewhere mentions blossoms can melt a demon's heart.

花の色も鳥の音惜む夕哉　宗牧 東國紀行
hana no iro mo tori no ne oshimu yûbe kana　sôboku -1545
(blossoms' color/eros-too bird's/s'/rooster's/s' sound regret evening tis) [?])

cockadoodledoo we regret the lost color of blossoms, too	a cock at dusk the blossoms' color another cause for regret	the cock's call and pink of the bloom a regretful dusk

I doubt that my translation will do. The original plays on the standard saw of lovers sobbing about having to part at dawn, but we need not hear a real rooster. Sunset fell in the center of the Sino-Japanese *Hour of the Cock* (6 pm for us) and the poet may simply refer to the vespers. The faint pink, is lost to the candle, torch or moonlight. My "pink" is color (*iro*) is beauty is eros in the original.

日栖・うそ誠はでにしぼるや花の暮　鳥兎
uso makoto hade ni shiboru ya hananokure　chôto -1759
(day-live/born // lie/s truth/s gaudily wrung-out/concentrated blossom's dusk)

lies and truths wrung out with aplomb blossom dusk	lies and truths all come down to this blossom dusk

The "dusk-blossoms" (*yûzakura*) found in Issa's chapterhead *ku* is a word, combining *yû* (evening) and *sakura* (cherry), while this *hana-no-kure* is a phrase meaning "dusk of the blossoms." If the former suggests evening blossom-viewing, the latter suggests the end of a day of viewing. Does the poet mean this is when men decide whether to go straight home, so they, retrospectively, told their wives the truth, or head for the pleasure quarters making the purpose of their outing a lie? Or, does it mean, less dramatically, that declarations made to buddies while drinking about the night's plans (sleep over or not, etc) suddenly are either carried out or forgotten? The untranslated preface may allude to an odd story involving a Buddhist saint, confusion about a woman's state (dead or alive) etc..

夕くれや花を離るゝ天の原　正名 花櫻帖
yûgure ya hana o hanaruru amanohara　seina ()
(dusk-dark: blossoms separate [from] heaven's plain)

twilight
the sky and blossoms
pull apart

This is about the purist evening blossoms *ku* that could be written. As noted elsewhere, I have experienced the thick blue sky over the cherry blossoms as a bottomless ocean and felt relief when it was replaced by the clearly visible firmament of night. To me, the starry heavens, though further to be sure, were less terrifying for being visible. I don't know what the poet felt. Perhaps the opposite.

it grows dark
and heaven falls away
from the bloom

Seina saw well. Buckminster Fuller was a fool for wanting us not to see/say "sun*rise*." We *should* see/say the sun *rises* as well as imagine the earth turning down, or heaven falling away. A good marriage of sense and intellect requires us to see inside out and outside in.

dusk

暮れてやゝ月に成迄桜見し 夜雪 花供養
kurete yaya tsuki ni naru made sakura mishi   yasetsu (1795)
(darkening [dusk+night falls: a while/smattering moon-into become-until cherries viewed])

after dark we view
blossoms for a while, waiting
for the moonlight

after nightfall
we blossom-view until
the moon wins

kept viewing
blossoms until we had
moon enough

A seemingly paradoxical but natural observation. "Until [the] moon-into become" means "until the (waning) moon rose high enough, or beat out the clouds, to create a *bona fide* moonlit night, safe for travel. If you wait for sunset, you do well to wait a while longer for the moon, not only for the sight of the blossoms in the moonshine, but to light your way home. The phase of the moon would have had a major influence on the behavior of blossom viewers.

人の散る程には散らず夕桜 梅室 アルス
hito no chiru hodo ni wa chirazu yûzakura   baishitsu (1768-1852)
(people scatter/fall degree-as-for fall-not evening-cherry/blossom[viewing])

evening bloom
people scatter faster
than the petals

petals scatter not
half so fast as people:
twilight *sakura*

Blossom-viewing in the evening gloom might be fine for the aesthetic elite, but most people are eager to get home or to the pleasure quarters for the lucky few. Then, there are those like young Issa:

夕桜家ある人はとくかへる 一茶 享三
yûzakura ie aru hito wa toku kaeru   issa (-1827)
(evening cherry home-have people-as-for already return)

dusk blossoms
everybody with a home
is long gone

dusk blossoms
all who have homes
leave quickly

We can imagine his evening blossom viewing was melancholy enough for any poet to wish for. This *ku* is spare and perfect, though not completely true, for there were doubtless some who stayed over for aesthetic reasons.

雨ならぬ夕も花の木陰哉 紹巴
ame naranu yûbe no hana no kokage kana   jôha 1523-1602
(rain become-not evening-even/too blossom's/s' tree-shade!/?/'tis)

even on nights
without rain, in the shade
of the blossoms!

This was a couple hundred years before Issa. The next is contemporary to him:

酒くさき人群来たり夕桜　車莫 花供養
sake kusaki hitomure kitari yûzakura　shamo 1795
(*sake*-stinking people-crowd/s coming evening-cherry/ies)

stinking of sake
people come in crowds
evening blossoms

evening blossoms
crowds of men drift by
stinking of sake

Evidently, there were some blossom-viewing sites where people not only were not kicked out at sunset but came to drink at night.

露は秋と思はし花の夕しめり　宗春 三籟
tsuyu wa aki to omowaji hana no yûjimeri　sôshun 1734
(dew-as-for, autumn-as think-not, blossoms' evening-damp)

who says dew
is best seen in the fall?
blossoms at dusk

dew means fall?
i think not: blossoms
after nightfall

Dew was officially an Autumnal theme. When another poet, observing the fullness of the bloom and the lively blossom-viewing, opined "Cherry hill: / Life sure doesn't seem / to be like dew" (花の山露とは見えぬ命哉　道院　鞭随筆 *hana no yama tsuyu to wa mienu inochi kana*　dôin (1759)), he was taking advantage of the fact dew didn't go with Spring, period. Sôshun told the truth. *I have seen it.*

人声にほっとしたやら夕桜　一茶
hitogoe ni hotto shita yara yûzakura　issa -1827
(people-voice-by bothered[by volumne]? evening-cherry)

have you too
had enough human voices
dusk cherries?

Today, *hotto shita,* which Issa used in the sense of "fed-up with" or "had enough of," means feeling relieved at the end of something. The translation was pulled up from between the lines. How pleasant to be in a crowded place when it empties out and silence returns with the fresh air. Issa did not write "you, *too,*" but I think he felt good and imagined the cherry trees felt the same.

にぎやかな桜の木の下から暮れてゆく　石川千晴 愛知県 安城西中 2
nigiyaka na sakura no ki no shita kara kureteyuku　ishikawa chiharu (contemp)
(lively/noisy/busy cherry tree's/trees' below/under-from darkening-goes/comes)

it grows dark
from below the lively
cherry trees

in the uproar
under the blossoms, night
comes first

I do not know of any studies of the relationship between perception of sound and light, but there is something to this observation of a middle-school student. The *ku* reminds us that we, too, have at one time or another experienced what English calls the *gathering* dusk. The "from" in the first reading (*kara*) is important. The second reading, which mimics the overall word-order of the original, loses it.

dusk

桜さく春に夕べはなかりけり 素丸　素丸発句集

sakura saku haru ni yûbe wa nakarikeri　somaru (1712-95)
(cherry/ies bloom spring-in evening/dusk-as-for, not[+emphatic])

<blockquote>
in the spring
when cherries bloom
there is no dusk
</blockquote>

<blockquote>
no twilight
in the springs we spend
with *sakura*
</blockquote>

Drinking in the bloomshade, the night can fall before you know it; and, with cherries blooming past the equinox the sun moves closer to perpendicular with respect to the horizon cutting the length of twilight day by day. Yet, for all this circumstantial evidence, at first, I thought that Somaru's *ku* might be read in a different way – that there is no *"last night"* in cherry time – for *yûbe* can mean *that*, as well as "twilight/evening," but a native speaker's intuition did not allow it and, on second thought, the fuzzy edge on the "not" (the *kari* in the *nakarikeri* that I cannot for the life of me translate) would be *why*. Declaring that there are no last nights would require a more forceful tone.

本降りのゆうべとなりし桜哉 一茶

honburi no yûbe to narishi sakura kana　issa 1804
(real-fall's evening-as become/became cherry 'tis)

<blockquote>
it only started
raining cats and dogs after
blossom dark
</blockquote>

<blockquote>
the real downpour
came after it grew dark
cherry blossoms
</blockquote>

<blockquote>
cherry bloom
after dark it falls
for good
</blockquote>

<blockquote>
the deluge came
after most went home
blossom-viewing
</blockquote>

Generally, *honburi* means the main body of the rain. There is a sprinkle now and then suggesting the sky is in a wet mood, then *it* falls for good. English has no such word. About all we can do to try to match it with description or idiom. I have never found it used for the falling petals, but it *could* be. Because Issa was young and had boasted (which is to say complained) about sleeping out, I think we are probably talking about a lone poet and, perhaps, other homeless, sitting out the rain all night.

城門の閉まるを告げて打つ太鼓
夕桜なほ燿ひてあり　初井しず枝 夏木立
jômon no tojimaru o tsugete utsu taikô / yûzakura nao kagayaite-ari　hatsui shizue (contemp.)

昔とは どこより昔 桜より
遠くは見せぬ春の曇りは 築地正子 鷺の書
mukashi to wa doko yori mukashi sakura yori / tôku wa misenu haru no kumori wa　chikuchi masako? (con.)

<blockquote>
*The big drums
beat out the closing of
the castle gate*

*the cherry blossoms
blazing all the more*
</blockquote>

<blockquote>
*what is ancient
is more ancient here than
anywhere else*

*this spring haze shows me
nothing beyond the cherry*
</blockquote>

These are two 20c tanka. The first mentions *yû* evening cherry (blossom-viewing). I imagine a closing at midnight or before. And I imagine torches and sparks as well as the full bloom that seems a shame to abandon. The second, dusky or not, reminds me of the *ku* with which we began the chapter.

Night Cherries
夜桜
yo-zakura

親なくば梢に寝たき櫻哉　萬翁 新選
oya nakuba kozue ni netaki sakura kana   manô 1773
(parent/boss-not-if tree-top-in sleep-want cherry!/'tis)

blossom bed

had i no parents,
you'd find me sleeping in
this cherry tree

as an orphan
i'd nest in the bloom
of the cherry

in the world alone
i'd sleep right a'top
the cherry bloom

It is not that an orphan could find no better place to sleep. Not having parents would free the young man from the obligation to remain home and care for them[1] and from worrying about the consequences of falling out of said tree, for the only casualty would be his own. Is this a John Muir-like desire to be rocked in the arms of mother nature,[2] or am I missing something (an allusion to the second floor of the pleasure quarters, maybe)?

春をわか木するにくらせ櫻はな　宗祇
haru o waka kozue ni kurase sakurabana   sôgi (-1502)
(spring[obj] young treetop-on live[imperative]! cherry-blossom/s)

live your spring
in the young tree-tops
cherry blossoms

cherry blossoms
in spring live on the tips
of young limbs

The night is not found in this old *ku,* here as a precedent for the previous *ku.* Both depend in part upon the untranslatable concept of branch-tips (*kozue*) for which "tree-top" is the closest English.

1. Caring for Parents   Unlike the case in most of the Occident, children tended to stay home and care for their parents in Japan. This care was, however, only natural because parents, for *their* part, did not cling to their power and riches until death, but retired in late-middle-age, turning over management of the family business and fortune to their children. (See *Topsy-turvy 1585*)

2. Rockaby John Muir   Muir, godfather of the Usanian national park system, spent a night high up a tree in a gale where, thinking about the miles of movement he enjoyed (?) – it's amazing he didn't get sea-sick! – realized that the fixed-fola-*vs.*-mobile-fauna concept was wrong: *trees travel as much as we do, they just make more short trips!*   Muir also ran out of his mountain hut in a major earthquake shouting his joy at being "rocked on Mother Nature's knee!" Obviously, he liked motion.

夜も見よ戸さしせぬ世の春の花　宗祇
yoru mo miyo tozashi senu yo no haru no hana sôgi -1502
(night, too, see-let's, door-lock-do-not!-world's spring-blossom/s)

view by night, too! the blossoms of spring are not locked up	at night, too, let's view so keep your gates unlocked for spring blossoms	view blossoms at night! the doors of spring are never closed

The expression, "a world unlocked," idiomatic for an ideal society where doors were never locked, is given a new twist in this *ku*. It is impossible to be certain whether the unlocked spring blossoms refer to all the blossoms or the portion that were so, but the "world (*yo*)" makes the former more likely.

言事のさわりそう也夜の花　素檗
iigoto no sawarisô nari yoru no hana sobaku -1821
(word-things' offend[gods/ruin-a-charm]-seems/could become night-blossoms)

charmed

night blossoms
something tells me to
watch my words

Issa's contemporary has found a fine way to express the preternatural beauty of blossoms seen by torchlight. I made many attempts at translation, but none worked well, for English has no equivalent for *sawari*, which means the bad luck (jinx), bad weather etc. resulting from something said or done that angers a tutelary god or the dragon gods or whatever. At first, I guessed the *ku* took issue with any words, but the OJD defines "word-thing" as vows, quarrels, complaints and such serious words.

ひきかへて花見る春は夜はなく　月見る秋は昼なからなむ　西行
hikikaete hana miru haru wa yoru wa naku tsuki miru aki wa hiru nakaranan saigyô
(reversing, blossoms-viewing spring-as-for, night is not; moon-viewing fall-as-for day/noon not!)

Contrary Play

the blossom-viewing spring
has no night
and the moon-viewing fall
it has no day

To spend the day/night viewing the moon/blossoms while drinking up a storm *and* enjoy the following night/day is hard for all not blessed with an extraordinary constitution. Because moon-viewing was a Buddhist activity, there is irony in the damage done to the working hours of the day: hence, there are more poems about *that* then about the effects of blossom-viewing. Still, Issa made one: *"My lethargy / I've been blaming it / on the blossoms* ひだるさを桜のとがにしたりけり 一茶 *hidarusa o sakura no toga ni shitarikeri*). He means *unfairly*. Since the cherries bloom as the nights grow short and the temperature rises, even people who do not go blossom-viewing might yawn. Not to worry, another poet observes: *"In the middle / of the bloom-roar, a true / lover of sleep"*(わやくやの花の中なる寝好き哉　旦理　小弓俳諧集 *wayakuya no hana no nakanaru nezuki kana*　tanri 1699). A fine *ku*, indeed. I do not count myself a lover of sleep, for I regret every minute taken from my waking life, but even *I* can attest to the pleasurable sensation of sleeping in the middle of a party. Tanri may be making a confession, which might better be Englished as follows:

do I love sleep!
right there amid the roar
blossom-viewing

how i love
sleeping with the blossoms
in the noise

I could not resist calling attention to this fun *ku*, but let us return to the proper subject, night:

同じくは月のをり咲け山桜花見る夜半の絶え間あらせじ　西行
onajiku wa tsuki no ori sake yamazakura hana miru yoha no taema araseji   saigyô -1190
(same[thing]-as-for/if, moon-time bloom[imper.] mountain-cherry/ies, blossoms view wee-hours break-not)

mountain cherries
if it's all the same to you
bloom with the moon!

we would view blossoms
all night long!

The cold winter moon and the cool summer moon and the hazy spring moon are all genuine *saijiki* terms, but *the* moon, i.e. the moon for the sake of the moon, is the Autumn moon. When it appears with cherry blossoms, the focus is generally not on the moon itself. Saigyô lived in a cottage up in the mountains, but this *waka* seems to put him outside all night. Keigu prefers to imagine a window –

月と咲け窓に光を山桜　敬愚
tsuki to sake mado ni hikari o yamazakura   keigu
(one-night's window moon with bloom mountain-cherry/ies)

a scholar's window

mountain cherries,
bloom with the moon, please
keep light coming!

A window where Saigyô could read the cherry blossoms a *sutra* in their own – the moon's – reflected light (Think of it: sun to moon to blossoms to wall to paper and up to Saigyo's eyes. *Skip the wall if you wish.*). Keigu alludes to the proverbial Chinese poet who studied by moon light reflected from snow banked by his window. Today, with abundant lighting, it takes a hurricane to remind us of the craft required to read with little light. A candle will do; but that light must be carefully gathered and directed.

山々をめくりて見るは花月哉　述貞 洗濯物
yamayama o meguritemiru wa hanazuki kana   jûttei? 1666
(mountain-mountain[obj] pivoting see-as-for blossom-moon!/?/'tis)

night tour

roving around
mountain to mountain
blossom moon

It is hard to say if the poet roams at night, the moon or both. Jûtei's *ku* is unique for treating blossom-viewing – or should we say cherry-hunting? – as a nocturnal activity. The *~zuki* "moon" puns as "~liker/lover" and unites the blossom-loving poet with the blossom-moon.

night

行すゑを花にさためん宿もなし 紹巴 大発句帳
yukusue o hana ni sadamen yado mo nashi   jôha 1523-1602
(going-end(destination) blossoms-by decide-will lodging-even-not)

no inn for me:	no reservations:
i'll let the blossoms pick	i'll let the blossoms
my destination	choose my inn

The poet may play on a 14c *renga* sequence by the monk Gusai *"At an unexpected place / I ask lodging for the night. // Going toward blossoms, / I let my heart take its course – / forgetting myself."* (*omowanu kata ni ...* Trans. Stephen D. Carter in *Traditional Japanese Poetry*).[2] Being *sans*-destination is metaphysically appropriate for viewing blossoms that leave their fate up to the winds, but it was not for lack of effort on the part of the inns. Another by Jôha: *"Road guides / are working near and far: / blossom inns"* (をちこちも道つたへあるや花の宿 紹巴 同*ochikochi mo michi-tsutae aru ya hana no yado* jôha). I suspect that not only were people guided directly to inns but to cherry mountains in the vicinity of the inn.[1] After all, a "cherry" (*sakura*) is a "shill" in Japanese. The original's "[I] have no inn" can be interpreted in two ways, as per my translations. With the above *ku,* it is impossible to tell if the poet plans to sleep out or simply has not reserved a room. Here, Jôha is clear:

宿からん花にまされる陰もなし 紹巴 大発句帳
yado karan hana ni masareru kage mo nashi   jôha 1523-1602
(inn/lodging rent/pay blossom-to [more than] excell shade-even not)

i won't take
a room! there is no shade
like a cherry's

If Jôha was not writing through his hat, he slept out and would have agreed with this later *ku:*

春の日に月夜を足して花見哉 棟戸
haru no hi ni tsukiyo o tashite hanami kana   tôko 1742
(spring-day-with moon[lit]night[obj.] adding, blossom-viewing!/'tis)

a clear spring day	spring sunshine
supplemented by the moon	followed by moonlight: that's
that's a *hanami!*	blossom-viewing!

In some parts of Japan, poets did not need to choose between room and tree: *"Not an inn / in the capital without / a cherry tree"* (花一本植ゑぬ都の宿もなし 智蘊？吾妻問答 *hana ippon uenu miyako no yado mo nashi*   chira (1470)). Japanese windows were as large as walls. If guests were allowed to sleep with open windows – not normal, for Japanese generally close not only their windows but the wooden storm shutters – they could enjoy their night-blossoms and the comforts of a good inn. An even older *ku* suggests where some inn trees may have come from: *"Plant blossoms / as you go, the poets' / inn spring"* うゑしうへは いく花鳥の宿の春 宗長 *ueshi ueba iku kachô no yado no haru* sôchô (1447-1532). The *ku* is not fully translatable for the "blossoms" in the original are part of the phrase *kachô,* "blossom/s-bird/s," shorthand for the professional world of poetry.

---

1. The Edo era soon to come was full of advertisement, from pretty girls who captured guests by promises of services, to free fans with inn rankings and maps drawn on them. Commercialism is hardly a Western invention.

2. The original, *omowanu kata ni / yado o koso toe; hana ni yuku / kokoro ya ware o / wasururan* was in the *Tsukuba-shû* (1356), the first collection of *hokku + tsukeku*, i.e. 17-syllabet lead verses and 14-syllabet links given in pairs outside of the broader linked-verse context. Carter points out that while the high-ranking courtier Nijô Yoshimoto is generally given full credit for the collection, this poet, his teacher Gusai, deserves to share it. The 7-7 start (*"At an unexpected .. night"*) of the sequence is the freshest part. The last part, ideally 5-7-5, does not English well. It can be smoothed up: *"The mind, heading for blossoms / would forget itself"* or, more directly translated (preserving the connections, not order) as *"Ah, the mind / that heads for blossoms! It would / forget about me* (the original actually splits 9-8, so irregularity is fine). The pronoun *ware* is problematic for *"itself=I=me=myself."* Carter's *"forgetting myself"* is masterful, for it suggests a lack of caution better than my translations; but his *"I let,"* is off, for the heart=mind desiring blossoms is, *itself*, in the driver's seat.

~~~~~~

夜ざくらや美人天から下るとも 一茶 文政三
yozakura ya bijin ama[ten?]kara kudaru to mo issa (-1827)
(night-cherry: beautiful-person heaven-from descend seems/even-if . . .)

<blockquote>
night blossoms!
like beauties come down
from heaven
</blockquote>

<blockquote>
they say angels
have come to earth
night blossoms
</blockquote>

<blockquote>
blossoms at night!
it wouldn't surprise me
to see an angel
</blockquote>

The word "beautiful person" (*bijin*) meant either a beauty (of either sex) or the ruler. In *Ora ga Haru* (My Spring=New Year), Issa mentions maidens (*otome*) descending from heaven (when an ancient Emperor played the *koto*, or zither, on Mount Yoshino) so we may assume he is thinking of pretty *female* angels[1] or maybe a picture of a beauty floating down with an umbrella parachute (from a kabuki play). The original *to mo* is an ellipsis that permits many readings. I enjoy combining the readings but most Japanese favor the first, alone. Blyth does too: *"Cherry blossoms at night! / Just like angels / come down from heaven."*). He follows it with one of Issa's more puzzling poems,

夜桜や天の音楽聞し人 一茶
yozakura ya ame no ongaku (otogaku?) kikishi hito issa
(night-cherry: heaven's music hears/d-person/people)

<blockquote>
blossoms at night
men who have heard
heaven's music
</blockquote>

– which he translates *"Blossoms at night! / People after hearing / heavenly music."* *Tengaku*, the usual term for "heaven's music," was heard on earth by a Buddhist just before – pardon my Occidentalism – the chariots come to carry you away. Blyth gives no explanation whatsoever, but in Issa's best known book, *Oraga Haru,* he tells of friends coming over to stay up all night and try to hear "Heaven's music," which so many people reported hearing that Issa joked that failing to do so could be taken as proof one was a sinner. Issa mentioned the ancient tales of maidens descending from heaven and dew sweet as nectar in passim, but still found heaven's music hard to believe in a literal sense, though he granted that it was also hard to disbelieve as totally groundless. He finally found it himself in the song of the warbler/nightingale (the call sounds like the name of a sutra) and found said maidens in the cherry blossoms seen at night. Blyth writes that Issa is using "heaven to describe the beauty of the cherry blossoms" (Blyth) in this *ku*, as in the previous one; but his translation seems, rather, to equate the enraptured faces of the cultists and the bloom. Perhaps Issa appreciated such joy. Or, could we be off-track? Could Issa really have had Saigyô's death-day in mind?

1. Angels in Japan Japanese are not so angel-oriented as Western people, with their sky-gods and their heavenly hosts. Still, there were heaven-flying beauties. Generally, they have thin scarfs and ribbons trailing them, but i have read of some boasting downy white wings, and wonder if it is these fluffy feathers evoked by the full bloom.

saigyô

night blossoms!
one man who heard
heaven's music

More on monk Saigyô (-1190), whose *waka* we saw pages back, and death elsewhere. Here, let me just say that Saigyô's sudden death and the manner in which cherry blossoms suddenly "let go" were greatly admired by all, but also helped to create fear of sudden death, if one were not enlightened:

花の陰寝まじ未来がおそろしき 一茶
hananokage nemaji mirai ga osoroshiki   issa -1827
(blossom-shade sleep-not [?] future/next-world [is] terrifying)

the bloomshade
i can't sleep for dread
of my next life

Mirai in modern Japanese simply means "future." It used to mean *the next world*. Issa felt guilty for writing instead of farming and fancied he would face retribution. Another version of the *ku* with further explanation is in chapter 36, *"Dying in the Bloomshade."* While not religious myself, I appreciate the powerful (not purely *personal*) emotion that belief brings to poetry. This *ku* belongs with "Rise, Ye Sea Slugs!" (*uke namako*), also by Issa, as one of the best Buddhist haiku.

花のもとに身をも浮世も忘れ寝や 乎焉 拍挙千句
hana no moto ni mi o mo ukiyo mo wasurene ya   koen (1782)
(blossom's base-by/at body/self and floating/woeful-world too forgetting-sleep?/!)

in the bloomshade   beneath a cherry
the sleep of forgetfulness   asleep, losing my self
no self, no world   and all my blues

While the sleep of forgetting has been identified with Buddhist nihilism by some in the Occident, this is probably secular. There is no woman-as-blossom here, either, for the "self" that is not is his "body." And, since drinking kills dreams – anyone sleeping by a tree has drunk, this sleep is as kind as death.

寒からぬ花の鏡や朧月 竹也 堅並
samukaranu hana no kagami ya oborozuki   chikuya ()
(cold-not blossom's mirror/[paragon?]: hazy moon)

a far from cold
blossom-viewing mirror:
the hazy moon!

Huh? Were those blossoms *breathing?* An old *ku*, that might be described as matter-of-fact to a fault, gives us the seasonal bare bones: *"At a blossom party / i see the first / hazy moon night"* (花の宴に見初る朧月夜哉 永次 毛吹草 *hana no en ni mi-somuru oborozukiyo kana* eiji (1645)). The cherry blossoms and the hazy moon coincide. Maybe that was news: the haze of the spring moon was traditionally attributed to the thick scent of the *plum* blossoms wafting up to the heavenly body. But, in reality, it usually waited for the cherries, and young Bashô (-1694) joked that the beauty of these blossoms *caused* the moon to become hazy (花の顔に晴うてしてや朧月 芭蕉 *hana no kao ni hareute shite ya oborozuki*), i.e., *bashful,* for haziness darkens (as in a blush) or hides it (as with hands over face). But to return to Chikuya's *ku,* the "cold-not" can modify the blossoms (*hot* at their peak) or the "mirror." Either way, the haze around the moon is associated with warmth. The hazy moon (*oborozuki*) is the *ku*'s main theme, but moon and bloom bring out each other's spring character.

下戸連は知らじ月夜の花の味 玉圃 句鑑
gekoren wa shiraji tsukiyo no hana no aji   gyokuho 1787
(abstainers-as-for know-not moon-night's blossoms' taste)

     non-drinkers   those teetotalers
can't appreciate blossoms   know not the taste of blossoms
     in moonshine   under the moon

True. Alcohol can keep some of us up as well as coffee! Does it slow the metabolism, dim the screen – or reduce the number of running processes – like a computer running on batteries? Or does it dull the feeling of being tired, as it dulls pain? For many, however, it does the opposite: they pass out.

酔覚て起れば月の山ざくら　蘭更
yoi samete okireba tsuki no yamazakura   rankô 1725-98
(drunkeness sobers wake-if/when moon's mountain-cherry)

when i come to
mountain cherry shining
in the moon-light

"Moonshine to moonshine"? Buds are pink but wide-open blossoms are generally white, hence *bright* in the moonlight.

寝残て暮に星見る櫻哉　尚白 反故集
ne-nokotte kure ni hoshi miru sakura kana   shôhaku 1649-1722
(sleep-remaining evening-in star/s see cherry[blossoms]!/?/'tis)

  remaining prone   still lying there
in the bloomshade, i saw   in the bloomshade i saw
  an evening star   the stars come out

驚くや花より出る夜半の月　松井 花七日
odoroku ya hana yori ideru yohan no tsuki   shôsei 1777
(surprised! blossom-from appear night-half(after midnight)-moon)

what a shock!
the moon pops from the bloom
after midnight

An indirect paean to profuse bloom. Were there several overcast days before, or was the poet so absorbed with the blossoms that he forgot what *day* it was (the day of the month would indicate the phase of the moon and that, the timing, so Japanese generally knew when to expect the moon)?

花に寝て月に驚く木陰哉 雪居 花桜帖
hana ni nete tsuki ni odoroku kokage kana   sekkyo
(blossoms-with/by sleeping moon-at surprised tree-shade/ow!/?/'tis)

    sleeping out
under the bloom: the moon
      pops through!

    sleeping out
surprised to see bloom-shade
      moon-made!

As my readings show, this poem is clearly ambiguous; shadow means many things in Japanese, as it once did in English.

花を照らし月又花にくもる哉　樗良
hana o terashi tsuki mata hana ni kumoru kana   chora -1781
(blossom[obj] illuminate moon again blossom-by cloud!/?/'tis)

the moon that
shows the blossoms, also
clouded by them

花に月何所からもれて膝の上　多代女
hana ni tsuki doko kara morete hiza no ue tayojo 1775-1865
(blossoms-with/in moon where-from leaking lap-on-top)

  bloom and moon
seeping in from somewhere
  light on my lap!

  blossoms at night
where-from this moon shine
   on my lap?

晴れわたる月も助かる花の雲　敬愚
hare wataru tsuki mo tasukaru hananokumo keigu
(clear-crossing moon even helps blossom-cloud/s)

   a full moon
the clear night is saved
   by blossoms

月よよしよしや花こそ春の雲　行助 大発句
tsuki-yo yoshi x2 ya hana koso harunokumo gyôjo 1644
(moon-night fine, fine blossom espec. spring clouds)

  hushaby, moon,
it's all right, this bloom
  is spring cloud

Bloom-as-cloud was generally a phenomenon of the daytime. Not here. Chora, through paradox expands a parallel. Keigu alludes to the Monk Saigyô and Kenko's observation that the moon is more interesting with clouds than without; and Gyôjo, if I read him right, has a lullaby of a *ku!*

閑さや花にそふたる庭の月　茶州 明からす
nodokesa ya hana ni soutaru niwa no tsuki   sashû 1773
(tranquility!/: blossom/s-to/with accompany garden's moon)

   how tranquil
blossoms in the company of
   a garden moon

   how peaceful
a garden moon with
   the blossoms

15 # 28~ 31

For a cherry time *ku*, Chashû's has more moon in it than any I know of, yet we still feel the centrality of the once-a-year presence, the blossoms.

渡月橋・月光西にわたれば花影東に歩むかな　蕪村
gekkô nishi ni watareba kaei higashi ni ayumu kana bûson (1715-83)
(moon-light west-to pass/cross flower/blossom-shadow/s/form east-ward walk!/?)

at moon-cross bridge

westward moon
as the blossom shadows
move eastward

the moon wests
and the blossoms creep
toward the east

as the moon wests
eastward crawl the shadows
of the full bloom

Besides shade cast in a recognizable form, shadows once included reflections and what we might call the sight of a thing today. The Chinese character used by Buson favors my second reading where the shadow "moving Eastward" is not shade but the sight of illuminated blossoms as the light of the Westing moon leaves the valleys and climbs the West slopes of the hills viewed to the East of the poet. The moon-light (月光) seems to mean the moon-as-a-light: it is just the moon.

しはらくは花の上なる月夜哉　芭蕉
shibaraku wa hana no ue naru tsukiyo kana bashô (1694)
(while-as-for blossoms-upon-is moon-night!/?/'tis)

lingering a while
above the blossoms, the moon
in the night sky

↑ trans. ueda, my centering ↑

The critical remarks translated by Ueda show magnificent disparity. Shiki thought the *ku* "has no profound appeal" for it was painted from the head, while Shûson praised the grand perspective capturing "the essence of a spring night," other critics appreciated it for depicting a view of blossoms wide open to the moon or seen from above like billowing clouds and one mentions the obvious allegory of fleeting beauty, a panorama made poignant by the soon-to-come departure of the moon, leaving the blossoms in the dark and another the poet joining the moon upon the bloom:

for a while
my eyes and the moon
on the blossoms

present a while
in the blossoms, tonight
the moon is out

Usually, a "moon-night" (*tsukiyo*) means a night when the moon stands out, i.e., the full moon. It rises near sunset and sets near sunrise. So why the *shibaraku,* which is only "a while?" Is this a moon too fat to be a crescent, yet not yet full? Or, is the cherry hemmed in by pine or cedar? Be that as it may, I like the leisurely yet not too long moon-strobe view of the fleeting bloom. The "ue-naru" can mean *"upon"* as well as *"above."* To bring that out, my alternate readings (Ueda's being the main one) uses "on" and "in." You might, more easily, change Ueda's *above* to *upon.* Either is equally valid.

西行上人五百年忌・はっきりと有明のこる櫻哉　荷分 あらの
saigyô jonin gohyaku-nenki // hakkiri to ariake nokoru sakura kana   kakei 1689
(saigyô-above-person five-hundred-anniversary // clearly morning-moon remains cherry/ies!/'tis)

on the five-hundreth year anniversary of saigyô's death

cherry blossoms
with the morning moon
still in the sky

still clearly seen
the *ariake* moon
cherry blossoms

the waning moon
still in the sky beyond
cherry blossoms

The broad meaning of *ariake* is the waning moon one finds in the morning that always surprises us for remaining so clear. There is something bone-like, even pathetic about it that would have been more touching before we knew the substance of the moon. It would have complemented the bloom and vice versa. My first two readings imagine the moon in light blue sky. A narrower definition of *ariake* (lit. is-[there-at]-daylight) is the slightly-past-full moon viewed at daybreak, with the colors changing with the sunrise from pinkish to white as was the case with many cherry blossoms including one called the *ariake-zakura* that Kuitert (*Japanese Flowering Cherries*) first finds in a 1681 catalog, i.e. eight years before the publication of the book with the above *ku*. My last reading assumes that most cherries already bloomed that year before Saigyô's deathday, but a certain *ariake-zakura* was still in full bloom, its large white petals reflecting the light of Buddhist Law, the moon.

のむ程に三日月かゝる櫻哉　万子 アルス
nomu hodo ni mikazuki kakaru sakura kana   banshi 1775
(drink-amount-as three-day-moon turn-on/bear-upon cherry!/'tis)

the more we drink
the closer the moon's cup
to the blossoms

after sunset
the moon and i toast
the blossoms

we drain our cups
as the moon's cup settles
on the blossoms

Kakaru has too many meanings to shake a stick at. Heavenly bodies *kakaru* (hang) in the sky yet *kakaru* also means "tilt", "come down" or even "rest upon." The crescent moon is already high in the sky by nightfall. I would love to find it tipsy, spilling slowly on the bloom, but actually it rights itself to settle in the West. A hard-to translate *ku:* "On cherry blossoms / we must leave to the night / the crescent moon" 暮をしむ櫻にしばし三日の月 胡柳 花櫻帖 *kure-oshimu sakura ni shibashi mikkanotsuki* koryû (?)). I coped with the "nightfall-regretting cherries" but lost a "momentarily"(*shibashi*).

夜櫻をひとりで見るや思ふまゝ　吟江 行雲日記
yozakura o hitori de miru ya omou mama ni   ginkô 1780
(night-cherry[obj] alone/single-by see: think/feel-just-like)

night cherry
viewing blossoms alone
as i please

Here, I assume the poet does not even have the moon for company so even the lighting is under his control. He swigs *sake,* sings, writes and decides how far to go to take a leak. But, how long can a man enjoy the blossoms alone? I would want at least a visit from a family of raccoon foxes (*tanuki*).

212 *night*

蝋燭の風に流るゝ夜の花 美角 続明烏
rôsoku no kaze ni nagaruru yoru no hana mikaku 1724-93
(candles' wind-in/by/with flow/ing night-blossoms)

night blossoms

in the draft
of the candle, petals
f l o a t i n g

drifting away	candle flames
in the candle's current	flowing with the wind
night blossoms	night blossoms

In the right weather, the draft of a candle can float petals. Or, does it just seem that way? Grammar also (barely) allows the less spectacular last reading.

隅ズミや灯とゝく庭ざくら せき女 花供養
sumizumi ya tomoshibi todoku niwazakura sekijo (1795)
(corner-corner!/: lamp/light/s reach/es garden-cherry[blossoms])

my lamp reaches	the lamps reach
every nook and cranny	every nook and cranny
garden cherries	garden cherries

We are not talking about total lighting from hundreds of lamps like a Haitian religious ceremony, but lamps/candles carried about by hand to shine light on the bloom from various angles. The poet is a woman. I almost titled the poem *"our blossoms, our selves."*

工夫して花にランプを吊しけり 子規
kufû shite hana ni ranpu o tsurushikeri   shiki 1899
(devise/create-doing blossoms-on lamp[obj] hang [emph.])

What pains i took,	HANGING THAT LANTERN
Hanging the lamp	ON THAT FULL WHITE
On the flowering branch!	BLOOMING BOUGH...
	EXQUISITE YOUR CARE!
trans. r. h. blyth	trans. peter pauper

I cannot *not* quote Blyth: "This seemingly subjective, ego-centric verse is really not so. The intense absorption with which he was hanging the lamp upon the blossoming cherry-tree is not only purely objective, but is used to praise the beauty of the flowers." The original is obviously "really not so," because *kufû shite* is far less dramatic than Blyth's "what pains . . .". and the idea may be less that Shiki took pains – though that might be true, too – than that he used a modern device, a *ranpu*, rather than a Japanese lamp (not called a *ranpu*) to further a traditional aesthetic aim> Hence, *"Improvising / I hang a lamp from / the blossoms."* This is, to use a modern art term, his *installation*. Shiki often baptized Western things in haiku. The "lamp" in the next *ku*, as was the case with the previous one by Sekijo, is a Japanese lamp, not half so bright as our kerosene or whale-oil fueled devices with screen about the wick and glass around that.

15 # 38~ 40

挑灯のてれんも見えぬさくら哉　巣桃
chôchin no teren mo mienu sakura kana　sûtô (?)
(lantern's tricks-too see-not cherry!/?/'tis)

> blooming cherry:
> the lamp with all its tricks
> cannot show you!

The *teren* is literally a handle, but figuratively a trick (handle→ manipulation→ trick?). The grammar is tricky, too, and I can only hope my guess (a cherry tree too large to fully illuminate) is correct!

木の股の哀なりけり夜のはな　乙二
kinomata no aware narikeri yoru no hana　otsuji (1755-1823)
([people born of]tree-crotch/es pitiful/plaintive are/become[+finality] night-blossom)

how pitiful the cherry tree crotches! night blossoms	night blossoms pity those born of a tree crotch

Cherry tree limbs are not especially beautiful, so the *ku* makes literal sense, but the primary meaning is figurative: to "be born of a tree-crotch" is to be *born without human feelings*, i.e., lacking a poetic sensibility. Such men would be bored with real night blossoms (as opposed to the pleasure quarters).

夜櫻や三味線引て人通り　蓼太
yozakura ya shamisen hiite hito tôri　ryôta (1707-87)
(night-cherry: shamisen-playing person/people pass)

night blossoms someone walks by playing on a shamisen	people playing shamisens stroll by night blossoms

A minstrel, or someone returning from an earlier party? Regardless, there is something strangely apt about this *ku*. The shamisen is a banjo-like instrument whose funky sound fits the cherry bash.

夜櫻に梟を追ふ礫哉　是岩　花櫻帖
yozakura ni fukurô o ôu tsubute kana　zegan ()
(night-cherry-in/at owl chase [thrown] rock!/?/'tis)

> night cherries
> an owl is routed
> with a stone

This off-the-wall *ku* was as unexpected to me as that stone must have been to the owl!

寝る隙の今更おしやちる桜　一茶
neru hima no ima sara oshi ya chiru sakura　issa -1827
(sleep time-off's now-doubly regretted! falling cherry[blossoms])

now most of all i regret having to sleep: the petals fall!	now more than ever who can afford to sleep the petals fall	doubly sorry for time lost sleeping as petals fall

By the time the petals begin falling in earnest, the poet, who has been there from the start, is exhausted from drink, song and blossom-glare. But, this is it: *the last act.* It won't do to crash quite yet!

寝惜みの二人出合ひぬ花に月　梅室
ne-oshimi no futari deainu hana ni tsuki baishitsu 1763-1852
(sleep-regretting-twosome meet blossom-to/with moon)

two who make
us hate to sleep meet up:
bloom & moon

This *ku* by Issa's long-lived contemporary has a light *haikai* flavor. You either love it or you hate it. I love it. The original has no clear "make us" in it. The facetious anthropomorphism is subtler.

moonlight	the moonlight	the blossoms
is fluttering about	flutters down in flakes	are falling as flakes
the cherry	cherry blossoms	of moonlight

I paraversed the above from Toshimi Horiuchi's *"cherry blossoms / falling with flakes / of moonlight"* (*Japan Times:* "Where there is yin there is yang" 6/20/1997), for it catches the magic of blossom-viewing in the moonlight beautifully. His essay included the words "fluttering down in flakes."

花に来て花にいねふる暇哉　蕪村
hana ni kite hana ni ineburu itoma kana buson (-1783)
(blossoms-to-come blossoms-with/to sleep leave-taking/leisure!/?/'tis)

i came for
the blossoms and found
time to sleep

quality time		***the poor servant***
coming to		coming to blossoms
the bloom i slept with		i take my leave sleeping
the bloom		beneath them

respite is mine!
i came to the blossoms and
slept with them

I came to the cherry-blossoms; / I slept beneath them; / this was my leisure.　trans. Blyth

The commentary in *Buson Zenshû*: "He came to the blossom-viewing, got intoxicated on the blossoms, and not viewing the blossoms, mostly dozed. Not sedulously gazing upon blossoms, how precious this quiet leisure!" Is the commentator one of the many Japanese who become drowsy when they drink? I, who find alcohol stimulating, view intoxication in a different light. Blyth goes deeper: "When we see that cherry-blossoms are something to sleep under, we have obtained a state beyond that of the average artist or poet" (*Haiku* vol 2 Spring). I like to read *itoma* as "taking leave" from a job or from this world. Has Buson just realized that blossom-viewing, *like New Year's Day,* was also ideal for sleeping? Or is blossom-viewing a type of work for a poet-painter like Buson, so that taking a nap *is* taking a break? Or, is he just confessing/boasting about the shamefully unemployed nature of an artist's life? While unsure of the reading, I feel a subtle humor in *itoma* (leave-taking/leisure).

night

寝て起て大欠して桜哉　一茶

nete-okite ôakubi shite sakura kana   issa -1827
(sleep-waking big-yawn-make cherry/ies!/?/'tis)

i sleep, i wake and, after a big yawn, the blossoms!	sleeping, i wake and yawning look up at the blossoms

i sleep i wake
i take a huge yawn
they've bloomed!

sleeping, waking yawning up a storm it's cherry time	i sleep, wake, yawn wide: petals in my mouth!

At first, I thought Issa's *ku* was a cross of Yayû's well-known New Year's haiku, *"I eat, sleep / wake up, look around and / it's new year's!"* (喰ふて寝て起て見たれば初日哉　也有 *kûte-nete okite-mitareba hatsubi kana*) and a *senryû* where snores replace the eating. That would make my first interpretation most likely. The last line, *the blossoms,* might be expanded to "and, I'm off for the blossoms!" The New Year was generally prepared for. It didn't just happen. Blossoms happen, but Spring is known for the sandman, so waking isn't easy. But the *ku* can also be read as a description of blossom-viewing days, for the most immediate precedent is *"Sleeping, waking / taking a big yawn / the cat's loves,"* " . . . a cat in love," " . . . my swiving tom,"etc. (寝て起て大欠して猫の恋　一茶 *nete-okite ôakubi shite neko no koi*) Yes, it is also by Issa and was written a year earlier about his cat in heat, or in a rut, if you prefer for describing the male. Only the last five syllabets differ.

花を踏みし草履も見えて朝寝かな 蕪村

hana o fumishi zôri mo miete asane kana   buson (-1783)
(blossom-treaded [fine]straw-sandals-even seeing, morning-sleep!/?)

i visited a friend

he sleeps late there are the sandals that trod on petals	i see sandals that tread upon petals sleeping in?

There are some long prefaces to the original which I abbreviated into a title. The sandals, *zori*, are good, tightly woven straw-sandals (not the wear-a-day, throw-away macramé *waraji*). Sleeping-in was a *fûryû* (hip, cool) thing to do, so the poem has a *bona fide* greeting element,[1] explains a Japanese annotator. That is to say Buson wrote it partly *for* his sleeping friend.

ちる花のわらじながらに一寝哉　一茶

chiru hana no waraji nagara ni hitone kana   issa (-1827)
(falling blossoms/petals' [crude]straw-sandals-while one-sleep!/?/'tis)

he dozes while petals fall with sandals still on his feet	i wake up petals falling, still wearing my *waraji*

nothing like
a nap wearing sandals
as petals fall

1. Sleeping In as Hip According to the 16c Jesuits, who had to adjust to being visited in the wee hours of the night by Japanese nobles wishing to discuss theology, the typical Japanese *hidalgo* (gentlemen) was a night-owl (see *Topsy-Turvy 1585*). In Japan as elsewhere the *fûryu* (cool) was and is copied from both the lower and the upper class and this would be an example of the latter. But note that essayists in matters of taste in the West also tended to sleep in. No Japanese that I know of has penned a defense of sleeping late that can match Lamb, who claimed "we choose to linger abed, and digest our dreams." (*The Last Essays of Elia*)

As parenthetically explained already, *waraji* are cheap, rough throw-away sandals. Adding the explanatory "straw" to "sandals" would hurt the translation – who would describe a cowboy's boots as "*leather*"! – but, it is important the reader can visualize what is what. This *ku* is a good picture of Issa's last spring before he inherited his own home (half-a-house, anyway). The "wake up" in the second reading takes account of the fact one cannot write a first-person poem about napping until one wakes up, but, on deeper thought, I felt it necessary to find a way to *stress* the nap, as *kana* does. Hence, the overly aphoristic third reading. Years later, Issa wrote: *"A small mat / a blossom-spent man / zonked out"* or: *"Small mats / blossom-spent men / zonked out."* (小むしろや花くたびれがどた／＼寝 一茶 *samushiro ya hanakutabire ga dotadota-ne*). Still later, he brought back those sandals:

花踏んだわらぢながらにどた／＼寝 一茶
hana funda waraji nagara ya dotadota-ne   issa (-1827)
    (cherry-trod *waraji*-while: collapsed/exhausted-sleep)

cherry sleep

wearing *waraji*
that trod upon petals
zonked out!

The title was added in case "zonked out" is not a clear enough indication of the fact our poet is in the arms of Morpheus. I cannot find a good English word for the "collapsed-sleep" (*dotadota-ne*). "Sleeping like a log" is too long, and "drunken slumber" too specific and not entirely right.

明の花しらぬ人には語られず 俳布 花七日
ake no hana shiranu hito ni wa katararezu daifu? 1777
    (dawn-blossoms know-not person-to-as-for tell-can-not)

you either know   the beauty
or don't know about   of dawn blossoms
dawn blossoms   cannot be told

Stylistically, the poem is like *"This longing / I can share with no one: / night blossoms"* (此思ひ誰に語らん夜の花　兎丈 *kono omoi dare ni kataran yoru no hana tojô*). Personally, I do not care for the "impossible to express" approach and prefer poets to hazard a metaphor. In either case, we do not know if the *ku* is straight or an allegory for loving a harlot. There are many such ambiguous *ku*: *"A moon night / the blossoms will remember! / I stayed over"* or, *"Staying over / A full moon the blossoms / will remember!"* (長居して花に名残の月夜哉　諷竹 淡ちしま *nagai-shite hana ni nanokori no tsukiyo kana* fûchiku (1698)). Maybe I am dirty-minded – *In Japan, I have a copy of all the poetry of Wilmot Rochester, unexpurgated!* – but I cannot help thinking about the homophone of moon (*tsuki*) meaning *poke* or *thrust*. Not knowing if the poet was young or tended to write risqué poems, or, to the contrary, never did, making a call on such a *ku* is impossible.

月も出て見るか見せるか夜の花　許一 四季発句塾
tsuki mo dete miru ka miseru ka yoru no hana　kyôichi ()
(moon-too/even comes-out see? show? night-blossom/s)

night-blossoms

the moon, too
comes out the better to see
or to be seen

night blossoms　　　　　　　　　　　　the moon, too:
moon's out, too, showing　　　　　　　a night to view blossoms
or showing off?　　　　　　　　　　　and be viewed

the moon's out
would they view or be viewed?
night blossoms

On a fabulous level, the moon either views the blossoms or shows off to them (or, the vice versa). But, the real subject might be women of the night as per the last reading. See *Book III* for that.

夜桜や人静まりて雨の音　子規
yozakura ya hitoshizumarite ame no oto　shiki 1894
(night-cherry: people quiet-down, rain's sound)

night blossoms　　　　　　　　　　　night cherries
when people quiet down　　　　　　　the sound of rain comes
the sound of rain　　　　　　　　　　with our silence

The rain may already have been falling unheard over the revelry. Good, but a bit too obvious a *ku*.

寝心に花を算へる雨夜哉　一茶
negokoro ni hana o kazoeru amayo kana　issa
(sleep-heart-for blossoms count rain-night!/?'tis)

a rainy night　　　　　　　　　　　　a rainy night
i drowsily count　　　　　　　　　　　i count blossoms
the blossoms　　　　　　　　　　　　to fall asleep

This *ku* has a strange attraction. Perhaps the soft sound of the rain-drops goes with the counting. Issa is probably counting the blossoms on a branch in his room rather than sleeping out.

桜花どつちへ寝ても手（の）とゝく 一茶
sakurabana dotchi e nete mo te no todoku　issa -1827
(cherry-blossoms whichever[way] sleep-even hands reach)

cherry blossoms　　　　　　　　　　　cherry blossoms
whichever way i sleep　　　　　　　　wherever we sleep
touching petals　　　　　　　　　　　within reach

"Whichever" is so long that it doesn't allow the "hands" to fit in. If the same *ku* were in a collection of *senryû*, it could describe a man sleeping with a bevy of beauties.

寝て見れと魂は寝入ぬ櫻哉　松水 反故集
nete-miredo tama wa ne-irinu sakura kana　shôsui (17-18c)
(sleeping-tried-but soul-as-for sleep-enter cherry[blossoms]!)

     i tried to sleep　　　　　　　　　　　　i tried to sleep
but my soul stayed up　　　　　　　　　but my soul kept racing:
   with the blossoms　　　　　　　　　　　cherry blossoms

i tried to sleep
but my soul wasn't in it:
cherry blossoms

My second translation, though the metaphor might be a bit off, has managed to keep pretty much the same ambiguity as that found in the original. The poet could be trying to sleep the night before the blossom-viewing, in the bloomshade during the day, or sleeping over.

魂は花に宿かる昼寝哉　如湖 蘆分船
tamashii wa hana ni yadokaru hirune kana　joko -1694
(soul-as-for, blossom-under/at noon-nap!/?/'tis)

    my soul lodges　　　　　　　　　　　　 taking a nap
with the cherry blossoms　　　　　　　while my muse hangs out
     while i nap　　　　　　　　　　　　　 in the blossoms

The Japanese concept of soul is complex and, unlike the case in the Judeo-Christian-Muslim world, no one really cares to define it. One sometimes reads of plural souls, where the soul that sleeps and the waking one are not the same. Poets take advantage of the unsettled concept to play with the soul as they please. Here, the soul would seem to be the one synonymous with the Occidental "heart;" and the poet does not think its absence will hurt his ability to sleep. But who needs people and their souls? The following *ku* about East Hiei-san, which is to say Ueno park in Edo (and still Tokyo's best blossom-viewing park today) is a panoramic expansion of the soul and definitely *should* be famous:

東叡山・人去て櫻群集の月夜哉 蓼太
hito sarite sakura gunshû no tsukiyo kana　ryôta 1707-87
(east hie-mountain: people left / cherries-mass/ing moon-night!/?/'tis)

East Mount Hiei

  the people gone　　　　　　　　　　　　the humans gone
this full moon is enjoyed　　　　　　a crowd of cherry trees
   by the cherries　　　　　　　　　　　in the moonlight

This next one probably should *not*, but it is a good end to our night:

明星の花眼ばゆしと消にけり 素丸
myôjô no hana mabayushi to kienikeri　somaru 1712-95
(venus's blossoms glaring and/because vanish[+emph])

i see her rise:
the blossoms are so bright
venus vanishes

16
The Blossom Zoo
花の動物園
hana-no-dôbutsu-en

花に寝ていかなることを鳥の夢　露川
hana ni nete ikanaru koto o tori no yume rosen (1660-1743)
(blossoms-in sleep what thing bird's dream?)

sleeping upon
blossoms what do birds
dream about?

Saijiki (haiku almanac) sub-themes by convention, start with the *heavens*, fall to *earthly phenomena*, then down to man (including rituals, life (largely food)), mammals, birds and, lastly, frogs, fish and the lowly bug. The animal order pretty much follows a chain-of-being scheme. Horses having babies or deer losing their horns come before cats in heat, though this feline phenomenon comes a month or two earlier. The cherries, as plants, come later, and I imagine that any animals found within those blossom *ku* should be listed in the same (prejudicial?) order. But I could not help putting Rosen's lyrical *ku* at the head of the chapter! What do birds dream about when they are *not* sleeping on blossoms?

人音や熊ののたりにちる櫻　轍車　小弓
hito-oto ya kuma no notari ni chiru sakura tetsusha (1699)
(people-sound!/?/:/& bear's/s' shuffle/scavenge-with/as/by scatter cherry[petals])

the sound of men　　　　　　　　　　　　　men coming!
as a bear shufffles off　　　　　　　cherry petals fly as
some petals fall　　　　　　　　　　　　　bears leave

cherry petals
falling to the sound of men
and bears moving

"Human sound" (*hito-oto*) can mean that raised by the presence of men or signify their arrival in a quiet place. *Notari* means scavenge, undulating movement, crawling-about. The *ni* leaves ambiguity.

籠かくや老馬の昔花の山　敬英　太夫櫻　再現
kago kaku ya rouma no mukashi hana no yama keiei (1680)
(basket/luggage-carrier: old horse's past blossom-mountain)

a pack-horse
long ago he raced up
cherry-mountain

How does a demoted old horse feel about such things, especially when he sees younger horses doing what he used to do?

大馬に尻こすらるゝ桜哉　一茶　文政三
ôuma ni [no] shiri kosuraruru [hikkosuru] sakura [no-ume]kana   issa -1827
(large horse-by['s] buttock-rubbed [rubs] cherry[plum]=tree=blossoms!/?/'tis)

cherry blossoms	a blooming cherry	the cherry tree
serving the big horse:	rubbed by the rump	and a large horse
a butt-scratch	of a big horse	rub rumps

All translations and readings I have seen of this *ku* put the rump on the horse alone. It makes sense for Issa has some marvelous horse rump *ku*. Offhand, I can recall young birds (sparrows?) using it as a base to practice flying and it becoming a prime target for a bucket of water in the heat of the summer. But, grammatically speaking, the rump *could be* the lower side of a large branch, too. This *ku* is almost identical to one where the big horse actively rubs his rump on a wild plum (in brackets above). If you ask me, both are pretty worthless *ku*. Issa wrote a *far* better one a decade earlier: *"The plum tree / pony rubs his neck on / is blooming"* (馬の子の襟する梅の咲にけり　文化四 *uma no ko no eri suru ume no sakinikeri*), or (*ni-keri* has many nuances) *"has bloomed! or "finally blooms!"* Why is it better? Because we feel Issa and the pony were both very familiar with that tree.

櫻咲頃鳥足二本馬四本　鬼貫
sakura saku koro tori ashi nihon uma shihon   onitsura (1660-1738)
(cherries blossom time birds legs two horses four)

discovery

again the cherry-buds
are bursting through:
horses have four legs!
birds have only two!

(stewart trans. ↑ *my decap/reparse/centering*)

while the cherries bloom
birds have two legs
horses four

Onitsura's *ku* is not really *about* the birds and beasts, but is by far the best known cherry blossom *ku* with them in it. As Blyth points out, it can be read to mean either that all else is prosaic when the cherries bloom, or that the sensational blossoms stimulate the mind's eye to see even ordinary things as remarkable, "full of their justness." Since Onitsura also wrote a *ku* captioned ***filial piety*** which goes: *"Eyes horizontal / nose vertical / spring blossoms,"* (孝行/ 目は横に鼻は堅なり春の花　鬼貫 *me wa yoko ni hana wa tate nari haru no hana*), Blyth guesses Onitsura meant the verse to be taken in the latter way. So, too, Stewart, who translates ***"An Ordinary Face** // Nose vertical, with horizontal eyes / On either side: yet spring flowers still surprise."* The blooming is only natural and that, like the ***"Discovery"*** of 4 & 2, is really something. All I can add to the discussion is that Chinese nursery rhymes mention the number of legs (eyes, tail, horns, etc.) on animals and Twain once reported *a four-legged cat* to his daughter. I suspect Onitsura may well be playing off something rather than writing from scratch. *But, what?* Could it be the same blossoms blooming every year need the same animals?

牛の背の花はき下る親子哉　一茶
ushi no se no hana haki-oriru oyako kana issa (-1827)
(ox's/cow's back's blossoms/petals sweep/swept-down parent-child!/?/'tis)

   sweeping petals   parent and child
   off the back of an ox   sweeping petals off
   parent and child   an ox's back

However you imagine it, this *ku* is doubly touching. Parents and children working together are always touching. So is the back of an animal, most animals, anyway, from the frog up to us.

道ばたの牛を飛する花見哉　蝶羽(-1741)   琴を嗅ぐ平家の牛や山ざくら　渭北 三河小町
michibata no ushi o tobasuru hanami kana chôu   *koto o kagu hiraya no ushi ya yamazakura* ihoku 1702
(roadside's ox/cow[obj] fly-make blossom-viewing!/?)   (zither[obj] smell/sniff hovel's ox/cow:/! mountain cherry)

   blossom-viewing   a working ox
   how the cows by the road   comes to sniff the zither
   do take to flight   mountain cherries

It is bovine nature to come over to check out anything odd not checking them out, in which case they flee instead. The above *ku* treat the timid and curious side of the cow, respectively. The ox in the original is a *flat-house* (hovel) ox. Not pulling the fancy carts of nobles, it is unfamiliar with zithers.

花の陰我は狐に化されし　一茶
hana no kage ware wa kitsune ni bakasareshi issa
(blossom-shade i-as-for, fox-to bewitched/changed-was)

   under the bloom   in the bloomshade
   the man who was me   i was, and by a fox
   turned into a fox   i was bewitched

花の世に穴ほしげなる狐哉　一茶
hana no yo ni ana hoshige naru kitsune kana issa
(blossom-world-in hole-want-become fox!/?'tis)

   in this world   i am a fox!
   of blossoms, remus   among blossoms, i come to
   seeks a hole   want a den

Both foxes and cherry blossoms bewitch us. Issa knew that (and how to look under his arm at someone who passed to tell if they were a fox or not) and he knew what it was to be without a den. At the time he wrote the first *ku* he had no home of his own and was burnt out of his rented shack on the outskirts of Edo. Though fox-possession did not necessarily turn one into a fox as per my second reading, Issa was one. He was a hungry fox spying on well-fed dogs. He knew but could not share the lives of his wealthy patrons. The second *ku* is later and may be an expression of sympathy for a fox disturbed by cherry-hunting or an old man's desire to curl up and die alone. Issa reminds me of Loren Eiseley, who, likewise, shivered through his life and felt for foxes (Read *Night Country*). Possession was usually related to emotion: *"After the spat / we split from the blossoms / two foxes"* 異見して花に別るゝ狐かな　支考 *ikken shite hana ni wakururu kitsune kana* shikô -1731). *Senryû*, however, generally describe men pretending they were possessed coming home from philandering.

池を呑犬に入あひ花の影　其角
ike o nomu inu ni iriai hananokage kikaku 1660-1707
(pond drinking dog-to vespers/mix the blossoms' shadow/reflection)

a dog drinks
from a pond reflecting
vesper bloom

This was "by the side of a pond at eidai[nagayo?] temple." The *ku* is a bit crowded. Dog, blossom reflection, sunset, ripples from lapping water spreading out with the boom of the bell.

来た犬の主得皃なりはなの下　嘯山　葎亭集
kita inu no nushi-e-gao nari hana no shita shôzan? 1717-1801
(came dog's master/owner gained/have/content[?]-face is blossoms-under)

a dog that came　　　　　　　　　　　a visiting dog
looks like he found a master　　　　delighted to find a master
beneath the blossoms　　　　　　　　in the bloomshade

in the bloomshade
an i-found-a-master face
on that stray dog

The "master-gained-face(=expression)" does not English well; nor, does a pun not worth explaining. What is good is the image of the dog we see moving from tree to tree before lucking out.

人音や犬の咎る山桜　沾峨　吐屑庵
hito oto ya inu no togameru yamazakura senga 1776
(person/people sound and/: dog's chastizing mountain cherry)

dogs barking　　　　　　　　　　　the sound of men
at the sound of people　　　　　and disapproving dogs
mountain cherry　　　　　　　　　mountain cherry

花見にも立たせぬ里の犬の聲　去来　　　　炭焼の犬人馴れつ櫻山　梅雨　反故集
hanami ni mo tatasenu sato no inu no koe kyorai -1704　　*sumiyaki no inu hito naretsu sakura yama* baiu 1783
(bloss.-viewing even excite-not home/country dog-voice)　　(charcoal-roaster's dog people used to cherry mountain)

blossom-viewing　　　　　　　　　　cherry mountain
their voices sound unchanged　　　the charcoal maker's dog
our local dogs　　　　　　　　　　　is used to men

The first *ku* is a cinch. The second is tough because *sato* means either a country town or one's hometown though it only be a string of houses on a roadway or scattered farmhouses. And, worst yet, the verb is ambiguous (depending whether it applies to the dogs or their voices) and I can only cross my fingers as to whether my reading matches Kyorai's intent. With respect to the third *ku,* the most common tree burnt for charcoal was cherry, so the dog would meet blossom-viewers year after year.

狗が供して参る桜かな　一茶
inukoro ga tomo shite mairu sakura kana issa
↓ (dog companion does visit[respectful verb] cherry!/'tis) ↓

open temple day

      a dog as escort   a dog escorts me
this pilgrim's progress   on the final stretch:
         to the *sakura*   cherry blossoms!

The *ku* seems to turn a trip to see the blossoms into a religious affair, but a preface notes that Issa is visiting a temple which had opened up its treasures to the public eye. As discussed elsewhere, the cherries usually bloomed at that time. I think David G. Lanoue's translation is perfect: *"The dog is escort / on the pilgrimage . . . – / cherry blossoms!"* I bury it in this paragraph only because dots and hyphens do not center well. I do not know if Issa had a dog at this date. My second reading assumes he does *not*, but a *ku* several years later suggests he *did*:

花に出て犬のきげんもとりけらし 一茶
hana ni dete inu no kigen mo torikerashi　issa (-1827)
(blossoms-at/to go/appear/ing, dog's mood/feelings too recover-fix/neaten

~~off to the bloom~~   at the blossoms
~~me and my dog putting on~~   even old dog tray
~~our best behavior~~   calms down

My first reading was guess-translated before I found out that *torikeru* (*torikerashi*) is a dialect equivalent of *torikatazukeru,* which means that *one's wild or upset elements fall under control.* "Is calmed down (by the blossoms)" might be more precise, but it doesn't read well. If Keigu wrote the *ku* it would be: *Blossom-viewing / after a while, Tray's hair / also lies down.*

.うしろから犬のあやしむ桜哉　一茶
ushiro kara inu no ayashimu sakura kana　issa -1827
(behind-from dog's [behaving] wary/suspicious cherry!/?/'tis)

   looking out from   my dog looks out   walking behind
behind the cherry tree   cautiously from behind me   the dog looks warily at
   a suspicious dog   cherry blossoms   the cherry tree

Our "wary" lacks a verb form like *ayashimu*. "Suspicious" has one, but "suspect" is not the active state of suspicion, is it? That, and no indication of *what* the dog is behind, challenge the translation.

犬どもやはねくり返す花吹雪 一茶
inudomo ya hanekurikaesu hanafubuki　issa -1827
(dog-sire: blossom spring/jump-repeat blossom/petal-blizzard)

     master dog   a petal blizzard
jumps and jumps again   our dogs are literally
  a petal-blizzard   flipping out

When a strong wind whips through the woods, mammals are simultaneously delighted at the novelty and jumpy. Terribly jumpy. They dash about and jump for joy, then suddenly start and cower. They have every right to be so hyped up. This is the time for windfalls (my cats went out baby-bird collecting), but falling limbs are second only to poisonous snakes as the cause of death for primitive humans and, I would guess, all animals who, like the proverbial bear, pee in the woods. Branches blowing in the wind also injure eyes. A dog experiencing its first cherry petal blizzard would be a sight!

おどされた犬のまねして花見哉　一茶
odosareta inu no mane shite hanami kana issa 1825
(scared/threatened dog's copy-doing blossom-viewing!/?)

      i imitate　　　　　　　　　　　　my hackles up
  a threatened dog　　　　　　　　like a cur in a corner
   blossom-viewing　　　　　　　　　blossom-viewing

This is one strange *ku*! Issa wrote it (and the next) only two years before his death. Are the blossoms giving him the heebie-jeebies? Is he bepissing himself? Is he growling to guard his bloomshade?

ぢゝ犬におどされて散る花見哉　一茶
jiji-inu ni odosarete chiru hanami kana issa 1825
(gramps/geezer-dog-by frightened fall/scatter blossom-viewing!/?/'tis)

   the petals fall　　　　　　　　　blossom-viewing
 scared by an old-dog　　　　　men fly like petals from
  blossom-viewing　　　　　　　　　a geezer dog

There may have been an old dog? But I am afraid that the second reading makes the most sense. Issa had health problems, had scared off his second wife a year or two before and was in a hard way.

酒のめと犬をあなとる花見哉　米仲　雪月花
sake nome to inu o anadoru hanami kana beichû 1736
(*sake*, drink! and[saying] dog[obj] despise blossom-viewing!/?/'tis)

   drink that *sake*!　　　　　　　　*drink up, rover!*
dogs treated with contempt　　blossom-viewing with one
   blossom-viewing　　　　　　　　　who bullies dogs

Anadoru means "despise;" the behavior described (*teasing* or bullying) would be a symptom of it. Are there men who think that the ability to drink makes us superior to other animals?

裏に猫表に犬や夕ざくら　虚吼　ホトトギス
ura ni neko omote ni inu ya yûzakura kyokô -1935
(behind-at cat front-at dog!/? evening-cherry)

    our cat in back
 and our dog in front
    dusk blossoms

髭のあるめをとめづらし花心　其角　五元
hige no aru meoto mezurashi hanagokoro kikaku -1707
(whiskers-having wife-husband [mates] rare blossom-heart)

cats or catamites?

  how rare to find
 a whiskered couple
  on mount cherry

I think Kikaku refers to cats, not catamites, but do not know enough about him to say. Blyth, not citing Kikaku's verse, elsewhere introduces 1734 and 1775 versions of a *senryû*, respectively: *"Both of them / with whiskers, – / cat spouses"* (*ryôhô ni hige ga aru nari neko no tsuma*) and *"~ cats in love"* (*~neko-no koi*). The first is closer to Kikaku's original. And I'd guess the *hana* (blossom/s) is cherry because cats generally do their blooming with the plum and here they are called "rare." Otherwise, this would be the only *ku* I know about gay men (as opposed to the usual combination of man and boy).

花に日のさして蝶噛む猫の声　百池
hana ni hi no sashite cho kamu neko no koe　hyakuchi 1757-1835
(blossom-on sun shines, butterfly chews/bites cat's voice)

<table>
<tr><td>

sun-lit blossoms,
the call of a cat chewing
up a butterfly

</td><td>

a cat mewing
sun on blossoms, butterfly
in her mouth

</td></tr>
</table>

When cats do appear with the cherry blossoms, it is usually with the butterfly. Cats make muffled sounds of contentment while chewing or call for others (feline or human) to come and see their catch. This would probably be the former sound and the scene is a quiet garden.

世のうさぎどちへやら走る花の波 不存 名越清水孫三郎
yo no usagi dochi e yara hashiru hana no nami　fuson 1651
(night's rabbits/hares where to? run/ning blossoms' wave)

all of the hares
whither do they go?
waves of petal!

This is probably not about the real thing, though crowds of men would scare hares. White crests and foam were generally called *nami-no-hana* (wave-blossoms) and, viewed at night, gained the livelier name of *moon-rabbits/hares*. It is hard to settle on a meaning, for "rabbit/hare" idioms abound: *gamblers*, something that abounded in cherry time, *half-wits* (we have that: *hare-brains*) and my favorite, *someone who sleeps-in and is late for something* (Aesop was translated in the early 17c), in which case, the poet up early enough to walk leisurely to the bloom, observes late-risers rushing about like idiots trying to catch the waves of blossoms. An easier *ku* from the same anthology: *"Shall we say / Mountains turn into the sea? / Waves of bloom!* (山も海に成と申さん花の波　正行 嵐山集 1651 *yama mo umi ni naru to môsan hana no nami*　masayuki (kzs)). *Mountains into sea?* In Japanese, that's akin to saying the magnificent bloom is as good as the end of the world. *See sakura and die?*

弥生山さくらに眠れ白兎　左江
yayoi yama sakura ni nemure shirousagi　sakô ()
(yayoi=third-month-mountain cherry-by sleep[imper], white rabbit

<table>
<tr><td>

the third month

white rabbit, sleep
below the blooming cherry
high in the hills!

</td><td>

mountain cherry

spring grows late
so, sleep, my white hare
below the bloom

</td></tr>
</table>

The Sinosphere months are terribly prosaic with their numerical "one-month," "two-month" names (our September-December, etc are saved by being in a foreign language, Latin). Luckily, the poets had other names to use. Rather than "*sangatsu*" (third-month), this *ku* uses the beautiful *yayoi* (the philology is uncertain, but what euphony!) which combines with mountain to mean those of late spring. The *ku* may play on a *waka* where the departing spring leaves the morning moon as a memento for such a *yayoi* mountain, as the rabbit/hare is identified with the moon (look at the moon and you can see the rabbit in it). If hare = white petals that fall to roots=ne=sleep, then there may be a wish for gentle weather.

花に寝ぬ春の鳥の心よ・花に寝ぬこれもたぐひか鼠の巣 はせを
hana ni nenu kore mo tagui ka nezumi no su　bashô (1544-94)
(blossoms-by sleep-not you/this[?],too, [same]type/ilk? mouse-nest)

to a nest of mice

so you, too,
are of the ilk that blossoms
keep awake?

A wife of the fickle Prince Genji compared him to a bird that can't settle on one cherry tree. Does Bashô borrow that allusion to explain the noise in the rafters of his lodge? More generally (and certain) Bashô expresses the ideas first expressed in ancient *waka*, that blossoms gave men cause for worry (for the classic expression: *shizugokoro naki* #46-2). Blyth handles the mice differently from me: *"Is it not like a mouse's nest, – / This being unable to sleep / For the flowers?"* He explains "the poet is unable to sleep at night because of the excitement of the cherry-blossoms, and compares his heart ot a nest of the mice who are squeaking and scuffing all night long." (*Haiku*: Spring). Since Bashô liked Saigyô, who once described *his* heart as a crying baby, Blyth may well be right (and my reading wrong). *Note:* the ambiguity is the result of the word *kore*. Literally "this," it can be first or second person! If Bashô is not alone, following Blyth's reading, I might compromise and put it like this: *"Unable to sleep / for the flowers, call us / a nest of mice!"* Regardless, the *ku* reflects well on Bashô. Instead of cussing, he turns noise into a sympathetic haiku.

物いはぬ花の機嫌やとりの声 政宣 崑山集
mono iwanu hana no kigen ya tori no koe　masanori 1651
(thing say-not blossoms' feeling/mood!/?/: bird's/rooster's voice/s/crow/s)

it's the spirit	catch the mood	the cock crows
of the voiceless bloom!	of the voiceless bloom:	that's how the voiceless
but hear the birds	the sound of birds	blossoms feel

Since the *tori* is written in phonetic syllabary, we cannot tell whether it refers to birds in general or a rooster. I wish "voices of the birds" worked in English. I resorted to "cock's crow," "hear the birds" and "sound of birds" because it does not, I think that the meaning probably is the cries, chittering, warbling, and singing of the birds, i.e. their various "voices."

花の木に鶏寝るや浅草寺　一茶
hana no ki ni niwatori neru ya asakusaji　issa -1827
(blossom-tree-in, chickens sleep!/?/: asakusa temple)

asakusa-temple:	roosters doze
do chickens sleep upon	upon the cherry trees
the blooming trees?	asakusa-temple

16 # 30 ~ 32

The roosters at Asakusa are known for their long – the longest in the world – tails. But, Issa doesn't write *ondori* or "rooster," but *niwatori* or "chickens." I visualize roosters, but the lower status of hens would give this more journalistic *ku* a bit of the incongruous and with it a *haikai* touch.

花さくや目を縫れたる鳥の鳴　一茶
hana saku ya me wo nuwaretaru tori no naku issa
(blossoms bloom:/! eyes[obj] sewn bird/s cries/cry/singing)

cherry blossoms
chickens with eyes stitched shut
are clucking

trans. lanoue

♪♪♪♪♪

cherries bloom:
a bird with sewn-up eyes
sings and sings

David G. Lanoue writes: "Jean Cholley notes that in the poultry market in the Muromachi district of Edo (today's Tokyo), the eyes of the doomed birds were sewn shut to keep them immobile while being fattened in their cages (Cholley, Jean. En village de miséreux: Choix de poèmes de Kobayashi Issa. Paris: Gallimard, 1996.) in his *Simply Haiku* article *Master Bashô, Master Buson ... and Then There's Issa* (Autumn 2005) (When centering I removed the hyphen after "blossoms."). Checking Issa's *Journal,* (publ. Shinano Mainichi Shinbun), I see an editor's note to the effect that the eyes were sewn shut on birds *used as decoys*. My reading is based on yet another assumption. I refer to the cruel practice of sewing a bird's eyes shut to make it stay put and sing more. So, we have *three* stories, all equally pitiful. This concludes our cherry birds. Note that not *one* nightingale/warbler (*uguisu*) – the bird most associated with blossoms – is in it. This bird is so strongly identified with the plum (*ume*) that to put it with a "blossom" (*hana*) alone would make that blossom a plum rather than a cherry,[1] so when it does go with cherry, the blossom is either specified as cherry or it is coupled with other sub-themes.

庭鳥の毛衣ふるへちりさくら　巴人
niwatori no kegoromo furue chirizakura hajin 1672-1742
(chicken's/s' fur-coat shake/ing! scattering-cherry(petals))

borrowed finery

chicken, shake
your pretty coat! hoh,
cherry petals!

An expert (Maruyama) believes that the use of "fur-coat" (*ke-goromo*) – not usually applied to chickens – here, suggests the poet is pulling the tail of elegant old *waka* where it refers to the beautiful coat of mandrake ducks. I expanded that into my title. The original is not so imperative as my reading.

憂きは只鳥をうらやむ花なれや　宗祇
uki wa tada tori o urayamu hana nare ya sôgi (-1502)
(sadness-as-for, only bird[+obj] envy, blossoms be!)

my gloom is only
because i envy the birds
these blossoms

trans. Steven D. Carter

1. Warblers in Plums vs Cherries. The *uguisu*, or bush warbler, not only begins to sing when the plum blooms, but skits about feeding from and knocking off blossoms (more from its wings than its tiny beak); and this is a delight to watch. Though this bird may still be around when the cherry blossoms, the song is no longer fresh – the gurgling, sucking-up part at the start disappears – and mixed in with other bird calls. Moreover, it cannot be visually enjoyed as much as with plum for the thicker limbs and profusion of the cherry's bloom hides it.

I chopped "my gloom" out from a linked-verse session, *Three poets at Yuyama* (cited by Higginson: *The Haiku Seasons* (1996)). The translation beautifully preserves the ambiguous yet understandable original.

鳥の音も花の底なる深山哉 宗祇 老葉
tori no ne mo hana no soko naru miyama kana   sôgi (-1502)
(birds' sound, too, blossoms' bottom becomes/are deep-mountain!/?/'tis)

deep in the hills
the sound of birds is part
of the last bloom

in the mountains
bird-song gives depth
to the blossoms

In the original, the bird sound first seems to underly the blossoms but, on further reading, turns reasonable: there are more leaves and more birds out when the late-cherries bloom in the comparatively cool hills.

花を糞て同しくよこす諸鳥哉   一雪 洗濯物
hana o fun de onajiku yogosu sho tori kana   issetsu (1666)
(blossoms[obj] shit-with/by same/likewise dirty/spoil various birds!/?/'tis)

various birds
shit up the blossoms
all the same

Objectively speaking, the welcome *uguisu* (warbler/nightingale), the taken-for-granted sparrow and the disliked crow all do it. The various birds suggest to me that the blossoms are cherry rather than plum, which is associated almost entirely with *uguisu* shit; speaking of which, all bird shit was not alike, for only that of the *uguisu* was used for improving the complexion . . .

鳥と共に人間くゝる桜哉 一茶
tori to tomo ni ningen kuguru sakura kana   issa (-1827)
(birds-with together, people slip/snake/creep-through cherry/blossoms!/?/'tis)

like song-birds
men slip through the bloom
what cherries!

bloom so full
men like birds weaving
through them

joining the birds
people weave through
these blossoms!

Issa does not exaggerate. Walking through trees with thick low-hanging bloom, I have felt like the pilot of an open cockpit plane slipping in and out of clouds. English lacks a good translation for the verb *kuguru,* meaning snaking through a maze, going through a hoop, creeping under a hedge or navigating clouds and branches. Perhaps *weave* is closest.

一日の巣は人にあり花盛　淡々
ichi nichi no su wa hito ni ari hanazakari　tantan
(one day's nest/web-as-for people-to is: blossom-acme)

鳥の巣に作り込れし桜哉　一茶
torinosu ni tsukurikomareshi sakura kana　issa
(bird's nest-into make-over cherry!/?'tis)

    full bloom
   for a day, people
    have nests

    a cherry tree
  madeover like a
    bird's nest

Tantan (1673-1761) also wrote: *"Fledgling humans / head up the mountain paths! / the blooming cherries!"* (巣はなれの人は山路へ花桜　淡々アルス *subanare no hito wa yamaji e hanazakura*). "Fledgling" is "nest-separated" in Japanese, so the idea is the same as that for the above *ku*. It may play with a saying: *"Blossoms are [suit the] mountain, people the flatlands"* (花は山人は里). Has Issa reified Tantan's tree-as-nest, put a tree-fort *in* a cherry, or prepared space below one for sleeping out?

花咲きぬ小雀も藪をわすれ顔　武玉川八
hana sakinu suzume mo yabu o wasuregao　senryû 1755
(blossom/s bloom small-sparrow/s-too thicket[+obj] forgetful-face)

   the cherry blooms:
there's no trace of thicket
    on sparrow faces

   the cherry blooms
who would guess sparrows
    live in the bush!

Because this is a *senryû*, the sparrows may refer to country kids, but it may just be a cheerful take on the dime-a-dozen birds at a luxurious venue! About a hundred years later Issa sketches their activity:

ちる花をざぶ／\浴る雀哉　一茶
chiru hana o zabuzabu abiru suzume kana　issa -1827
(falling/scattering-blossoms splish-splash bathe sparrow!/?/'tis)

    sparrows
 bathing noisely in
  cherry petals

   splish-splashing
about in a petal deluge
   some sparrows

木兎の面はらしたる落花哉　一茶
mimizuku no tsura harashitaru rakka kana　issa
(owl's face relief-be/doing fall-blossom[petals]!/?/'tis)

  the owl's face
how it brightens up
 when petals fall

  fallen blossoms
the owl's countenance
  has cleared up

With petals flying about, the owl could not hear the field mice, I think. Could that be it?

烏だに夜明はうれし初櫻　保吉
karasu dani yoake wa ureshi hatsuzakura　hôkichi ( )
(crows even daybreak-as-for delighted first-cherry/ies)

  even the crows
sound delighted at dawn:
  first blossoms!

   first blossoms
i'm even happy to hear
   a raven at dawn

Have you noticed the difference between "bird" 鳥 and "crow" 烏? No eye can be seen on a crow's jet-black face!

うれしいか花に明けゆく烏飛 蓼太 再現
ureshii ka hana ni akeyuku karasu tobi   ryôta 1707-87
(happy? blossoms-to light-[dawning]-proceeds, crow flies)

are you happy? as the *hanami* day dawns the crows fly	are you happy? as dawn meets the bloom a crow leaves

This is a good example of a *ku* that makes a translator sob. The initial question, *ureshii-ka* = "are you happy?" (with no unnatural "are" or "you" in Japanese) is stunningly effective in the original, while the crow can also be modified by the phrase of dawning/brightening with the blossoms.

うかれ烏友よぶ声や花心　沾峨　吐屑庵
ukarekarasu tomo yobu koe ya hanagokoro   senga (1776)
(high/excited crow/s friend/s calling voice: blossom[-viewing –mind/heart])

blossom crazy hear that crow calling his friends	high on blossoms giddy crows calling one another

Is this a subjective judgment about the voice of the crow based on the poet's excited state of mind? I doubt it. Crows are bright enough to get a kick out of cherry blossoms and blossom viewers. They remember the previous year. Any crow over a year old would be *thrilled* to see it happening *again*(I have noticed old crows reassuring young ones on New Year's Day, when it is far quieter than usual).

花の跡なれや烏はいつも啼く 鋤立 其角袋
hana no ato nare ya karasu wa itsumo naku   joritsu (18c)
(blossoms' aftermath: crow/s-as-for always cry/ies)

in the aftermath of the blossoms: a crow always caws	on the trail of a blossom-thief, a crow always caws

Reading one: *See you next year? Thanks for the garbage? It's safe now, everybody?* I would not be surprised to learn that crows caw to divide all sorts of times – not just the day-*vs*-night-time the cock marks – but more subtle divisions such as those made by human activity. Reading two: the trail is that of one who carries a broken-off branch of bloom. We will have a chapter about that activity.

木啄や（の）枯木をさがす（探すや）花の中　丈草
kitsutsuki ya [no] karegi o sagasu [karegi sagasu ya] hana no naka   jôsô (1643-1704)
(woodpecker:/!/[or, 's /s'] dried/dead tree search: blossoms' among)

a woodpecker searching for dead wood in the blossoms	among blossoms woodpeckers searching for dead wood

Jôsô had an eye for birds. He is known for: *"A duckling / looking like it just found / the lake bed."*

十二羽の雉の子供や遅櫻　浪花 アルス
jûniha no kiji no kodomo ya osozakura　rôka -1703
(twelve pheasant children/chicks!/: late-cherry/ies)

twelve baby
pheasants string along
late-cherries

The plush bloom of the late-cherries and a train of baby birds bring spring to a comfortable end.

仁和寺にて・花を踏て蛇のうへ行人の声 大江丸 俳懺悔
hana o funde hebi no ue yuku hito no koe　ôemaru 1722 - 1805
(blossoms[obj] treading snake/s-upon/over going people's voice/s)

the voices of men who tread on cherry blossoms going over snakes	treading petals the voices of men passing over a serpent

This was at a Buddhist temple on Big Within Mountain (大内山). Are people making such a clamor as they tread the petals that one might *think* there was a snake or stepping over passed-out drunks (called snakes), or climbing blossomed limbs to escape from a real snake that came out from the roots? Or, did the temple have Shintô connections and boast one or more propitious white snakes? Or, is there a legend I have missed? Regardless, it is a fact that large snakes *are* up and about every Spring because there are many eggs and baby animals to eat, and there is a *ku*: *"If not for snakes / i'd spend the night out / cherry-hunting"* 蛇なくば一夜あかさん桜がり 桃隣 *hebi nakuba hitoyo akasan sakuragari* tôrin (-1719, or -1806)). In 1585, Luis Frois, S.J. wrote, as one of his 611 ways Europe and Japan were contrary, that, unlike "us," Japanese did not fear snakes, and even picked them up and ate them (see *Topsy-turvy 1585*); apparently, it did not hold true for all Japanese.

うれしいか櫻かぶりて飛蛙　史流 未来記
ureshii ka sakura kaburite tobu kawazu　shiryû 1765
(happy? cherry/petals wearing [on top] jump/ing frog/s)

are you happy,
hopping frog with petals
on your back?

Yes, it is the same start as we saw in Ryôta's *ku*. Chances are the expression "[Are you] happy?" (*ureshii ka*) was used in *kabuki* or some other drama and became faddish.

ちる花を思案して見る蛙哉 東鵝 古選
chiru hana o shian shite miru kawazu kana　tôga 1763
(falling blossoms[obj] pondering/worrying looks/ing frog!/?/'tis)

seemingly lost in thought, frog views falling petals	pondering the falling petals a frog	frog, a penny for your thoughts about the falling petals

The poet may just be observing the thoughtful stance of the frog, as Issa was later to do.　But I imagine a frog experiencing difficulty separating potential food from the petals.

細声や花ちる水を行蛙　成美
hosogoe ya hana chiru mizu o yuku kawazu　seibi (-1816)
(thin/weak voice: blossoms-falling water[obj] go/es frog/s)

<table>
<tr><td>that plaintive peep
a frog wading through water
full of cherry petals</td><td>such faint voices
from frogs parting the water
petals fall into</td></tr>
</table>

ちる花をかつぎ上たる蛙哉　宗波
chiru hana o katsugi-agetaru kawazu kana　sôha (fl 1700?)
(falling blossom/s carry-raising frog/s!/'tis)

<table>
<tr><td>a fallen petal
raised by the back
of a frog</td><td>fallen petals
shouldered by frogs rise
from the pond</td><td>falling petals
carried back up
by frogs</td></tr>
</table>

I cannot recall if a *ku* about a water-bird parting the petalled water antedates or postdates Seibi's *ku* and cannot say whether the frog's feat is just that or an aqueous reflection of the famous *ku* about the petal that returned to the branch but really was a butterfly. The "pond" reading is my invention.

つく／＼と蛙が目にも桜哉　一茶
tsukuzuku to kawazu ga me ni mo sakura kana　issa (-1827)
(intently frog's eyes-in also/even cherry/petals!/?/'tis)

<table>
<tr><td></td><td>searching i spy
the cherry petals even
in frogs' eyes</td><td></td></tr>
<tr><td>the frog's eyes
also intently reflect
the blossoms</td><td></td><td>looking closely
i see the cherry's bloom
in frog's eye, too</td></tr>
<tr><td></td><td>focus and find
cherry petals even fall
into frog eyes</td><td></td></tr>
</table>

With eyes placed considerably higher than ours, frogs are well made for seeing *and* reflecting the bloom; but who knows if Issa or frog looks intently (*tsukuzuku to*) or if this is about bloom or petals! The later reading would follow Bashô's famous petals, petals, everywhere, i.e., fish salad *ku* (32-14).

花喰に鮎ものぼるかよしの川　蓼太
hanakui ni ayu mo noboru ka yoshino kawa　ryôta -1787
(blossom/cherry-eat-as sweet-fish, too, climb[go up]? yoshino river)

<table>
<tr><td>sweetfish, too
climb up yoshino river
to eat blossoms?</td><td>sweetfish climbing
yoshino river, do they too
seek blossoms?</td></tr>
</table>

Ryôta's "too," implies that in some psychological way, humans climb cherry mountains to "eat" blossoms ("You're so beautiful, I could *eat* you!"). Another *ku* captioned "Yoshino River" puts the eating in a different context: *"Tiny sweetfish, / is the dew on the bloom / your milk* [=mother's breasts]?" (よしの川・鮎小鮎花の雫を乳房かよ　素堂 *aya ko ayu hana no shizuku o chibusa ka yo* sôdô (1641-1716)).

口びるを魚に吸るゝ櫻哉 其角 五元集
kuchibiru o uo ni suwaruru sakura kana   kikaku -1707
(lips[obj] fish/es-by sucked cherry!/?/ 'tis)

<table>
<tr><td>cherry blossoms!
so your lips are smacked
by sweet fish?</td><td>it lets its lips
be osculated by fish
the cherry tree</td></tr>
</table>

Most cherry petals have what seems like lips on the outside end. In Japanese, kissing is called "sucking." I found a "puckering up" *ku* but I think it means this: *"Mountain cherries / keep your lips closed . . ."* (人に口すほめ居てよし山櫻 川石 *hito ni kuchi subome ite yoshi yamazakura* senseki (?)). Petals are generally chided for clogging up rivers and bothering anglers. As far as I know, Kikaku's perspective is a completely fresh one. Speaking of which, Issa has a strange *ku*: *"I tried lifting / one up with a fishing hook: / the sakura"* (釣針に引上て見る桜哉 一茶 文政一 *tsuribari ni hiki agetemiru sakura kana*). At first, I thought of those cherry-petal lips, but it is more likely Issa means he invented a new way to display a spray of bloom (I, too, have hung things from fishing hooks in *my* room . .)!

蝶鳥も順の舞せよ花の庭   氏重 犬子
chô tori mo junnomai seyo hana no niwa   shijû (1633)
(butterflies birds, too, [take]turn-dance do! blossom-garden)

<blockquote>
blossom garden
butterflies, birds, it's your turn
at jun-no-mai
</blockquote>

Jun-no-mai (lit., dancing in order) is a party activity where people take turns showing off (singing, dance or magic). As shy Western visitors learn to their dismay, *everyone* is expected to participate.

天人も舞ふ日やこゝに花の蝶   菟玉 文星観
tenjin mo mau hi ya koko ni hana no chô   togyoku 1732
(heaven-person, too, dance day! here-at blossoms' butterflies)

<table>
<tr><td>the day the angels
come to dance: butterflies
and blossoms!</td><td>the day the angels
dance here in the blossom court
of the butterflies</td><td>the day heaven
and men dance: butterflies
visit blossoms</td></tr>
</table>

A fine *ku* about a tipsy day, where the butterflies are the bubbles of the champagne – *the cosmos is united and it is dancing!* But, not so fast. The words "heaven-person" can be pronounced *tenjin* and mean 1) men and the cosmos; or *tennin* and mean 2) beautiful angels or, as argot, 3) "stealing things left outdoors." Also, butterflies can mean *thieves* and modified with blossoms, pretty ones. Still, such a reading is *unlikely*. Reading 2, with "butterfly" pun-doubling as "realm/court," is far more probable.

たのしみよ胡蝶も花に一勢   有貞女 玉藻
tanoshimi yo kochô mo hana ni hito-ikioi   yûteijo 1774
(pleasure [it is]! butterflies, too, blossoms-to one-power/force)

cherry blossoms

<table>
<tr><td>what a joy
the butterflies also
out in force!</td><td>this is pleasure!
the butterflies are also
coming in waves</td></tr>
</table>

> blossom-viewing
> what fun to find crowds
> of butterflies, too

The suggestion of collective energy in the word *ikioi* (power/force) is perfect for describing the assault of butterflies. I dare say *if you watch enough butterflies up close,* you can even find individuals so full of nervous energy – some twitch! – that it is *spooky*. If only *"butterfly"* were not so damn long, blossoms might have fit into the first two readings. The "too/also" makes the poem. They, *like us,* do this.

飛ぶ蝶はまいまい虫か花の波　梅盛
tobu chô wa maimai mushi ka hananonami baisei 1613-1702
(flying butterfly-as-for, waterskaters? blossoms' waves)

> are they whirligigs,
> these butterflies flitting about
> the blossom waves?

"Waves" also means *water-surface* in Japanese (for example, Issa has a *ku* where a captain is told to forbid pissing overboard because the "moon is on the waves") so the water-skater analogy based on the waves trope is more natural in the original. My first line comes from Blyth, who tells us that the work of this disciple of Teitoku, were criticized as "neither good nor bad; Buddha's excrement mixed with flowers."

花一ツよそ心なき胡てふ哉　作者不知 毛吹草
hana hitotsu yosogokoronaki kochô kana   anon. 1645
(blossom-one other/aside-heart/feeling-not butterfly!/?'tis)

> the butterfly   only blossoms
> perfectly occupied with   occupy the mind of
> one blossom   the butterfly

Paradox: the butterfly flits promiscuously between blossoms *and* it is faithful to the blossoms alone.

花の露吸ふに下戸なき胡蝶哉　梅霞 蘆別船
hana no tsuyu suu ni geko naki kochô kana   baika 1694
(blossom's dew suck-regarding, teetotaler-not butterflies!/?'tis)

> blossom dew   the butterflies:
> not a teetotaler among   no blossom dew-sucker
> these butterflies   ever abstains

While it is true that butterflies must drink, they are also more complex than most might think. I love to see them flitting back and forth between a potential mate of their own species and a delectable flower.

花ぶさをちぶさにそたつ胡蝶哉　望一 毛吹草
hanabusa o chibusa ni sodatsu kochô kana   môichi (-1643)
(blossom-corolla[obj] breast/milk-corolla-as/by raised/grow butterfly/ies!)

> these butterflies
> nursed on the corolla
> of the cherry

If budding blossoms nurse the udders of rain clouds, butterflies suck the blossoms' "nipples." And, doesn't a bobbing force of butterflies remind you of piglets roughly butting mama sow's belly? (If you haven't seen it, let us just say, evolution has created ferocious babies).

月の夜の櫻に蝶の朝寝かな　千代
tsuki no yo no sakura ni chô no asane kana　chiyo-ni 1701-75
(moon-night's cherry/blossoms-in/on butterflies' morning-sleep/sleep-in!/?'tis)

morning scene

butterflies still
on blossoms sleeping off
the moonshine

after a full moon
of blossoms sleeping in
butterflies all

The original is not alcoholic as per my moonshine. Butterflies cannot fly until they heat up, so they have no choice but to sleep in, but I doubt they were up to begin with, so the poem may be a metaphor.

花に蝶ねふるは一のらくね哉　作者不知 毛吹草
hana ni chô nemuru wa ichi no rakune kana　anonymous (1645)
(blossoms-on butterfly sleep-as-for first/one's easy/comfortable-sleep!/?'tis)

of all sleep
the best is a butterfly
on a blossom

most comforting
of all sleep? – psyche
upon her flora

Fluffy clouds of blossoms would seem a heavenly bed. Sappho might have liked my second reading.

寝て待し果報か花に飛こてふ　作者不知 毛吹草
nete-machishi kahô ka hana ni tobu kochô　anon. (1645)
(sleep-waiting, reward? blossom-to fly blossom)

sleep and your dreams
will come true? a butterfly
flies to the blossoms

Are blossoms beautiful women and the butterfly a male dreamer? *"My dream-world: / to be a butterfly living / on/among blossoms"* (夢の世と花でくらするこてふ哉　重供 毛吹草 *yume no yo to hana de kurasuru kochô kana*　shigetomo 1645)? But the anon. *ku* is trickier than it looks. It turns a saying about *sleeping on ones wishes to make them come true* into a question. Is the reply 1) Butterflies don't sleep, they *fly themselves* to their reward? 2) Butterflies, having trustingly slept in their cocoons, awake to fly over to their waiting reward? 3) The Chinese man who slept and dreamed he was a butterfly had the right idea? I favor 2) *and* 3).

花の夢聞たき蝶に聲もなし 鈴竿 古選
hana no yume kikitaki chô ni koe mo nashi　reikan (1763)
(blossom's/s' dream/s hear-want butterfly/ies-to voice-too-not)

The butterfly's dream of flowers
I fain would ask, –
but it is voiceless.

Blyth trans.

△△

sleeping on blossoms
if only butterflies could
tell us about it!

blossom dreams
if butterflies could only talk
i'd listen

I love Blyth's "*fain,*" but neither he nor I can capture the blossom-dream (*hana no yume*) of the original, for it is not only a "dream *of* flowers," i.e., "about flowers," but a *flowery,* or particularly beautiful dream, even sleeping with a courtesan, in which case the poet may be chuckling "if only you could tell me about it, you lucky butterfly!" Here we are reminded of Lady Daibu (　) wishing she could hear the Star Lovers enjoying their once-a-year rendezvous (IPOOH-fall-star). The more probable allusion is to the Chinese poet Chuangtse (Sôshi in Japanese, Chuang Chou, Chuang Tzu, or whatever in the Chinese pronunciation) who dreamed he was a butterfly and vice-versa. That is why Blyth's butterfly is single, and it also implies the "blossom-dream" is Chuangtse's life.

画賛・道くさに蝶も寝させぬ花見哉　千代
michigusa ni chô mo nesasenu hanami kana   chiyoni (1701-75)
(road-grass/diversions-by butterfly/ies-too sleep-let-not blossom-viewing!/?/'tis)

what a picture!

road-side butterflies　　　　　　　　butterflies, too
get no sleep when we play　　　　get no sleep when humans
at blossom-viewing　　　　　　　　view blossoms

blossom-viewing
humans wander and
even butterflies can get no sleep

A touching *ku* of the type most would associate with Issa. Even butterflies on weeds have no place to hide when humans paint the fields red. "Road-grass" idiomatically means "diversion/entertainment."

胡蝶もや寝ん猫ねむる花の陰　弘永 毛吹草
chôcho mo ya nen neko nemuru hana no kage   kôei 1645
(butterfly/ies too! sleep/s-would! cat sleeps blossom-shade)

the butterflies, too　　　　　　　butterfly, you, too
would sleep while cat naps　　　go to sleep! kitty naps
in the bloom-shade　　　　　　　in the bloom-shade

This early *haikai* sympathy for insects is more common later. The second reading is highly unlikely.

見る人の魂飛出てや花の蝶　愚候？侠？洗濯物
miruhito no tama tobi-dete ya hana no chô   gukô/kyô? 1666
(looking person/people's soul/s fly-out: blossom's butterfly)

the viewers' souls
fly out! blossoms joined
by butterflies

The butterfly-as-soul – psyche – idea is found East and West. Usually, "heart" (*kokoro*) rather than "soul/spirit"(*tama*) is associated with cherry blossoms, but when the butterfly is involved, the latter word is used. The soul's absence puts one in a sort of suspended animation. When the blossoms are done falling, people's souls return to their bodies, as can be confirmed by the absence of the butterflies.

ちる花に姿習ふてこてふ哉　吟江 古姿
chiru hana ni sugata naraute[?] kochô kana　ginkô 1775
(falling blossoms-by shape/form/appearance learned butterfly!/?/'tis)

its earthly form taken from a cherry petal: this butterfly!	their moves learned from falling petals the butterflies

Why are butterflies so beautiful? To mimic the brilliant color of the most poisonous? *Perhaps*. But, it could be camouflage, to mix safely with the blossoms. And that means mimicking the blossoms' "behavior," too. How successful are they? Moritake's well-known *ku* –

落花枝に帰ると見れば胡蝶かな 守武
rakka eda ni kaeru to mireba chôcho kana　moritake 1472-1549
(fallen-blossom-to return-as see/appear-when butterfly/ies!/?/'tis)

the fallen flower
returns to the branch?
it's a butterfly!

chamberlain+me

– is the proof. *If,* that is, *you believe it*. Blyth translates "A fallen flower / *Flew* back to *its* branch! / No, it was a butterfly." (*Haiku*: Spring) The *italics* are mine. He writes "there was a momentary mistake, with disillusionment, expressed in the third line, and as such, this is not poetry;" then, gratuitously adds, "nevertheless, we feel that Moritake, like Alice, has peeped into the garden he could not enter." I'd say the "flew" in the translation suggests Blyth *himself* had trouble peeping. Imagine: *You are seated there, giddy with drink. The warmth rising from the ground causes petals fluttering sideways in the occasional gusts to shoot upwards at times and the wee dust devils sometimes sweep petals up into the air. You have seen some birds (you always see some birds, for they are not about to miss the fun), but not any butterflies. None (that, too, is often the case, for the previous day is often chilly). Believe me, if the butterfly is close in color to the petals (and there are yellowish tinged blossoms), you would be fooled for a moment.* Who is to say that is not poetic? As we have already noted, blossom and petal are the same *hana* in Japanese, moreover, there is no zoomorphic verb such as "fly" in the poem. Blyth follows the tendency of Japanese to criticize this poem, though their complaint is generally that it is purely logical play with a Chinese saying (*the flower returns not to its branch*). Call me naïve, but I prefer to give Moritake the benefit of the doubt.

この頃やあとさきしらす花に蝶　猿推 泊船
konogoro ya atosaki shirazu hana ni chô　ensui -1704
(this time: after-before know-not blossoms-to/and butterfly)

in this season
who knows if butterfly
or cherry leads!

Unlike early spring, when things appear one at a time, it is now hard to catch what is happening.

小筵や銭と小蝶とちる桜 一茶 文政七
komushiro ya zeni to kochô to chiru sakura issa (-1827)
(small [straw] mat: (small denom.) coins & small butterflies & falling cherry)

a small mat:
small change, small butterflies
falling petals

I was not sure if this described gambling, begging or Issa's change ready for passing vendors – in which case, change "a" to "*my* small mat" – so I put it here. The "and's" were dropped because "butterflies" ate up too many syllabets. No matter. In translation, it is better without them.

塵塚や櫻の中の蝶のから 句空 北の山
chirizuka ya sakura no naka no chô no kara kukû 1692
(trash-heap/s: cherry/petals among's buttterfly's/ies' shell/s/remain/s)

in the trash pile   in the trash-pile
mixed in with cherry petals   bits of butterfly among
a dead butterfly   the cherry petals

Damn the pushiness of English number! How I hate being forced to choose between *butterfly* and *butterflies!* The second reading avoids the problem. Butterflies and blossoms, an ephemeral blend.

花に寄る蜂追にけり追れけり 無關 俳諧古選
hana ni yoru hachi oinikeri owarekeri mukan (1763)
(blossoms-to approach wasp/s/bee/s chase-off, chased off)

chasing off   i chase a bee
bees from blossoms and   that came to the bloom
being chased   he chases me

This predates Issa's well-known *ku* about a kitten chasing and being chased by fallen leaves.

人追ふて蜂戻りけり花の上 太祇
hito oute hachi modorikeri hana no ue taigi -1772
(people chase/d bee/wasp return[finality] blossom-upon)

a wasp chases
people, then, returns
to its blossom

Wasp *ku* are more interesting than butterfly *ku* because the stinging insect keeps the poet attentive. They are not afraid and will sip anything sweet you are drinking if you let them. You can observe the same individual returning at fixed intervals as it transfers your drink a drop at a time to its hive. If you time it and predict the next arrival, your friends will think you are a genius.

花に舞ふ蜂は針なき心にや 和角 蘆別船
hana ni mau hachi wa hari naki kokoro niya wakaku (1694)
(blossoms-at dance bees/wasps-as-for needle=tension-not heart/mind [informal "is"])

        the bees dancing
     in the blossoms have left
       their sting behind

Bees and wasps partaking of blossoms seldom sting. They, too, are harmless drunks, blossom drunks. There is a pun: "no tension = *hari*" written with the character for "needle/stinger." A later *ku* expresses the same idea less cleverly: *"All of us, even / the birds and the bees relaxed / in the bloomshade"* (蝶鳥もみなやすげなり花のかげ 士朗 *chô tori mo mina yasuge nari hananokage* shirô (-1813)).

初花に人来べきかも下り蛛 鏡平 花供養
hatsuhana ni hito kubeki ka mo sagarikumo kyôhei 1795
(first-blossom/s-to people come-ought-maybe descending-spider)

    so, is someone   i'll bet someone
coming for the first blossoms?   calls on your first bloom:
    dangling spider   a dangling spider

Whether they attached a web-stay to your hanging robe or just dangled down from a tree limb near your door, spiders in classical song and poetry prognosticated the coming of a lover. The association of blossom-viewers and lovers is a good one.

振舞のしげきや蛛の家桜 長頭丸 崑山集
furumai no shigeki ya kumo no iezakura teitoku 1651
(shake-dance[behavior]'s frequent! spiders' house-cherry)

     how spiders   what spastic
dance about a house   moves! my spidery
   cherry in bloom   house-cherry

An *ie-zakura,* or "house-cherry" is one growing by your home. Spiders like to live near us for the light at night and smells by day attract bugs, and buildings are good web support. *Have you ever seen a spider coping with petals falling on its net?* At first, they shake their feet to help objects stick to the web, and rush to investigate. If the catch is not worth sucking or wrapping up for later, the spider drops it by cutting out that section of the web. A spider given junk over and over shakes the net in another way to try to flick it off instead of entangling it. Each spider accomplishes this at its own pace (Time it, and impress someone by making predictions!). A rain of petals would drive a spider bananas. Eventually, it would desert net; so this would be when the petals were just starting to fall. *Since spider movement, it might also mean the cherry will receive many calls from blossom-lovers.* Unfortunately, the first reading is *almost surely wrong.* Chances are Teitoku describes a double-petaled pendulant tree, what Japanese would call an eight-fold thread-cherry. Their hanging limbs seem like daddy longlegs: *"This bloomshade / I cannot sweep: my spider / house-cherry"* (掃除せぬ木陰やくもの家櫻 廣直 犬子 *sôji senu kokage ya kumo no iezakura* hironao 1633). It was taboo to mess with spiders.

物皆自得・花にあそぶ虻なくらひそ友雀　芭蕉
hana ni asobu abu na kurai so tomo suzume　bashô (1654-94)
(things-all-self-get: blossoms-in play horsefly/ies not-kill! friend-sparrow/s)

horseflies at play　　　　　　　　　　　brother sparrow
in the blossoms: brother　　　　　eat not the horsefly at play
sparrows let them be　　　　　　　　　in the blossoms

Although I like and often make up titles, I agree with critics who skip the preface, meaning, roughly, "what you sow you reap," because it diminishes the poetry. Without it, we have a natural Issa-like *we are all in it together.* We have the love for all things that naturally arises in a good person who is drunk (It may seem maudlin to those who have not experienced it, but, if that be the case, then *all* love is maudlin). With it, the *ku* would indeed seem didactic. But even then it beats this: *"Seeing blossoms – / In my former life was I / a horsefly?* (花を見て我前生は虻やらん　青亜 *hana o mite waga zensei wa abu yaran*　seia (?)). Unless I am missing something, that is *awful!*

手のひらに虱這はする花の陰　芭蕉か 猿蓑
te no hira ni shirami hawasuru hana no kage　bashô
(palm-on lice crawl-let blossom's/s' shade)

on my palm
i let a louse crawl
bloomshade

Some might think this precious, but I *like* it. The commonplace that lice accompanied the saint – not just Buddhist, for Saint Xavier scored brownie-points with his in the mid-16c – and the existence of the term "blossom-viewing lice" (*hanamijirami*) which will be defined elsewhere, is less important to me than the mood so wonderfully expressed. Blossom-drunk in the bloomshade, we can even feel for a louse. This *ku* would go well with Bashô's *ku* about noticing a violet on a mountain path. We will encounter it again, as we have a whole section on "blossom-viewing lice" in chapter 64

島の花人なつかしき風情哉　紀州 枕石 花供養
shima no hana hito natsukashiki fujô kana　kishû 1795
(island's blossom/s person familiar mood!/?/'tis)

island blossoms
everything around seems
so familiar

island blossoms　　　　　　　　　　　island blossoms
all the cherry trees　　　　　　　　here is something
seem so tame　　　　　　　　　　　　friendly to man

blossom-viewing
on an island what is
this friendliness

The expression "*hito-natsukashii*" is most commonly used to describe a dog or a wild animal that acts like it knows you and does not run away. In other words, it *likes* you. I wonder if the way island animals tend not to fear people was known in Japan at this time. If so, then this is a truly remarkable *ku* about the cherry *tree/blossoms-as-animal.*

Blossom Clouds, Cloud Blossoms
花の雲
hana-no-kumo

よしの山人に心をつけがほに花よりさきにかかる白雲　西行
yoshino yama hito ni kokoro o tsuke gao ni hana yori saki ni kakaru shiragumo　saigyô
(yoshino mountain, person-to mind/spirit[+obj] put face-for blossom ahead-of cover white clouds)

mount yoshino
puts on a face to prime
the hearts of men:

why else fluffy clouds,
before the cherries bloom?

these white clouds,
before the cherries bloom
mount yoshino

would wet the appetite
of blossom-lovers

Saigyô (1118-90) covers his favorite subjects, of which cherry blossoms were one, from every possible angle. If cherry blossoms look like clouds, then, clouds look like blossoms and . . . .

花になる雲も出始や山の春　馬光
hana ni naru kumo mo dehajime ya yama no haru　bakô -1751
(blossoms becomes/are cloud, too appears-begins: mountain's spring)

clouds that will
be blossoms, too, appear:
mountain spring

The cloud metaphor might better have been portioned out between other sub-themes dealing with various stages of blossom blooming, viewing and falling in this book. But, considering the ample number of poems for most of these themes, I felt it might be interesting to divert a portion of the clouds into a separate chapter. Bakô's *ku* was captioned "New Year" – blossoms are a celebratory theme and spring was synonymous with the New Year – and must refer to *ume* (plum) rather than cherry, but the ambiguity of cloud and blossom is well expressed and that principle is the same.

万天の雲もさくらの蕾より　哲亜?寛美万句?
manten no kumo mo sakura no tsubomi yori　tetsua 1798
(ten-thousand/myriad clouds, too cherry's buds-from)

the clouds of
a thousand skies from
cherry buds

It would make more sense to say the buds were for clouds on myriad *mountains*. The hyperbole that allows the buds to bear the clouds in the sky as well as those on the limbs of the trees reflects the close relationship of the plant and season: "The spring? / the blossoming hills / are *it!*" (春といふはこれらなるへし花の山　蜊口　*haru to iu wa korera narubeshi hana no yama*　rikô()).

今植ゑし櫻や世々の春の雲 也有
ima ueshi sakura ya yoyo no haru no kumo　yayû 1701-83
(now planting/ed cherry/ies!/: world/age-world/age's spring-cloud/s)

<table>
<tr><td>the cherry tree
i just planted: generations
of spring clouds!</td><td>the cherry trees
we just planted: spring cloud
for centuries</td></tr>
</table>

What a sweet *ku!* The next *ku* is less personal, but fine for binding heaven and earth:

白雲の根をおろしけり櫻苗 眠獅 花櫻帖
shiragumo no ne o oroshikeri sakura nae　minshi? ()
(white-cloud/s' root's/s' lower/sink-down[+emph.] cherry seedling)

white clouds
have begun to take root:
cherry seedlings

白雲は幾代の花の歌ぶくろ 鬼貫
shiragumo wa ikuyo no hana no utabukuro　onitsura 1660-1738
(white-clouds-as-for [how] many-ages' blossoms' song-bag/[*also* frog-throat])

<table>
<tr><td>white clouds
song-pouches for ages
of blossoms</td><td>white clouds
how long have they held
blossom poems?</td></tr>
</table>

one for the song-bag!

blooming clouds
like the throats of ancient
singing frogs

The "song-pouch" was a container usually tied up to the main pillar of a poet's house into which scraps of paper with drafts of songs/poems were dropped It also is the balloon-like throat of the frog, a proto-poet according to the preface to Japan's second oldest major poetry collection, the *Kokinshû* (905). Onitsura may be chuckling: *How many generations of cherry blossom poetry have been served by this cloud conceit?*

落陽　歌一首もたぬ山なし花の雲 蓼太 蓼太集
uta ishû motanu yama nashi hana no kumo　ryôta 1707-87
(song/poem one have-not mountain not, blossom-cloud/s)

<table>
<tr><td>not a mountain
without a poem to its name
blossom clouds</td><td>every mountain
deserves a song today!
blossom clouds</td></tr>
</table>

Here it is safe to say we are talking about blossoms and not clouds. Like Onitsura, Ryôta writes of *uta* or "song," meaning *waka*, longer traditional poems usually associated with romance, which even included anthropomorphic mountains. His *ku* plays with Basho's *ku* about spring haze making even a no-name mountain precious (*haru nare ya na mo naki yama . . .*) – a caption specified an area just East of Kyôto where Bashô had been – and both *ku* remind us of the following *waka* by Saigyô (1118-90).

雲もかかれ花とを春は見て過ぎむいづれの山もあだに思はで 西行 山家集
kumo mo kakare hana to o haru wa mite sugimu izure no yama mo ada ni omowa de saigyô

<blockquote>

clouds, you, too
rise up for the spring
expects bloom

and i would have no hill
without its own dream!

come, clouds!
in spring i would view
you as bloom

i don't want to imagine
even one barren hill!

</blockquote>

よしの山櫻にまがふ白雲の散りなん後は晴れずもあらなん (む) 西行
yoshino yama sakura ni magau shirogumo no chirinan ato wa harezu mo aramu saigyô

<blockquote>

oh, ye clouds
mixing with blossoms
on mt yoshino,

must you clear up
after the petals blow?

</blockquote>

Is the *Manyôshû* (8c), the poets *beg* the clouds, if they have a heart (i.e. sympathy) to vanish and not block his or her view of this or that mountain. In these *waka*, Saigyô, conversely, welcomes clouds as mountain equalizers(?), or should we say *cosmetics?*

むら／＼と杉を埋むや花の雲 傘下 小弓
muramura to sugi o umemu ya hana no kumo sanka 1699
(gathering/irresistably cedar/s[obj]:/! blossom-cloud/s)

<blockquote>

great cedars: would
the gathering clouds of bloom
bury them?

</blockquote>

Yes, there are other trees on most mountains, so it is not really right to call those without cherry blossoms "barren" (as in Saigyô's first, above). A cedar is taller than a cherry, but many blossoming trees seen from below can pretty much block the cedar from our view.

樫の木の花にかまはぬ姿かな 芭蕉
kashinoki no hana ni kamawanu sugata kana bashô -1694
(mountain-hut // oak tree's blossom-in concern/interest-not form!/?/'tis)

(on visiting someone's mountain hut)

<blockquote>

the oak tree:
not at all troubled by things
like blossoms

</blockquote>

> **the oak**
>
> the appearance
> of not giving a damn
> for blossoms!

> the oak tree:
> not interested
> in cherry blossoms
>
> trans. hass

In this famous *ku*, Bashô praises the austere hut and its aesthete inhabitant (poet Aki-no-bô). The Japanese oak in question is an evergreen and by itself might have trouble fitting into the haiku almanac. Not only are all oaks hard, the angle which the large limbs of some varieties attach to the main trunk is close to 90%. I think this, too, gives the tree a singular power and an upright character. *Back to the clouds!*

まがふ色に花咲きぬれば吉野山春は晴れせぬ峯の白雲　西行
magau iro ni hana sakinureba yoshinoyama haru wa haresenu [?] mine no shiragumo　saigyô

> *cherry blossoms*
> *so full of pretense on*
> *mount yoshino!*
>
> *not a clear day this spring*
> *white clouds on each peak*

◎

w^hat is t^his c_on_st_ant ov_erc_ast?

> *not a clear day*
> *of spring on mt yoshino*
> *cherry blossoms*

Clouds, because they change, were traditionally *devious*. Saigyô's joking about clouds of bloom preventing clear weather in spring is pure *haikai* hundreds of years too early. I couldn't help trying turn Saigyô's *waka* into a *ku*. But let us get to the real thing:

花や孕む大原山の雲の帯　重供 鷹つくは
hana ya haramu ôhara-yama no kumo no obi　shigetomo ( )
(blossoms! pregnant/swollen ôhara (big-field[=belly])-mountain's clouds' belt)

> **quick spring**
>
> blossom clouds:
> lo, big belly mountain
> wears a belt!

I had to veer away from the original syntax to make an understandable translation. The cloud-as-belt was a classic conceit. The verb *haramu* combined with the suggestive name of the mountain turns that belt into the special belt used by pregnant women.[1] The "big-field" = belly pun is very common in old haiku: eg., *"Big-belly-field / more room than wine / under the bloom"* or *"Big-belly Field: / Not enough drinkers here / under the bloom"* (大原や酒呑たらぬ花の下　無記名 犬子　*ôhara ya sake nomi taranu hana no shita*　anon. (1633)). "Under the bloom" is a pun for "below-the-nose," which has metaphoric meanings including . . . . *Enough*. Clouds, again:

1. Pregnancy Belt. In what may be the world's first clear exposition of cultural relativity, Valignano, Jesuit Visitador for the Far East at the end of the 16 c, paid great attention to the pregnancy belt when describing ways in which not only arbitrary European and Japanese cultural *artifacts* but *behavior*, that we assume to have empirically proven origins, could be contrary. He testified that European women loosened their belts when pregnant, using them as a loose sling, while Japanese cinched theirs up tighter than ever and both claimed to know through *experience* that their way was good for themselves and the growing fetus (see my TOPSY-TURVY 1585).

帯をとけ花をぬすみし峰の雲 強永 毛吹草
obi o toke hana o nusumishi mine no kumo kôei 1645
(belt loosen blossom steal/ed peak's cloud/s)

> girdle undone
> the blossom is stolen
> clouds on peaks

Banner clouds (streaming from the peak, breaking and drifting off) are read as blossoms stolen from the mountain. Spring mountains were often eroticized in old haiku, with blossom clouds, as we have seen, signifying a woman's *obi*, usually translated as "belt" or "sash". I *girdled* it because the "stolen" aspect suggests the *shita-obi*, the "under-belt" guarding a woman's privates. Blossoms suggest personal charms as fruit does in the Occident (including the so-called "Middle East"): *"Does it hide / the charms of [her]blossoms? / Morning mist"* (みてる色をかくすか花の朝霞 宗養 *miteru iro o kakusuka hana no asagasumi* sôyô (1538-63)). *"Cherry blossoms / behind the mist: it makes you / want to grope"* (かすむ花探つて見たき心哉 快風 小弓 *kasumu hana sagutte-mitaki kokoro kana* kaifû (1699)). Fun, but let us see something classier by Tsurayuki, the editor of the *Kokinshû*:

みわ山をしかもかくすか春霞人にしられぬ花やさくらむ つらゆき 古今集九四
miwayama o shikamo kakusu ka harugasumi hito ni shirarenu hana ya sakuramu kokinshû 905

> Mount Miwa
> would you, too, veil *it*,
> Spring Mist?
>
> i'll *bet* something blooms:
> blossoms unknown to man!

見ぬ花もおもかけにたつ霞哉 宗祇
minu hana mo omokage ni tatsu kasumi kana sôgi
(see-not blossoms-too phantom/visage-on appear mist!/?/'tis)

> this rising mist: mist on the hills
> blossoms unseen appear   unseen blossoms move
> before my mind   a lover's brow

Miwa was a sacred mountain where even the clouds were addressed by ancient poets who begged them to prove they had hearts by not blocking their view. I changed the emphatic *shikamo* (closer to "even" [Mt. Miwa]) in Tsurayuki's *waka* into "too" in reference to the implicit allusion to the *clouds* addressed by the first 12 syllabets of *Manyôshû* (8c) song #18, which Tsurayuki borrows word-for-word. I do not know if Sôgi's *ku* owes anything to Tsurayuki's *waka*. In Sôgi's original, *tatsu* (appear, rise) is a pivot word serving both the mind [mind's eye]/visage and the mist, in turn. The first reading is the main one, but the second – no allusion to love, *per se*, but to the Chinese tradition of reading the expressions of beautiful women – is also possible. Even so, this is already the nature-centered world of haiku, the posited beauty's interest is in the blossoms of nature. A later *ku* turns the mist+blossoms into simile: *"Somewhat like / unseen love, blossoms / in the mist"* (見ぬ恋にちと似かゝりぬ霞花 海角 蘆分船 *minu koi ni chito ni-kakarinu kasumibana* kaikaku (1694)). And, another treats it as a stage prop: *"The mist is here: / Let it serve as a curtain / for blossom-viewing"* (花見には前ぎりをせよたつ霞 立圃 空礫 *hanami ni wa maegiri o seyo tatsu kasumi* ryûho (1594-1669). Blossom viewers often erected screens around their party. Ryûho plays against an older *haikai* conceit of the Spring mist pulling down a curtain on the Old Year to set off the New one (*The Fifth Season*).

花なきも霞にかゝる老木かな　宗春
hana naki mo kasumi ni kakaru rôki kana sôshun (c1734)
(blossom-not/less-too, mist-by place/cover old-tree!/?/'tis)

not a blossom
but the mist still veils
that old tree

This is true, and a response to the tantalizing mist conceit. Please forgive my ambiguity; there should be a comma after the "blossom." Enough mist, the clouds can draw on their own:

花の雲あちらの山も気にかゝる　雨青 類題
hana no kumo achira no yama mo ki ni kakaru usei (1774)
(blossoms' cloud over-there's mountain too attention/concern catches)

blossom clouds i am drawn to the mountain over there, too	blossom clouds the mountain over there also appeals

The *mo* (too) is effective here, for it tells us the poet is sitting at *one* blossom-viewing peeking out across a valley to another. *The bloom is always pinker on the other side?*

遠山や花と見るより道急ぐ 一茶
tôyama ya hana to miru yori michi isogu issa (-1827)
(far-mountain!/: [cherry]blossoms as see-from road-hurry)

distant mountain
seeing the clouds are blossoms
we speed up!

The word "cloud" is not mentioned in the original, but Issa's seeing an un-named something *"as blossoms"* allows it. A much older renga includes the following 5-7-5+7-7: *"Our destination / far-off yet how / we hurry! // Looking o'er the bloom / from the Mt. Shiga Pass"* (行末の遠き道をや急ぐらん / 花を見すぐる志賀の山越 元亨三年四月亀山殿百韻の連歌に (*yuku sue no tôki...* (1324)) But a more likely reading of Issa's *ku* would take the something to be the *mountain* or the (cherry) trees on it:

a distant hill seeing it's in bloom i step on it!	a distant mountain i whip my shank's mare on seeing the bloom

"Step on it" is automobile slang, "shank's mare" won't fit in mid-*ku*, "pick up pace" would bore . . . .

指さした雲に近つく櫻哉 仙鼠 鹿島立
yubi sashita kumo ni chikazuku sakura kana   sensô ()
(finger pointed cloud/s-to near/s cherry[tree/s]/ies!/?/'tis)

>we draw near
>the cloud i pointed at:
>a cherry tree!

Perhaps a clever way to say *"I found it first! See, I was right!"* But I *like* it.

遠山と見しは是也花一木 一茶
tôyama to mishi wa kore nari hana hitoki   issa -1827
(far-mountain as? saw-as-for, this is/beco/ame blossom[cherry] one tree)

>what i thought
>a distant mountain, this:
>one cherry tree!

Issa has many *ku* playing with perspective (One I recall has rice seedlings thrown over Mt Fuji), but is mistaking a large cherry tree covered with white blossoms for a mountain believable? Perhaps, if one is tired and near-sighted. Another of Issa's single-tree *ku* is explicitly nebulous: *"Highwell field / just one standing / blossom cloud"* (高井の（野）や只一本の花の雲　一茶 *takaino ya tada ippon no hana no kumo*) where a counting term *hon* (*pon*) used for stick-like objects – including trees – with a fluffy cloud, that should take a different counter, though I know of none specifically for clouds (unless it is "peaks" (*mine*), but that only refers to those in what we call *banks*)!

空色の傘〔の〕つゝく也〔や〕花の雲〔盛り〕 一茶
sora-iro no kasa tsuzuku nari hana no kumo (or, *sakari*)   issa (-1827)
(sky-color's umbrella/sunbrella continues/extends-is/becomes blossom-cloud/s)

>the sky-color
>parasol extends beyond
>blossom clouds

～

>A vast sky-color umbrella:
>above the clouds of bloom.

The sky as a surreal parasol!? I only translated the "cloud" version. Another has *full-bloom*, instead.

白雲の土から光る櫻哉 寄園 春遊
shiragumo no tsuchi kara hikaru sakura kana   kien 1767
(white-clouds' earth-from shine cherry!/?/'tis)

>white clouds   white clouds
>shine up from the ground   glow upon the ground
>cherry bloom   cherry petals

Such albedo! If they bloomed year-round, our concern might be snow-blindness rather than global warming. And, if the "ground" were 地 rather than 土, the first reading would be certain. As it is . . .

1. Counting Terms. Japanese has scores of counting terms. English lacks counters for most things, but does number bread in *loaves* and cabbage in *heads*, so we can understand the concept. On the other hand, English has far more collective terms such as "school of fish," and "pride of lions" which Japanese cannot match.

しら雲やはななき山の恥かくし 杉森信盛 = 近松門左衛門
shiragumo ya hananaki yama no haji kakushi chikamatsu -1724
(white-clouds:/! blossomless mountain/s' shame-hider)

white clouds, good
to hide the shame of hills
without blossoms

This, most ridiculous and literally ironic of all *hana* cloud *ku,* found by the fun-loving Katô Ikuya (市井風流), is by none other than Chikamatsu Monzaemon, Edo's top popular playwright!

草庵　花の雲鐘は上野か浅草か　芭蕉
hana no kumo kane wa ueno ka asakusa ka bashô -1694
(grass-hut [at] // blossom-cloud/s: bell-as-for ueno? asakusa?)

(miyamori trans.)　　　　　　　　　　　　**(w. g. aston trans.)**

a cloud of flowers!　　　　　　　　　　　　a cloud of flowers!
an evening bell booms.　　　　　　　　　　is the bell ueno
at ueno or at asakusa?　　　　　　　　　　or asakusa?

(stewart trans.)

FROM MY WINDOW AT TWILIGHT

A cloud of flowers. A booming temple-bell.
Ueno's or Asakusa's? Who can tell?

(blyth trans.)　　　　　　　　　　　　**(hass trans.)**

a cloud of cherry-blossoms;　　　　　　　clouds of blossoms –
the temple bell, –　　　　　　　　　　　that temple bell, is it ueno?
is it ueno, is it asakusa?　　　　　　　　　asakusa?

grass hut

clouds of bloom
is that bell ueno's?
or asakusa's?

This, as the multitude of translations (my centering) shows, is the most well known blossom cloud haiku. The original prefaces the poem with the location. Miyamori wrote: "The theme is a distant view of the cherry-blossoms on both banks of the Sumida River, seen from the poet's hut . . . . Mukôjima, Ueno and Asakusa are wrapt in clouds of cherry-blossoms veiled in a thin haze. The poet, casting his gaze out of the window, is spellbound by the sight. At that moment the boom of a great evening bell resounds . . ." (*Haiku Poems Ancient and Modern*). Despite blossom *clouds* in his explanation, Miyamori follows older translations using the singular cloud, as does Stewart (1960), rhyming. Hass (1994) follows Ueda (1991), dropping only one word, an "or" before Asakusa and dashing the dots. Ueda cites a poem in Chinese by Sugiwara Michizane where Kannon is identified by the sound of its bell alone and a commentary by Higuchi Isao which amazes me though I do not know if I agree with it: "Normally the poet could tell which temple bell it was, but in the cherry blossom season, when all was enwrapped in tinged haze, he *felt as though* it was impossible to tell." (*Bashô and His Interpreters*).

CENTRE OF OUR WORLD   trans. Stewart

Now springtime clouds Japan with cherry-flowers,
Mount Fuji in the midst supremely towers.   – shô-u

Without seeing the original (Stewart does not give it), I cannot tell if we are talking about clouds of bloom, or the so-called "blossom-overcast" (*hanagumori*), which is to say a haze often seen when the cherry blooms. Regardless, Stewart's use of the English verb "clouds" is good, for it suggests the paradox inherent in the term "blossom clouds" which Japanese poets played with.

鹿島根本寺 憎まれぬ花の雲也月の寺 柳几 鹿嶋立
nikumarenu hana no kumo nari tsuki no tera   ryûjin ()
(hated-not blossoms' clouds become/are moon's temple)

cherry blossom clouds are not hated here the moon-temple	welcome clouds: blossoms below a temple in the moonlight

Despite Kenkô's observation that a modicum of clouds improved moon-viewing, clouds were generally hated for blocking views of the moon or of mountains. I know not why the location, Shikajima Nehonji (temple), matters, but give it in Japanese, above, in case anyone else does.

月よよしよしや花こそ春の雲 行助 大発句帳
tsuki yo yoshi yoshi ya hana koso haru no kumo   gyôjo? 1624/44
(moon-night good! good! blossom especially spring's clouds)

a moon-lit night good! good! spring clouds of cherry blossoms	the full moon rah! rah! with blossoms the clouds of spring

a full moon night
don't you cry, the clouds
are only blossoms

(Second go for this *ku*). Outside the bloomshade, these *clouds* would illuminate rather than darken the world.

送別・門口の櫻を雲のはしめ哉   蕪村
kadoguchi no sakura o kumo no hajime kana   buson -1783
(gate/door-opening's cherry[obj] cloud/s' beginning!/?/'tis)

in parting

that cherry tree
by my front gate: the start
of our clouds

Had Buson not written a preamble, I would have thought the poet fancied himself a Johnny Appleseed of the clouds, starting at home. Actually, Buson is using traditional trope, the cloud as something that lies between desire and the longed-for object. He and his friend will soon be separated by many clouds of which the cherry bloom is only the first. As the preambles of less highly respected poets rarely remain with the *ku*, their *ku's* real meaning, unlike that of this *ku,* must remain cloud-hidden.

花盛雲にかさなるいらか哉　紹巴 三崎志
hanazakari kumo ni kasanaru iraka kana　jôha (1523-1602)
(blossom-peak/heat cloud/s-with double/pile/overlap [roof] ridge/tiles!/?/'tis)

<blockquote>
the bloom-peak
an overlapping range of
tile and cloud
</blockquote>

English lacks a perfect verb for aesthetic overlap. The Japanese *kasanaru* (layer/overlap) works well because the traditional clothing of the nobility was multilayered (up to twelve layers) yet a bit of all the colors could be seen. Cherry blossoms look very good either with the indigo blue tiles of samurai dwellings or the thick finally woven straw roofs of the common folk. *Iraka* means either the roof ridge of any type of roof or tiles. Since tile roofs tend to be higher, that would be the case for the above *ku* and this: *"The bloom peak: / roofs rising higher / than the clouds"* (花盛雲より高きいらか哉　宗養 大発句帳 *hanazakari kumo yori takaki iraka kana*　sôyô (-1563))

隣／＼屋根の上より花の雲　子規 明治廿九
tonaridonari yane no ue yori hana no kumo　shiki 1896
(neighbor-neighbor rooves' above-from blossom-cloud/s)

<blockquote>
our neighbors
peeking over the roof-tops
blossom cloud
</blockquote>

Pardon my overly dramatic "peeking." Shiki lived in a good neighborhood, where each house had a cherry tree. But, as a rule, home was not the place where men became familiar with these clouds:

雲へ入人を出て見ん花の山　沾山 雪月花
kumo e iru hito o dete min hananoyama　tenzan 1669-1739
(clouds-to/into enter people leave-see blossom's/s' mountain)

<blockquote>

i'd leave man and enter the clouds on mount cherry	i'm off to see people who enter clouds mount cherry	into the clouds leaving man's world i'd see mt blossom

</blockquote>

Mount Cherry (*hananoyama*) usually is a urban park of cherry trees, but the mountain metaphor matches the clouds of bloom. As such a place would be crowded, I favor the middle reading.

雲ばかり見るまで入ぬ花の奥　梅室
kumo bakari miru made irinu hana no oku　baishitsu 1768-1852
(cloud/s only see until enter blossom's/s' innermost/farthest-recesses)

<blockquote>

climbing until clouds are all that i see, the inner bloom	deeper and deeper until all i see are clouds of cherry blossoms

</blockquote>

17 # 37 ~ 41

Oku, the most distant recesses of a home, forest, or country has no good English equivalent.[1]

白雲と一つにありく櫻哉　枯藤 蘆分船
shiragumo to hitotsu-ni ariku sakura kana　kotô 1694
(whiter-clouds-with one-as walk/ing cherry/blossoms!/?/'tis)

walking about
at one with the white clouds:
cherry blossoms

"At one with." While, I've felt *like* an airplane going through a maze of clouds, as already mentioned, I haven't ever fused with blossoms. With a few trees, yes. With the blossoms, no.

人々や笠きて花の雲に入　一茶
hitobito[ya] kasa kite hana no kumo ni iru　issa (-1827)
(person-person(people) hat-wearing blossom-cloud/s-into enter)

wearing hats
people enter the clouds
of blossoms

Hats were standard traveling/picnic/blossom-viewing gear. Pointed out like this, however, I believe they increase the enchantment, for Japanese legendary treasure ships (put under the pillow New Year's Eve) included a magical hat which allowed its wearer to fly.

見る人に雲は花のあまり哉　和推 雪月花
miru hito ni kumo wa hana no amari kana　wasui (1736)
(see person/s-to cloud/s-as-for blossom's/s' excess/extension/left-over!/?/'tis)

    to viewers　　　　　　　　　　　　to viewers
the clouds above extend　　　　　　the clouds are blossom
     the bloom　　　　　　　　　　　　 leftovers

Simple, but well put. When we would view something, we find it everywhere.

しら雲を枝にやつぎ木花盛　吹白 崑山集
shiragumo o eda ni ya tsugiki hanazakari　suihaku 1651
(white-cloud/s branches-on! grafted blossom-acme)

white clouds
are grafted on the limbs:
full blossom

---

1. *Oku* Usages. Another person's wife is, even today, called *oku-san* or *oku-sama,* "ms inner-recesses." It used to refer to the upper-class consorts of the lords, who lived a harem-like existence in the inner recesses of the palace. As a common term, its etymology means practically nothing to those who use it. A more specific usage is in the title of haiku's most famous travelogue, Bashô's *Oku-No Hoso Michi* (deep/recess's narrow-road), usually Englished as *Narrow Road to the Far North* or simply *Narrow Road*. Miyamori explains that the *oku* also was an abbreviation of the place name Michinoku, also called Ôshû. (Personally, I'd call it the "boondock trail.") And, the furthest reaches of Issa's Shinano, *oku-shinano* are often translated as "inner Shinano."

花は櫻まことの雲は消にけり　千代女 千代尼発句集
hana wa sakura makoto no kumo wa kienikeri chiyojo 1701-75
(blossoms-as-for cherry genuine clouds-as-for dissappear[+finality])

    say "blossom" and　　　　　　　　　　cherry's the blossom!
you say *cherry:* the real clouds　　　　　　　all the real clouds
     have all vanished!　　　　　　　　　　　have vanished

Chiyo plays on the idiom, "for blossoms, the cherry; for men, the warrior (*bushi*)." The implication is that the magnificent clouds of cherry vanquish the less substantial ones in the sky.

白雲の桜をくぐる外山哉　一茶
shiragumo no sakura o kuguru toyama kana issa -1827
(white-cloud/s cherry/ies snake/duck-through outer-mountain!/?/'tis)

white clouds
wind through the cherries
in the foothills

An observation of what happens on a mountain-side (mountain nearest to the view) when clouds come to earth or (the long-shot) a slow-motion description of cherries that do not bloom simultaneously.

雲の中にあそふ仙あり櫻山　府月 靱随筆
kumo no naka ni asobu sen[hijiri?] ari sakura yama fugetsu 1759
(cloud/s' inside/among play sage/hermit/s is/are cherry mountain)

   cherry blossoms　　　　　　　　　　some hermit sages
so that's how mountain sages　　　　　really play in the clouds
  play in the clouds　　　　　　　　　　mountain cherries

A new tooth on the old saw? The mountain sages of legend had the power to commandeer clouds.

花の山や雲の街の人通　百童 百堂千句
hana no yama ya kumo no chimata no hito tôri hyakudô 1775
(blossom/s' mountain: cloud/s' town's people pass)

cherry mountain
people pass through a town
made of clouds

If I ever put together a collection of surreal haiku, this will be in it. For some reason, I keep thinking of a ghost-town, tumbleweed and all.

さく花の雲の上にて寝起哉　一茶
saku hana no kumo no ue nite neoki kana issa -1827
(blooming blossom/s' cloud/s above-on sleep-wake!/?/'tis)

   sleeping and　　　　　　　　　　　 upon clouds
waking above clouds　　　　　　　　of cherry in full-bloom
   of blossom　　　　　　　　　　　　 i sleep i rise

みよしのや寝起も（ねころぶ）花の雲の上　一茶
miyoshino ya ne-oki mo[ne-korobu] hana no kumo no ue   issa -1827
(pretty[honorific]-yoshino! sleep-wake-even[or, sleep-roll] blossom-cloud/s'-on)

ah, yoshino!
sleeping and waking on
clouds of bloom

sweet yoshino!
rolling about on a cloud
of blossoms!

花の雲の上にて寝物がたり哉　一茶
hana no kumo no ue nite nemonogatari kana   issa
(blossom-cloud's-above/on sleep-thing-talk(nothings)[?] tis)

lying upon
a cloud of blossoms
bedtime tales

Issa was delighted to find a gap in cherry blossom poetry. Because there were few *ku* about sleeping on clouds of blossoms, he composed many. *Bedtime Tales* was the name for a region bordering on Minoguni and Chikaeguni famed for the nightlife, so there are possible allusions, too.

山寺や寝聳べる下の花の雲　一茶
yamadera ya ne-soberu shita no hana no kumo   issa
(mountain-temple! sleep/lie=loom[over] below's blossom-cloud/s)

a mountain temple
lying on top of the world
above bloom clouds

a mountain temple
clouds of blossom below
my exalted sleep

There is a unique Issa-style pun here. The double verb *ne-soberu* means *to sleep in a sloppy way*. *Soberu* is generally written in phonetic syllabary but Issa replaced the *sobe* with the Chinese character for *sobieru* which means to loom high, even magnificently, over the surroundings. This *ku* was written only a year before Issa's death. It is nice to think he was above it all.

花に来て花なき花や峰の雲　昌叱 大発句帳
hana ni kite hana naki hana ya mine no kumo   shôshitsu 1540-1603
(blossoms-to come blossom/s-not blossoms! peak/s' cloud/s)

arriving, we find
the blossoms aren't blossoms:
mountain clouds

Perhaps I should have put Shôshitsu's *ku* into the cherry-hunting chapter, for being fooled, or rather fooling oneself, is one of the pleasures of the hunt (so long as it does not end in tragedy!). But it is nice to have a reversal of the usual vector of which the following is typical: *"Before we realize / they have turned blossom / clouds on the peak"* （いつとなく花になりけり峯の雲　梅室 *itsu to naku hana ni narikeri mine no kumo* baishitsu (1768-1852)). That the first part of Baishitsu's *ku* may play upon the idiom of people growing up only makes the boring worse. Unless . . . *Unless* it is the case that clouds were so disliked we can imagine the much despised ugly duckling clouds turning into magnificent cherry blossom swans? *Just like that / they turn into blossoms! / hilltop clouds!*

白雲の花の上行く嵐哉　今江
shiragumo no hana no ue yuku arashi kana   ginkô c1780
(white-cloud's blossom's-above go storm!/?/'tis)

this storm
rushing over white clouds
of blossoms!

what a storm!
stupid white clouds rush
over blossoms

Are the white clouds blossoms or part of the storm? Since storm clouds tend to be gray, I suspect the former; but who knows? When one encounters a chain of modification in Japanese, it is hard to be certain what modifies what. My unlikely "stupid" reading follows the homophonic pun-derived conceit of *white* as *unknowing* or *ignorant*.

白雲の風にほぐるゝ櫻哉　亭水 春遊
shiragumo no kaze ni hogururu sakura kana   teisui 1767
(white clouds' wind-by/in unravel/ing cherry/blossoms!/?/'tis)

white clouds
unraveled by the wind:
cherry blossoms

the white clouds
unknit by the wind were
cherry blossoms

The original allows for two readings, which can only be Englished separately.

一天の雲吸ふ山の桜かな　亀洞
hito ten no kumo suu yama no sakura kana   kidô fl. 1690
(one-heaven's clouds suck/ing mountain's/s' cherry/ies!/?/'tis)

hungry bloom

they've sucked up
all the clouds in the sky:
mountain cherries!

the hill's sucked up
all the clouds in the sky?
what cherry bloom!

cherry blossoms
on a hill puffing in and out
all those clouds?

The ambiguity of the party doing the sucking does not translate. "Suck" also meant smoke/puff, as on a pipe, and even "kiss" as we have already noted.

.

雲を呑て花を吐なるよしの山　蕪村
kumo o nonde hana o hakunaru yoshinoyama   buson (1715-83)
(cloud-drinking/swallowing, blossoms/petal-spitting/spewing yoshino mountain)

mount yoshino
drinks up clouds and
spews out petals

Did Buson know Kidô's poem? Or was it enough to entertain an image of caves up on mountains housing the wind and breathing clouds? Has he turned the cloud-factory (The ancient Greeks and Japanese shared the general idea; I borrow Thoreau's term based on the latter) into a blossom processor?   Note that the *drinking+spewing* metaphor suggests the greater metaphor of bloom-as-inebriation. Stewart translates *"Mount Yoshino has swallowed up the clouds, / And now spits cherry-petals forth in crowds."* Rightly or wrongly, the metaphor is different. It doesn't hiccup. Strangely enough, neither he, nor the Japanese give equal time to the reverse vector. The cloud-factory, blossom-processor evidently has two settings:

花を呑で雲を吐なりよしの山　蕪村
hana o nonde kumo o haku nari yoshino yama   buson 1782
(blossom/petal-drinking/swallowing cloud-spitting/spewing yoshino mountain)

mount yoshino
swallows blossoms and
disgorges clouds

Buson's preface for both this and the previous *ku* mention violent wind and rain on the day he left Yoshino which had been in the peak of bloom, and end with the observation that, with the flight of the petals, "none of spring remains" (飛花、春を余さず). I cannot be sure why one *ku* was so strongly favored by the critics and can only guess that it had the advantage of alluding to the sleight-of-hand artists who swallowed things and spewed forth petals (or, for that matter butterflies!), though none of this is mentioned in the annotations I have seen. The combination of swallowing+spewing was not Buson's invention. An older *senryû* quips: *"The spewed cloud / and the swallowed cloud, both: / A fall peak"* (吐く雲も呑み込む雲も秋の峰 武玉川十一 *haku kumo mo nomikomu kumo mo aki no mine* 1757). Both may be based on yet older *ku* such as:

い〔ッ？〕へんの雲を吐くなり花の庭　正隣 洗濯物
ippen [?] no kumo o haku nari hana no niwa   seirin 1666
(one-piece of cloud spewing blossom/s'/tree's garden)

a scrap of cloud   part of the clouds
spat out by the garden   disgorged by our own
cherry tree   blossom garden

This probably plays with the "one-sky" (*itten*) meaning "the whole sky" found in an earlier *ku*. It is also possible that some editor used the wrong Chinese character for *haku* and the "spew/spat/disgorged" should be "rake up" (掃く, not 吐く!), in which case the "by" should be "in."

面白や理くつはなしに花の雲　越人 あらの
omoshiro ya rikutsu wa nashi ni hana no kumo   etsujin 1689
(interesting! rationalizing-as-for not-with, blossom-cloud)

look at that!
an honest-to-goodness
cloud of blossoms!

Is Etsujin talking about cherry blossoms in a sun-warmed tree giving off vapor after a sudden chill? Or is it literal clouds of petals that have been swept up by the breeze and ascended, as gliders sometimes do in rising warm air? Or does he just mean that the magnificently blooming cherries really look like clouds, unlike the petaled clouds of Buddhist catechism?

雲と見し高ねに帰る花も哉　智蘊 大発句帳
kumo to mishi takane ni kaeru hana mogana chiun 17c
(cloud-as see, high-peak-to return blossom wish-for)

    oh for a blossom
    that passing for a cloud
    returns to heaven

山の花誠の雲に成なかし　犀角 蘆分船
yama no hana makoto no kumo ni naringashi saikaku 17c
(mountain blossoms, genuine cloud-as/into become-flow[away])

    mountain blossoms
    become real clouds
    and float away

Petals don't fall, they just float away. The first *ku* plays with the stereotypical blossom returning to its *roots*, homophonic with *peak* (*ne*).   Regarding the second, clouds *do* come and go in thin air.

出し入レは雲の仕事や山櫻　睡雲 新選
dashi ire wa kumo no shigoto ya yamazakura suiun 1773
(taking-out-bringing-in-as-for clouds' work!/?/: mountain cherries)

    pick up and delivery
    is the work of the clouds
    mountain cherries

This is not quite blossoms-as-clouds *or* the vice-versa, and far gentler than Buson's vomiting or expectorating metaphor.   I think it a brilliant take on the *calling* of real mountain clouds!

花の山又雲にして戻りけり　其水 芭蕉庵再興集
hananoyama mata kumo ni shite modorikeri kisui 1771
(blossom-mountain again cloud-into make return[+emphatic])

    mount cherry   again we help
    once again comes back   cloud up mount cherry
    to us as cloud   and go home

Unsure of whether blooming here makes clouds or scattered petals return us to them, I favor the latter.

夕くれや雲にまきれて散櫻　鳥跡 花七日
yûgure ya kumo ni magirete chiru sakura chôseki (1777)
(evening: clouds-with mixed-up fall/scatter cherry/ies/blossoms/petals)

    this evening
    falling petals confused
    with clouds

    what an evening!   what a sunset
    as cherry blossoms fall they   the falling cherry petals
    mix with clouds   mixed with clouds

雲と咲雪と散り行櫻哉　峯鳥 安永四
kumo to saku yuki to chiri yuku sakura kana hôchô 1775
(cloud as bloom, snow as fall/scatter-go cherry/blossoms!/?/'tis)

    they blossom
    as clouds and fall as snow:
    cherry flowers

While we have examples enough of falling petals joining the cloud metaphor, a blizzard is the standard conceit. There is also the cataract:

雲払ふ木の間／＼や花の瀧　湖石 月影塚
kumo harau konoma konoma ya hana no taki　koseki ()
(cloud-clear-up/sweep tree-space/between x2 blossom-cataract/s)

    sweeping out
   clouds tree by tree
    petal cataracts

a cloud empties   cloud suicide
between the cherry trees   cataract after cataract
a petal cataract   of cherry petals

    blossom rapids
  cleaning out tree after
    tree of cloud

My translations fail to achieve the brilliance of the original. Please forgive the suicide.

竜に成てのぼらん物や花の雲　賢之 崑山集
taki ni narite noboran mono ya hananokumo　kenshi 1651
(dragon-into become climb/rise-would thing! blossom-cloud/s)

   believe me, they
  would rise up as dragons!
   blossom-clouds

Some, not all, cherry trees seem buoyant. *Noboru* means both *rise* and *climb*. A kite in the sky and a carp in a river (or waterfall) do it. "Rise up" is not quite right, but what can I/English do?

浮雲はあだなる花のかたみ哉　南佛 つくは
ukigumo wa ada naru hana no katami kana　nambutsu (1356)
(drifting/floating clouds-as-for ephemeral/empty/vain blossoms' *memento mori*!/?/' tis)

   memento mori
  for the short-lived bloom:
   drifting clouds

Intended or not, *katami*, or "*memento mori*" is homophonic with "solidity." Clouds were traditionally identified with the souls of the recently cremated. Is there an allusion to someone who died young?

菩薩こそのりうつります花の雲　立圃 花見記
bosatsu koso nori-utsurimasu hana no kumo　ryûho 1594-1669
(saint especially ride/mount change/move/die blossom's/petals' cloud/s)

   swing low

   just the thing
  for a saint to mount
   blossom clouds

Buddhist saints were carried off by five-color scented clouds. I do not know if the original refers to the blossoms on the trees or (less likely) petals in the air. Old Issa wrote something similar: *"Saints, please / make an appearance / blossom clouds"* (菩薩達御出現あれ花の雲　一茶 文政四 *bosatsu-tachi goshutsugen are hananokumo*).

持て贈るみやげの雲や山桜　也有 アルス
mochite okuru　miyage no kumo ya yamazakura　yayû (1701-83)
(bringing-give [return mistake?], present-cloud! mountain cherry)

this cloud i bring
as my present to you?
mountain cherry!

A charming accompaniment for a flowering branch, a sack, or a sleeve-full of petals.

家つとに雲の折らるゝ櫻哉　梅志 春の遊ひ
iezuto ni kumo no oraruru sakura kana　baishi 1767
(home-gift-as cloud-broken cherry!/?/'tis)

cloud torn off	a bit of cloud
for a take-home gifts	broken off for a present
cherry bloom	cherry blossoms

Japanese has an extremely large vocabulary for *giving and receiving*. Not only is there a great variety of verbs for both, depending upon who gives what to whom and the circumstances, but there are more categories of what we can only call "gifts" or "presents." An *iezuto*, or gift to take home, is one such.

文遣すとて・ひとつかみ白雲おくる櫻哉　蓼太
fumi yarasu tote// hito-tsukami shirakumo okuru sakura kana　ryôta 1707-87
(writing send/entrust-as // one-grab/clutch [of] white-cloud sending cherry!/?/'tis)

told to add words

one handful of
white cloud delivered:
cherry blossoms

The poet had to invent a good term for a "piece" of cloud, and came up with the grab/clutch/handful. It makes the poem.

ちりひぢて雲を手に取花見哉　哲阿彌？
chiri hijite kumo o te ni toru hanami kana　tetsua? 1798
(rubbish snatching cloud/s hand-in take blossom-viewing!/?/'tis)

blossom-viewing	though rubbish
the rubbish we snatch up	it is your own cloud:
clouds in hand	gathering petals

If *a cloud in hand* is not proverbial, it should be. The second reading is a loose one. Let's come back to ground with what should be a classic, though I believe it is as unknown as any *ku:*

物干や夜着かかへ出て花の雲　岱水
monohoshi ya yogi kakae-dete hana no kumo taisui (early 18c)
(thing-dry[clotheshorse/clothes-line/clothes-pole])

<table>
<tr><td>

time for drying!
i carry a quilt outside
blossom clouds!

</td><td>

blossom clouds!
out i go hugging the quilt
it's time to air

</td></tr>
</table>

As I first read this *ku,* I saw a bamboo pole (the most common drying device in Japan) and clothing against a background of summer clouds, a combination every bit as sublime as Niagara Falls. But, chances are the *monohoshi* at the start of the *ku* refers to an activity instead of the *thing* it usually means, though the second reading saves the thing by imagining the poet roused to bring out the quilts by spotting the bare pole against a background of . . . . . I also wonder if by throwing the quilt over the pole, the beautiful sight will be lost to the poet who returns to his desk by the window.

送られし狼鳴くや花の雲　一茶
okurareshi ôkami naku ya hana no kumo issa
(sent wolf/wolves cry!/: blossom-cloud/s)

<table>
<tr><td>

sent into the hills
i hear wolves howling
clouds of bloom

</td><td>

sent out ahead
i hear my wolf cry-out
a bloom cloud

</td><td>

they send me
when the wolves howl
clouds of bloom

</td></tr>
</table>

At first, I thought this Issa's version of Buson's man sent to scout out the cherry trees (*#1-39.*) and my task was relating the wolf/wolves' "cry/call" to the bloom cloud/s. Then, discovering the existence of a once widely held fiction of *okuri-ôkami,* a pair of wolves imagined to lead and trail people walking in the wilds, my problem was the passive voice of *okurareshi*. I guess that it applies to Issa being sent out *and,* by allusion, to the imagined nature of the wolf/wolves he heard. Note that these *sending-wolves* (people were often accompanied for a spell when leaving, so "send" in Japanese also means *accompany*) ate people who fell – indirectly helping travelers by causing them to watch their footing – but, otherwise, defended them from wolf-packs and pointed out good things, like the blossoms Issa sought, I guess.

田上の尼へ花見にまねかれて
海を見る目つきもいでず花の雲　去来 ～句集
umi o miru metsuki mo idezu hana no kumo kyorai (-1704)
(sea[obj] see eye-look even appears-not blossom's/s' cloud/s)

on being invited to a blossom-viewing at nun tanoue's

no eyes amazed
to view the sea below
blossom clouds

My first attempt to make sense of this (*blossom clouds / i prefer the way you look / gazing at the sea*) failed to convince my best reader, but she had no alternative. Then, recalling how Issa wrote of women thrilled to view the sea on the one day a Sacred Mountain was open to female visitors, . . .

Blossom Overcast, *or Haze*
花曇り
hana-gumori

のとかさの満るを花の曇り哉 亀全 (入+王) 拍挙千句
nodoka(e?)sa no michiru o hana no kumori kana   kizen 1782
(calmness' filling[obj]: blossoms-haze/overcast!/?/'tis)

a calmness
fills the air: call it
blossom haze

Or blossom *daze*! Unlike blossom clouds, this overcast is not a metaphor but *a type of weather* not uncommon when cherries are in bloom. Buson (-1783) placed the phenomenon in precise seasonal time-frame: *"Blossom haze / an evening close to / a hazy moon night"* (花曇朧にちかき夕かな 蕪村 *hanagumori oboro ni chikaki yuube kana*). Many poems credit the scent of the plum with hazing the spring moon, but Buson may be more accurate, for the humidity usually does not rise in time for the plum. I will use "haze" more than "overcast" because it is shorter.

あつらへの天気なりけり花曇 史邦 ありそ海
atsurae no tenki narikeri hanagumori   shiho (1695)
(made-to-order weather is[+emph.] blossom-overcast)

this weather
is made to order!
blossom haze

Two less successful *ku* saying, I think, the same thing: *"As the blossoms / themselves would have it: / a cloudy haze"* (此空を我と曇りて櫻哉 之由 三千花 *kono sora o ware to kumorite sakura kana* (shiyû (1725)); *"A hazy day / reflecting the hazy / cherry blossoms"* (曇る日は曇る姿の櫻哉 吟江 心花 *kumoru hi wa kumoru sugata no sakura kana* ginkô (1776)). While the blue sky is refreshing, the blossoms and blossom-viewers will probably hold up better with something between them and the sun.

曇る日は一日花に照れけり 挙白? 雑談
kumoru hi wa ichi nichi hana ni terarekeri   kyôhaku (-1696)
(overcast-day/sun-as-for one-day[all day-long] blossoms-by lit[+emphatic])

an overcast day   an overcast day
dawn to dusk , sunshine   dawn to dusk, in the light
on the bloom   of the blossoms

Sunshine may seep through the haze *all day long*, unlike the case where a brighter sun and clouds share the sky so that the shine is *on & off*. My first reading of *hi* is "sun," my second "day."

ひとつ脱こころしきりや花くもり 市原多代女
hitotsu nugu kokoro shikiri ya hanagumori tayojo 1775-1865
(one/a bit strip/undress/peel-off heart intently blossom-haze)

blossom haze we feel like peeling off at least a layer	how i feel like stripping down! blossom haze	an overcast day people and cherry trees feel like stripping

The balmy day makes everyone – but, especially women: the poet is female – feel overdressed. I imagine a full bloom with the blossoms just beginning to shed their petals. At the same time, cradled in the hazy envelope of bloom, the *kokoro* (body/mind) is at peace and we shed a layer of body armor.

息杖の音や鈴鹿の花曇 狸唾 小弓
ikizue no oto ya suzuka no hanagumori rida 1699
(breath-cane[porters' staff]'s noise! bell-deer' blossom-overcast)

blossom haze on belldeer peak the sound of porter staffs	is that the sound of lug staffs? blossom hazy belldeer peak

At first, I imagined a shrine in Nara (famous for tame deer): *Blossom haze / the sound of porter staffs / and deer bells*. But something seemed off. I overlooked the name of a peak. And, there may be more. Emitting a noise in Japanese is making it "stand," and porters had the practice of *standing* their belled staffs (used for carrying things) up and pounding the ground to get money for *sake* (tips) from their charges. Haze cuts down on some noises, calling our attention to others. Ground noise might do well.

ごろ／＼と車の音の花曇 (付句) 李由 韻塞
gorogoro to kuruma no oto no hanagumori riyû (1697)
(rumble/thunder-rumble/thunder-with car-sound-blossom-overcast)

a blossom haze
of the rumbling sound
of the ox cars

The haze and soft blossoms filter out high sounds, leaving the low rumbling sound of the carts full of nobles or elderly on their way to blossom-viewing. The original is a typical Japanese chain of modification for the subject of the sentence, the *hana-gumori,* or "blossom-overcast," at the end.

頭痛にもにくまれぬ名や花曇 也有
zûtsû ni mo nikumarenu na ya hanagumori yayû -1783
(headache-as-even hated name: blossom-overcast)

beyond reproach the name for my headache: is *blossom haze*	a word not even headaches can make us hate *blossom haze*

Apparently, this overcast included smoke, dust and pollen. Allergies are common at this time.

本町の埃の末は花曇（つけ句）木導 韻塞
honchô no hokori no sue wa hanagumori   mokudô (1697)
(main-town[a street in the business district of edo]'s dust's end-as-for blossom-haze)

blossom haze:
where mainstreet's dust
comes to rest

mainstreet dust
on the far side of town:
blossom haze

The more natural "ends up" would be more accurate, but sound dictated "comes to rest." I see a hazy cherry tree'ed hillside across town, with dust rising from the streets because of heavy traffic to and fro the blossom viewing. Pollen and pollution (things out of place, like dust in the air) reinforce each other, hence the headache.

出て見れば出ぬ人はなし花くもり 濱馬 句鑑
detemireba denu hito wa nashi hanagumori   hinba (1777)
(going-out-seeing/checking leaving person/s -as-for not: blossom overcast)

i came and saw
not a person missing
blossom haze

blossom haze
i came and saw that no one
was not there

i came and saw
the whole world was out
blossom haze

Depending on context, *denu* can be positive or negative. Here, it is more interesting positive.

もし降らば天津乙女ぞ花曇 一茶
moshi furaba amatsu otome zo hanagumori   issa -1827
(if falls, heaven firmament/shoals[?] princess [emphatic]! blossom-overcast)

heaven's cherries
:

blossom-overcast
if something comes down
expect maidens

when it settles
on us, i think *angels:*
blossom-haze

Allan Watts once quipped, "what is this "it" that rains?" Whatever *it* is, English's need for such a pronoun hurts haiku such as the above. Adding "something" left me no room to modify the maidens as heavenly. The second reading is as impressionistic as the original, but not the same.

花曇り誠になりぬ山櫻 沾峨 吐屑庵
hanagumori makoto ni narinu yamazakura   senga 1776
(blossom-haze/overcast truly become/s mountain cherry/ies)

this blossom haze
has become the real thing
mountain cherries

mountain cherries
the so-called blossom haze
is tangible here

Finding actual trees in bloom makes the "blossom haze" more than a calendrical fiction. The second, less likely, reading puts the poet up the mountain.

18 # 11 ~ 14

雲雀にもしをりつけてや花曇　李仲 三千花
hibari ni mo shiori tsukete ya hanagumori   richû (1725)
(lark-to-even, melancholy attach/add/ing!/?/: blossom-haze/overcast)

are larks too
marking their paths?
blossom haze

for larks too
a poetic patina?
blossom overcast

blossom haze
the lark's calls take on
a plaintive air

I am torn between two different *shiori* here. The first reading takes the common term, meaning broken twigs or branches marking a path as the poet's intent. Presumeably, the calls serve for markers. The less common term is an elegant sort of melancholy (sadness+beauty). In Noh drama, *shiori* is the way to cry, to "cloud" the mask, when an actor bends down slightly and hold his hands over his eyes. In *haikai*, it refers to an idea from Bashô's late period where the subject of a *ku* is not in itself melancholy but still moves us in such a way. His disciples later found this made most sense when applied to sequential *ku* in linked verse. My respondent warns me about going too deeply into such hidden meanings, but I feel the information and secondary readings indirectly enrich the first one.

忘れぬる笠はそれ迄花くもり　柳童 句鑑
wasurenuru kasa wa sore made hanagumori   ryûdô 1777
(forgotten hat-as-for then/that-until blossom-overcast)

my cherry hat
forgotten, forgotten:
blossom haze

that's the end
of my blossom hat!
pink overcast

I think the idea is that the haze is so heavy the hat, probably dangling from a limb in the bloomshade, is not missed until it is too late to walk back for it. At the same time haze suggests a daze, where forgetfulness is *de rigor*. In the second reading, the poet glances back at the blossoms from a distance and thinks that while he may miss his hat, his hat has come to a singularly fortunate end.

U·N·S·O·L·V·E·D

鍋の尻朝にうれし花曇　陳次 雑中
nabe no shiri ashita ni ureshi hanagumori   chinji ()
(kettle/s[name-for-maid] butt/s morning-on delighted blossom-overcast)

How delightful the kettle butt this morning – blossom overcast.
Does the poet enjoy the dull reflection of the bloom on kettles washed and laid out to dry?

The maids' rumps so happy this morning – blossom overcast.
Would the delight of the maids, called kettles (*(O)nabe*), be noticeable in their movement?

This morning, joyful scouring the kettle butts – blossom overcast.
Is this Kyôto, where a *zappai ku* claims they polish their kettle butts morning *and* night?

The problem is identifying the butts and relating them to the overcast day for blossom-viewing. 誰か?

19

Other Trees
松柳等

一花におもひやらるゝ木草哉　紹巴
hitohana ni omoiyararuru ki kusa kana　jôha 1523-1602
(one blossom-to/by/for thought-of tree-grass[all-plants]!/?)

cherries bloom
and men think about
all plants

for one flower
our hearts go out to all
the other plants

in one blossom
all plants big and small
remembered

do all plants
gain from our compassion
for one flower?

The passive *omoiyaruru,* "longed/sympathized-for/with" linking the blossom, presumably the generic cherry with the plants Englishes poorly but the idea translates well enough. It contradicts an earlier *ku* in a 1561 anthology Jôha edited: *"Cherries bloom / in Spring other plants fail / to attract us"* (櫻さく春は色なき草木哉　兼載 大発句帳 *sakura saku haru wa ironaki kusaki kana*　kensai -1510).

梅こほれ櫻にうつる柳哉　竹亭 芋環
ume kobore sakura ni utsuru yanagi kana　chikutei ()
(plum/s spill/s, cherry/ies-to shift/catch willow/s!/?/'tis)

after plums blow
they bow toward the cherry
weeping willows

the plum blossoms
spilling, the willows turn
to the cherries

the plums done
cherries gain the affection
of the willows

Pine is also noticed against the plum and cherry when they blossom, but the willow is newly green and sways back and forth, allowing the poet to play with the verb *utsuru*, i.e. "shifting" from one to another, playing the intermediary between the plum and the cherry, whose bloom miss one another – *and* providing a risqué hint of a transfer of affection. Japanese willows do not really weep.

花のうへにふくとも風の柳かな　紹巴
hana no ue ni fuku to mo kaze no yanagi kana　jôha
(blossom/s-above blow/ing even wind's willow!/?/'tis)

that willow
blowing over the blossoms
is the wind

though it blows
o'er cherry bloom, willow
belongs to the wind

Grammar makes my "wind-as-willow" idea unlikely. The second reading is almost surely right and serves as a fine retort to the previous *ku*, though it probably antedates it.

花過てもとの柳にもとりけり 荷翠 真木柱
hana sugitte moto no yanagi ni modorikeri   kasui 1697
(blossom past-even, original willow-as/to return[+finality])

the blossoms past
the willows once again
become willows

the bloom passes
and the willows return
to willowhood

A good translation is *impossible* because of the English requirement for number. The untranslated alternative reading is "*Her* bloom past, / the willow once again / only a willow." *I.e.*, an allusion to a woman who spent time as a courtesan in the flower (cherry blossom) of her beauty.

こきませる柳の枝や絲櫻　乙州
kokimazeru yanagi no eda ya itozakura   otokuni -1720
(stir-mixing willow's/s' limbs!/?/: thread-cherry/ies)

willow limbs
tangled up with thread
cherry limbs

their limbs mixing
promiscuously, weeping
willow and cherry

We have a whole chapter for the "string/thread-cherry," usually Englished as "weeping cherry." The original *ku* is no more anthropomorphic than the first reading.

地謡や花の外には松はかり　其角 五元
jiutai ya hana no hoka ni wa matsu bakari   kikaku -1707
(earth-song/chant[noh-chorus] blossom/s-other-than, pine/s-only)

a noh chorus
besides cherry blossoms
only the pine

The *jiutai* is a background song in noh, sung by a chorus. My respondent notes the décor is simply pine trees, but sometimes, cherry blossoms, too. Kikaku may allude to lazy samurai (*jiutai-bushi*) who fritter away time with women=blossoms while waiting=*matsu* = pine (pun).

まつ風のはなより出るゆふへかな 紹巴
matsu kaze no hana yori ideru yûbe kana   jôha 1523-1602
(waiting wind's blossoms-from-come-out evening!/?/'tis)

this dusk when
the pine breeze comes out
of the blossoms

the pine breeze
emerges from the bloom
in the evening

The "pine breeze" (*matsu-kaze*) is green and fragrant in the spring, cooling in the summer, melancholy (like the high and lonely sound of bluegrass) in the autumn and cold in the winter. The idea of a breeze that resides here and there, is refreshing. The "blossom-breeze" (*hana-kaze*) later, we shall meet later is an altogether different animal.

さくら咲遠山松の曇かな 柳眉 花供養
sakura saku tôyama matsu no kumori kana ryûhi 1795
(cherry[blossoms] far-mountain's/s' pine/s overcast!/?/'tis)

cherries bloom
pine on distant mountains
are overcast

cherries bloom
on the distant mountain
haze, *pine* haze!

I cannot tell whether the idea is that the blossoms are clouds that block view of the pine or that there is *pine* haze as well as blossom haze. Regardless, it is a pleasant *ku*.

夜ざくらや暫眠る松の陰 㻌卜
yozakura ya shibaraku nemuru matsu no kage futo ()
(night-cherry/ies!/: a-while sleep/ing pine-shade)

night blossoms
i get to sleep for a while
under a pine

The pine typically offered a refuge in the day. This is new. In a park that was solid cherries, anyone trying to sleep might get stepped on by dancing drunks, so . . . Or is it a John waiting (also *matsu*)?

遠山の松やさながら花のしん 弘嘉
tôyama no matsu ya sanagara hana no shin kôka ()
(distant-mtn's pine/s!/: so-being-even, blssm's core/heart/style/stigma)

pines on distant mountains
should we call them
blossom styles?

distant mountain
pine trees: the backbone
of the blossoms?

are they the hearts
of the cherry blossoms, pines
on distant mountains

Shin suggests the heart or core of something. I wish I knew what terms were natural in English before science took over the language. Would a blossom's central male-part be better called "prick" rather than a "heart" or a "style"?

春いく世松にあひ生の山さくら 宗祇
haru ikuyo matsu ni aishô no yamazakura sôgi 1420-1502
(spring how-many ages/generations pine-to congenial's mountain-cherry)

how many springs
has the ancient pine enjoyed
this mountain cherry?

how many springs
have these mountain cherries
cheered the old pine?

I appended "ancient" to the pine because the original's "spring, how many realms/ages" failed to English. In the original, the cherry comes at the end as per the first reading, but the subject is the cherry tree, or trees, as per the second. Pines in the mountains could live for what seemed forever and the mountain cherries were themselves known to live for centuries, so this is an old friendship, indeed.

other trees

松葉拾ひちろりや埋ム花の雲　露言 新道
matsuba hiroi chirori ya umemu hana no kumo　rogen ()
(pine needles gathering sprinkle[mimesis]!/: bury-would blossom-cloud)

blossom clouds i'd bury with a sprinkling of pine needles	i gather pine needles and sprinkling them bury my blossom cloud	pine needles sprinkled over the fallen cherry clouds

The original has a "would-do" feeling that I found impossible to fit into all the readings. While the blossom clouds might be on the tree/s, the mimesis *chirori* suggests needles falling lightly upon the fallen petals and I cannot imagine throwing the needles into the air. (Didn't Yoko Ono once bury a cloud?)

梅・柳・松・杉

These are the four other trees mentioned in this chapter, the plum (flowering apricot), willow, pine and cedar, respectively. There would have been more trees and more of each had the idea for a chapter come earlier. As it is, they are scattered through the book. The only plant *often* mentioned in connection with the cherry not found in this chapter is the wisteria, which is a vine and not a tree, and, as we have seen with the *Late Cherries,* starts the summer. While there are some cedars mentioned elsewhere in this book, I am afraid there are not enough of them with respect to pine, for cedar is *the* shrine tree and, with its straight trunk without noticeable limbs, offers a greater contrast to the cherry than the pines which (like the Scot pine) have strong individual character. Then again, it may be that personality is what endeared pine to the poets. Be that as it may, let us see one good cedar *ku:*

花の気を杉の林にさましけり 子規
hana no ki o sugi no hayashi ni samashikeri　shiki 1898
(blossom-feeling/spirit[obj.] cedar grove-in cool down[+emph])

i cool down
my blossom fever
in the cedars

A grove of cedar rather than the usual cool pine suggest Shiki is on (or imagining) a mountain with a shrine as well as a temple whose grounds probably had the blossoms.

~~~~~~

<div align="center">
南殿桜樹者, 本是梅樹也
That cherry tree of Sir South, once was a plum, none doubt.
</div>

This legend-in-a-line comes from an early 13c story (「古事談」源顕兼の編) about a tree which had been transplanted from the old capital Nara to the new one we now know as Kyôto. It did not take to the new soil and pined away (if one can say that of a plum), but since the tree that replaced it was later replaced and that too was replaced, who knew exactly when the switch from plum to cherry was made! This tale indirectly celebrates the pleasure of not knowing and it is a perfect reflection of the problem with old poems which was broached in the introduction – it is hard to say when a blossom changes from being a plum (flowering apricot, say sticklers for botany) to a cherry. This is one reason why I want another chapter with about ten plum *waka* and fifty plum *ku* for comparison if a publisher brave enough to venture an enlarged book at a decent price can be found.

20 Other Things

> The artistic character of the people is indicated in many ways – in trifling matters even. If a child accidentally punches a hole through the paper screen, instead of mending it with a square piece of paper, the paper is cut in the form of a cherry blossom. Seeing this pretty way of mending holes in screens I recalled the broken windows in our country mended with an old hat or a stuffed bag.   Edward S. Morse: *Japan Day by Day* (re.1877-8, publ.1917)

This paragraph from Morse's enlightened late-19c book noted the clean-swept walks, tasteful houses with beautiful grained panels, odd knots from trees and woody fungus hollowed out to hold flowers, all of which, most remarkably, could be found "in the houses of common country farmers."

The Japanese equivalent of our Romeo and Juliet would be the 1771 *jôruri*=ballad-play (shamisen accompaniment) by Chikamatsu Hanjiya (半二也 = not to be confused with the even more famous Chikamatsu Monzaemon, who wrote *ku* #17-31) called 妹背山婦女庭訓 = little-sister-back-mountain-woman-garden-lesson, or, *My Sweet Baby Mountain, A Cautionary Tale for Housewives.* The youth, naturally, a handsome samurai, dies to save the family of his beloved, whose name translates as Separated-bird. Not having read the play, I do not know exactly why, but suffice it to say that "duty runs deepest when relationships are unclear" (不知な中程義理深し) – this makes about as much sense as "freedom is another word for nothing left to lose," and the equivalence of a warrior to the cherry blossoms of Yoshino is invoked as he dies, maybe at his own and maybe at the hands of her father, a judge, and bloody tears at the waste of a young warrior's life fall on a branch of a blooming cherry that is tossed into the Yoshino river, and floats down to the sea, where Separated-bird sees it. I guess the blood was washed off, for she took it for a sign that her sweetheart *survived*. So, she wishes him the best, that he lives a thousand or ten-thousand years, etc. and kills herself so she can be his wife in the next world (after rebirth). I guess that if the youth died, she would have stayed alive to pray for his soul! The reason she killed herself is not that of Romeo or Juliet but, East or West, the hero and heroines die for tragic – due to *the inexorable working of things* (G.H.) – reasons.

The snow-princess gathers up dark cherry petals with her feet, grinding them into ink with her tears for water. Her toenails do for a brush. Her heart goes into the painting. Rustling. Is it a breeze? The blossoms turn into white mice that gnaw through the vines binding her . . . Abbrev. from a 1757 ballad-drama *Kinkakuji*.

I once visited England and was delighted to get double the usual three months for a tourist because, the immigration official told me (after hearing why I was there and seeing my hand-made PET-bottle fiddle), "We English like eccentrics." Japanese, like the English, have many books about interesting eccentrics and one such book dated 1790, introduces one Arima Ryôkyû, who loved cherry blossoms so much he went into debt to buy a huge tree. When it was delivered, he found it was too big to plant in his garden. People asked him *"What will you do?"* And he replied nonchalantly, *"I'll just have to make this a-cherry-tree-for-viewing-as-I-lie-on-my-side."* So says the abbreviated version I have seen (in 季語の底力), but the explanation that there was no space makes no sense. Could it mean that he would only see the trunk from inside his house because the branches would spread over his roof?

☆ I hope to have many more, and longer, stories, some about *specific old trees*, if circumstances permit a larger book.

BOOK I

postscript
13+ Derivations of *"sakura"*

As you may see in the selected bibliography, my favorite research aid is the Japanese National Language Large Dictionary (*Nihon Kokugo Daijiten*), a twenty-volume set – mine is reduced print ten-volume – which I call the OJD, that is, *"Only Japanese Dictionary"* or *"Old Japanese Dictionary."* While it is not as good at putting dates on first usages as the OED, it is more fun because usage examples are often complete haiku or senryû (in that, it beats Samuel Johnson's Dictionary, too!) and because of the enormous number of largely absurd etymologies given for most basic words. Many are so hilarious that I have long wished to compile them into a book. Unfortunately, none of the 13 (!) derivations of *sakura* (the cherry tree and/or its blossom) include anything as ridiculous as the plum, or *ume,* which one benighted scholar claimed was a fusion of the first syllabet of *utsukushi,* meaning "beautiful" and *mezurashi,* meaning "rare/precious;" but the *sakura* philology is remarkably full of significance and some of the old derivations are taken seriously today, for they confirm the folklore – which is to say *natural history* – of the cherry, something that goes back to a time when Japan had no written records. All brackets are mine.

    1. It [*sakura*] is a corruption of *sakuya* of *sakuya-hime,* the "blooming" or "opening princess" [depending on the Chinese character used for her name] who was the spirit of the cherry.

    2. It is an abbreviation of *saki-muragaru,* "blooming-crowd/swarm." [*~ra* is a pluralizer]

    3. It signifies *saki-ura,* "blooming-beauty." It signifies *saku-uruwashi-gi,* "bloom-beauty-like-tree." [different sources, and the second involves abbreviation, but basically the same idea]

    4. As the most beautiful of myriad blossoms, it is an abbreviated corruption of *sakihaya,* "blooming-light-glow/reflect." [in ancient Japan, the truest beauty glowed from within; one lady glowed right through her clothes!]

    5. A corruption of *sakuru,* "burst/crack," because the tree's bark cracks horizontally.

    6. An abbreviation of *sake-hiraku,* "splitting-open" [the bark? the bloom?].

    7. It signifies *saki-kumoru* [with vowel-shift], "blooming-clouds-over" because it becomes cloudy/hazy [with blossoms? meteorological coincidence?] when they bloom.

8. A derivation of *saki,* "fortune/luck/bounty." The *ra* from *katsura,* "crown" [laurels not necessarily laurel, a head decoration or temporary crown] as in *hana-katsura,* "blossom-crown" [an old poem has ancients adorning their heads with cherry-blossoms].

9. Because it is an especially superior blossom, the keen prefix *sa,* "beautiful/godly/precious," is used, followed by *ku,* meaning "separated" and *ra,* meaning "to open."

10. From *shirakarura,* "whitening/lightening(+plural *ra*)" [the color turning gradually whiter (from pink) being a characteristic of the bloom].

11. A derivation of *sakuwau [sakuô],* "opening king." [A colorful place as an opening for the underworld or the tree that opened more blossoms than any other?]

12. From being beautiful and shiny, a different pronunciation [*betsu-on*] of *shakushaku,* "[to] shine brightly glowing"[an adverb applied to blooming], SakRa [there is no explanation for this, but a type of peony called a *shakuyaku,* seems to be derived from a less tenuous mutation of the same].

13. The *sa* from the *sa* in *sagami,* "field-god" [a word not in the OJD], signifying "grain" (*kokumotsu*). *Kura* is a seat [place/object] possessed by the gods, though this was not only true for the *sakura.*

Were I to philologize, I would say that the homophony of "bloom" with "splitting (open)," both *saku,* as suggested in (5) and (6) is enough, with the plural suffix *ra,* to cover the semantics. But the etymologies most commonly encountered are the legendary (1) and the ethnographic (13), while my idea of putting a plural suffix on a verb is ridiculous to Japanese, as it is never done. As a supporter of the original language argument in Plato's *Phaedras,* I would like to offer my purely sound-sense etymology, which you may compare to (9), *Sa,* a surprisingly, swift, splitting motion expresses the quick opening of the blossoms, stopping-pat with the in-your-face punch of the *k,* given the emotional impact *u* (as in *ooooogh!*) followed by the trembling *r* (which may carry forward to the falling blossoms) and the awed, or possibly relieved *ah* or *a.*

Sakuya-hime, the cherry sprite in derivation 1), appears in full bloom around 1770 (as noted in connection with Issa's angel *ku*). It made sense as far as it went, but it would seem that the legends in which she appeared dated back to a time and place where the cherry was not cited in anything else – i.e., to the *ume* or "plum" – and most contemporary scholars assume she was retroactively *sakura*-fied after the blossom became popular among the literary class. The research is complicated by the fact that the character now assumed to apply to *sakura*=cherry alone, once applied to a number of blossoming fructiferous plants, etc. And, come to think of it, why should a plant be named for its spirit rather than vice-versa? Or does this question reveal my bias with respect to the relative importance of plants and gods?

The last derivation, cherry as the sacred grain-seat, has been the darling of the scholars in the second half of the twentieth century, when the bold work of pioneering ethnologists in the first half of the century was resurrected and expanded upon. If I get this right, Origuchi, a progressive but nationalistic maverick scholar, first claimed that the cherry's bloom was used to foretell the crop because it bloomed as a manifestation of the field/crop god's descent just before it was time to plant the rice. Indeed, he wrote, the *sakura* was only used for the practical purpose of prognosis and not appreciated as a flowering plant in Nara. The *Manyôshû* poems he gave as proof (#1546, etc.) are insufficient, as is his forced connection of the desire for the bloom not to fall quickly to farming concerns. Inspired by this, nonetheless, later scholars (perhaps starting with Wakamori Tarô in 1951) invented the *sa-kura* etymology that today is ubiquitous enough to be considered standard, though some doubt is also standard!

There is no question that the blossoming of this fruit-wise barren tree are used by farmers in parts of Japan. Ono Sawako (『江戸の花見』) notes "rice-nursery-cherries" or *nawashirozakura* (苗代桜), whose blossoming determines the date for sowing the rice seeds, and "harvest-see-cherries," or *sakumizakura* (作見桜), also "world-within-cherries," or *yononakazakura* (世の中桜) cherries whose bloom (quantity) foretold the size of the harvest. At one shrine, a fine blossoming of South-side cherries meant that fields to the South of the shrine would prosper that year while those to the North would suffer wind and rain damage, so we can imagine a variety of ways the blossoming trees were read in various places. She also points out that the *wisteria* rather than the cherry was relied upon in some localities. Since Japan is latitudinally long, one would expect such difference. At any rate, I am not one to deny the possibility that Origuchi's intuition might ultimately be proven right. The *sa* sound does begin several rice-planting related words while *kura* can mean a place where god's (or an oracle) dwell, but, as Shirahata Yosaburô – this short essay relies heavily on chapter 1 of his 『花見と桜』(PHP:2000) – points out, *all of this is taken on faith with precious little investigation.* I did find *one* ku indirectly supporting Origuchi:

いなづまのやどり木なりし櫻哉　其角
inazuma no yadorigi narishi sakura kana　kikaku -1707
(lightning's perch[lodge-tree] becomes cherry!/?/'tis))

it serves as
a perch for lightning
the cherry

Lightning in Japanese is "rice-mate"(either husband or wife) and the first etymology given in the OJD is that folklore credits the lightning for making the rice plant with child, if it were. The only problem is that, as we will discover later, one variety of cherry was called the fire-cherry (hizakura), so it is possible Kikaku was celebrating one of them instead of all *sakura* (其角の研究家諸君、ご意見下さい！). But, as Shirahata most correctly points out, the philology of the *sakura* and its historical significance *is not nearly so interesting as what Japanese have come to do with it* (indeed, even the "fire" is, according to experts, rightfully "scarlet.*"*) The contributions of *sakura-ron,* i.e., theories and debate on the nature of cherry blossoms and the accompanying explanations of the nature of the Japanese soul, have not been all for the good. The cherry blossoms have been anthropomorphized, emotionalized and, worse, appropriated for nationalistic and militaristic agenda. Far better, he argues, to concentrate on something that would seem to be genuinely unique to Japanese culture: *the phenomenon of blossom-viewing.* To that, I say *amen!* The *hanami* (blossom-viewing) will be the focus of Book II.

..

BOOK II

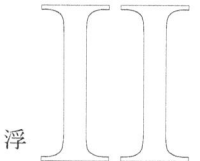

夜明哉淡々立つ花の浮貝にらほ

drinking with

影に来てまぼろしでなし花の神　琴風
kage ni kite maboroshi de nashi hana no kami kinpû
(shadow-to coming, phantom[is] not, blossom-god/s)

..

coming to the bloom
no phantom he
the blossom
god
▽

Flowers

△ 芭蕉句＜猶見たし花に明行神の顔＞で有名、醜ききわまる神とそっくりの琴風？

花見酒

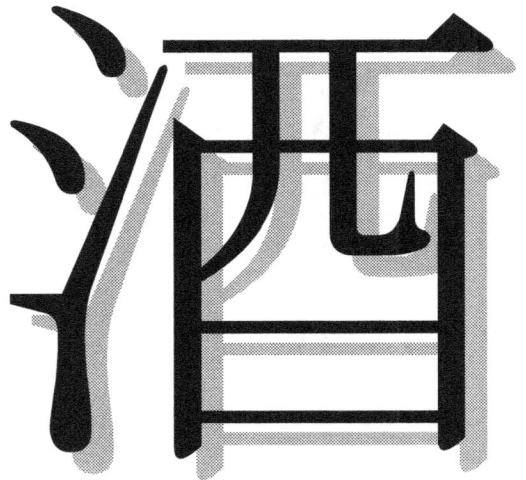

poetic   preface
To Be Alive

活て居る人をかぞへて花見哉　一茶
ikite-iru hito o kazoete hanami kana   issa   西記書込
(living/lively-are people[obj] counting, blossom-viewing!)

blossom viewing
i count the people who
are truly alive

Were Issa an old man when he wrote this, I might have thought he was tallying up his buddies who survived to enjoy one more spring and translated: *"Blossom viewing / i count the men who / are alive;"* but this is one of his early poems, so I think he means that all folk with gumption are out viewing the blossoms, where they are further charged by the pink electricity – all those petals brushing against each other must build up some static energy, right? – while those who miss the experience do not know what it is to be *so* alive.   A century before, a lesser-known wrote:

死さうな人ひとりなし花の山　祇徳
shinisôna hito hitori nashi hananoyama   gitoku 1763 古選
(die-seeming person one not, blossom's/cherries' mountain)

mount cherry   not a person
not a man here looks   looks mortal here on
likely to die   mount cherry

Is the blossom park, paradise, then? Young Issa's somewhat obnoxious *ku* is more personal and fresh. Years later, he wrote in a more mature vein:

斯う活て居るも不思議ぞ花の陰　一茶
kô ikiteiru mo fushigi zo hananokage   issa -1827
(thus living/lively-being-too/even strange! blossom-shade)

how strange it is   the bloomshade:
to live and live like this!   how strange it is to be,
below the bloom   and be alive!

how strange
to be alive like this
beneath the blossoms

Book II preface 1-3

276 *Book II preface*

The Chinese character used for "live/alive" in both the *ku* is not the most common one 生, but a slightly more complex one 活 that suggests liveliness and activity or, in the case of this *ku*, perhaps, that our life is as tenuous and temporary as that of a cut flower, for the character is that used for the *ike* in *ikebana*活花 (flower-arrangement) literally "lively-flower/s" or flowers kept alive. The "to be, and be alive" is borrowed from a creative translation by Jack Stamm[1] of a modern *tanka* by Tawara Machi. My last translation is closest to the original and to Blyth's *"What a strange thing, /to be thus alive / beneath the cherry blossoms"* (Good, but note that Issa's *kô* and *zo* are so colloquial that a *thus*, seems out of place). While I prefer *viewing* my clever readings, simple is best for such a moment. So, I prefer my last reading, which I'll reprint in a manner reflecting the miraculous anti-entropy of life:

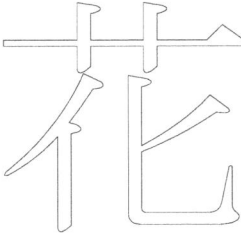

beneath the blossoms
to be alive like this
how strange

~~~~~~

1. *To Be, and Be Alive* Jack Stamm's translation of a *tanka* (5-7-5-7-7) by Tawara Machi from her best-selling *Sarada Kinenbi* (salad anniversary): "Shower shelter / under a little street-stand, / a glass of sake / what a happy, happy thing, / to be, and be alive."(publ. Kawade) That particular phrase was not in the original. Julia Carpenter's translation of the same: *"Escape from a shower into a street stall / and drink a glass of cheap sake – / fun to be alive."* (publ. Kodansha). Tawara Machi used the standard Chinese character when she expressed her delight to be alive (*hito ikite-iru koto no tanoshisa*). It was not in the original, but it made that *tanka* one of Jack's best translations. Remember that, on the whole, so much is lost in translation that something must be added to even the balance. And, damn it, I wish Jack were here to enjoy my translations (and better yet criticize them)!

foreword
Blossom Viewing
- the Significance of it -

Let me explain the difference between lyrical feelings for [cherry] blossoms and the behavior of admiring them as ornamentals [both common in the West] and the *hanami* [(cherry)blossom-viewing] about which I speak. To be blunt, this *hanami* includes three things: *gunô* [a stand of cherry trees 群桜, as opposed to just one or two], *inshoku* [food and drink, generally hard], and *gunshû* [massive crowds] . . . . . When these three prerequisites are fully met, we have a [genuine] Japanese blossom-viewing. Accordingly, we must say that *hanami* exists nowhere else in the world.[1]

– Shirahata Yôzaburo (HMS: 2000)
『花見と桜＜日本的なるもの＞再考』白幡洋三郎

Book I, *The Cherry Hunt,* got all of the trees into bloom and brought you to the cherries. It also introduced a variety of cherry blossom types and set the mood for Book II, *Drinking with Flowers,* by jumping the gun with chapters on blossom intoxication and "bloompeak" frenzy. Some chapters in Book I, such as those concerning dusk and night blossoms, describe peripheral aspects of the blossom-viewing, because the entire viewing – or, "cherry-bash," as I sometimes call it in light of the carnival-like nature at some of the large "cherry mountains" – is too much for one book.

Not only are there too many *ku* on cherry-blossoms to squeeze into one book, but even the number for some sub-themes is so large that one feels tempted to turn sub-sub themes into chapters and chapters into books. It would not be hard to make a hundred different books on the cherry blossom experience. It was hard, very hard, to make only three, and dividing their content into chapters of a reasonable length was torture. Particularly in this Book II, which purports to concentrate on the single happening, the blossom-viewing, both the categories chosen or created (sometimes my sub-categories are not found in any previous *saijiki*) and their order tend to be arbitrary, so I would be surprised if any reader goes along with all my calls, for I myself am far from satisfied with them . . .

Yet, even as I complain, I lie by omission, for it is exactly that, the fact there is no editorial challenge so great as selecting and arranging haiku, that draws me to do it over and over again. Eventually, when I can afford a large screen, a computer powerful enough to keep the entire book in a single file (I have to split it into 6 to prevent freezing), ink enough to print out what I write, and the time to read it, I hope to do a better job. For now, this will have to do.

In Book I, I claimed the bloom of the cherry was sublime as Niagara Falls. To readers who have never enjoyed a blossom-viewing, let me add more simile: the heavy clouds and eventual blizzard of light pink blossoms is as sense-shocking and mind-blowing *as fireworks experienced up close.* It resembles white-water kayaking, where you ride the roaring torrent in utter silence aware of infinite time *and* the absence of it when an occasional rock or snag is not seen until it swooshes by. I must confess that I do not know if one has to be experienced in blossom-viewing to truly appreciate the *hanami* haiku; I *had* that experience before reading the poetry.[2] For readers who have *not* had that experience, here are two testimonials in vintage nineteenth century prose:

> If the plum invited admiration, the cherry commands it; for to see the *sakura* in flower for the first time is to experience a new sensation. Familiar as a man may be with the cherry blossoms at home, the sight there bursts upon him with the dazzling effect of a revelation. Such is the profusion of flowers that the tree seems to have turned into a living mass of rosy light. No leaves break the brilliance. The snowy-pink petals cover the branches so completely that one is conscious of a bridal veil donned for the tree's nuptials with the spring. (Percival Lowell: *The Soul of the Far East*: 1888)

> With us, a plum or cherry tree in flower is not an astonishing sight; but here it is a miracle of beauty so bewildering that, however much you may have previously read about it, the real spectacle strikes you dumb. You see no leaves − only one filmy mist of pearls. (Lafcadio Hearn: *Glimpses of Unfamiliar Japan*: 1894

Lowell prefaced the above with doubt as to whether he could do justice to what was "perhaps as superb a sight as anything in this world." I doubt any Twentieth or Twenty-first century writer could describe the miracle of cherry blossoms in Japan as well as he or Hearn did.

Here is Lowell on the blossom-viewing:

If the anniversaries of people are slightly treated in the land of the sunrise, the same cannot be said of plants. [3] The yearly birthdays of the vegetable world are observed with more than botanical enthusiasm. The regard in which they are held is truly emotional, and if not truly individual in its object, at least personal to the species. Each kind of tree as its season brings it into flower is made the occasion of a festival. . . . (Ibid)

But wherever the tree may be, there at their flowering season are to be found crowds of admirers. For in crowds people go to see the sight, multitudes streaming incessantly to and fro beneath their blossoms as the time of day determines the turn of human tide. To the Occidental stranger such a gathering suggests some social loadstone; but none exists. In the cherry trees alone lies the attraction. (Ibid)

Calling the annual blossom-viewings *birthdays* and the participants "crowds of admirers" is a brilliant way to explain the nature-centric East to the human-centric West, but Lowell fails to sufficiently appreciate the attraction of the crowd *for itself* – hanami as a human happening – and the fact that most of the "admirers" are *drunk* or *drinking* – with the accompanying singing, reciting, dancing, eating, etc. – under the bloom. As Shirahata Yôzaburo noted with respect to other more well-known writers on Japan, the heart of the *hanami* evaded even most sympathetic Western observers.[4] The exception was Lowell and Hearn's contemporary Eliza Scidmore – the person most responsible for the idea of bringing cherry blossoms to Washington DC – who described the real thing, giving ample and sympathetic attention to *sake,* but we shall save her words for the chapter on *drinking in the bloomshade*.

Now, let us join the poets and view the cherry blossoms and see what goes on under them, saving only their falling and allegorization, mostly as women or warriors – the most exciting stuff is kept for last to ensure readers don't stop with the first two books – and the blossom viewers' return for the third book.

1. *Only In Japan* The claim that [cherry] blossom-viewing is peculiarly Japanese may seem silly, but Shirahata did make a valiant effort to check out the situation around the globe. Many places meet one or even two of the requirements, but none enjoy all three. The *hanami* would seem to belong to Japan alone. Many varieties of cherry have been exported with success, but the cultural particulars did not accompany them. The Harvest Moon festival in Korea bears resemblance to blossom-viewing in that great numbers of people go out to sit outside picnicking (including drinking and (more) dancing), but hey do this in graveyards and enjoy wild flowers and fruit of trees. Perhaps the July 4 barbecue is the Usanian equivalent, though the grass is more appreciated as a playing field than a thing of beauty.
2. *Virtual Blossom-Viewing* If you have not experienced a cherry blossom viewing bash in Japan, go to the world-wise web and do an image search on "hanami."
3. *Lowell on Birthdays* The main tenet of Lowell's book was that Western man was individual, while the East was collective. Not knowing that the Chinese were into birthdays before the West (as suggested by remarks about China by Portuguese visitors in the 16c), Lowell relied heavily upon the presence/absence of birthdays. Personally, I find the emphasis on *death*days in the Far East far more individualistic than our emphasis on *birth*days, because our deaths tell much more about us than our births (Elvis Presley being a good example?).
4. ***Hanami* evaded** As Shirahata points out, even Chamberlain's magisterial *Things of Japan* gives much less attention to the blossom-viewing than its importance in Japanese culture dictates. Lowell, to his credit, recognized its importance and only failed to give sufficient weight to the vulgar part of it.

280

 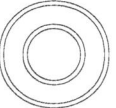

21

Blossoms as Medicine
眼の薬・気の薬
me-no-kusuri & ki-no-kusuri

第一に気の薬也花の山 一茶 1824
dai ichi ni ki no kusuri nari hananoyama issa
(first-as spirit/*qi*'s medicine is/becomes blossom-mountain)

and first of all
tis medicine for the soul
cherry mountain

When I first read Issa's poem, I had not yet read tens of thousands of old haiku and naively assumed the "medicine for the *ki* (spirit/mood/soul)" was a phrase of Issa's invention. I had only come across one similar expression, and it was in a *Chinese Mother Goose* poem, where a big boy baby is the parent's "open-breast-circulate-pill" (開胸順気丸).

.

My big son, / My own boy, / Baby is a sweet pill / That fills my soul with joy."

As translated by I. T. Headland, the spirit pill is sweetened for the consumption of English speaking children and, for rhyme's sake, the circulatory benefit (exhilaration) is turned into pure and simple "joy". Subsequent reading turned up dozens of similar, mostly older, poems. This chapter samples them.

見る度に薬と思ふ櫻哉　宋屋 新選
miru tabi ni kusuri to omou sakura kana sôya 1773
(see [each] time medicine-as think cherry[blossoms]!/?)

cherry blossoms!
whenever i see them,
i think: medicine!

Compared to Issa's poem, with its fresh vernacular "first of all," this poem seems lacking. It may allude to women. Like Issa's poem, its subjective and aphoristic style is not very popular today. The freedom to write such unabashedly philosophical poems is one thing that draws me to old haiku. I am not yet certain what the *ku* are based upon. Japan's most prolific writer on cherry blossom history, Ogawa Kazusuke claims that "the beauty of the cherry blossom exorcises all bad things," that gathering below the tree in bloom "ensures a tranquil and prosperous year to come," and, again, that "the beauty purifies all ugliness and evil" (日本の桜、歴史の桜). These next four *ku* are from well-known anthologies predating Issa by centuries:

善峯の花や目薬気の薬　宗治 毛吹草
yoshi mine hana ya megusuri ki no kusuri   sôji 1645
(yoshi peak's blossom/s!/: eye-medicine, spirit-medicine)

cherries blooming
on yoshi peak: medicine
for eyes and soul!

Yoshi-mine is the most admired peak of Mount Yoshino, the prime cherry-blossom viewing spot (ch 58) and ancient spiritual property. As we have noted elsewhere, the cherry trees were said to be planted to guard capital cities – first Nara, then Kyoto – i.e. charm prosperity and ward off disaster. Haiku make such macro-medicine personal. The *eye* part of the *ku* is clarified by the next *ku* (credited to Tôshin 當信 in *Taka Tsukuba* (1642), and Sôji 宗治 in *Kebukisô* (1645)).

見る花や目薬入の櫻貝　當信 鷹つくは
miru hana ya megusuri ire no sakuragai   tôshin 1642
(see blossoms!/: eye-medicine-container's cherry-shell/s)

blossoms for sight
cherry-shells filled with
eye medicine!

The "cherry-shell" (*sakura-gai*), according to my dictionary, is "a kind of carpenter's tellin" (*Nitidotelina nitidula*). Even the *OED* doesn't say what a *tellin* is, so the metaphor in "our" name is lost on me! The shell most commonly used for medicine, particularly that presented to someone, was the *clam* – a beautiful shell in the Far East, unlike our thick and ugly ones that literally make me sick! – but other shells, including the cherry's namesake, were also used. One *ku* seems to express doubts: *"They're white / but medicine to the eyes, too / cherry blossoms!"* (白けれと目にも薬の櫻哉　来儀 鞭随筆 *shiro keredo me ni mo kusuri no sakura kana* raigi (1759)). Bright white snow was a real killer of eyes and blind eyes are often white; cherry blossoms were the exception.

御堂にて・色々の花をみ堂や目極楽 空存 夢見草
midô nite / iroiro no hana o midôu ya me-gokuraku   kûzon 1656
(honorable hall // various blossoms see→honorable-[temple] hall! eye-paradise)

what a variety of flowers at the temple! eyeball-paradise	heaven for eyes promiscuous blossoms at the prayer-hall

The "honorable" prefix "mi" functions as a pivot word here: it means "to see" until the next word tells us it must be a prefix. I suspect the poet is viewing female worshippers and/or pretty boys rather than cherry trees, but I could be wrong. As noted already, temples used cherry blossoms to draw people in to see Buddhist treasures and make contributions. Their gardens often had and still have many fine flowers (azalea, wisteria, peony, lotus, chrysanthemum, etc.) and draw crowds. I recall going to see a great show of hydrangea (*ajisai*) at one large temple. Centuries ago, churches in Europe were known for their extraordinary flower gardens, but they were primarily for cutting and bringing into the church. How many churches do you know in the USA that can boast extraordinary botanical gardens? Another *ku* from a poetry collection with a name that translates as "dream-seeing-plant" shows that describing flowers as medicine was not limited to tree blossoms: *"Smelling salts / for the eyes, they are! / Chinese violets"* (気のつきし目の薬也から菫 満家 夢見草 *ki no tsukishi me no kusuri nari karasumire* manka (1656)) The original does not mention "smelling" although the nose is, of course, what a medicine helping one revive would work through. Issa's contemporary Baishitsu was also a believer of the healing power of nature: *"Spring grasses / even treading them is / good medicine"* or *Spring herbs! / To tread upon them also / saves your life"* (春の草踏むも命の薬哉 梅室 *haru no kusa fumu mo inochino kusuri kana* baishitsu (1768-1852)). That is, the mouth and eyes are not the only portals through which medicine can be absorbed. But, why, so much medical metaphor? My guess is that creative advertising of medicine by myriad street vendors in the Tokugawa era (my favorite is the toothpaste vendor with his demi-masks) caught the attention of the poets.

ひし／\と心に花のひゝき哉　乙二
hishihishi to kokoro ni hana no hibiki kana otsuni -1823
(thick/squished [mimesis] heart-in blossoms' echo!/?/'tis)

<blockquote>
thick and fast
within my heart the sound
of the blossoms
</blockquote>

I do not know what the echo/sound of the blossoms means. Is it the rustling of petal against petal in the wind? When falling? The birds? The din of the blossom viewing? A turning of emotion that is not sound into sound? Whatever it is, Otsuni is attempting to objectively describe the effect viewing had on him – I am reminded of white water kayaking. How the surreal roar, both extraordinarily loud and silent remains. I think that Otsuji was thinking of the effect of blossoms on the spirit in a way we might now call medical, for he also wrote this:

脈取て見るや花の夜只ひとり　乙二
myaku totte miru ya hana no yoru tada hitori otsuni
(vein/pulse-taking-see!/?/: blossoms' night just alone)

<blockquote>
taking my pulse
just to see: at night alone
with the blossoms

trying to find
a pulse: blossoms at night
all by myself
</blockquote>

I think Otsuni is checking to see if the cherry blossom quickens his pulse. That is to say, whether or not they act as a stimulant. But it is at least *possible* he is simply observing the blossoms very carefully, for such an idiomatic usage was not unknown. Otsuni, a Buddhist abbot, was a teacher of Issa's employer, Seibi and it is a good bet Issa knew the *ku*. Chinese medicine had varieties of pulses unknown to Occidental medicine, but I cannot say exactly what is being measured here,

ちかつきになりてくつろく花見哉　正秀
chikazuki ni narite kutsurogu hanami kana masahide ()
(nearing becoming/became relax blossom-viewing!/'tis)

<blockquote>
as we approach
the relaxation mounts
blossom viewing

the *hanami*
as we near, mounting
relaxation
</blockquote>

梅に折る膝を伸たるさくらかな　哲亜彌
ume ni oru hiza o nobitaru sakura kana   tetsua? -1798
(plum-for folded knees[+acc] stretch cherry[blossoms]!/'tis)

the knees neatly   knees that bent
folded for the plum, stretch   for the plum relaxed:
for the cherry   cherry blossoms

The plum as the first bloom of the year is treated politely. We have seen the cherry blossoms treated as a stimulant and a relaxant. This is one of the latter expressed in terms of viewing posture.

見る人に笑ひをうつすか櫻花　次推 蘆分船
miru hito ni warai o utsusu ka sakurabana   jisui 1694
(see/ing person-to laugh/smile[acc.] spread? cherry-blossoms)

cherry blossoms   do you spread
do we all risk catching   your smile through our eyes
your sweet smile   o, cherry tree

do all who view
catch your laughing spell
cherry blossoms

悟をもひらくか花のわらひ顔　一治 嵐山集
satori o mo hiraku ka hana no waraigao   ichiji 1651
(enlightenment[acc]-even, open? blossom's/s' laugh/smiling-face)

is that how we   smiling blossoms
are enlightened? the blossom are we watching the crack
cracks a smile   of enlightenment

enlightenment
does it open laughing
like blossoms

We will enjoy half a dozen laughing/smiling cherry blossoms in *Mountain Cherries*. Hills turning green in the Spring are commonly said to smile/laugh, while it is rare to speak of plants doing so, and, when they do, it generally refers to their shiny leaves (*ha*) which are homophonic with "teeth."

観音のあらんかぎりは桜かな　一茶 文化七
kannon no aran kagiri wa sakura kana   issa (-1827)
(kannon's existing-not extent-as-for cherry[blossoms]!/?/'tis)

in the absence   so long as she
of the goddess of mercy   kuan-yin is not to be seen
cherry blossoms   a cherry tree

The Japanese Buddhist deity of mercy, Kannon (Chinese: Kuan-yin; Sanskrit: Avalokitêsvarta) is male, female or something in between. S/he is always both beautiful and gentle. In a word – *soothing*.

bathed in a blizzard
of petals, does the tree too
know catharsis?

Keigu wrote the last *ku* after googling across a blog where someone who had been under treatment for a mental disorder pointed out to a fellow soul that comedy could be cruel while tragedy could help the patient achieve the desired catharsis. (Aren't country weepers far more consoling than happy pop when you're down?). A cherry tree visible from the hospital window was mentioned that made me rethink *why* and *how* blossoms become medicine for the soul. I suspect homeopathy plays a role here, too. Could not the sadness of losing the bloom be as healing as the smile shared with it?

Miira, also called *The Divine*, but usually just *Mother* by the followers of Sri Aurobindo lived in Japan from 1916-20. "For four years," she wrote, "from an artistic point of view, I lived from wonder to wonder." I can not resist including "The Cherry-Tree Experience" as the words whispered to Miira happen to touch upon the nature of Issa's *cherry-blossoms-as-medicine*. (Note: *sakura* was in the air. The first issue of the magazine *Sakura*, the official organ of the Sakura-no-Kwai, a society for promoting cherry trees, and a phenomenal cultural achievement in its own right, came out in 1918.)

The Cherry-Tree Experience

A deep concentration seized on me, and I perceived that I was identifying myself with a single cherry-blossom, then through it with all cherry-blossoms, and, as I descended deeper in the consciousness, following a stream of bluish force, I became suddenly the cherry-tree itself, stretching towards the sky like so many arms its innumerable branches laden with their sacrifice of flowers. Then, I heard distinctly this sentence:

Thus hast thou made thyself one with the soul of the cherry-trees and so thou canst take note that it is the Divine who makes the offering of this flower-prayer to heaven.

When I had written it, all was effaced; but now the blood of the cherry-tree flows in my veins and with it flows an incomparable peace and force. What difference is there between the human body and the body of a tree? In truth, there is none: the consciousness which animates them is the same.

Then the cherry-tree whispered in my ear :

It is in the cherry-blossom that lies the remedy for the disorders of the spring.

22

Blossom Viewing
花見
hana-mi

あれ見さいこれを見やうの花盛　立甫 花見記
are misai kore o miyô no hanazakari ryûho 1594-1669
(that look[polite imper.]! this look!'s blm-acme/full-blm)

my, look at this!
hey, look at that! cherries
in full bloom

見て居れば物いひたげに桜かな　素丸
mite ireba mono iitage ni sakura kana somaru 1712-95
(seeing-am/sitting something/words say-wanting cherry!/?/'tis)

      viewing them   as i sit and view
you feel like speaking out   i feel like saying something
     cherry blossoms   to the *sakura*

At first, there was no chapter on *hanami per se.* I had one on *people*-viewing but none for the *blossom*-viewing. This was because blossom-viewing, as the main theme, is found to a degree in *all* the sub-themes. But that is not the whole story. It is partly because sublimity tends toward wordless awe and partly because most *ku* where blossoms are carefully examined are about first-blossoms (*hatsu-hana* ch.4). Once the blossoms have opened and the marriage between viewer and tree consummated, they may be taken for granted and overlooked in the party. Obviously, that, too, is an oversimplification. The full-bloom was impressive enough to call attention to itself, and even the blossom-sated drunk had to notice it now and then.

見あぐれば見おろすよりも桜哉　素丸
mi-agureba mi-orosu yorimo sakura kana somaru 1712-95
(look-up-if/when look-down-[more?/better?]-than cherry[blossoms] 'tis)

    cherry blossoms: for the real cherry
better looking up at them   blossom-viewing experience
   than looking down   look up not down

how to view blossoms

      looking up   you find it
beats looking down   looking up not down
     on cherries   the real cherry

I could be wrong about the drunk idea, but looking up does have its shortcomings.

首の骨何そみをのをや木々の花　幽閑 新道
kubi no hone nani zo mi o no ya kigi no hana yûkan ()
(neck's bone what [+exclam.] look-let's!? trees' blossoms)

なかむとて花にもいたし頸の骨　宗因
nagamu tote hana ni mo itashi kubinohone sôin
(gaze-[say/s] blossms-by-too hurt neck-bone) 1604-82

oh, my neck!
what is this call to view
tree flowers!

he'd have us gaze
but even blossoms hurt
my poor neck

These poets should have drunken more and viewed the blossoms on their backs. The first *ku* may react to Ryûho's call to *look* at this and that, but the second is prefaced in the original to lay the blame on the blossom-lover's blossom-lover, Saigyô, who "spent the whole day under the bloom." Sôin (1604-82) takes 11 syllabets from one of Saigyô's more boring blossom-viewing poems (SKS#126), and pretends the intensifier *itaku*, used in the context of becoming "*extremely* close to" the bloom, means its homophone, "painful." The first *ku* is the only one I know of specifying "*tree* flowers." I cannot help wanting to contrast them with those on or near the *ground* that Occidentals typically look at. *Could neck-fatigue help explain one reason why a tree-blossom-loving culture came up with the idea of sitting or lying down under the blossoms rather than walking about bending over and sniffing?* If my interest in these *ku* seems excessive, it is because I, too, have a bad neck. Viewing blossoms, I find myself tilting my head from side to side like a bird, speaking of which, the only time the cherries got to my neck was when I spent too much time looking at the little birds in them, trying to figure out how many petals were knocked off by their feeding and how many by accident when they came and went (the latter was far more deadly). While I was seated, I am afraid I was not drinking as I should have been for I was on a university campus (Komaba Tôdai) on my way to work. At that time, I also discovered that cherry blossoms are urbane: they look fine against buildings.

あまり見ば果や目ぼしの花盛　貞成 犬子集
amari miba hate ya meboshi no hanazakari sadanari 1633
(excessive-see-if/when, end/result: eye-stars' blossom-acme)

gaze too much
and the bloom-peak ends
in seeing stars

Japanese and English are in full accord about the idea of "seeing stars" when one strains or feels faint.

花桜是にさへ人の倦日（哉）　一茶 西紀書込
hanazakura kore-ni sae hito no aku hi kana issa -1827
(blossom-acme this-with even people tire-of day ('tis))

cherry in blossom
a day comes when we
tire, even of this

cherries in bloom
even this eventually
is yawned at

As short as the bloom is, there are people who find it too long. Issa's "bored-day" puns as *akubi*, or "yawn." If young Issa met a man who complained of his own wife's sexual demands, there may be a B-side reading. As a single young man, I recall being *astounded* to hear a married man complain about too much of something I was starving for. Note: in Issa's day, when there was more variety in trees than today, the local cherry-viewing season generally lasted about a month!

 # 22 - 4~7

花の山日中の月を見付けたり 梅塢 花供養
hana no yama hinaka no tsuki o mitsuketari   baiu 1795
(blossom-mountain day-while/among moon[obj] see/find[+repeat])

cherry mountain
finding the moon above
in the daytime

cherry mountain
now and then we see
a jellyfish moon

Japanese, unlike their neighbors, the Koreans who walk ramrod straight, tend toward a posture they call "cat-backed" – we call it hunch-back – and do not, therefore, pay much attention to the heavens. Hence, the daytime moon would generally have passed unnoticed. Yes, the *jellyfish* is all mine.

日盛や平たく見ゆる花の山 素丸 百番句合
hizakari ya hirataku miyuru hana no yama   somaru 1712-95
(day/sun-acme:/! flat [is] seen blossom-mountain)

it's high noon
and it seems to flatten out:
cherry mountain

At high noon, shadows are tucked under the trees. Seen from above, the intaglio effect would vanish. That is the rationalization, but I love the poem on a different level: *I feel I have seen it but can't say when.* I have stepped out of a bloomshade, before my eyes are adjusted and the world looks unreal.

年〴〵やまだ見定めぬ花の色 泰渓 花供養
toshidoshi ya mada mi-sadamenu hana no iro   taikei 1795
(year-year!/: still see-determine-not blossoms' color/eros)

year after year
i just can't pin it down
blossom color

year after year
still can't tell why blossoms
are so sexy

Roses are red and violets are blue, but cherry blossoms? This would indeed be hard, for no cherry tree has blossoms all the same color and no blossom has petals all the same color and I am not even sure if all petals are themselves one color and there is a tendency for petals to start dark pink and turn white. And if this were not enough, there were shades of yellow and green and grey and even (rarely) blue!

下手な絵のやうに咲たる櫻哉 白雪
heta na e no yô ni sakitaru sakura kana   hakusetsu c1700
(poor painting/picture/print-like bloom/s cherry/ies 'tis/!/?)

it blossoms
like a cheap painting
this cherry!

a cherry tree
in bloom looks like
a cheap print

the cherry trees
too much bloom for
a good picture

In a picture, such a tree would be a light-pink blob, but up-close in reality it might be very pleasant. I think the poet intends his *ku* as praise for a profusely blooming tree (or grove of trees).

#22 - 8 ~ 11

あるが中に花見の欲や遠眼鏡　仙丈 花供養
aru ga naka ni hanami no yoku ya engankyô senjô 1795
(is/have-the among blossom-viewing-greed!/?/: telescope)

amid plenty
blossom-viewing greed
a telescope

The *ku* is saved by the possibility this telescope is being used for spying out trees rather than people. Read *greed* in the context of the catechism that loving blossoms is less sinful than loving women.

又類さくらに月の表かな　光暁 花供養
mata tagui sakura ni tsuki no omote kana kôgyô? 1795
(again, [a] relation [= same type] cherry-to/and moon's face!/?/'tis)

here, too, kin	this, too, alike
cherry bloom and the face	the bark of the cherry
of the moon	and the moon

I favor the second reading, but no "bark" is specified, so the wax and wane comparison is the likely.

身に瘤のありとは見へぬ桜哉　求我 花供養
mi ni kobu no ari to wa mienu sakura kana kyûga (1795)
(body-on wen/bump/s are-as-for appear-not cherry[tree/blossoms]!/'tis)

you wouldn't think
it was covered with welts
the flowering cherry

Wart came to mind, for a *kobu* is an ugly bump; but that would be unnatural on a *tree*, so I requisitioned *wen*, a word old enough to no longer seem specific to any part of nature, then changed to *welt*.

枝なりはともあれ花は櫻哉　梅室
eda nari wa tomoare hana wa sakura kana baishitsu 1768-1852
(limb-shape-as-for however-are, blossoms-as-for cherry!/'tis)

however its limbs	however the limbs
this is not just a flower	no blossoms can compare
it's my cherry	to the *sakura*

Some varieties of cherry have unattractive limbs and individual trees may have misshapen ones, but these are compensated for not only by the profuse bloom, but the autumn colors.

一樹／＼我魂うつす桜かな　晴山 花供養
hito ki hito ki waga tama utsusu sakura kana seizan 1795
(one tree one tree my soul transfers cherries!/'tis)

i feel my soul
move from tree to tree
cherry blossoms

blooming cherries
my soul comes and goes
tree by tree

my heart-strings
tied to tree after tree
cherry blossoms

tree by tree
my heart leaves me
for the cherries

Reading *Fanny Hill* at an impressionable age, I recall souls once moved from body to body in English, too, if only in metaphor. We do, however, find a hint of moving spirit in the word "sweetheart," which reminds us that lovers once exchanged hearts. Since it does not make sense to call one's own heart "sweet," logic dictates that one's sweet-heart is the heart within one's own chest which belongs to the other party. Confusing? Read Shakespeare's love sonnets if you want more of it.

一日もかけずに来てや散さくら　蘭更
ichinichi mo kakezu ni kite ya chiru sakura　rankô 1726-99
(one[all]day even lack-not coming!/: falls/ing cherry/ies [blossoms])

not a day
have i missed!
falling petals

i have come
every day, every day!
falling petals

人去て暮る間しばし花見哉　五立 花供養
hito sarite kureru ma shibashi hanami kana　goritsu 1795
(people leaving/left darkening-a-while blossom-viewing!/?/'tis)

the people leave
as night falls, for a while
i view blossoms!

Rankô stays for breakfast if it were, *and* it is his just reward (Obviously, I've screwed up those metaphors!). Ostensibly describing his blossom-viewing, the *ku* makes the falling petals significant in an indirect and masterful manner. If Goryû's *ku* only pointed out the fact people-viewing, though part of blossom-viewing, may detract from the attention given to the real thing, that would be fine, but there is much more. The simple *ku* seems to me an unsong masterpiece of time and space.

ちる音ハかせなきはなの夕かな　宗祇
chiru oto wa kaze naki hana no yûbe kana　sôgi 1420-1502
(falling-sound-as-for, windless blossoms' evening!/?/'tis)

for the sound
of falling blossoms
a windless dusk

朝ひとり見直しに行桜哉　竜山 花供養
asa hitori minaoshi ni yuku sakura kana　ryûzan 1795
(morning/tomorrow see-over-to go/come cherry/ies!/ 'tis)

in the morning
coming back alone
to see the blossoms

at dawn alone
coming for a new look
cherry blossoms

22 - 17 ~ 20

There are some, who could not come back because they do not deliberately go to view the blossoms to begin with. We will meet more in chapter 33, *Vendors*, but here is one:

柴刈も見返る峠の櫻哉　　那李　藤首途
shibagari mo mikaeru mine no sakura kana　nari 1731
(firewood-hunter looks-back peak 's/s' cherry!/'tis)

even the firewood man
looks back at the cherries
blooming on the ridge

For such a man to pay attention to the trees with which he is intimate is not so much a statement about a common man with aesthetic sense (for, unlike the Occident, all classes unabashedly worshipped beauty, this was taken for granted in Japan) as indirect praise for the cherry or cherry trees.

思ひこめて見るべき花の青葉哉　　宗因　産籟
omoikomete mirubeki hana no aoba kana　sôin 1604-82
(think-entering view-should blossom's/s' gree/new-leaves!/?)

make a point　　　　　　　　　　　　　the new leaves
of viewing the blossom's　　　　　　　of the bloom: we should
new leaves!　　　　　　　　　　　　　notice them

There is a tendency to concentrate on the bloom and dismiss the leaves as impediments to the perfect vision. Though a bit plain, the *ku* is iconoclastic and positive, a pleasant combination. I have a feeling that had Bashô written it, it would be well known today. At the time, Sôin was as important for the development of *haikai* in the "West" (Osaka and Kyoto etc.) as Bashô was soon to be in the "East."

成美亭・年々に花の見やうのかはりけり 士朗
toshidoshi ni hana no miyô no kawarikeri　shirô 1742-1813
(year-year-with blossoms' appearance/way-of-viewing's changes[+emph.])

blossom-viewing at seibi's

year by year　　　　　　　year by year　　　　　　　year by year
the blossoms look　　　　the way we see them　　　something is different
is different　　　　　　　 is different　　　　　　　　about the bloom

The ambiguity of the *miyô* – either how we look or how they look – cannot be carried over, that is, *translated*.

淋しかれとけふこそおもへ花のかげ 士朗
sabishikare to kyô koso omoe hana no kage　shirô 1742-1813
("melancholy/lonely" today especially think [of] blossom-shade)

pink melancholy

yes, *loneliness*
was meant for this day
this bloomshade

To me, this *ku*, with its "today," is more impressive than the aphoristic one preceeding it about how the blossoms look different every year. Shirô's *sabishikare* reminds me Bashô's famous *sabishigarase* = "make me lonely!" cuckoo *ku* that actively courted melancholy. English has no single *verb* for the condition of being lonely or melancholy, such as the verb in this *ku*, much less in the Bashô's imperative usage meaning *"be pensive and sensitive in a melancholy way!"* Still, we have our Burton.

外ならぬ淋しさもまた桜かな　素檗
hoka naranu sabishisa mo mata sakura kana   sobaku 1758-1821
(other-is/become-not loneliness also cherry[blossom-viewing]!/' tis))

a loneliness
found nowhere else, that
too, is <i>sakura</i></p>

Trite or a masterpiece? I think the latter. Sobaku was more famous than Issa in their day, partly because of his marvelously droll paintings. Like Issa, he studied under Shirô, but longer. Shirô had a straightforward style, hopelessly plain, but was, I think, a good influence on others.

故主蟬吟公の庭前にて・さま／＼な事思ひ出す櫻かな　芭蕉
sama-zama-no* koto omoidasu sakura kana   bashô 1644-94
([late cicada-song's garden-in] sorts-sorts-of thingd remember cherry!/'tis))

How many, many things
They call to mind,
These cherry blossoms.

Trans. Blyth   (Haiku vol.2 Spring)

Sengin was Bashô's lord, best friend, a talented poet, and the son of the man in charge of Ueno castle (a place famed for high-class blossom-viewing in Edo). When he died, 23 year-old Bashô renounced the world. He wrote the above twenty years later. Blyth's translation is perfect, though he failed to put the preface *"in front of the ___ Sengin's garden"* before it, perhaps because English has trouble with the <u>ko</u> = *"dead/deceased/departed/poor/late"* pegged on a name. With such a passage of time, "the *late* Sengin" doesn't work, neither does the more pretentious "deceased" or "departed," while "poor" is maudlin and "dead," crude. But Blyth may not have wanted to pre-judice the reader. *Does it not seem that the poem is belittled by particular circumstances? One, then, wonders, what if it were written by an unknown poet? Would it still be considered good?* How does it compare to Issa's *ku* on the 17th anniversary of one of *his* first master's, the poet Chikua's passing: *"As if to say / do not forget old times / the cherry blooms"* (（竹阿十七忌）古き日を忘るゝなとや桜咲　文化三*furuki hi o wasururuna to ya sakura saku*   1806)? Blyth also appended a beautiful and apt stanza from "the mouth of the Wanderer" of Wordsworth (I'll let you find it in Blyth or Wordsworth, so as not to borrow too much) and, one by Shiki that might not be as similar as he thought. To wit:

我病で桜に思ふ事多し　子規
ware yande sakura ni omou koto ôshi   shiki 1898
(i sickening cherry[blossoms] with/about think/feel things many)

<table>
<tr><td style="text-align:center;">seriously ill
the blossoms give me much
to think about</td><td style="text-align:center;">in my illness
cherry blossoms fill me
with thoughts</td></tr>
</table>

1. Many, many = *samazama*. I suspect more is going on with Bashô's *ku* than meets the eye. I would bet he recalled how Sengin shared his love for Saigyô, who used the term *sama-zama* ("many, many" "various" "all sorts") more than any other poet. One eg.: "Tell my friends there are all sorts of /melancholy: / deep in the mountains, fall draws to a close" (samazama no aware aritsuru yamasato o hito ni tsutaete aki no kurekeru).

~~~~~~

Blyth translates Shiki's *ku*, *"The cherry blossoms: / Being ill, how many things / I remember about them."* but I doubt *omou* (as opposed to Basho's *omoidasu*) is purely memory. Shiki had a strong imagination and may be saying that if he can not be out there enjoying them, by god, he could turn them over make them bloom in his fertile head – or, more likely, he may be thinking of life and death.

<div align="center">
我病んで花の句も無き句帖かな 子規
ware yande hana no ku mo naki kuchô kana shiki 1902
(i/me sickening blossom/flowery ku even not ku journal!/'tis)
</div>

<div align="center">
wasting away
not a single blossom-*ku*
in my poem-pad
</div>

This is the same *ware yande* found in the last *ku;* but, by this time (4 years later), Shiki's condition had worsened – he died later that year – so I translated the first line differently. Since "blossom" also means *flourishing*, the poem also suggests that all his *ku* lack their old ebullience.

<div align="center">
泣に来て花に隠るゝ思ひかな 蕪村
naki ni kite hana ni kakururu omoi kana buson 1715-83
(crying-for coming blossoms-in hide thoughts/feelings!/'tis)
</div>

<div align="center">

coming to cry	in the blossoms
i hide my thoughts	i can cry and hide
in the blossoms	my feelings

</div>

People warmed up with sake are often overcome by undifferentiated emotion as they sit within the overwhelming beauty of the cherry blossoms. Moist eyes are common enough that a man could hide his tears there. Buson is mourning someone specific, the poet and eccentric Tairo[1] who died the year before. Unlike Bashô's poem, I feel we do not need to know that to fully appreciate it. *Does that make it a better poem or a worse one?* Here is an earlier example of thinking under the bloom.

<div align="center">
見るうちにあらぬ思の色ぞ添ふ花に夕や深くなるらん 心敬 百首和歌
miru uchi ni aranu omoi no iro zo sou hana ni yûbe ya fukaku naru ran shinkei (-1475)
</div>

<div align="center">
Even as i view
hitherto undreamed of
hues of thought

come with the blossoms
as the dusk grows deep
</div>

~~~~~~

1. Tairo. I seldom find the representative *ku* of a poet interesting, but all three by Tairo (-1778) in my dictionary of haiku poets (*haikujinmeijiten*) are: *"Falling plum blossoms / the end of the spring / has begun"* (plum being the first flower); *"Cutting a peony / how fondly I recall / dad's anger!"* (at his damaging a peony when a kid) and one concerning our cherry: *"To each his own: / some come to the blossoms to play / some not to."* (蓼喰ふ虫花

に来て遊ぶか遊ばぬか　大魯 *tade kuu mushi hana ni kite asobu ka asobanu ka*　note: the original is a bit long). This free spirit died at the young age of 54, and his master Buson must have come *not to play.*

おもうこと花にまびれて何もなし 成美 再現
omou koto hana ni mabirete nani mo nashi　seibi (1748-1816)
(thinking/feeling/loving-things blossoms-in/with swarming anything-even-not)

my thoughts	my thoughts
plastered by blossoms	covered with petals
a pure blank	disappear

Thinking this *ku* described something like love, when one can not think because countless thoughts zip back and forth, I first translated *"My thoughts / swarm the blossoms and / nothing remains."* Grammatically speaking, that did not hold up. Here, it is the blossoms that have blown the *poet's* mind.

何事もなくて花見る春も哉　一茶 文政四
nanigoto mo nakute hana miru haru mogana　issa -1827
(anything-even-not-being blossoms[acc] view spring wish)

ничего

oh, for a spring	my dream: viewing
when nothing happens	blossoms some totally
to view blossoms	peaceful spring

Issa's humble wish reminds me of the Russian *nichevo,* or "nothing," the equivalent to the English response *"fine,* thank you." Many more *ku* on thinking in the broadest sense, i.e. observing the state of the mind, are found in the final chapter of this *Book II, hana no kokoro* = "blossom-mind/heart." Many are not as sad as those we see here, though it seems that when the *words* "thinking" (*omou/omoi/ omoe*) and "thought" (*omoi*) are in a poem, they tend to be melancholy. I do not know whether or not Issa read Shinkei's *waka "Oh for a world / when i could gaze upon / the blossoms / and forget about / both of our plights!"* (ながめつゝ花とふたりのあはれをも忘るゝ程を此世共がな 心敬 百首和歌 *nagametsutsu hana to futari no aware o mo wasururu hodo o kono yo to mogana* (-1475)). Because Shinkei, referring to the savage civil war also questioned whether a tempest of warriors would leave a single tree of bloom behind in the capital (一本の花やは残ものゝふの荒山おろし騒ぐ都は　同　*ippon no hana ya wa nokoru mononô no arayama oroshi sawagu miyako wa*), I feel he may be alluding to women, but who knows? Though rarely cut down, many trees did burn to death.

むつかしや花の上にも小言あり 嘯山
mutsukashi ya hana no ue ni mo kogoto ari　shôzan -1800
(difficult! blossom-upon-even small-words/complaints exist)

mixed feelings	it's hard to believe
about people criticizing	there are even those who
cherry blossoms	grumble at blossoms

what can i do?
i can't even hold my tongue
for the blossoms

Some people, overwhelmed with emotion grow critical rather than melancholy. Judging from Shôzan's poetry, he was a hell of a wit. That implies a poison tongue, hence, the last reading.

 # 22 - 31 ~ 35

よきことはいひたきものよ花のかげ　士郎
yoki koto wa iitaki mono yo hananokage shirô 1742-1813
(good thing/s-as-for say-want-to things! blossom-shade)

<table>
<tr><td>

the bloomshade:
here, you really feel like
saying good things!

</td><td>

good things
just asking to be said
bloomshade

</td></tr>
</table>

ものいふもいやなりけふは花の陰　成美
mono iu mo iya nari kyo wa hananokage seibi 1748-1816
(thing-say-even dislike-become today-as-for, blossoms-shade)

<table>
<tr><td>

grumbling is not
what i would hear today
in the bloomshade

</td><td>

bloomshade
today, i will hold
my tongue

</td></tr>
</table>

Being treated to such beauty, one feels obligated to be good. Should these reflections have been included in the chapter on blossom *intoxication* or the one on *equality* to balance the rosy picture?

桜見て歩く間も小言哉　一茶
sakura mite aruku aida mo kogoto kana issa -1827
(cherry/ies seeing walk while even small-things=complaints!/'tis)

<table>
<tr><td>

bitching, bitching
even as they walk about
viewing blossoms

</td><td>

my complaining
doesn't stop though i walk
through blossoms

</td></tr>
</table>

夕過や桜の下に小言いふ　一茶
yû sugi ya sakura no shita ni kogoto iu issa -1827
(evening past: cherry-below-at complaints say)

after nightfall
i admit to bitching
below the bloom

How can one complain in paradise? Are we talking about the poor etiquette of blossom-viewers or the confession of a malcontent? I would *guess* this poem is also autobiographical, but I do not *know*. The "I admit" is mine; but the idea of the *ku* that takes it a step beyond the other complaining-under-the-blossoms *ku* (including Issa's) is the emphasis on "after nightfall." We can feel how Issa was on his good behavior during the daytime and this turns the *ku* into a temporal panorama.

達磨賛・ちる花を屁とも思はぬ御顔哉　一茶
chiru hana o he to mo omowanu okao kana issa (-1827)
(falling-blossom/s[+acc] fart-even-as think-not honorable-face 'tis)

in praise of daruma

<table>
<tr><td>

falling petals
and a face that does not
give a damn

</td><td>

this is a face
that cares not a fart for
falling petals

</td></tr>
</table>

22 - 36 ~ 40

The *daruma* (Bodhidharma) was originally a saint who decided to stay around and help us rather than cashing in his enlightenment to live in the godhead, paradise or whatever. The mouth is generally drawn in a straight line or even a slightly down-turned one looking like the letter *he* へ (see pic. at bottom of page). But why is this a subject for praise? Note, here, that we are not talking about the any part of the blossom-viewing but the petals falling. If you think that trusting in the Buddha and letting go of life (as the petals do) is good, then I suppose there is no call to regret their passing. And, is there not something poignant about a straight-man? This is the type of *ku* one wants a picture or introductory sentence with, because in Issa's day, a *daruma* could also mean a monk or a prostitute (a common form of daruma doll was what we might call a roly-poly, and these women were noted for taking tumbles).

道楽といはれて花に二度三度 士郎
dôraku to iwarete hana ni nido sando shirô -1813
(hobby/debauched-as said blossoms-to two times three times)

debauched, they say
i view the blossoms
more than once

I do not know enough about Shirô to say for certain who thought poorly of his repeated blossom-viewings. He was a physician and the best known haikai poet in Nagoya, a city of merchants.

一本のえだで惚々花見かな 杜若
ippon no eda de horebore hanami kana tojaku -1729
(one-stick[of]limb-in/with love/besotted blossom-viewing!/'tis)

just one limb	blossom-viewing
and i am captivated	how enthralled we are
blossom-viewing	with but one limb

One stolen or presented branch? Or could it be that someone sitting and drinking at a blossom-viewing generally sees but one branch? If you think about it, *this entire book* is about thinking under the blossoms, or, at least the portion of haiku that was really composed in cherry time, whether or not thinking or thoughts are actually mentioned. Had I done this chapter early rather than late, it might have had more *ku*.

荒果し垣根ゆかしき櫻哉 信規 月影塚
arehateshi kakine yukashiki sakura kana shinki ()
(dilapidated wall charming cherry[tree/blossoms]'tis)

old and crumbling
the wall is charming now
cherry blossoms

23

Buddies in the Bloomshade
花見連
hanami-ren

活てあふけふも桜の御陰哉　一茶
ikite au kyo mo sakura no okage kana issa -1827
(living-meet today, too, cherry's favor/grace/patronage/shade!/'tis)

bloom-shade

that we should live
and meet today! let us
thank the cherry!

Like all social events, blossom-viewing provided an opportunity for getting together with old friends. If some people enjoyed the anonymity of the crowds to play the *flâneur* – an unnoticed people-watcher with broader interests than the voyeur – others sought the comradery of the bloomshade. Issa's *ku* plays on that bloomshade, for the "favor," *i.e., okage*, transliterates as "honorable-shade."

めくりあふはまれなる花の都かな 紹巴
meguri-au wa mare naru hana no miyako kana jôha 1523-1602
(happen-to[luckily] meet-as-for rare-is blossom-capital!/'tis)

a chance meeting
rare indeed in the capital
city of blossoms

blossom capital
so many trees i can't find
a single friend

blossom capital
how rare to meet up
with a friend

Judging from what Issa wrote, it is clear that several hundred years later at popular blossom-viewing parks in Edo, people who came alone could just crash a party and make friends. But that is not the same thing as finding someone you know, and, at the time Jôha wrote, I do not know how much party-crashing was acceptable. Be that as it may, I read the *ku* as a description of how expansive the blossom-viewing grounds were in Kyôto, or, rather around Kyôto. When you add it all up, I bet there were over a hundred square miles with enough cherries in bloom to draw tens-of-thousands of blossom-viewers. Jôha was a hyperlogical poet who could not overlook that.

知る人はあはじ／＼と花見哉 去来 猿峰 -1704
shiru hito wa awaji awaji to hanami kana kyôrai
(know-person-as-for meet-not x2 - blossom-viewing!)

where's someone!
where's someone i know!
blossom-viewing

ふらここや花を洩れ来る笑ひ声 嘯山 -1801
fura koko ya hana o morekuru waraigoe shôzan
(halloo, here!/: blossom[acc] leak-come laughing-voice)

ho! over here!
voices of cheer leaking
out of the bloom

These *ku* are in the lively vernacular style Issa would adopt. By this time, the capital (now, *old* capital!) was not the only place with large crowds. The population, human and cherry, of Greater Edo (new capital, i.e., seat of the *de facto* government) had increased ten-fold. A book published in 1683 (Kyôrai would have been in his thirties), mentioned over 300 proper curtains (*maku*) – affluent blossom-viewers hung curtains partially around the trees – not to mention robe-like overcoats (*haori, kosode*) hung from the limbs of periphery trees by individuals and small parties (戸田茂睡「紫のひともと」in 白幡『花見と桜』) at one place. Considering the size of the crowds, fortuitous meetings were probably not that common unless one belonged to a group that frequented the viewings:

花守や白きかしらを突あはせ 去来 炭俵
hanamori ya shiroki kashira o tsukiawase kyorai -1704
(blossom guards!/?/: white heads/crowns[acc] thrust-meeting)

blossom guards   blossom guards
putting their solid white   white head and white head
heads together   come together

Usually, there is something pitiful about elders meeting, but this is different; we imagine these guards are outdoor men with tan skin setting off that white hair. I see them enjoying a sip of tea or *sake* as they gather to talk. Three or four would seem the right number. Compare the *ku* to a less well known one that is too general: *"This year, again / blossom-viewing heads / come together"* (ことしまた花見の顔を合せけり 召波 春泥集 *kotoshi mata hanami no atama o awasekeri* shôha -1771). Those of us who lack such comradeship feel a bit jealous of the guards, though we might not wish to exchange lives.

名を知らで知つた顔ある花見哉　沙月
na o shira de shitta kao aru hanami kana sagetsu (or, zamei -1727?)
(name[+acc.] know-not-with known face/s is/are blossom-viewing!/'tis)

and there are faces
i know with names i don't:
blossom-viewing

A blossom-viewing would be the ideal place to test people for their visual and verbal memory!

きのふあふた人に又逢ふ花見哉 稲音 新選
kinô auta hito ni mata au hanami kana inane 1773
(yesterday met people-to again meet blossom-viewing!/?/'tis)

meeting the man   meeting the men
i met yesterday, again,   i met yesterday, again,
blossom-viewing   blossom-viewing

A remarkably good minor ku about a remarkably insignificant happening. The original does not specify whether the poet speaks of one or many. I favor one because it would be humdrum to meet up again with a group, while the idea of running into a certain person and recognizing him in a large park is *somewhat* interesting, for it sets us to wondering what happened between the two or whether the man simply looks unique, and, if so, how. With a large planting of cherry trees – hundreds at the newly public (as of 1737) Mt. Asuka, just North of Edo, and over a thousand within the Edo castle in the early 18c (白幡：『花見と桜』第四章), the cherries would have been impressive in the decade before 1773, when the above *ku* was published and we can imagine crowds in the tens of thousands.

又とみぬ人は一花心哉　心敬 毛吹草 崑山集
mata to minu hito wa hitohana kokoro kana shinkei -1475
(again see/meet-not person-as-for, one-blossom heart!/?/'tis)

each blossom
at heart a person we shall
not see again

each person
we will never see again
is a blossom

This old *ku* (found in many *haikai* anthologies) is a wonderful nature poem, where the poet is unashamed to feel emotional about each and every blossom, or it is less poetic for being pure allegory. Traditional criticism would say the opposite, as the former would be identified as *pathetic fallacy*, while the latter would be called *romantic*. Grammar favors the latter reading; and Shinkei (whose name means "heart-respect") was a master of metaphor who reminds me of the English metaphysical poets, eg.: *"Here, all / i think of is flying / into the sky – // but old age turns us into / birds without feathers/wings!"* (大空に飛立つばかり思へども老は羽無き鳥と成ぬる 心敬).

華の友に又逢ふ迄は幾春や　一茶 寛三
hana no tomo ni mata au made wa iku haru ya issa -1827
(blossom/s-friend-as again meet-until-as-for howmany springs?)

how many springs
before i meet my blossom
buddies once again?

The blossom-viewing as a place of meeting was also a place of parting, meeting again or, maybe not. 29 year-old Issa covered a lot of ground that year and would have met people and trees he knew he would not see for a long time. His *ku* is similar to Shinkei's, but more natural.

にくい奴花の陰にて逢にけり 成美
nikui yatsu hananokage nite ainikeri seibi -1816
(spiteful guy/s bloom-shade-as meet/met[+finality]))

and i end up
meeting my nemesis
in the bloomshade

in the bloomshade
i come across someone:
my nemesis

The adjective *nikui* means someone who is "hated," usually for being better looking or more talented than oneself. It suggests envy if not attraction for the same and is the flip-side of love – in old Hollywood, too, we guess that a woman loves a man when she says *I hate you! I hate you! I hate you!* and pounds her dainty fists on the silent type's chest. I wrote "nemesis," for Seibi may well be referring to his wife and, was it not sometimes used in English by men to describe their wives?

待/\し桜と成れどひとり（or, 田舎）哉　一茶
machi machishi sakura to naredo hitori [inaka] kana issa 1813
(wait-waited cherry [blossoms] became but alone [or, the country]!/it's)

the cherry blossoms
i waited and waited for, yet
here, i'm all alone!

the cherry blossoms
i waited and waited for, yet
i'm in the sticks!

Issa, still single at age 50, came back to the town of his birth after finally making it – participating in *haikai* events, publishing and being well enough known to be listed at rank 27 in a national ranking of popular *haijin* (矢羽『一茶大事典』) – enough to press his claim to share half-a-house with his half-brother. He was back to the beginning, his spring, yet, still without a wife and friends at home. I assume he also has encountered a blossoming cherry and this is not purely allegorical flourishing.

花咲や牛は牛連馬は馬　一茶
hana saku ya ushi wa ushizure uma wa uma issa (1821)
(blossoms bloom!/: cows-as-for cow-companions, horses-as-for horses)

cherries bloom
cows have cows and
horses horses

With half-a-house and a bit of a name, Issa soon had a wife; but he had to stay on the road to make a living, teaching, editing, judging poetry competition and spreading news for patronage. So, at times, he still blossom-viewed alone and feel the loneliness humans create for themselves. Could the *ku* play on Onitsura's animal eg-count (#16-5), by giving the emotional rather than phenomenological view?

小言いふ相手もあらば花筵　一茶
kogoto iu aite mo araba hana-mushiro issa 1824
(complaint say companion even was-if blossom-mat)

ah, how i miss
my nagging mate, today!
the blossom-mat

the blossom mat
if only i had someone
to grumble to

Issa's upper-class patron Seibi may have preferred not to take *his* wife blossom-viewing, but Issa, as a well-off peasant, enjoyed more equal relations and, when he was home, took his wife viewing with him.[1] The preface to earlier versions of the *ku* written the previous fall* suggest the "small words" (bitch/complain/grumble) are *from her to him*: "This year, the noisy old wife's not here" (*yakamasikarishi rôsai kotoshi naku*); but grammar permits either reading and Issa has one *ku* where the other party is a *wall*. Because Issa mentions the mat, which was carried to the viewing, rather than the bloomshade, he may be inside his home looking at it. As an old man with a bad leg to boot, he would not have carried a mat, but sat on the mat his *young* wife – she died in her mid-thirties – carried for him. In cherry time, it would become a *memento mori*. Or, he might be sitting on a mat blossom-viewing, gazing upon the extra space, feeling the absence of what once was on it: the cool derriere he rested his head upon viewing the moon one summer (so records my favorite unsong *ku* of his).

@ Gender In/equality and Class The lower down the social ladder you went in Japan, the *more* egalitarian the male-female relationship. This was the opposite of the case in much of the West where poor men were known for insisting on superiority in their only castle (For a long discussion, see *Topsy-turvy 1585*.)

1. Fall Versions? The cherry blossom haiku is a close paraverse of these two *ku* where only the last five syllabets differ: *"Ah, how I miss / my nagging old mate / today's moon"* (~*kyô-no tsuki*); and, *" " " / chrysanthemum wine"* (*kiku-no-sake*). The moon is *the* moon, the harvest moon which might best be called the Buddhist moon, for viewing it was a quasi-religious experience. The mum wine was drunken on 9-9 in the hope of health and a long life, moreover, Chrysanthemum (Kiku) was her name (which can make it hard to sort out the real mum from her). Two others: *" As fall ends / how i want someone / to scold me! (kogoto iu aite no hoshi ya aki-no kure).* Instead of the more subtle "if [only I had]" this earlier version had "[I] want." I reversed the syntax; the original resembles the blossom-mat, moon and mum *ku*. These are what I call *paraverses*, different takes on what is, at heart, the same thing. Another version replaces the *middle 7* syllabets: *"As fall ends / my nagging mate is / the damn wall!"* (~*aite-wa kabe zo~*). Here, Issa must complain to the wall, so maybe I should retranslate: *"As fall ends / i grumble, my mate / the damn wall."* Issa would have loved Willie Nelson's *Hello Walls*.

人来ればひとりの連や花の山 一茶 文政八
hito kureba hitori no tsure ya hananoyama issa 1825
(person comes if/when, one companion! blossom-mountain)

one more man
means one more buddy:
cherry mountain

This probably paraverses Issa's well-known "there-are-no-strangers" *ku* (#8-6), but might also mean the old poet is alone: "If anyone comes / I'll have *one* companion . . ." The original's parallel rhetoric ("one man comes: one companion becomes") is far more poetic than "means," but does not English.

人選して一人也花の陰　一茶
hito-erami shite hitori nari hananokage issa
(people-selecting-doing alone become bloomshade)

よりあきてもとへもどるや花の陰 一茶
yori-akite moto e modoru ya hananokage issa
(approach-tiring origin/start-to return! bloomshade)

being choosey
i end up all by myself
in the bloomshade

tired of trying
to join others, i'm back
in my bloomshade

By Issa's day, large viewing spots had huge crowds. Issa did not visit such a place the year he wrote the first *ku*, and may have failed to find a tree with other poetry-lovers. The original term "person/people-selecting" (*hito-eram[b]i*) means being discriminating with respect to people, and is only slightly more neutral than being "stuck up." The second *ku* written two decades earlier, shows that Issa, being poor, did not need to wait for old-age to experience marginalization/rejection.

つき合いはむりにうかるゝ桜哉 一茶
tsukiai wa muri ni ukaruru sakura kana issa 1825
(socializing-as-for forced floating/high cherry[blossoms]!/'tis)

so-ci-a-li-zing:
and so we overdo it
blossom-viewing

fellowship is
pretending to be high
blossom-viewing

The term "attach/stick-meet/associate" (*tsuki-ai*) is fine vernacular for which the Latinate equivalents given by the dictionary – *socialization, association, intercourse, social obligations* and so forth – are horrible matches. But the Anglo-saxon "fellowship" and "friendship" are too restricted. How about "for the company"? This is a rare perspective: a poet not in the mood for a *hanami*. The first reading hints that drink is used to fake it. The second, that the poet just gamely went along with the others.

遊びやう互いにかわる花見哉　がいん 雅因?
asobi yô tagai-ni kawaru hanami kana   gain -1818? 再現
(playing-style, each-other-with change blossom-viewing!/'tis)

<table>
<tr><td>

how we party
depends on our playmates
blossom-viewing

</td><td>

blossom-viewing
we all play differently
with one another

</td></tr>
</table>

Partying with different people brings out different faces within us. I like to think this mutuality extends to the trees, that new bloom brings out a different sort of play than full bloom and the later petal blizzard.

花咲いて思ひ出す人皆遠し　子規
hana saite omoidasu hito mina tôshi   shiki 1896
(blossoms blooming remember people all far-away)

cherries blooming
everyone i think of
is far away!

Beauty makes one think about others with whom to share it, but Blyth, who translated *"The cherry-blossoms blooming / those i remember / all far away,"* makes a necessary point: "This becomes poetry only when we keep our eye steadily on the cherry-flowers."

山峡に咲ける桜をただひと目君に見せてば何をか思はむ　大供池主 万葉集#3967
yamagai ni sakeru sakura o tada hitome kimi ni miseteba nani o ka omowamu   manyôshû 8c

anatomy of melancholy

<table>
<tr><td>

just one glance
of the cherries gorgeous
in this ravine
i would be content just
to give it to my divine

</td><td>

if i could but
give you one glance
of the cherries
blooming in the hollar
my heart would quiet!

</td></tr>
</table>

The allusion to a poet needing but a glimpse of the beloved is lost in the second reading, but the poem, as a whole, suggests the bowerbird fantasy: *if only something beautiful could be shown to the beloved, she would be taken by it and* (this part that doesn't necessarily follow, for most human females are not bowerbirds) *fall for him.* A lovesick man may experience something akin to bipolar disorder when he encounters natural beauty: extreme elation and utter despair – *With this beauty, who needs a woman! Without a woman, this is a waste!* One of the earliest poems showing cherry blossoms were highly appreciated, song #1752, with its simpler *"if only I had a girl to show these cherry blossoms to!"* (桜の花を見せむ児もがも) may be more representative of the *Manyôshû*, but the above #3967 is better.

山桜ひとり見に来てすまぬもの　千代
yamazakura hitori mi ni kite sumanu mono   chiyo 1701-75
(mountain cherry.ies alone view/see-to coming closure-not thing)

mountain cherries:
i came alone to see them
and it was a shame

Obviously, the feelings I explained from my (male) experience are not only male. When Chiyo went blossom-hunting alone and felt what she found deserved more praise than she alone could provide, she must have felt it too. And this was Chiyo, who usually was delighted not to meet a soul:

山彦や見ず見られずに花戻り 千代 松の声
yamahiko ya mizu mirarezu ni hanamodori chiyo 1701-75
(echo! see-not seen-not-with blossom[viewing]-return/ing)

cherry huntress

call me "echo"! seeing no one, back unseen from the blossoms	am i an echo? seeing no one, back unseen from the blossoms

A hike through the hills? In Japanese, the *yamahiko* or "echo" includes the word "mountain" in it.

人先に来て又ひとり花戻り 千代 松の声
hito saki ni kite mata hitori hana-modori chiyo 1701-75
(person/people ahead-of coming again alone/single blossom-return/ing)

blossom-viewing

coming ahead
of the crowd, alone again
on the road back

Chiyô's ability to go it alone, to find solace within even as she viewed nature without, exceeds that demonstrated by the other major haiku poets until the early 20c wanderer Santôka.

いつとなくさくらが咲いて逢うてはわかれる 山頭火
itsu to naku sakura ga saite atte wa wakareru santôka -1940
(sometime[not-obviously] cherries bloomed meeting-as-for [we] part)

well, the cherries they blossomed in a wink we meet, we part	i almost missed the cherry's bloom: soon as we meet we part

Santôka did not so much *hanami* with people as meet with the blossoms, themselves.

桜花咲きかも散ると見るまでに誰かも此処に見えて散り行く 万葉集#3129
sakurabana saki ka mo chiru to miru made ni tare ka mo koko ni miete chiriyuku *manyôshû* (8c)

cherry blossoms
as soon as they blossom
you see they'll fall

and all whom we see here
now gathering, will scatter

"Meeting is departing" says a Japanese proverb. The *Manyôshû* poem shares the *bloom: meet+fall:depart* idea with Santôka, but the blossoms are probably metaphor for a send-off party.

#23-24~26

花が葉になる東京よさやうなら　山頭火
hana ga ha ni naru tôkyô yo sayônara　santôka -1940
([cherry]blossoms-the leaves-into become tokyo goodbye)

sayônara

the blossoms
have become leaves so
tôkyô, *i* leave

hey, tôkyô
your blossoms are leaves:
good-bye!

This is later than the others, early 20c. Is Santôka, Mr."Mountain-head-fire," leaving for the cool hills where he will find wild cherry still in bloom? I love his bold direct address.

見る人の花に見られて帰りけり　長久 欅炭木
miru hito no hana ni mirarete kaerikeri　chôkyû ()
(seeing person's blossom/s-by seen return [+emph.]))

the viewers
seen by the blossoms
go home

blossom-viewers
seen blossom-viewing
head for home

the viewers
seen with the blossoms
go home

This, last old people-viewing *hanami ku,* seems to come from a blossom-centric perspective, though it may be allegorical: The second reading takes the blossoms for the viewing and sees blossom-viewing as a time to view and be viewed by others, but I would *like to think* the ostensible reading, the first, was also on the poet's mind . . . As that is dubious, the *"by"* is less likely than the *"with."*

こぬまても花ゆへ人のまたれつる春も暮ぬるみ山辺の里　藤原伊綱　新古今集#170
konu made mo hana yue hito no mataretsuru haru mo kurenurumi yamabe no sato　shinkokinshû (1205)

*this mountain
where blossoms made me
wait for men*

*(unexpected, they never came)
comes to the end of its spring*

*back in the hills
not expecting a soul i still
thought someone*

*might visit the blossoms
before spring finally left*

24

People Viewing
人見
hito-mi

年ことの人しもうれし花の陰　宗因
toshigoto no hito shi mo ureshi hana no kage   sôin 1604-82
(year-each's people[+emph.] too delighted/ful[to me] blossom-shade)

    the humans, too   the yearly sight
delight us every year   of men, too, delights!
   below the bloom   the bloomshade

every year
i thank the bloom for
people, too

While the cherry trees are the stars, people-viewing was and still is a large part of the blossom-viewing experience. My last reading takes the secondary, idiomatic usage of shade, "thanks to" and twists it further into "i thank," though it is not obvious (or likely), as with the last chapter's lead *ku*..

世の形花に先見る千人哉　宗春 三籟
yo no katachi hana ni mazu miru sennin kana   sôshun 1734
(world's shape blossoms-in/through/by first see thousand-people!/'tis)

  state of the world?   worldly fashion
first look at a thousand   first seen by the crowds
  blossom viewers!   blossom-viewing

In Japan, it is said that the first few days of the New Year reveal the entire year to come, but that is probably less true than this observation. I felt tempted to title the poem *Fashion Show,* but the scope of the "world," i.e., society that is revealed might include the economic and physical health of the people as well as the fads. I wonder if you could substitute "opera" for "blossom" and describe Europe of that time (or shortly thereafter, as opera was not yet developed).

見る人を見るや都の花盛　紹巴　大発句帳
miru hito o miru ya miyako no hanazakari   jôha 1523-1602
([blossom-]viewing people[obj] viewing /watching!/: capital's blossom-peak)

   kyôto blossoms: the bloom-peak
you view the people   in the capital: people
   viewing them!   viewing people!

The capital was full of princes and princesses, the beautiful people. With opera or *kabuki*, I find watching people 99% of the fun. Cherry blossoms are far more interesting than men, East or West, who sing in high-strung voices, but even so, people are always a sight to behold.

金の糞しそうな犬ぞ花の陰　一茶 文化三
kin[or, *kane*]*no fun*[or, *hako*] *shisôna inu zo hananokage*　issa 1806
(gold/golden/coin-shit/poop do-would/so/seems-dog/s! blossom-shade)

in the bloom-shade
a dog that looks like it
would shit coins!

bloom-shade scene:
lap-dogs that probably
poop pure gold

Reading the original for the first time, I imagined exactly what DL must have when he (also, once) translated *"that dog's pooping / pure gold! / blossom shade;"* i.e., a surreal mood, soft light slipping through blossoms creating a happy Midas of the mind. Unfortunately, the grammar won't quite support a poop-in-progress. Issa's *ku* is not *that* good. It is about the in/equality we saw already (ch.8) and people-watching. As Kaneko Tohta (『一茶句集』) points out, the coin=money reading is probably correct, for Issa has many poems criticizing the "money is everything" world of his times. But, he *also* feels that a less likely *kin*, or "gold" pronunciation of the same would raise this *ku*, probably satirizing a lap-dog – pampered by women in luxurious dress (the year before, an Issa *ku* says speech is lost before the gorgeous blossom(-viewing) dresses （ことの葉も天ゝたらん花衣 *koto no ha mo ô ô taran hanagoromo*) – beyond banality, by giving us a *hint* of surrealism. I would only add that young Issa would have seen prints of the wealthy literally vomiting and shitting gold coins when the great leveler shook up their guts. (*The leveler?* The supernatural catfish, held responsible for earthquakes, was thought to act partly out of moral concern for excessive avarice.)

いそかしき花見る花や花盛　春峰 安永六
isogashiki hana miru hana ya hanazakari　shunpo 1777
(busy/ily blossom-view/ing-blossoms!/: blossom-peak)

a bustling scene:
blossoms viewing blossoms
in full bloom

The ones doing the viewing are human blossoms, beauties. I am afraid English has no equivalent generic expression: "English roses" observing roses would not do here. *Women watching women* are quite common in haiku. Men watching men are not, though, from Frois (*Topsy-turvy 1585*), we know that Japanese men, unlike Europeans, preened themselves before mirrors.

始めて都の花に遊ふ・櫻にも人にもうつる心哉　蘭更
sakura ni mo hito ni mo utsuru kokoro kana　rankô　(1726-99)
(cherry[blossoms]-to-even [and] people-to-even transfer heart!/'tis)

first capital blossom-viewing

it jumps ship
for cherry trees and men
my own heart

my heart, my mind
it leaves me for the blossoms
and the people!

The soul drawn out its own window? Rankô is drawn to the beauty of the blossoms *and* the people viewing them (the *men* is generic, used to save syllables).

people

いろ/\の人見る花の山路哉　小いと 花櫻帖
iro-iro no hito miru hana no yamaji kana   koito ()
(color x2[various] people view blossoms' mntn-path)

all sorts of people
to view on this path to
mountain cherries

this mountain trail
to the blossoms full of
people to view

On a mountain trail, we might meet wood-cutters, charcoal makers, monks, poets . . . but, when the cherry is in bloom, there is no telling what we will see. One could sit by the path and people-view all day. The haiku collection's editor noted the poet was a woman.

さま/\の人にもあかぬ櫻哉　野馬
samazama no hito ni mo akanu sakura kana   noma ()
(styles-styles[various] people-to/with-even tire-not cherry!/'tis)

cherry blossoms!
the variety of men, too
holds our interest

we're not bored
with our variety, either:
blossom viewing

The *mo* (also/even/too) makes the *ku*. It indirectly notes the variety of the blossoms while playing lightly on an older saw about cherry blossoms never cloying our senses, thanks to the brevity of its bloom.

向島の絵に 同じ人もなくて日毎の花見かな 子規
onaji hito mo nakute hi goto no hanami kana   shiki -1896
(same person even not day-each blossom-viewing!/'tis)

the same people
not around: day-by-day
blossom-viewing

The original is prefaced *"On a picture of Mukojima,"* the popular viewing place noteworthy for its blossom-viewing boats. Apparently, sleeping under the bloom was not allowed and lodging was dear, so locals saw different visitors each day. It is a remarkably imaginative *ku* for a picture.

御殿山 花の陰口きく人やいはぬ人 成美 手習
hananokage kuchi kiku hito ya iwanu hito   seibi 1748-1816
(bloom-shade mouth work/ing people and say/ing-not people)

the bloomshade:
talkative men and
taciturn men

some complain
some do not in the shade
of the blossoms

All men appreciate cherry blossoms, but not all appreciate other men. Or, paradoxically, do the latter enjoy crowds, because a crowd is a good place to hide from men? Did Seibi notice that there is no in-between; that men when moved by beauty (as by danger) tend to respond by blabbing or clamming up? The original is prefaced by a location, Goten-yama. This was a hunting preserve for the Shôgun Iemitsu to the North of Edo that was planted with cherries and famously good by Seibi's time. The shade (*kage*) can pun into the mouth, hence the second reading which may be bunk.

他の為に花見る顔そ哀なり　姿仙 新虚くり
hoka no tame ni hana miru kao zo aware nari shisen 1777
(other[things] for blossoms view face/s [+emph] pitiful become/are)

wretched faces!　　　　　　　　　　someone viewing
men with ulterior motives　　　　blossoms for other reasons
blossom-viewing　　　　　　　　　　is a pitiful sight

This is a hell of a poem for it tempts each reader to conjure up a story. Is it an abbot thinking of the blossom's draw, i.e., more contributions from visitors; or gamblers out to rob the suckers blind; or pimps, seeking new women to induce into the trade? I prefer a broad take: men looking at women as objects for sex rather than objects of beauty. The first line might also be: *how pitiful looking!*[1] and it is not clear whether the intent is sympathetic or critical. On second thought, my view may still be far too narrow. Take this sentence from *"Five Sex-loving Women"* a novel by Saikaku that antedates the above *ku* by about a hundred years:

> The cherries on the Takasuna ridge are blooming. Married women proudly exhibit their beauty, mothers show off their attractive daughters. Nowadays, people are only interested in gadding about to be viewed rather than viewing the blossoms. (「好色五人女」1686)

As a cherry-blossom lover, all I can say is that there is no excuse for neglecting the real thing, for the bloomshade, blossoms and all, is far more interesting then, say, the stage of an opera, where anyone with good sense would turn one's spy-glasses (and ears) away from the stage.

知足亭・見直すやかゝる男も花の陰　組月 千鳥かけ
minaosu ya kakaru otoko mo hananokage sogetsu 1712
(look-afresh!/: such-a man/men also blossoms-shade)

at know-legs inn

i'll be damned
that man's ok! he was there:
in the bloomshade

It is possible to English the verb *minaosu* or "[i] see-correct/afresh" with respect to a person as "[i have] come to have a better opinion of;" but try to put that into a haiku! Many Occidental visitors to Japan have marveled together with Lowell at the "so complete and so universal" appreciation of Japanese for cherry blossoms:

> Appreciation is not confined to the cultivated few; it is shown quite as enthusiastically by the masses. The popularity of the plants is all embracing. The common people are as sensitive to their beauty as are the upper classes. (*The Soul of the Far East:*1888)

Good or bad, an outside view tends to homogenize a population. Seen from the inside – *viz* Sogetsu's poem – it was obvious that whatever the class, some people appreciated the cherry blossoms more than others. Yet, Lowell does point out a real difference between the culture of Japan and that of the Occident. Most Japanese appreciated the more delicate things of life; poor or not, they were cultivated. When the Russian Captain Golownin spent a couple years captive in Japan about eighty years before Lowell, he was *astounded* to find guards and soldiers reading books and playing the Japanese equivalent of chess (*shogi*) and the even more difficult game of *go*. I dare say that Japan's level of culture in the 19c compares favorably with ours today (and the gap is growing).

24 - 12 ~ 13

1. Pitiful Men I once saw a stark naked *avant garde* drama on the grounds of the French Embassy in Tokyo (the Ambassador allowed it to protest the maltreatment of the nude photography of a French photographer at the hands of the Japanese Customs for, at the time, pubic hair was censored). The bare hemp rope used for the tug of war held between bare legs was raw art, I guess; but how could I appreciate the French woman (one in an otherwise Japanese troupe) writhing on the ground *as art*, when my mind was lost in the soft country between her full thighs? A lonely man cannot appreciate such beauty as beauty. The performers are fine, I thought: they are f__ing someone. I am not. I left before the end of the performance. To me, condemnation on the part of the sexual *haves* of *have-nots* looking at women as they do shows a remarkable lack of sympathy.

~~~~~~

我らさへ腹のふくれる花も見る　一茶
warera sae hara no fukureru hana-mo miru issa 1812
(we-even blossoms' swell/bloat blossom/s too view/see)

even we saw enough blossoms to feel satiated	even us poor get to see blossoms with fillable bellies	even us poor see blossoms that make us feel wealthy

Fukureru can mean a belly full of food i.e., *content*, or one full of yet unvoiced complaint i.e., *discontent*. Hence, reading one and three are contrary. The middle reading guesses that Issa alludes to women! I save most woman=blossom *ku* for Book III, but we will see some about "viewing" here.

寝並んで遠見ざくらの評義/議哉　一茶
nenarande tômi-zakura no hyôgi kana issa -1827
(sleep/lie-lined-up far-view-cherr/ies' evaluation/conference!/'tis)

we lie in a row critiquing blossoms viewed afar	lying in a row we collect intelligence: distant cherries

Love this one. The question here is whether the cherry blossoms in the distance are the *bona fide* thing on mountains the poets didn't feel up to climbing, or women. Likewise, for this later *ku:*

我／＼も目の正月ぞ夜の花　一茶
wareware mo me no shôgatsu zo yoru no hana issa 1818
(us too/even eye[=woman]'s new-year! night-blossoms)

we also get
a feast for our eyes:
night blossoms!

Despite the fact Issa's only earlier "our eyes" (*wareware no me*) *ku* is about the refreshing sight of streetwalkers, Kaneko Tohta thinks this may be a straight *ku* by a man old enough to appreciate blossoms as blossoms. The OJD gives an older *ku* where a plum blooming in a mid-winter warm-spell is called an "eye-new-year" (小春にも梅の花見や目正月　伊人　嵐山土塵集), so, there is precedent; but another version of Issa's *ku*, written two years before, has "elderly" rather than "we" and a caption *specifying* "Yoshiwara," i.e, "the pleasure-quarters" (吉原 としよりの目〔の〕正月ぞさくら花 *yoshiwara // toshiyori no me[no] shôgatsu zo sakurabana*). The "Eye-New-Year" is idiomatic for the New-Year-as-the-year's-greatest-spectacle, but there is also at least an off-chance that Issa means "we *men*" and alludes to blossoms on the woman's New Year (on the full-moon, the 15th), sometimes called *me[=female]-shôgatsu*. In Issa's snow country, there was precious little bloom on New Year's

Day. The *ku* before the Yoshiwara *eye-new-year* in Issa's journal has him picking greens (a New Years' ritual) within the distance his *onjaku* (a stone carried as a heater) stayed warm!

花の咲くころはどちむく春の神　二松 淡路嶋 再現
hana no saku koro wa dochi muku haru no kami   jishô 1698
(blossom blooms time-as-for, wherever face spring's god/s)

~~flowers bloom:~~ ~~cherries bloom~~
~~the deities of spring~~ ~~wherever you look it's~~
~~are everywhere~~ ~~princess sao!~~

when cherries bloom
the god of spring no longer
knows where to face

At first, I failed to realize that the "faces" modifies the god/dess/e/s? The wit is in the *any-which-way-ness*, because the God of the Spring would be associated with one direction (East) and certain directions were propitious at certain times. With blossoms all about, any way is fine!

見る若衆見らるゝ花よ仇くらべ　幸佐
miru wakashu miraruru hana yo ada kurabe   kôsa () 芋環？
(looking young-crowd, looked-at blossoms! cheating/vanity-comparison[contest])

vanity competes:　　　　　　　　　　　　　　gay boys viewing
the gay boys viewing and　　　　　　　　cherries viewed, hey, who's
the blossoms viewed!　　　　　　　　　　the ficklest of you?

Ada-kurabe means either a comparison of the relative transience of two or more parties, or vying to put down the other as the biggest cheater (a type of ancient cut-down contest). Since *wakashu* lose their boy beauty quickly, the second is possible, but, if cherry blossoms alludes to harlots or wives, the second is also possible. The *ku* indirectly praises the "young-crowd," with its fancy dress and coiffure, vies with the blossoms in splendor. In a sense, these pretty young men who sold their favors to older men[1] were not transvestites, for the Japanese culture allowed men to participate in the beauty game, but dressy in their own right. In the 17c and early 18c, they were so popular that female prostitutes whose features were not fine in a feminine way, were known to deliberately pass as "young-crowd." If you do not like "gay boys, please use the transliteration, "young crowd," if you wish. If you like being direct, change the "ficklest" into "sluttiest." What makes the *ku* interesting if not good, even with my bad readings, is the contrast of look/looked-at (*miru . . . miraruru*). The gay boys, as literal lookers, play the male part, though they may play the female (socket) role in sex.

観想・廿とせの小町か眉に落花哉　几董
hatatose no komachi ga [ka?] mayu ni rakka kana   kitô -1789
(twenty-year[old]-komachi's [or, "?"] eyebrow/s-on fallen-petal/s!/?/'tis)

a cherry petal　　　　　　　cherry petals　　　　　　　am i komachi
drops on the eyebrow　　dropping at a glance from　　at twenty? there's a petal
of a young komachi　　　　a young komachi　　　　　　on my eyebrow

Probably a picture of *a* Komachi, *i.e.* young beauty. Does the petal's location hint at the fate of this coy poetess of love, who, legend has it, died in the marsh, alone, where she was found with a blade of saw-grass growing through her eye-socket? My bold last reading is the most *haikai*. The poet is male.

24 - 18~ 20

1. Men and Boys. Men in many cultures, not just the classic Greeks, love boys. This does not make them homo-sexual, at least not in their opinion. If anything, they think of themselves as *macho*, or hyper-masculine, because poking into things, whatever the sex (or, in some cases, species) is masculine. Men were not ashamed to be seen with boys in public. In the well-known book of lists (*mono-wa-zukushi*) *Inu-makura*, written at the end of the 16c, but read mostly in the 17c, the last of the six "Interesting Things" (*omoshiroki mono*) listed was "Walking with the young crowd (gay boys) at a blossom-viewing" (*wakashû to hanami ariki*).

ちる花や今の小町が尻の迹　一茶 文化十
chiru hana ya ima no komachi ga shiri no ato issa 1813
(falling/scattering blossoms: now's komachi's butt's print/after)

<blockquote>
falling petals:
ass-prints of the latest
komachi girls
</blockquote>

<blockquote>
petals scatter
in the wake of the ass
of a komachi
</blockquote>

<blockquote>
petals fall and
a modern day komachi's
ass-print vanishes
</blockquote>

酒を妻妻を妾の花見かな　其角
sake o tsuma tsuma o mekake no hanami kana kikaku -1707
(sake[obj] wife/nibbly, wife[obj] mistress's blossom-viewing 'tis)

<blockquote>
sake for my wife
and my wife for my mistress:
blossom-viewing
</blockquote>

I do not know what my first reading of the first *ku* means, but my respondent favors it. The second *ku* suggests spouses who know how to enjoy themselves, but the wife=nibblies pun is lost in translation.

妻つれて妾つれて人の花見哉　子規
tsuma tsurete mekake tsurete hito no hanami kana shiki
(wife taking mistress taking people's blossom-viewing)

<blockquote>
their wives in tow
mistresses in tow, other men
blossom-viewing
</blockquote>

奇麗のがそろり／＼と花の山　子規 明治27
kirei-no-ga sorori-sorori to hananoyama shiki
(beautiful-ones many/slowly x2 blossom-mountain)

<blockquote>
beautiful ones
slowly flow past me:
cherry mountain
</blockquote>

Issa has a New Year's *ku* similar to Shiki's 19 syllabet first *ku*. It is lonely enough to be poor, sick, ugly and sleeping alone year after year. But, to watch the fortunate ones . . . Or, am I over-reading from *my* situation? Is this the studious male poet *vs.* ordinary Joes with lives? The second *ku* is more poetic *and* philosophical (達観). *Sorori-sorori* means both "many, many" *and* "slowly." This next is nothing much, but, I find it charming. In cherry time, even Japanese could turn into Lafcadios:

花の山浮世画の美人来る哉　子規
hananoyama ukiyoe no bijin kitaru kana shiki 1894
(blossom-mountain floating-world-prints' beauty/ies came!/?)

<blockquote>
cherry mountain!
will we see one of those
woodcut beauties?
</blockquote>

<blockquote>
cherry mountain!
did those beauties come
from a woodcut?
</blockquote>

<blockquote>
cherry mountain!
here come beauties right
from a woodcut!
</blockquote>

駕かきは女也けり花の山　一茶 文政一
kagokaki wa onna narikeri hananoyama   issa (-1827)
(basket=satin-as-for woman become/was[+emph.] blossom-mountain)

      the sedan man
   turns out to be a woman
      on mount cherry

Unlike the *ku* so far, this is straight reporting. Issa has at least a half-dozen such women-in-unexpected-places *ku* in his journal. I think of it as a form of ethnographic journalism.

京女花に狂はぬ罪深し　虚子
kyô-onna hana ni kuruwanu tsumibukashi   kyoshi 1893
(kyoto women blossom-at/with rave-not sin grave)

    the greatest sin   kyôto women:
of kyôto women: not catching   failure to fall for blossoms
      blossom fever   is a grave sin

Kyoto women were considered ideal, hence poets hunted for their flaws (*Senryû* point out that they had a tendency to pee while standing. That was true, for fertilizer-related reasons I give in *Topsy-turvy 1585*).

まもられてはづるか赤き花の顔　長昌 毛吹草
mamorarete hazuru ka akaki hana no kao   chôshô 1645
(protected release/open?/ed red blossom's/blossoms' face/s)

    the red-tinged faces
  are the blossoms just out
   from their cloisters?

Since only tiny buds are sepal-guarded the metaphor is weak. There are other flowers that would fit the bill better. It is hard to say if the redness owes more to bashfulness or sun-burn.

花の陰朧に見ゆる女かな　吐江 芭蕉庵再興集
hananokage oboro ni miyuru onna kana   tokô 1771
(bloom-shade hazily seen/seeable woman/women!/'tis)

   dimly made out   in the penumbra
through the bloom-shade   of the bloom, i barely
    some women   see: a woman

There are good, bad, beautiful and ugly words for vagueness. *Oboro* is a poetic one.

疱瘡の跡まだ見ゆる花見哉　傘下 あらの
hôsô no ato mada miyuru hanami kana   sanka 1689
(small-pox-marks still see-able blossom-viewing!/'tis)

  the small-pox scars
are fresh and still stand out
   blossom-viewing

Smallpox usually struck in the winter. It did not kill as many people in Japan as measles, but ravaged their faces. Made-up or not, those who survived would reveal their fresh scars when they went out for the first time in the spring. Think of the cracked tree bark, soft pink-white blossoms and fine clothing.

花笠や母の見をくるかゝへ帯 虎女 淡路嶋
hanagasa ya haha no mi-okuru kakae-obi　torajo (1698)
(blossom-hat!/: mother's sending-off supporting-belt[pregnancy])

off to the hanami!

her cherry hat!
her mother's eyes send-off
her gravid form

While good poems often fail to translate, this is exceptionally poor. Problems: 1) pronouns, none of which are needed in Japanese; 2) the untranslated "holding-belt," a special sash worn when a woman was pregnant; 3) the compound-verb "see-send" requiring "eyes" in English; and most important, 4) *why* she heads off to the blossom-viewing despite being with child: the Japanese reader would see an *odori-ko,* a dancing-girl, who learned her trade from her mother and will raise her girl to carry on her trade. The poet's name, *Tiger-woman,* is female, but the *ku* may well be written by a male poet, for Japanese were not adverse to writing in the guise of the other sex.

誰が母そ花に数珠くる遅櫻　祐甫 炭俵
daga haha zo hana ni juzu kuru osozakura　yuhô? 1694
(whose mother[+emph] blossoms-at/with/for prayer-beads move late-cherry)

whose mother　　　　　　　　　　　　whose mother
below the late-cherry　　　　　　　is that praying below
doing her beads　　　　　　　　　　　the late-cherry

A late-cherry implies warm weather and an old woman. It also might signify her, as she "counts" her Buddhist prayer beads for her own soul that has hung on after her husband died and she became a nun, or for the success of her children, who might be in a perilous situation.

母らしき人の居にけり花むしろ 嘯山 葎亭
haha rashiki hito no inikeri hanamushiro　shôzan 1717-1801
(mother-like/resembling person's being(there)[+finality] blossom-mat)

blossom-viewing
on a rush mat, someone who
looks like mom

This is what I call an 温句 *onku,* or warm(hearted) verse. The next is another matter!

妻にもと幾人思ふ花見かな（櫻狩）破笠 続虚栗
tsuma ni mo to ikunin omou hanami kana[sakura-gari]　haryû (1687)
(wife-as-even how-many people think/consider blossom-viewing!/?/'tis)

blossom viewing:　　　　　　　　　　oh, how many
any number of women　　　　　　　　woman i would mate!
you would swive!　　　　　　　　　　cherry hunting

The original *tsuma* can signify a male mate as well as a female one, but considering the sex of the poet and the cherry blossom at this time, women are the likely objects of desire in this semi-famous *ku*.

どこぞから引れたがるも花見哉　りん女
doko zo kara hikaretagaru mo hanami kana rinjo (1673-1757)
(where[+emph./exclam.]-from pull-out-wanting also blossom-viewing)

> wanting freedom
> from *that* place is also
> blossom-viewing

Somewhere-from pulled-wish-too blossom-viewing? The original *ku* had me stumped. Since I like Rinjo (expect scores of her shell *ku* in a book of lubricious marine poetry), I convinced myself it meant something like "Wanting someone / to pick me up; that too's / blossom-viewing;" "Wanting to fall / for something! that, too / is my *hanami.*" But, I was wrong. The emphatic *zo* between "somewhere" and "from," suggests a specific place, a dreadful place one might not want to mention, namely, the so-called "pleasure quarters." Next edition, expect the *ku* to *move* to chapter 59.

羽折著て花折りさうな女哉　梅室
haori kite hana orisôna onna kana baishitsu (1768-1852)
(haori[light overcoat] wearing blossom[branch] break/steal-likely woman!)

breaking blossoms

> something about
> that woman in a *haori*
> says she'll do it!

the look

> see that woman
> in a *haori*? i bet she'll
> break off a spray!

The *haori* is a silken thigh-length overcoat, generally plain on the outside but ornate on the inside. Like most clothing, it cannot translate in a word. Judging from Bashô's older *ku*: *"Blossom-drunk, / a woman puts on a haori / and a sword"* (花に酔へり羽織着て刀さす女　芭蕉 *hana ni eeri haori kite katana sasu onna*), it would seem that samurai were the most likely to wear *haori* at blossom-viewing. It is hard to say why cherry blossoms made women gallant, but they did. Bashô is echoed by two women, Kikujo (?) *"In the bloomshade / who bears a sword? / it's a woman!"* (花の陰刀もちたる女かな　きく女 *hananokage katana mochitaru onna kana*), and Kasanjo (10-4). Baishitsu's *ku* is more interesting than all of these, for we can see the woman's eyes, intent on possession. We will have a whole chapter on the practice of breaking off branches, for now, suffice it to say it is not as bad as it might seem.

盛りぢゃ花に坐浮法師ぬめり妻　芭蕉
sakari ja hana ni sozoro bôshi numerizuma bashô -1694
(acme it's! blossoms-to sit-float-priest/s slippery-wife/wives)

> it's full bloom!
> priests float from their mats
> wives slip about

Buddhists priests and wives generally remained in place, *their* place. A book of Basho's *ku* explains that a *numeri-zuma* (slippery-wife) is one acting "like a dandy," but the OJD (which uses the poem for its example) has her acting sexy (*namamete*). Imagine a woman, or women, face/s flushed, leading men on and using a body language usually kept under tight wraps. (Note how I verbed two adjectives!).

people

うかれよる人こそなかれ茶の花見　千川
ukareyoru hito koso nakare cha no hanami   chisen (17-18c)
(floating[crazed] people especially not tea's blossom-viewing)

no people come
floating o'er: a tea master's
blossom-viewing

Alcohol helped the normally reticent Japanese float about from tree to tree. It is not so much that tea does not here, as that tea parties are not crash-able. This next *ku* adds a corollary to Bashô's.

櫻の陰のうかれ妻・傾城の花にからるゝ浮世哉　空我 権の葉
sakura no kage no ukarezuma // keisei no hana ni kararuru ukiyo kana   kûga 1795
(beauties/harlots blossoms-at/with/by wither/hunted/chided floating[woeful/hip]-world!/'tis)

(merry wives in the bloom-shade)

prostitute beauty withers before the blossoms *ukiyo*, indeed!	the whole world crazy in cherry-time: pity the poor whores

When wives behave licentiously, women who sell their sexual charm are in trouble. The *keisei* (tip-castle) originally meant a concubine that could cost a man his castle, but by mid-Edo era it meant *a good-looking courtesan* or even a beautiful street-walker. *Ukiyo* (floating world) is hell to translate for it evokes both the troubles and the romance of the entertainment classes. *Kararuru* in phonetic syllabary is also hard to pin down: "withering" "hunted," as *gareru*, "chided," etc.. The keisei could even be hunted by the crazed wives, and floating wives (*ukarezuma*) was also argot for *keisei,* so there might be no wives here, period! My first reading is my best guess, but it is a guess!

花見さと下女軽石で手を磨き 川柳 *hanami sa to gejo karuishi de te o migaki* senryû () (bl-vg[+snide] maid pumice-with hands polish)	屋形船花見ぬ女中出にけり 其角 *yakatabune hana minu jochû idenikeri* kikaku (roof-form-boat b-vg maids out[+fin.+emph])
"blossom viewing!" replies the maid, scrubbing her hands with pumice	roofed boats the maids are all out blossom-viewing

Servants generally had to catch the tail-end of the blossom-viewing. The "maid" in the first *ku* (as in most *senryû*) is written "under-woman" 下女 and pronounced *gejo. Haikai* usually use the proper term "woman-among," *jochû* 女中. Compare my translation with a more polite one by Blyth: *"We're going cherry-blossom viewing!" / Replies the servant, / Scrubbing her hands with pumice."* If the *senryû* were not meant to poke fun at the stereotypical maid with her calloused hands presuming to join in a cultured activity, it would be a fine *ku*, less vulgar than many old *haikai*. The second *ku* is what I call a journalistic *ku* (記句). But, what unites *maids* with *boats?* Ueno, with only a small pond was upper-class and real mountains outside of Edo were too far to walk for hard workers on a holiday. Sitting in a boat, doing nothing but enjoying the blossom-viewing at Mukojima must have been heavenly to them. The fact they were affordable speaks well of the economy of what was the world's greatest city! I have come across many maids in boats in *senryû*, but the main interest of those poets (?) was the clay jugs the maids brought for peeing into. Kikaku's *ku* is not poking fun at the maids but smiling at the roofed boat, once used for parties of nobles, now serving maids.

今ぞ上野女中のため息花曇　実定 俳諧坂東太郎
ima zo ueno jochû no tameiki hanagumori　jittei (1677/9)
(now[+emph./exclam. ueno maids' sighs blossom-overcast)

ueno, right now
the rising sigh of maids:
a blossom haze

上野にて・松原や天人のむかし女中の花　調泉子 江戸広小路
ueno nite – matsuhara ya tenjin no mukashi jochû no hana　chôsenshi 1678
(ueno-at /// matsuhara[pine-field:heaven-peoples'past/ancient maids' blossoms)

at ueno

this pine meadow	oh, pine meadow
of angels on old now	once the angels' playground
blooms with maids	the maids' blossoms

Obviously, the maids eventually made it to Ueno. Ueno, literally "high/upper-field," the high ground of Edo, once the wooded haunt of the nobility and samurai alone, heaven forbid, was being polluted by the presence of all those working women!

櫻見て鏡をぬくふ女哉　一笛 小弓
sakura mite kagami o nugû onna kana　itteki 1699
(cherry/ies seeing mirror[+acc] wipe woman/womens!/?/'tis)

after seeing	after she views
cherry blossoms women	the blossoms a woman
wipe their mirrors	cleans her mirror

Could this mean women who see the courtesans (called *sakura* sometimes) that are the paradigms of beauty in the society polish up their mirrors to see how they compare or improve their make-up? A higher reading would take the mirror in a metaphysical Shintô sense. The women encountering totally beautiful and giving cherry trees go home and reflect upon their own purity of mind (not to be confused with *chastity*).

おれハ／＼と斗むこ花の山　柳多留
ore wa ore wa to bakari muko hananoyama　yanagidaru 24-27
(i-as-for, i-as-for [me! me! = hear! hear!] only son-in-law blm-mountain)

ore wa ore wa
that's all of the son-in-law
cherry mountain

There were far more males in Edo than females (60-80%, depending on the source), but the maids enjoy/suffer – the lion's share of the *senryû* and haiku. Partly, it is because lonely men tend to pick on what they cannot get, partly because the weak are easily kidded and partly because the humanity of the maids was the more easily felt. One male group often stereotyped was the *muko*, "groom" in a wedding situation, but in *senryû* always a man married into his wife's family. In this case, he was the social inferior of his wife, for life (See *Topsy-turvy 1585* notes to the chapter II, on Women, for details). The male first-person singular *ore* has a tougher ring than any pronoun a woman might use, but the article[?] "*~wa*" (often translated "as for") following it, repeated to boot, makes it clear that this husband at the beck and call of his wife and her family keeps *trying* to interject his opinion on what *he* would like to do, *but no one pays him heed*. Other men wouldn't need to say "I this or that," they would just *do it* or *command* it done.

一僕とぼく／＼ありく花見かな　季吟
ichi boku to bokuboku ariku hanami kana　kigin 1624-1705
(one-servant-with clip-cloppily[mimesis] walk blossom-viewing!/'tis)

a servant and me
strolling slowly about
blossom-viewing

The *bokuboku* mimesis of the well-known original puns on the *boku, or,* servant, and evokes the leisurely clip-clop of the clogs. An unknown *ku* improves the lot of the servant even more: "The next day / it trickles down to the footmen: / bloomshade *sake*" (翌？も花僕に酒もる木陰哉　一笑　古選 *asu?? mo hana boku ni sake moru kokage kana*　isshô -1688). An even better known *ku* with a servant:

惜花不掃地・我奴落花に朝寝ゆるしけり　其角
waga yakko rakka ni hirune [or, *asane*] *yurushikeri*　kikaku -1707
(my servant falling/fallen blossoms/petals-for/to sleep-in allow/forgive[+emph.])

for blossoms' sake

my servant:							my servant man
while petals fall may				allowed to sleep-in: petals
enjoy a nap							on the ground

my footman
petals litter the ground
i let him sleep

Kikaku's original comes in two versions, one for a "day-sleep" or nap, and one for sleeping-in. My title reflects the five Chinese words prefacing his *ku,* "regret-blossom-not-sweep-ground."

散るときに箒のいらぬ桜哉　桃種 芭蕉庵再興集
chiru toki ni hôki no iranu sakura kana　tôshu (1771) 再現
(falling time-in/when broom need-not cherry[blossom petals]!/'tis)

when they fall
no broom is needed
cherry petals!

Usually, wealthy Japanese kept their grounds – including sand and, well, dirt! – immaculate, but cherry petals were allowed to mess-up that perfection, for a while.

指切や対の禿の初ざくら　りん女
yubikiri ya tsui no kaburo no hatsuzakura　rinjô 1673-1757
(finger-cut[person]!/: partner-baldy's first-cherry[blossoms])

a pinkie-less
with her handmaiden:
first blossoms

a pinkie-less
first blossoms for her
little helper

The "pinkie-less" is a *yûjo*, literally "play-woman" or, as generally translated, *courtesan*. She has, at some time in the past, pledged everlasting love, mourned, or apologized for something serious by cutting off the tip of her pinkie. The *kaburo* is a girl – pre-apprentice – who helps the courtesan with little things (errands, lifting hems, diverting guests, etc.) and generally reminds one of *a doll* (As the gloss shows, *kaburo* is written with the character for "bald." Why? Because it is used for babies, as well) The *first-blossoms* hint she is *coming of age*. The fact this observation was penned by a female poet matters. Why, I do not know. I wonder if the *ku* was well-known enough to explain Koppô's *"In those days, too / people cut their finger tips! / the blossom spirit"* (当代も指切事や花ごころ 兀峰 *tôdai mo yubikirukoto ya hanagokoro* (-1694)). Sacrificed finger-tips and cherry blossoms: a fine match!

もとかしや花にも笠をとらぬ姫　良詮 kyôsui?
modokashi ya hana ni mo kasa o toranu hime　ryôsen (?)
(bashfulness!/: blossoms-for/at even hat[+acc] take-off-not-princess)

so, so bashful
with the blossoms, princess
keeps her hat on

While Japanese women were *less* cloistered than those of much of Europe at this time, the upper class did hide their faces. The *bashfulness* suggests to me a young woman, not a noble but acting like one, because she is very pretty and the commotion her beauty causes makes her reluctant to show her face. While women may be as curious to see each other's faces as men are, the fact most olde *ku* were by men has greatly skewed people-viewing *ku* on the men-view-women side. Of the rare, clearly female perspectives on blossom-viewing, my favorites are Chiyo's *"these footprints / belong to a man:.."* (4-72), and this, very different style of *ku*, by her less well-known, but formidable predecessor, Rinjo:

片言の人にもまれしさくら哉　りん女
katakoto no hito ni momareshi sakura kana　rinjo 1673-1757
(broken-words people-by rubbed cherry[blossoms!/'tis])

mumbling men
always bumping into me
blossom viewing

cherry blossoms!
with blathering people
running into me

jostling with
incoherent people
that's *sakura!*

One might expect the poem to end in *hanazakari*, when the bash reaches its boisterous crescendo, but instead it is a plain "*sakura* 'tis!" From start-to-finish, the blossom-viewing is wild. It may be that the *sake* has reduced the power of speech of the revelers who stay as she tries to make her way through them to return to her inn or home, but I also imagine men making comments like those recorded in the following passage from Issa's journal:

If there are those who silently endure the loneliness of dawn, like the old priest with his dry-plum-lined face, sitting on a *daikon* [huge radish=root, suggestive of something?] killing the coals of his hand-warmer, a woman, apparently no amateur, strains her face as she lights her pipe, grumbling "Yeah, yeah always criticize the cherries [women?] you *wish* you had!"(*atara-zakura-no toga-ni zo*)! She starts off without shaking the petals from her hair, cleaning her teeth with a twig, enameled clogs clattering, zigzagging here and there, looking voluptuous enough to wear out ten husbands. Meanwhile, five or six men down the hill tied night-soil buckets to their carrying poles fore and aft while yapping and squawking as loud as the local crows; and, coming up to the grove, passed nearby the woman, murmuring things like "What's a mountain-god [wind-bag, talkative old married woman, feared by courtesans and husbands alike?] doing up so early? Oh boy, red sky in the morning . . ." which she caught [ref. to on the rag? or just grumpy?] immediately and replied in an unwomanly way, "Look who's talking! You just try insulting me! I'll snap your necks! I'll break your legs!" and all of this foulness blew about as lightly as the snow of blossoms, all was but part of the spring landscape below the cherry trees. (文化 8-1)

I would not bet on my translation being more than, say, 80% right, for I can do no better with old Japanese prose than, say, "our" Chaucer; but, speaking of Chaucer, there is no question that Japan had sassy women, too. Cherry Blossom and *ku*-wise, I am afraid there is a whole body of *ku* I have overlooked which might have reflected this. According to Katô Ikuya (市井風流), a 1734 anthology by Onoe called *sakura-kagami* 桜鏡, or "cherry-mirror," included over 300 *ku* by singing girls (妓 utaime) and courtesans (遊女). Two of the three *ku* he cites (the other is *ku* #36-15 by Onoue 尾上 give what seems to be a woman's view: *"Blossom viewing / who needs a servant / with a long-sword!"* (花見にやいらぬやつこの長刀　似休　*hanami nya iranu yakko no nagagatana* nikyû); *"While viewing i think / samurai just despicable: / cherry blossoms"* 見る中に侍にくき桜かな　不干　*miru uchi ni samurai nikuki sakura kana* fukan). If the servant in the first is her own, rather than a guests, "a bouncer" might be more fun as a translation. With respect to the second *ku*, it also means *"Cherry blossoms: / I can't stand samurai / when they look,"* which suggests she does not like the male gaze directed her way. I repeat: in Japan, it is almost impossible to be sure about what is by women or men writing as women. Lacking documentary evidence, we cannot swear the *ku* were by honest-to-goodness women of the pleasure quarters. Rinjo is another matter:

道草にはてぬ女のはな見かな　りん女
michigusa ni hatenu onna no hanami kana　rinjo 1673-1757
(road-grass-as exhaust-not woman's/women's blossom-viewing?/'tis)

blossom-viewing a woman always finds countless diversion	when we women go blossom-viewing we view everything!

I love the idiom *michigusa*, road/path-grass, meaning to stop and enjoy the things one happens across on the way somewhere. To reverse this *ku*, could we say that men, with their one-track, or jaded (they've been around) minds, just want to hunt blossoms, get to blossoms, sit down and start guzzling *sake*, while women found the trip equally interesting? My interpretation echoes Blyth in *Japanese Life and Character in Senryu*. The off-beat *senryû*: *"If it's cherry-blossoms, / Then cherry-blossoms; if play, / Then play!"* (花なら花さあそひならあそびとさ　柳多留 11－14　*hana nara hana sa asobi nara asobi tosa*　1776) is followed by this: "The man wants each separately, art or sex. A woman wants a little of each, beauty and love; and she wants them mixed." With this, we see Blyth is not so mysogynist as he is sometimes regarded. Who knows if there is anything to this. I suppose we could link this to scientific research findings to the effect that women tend to have thicker *corpus callosum* than men , something suggesting more conversation between the hemispheres . . .

25

House-Sitting in CherryTime
花の留守
hana-no-rusu

猫に逃ヶ猫を追日や花の留守 江斎子 小弓俳諧集
neko ni nige neko o ou hi ya hananorusu esaiko (1699)
(cat-from flee cat [obj] pursue day! blossom's stay/absence)

cherry-house-sitting	***while others view blossoms***
a day to chase	a day to chase
and be chased by the cat:	and be chased by the cat:
hana-no-rusu	house-sitting

"When cherries bloom / in the spring, not a soul / stays home" (櫻咲く春は宿守る人もなし 心敬 *sakura saku haru wa yado moru hito mo nashi*) wrote Shinkei (-1475)); but not everyone gets to attend the blossom-viewing. Some must stay home, and they, too, are part of the larger picture. "Cherry-house-sitting," "home-keep," or whatever we can come up with for *hana-no-rusu,* is awkward to say the least. *Rusu* usually means "being out/away," but also is short for *rusuban,* or "absence-guard," or remaining home when another goes out. English can squeeze by with "house-sitter/ing," or the obsolete term *home-keeper/ing* (guard-dogs once were called this)*;* but, add "blossom" (*hana no*) to signify one who remains home when others go blossom-viewing, and English can only throw up its hands or turn seventeen syllabets into an epic to get it all in, as Blyth demonstrates when translating a *senryû*: *"The better the weather, the angrier he is, / looking after the house / while the others are flower-viewing."* 好い日和ほど腹の立つ花の留守 柳多留 *ii hiyori hodo hara no tatsu hananorusu* yanagidaru (18c? Cannot find it). Here, the standard 7-beats expand over 50% to 11-beats to accommodate two whole lines of explanation. Is it any surprise haiku with *hana-no-rusu* are rarely translated? "The only way not to be miserable is to think of others more unfortunate than ourselves" explains Blyth. Sure, sad songs do more for me than happy ones, but this *senryû* also reflects a sad truth: *the weather clears when one must stay home and beautiful blue-sky mornings always come when you have a bad hang-over.* The charming old *ku* at the head of the chapter must not be well known, for I have yet to see it mentioned alongside of Issa's famous kitten chasing and being chased by leaves. The lengthening spring days make staying home particularly yawn-inspiring, so the poet was lucky to have lively companionship!

花の留守やつぴし雛へ手をのばし 柳多留 12-39
hananorusu yatsupishi hina e te o nobashi senryû yanagidaru 1777
(blossoms-absence/remaining over-and-over doll-to hand[acc] stretches)

cherry-house-sit	cherry keep-home:
she picks up the dolls	how many times she reaches
over and over	for her chickadee

house-sit 321

Blossom-viewing and the Doll Festival (3rd month 3rd day) could coincide. Were this a haiku, we could assume the lonely house-keep is playing with dolls (or, less likely, chicks; both are called *hina*). Because it is a *senryû*, however, we cannot ignore the possibility that *hina* is short for *hinasaki* and means the button I chose to call a *chickadee*, i.e., the house-sitter consoles herself.

うか〴〵と来ては花見の留守居哉　丈草
uka-uka to kite-wa hanami no rusui kana　jôsô (1661-1704)
(absent-mindedly/lackadaisically coming-as-for, blossom-viewing's stay-guard!)

just dropping in
at someone's place, i end up
a cherry house-keep

At a time when all wanted to be out, it must have been hard to conscript house-sitters (thanks, OM).

花の留守聟つゝしんで相つとめ　柳多留 24–15
hananorusu muko tsutsushinde ai-tsutome　yanagidaru senryû 1891
(blossom's-absence groom humbly sequential-duty/working)

cherry-home-keep:
mr married-in humbly
does it again

The *muko,* or "groom" here means a man who marries into a wealthy woman's family, rather than taking an economically equal or inferior wife into his (parent's) family. In this case, the man was, stereotypically at least, pushed around by everyone in the house, including his wife. We can't help wondering whether or not the henpecked man enjoys the opportunity to be lord of the castle, alone.

断酒弁　花あらは花の留守せん下戸一人　也有　鶉衣
hana araba hananorusu sen geko hitori　yayû (1701-83)
(blossom/s are/have-when/if blossoms'-absent-would teetotaler one)

~~when the blossoms are out~~   　had i blossoms   　~~when cherries bloom~~
~~i'll keep the fort alone~~   　i'd gladly guard the house   　~~and someone must stay home~~
~~teetotaler me~~   　sober, alone   　~~dry is best, alone~~

My first translations were titled respectively, "a word for sobriety" and "the teetotaler's defense." I wondered: Has Yayû laid off the *sake*, and wants to stay home to avoid temptation? Or, does he want to avoid the possibility of a home-keep who drinks himself silly out of chagrin for missing the flowers? But, those readings would have belied Yayû's usual good-natured take on life.

世は花見留守居ひとりや酒はつれ　福富
yo wa hanami rusui hitori ya sake wa tsure　fukuhô (?) 雑中
(world-as-for blossom-viewing-stay-guard alone/single:/! *sake*-as-for companion)

the world is out   　　　　　　　　　all view blossoms
viewing blossoms, the wine   　　　house-sitting alone, just me
and i home-keep   　　　　　　　　and brother wine

While drinking is understandable, it defeats the purpose of leaving someone home.

ぬけがらが（の）いくつも（か）出来る花の留守　柳多留 9-11
nukegara-ga[no] ikutsu mo[ka] dekiru hananorusu　yanagidaru ()
(empty shells how many can [make] blossom's-absent[for]/[-guard?])

<blockquote>
several cast-off skins
left behind: ---
out for the cherry-blossoms.

trans. blyth
</blockquote>

The people of the house were in a hurry, and changing into their best clothes, shed their ordinary ones on the floor. The empty rooms are dotted here and there with the cast off skins of human beings, like those of snakes or cicadas. (*Japanese Life and Character in Senryû*)

Since *hana-no-rusu* can refer to absence-during-the-blossoms (i.e. *an empty house*) as well as whoever keeps the place at that time, Blyth's charming reading is *possible*, though I think it equally or more likely an Edo era Japanese reader would read the *senryû* in one of the following two ways:

some houses are cleaned out when men go blossom-viewing	how many men will lose their minds keeping home for *hanami*

Many *senryû* have two readings, the ostensibly right wrong one and clever right one. I have no idea which is which here. *Nukegara*=empty-shell can mean a burgled house or someone out of his mind. The later recalls a popular Kyôgen play where the servant, Tarô (太郎冠者) found drunk by his master, becomes a *nukegara* after seeing his face reflected as a demon in the water (the master stuck a mask on it). The *dekiru* (able to do) in the *senryû*, might then imply, *Who needs playwrights, when we can produce plenty of such Tarôs, naturally, by this cruel practice of making people stay home?* Blyth's reading probably came from his knowing a later *ku* by Seibi about going out for the New Year sunrise with the sloughed off skin of the previous year, his night clothes, left as-is on the *tatami*. (My Japanese friends tend to favor Blyth here, but all my friends are connoisseurs of haiku, not *senryû*.)

死んだとも留守とも知れず庵の花　丈草
shinda to mo rusu to mo shirezu io no hana　jôsô -1704
(dead or absent/out which know-not hut/atelier's blossom)

in absentia	***the poet's hut***
dead, or out? the cherry tree blooms by his shack	cherry blooms not knowing if he's dead or simply out

If the man is home, his friend reasons, he would be sitting under the blossoms. Since he is not, he must either be out viewing other blossoms or dead.

夜櫻よ留守する妻の心もて　蓮之　綾錦
yozakura yo rusu suru tsuma no kokoro mote　renshi 1732
(night-cherry/ies!/: absent[guarding in my absence] wife's heart having)

lo, night cherries my wife is home and i am here with her heart	night-cherry crowd your wives mind the house so mind your manners!

Having her heart would mean keeping her wishes in mind, and not overdrinking or buying whores.

只一人花見の留守の地震かな　子規
tada hitori hanami no rusu no jishin kana   shiki 1896
(just-one[person]-blossom-viewing-keep/guard-earthquake-'tis/!)

all by myself
cherry-home-sitting:
an earthquake!

an earthquake
with me home alone
cherry-sitting!

How I wish I could translate the original's chain of possessives where the earthquake is modified by all that comes before it! *Look at the hyphens in the gloss and reflect on the difference between Japanese and English!* Putting the quake first and adding "with" (or "and," if you prefer) restores the single flow but the punch is gone. When the earth quakes, we always wonder if this will be *it,* the Big One, and, in that instant, reflect upon the metaphysical significance of the place/time that may be our last, or, less nobly think, "Damn! If only this or that, I wouldn't be here, where they will find me!" Poor sick Shiki! How much more fun to be sitting under a cherry tree in full bloom where one could see how many petals were shaken off by the quake! The only better would be a plateau by a grand canyon at night. John Muir has described the magnificent fireworks (noise and light) caused by the earthquake-induced rock-fall.

母ノ花見ニ行き玉ヘルニ・たらちねの花見の留守や時計見る　子規
tarachine no hanami no rusu ya tôkei miru   shiki (明治= Meiji 35 = 1902)
(dangling-breast[mother]'s blossom-viewing absence!/: clock[obj] view)

on the occasion of mom going blossom-viewing

when mother's out
blossom-viewing, i stay
and watch the clock

when mom goes blossom-viewing

the time when mom went to the hanami

while mother is out
viewing blossoms, i keep
watch on the time

mother is out
blossom-viewing: i am
clock-viewing

The "mother" in the original is a respectful ancient – and for hundreds of years obsolete – word, that was usually written with the Chinese characters "droopy-breast-root," but also "many-good-knowledge" and other ways. It is not often encountered in haiku. I have no idea why Shiki uses it other than to easily gain the right number of syllabets or provide a shocking contrast of old and new (the wall-clock).   While I played a bit with the last two readings, the original suffices: a man so weakened by the disease that would soon take his life that *he* stays home and guards the house while his mother goes out. And remember that poets put special stock in blossom-viewing. I dare say no one will find another example of this in all the previous haiku *and* senryû. Illness constricted Shiki's life, but it opened up new possibilities for poetry.

26

Drinking in the Bloomshade
花見酒
hanami-zake

酒の徳何といふても花に在　任口 古選
sake no toku nan to iutte mo hana ni ari ninkô 1605-86
(sake's/wine's virtue whatever say-even, blossom-in/within/by is)

    in the blossoms   wine's good grace   the good of drink
more than anywhere else   i feel it most among   nothing brings it out
     the virtue of drink   the cherry blossoms   like blossoms

Drink has been praised and criticized from ancient times in the East as in the West. Here, the praise comes from an unlikely source: Ninkô, is a monk. Could he mean that with the help of alcohol and the example of the cherry petals, we behave as if we are enlightened, letting go rather than clinging to life and this illusionary world? Or, is it a personal discovery, as per the second reading? Two hundred years later, Eliza Scidmore described the mass blossom-viewing at Mukojima (remember the maids?), on the East bank of the Sumida River in Edo =Tokyo:

> Every reveler has his saké gourd, or tiny tub slung over his shoulder, which he empties and refills, as long as his money and consciousness last. Every man offers friend, neighbor, and stranger a cup of the cheering spirit. (*Jinrikisha Days in Japan:* 1881)

Have you ever read such a favorable review of prodigious drinking in the Occident? And, note that Edoites were famous in Japan for being quick to quarrel! Had Scidmore collected and translated haiku, she might have offered the next three to illustrate her last sentence:

醉て猶眼涼しや桜人　几董 アルス
yotte nao manako suzushi ya sakurabito kitô -1789
(drunken still eyes cool!/?/: cherry[blossom-viewing]people)

         drunken, still
       their eyes are cool
          cherry people

This is my only encounter with "cherry people." Blossom-viewers, obviously. I could not make-out the entire preface, but *beautiful youth* (美少年) and a *blue sky* (青天) are part of it.

drinking

十二三日棒もつかはず花見哉 斗入 アルス８５
ju ni san nichi bô mo tsukawazu hanami kana tônyu ()
(twelve,thirteen-days, staff use-not blossom-viewing!/'tis)

     for a dozen days
   all the billy clubs rest
      blossom-viewing

棒突に盃をさす花見哉　大祇
bôtsuki ni sakazuki o sasu hanami kana taigi -1772
(stick-poke-to *sake*-cup reach-out/offer blossom-viewing!)

     a cherry guard
  is offered a cup of *sake*
    blossom-viewing

The "staff" or "sticks" or "cudgels" refer to what temple or park-guards carry and their nick-name, "pole-pokers." The original of the first *ku* says simply they "are not used." The second, better known *ku,* suggests why. Once a year, Buddhists earned karmic brownie points by setting up booths and giving strangers tea. This was commonly done to teach children the joy of giving. Blossom-viewing, we see this occur *spontaneously*. There is, however, a fine line between giving and *forcing.*

知らぬ人に盃強ひる櫻かな　子規
shiranu hito ni sakazuki shiiru sakura kana   shiki 1896
(know-not people-to sake-cup force cherry[blossom-viewing]'tis)

   cherry blossoms
 forcing cups of sake
    on other men

    pushing sake
 upon utter strangers
    it's *sakura*

In the late-16c, Jesuits recorded how Japanese forced others to drink though they themselves admitted it was a sin. An older *ku* confesses: *"Pushing food / that, too, is part of / the blossom capital!"* (喰物をしいるも花の都哉　李由 *kuimono o shiiru mo hana no miyako kana* riyû (-1705)). The "too" implies pushing *drinks* was taken for granted. The ancient capital was a genteel place, but we can have too much of such kindness. The great playwright Saikaku (1641-93), known to polish off a thousand *ku* in a night, complained in metaphor: *"A flat keg / born without a handle / blossom-viewing* sake" (平樽や手なく生るる花見酒　西鶴 *hiradaru ya te-naku umaruru hanamizake* saikaku). Handles and hands are both *te* in Japanese, so the metaphor is natural, and those who force others to drink were doomed to be reborn limbless. With monks, this punishment was supposed to last for five hundred generations! Clever Saikaku has them reborn as kegs. Others turn them into sea cucumbers! (See *Rise, Ye Sea Slugs!*)

酒買にある日は下る山桜　千条 俳諧天狗問答
sake kau ni aru hi wa oriru yamazakura senjô (1773)
(sake buying-for particular-day-as-for descend mt-ch)

    to buy *sake*
 he descends one day
   mountain cherry

    a certain day
 they come down to buy *sake*
    mountain cherry

In the first reading, I take this for a mountain sage or even an adept because the title of the collection it comes from is "Question and Answer for Tengu," *tengu* being a goblin with a long erect red nose or slang for wizard-like mountain priests (occasionally *monteblanc*). It also makes me recall one of Ôtomo no Tabito's 13 poems 讃レ酒十三首about drink in the *Manyôshû* (#338 ~ #350). Some of them, such as *"Ancient sages / called wine "sage." / What the hell / is the matter, then / with our age!"* (the rhetoric and rhyme is mine) suggest that foreign morals (Confucian) or religion (Buddhism[1]) put heavy drinkers in Japan on the defensive. His basic advice, which might be summed up as *"Don't think / Drink!"* would have gone double for cherry-time. The second reading supposes sharp-eyed townspeople finding the first blossoms by observing mountain dwellers trickling into the *sake* shops.

1. **Buddhist Drinking.** With noteable exceptions, Buddhist monks were expected to drink tea and shun *sake*. Besides the obvious association of tea with attentive meditation and drinking with loose living, *sake* was associated with the native religion, Shintô, and tea with China, where Japanese Buddhism came from. A late 16c farce called "Blossom-breaking" (stealing a branch 出家座頭狂言 花折) plays upon the religious mix. Monks who were not allowed to have a blossom-viewing within their temple grounds, notice people enjoying one just outside their walls. One calls out *"Hey, what are you doing! You may be on the outside just looking in, but the blossoms are ours! If you want to view them that much, you had better make an **omiki*** (offering of "god/s-*sake*," a Shintô practice) *to the cherry tree!"* Before long, the party is allowed in and the now drunken monks even let them break off branches of the tree they were supposed to be guarding, to take home as souvenirs.

~~~~~~

花に酒武蔵野坊は山櫻　春舟 太夫櫻
hana ni sake musashi-no-bô wa yamazakura shunshû 1680
(blossoms-with/and *sake* mushashino-monk/boy-as-for mountain-cherry)

broads and booze　　　bloom and booze　　　bloom and booze
the great warrior benkei　the real monks of musashino?　to fill a musashi monk
a mountain cherry　　mountain cherries　　　mountain cherries

I thought Musashi-bô, the great monk-samurai Benkei (not to be confused with the great lone swordsman Miyamoto Musashi), was known for sober celibacy, but my respondent points out he was also famously drunk and rumored to have a girl. Musashi-No, was a huge field and metaphorically meant something too big to completely take in (most commonly, a sumo-sized cup of sake). My OJD has Musashi-bô and Musashino, but no Musashi<u>no</u>-bô, so it is hard to know what is what. Either way, we have a gargantuan fiction, a rip-roaring mountain-cherry blossom-viewing. The last reading is safest.

濁酒やのまねは其名山櫻　仙舟 太夫桜
doburoku ya nomaneba sono na yamazakura senshû 1680
(cloudy-wine:/! drink-not-if/must-then, that/your name mountain-cherry)

home-made brew!　　　*ah, cloudy sake!*　　　this cloudy *sake*
if you do not drink you are　up here, only the mountain　if you'd drink it you are
a mountain cherry　　cherries are dry　　　a mountain cherry

Is *mountain cherry* here a drinker, non-drinker, yahoo, hillbilly girl, monkey or the trees? Next edition.

山櫻昼から下戸はなかりけり　風睡 小弓
yamazakura hiru kara geko wa nakarikeri fûsui 1699
(mountain-cherry daytime/noon-from teetotaler-as-for not[+emph]))

mountain cherry
after noon, you can't find
one dry soul

予は酒と討死するそ山櫻　自逐力 蘆別船
yo wa sake to uchishi suruzo yamazakura jichikuriki 1694
(i-as-for wine-with fight-die do/will! mountain-cherries)

mountain cherry,　　　　　　　　　　hoh, i'll duel
my death-match will　　　　　　　　to the death with *sake*
be with *sake*　　　　　　　　　　mountain cherry

Or, in looser translation: *"I'm climbing up / mountain cherries, to have it out / with cloudy sake!"* Some did not make it that far:

松原や花迄行（ゆか）で大上戸　青人 野梅集
matsubara ya hana made yuka de ôjôgo seijin 1687
(pine-field!/: blossoms-until go-not-as big drinker)

at matsubara not reaching the blossoms a heavy drinker	out on matsubara before reaching the blossoms drink in full bloom

Matsubara, or pine-meadow, was crossed to get to the cherry mountain. Some who fueled their legs with alcohol never got that far. If an allusion to a line in *The Tale of Genji* where blossoms and red leaves (*hanamomiji*, the latter slang for a red-faced drunk) are said to fall and mix with the green of a pine-meadow was intended, the first reading has it.

盃の逆にも廻れ花筵　沾峨 吐屑庵 *sakazuki no gyaku ni mo maware hanamushiro* senga (*sake* cup's reverse-in too circles blossom-mat-1776)	花に酒や左の御手にて六七杯 幽印 大夫桜 *hana ni sake ya hidari no mite nite rokunanahai* yuin (bloom-with *sake!*/: left hon. hand-with 6, 7 cups - 1680)
the *sake* cup passed in reverse, too the blossom mat	*sake* with blossoms! drinking from the left hand six or seven cups

People in the Sinosphere often take turns drinking, passing one cup (and jug) around a circle. Generally, one waits for the cup or bottle to come full circle, but here . . . Perhaps the next edition can explain more of what is happening with the left-handed *ku* other than the obvious, *glug, glug, glug!*

その花にあるきながらや小盃　其角 *sono hana ni arukinagara ya kosakazuki* kikaku (those-blossoms-in walking-while: small sake-cup)	蛇とならふより蝶となれ花の陰 也有 *hebi to narabu yori chô to nare hana nokage* yayû (snakes-with line-up rather butterfly become bloomshade)
walking among those blossoms carrying a small sake cup	forget the snakes and become a butterfly below the bloom

The snakes in the second *ku* mean heavy-drinkers, who will swallow a lot of *sake* and swollen-up like a full snake, sleep it off. Much more pleasant to imagine a sole poet flitting about like a butterfly with a tiny *sake* cup in order to exchange drinks from more tree parties than might otherwise be possible. Unfortunately (to my, modern mind), there is a preface to Kikaku's *ku* mentioning a *sake*-server (*gi-ko*) walking with him. Kikaku (-1707), not necessarily the best but clearly the most outrageous poet near to Bashô, was often criticized by the others for drinking too much. After his death, the husband of the woman supposed to have composed the famous *ku* about the dangerous well-side cherry (#9-32) warmly quipped: *"We won't mention / his drinking today: / the blossom ghost"* (申すまい酒の異見を 花の霊　寒玉 *môsumai sake no iken o hana no rei* kangyoku). But, who could criticize such wandering, reminiscent of a begging monk, learning to be humble enough to rely on others and trust to luck, which is to say heaven? I can think of no other *ku* so successful in exalting the tiny, tiny, Japanese *sake* cup than Kikaku's masterpiece. Someday I hope to learn for sure what "those" (*sono*) refers to. Now, I can only guess the *ku* was written after Bashô died and Kikaku has chosen a small cup – as opposed to the large one he preferred to use – in honor of his spirit of moderation.

盃を袂に入て櫻哉　空牙 皮こすり
sakazuki o tamoto ni irete sakura kana　kûga 1699
(sake cup[obj] sleeve-into putting, cherry[blossom-viewing]'tis)

a *sake* cup
in my sleeve, i go
to *sakura*

blossoms await
first i drop a *sake* cup
into my sleeve

dropping a *sake* cup
into my sleeve, i'm off
to the cherries!

The dangling sleeve-tip is partially closed and serves as a pocket. Next to Kikaku's, it is my favorite *ku* in this chapter. Note the alliteration between the cup (*sakazuki*) and the *sakura*.

花の酔かくまで涙もろきかな　桂史
hana no yoi kaku made namida moroki kana　keishi
(blossom-drunk such-until tear-maudlin!/?/'tis) 蝸牛社「酔」)

blossom drunk　　　drunk with the blossoms　　　blossom-viewing
why do i become　　to think i am such　　　why does drinking here
so teary eyed　　　a cry-baby　　　make me cry

土産にはならぬ涙や花の酒　淡々
miyage ni wa naranu namida ya hana no sake　tantan
(gift-as-for become-not tears!: blossom *sake*) 1673-1761

all these tears
won't serve for a gift
blossom sake

Mix blossoms and *sake* and you get maudlin. We have read about "cool-eyed" drunks, but I think this is just as common. The usual gift – something the Chinese characters for *miyage* 土産 connect with place (lit. earth-birth/produce) – from a blossom-viewing would be broken branches of blossoms or pieces of paper with poems and pictures. Perhaps these men should bring little bottles for their tears.

酒　其人の癖あらはして花見哉　浙江
sake // sono hito no kuse arawashite hanami kana　setsue ()
(that person's mannerisms/faults/peculiarities come-out: blossom-viewing!/'tis)

en vino veritas

blossom-viewing
when you show yourself
for what you are

The buds expose themselves and so do we who drink. The original *ku* is prefaced by a single word "*sake*," and, thank goodness, we have that fine Latin phrase to translate it with! In a society where people hid their emotions from each other as closely as the Japanese did,[1] this yearly release was probably far more valuable than it would be for a people whose emotions ordinarily fly in your face.

↑ 1. *Japanese Emotions*. See items 14-2, 14-4, 14-35, 14-36 and 14-57 in Topsy-turvy 1585 for the whole picture.

花見酒凡夫の旨い所哉 (也?) 嘯山
hanamizake bonpu no umai tokoro kana (nari?) shôzan 1717-1801
(blossom-viewing-sake common-man's good/lucky/fine place/thing!/'tis)

hanami sake
when the ordinary man
is the lucky one

drinkin' and viewin'
the time when it's good to be
an ordinary guy

The life of the common man in 18c Japan was nothing to be jealous of, but cherry-blossom-viewing on this day, unlike his superiors, he didn't have to wear stiff formal clothing and could pass-out in comfort, not worrying about losing the face he didn't have. The man who wrote *"Not a day / when i can't drink my fill / blossom-viewing sake"* (心行て呑ぬ日ぞなき花み酒 信政 *kokoro yukite nomanu hi zo naki hanamizake* shinzei) was probably not a samurai.

花に世をとりて七日の上戸哉 大江丸 俳懺悔
hana ni yo o torite nanuka no jôgo kana ôemaru 1719-1805
(blossoms-to/at world takes/conquers seven-day-strong-drinker 'tis)

below the bloom
we drinkers rule the world
for seven days

As we have seen, seven days is the standard duration of the bloom when speaking of a single tree. If the poet were to tree-hop, he could rule the world from the bloomshade for a month.

花見迚余所の酒買ふ酒屋哉 露汀
hanami tote yoso no sake kau sakaya kana rotei ()
(blossom-viewing regarding, others' *sake* buys *sake*-shop/dealer 'tis)

that's a *hanami*
the *sake* dealer buys *sake*
from another

Japanese does not differentiate between a producer, retailer or bar, all are *sakaya*. At first I thought the pro chose not want to carry much, but that would not make the behavior *hanami*-like enough for the syntax. The blossom bash is about equal intercourse and that includes topsy-turvy relationships.

猿の寄る酒屋きはめて櫻かな 其角
saru no yoru sakaya kiwamete sakura kana kikaku -1707
(monkey/s[macaque/s] approach bar/*sake*-vendor acmes cherry!/ 'tis)

monkeys come
as the bar scene peaks
a cherry bash

Among Otomo Tabito's 13 poems in praise of drink is one I translate *"Teetotalers / how they arch / their brows / looking smart / as apes."* I title it *"A Red-faced Riposte."* Strictly speaking, Japanese simians are not *apes*, but neither are they *monkeys*. They are red-faced *macaque*. Since almost half of Japanese turn red drinking, the connection is a natural one. But *saru* is a general term, so my translation had to be "monkey" or "ape."

<pre>
            the monkeys come
        when cherries bloom and sake
            sells like bananas!
</pre>

Please excuse my *bananas!* I could not help having fun with Kikaku, who was known to re-preface his own poems to completely change their meaning. I would guess he would laugh and say, *Read it as you like, I am only saying that around four in the afternoon (the hours had animal names and* monkey time *was late afternoon) was when the drinking got heavy*. Sonojo, who was close to Kikaku, and quite the character herself, also gets into monkey business, with her *ku*: *"Though it be / horn-keg monkey brew, give me / cherry spirit!* 角びしの猿の酒でもはなごころ 園女 *tsunopishi no saru no sake de mo hanagokoro*). The keg in question has two long handles for carrying from bamboo-poles. The only monkey-*sake* mentioned in the dictionary, *saruzake*, was a rare gourmet treat found inside some indented or hollow trees or years with abundant fruit (kumquat, persimmon, pear) when the macaque stored what they could not immediately eat. The natural fermentation was said to create a weak wine, so I would guess Sonojo means some fruity tasting home-brew.

樽があるく上野の花の夕哉 曲言 江戸通り町
taru aruku ueno no hana no yûbe kana kyokugen 1678
(barrel walks/ing ueno's blossoms' evening!/'tis)

<pre>
           this evening
        at ueno in cherry-time
           walking kegs
</pre>

Soused men? One of Tabito's thirteen *Manyôshû* (8c) *waka* that I title *"Moderation, you say?"* recalls Fitzgerald's Khayyám: *"Rather than be / a half-hearted lug / let me / soak in wine, / a jug!"*

山や花垣根々々の酒はやし 亀洞 春日	畠縁りに酒を売也花盛 一茶
yama ya hana kakine ne ne no sake hayashi kidô fl 1690~	*hataberi ni sake o urunari hanazakari* issa -1827
(mountain & blossom, hedge/fence-base-base's *sake*-woods)	(plot/field-edge *sake* sell becomes/is blossom-peak)
hill and bloom every fence, wall and hedge a grove of *sake*!	*sake* is sold by fields newly hoed: cherry bash!

Kidô and Issa, note how folk living miles around took advantage of the yearly bashes to make cash selling home-brew. English lacks a word for fields used specifically for agriculture, so I added "newly hoed" – season-wise correct in some districts (in others, hoeing starts right after the blossom-viewing) – to Issa's *ku*..

花ちるや日傘の陰の野酒盛 一茶
hana chiru ya higasa no kage no nozake-sakari issa
(blossoms scatter/fall/ing!/& parasol's shade's field-sake peaks/ruts)

as petals scatter parasols shade the full bloom of the farm *sake*	the petals fall moonshine's in full bloom under parasols

26 28~32

No-zake: field-*sake*. As the increase in heat lags that of sunlight, the pitch of drinking lags the bloom. With the trees bare, is Issa joking about the "*field*-sake"? Or does this mean the stands are literally out in the fields? Regardless, I think we are talking about *moonshine*.

酒なくて何のおのれが桜かな　無名
sake nakute nan no onore ga sakura kana   anon.
(sake without/lacking, what's "*my* cherry!" /'is)

<blockquote>
without <i>sake</i>
who the hell would sing
about cherries!
</blockquote>

<blockquote>
without <i>sake</i>
who would lay claim to
a cherry tree!
</blockquote>

This *ku* pops up a lot. I do not know exactly what "*my* (*onore*) cherry [blossoms]" means. Or, is it Without *sake* / who would fight over / cherry trees?   This later *senryû* is easier to understand:

酒なくて見ればさくらも河童の屁 柳多留 71-14
sake nakute mireba sakura mo kappa no he   yanagidaru late-19c
(sake-without see-if/when, cherry/s, too/even [is/are] kappa's fart)

<blockquote>
without <i>sake</i>
the blossoms aren't worth
a kappa's fart
</blockquote>

A kappa was a legendary semi-human creature who dragged people into the water to either drown them or condemn them to waste away by sucking out the plug to their anus.[1] Fart as metaphor is something worthless.

桜も無雅で散りうせし禁酒寺　柳多留 153
sakura mo muga de chiri-useshi kinshudera   yanagidaru 19-20c?
(cherry-too no-elegance/style-with fall/scatter abstinence-temple)

<blockquote>
even cherry petals
lack class when they fall
at a dry temple
</blockquote>

<blockquote>
at a dry temple
even cherry petals drop
as plain as pie
</blockquote>

Cherry blossoms falling are supposed to be a *haute culture* experience. If, *sake* was as important as poets claimed, petals falling without it, would lack grace. The false anthropomorphism gives the *senryû* the charm of an olde haiku. The *muga* (lacking-elegance) was a common modifier for a plain monk and may evoke its homophone, "lacking-self," a desirable condition in Buddhism.

酒うらぬ山かたふとし花盛　専吟
sake uranu yama ga tôtoshi hanazakari   sengin ()
(sake sell/s-not mountain/s [is/are] valuable blossom-acme/peak/heat)

<blockquote>
the bloompeak
mountains not selling sake
are so precious!
</blockquote>

In the white heat of the blossom bacchanalia, a mountain/park *without sake* would be a cool refuge, valuable not only for allowing *sake* to be sold, but for resembling the bloom, i.e. something sought for its rarity (As the ancients asked, *Who would chase after cherry were it blooming year round!*).

1. The Kappa's Aim If the Japanese thunder-demons went right for the navel – which little children in Japan cover to this day at the first sound of thunder – the kappa apparently attacked the anus, or more precisely something which humans are supposed to have there called a *shirikko-dama,* or butt-gem. Although people engaged in folklore studies have been known to "bet their butt-gems," the OJD has no good explanation or etymology for this riddle of a word. Since the *tama* (gem/bead/ball) is not always round as it is assumed today, but once included macaroni shaped hollow gems or "beads" – if we call all precious things strung "beads" and fetus-shaped "bent-gems" (*mage-tama*) – my guess is that someone discovered *the sphincter muscle* long ago, and then it was lost again. Strangely enough, old prints show people warding off kappa by "shooting" fart-balls (Japanese terms, not mine!) at them, where one might assume their loincloths should be kept tightly closed!

~~~~~~

酒うけてちらば今なり花の下　長虹
sake ukete chiraba ima nari hananoshita chôkô fl late-17c
(sake received, fall-if/would now becomes blossoms' below)

the stage is set

i'm sitting below
sake in cup: if you'd fall,
blossoms, fall now!

below the bloom

my sake's poured
if you'd fall, fall now,
cherry blossoms!

my cup is full
now is when i would fall
below the bloom

Ancient *waka* poets wanted the trees to wait for their friends. With *haikai* poets, *sake* in a thimble-sized cup suffices. I feel, however, that there is more here. Like the painter who grinds up a batch of *sumi,* or the writer who whittles a pencil (I play my computer a quick game of *go* (手談)before starting to write), the blossom-viewer is warming up to the pleasurable business of witnessing the world, holding a cup of *sake,* breathing in its fumes and imagining a petal will soon float in it.

扇にて酒くむかけやちる櫻　はせを
ôgi nite sake kumu kage ya chiru sakura bashô (-1694)
(fan-by *sake* scoop/cup-up/draw shade/reflection! scatter/fall cherry[petals])

using my fan
to scoop up *sake* as
the petals fall

petals are falling
in the bloomshade a fan mimes
a wine scoop

the petals fall
reflected in the *sake*
a fan ladles

I thought of children at a fair trying to scoop up goldfish with tiny fan-shaped paper "nets," but the Japanese annotators say the gesture is borrowed from fan dances in Noraku plays. Celebratory *sake* was ladled from open kegs, so one reading imagines Bashô seeing or imagining a reflection.

瓶に酒さくらの宿と答けり　官橋 花供養
bin ni sake sakura no yado to kotaekeri kankyô 1795
(bottle-in *sake* cherry-lodging [is what] reply[+emph.])

a flask of wine
it's my blossom lodge
was the reply

In other words, drink enough and one can sleep under the cherry tree, oblivious to the world. No one with *sake,* or to use the generic, *wine,* enough to allow them to sleep is homeless.

drinking

蛇出て兵者を撰る花見哉 一茶 寛五
hebi idete tsuwamono o eru hanami kana issa
(snakes come-out warriors[acc] select *hanami*!/'tis)

蛇之介か恨みの鐘や花の暮 常矩 歴代滑稽伝
janosuke ga urami no kane ya hana no kure tsunenori
(snake-guys-the begrudge-bells!/: blossom-dusk)

    the snakes are out
  rounding up their minions
     blossom-viewing

    the bell so hated
  by all the snake guys
     blossom dusk

At first, I thought "snakes" were gamblers (who share their spooky eyes and tended to carry snake-eye parasols (*janome-kasa*), but it is far more likely we are talking about drinkers, often called *hebi-no-suke,* or "snake-guys" rounding up their fellows to engage in *bouts* of heavy drinking. Issa's *ku* has a heart. No one can use the word *tsuwamono* without recalling the warriors lying under the grass in Bashô's famous *ku*. We think of the mortality of the participants in their flower. Note that the relationship of snakes to drinkers is not simply the obvious one I have already explained. Some say it derives from a mythic leviathan, a gigantic serpent named Orochi, who gobbled up maiden tributes, until he was killed by a hero who managed to get him drunk. (See the *ku* "subin ikutsu" in *Rise, Ye Sea Slugs!*) As noted, some cherry mountains, i.e. parks, closed for the night. Here, too, I first thought of gamblers forced to quit rather than going all night as might have been the case elsewhere. Drinkers also hate to stop.

花見酒始はありて終なし 一具 一具庵俳句拾遺
hanamizake hajime wa arite owarinashi ichigu -1853
(blossom-viewing-*sake* beginning-as-for is, end-not)

     hanami wine
  there is a beginning
     but no end

ねごき人たゝきておこす花の枝 貞徳
negoki hito tatakite okosu hana no eda teitoku? 1642
(sleep-heavy person hitting-wake blossom-branch)

寝むしろ桜にさます足のうら 一茶
nemushiro ya sakura ni samasu ashinoura issa
(sleeping-mat: cherry[petals]-by wake foot/leg-back)

   the heavy-sleeper
 beaten until he wakes:
   a blossom bough

   the straw mat
 awakened by petals
   on my soles

Issa's *ku* does not mention drinking, but doesn't it complement the earlier *ku* well? (「新増犬筑波集」)

貴賎くんつころんつ酔や花見酒 一雪
kisen kuntsukurontsu ei ya hanami-zake issetsu -1680
(noble-poor jumbled-together drunk!/: blossom-viewing-*sake*)

   noble and pauper
 all jumbled up drunk
  blossom-viewing wine

Waka and *haikai* are credited with creating equality below the bloom. I would bet that had illiterates written history, poetry would get less credit and *sake* more. Strangely, I found no *ku* about giving the cherry trees a drink unless it is this: *"No wine around? / I guess the cherry blossoms / can drink me!"* (酒遠し花にのまれんさもあらはあれ 重似 雑中 sake tôshi hana ni nomaren sa mo araba are jûji (18c?) – An attempt at idiom-preserving accuracy: *". . . / I guess I'll just be overwhelmed=drunken / by the bloom!"*)

27

the Cherry Bash
人盛り
hito-zakari

気の古い人にな見せそ花の山　左簾 句鑑
ki no furui hito ni na mise so hananoyama saren -1779
(feelings/spirit-old person-to show not blossom-mountain)

don't show it to
old-fashioned people!
cherry-mountain

In the 18c, blossom-viewings at parks planted for that purpose became increasingly like carnivals and horrified conservatives; but let us not imagine a simple slide from genteel to gross. History moves in somersaults.　If you go back yet another generation, Kikaku had the opposite lament:

花は都物くるゝ友はなかりけり　其角 五元
hana wa miyako monokururu tomo wa nakarikeri kikaku -1707
(blossoms-as-for capital, thing-craze[go crazy] friends-not[+emph.])

nobody wants to get high in kyôto

cherry blossoms are
royal, indeed: not one friend
to get down with!

gentle capital
of bloom! where are all
my rowdy friends?

In Book I, we came across the cherry tree in bloom as the capital. Yet "capital" was first and foremost Kyôto, where people were gentle and exercised some self-control even in their celebrations (or did at this time, at any rate). Kikaku combines the idiom and stereotype to lament a lack of rowdy friends to paint the town, or rather, the hills in cherry time there. I think of Hank William jr's *"all of my rowdy friends have settled down . . . nobody wants to get drunk and get loud"* complaint.

はぢかきに行まいかさあ花にさあ　壺中
haji kaki ni ikumaika saa hana ni saa kochû 17c?
(shame-making-to go-shall? yeah, blossoms-to, yeah)

let's go and
do shameful things! let's go
blossom-viewing

to the bloom!
let's go and let's make
fools of ourselves:

I have not dated this yet but would guess it was mid-to-late-17c, a bit after the next one:

the bash

花の下にこぞりて座をや作りひげ 夕翁
hananoshita ni kozorite za o ya tsukurihige   yûô 1651 崑山集
(blossoms' below-at gathering/plotting group!/?/: artificial whiskers)

below the bloom
a whole group boasting
false whiskers

in the bloomshade
painted whiskers
on every cat

In the mid-19c, there was a fairly well-known demi-mask fad. Was it was done already in the 17c?

花咲て阿房仲間のふへにけり 一茶
hana sakite ahô-nakama no fuenikeri   issa 1815
(blossoms blooming, fool-companions' grow[+fin./emph.])

the cherries bloom
my friends in foolishness
multiply like crazy

with the blossoms
my mates in horseplay,
have increased

I love the expression *ahô-nakama* and regret doing no better than "friends in foolishness" and "mates in horseplay." Issa, poet, was a bit crazy all the time, but most people need an excuse to play the fool. I first imagined a big bash, but Issa may just mean that he finds his new wife a fun companion, for his journal records their blossom-viewing in the garden on what we would call April Fool's Day. An earlier *ku* is a bit too didactic for me: *"Where he who / plays the fool is bright: / the bloomshade"* (うつけたる人はかしこし花の陰 羽笠 *utsuketaru hito wa kashikoshi hana no kage* uryû 1642-1726).

御山や人よばるにも花礫 一茶 文政七
onyama ya hito yobaru ni mo hanatsubute   issa 1824
([honorable]-mountain! [other's]people call-for-even, blossom-ball)

honorable mountain:
calling each other's attention
with blossom-balls!

Blossom bash behavior not quite as elegant as Bashô's fan dance: an *ishi-tsubute* is a thrown rock, a *yuki-tsubute* a snow-ball and, by extrapolation, Issa has fashioned a *hana-tsubute* or blossom[petal] ball, perhaps held together by some mud. Issa wrote (and did?) this in his sixties. I have no idea whether it is real or imagined. Another try at translating this odd *ku* of *haute culture*:

sweet mt. cherry!
here, we call each other
with petal-balls

On is an honorific English cannot translate. "Honorable" is a sorry translation. So is "sweet."

花さくや榎にはりし火の用心 一茶
hana saku ya enoki ni harishi hi[no]yôshin   issa 1812
(blossom/cherry blooms! chinese-nettle-tree-on posted fire-caution)

when cherries bloom:
signs posted on the nettle trees:
don't play with fire!

when cherries bloom
signs are fixed to the *enoki*
be careful with fire

336   the bash

The major highways of Japan were planted with Chinese nettle tree (*enoki*) at measured intervals (about a mile) from one end of the country to another. Besides keeping track of the distance, these trees provide a shady rest-stop, a visual homing device in the snow and a bulletin board! When the cherry blossoms drew people to play, the *enoki* had to work. Making fires when under the influence – since *sake* was often heated – was dangerous. Because almost all Japanese houses were made of wood, and many were covered with thatching as well, a license was required to carry fire-making equipment (See 14-1 in *Topsy-turvy 1585* for details!) and there were draconian laws in place throughout the Tokugawa era. Even today, in the dry winter, warnings to be careful of fire (heaters) are blasted by loudspeaker and sound-truck. To my mind, Issa's way of including a working tree, the *enoki*, in cherry-time beats Bashô's oft quoted stalwart, blossom-less oak *ku* hands-down!

あり切の音ぼねを出す野かけ道 柳多留川柳年中行事
arikkiri no otobone o dasu nogakemichi   yanagidaru (6-16: 1771)
(every-bit-of-sound/noise[+acc] make field-through road/trail/path)

<blockquote>
men making
every sound possible
picnic paths
</blockquote>

This *senryû* found in Ono Sawako's book about Edo blossom-viewing does not specify that anyone is headed for the cherries – another picnic is as likely – but it suggests how city folk might behave when they set foot in the country. The original beats my translation hands-down.

娘の火借りて野掛のやかましさ
musume no hi karite nogake no yakamashisa __?__
(girls fire/light borrowing field-path's noisiness)

<blockquote>
borrowing a light
from girls, how noisy
this country road
</blockquote>

真っ黒な煙管を借りる野掛道
makkurona kiseru o kariru nogakemichi __?__
(pitch-black pipe[+acc] borrow field-path)

<blockquote>
getting a light
from pipes black as pitch
the farm path
</blockquote>

すひ付けてけむをいただくのがけ道 柳多留 二
suitsukete kemu o itadaku nogakemichi yanagidaru (1767)
(suck-attaching smoke[+acc] receive [gratefully] field-path)

<blockquote>
sucking up
for a hit of smoke
picnic path
</blockquote>

Though I just mentioned licenses for carrying fire-making devices, that apparently was only true in urban areas, where smoking in the street could get one arrested. With the first *ku*, above, we imagine the request a pretext for flirting, and banter turning into loud kidding back and forth as the parties part. In a city, such an exchange would be rare, for it might be taken for rudeness rather than fun. With the second, we imagine an old farmer with his incredibly sooty pipe, nothing like the shiny ones used in the city. With the last (unlike the other two, I looked it up in the original source and used that transcription, harder to read for having less Chinese characters), the vernacular *kemu* hints at a farmer-urbanite meeting but it is hard to see who is asking whom. The pun falls short, for in Japanese, a pipe or cigarette is "sucked" (as are lips = kissing). As Ono notes, this traveling across fields was not restricted to *hanami*, but the blossoms were the most common excuse to get out and get rowdy, so I, too, include these *ku* that show an area where *senryû* poets clearly observed better than *haikai* poets did.

花のない山へも登る花見かな 汀石 園圃録
hana no nai yama e mo noboru hanami kana   teiseki 1741
(blossoms-without mountain/s-to also climb blossom-viewing'tis)

blossom-viewing
i climb up a mountain
without blossoms

we climb hills
without blossoms, too
blossom-viewing

In some localities more than others, the word *hanami* or "blossom-viewing" was used not only for viewing blossoms other than cherries (such as azalea and wisteria) but for *any* outing. Poets noticed this and played upon it. At the same time, I can't help but wonder whether Teiseki is viewing distant blossoms or blossom-viewing parties.

花盛あちないものはなかりけり 尚白 雑中
hanazakari aji nai mono wa nakarikeri   shôhaku -1722
(blossom-peak/excitement flavor-not thing-as-for not[final])

the bloompeak
there is nothing, nothing
lacking flavor

Read on a low level, this either makes the blossom-high something like a marijuana high when any*thing* tastes equally good or rutting, where any*one* tastes equally good. On a high level, we imagine the crisp blue air, new leaf, bird call . . . all felt with more intensity than usual. One would have to know the poet to guess what lies between the lines.

青くさきたばこ吹かける桜哉 一茶 花見の記
aokusaki tabako fukikakeru sakura kana   issa 1808 文化五
(green/raw-smelling tobacco[smoke] blowing-on cherry/blossoms!/'tis)

me, blowing raw
green tobacco smoke
on the blossoms

さく花にけぶりの嗅いたばこ哉 一茶
saku hana ni keburi no nioi tabako kana   issa 1811
(blooming blossoms-to/with smoke's smell tobacco!/?/'tis)

the smell of smoke
with cherry blossoms
it's tobacco!

oh, tobacco!
the smell of smoke with
cherry blossoms

The second reading reverses the syntax, but if we assume Issa was the smoker, the positive emotion ("oh," as opposed to "it's"). Though *haika* masters, linkverse teachers, or whatever you'd call them, officially made a living by judging linkverse-jams and hosting poetry parties for patrons, like the bonzes whose garb they often borrowed (or shared by temple affiliation), they were also important purveyor of news and, at least in Issa's case, a trafficker in tobacco. But these poems speak of the pure visual, tactile and olfactory pleasure of the mix: delicate pink blossoms and powerful smoky new tobacco,[1] the raw joy of cherry-time. I put this in the "bash" for we put tobacco with alcohol, but Issa is just as likely *alone,* savoring the moment in the way that a wee bit of smoke encourages us to do.

1. The Joy of Tobacco. Good tobacco, like any good smoke is magical, but what passes for tobacco – the cigarettes smoked by most people in the West and in Japan – today stinks of chemicals and has far too little resin to appeal to a person of taste. Do not dare let the smoke of such a cigarettes pollute a blossom-viewing! Because international law is made for the 99% of the people who do not love tobacco (and that includes almost all smokers), I cannot obtain the classic Garam cigarettes (unfiltered resin-rich tobacco in clove flavored paper) I like – I had a pack-a-year habit – for over ten years. Perhaps, I should buy a pipe, for there may yet be good pipe tobacco, but that would be quite an expenditure for blossom-viewing.

わらの火でたばこむまがる花見哉 万平 旅袋
wara no hi de tabako mumagaru hanami kana manpei 1699
(straw-fire-with tobacco enjoying blossom-viewing!/'tis)

burning straw
for a light, good smoke
blossom-viewing

straw for my light
a damn delicious smoke
blossom-viewing

blossom-viewing
a lip-smacking smoke
straw for a light

吹出した雲は花とよ朝たばこ 吾仲
fukidashita kumo wa hana to yo asa-tabako gachû -1733
(puffed-out cloud-as-for blossom as hey! morning-tobacco)

look, blossoms!
puffing out a cloud: my first
smoke of the day

my first smoke
of the day: i make a cloud
call it *blossoms!*

As you can see, Issa wasn't the first *haijin* to appreciate the aromatic leaf. Manpei, in (or before) 1699, notes the type of thing Issa would later: *local detail*. I like to imagine Gachû actually *did* what he says, turned the blossom-as-cloud conceit into an impromptu joke, saying that outloud to his buddies or his family. I removed another *ku* (*Whose hut is it / filling the air with smoke / among blossoms?* 誰が庵そ烟のこもる花の中 箕夫 *tare ga an zo kemuri no komoru hana no naka* kifu (1777)) because I was unsure if the smoke was *that* smoke. Once one starts seeking something – or, at least once *I* start seeking something I find it everywhere, even where it isn't, and tobacco smoke was, after all, ubiquitous in novelty-loving *haikai*.[1] But, back to the cherry bash, described in more detail by Issa than any other poet I know of :

赤髪にきせるをさして花見哉 一茶 文政三
akagami ni kiseru o sashite hanami kana issa 1820
(red-hair-in pipe thrust/stuck-in blossom-viewing!/'tis)

sticking a pipe
into her sun-burnt hair
blossom-viewing

with a *kiseru*
stuck in her red hair
blossom-viewing

Issa himself had solid white hair, shaved too often to hold the long thin pipe called a *kiseru*.[2] Another *ku* that year mentions blossom-viewing friends white of hair and whisker (髪髭も白い仲間や花の蔭 *kami hige mo shiroi nakama ya hananokage*). His wife, Kiku, worked outside enough to have the sun-reddened hair identified with brash women (eg. *kinpira* means blond/redhead & tomboy). Women in Japan did not wear rings, necklaces and ear-rings, but filled their hair with chopstick and pipe-like hair-pins.

1. **Haikai Tobacco** I could write a book on it. Take this 7-7 from the *Enokoshû* (1631-3): *"This smoke in the breast, / it could make you sick //* (a few *ku* back there was mention of sucking eye, nose and mouth, which suggested love-making, but turned into chowder (yes, fish-heads), followed by a 5-7-5 alluding to *lovesickness*, where overheated hearts were known to burn one's clothing unless tears dripped down to put the fire out): ~ *"Don't swallow! / Just puff for pleasure / on that tobacco"* (The smoke turned into tobacco and the danger of tobacco smoke inhalation was, in fact, already part of the Sino-japanese medical literature, and puff = suck).

2. **Japanese *Kiseru* and Pipe** The Japanese *kiseru* has a thimble-sized bowl with a straw-length neck. It is similar to pipes used by Europeans at the time tobacco was introduced into Japan (16c). One can still find them used, but rarely, and as often or not in a very weird way = as a cigarette holder with the cigarette standing on end! (The word is also slang for buying tickets for the start and finish of a long trip (using ones rail-pass) but not the middle. That is because the metal tips were expensive while the long cane in-between could be had for free.) Modern large-bowl, Western-style pipes are called *paipu* (pipes) in Japan. To me, this parallel existence of two names and two different designs is representative of what makes Japanese culture richer than that of the West (or, at least the Usania I know) where the carpet rolls up behind leaving only one new fashion as *the* reality.

~~~~~~

花の中早世わたりの烟かな　多代女
hana no naka haya yowatari no kemuri kana tayojo 1775-1865
(blossoms-among quickly world-crossing [socializing] smoke!/?/'tis)

<table>
<tr><td>

within the bloom
already the blue smoke
of socializing

</td><td>

among blossoms
men already living
off of smoke

</td></tr>
</table>

among the blossoms
smoke says men already
make a living here

At first I was just thinking smoking, for business is done over a smoke, but simplicity votes for food and drink vendors setting up shop, i.e., the third reading.

見つれて (は?) 花見にまかり帽子哉 太祇
mitsurete [wa?]hanami ni makari bôshi kana taigi -1772
(see-accompany-as-for, blossom-viewing-to go[forth] hat/s!)

<table>
<tr><td>

bringing us along
they're off to the *hanami*
the cherry hats

</td><td>

coming together
to view the blossoms
our sombreros!

</td></tr>
</table>

The blossom-viewing hat as actor. This is a charming (not pathetic) fallacy. Think of any outdoor event. Doesn't the head-gear stand-out? Solemn events bring uniform hats or none, but any bash boasts a variety of hats, including the proverbial lampshade. (A late-19c sketch by Edwin Morse shows a Japanese man walking by with the carapace of a large crab for his hat. Morse was impressed because the Japanese tolerated eccentricity that would have given ruffians an excuse to use violence in the USA.) Generally, serious hats were a cross between a frisbee and upside-down salad-serving bowl, but women's blossom-viewing hats in the 16-17c usually boasted witch-like cones in the center.

花の山仏を倒す人も有　一茶
hananoyama hotoke o taosu hito mo ari issa -1827
(blossom-mountain buddha/sculpture[acc] tumble people even are)

on mount cherry
there are even men who
topple buddhas

I imagine drunks rough-housing or standing on statue heads (Buddha statues are usually sitting) to reach a branch to break off or climb into a tree and knocking them over by accident. But, who knows? It may be that some wooden ones were used to fuel fires on a cold night.

閻魔王も目をむき出して桜哉 一茶
enma-ô mo me o mukidashite sakura kana issa 1815
(demon king even eyes[+acc] bare-stick-out-doing cherries!/'tis)

cherry blossoms
the demon king's eyes
also pop-out

Enma, Indo-Europeanized as Yama, is the King of Hades. You may find him on the fake money Chinese burn. People do not worship him, but they do not think badly of him, either. They only want him to facilitate things in the next world. Yama punishes the bad, *but he is not himself bad.* Unlike the sadistic, seductive, power-hungry, clearly evil Christian Devil, he is not engaged in a contest with any God or Gods to gain more souls for his domain and, consequently, has no interest whatsoever in making men bad. If he terrifies, it is only to scare people into *not* being bad. Indeed, one reason his eyes bulge, as they always do, is that even though he torments the bad for the sake of making people good, doing so is still a sin, for which he must atone by swallowing molten iron over and over. At first, I thought Issa meant Enma was upset at the cherry bash, but the "also/too" would be weak (meaning, *like the abbot*), so, chances are, Issa means, "like us, eyes wide with amazement."

酒と名のる鬼も逃たり花の山 有佐 雪月花
sake to nanoru oni mo nigetari hananoyama yûsa 1736
(*sake* [as] name-announce demon/s even flee blossom-mountain)

sake challenges and even demons flee cherry mountain	even the demon who calls himself *sake* flees cherry mountain	cherry mountain even the demons flee when *sake* raises its voice

Grammar favors the middle reading, but it is hard to make sense of it. Does *beauty* cow drink? Or, is this about a bash so dreadful that even the unashamed demon of drink runs away? Or, is it a clever way to complain about running out of *sake?* Warriors challenging others in Japan used to loudly proclaim=name themselves. Unfortunately, "when demon wine drops his gauntlet" would not work.

山ひとつ陰打にしてさくらかな 素丸
yama hitotsu kageuchi ni shite sakura kana sômaru (1712-95)
(mountain one shade-strike/beat[accompaniment]-as doing cherries!)

backing the blossoms

a whole mountain
provides the shade-beat
for the cherries!

Were *kage-uchi* not a *kabuki* term for the practice of beating out accompaniment to the actors' movements from an unseen part of the stage, "shade-beat" would be "shadow-noise" to better match the magic of voices heard in the woods. Another *ku* about the ruckus we make is not quite specific enough for my taste: *"Human voices / can be heard from afar / inside the bloom"* (人声や遠く聞ゆる

花の中　野乙　年尾 hito-goe ya tôku kikoyuru hananonaka   yaotsu (1772-80)). This probably describes a poet in the bloomshade hearing people coming or partying far off, but one might hear the loud voices of revelers in the distance as one approached a grove of bloom on a mountain.

蝉の鳴く木は花よりも静なり 嵐外
semi no naku ki wa hana yori mo shizuka nari rangai -1845
(cicadas' crying tree-as-for blossoms more-than quiet becomes)

a tree-full of
cicada is quieter
than blossoms

A "cicada storm" (*semi-arashi*) can be deafening – almost as bad as a leaf-blower – so this poem is testimony to the enormous noise made by blossom-viewing revelers. It is not heard by those making the noise, so we imagine a sober Rangai on the outside, poking his head into the bloomshade as one might poke one's head into a house-party. The *ku* works best if you have *experienced* a large tree full of cicada. They are so loud you can see the color of the sky change as you approach.

えどを見に上る人哉花の山 一茶
edo o mi ni agaru hito kana hananoyama issa 1823
(edo/corruption[acc.] see-for climb-up people!/: blm-mtn)

men climb up it
to get a view of *edo*
cherry mountain

Edo may be written in two ways. As "inlet-door" 江戸 it is Edo, at that time, the greatest city in the world; but, as "filth-dirt/land" 穢土 it is a Buddhist term for the corrupt world. Issa purposefully confuses things here by writing with the phonetic syllabary えど. On the one hand, the bash may be rowdy and even raunchy, a veritable *edo*. On the other hand, one *could* get a view of the city, Edo. Or, could Issa mean that the blossom mountain is heaven and the city viewed in the distance is hell?

小泥坊花の中から出たりけり 一茶
kodorobô hana no naka kara detarikeri issa 1814
(petty/child-thief/ves blossoms-within-from leave[repeated +emph.])

petty thieves
ducking in and out of
cherry blossoms

今の世や花見がてらの小盗人 一茶
imanoyo ya hanamigatera no konusubito issa 1822
(now's-world! blossom-viewing-on-the-side-petty/small/child-thieves)

what's the world   nowadays, sir,
coming to! petty thieves   some folk blossom-view
blossom-viewing?   *and* pick-pocket

what times these!
children stealing the very
bloom they view

342 the bash

The second *ku*, written but a year before the veritable *edo ku* is one reason the *edo*=fallen-world reading of the *edo ku* could not be overlooked. The fact the world/times is brought into the *ku* tells us that we are probably talking about something more serious than innocent children stealing bloom. If it is children, they are going about breaking off branches here and there for sale, probably doing the work for bosses who could not get away with it. Yet the ~*gatera*, suggesting that the thieves really were blossom-viewing makes it more likely we are talking about other types of theft.

泥坊や花のかげにてふまれたり 其角
dorobô ya hananokage nite fumaretari   kikaku -1707
(thief/thieves!/: blossom-shade-at/in stepped-on, etc.)

thieves
get trampled
in the bloomshade

At first, I thought, hmm, was it *that* crowded in Kikaku's time? Then I came to my senses and realized that, unlike Issa's petty thieves, these would be honest-to-goodness burglars and robbers who worked at night and, therefore slept during the day!

花の陰隙ぬす人ぞたのもしき 一茶
hananokage hima-nusubito zo tanomoshiki   issa 1820
(blossom-shade free-time-thief/thieves[exclam.] reliable/desired)

in the bloomshade   the bloomshade:
you who'd steal my time,   here, the thieves of time
are welcome to it!   rest content

hours for the taking

~~bloomshade:~~   bloomshade:
~~here, stealing time~~   here, stealing time
~~is my pleasure~~   is no sin

sanctu temporalis

in the bloomshade   in the bloomshade
my thieves of time, you   all you thieves of time
are expected   are my guests

I have asked Japanese acquaintances to tell me which translations they feel are closest to the original. As you can see, one was not acceptable. This *ku* might be too quiet (?) for the carnival atmosphere we are discussing. Think of it as quiet at the heart of the storm. Back to the criminal elements:

修羅・穴一のあなかしましや花の陰 一茶
shura // anaichi no anakashimashi ya hananokage   issa 1812
(ashura [scene of carnage and bloodshed] // hole-one's [emph.] noisiness! bloomshade)

ashura

the crap shoot
is as noisy as hell:
bloomshade

27 32~34

The type of gambling mentioned here is literally "hole-one." Participants stand back a yard or so and try to toss coins into a tiny hole. Like pitching pennies, it was a children's game indulged in by adult gamblers. This *ku*, part of a series of six Buddhist cherry-blossom *ku* – the *shura* or scene of carnage is a hellish level of carnation – is but one of many Issa wrote about gambling in the bloomshade, something I find ironic considering the fact that the first large-scale gambling under the bloom probably had to do with *poetry* (as we shall see later). Years later, Issa wrote another *shura,* or *ashura* poem that literal translates "voice-voice-by, blossom's tree-shade's gambling 'tis" is ambiguous. My first reading was: *"You can tell / by the voices which cherries / shade gamblers,"* (声々に花の木陰の ばくち哉 一茶 文政番 *koegoe ni hana no kokage no bakuchi kana*); but Blyth, who translates *ashura* as "Malevolent Nature-Spirits," beat my paraverse with his formally flawed (excessively long!) but semantically brilliant *"Under the shade of the cherry-blossoms, / Voice against voice, / The gamblers."* The *koegoe* or "voices-voices" is the problem. I believe the classic term indicates the various voices of beasts and suggests the *kowagowa,* or the fearsome loud quality of the shouting.

花咲くや桜が下のばくち小屋 一茶 文化五
hana saku ya sakuragashita no bakuchigoya issa
(blossoms bloom: cherries below gambling small-shops)

cherries bloom
and below the trees
gambling sheds!

けふこそは地獄の衆も花見哉 一茶 文化九
kyô koso wa jigokunoshû mo hanami kana issa
(today especially-as-for hell's-crowd also blos.-viewing!)

today of all days
the hell-bound crowd, too
blossom-viewing

傘持はばくち打花の陰 一茶 文政五
kasamochi wa bakuchiuchi nari hananokage issa
(parasol-bringers-as-for gambler is blossom-shade)

the bloom-shade
the ones with umbrellas
are the gamblers

傘で来し人をにらむや花の陰 一茶 文化四
kasa de kishi hito o niramu ya hananokage   issa
(parasol-with came people [+acc] stare: blossom-shade)

glares for men
who come with parasols
the bloomshade

Some gamblers set up instant gambling halls within the blossom-viewing grounds. Are the parasols carried because the gamblers wake up late and travel at mid-day? Or is it gang identification? I recall an old print of *kabuki* actors outfitted as a gang of cool/dashing/debonair high-class robbers (like Chicago gangsters?) called *shirabôshi,* or "white-caps" (such waves mark reefs?), each of which held a large snake-eye parasol (◉ with the middle solid black). These parasols went in and out of fashion for *centuries.* Shiki (-1902): *"Ah, Yoshiwara! / Night cherries in the rain, / snake-eye umbrellas"* 吉原 や雨の夜桜蛇目傘　子規　明治 32 *yoshiwara ya ame no yozakura janomegasa*) and, *"Is spring rain / falling in the backstreets? / Snake-eye umbrellas"* (*uramachi-wa harusame furu ka janomegasa*). But to return to Issa's *ku,* note the *glares?* Issa elsewhere describes farmers lynching gamblers.

散花もつかみ込けりばくち銭 一茶 文化十三
chiru hana mo tsukamikomikeri bakuchi zeni issa
(falling blossoms too grab-put-in[emph] gambling-coins)

falling petals
grabbed up along
with the bets

日本はばくちの銭もさくら哉 一茶 文化十三
nihon wa bakuchi no zeni mo sakura kana issa
(japan[?]-as-for gambling-coin/s too cherry!/'tis)

in our japan
even the bets of gamblers
cherry petals

My "bets" are "gambling-coins." The compound verb won't translate, so "grabbed up" had to do for "grab+put-in," i.e., into a sack. The second *ku* is, I think, a fancy paraverse of the first. I have seen it identified as nationalistic, *a strange boast!* Or, is Issa reminiscing about the Nara area (called Nihon, or Japan), in which case such a reading would be wrong?

さかりにはいやが上野の花櫻　一貞 綾錦
sakari ni wa iya ga ue[-]no no hanazakura　ittei (1732)
(acme-as-for/during, no!-above/despite=ueno's blooming-cherries)

at the bloom-peak
you love ueno's cherries
despite yourself

at bloom-peak
ueno's cherry blossoms
are to die for

Pity your translator! The place name Ueno is punned as *"above/despite"*-the-*iya*. Do you remember the last *Late-Cherry ku* where the repeated *iya,* or "No!" signified applause? Here, I think it means *"despite myself, I/we can't help being smitten by the beauty."* Why the negative rhetoric, the "despite myself?" I think it is because Ueno's bash was as noisy as cats in heat (*koi-zakari*), far from the lyrical ideal. I have seen prints of horses raced around a pond – a regular circular track! – *within the park* while cherries were in bloom – *"Among the blossoms / every damn person heads for / the horse race"* (花の中競馬見に行く人のみぞ　竹の門　新俳句 *hana no naka keiba mi ni yuku hito nomizo* takenomon (19c?)). At the same time, it is generally agreed that Ueno was *not* the most vulgar place for blossom-viewing because many viewers were upper-class and part of the grounds belonged to a temple where drinking and instrumental music were forbidden. Mukôgajima, where the masses swarmed in boats and, within a decade or so, Mount Asuka, to the North of Edo, hosted the real bashes. At the latter, not only were there so called water-tea-shops, with the accompanying prostitution (remember that, in Japanese, *water-trades* = the low life), but archery booths (*agekyûba* 楊弓場), where men were allowed to shoot at the padded butts of the women picking up the blunt arrows they shot at targets for prizes, and unfired-pottery-throws (*kawaragenage* 土器投), where saucers were thrown off mountains to see how they played with the wind.[1] Still, more haiku mention Ueno, for it was to Edo what Mount Yoshino was to the old capital, Kyôto, and this attention continued in modern times, partly because Ueno was reinvigorated by blood (the last uprising against the new Order by loyalists in 1868). [2]

病中寝て聞けば上野は花のさわぎ哉　子規
nete-kikeba ueno wa hana no sawagi kana　shiki 1896
(sleeping/lying hear-if ueno-as-for blossoms uproar!/'tis)

a sick haiku

lying in bed
i hear ueno's blossoms,
their uproar!

Lacking a large enough collection of *ku* by the generation after Issa (mid-19c), I cannot properly haiku the historical peak of the blossom bash. Ono Sawako's *Edo no Hanami* describes a topsy-turvy carnival atmosphere with political satires occasionally getting people arrested and humor gross enough to remind us of television game shows. At the 1840 Mt. Asuka blossom-viewing, for example, a four-person drama troupe at a bloomshade party created an uproar by pretending a woman was about to give birth and calling loudly for a doctor. Sure enough, a doctor came running up. Opening his medicine pack, he pulls out . . . dishes of *sashimi* (raw fish) and other goodies. Then, the woman groans loudly and gives birth. What is it she delivers? A three *shô* (about 2 gallon) barrel of *sake*. At this happy moment, another actor jumps up with a *shamisen* (Japanese banjo) and yet another starts dancing. And, if that is not crazy enough, in 1849, not long after an epidemic of small-pox, a line of children's caskets snaked into the blossom-viewing grounds. What was in them? *Lunch boxes!*

↑ 1. *Flying Saucers in Japan*. Saucers is not quite right because our saucers tend to have broad rims and are made for setting cups on, while the Japanese ones I have seen are more like very shallow soup bowls – and were, when not thrown, used for drinking sake. The description of the saucer-throwing from Asuka (found at a website and in Ono Sawako's book) makes it seem like a precursor to the frisbee, i.e., pure fun, but all the other descriptions of the practice locate it at, or near a mountain temple, which loaded them with supernatural significance. Most commonly, they were thought to rid one of bad luck or help ward off disease and whatnot, for which reason, the characters 厄除 were inscribed on them. Almost as commonly, it was explained that the more beautifully, or the longer they could be thrown the more successful one would be with whatever endeavor one made a wish about. At one temple, the same saucer that warded off bad luck brings good luck if it passes through a hoop dangled from a tree near the cliff. The prices range from tiny unlettered (possibly unfired) saucers at 7 for 100 yen (about a dollar) to larger saucers at 2 for 300 yen. Keigu wrote a *ku* about this: *"Cherries bloom / to clay saucers tossed / by young and old"* (老若の土器投にさくさくら　敬愚 *rônyaku no kawaragenage ni saku sakura*).

2. *Ueno Cherries*. Someone could write a whole book about these cherries. Let me just introduce two of Shiki's *ku*: *"Ueno" // How plaintive / the Tokugawa cherries / still here"* (徳川の桜残りてあわれなり＝再現　明治 34 *tokugawa no sakura nokorite awarenari*) and *"Just Tokugawa / cherry trees, Meiji / cherry trees"* (徳川の桜明治の桜かな　子規　再現　明治 35 *tokugawa no sakura meiji no sakura kana*). These will mean something to all who know Japan's early modern history, nothing to others.

花を見る人の袂に墨つけん　移竹　続明からす
hana o miru hito no tamoto ni sumi tsuken　ichiku 1776
(blossoms[acc.] view/see person/s' sleeve-on ink mark-would/let's)

let's ink-mark their sleeve-tips: all who view blossoms	they would mark the sleeves of all who view blossoms with ink

Would the poet wish for all who have viewed the blossoms that year to be instantly identifiable even in town after descending the mountain or leaving the park? Or would inky sleeve-tips make it look like all engaged in literary endeavors in the bloomshade? My first thought was the second reading, that this was an arrangement to mark people who paid entrance into a "cherry mountain" in an urban area, or an indirect protest against such a practice, started to cope with increasingly large crowds; but I found no information about marking sleeves, and the wishful or even willful ending on the verb favors "let's" over "they would."

やう／\と夜中の櫻静か也　和賎　蘆分船
yôyô to yonaka no sakura shizuka nari　wasen 1694
(finally/by-and-by midnight's cherries quiet become)

at long last midnight and the cherries know silence	and finally the late-night cherries grow silent

花の頃太鼓にしたし時の鐘　松鶯　蘆分船
hana no koro taiko ni shitashi toki no kane　shôo 1694
(blossoms' time drums-as/into make time's[hours] bell)

in cherry time
i'd like to make them drums
the clock bells

28

Cherry Song
桜、桜
sakura, sakura

花の山歌よむ人や踊る人 友尚 類題発句集
hananoyama uta yomu hito ya odoru hito yûshô 1774
(blossom-mountain song read/ing people and dance/ing people)

on mount cherry
there are those who sing
and those who dance

mount cherry: mount cherry:
song-reading people &   some recite poems
dancing people   others dance

While nursery rhymes such as "Mary Has a Little Lamb" and "Three Blind Mice" are *songs* as well as verses, to the English-speaking mind, it sounds odd to "*read* songs" (*uta yomu*). While the Chinese characters for *waka* ("peace=japan+<u>song</u>") include "song," they are *still* said to be "read." More readings are possible, for "read" (*yomu*) in poetic context can also mean *compose* or, even *write*.

目を閉て四方の花見る歌人哉 芳重 古選
me o tojite yomo no hana miru kajin kana hôjû (1763)
(eyes[acc.] shutting four[=all] sides blossoms view song-person!/'tis)

closing their eyes   the *waka* poets
they see blossoms everywhere   eyes closed they view
the waka poets   the world's blossoms

The *haikai* poet is criticizing "song-people," ie. *waka* poets, for ignoring the real world and writing desk-top poems. But the *ku* itself is hardly naïve. It references a proverb: "The songman (*waka* poet), staying home knows famous places" (*kajin wa inagara meishô o shiru*), or "Songman knows the world without going there," (*kajin wa ikazu-shite meishô o shiru.*)

歌の題は詞の花の蕾かな 重方 毛吹草
uta no dai wa kotoba no hana no tsubomi kana shigekata 1645
(songs' theme/s-as-for word-blossoms-bud/s!/?/'tis)

our song theme   song themes
a bud for the blossoming   each a bud for the bloom
of our words!   of our words

"*Song* themes" are subjects for *waka*. The *ku* is a boring for being nothing but metaphor, but after the insulting attitude of the last poet toward *waka*, I thought it would be nice for balance. A *ku* from a slightly later anthology explains where these blossoming trees originated: *"Beautiful Yoshino! / the garden where the tongue / of Yamato blooms"* みよし野や大和詞の花畑　休安　夢見草 *miyoshino ya yamato kotoba no hanabatake* kyûan (1656)). That bloom was *waka*. As will be explained later in the chapter, *waka* was not all closed-eye, indoor blossom-viewing. The type of linked-verse that eventually led to haiku was probably born under the blossoms.

見るよりもまさる言葉の花し哉　貞継　鷹つくば
miru yori mo masaru kotoba no hanashi kana　teikei? (1642)
(see-more-than beat/excell language[word-leaves] talk=blossom, too!)

beating even
what we see, the flower
of our words

beating even
those we view: but hear
words bloom!

The early *haikai* poets were not afraid to own up to enjoying their comradery – *kotoba no hana* = word blossoms – more than the cherry blossoms that provided the excuse to meet. The translation is a total re-creation of unEnglishable puns. Note that the second character of *kotoba* 言葉, or "words/language," is normally written "leaf," 葉, where the "flower"(*hana*) in the *hanashi*, "talk," is not a *bona fide* part of the word, but just two syllabets of homophonic coincidence.

ひらきぬる哥書は詞の花見哉　正良　毛吹草序
hirakinuru kasho wa kotoba no hanami kana　seiryô 1638
(open song-book/s-as-for words' blossom-viewing!/?)

歌塚やたとへは言葉の花の山　近之　洗濯物
utazuka ya tatoeba kotoba no hananoyama　kinshi 1666
(song-mounds metaphored words' blossom-mountain)

open song-books:
is this a blossom-viewing
of the word?

song-mounds:
as simile how about
mt word-bloom?

Other than "song" meaning *waka*, the first *ku* needs no explanation. The second does. During WW II, Japanese stand-up – or, rather, sit-down – comics (*rakugo-ka*) who were ordered not to tell jokes (generally 5-30 minute stories with many sound-effects and a good *punch*-line) about *adultery* and *drunkenness* because it was unfair for the soldiers on the front who would worry about the first and miss the second and otherwise hurt the national spirit. The scripts for the retired jokes were ceremoniously buried at a Buddhist temple and a plaque erected on the mound (No joke: I *saw* one). This *uta-zuka,* or song=*waka*-mound, however, does not appear in my dictionary and no one I asked could guess what the *ku* was about. I would have preferred *"A song mound! / the blossom mountains / of our word,"* or, better yet, to turn the direction of the simile around to make a blossom mountain into a living *stupa* of poetry=song, or to reflect on all the poetic words spoken but not recorded and left buried forever under the petals: *"Old poem mounds / the equivalent of words / left with the blossoms."* But, it was not my poem.

隔るや花に弁慶か筆の海　未学
hedataru ya hana ni benkei ga fude no umi　migaku
(separate[emph] blossoms-at benkei's brush-ocean)

花の木のならふは筆の林哉　義政　新つくは
hananoki no narabu wa fude no hayashi kana　yoshimassa
(blooming-trees line-up-as-for brush-grove!　1643)

keeping my distance
the sea of brushes by the bloom
benkei's armory

flowering trees
that compete abreast?
a grove of brushes

If I read the first *ku* right – a big *if* – the allusion is to the large assortment of weapons that turned the mighty warrior Benkei into a veritable porcupine. There are so many poets out that you had better be careful not to be blinded by the handle of a brush. The second *ku* does not say "compete" outright, but it was implied by line-up, for that was a term used for ponies rode abreast, and the "grove" puns for loud bantering. In all of these *ku*, one feels the literary forest of which poems are the blossom.

文台に扇ひらくや花の下　惟然
fumidai ni ôgi hiraku ya hananoshita   izen (-1711)
(writing-desk-as fan open!/: blossom[ing cherry]-below)

花の陰硯にかはるまる瓦　存疑芭蕉
hananokage suzuri ni kawaru marugawara   ?bashô?
(bloomshade inkstone=well-for change, round[roof]tile)

    opening my fan
  for my writing desk
    below the bloom

    the bloomshade
  a roof tile serves well
    for an inkstone

After half a dozen abstract poems, relief. Writing and roof-tile may have come from China, but the folding fan is one of a few "Japanese" things that truly is a Japanese, not Chinese, invention.

無筆には縄ばりしたるさくら哉　也有
muhitsu ni wa nawabari-shitaru sakura kana   yayû 1701-83
(no-brushes[illiterates]-for cordon-off-want cherry[trees]!/'tis))

    ah, cherry trees
  i'd keep them off-bounds
    for illiterates

    the unlettered
  i'd cordon off from these
    fine cherry trees

Though the rate of literacy was higher in Japan than in the Occident, the gap between literate and illiterate was deeper because it was not merely a matter of skill but of social status and *aesthetic* sense. There were perfectly respectable Englishmen who could not read or write, and our "calligraphy," "beautiful-writing," is child's stuff compared to the Way of Writing (*shodô*). Considering this, the idea that visual bias is peculiarly Occidental is absurd. Yes, there was equality. A songman (*waka* poet) wrote: "the songman, though not noble, rubs shoulders with the highest rank." (*kajin wa tôto karazu-shite kôi ni majiwaru*). Another wrote, "in the practice of *waka*, even the gods deign to permit access." (*waka no michi naraba kami mo yurushi owashimase*" 車屋本謡曲・鸚鵡小町). But, that was equality among the literate. This equality came to be particularly important for *haikai*, for the first poems associated with the link-verse (*renga*) tradition that bore it involved nobles and commoners![1]

Noble-commoner Exchanges. As Hiroaki Sato points out (*One Hundred Frogs:* 1983), the editor of the *Tsukuba-shû* (1356), Nijô Yoshimoto, noted that a 12c scholar opined the origin of *renga* (linked verse) was found in the *Nihon Shoki* (History of Japan: c720), when a torch-bearer answered a question from the Prince about how many nights were slept on a journey they had taken. To me, it is not poetry but poetically expressed prose; but the point is *we already have royalty rewarding the lowly for speaking up with well-chosen words.* In a treatise on *renga* written after the *Tsukuba-shû*, Yoshimoto "pushed the date of the origin further back to the first words exchanged between Izanami and Izanagi, the first male and female deities in Japanese mythology." (Sato: Ibid) If so, I would add, "renga" had a very *haikai* start, for this is where the male deity discovers he has *an extra part* and nowhere to put it, and she discovers she has *a missing part*, or place, that could use a supplement. (It is hilarious to read the Vic-torian era translations of this, but that for another book!) Japan's first poem collection *Manyôshû* (also 8c) also has a close call, with a 5-7-5 by an un-named nun (not neces-sarily a commoner) wondering what to do with a paddy of rice, capped by an 8-7 by a noble poet, who suggests the first crop should be eaten by the planter herself. The first part, by itself, is clearly unfinished, which was why the second poet's help was called for); this is more an example of the type Sato calls a "half-song." A treatise of poetry written in an early 11c book of poetry has a decent 5-7-5 (17 syllabet) start, *"When it snows / Mount Stallion / looks piebald."* (Sato trans., my slashes) Because this is, by itself (barely), a poem, the punning 7-7 cap added by "a lowly samurai" improves it. Another precedent from about pretty much the same time, but only reported 800 years later, by a modern scholar who looked "into renga systematically," has a young man (I'd guess a noble, or of a high-ranking samurai background) noting aloud: *"A chickadee has gone into the travel casket"* (this 6-7-5, in the Japanese original, at least, is a real *ku*), challenging the old pilgrim with said travel casket to cap his verse. The 7-7 reply *"I'd like to know the road to Wakasa"* is *masterful*, because the above-mentioned first part (*shijû-kara wa oi no naka ni zo irinikeri*) sounds like *"From forty (shijû kara)/ you enter old age / by god!* (I add the "by god" because English lacks a grammatical way to be emphatic) and the reply (*wakasa ni kaeru michi ga shiritai*) can be instantly recognized as also meaning *"I'd like to know / the way back to youth."* (The last two punning translations are mine: for some reason Sato, who generally is more thorough than I am, missed it, despite the verb being clearly "return" and not just "go."). The young man clapped his hands in delight – and gave him the directions. I suspect the exchange is apocryphal for the punning is just too damn perfect, but I like it for suggesting that the vaunted equality in the world of ancient Japanese poetry may have been primarily a matter of wit (rather than esoteric talk about the sacred spirit of the Japanese language some harp on). Put this way, this Japanese trait becomes more universal:

Remember how the princess marries the commoner who made her laugh?

~~~~~~

Not all was equal always. There were *two* major types of poetry parties in the centuries before linkverse as we know it today – or, something close -- came into its own. One was indoor (*shitsunai renga*), with only high-ranking aristocrats engaged in very long chains of linkverse (*naga-renga*). It was also called court link-song (*tenjô-renga*). The other was outdoor, derived, at least in part from the ancient folk tradition of "song-walls," or *utagaki*, and other events where young men and women bantered back and forth attracting and repelling one another. This *utagaki* was supposedly egalitarian, though I cannot imagine peasant men trying to win the hearts of noble maidens and suspect the reality was more complex and segregated. The *utagaki* is romantic, so I could hardly not mention it, but I would guess the equality came more from the actual manner in which the outdoor link-verse started, which is said to be that poetry-lovers whose rank was too low to be promoted into the court with its *indoor*-linkverse started holding their own link-verse parties outdoors and the favored spot was under cherries in bloom at major temples in Kyôto, Nara and elsewhere. These outdoor linkverse parties, generally called *hana-no-moto-renga,* or "*renga* under the blossoms" were presided over by *jige-renga-shi* or "underground renga masters" (*underground* because of their low rank and/or because the parties were not held within the exalted court), gained in popularity year to year, decade to decade and century to century, (though, if the truth be told, Japanese did not have centuries). With a promiscuous audience liberated from buildings, these parties turned into occasions for major carousing. Yoshida Kenkô, the noble-turned-priest who invented the canon of the subdued, was horrified of:

> ". . . rustic boors who take all their pleasures grossly, squirming through the crowd to reach the trees, stay and possess them, drinking sake, *doing link-verse* and, as they go, heartlessly breaking off large branches [to take home]. (*Italics, mine*. Some ideas borrowed from Keene's translation: *Essay in Idleness.*)

This was about the period between 1310-30. We only miss *Prizes* (other than broken limbs!) and *gambling*. A famous broadside of 1334 posted at Kyoto's Nijokawahara, put it like this:

> In places as diverse as Kyoto and Kamakura (a religious center close to a martial region, near what came to be Edo), there is an epidemic of un-standardized fake renga (renga not following the rules of the aristocracy?) and local (hick?) *renga*, and everyone pretends to be a judge. (二条河原落書)

I use the word broadside for it is called a *rakugaki,* but I suspect it was a warning posted by the authorities. The "judge" in the original is a *tenja,* literally: "pointster" (the same *ten* = "point" found in Issa's *ku*). The underground renga masters must have been in high demand as good judges, for, to quote Lewis Cook's introduction to the *Tsukubashû* (online at the Virginia Text Initiative), "they were indispensable to competitive renga played by individuals who pooled their money and gambled upon the outcome, to be awarded to the participants who composed the largest number of verses accepted by the judge." In some cases, the winners also won clothing, fans, combs and other goodies. In high tradition poetry, rewards were given to winning poets or teams of poets. If there was some informal wagering at the court, as might be expected at a place where money and clothing was changing hands, there was gambling. Betting on winners spread to bystanders. There were, as might be expected, irregularities – Can you not imagine judges being bought and poets who bet against themselves producing bad poems? -- and two years after the above-noted broadside, the authorities cracked down, and, quoting Cook, again: "the second article of the Kenmu legal code of 1336 called for the suppression of renga parties under a measure to prohibit drinking in crowds and disorderly carousing in public." (I love the expression "group-drinking" = 群飲 = used by the authorities). The crackdown was very thorough, for it even qualified "whether called *tea get-togethers* or *renga parties*."

This did not, however, dampen the spread of *renga* under the blossoms for by this time, the aristocracy was already crashing the blossom bashes – or, that was the real reason *why* there was a crackdown, fear that the upper classes were being corrupted – and in 1366, none other than a Minister of Defense (守護大名), Sasaki Dôyo (道誉), held the cherry bash to beat all, the Ôhara No, or Big Meadow Field Blossom Viewing. It started when rival Minister of Defense (they had two?!) announced a blossom-viewing party at the Shôgun's residence. Dôyo slyly said he would attend and simultaneously prepared his own, "dragging" all the renga masters and dancing girls that could be found in Kyoto out to Big Meadow Field. It is recorded in the War Chronicles called the *Taihei-ki* that participants were throwing the dancing girls *ko-sode*, a type of kimono, and *ôkuchi*, a type of *hakama* trousers. It is not recorded whether these trousers were pulled off on the spot, but neither is the content of the poems . . . (Most of this information came from Shirabata Yôzaburô: *Hanami to Sakura* (Blossom-viewing and Cherry Trees))

Bearing this little history in mind, we must chuckle at the gambling observed by Issa (*ku* # 27- 34~42 in the *Cherry Bash*) It was always there. The only difference is that by the 18 or 19c, it was not all about poetry. The blossom-viewing did not fall into gambling, the gambling at the blossom-viewing fell from elegant *waka* poetry to intelligent board-games to plain ole dice to stones tossed into holes. But, let's return to the poetry that did continue, as expressed both by participants in link-verse meets and poets composing alone.

花にあかぬ嘆やこちのうたぶくろ 芭蕉 如意玉珠
hana ni akanu nageki ya kochi no utabukuro bashô -1694
(blossoms-to open/tire-not troubles/lament!/?/: self/eastwind's song-sack)

blossom problems
indeed! my sack of song
just won't open up

This *ku* by 24 year-old Bashô already bears one mark of greatness: *translation-defeating density*. 1) It is a *meta-ku* confessing his trouble composing a *hokku*, a proper *ku* for starting, or strategic parts of a link-verse. 2) It pokes fun at the romantic fixation of the *waka* poets, of Ise (c 880), anyway, for the first half of the *ku* mimics a line that lamented troubles resulting from his (Ise's) never growing tired of blossoms=women: *Ise, you think you had it hard!* 3) While the lines are phonetically identical, Bashô's *akanu* primarily means "opens 開-not," while Ise's meant "tires 飽-not;" yet, the trace of Ise's idea allows Bashô to indirectly express his love for blossoms, too. 4) *Kochi* is a polite self-reference (this-one) yet also means the East Wind, and that, A), links to the song-sack, for wind deity carried breeze in sacks, and, B), shows he was a participant from the East in the link-verse meet in question.

どこそこや点かけておく花見の日 一茶
dokosoko ya ten kakete-oku hanami no hi issa (1821)
(where-there!/: points placing blossom-viewing day/s))

<table>
<tr><td>

blossom-viewing
today, i'm here and there
giving out points

</td><td>

here and there,
i hand out points
hanami day

</td></tr>
</table>

I first thought Issa, with his experience as a nurseryman – especially raising chrysanthemum which were contest plants – could not help but judge the trees, but the second reading is more likely: *he is judging poetry at linkverse contests.* By this time, Issa was a well-known pro and his services would have been in high demand in the bloomshade. I can imagine the frustration he must have felt with all the high-paying work coming at the same time. It is also a delight to know that the tradition of verse contests in the bloomshade not only survived that long but did so amid raucous festivity of the sort usually not identified with poetry in the West.

短冊も我一ひらや初桜 梅室 (1768-1852)
tanzaku mo ware hitohira ya hatsuzakura baishitsu
(poem-strip-even i/me one-petal: first-cherry)

それ花につらき物にや小短尺 風音 太夫櫻
sore hana ni tsuraki mono nya kotanzaku fûon (1680)
(that blossoms-to painful thing!/? small poem-strip)

<table>
<tr><td>

tanzaku, too
for me, one petal will do
first cherry!

</td><td>

isn't that hard
on the blossom, a little
bitty *tanzaku*?

</td></tr>
</table>

Poems hung from trees were written on *tanzaku*, strips of thick paper that look like the tongue of a wind-chime. Does Baishitsu's wish for a single sheet reflect the delicate nature of first bloom or a preference for single petal cherries? The "A" side of the second *ku* kids that a pretty tree may not feel a *ku* written small sufficient token of the poet's affection, while the "B" side reading (abetted by the character 尺) suggests that said blossom-as-woman may want something more filling.

他の耳を驚かす句も花の音 青流 類柑子
hoka no mimi o odorokasu ku mo hana no oto seiryû 1707
(other ears[+acc] surprise/shock *ku* even blossom's sound)

<table>
<tr><td>

poems that shock
other ears, that, too, is
blossom-viewing

</td><td>

the sound of blossoms
it includes poems to make
your ears start

</td></tr>
</table>

With the blossoms (and *sake* and competition) bringing out the poet, however bad, in every man, the cherry mountains of Japan must have produced tons of atrocious poems per year. The "*other* ears" suggests that the poet is laughing at himself, but it might be that he means all these drunk poets come up with things that shock one another. Note the *ku* uses the word *ku*.

落書の一句拙し山ざくら 一茶 西国紀行
rakugaki no ikku tsutanashi yamazakura issa -1827
(fallen/left-behind writing one-*ku* naïve mountain-cherry)

<table>
<tr><td>

a *ku* left hanging
is delightfully naïve
mountain cherry

</td><td>

a wild cherry
with one messy poem
childish indeed

</td></tr>
</table>

We will explore the mountain, or wild cherry later. The context of Issa's *ku* (野辺を逍遥す。折から住吉の宮に詣て) escapes me, but I love the words *rakugaki,* which means "graffiti" today, and *tsutanashi,* which translates as "naïve" or "childish" in a charming way.

一抱へさくらにたまる反古（故）かな 紫白女
hitokakae sakura ni tamaru hanko kana shihakujo (-1719)
(one-embrace/clutch cherry-by accumulate scrap[paper]!/'tis)

a whole armful
piles up by the cherry tree
my scrap-paper

Because I think *while* I write instead of *before* I write, I, too, wasted paper before the age of computers. Have you seen prints the crumpled up paper on the tatami of a courtesan=*sakura's* room?

なまけるないろはにほへと散桜　一茶
namakeru na iroha[wa]nihohedo [=to] chiru sakura issa 1818
(slack-off-not! beauty-as-for[=colored-leaves] glows but/as falls cherry[blms]))

vida brevis ars largis

don't slack off!   keep studying
i-ro-ha-ni-ho-he-to   **A**ll **B**eauty **C**onceals **D**eath
the petals fall   the petals fall

The middle of Issa's *ku* is pun upon allusion upon coincidence. It is the start of a syllabary song supposedly by the Monk Kukai (also Kobo Daishi), based on a sutra and using each syllabet once that translates "colored leaves are beautiful but . . ." or "beauty glows[has good scent] but" (it puns, too!). As English's *ABC's* are synonymous with reading and writing, so, too, the *i-ro-ha*.

声よくば謡はうものを桜散る 芭蕉
koe yokuba utaô mono o sakura chiru bashô -1694
(voice good-if sing-would thing [+contra. emph.] cherry[petals] fall)

were my voice   i would sing
only good i would sing   now, if i had a voice
the petals fall   the petals blow

This is simple *ku* is one of my favorite by Bashô, for I like haiku about what might or should be. The song he imagines could be anything from a sing-song *waka* to a real folk-song.

櫻々と唄はれし老木哉　一茶
sakura sakura to utawareshi rôki kana issa
("cherry cherry" sung old-tree!/'tis (1819))

sakura sakura
once they sang about
this old tree

Sakura Sakura is the start of the song that today is almost synonymous with Japan. It is majestic, but, like the Japanese national album, tends to drag (the cure is mixing it with flamenco, if you can improvise, try it!) and every time I hear it, I envision a gnarly, very old tree. So, with the help of the slight grammatical fudging only possible for one who is not a native speaker, I first misread Issa's poem as "*Sakura, sakura* / it should be sung to / an old tree!" The only problem is that the song (melody+words) we are familiar with only dates back about a hundred years.

"cherry-flowers, cherry flowers . . ."
it was sung of,
this old tree.

trans. blyth
(my centering)

Blyth notes that the *Sakura, sakura* part of Issa's *ku* comes from a *naga-uta* (lit. long-song) called *Dôjôji* (道成寺, lit. Road-Become-Temple), composed in 1753 (*Haiku* spring). *Issa is imagining that the old cherry was feted with the song when it was a pretty sapling in its first bloom.*

さしあたる古歌も覚えず山櫻　吟江　夢占
sashitaru koka mo oboezu yamazakura   ginkô (1780)
(appropriate old-song even remember-not mountain-cherry/ies)

     i can't recall   mountain cherry
the right old song for it   i can't quite recall that
     a wild cherry   perfect old poem

馬方の桜見かけて唄ひけり　子規
umakata no sakura mikakete utaikeri   shiki (1893)
(horse-boy/groom's [blooming]cherry see-catching sings[emph.])

the horse-boy
seeing cherry blossoms
bursts into song

What I Englished as "horse-boy" is a man who cares for and runs with – usually in front of, to clear a way or hold the bridle! – the horses. This is the type of thing Lowell must have encountered when he wrote about "the chronic state of flower-fever" he found in Japan when Shiki was a boy:

> The intense appreciation shown the subject [plants] is something whose very character seems strange to us, and when we consider that *it permeates the entire people from the commonest coolie to the most aesthetic courtier,* it becomes to our comprehension a state of things a little short of inexplicable. To call it artistic sensibility is to use too limited a term, for it pervades the entire people; rather it is a sixth sense of a natural, because national description; . . . . Their care for tree flowers is not confined to a cultivation, it is a cult." (Lowell: 1888 *italics mine*)

Eliza Scidmore, who, I might point out, wrote more about her "horse-boy" and his beautifully turned legs – until the twentieth century, a man's legs were the pride of a man of parts in the West – than any travel writer before or since, as we have seen, put this same idea more poetically (see ch 8 *"Equality under the Bloomshade"*). The interesting thing about Shiki's *ku* to me is that Japanese themselves seem to have been surprised at the aesthetic sensitivities of their "commonest coolie." Or, at least they were by Shiki's time after encountering Europeans who marveled at it. Or, I have that wrong, and Shiki is only pointing out a fact.

虻も来て何やらうたふ花見哉　杏村 古選
abu mo kite naniyara utau hanami kana　kyôson (1763)
(horse-fly/flies too coming/came somethingorother sing blossom-viewing!/'tis)

blossom-viewing
the horse-flies also come
to sing something

This is not the usual complaint about the vulgarization of blossom-viewing. The colloquial *naniyara* ("something or other" or "whatever" are close but not right) makes this *ku* by a little known poet *perfect!*

鶯や咽鳴やぶる花の中　亀洞
uguisu ya nodo nakiyaburu hana no naka　kidô (c1700)
(warbler/nightingale/s! throat sing-burst blossoms-within)

a bush warbler	the nightingales
in the blossoms singing	are busting their throats
its throat out	in the blossoms

Since the nightingale – "Japanese bush warbler," if you prefer accuracy to convention – is both bird *and* professional singing women, it is hard to tell one from another. Today, *uguisu* is most commonly used with respect to the women riding about town in vans sweetly loudspeakering for politicians.

三味線や借あふ花の幕隣　柳士 古句を観る
shamisen ya kari-au hana no makutonari　ryûshi (c.1700)
(shamisen! borrow-meet[mutually] blossom's curtain-neighbors)

the cherry curtain

one samisen
back and forth from blossom
party to party

The stage is probably one large tree with the ground beneath divided into several parties by curtains hung from the lowest branches. Another translation: *"Blossom-viewing / curtain-neighbors sharing / a shamisen."* The banjo-like instrument could have come with a female performer, but it is more likely it was loose, for many could play it.

花さくや田舎鶯いなか飴　一茶
hana saku ya inaka uguisu inaka ame　issa -1827
([cherry]blossoms bloom!/: country warbler country sweets)

cherries bloom	they're in bloom
country nightingales and	hick nightingales and
country candy	hick lolipops

Issa's country *ku* tend toward self-denigration, contrasting his rural condition and the classy city. Here we also have the cherry as blossom among blossoms *and* what follows, though the "blooming" also suggests a plentiful supply of song and sweets. There were uguisu mimicing devices sold, too; but I feel that the contrasts in the *ku* come alive only if we assume the birds are human singers.

song

三絃で親やしなふや花の陰　一茶
samisen de oya yashinau ya hananokage　issa -1827
(three-string banjo-with parent/s support!/: bloomshade)

<table>
<tr><td>

using a banjo
to support her mother
bloomshade

</td><td>

one shamisen
to support two parents:
the bloom-shade

</td></tr>
</table>

Often, raised and apprenticed to their mothers, more entertainers were female than male. They also turned tricks, called "stumbling." *Senryû* details: *"Revealing just / a bit of (transparent) crepe, she plays / her shamisen"* (*hijirimen sukoshi dashite shami o hiki*); *"Her shamisen / for her pillow she sleeps / embarassed"* (*samisen o makura ni shite wa hazukashi*). This is far from embarrassed in the Spanish sense of the word (*embarasado* means impregnated); quite the contrary, it means she failed to induce a customer to sleep with her. The bloomshade seems to pun as "thanks to the blossoms."

尾部山・三弦の拍子にかゝる櫻哉　園女　玉藻
sangen no hyôshi ni kakaru sakura kana　sonojo (1663-1726)
(three-strings' rhythm-to catch cherry[tree/blossoms]!/'tis))

tail mountain

catching the rhythm
of the three-string fiddles
the cherry petals

The *shamisen* (or *samisen*), a relatively new instrument in Japan – probably influenced by the African trade of the Portuguese as was "our" banjo – was as popular in the Edo era as the guitar is today. It is rarer to find this fiddle, a less raucous and more difficult instrument to play, in haiku, for its star fell quickly in the Edo era. Its musical niche was too close to that of the *shakuhachi* (the large bamboo flute with complex grainy notes) and its virtual extinction demonstrates the law of competitive exclusion applied to culture. The slow undulation of the full bow-stroke with a throbbing vibrato is the perfect accompaniment for petals falling in scarcely discernable waves. This is a much more subtle phenomenon than one where each strum of the shamisen strums knock off petals wholesale.

櫻々帰りは醉ふて白拍子　子規
sakura sakura kaeri wa youte shirabyôshi　shiki (1896)
(cherry cherry return-as-for drunken white-beats[musical harlots])

<table>
<tr><td>

sakura sakura
on the way back, a troupe
of drunken singers

</td><td>

sakura sakura
a troupe of drunk harlots
heads for home

</td></tr>
</table>

The *shirabyôshi*, literally "white-beat(rhythm)-child" were originally *kabuki* actresses whose profession died out by the end of the 16c as males completely took over the theatre (I oversimplify, see more in *Topsy-turvy 1585*). They survived and multiplied as prostitutes who sang and put on skits. My "troupe-harlots" is an ad-hoc translation for these women who have fused the world's first and second oldest professions. My dictionary suggests courtesan or hetaera. But that is neither here nor there.

What a fine way to indirectly record a cherry blossom high! Exhausted from days of playing/working on their feet and off, they walk back home singing *sakura sakura!* I love the above *ku* and find it much better than, say, Buson's *"The white-beats / How hateful they should leave / without dancing! "* (花に舞はで帰るさ憎し白拍子　蕪村 *hana ni mawa de kaerusa nikushi shirabyôshi*　buson (-1783)).

三味ひくや花に埋れて瞽女一人　虚子
shami hiku ya hana ni umorete goze hitori　kyoshi 1902
(shamisen play!/: blossom-by buried *goze* (blind female singer))

a blind singer	she strums on!
buried under petals, plays	buried by the blossoms
her shamisen	a lone blind singer

Strumming on her banjo-like instrument may not make many petals drop, but it *seems* there is a causal relationship. Is it possible that her not knowing the beauty of the blossoms is not as affected by by the falling petals as the poet? Or, to the contrary, does she feel them more because of her hypersensitive touch? Like Shiki's above *ku,* this one by the other father of modern haiku is a helluva image.

花に鳥青葉の笛の音色哉　行次 太夫櫻
hana ni tori aoba no fue no neiro kana　gyôji 1680
(blossom-with birds new/green-leaf's sound-tint!/'tis)

blossoms and birds:	blossoms and birds
the nature of the sound	the sound of new leaves
of a leaf-flute!	played as flutes!

花の形見残す青葉や笛の主　栄行 太夫櫻
hana no katami nokosu aoba ya fue no nushi　eikô (1680)
(blossoms' memento left-over new-leaf/ves!/: flute's master)

this young leaf
a blossom memento
of the flautist

But, I am more delighted with these old *ku* about a fresh, totally untraditional, yet ageless music. Note that both date from Bashô's time. Because these two poets were not disciples of Bashô, their poems remain as neglected and unknown as they are. I am delighted to be able to bring them and others out.

笛の音や惜み帰りや花の友　明網 太夫櫻
fue no ne ya oshimi kaeri ya hana no tomo　meimô 1680
(flute's sound!/& regretful return!/& blossoms' friend/s)

that flute sounds	hear that flute!
like someone who regrets	do we have to go home!
leaving the blossoms	blossom friends

the regretful notes
of a flute going home
a blossom lover

Unlike the last two *ku,* this is probably about a wooden flute, or *shakuhachi*, not a leaf. The last reading ran roughshod over the syntax in an effort to come closer to the heart of the original.

青葉笛・須磨に音を残して散るや兒櫻　蟻道
suma ni oto o nokoshite chiru ya chigozakura   arimichi -1711
(suma-in sound[+acc] leaving fall/scatter!/: boy-cherry)

a young leaf-flute

<table>
<tr><td>

the boy cherry
leaves a ♪ behind and
falls in suma

</td><td>

leaving a ♪
in suma, boy cherry's
petals scatter

</td></tr>
</table>

♪ = *note*. This is about the sixteen-year-old samurai who lost his life in Suma because he would not leave his flute behind (see the *Boy Cherry* chapter).

念仏踊・花さくや三味線にのる御念仏　一茶　文政二
nenbutsu-odori・hana saku ya shamisen-ni noru on-nenbutsu   issa -1827
(devotions-dance // blossoms bloom!/:& three-string-to groove devotions)

devotional dance

<table>
<tr><td>

cherries bloom
and we chant amithaba
to the shamisen!

</td><td>

cherry blooms
and our prayers to buddha
ride the banjo

</td></tr>
</table>

Not all music under the blossoms was secular. Issa, who has more *ku* about Buddhist expression found in, or shared with, nature than any other Japanese poet – his nightingale sutra was old hat, but his mosquito larvae dancing out sutra and flies doing prayer beads were unique – notes what is the equivalent of accompanying church hymns with an electric guitar in some bluesy 20c Usanian churches. Some Buddhist sects in Japan literally danced their devotions, but that was more common centuries earlier.

寺／＼や拍子抜してちる桜　一茶
teradera ya hyôshi nukeshite chiru sakura   issa -1827
(temple temple!/: beat lacking falling/scattering cherry[petals]))

<table>
<tr><td>

temple after temple
the cherry blossom petals
listlessly falling

</td><td>

the beat is gone
at temple after temple
cherry petals fall

</td></tr>
</table>

Why include this *ku* here, with song and poetry? Because the idiom meaning "without-tension" or "listless" is literally "beat-less" and any observation about the absence of music is also one about music: One might think petals falling easily a plus, for, as we shall see in later chapters, Buddhism was all about dying, i.e. *letting go.* Did Issa suddenly realize the aesthetic value of tension? Or, does the end of the bloom mean smaller crowds at the end of the most profitable season for the temples?

<table>
<tr><td>

硯石かはく間もなし花ざかり　立志
suzuriishi kawaku mamonashi hanazakari   ryûshi -1681
(inkstone dry interval-even-not blossom-acme)

the full bloom
inkstones have no time
for drying out

</td><td>

三味太鼓花見の舟の花も見ず　子規
shami taiko hanami no fune no hana mo mizu   shiki 1896
(samisen drums hanami boat's blossoms-even see-not)

shamisen, drums,
a blossom-viewing boat:
blossoms, you say?

</td></tr>
</table>

An inkstone is a slope upon which brushes are wiped to adjust the amount of ink in them and the dry inkstick is rubbed/ground, with a cavity to hold water which becomes ink when said inkstick rubs up and down the slope dipping into the pond each time. Another reading: *"Not a moment / the inkstone well is dry /it's full bloom!"* The *ku* is very *haikai,* for it plays on old *waka* where the tear-soaked sleeves of lovers with no time to dry out is a rock/stone in the ocean. The second *ku* ends in a plain "blossoms-even-see-not" in the original. If I improved Shiki's final line by making it colloquial, it is only right for me to do so for we have lost something else in the Englishing of the *ku.* It has waves (*nami*) and water (*mizu*) hidden in it. Japanese boat-outings were orgies of song, dance and – though there was no room in this *ku* for them – drink and food. To compare these two *ku* is to think about the difference between composing poetry and enjoying popular music at a *hanami.*

葉桜に屁のやうな句がぶら下り 柳多留 32-28
hazakura ni he no yô na ku ga burasagari   yanagidaru 1830's
(leaf-cherry-on fart-like *ku [is/are]*hanging)

a blown cherry
dangling its fart-awful
pieces of doggerel

dangling down
from the leafy cherry
excremental *ku*

The leaf cherry, leafy *sakura* is a tree that has lost many or most of its blossoms and is starting to look green. It is also idiomatic for a woman over-the-hill. One *ku* points out cruelly: *"The leaf-cherry / no one steals from it / no one guards it"* (葉櫻や盗人もなし番もなし 嘯山? 葎亭句集 *hazakura ya nusubito mo nashi ban mo nashi* shôzan? (1717-1801))   I do not know if the *ku* referred to in the *senryû* was thought to remain dangling from the tree for days or weeks, somehow surviving the dew and rain to outlast the blossoms or if someone hung it up for fun.   I have yet to read anything about the percent of poems hung from trees that were left hanging as opposed to those removed and taken home.   It is not the type of thing people calculated and recorded hundreds of years ago.
..

俳諧の口過ぎに〔さく？〕さくらかな 誤一茶？再現
haikai no kuchisugi ni [saku?] sakura kana   allegedly issa
(haikai's living [daily food]-as/for [bloom?] cherry!/?/'tis)

~~cherry trees~~
~~blooming: bread for~~
~~haikai poets~~

Max Bickerton (1932), translated this as "Cherry blossoms made for *haikai* poets to exploit," according to Faubion Bowers (*Haiku An Anthology* Dover:1996), who calls it "a veiled attack on haikai poets who see flowers only as excuses for making pretty poems." Thinking someone lost two syllabets from the mid-7, I added *saku,* or "bloom," guessing that one *saku* was taken for a mistake and dropped by a typesetter. Because Bickerton gave Issa credit for a *ku* poking fun at sea slugs as hardly Japanese by his employer, Chikua (it was mistakenly published as such in Japan), I guessed the above was also by Chikua, until finding the following two *ku* in Issa's Journal: *"A whole county / makes a living off it: / that cherry tree!"* (かいは（わ）いのくちすぎになる桜哉 一茶 文化二<u>kaih(w)ai no kuchisugi ni naru sakura kana</u>). *"A whole county / feeds off of that cherry / now blooming!"* (一里の身すぎの桜咲にけり 同*hitozato no misugi no sakura sakinikeri*).   Unless there was a radically different third version I have not seen, it would seem that Issa's old spelling of *kaiwai* (界隈), a bounded fairly large local area, as *kaihai*, reversed itself as *haikai!* Note: there was indeed a *huge* pendulant cherry tree in Issa's part of Shinano that doubtless gave business to scores of backyard *sake* sellers and inns and restaurants and souvenir venders, etc. The *ku* belongs in the *Vendors* chapter, but I put it *here* to correct that mistake.

itozakura, shidarezakura

Thread Cherry
糸桜・垂桜

まゆひらけ花さく柳さくらかな　宗祇
mayu hirake hana saku yanagi sakura kana sôgi 1420-1502
(eyebrows opening, blossom bloom willow cherry!/'tis)

eyebrows raise
the blooming willow
is a cherry

The thread-cherry, *itozakura*. Its blossoms, close to its willowy branches, seem to be strung up on the threadlike limbs. The tree, or rather trees, for there are weeping versions of many unrelated species of cherry, are also called dangle/hanging/showering cherry (*shidarezakura*) and, more rarely, willow-cherry (*yanagizakura*). While English speakers have every right to call them *weepers* – "the thin branches weep because of their fast growth and supple characteristics, and not because of differences in growth speed between upper and lower sides of a spreading branch" (Kuitert) – we cannot bring "weeping" into the translation of most of the *ku* and be faithful to the metaphorical sense of the original, for, in Japanese, pendulant plants are not said to *weep*. Strangely enough, there is a reverse metaphor, from the plant to person. When men urinate describing large arches, they are said to do it in a willow-style (*yanagidare*). The willow, not cherry, is the archetype for the pendulant limb-form, as demonstrated by countless poems. In the above *ku*, Sôgi combines the classic conceit of eyebrows like willow leaves with blossoms that may be punned as nose (both being *hana*) to get (phonetically only!) *"Split your eyebrows! / blow your nose! the willow / blooms a cherry tree!"* This gets us nowhere in English, as the English idiom (raising one's eyebrows) I used to re-create the *ku* would not translate correctly back into Japanese. But there is more. Sôgi has also created a fresh metaphor with a homophone: *mayu* means "cocoon" as well as "eyebrow/s."

open cocoon!
that willow blooming
is a cherry!

holy cocoon!
is that willow tree now
a blooming cherry?

Turning an eyebrow conceit into a fresh metaphor to conflate trees is the type of antic we associate with the *haikai* poets two hundred years later. I can understand why Sôgi did it. His straight version is boring: *"A thread cherry: / look at it and you see / a blooming willow"* (糸櫻みれは花さく柳哉 宗祇 *itozakura mireba hana saku yanagi kana*). A willow covered with butterflies might have been more original. Later, in the heyday of *haikai,* the thread-cherry as a blossoming willow conceit was turned around to better effect:

花のまたしき頃木陰に立寄て・柳にやさかてまかひの絲櫻　慶友
yanagi niya saka de magai no itozakura keiyû (1633) 犬子
(willow-so-then? bloom-not-from suspect thread-cherry)

– approaching the tree at a time when blossoms were anticipated –

<table>
<tr><td>

are you a willow
no-bloom makes you a fake
thread cherry

</td><td>

willow, bloom not
and i suspect you are not
really a cherry

</td></tr>
</table>

Insults and threats to plants are found around the world. Yet, weren't all mentioned by Frazer (*The Golden Bough*) fruit or nut trees? Here, a non-bearing tree is being shamed into *blossoming*. If you prefer similitude to be handled in a sweeter way: *"Green willow / has a pretty niece / thread cherry,"* or, if you do not mind using a non-Japanese metaphor, "weeping cherry" (青柳はよい姪もてりいと桜　桃先　きれぎれ *aoyagi wa yoi meiko moteri itozakura* tôsen (1701))

羽衣のかかり所や絲ざくら　りん女♀
hagoromo no kakari tokoro ya itozakura rinjo 1673-1757
(feather-robes hang-up place!/?/: thread-cherry/ies)

<table>
<tr><td>

the place where
feather-ropes are hung
a thread cherry

</td><td>

it's where they
hang their feather robes
thread cherries

</td></tr>
</table>

The Japanese had a concept of flying women with downy white wings. They were heavenly, but not angels serving any god that I know of. In fact, I am not sure what, if anything, they were *for*. At this point, all I know is that they *were*. I wish I knew if Rinjo knew Sôgi's eyebrow=cocoon *ku*. With the thread connection, this is a bit cleverer than Issa's angelic night cherries we have already seen.

佐保姫のあやとる庭や糸桜　楓色　(秋田女) 花供養
saobime no aya tori niwa ya itozakura fûshiki ♀ (1795)
(sao/saho princess's cat's-cradling garden?/: thread-cherry)

a garden where
spring plays cat's cradle
the thread cherry

The original personifies Spring as Saho-hime, Princess Sao. Write her in, if you wish.

絲櫻すなはちこれが花の雨　淡々
itozakura sunawachi kore ga hana no ame tantan (1673-1761)
(thread-cherry, viz [videlicet] this is blossom-rain)

<table>
<tr><td>

weeping cherries
this is what i'd call
a blossom rain

</td><td>

prunus pendula
so this is the *it* that rains
cherry blossoms

</td></tr>
</table>

As we saw in chapter 6, *"blossom rain"* was a standard term for rain that fell in cherry time. This poet has noted that strings of bloom, or thin hanging limbs, resemble the streaking lines of falling rain, or the blossoms, raindrops, dripping down a thread. The second reading is for Alan Watts.

絲櫻賛・行きくれて雨もる宿や絲櫻　蕪村
yuki-kurete ame-moru yado ya itozakura buson (-1783)
(going-darkening rain-leak-lodge: thread-cherry)

in praise of thread cherries

<blockquote>
the lodge where
i stop for the night leaks
a thread cherry
</blockquote>

<blockquote>
walking until dark
we find a leaky roof
thread-cherry inn
</blockquote>

<blockquote>
the rain leaks
my last-minute inn's
a weeping cherry
</blockquote>

Buson wrote this for a painting of a thread cherry. It is a take-off on a *waka* found in the *Heike Monogatari* (1219) a war chronicle: "Going 'til dark, we made tree shade our inn and so doing the blossoms become our host for the night." (*yuki-kurete ko-no-shita kage o yado to seba hana ya koyoi no aruji naramashi*).   Buson fused traditional Chinese love for leaking roofs with the thread cherries for reasons obvious with the last *ku,* possibly intended the "thread" to sew up the leaks=holes, and surely plays upon Japanese trope of willow-as-shelter from the sun or rain. This brings us to back to the first linked-verse under the blossoms, *hana-no-moto-no-renga*. Since formal *renga* had been indoors, we may assume that only the *roomiest* trees were able to lure the nobles outside, and no tree in Japan offers a roomier shade than the large pendulant cherry. The fact that 花下 "under the blossoms" was pronounced *hanano<u>moto</u>* rather than *hano<u>shita</u>* suggests a gathering *around* these trees, usually found only at major shrines and temples (I imagine they were liable to be killed by fires elsewhere). The first compilation of *renga*, the *Tsukubashû* (1356) includes this exchange between a big shot (前大納言為世 1250-1338) and an un-named person from among the blossom-viewing crowd (花見る人の中に) :

絲櫻のはなのぬひよりほころびて・霞のころも立ちもはてぬに 筑波集
itozakura no hana no nui yori hokorobite / kasumi no koromo tachi mo hatenu ni

<blockquote>
*the thread cherry
unravels from the stitching
of the blossoms*

*still her robe of mist
shows no loose ends*
</blockquote>

The outsider puts the thread-cherry's unraveling into a broader perspective. With *haikai,* the metaphors of *waka* would multiply like crazy. We have not yet seen the half of them:

道はたはおりてや多き絲櫻 重次 犬子
michibata wa orite ya ôki itozakura chôji (1633)
(road-side=loom-as-for descend=weave: many thread-cherries)

<blockquote>
thread cherries
weaving back and forth:
the hill looms
</blockquote>

<blockquote>
people shuttle
back and forth between
thread cherries
</blockquote>

The original has neither looming hills nor shuttling. It has two puns – *road-side=loom* (*michi-bata=hata*), *dismount/descend=weave* (*orite*))   – I dropped in favor of the puns English provides.

見る人は機へる如し絲櫻 吉政 毛吹草
miru hito wa hata heru gotoshi itozakura kissei 1645
(see/ing people-as-for loom weave like thread-cherry)

blossom viewers
weaving about like shuttles
thread cherries

blossom-viewers
make the woof in the warp
of a thread cherry

My grandmother was a weaver, hence the details in the second reading. In my grandmother's loom, the warp was always thread/yarn/string, but wheat and other folia was sometimes used for the woof.

山遠しあやしや瀧の絲櫻　宗因
yama tôshi ayashi ya taki no itozakura sôin 1604-82
(mountain/s far suspicious! cataract/s of thread-cherry)

distant mountains
dubious waterfalls dubious
thread cherries

so far to go
are those thread cherries
or waterfalls

The second reading takes the mountain for granted. About the resemblance nothing needs to be said. Artists are invited to tie helium-filled salmons to a pendulant cherry (or a weeping willow, for that matter).

透きて見るや花すくふ網の絲櫻 吉隆
sukite-miru ya hana sukuu ami no itozakura yoshitaka ()
(transparent[v.!]-see: blossom scoop-up net-of[a]thread/string-cherry)

looking through
it seems a net for blossoms
the thread cherry

the thread cherry:
it looks like a net for
catching blossoms

If waterfalls are seen from afar, a net may be found up close. The thread-cherry is like a beaded curtain or a screen. Standing under the canopy, close to the edge, you can see out far better than a passerby sees in. I wish English had a good verb for viewing through something, as Japanese does.

山川に人魚つるらん糸さくら 丸尺
yamakawa ni ningyo tsururan itozakura ganshaku ()
(mountain stream/s personfish[mermaid] fish [hypoth.] thread-cherry)

would they fish
for mermaids in alpine streams?
string cherries

string cherry, say
are mermen what you catch
in the mountains?

do they angle
mermen in mountain streams?
string cherries

String is within the scope of "thread" in Japanese. A kite string, for example is called an *ito*. In English, only a tailor or seamstress stranded on an island might fish with *thread*, so translation demanded a "*string*-cherry." Most Japanese today would make the *ningyo* a mermaid, but in pre-modern times, when (?) fish-human artifacts were sold to the gullible (or oddity-loving?) Occidentals throughout South-east Asia, the mer*man* was more common (monkey heads made better *men* than *women*).

風にうこく枝やあやつる絲櫻　徳元 犬子
kaze ni ugoku eda ya ayatsuru itozakura　tokugen　1633
(wind-to/by move branches! handle [as-a-puppet] string-cherry)

branches moving
in the wind: string cherry
puppet-masters

string cherries
dancing to the puppet
master wind

String again; we cannot "pull *threads*." The *ku* makes *some* sense if we think of this puppet-tree as a ghost, octopus, or – *"Wind and petals: / the spidery thread cherry / spins up a storm"* (風に花やちりかい蜘の絲櫻　直行 洗濯物 *kaze ni hana ya chirikaikumo no itozakura* naoyuki (1666)). The spider, by virtue of homophony (like "cloud," it is *kumo*) plays on the traditional conceit of scattering-mixing-clouds 散交曇 (dust and scatter both *chiri*) and alludes to *waka*, such as *Kokinshû* #349 (see ch. 49, *Petal Cataracts*). （方言には「塵飼い蜘蛛」って、いないかな？）. Another plays on the idiom "spider(multi-directional)-hands": *"Blooming eightfold / this is a spider-legged / thread cherry"* (八重に咲く花や蜘手の絲櫻　正平 鷹つくば *yae ni saku hana ya kumode no itozakura*　shôhei (1642)).

一丸にからみて散るな絲櫻　定時 毛吹草
hitomaru ni karamite chiru na itozakura　teiji? (1645)
(one-ball/clump-as gather/tangling fall-not, thread-cherry)

gather in a ball
so as not to fall
yarn cherries

Yarn, for our thread is spooled rather than balled. There are more *ku* in this vein. One I will not even attempt to properly translate puns: *"Viewers come=wrapping-around like crazy=spools: yarn-cherry"* (見る人やわくやうにくる絲櫻　無名 犬子 *miru hito ya waku yô ni kuru itozakura* anon. (1633)).

風袋口ぬひとめよ絲櫻　光貞妻 犬子
kazabukuro kuchi nui-tomeyo itozakura　kôtei's wife 1633
(wind-bag mouth sew-stop[+imperative] thread-cherry)

thread cherry,
sew up the big mouth
of the windbag

sew up the mouth
of the old wind bag
thread cherry!

Wind in Japan was generally thought to reside in caves. The bag may come from China. We will sport with the wind in a later chapter; for now, let us just observe the use to which the threads=whip-like limbs are being put to by the poet's imagination. The *dog cherry* was warned to bite anyone who tried to break his limb. Now, this tree is assumed to defend itself. Threads were also used for snares:

花散す小鳥わなかけよ糸桜　辻猿子 嵐山集
hana chirasu kotori wana kakeyo itozakura tsujienshi (1651)
(blosom/s scatter small-bird trap/snare set [imperative/exclamatory] thread-cherry)

set a trap, a snare
for bloom-scattering birds,
my thread cherry!

夕風やおのが花はく絲櫻　乙由 麦林集
yûkaze ya onoga hana haku itozakura otsuyû (-1739)
(evening-wind: its own blossoms sweep thread-cherry)

an evening breeze
the thread cherry sweeps up
its own blossoms

This is ridiculous enough to be good. It plays on standard willow conceit, which treats the droopy branches as brooms and the corollary thread-cherry-as-rake. Were Japanese *haikai* masters using English, they might have made that *itozakura* into a gallant dressed up to kill the ladies: *My ladies, beware: / that weeping cherry in your hair / is really a rake!*

下臥につかみ分ばや絲櫻　巴風 錦繡段
shimobushi ni tsukami-wakabaya itozakura hafû (1698)
(prostrated-as grabbing-part-would[wish-for] thread-cherry)

~~have a retainer~~	lying flat below	~~i'd have a lackey~~
~~clutch and split them~~	i'd grasp and part her limbs	~~grab hold and part the skirt~~
~~thread cherries~~	the weeping cherry	~~of a thread cherry~~

I first imagined a nobleman poet wouldn't want a wet thread-cherry to dampen his own fine threads; but the pronunciation of the characters 下臥, a low-down retainer, had 3 syllabets which, with the *ni*, added up to 4, one short of the needed 5. Later, I found a 4-syllabet pronunciation meaning *prostrated*.

寝て居ってひっぱりて見ん糸桜　是相 草庵集
nete-itte hipparite-min itozakura shisô (1700)
(sleeping-being pull-try-would thread cherry)

no harm in trying	*(a princess, perhaps)*	*no harm in trying*
i'd sleep there	sweet thread cherry	sleeping below
and try pulling her string:	let's pull on a limb to see	i'd tug her limbs just for fun:
the *ito-zakura*	if she's sleeping	a thread cherry

I like the fantasizing, in this, as in the last *ku*. If the Egyptians slept under the naked sky goddess Nut, well, the Japanese poet can sleep below the lithesome *itozakura*. The grammar of the original does not support the center reading, though, at first, I thought it had to be right because the *ku* is much better that way – and, don't pendulant trees appear to be *sleeping* (rather than *weeping*)?

花見酒や舌ももつれるゝ絲櫻　遊流 洗濯物
hanami-shû ya shita mo motsureruru itozakura yûryû (1666)
(blossom-viewing-wine and tongue even lisp/tangled thread-cherry)

i'm tongue-tied
by blossom-viewing *sake*
& thread cherries

In Japanese, the tongue is "tangled" (*motsure*) when it fails to succeed with a tongue-twister, simply slips up, or stutters, which is not quite the same as tongue-tied, but who could resist it with the thread?

花は根に帰る筋目か絲櫻　定次　毛吹草
hana wa ne ni kaeru sujime ka itozakura teiji? 1645
(blossoms-as-for roots-to return pedigree? thread-cherry)

"Blossoms return to their roots?"
only the thread cherry
is bred for it!

Of course, the others do, too, but only as petals that drop down dead to rest upon their roots.

blossoms
return to their roots
only the thread cherry really does it

Which way do you prefer the *ku*? Shiki reminds us that viewed in slow motion the thread cherry shows us another directional vector altogether:

糸桜下の方から咲きにけり　子規
itozakura shita no hô kara sakinikeri shiki (1893)
(thread-cherry below-direction-from, bloom(emphatic/finality))

discovery:　　　　　　　　　　　　　　　it blossomed
thread cherries　　　　　　　　　　　from the bottom up
bloom from below　　　　　　　　　　a thread cherry

The "discovery" can be dropped if you don't mind a two-line minimal translation. This is that it is not only real but a real good observation. Keigu, plod that he is, would take it one step further:

花と鼻あわせ初花糸桜　敬愚　　　　　　火の子投げながら火縄の糸桜　敬愚
hana to hana awase hatsubana itozakura　　*hinoko nagenagara hinawa no itozakura*

flower and nose　　　　　　　　　　　petals sparking
meet: the weeping cherry's　　　　from the burning fuses:
first blossom!　　　　　　　　　　　　thread cherries

まさをなる空よりしだれざくらかな　風生
masao naru sora yori shidarezakura kana fûsei (1893-1979)
(pure-blue-is-sky-from dangling-cherry[blossoms]!/'tis)

drooping down　　　　　　　　　　　　out of the blue
from the pale blue sky　　　　　　a spray falls on you
cherry blossoms　　　　　　　　　　　weeping cherry

The original turns the first part of the cherry type, *shidare*, into a link-word, which first works as a verb, "dangling," *then* modifies the -cherry that follows. The pendulant bloom can be seen ascending or descending, *as you please*. Because the blossoms on the tip, or lower ends of the hanging branches first open and fall, the bloom may be seen *in time*, as Shiki depicted it, *ascending*. But, viewed in full bloom, before the petals start to blow, the blossoms at the tip will be wider open and whiter than those above, so the instantaneous image will be something dripped from above that broadens *as it descends!*

大象もつなぐけふりや糸ざくら 一茶
ô zô mo tsunagu keburi ya itozakura issa (1822)
(big elephant even tie/fasten manner/bearing: thread-cherry)

you could hitch
a behemoth to a strand
of that *itozakura*

a thread cherry
that could tie up a herd
of elephants

Though the thread cherry can be so huge it seems a sort of World Tree – very different from the dwarf varieties of pendulant cherry common in the Occident – the limbs closest to the viewer are slight. Issa plays with the conceit of a single strand of a beauty's hair being strong enough to hold an elephant. The power of pulchritude is similarly expressed in the Occident (Pope: *And beauty draws us with a single hair.* Howell: *One hair of a woman can draw more than an hundred pair of oxen.*). Issa may also allude toward the direction of the bloom (as mentioned later by Shiki, above), for *keburi,* ostensibly 気振, a general impression of how something looks, has a homophone, *smoke,* which in the classic poetry suggested ruddy-leafed grasses and shrubs *burning from below* (下燃), hence, a strong longing in one's breast. He may also have been aware of a third homophone, a *keburi* neither appearance nor smoke: 毛振り or, "hair-form." The word does not exist, but can be imagined from *edaburi,* or "limb-form," a *bona fide* word we encounter elsewhere in this book, and would enhance the conceit. This *ku* is probably a paean to a beautiful and famously large thread-cherry in Shinano, Issa's province.

折枝を引や小弓の絲櫻 次广都 洗濯物
ori-eda o hiku ya koyumi no itozakura jigento 1666
(broken branch[acc.] pull: small-bow of/as thread-cherry)

you can draw
a stolen limb like a bow
string cherry

a broken branch
that draws like a bow
string cherry

To be strung, the thread had to be *string* here! It seems the flexible limb serves for both bow and string. We will have a whole chapter on the practice of breaking off blossoming boughs, later.

☆

けいせいは骨であゆむよ糸ざくら 素檗   有難や同生はちす絲櫻 正冬 太夫櫻
keisei wa hone de ayumu yo itozakura sobaku -1821   *arigataiya dôsei hachisu itozakura* shôtô 1680
(harlot/beauty-as-for bones-with walk! thread-cherry) (grateful-thing! same-birth lotus thread-cherry)

sexy beauty
walks from the hipbone
itozakura

let us rejoice,
the lotus is not alone!
a thread cherry

Two fancy metaphors. The first, depending upon your frame of mind, is beautiful or crass. A sexy woman does not use leg muscles for her hips are flexible. The round top of the pendulant cherry is the "hip." It would meet more wind than the lower branches, so limbs would *swing* rather than bend. Or, at least, that is *my* reading. My respondents will not even guess! The second references the circular bloom-shade, with its all-in-it-together atmosphere suggesting common birth in Paradise. If the blessed sat on lotuses, the otherworldly upside-down bloom puts the viewers on top of the cherry blossoms, while the floating plant was called "lotus lodge" (蓮の宿), and something called the lotus-*thread* (*hachisu-no-ito*), found within its root, was thought to bind us to the other world. **Warning to thread cherry owners:** According to testimony on the net, a gardener pruned one and the result was the top grew straight up (no weeping and no bloom!) creating what might be called *a mullet haircut!*

30

Life-Laundry or, Cherry Catharsis
命の洗濯
inochi-no-sentaku

けふ（これ）までの日はけふ捨（終へ）てはつ桜 千代
kyô(kore) made no hi wa kyô sutte [oete] hatsuzakura chiyo -1775
(today[this]-until's day-as-for, today abandoning, first-cherry/blossom)

first blossom:
the days up to now
thrown away!

Here, Chiyo the nun would seem to jump the gun. The New Year, proceeded by a Year-Forget Party, *starts* as a blank, an empty mind, but blossom-viewing is supposed to *end up* blank *after the catharsis* of the cherry bash. For that reason, this *ku* might best be read as the dramatic "first-bloom" *ku* of the allegorical "blossom-as-woman" we will see in *Book III*. However, we can also read it as her treating the first blossom of the cherry as *a sign of the start of the earthly Spring New Year*, a terrestrial, biological equivalent to the rising of that First Sun.

何もかも今日は忘れて花見哉 東鴬坊 恒誠
nanimokamo kyo wa wasurete hanami kana tôyôbô ()
(everything, today, forgetting blossom-viewing'tis)

| today is when
we forget everything:
blossom-viewing! | | today, let us
all forget everything!
blossom-viewing |

yes, let's forget
everything today and go
blossom-viewing!

The original is unclear as to whether a blossom-viewing is in progress or the poet is on the point of departing for one. I think it is probably the latter because of my childhood. When there was preternaturally beautiful weather, my mother would sometimes call a stop-day and head for the beach with us kids (three), dalmation and raccoon in tow. On those days, we skipped school to play with the sea horses, or bear witness to nature (though we did not think of it like that). So I see the poet "forgetting" all of his duties to answer to a higher one: *blossom-viewing*. Again, catharsis jumps the gun. It is like cleaning off *before* stepping into a sacred stream for the deeper cleaning.

30 1~2

耳よりも心の垢や花の瀧　雲巾 三千花
mimi yori mo kokoro no aka ya hana no taki unkin 1725
(ear rather-than heart/mind's crud!/: blossom-waterfall)

pink ablution

cleaning crud
from the heart, not ears:
petal cataract

Ear crud (wax) is nothing to us, but in Japan where mothers and wives use tiny wooden spoons to clean the ears of their families, it is a bi-product of social grooming. The cleansing of the soul was always central to Shintô and ablution was also given Buddhist meaning. Unlike the case with cherry petals, it could be painful. The more suffering endured, the more help for the party one prayed for, who, was generally not oneself (as was the case with bloody Christian self-flagellators). The colder the water the better, ideally splashed hard from a bucket drawn from a deep well or falling from a waterfall directly down upon one's bare head (my impression from television, anyway).

花（の）山命のせんたく所哉　一茶
hananoyama inochi no sentakudokoro kana issa -1827
(blossom-mountain, life's laundry place!/?/'tis)

mount cherry: the place where i go to wash my life		cherry mountain: this is where our lives get laundered!
	mount cherry here is where we sow our wild oats	

In this context, "life/lives" is more or less synonymous with the far more common *kokoro,* or "heart/mind/soul." I love the phrase "life's laundry," meaning simply "to refresh one's life" or "recreate oneself" by letting everything – one's "bad blood" or "vexations," to use dictionary words – come out. It is what Japanese mice would do when the cat is out. The *laundry* metaphor seems odd even to Japanese. As one book of drollery (*kokkei-bon: ukiyo-toko:* 18c?) put it: *"Before laundering your life, how about washing that loin-cloth!"* (*inochi-no sentaku yori wa fundoshi-no sentaku demo shiro*). The idiom is not new to *haikai.* The *ku* *"Even lives / may be laundered / year-forget[party]!* (命さへ洗濯すなり年忘　野坂 *inochi sae sentaku sunari toshiwasure* yaba (1663-1740) predates Issa's and I would bet there are more; but combined with the petal-bathing atmosphere, the literal washing aspect of the idiom *itself* is revitalized. Here are three paraverses for Jeremy Riftkin:

mount cherry where life pukes up its entropy	mount cherry because life needs a place to lose entropy	mount cherry we climb up to leave entropy behind

What delighted me about the Japanese idiom was that not the heart/mind but "life" is washed. I am reminded of the anti-entropic magic of living and of the mess that life makes in order to keep clean, i.e., healthy inside. This catharsis should not be conflated with the ablution and purification we have seen, but it may be compared, for the results are similar. Issa's teacher, Somaru (1712-95), had a non-cherry *ku* about the benefits of getting out: *"What long days! / The mountains and the sea / wash our lives"* 永き日や命を洗ふ海と山 素丸*nagaki hi ya inochi o arau umi to yama*). It doesn't work in English, does it? Would the following be better? *Summertime: / the forest and the sea / keep me sane!*

咲ぬ間や長屋で暮す江戸桜　之方 俳諧当世男
sakanu ma ya nagaya de kurasu edozakura   shihô (1676)
(bloom-not period! long-house [worker's flats] -in live edo-cherry)

<blockquote>
between blooms
living in our long flats
edoite <i>sakura</i>
</blockquote>

150 years after this *ku*, Issa experienced the low life in Edo and became conscious of the blossom-viewings as a place to let out his "heart's demons" (we'll see the *ku* below). Old Issa decided to drop the demons for the life-wash idiom he may have avoided as a young poet for fear of sounding corny.

数々に忘れて行もさくらかな　素檗
kazukazu ni wasureteyuku mo sakura kana   sobaku -1821
(number-number-by forgetting-go even cherry!/'tis)

this, too

cherry blossoms mean getting lost among the multitudes	losing oneself in the crowd is part of blossom-viewing

Cherry blossoms bloom in masses and people come to see them, likewise in masses. This *ku* offers a unique explanation for the forget-it-all, wash-the-soul phenomenon: *numbers*. Blossom-viewing as a tumble in the multitudes. I had no room to fit the "too/also" into the translation so I titled it, instead.

独り行て物忘れせん花のもと　蕉國 花桜帖
hitori yukite monowasure sen hana no moto   shôkoku ()
(alone going thing-forgetting-do-would blossoms-around/below)

and i'd go alone the better to lose myself below the bloom	i'll go alone there are things i'd forget below the bloom

The second reading is correct. The first just popped out of my head. "**X**" it out if you wish.

花にきてうつくしくなる心哉　たつ あらの
hana ni kite utsukushiku naru kokoro kana   tatsu 1689
(blossom-to come beautiful become heart/mind!/'tis)

blossom-viewing how beautiful it becomes: my own heart!	with blossoms my very soul becomes more beautiful

An older *ku* laughs about "fixing," i.e., *softening*, a (ferocious) Enma (Hell's judge) face by showing him a thousand blossoming trees (a reference to the thousand-armed, sweet-faced Goddess of Mercy). It does not translate (千本の花見せ直て閻魔顔　重供 毛吹草 *senpon no hana mise naote enma-gao* shigetomo 1645). As noted, Enma's expression was not just stern but excruciating, for the punisher was himself punished. It is a commonplace that beauty can soften anger, but pain? Be that as it may, an Enma face *idiomatically* meant someone who had a stern if not downright terrifying face. While two deity are referred to in the *ku*, the blossoms are affecting a human and not a statue.

花はさかせ心気はちらせ春の風　一井　嵐山集
hana wa sakase shinki wa chirase haru no kaze　issei (1651)
(blossoms-as-for [make]bloom! [heavy]heart scatter! spring wind)

spring wind!
make buds bloom and blow
away my blues

oh, spring wind
open the blossoms and
free our spirits

make them bloom
and lighten my heavy heart!
oh, spring wind!

winds of springs
pry the buds open and
blow my mind

散る桜心の鬼も出てあそべ　一茶
chiru sakura kokoro no oni mo dete-asobe　issa -1827
(scatter/falling cherry[petals] heart/mind's demons too come-out play!)

blooming cherries:
demons of mine, you, too
come out to play!

falling petals
mind demons, you, too
are free to go!

the petals fall:
demons of my heart
you, too, leave!

If our minds are beautiful and relax when cherries blossom, this may be *because* they let their demons out to play. However, "play" was also a polite way to request something of a superior. Another version locates the demons in his guts (~ 腹中の鬼も出てあそべ　一茶　*fukuchû-no oni-mo idete asobu*). No matter. It's the same place. And the demons have a "laundry" association, a proverb: *"when the devil is out, laundry,"* which means, when the demon (a tough boss) is away, the workers let it all hang out. But, why is *laundry* equated with uncontrolled behavior? The *wash=refresh* equation seems reasonable enough to me, but there is a contrary explanation, namely, that dirty laundry is allowed to build up in the absence of oversight. Yet another historical guess is that the practice of taking apart kimonos to wash them is behind it! *Deconstruction as catharsis?* (Sorry to be so confusing!)

鬼の角ぽっきり折るゝ桜哉　一茶
oni no tsuno pokkiri oruru sakura kana　issa -1827
(demon's/s' horns snap-with break cherry[blossoms]!/'tis)

cherry blossoms:
the power to snap off
demon horns!

The saying "even the devil (even demons) breaks his/her horns" means that even a bad person occasionally turns into a good one. The blossoms provide that occasion, though the "power" is added in translation. Japanese demons, themselves, are not *that* bad, even *cute*. They sit up on clouds playing with fireworks (thunder and lightning). If I sometimes call them "devils," it is because they have horns. Within us, they can be what Freud called the *Id* and some call *gremlins*. Japanese have long personified the psych. One *kibyôshi* cartoon novella from Issa's time has good and bad souls (with *round* heads, for soul and ball are homophonic: *tama*) pulling the protagonist's arms in opposite directions (interestingly, there is but *one* Goody and three Baddies!). This next *ku* treats such internal demons:

散る桜心の鬼も出て角を折る 一茶
chiru sakura kokoro no oni mo tsuno o oru issa
(falling cherry[petals] heart/mind's demon/s too horns break)

falling blossoms
my mind-devils, too
break their horns

falling petals
my own demon horns
also fall off

Further to the above-mentioned saying, we have horny idiom. "Breaking horns" means losing one's ornery edge, or mellowing one's mulishness. The "too/also" means *inside as well as outside*.

紅葉には落さぬ角を櫻哉 琴馬 月影塚
momiji ni wa otosanu tsuno o sakura kana kinba ()
(red[fall] leaves-with-as-for, drop-not horns[contradict.] cherry!/'tis)

though the horns
drop not for fall leaves:
cherry blossoms

Because of deer. One might expect the horns to fall off after the deer finish rutting in the Autumn but, no, they hold up until cherry time (like bamboo dropping their leaves just in time for the shoots!).

角入れし人をかしらや花の友 丈草 続猿みの
tsuno ireshi hito o kashira ya hana no tomo jôsô -1704
(horn put-in person[acc.] head/leader!: blossoms' friends)

cherry buck

wearing horns
a man heads a party of
blossom-viewers

finding horns
he's head of the friends
of the blossoms

Imagine a man pink with drink, finding some deer horns, holding them to his head and dancing! Or, did some people bring them along for that purpose? Nah, that would be too contrived.

ちる迄はうか／＼暮す江戸の花 柳多留 124-18
chiru made wa uka-uka kurasu edo no hana yanagidaru ()
(fall until-as-for ship-shod live/living edo's blossoms)

until they fall
life is out of control
edo's blossoms

careless until
the day they fall
edo blossoms

until they fall
time is just whiled away
edo's blossoms

I have trouble with *uka-uka,* for it means excited, not in a tense way, but one that prevents concerted activity. Running about like a chicken without its head, but comfortably. As a *senryû*, a form that pretty much dealt with stereotype, this can either refer to Edo's blossom-viewing mania, or, as per the last reading, the lifestyle of Edo's cool crowd. The last line can be changed to "the *flowers* of Edo."

きの楽さ花みやみなは桜の木　理重 夢見草
ki no rakusa hanami ya mina wa sakura-no ki　rijû 1656
(feeling's ease blossom-viewing!/: everyone-as-for cherry tree/s)

ah, what ease!
blossom-viewing, we are
all cherry trees!

Let it all hang out – let petals fly! There is a pun in the last *ki*, so *tree* and *spirit* may substitute for each other, as indeed they *do* for an odd reason: the *ku* is a palindrome.[1]

大の字に踏んぞり返て桜哉　一茶
dai no ji ni funzorikaete sakura kana　issa
("big"大 letter-in treading-turning cherry!/'tis)

sprawled out
under the bloom, i make
the letter "large"

large the letter
i make lying on my back
it's cherry time

ふんどしのゆるんで暮るる花見哉　子規
fundoshi no yurunde kururu hanami kana　shiki 1894
(loincloth's/s' loosened/ing live blossom-viewing 'tis)

when we live
with loosened loincloths:
blossom-viewing!

Issa's stretched-out posture, *literately* depicted in the first *ku*, evokes relaxation, toleration and being open to the cosmos. In that sense, it is a good-to-be-large *ku*. A loincloth (*fundoshi*) was typical male underwear, but *also* worn alone by many outdoor workers. Shiki, like Issa, has many loincloth poems. What better expression for *letting it all hang-out* than this? The "live" – Japanese has half a dozen nouns and verbs for various aspects of *living* – the one in this *ku* means humble day-to-day existence.

---

1. **Japanese Palindromes** If the reader cannot see how *ki-no rakusa* is *sakura-no ki* backwards, remember that most Japanese syllabets combine a vowel with a consonant. Ask a Japanese to say *sakura* backward and he or she will say *rakusa* rather than *arukas*, as an English-speaker would. Why? Because, thinking in syllabets, sakura is さ・く・ら *sa-ku-ra*, not s-a-k-u-r-a. So, *ki-no-ra-ku-sa-ha-na-mi-ya-mi-na-ha-sa-ku-ra-no-ki* works as a Japanese-style palindrome. Because syllabets including consonants do not individually reverse, Japanese palindromes are further from phonetic reality than what a reversed sound recording would show. But the difference with English-style palindromes is a matter of degree: consider the well-known palindrome "Evil I live;" not only is the "e" pronounced differently in *evil* and *live*, but the syllable count differs.

花ふゝき泥わらんじで通りけり 一茶
hanafubuki doro-waranji de tôrikeri issa (-1827)
(blossom/petal-blizzard mud-[straw]sandals-in pass[emph.])

petal-blizzard
some muddy flip-flops
pass on by

This could be first-person, but I prefer to third-person it and, sitting, see the *waraji* (*waranji* is dialect) go by in front of my eye. *Waraji* are not, of course, rubber flip-flops. They are crudely fashioned (macramé-like braid) straw sandals, equivalent only in that they are cheap and expendable. Travelers wore through them in a day or two. *De rigueur* for pilgrimage, they were clearly informal/relaxed in contrast to the square formal footwear, fancy painted footwear and finely woven footwear.

わらんじのぐあひわろさよ花一日 一茶   わらんじのぐあひ苦になる花見哉 一茶
waranji no guai warosa yo hana ikka issa   *waranji no guai ku ni naru hanami kana* issa
(strawsandals' condition badness! blossoms one-day)   (strawsandals condition pain-into become bloss.vwing)

a day of blossoms   blossom-viewing:
what grief they bring me,   the state of my sandals
my *waranji*!   is an affliction

Waraji were not expected to last more than, say, 20-50 miles and muddy hillside paths would test their strength. If Issa made his own, they might be lumpy, too. That might be stimulating for walking back and forth to the outhouse or in his garden, but could start hurting if worn for a day.

女殿はわらん（ぢ）がけの花見哉 一茶
onadomo wa waranjigake no hanami kana issa (1813)
(women/ladies-as-for strawsandal-style blossom-viewing)

and the women
are out for a straw sandal
blossom-viewing

These women are ready to climb muddy trails, ready for serious cherry blossom hunting. Most female footwear described in haikai is either the upper-class *zôri*, finely woven sandals, or the *bokkuri*, lacquered clogs, of the dancer. Upper class men also wore *zôri,* which were carried by their Ozô (お草 (取り)) or, Honorable-grass, who carried them while their masters rode and kept them when he removed them to enter the mat-covered bloomshade (花の山いまだ御ぞうが氣ハしれす 柳多留 10-8).

売わらじぶらり（と）下る桜哉 一茶
uru waraji burari to sagaru sakura kana issa (1814)
(selling strawsandals dangling down [flowering]cherry!/'tis)

sandals for sale
dangling from the branches
of a cherry tree

Rough straw sandals would reflect the vagabond life even without the cherry tree, which, unless otherwise stated, is in full bloom; and they look better hanging from a tree than leather ones would.

花踏だ香に捨かねるわらぢかな 也有
hana funda ko ni sute-kaneru waraji kana yayû (1701-83)
(blossom[petals] treaded scent-from throw-away-hard strawsandals!/'tis)

> how hard to chuck
> my sandals bearing the scent
> of blossoms we tread

Sandals that would be matter-of-factly thrown away on return are kept for a while as a memento of the *hanami*. This is more romantic than relaxed or cathartic. I keep it here, for once I started with the sandal poems, I found it hard to stop. Had I held my horses and shuffled *ku* a bit longer, I might have ended up with a separate chapter for all items worn blossom-viewing.

櫻にも人にもうつる心哉 蘭更 新五子
sakura ni mo hito ni mo utsuru kokoro kana rankô 1726-99
(cherries-to-even, people-to-even transfer heart/mind!/'tis)

> cherry blossoms   ah, my heart!
> and human beings all   lost to the cherries
> lose their minds   and the people

This is a translation of which only Humpty Dumpty could approve, provided it was his. Yes, you have seen a completely different reading in the *People Viewing* chapter! *These are probably wrong.* Indeed, I do not even mean for the English idiom to mean what it does. Here, and only here, "lose their minds" means that all the thoughts, all the preoccupations and frustrations of the viewer, like the life-force or energy fields of the blossoms, scatter away with the petals.

弁慶は花見るまでも具足哉 重徳 秋津島
benkei wa hana miru made mo gusoku kana shigenori 1690
(benkei-as-for blossoms viewing up to even arms/armor!/'tis)

> brave benkei
> even blossom-viewing
> wore his arms

This is the only exception to the rule. Someone who resists the blossoms. Benkei, the faithful giant, the bonze-samurai famous for his loyalty to his master, for sleeping in full armor (*senryû* describe him as resembling a watermill – the Ferris wheel-like shape with moving buckets like his bristling collection of weapons – and imagine the damage he would do to a mosquito net, prints show him with weapons I cannot begin to name, etc.), and remaining virgin (except for one escapade shortly before he died). Armored or not, Benkei ends up with more arrows in him than a porcupine has spines, but that is another story. The *ku,* if written a century later, would have been called a *senryû*.

ぶら／＼と不断の形で花見哉 一茶
burabura to fudan no nari de hanami kana issa (1824)
(loitering/fiddling-around ordinary shape/style-in blossom-viewing 'tis)

> just hanging out
> in my usual clothes and face
> blossom-viewing

catharsis

This may be intended as a bohemian boast of the sort Issa was wont to make, but I feel the *ku* resembles that about those women in *waranji* (rather than fancier *zori* or *bokkuri*) in that it describes what is not noted in other *ku,* yet must be fairly common. Neither *ku* is found in the most well-known 2000 *ku* anthology (Iwanami) of Issa's work. I put this one into this chapter because it does *not* fit the need-for-catharsis mold, i.e. for the balance. As I see it, old Issa – this was a few years before his death – was his own man and no longer uptight, no longer concerned about keeping up appearances.

花に気のとろけて戻る夕哉　杉風 アルス
hana ni ki no torokete modoru yûbe kana　sanpû 1646-1732
(blossom- with/by spirit/energy melted/bewitched returning evening!/'tis)

returning at dusk
all my armor melted
into blossoms

the walk home
at night all our blossom
spirits . . . spent

all my spirit
melted into blossoms
a dusk return

The etymology of "catharsis" is *cleansing/washing,* but the concept includes a release of pent-up spirit and dissolution. Aside from Issa's single *ku* on Mount Cherry being a place for laundering the heart, my chapter head does not appear anywhere as a proper seasonal term and the theme most similar to it is not found among the blossoms or even the Spring but, as we have seen, the Year-Forget Party (*toshiwasure,* a favorite theme of mine) at the end of Winter. I invented *cherry catharsis* for this book because it floated up naturally when I read Issa's 800 odd blossom-viewing *ku.*

見て来てハ心にあびる桜かな　素檗
mite-kite wa kokoro ni abiru sakura kana　sobaku (-1821)
(seeing-coming-as-for, heart/mind-on pour/bath cherry!/'tis)

~~that's why i came:~~
~~for the cherry blossoms~~
~~to bathe my heart~~

~~having come to see~~
~~the cherry blossoms~~
~~they rinse my heart!~~

~~how they clean~~
~~my heart: the blossoms~~
~~i came to view!~~

~~i saw, i came~~
~~my soul got washed:~~
~~cherry blossoms~~

Were the て only に, the above translation would be correct. It would have been a "coming-to-see" *ku.* If you are a more thorough reader than I am a writer, you might note that the second page of this chapter is a cherry *ku* short of the numbers given (non-cherry ku are not numbered). I had this *ku,* by Issa's fellow countryman and contemporary, Sobaku, at the number 4 spot, to put Issa's similar *ku* into perspective. But the grammar and my reading were a poor fit, so I bounced it off a native speaker. Sure enough, my conceptual bias, or wants, had led me astray. As it stands, "seeing-coming" (*mite-kite*) means to have viewed the blossoms and come home. We have a good end *ku,* instead.

back from viewing
my mind is still awash
cherry blossoms

back from viewing
is when they shower my heart
the cherry petals

basking in the bloom
after returning home from
blossom viewing

Fighting Below
花の喧嘩
hana-no-kenka

> Mukojima's carnival rivals the saturnalia of the ancients. . . . Men dance like satyrs, cup and gourd in hand, or, extending a hand, make orations to the crowd --- natural actors, pantomimists every one of them. But, with all this intoxication, only glee and intoxication manifest themselves. No fighting, no rowdyism, no rough words accompany the spring saturnalia . . .
>
> Eliza Scidmore: *Jinrikisha Days in Japan* (1891)

The greater self-control of the people of the Far East was noted in the 16c not only by the Jesuits but by the adventurer and story-teller extraordinaire Mendez Pinto. Compared to these people, they observed, we Europeans are like children who cannot hide their emotions or refrain from acting on their impulses. In the 19c, despite the assassinations of foreigners by nationalist *ronin* (unemployed samurai [an oxymoron, for samurai, by definition, had masters]), the heart of Japan was, as ever, found to be less violent than that of the West. Yet, blanket statements such as Scidmore's *no this* and *no that* are wrong. Exceptions are, after all, the rule:

花の時は腕に生疵絶なんた　宗因
hana no toki wa ude ni namakizu taenan da　sôin 1604-82
(blossom-time-as-for arms-on fresh-bruises end-not[+emph.])

in blossom time
our arms are always
black and blue

in cherry time
my arms never run out
of fresh bruises

Edoites were famed for their quick tempers. I had even thought to title this chapter Edozakura; but Sôin was *not* an Edoite. He was the founder of the Ôsaka *Danrin,* or "chat-woods" school of poetry which rivaled Bashô's in importance. Ôsakans rarely lost their tempers and punched or drew weapons – most being (stereotypically – for I know more about images than realities) merchants whose weapon was money and words. The *Yanagidaru* senryû *"The first punch: / thrown by the man with / the losing tongue"* (*ii-maketa hô kara butte kakarunari* Y12 1777) would apply to Edoites, or more generally, the Kantô area where the more militaristic ego was quickly bruised and real fights broke out. In the Kansai (Ôsaka-Kobe) area, both parties wax hyperbolic and, as far as I know, never lose, or at least never admit they do. So the physical bruises stymie me. Did they, perhaps, grab each other's upper arms as they argued – I have seen such rough physical contact between men and women shouting at each other in public in Korea – or, did they have some sort of game, no longer remembered, where losers in poetry competition socked each other on the arm, or, is Sôin writing as an old man who bruises easily when he bumps people in the crowds? If the last is the correct interpretation, the *ku* is in the wrong chapter, unless Sôin was writing about Edo, for he has *ku* showing he was there and was impressed, such as this send-off: *"If I could part / with one eye, it would go with you / to blooming Edo"* (別らるるものなら片目花の江戸 梅翁 再現 (*hito no azumabushi e omomuku o okuru*) *wakararuru mono nara katame hana no edo*). Sôin's separate eyes parody the antics of the *waka* poet's blossom-infatuated hearts (see ch. 46). *"Let's follow Edo / in this: its cherry blossoms / and its sake"* (江戸を以て鑑とす也花に樽　梅翁 *edo o motte kagami to su nari hana ni taru*). *Kagami*, as written, means "paragon." The poet's intent? *"In this alone / let's be Edoites: bring kegs / blossom-viewing!"*

何ことぞ花見る人の長刀　去来 再現
nanikoto zo hanamiruhito no nagakatana　kyorai -1704
(what thing! blossom-viewing-people's/s' long[battle-use]-swords)

What insanity!
men out blossom-viewing
with long-swords

Samurai always carried arms; a short sword and dagger might be expected, but this serious weapon was out of place. It would frighten everyone, including the man who carried it. The long scabbard might bump into people and the loss of a valuable sword (what if the samurai passes out from drink?) might cost the man his position (or, in the worst case, he might have to kill himself to atone for it). A *senryû* shows that heavy drinking and swords was not taken for granted *"'Drunken samurai!' / A wet blanket drops on / the blossom-viewing"* (侍が酔って花見の興がさめ　川柳評万句合わせ再現 *samurai ga yotte hanami no kyô ga same* 1767) The first line was borrowed from Ueda: *Light Verse* 1999)

花に鐘そこのき給へ喧嘩買　其角　五元
hana ni kane soko noki tamae kenkakai　kikaku -1707
(blossoms-with bell/s there! get-back please! fight-buyers)

bell peal in the bloom:　　　　　　　　　　　bells to the bloom
you'd better get out of the way!　　　　　*out of there! out you go!* that's
here comes a fight!　　　　　　　　　　　　asking for a fight

Did the bell happen to sound right when a fight-monger passed by? Or, were bells used as a warning, much like they were used for fires? If so, I am afraid it would backfire for people run *to*, not away from, fights: *"Ignoring even / the horse-race, how men run / to the fight!"* (けい馬をは見ずにけんくわへ人（客）たおり 柳多留十六 *keiba o ba mizu ni kenka e hito[kyaku] taori* yanagidaru 1781), as this *senryû*, poking fun at an earlier *ku* about viewing the horse race rather than the blossoms, confirms. Or, is someone chasing people from the bloomshade upon hearing the vespers, the official time to leave?

男伊達に逢うて懲りたる花見哉　樗良
otokodate ni aute koritaru hanami kana　chora 1728-1780
(machopunks-with meeting fed up with blossom-viewing 'tis)

edo cherries?

meeting up with　　　　　　　　　　　　　too many punks
macho jerks, fed up with　　　　　　　　　makes blossom-viewing
blossom-viewing　　　　　　　　　　　　　tough to take

meeting up with
would-be toughs, i'm sick
of blossom-viewing

378 *fighting*

In the Edo era, there wasn't much opportunity for men to do battle. A hyper-masculine persona may be explained as compensation or cover up, as you wish. Good translation was hard for lack of a word for *would-be* tough-guys in English. This poet evidently went to a blossom-viewing, where these men strutted their stuff (I imagine obnoxious drunks like some who pushed their *yamato-damashi* = Japanese soul = absolute sincerity+courage = stuff on me in Tokyo area honkytonks in the heady 1970's and 1980's). My guess is that Chora, who ended up in the city of gentle men, Kyôto, and wrote: *"Endangered / by my staff exercise / morning glories"* (*asagao ni abunaki bô no keiko kana*) was turned off by *cock-a-doodle-doo* Edoites. He must have felt tempted to dust them down with his staff.

上野とあり・隙あれや桜かざして喧嘩買　一茶
hima are ya sakura kazashite kenka kai   issa (1814)
(leisure let-there-be! cherry adorned fight-buying)

ueno scene

i've got the time:
decked with a sprig of cherry
off to pick a fight!

time on their hands
with blossoms in their hair
they pick fights!

The first 12 syllabets come from *Shinkokinshû* (1205-10) *waka* #104, mis/attributed to Yamabe Akahito, a *Manyôshû* poet, which describes the elegantly attired courtiers *living* (that is, passing their days = *kurashi*), rather than fighting, with blossoms adorning their hair. Said *waka* is, itself, a paraverse of a *Manyôshû* (8c) poem in which the blossom is the one favored by the court at *that* time: a plum. Knowing this does not solve the ambiguity of Issa's *ku*. The first reading is that of Japan's most prolific 20c novelist, Tanabe Seiko. In her fat historical novel *Warped Issa* (『ひねくれ一茶』), she wrote that Issa may have been "self-deprecatory, but when he felt someone looked down on him, his fighting spirit was immediately aroused." She imagines him challenging other poets. Coming across anyone who sez he's the better haikai-man, Issa would crash their bloomshade and join the verse-jam. I feel this unlikely, for Issa lacked the sharp memory needed to be an aggressive verse-jammer. His journals reveal a sit-down-and-work-out-the-possibilities type of mind. The first-person reading is delightful, but the *ku* is almost certainly about pugnacious Edoites. It is supported by the nuance of ~ *are ya*, which seems to concern others, i.e., *"they must have* time to spare." And, as Ueda notes, "it is an ironic comment on the different ways of spending a spring day, then and now." (*Dew on the Grass*)

喧嘩買花ふんづけて（けちらせて）通りけり　一茶
kenkakai hana funzukete (kechirasete) tôrikeri   issa (1817)
(quarrel-buyers blossoms treading [kicking-scattering] pass [emph.])

looking for fights
men trample on blossoms
as they pass by

fight-mongers
pass by, kicking about
the pink petals

ちる花に喧嘩買らが通りけり　一茶
chiru hana ni kenkakaira ga tôrikeri   issa (1814)
(scattering blossoms-with/in fight-buyers-the pass[emph.])

fight-mongers
pass by as cherry blossom
petals scatter

Though English-speaking cultures have never lacked men looking for a fight – young bullies trying to make you "dis" them to provide an excuse for their cruelty – we lack a term for *people eager to pick fights who are not necessarily bullies, for they welcome resistance.* Japanese, on the other hand, is problematic for failing to distinguish between a *fight*, and an *argument*, all of which are called *kenka*.

情強を蒔そこなふ (や) 花の山 一茶
jôgowa o makisokonau ya hananoyama issa 1818
[emot.strong/ pushiness[acc] sow-mistake!/:blossom-mountain]

<table>
<tr><td>

pushiness pushed
in the wrong place
cherry mountain

</td><td>

the wrong place
to be an obstinate fool
cherry mountain

</td></tr>
</table>

Issa wrote this as an old man. It could be self-reflective. Or, it might mean Issa was tired of men who could not see the flowers for the fights, or, more subtly, that pushy behavior did not find purchase, as most people were hanging loose. Of course, some *welcomed* it. A *senryû not* about blossom-viewing puts it well, *"Back to fight me? / Is that why you've come? / Buddy talk."* (又けんくわしに来たといふ中のよさ 柳多留 12-39 *mata kenka shi-ni kita to iu naka-no yosa* yanagidaru 1777).

谷中・日ぐらしや花の中なる喧嘩買 一茶
higurashi ya hana no nakanaru kenkakai issa 1818
(day-livers!/: blossoms-among-is fight-buyers)

in the valley

<table>
<tr><td>

day laborers
among the blossoms
seeking fights

</td><td>

day laborers
here among the blossoms
buying fights

</td></tr>
</table>

You might think day-laborers (*higurashi* – lit. day-living) a modern invention, but they are just one of the many *modern elements* of Edo. Could Issa's *ku* play with a phrase in *Manyôshû* song #3324, *"smoke rises from spring day living"* (*kemuri-tatsu haru-no hi-gurashi*), where the image is one of tranquility?

江戸声や花見の果のけん花かひ 一茶
edogoe ya hanami no hate no kenkakai issa (1824)
(edo voices!/?/: blossom-viewing fruit/end's fight-buyers)

these edo voices
after the blossom viewing
they pick fights

<table>
<tr><td>

edo voices!
blossom viewing ends
in quarrels

</td><td>

the voice of edo
after blossom-viewing
fight! fight! fight!

</td></tr>
</table>

edoite voices:
are quarrels the fruit of
blossom-viewing

The *hate* means at the end of something, but "ends" does not do it sufficient justice, for it also means "result" and poetically "horizon." Would the Spanish *disfrutarse* be better? *"Vozes de Edo / se disfrutan luchando: / los miraflores."* I just made up *miraflores* and have no idea if it is a real word!

江戸声やあたり八間花の山　一茶
edôgoe ya atari hakken hananoyama issa 1825
(edô-voices:/!roundabout-8-mats blossom-mountain)

fight! fight! fight!

edoite voices
don't even go to look!
cherry mountain

cherry mountain
curiosity killed the cat
edoite voices

The idiom "near-eight-mats" (a version of "near-neighborhood"(*atari-kinjô*)), was used in the sense that one should not even get *near* to conflict.

江戸衆に見枯らされたる桜哉　一茶
edoshû ni mikarasaretaru sakura kana issa 1825
(edoites-by see-drying/dried-up cherry[blossoms]!/ 'tis)

cherry blossoms
withering under the gaze
of those edoites

On the one hand, Issa is just describing a blossom-viewing coming to an end, perhaps in dry weather; but, I believe the ferocious (?) Edo gaze is implied.[1]

あつさりとあさぎ頭巾の花見哉　一茶
assari to asagi-zukin no hanami kana issa (1825)
(crisply light-yellow/scallion-headcloth's/s' blossom-viewing'tis)

blossom-viewing
my scallion bandana
crisply starched

a new bandana
asagi cool and crisp
blossom-viewing

The color *asagi* is "light-scallion" 浅葱, "light-yellow" 浅黄 or, "corn color!" (my dictionary forgets to specify husk or cob). Further defined as *the pale green of young shoots*, it connotes: 1) *A clean-cut refreshing look* – far from the sogginess of old age – "speaking in *asagi*" (*asagi ni iu*) meant to speak forthrightly without mincing words; 2) *Inexpensive cool fashion* – whereas the fashionable was generally expensive – as mentioned in this *senryû*, "Mt Asuka: / the asagi bandanas, / a cheap cool" (*asuka yama asagi no zukin yasui share* yanagidaru 3-7 = 1768); 3) Wearing said bandana was *a way to enjoy one's anonymity*, not in secret, but together with others under the blossoms. Adjectives like "pale" or "light" weaken poetry. If *scallion* bothers you, make it "turquoise" or "sky-blue." They are cool and pale green is *also* blue in Japanese. I include the *ku* in this chapter, for *refreshing crispness* is an Edo-like characteristic and reminds us that Issa had become *somewhat* Edoized during his long stay. The *ku* is also interesting considered against a more famous New Year's *ku* where he mentions the sky of that color (*asagi*) as "lucky/auspicious." *There*, he is graced by the gods or nature. The old poet brings his own luck, pluck, and spirit to the blossom-viewing.

---

1. Edo Gaze, Japanese Gaze The Japanese are collectively known for *not* fixating on eyes the way Occidentals are taught to do. Books for Japanese tourists advise them to stare at an Occidental's nose or forehead if they find it hard to look straight into the eyes. (See *Topsy-turvy 1585* for more) There is, however, a difference *within* Japan; the more pushy Edoite is more likely to stare than the retiring Kyotoite. Western tourists might be taught to avert their eyes so as not to frighten people or give them an impression of being aggressive.

山桜きのふちりけり江戸〔の〕客 issa (純和三)
yamazakura kinô chirikeri edo no kyaku issa (純和三)
(mountain cherries yesterday scatter[emph] edo-guests)

    mountain cherries
    yesterday the edoites
    all scattered

花の木をうしろになして江戸びいき一茶
hana no ki o ushiro ni nashite edo biiki issa (文政六)
(blossom-trees behind-at becoming edo-drawn/lover)

    leaving behind
    trees still in bloom, i play
    the edoite

What did the snappy Edo spirit bring to blossom-viewing besides pizzazz and fights? *Speed*. They tended to contract into mobs as fast as a fist is clenched, then explode like the big bang. Cherry blossoms may scatter quickly, but not nearly so fast as blossom viewers from Edo (who, we might add, are still found *doing the world* in three days, etc). Perhaps this came from Samurai manners – Edo's martial air encompassed far more than the actual *bushi* class – that praised a man for doing *everything* (even taking a shit) with dispatch. Young Issa had mixed feelings about that. The *edo-biiki* in the second *ku* is an Edo-lover or someone filling in for, or being a representative for an Edoite. Issa, old and ill, has found a witty way to excuse his having to go home early from a cherry-viewing.

江戸桜花も銭だけ光る哉　一茶
edozakura hana mo zeni dake hikaru kana   issa 1820
(edo cherries blossoms even [small-]change[coins] only shine!)

    edo cherries
    even among blossoms
    only coins shine

    cherries in edo
    the only thing that shines
    is small change

If the last *ku* showed mixed feelings for Edo, this one *seems to be* critical; but I hope I'm wrong and Issa means that shiny hair-decorations and bright clothing including silver or gold thread seen at blossom-viewing in Kyôto are not seen in the more masculine, subdued blossom-viewings in Edo. This is a good example of a *ku* where reading is not just reading.

船で見る櫻の中の喧嘩かな　桃雨
fune de miru sakura no naka no kenka kana   tôu (c.1900)
(boat-on/from view cherries-among-fights!/'tis)

    viewing a fight
    among the cherry blossoms
    from our boat

Here, we have no connection with a given locality but, instead, a moving picture. With a moat between the poet and the ruffians, this is almost like watching a fight on television, but the water has metaphorical suggestions: all life is, in a sense, written on it.

Eating in the Bloomshade
花見食
hanami-shoku

初桜弁当もなく見る日かな 尺樹 花供養
hatsuzakura bentô mo naku miru hi kana shakujû 1795
(first-cherry/ies lunchbox-even-without view/ing day!/'tis)

first blossoms
today i view them
bentô-less

first blossoms
we view though the bentô
are yet to bloom

Japanese *bentô*, or box-lunches, have variety enough to fill a large museum. Those sold outside of restaurants are made of thin wood today and are throw-away, while those used by households and restaurants for meals delivered to offices and other clients are generally lacquerware (tough but light, like the plastic fakes that abound today). Unlike crude occidental "boxes," these containers, with built in or removable dividers, serve as dishes, holding food directly. They are even common *inside* restaurants because they facilitate quick and fair proportioning of food and a high waiter/customer ratio. The above *ku* might concern bentô sold on the grounds, but preparing them at home was a standard start to the blossom-viewing and, like putting tinsel on Christmas Trees on Christmas Eve, enjoyable to some. The author of *Edo no Hanami* (Edo blossom-viewing), notes this as one sign, or proof that blossom-viewing was a dramatic event, for such *bentô* were most commonly prepared for theater (See *Topsy-turvy 1585* on the extraordinary length of these!). One *senryû* demonstrates the truth of the parallel: *"If it rains, / just take them to theater / double-deck boxes"* (もし降らば芝居にしなと重へ詰め 川柳年中行事（江戸の花見から）*moshi furaba shibai ni shi na to futaezume* (pre-1918)) I would add to drama one more occasion, *the New Year*; for *bentô* were prepared at the year's end because no one was supposed to cook on that day.[1] Apparently, the first blossoms took almost everyone by surprise. I say *almost* because of this 1674 *ku*: *"A sputtering / of box-lunches, too – / first blossoms"* (弁当もちらり／＼やはつざくら 広寧 桜川 *bentô mo chirari-chirari ya hatsuzakura* kônei).

弁当がひらかぬ内が花見哉　一吟 八束穂集
bentô ga hirakanu uchi ga hanami kana ichigin 1680
(lunch-boxes-the open-not-while blossom-viewing!/?/'tis)

before we open
our lunch boxes is
the blossom viewing

blossom viewing
only until we open
our lunch boxes

Is this poet a purist who thinks food ruins blossom viewing or does he just wish to point out how hungry all that hiking makes people?

↑ 1. **New Year's = Blossom-viewing Parallels.** Besides the bentô, we have the common inebriation of spirit and drinking (not true for watching drama, for no one wanted to get up and pee), dressing up, and going out early, to see the sunrise on New Year's or get to the blossoms and claim a place before it gets hot (partly because of the clothing) in the latter case. The same old *waka* about a ship disappearing into the mist was used for an alarm clock, too: "Between the 14 / and the 17 you sleep / for the hanami" (十七と十四のあいへ花見寝る 川柳年中行事 *jûnana to jûshi no ai e hanami neru*) as a senryû put it, for the method was to say the first part of the *waka* (17 syllables) before falling to sleep in which case the spirit of the poet would wake you up in the dawn (before the sunrise) for the remainder (14 syllabets). Another senryû puts it like this: "Blossom eve / reservations are made / for one ship" (花の宵舟を一艘（そう？）とっておき *hana no yoi fune o isseki totte-oki*). Interested readers may find pages devoted to the alarm clock poem in *Rise, Ye Sea Slugs!*

―――――――――――――――――――――――――――――――――――

花に浮世我酒白く食黒し　芭蕉
hana ni ukiyo waga sake shiroku meshi kuroshi bashô 1684
(blossoms-with/in floating-world my *sake* white, rice black)

the world's high
on blossoms: my sake's white
my rice black

high on blossoms
life goes on: murky wine and
unpolished rice!

This poem was prefaced by a Chinese poem by one "white-pleasure-heaven" to the effect that *if you know sorrow you know wine is divine and if you become poor you know the value of money.* The title of the first reading follows Japanese annotator Kon Eizô: "in this happy world high on blossoms, here I am living in depressing poverty (a homophonic pun on *uki* (floating/high *or* depressed/melancholy) with my raw wine and unpolished rice. I think Bashô was not so much complaining as *boasting* about his voluntary simplicity, ie., the world may be high on blossoms, but i'll stick to my raw *sake* and black rice, which, thanks to their rough texture, go well with blossom-viewing, aesthetically speaking! Poor is beautiful, *sometimes*! This is one of Bashô's three most famous food+blossom-viewing *ku*.

一日は米の飯食て花見哉　吾人 花供養
ichinichi wa kome no han kutte hanami kana gojin 1795
(one-day-as-for rice's meal eating/ate blossom-viewing!/'tis)

the first day
each meal graced with rice
blossom-viewing

for one day
we eat rice with each meal
blossom-viewing

While Japan was officially a rice economy – land was measured by rice-production capability and taxes paid in it – most Japanese could not afford it and generally had to settle for buckwheat noodles, sweet potatoes, etc.. What rice they could afford was unpolished. I.e., the "black" rice of Bashô.

四つごきの揃はぬ花見ごころ哉　芭蕉
yotsu goki no sorowanu hanamigokoro kana bashô -1694
(four-[formal-set of]-dishes gather/match-not blossom-viewing-heart!/'tis)

not even
a four bowl set
our blossom-viewing

Bashô prefaced the *ku*: "Going to the blossom-viewing at Ueno, [I/we saw] various people had curtains raised and were partying up a storm, making lots of noise including various voices singing popular ditties. I begged permission to use the shade of a pine tree off to one side." The four-bowl set (different sizes, one within the other) is carried by begging monk and suggests Bashô is content with a humble blossom-viewing. I follow the accepted interpretation, above, but cannot refrain from wondering if he might have meant: *"Unlike a beggar / my mind is not together / blossom-viewing."*

家中の常器集めて花見哉 吹衣 淡ちしま
iejû no jôki atsumete hanami kana   fui 1698
(house-within's usual utensils gather blos.viewing!/'tis)

we gather up
all the cups, jugs and pots:
blossom-viewing!

gathering all
the vessels in my house:
to the cherries!

The aesthetic value expressed by Bashô (voluntary poverty) may be more admirable than the plain proof of poverty (living with minimal possessions), but this *ku* is, to my mind, better than Bashô's.

拾ひたる金有合の花見哉　抱月 小弓
hiroitaru kane ariawase no hanami kana   hôgetsu 1699
(gathered coins are-combined blossom-viewing!/'tis)

gathered coins:
blossom-viewing with
what's on hand

This *ku*, like the last one and Ginkô's transport-borrowing *ku* (#8-59) in the *Un/equality* chapter may have been influenced by Bashô's four-dish *ku*. Food is not the only measure of have and have-not.

あり合を人にまかせて花見かな　紫貞女
ari-awase o hito ni makasete hanami kana   shiteijo (-1751)
(are-combined[acc. – taking?] people/others-on relying blossom-viewing!)

with only what was
on hand, counting on others
blossom-viewing

i'm content with
whatever others scrounge up
blossom-viewing

coming here with
only what was on hand
i am now in the hands of
other blossom-viewers!

The second reading of the Shiteijo's *ku* may be off a bit, but I am unsure and leave it. Regardless, I like a happy-go-lucky *woman*. If the blossoms fall without worrying for *their* future, why should we, male or female, plan *ours*? A leave-it-to-providence approach seems metaphysically fitting here.

喰物に喰ひ入るやつも花見哉　嵐蘭 ありそ海
kuimono ni kuiiru yatsu mo hanami kana   ranran (-1689)
(eat-stuff[food]-into eat-into guy too blossom-viewing!/'tis)

there are some
with eyes for food alone
blossom-viewing

& there are guys
who come for your food
that too's *hanami*

I would guess both readings are correct and we are talking about freeloaders.

花見・木のもとは(に)汁も鱠も櫻かな　芭蕉
konomoto wa(ni) shiru mo namasu mo sakura kana   bashô (1690)
(tree-beneath[one-tree-base]-at/by soup-too catfish-too cherry!/?/'tis)

blossom-viewing

under the tree
soup and fish salad
solid petals

Namasu, the "salad" in question, was a mixture of lightly marinated meat, fish and shellfish. Blyth, who translated *"Under the cherry-trees, / on soup, and fish-salad and all, / flower petals,"* writes that there is "perhaps a feeling of the way in which all things are blended with one another through some particular agency;" Japanese annotators concentrate on something else, namely, this *ku* was the first Bashô explicitly called an example of *karumi*, or "lightness," the style of haiku he touted in his final years. As such, it is the most famous *ku* about food under the blossoms. The original is spare in the sense that it does not specify whether the *sakura* is "on," or "in" the food, or whether the food has turned into *sakura*. At first, I imagined a strong wind, but Bashô is said to have disliked a *wakiku* (following verse) to the effect that the people who came the next morning people would be disappointed to find no spring=petals remaining, partly because it merely parroted a *waka* and partly because he had not intended to emphasize the loss of petals but to depict an idyllic or even magical scene. He was much happier with the *wakiku* provided for his same *hokku* (lead verse of the sequence) at another *kasen* (poetry-jam): *"Tranquil in the westing sun / it is fine weather."* Not knowing the character for *namasu*, I first thought it an old way to write *namazu* 鯰, or "catfish," and drew a picture of one in a bowl, peeking out of the soup with the little heart-shaped petals falling on "his" whiskered (feelered) face. How poetic, I thought, that the creature whose supernatural counterparts caused earthquakes should make trees tremble and shed their blossoms upon it! *Oh, well.*

冷汁にふたをつけたる櫻哉　浪花
hiyajiru ni futa o tsuketaru sakura kana   rôka (-1703)
(cold soup-on lid[+acc.] placed cherry[blossoms]!/'tis)

keeping a cover
on a bowl of cold soup:
cherry time

This is what I call a *riddle ku*. You read the first twelve syllabets and guess the answer. Of course, that is obvious in the context of *this* book; but imagine it in another context.

二の膳やさくら吹込む鯛の鼻　子珊
ninozen ya sakura fukikomu tai no hana   shisan (-1699)
(second dish: cherry[petals] blow-into snapper's nose)

the second dish
cherry petals blow into
a snapper's nose

はら／＼の飯にまぶれる桜哉　一茶(1818)
harahara no meshi ni mabureru sakura kana   issa (1818)
(fluttering rice/food-to swarm cherry[petals]!/'tis)

fluttering they
crowd 'round the rice
cherry petals!

Does anyone know if the first *ku* was written before or after Bashô's *ku*? The snapper (red sea bream) is uniquely appropriate – we will have a whole chapter on the "cherry-snapper." Note in the second, how the same *sakura kana* I translated as "cherry time" two *ku* back is, again, "cherry petals," and animistic ones at that. *Have you ever seen fine bonito flowers (flakes) squirming upon hot food?*

財布から焼飯出して桜哉　一茶
saifu kara yakimeshi dashite sakura kana　issa (-1827)
(wallet/purse-from fried-rice removed cherry[blossom-viewing]!)

picking out grains
of fried rice from my purse:
that's cherry time

Cherry petals are not the only thing ending up everywhere. Issa has managed to find something coming from the human side. Gonsui (-1719), playing upon the stereotype of drinkers and non-drinkers had haiku'ed: *"Fried rice! / The heavy drinker laughs at / teetotalers' cherry"* (焼飯 や上戸 の笑ひし下戸の花　言水 江戸新道 *yakimeshi ya jogo no waraishi geto no hana*). Issa, however, both drank more than his fill (the journal includes episodes of passing out, etc.) *and* still ate like the proverbial man from Shinano. Issa's "fried rice" may be *sakura-meshi* (cherry-rice), *i.e.,* rice sautéed in soy sauce and *sake,* which usually included some crosswise cut slivers of boiled octopus leg.

水藩留別・花に来て結ぶもあはし水の味　柳几 鹿嶋立
suihan? ryûbetsu // hana ni kite musubu mo awaji mizu no aji　ryûki? ()
(leaving sui feif // blossom/s-to-coming, cup[hands-together]-even meet/fit-not water's taste)

blossom-viewing　　　　　　　　　　　　　with the blossoms
even fresh spring-water　　　　　　　　even hand-cupped water
doesn't satisfy!　　　　　　　　　　　　　is short of flavor

While coming yet not uniting – moreover, "water" connotes a lack of a relationship – may have erotic undertones, I think the poet's point is that the cherry-bash raises the threshold of stimulation so that mere water, even that *cupped* ("joined" in Japanese, for hands meet) from pure spring water, will not do and we must have green tea or strong *sake!* Also, the poet just left a place with "water" in its name.

花盛あちないものはなかりけり 尚白 アルス　　　　喰ひ(へ)共味ひしらぬ桜哉 一茶 1821
hanazakari ajinai mono wa nakarikeri　shôhaku (-1722)　*kui/e-domo ajiwai shiranu sakura kana*　issa
(blossom-flourish/peak/heat flavor-not thing-as-for not [+final])　(eating-but/nevertheless flavor know-not cherry!/'tis)

the bloom-peak　　　　　　　　　　　　　you eat but
today, there is nothing　　　　　　　　cannot tell the taste:
lacking flavor!　　　　　　　　　　　　　　cherry time

These clearly contradict, yet both are true. Together, they sum up eating under the cherry blossoms.

君が世の大飯喰ふてさくら哉 一茶 文政
kimigayo no ôhan kuute sakura kana　issa (1820's)
(lord's reign/era's big-meals eating cherry[blossoms!/'tis)

good times are here:　　　　　　　　　　these, our times,
we eat big meals then　　　　　　　　　we eat big meals with
view the blossoms!　　　　　　　　　　　cherry blossoms!

As a celebration of a nation living the good life, thanks to a good harvest the previous year or the beneficent policies of the rulers, this *ku* reminds me of a typical New Year *ku*. But, as the second reading suggests, it *may* be critical of the pigging out under the blossoms as lacking good taste. Drinking with or without *hors de oeuvres* was, after all, the correct way to view blossoms. Yet, blossom *viewing* was always blossom-*eating*, too: *"Our hairdos / and our food are festive: / blossom-viewing"* (髪かたち飯もはれなる花見哉　嘯山　葎亭句集 *kami katachi meshi mo harenaru hanami kana* shôzan (-1801)). Indeed, a hundred years before, women were already downright competitive with their box-lunches: *"Women shamed by food / among the blossoms,"* as one 7-8 *ku* put it! (食事に女の恥る花の中　松星　（付句）小弓俳諧集 *shokuji ni onna no hajiru hana no naka* shôsei (1699)).

重箱に鯛おしまげて花見哉　成美 ~家集
jûbako ni tai oshimagete hanami kana seibi (-1816)
(double-box-in snapper push-folding/ed blossom-viewing!/'tis)

snappers crammed
into our lunch boxes
blossom-viewing

folding a snapper
into a lunch box, i'm off
to view blossoms

This *ku* by Issa's patron/employer is superb. The luxurious fish crammed into the box – I imagine its tail doubled back – strikes a chord though we do not know if it is because the preparations are rushed or because lunch boxes are not made for such big fish. If only I could English the splendid compound verb *oshi-mageru* (cram-fold) and fit the "two-layer" (double-deck?) modification of the box (it is a particular type of lunch box) into the translation. The rice fills in the bottom half of the box (horizontally, rather than vertically wide) and a floor(?) inserted above it holds the condiments.

花よりもよしや吉野の葛団子 失名失典 17c?
hana yori mo yoshi ya yoshino no kuzudango　lost name
(blossoms more-than good!/: yoshino's arrowroot dumplings)

ho, they beat
the blossoms! yoshino's
kudzu dumplings

Japanese enjoy a range of soft cooked round steamed or boiled items made of one or another type of flour. Translations such as "dumplings" for those made of wheat or *kudzu* (the starchy arrowroot), ie. *dango,* or sweet-rice "cakes," i.e. *mochi* for those made of a special highly glutinous rice, do not work for we are talking about *different textures* of food. Be that as it may, the Yoshino dumplings must be very good, for Yoshino's blossoms were said to be beyond words. This *ku* builds upon a saying, "dumplings over blossoms" (*hana yori dango*　lit.: "*blossoms-more-than, dumplings!*").

まん十はおくある花のもたせ哉 長頭丸 崑山集
manjû wa oku aru hana no motase kana　teitoku (1651)
(beanjam-bun-as-for depth/recesses-have blossoms' hospitality!/?)

what you find
way back in the blossoms:
a bean bun

bean-jam-buns
what you find in blossoms
with real depth

so bean buns
are what blossoms serve
to a tea-master

A *manjû* is a soft bun occasionally filled with minced meat – today, it comes with many fillings, including curry and pizza! – but sweet bean-paste was standard. I would guess the *ku* is risqué for this bun was synonymous with a plump *mons veneris* and *oku aru*, literally "having a recess," could mean the inner shrine of the blossom recess, the vagina. I was tempted to translate: *"A bean bun: / Blossoms with a real heart / give it to you!"* However, *manjû* also was an abbreviation for a wicker hat shaped like half-a-bun which monks might wear and, in some dialects, a mushroom that sprouts under a tree. I believe the A-side reading is aesthetic depth, a blossom-viewing *cum* tea ceremony.

花中尋友・饅頭で人をたづねよ山桜　其角
東叡山 *manjû de hito o tazuneyo yamazakura*   kikaku -1707
(bean-bun-with person[obj] call-on/ask-for! mountain-cherry/ies)

calling on someone among the blossoms at ueno

take this hot bun
and go find someone!
mountain cherries

Responding to his contemporary, Kyorai's befuddlement, Kikaku explained he gave a bun to someone to eat as he sent him off to hunt for friends. A modern scholar calls it an example of a failed *ku* that only pleases its own author (「其角の一人よがり」=『名句事典』). *Perhaps*. But, can not the same be said for many of Bashô's poems if they are not explained? I added the *hot* for, in a magical world, that would help Kikaku's servant find his friend quickly. The location was Tôeizan (East Hie Mountain), the Ueno hills in Edo, so the "mountain cherries" would be the type of cherries the friend was expected to be under. Could the food in question match the type of cherry?

山里に食ものしゐる花見哉　尚白 あら野
yamazato ni tabemono shiiru hanami kana   shôhaku 1689
(mountain-country/home-in food stock blossom-viewing ' tis)

back in the hills
they force food on you
blossom-viewing

At first, thinking *shiiru* might be a literate term for *shiireru*, I translated: *"Up in the hills / it's time to stock up food / blossom-viewing"* implying they were poor and gathered food from the visitors. Late spring was not an easy time food-wise. Young Issa wrote *"My rice bags / are empty but the cherries / are in bloom,"* or, if I dare wax poetic in an English manner: *"My rice sacks / are a void – Thank God / for the cherries!"* (米袋空しくなれど桜哉　一茶 *komebukuro munashiku naredo sakura kana* issa). But I came back to the less forced "force" reading (though that, too, is uncertain) and now wonder whether: 1) the poet contrasts the usual blossom-viewing in a park where one was pushed to *drink*, with a viewing back in the hills where one was plied with food (precisely because it was valuable) or, we have 2), country folk paying poets in food-stuff (not easy to carry back) rather than money.

木の下に杓子とるなり花の料　春来 古選 再現
ki no shita ni shakushi toru nari hana no kate   shunrai 1763
(tree-below-at ladle take [server role] become blossoms' food)

beneath the tree
i find myself holding the ladle
blossom food

In many cultures, a young wife accepts a ladle when she assumes her domestic duties, or, as was the case in Japan, inherits authority from the husband's mother after years of service in the household. Does this male poet note the topsyturviness of cherry-time? 料 *kate* = "food" can pun as *toga* = punishment.

ばゝが餅爺が桜咲きにけり 一茶 文化四
baba ga mochi jijii ga sakura sakinikeri issa (1807)
(old-lady/ies rice-cake old-man/men's cherry bloom[+fin.])

<blockquote>
old lady's <i>mochi</i>
and old man's cherry
bloom away!
</blockquote>

The old man who makes a tree bloom is legend and women made artificial blossoms of sweet-rice cake/dough. Had Issa done this a decade later, I would have thought he alluded to the cherry tree he planted is blooming and the sweet-rice his wife Kiku has pounded and cooked was ready to eat. As it stands, I am puzzled. He may refer to drunken old men releasing steam, while their wives had tea with their rice cakes which heated expand like marshmallows.

桜餅みんな禿にたゝとられ 柳多留 93-11
sakuramochi minna komuro ni tada torare yanagidaru 19c
(cherry-rice-cake all komuro[geisha's helper]-by just taking/en)

<blockquote>
cherry-leaf <i>mochi</i>:
the sweet <i>komuro</i> get
all of the cakes
</blockquote>

A *komuro* is a little girl indentured in the pleasure quarters, where she serves the geisha, running errands, amusing waiting guests, and so forth. She was the embodiment of that class of charm called pure cuteness. Being so cute, she naturally managed to appropriate all the sweets for herself; as *senryû* attest, pretty girls tended to become obese. The cherry-sweet-rice-cake is a piece of lightly pounded *mochi* rice (the grains can still be sensed) wrapped in a cherry leaf. The leaf, like its closest competition, the grape-leaf, is briny with a subtle and, to my mind, elegant, taste. It was generally made from the leaves of certain varieties of Ôshima cherry trees, but as one who has cooked with wild grape leaves, I would bet that this would be a case where close will do. A fourth-grade child writes *"Cherry-leaf mochi: / you can gobble up / the taste of spring;"* or, *"Sakura-mochi / i gulp down the taste / of spring-time"* (さくらもちパクッとたべる春の味　佐藤　滋　宮崎県　北六番丁小*sakura-mochi pakutto taberu haru no aji* satô shigeru 4th grade). The idea of something representing the taste of spring is old, but most adults would pick the preternaturally fresh plant scent of the young *seri* (dropwort: *Oenanthe javanica*), *udo* (*Aralia cordata*) or *yomogi* (mugwort: *Artemisia indica*), none of these eaten in the West (**Note: most of the best Japanese vegetables are not found in *sushi* bars or even in the best Japanese restaurants!**). But the cherry, because of its blossoms, represents the spring, so you could say this child's haiku gives us the most suitable symbolic taste of the season.

餅さめて臍のさびしき花見哉 HOUROU MUSHU (失出典)
mochi samete heso sabishiki hanami kana Hôrô Mushu? (contemp)
(sweetrice-cake cools/ing navel lonely blossom-viewing!/'tis)

<blockquote>
the <i>mochi</i> cools and   the <i>mochi</i> turns cold
loneliness fills my navel   and blossom-viewing's lonely
blossom-viewing   down to my navel
</blockquote>

What exactly is a "navel-lonely" blossom-viewing? Does the rice-cake remind the poet of his mother, who is associated with the umbilical chord which is kept in Japan? Japanese are not only big on *farts* and *poop* (As you know from translated children's books?); I have a large old book all about *belly-buttons!*

有様は我も花より団子哉　一茶
ariyô wa ware mo hana yori dango kana　issa 1814
(appearance-as-for i too blossoms more-than dumplings!/'tis)

<table>
<tr><td>

truth be told
i, too, take dumplings
over blossoms

</td><td>

the plain truth
even a poet picks pie
over flowers

</td></tr>
</table>

花に背をむけてたんこを食て居る　柳多留
hana ni se o mukete dango o tabeteiru　yanagidaru 10-13
(blossoms-to back face dumpling[acc.] eating)

としまかりよれば花より団子哉　一茶
toshi makari yoreba hana yori dango kana　issa 1824
(age comes-when blossoms more-than dumplings!)

<table>
<tr><td>

turning his back
toward the cherry blossoms
eating a dumpling

</td><td>

when old age
is upon you, dumplings
beat blossoms

</td></tr>
</table>

Tanabe Seiko *(Warped Issa)* made a big deal of Issa's preference for strapping "food-pilers" (*meshimori-onna*) who washed an inn guest's feet, sewed his clothes, cooked his food, made his bed and, if he desired . . . over the useless courtesans=blossoms (he couldn't afford). The proverb *hana yori dango* in the first *ku* means the substantial should be preferred to the pretty. As Issa would marry for the first time within months, he may have decided upon a dumpling who could help put food on his table over a pretty young thing. He is owning up to his birthright in a province noted for ravenous men and playing on his *far-from-lyrical-me* rhetoric. Two years before he wrote: *"To tell the truth / all i feel is it's cold: / the first time-rain"* (*ariyô-wa samui...*). Haikai poets were supposed to cherish these early winter showers. Issa's second *ku* is ironic in retrospect, for later that year, Issa would remarry the daughter of a samurai who would ditch him in a week! The 18c *senryû* is thrown in for good measure.

としよりの身には花より玉子哉　一茶
toshiyori no mi ni wa hana yori tamago kana　issa 書簡
(elderly body/self-for-as-for blossoms more-than eggs!/'tis)

<table>
<tr><td>

for old men
with old bodies, eggs
beat blossoms

</td><td>

for old bodies
eggs beat buns beat
pretty flowers

</td></tr>
</table>

This *ku* thanks a friend (student?) who sent Issa bottles of *sake* with eggs in them. The health of mother and father effects their progeny. Could this explain why Issa's last child, conceived only months before he died a few years later, was the first strong enough to survive and pass on his genes?

花の山団子を焼もさくら炭　柳多留 131-29
hananoyama dango o yaku mo sakurazumi　yanagidaru (19-20c)
(blossom-mountin dumpling[acc.] roast even cherry-charcoal)

bloom mountain:
dumplings are toasted with
cherry charcoal

This post-Issa *senryû*, linking blossoms and dumplings rather than contrasting them, chuckles about the cherry cooking its antithesis. Another *senryû* was soon to copycat the same for tea rather than dumplings (花の山茶をせんじるも桜炭　柳多留 166-31 *hananoyama cha o senjiru mo sakurasumi yanagidaru* 20c). Though tea fits charcoal and is classier than dumplings, the wit misses the allusion.

奈良漬を丸でかぢりて花の陰　一茶
narazuke o maru de kajirite hananokage　issa 1804
(nara[daikon] pickle[acc.] whole chewing bloom-shade)

here, i munch	in bloomshade
on a nara pickle, whole:	munching a rusty gold
the bloomshade	pickle of nara

We will return to this pungent pickle, the *narazuke,* again in *Book III*, with eight-fold (double) cherries, a variety identified with the ancient capital of Nara. Here, the point would seem to be the contrast between the crude behavior of chewing on a *daikon* (huge radish) pickle, normally eaten in small slices, with blossom-viewing etiquette. The *ku* is a pleasant contrast to his rather fulsome "Cherries in bloom: / My food the type allowed / by our founder [i.e., Bashô]" (花咲て祖師のゆるしの肴哉　一茶 *hana saite soshi no yurushi no sakana kana* issa (1811)).

塩鱈やしほうれしかる山さくら 鼠弾 三歌仙	人も我も栄（?）螺喰ひや花ざかり　句空
shiodara ya shio ureshigaru yamazakura　sôdan (1775)	*hito mo ware mo tanishi kui ya hanazakari*　kukû (-1714)
(salt-cod!/: salt delighting/delighted mountain-cherry)	(people and me too snails eat!/?/: blossom-acme)
hard salted cod:	me and others
how they love the salt,	are eating mud snails
mountain cherries!	the bloom-peak

Salt was hard to come by in the hills so things like sea-weed, dried sea cucumber or cod were valued as much for their salt as their protein value. I translated "they," for the cherry trees and their namesake, the mountain folk, but there is a tiny possibility it means "we," for the poets may have lost enough sweat on their climb up to appreciative salt more than they would have at home. The second *ku* may mean people out at the height of the blossom-viewing are so intoxicated by the bloom and the booze that they eat food they would normally avoid. The *tanishi* are snails found in the paddies being prepared for planting rice. There may be an allegory here for blossom-viewers wallowing in a park that has experienced enough rain to muddy the ground.

何人のぬくめし石そ櫻花　言水 (付句) 反故集
nanibito no nukumeshi ishi zo sakurabana [tsuke-ku] gonsui 1719
(what-person's warm-food-rock?[emph.] cherry blossoms)

cherry blossoms:	who left that
whose food-warming rock	food-warming stone
is that there?	cherry blossoms

Heated rocks were carried about to keep food warm. *Odd?* We carry ice to keep food cool and ice is not light either. Japanese did not use many hot spices so warmth was particularly important. As described in the next chapter, there were vendors at blossom-viewings, so chances are this is an isolated tree or a grove too small to draw multitudes. One wonders how far rocks might be carried.

一夜さは花には喰もしてみたい　花賛女
hitoyasa wa hana ni wa kuu mo shite mitai　kasanjo 1807-1830
(one nightness-as-for blossoms-with/at eat even do try-want)

for just a night
i'd like to try eating
below the bloom

This *ku* reminds me of how much has *not* been covered in this chapter. *Eating at night.* As a young woman (she died at 23, so we know that), Kasanjo may never have had the opportunity to sit and, as in the daytime, eat below the bloom at night. In poetry or song, "one night" generally had sexual implications, so the *ku* seems a bit risqué, but I think she really has her mind on a feast.

~~~~~~

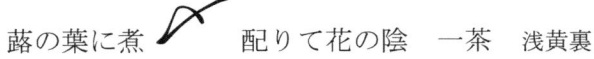

steamed rice wrapped in a butterburr leaf passed out in the bloomshade

＜次版あれば、蒟蒻もアップしたいと思います＞

「花咲て妹がこんにやくはやる也」一茶　文化四
「櫻蒟蒻いかなる人の何を以て〔似て?〕櫻?」杉風
「蒟蒻に月の名はなし山桜」馬泉　三千花

33

Vendors of Cherry-time
花見の商売
hanami no shôbai

種芋や花の盛りに売り歩く 芭蕉
tane-imo ya hana no sakari ni uriariku bashô -1694
(seed-potatoes!/?/: blossoms' acme-during selling-walk)

seed potatoes!
a man is selling them
in cherry time

"seed potatoes!"
they walk about selling them
in the bloompeak

Were the cherries always blooming at the time farmers were ready to plant potatoes, or was it a rare occurrence? I wish Bashô noted whether he saw one salesman or many. Is there any humor in the homophony of potato (*imo*) and younger sister, i.e. sweetheart sold with beauty all around? Probably not. If there is wit, it is more likely in the fact that digging, eating and farting potato was a typical Autumn theme. We see the seeds of the opposite season sold in the flowering of this one.

殿は狩ッ妾餅売る櫻茶屋　嵐雪 -1707
tono wa karitsu mekake mochi uru sakura chaya ransetsu
(master-as-for hunts [his] mistress rice-cake sells cherry teashop)

a cherry tea-room:
while master hunts, mistress
sells her *mochi*

But, this *ku* by one of his disciples is risqué. *Mochi* cakes were a standard blossom-viewing food, but most male readers will imagine a good-looking mistress, here – for, unless otherwise specified, mistresses are presumed to be beautiful – selling her smooth white sweet-rice skin (*mochi-hada*).

藪道や新し茶屋も花の時　龍昇 拍挙千句
yabumichi ya atarashi chaya mo hana no toki ryûsho 1782
(thicket-path!/?/: new tea shop/s also [cherry] blossom time)

a thicket path!
new tea-rooms, too,
mean cherry-time

a thicket path!
new tea-rooms are part
of cherry-time

This *ku* would be well known if Buson wrote it, for anyone who knows Japanese thickets will immediately picture and feel a virtual nostalgia for the path. Issa wrote many instant tea-room *ku*:

茶屋村（の）出現したるさくらかな　一茶
chayamura no shutsugenshitaru sakura kana   issa 1819
(tea-room/shop-town's appearance/advent-does/is cherry!/'tis)

the advent of
new tea-room villages:
cherry blossoms

it's cherry-time,
tea-room towns appear
from nowhere!

茶屋村の一夜に出来し花の山　一茶
chayamura no hitoyo ni dekishi hananoyama   issa (1819)
(tea-shop-town/s' one-night-in made blossom-mountain)

tea-room towns
sprouting up in a night!
mount cherry

What speed! *Mushrooms?* Since they disassemble and move about, I'd say *slime mold!*

担ひ茶屋も花見る人になりにけり　可全
ninaichaya mo hana miru hito ni narinikeri   kazen ()
(shoulder/back-carrry-teashop even blossom-viewing person into became [finality])

a portable tea-shop
turns into a person
blossom-viewing

a tea peddler
turns into a person
viewing blossoms

I was tempted to use the smoother "tea-peddler;" but that would suggest someone selling tea leaves rather than a man or woman shouldering stove, kettle, table and what-not needed for serving tea.

団子など商ひながら花見哉　一茶
dango nado akinainagara hanami kana   issa 1821
(dumplings etc. selling-while blossom-viewing!/?/'tis)

hawking dumplings
and stuff, all the while
blossom-viewing

Our last tea vender either took a break or sold out and switched to a blossom-viewing mode. In this *ku*, the vender does both at once. The antithesis between blossom and dumpling has been overcome.

一銭の茶も江戸ぶりや花の陰　一茶
issen no cha mo edoburi ya hananokage   issa 1824
(one-penny-tea even/also edô-manner!/: blossoms'-shade)

bloomshade:
one penny of tea
is very edo!

one-cent tea
how very edo this
bloomshade

Edo, a city of bachelors, pioneered the art we now denigrate as fast-food though *speed* is but half of the equation. The other half is selling food in individual *portions*. In Edo, watermelon was sold on the street *by the slice*, whereas, even today (when individualism is alternatively vaunted and bemoaned in Japan), it is usually sold whole or in family-size pieces (when I suggested smaller pieces for single people, Japanese grocers told me that only individualistic Americans would even think of it!).

素湯売も久しくなるや花の山　一茶
sayu-uri mo hisashiku naru ya hananoyama　issa 1805
(plain-hotwater-vendors also [it's been a] while!/: blossom-mountain)

hot-water venders,
it's been a while for you, too!
cherry mountain

hot-water men,
how long has it been?
cherry mountain

Hanami is a totality. Not only the blossoms but the rarely encountered vendor warms the poet's heart. Japanese has a special word for "hot-water" (*sayu*), but I doubt it improved the taste!

水茶屋の人や数へん初櫻　鶴介 安永六
mizujaya no hito ya kazoen hatsuzakura　tsurusuke 1777
([cold]water tea-shops' people!/: count-let's first-cherry[blossoms])

let's count
the people in cold tea-shops
first-blossoms

"Mizu=Water" means "cold," for warm water had a different name. Tea was chilled but iceless. Some may have been roasted barley water; it is drunken warm in Korea and chilled in West Japan. Most "cold" tea-shops also served it hot and had girls snag passing men. I do not get the point of the *ku*.

花の山小便に似た茶もうれる　柳多留 80-29
hananoyama shôben ni nita cha mo ureru　yanagidaru 19c
(blossom-mountain piss-to resemble tea even sells)

mount cherry:
they even buy tea that
tastes like pee

mount cherry:
even tea like piss
sells just fine

mount cherry:
they even buy tea that
looks like pee

Who knows if the piss refers to the color or the taste! I have also read that *sake* venders sometimes watered down their product for drunken customers. Because the cherry bash involved strangers selling to strangers, irresponsible behavior was inevitable. But even awful tea was welcome. In parts of the country, people were so poor they had no tea for themselves, much less any to sell: *"Water in the country / where we meet up with no tea / also is* sakura*,"* i.e., part of the experience (茶にあはぬ田舎の水も桜かな　亀洞 *cha ni awanu inaka no mizu mo sakura kana*　kidô (fl. 1690)) as one *ku* puts it.

茶酒売る人や櫻に銭まうけ　在貫 年尾
cha sake uru hito ya sakura ni zeni môke　zaikan 1772-80
(tea *sake* sells person!/?/: cherry-at/from [small] coins earning)

those who sell
tea and *sake*, make money
off the cherries

Oh, the scandal of it! But, as Issa points out in many *ku,* so did the temples.

花は根に出茶屋幾度なま欠　雅計 功用群鑑
hana wa ne ni dejaya ikutabi nama-akubi gakei (1681)
(blossom-as-for root-to tea-vendor how many times fresh yawn)

when petals drop

a tea vendor
at the foot of the tree,
yawns & yawns

A Japanese annotator thinks the original plays on an old *waka*: *"Blossoms to their roots / birds to their old nests / all return: / But what man knows / where [his] spring goes?"* (花は根に鳥は古巣に帰るなり春のとまりをしる人ぞなき ＝ 崇徳院御製 千載集 *hana wa ne ni, tori wa furusu ni kaerunari haru no tomari o shiru hito zo naki* senzaishû 1188); I think it may be enough to cite the saying about blossoms returning to their roots – common trope because blossom=woman and roots=sleep (the homophone *ne*). Regardless, we imagine some petals slowly drifting down as the blossom-viewing starts going downhill while our exhausted vendor, not drinking enough of his own goods, fights off sleep.

のどけさや出茶屋の烟土手の人　子規
nodokesa ya dechaya no kemuri dote no hito shiki 1896
(tranquility! out-tea-shop's/s' smoke embankment's person/people)

what tranquility!
smoke from the tea vendors
people on the levee

Tea venders mean *cherry time*, whether stated or not. Unlike the loud streets and louder bridges, embankment paths are often quiet even though heavily traveled. Nothing shows the calm – one of the standard weathers for this season – so beautifully as smoke.

茶碗出ス柄杓は長し花の下　艶士 字の筆
chawan dasu hishaku wa nagashi hananoshita enshi ()
(tea-cup/bowls put-out ladle/palette?-as-for long bloom-below)

bowls held out　　　　　　　　　　　under the bloom
the ladle is long indeed　　　　　the cup server handle
under the bloom　　　　　　　　　　is long indeed

Because I happen to know that horse stale was caught by a long-handled ladle (see *Topsy-turvy 1585*): they had to protect the wooden floors in the stables – this reminds me of the *senryû* on tea like piss though I doubt that was the poet's intent. The second reading is a guess: grammar favors a "ladle" that handed out cups/bowls, but no such *hishaku* is found in my dictionary. As such, it would be a vendor's.

棒突も餅をうりけり山桜　一茶
bôtsuki mo mochi o urikeri yamazakura issa (1804)
(staff-pokers too/even rice-cake[acc.] sell[emph] mountain-cherry)

mountain cherry
even gendarmes sell
sweet-rice-cakes

Issa has a short preface (月船と登東叡山) about climbing East Hie-zan with his friend/student Gessen, literally, Moonboat. How poetic to climb a mountain with the moon; but, if the moon is not real, neither is the mountain: this, again, is the Ueno cherry-park in Edo.

さびしき故其花をうるや櫻飴　梅雫 太夫櫻
sabishiki yue sono hana o uru ya sakura-ame　baida 1680
(lonely because that blossom[acc] sell?/:cherry[blossom?]candy)

> selling her blossom
> out of sheer loneliness?
> *sakura* candy

My dictionary says cherry candy (sakura-ame) was red, round, hollow in the center and sold in Osaka. Considering the rarity of the *fruit* cherry, this is puzzling and I cannot help wondering whether the lack of a word for "pink" may explain the "red" and, given the allusion to the seller's body, whether the "round" might not be ring-like and the hollowness a whole, *i.e.*, whether we might not have a life-saver here. (evidently not). Black blues have a Candy-man. Is this the pork? Or, is cherry candy merely allegory for a sweet young thing? If it is, that, too, would be rare, for Japanese generally do not associate sweetness or sweet food with love and loveliness as English-speakers do.

一軒は花のしら雲男茶屋　寒露
ikken wa hana no shiragumo otokojaya　kanro 増補をた巻?
(one house-as-for blossoms' cloud man=homosexual=tea-shop)

> one shop boasts
> white blossom clouds
> a gay tea-shop

Despite the erotic undertone, this is mild, even lyrical. Compare it to a *ku* titled *"Red Bangs"* (for women working in the water-trades, *i.e.* entertainment, often dyed their hair): *"You enter hugging /and light your lamp at these two / blooming tea shops"* (赤前垂・抱き込め火とほす花の二軒茶屋　知里　宝暦 11 *akamaedare // dakikome hi tobosu hana no ni ken chaya*　chiri 1647-1716). I am not sure whether anyone bothers to drink tea at such a place, which reminds us of the modern "love-hotel." Another strange *ku* is titled "Bright tea shops not making the usual profit at Ueno" and seems to read *"In the bloomshade / we can't drink advertisements: / portable tea-shops* (上野花見に例常もうけもなくかしこの出茶屋にて・花の陰ちらしはのまし荷ひ茶屋　近之　洗濯物 *ueno hanami ni reijô môke mo naku kashiko no dechaya nite // hananokage chirashi ha nomashi ninaichaya*　kinsuke (1666)). Is the shop seeking long-term publicity?

絹売の色尋とるや花ざかり　紫貞女
kinu-uri no irotazune toru ya hanazakari　shiteijo -1751
(silk-sellers' color[styles]-asking pass!/?/: blossom-acme)

it's full bloom there go some silk merchant trend-spotters	design spies from silk sellers pass by the bloom-peak

We tend to feel that people making a business of sniffing out fads is a modern phenomenon. In Japan, it goes back centuries. If you recall, there was an earlier *ku* about blossom-viewing setting the fashion for the year. This was noticed by the pros.

花の山土鉢売も登りけり　沾圃
hananoyama dôbachi uri mo noborikeri senpo -1730
(blossom-mountain earthen pot vendors also climb-up[emph.])

<blockquote>
cherry mountain
even clay pot vendors
have climbed up
</blockquote>

At first, I thought the "climb" extending the metaphorical mountain (this would be a blossom-viewing park) was the point of the wit, for a real mountain would not be scaled by a vendor with cheap and heavy goods. But, who knows? There was a practice of throwing light pots off real mountains near cities which we will discuss later if we have not already.

花咲ばつげむというや松葉うり　傘下
hana sakaba tsugemu to iu ya matsuba-uri sanka c1700
(blossoms blooming-when connect-not? says!/?/: needle-seller)

<blockquote>
"the cherries bloom   sew 'em up one and all
sew them up before they fall!" before the cherry blossoms fall
a pine-needle man   says the needle vendor
</blockquote>

Needles (*hari*) in Japanese were sometimes called "pine-leaves" (*matsuba*). English makes the wit a bit too obvious because the pine leaf is already called a needle! What we have here is a clever vendor taking advantage of poetical conceit (probably found in popular song as well as classic poetry) about sewing petals back on blossoms and blossoms back on boughs. Or, we have a poet fantasizing about what a needle vendor should say. Because Japanese pine needles are generally twin, they also stand for fidelity/mates, so I suppose the real needles could make propitious gifts.

34

Blossom Guards
花守
hana-mori

花守やむかしは烏帽子今は棒　嘯山 葎亭句集
hanamori ya mukashi wa eboshi ima wa bô shôzan (-1801)
(blossom-guards!/: olden-times-as-for eboshi[headgear] now-as-for staff)

blossom guards
they used to wear top-hats
now it's cudgels!

Like the vendors, blossom guards were once an integral part of the *hanami* experience. I am still not sure exactly who they were and what they did. Up in the mountains, some were gillies, protectors of nature for the Lord's hunts. Others may have found and kept watch on trees for the big-shots who claimed them before a blossom-viewing and kept them reserved for more than one day, and finally others may have been security guards hired by the temple or a city to keep order, i.e. deputized police, though these were usually called *bôtsuki,* or "staff-pokers" (see below). The original hat is a "crow-hat," short for "crow-barnacle-hat," for these hats were shaped like barnacles yet black in color like crows. They were only worn by the elite or, in the case of ancient blossom guards, those doing the elites' bidding. This *ku* reflects the popularization of Japanese culture, and the change from an elegant classical society to the boisterous world of the Tokugawa era (1603-1867).

花守となりて棒つく坊主哉　蘭更 三籟
hanamori to narite bôtsuku bôzu kana rankô (-1799)
(blossom-guard, becoming/became stick/cudgel-poke/ing-monk!/'tis)

becoming a blossom-guard the monk is now a stick-poke	loh, a monk with a billy club! he became a blossom guard

Once, there were whole mountains of fighting monks with cudgels, maintaining their independence as ferociously the Swiss, attacking each other at times and even hiring out as mercenaries, before they were utterly obliterated by the unifying Shôguns just prior to the start of the Tokugawa. When Rankô wrote this *ku* hundreds of years later, the remaining monks were uniformly pacifistic. There was no *billy club* but a "stick," called *bô* (a word martial art enthusiasts in Usania know), that alliterates nicely with *bôzu,* or monk. Generally, a stick-poke (*bôtsuki*) was a crossroads or temple guard. Real city cops carried *jûtei,* thin iron clubs with hooks to catch sword blades (and break them when twisted) Another *ku* even harder to translate: *"A mountain monk / becomes a blossom guard / and looks the part."* Or *"A mountain monk / becomes a blossom guard / an avid one."* (山僧や花守になり見てに成　申候　伊達衣 *yama sô ya hanamori ni nari mite ni nari* shinkô 1699)

棒突が腮でをしゆる桜哉　一茶
bôtsuki ga ago de oshiyuru sakura kana　issa -1827
(stick/staff-poke[the] chin-with teach/es cherry[blossoms]!/'tis)

a poke-stick
points 'em out with his chin
cherry trees

the poke-stick
chin-points a party
blossom-viewing

One might expect the stick to point the way. This poke-stick may well have been a regular cop on duty rather than a blossom guard. It is hard to say what he points at. A tree? A certain party? And, why the preface, explaining that it is 3-3, doll day (御所三月三日)?

花もりや人の嵐は昼ばかり　千代
hanamori ya hito no arashi wa hiru bakari　chiyo -1775
(blossom-guard/s: people-gale-as-for daytime only)

blossom-guards:
the storm of humanity
comes by day!

blossom-guards:
for human tempests come
by day alone

The storm is the bad guy (ch.48) who would rape the blossoms –in the old sense of carrying off or *ravishing* – and, sometimes, rip-off whole branches, as men did. The stereotypical onslaught took place at night. With blossom-viewing, however, crowds gathered in the daytime, hence, that is when the guards were active. I must confess to confusion regarding the *status* of the guards. A 1645 *ku* declares: *"Not a man / is not humble before / a blossom guard"* (花守にがを折詫ぬ人もなし 一正毛吹草 *hanamori ni ga o ori-wabinu hito mo nashi*　issei) The original language is "self-break-not man even not" and, if I read it correctly, implies that men felt guilt about the practice of breaking off sprays of bud and/or bloom and this made them obedient to the blossom guards: *"All men / break-off breaking before / a blossom-guard."* A little over a hundred years later, a poem of Buson's suggests the blossom-guards no longer commanded quite so much respect:

花守の身は弓矢なきかゝし哉　蕪村
hanamori no mi wa yumiya-naki kakashi kana　buson -1783
(blossom-guard's body/situation-as-for bow-arrow-not scarecrow!/'tis)

a blossom-guard
is a scarecrow without
his bow and arrow

Japanese scarecrows – with nothing about "crows" in the name – were generally equipped with a bow and arrow. But, Buson's contemporary, Yayû, tells us that some of the guards still made good scare*men*:

花守が下戸で折らせぬ櫻かな　也有
hanamori ga geko de orasenu sakura kana　yayû -1783
(blossom-guard-the teetotler-because break-let-not cherry!/'tis)

the blossom guard
stuck to tea, so i left
this branch as is

the blossom-guard being a teetotaler, i couldn't break off a spray	the blossom guard was sober, so i leave you this cherry spray

a would-be blossom-thief's lament

a teetotaler
blossom guard so i
let them go

"*Because the guard / was sober breaking one off / was not allowed.*" The implication is that drunken blossom-guards might overlook the poet's taking a little spray back home for his study or a gift. I imagine Yayû's *ku* on a painting of a branch one could not take home or written at a blossom-viewing, hung from a branch and left for the guard to read and keep!

花守や花の木陰にあちら向　荷卒 類題 1774
hanamori ya hana no kokage ni achiramuki kasotsu 1774
(blossom-guard/s blossoms' tree-shade-in overthere-facing)

a blossom guard in the bloomshade, looking the other way	blossom-guards in their blossom shades looking elsewhere

the blossom guard
in the bloomshade, views
the other party

I cannot tell if the poet is thinking, *A fine guard that is, he doesn't even notice me!* or *Hey, i wonder what that blossom guard is watching over there?* or, *Is the poor blossom guard, keeping his eyes peeled for would be space-stealers and blossom-thieves, to busy to view the bloom he sits under?* Or, *Is our party of poets that much more boring than the* party *next door, excuse me, next* tree?

花守は花あるうちを気詰哉　盲探 蘆別船
hanamori ya hana aru uchi o kizume kana môtan 1694
(blossom-guard:/! blossoms are while[obj.] feelings-cramped!/'tis)

cherry-time anamoly

blossom-guards: all tensed up so long as there are blossoms	cherry blossoms bring *them* no catharsis: blossom guards!

I love this poet's *haigô* (*haikai nom de plume*) "groping," literally: *blind-search*. As we have seen, cherry-time was identified with letting it all come out, blowing off one's steam. Not so for the poor guards. I hope they gather and drink themselves under the table *after* the blossoms fall!

今日も亦花に酔たる花の番　魚道 宝暦十一
kyo mo mata hana ni yoitaru hana no ban gyodô 1761
(today too again blossoms-by drunk blossoms' guard)

today once again the blossom-guards are drunk on the blossoms	guarding blossoms, today, once again drunk on the bloom!

The words "*hana-no-ban* = blossom's turn/duty/guard" rather than the official *hanamori* = blossom-guard" suggest that the poet himself may be the guard.

花守は寝ころんだとき花見哉　斗孝　雁風呂
hanamori wa nekoronda toki hanami kana　tokô 1794
(blossom-guard-as-for sleep-tumblingabout time blossom-viewing!/'tis)

blossom guards
taking naps is their time
to view blossoms

This is a superb observation, but something tells me it might be considered a *senryû* today.

よき犬や此植木屋の花守り　揚水　雑談　　　　　花守と成る古雛や棚のすみ　哲亜
yoki inu ya kono uegiya no hanamori yosui (?)　　*hanamori to naru furuhina ya tana no sumi* tetsua (-1798)
(fine dog!/: this nurseryman's blossom-guard)　　(blossom-guard as become old-doll!/:shelf's nook)

what a fine dog!　　　　　　　　　that old doll
this nurseryman has *his*　　　　in the corner of the shelf:
blossom-guard　　　　　　　　　　my blossom-guard!

The first *ku* had a preface "Checking on blossoms" 尋花. I guess the poet visited a pro who knew that aside from pooping and peeing where we would sit, dogs make far better guards than men. They can keep their ears *semper paratus* even in their sleep. Imagine a sprig of blooming cherry in a vase, and the idea of doll-as-blossom-guard is strangely heart-warming. *So is this:*

花守や白きかしらをつき合せ　去来
hanamori ya shiroki kashira o tsuki-awase kyorai -1704
(blossom-guards: white heads[acc.] thrust-out-meeting)

blossom guards
putting together
their white heads

Feeling the guards' friendship, I put this *ku* into the "meeting people under the bloom" chapter, but must at least mention it here, too, for it is the most famous blossom-guard *ku* of all, if for no other reason than that Bashô praised it as an example of *sabi,* one of those words that does not English well. (Ueda's definition starts: "Lonely beauty cherished in the Bashô school of *haikai*. Elements of sadness, old age, resignation, tranquility, and even happiness can also be found in it . . ." (1992)) Another *ku* jokes *"The whiskers upshot: a face that could be chosen / for a blossom guard"* (花守にゑらるゝ顔や髭のはて 落霞 蕉尾琴 *hanamori ni eraruru kao ya hige no hate* rakka (1701)); but I feel the years of self-discipline that once went into growing up Japanese and the strength of character of these elders.

年々や花守る宿の薪一駄　士朗
toshidoshi ya hanamoru yado no maki hito-da? shirô -1812
(year-year!/: blossom-guard-inn's firewood one-stack)

every year in front　　　　　　　　year after year
of the blossom-guard house　　　by the bloomguard's hut
the same firewood　　　　　　　　firewood, one bale

One *da,* of firewood is the load of a working horse or nag, *daba*. Perhaps the blossom guard always started cherry time with just one such load left because he timed the winter perfectly. Perhaps it was a tax he gathered from the cherries he guarded, part of his salary, or a present. Regardless, I feel the firewood would *seem* the exact same firewood, year after year! I recall such cottages on a Japanese mountain near Tokyo where I attended a bluegrass festival every year (I was most impressed to see that the cheap throw-away plastic bags were all washed in the stream and hung up to dry on clotheslines!). If Bashô wrote the *ku,* it would be famous. It is, I think, *that* good.

見しられて花守招く木陰哉　良水 年尾
mishirarete hanamori maneku kokage kana ryôsui (1772-80)
(see-known, blossom-guards invite bloomshade!/'tis))

       i'm known!   bloomshade
the blossom guards call me   a blossom guard i know
          into the shade   invites me in

The minimal grammar also allows the poet to recognize a guard, but I'll bet it was the other way around.

この頃の歌はきかぬか櫻守り 櫻角 蘆分船
konogoro no uta wa kikanu ka sakuramori ôkaku 1694
(this/these time/days' song/s-as-for hear-not? cherry-guard)

  cherry guards   cherry guards   cherry guards
don't you ever hear   don't you have anything   why do we only hear
  a new song?   popular to sing   old songs?

Does the conservatism of the blossom guards, then, extend to their musical taste?

花守や夜は汝が山桜（八重桜） 一茶 文化八/政三
hanamori ya yoru wa nanji ga yama[yae]zakura issa 1811/20
(blossom-guard/s!/: night-as-for your mountain'[eight-fold]cherry)

   blossom guards   blossom guards
at night your very own   at night, you rule the hills
  mountain cherries   of wild cherry
                blossom guards
      at night, eight-fold cherries
         you talk up a storm
   blossom guards   blossom guards
night is when your days   night is when you let
  really blossom   your petals fly

Because "mountain cherries" and not "blossom-mountain" are referred to in the old version of the *ku*, this may be a genuine mountain off-limits to campers. The extremely formal, archaic "you/r" = *nanji* is a mystery to me. The last three translations are my reading of a later version mentioning the *yaezakura*, a double-petal (or quadruple, sextuple, octuple . . .) cherry with profuse bloom, most commonly used idiomatically for many types of profusion. Here, it means what we might call *talking up a storm*. Apparently, the guards get together and shoot the breeze after the viewers leave. Or, am I wrong? Could it mean they are plentiful and *all eyes,* if it were, lest people creep in to reserve spaces for blossom-viewing the next day. *I do not know.*

a Single Tree
壱本桜
ippon-zakura

世に一木さかは都や花のかけ　兼載 大発句帳
yo ni hitoki sakaba miyako ya hananokage　kensai -1510
(world-in one-tree bloom-when capital!/: blossoms' shade)

one tree blooms
and the world's capitol?
this bloomshade

one tree blooms
in the world and its shade
is our capitol

one tree blooms
and the world's a cherry
blossom palace

If one robin makes the spring, one tree can set the stage. It cannot, however, make the quintessential Japanese *hanami*, for, as already explained, that requires a *grove*. One-tree blossom-viewing was found in China, Korea or anywhere people went on picnics. Tiny in scope, it is actually the more cosmopolitan practice, though this (my thought) is hardly what was on the mind of the poet! "Capital" as a synonym for beauty and high culture doesn't work well in English, so I used "palace" in one reading (necessitating a change in the way world was used, too) and replaced the "a" with an "o," for it looks grander, more **O***pulent* – who says (other than Webster, a Usanian, himself) that Washington DC has a right to monopolize "capitol" with an "o;" it is bad enough we take the name of the continent for our own!

千里をも一木に見るや春の花　昌叱 大発句帳
senri o mo hitoki ni miru ya haru no hana　shôshitsu (-1603)
(thousand leagues/miles even one-tree-as see!/?/: spring's blossom/s)

a thousand miles
seen in a single tree!
spring blossoms

Can you feel the expansive mindset of these old poets? There is a pun here playing on a saying where a thousand leagues/miles (whatever) begin with a single league/mile (*hito-ri* vs *hito-ki*, or "one tree"). What makes the *ku* so good is the fact that it is not just a Tennysonian moment where the *little flower – but if I could understand* . . . encompasses the infinity of space, but one embedded in time. Looking upon a blossoming cherry, we can chart that point in the time and place of the cherry-blossom front and, further, the entire seasonal parade.

one tree

一本の日数をためす櫻かな 吟江 行雲日記
ippon no hikazu o tamesu sakura kana   ginkô 1778
(one-pole[tree]'s day-number[acc] test/try cherry!/'tis)

counting the days
one tree stays in bloom:
it's cherry time!

One can walk a mountain and find cherry trees in various stages of bloom in a single day. Sticking with one tree takes time. We are talking about an experiment that will take at least a week. Such a simple but luxurious idea! My imagination immediately thinks of putting a tree within a screened-in patio, *counting the petals* that fall year by year and comparing their number and weight to that of the leaves it loses in the fall. The original may only mean that Ginkô stayed home with his garden cherry.

一木さく花や守る人初桜 宗養 大発句帳
hitoki saku hana ya moru hito hatsuzakura   sôyô -1563
(one-tree blooms blossoms !/?/& guard[or witness] person / first-cherry)

<table>
<tr><td align="center">one tree blooms
a blossom it's guarded
my first cherry</td><td></td><td align="center">first blossoms
someone guards the bloom
of one cherry?</td></tr>
<tr><td></td><td align="center">one tree blooms
with it's blossom guard
first sakura</td><td></td></tr>
<tr><td align="center">one tree blooms
first blossoms for cherry
and the witness</td><td></td><td align="center">one tree blooms
as a first and as a cherry
it has a guard</td></tr>
<tr><td></td><td align="center">one tree blooms
the blossoms and their keeper
first-flowering</td><td></td></tr>
</table>

The large number of readings reflect my puzzlement with the original which is, grammatically speaking, so loosely tied it seems to be in pieces as per the first and last readings. Could this be an allegory for the coming of age of a girl at the home of her protector who will become her husband?

はな一木遠近ひとのせき路かな 紹巴 大発句帳
hana hitoki ochikochibito no sekiji kana   jôha 1523-1602
(blossoms one-tree far-near[or, present/future] people's customs -road!/'tis)

<table>
<tr><td align="center">one blooming tree
a border road for people
present and future</td><td align="center">one tree in flower
along the road to the barrier
people here and there</td><td align="center">one cherry tree
the checkpoint for travelers
near and far</td></tr>
</table>

trans. earl miner

Modern English has no equivalent for *sekiji*, "customs roads" that lead to and fro the many checkpoints between fiefdoms. My second reading of this fine *ku* makes the tree itself a checkpoint, for, objectively speaking, both are crowded places in the middle of nowhere. Miner's straight melody of a translation (*Japanese Linked Poetry*) allows me freedom to sing harmony. Another blossoms+checkpoint *ku*: "*Fuji is snowy: / a clean view from the blossom / barrier road*" (富士は雪清見は花の關路哉　宗因 *fuji wa yuki kiyomi wa hana no sekiji kana*   sôin (1604-82)). I don't get it, but still imagine many people in beautiful dress waiting their turn at a location with a panoramic view.

一本をくるり／＼と花見哉　浪花
ippon o kururikururi to hanami kana   rôka -1703
(one-pole=tree[acc]circling-circling-as/with blossom-viewing!)

circling 'round
and 'round a single tree
blossom-viewing!

If someone follows the shade, they might move from one side to the other of the tree, but circling around a tree is rather extraordinary. I suppose it *could* be a bottle of *sake* doing the moving, for the same counter (*~hon/~bon/~pon*) is used for trees and bottles. The poem was written about the same time as Bashô's famous *ku* about circling a pond while moon-viewing. I wish I knew which came first.

千も萬もいらし一木の花盛　忠利 洗濯もの
sen mo man mo iraji hitoki no hanazakari   tadatoshi 1666
(thousands even ten-thousands even need-not one-tree's blossom-acme)

no need for   a thousand trees
a thousand: this one tree   a million: who needs more than
in full bloom!   one in full bloom

The wonderful word *sakari,* full-bloom with a hint of sexual ripeness favors the original.

咲満て一木の花のくもり哉　十境 花七日
sakimichite hitoki no hana no kumori kana   jûkyô 1777
(bloom-overflowing one-tree's blossoms' overcast/haze!/?/'tis)

profuse bloom!   profuse bloom!
call it one tree-worth   one tree brings a spell
of cloudiness   of blossom haze

The "cloudiness" – actually the haze that sometimes accompanies the cherry blossom "front" – rather than the usual blossom "cloud" is fresh hyperbole.

一本は（の＝文政九）桜もちけり娑婆（の）役　一茶
ippon wa [no] sakura mochikeri shaba [no]) yaku   issa (1809[26])
(one-pole=tree-as-for cherry <s>bring-return</s> have[+emph.] sahâ role)

<s>i carry it home!</s>
<s>one cherry tree, *shaba*</s>
<s>my very own</s>

<s>this one tree,</s>   <s>one cherry tree:</s>
<s>i bring home for a prop</s>   <s>brought home with me</s>
<s>my own *shaba*</s>   <s>her role is sahâ!</s>

<s>a world of woe</s>
<s>brought home with me!</s>
<s>one cherry tree</s>

i have one tree   i have my own,
a cherry to play the role   a cherry, one tree-worth
of *sahâ* for me   of fallen world

Ten years ago, I misread *mochikeri* as *mochikaeri,* and *just* caught it, now, in the final proofing! If Issa conveys the drunken bash in exceptional detail, he is also the deepest poet of single cherry trees. We saw one as a stick of cloud in *Bk I*. Another simply observes: *"One cherry tree / in a wind-swept place / blooms away"* (風所の一本桜咲にけり *kazadoko no ippon-zakura sakinikeri* issa 1809). By using Buddhism to dramatize his seedling, Issa made his cherry more than just a cherry.

花一ッ里のきづ也花盛り 一茶 文政六
hana hitotsu sato no kizu nari hanazakari issa 1823
(blossom[ing tree] one hometown/countryside's scar becomes bloom-acme)

in full bloom one cherry tree scars my home-town	rampant bloom! my cherry tree a blemish on the countryside

Sato, usually translated "hometown," is the place one comes from or a rural locality. I felt tempted to change it to "farm-village," for farmers, jealous of their productive land and sunlight, tend to be the least tree-friendly people in the world, but the best I could do was "countryside." I vaguely recall a European botanist who despaired of finding weeds in the fully farmed countryside of Japan.

春の野のけしきそ無為の初桜 浦京 新虚くり
haru no no no keshiki zo mui no hatsuzakura hôkyô 1777
(spring's fields' appearance/sight[+emph.] not-useful's first-cherry)

the spring field now there's a sight: useless first-blossoms	the spring field pretty as a picture, for what *hatsuzakura*

The *mui* (useless) here may echo Zhuangzi, but suffice it, here, to note Issa's *ku* had a predecessor.

一本に野なる草木や花のいろ 紹巴
ippon ni no naru kusaki ya hana no iro jôha 1523-1602
(one-pole=tree-in field becomes/is grass=plants-trees: blossoms' color/eros)

with just one tree all the plants in the field blossom-charged	one tree blooms and a whole field of plants is tickled pink

The original says all the plants are "blossom color," but color is too concrete in English. Reading this old *ku* with Issa's, we wonder: *Did the farmers feared temptation?* Or, am I being absurd about this?

畠中にのさばり立る桜哉　一茶 遺稿
hatanaka ni nosabaritatsuru sakura kana issa -1827
(fields/plots-in brazenly-stand [flowering]cherry!/'tis)

in mid-plot,
it stands brazenly:
the cherry tree

The first part of the compound verb had to become an adverb, "brazenly" in English. The verb *nosabaru* means "have everything one's way," "throw one's weight around" and other such things.

Elsewhere, Issa used it to describe the presence of a big toad! In this *ku,* one of a small (undated) number found after Issa's death, I think *nosabaru* means that this noble beauty is, to use recent slang, "in the face of" the farming community. Think of it as *a poet's last laugh* or a *cherry tree swan song!*

一本も山路のはく木家櫻 周桂 大発句帳
ippon mo yamaji no haku ki iezakura   shûkei (-1544)
(one-tree even mountain-path's sweep tree house-cherry)

一本もやまちのいくきいゑさくら 周桂 同
ippon mo yamaji no ikuki iezakura   shûkei (-1544)
(one-tree even mountain-path's go-come hse-cherry)

      i could use one
to lodge on a mountain path
       the house cherry

      one of them up
and down the mountain path
      my house cherry

The same *ku,* allegedly from the same source, one in Shiki's *Categorical* (分類別) and the second in a more recent reproduction (古典文庫). Both are hard to read. I first read them to mean:

just one cherry
by my hut and a mountain path
beats to and fro

let one of them
sweep the mountain path
a house cherry

just one cherry
and the hilly trail to my hut
boasts traffic

To tell the truth, I would not bet on any of my five readings. The different transcriptions suggest that even Japanese experts were equally befuddled. This single house-cherry is a good example of an old *ku* that must be worked and reworked like a puzzle, though it may never be solved beyond doubt. Some of us find *joy* in that, others find it not only worthless, but frustrating to no end.

おもひやれとはゝ一木の春のはな 宗祇
omoiyare towaba hitoki no haru no hana sôgi (1420-1502)
(thoughts-send/sympathize! inquire-if/when, one-tree's spring-blossoms)

   if asked how
to lose the blues: one tree
   of spring bloom

   what is caring?
suffice it to see one tree
   of spring bloom

I bet on my first reading, where *omoiyare* takes the classic meaning of sending off, or excorcizing unsatisfied longing and other troubling thought. Blossoms might be played against Tabito's advice to drink away one's blues in the *Manyoshû.* The second reading follows a respondent's. At first, I waffled with a paraverse: *"All for one / one for all, spring blooms / in this tree."*

出かけには一樹にきそふ花見哉 太祇
dekake ni wa hitoki ni kisou hanami kana   taigi (-1772)
(departure-at-as-for one-tree-for compete/dress-up blossom-viewing!/'tis)

   from the get-go
we compete for one tree
   blossom-viewing

   setting out for
the *hanami* all hearts
   seek one tree

At first, I *wanted* this: "I'm going out / dressed up for one tree. / Yes, a *hanami!*" but the suffix on the "departure" does not fully warrant such a reading. Taigi's *ku* is puzzling. Did each blossom-viewing site have its prize tree, or does the *ku* allude to a specific location? Or, am I thinking too small? Could we have an *ideal tree,* equivalent to the eternal feminine, the ideal beauty sought in the West?

36
Dying Under the Bloom
花死
hana-jini

骸骨の上を粧ふて花見かな 鬼貫
gaikotsu no ue o yosôte hanami kana   onitsura
(skeleton/s-on-top-of costumed blossom-viewing!/?/'tis)

my skeleton
plumped in pretty silk
views blossoms

blossom-viewing
costumes without belie
the bones within

bones, old bones
dressed up like the trees
blossom-viewing

B. H. Chamberlain: *"Oh! flower-gazers, who have decked / The surface of their skeletons!"* Miyamori Asataro, until Blyth the leading haiku translator, wrote, *"Their skeletons / Wrapt in richest silks, / The people are viewing cherry bloom,"* and snorted: "This verse, although very famous, seems to be of little value." The editor of a book of famous *ku* (名句辞典), is harder yet on Onitsura, claiming the *ku* is simply an application of the Buddhist platitude of men as meat (flesh) and skin on bones where all color (beauty=eros) is an illusion to the beautiful people he saw blossom-viewing. "Not only is this shallow rationalizing (*rikutsuppoi*) but the example used is banal (*chinpu*)." *Bullshit.* The ku *deserves* its fame. The blossom-viewing experience makes us *feel our mortality*, even more strongly than we do in the fall, facing colored leaves; and who says Onitsura did not experience what he wrote and suddenly see *skeletons in drag* viewing cherry blossoms? We should not forget, too, that *many cherry trees have no leaves when they bloom*, so we view what are, literally, *skeletons bedecked*. Note that the original is subtle, as may be surmised from the word-by-word rendition and further translations in the front of this book. With scores of previous translations, I felt free to play.

花に行心も秋の寝覚哉 宗因
hana ni yuku kokoro mo aki no nesame kana   sôin 1604-1682
(blossom-to going heart/mind/feeling too autumn's sleep-waking tis)

going to view
the blossoms feels like
waking in the fall

Waking up in the fall. The indolent body of summertime – when the living is easy (if hot) – suddenly comes to its senses. *Bracing.* The air is dry and the barometer high. *Refreshing.* Yet, in the morning chill, we also feel the cold to come and know that life, in the long run, runs down.

来年はなきものゝやうに桜哉　一茶
rainen wa nakimono no yô ni sakura kana issa (1804)
(next year-as-for not-thing-like-as cherry[tree/s/blossoms]!/?/'tis)

the cherry trees　　　　　　　　　　　　　as if this year
blooming like this year　　　　　　were their last one, behold
is their last　　　　　　　　　　　　　　those cherries

the whole world
has no tomorrow now
cherries bloom

Are we talking about the cherry trees (my first guess) or the viewers? Young Issa's *ku* is banal but it makes us consider the paradox of living as if there is no tomorrow: it both respects and disrespects life. Danish poet-mathematician Piet Hein put it like this, *"We ought to live each day as though / it is our last one, here below, / but if I did, alas, i know / it would have killed me long ago!"* (a grook, from memory). We react to blossoms in a bipolar way. Everything is more precious, yet all can be given up. Issa tries to express it with the next *ku* we saw in the foreword to this *Book II*.

斯う活ているも不思儀ぞ花の陰　一茶
kô ikite-iru mo fushigi zo hananokage issa (1810)
(this[way] living-am-even strange/wondrous! blossom-shade)

how strange　　　　　　　　　　　　　　　it's a miracle
to be alive like this!　　　　　　　　to be alive and here!
blossom-viewing　　　　　　　　　　　　the bloomshade

how strange it is
to be alive, alive like this!
under the blossoms

What more can be said about what we feel in the bloomshade? As a bridge to the next *ku*, Pascal's *pensée* #213: *"Between us and heaven or hell there is only life, which is the frailest thing in the world"* (trans. William Finlayson Trotter).

世 [の] 中は地獄の上の花見哉　一茶
yononaka wa jigoku no ue no hanami kana issa
(world-among-as-for hell-above's-blossom-viewing!/'tis 1812)

what is life?　　　　　　　　　　　　　the whole world
it's blossom-viewing　　　　　　　is out blossom-viewing
on top of hell　　　　　　　　　　　　on the roof of hell

in this world
we sit on the roof of hell
gazing at flowers

Popular Buddhism in Japan had a hell, or rather, hells, every bit as frightening as that/those of Christianity. The idea that one could fall through at any time, that darkness was but one inch away (*issun-saki-no yami*)[1] was as understandable to these Buddhists as to the Calvinists in New England. The last translation is borrowed from R. Hass's *The Essential Haiku* with one change: *walk → sit* (As the reader doubtless realizes by now, blossom viewings were, for the most part, *sitting,* not walking, affairs!). Issa's *ku* is one of the ten or so most famous blossom-viewing *ku*.

1. Hell Near By Early haiku and *senryû* found *jigoku = hell* fun to play with. A *ku*: "Does hell then lie / under your fiery shoots, / my devil-thistle?" [a plumed thistle, *Cirsium nipponens*] (もへ出る下は地ごくか鬼あざみ　無記名　嵐山集　*moe-izuru shita wa jigoku ka oni-azami* anon. 1651?). The best known hell *senryû* has a Buddhist priest assuring his mistress that it does not really exist (so she need not fear punishment for corrupting a priest). In regard to the closeness of hell, how about this less enlightening but all too true later *senryû*? "Hell's not far off: / on opposite sides of a wall / between neighbors" (地獄遠きにあらずして壁どなり　柳多留 123 別 6　*jigoki toki ni arazu shite kabedonari* Y 20c?). Imagine this "wall" as a paper-thin partition between the adjoining apartments in a tenement, not the thick outdoor walls between that keep friendship green.

心から地獄に近き桜かな　亀世　再現
kokoro kara jigoku ni chikaki sakura kana　kisei c1700
(heart/mind-from hell-to close [blossoming] cherry!/?/'tis)

the mind is what
brings cherry blossoms
so close to hell!

our own minds
put us close to hades
blossom-viewing

Were it not written about a hundred years earlier, you might think this *ku* a reply to Issa's sitting-on-hell *ku*! Could we, then, describe Issa's as a question written to match the answer of an unknown *ku*?

人に花大からくりのうき世哉　一茶
hito ni hana ôkarakuri no ukiyo kana　issa 1818
(people-with/and blossoms big automatum's floating-world!/?/'tis)

people and flowers:
it's a huge automatum,
this floating world!

people and flowers:
this world's a machine,
an automatum!

To my mind, this virtually unknown *ku* is far more impressive than the "over-hell" one. The *automatum* is no mere metaphor, it is an epiphany. Issa has finally found the right word for the wonder and terror found, respectively, in his earlier *ku*. Japanese *senryû*, are full of *karakuri*, or automata,[1] for the people of the Tokugawa age enjoyed clever devices (including watches that adjusted to the varying length of the day and night-time hours). One thinks of Descartes, but Issa's observation is not purely philosophical as it might seem in English; the "floating world" is a religious concept. Were it not illusory, "the world of woe" would be a better translation.

旅駕にうしろ窓なし花の中　梅室
tabikago ni ushiro mado nashi hana no naka　baishitsu 1768-1852
(traveling-basket=sedan-in back-window not, blossoms among)

a traveler's sedan
with no back-window goes
through the blossoms

Living for the day is *not looking back,* as well as not looking forward. Did Issa's highly respected contemporary actually observe this fine metaphor echoing that of the petals *falling without regret?*

---

1. ***Automata*** **in** ***Senryû.*** I have seen maybe a dozen *senryû* on *automata*. In each, the word *karakuri* needs a different translation. Eg. 1. *"The dreams we think / we see? Our organs are / the puppeteer"* (*omotte-miru yume-wa go-zô-ga karakuri-shi*: think-see-dream-as-for, five-organs are automata-master). The "automata master" mentioned in this *Mutama* 5 (1753) *senryû* is a sort of magician, a mechanical sleight of hand artist who entertains with his devices, but poetry dictated it become "puppeteer." Eg.2: "The artificial persona *A pock-marked face / is not left to / its own devices*": *abata-ga areba kao-mo karakuri* (pockmarks have-if/when, face-even automatum/artifice). This *Mutama* 17 (1773) *senryû* uses *karakuri* in its broadest sense as artifice, a made-up, or apparent reality.

~~~~~~

花盛こゝで死たき心哉　捨童　花七日
hanazakari koko de shinitaki kokoro kana　shadô 1777
(blossom-peak here-at die-want heart/feeling is)

the bloompeak
here, right here, where
i want to die

the bloompeak　　　　　　　　　　　　　　the bloompeak
this is where thought　　　　　　　　　　here is where i feel
turns to death　　　　　　　　　　　　　　i want to die

the bloompeak
when we feel so good
we want to die

The only question in this otherwise simple poem is whether the "here" should be taken literally or not. The last reading is my re-creation, or paraverse. In the third-person, such a *ku* seems more like a *senryû*: "*The blossom-viewing / of a man who insists / he wants to die!*" (死にたしというたる人の花見哉　在亜　発句題業 *shinitashi to iutaru hito no hanami kana*　zaia (1820)).

しなばやと櫻におもふ時もあり　成美
shinabaya to sakura ni omou toki mo ari　seibi -1816
(die-would, cherry-at/with [i] think times even are)

and sometimes
when the cherries bloom
i feel like dying

I like Seibi's *ku* for the refreshingly honest qualification "sometimes" (lit.: "times-even-are"). I can vouch for having felt the same, *sometimes*. It is worth noting that the feeling is not martial, Buddhist or Zen: it just *is*. A modern Japanese man is more analytical:

> The cherry blossom is ominous [petals falling quickly portend an early death]. So why am I, who feel that way, enraptured with the cherry [blossoms] every year? Is it not because somewhere in me there is this longing for death? (takagishi: hana-saka jisan 2000-01-10 googled)

This "longing for death" is the death-wish Freud thinks we have. To say it is what draws us to the bloom like so many moths to a flame is quite different from Seibi's observation, or this similar, but more dramatic *ku*:

脇さしはけふもささぬか花さかり　花賛女
wakizashi wa kyo mo sasanu ka hanazakari　kasanjo 1807-1830
(side-stick[short sword]-as-for today, too/even stab-not?/! blossom-peak)

~~cherries in full bloom~~　　　　　　　　　once more, today
~~my dagger, today, too,~~　　　　　　　　　should i sport a sword?
~~i feel like using it!~~　　　　　　　　　　it's the full bloom

I called the short-sword a dagger to suggest suicide: one way to express the elation of cherry-blossom time: *I'm so high I could die!* Unfortunately, the "stab" (*sasanu*) here is surely idiomatic for stabbing the sword into one's sash, i.e. *wearing it*. Kasanjo means to experience the joy of gallantry, of wearing and perhaps even brandishing a sword. Because she died young – twenty three – a suicide popped into my mind. An older *ku* gives us a picture of what can happen to these weapons at blossom-viewings: "*Putting a label / on the short-sword / cherry-time!*" (脇差へ札つけて置さくらかな 尾上 さくらかゝみ *wakizashi e fuda tsukete-oku sakura kana* ojô (1734)). I cannot tell if this labeling is preparation lest it be lost or information attached to one found there. Probably, it is the latter.

春死なば花に迷はん後の闇　許六
haru shinaba hana ni mayowan ato no yami kyoryoku -1715
(spring-die-if blossoms-by confused/seduced-let's/i'll following-dark)

> come what may
> spring is the time: blossoms
> are to die for

> heaven's a blank
> if spring has your number
> fall for blossoms

> die in the spring
> and no grief will come from
> loving blossoms

> who knows what
> comes next: love the blossoms,
> die in the spring

A saint might ride a cloud of blossoms from this world to the next, but such worldly beauty was generally associated with sin. Ah, but there was a paradoxical saying: *You can't be enlightened unless you stray* (迷わぬ者に悟りなし). Is that it? The *ku* is clever: "afterward-dark" which *means* that none knows what comes after death, plays on an idiom parallel to *straying with the blossoms* (i.e. women) *straying in the dark*. So saying, the above readings are not only loose, but miss the point, to wit:

post mortem nihilo est

> dying in spring?
> first, i'd have a fling
> with the blossoms

To understand *why* that would be witty, however, you would need to know this famous *waka*:

願はくは花のしたにて春死なんそのきさらぎの望月の頃　西行 skks #1845
negawakuba hananomoto nite haru shinamu sono kisaragi no mochizuki no koro saigyô (1118-90)

> if i had a wish
> my wish would be to die
> under a cherry
>
> at full moon, moon two
> in the bloom of spring!

> my plea is this
> to die in spring dress
> below the bloom
>
> a flowering cherry
> in the light of the moon

Saigyô's *waka* has three seasonal words, spring, blossoms and the month. For *haikai* this would be horrendous overkill. However, it is not mere redundancy. Spring = with youth remaining, blossoms = fellows in death, and, among the fourteen etymologies (OJD) for the month called *Kisaragi* is the one reflected in my last reading: 衣更着 lit. "robe-again-dress," or *the month of redressing*.

願はくは花のもとでや生とをり 塞佐 真木柱桂
negawakuba hananomoto de ya ikitôri kisa 1697
(wish-if blossoms-under/by!/?/: live-capture)

the redress

"my plea is this"
beneath a blooming tree
a protest-suicide

This is in a collection of *haikai* but had it been written a hundred years later, it would surely have been a *senryû*, unless the author really did the act. The first five syllabets of the twelve taken from nobleman-turned-monk Saigyô's *waka* can be construed as the opening for the request accompanying such a suicide. It is also fitting because the message could be put on strips of paper and dangled from the tree just like poems were.

いざさくら我もちりなむひとさかりありなば人にうきめ見えなむ そうく法し 古今集#77
iza sakura ware mo chirinamu hitozakari arinaba hito ni ukime mienamu monk sôku 905

cherry blossoms,
i'd fall here with you!
for a man's life

after the bloom is gone
is an ugly sight!

This man, like Saigyô, a Buddhist priest, would drop dead in the full bloom of life, as the blossoms do. But this idea of living beyond one's peak – *i.e.*, becoming old – as something shameful if not gross is not so much Buddhist as ancient Japanese. It is the desire of a people that admired a martial demeanor and boasted lovers with energy enough to rove about like tom-cats. Sôku seems more connected to this culture of courage and prowess than to the idea of non-attachment. Saigyô's later *waka* is better for having none of this negativity – in the original, the month's name *Kisaragi*, also provides refreshing psychological mimesis (it suggests *sarari to* = freshness = one of its (probably spurious) etymologies) – and a chuckle in the precision with which he bears down upon a season, a month, a day and a tree – *i.e.,* a splendid target for dying.

はづかしや畳の上の西行忌 西馬 俳諧裾野集
hazukashi ya tatami no ue no saigyô ki saiba (1848)
(embarassing!/: mat=floor-upon's saigyô memorial-day)

how embarassing
saigyô day and i'm here
seated on tatami

Nothing said about our cherry blossoms, but the implication is that they are in bloom yet the poet sits inside, at home. Saigyô's Day, of course, is the anniversary of his death. Since Saigyô whose name literally translates as West-go/ing (West being the location of the Buddhist's paradise, rather than, say, the Yellow Springs, below) lived to be 73, I suspect the poet, whose name means West-horse, was also getting on in years when he wrote this *ku*, for the wit comes partly from its *not* being about the anticipated shame, that of staying alive too long rather than letting go like a blossom, like Saigyô.

dying

花に死ん願ひは欲の鏡哉　白雄 ｱﾙｽ

hana ni shin negai wa yoku no kagami kana shirao -1792
(blossoms-with/at die-would wish-as-for greediness's exemplar!/?/'tis)

thanatos considered

wishing to die with the blossoms: that too is attachment	wishing to die under the bloom: that, too, a sinful desire

Either last line may be changed to "greediness." Lack of fear of dying is a mark of enlightenment, but such a wish is not. If Shirao's *ku* were by a *senryû* poet it would be a *senryû*, because he seems to poke fun at Saigyô. And did I say that Saigyô's wish came true?

是 (それ) てこそ命をしけれ山櫻 (櫻花)　智月 玉藻

kore(sore)de koso inochi oshikere yamazakura (sakurabana) nun **chigetsu** 1622-1706
(this(that?)-from especially life regret[want-to-keep] mountain-cherry[cherry-blossoms])

cherry blossoms they only make me want to stay alive!	because of them i love life all the more mountain cherries

Chigetsu's Buddhism serves as an invisible foil to bring out the joy of living. Saigyô would have liked this more than Shirao's *ku*, for he admitted to mixed feelings: some of his *waka* confessed that his mountain retreat – supposedly a refuge from worldly attachment – brought him closer to nature, and that natural beauty, even the moon that symbolized the Buddhist Law, was a form of attachment.

たからとは今日の命ぞ初さくら　千代

takara to wa kyo no inochi zo hatsuzakura **chiyo-ni** 1702-75
(treasure-as-for, today's life! first cherry/blossom/s)

first blossoms! the real treasure is living today	the treasure is this: today's life first blossoms

what's treasure?
life today, by buddha!
first blossoms

I fear that this *ku* translates as poorly as the previous one by Chigetsu-ni translates well (There is something we may call *the luck of translation* which has less to do with the skill of the translator than the presence or lack of equivalent idioms and syntax suitable to do justice to the original when it is re-created). Buddhist law is usually considered the most important "treasure." Yet this widowed nun and most famous female haiku poet of all time, found the fleeting blossom taught her to appreciate the gift of life. This consciousness of living is always accompanied by its opposite, consciousness of dying. Her emphatic *zo is*, as always, a problem for English, with its specific word- or phrase-based way to express excitement. It is a shame but, in English, *we must be profane to be human*. Profanity (including, its child, *euphemism*) is the only spice we have! Japanese need not say "by Buddha," as we must say, "by God." In English, only preachers, who can use His (or Jesus') name liberally are free to speak dramatically without violating good taste or religion. (For a rarely effective use of religion as rhetoric by a layman, see Annie Dillard's, *A Pilgrim at Tinker Creek*. Edward Abbey, in most ways a wise man, was wrong to criticize her for excessive use of the capital "G" word.)

遊台嶺・上もなき此世の櫻さきにけり 暁台
ue mo naki kono yo no sakura sakinikeri gyôtai -1792
(above-even-not this world's cherries bloom[+finality])

on playtop peak

nothing above
the cherries of this world
blooming now

The name of the peak the poet saw or stood on actually translates as play-stage-peak. The original syntax requires a modifying clause to English – the cherries of this world, *above which there are none*,[1] have blossomed. Such wordiness kills poetry, so I killed *it*. I wish it were true, our *love for blossoms*; for, unlike beautiful women (or handsome men) on earth, who only give themselves to the lucky few, the *sakura* is here *for all of us to enjoy*. But, I am afraid most of us would give up the most beautiful flower in the world to enjoy a beautiful human and, needless to say, promises of a higher reality cannot compete with even the former unless you really believe them.

寝たるまをほとけと言わじ花盛　強氷 毛吹草
netaru ma o hotoke to iwaji hanazakari kôei 1645
(sleep-while[acc] buddha/corpse say-not blossom-acme)

the bloompeak	you can't claim
passed out does not	buddhahood sleeping out
a buddha make	the bloom-peak

To become still – *i.e.* dead – is to become a buddha, which is to say enlightened; but sleeping (passing out?), the poet chuckles, does not count. Or, do I misread the *ku?* Could it mean the following?

when they sleep	sleeping the trees
don't say they're dead	were not dead : now blooming
the bloompeak	they die, instead

In other words, before bursting into bloom, the cherry trees looked as good as dead, but now, the full bloom sets the real stage for death to fall, for the blossoms to turn into petals, into Buddhas.

落花・又一つ花につれ行命哉　鬼貫
rakka // mata hitotsu hana ni tsureyuku inochi kana onitsura
(falling petals) again one / blossoms/petals-by accompanied-go/leave life!/?/'tis)

falling petals

off goes yet	i wouldn't mind
another life with	another life to lose
the blossoms	on the blossoms.

~~~~~~

1. *Nothing Above* The phrase "nothing above" describing the cherry blossoms may allude to the anonymous poem #70 of the *Kokinshû*: *"If saying "Stay!" / could only stop / their falling . . . / how could i possibly / love blossoms more!"* – trans. lc+rdg (*mate to iu ni chira de shi tomaru mono naraba nani o sakura ni omoimasamashi*) which implies that cherry blossoms are as beloved as beloved can be. A less accepted reading interpreting the last two lines as "what could possibly / be dearer than blossoms? (trans. lc) brings this out even more. But the poet may only be expressing his appreciation of blossoms, in which case, my metaphysical speculation is moot.

a falling petal

another life
is carried off with
the blossoms

Onitsura is as difficult as Donne. Is this a magical confluence of man and bloom? Or, is each falling petal imagined in the same way meteors are by many cultures? A contemporary poet uses words from the song "Sakura" (it begins, *sakura sakura*) to bring out this ghostly element in a beautiful *ku*:

さくら／＼今宵は誰を連れてゆく　黛まどか
sakura sakura koyoi wa dare o tsureteyuku　mayuzumi madoka (contemp.)
(cherry[blossoms], cherry[blossoms], this-evening-as-for who[obj] accompany-go/ing)

sakura, sakura
who will you take with you
this evening!

Sound-wise, I would have liked to change "take with you" to "carry off," but meaning demurred. The poet [1] explained that the theme was "death," but failed to mention Onitsura's poem. Perhaps she did not know it, for the *ku* is not so famous as his skeletons in finery *ku*. It should be.

睡布袋讃・此眠りさます人なし花の陰　蓼太
kono nemuri samasu hito nashi hananokage　ryôta 1707-87
(sleep-clothbag-praise // this sleep awaken person none bloom-shade)

in praise of sleeping hotei

~~from this sleep~~	this is a sleep	~~from this sleep~~
~~none awake: in the shade~~	no man would disturb	~~there are none who wake~~
~~of the blossoms~~	the bloomshade	~~the bloomshade~~

This *ku* belongs does not belong here! I *literally* misread the name of Hotei the rotund Chinese God of Happiness as a "sleeping bag" intended as a shroud for possibly dying in one's sleep and mistook the mood to read "none who wake" rather than no one to wake the fat and happy god.

狩り暮れて花おそろしくなる日哉　蘭更
karikurete hana osoroshiku naru hi kana　rankô 1726-99
(hunt-nightfalling, blossoms terrifying-become day!/?/'tis)

hunting until
night falls: the blossoms
turn terrible

Cherry blossoms became associated with death, but not everyone was eager to die. The hunters in this *ku* are especially anxious as they have just earned themselves some bad karma.[2]

~~~~~~

1. *Mayuzumi Madoka* This young beauty-queen-turned-poet writes extraordinarily good haiku for one who does not seem well-versed in older material. She has a haiku magazine for young women called "Audrey" with a picture of Audrey Hepburn on the cover. That she wears dresses with frilly collars and stands up for everything sweet and the cute is to her credit. In a world dominated by muscular Occidental culture, where only square-jawed Katherine and her obvious toughness is admired, where women have asserted their equality by turning *macho* themselves rather than standing up for the value of softness, I find Madoka's anachronistic femininity delightful (though her beauty-queen prim can be as fulsome as Arnold's muscleman smug – Oh well, who's perfect? – she is on the right side of life). Were I not penniless, I would have sent Madoka a splendid potted plant called the falling-star as a reward for her *ku*.

2. **Hunting Karma** In the oldest anthology of Japanese poetry, when Yamanoueno Okura (660?-733?) laments his illness – presumably a tumor, for he wishes for the Chinese doctors of old who knew how to cut things out of people! – he blubbers that it is hardly fair, for even hunters and especially cormorant fishers who have taken countless lives and earned bad karma live on, while *he* has been so very careful to be good. Okura's Buddhism was a bit odd. Isn't bad karma earned by taking lives supposed to manifest itself in the *next* life, where the hunter might become, say, a stag?

死下手と又も見られん桜花　一茶
shinibeta to mata mo miraren sakurabana　issa 1808
(dying-poor-at, again-even seen: cherrry blossoms)

this poor dier would see the blossoms once again!	cherry blossoms and we who fail to die appear again

Mr. poor dier, Issa, enjoys seeing the good diers once again. There is humor in this combo.

死下手の此身にかゝる桜哉　一茶
shinibeta no kono mi ni kakaru sakura kana　issa 1809
(dying-poor-this[my]-body-on/to fall/stick cherry[blossoms/petals]!/'tis)

rubbing it in?

cherry petals! stuck to the body of this poor dier	they plaster a poor dier's body cherry petals!

Such self-denigration from a poet yet in his mid-forties, is less interesting than nun Chigetsu's confession (*they only make me want to live*); but the colloquial term *shinibeta,* "poor-dier" has a nice ring to it and sticking petals provide pleasant irony. The following year, Issa wrote:

たゞ頼め桜ぼた／＼あの通　一茶
tada tanome sakura bota bota ano tôri　issa 1809
(just trust/request cherry[blossoms] tumbling/trickling that way)

simply believe like the cherry petals tumbling down	just have faith cherry petals let go just like that

This Buddhist homily would also be a lousy *ku* if Issa were not addressing himself most of all. The mimesis, *bota bota,* is a translator's nightmare. The dictionary describes it as a heavier version of *pota pota.* If the transcribers misread Issa's "*po* = ぽ"as "*bo* = ぼ," "trickling down" might work but for its failure to capture the *mimetic* plop-down. Drip-dropping could, but only liquids are allowed to do that in English – a pity, for Issa probably intended a hint of *petal-as-dewdrop*, the classic symbol of transient life and a favorite theme for Issa. *Bota-bota* also includes a measure of irregularity, and that is one reason I decided to let the petals take a *tumble*. Another version of the *ku* has "*hara-hara* (fluttering down)" instead of *b/pota-b/pota*. It is good if we change it to "floating down."

いざゝらば死げいこせん花の陰　一茶
iza saraba shinigeiko sen hananokage   issa 1808
(whenever if, dying practice/lessons do-let's! bloomshade)

bloom-shade school

be prepared,
take lessons for dying
from the cherry

what better place

who knows when:
so practice, practice dying
under the bloom!

Does Issa mean watching the blossoms self-destruct and scatter their petals is a good lesson? Or, that being covered by petals might be good practice for being buried, too. Then, again, who can practice being *dead,* rather than *dying?* And, who needs the petals to fall? Just sitting or lying under the low-slung blossom-covered branches is enough to get the idea. Issa made many paraverses of this *ku.*

死支度致せゝと桜哉　一茶
shinijitaku itase itase to sakura kana issa 1810
(dying-preparation do it! do it! [says] cherry [blossoms]!/'tis)

"prepare to die!
prepare! prepare!" imply
the cherry blossoms!

cherries tell us
get ready, get ready, get
ready for death

Issa gave new teeth to an old saw with expressions such as "dying *practice*" (*shini-geiko*), where this "practice" usually referred to lessons in music, tea-ceremony or like arts, above, and this "dying-*preparations*" (*shini-jitaku*), where the "preparation" was associated with hunkering down for the winter or fitting up for travel. The original has no "imply" or "tell," just a grammatical indication or sign, the spirit of which is *as-if-to-say.* While I read this as a constructive Buddhist *ku,* Ueda reads it as an example of middle-aged Issa's "pessimistic outlook on life . . . projected even onto animals and plants" (*Dew On the Grass*). He may have something there.

なむゝと桜明りに寝たりけり　一茶
namu namu to sakura akari ni netarikeri   issa 1816
(*"namu-namu"* cherry[blossom] light-in slept.etc.[+emph])

praying aloud
in the blossom glow
i fell asleep

praying for mercy
i fell asleep among gleaming
cherry blossoms

praise be! praise be!
i pray while falling asleep
in the blossom-light

The first translation does not read the poet's mind. The second was my guess based upon Issa's fearful side. The third is KS's reading: the poet, as a religious man, *feels something holy in the glowing blossoms, as if he was in the presence of Buddha.* The last line might also be "in the glow of the bloom." Since Issa saw the night blossoms as beauties descended from heaven (15-17, 48-69) – and light was not frightening but reassuring – this is probably the correct reading and the *ku* doesn't belong in this chapter unless we are to think *"See the cherry blossoms and die!"* in the sense of that phrase about Venice. Issa did write such a *ku*: *"Having seen all / the blossom world, he dies: / Buddhahood!"* (華の世を見すまして死ぬ仏哉 *hana no yo o misumashite hotoke kana* 1826). Since the words of the prayer only evoke the name of the Buddha, they were of little help with the reading.

けふは花見まじ未来がおそろしき　一茶
kyo wa hana mimaji mirai ga osoroshiki　issa 1818
(today-as-for, blossoms see-won't future-is terrifying)

花の陰寝まじ未来がおそろしき　一茶
hananokage nemaji mirai ga osoroshiki　issa 1826
(blossoms' shadow sleep-won't future-is terrifying)

<blockquote>
i dare not view
the blossoms today: for fear
of my next life!
</blockquote>

<blockquote>
i cannot sleep
in the bloom-shade, for fear
of my future
</blockquote>

The word translated as "future" had strong supernatural connotations in Issa's day, *i.e.* the next world/life. The first *ku* is from his fifties, the last, his sixties, the year before his death. A preface expresses his fear that a lifetime of eating without farming and wearing clothing without weaving earned him bad karma.[1] Old man Issa's faith gives his *ku* a power not felt in his youthful oeuvre.

醉死なぬ先から花の埋みけり　丈草
yoishinanu saki kara hana no uzumikeri　jôsô -1704
(drinking-die-before-from blossoms'/petals' buried[finality])

<blockquote>
if the *sake*
don't kill me i'll be buried
by the petals
</blockquote>

<blockquote>
before dying
the dead drunk is buried
by the petals
</blockquote>

The odd grammatical construction doesn't translate and might best be described as close to that found in *Rye Whiskey* (*"If the Whiskey don't kill me, I'll live 'til I die!"*).

花に埋れて夢より直に死ん哉　越人
hana ni umarete yume yori sugu ni shinan kana　etsujin -1702
(blossoms-by buried dream-from immediately die-would!/?/'tis)

<blockquote>
as soon as petals
bury me, dream over
i would die!
</blockquote>

my dream

<blockquote>
as soon as
the petals bury me
i would die!
</blockquote>

cherry petals

<blockquote>
i would die
as soon as they finish
burying me
</blockquote>

<blockquote>
i would die
as i finish dreaming
of being buried in petals
</blockquote>

Is this man and nature in close embrace? Would he die for real, as the princess of spring sheds her petals in the throes of *petit mort?* Or, is this just desire expressed in metaphor? In a haiku blog a man recently expressed the desire to die *that* way. Though indirectly expressed in a *ku*, one female participant couldn't resist writing that the "male's real-desire" had slipped out (sex in another chapter).

@ Poet as Parasite? Years before Issa, Sonojo (d.1726) wrote *"Change of dress / how deep my sin for not / weaving myself"* (*koromo-gae mizukara oranu tsumi fukashi*). There would seem to be three ways the religious rationalize not laboring. The *first* is to behold the Lilly and see labor as degrading complicity in worldly affairs when one should be whole-heartedly interested in more lofty things. The *second* is to feel guilty about not suffering as other folk are and hope your good works (religious or poetic) can justify your life. The *third* is to have no opinion, but simply accept that whatever *is* is right, *i.e.*, your good fortune. Issa was particularly hung up on 2), but I think a bit of each of these idealistic, compassionate and tragic approaches may be found in all old haiku poets.

御室・埋むとも木陰は去らじ散る櫻　蘭更
(uzumu to mo kokage wa saraji chiru sakura　rankô 1726-99
(buried-even-though, tree-shade-as-for depart-not falling cherry/petals)

god's chamber　　　　　　　　　　　　　　**falling petals**

though i should　　　　　　　　　　　　　　though i should
be buried, i'll stay under　　　　　　　　be buried alive i'll stay
the falling blossoms　　　　　　　　　　　in the bloom-shade

The preface is *mimuro:* literally "honorable-room," a beloved room or grotto keeping, perhaps, a saint or a god. The *ku* can be taken for facetious bravado *and* tender feeling toward the beautiful space the poet occupied. I like the idea of a *hanami* to the end! Mimuro is also a Mountain's name.

追善・二月や死て朽せぬ花の下　湖十　父の恩
tsuizen // kisaragi ya shinde? kuchisenu hananomoto　kojû (-1738/46/80/89?*)
(memorial // second month: dying rot-allow?-not blossom-below // * There are 4 poets so named,)

requiem　　　　　　　　　　　　　　　　　*requiem*

the second month　　　　　　　　　　　　　dressing month
dead yet not rotting　　　　　　　　　　　dying yet he will not rot
under the petals　　　　　　　　　　　　　below the bloom

The poetic name for the second month, *kisaragi,* is beautiful to the ear. One etymology has clothing in it, hence the second reading. Saigyô and his exemplar, Gautama, died: right in the middle of that month, dead-center of the spring (more or less the same time chosen by Christ). The *ku* comes from a book written in gratitude toward the poet's father and suggests he was a good if not saintly man.

散花の下にめでたき髑髏かな　星布尼
chiru hana no moto ni medetaki dokuro kana　seifu-ni 1732-1814
(fall/scattering blossoms' below-at/in celebratory/joyful skull!/'tis)

lying below　　　　　　　　　　　　　　　　below falling
the falling blossoms　　　　　　　　　　　cherry petals a skull
a lucky skull　　　　　　　　　　　　　　　is cheerful

falling petals
this skull has something
to celebrate

Or, "a skull / looks happy"? Does Star-cloth nun contrast the happy end of Saigyô (she copies his *waka* before it) with the sad one of the poetess beauty Komachi, with her sawgrass violated orbit/s?

成仏の棺ゆくらん花ざかり　蓼太
seibutsu no hitsugi yukuran hanazakuri　ryôta 1707-87
(become-buddha[corpse]'s casket goes! blossom-acme)

the bloom-peak:　　　　　　　　　　　　　they carry off
there goes the casket　　　　　　　　　　one who really made it
of a lucky one　　　　　　　　　　　　　　in full-bloom

Someone has died at the perfect time. He or she is called "become-buddha." All who die may be called so, but the term suggests that this is one of the lucky ones who graduates from the chain of suffering. Imagine cherry petals blowing over the casket, some sticking to it for the ride.

其まゝに花を見た目を瞑がれぬ　子規
sono mama ni hana o mita me o fusagarenu shiki -1902
(just like that blossoms saw eyes[obj] shut[cover?]-can-not)

who can close
eyes that just viewed
the blossoms?

This is one of the best death *ku* (for someone else, as opposed to the more plentiful ones for the poets themselves) I know. Nothing in it is not fresh. I suspect "the blossoms" allude not only to the season, but to recent marriage or achievement that, for the first time, gave the deceased the promise of a life. I forgot to copy the preface which probably had such information, but it does not matter.

散る花や跡は阿弥陀の爪はちき　礎江　葛松原
chiru hana ya ato wa amida no tsumahajiki sokô 1692
(falling blossoms! afterwards, the merciful-buddha's fillip)

petals falling	the petals fall	the petals fall
the merciful buddha's	the fillip of the buddha	will merciful buddha now
fillip remains	waits unsprung	flick them away

Or, *us* away? A *tsumahajiki* is a *fillip,* the mini-motion of tensing the tip of the index or middle finger against the belly of the thumb, then allowing the finger-tip to spring forward. It is also the position of the fingers (before the actual flick), a Zen meditation posture found on some of Buddha's images.

西上人五百年忌・はっきりと有明のこる櫻かな　荷分　アルス
saijônin gohyaku-nenki // hakkiri to ariake no nokoru sakura kana kabun (18c)
(saigyô five-hundred year-memmorial // clearly have-light remains cherry!/'tis)

five hundredth saigyô deathday

the morning moon
how clearly we see it
and the blossoms

If the natural association of death with gorgeous bloom and falling petals were not enough, the poetry and death of Saigyô made it official. It is hard to tell whether moon or blossoms remain. Let us see some more ku about the man famous partly for dying as he wanted.

西行忌・其望の日を花くもり　鳥酔　アルス
saigyô-ki // sono mochi no hi o hanagumori chôsui 1700-1769
(saigyô's memorial // this hope=full-moon-day-despite blossom-overcast)

his anniversary	blossom haze
a full moon day overcast!	on that full-moon day
clouds of blossom	of dear saigyô

The full moon specified by Saigyô as ideal for dying was the *mochizuki,* or "hopeful" one (of many synonyms). While his deathday is the given theme, this is really a clever take on blossom overcast.

東風吹ばどれも西行ざくらかな 丸川 一茶留筆
kochi fukeba dore mo saigyô sakura kana   gansen 18-19c
(east-wind blow-when each saigyô cherry-tree/blosssoms/petals!/'tis)

an easter blows
and every cherry becomes
a saigyô tree

One name for the *higan-zakura* (equinox[-blooming] cherry tree) is *saigyô-zakura,* but this more likely refers to a grove of cherry trees near Hôrinji Temple in Saga (Kyôto) supposedly so named from a poem of Saigyô's about the sadness of parting from blossoms one has become accustomed to (*nagamu tote hana-ni mo itaku narinureba* . . .). Since Saigyô translates as "West-going" – the West, as noted, being the location of paradise – should we think *westward ho!* when the East Wind blows?

年をへて又みん西行桜かな 保友 崑山集
toshi o hete mata min saigyô sakura kana   hoyû 1651
(year passes again see-let's saigyô cherries/blossoms!/?/'tis)

after a year
let's see them again!
saigyô cherries

The message of this *ku* alluding to Saigyô's *waka* expressing the pain of parting from the falling petals, his deathday and said cherry is that the "death" of blossoms and men cannot be compared but may be celebrated together. As an anonymous *Kokinshû* (905) *waka*, in loose translation, reminds us, "*Every Spring / the cherry blossoms / do their thing // but you need a ticket / to view them: your life!*" 春ごとに花のさかりはありなめど あひ見むことはいのちなりけり よみ人知らず 古今集#97 *harugoto ni hana no sakari wa ari namedo aimimu koto wa inochi narikeri*). But trying to catch the Saigyô cherries in bloom on the right date was tricky, for not only did the climate change year to year but the solar date varied as the calendar followed the moon. Then, there were topographical elements: *"A north slope / the saigyô cherries / blossom late"* (北面や遅き西行さくらばな 保友 崑山集 *hokumen ya osoki saigyô sakurabana*   hoyû 1651). The North was the side of death and impurity, things Shintô was happy to leave to Buddhism, so there are many temples on Southern-facing slopes to the North of cities. A temple on a Northern slope would probably be on the farside of the mountain and lack warmth from the city as well as sunlight. This could make the bloom late for Saigyô's deathday.

花の陰此世をさみす人も有 一茶
hananokage kono yo o samisu hito mo ari   issa 1806
(blossom/s-shade, this world[acc.] cramped/despicable person/s, too/even is/are)

below the bloom	magical bloomshade	the bloomshade
even men who look down	to think there are men who feel	and there are men who think
on this world	cramped in this world	this world sucks

This *ku* rightfully belongs with the blossom-viewing attitude *ku* in ch. 22. I convinced myself *samisu* was an obsolete form of the verb for being lonely (*sabishigaru*), imagined Saigyô waiting for the sweet chariot. I even came up with a contrary *ku*: *"There are lovers / of this world who watch / the autumn moon,"* the light of Buddhist Law. As it turns out, *samisu* is a rare old verb for *thinking something cramped or despicable, generally because of one's own shortcomings.* I'd bet on my second reading.

西山や花の朧に日の落る 士巧 花櫻帖
nishiyama ya hana no oboro ni hi no ochiru shikô ()
(west-mountain/s! blossom's haze/cloudiness-in sun's fall)

western hills
the sun sets in a haze
of blossoms

Nothing about the Western paradise or death, here, but the presence of such things cannot help but enrich *and* pollute the *ku*.

夜桜や天の音楽聞し人 一茶
yozakura ya ama no ongaku kikishi hito issa 1819
(night-cherries/blossoms: heaven's music hearing person/people)

| night blossoms:
men who have heard
heaven's music | night blossoms!
with men who heard it
heaven's music |

Blossoms at night!
People after hearing
Heavenly music.

– trans. Blyth

Night seems closer to the Other World than the day. Heavenly music was heard when Gautama was about to be translated. A pious Buddhist sleeping under the blossoms might hear it. Especially, in the year Issa wrote his poem, *when a whole lot of people claimed to be hearing it from New Year's on* (two or three months before the cherries bloomed). Issa even had friends over to stay up until they heard the music, but, as far as I know, he never heard it. Blyth had not read Issa's journals and thought Issa was just using "heaven to describe the beauty of cherry blossoms;" but how brilliant his re-creation of the verb as "after hearing!" *Forget my translations!* But what does it *mean*? Did Issa view the blossoms with the elect? Was he so impressed by their blissful faces he drscribed the bloom with them? Or, does he have mixed feelings? Could he mean that the sight of a large cherry partially lit by torch and/or moon is wonderful, but also spooky and, lacking the full color palette of one seen by day, unnatural? Or, are the elect, unafraid of death, the only ones there late at night?

鰒の夜に似たる花見の戻り哉 蝶羽 再現
fugu no yo ni nitaru hanami no modori kana chôu -1741
(swellfish-night-like resemble blossom-viewing-returning!/'tis)

| the return trip
from blossom-viewing is like
a puffer night | something feels like
a swell-fish night: returning
from the *hanami* |

After eating the fish that might kill you with your equally courageous buddies, you go to sleep wondering if you will awaken in this world or the next. *That* is a "swell-fish night." But swell-fish also was *a warming food* eaten when it snowed – the very name (鰒) combines "fish" (魚) and "summer" (夏) . The blossom viewer might be still feeling a glow from the *sake*, yet be a bit dazed, zombie-like, as a tiny trace of blowfish poison would make someone feel (Please enjoy *Swellfish Soup*, if I ever finish and publish it. Sorry, WSW-san for taking so damn long!). The *ku* is a masterpiece.

極楽へゆけば蓮より櫻かな　葵足
gokuraku e yukeba hasu yori sakura kana kizoku
(paradise-to go-if/when lotus-rather-than cherry!/'tis)

<blockquote>
if you'd go
to heaven, cherry
beats lotus
</blockquote>

Buddhist saints are often shown seated upon lotus blossoms. This pure white blossom rising from mud is a reification of enlightenment. Moreover, in Japanese poetry, the globules of water on the leaves pun souls (both being *tama*). But, Buddha's deathday fell in cherry-time – lotus is mostly summer in haiku – and the blossoms' easy release from attachment was taken as Buddhist catechism, so why not induct it into paradise? This *ku* may also have a B-side reading, for *hasuppa*, or lotus leaf was a tart who could be enjoyed on the cheap, while *sakura*, or cherry-blossom, was an expensive "play-woman" (courtesan) in the pleasure quarters, widely called *gokuraku*, "extreme-ease," *i.e.*, "paradise."

生死ふたん人間しらす花の山　混夫 新虚栗
seishi fudan ningen shirazu hananoyama konpu 1777
(life-death generally, humans know-not blossom-mountain)

<blockquote>
cherry mountain　　　　　　　　　　　　　　mount cherry
where all men catch sight　　　　　　　　where life and death
of life and death　　　　　　　　　　　　　　no longer hide
</blockquote>

Fudan can mean either *unbroken/indivisible* or, *ordinary*. Lacking a short word for "generally," I was forced to write "all" in one reading and reverse-translate both readings as positive rather than negative.

何所の花何所の芝居か死処　乙二
doko no hana doko no shibai ga shinidokoro otsuni -1823
(where[what place]'s blossom, where's theater-the/is dying-place)

<blockquote>
where the blossoms
where the playhouse to be mine
my place of death
</blockquote>

Saying has it that any green mountain will do for a final resting place. Otsuni would seem an optimist in death.

花咲て死とむないが病かな　来山
hana saite shinitomunai ga yamai kana raizan -1716
(blossom/s blooming die-want-not disease!/?/'tis)

<blockquote>
they bloom　　　　　　　　　　　　　　　　　cherries bloom
not wanting to die　　　　　　　　　　　　you are sick if you don't
is a sickness　　　　　　　　　　　　　　　　want to die
</blockquote>

土になる土に寝て見ん花の陰　六窓 芭蕉庵再興集
tsuchi ni naru tsuchi ni netemin hananokage   rokusô 1771
(earth-into become earth-as sleep-try-would bloomshade)

the bloomshade
i would become dust
and sleep in dust

i would be dirt
and sleep in this dirt
under the bloom

花の山どなたの墓とくそだわけ 柳多留 69-1
hana no yama donata no haka to kusodawake   yanagidaru 19c
(blossoms' mountain whose grave [asks] shit=utter-moron x2, also # 6-46)

cherry mountain:
"is this someone's grave?"
asks the moron

Traditional graves were mounds and often planted with flowers or blossoming trees. This is a *senryû*, but it could be a haiku, for someone not right in the head might see all those flowers and wonder aloud who was under the mountain, or hill. Given the mindset of our poets, the moron was not completely off the mark! (By explaining the *ku* in terms of ideas, I may have undeservedly elevated the humor. The moron may be stumped by the *word* "blossom-mountain, in which case we have "false" rather than "true" wit, according to Locke.)

The idea of flowers teaching men to welcome death was hardly Japanese, much less oriental alone. Hearn quotes a "sermon in verse" by the English bishop Henry King (b.1592) called *A Contemplation Upon Flowers*. It is not the usual dour reflect-upon-your-mortality-and-repent preaching, but something akin to Issa's celebration of the flower's goodness. I telescope the poem to save space:

> *Brave flowers – that I could gallant it like you, / And be as little vain! / You come abroad, and make a harmless show, / And to your beds of earth again. / You are not proud: you know your birth: / For your embroider'd garments are from earth.*

> *You do obey your months and times, but I / Would have it ever Spring: / My fate would know no Winter, never die, / Nor think of such a thing. / Oh, that I could my bed of earth but view / And smile, and look as cheerfully as you!*

> *O teach me to see Death and not to fear, / But rather to take truce! / How often I have seen you at a bier, / And there look fresh and spruce! / You fragrant flowers! then teach me, that my breath / Like yours may sweeten and perfume my death.*

To be gallant was to cut a pretty picture, to be dressed to kill. As Hearn pointed out, only the last lines alluding to conduct in speech suggest a Bishop: otherwise, the ideas are common to "any civilized country" (*On Poetry* 1934). Belief in an Afterworld is fine, but nothing beats example, *i.e.*, flowers. Note, however, that not *all* flowers die gracefully. That is why some must be *dead-headed*.

Gods' Own Cherry
伊勢桜
ise-zakura

奥山は内宮なれや伊勢桜 定重 嵐山集
okuyama wa naigû nare ya isezakura   teichô 1651
(remote[recessed] mountain-as-for, inner-shrine/temple be! ise-cherry)

    deep mountains
become inner shrines
    ise cherries bloom

    ise cherries!
remote mountain be thou
    an inner shrine!

    back in the hills
we find inner shrines
    the ise in bloom

The Inner Shrine brings to mind the Grand Shrine at Ise, on the sea-side of a small peninsula. If the cherry blossom of transience and mortality is associated with Buddhism, the beautiful bloom of the mountain/wild cherry tends to be identified with nativism. This is something else, a variety of cultivated cherry (*satozakura*) with a *nominally* Shintô pedigree. While Ise Shrine *does* have a cherry blossom festival, it is not the source of this cherry. One explanation has it coming from Iseji (literally "Ise temple," a place just North of Ôsaka named after a *waka* poet named Ise), another credits a place of the same name in 摂津 and yet another wonders if it was named for its relatively late bloom as Ise Shrine generally came near the tail of a pilgrimage (OJD)! Very light pink, it was whiter than most light cherries and that trait (whiteness=purity=sacred) is also Shintô. If we had a flowering cherry called the Vatican Cherry, the discovery of one in an Ozark hollar (a valley back in the mountains) would turn it into the Holy See, or Holy Sees (as, always, we have the number problem).

神そ／＼日本一のいせさくら 静壽 鷹筑波
kami zo kami nippon ichi no isezakura   seiju 1642
(god/s[+emph] god/s sun-source[jap.] first ise cherry)

    god, it's a god!
number one in japan
    this ise cherry

    gods, by god!
nippon number one
    ise cherries

Does the poet refer to Ise cherry trees as a class or a single tree? The only real defense for a poem like this (you wonder if nurserymen knew about these *ku* and used them for publicity!) is one given by an English, Scott or Irish poet, whose name I forget, with a friend, whose name I likewise forget, who wrote doggerel praising the beauty of a girl. When his friends told him the poem stunk, he replied that had they, too, seen this maiden, who was no dog, they would think differently.

↑ **1. *Oku-yama* Translation** The word/character *oku* connotes a place deep within, out of reach and secreted from view by barrier after barrier. Some relate it to the heart of Imperial Japan – nothing within nothing within nothing – as opposed to the visible throne of the Western monarch. It is also the character used for another's wife, "*oku-sama*." For a similar *ku* I use a hillbilly term: "*Even the hollars / when the cherries bloom, / our capital! /* 奥山も花の時には都哉　作者不知　毛吹草 *okuyama mo hana no toki ni wa miyako kana* anon 1645).

~~~~~~

日本の花のあるじかいせ桜　無記名 崑山集
nippon no hana no aruji ka/ga isezakura   anon. 1651
(japan's blossoms' master/owner/boss/host-the/? ise cherry)

<div style="text-align:center">

paterfamilias　　　　　　　　　　　are you lord
of japan's cherry trees?　　　　　　of all japan's flowers
ise-zakura　　　　　　　　　　　　*ise cherry?*

</div>

East or West, all the creatures of the world were once divided into groups (plant/four-legged/ flying/ swimming etc.) and given their respective heads. The cherry was considered the chief-flower in Japan and the poet goes one further by creating a chief-in-chief. The original could be statement or question.

海老腰に成てあがめよ伊勢ざくら　長頭丸 崑山集
ebigoshi ni narite agameyo isezakura   teitoku 1570-1653
(shrimp-hips/back-into become, worship! ise-cherry)

<div style="text-align:center">

bend yourself　　　　　　　　　　the ise cherries
like a shrimp and worship　　　　　i'd become an old shrimp
the ise cherry!　　　　　　　　　　and worship them

</div>

The Ise Grand Shrine is by the sea and has many marine connections. A shrimp was a symbol of longevity because of its hunch-backed posture combined with spry movement and turned auspicious red when cooked. Aspects of both readings, the posture as suitable for expressing reverence and the wish for the reader to reach old age (he *did*) and enjoy a leisurely pilgrimage are in the original.

見あかぬは日本の神ぞ伊勢櫻　良徳 犬子
mi-akanu wa nihon no kami zo isezakura   ryôtoku 1633
(see-tire/get-bored-as-for japan's god/s! ise-cherry/ies)

<div style="text-align:center">

we never tire
of seeing our deities
the ise bloom

</div>

物がたりの人も待ちけり伊勢櫻　宗因
monogatari no hito mo machikeri isezakura   sôin 1604-82
(legends/tales' people too wait[+emph] ise-cherry)

<div style="text-align:center">

i also await　　　　　　　　　　and we wait
the folk in the tales　　　　　　for the folk in the tales
ise cherry　　　　　　　　　　　ise in bloom

</div>

A boring but somewhat similar *ku*: "*Ise cherry / petals scatter: we recall / old folk tales*" (伊勢桜散てやむかし物がたり　種栄 崑山集 *isezakura chirite ya mukashi-monogatari* shuei 1651).

花の上に海少しあれ伊勢櫻　暁台アルス
hana no ue ni umi sukoshi are isezakura gyôtai -1792
(blossoms' above sea a-little [let]-be! ise-cherry[blossoms])

a bit of sea
peeks over the bloom
ise cherries

let there be
a bit of sea upon ise
cherry blossoms

Gyôtai viewed a stand of Ise cherry from a peak (鈴鹿峠（とうげ）は伊勢と近江にさかふ) and saw the sea with them. Who says there is no poetry in the match of name and nature?

花に蝶のまふは神楽そ伊勢櫻　良徳 犬子
hana ni cho no mau wa kagura zo isezakura ryôtoku 1633
(blossom-with butterfly's/ies' dance-as-for *kagura* (shintô play)! ise-cherry)

it's kagura!

butterflies
dance at gods' pleasure
ise cherry

The title comes from the body of the original poem. *Kagura,* literally "god-fun,"[1] might be defined as sacred Shintô musicals or short plays of Japan's dream-time performed at shrines. Another *ku* less poetically, but more lyrically, sees *butterflies* about blooming Ise cherry trees as shrine maidens, "Ah, the *miko* dance! / the butterflies Ise / cherry blossoms" (神子の舞するやこてふのいせ櫻　重弘 鷹筑波 *miko no mai suru ya kochô no isezakura* shigehiro 1642).

風の神しづめ給へや伊勢桜　無記名 崑山集
kaze no kami o shizume-tamae ya isezakura anon. 1651
(wind-god[+acc.] quiet/pacify[polite imperative]! ise-cherry)

for all blossoms

please pacify
the god of the wind
o ise cherry!

Shintô's pantheon includes a Wind God, who may well be the representative *native* god, for the old chronicles portray him (Susano) as unruly, rioting against changes which the new regimen brings. Any cherry with an Ise connection would be the perfect way to get his ear. A village head called Winluck appealed: "Bad winds, too / become the *kamikaze!* / Ise cherries" (悪風も神風となれいせ桜　勝吉　越後新潟西村長蔵　崑山集 *akufû mo kamikaze to nare isezakura* shôkitsu 1651). *Kamikaze* is the "God-wind" credited with saving Japan from the Mongols not once but twice!

---

1 *Go(o)d-Fun?* I have seen *kagura* performed at a Buddhist temple with a Shintô connection. While the Grand Shrine, taken down and rebuilt every 17 years, is eternal and new, unfortunately, the language is not. Most people watch a bit and doze off a bit, sit still for five minutes and wander around the grounds five minutes, chatter yet rarely raise their voices in excitement. At the very least, *kagura* needs to be spiced up with puns contemporary Japanese can appreciate. (I, a foreigner, thought of many ways to improve it as I listened!).

38

the Buddhist Cherry
世捨桜
yo-sute-zakura

釣鐘を扇で叩く花の寺　冬松　あらの
tsurigane o ôgi de tataku hana no tera　toshô 1689
(hanging bell[obj] fan-with strike blossoms' temple)

i strike a bell
with my folded fan
blossom temple

This *ku* is nothing much, but portrays the mood of a temple (visitor or resident?) in cherry-time well. Usually a pole the size of a battering ram is swung into the bell. The poet may be mimicking.

散る花を南無阿弥陀仏とゆふべ哉　守武
chiru hana o namu-ami-dabutsu to yûbe kana　moritake 1452-1549
(falling-blossoms[+obj] south-nothing-initial-name-buddha [a sutra] say/evening 'tis)

as blossoms fall this evening i chant a buddhist sutra	as blossoms fall this evening: *namu- ami-dabutsu!*

Moritake, sometimes considered the first master of the line of *haikai* that became haiku, was the hereditary chief priest of the head Shinto shrine at Ise. The North-eastern part of the shrine precinct included a Buddhist temple where he viewed the scattering cherry blossoms and made this poem, a tribute to the long-lived symbiosis of Shinto and Buddhist facilities and consciousness. Moritake's pun of "say" and "evening" came to be very common in haiku.

寺法師いかゞみるらん山ざくら　長頭丸　崑山集
tera h[b?]ôshi ikaga miruran yamazakura　teitoku 1570-1653
(temple-priests how do you see/view [them]? mountain-cherries/blossoms)

buddhist priests,
so what do *you* see in
mountain cherries?

This is a good question. Then again, I love question *ku*. What a time I had playing with Ransetsu's *"So, my monks / do you think it dirty / to eat sea slugs?"* in *Rise, Ye Sea Slugs!* Be that as it may, various answers will appear in the course of this chapter.

花々のつぼみは浮世袋かな　無記名　嵐山集
hanabana no tsubomi wa ukiyo bukuro kana anon. 1651
(blossom-blossom's bud-as-for floating[woeful]-world-bag!/'tis)

metaphysical

cherry buds,
each one a bag full
of mortality!

prunus pandora

blossom buds:
each one holds a whole
world of woe!

woeful world

blossom buds
each one packed with
an empty dream

ss vanity

blossom buds
each afloat in this
world of woe

The promise of the blossoms – and this *ku* may not be only about the cherry – is that of the *ukiyo,* our floating world, in its joy and sadness, apparent beauty and, according to Buddhism, vanity and inherent woe. My last reading supposes a pun on *ukibukuro,* "a float."

盛なる花にも絶ぬ念佛かな　鬼貫
sakari naru hana ni mo taenu nenbutsu kana   onitsura 1660-1738
(full-bloom/peak/heat blossom-to-even stop/pause-not prayer!/?/'tis)

cherry blossoms
in full bloom, yet still
our prayers go on!

though cherries
bloom, there is no end
to their prayers

This is a good example of a *ku* that could use a preface. I prefer the second reading – others concerned for the next world while this one is in full bloom do *not* include the poet; but nothing prevents the first reading, including the poet. Had I all of Onitsura's *ku,* dated, as is the case with Issa, I might judge his intent. There is also a slight chance he means neither "my" nor "our" nor "their" but simply prayers and poses a riddle for which the answer is the *uguisu,* a bush-warbler conventionally translated as a nightingale: *"'Blossom garters / open up!' – that sutra? / a bird's voice"* (花の紐もとけ法花経の鳥の声　一正　毛吹草 *hana no himo mo toke hôkekyô no tori no koe* issei 1645). This nightingale's call is said to resemble the *Hôkekyô* sutra. Could it not be among the blossoms?

夕暮や下手念仏ぎらひ哉　一茶
yûgure ya heta-nenbutsu mo sakura chiru issa
(dusk: poor praying/chanting even cherry[petals] fall)

dusk falls and
even the poorest prayers
loosen petals

素人の念仏にさへ桜ちる　一茶
shirôto no nenbutsu ni sae sakura chiru issa
(amateur's prayers/chanting-to even cherry[petals] fall)

even the prayers
of a rank amateur help:
falling blossoms

Seeing petals fall, the standard response is the Buddhist equivalent of, *there but for the grace of God goes I.* Here, however, Issa suggests that prayer helps the blossoms lose what little attachment they have to the world, relax and fall. Why, even a bit of poorly mumbled prayer works, see!

一番の弥陀からぱつと桜哉　一茶
ichiban no mida kara patto sakura kana   issa 1818
(first "mida" –from suddenly/bingo! cherry!/'tis)

at the very first	at the very first	at the very first
mida, all the cherries	*mida*, shazam! there goes	*mida* they bloom like that
burst into bloom	the cherry tree!	cherry blossoms

The *mida* is the *na-mu-a-mi-da-butsu*...repeated in the simplified sutra, where only the name of the Buddha is repeated over and over. Facetious causality is fun to read, but what is happening? *Pa'tto* is more likely to mimic the *opening* of a blossom than the falling of one, though things could vanish *patto!* The most common psychological mimesis for the ideal death, dying in a jiffy, is *po'kkuri to*. By fusing Buddhist color and instant blooming here, we get blossoms enlightened as they open rather than when they fall. Issa expresses this plainly in a lesser *ku*: *"Oh, Buddha, / he makes the blossom of death / bloom pa'tto!* (死花をぱつと咲せる仏哉   *shinibana o patto sakaseru hotoke kana* 1820)

散花につけても念仏ぎらひ哉　一茶
chiru hana ni tsukete mo nenbutsugirai kana   issa 1822
(falling blossoms-respecting-even prayers-dislike!)

even falling blossoms
don't get a prayer
out of me

Because this *ku* comes shortly after the death of his wife and children, it would not be surprising if Issa lost faith, but the term *nenbutsu-girai*, or "prayer-hater" suggests *character*, i.e., that, religious or not, Issa was not one for praying aloud. But, Issa's *ku* include many prayers=*nenbutsu* (see F*ly*-ku*!* for ones accompanying fly-swatting) and it is hard to know if this is "out of me," or "him/her."

神事の跡はほとけの二月哉　蓼太
kamigoto no ato wa hotoke no nigatsu kana   ryôta 1707-87
(god-things[ceremonies/rituals]-after-as-for buddha's second-month!/?/'tis)

after the gods
the buddha gets his due
in month two

Ontogeny recapitulates phylogeny. Japan's first religion, Shintô, a religion of beginnings, gets the New Year, while Buddhism captures the Spring. While Autumn might seem to fit a death-oriented religion, this, too, makes sense, for Shaka (Gautama) left his wife, child and riches in the Spring of his own life. His death date, which is to say Enlightenment, is at the Equinox. No blossoms in the Ryôta's *ku*. It is here to set up what follows:

ちる事を花に教へてねはん哉　吟江 心花
chirukoto o hana ni oshiete nehan kana   ginkô 1776
(fall-thing[acc] blossom-to teach: nirvana/buddha's-death meeting/picture)

teaching blossoms	teaching flowers
how to fall? it's a matter	about dying on this day
of buddhahood	of enlightenment

Buddha's death, concurrent with his Enlightenment, is both celebrated and mourned. Nehan thus unites the passion of Good Friday and triumph of Easter. But the Buddha also leaves us graciously and without regret, as blossoms are always said to fall. I find it funny to have flowers learning from us rather than vice-versa and am reminded of an old Russian cartoon where an old maid preaches love to the young in the Spring. I hope the poet is chuckling, but he could be serious.

木のもとをすみかとすればおのづから花見る人になりにけるかな　花山院御製 詞花和歌集
kinomoto o sumika to sureba onozu kara hana miru hito ni narinikeru kana kotobana wakashû 1151

(asked to read a poem while resting below a cherry in full bloom after hike austerities)

a bona fide way

*if i could only
build a hut right here
below the tree

i could view blossoms
naturally, from within*

If looking at blossoms came from the self/naturally (*onozu-kara*), as opposed to seeking them out of desire, vows of Buddhism would not be violated, if I understand the poet, retired Emperor Hanayama (968-1008), correctly. The *waka* plays with the idea of Enlightenment under the tree, *ala* Shaka, at the same time. The next *ku*, by someone whose name translates as Fish-path has the trees participate.

花も灯を枝に手向ん涅槃像　魚道
hana mo hi o eda ni tamukan nehanzô gyodô 1761
(blossom-even lamps[acc.] limbs-on/from offer enlightenment image/s)

even blossoms   lamps on limbs
bring lamps on their limbs   even blossoms bear gifts
for enlightenment   for the buddha

戸をあけて咲く花見せん仏達　知月尼
to o akete saku hana misen hotoketachi chigetsu-ni¹ 17c
(door[acc.] opening bloom blossom show-would buddhas)

i open the door
to show the cherry blossoms
to my buddhas

The second *ku*, by the nun Chigetsu=Know-moon, reminds me of a better known *ku* by Sôkan (1465-1553) who shows the full moon to a similarly round and reflective sweet-rice-cake. The statues should be delighted to see their philosophy of non-attachment embodied in the blossoms soon to fall. Or, should I imagine an urn with the ashes (the throat-buddha = Adam's apple included) of her dead husband, or, corpses awaiting burial at a temple funeral hall?

---

1. Poet Nuns Chigetsu was known as Chigetsu for much of her life as a married poet and became a nun after her husband died. Because husbands tended to die first, and new husbands willing to support a poet were rare, we find many – perhaps half of all – female *haikai* poets were nuns by the time they were published. Because female names sometimes had a "*jo*" (woman) attached as well as "ni" (nun), *inconsistency with names is the rule*.

國々の開帳も花の徳とかや 沾涼 古今句鑑
kuniguni no kaichô mo hana no toku to ka ya tenryô 1679-1747
(country-country's open-ledger[temple-day]-too blossom's credit, yeah)

the temples open
everywhere: this, too, proves
blossoms good

bless blossoms
for this, too: revealing
holy treasure

Buddhist temples did not generally exhibit the inside of most of their buildings, so the greater part of their sculptures, paintings and relics, if any, may only be seen periodically. These open-temple days held every few years were called *kaichô*,[1] or "open-ledger," presumably because the books were opened to record large donations made at that time. One meaning of *sakura* is "shill/decoy," for nothing draws people like cherry blossoms. Temples took advantage of this. The careful reader may wonder about the "too." It may allude to medicine of the spirit (*ki no kusuri*), but is more likely to refer to the *other* blossom's virtue, namely giving birth to Buddha.

三人上戸 とゝ喰た花と指す仏哉　一茶
toto kuuta hana to yubisasu hotoke kana issa -1827
("finally ate blossom" [as-if-to-say] pointing buddha!/'tis)

three heavy drinkers

hah, you finally
ate that blossom! says
buddha's finger

buddha points
as if to say "you finally
ate the blossom"

Three men are evidence enough of a tiger. The Buddha handed a blossom to his favorite disciple without a word. This was the first Daruma, legendary founder of Zen, pictured seated and sculpted as a roly-poly doll (universal drunk?). The silent Buddha is often depicted giving the world his (index) finger. I would guess Issa and two friends drink by such a statue. Who knows what this *ku* means!

咲く花に浮世の人や神せゝり 去来 今日の昔
saku hana ni ukiyo no hito ya kami-seseri kyorai -1704
(blooming blossoms-with/at floating-world's people? god-kidding)

cherries bloom
and folk of this world
toy with the gods

Kami-seseri, or, *kami-ijiri*, is literally "kidding the gods," but *means* pretending to make pilgrimages out of devotion when one's motives are not really religious at all. People visiting temples and shrines are more interested in their blossom and the people-viewing than matters supernatural.

---

1. Slang-readings of *Kaichô*. Erotic Buddhist metaphor often unites with blossom metaphor. *Nehan*, the Enlightenment/Death-day *also* means the bliss of sexual union; and, *kaichô* (which can *also* mean organized gambling) is slang for the kindly exposure of the female genitals to the starving gaze of the male. And, remember that sutra bird? Here is another bringing Buddhism to cherry-time: *"The blossom girdle / when the truth is freed: / hokkekyô!"* (花の紐真実とくやほつけ経　元辰　崑山集 *hana no himo shinjitsu toku ya hokkekyô* genshin (1651)). As with the other *ku*, the undoing (?) of the bud is allegorized as the "below-belt" (today's panties) and the name of the sutra is shouted in joy, one associated with dying (Not only is *la petite mort* a Japanese concept, but dying was thought of as something for the monks to mind). Yet, the *ku* simply depicts a natural event, the call of the *uguisu*, coming after the cherries blossom. Note: *Kaichô* can also mean the start of gambling operations!

buddhist

花に来てついでがましや神佛 馬光 -1751
hana ni kite tsuide gamashi ya kami hotoke bakô
(blossoms-to coming, next/secondarily/: gods buddha/s)

visiting blossoms
then, as an after-thought,
shrines and temples

高山や花見序の寺参り 一茶 -1827
takayama ya hanami tsuide no teramairi issa
(high mountain! blossom-viewing next temple/s-visit/s)

a high mountain
blossom-viewing leads us
to the temples

Bakô's *ku* is mildly critical; Issa's simply states what was. Be that as it may, no one wrote as many *ku* linking temples, blossoms and money as did Issa.

開帳の目当に立し桜哉 一茶 1820
kaichô no meate ni tachishi sakura kana issa
(open-[temple]'s beacon/tool-as stand/s cherry/ies!)

kaichô day

cherry trees
beacons guiding us
to the temple

さい銭にあおり出さるゝ桜哉 一茶
saisen ni aori-dasaruru sakura kana issa 1820
(offeratory-to/for/as fan/stimulate/inflame cherry/ies!)

jôjô-tera

cherry trees
all whipped up for
the offertory

御仏や寝てござっても花と銭 一茶
mihotoke ya nete-gozatte mo hana to zeni issa 1819
(honor. buddha!/: sleeping[+honorific]-even blossoms & coins))

windfall

blessed buddha
lying still is showered
with blossoms and money

dear buddha
even lying eyes closed
petals and coins

Clearly, trees helped out the temples and some temples *used* them. Each of the three above *ku* finds a different metaphor to express the participation of the blossoms in the temple opening. My favorite is the second, with the excited blossoms. The third *ku* is not so much rudely ironic (as a famous Japanese *ku* annotator would have it), as facetiously jealous. Issa was poor and never forgot it. The pictures and/or sculptures of the Death=Enlightenment of Sakyamuni (Gautama) often showed him supine.

欲面へ浴せかけたる桜哉 一茶 遺稿
yokuzura e abise-kaketaru sakura kana issa -1827
(greedy-face-to showering-upon cherry[blossom petals]!/'tis)

catechism

dumped upon
avaricious faces:
cherry petals

showering down
upon greedy faces
cherry blossoms

A shower of short-lived petals is a metaphysical glass of cold water. Issa has a similar *ku* which is better, but hard to translate: *"Upon the dirty / nape of this sinner's neck: / cherry petals!"* (慾垢のほんの凹へも桜かな 一茶 文政二 *yoku-aka no hon no kubo e mo sakura kana* 1819). The original ("greedy-lint/dirt's hollow[on both sides of nape of the neck]-to-even cherry[petals] tis!") suggests a self-portrait, for Issa was always referring to his shivering nape. Hence, *"this* sinner."

開帳の庭にほしがる櫻かな 也有 -1783
kaichô no niwa ni hoshigaru sakura kana yayû
(open-ledger's[temple's] garden-in want cherry/ies!/'tis)

無掃除の日を来て見たし寺の花　也有
musôji no hi o kitemitashi tera no hana   yayû
(not-cleaning day come-want/see temple-blossoms)

    on *kaichô* day
a temple's garden should
     have a cherry

    i'd like to come
on an unswept day:
   temple blossoms

Two refreshingly straight and unaffected *ku*. When Yayû comes to view the temple's treasures, he also wants a cherry, by god; and, isn't it true that there always seems to be a monk out sweeping or raking leaves to preserve the perfect cleanliness of sacred grounds?[1]

小坊主や親の供して山桜　一茶
kobôzu ya oya no tomo-shite yamazakura   issa 1808
(small monk/s!/: parent/s' companion-doing mountain-cherries)

  mountain cherry
parents are lead about
  by their acolyte

  the little monks
accompany their parents
  mountain cherries

The term "small-monk" (*kobôzu*) can mean only a little boy, but the location tells us this boy or boys is/are apprenticing at a temple. A child away at Buddhist school might only see his parents once or twice a year. Mountain cherries are often found within or near temples for reasons already given.

花咲きぬあそこは社こゝは寺　子規
hana sakinu asoko wa yashiro koko wa tera   shiki 1896
(blossoms bloom overthere-as-for shrine here-as-for temple)

  the cherry blooms
a shrine is over there
   a temple, here

四向寺・地に落つる花や佛の目の前に　成美　手習
shikô-ji? chi ni otsuru hana ya hotoke no me no mae ni   seibi -1816
(four-directions-temple ground-to fall blossom/petals:/! buddha/statue's eyes-before)

  at shikô-ji

cherry petals
falling to the ground
before stone eyes

  shikô temple

cherry petals
fall to earth before
  idol eyes

  four-way temple

a bronze buddha
watches the cherry petals
  fall to the earth

The ambiguity of *hotoke* (Buddhist statues) does not English. *Idol* is insulting for it is colored by Judeo-Christian-Muslim ignorance and prejudice – I use it in Reading Two for the unjustified but irresistible pun on "idle," and because "statue" would be too classically Western. We cannot know what Seibi saw. My "stone eyes" favor *rakkan* or arhat, minor *hotoke*, saints who stayed to help.

↑ **1. Raking Petals** The seemingly obsessive cleanliness of Buddhist monks in Japan astounded the Jesuits in the 16c, who contrasted it to their filthiness within (as opposed to the Jesuits who were clean within yet dirty without). The usual explanation for the constant raking has to to with mindfulness and the shut-out of distraction, etc.. My theory is different. Staying over at a temple, I noticed it was full of clocks and wrist-watches, not to mention bells and wooden blocks keeping time around the clock. Maybe that was only a remnant of the temple's old duty of keeping time for the community, but I couldn't help but wonder if it was a clever trick: by rubbing your nose in time, they break your addiction to it. Constant raking of what will only return to the same condition within hours would seem to me to have a similar effect. You see less rakes at a Shintô temple, though cleanliness is the only catechism (if we call it that) there. Partly, this is because more of the grounds are natural forest, but that, too, is choice: it reflects the naturalism, as Shintô is also a fertility religion. Baishitsu seems to reflect a Buddhist monk's sensibility when he writes: *"Half-assed / the blossoms become litter / in gods' forest"* (なまなかに花は塵也神の森　梅室 *namanaka ni hana wa chiri nari kami no mori*). But I'm not sure I get it.

大佛膝うづむらむ花の雪　其角
daibutsu hiza uzumu ran hananoyuki kikaku -1707
(big-buddha[colossal] lap buried, hey! blossom-snow)

daibutsu's lap
completely buried by
a petal snow

大佛を見に行く花の小道哉　子規
daibutsu o mi ni yuku hana no komichi kana shiki
(big-buddha see-for go blossom-small-road!/'tis 1896)

that small road
below the blossoms leading
to the daibutsu

going to see him,
the *daibutsu*: a blossom
covered path

華頂山・そこ／＼に佛を拝む花見哉　畝司 花七日
sokosoko ni hotoke o ogamu hanami kana　bôshi ?hoshi? 1777
(there, there-at buddha[acc] worship blossom-viewing!/'tis)

cherry-top mountain

blossom-viewing:
here and there prayers
to the *hotoke*

The *daibutsu* is a huge sculpture of Buddha, seated, called "The Colossal" by 19c writers. Like the best *ku* of Buson, Shiki's small path brings us back to our childhood. Even if the scene is not one we literally saw, we *feel* we know it. The "blossom-path" is a problem for English, as we don't think "tree." Perhaps the second reading could end: *"~ a path / through the cherries."* Tired of *idols* and *buddhas,* for not all the Buddhist sculptures called *hotoke* are that, I just used the Japanese.

神前寺・百度や花より出て花に入　一茶
ohyakudo ya hana yori idete hana ni iri issa -1827
(100-times worship: blossoms-from leaving, blossoms-to entering)

pleading prayers
a hundred times in and out
of the blossoms

a hundred times
into the blossoms and out
asking his help

Hyakudo-mairi ("hundred times worship") means someone goes back and forth on a fixed route making prayers in front of the main temple building which may or may not house a manifestation (some male, some female: it could be *Her* help) of Buddha. The route tends to stay within the temple or shrine grounds. Issa gave the name of a temple facing a shrine, so both may be involved here! According to television Easterns, it was usually done of desperation, in the hope of divine intervention for a sick child, etc. or to fulfill a pledge. "In and out of blossoms" plays on the phrase "in and out of *darkness*" from a *waka* by Murasaki Shikibu (author of *Tale of Genji*), not in parody but in all seriousness.

世を捨にありくさくらの山路哉　士朗
yo o sute ni ariku sakura no yamaji kana　shirô -1813
(world[acc] abandon-in walking cherry[blossoms]' mountain-path!)

```
     forsaking man                          he walks away
he walks on pink blossoms              from the world on a trail
     in the mountains                       of wild cherries
```

Too bad English cannot say "abandoning the world" in two-beats or describe "a mountain trail to, between, and among cherry trees that are presumed to be blossoming" in two words as in Japanese! I think of the mountain cherry as a nicotine patch for monks. Loving a woman would be an "attachment," Buddhist for what we might call "addiction," which could result in more attachments called children, but blossoms were alright, for they faded or fell as quickly as they bloomed.[1]

聖人に見放されたる桜哉　一茶 1804
seijin ni mi-hanasaretaru sakura kana　issa
(holy-man-by abandoned cherries!/'tis)

```
  cherry blossoms              abandoned              cherry blossoms
abandoned by a saint         by the holy man:       abandoned, down comes
    to save humans              cherry trees            the holy man
```

Issa's preamble mentions a saint by the name of Atsune Azari (篤音あざり) who lived in the wild since childhood eating nuts and berries and roots, and preached to the beasts of the mountains. Issa writes that the Saint, *whom he was thrilled to have actually met,* descended the mountain (identified with the flowery beauty usually associated with the capital city) to help the denizens of the "murky-world" (濁世). Upper-class Japanese thought of their capital city as *the world* (much like Usanian soldiers in Vietnam who spoke of leaving as "going back to the world," and more generally used it to describe the society of man, as opposed to the woods. There is wit in Issa recording the reverse vector, where it is the mountain that is left behind and in adding a plant to the beasts in this *ku*. Issa described Atsune's voice as *wind blowing through bamboo* and testified that he was something otherwise found only in ancient tales (昔物がたり)! Issa's annotators give Atsune Azari's date of birth and death and add only that became a priest of the Pure Land sect at age 25. My OJD does not even mention him.

---

1. Attachments and Nature. The *women-out-blossoms-in* idea is not entirely valid, for once the cherry blossoms fall, others appear and even when there are no flowers there is always something attractive in nature. I once read *Hojô-ki* – translated as "A Description of My Hut", "A Description of My House" "Notes from a Ten Feet [sic] Hut" "Ten Foot Square Hut" "Hojoki: Visions of a Torn World," etc. – by Kamo-no Chomei (13c) hoping to find a Thoreau of the East. He went to the mountains where the beauty of the natural world helped wean him from the human one (though he seemed disenchanted already with its war, famine and plague – but stopped short of becoming a nature essayist, as it were, because he feared his growing attachment to that world, including the moon, generally considered a Buddhist symbol, his "grass-hut" and even the serenity of writing, which he called a "distraction" (*sawari*) from his job of, shall we say, abstracting himself?

buddhist

花の世に西の望はなかりけり　一茶
hana no yo ni nishi no nozomi wa nakarikeri　issa 1822
(blossoms' world-in/for west=paradise's hope/thought not[emph.])

<table>
<tr><td>in this world
of blossoms what hope
for the west?</td><td>in this world
of blossoms, who thinks
of the west?</td><td>not a chance
for the blossom world
of going west</td></tr>
</table>

West is Heaven, the Pureland paradise. If cherry blossoms embodying transience advertise Buddhism, they also advertise the physical beauty of this world. My first reading assumes Issa sees no hope for the millennialism he had shown interest in years before. The second uses *hana* in the metaphorical sense as luxury (i.e., the Buddhist version of what, like a camel, will not pass through the eye of the needle).

さく花に都てえど気の在所哉　一茶
saku hana ni subete no edo-ki[ke?]no arike kana　issa 1810
(blooming blossom/s-to/with all the mundane/foul spirits whereabouts!/?)

<table>
<tr><td>blooming cherries
the whereabouts of all
things mundane</td><td>blooming cherries
the place to find all of it:
the edo spirit!</td></tr>
</table>

The phonetic *Edo* can mean either "dirty/foul/mundane land" *or* the largest city in the world, with residents boasting an explosive temper and love for spending it all at one time. Though the character of the men may match that of the blossoms, Issa may refer to behavior at the cherry bashes. I hope my second reading is correct though that would mean this *ku* belongs elsewhere in this book.

さく花の中にうごめく衆生哉　一茶
saku hana no naka ni ugomeku shujô kana　issa 1812
(blooming blossoms-among squirm masses!/'tis)

humanity

<table>
<tr><td>within the heart
of the cherry blossoms
squirming masses</td><td>squirming life
among the blooming
cherry trees</td></tr>
</table>

The verb *ugomeku* suggests the writhing of larvae or squirming of maggots. Does Issa see larvae ready for apotheosis or maggots in a rotten world? Either way, it is not a pretty picture (especially if you imagine *everyone* naked). The *ku* was one of a series of six *ku*, representing the six worlds one might be born into. Because the same Buddhist term, *shujô*, can mean both the sentient masses (all animals) *and* humans I was tempted to title it *animals*. Blyth titled his translation – *"We human beings, / Squirming among / The flowers that bloom"* – simply "Men." His bold "We human beings" is fine for picking up on the emphatic *kana*, but the last part is *awful:* Are there flowers that do *not* bloom?

末世末代でもさくら／＼哉　一茶
masse matsudai demo sakura sakura kana　issa -1827
(end/last-world end/last-age even/though "sakura sakura"[lyrics] 'tis)

though the world
should come to an end:
sakura sakura!

Sakura sakura again. I hope to get more of the words for a future edition. Issa may mean "though we live in fallen times nearing the end of the world, we still enjoy ourselves beneath the cherries."

此やうな末世を桜だらけ哉 一茶
kono yô na masse o sakura darake kana issa 1814
(this type-of end=corrupt/world[contradic.] cherry-plastered!/'tis)

| this rotten world completely plastered over by cherry petals! | a fallen world, this but have you ever seen so many blossoms? | these end-times why, then, so damn many cherry blossoms |

This was written after a long winter following a poor harvest, rising prices, riots and starvation, which had some Buddhist cultists looking forward to the end of the world. Years later a grieving Issa wrote: *"A world of pain / whether the cherries should / bloom or not!"* or, *"World of woe, / whether the cherry buds / open or not;"* // *"This world of pain / the cherries have bloomed / they bloom and yet . . ".*(苦の娑婆や桜（花）が咲（開け）ば咲いた（ひらく）とて 一茶 1819 *ku no shaba ya sakura ga sakeba saita[hana-ga hirakeba hiraku] tote*). The "world" in the original (*shaba*) is "the place where the masses who can't free themselves from desire continue to live while enduring suffering."

嘆かずやかくおとろふる世の中に昔なあらの花の色哉 心敬 百首和歌
nagekazu ya kaku otorouru yononaka ni mukashi nagara no hana no iro kana shinkei -1475

| don't they care about the fallen state in which we live? | don't they lament this god-forsaken world? how can blossoms |
| how do the blossoms glow like they did in better days? | glow as beautifully now as in the good old days? |

I realize that "God-forsaken" is culturally speaking all wrong – and the poet Shinkei was a Buddhist priest – but the feeling is right. My problem with this *waka* that seems a predecessor of Issa's *masse*, or "end-world" *ku*, is whether it really is about cherry blossoms. The poem immediately following it is: *Though familiar / how unfathomable the mind=heart / of a blossom // not to give up and bloom / in a world like this!* (なれてだに知らぬは花の心哉かかる世にしもあかず開らん 心敬 *narete dani shiranu wa hana no kokoro kana kakaru yo ni shi mo akazu sakuran*). Does Shinkei 1) love blossoms like people? 2) treat them purely as religious trope? or, 3) is he still hooked on female beauty?

花咲て娑婆則（即）寂光浄土哉 一茶
hana saite shaba soku jakukô jôdo kana issa 1825
(blossoms blooming saha [fallen-world] instantly illuminated pureland!)

illumination

cherries bloom
and this world below is
the pure-land

This last *ku*, written less than two years before Issa's death, reflects the esctasy of blossom-viewing. The "serene light" (寂光) in the original is often appended to "Pure Land." I imagine a quiet, late afternoon viewing and the magical illumination only seen once in a while.

花見れはたゝゆいしんの浄土哉 失名 毛吹草
hana mireba tada yuishin no jôdo kana   lost name 1645
(blossoms-see-if/when, just only-heart/mind-argument's pure-land!)

    viewing blossoms   these blossoms:
the pure land appears   none other than paradise
   in the mind's eye!   within seen without!

                      seeing blossoms
                 does the pure land not
                    bloom within us?

Yuishin-ron means "mentalism" or "spiritualism," the belief that the Pure Land and other Buddhist reality is in the heart/mind. But, that is little help for interpreting the poem.

佛とはさくらの花に月夜かな 其角
hotoke to wa sakura no hana ni tsukiyo kana   kikaku -1707
(buddha/corpse/bliss-as-for cherry blossoms-and [full]moon-night!/'tis)

                        the buddha is
               cherry blossoms and moonshine
                    on a clear night

   what is bliss?   what's paradise?
cherry blossoms with   cherry blossoms with
   a full moon!   a full moon!

Hotoke has too many meanings to shake a stick at. It is even used for the saying "ignorance is bliss."

剃すてゝ櫻の奥の月夜哉 田旦 鞭随筆
sorisutete sakura no oku no tsukiyo kana   tadan? 1759
(shave-abandoning/ed cherry's recesses/beyond moon-night!/'tis)

    shaven locks   leaving his locks
left behind, a moonlit night   a night of the full moon
   beyond the bloom   deeper than cherry

First I saw a newly shaven=initiated retiree way out in the hills, beyond the cherry pale. But, then, recalling how the blossoms and the moon, though gently at odds, complement one another, I saw the new monk experiencing the moon seen through the blossomed branches as he never had before.

頭巾きて髪ある真似の花見哉 沾峨 吐屑庵
zukin kite kami aru mane no hanami kana   senga 1776
(head-cloth wearing hair-have mimicking blossom-viewing!/'tis)

   blossom-viewing   wearing a scarf
with a headwrap: i could   pretending i've hair to hide
   still have hair   blossom-viewing

It is more likely the poet is a monk than a bald man, for the pretension is deeper and more satisfying that way. This is less likely to be the case for Issa's "Mountain cherry / a man without hair is / adorned with it" (山桜髪なき人にかざゝる　一茶　*yamazakura kaminaki hito ni kazaruru*).

山櫻鏡こひしき僧あらん 其角
yamazakura kagami koishiki zô aran kikaku -1707
(mountain-cherry mirror dearly[recall] monk is not [?])

~~mountain cherries~~
~~when they bloom no bonze~~
~~misses his mirror~~

mountain cherries
aren't there any bonzes who
miss their mirrors?

Etiquette required samurai to make up before going out. Most monks were retired samurai. My first reading supposed that with the cherries in bloom, none missed human beauty, for they had a good substitute. But, on second thought, when the cherries bloom, isn't it natural to think about *our* looks?

ねたるまを佛といはし花盛 弘永 毛吹草
nedaruma o hotoke to iwaji hanazakari kôei 1645
(sleeping-daruma[dative] buddha-as say/call-not blossom-acme)

sleeping daruma
cannot be called buddhas
the bloom peak

you can't pretend
to be enlightened passed out
the bloom peak

花の塵は中々清し寺の庭 昌察 三籟
hana no chiri wa nakanaka kiyoshi tera no niwa shôsatsu 1734
(blossom-litter[petals]-as-for really fresh/pure temple-garden)

blossom litter
looks downright pure
a temple garden

花ちつてどつとくづるゝ御寺哉 一茶
hana chitte dotto kuzururu [kutsurogu] otera kana issa
(blossoms fall/en suddenly[mimesis] crumble[relax] [hon.] temple!/'tis)

blossoms fall
and a temple suddenly
lets out its breath

bloom over
it instantly unwinds
the old temple

Kôei's *daruma* might be a prostitute, but *passed out* works better. The first version of Issa's original is unclear as to whether the collapse (*kuzururu*) refers to activity at the temple or the visitors, or rather, their dispersal. His second version, using a more specific verb, *kutsurogu*, shows a temple humming with activity – visitors keep all the monks busy – suddenly *relaxing*. The viewpoint is temple-centric.

遠山の花に明るし東窓 一茶
tô yama no hana ni akarushi higashimado issa 1820
(far-mountain/s' blossoms-by bright east-window)

my east window
bright with cherry blossoms
of far-off mountains

Does the light from the sun setting in the Pureland West illuminate Japan's East?

39

White Elephant Cherry

普賢像桜
fugenzo-zakura

獣の雲にのぼるや普賢象　如貞 嵐山集
kedamono no kumo ni noboru ya fugenzô　nyotei 1651
(beasts clouds-in/into climb-up! samantabhadra-elephant)

ho! beasts rising
in clouds! samantabhadra's
white-elephant

Cherry bloom, as we have seen, was metaphorically speaking *cloud*. The kind and powerful *Samantabhadra* – Fugen in Japanese – sat at the side of the Buddha, upon his wise-looking white elephant. Another *ku* from the same anthology more simply notes: "*In white clouds / behold the Blossom of Law! / Fugen's elephant*" (白雲に法の花哉普賢象 貞徳？嵐山集 *shirakumo ni nori no hana kana fugenzo* teitoku 1651). Simple, though *nori* (Law= Buddhist scripture) is a pun for "riding."

我と花の匂ひをやかぐ普賢象　重弘 鷹筑波
ware to hana-no nioi-o ya kagu fugenzô　shigehiro 1642
(self-by blossom's scent smells! samantabhadra's elephant)

the white elephant
of samantabhadra smells
his own blossoms

This cherry with ivory-white white flowers has two leafy stamens that protrude from the petals far enough and with just enough bend to resemble an elephant's trunk. Did the poet perhaps note the bend in the stamen that makes it seem like it sniffs its own bloom? I confess to guessing the elephant's sex, for no elephant is an "it." So far, the *ku* for this cherry tree have had minimal information, so there was space for the long name, but that is not the case for the next *ku*. We will have to abbreviate.

普賢象のはなにまかれぬ人もなし　一正 毛吹草
fugenzô no hana ni makarenu hito mo nashi　issei 1645
(samant.'s elephant's trunk=blossoms-by wrapped/buried-not person-even not)

not a man not
wrapped up in the trunk of
saman's elephant

not a man not
buried in the blossoms of
saman's elephant

Corpses were once wrapped in mats; "buried" may be one of the connotations of "wrap" in Japanese. The "nose=blossom" homophone (*hana*) includes the elephant's trunk, for "trunk" is "nose" (*hana*) in Japanese. If you wish to go further and abbreviate all the way to "Sam," please do!

普賢象の陰も恐るな犬櫻 長吉 犬子
fugenzô no kage mo osoru na inuzakura chôkichi 1633
(samantabhadra's elephant's shade-even fear-not dog-cherry)

fear not the shade
of samantabhadra's elephant
my dog-cherry!

This silly *ku* is the only white elephant cherry I find over and over again in old anthologies.

ちへさかば文殊とやいはん普賢象 正朝 崑山集
chie [=chi e?] sakaba monju to ya iwan fugenzô shôchô? 1651
(1000-fold=wisdom blooms -if stupa-as-for call [it]! samant.'s elephant)

call it a *stupa*!   just stupendous!
a 1000-fold=wisdom blooms: this blooming stupa is no
the white elephant   white elephant

A *great* pun. Too bad it won't translate (My second reading is sheer nonsense. English speakers who are not Usanians should note, and then forget, the negative meaning of the white-elephant in it). This cherry is lushly peteled. Thirty layers are not exactly a thousand, but Indian concepts and big numbers go together. A *stupa* is an edifice containing a stupendous quantity of *sutra*=prayers. Enormous? Some, I have read, hold millions of short *sutra*. Walk around one and you are credited with saying them all. I think of it as *fast-food prayer*. A hundred times around and you could get a lifetime of praying accomplished, a thousand and you have prayers enough for the whole world. In Tibetan Buddhist countries, you might not even need to walk. Waterwheel *stupas* and heavily lettered flags let the wind flap them out for you. You've heard about the day when we no longer need to work because technology will? Well, in the Sinosphere they did the same thing for prayer thousands of years ago. Now, can you imagine each petal as a prayer and each tree as an organic stupa?

普賢象散りてや庭の土佛 正虎 洗濯物
fugenzô chirite ya niwa no tsuchibotoke masatora 1666
(samantabhadra's elephant falling: [the] garden's dirt/mud buddha [sculpture])

demonstration

saman's elephant
scatters in the garden
a mud-buddha

What a union: *two symbols of non-attachment!* The *tsuchi-botoke,* literally, "mud-Buddha" is an image of Buddha or other Buddhist gods, saints or whatnots made of dirt or mud, that might be fired or simply left to dissolve like a sand-castle. A slightly earlier *ku*: *"The snow-buddha / vanishes, leaving in its stead / a mud-buddha"* (雪仏消えてのあとや土仏　重方　鷹筑波 *yukibotoke kiete no ato ya tsuchibotoke* shigekata 1645). "Snow-Buddha" was what English, more secularly, calls a "snow-man." Today, this term is obsolete in much of Japan, where you need to call the snowman a "snow-Bodhidharma," or *yuki-daruma*. I do not know if the same holds for mud.

草木も成佛の縁か普賢象　氏重 犬子
kusaki mo seibutsu no en ka fugenzô shijû 1633
(grass-tree =plants even become-buddha=saved's affinity? sam's eleph)

are even the plants
brought into buddha's fold?
saman's elephant

If cherry petals "falling without regret" can be put to use as metaphor of Buddhist non-attachment, the tree deserves something for providing us with such catechism, no? How about a rung up the ladder of reincarnation putting it within striking distance [1] of Buddhahood?

潮来・わが目には遊女も見えて普賢象 柳几 鹿嶋立
itako // waga me ni wa yujô mo miete fugenzô ryûki? ()
(my eyes-to-as-for, play-woman [courtesan]-even see, sam.'s elephant)

~~high bloom-tide~~

my eyes can see
a woman of pleasure, too
saman's elephant

Elephants and most Buddhas enjoy folds of flesh,[2] the *sine qua non* for voluptuous women around the world. The poet saw the lush bloom, the amplitude of this heavily petaled cherry as a courtesan, and was brave enough to admit it. The subtle "too" raises the *ku* a cut above the simpler iconoclasm of the *senryû* which finds *not this but that* (usually sex) everywhere. I mistranslated the "Itako "prefacing the *ku* by reading it literally ("tide-comes"), when, it turns out to be a place well-known for a popular three-shrine pilgrimage. Unfortunately, I cannot yet find any connection between that place and the content of the *ku*.

---

1 Striking Distance? While I am not Jewish, Christian or Muslim, facile contrasts of such patriarchal beliefs and gentle equality-loving Buddhism are unfair. As elaborated in *Orientalism & Occidentalism* and *Topsy-turvy 1585*, some Buddhist beliefs can be even more hierarchal than Christianity. Reincarnation as climbing rungs of a ladder favors our species and favors the elite. Plants were not only below man but below animals. In Japanese Buddhism, we even find a tendency toward believing that women had to die and be reborn a man before having a go at the next step up: Enlightenment. Some sects even had prayers for women to try to change sex as they died to skip the extra life before paradise.

2 Folds of Flesh   Most cultures have long appreciated the beauty of soft excess. Neck-creases and back-folds are perhaps representative of this. The first also indicates the good finishing more common to over-term than under-term babies, while the latter is peculiar to women blessed with bounty. Both of these are found fully developed in Indian art yet are virtually unrecognized in the West, where hard muscles have – with a few notable lapses – been worshipped since Classical times. Because excess muscle is anti-ecological, one of my pet projects is deconstructing and eventually destroying this Greco-Roman fetish. *Why is muscle bad?* Calorie-wise, it is costly to maintain; it is conspicuous consumption because seldom put to use; and it represents a belligerent culture. Given the limits of our planet, driving to gyms (instead of walking places, using push-mowers, whacking weeds, carrying things and playing in the neighborhood, etc.) is no misdemeanor: it is a real crime.

Breaking One Off

折花・手折り桜
ori-bana, taori-zakura, etc.

紙きぬのぬるとも折らん雨の花　はせを
kamiginu no nuru to mo oran ame no hana bashô -1694
(paper-silk=clothing's wets even break-would blossom-rain)

<table>
<tr><td>

wearing paper
i'd still go out to break
a blossom in the rain

</td><td>

though rain wets
my paper robe, i'd have
these blossoms!

</td></tr>
</table>

The paper kimono is a seasonal word in its own right, a winter theme, for they were warm (the homeless know what they are doing with those newspapers) and Japanese winters are dry. Even shellacked, however, the glue used to cement the seams was not rain-proof. Blossoms in the rain, unless demolished by a strong wind, are a particularly luscious sight and Bashô couldn't resist them, as he couldn't resist attending the haikai jam-session, to which this was presented as a greeting and first poem, a *hokku*. My "break" *by itself* is not proper English, but even if an "~ off" were added (losing the poetry in the process, by narrowing down the metaphorical associations), we would still have the blossom/blossoms to deal with, for we are talking about blossoms attached to anything from a sprig suitable for a hair-pin, to a bough large enough to stick in the ground and sit under. Unfortunately, "to break off a branch of blossoms" is, by itself, over half a *ku* in length. Such accidents of language not only make translation hard; they decide what is and is not translated. In Blyth's *Haiku* (Spring) there are about 70 cherry blossom haiku, but none about "blossom-breaking." He does have several in the *plum* blossom section. One of these, by Issa, I consider *cherry* and include in this chapter: *"Failing strength: / Even in breaking off this flowering spray, / a grimacing mouth."* Note: the middle line in the original is simply *hana o oru*, or "blossom/s[obj.] break." Blyth's other broken-off and stolen *plum*-blossom/s became, respectively "the flowering branch of the plum," and "this branch of flowering plum-tree." Grammatically and semantically speaking, Blyth did right; but he gave himself more feet than I allow, for he did not dwell on sub-themes long enough to justify using a special abbreviated vocabulary as I do. *As far as I know, no one does. It is my invention for translated poetry and I hope others who would introduce poetry from foreign languages will rip me off and use it!*

折るは木の為か折られし花の為か　敬愚
oru wa ki no tame ka orareshi hana no tame ka keigu
(breaking-as-for tree/s-for[purpose]? broken blossoms-for?)

breaking them
is it for the blossoms
or for the trees?

breaking

With good pull-teeth saws and all those swords out there, why is it always *"break"* and not "cut?" The answer is found in a Japanese proverb: *"Fools cut cherries; fools don't cut plums"* (桜切る馬鹿梅切らぬ馬鹿 *sakura kiru baka; ume kiranu baka*). That is just how it is. Broken branches of cherry and sliced or sawn-off branches of plum apparently suck up water better. So "breaking them" is better for the blossoms on the branch you take. Whether it is better for the trees, too, I do not know.

手折らぬをうけよ神路の山櫻　宗祇
ta oranu o ukeyo kamiji no yamazakura   sôgi 1420-1502
(hand-broken-not(one) [acc.] accept[imper.]! god/s-path's mountain cherries)

the offering

unbroken blossoms:
kami, please accept this
whole mountain!

mountain cherries

bearing nothing
to the shrine: please take
them in place

spring oblation

on the gods' path
i bear a gift unborn:
mountain cherry!

The idea of ripping off branches of blossom for offerings seems cruel until we remember that when we pluck flowers most of them matter more to the plant they were plucked from than the branch does to the tree, right? This *ku* is not wholly original, for it plays upon *Kokinshû* poem #420, where the "brocade" (colorful mountain-side vista) made of fall maple leaves is offered in lieu of a proper oblation, but Sôgi's *"ta-oranu"* (unbroken [ones]) is bold, original language and *"ukeyo"* (take!/accept!) is powerful in the abrupt colloquial style later to mark many of the best *ku*.

折に殺生偸盗あり あた也と花に五戒の櫻哉　其角 墨俵
ada nari to hana ni go kai no sakura kana   kikaku -1707
(futile becomes and blossom-for/to 5-infractions' cherry!/'tis)

viewed in vain
the cherry is the most
sinful blossom

done for the hell of it
blossom-breaking breaks
the five taboos

fail to get one
and cherry of all blossoms
is most sinful

Buddhism's Five-Taboos, or Commandments if you prefer, forbid *killing, lusting, stealing, lying* and *gluttony* (drinking included). There is a preface to the *ku*, "sometimes there is killing, stealing" that may also be read "in breaking [off a branch], there is killing, stealing, "*i.e.,* greed for blossoms (possibly, meaning *women,* too?) sometimes gives rise to such behavior. The first reading assumes a drunken blossom bash damned by the failure to get some good prayer, or, poems out of it by which to compensate for those sins the beautiful cherry blossoms (women?) cannot help but engender; the second reading means that if you *break* something, you better do it well (Chinese novels on adultery come to mind); and the last allegorizes along the lines of Joane Sharpe's *Defense of Women.*: *"They say, women are proud, wherein made they trial? / They moved some lewd suit, and had the denial: / To be crossed in such suits, men cannot abide, / And thereupon we are entitled with pride"* (From Angeline Goreau: *The Whole Duty of Women,* a stupendous book about the 17c Battle of the Sexes in England packed with primary material). Be that as it may, Buddhists knew the difference between animal and vegetable life. Hokushi (-1718) recorded "playing at a mountain temple," where he observed: *"Blossoms inside / white tapa cloth: doling out / cherry limbs"* (山寺に遊ぶ）白妙に花や櫻の枝くばり 北枝 *shirotae ni hana ya sakura no eda-kubari*). Wrapped up in classy traditional paper mulberry cloth to go!

所思・折は折れ遅かれ疾かれちる櫻　暁台
oraba ore osokare tokare chiru sakura　gyôtai -1793
(break-if/when break[+imper.] later sooner fall/scatter cherry)

if you'd break it break it! sooner or later blossoms blow	if you'd take it break it! sooner or later blossoms fall

The reader may substitute "take" or "have" for "break," as desired. Thinking about the metaphysical and cavalier poets of England, who wove far more complex (and witty) poems of the same logic, I am not impressed, though the original claims to be "on the spot thought 所思." Likewise with, *"This heart that / would break off a limb / above the clouds* [i.e. a noble woman]" (雲の上の花も折取る心哉　紹巴 大発句帳 *kumo no ue no hana mo oritoru kokoro kana*　jôha (1523-1602)); *"The limbs left / unbroken are a cherry's / sour grapes* [flower on a peak = unattainable object (girl)]" – 折残す梢は花の高ね哉　昌叱 *orinokosu eda wa hana no takane kana*　shôshitsu (1540-1603)); *"Cherry blossoms: / broken only as far as / we can reach"* (手のとゝく程は折らるゝ櫻哉　一橋　あらの *te no todoku hodo wa oraruru sakura kana*　ikkyô 1689). There is something to be said for the penultimate *ku* (at least with my substitution of sour grapes for the boring "high-peak" (*takane*) but they are all too thin to chew on.

一枝は折らぬもわろし山櫻　尚白
hito-eda wa oranu mo waroshi yamazakura　shôhaku -1773
(one-branch-as-for break-not even bad-would[be] mountain-cherry)

mountain cherries
i'll break one: it would
be rude *not* to!

Breaking off a branch of blossoms is, obviously, a bad thing. But, not to break off at least one branch as a keepsake would insult the mountain cherry; as it would be discourteous for the man staying at the local inn to refuse the services of the local women, both (cherry trees and women) of whom were sometimes denigrated by the elite from the capital as *yamazaru,* "mountain monkeys." This *ku* is simultaneously a cruel *senryû* and a kind haiku. Or, does the poet really mean that he has an obligation to bring a spray home for others to see. Some men took their responsibility seriously, too. There is a story in Yamada's 1941 classic *Sakura Shi* (cherry history) of a man who, despite the saying *an infatuation lasts but three days* (耽恋三日), fell so hard for the blossoms of Mount Yoshino that he brought back a limb in 1772 and, after it finished blooming, kept it by his side *for life*, as a cane!

折らずんば空し宝の山櫻　重頼　毛吹草 1645
orazunba munashi takara no yamazakura　shigeyori 1601-1680
(break-not-if empty/worthless treasure-of[-a-]mountain-cherry)

treasure is vain, if you can't bring it back: mountain cherry	who wants treasure you can't make your own? mountain cherry

Kindly interpreted, this is a good *ku*, for when we see something beautiful, we want to share it with a loved one or someone we admire for sharing our aesthetic taste (or, some would have it, to make a rival jealous). The more beautiful the discovery, the bluer it makes us, unless we are lucky enough to have a fine camera on hand to "break off" the scene and take it home). Meanly interpreted, we have a smuck who must show off something to enjoy it. Here is what may well be its *waka* predecessor:

breaking

山のさくらを見てよめる・見てのみや人にかたらむさくら花てごとにをりていへづとにせむ　そせい法し 古今集 55
yamazakura o mite yomeru // mite nomi ya hito ni kataramu sakurabana tegoto ni orite iezuto ni semu kokinshû (905)

◎ composed while viewing mountain cherries ◎

cherry blossoms:
a picture you can hardly
put into words
break off a bough of each
for show & tell back home

for eyes alone!
no tongue can share them:
cherry blossoms
if i could i would break off
and bring back all of them!

can i only look
and tell not a soul of these
cherry blossoms?
what but break each one i see
to take them home with me?

The preceding poem (#54) has someone upset about being unable to cross a rapids to take bloom for those who cannot be there to see them. This could be altruistic vandalism (gifts for others) or egotism (trophies). The Rodd+Henkenius reading ends *"let us gather armfuls to / carry home as souvenirs."* The "gather" is a funny way to skirt the "break" translation problem but "souvenirs" is perfect !

いざ折て人中見せん山櫻　来山？一鐵 = 木桂？続錦？談林十百匂
iza orite jinchû misen yamazakura raizan?-1716 ittetsu? f.1675 confused but 17-18c
([if it turns out you] break [one] men-among show-would mountain cherry)

temptation

i almost feel like
beaking one to show people:
mountain cherries

country matters

i'd like to break one
and show it to other humans?
mountain cherry

breaking off a spray

if you can't take
people to the mountain,
take it to them

I did not translate *iza*, meaning *"on-a-whim/in-an-emergency/worst-case-scenario//if-i/you-really-must."*

手折とて宿にぞかざすさくらばな梢は風のうしろめたさに　權中納言國の信　新千載集
↓ *taori tote yado ni zo kazasu sakura-bana kozue wa kaze no ushirometasa ni* shinsenzai-wakashû 1359
吹風も治れる世は音もせでのどかに匂ふ花ざくらかな　藤原光経集
fuku kaze mo naoreru yo wa oto mo se de nodoka ni niou hanazakura kana fujiwaranomitsutsune-shû? ↓

cherry blossoms
broken adorn the brow
of our lodging:
but hear the old wind
whining in the boughs

a world where
even the blowhard wind
holds its tongue:
in tranquility, beautiful
blossoming cherries!

Not all breaking was benign. Big-shots had contests called *hana-awase* (花合), or "blossom-meets." Poetry may have been involved, but my impression is that the main thing was contesting the trophies brought down the mountain (as one might the point-spread of antlers or length of tom turkey's beard). I read of a branch revived by being thrust into a spring, of another so large three men were needed to carry it that ended up stuck into a pond – no vase being large enough? – and so forth. I can imagine a show-off element in the limb adorning the lodge. The second *waka* is not obviously about stolen branches but it does "celebrate a contest between the Emperor's wives." So, I guess, they, too, *took* trophies.

おりとらばをしげにもあるか桜花いざやどかりてちるまでは見む　　よみ人しえあず　　古今集#65
oritoraba oshige ni mo aru ka sakurabana iza yadori karite chiru made wa mimu　　anon. kokinshû (905)

     we would regret　　　　　　　　　　　　but it would be
  breaking off a branch of　　　　　　　　　a shame to steal a limb
      cherry blossoms　　　　　　　　　　　　cherry blossoms
if we must, let's take lodging　　　　　　　i'd rent a room and stay
and view them until they fall!　　　　　　　to see them through

This follows one advising us to break off a keepsake, lest our longing be left with petals of nothing. Call it the dialectics of the *Kokinshû*. If following the process from start to finish leaves us content to refrain, what about walking a mountain to view the whole sequence from bud to fallen petal in many cherry trees in a day? Still, it is not the same as seeing one tree through, which can be done by taking home a budding limb. Yet, I have yet to find a *waka* giving *that* as the reason for breaking off a limb. Perhaps the *oddest* of the "reason-for-breaking" *waka* I know is *Kokinshû* #100, where the excuse given by the anonymous poetess is the failure of a person to call: *"Because I await / one who does not call / I've broken off / this flowery limb / visited by its warbler"* (まつ人もこぬ物ゆゑにうぐひすのなきつる花ををりてけるかな　*matsu hito mo konu mono yue ni uguisu no nakitsuru hana o oritekeru hana*). But, why, the "because"? Rodd & Henkenius, with their *"... spray of blossoms / over which the mountain thrush / had wept tears and sadly sung"* make it seem like she wants a memento of her grief (*naku* can mean "weep" or "sing," hence the odd melodrama). Carter, has her do it *"though"*(?) he didn't show, to *"a branch of the flowering tree / the warbler begged me to spare."* I like the allusion ("woodman, spare this tree,"), but really! He speculates the action could be "out of spite toward the warbler, whose song reminds" her he hasn't come, or from "resigned determination to enjoy the blossoms whether the man comes or not." My first two guesses are that it was either envy toward the *blossoms* (plum/cherry tree) who met *their* (its) lover (the bird), or chagrin at having no one to share the bird's visit with.

新発意か花折跡や山おろし　嵐雪
shinhatsui ka hana oru ato ya yamaoroshi　ransetsu -1707
(new-launch-mind/will? blossom-break-after! mountain-gale)

    turned on again　　　　　　　　　　　renewed libido
by the broken blossoms?　　　　　　seeing the cherries' scars?
    a mountain gale　　　　　　　　　　　a gale descends

A witty (and very male) explanation of a late gale. The wind plays havoc on the blossoms. Seeing humans break off whole branches of bloom, the wind, its salacious appetite newly wetted, charges down the mountain. It helps to know that "gale" in Japanese is called a "mountain-descender."

花瓶にしいけどりにするや花軍　貞好 嵐山集
kabin ni shi ikedori ni suru ya hanaikusa　teikô 1651
(flower-vase-in done live-capture-as do:/! blossom-uprising)

    put in a vase
they are taken alive!
   the blossom war

Not all cherry blossom metaphor was female and/or sexual. There is an alternative concept of the blossom-as-warrior. The common trope *ikusa,* or uprising, is cleverly expanded to include a vase. *Ikedori,* or being taken alive, suggests *ike-bana,* flowers kept alive (Englished as "flower-arrangement")!

折る人に鳥なく花の山路哉　宗祇 毛吹草
oruhito ni tori naku hana no yamaji kana　sôgi 1420-1502
(breaking person-at bird/s cry/cries blossoms' mountain-trail!/'tis)

up in the hills
a bird cries at a man
blossom-breaking

This gentle depiction is, in its naturalness, more modern than most chronologically later *ku*.

花折て蜂に追るゝ山路哉 狂風 蘆別船
hana otte[orite?] hachi ni owaruru yamaji kana　kyôfû 1694
(blossoms breaking wasp/s-by chased mountain-trail!/'tis)

mountain path
a blossom thief flees
pursued by bees

breaking one off
i get chased by wasps:
a mountain trail

The accidental poetic justice needs no elaboration. I hope the reader will pardon my short-hand: "breaking one off." Call it a contrived colloquialism or *ad hoc* vernacular.

跡追し虻もみやけや山櫻　呉竹?
ato-oishi abu mo miyage ya yamazakura　gochiku? 1777
(after-chasing wasp/s also gift!/?/: mountain-cherry/ies)

mountain cherry:
the horsefly chasing after
is part of the gift

mountain cherry
are the pursuing horseflies
part of the gift?

The "mountain-cherry" is, of course, a broken-off branch of bloom. Here is humor not dependent upon punning or metaphor.

蝶一羽花ぬす人を追えけり 松波 三千花
chô ichiwa hananusubito o ôekeri　shôha 1725
(butterfly-one bloom-thief/ves[acc] chase[emph])

one butterfly
still chasing after
a blossom thief

蝶々や花ぬす人を付て行く　也有
chôchô ya hananusubito o tsuiteyuku　yayû -1783
(butterfly'ies!/: blossom-thief-after clinging-go)

the butterflies
fly away with
the blossom thief

The single butterfly in Shôha's poem is touching. The "still" is my way to try to match the emotive force of ~*keri*. The number of butterflies and thieves in Yayû's *ku* is anyone's guess.

花どろぼ蝶は無言で追かける 柳多留 63-9
hanadorobo chô wa mugon de oikakeru　yanagidaru 1830's
(blossom-thief butterfly/ies-as-for no-words-with chasing)

a blossom thief
chased by a silent
butterfly

blossom thief!
chased by a silent posse
of butterflies

Something is gained by specifying the obvious voicelessness of a butterfly. The original term *mugon* (no-words/silent,) has a human scent (eg. a monk who took *vows of silence*), so I don't feel my *posse* is out of place in this *senryû* that may or may not be a paraverse of the previous two haiku.

山の月花ぬす人をてらし給ふ 　一茶
yama no tsuki hananusubito o terashi tamau　issa 1819
(mountain's moon blossom-thief[acc.] shine[+polite imperative])

mountain moon,
shine down and illuminate
the blossom thief!

In a better-known *ku*, Issa has the moon *pointing out* a limb of plum to break/take, so it would be simplistic to assume the Buddhist moon is simply policing the mountain.

手折ても他國へ見せよ江戸の花 　理帆
taorite mo takoku e miseyo edo no hana　rihan 鞭随筆 1759
(hand-breaking-even other-country-to show[+imperative] edo's blossom)

break 'em off	even if you must
and show them abroad!	break a branch: show the world
edo blossoms	our edo's flower

Branches of cherry blossoms were typically broken off in the mountains and carried *in* to the big city, Edo. Call it domestic cultural imperialism – "other countries" means the rest of Japan – if you wish, but Edoites of all classes were rightly proud of the cherries of Edo, so, why *not* the reverse?

花を折る曲者見れば我子也 　梅室
hana o oru kusemono/kyokusha mireba waga ko nari　baishitsu 1768-1852
(blossom/s[acc.] break skilled-performer saw-when my child was[turned-out-to-be])

i looked and saw	i finally caught
the blossom-breaking knave	the master blossom-thief
was my own kid	it was my son

My unlikely second reading improves Kikaku's much better known *ku* about a blossom thief found to be "my son" (折とても花の間のせがれ哉　其角 *orutotemo hana no aida no segare kana* -1707), itself based on a story about a fair magistrate who catches a burglar who turned out to be his own son.

花の山常折てふる枝もなし 　一井 あらの
hana no yama tsune oritefuru eda mo nashi　issei 1689
(blossom-mountain normally breaking fall?/touch? branches[+stress] not)

blossom mountain:	the cherry park
you don't find branches that	no branches here for easy
just break and fall	break and touch

The 1st reading: Blossom-branch-breaking requires an act of will. I have seen large limbs break-off a snow-covered late-blooming eight-fold (possibly chrysanthemum = *kikuzakura*) petal cherry, but never from others. *The 2nd reading:* the easily broken branches are no longer there and breaking forbidden.

breaking

花折て人〔市〕の礫にあづからん 其角 続虚栗
hana orite hito no tsubute ni azukaran kikaku -1707
(blossom[branch]-breaking, peoples' stones despite/for keep-would)

    i'll break off   i'll break a bough   stealing blossoms
my blossoms though people   and use the bloom to ward off   i'll bring 'em to town though
    should stone me   the stones they throw   they stone me for it

In the original, this is prefaced by 日々酔如泥 *"day after day as drunk as mud."* I think Kikaku means to use the blossomy bough to protect himself from people tired of seeing him staggering about the street market (one version has "market" for "people"). Two Japanese advisors take the first and third reading, which have the drunken monk drawing fire for breaking or parading the blossoms (possibly women, for Kikaku as a bonze was forbidden *that?*) – through town. I still favor my improbable reading.

生酔をふみ台にして花を折 柳多留 10-2
namayoi o fumidai ni shite hana o oru yanagidaru 1775
([a] drunk-for stepping-stool-as using blossoms[acc.] break)

   foot-stool   ***sin upon sin***

   stepping upon   using drunks
a drunk to break off   as stepstools they would
   a cherry spray   steal the bloom

This *senryû* is not about women but the real thing. The first reading is more haiku than many *haikai*.

しばられるともよき花を盗なん 竹房 新選
shibarareru tomo yoki hana o nusumunan chikubô 1773
(tied-up though good/beautiful blossom/s[acc.] steal-would)

if i get tied up,
i get tied up! i'm off
to steal blossoms!

Being tied up (for ransom to be paid by employers, wife, etc) was one of two standard ways of handling a customer who didn't pay for his play in the pleasure quarters (If I recall correctly, the other was a cage in the street near the gate). The poet uses the expression to show his determination to bring home a blooming branch. I dropped the *yoki* good=beautiful. A blossom is that by definition, but it makes the allegory of a man enjoying a courtesan he cannot afford work better in the original.

折人を木にやくゝしの糸桜 無記名 嵐山集
oru hito o ki ni ya kukushi no itozakura anon. 1651
(breaking person[acc] tree-to! bind's thread[pendulant]-cherry)

  blossom thieves: a limb-breaker
bind them to the trunk   tied to a trunk by strings
  of string cherries   of *itozakura*

This *ku* plays with the name of the *thread*=weeping cherry (ch 29) and, unlike the last *ku,* can not be allegory. It is kinder punishment than what the Druids did to men who harmed oaks (The *Golden Bough*).

行心手折りて帰る花もかな（もなし）宗伊 新つくは
yuku kokoro ta-orite-kaeru hana mogana [mo nashi] sôi 1417-85
(going heart hand-breaking-return[-able] blossoms wish[for])

    ah, for a blossom
   my heart alone could break
     and bring back!

This lazy poet would have his blossom without going out to break it himself. Another version of the *ku* ends by saying such blossoms don't exist. The "wishing" *mogana* is better. Three hundred years later, Buson fantasized a pot of *sake* that would heat itself and walk over to him in mid-winter.

舟よせてさくらぬすむや月夜影 太祇
fune yosete sakura nusumu ya tsukiyo kage taigi -1772
(boat/s approaching cherry[blossoms] steal!/: moon-night image/shadow)

  pulling up by boat   pulling up by boat
to steal some cherry bloom   to steal some *sakura*
  against a full moon   moon shadows

The *kage* is ambiguous for it can mean a moonlit image *or* shadows. I am torn between a visible boat and passengers, a back-lit silhouette and the shadow cast by the people, boat and trees on the water.

ゆさ／＼と桜もて来る月夜哉 道彦
yusayusa to sakura motekuru tsukiyo kana michihiko -1819
(rustling-with [blooming] cherry[bough] bringing-come moon-night!/'tis)

   a cherry branch   the full moon:
lumbers home rustling   a large limb of cherry
    it's full moon   lumbers home

The psychological mimesis *yusa-yusa* suggests something *large* swinging/rustling/dangling (eg., a the balls of a bull walking through the grass). Hence, my lumbering translations. Only a tipsy man would have done such a thing at this time in history: as noted already, centuries earlier noble blossom thieves broke off limbs so large it took a party of men to carry them.

酔さめて土手に突きさす櫻かな 梅室 アルス
yoi-samete dote ni tsukisasu sakura kana baishitsu 1768-1852
(drunk-sobers/awakes levee/bank-into stick-in cherry!/'tis)

     sobering up
he sticks his cherry branch
     into the bank

If one is too drunk, one might not make it home at all. Sobering up, a large branch would not only start to feel heavy but be an embarrassment, for it would say "I am a vandal." This man sticks it into the bank of the levee (commonly used as roads in Japan, they are wonderful for one can enjoy an excellent view and, in the summer, be cooled by the breeze as one walks: if you are in Tokyo, be sure to walk on top of the embankment near Sophia University and give my best to the old pine trees) and, if he rationalizes as I do, tells himself he has done his work to decorate the world, and goes home.

breaking

折かへる袂は花のみやま哉　紹巴
ori-kaeru tamoto wa hana no miyama kana jôha -1602
(broken-return bosom-as-for blossoms' deep/honorable-mountains!/'tis)

my bosom full of broken limbs returns: a blossom mountain!	their bosoms full of broken limbs return: blossom mountains!

Japanese at this time were astounded at the amount of (smuggled) goods that could fit into the Portuguese pantaloon (our so-called "thunder-thighs" look like bird-legs next to these huge *globes* favoring the bow-legged) and the Europeans, for their part, were impressed with what Japanese could stuff into their *kimono* breast and sleeves (see *Topsy-turvy 1585* for the *astounding* details!).

花にきてをる人いそぐかへさ哉　紹巴
hana ni kite oru hito isogu kaesa kana jôha 1523-1602
(blossoms-to coming break person/s hurry return!/'tis)

how people who
come to break blossoms
do hurry home!

Jôha, the top *renga* master of his time, like Sôgi, the top *renga* master of the previous generation, may have been strongly against the practice of tearing off boughs of bloom – why I suspect my first-person reading of the last *ku* is less likely than the third-person one (though he may have changed his attitude with age) but, unlike Sôgi, sometimes let his temper get the better of his wit:

花の枝を折れは香もなく色もなし　紹巴 *hana no eda o oreba ko mo naku iro mo nashi* jôha (blossoms' branch[acc.] break-if/when scent-not color-not)	またれしもうへなる花の色香哉　紹巴 *matareshi mo uenaru hana no iro-ka kana* jôha (waited-for even planted-are blossoms' scent-color!/oh)
when you break a blossom branch, it has none: no color, no scent	wait you must, but oh, the scent and color found: blossoms you plant

As Wilde put it, *"all bad poetry springs from genuine feeling. To be natural is to be obvious, and to be obvious is to be inartistic."* Jôha's "How people . . ." *ku* says something about the character of people who break blossoms and make women. They are not much on afterplay. But, as we shall see, many branches were broken not for lovers but for the sick and decrepit at home, so it is unfair to paint with a broad brush. Jôha knew this. So I have a faint suspicion he was not really upset about people taking some branches home, but, rather, was *furious* about the wife-stealing habit of Hideyoshi. The shôgun did horrible things to more than one good man (dispatch them to Korea, make them commit suicide for a trumped up charge) to obtain the object of his lust. The famous lover, Hikaru Genji, did not do this sort of thing. Failing to find the perfect woman (one as beautiful and brilliant as he, himself, the Shining Prince?), he adopted a ten-year-old, educated and married her at fourteen. And there are many examples of "planting" them much younger. Contemporary Usanian readers may not find *growing your own* much better than breaking/taking older women who might have their own (different) ideas. For the sake of East-West fairness, let's note the same sort of thing happened in Europe, though the girls were not educated as well as in Japan where the literacy of both sexes was considered important. The second *ku,* above, has a good pun in it: *ue-naru* means both *to plant* and to *be better*. If I should learn that these *ku* were written by Jôha before Hideyoshi took power and lovers, then I will, in some future edition, admit to being wrong and come up with something else.

藤原朝臣広嗣の桜の花を娘子に贈れる歌一首・この花の一枝のうちに百種の言そ隠れるおほろかにすな
kono hana no hitoyo no uchi ni momokusa no koto zo komoreru ôroka ni su na   manyôshû #1456 (8c)
娘子の和へたる歌一首・この花の一枝のうちは百種の言持ちかねて折らえけらずや   万葉集 #1457
kono hana no hitoyo no uchi wa momokusa no koto mochikanete oraekerazu ya   manyôshû

– one song from fujiwara-no-hirotsugu to a young lady he sent cherry blossoms –

within this single
blossomed limb reside
the seed of countless words:
don't you take it lightly!

– a song from the maiden in reply –

really! so this limb
of blossoms was so heavy
with the seed of all those words
that the poor thing broke off?

I introduce these *waka* (in awful translation, *sorry!*) not just to give an example of the broken-bough message complete with something *haikai* lack – a reply – but because they were given as proof the *sakura* foretold the harvest by ethnologist-critic Origuchi, who asked rhetorically "If it wasn't customarily believed in the Nara Era (8c) that cherry blossoms held a secret message, how could these poems have been written?" Origuchi could be a ridiculous literalist. The Chinese character for "hide" was used, but it meant *pregnant with*, or *full of*. Were cherry blossoms the only sent objects invested with messages at the time, his claim *might* have held water, but that was hardly the case.

文は跡に櫻さし出す使哉 其角
fumi wa ato ni sakura sashidasu tsukai kana   kikaku -1707
(letter-as-for afterward cherry thrusting-out messenger'tis)

the page thrusts forward a spray: "the letter will come later"	"the letter will be forthcoming" the page hands me blossoms

The page is not all I see. I see the sender having too much fun on cherry mountain to write a letter. But was Kikaku really on the receiving end? Or, did he attach this *ku* to blossoms he sent back? The *ku* reminds us that blooming branches were part of Japan's gift-circulating culture.

馬士にゆるされて折櫻かな 梅室
umanori ni yurusarete-oru sakura kana   baishitsu
(horse-gentleman[samurai]-to permitted, breaking cherries!)

our horsemen have full rein to break them cherry blossoms	cherry blossoms what knights are granted to break an' take

Issa's contemporary Baishitsu plays with the right to take women (an unofficial *droit du seigneur*), but don't be fooled: the real wit lies in the high status of the *sakura* as the equal or proper mate of the *samurai* (recall the saying that one is to men as the other is to flowers: the *best*) and a pun where the polite part of the verb "permitted" (*oru*) turns into "break" by fiat, confirmed by Chinese character.

breaking

羽織きて花折さふな女かな　梅室
haori kite hana orisôna onna kana baishitsu 1768-1852
(*haori*-wearing, blossom break-appears-woman!/'tis)

ah, her *haori*	*that* woman
says that woman will	in a coat, looks likely
break a blossom	to take a spray

A *haori* is a thin but beautifully lined piece of dress worn over a kimono. Relatively short of sleeve and loose, it might be called a cross between a shawl and an overcoat. We are talking about a woman of samurai (*bushi*) class or a noble. Granted, if every footman and peasant woman were allowed to do the same, it would have been an ecological disaster.

輿の花盗人よぬす人よ　一茶 1813	夕月や花泥坊の迎ひ駕　一茶 1806
norimono no hananusubito yo nusubito yo issa	*yûzuki ya hanadorobô no mukai-kago* issa
(sedan's blossom-thief hey/! thief hey/!)	(evening-moon!/: blossom-thief's meet-basket)

hey, blossom-thief	evening moon:
in the sedan, a blossom	a sedan pulls up for
thief is a thief!	the blossom thief

Who can doubt that blossom guards picked on poor "thieves" more than wealthy ones! An evening moon is a waxing one that will not last out the night. The wealthy man who prefers breaking to planting trees is safely and regally escorted home before the light is lost.

脇息にあの花折れと山路哉　其角 末若葉	手折せ手を花瓶や御駕脇　百萬 新選
kyôsoku ni ano hana ore to yamaji kana kikaku -1707	*taorose te o hanabin ya okagowaki* hyakuman 1773
(armrest-to "that blossom break[imp]" mountain path)	(hand-breaking hand blossom-vase: sedan lackey)

the imperative	*sedan sidekick*
from his armrest	the hand, made
"break me that blossom!"	to break a spray, made
a mountain road	into its vase

Kikaku was accompanying a lord to a hot-spring resort(行露公あたみへ御浴養の餞). Did the lord in the sedan have a footman do *his* bid, or if Kikaku also was carried, in which case "*his* → *my* armrest."

わか役に花盗しもむかし哉　一茶
wakayaku ni hananusumishi mo mukashi kana issa 1822
(young-role/duty-as blossoms-stole also long-ago!/'tis/oh-so)

that, too, long past	blossom stealing
my juvenile duty of	as a young sidekick, even
blossom-stealing	*that* was long ago

Wakayaku implies Issa was not misbehaving on his own but expected to do daring things because of his youth. Possibly he was prompted to do it for his employers as depicted in Kikaku's *ku*. As far as I know, blossoms and an unmarried woman's love were the only thing that could be stolen without risking a death penalty in old Japan (See *Topsy-turvy 1585* re. the harshness of the law).

手折ては水こそ花の命なれ 六條内大臣 つくは
ta-orite wa mizu koso hana no inochi nare   interior-minister rokujo 1356
(hand-breaking-as-for water especially blossoms-life becomes/is)

after it's broken water is what becomes a blossom's life	a stolen branch the blossoms' lives are now pure water

呑み明けて花生にせん二升樽 芭蕉
nomi-akete hana-ike ni sen ni-shôdaru   bashô 1694
(drink-emptied blossom-arrangement-as-do-let's two-shô keg)

this gallon jug
let's drink and refill it
with blossoms

One wonders what the metaphorical implications, if any, are of the water in the first *ku*. Bashô did his impromptu, and, for him, perhaps, thin, thank-*ku* after receiving gifts of *udo* (a soft plant with shoots that taste like spring itself [1]), "thick *sake*" and "one type of tea" from his followers. I could not match "*nomi-akeru*," meaning both "drink until empty" *and* "drink all night," in English.

おりおこせむかしかたらんうばざくら 園女
ori-okose mukashi kataran ubazakura   sonojo -1723/ 26?
(breaking[puns on ~~awaken?~~] send old-times tell-would/let's auntie-cherry)

~~break, wake and~~ ~~make her speak of olden times~~ ~~the auntie cherry~~	steal me a spray and i'll tell tales of past days granny cherry	~~i'd break awake~~ ~~past memories, let's talk~~ ~~auntie cherry~~

"The idea of breaking one off to catch the old tree's attention is outrageous." So was my ~~old~~ reading. My new one assumes an elderly Sonojo = auntie/granny cherry. As a young woman, she knew Bashô and his tamer *ubazakura* (#7-21). Another of her *ku* more than matched his two *shô* jug (#40-51):

山人の薪に花を折添て 園女 無俳言
yamahito no maki ni hana o orisoete   sonojo -1723?26?
(mountain-person's firewood-to blossom break- adding/ed)

flower arrangement in the hills

i add a bough to a bundle of firewood broken bloom	adding a spray to firewood on the back of a woodsman

As described in Book I, (ch 5), Sonojo was known for her impromptu art. I do not know if the firewood was by the house or left momentarily atop an A-frame back-pack (still found in Korea).

---

1. Udo   The scent of this plant (*Aralia cordata*) is unique and cannot not be described in terms of any other. The great plant collector David Fairchild, whose mother-in-law, Mrs. Alexander Graham Bell, succeeded in growing it in Nova Scotia, wrote: "I was delighted with the delicate flavor," but did not even try to describe what that flavor was. *Udo* is only one of many plants which the West has continued to overlook. *Myôga* (*Zingiber mioga* – a ginger), *mitsuba* (*Crytotaenia japonica* – a honewort or stone parsley) and *seri* (*Oenanthe javanica* – a dropwort or Japanese parsley) and *gobo* (burdock, damned doc, or cockle-burr) are only some of the most popular vegetables which are common in Japan but strangely missing, even from most supposedly Japanese restaurants in the USA, which tend to use only food Usanians are familiar with!

~~~~~~

折らで帰る人なまめかし山桜　漢甫 花供養
ora de kaeru hito namamekashi yamazakura　kanpo 1795
(breaking-not-with return people bewitching/voluptuous mountain-cherry)

mountain cherry (or, returning from the wild sakura without a trophy)

| how bewitching
those who break off without
breaking bloom | people returning
without broken blossoms
are voluptuous | mountain cherries
the beauties return without
stolen blossoms |

Shirô asked *"I'd like to know / what blossom thieves feel / for the blossoms"* (問ひたきは花盗人の心かな 士郎 *toitaki wa hananusubito no kokoro kana* -1813). An older *ku* replies: *"Cherry blossoms / broken off and kept by / short-sighted men"* (折りとるははなのさきなる心哉　弘永 毛吹草 *oritoru wa hana no sakinaru kokoro kana*　kôei -1645). It echoes a proverb, "conclusions made before the bloom reach not the guts," (花の先の合点は腹の底まで通らぬ *hana no saki no gatten wa hara no soko made tôranu*), *i.e.*, are not taken to heart. So, alacrity may not make us wise, but can forbearance really make us sexy?

な折そと叱るに一枝花の庭　梅翁
na ore so to shikaru ni hitoe hana no niwa　sôin 1604-82
("break not!" scold-despite[=yet] one bough, blossom-garden/yard)

| the blossom garden:
don't break one! he scolds
handing me a spray | scolded, he still
breaks one off: a whole
garden of bloom |

The first reading. *We all have a warm memory like this, of being chastised lightly yet given something we wanted.* The "scold=*shikaru(ni)*" is homophonic with "yet" (然るに) and plays on a song 謡曲 called Banana/ Bashô「芭蕉」with the same "yet" in it「然るに一枝の花を捧げ」. *Yet,* the second reading may be as common. The beautiful blossoms are irresistible to the child/youth who creeps back to steal them despite being scolded. I added "a whole," because a child who saw yard-full of trees would be able to rationalize his action more easily. Would the owner miss just *one* branch?

おれ／＼と折せて花のあるじ哉　蓼太
ore ore to orasete hana no aruji kana　ryôta 1707-87
("break! break!" and break-allows/has blossoms' host!/'tis)

| break one off!
break one off! he shouts:
the blossom host | the blossom host
go ahead! go ahead!
break one off! |

手折もて見つ我宿の櫻哉　宗因 三籟
ta-ori mote mitsu waga yado no sakura kana　sôin 1604-82
(hand-broken[one] bringing see[it], my dwelling's cherry!/?/)

| a stolen spray
it turns out to be from
my own garden | i break-off and
bring one in to view: that's
my house cherry | i break one off
for viewing, a cherry
from my garden |

How convenient to have your own cherry tree nearby to "break" for yourself or others! It is a fountain of gifts, though not so prolific as the plum: a small tree sprouts hundreds of budded stems every spring. If the first reading is correct, we must try to guess who did it. A proud young son? A lazy servant? Or, was it bought from a stranger? The second is clever. My respondent votes for the third.

折よしと花もほゝゑむ軒端かな　鬼貫
ori yoshi to hana mo hohoemu nokiba kana onitsura 1660-1738
(break fine-as blossoms also smile/smiling veranda!/'tis)

sure, break me!
the cherry tree smiles
by the veranda

Had Onitsura used the standard "smile" for flowers and mountains, *warau*, the implication that the cherry blossom was his wife or a maid would be too strong. This *hohoemu* is a cheerful and wholesome round-cheek smile that tells us Onitsura is indeed writing about a sweet and willing *tree*.

盗まれて笑ふも花のあるし哉　近江朽 木社中? 新選
nusumarete warau mo hana no aruji kana kinkôkyû 1773
(stolen laugh [person+emph.] blossoms' owner!/?/'tis)

the one laughing
about the theft is the owner
of the blossoms

A magnanimous owner is a pretty picture; and one that gets a kick out of watching the thieves is a masterpiece. This *ku* reminds us of *how pleasant it is to be an owner*. I dreamed of a house and planting fruit trees as a teenager and here I am, old, with no real estate, nothing growing and nothing to guard or give away. Old Issa so enjoyed his few years of ownership, he guarded even his bitter persimmon tree just to tempt kids to try to steal the fruit! *Ownership*. As I write, the heartless cabal of Greedy Old Plutocrats (the GOP) say we all should enjoy "the ownership society" while taking what little we own for themselves. They lie through their teeth, doubtless because they agree with Plato that the ruling class has that right: *"He can say / whatever he likes: lord / of the cherries"* (我まゝを いはする花のあるじ哉　路通　アルス *wagamama o iwasuru hana no aruji kana*　rotsû 1649-1738). Pardon my getting off-track. It is spring and I am feeling my poverty. The translation of these *ku* is difficult because *aruji* (sometimes pronounced *nushi*) is "host" for a blossom-viewing yet also "owner," "lord" "master" and/or "boss."

木々はあれと櫻を春の主哉　宗因 三籟
kigi wa aredo sakura o haru no aruji kana sôin 1604-82
(trees-trees-as-for are-but cherry[dative?] spring's host!/?/'tis)

trees there are many,　　　　　　　　　　of all the trees
but it is the cherry i call　　　　　　　　you might say cherry
lord of the spring　　　　　　　　　　　owns the spring

Oddly enough, "owner" would never work for a cherry, but "own" does! Respecting blossom-thievery we should not overlook the party actually harmed. Whom, we might ask has been robbed? For a garden, the owner, for a mountain, the public (or Shôgun if it is his preserve); but, in all cases, it is the trees – the true *Lords of the Spring* – themselves. It goes without saying that broken limbs can give dastardly bugs or insidious disease a foothold. Yet, is it not true that breaking relatively small branches may, by increasing a tree's resistance (flora engage in chemical warfare, defensive and offensive) help protect it from damage when larger limbs break in gales? Also, the result can be aesthetically pleasing, while less growth can increase a tree's longevity by slowing it down. Botanists are invited to gloss this for a future edition. *Haikai* generally does not touch these matters, except in allegory (their consolation is being loved or being shown off) and complaint (when it's a sorry sight).

炭売も一重さくらのあるじ哉 野水 続虚栗
sumi-uri mo hitoezakura no aruji kana yasui 1687
(charcoal-seller too single-petal cherry's master!/'tis)

櫻咲てあるじ二人の庵かな 存疑芭 翁反古
sakura saite aruji futari no iori kana ?bashô? 1783
(cherry blooms/ing master two's hut/atelier)

    the charcoal-man
himself the proud lord of
    a *hitoe-zakura*

    the cherry in bloom
this is now a cottage
    with two masters

Why *hitoezakura?* Because "single-petal cherry" is a beat too long and *monotonous,* as description tends to be. My poetic license added the "proud." The cherry with a modest bloom might *also* be his wife or daughter, accompanying him on his rounds selling a product which, as it *not incidentally* turns out, was generally made from cherry. Could one tree, safe from his ax, bloom outside his hovel? The second *ku* was said to be by Bashô (1544-94). Perhaps, or perhaps not. It, too, has two masters/hosts.

山桜花の主や石仏 一茶
yamazakura hana no aruji ya ishibotoke issa 1805
(mountin-cherry blossom's master/host?/!/: stone-buddha)

    mountain cherry
the lord of these blossoms
    a stone buddha

    mountain cherry
is *that* the blossom host?
    a stone buddha

I write "buddha" but it could be a saint, arhat, any type of buddhist statue.

草臥れて寝にかへる花のあるし哉　蕪村
kutabirete ne ni kaeru hana no aruji kana buson -1783
(exhausted sleep[= roots]-to return blossoms' master/host'tis)

    exhausted he
leaves us to go to sleep
    the blossom lord

    the petals seek
their roots while master
    falls asleep

This *ku* refers to and is dedicated to Bashô, who wrote of being tired out from officiating at *haikai* events at tree after tree. Buson combined an idiom based on the commonplace pun of sleep=roots (*ne*), "return to sleep=roots" (for petals fall there) with a gloss on the following *ku* by Bashô: *"When, exhausted, / we lease room at a lodge, / the wisteria"* (*kutabirete yado karu koro ya fuji no hana*). Wisteria bloom immediately after the cherries finish. But, I like to forget all that and imagine the master doing his rounds, a day with this blossom, a night with that, like a tom-cat when the feline community is in heat ...

少年行・花手折美人縛らん春一夜　几董　井華
shônen-yuki // hana ta-oru/ori bijin shibaran haru hitoyo kitô 1789
(youth/s go/leave // blossom/s hand-break/ing beauty tie-up-would spring one-night)

    let's tie and keep
 that pretty blossom-thief
     one spring night

                                 let's tie and keep
                             a blossom-stealing lad
                                  a whole night

               let's break a bloom
       and tie up the beauty for
             one night of spring

The Chinese preface is telegraphic: *"youth/s go forth!,"* or *"youthful action."* Traditionally, either sex could be a "beauty" (*bijin*) in the Sinosphere, and beauty was proverbially short-lived. With my first two *ta-oru* readings (where the blossom-breaker/stealer is the beauty), the desire to keep one's youth = the spring = fuse with keeping *a* youth (homo-eroticism). With the last *te-ori* reading (where a branch of bloom is broken which is the beauty), the metaphor, if "she" is a metaphor, is female, for the cherry was generally considered so. Imagine "her," if you will, bound to the main pillar of a house holding a blossom-viewing poetry fest. *Hitoyo* ("one-night") puns on "one branch." (専門家の欄外注、求め！)

掃く人の折る人叱るさくらかな　也有
haku hito no oru hito shikaru sakura kana yayû 1701-83
(sweeping person's breaking person scolds cherry[petals]!)

     the raking man
 scolds the breaking man:
     cherry blossoms

                                     the breaker
                                tells off the raker:
                                   sakura rules

Since word order matters little in Japanese and the *ku* lacks grammar signs, who can say who scolds whom? There is humor in a lowly raker telling off his better or in a thief scolding someone for committing an aesthetic *faux pas* – cherry petals should be left on the ground to blow away on their own. *I* favor the second reading; my respondent advises against it, and thinks I think too much.

おれぬすめとても花には狂ふ身ぞ　成美
ore nusume totemo hana ni wa kuruu mi zo seibi -1816
(break! steal! completely blossoms-to-as-for crazy body/self!)

   break 'em! steal 'em!
 when it comes to blossoms
     this man is mad!

                                break 'em! steal 'em!
                              you might say i get crazy
                                around blossoms

A drunk caught up in what we might call blossom-rut, egging on others acting on their lust, or a strange self-portrait of a metaphysically dirty old man? Probably the latter, because of the *mi*=self.

花を折こゝろいく度もかはりけり　成美
hana o oru kokoro ikutabi mo kawarikeri seibi -1816
(blossoms[acc.]-break heart howmany-times-even changing[emph.])

    breaking bloom
  my mind changes
    over and over

                                    half a mind
                                to break one off
                                  half a mind

To break or not to break, that is the question? Timidity? Pangs of conscience? Aesthetic qualms over the choice of limb? Hesitation over the relative strength of branch and arm? *Resolution* brings health:

花を折拍子にとれししゃくり哉　一茶
hana o oru byôshi ni toreshi shakuri kana issa 1818
(blossom[acc.] break moment-in took hiccups!/that-is)

the moment i broke
the blooming branch, there
went my hiccups!

おとろへや花を折にも口曲る　一茶
otoroe ya hana o oru ni mo kuchi magaru issa 1817
(weakening!/: blossoms[acc.]-breaking-at/with-even mouth distorts)

marks of aging
he can't even break one off
without grimacing

going downhill:
just breaking off a sprig
makes me grimace

Both *ku* could be self-portraits, for Issa is in his mid-50's. But the second, with that "grimace" (lit. mouth-bend) more easily seen than felt *might* well be about Issa's patron Seibi, or another old man.

春の花今は盛りににほふらむ折りて挿頭さむ手力もがも　大半家持 #3965
haru no hana ima wa sakari ni nihofuramu orite-kazasamu tajikara mogamo manyôshû 8c

spring blossoms
so beautiful in the peak
of their bloom:

had i but strength enough
to break and wear them!

Before reading that the author of the poem, recovering from a serious illness and too weak to go outside even with a cane, wrote it to apologize for not being able to attend a blossom-viewing, I treated the poem a bit too cavalierly:

Unlike the case with haiku (post-Bashô *haikai*) where breaking one off usually has no allusion – as confirmed by the details in Issa's and Seibi's *ku* – and we assume innocence unless proven guilty, we hold generalizing old *waka* [1] guilty if not proven innocent. The old and sick *Manyôshû's* main editor, Ôhan Iemochi was a famous womanizer. There is, of course, an off-chance he just misses ripping off branches of willow to wrap around his crown or cherry to deck himself out, however such was done,[2] but, chances are, he means that he still has eyes for beautiful women but is too decrepit to properly swive them (forgive my olde English).

---

1. Generalizing Old Waka While *haikai* may generalize, *waka* only occasionally do *not*. Here, is one exceptionally concrete cherry in unpoetic translation: *Above the waterfall on cloud-covered Mount Tatsuda, blooming on Ogura Peak, where the mountain wind and rain never cease, the blossoms have blown from the top branches, but those on the lower branches had better not fall and get messed up until my traveling lord returns!" Manyôshû* #1747 (*shirakumo no tatsuda . . .*) The envoi advises the Wind God to hold his breath for seven days. Cherries do bloom top down and the upper branches would catch more wind.

2. Blossoming Heads WWII pilots had sprigs of blossom stuck in their twisted cloth headbands. I read that willow was used for the supporting headbands at these old blossom-viewings but do not yet know the whole *style*.

花のある枝てはないか斧の音 道悠 恒誠
hana no aru eda de wa nai ka ono no oto dôyû ()
(blossoms are/have branch is it not? axe's sound)

<blockquote>
now, is that not
a branch with blossoms?
the sound of an axe
</blockquote>

An axe chopping firewood would make a drier sound. One chopping down a living branch would thud. This is not the accepted way to obtain a flowery branch unless we assume it to concern a plum rather than a cherry, but that is unlikely because thin green plum shoots cut so easily they make little noise.

鎌できる音やちよい／＼花の枝 露節 貝掩ひ
kama de kiru oto ya choichoi hana no eda rosetsu 1672
(hoe-with cut sound:/! now and then blossom-branch)

<blockquote>
again the sound   now and then
of a hoe chopping off   the hacking sound of a hoe!
a cherry limb   blooming limbs
</blockquote>

This *sounds* horrid and brings to mind a piece of reporting by Issa of farmers lynching gamblers who thought to take advantage of them. Farmers can be far scarier than samurai because they kill things in crueler ways. Not all branches can be wrested off a tree even by strong men (Gorillas do much better, but then again, they do it every night to make their beds, some of which must be flowery!). It is hard to say if hoes are being put to a new use for aesthetic reasons (wanting to take a branch home) or blossom-laden limbs are begrudged the shade they cast on the fields. Change "limb" to "branch" for less sadism.

いらぬ花折たく成るが手癖哉 一茶
iranu hana oritaku-naru ga tegusa kana issa 1822
(unneeded/superfluous blossom break-want become-is hand-habit!)

<blockquote>
my natural bent: i cannot see
to reach out and snap off   extraneous bloom but
superfluous bloom   i would break it
</blockquote>

Issa was a bit of a nurseryman, though he mostly confined himself to the gentleman's flower, Chrysanthemum. Be that as it may, Issa's "natural bent" is not representative of the practice of breaking off branches to present to people, or to bring back home. This is a one-of-a-kind *ku*, precious for reminding us that breaking can improve the shape of the tree, the *eda-buri* (branch-style).

どこそこや点かけておく花見の日 一茶
doko soko ya ten kakete-oku hanami no hi issa 1821
(where[here?]-there!/:points placing blossom-viewing day/s)

<blockquote>
this tree, a ten!   *popular poet-master*

here, there and   leaving points
everywhere i grade them: here and there, my day of
blossom-viewing   blossom-viewing
</blockquote>

40 73-76

I once was *sure* Issa was either critiquing the trees or the women viewing them; but, now, think it more likely he went from tree to tree grading (putting points on) *ku*. As mentioned before, cherry-blossoms meant poetry matches and this was written at the time Issa became popular enough to have been in demand as a judge. Still, Issa *did* think about the quality of individual trees. Once, he even expressed this inversely: *"After leaving them / every cherry tree gets / a high mark"* (*sareba koso daihyôban no sakura kana* さればこそ大評判のさくら哉　一茶). Someone, perhaps on Prarie Home Companion, sang a parody of Julio Iglesias and Willie Nelson's romantic hit: "To all the *cats* we loved before." Issa might have sung: "To all the *trees* we've loved before."

持て贈るみやげの雲や山櫻　也有
motte-okuru miyage no kumo ya yamazakura　yayû 1701-83
(bringing give gift-cloud!/: mountain-cherry[blossoms])

<table>
<tr><td>

mountain cherry
carried down, the perfect
gift of a cloud!

</td><td>

call this gift
a cloud from the peaks
cherry blossoms

</td></tr>
</table>

ひとつかみしら雲贈る櫻かな　蓼太
hitotsukami shirakumo okuru sakura kana　ryôta 1707-87
(one-grab white-cloud give cherry[blossoms]!/'tis)

<table>
<tr><td>

here's a handful
of white cloud for you:
cherry blossoms!

</td><td>

i'm sending you
a clutch of cumulous
cherry blossoms

</td></tr>
</table>

A preface for the second *ku* explains that the poet gathered petals from various famous spots in the Yoshino cherry hills to send to a friend accompanied by the *ku*. I imagine the "one-clutch/grab" of petals was actually enough to fill a couple kimono sleeves, which is to say a gallon or two.

花をけふつみてしほれぬ袖もなし　紹巴
hana o kyô tsumite-shiborenu sode mo nashi　jôha 1523-1602 x2
(blossoms[obj] today stuffing-wring-not sleeve-even-not)

lacrima cerasum

today, all of us
wring our sleeves, stuffed
with cherry petals

This *ku* (also in the *Equality,* ch.8) describes a benign alternative to breaking branches: scooping up blossom petals and carrying them home. It is metaphorical – or, *metaphysical* – for sleeve-wringing is idiomatic for crying (like "our" handkerchief-wringing), and dyeing. Jôha, the kind-hearted master of link-verse, was, however, disappointed to find that most of the people in his war-wracked era, as might be expected, tended to lack or repress deeply felt emotion toward each other or toward the blossoms. *"Oh,"* he lamented, *"for the darkly / dyed sleeves of old to bring out / the blossom's beauty!"* (花の色にむかしのこさの袖もかな　紹巴 *hana no iro ni mukashi no kosa no sode mo gana*).

◎ Sour◎Grapes◎Again◎

> Apparently there have been some foreign tourists of the brutal class in this place, since it has been deemed necessary to set up inscriptions in English announcing that it is forbidden to injure the trees.   Lafcadio Hearn (*Glimpses of Unfamiliar Japan*: 1894)

Japanese did not mind breaking off branches, themselves. They would, however, know where they could or couldn't get away with it. That much the visitor might not know.

折のこす木末ははなのたか根かな　昌叱
orinokosu kosue wa hana no takane kana shôshitsu -1603
(breaking-leave tree-tops-as-for blossoms' high-peak?/!/'tis)

> so, are the limbs
> not broken the proverbial
> blossoms on high?

The proverbial "high-peak-blossom," the high-class beauty you can't touch, is now part of the same ravaged tree. *That* is a metaphor to consider! (Yes, I *know* I introduced this *ku* eighteen pages ago. If you can't step into the same river twice, you can't drop a *ku* into the same brain twice, either.)

凹 & 凸 "Ravishing"

Aside from the problem with vocabulary which forced me to present the reader with crudely "broken blossoms" and other awkward coinage, I am afraid some if not all readers may have had a hard time appreciating some of the pro-breaking poems in this chapter due to a cultural difference in perspective with respect to what we might call the role of the active party and the role of the blossom. It is not so much a difference between Japan and Europe as between contemporary culture and that of the past. Consider the following passage from the essay "A Bit of Seaweed" by/in *Alpha of the Plough* (1920):

> I do not know what the lilac says to you; but to me it talks of a garden-gate over which it grew long ago. I am a child again, standing within the gate, and I see the red-coated soldiers marching along with jolly jests and snatching the lilac sprays from the tree as they pass. The emotion of pride that these heroes should honour our lilac tree by ravishing its blossoms all comes back to me, together with the old home and the vanquished faces . . .

☆ Another Choice

強ひて手折らまし 折らでやかざさましやな 弥生の永き春日も なほ飽かなくに暮らしつ 閑吟集
shiite ya taoramashi ora de ya kazasamashiya na yayoi no nagaki harubi mo nao akanaku ni kurashitsu kanginshû 1518

> *Should i grab and break one off,*
> *or, rather, wear one on the tree?*
> *Though the days of spring are long,*
> *they can hardly bore a man like me!*

Like Issa's *ku* #31-10, this song plays upon older *waka* about living the good-life with garlands of bloom on one's head. The idea of wearing the bloom *in situ* is novel. It belongs with Sôgi's *ku* #40-2, offering the gods cherry blossoms growing *on the mountain,* but the book with it (which cost a pretty penny) arrived at the last minute, and it was too much trouble to break and remake the pages.

41

Nirvana Cherry

彼岸桜
higan-zakura

彼岸とて慈悲に折らする花も哉 重頼 犬子 維舟等
higan tote jihi ni orasuru hana mogana   shigeyori 1601-1680
(equinox/paramita-as/because mercy-for break-let blossom wish-for)

<blockquote>
breaking her would be
a blessing: how i long for
an equinox cherry!
</blockquote>

equinox cherry

oh, for a flower
that even i could take
for mercy's sake

equinox cherry

oh for a flower
who would give herself
out of mercy

equinox cherry

for mercy's sake,
won't anyone break off
a blossom for me!

The Equinox in Japan is the Enlightenment, that is, the time to celebrate the translation from our wretched bank of the proverbial river (or sea) to the other shore, the *higan,* which is homophonic with 悲願 *a sad plea*, i.e. a prayer for the sake of mercy, and includes the connotation of *a cherished goal*. The poet plays with all of this and more, for a song 謡曲＜田村＞mentions "the merciful blossom/s of spring" (大慈大悲の春の花). By the common law of synchronicity (no Jung needed in Japan!), dying in that period (like a blossom's life, seven-days) made it easier to know Nirvana, so this *ku* can be seen as both a plea on the behalf of the poet *and* a rationalization of the act of breaking a bough as mercy for the blossoms. The poet's wish is practical in one sense, for there was and still is a cherry variety called Higan-zakura. Blyth's translation (*"It is the spring equinox; / The compassion of Buddha / Allows us to break the flowering branches"* History of Haiku) and explanation that, on this day, "The Buddha is merciful enough to let us break the Buddhist law together with the branches, for the sake of beauty" overlooks something: the *mogana,* a classical emphatic signifying desire for something (usually a member of the opposite sex) that one lacks and is not likely to get, i.e., wishful thinking, and, with it, the poet's chuckle. Perhaps, I should add that in his *History of Haiku*, Blyth gives over a page to Shigeyori (also called Isshû), but only includes one of his *ku* in *Haiku*. I feel Shigeyori deserves better; but, for all of his love for zany, or should I say, Zeny nonsense, Blyth followed the Japanese lead and shortchanged the playful Teimon school in favor of conventional Bashôism.

二季に咲く彼岸櫻の種もかな 貞徳 犬子
ni ki ni saku higanzakura no tane mogana teitoku 1633
(two seasons-in bloom, equinox-cherry's seeds wish-for)

秋もさく彼岸櫻の花も哉 時之 鷹筑波
aki mo saku higanzakura no hana mogana jishi 1642
(autumn also bloom equinox cherry's blossoms wish-for)

<blockquote>
oh for the seed of
a nirvana cherry that would
bloom in two seasons!
</blockquote>

<blockquote>
if only we had
an equinox cherry that also
bloomed in fall
</blockquote>

I sometimes translate *higan* one way, sometimes another, but it always means *both* and, found with blossoms, the cherry tree by that name. As a matter of fact, one of these *higan-zakura* may have granted the poets' wishes for Kuitert mentions one "autumn-flowering higan cherry, the *jugatsu-zakura,* or "tenth-month cherry" a sub-variety of *Prunus x subhirtella*. I must say, however, that it confuses me because one of its names is Oeshiki-zakura, from the name of a ceremony on the deathday of Nichiren on the 13th day of the 10th month which should make it early *Winter* by the old calendar, yet Kuitert writes it is said to "profit from Japan's "October spring" a *fall* warm spell that occurs quite commonly." (*Japanese Flowering Cherries:* my *italics*). The Kodansha *saijiki* puts "small spring" (*koharu*) in early winter where it belongs but, translates Nichiren's deathday to the Fall (perhaps, following the practice of Nichiren believers?). No wonder Kuitert was confused. It is too bad he was not right, for the real old date would put the bloom well past the Fall Equinox.

雲を花とまかふは彼岸櫻哉 重雅 鷹筑波
kumo o hana to magau wa higanzakura kana shigemasa? 1642
(clouds[acc] blossoms-for mistake-as-for equinox-cherries!/it's-the)

<blockquote>
those clouds that
are taken for blossom?
nirvana cherry
</blockquote>

<blockquote>
when are clouds
mistaken for blossoms?
equinox: cherries
</blockquote>

The usual blossoms taken for clouds are reversed to clouds posing as blossoms. Buddha's ascension on the equinox involved five-colored clouds of flowers.

衆生縁あるから彼岸櫻哉 岩芝 類題
shujô en aru kara higanzakura kana ganshi? 1774
(masses-link have-from/because equinox cherries!)

<blockquote>
nirvana blooms
because we all have one
a buddha link
</blockquote>

<blockquote>
because we all
have a lifeline to buddha
nirvana cherry
</blockquote>

This *ku* conflates the cherry and Enlightenment. The "lifeline" is just a "connection," but it refutes a narrow-way saying that those who do not know Buddha will not be saved even though he is merciful.

彼岸にて彼岸櫻のちりにけり 彫棠 句兄弟
higan nite higanzakura no chirinikeri chôtô 1694
(equinox-on equinox-cherry[blms] fall/scatter[finality])

nirvana-bound

on the equinox
the equinox cherry
lost its petals

nirvana

うたがはす花は開きし彼岸哉　李友
utagawazu hana wa hirakishi higan kana riyû
(doubt-not blossoms-as-for opened equinox!/'tis)

who can doubt it
the blossoms have opened
nirvana cherries

鐘撞てさかせる彼岸櫻哉　風草 類題
kane tsukite sakaseru higanzakura kana fûsô 1774
(bell-striking bloom-make equinox-cherries!/'tis)

brought to bloom
by our striking the bells:
nirvana cherries!

The first *ku* makes us think of the blossom of Enlightenment, but rhetorically speaking, it follows a convention of ancient Japanese poetry, making a big thing of whether something proved true to its name or not. With respect to the second *ku,* it was the practice to sound temple bells on the equinox to celebrate Buddha's Enlightenment, which, like the Christ's "dying for our sins," was potentially for all of us. People gathered to hear religious talks and buy objects of devotion and pray. Whether "brought to bloom" or "made to bloom," any Englishing would be forced in comparison to the Japanese where the verb bloom/blossom, like many Japanese verbs, is blessed with a simple transitive case.

寺古りて櫻一木の彼岸哉　枝静 句鑑
tera furite sakura ippon no higan kana shisei 1777
(temple aged cherry one-pole=tree's equinox!/'tis)

an old temple   the temple aged
just one equinox   its one blossoming tree
cherry tree   a nirvana cherry

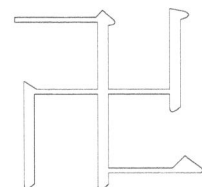

卍　No, it's not *that* swaztica. It is the *manji,* or, "man-letter" and is used on maps to indicate Buddhist temples.　卍

Ambiguous Mountain Cherry

山桜
yama-zakura

花ならていつ見し雲そ山櫻　性遵 つくは
hana nara de itsu mishi kumo zo yamazakura　seijun 1356
(blossom is-not-because when saw clouds! mountain-cherry/ies)

are these blossoms
or clouds i've seen before?
mountain cherries

"Cherry mountain" in Japanese (*sakura yama* or *hana no yama*) means any place where people gather to view cherry-blossoms, i.e. a park. Reverse the words to "mountain-cherry" (*yama-zakura*) however, and we are talking about cherry trees on real mountains, or, more rarely, the single-petal wild cherry. Shiki played with this reversal: *"Mountain blossoms / seen from below / blossom mountain"* (山の花下より見れば花の山　子規 *yama no hana shita yori mireba hana no yama*　shiki 1889).

山の名を聞て見直す櫻哉　花渕 藤首途
yama no na o kiite-minaosu sakura kana　kaen 1731
(mountain's name[acc.] hearing-see-afresh [blooming] cherries!)

i take a new look　　　　　　　　　　　on being told
at the blossoms, on hearing　　　the hill's name, the blossoms
the mountain's name　　　　　　　　are reappraised

Rewritten in the third-person, the haiku is a *senryû*. *Saijiki* would not have this *ku* with *yamazakura*, mountain cherries, because the *word "yamazakura"* is not in the poem.

天井に首はつかへて山櫻　李由 風俗文選
tenjô ni kubi wa tsukaete yamazakura　riyû -1705
(ceiling-against head-as-for blocked mountain-cherries)

with my head
pressed against the ceiling
mountain cherry

The cheapest sedans, if a "basket," or box-car shouldered by two men can be called that, were little more than slings. This would be a medium-size, covered sedan. The poet sits up straight to use his legs as shock absorbers over the rough paths. Like "ceiling," a touch of sky/heaven is felt in the Japanese *tenjô* and this metaphysically fits the location. A fancy sedan would have a higher ceiling.

山桜銭をつかへば阪もなし　尚白　アルス
yamazakura zeni o tsukaeba saka mo nashi shôhaku
(mountain-cherry coins/cash use-if slopes not 18c)

山桜見つゝ我腰のいたき哉　玄茂　境海草
yamazakura mitsutsu waga koshi no itaki kana genshi
(mt-cherries viewing-while my hip/back hurts! 1660)

    mountain cherries
    use money and forget
    about the slopes

    mountain cherries
    as i view them how
    my hip aches!

駕籠下りてこれからかほんの山櫻　二逐　恒誠
kago orite kore kara ga hon no yamazakura jichiku ( )
(basket/sedan descending this/now/here-from is real mountain-cherries)

    leaving the sedans,
    now it's time for the real
    mountain cherries!

    leaving my taxi
    from here the real mountain
    cherries blossom

The first *ku* suggests that money could replace good legs. The second, while describing a real problem for elderly viewers, *may* be risqué, for the *koshi* was *also* the lower-back stereotypically affected by overdoing it in sex (with a country maid back at the Inn), but this is not likely. The third notes that mountain cherry at their best are not only beyond the reach of animal transport, but beyond that of human-powered sedans. As one poet put it: *"From now on / it will be all men [male] / mountain cherries"* (是からは男許りや山櫻　富水　新選 *kore kara wa otoko bakari ya yamazakura* fûsui 1773).

人声の雲に登るや山櫻　来鴎　春遊
hitokoe no kumo ni noboru ya yamazakura raiô 1767
(human-voice's clouds-on/in climb?/!/: mountain-cherry)

    human voices
    climbing through clouds
    of wild cherry

    mountain cherry
    human voices climb
    upon the clouds

    mountain cherry:
    are those voices of men
    climbing clouds?

人音にまた分入や山櫻　雲子　花七日
hito oto ni mata wake-iru ya yamazakura unshi 1777
(person-noise/sound-into part/split-open-enter! mountain-cherries)

    slipping once more
    into the sound of men
    mountain cherries

    diving and diving
    into pockets of our noise:
    mountain cherries

Slipping and *diving* was the best I could do for the splendid compound-verb "parting-entering" (*wake-iru*), meaning the way we make our way through thick foliage parting it as we go. Either the poet re-enters the human bubble after a long hike, or finds himself scooped again and again (In which case, it must have been pleasant exchanging drinks with the party under each tree).

人の目にあまるものなし山ざくら　来山
hito no me ni amaru mono nashi yamazakura raizan -1716
(man's eyes-in/to exceed/left-over thing not/none mountain-cherry)

not one thing
escapes the eye of man:
mountain cherries

見ぬ奥の猶ゆかしさよ山櫻　思温 翁反故
minu oku no nao yukashisa yo yamazakura shion 1783
(see-not recesses yet-more charming! mountain cherries)

the yet-to-be-seen　　　　　　the hollar beyond
fascinates all the more!　　　holds even more charm:
mountain cherry　　　　　　　mountain cherries

I doubt Raisan's *ku* holds true for some blossoms not feted so much as the cherry. We get the idea but the best thing about mountain cherries is that there are always more (or, *were* before the monoculture of modern forestry). I had to radically re-create the first line of Shion's *ku* for English lacks a word for *oku*, somewhere beyond what we see, an inner recess or back-woods, deep in the hills, house, or brain.

外の木に押されし痩や山櫻　雨谷 新選
hoka no ki ni osareshi yase ya yamazakura ukoku 1773
(other trees-by pushed thin!/?/: mountain-cherry/ies)

crowded by
other trees, how thin
these mountain cherries!

To be thin in the Sinosphere was to be sick. The Chinese character for "thin" (痩) attests to it, for the radical 疒 means disease. This hard-boiled reportage is the opposite of the dreamy first *ku* of the chapter. I can attest to its accuracy, for I have witnessed not just the harassment and thinning (loss of major limbs), but the final takedown of such a cherry at the hands of a ravenous pack of bamboo.[1] In a park, each cherry tree has plenty of space and only enough evergreen companionship to salve the eyes in the winter and improve the pink of the bloom are allowed close by. Mountain cherries, on the other hand, must fend for themselves. Only a few fortunate ones grow fat and happy.

松伐たあとの日なたや山櫻　几董 其雪影
matsu kitta ato no hinata ya yamazakura kitô 1789
(pine/s cut after/mark's sunlight!/: mountain-cherry)

mountain cherry
bathing in sunlight where
a pine was cut

This would be a *ku* about one of the fortunates. Because the pine is a symbol of longevity and the cherry of mortality, this sunny space is paradoxical. There is an untranslatable cherry+pine *ku* that is too entertaining not to introduce: *"Blown into / the song-trash [doggeral] pine: / mountain cherry [petals]"* (歌屑の松に吹れて山櫻　蕪村 *utakuzu no matsu ni fukarete yamazakura* buson). The pine tree in question comes from a *waka* considered representative of a hackneyed poem. So, the mountain cherry, essence of the wild and pure, litters the trashy pine.

↑ 1. *A Cherry Tree Killing*   Snow-bent bamboo criss-crossed the tree's crotches(?) and, with the weight of that snow, toppled the cherry, whose roots it had already invaded, and almost took out my apartment! Details of this literally earth-shaking event will be in one of my books to come, probably about the *tanuki* (raccoon-faced foxes) who made the "beast trails" (*kedamono michi*) with public W.C.s criss-crossing the bamboo forest.

~~~~~~

山里にさけるを花の心哉　宗祇 老葉
yamazato ni sakeru o hana no kokoro kana   sôgi 1420-1502
(mountain-country-in bloom [is] blossom's-heart/mind/essence!/?)

<div style="display:flex;justify-content:space-around;">

to bloom at home
in the mountains: that's
true blossomhood

to blossom
in the wild is to be
a cherry tree

</div>

The mountain cherry, as the original, is most revered of cherries. Blooming late would not endear it to moderns, but early *haikai* admired *"The blossom / in the heart of men who wait: / mountain cherries"* (待人の心の花や山櫻　宗祇 大発句集 *matsu hito no kokoro no hana ya yamazakura   sôgi*). It came to be identified with Japaneseness, as we shall see in *Book III*.   When that happened, the prevalent female beauty took a backseat to male bravado: *"When petals fall / the spirit is male: / mountain cherry"* (ちる時は男氣のあり山櫻　立些 *chiru toki wa otokoge no ari yamazakura   rissha?* ()).

慰に浮世すてばや花の山　風律 続明烏
nagusami ni ukiyo sutebaya hana no yama   fûritsu 1776
(for-consolation/fun-for floating/woeful-world[acc.] abandon-would! blossom-mountain)

<div style="display:flex;justify-content:space-around;">

~~beauty in the wild~~
~~abandoning men~~
~~for a mountain retreat:~~
~~cherry blossoms!~~

~~spring surprise~~
~~leaving the city~~
~~for the dark silent woods~~
~~a blooming hill!~~

</div>

modern retirement

<div style="display:flex;justify-content:space-around;">

cherry mountains
now i can ditch the world
and have some fun

i'd leave my life
but still console myself here
a cherry mountain

</div>

Mountains were synonymous with *wilderness* and a quiet life free of social problems yet hard for being lonely. The presence of beauty was an anomaly. Since *nagusami* can mean calming oneself, as well as having fun, my crossed-out translations made sense but for the date of the *ku*: "blossom-mountain" in the mid-18c meant parks where *hanami* were held, *not* real mountains. I missed that at first. The *ku* is a parody of the idea of the mountain as a place to escape man.

西行に逢ぬばかりよ山桜　可休 物見車
saigyô ni awanu bakari yo yamazakura   kakyû 1690
(saigyô-with meet-not only! mountain-cherry/blossoms)

mountain cherries:
the only thing missing:
saigyô himself!

Born in the highest circles, Saigyô retreated to the mountains, where he could not help becoming attached to the beauty of nature. If cherries in full bloom suggest Saigyô's desired and achieved perfect death, an all-but-perfect mountain cherry blossom viewing experience brings him to life.

山桜人に見よとて散りやせん 一茶
yamazakura hito ni miyo tote chiri ya sen issa 1816
(mountain cherries people-to "look!" [saying] fall?-as-for do-not)

the natural

these blossoms
don't say "look!" when they fall
mountain cherries

mountain cherries:
you can't say that they
fall for us men

Mountain cherries cannot be faulted by those who fall for them because their beauty was not meant for human eyes. The traditional occidental equivalent is the conceit of the rose that blushes unseen in the desert – the "desert," of course, meaning the wilderness, which in the Sinosphere is the mountain. But why "fall" instead of "bloom" here? Because, as we have seen, that was where Issa's Buddhist cherries had something to teach: *how to fall without regret.* It was where they could show off: *I am more faithful than you!* Other *ku* expressing the solitary nature of these cherry trees: *"We speak not / and cry in our hearts: / mountain cherries"* (輪門様夢御?・物いはす心になかん山さくら 不角 其袋 *mono iwazu kokoro ni nakan yamazakura* fukaku 1652-1743), which could also be read: *"They speak not / and cry in their hearts: / mountain cherries."* A bit less clear: *"There are no men / biting their nails waiting / mountain cherries"* (指噛でまつ人やなき山櫻 二柳 新選 *yubi kande matsu hito ya naki yamazakura* niryû 1773)? It *seemed* clear until I noticed the preface: *"Grieving for Shôzan's mother"* (嘯山老母を喪せしを弔ふ). Shôzan is a favorite poet of mine, but I do not get it.

すか／\と咲てちるよし山桜 松辷 物見車
sukasuka to saite-chiru yoshi yamazakura shôshin 枩逗 1690
(freely/gently blooming fall fine/OK mountain cherry/ies)

free to bloom
or blow at their own pace
mountain cherries

The original *mimetic* adverb *suka-suka* escapes translation. I have heard it used for *baby's breath*. Trees in parks or gardens probably did not suffer warm water on their roots or other such tricks, but we can imagine they were *implored* to bloom fast or slow, while the wild cherries suffered no such duress. Or, is it that, with less crowding, there was less peer pressure from fellow trees (even plants can chemically impinge upon one another's freedom)? Bashô had a *ku* indirectly expressing the idea of independent mountain cherries: *"How delightful! / North of our world of woe, / mountain cherries!"* (うらやまし浮世の北の山櫻 芭蕉 *urayamashi ukiyo no kita no yamazakura*). Actually, he had "I'm *jealous*" rather than "how delightful," but that does not English despite our agreement about envy proving admiration. Bashô's friend had the good fortune to retire in a place with many cherry trees, "Egg-dragon-mountain" (卵竜山). The character for "North 北" has half of "back 背" in it, echoing the idea of turning one's back on the floating world (of woe). If the pleasure quarters of Yoshiwara were North of Edo, this was further North and, by analogy, a pleasant place for a man to be.

咲くも散るも一木つゝせよ山櫻 挙白 続?の原
saku mo chiru mo hitoki zutsu seyo yamazakura kyohaku -1696
(bloom-and-fall-even one-tree-each[at-a-time] do! mountain-cherries)

so bloom ye, and
blow ye, a tree at a time
wild cherries!

bloom and scatter
tree by tree, time is yours
mountain cherries!

I love this *ku* in blatant contradiction of the usual desire for a mass detonation. Come to think of it, non-conformity marks mountain folk as well as trees.

斧の音の響にちるや山櫻　露蝶
ono no oto no hibiki ni chiru ya yamazakura　rochô 1775
(axe's sound's echoes/vibrations-by/with fall/scatter?/!/: mountain-cherry)

mountain cherry
petals fall with each thud
of a far-off ax

its petals fall
to the ax's report
yamazakura

The "ax's sound's echo/shake/effect/vibration" in the original is difficult to translate. The "sound" suggests the ax is chopping in the distance and the effect largely psychological.

炭やきの心かはりや山櫻　悠川 アハチシマ
sumiyaki no kokorogawari ya yamazakura　yûsen 1698
(charcoal-burner's[maker/seller's] heart-change! mountain cherries)

the charcoal maker
has a change of heart!
mountain cherries

Cherry is a favorite wood for charcoal, which Japanese burnt in braziers used to warm fingertips and tea-water. The poet imagines that seeing the blossoms, even the man whose profession is hunting down and burning cherry trees regrets the beauty he destroys. Another *ku* more subtly notes that the smoke from a charcoal kiln disappears when mountain cherries bloom. (炭窯の烟もきえて山櫻　路景　花櫻帖 *sumigama no kemuri mo kiete yamazakura*　jikei?()) Was it because the charcoal-maker was out blossom-viewing? Or did he feel it was wrong to bathe blossoms in their relatives' smoke?

◎

見るやいかに塵の外なる山櫻　宗因 三籟
miru ya ika ni chiri no hoka nari yamazakura　sôin 1604-82
(viewing! how-much dust-outside is/becomes mountain-cherry)

behold how far
the mountain cherries
are from dust!

Can I get away with *that* translation? Dust=trash=mortal=vulgar-world *in a word* is hard in English.

人声の雲に登るや山桜　来鴎　春遊
hitogoe no kumo ni noboru ya yamazakura　raiô 1767
(person's voice's clouds-into/within climb!/: mountain-cherries)

the sound of voices
in the clouds! men with
mountain cherries

human voices
climbing the clouds!
mountain cherries

In a culture where the circle of nobility was called the "ninth-cloud," height meant status. At the same time mountains were *wilderness*, contrary to culture. And, they were one more thing: *magical*.

山々の風流か木々の花盛　立圃 空礫
yamayama no fûryû ka kigi no hanazakari　ryûho 1649
(mountain-mountain'stylishness? tree-tree's blossom-acme)

haute culture of the hills? every tree in full bloom	every mountain a fashion capitol: cherry trees in bloom	the full bloom of each tree: is that what's hip in a hill?

風流の國守なるらん山さくら　北枝 アルス
fûryû no kokushû naruran yamazakura　hokushi - 1718
(fashion's national guardian is[+emph.?] mountain-cherry/ies)

they really are the national fashion guard! mountain cherries	mountain cherries you really are guardians of what is cool

What is *fûryû* is stylish, not only in the sense of being elegant (the usual understanding) but in the sense of being timely, *with it*. For a while, the wild cherry trees head the fashion parade, or, rather, each mountain/hill becomes a stage. I think the second *ku* may play with Bashô's *ku* on rice-planting songs as the font of true fashion, but it may, instead applaud the relatively subdued single-petaled bloom, or, again, the trend for people in mountainous reaches to conserve old traditions. (求御異見！)

山里の花にわするゝ都哉　元就 春霞	四五日の都ありけり山櫻　利次 雑中
yamazato no hana ni wasururu miyako kana　genshû ()	*shigonichi no miyako arikeri yamazakura*　riji? ()
(mountain-country's blossoms-in forget capital!/'tis)	(four, five days' capital is[emph] mountain-cherries)
the capital is all but forgotten when cherries bloom in the hollar	for five or six days, this is the capitol: mountain cherries!

Miyako means the "capital," Kyoto, "the world" of high culture. "Hollar" brings out the connotation of "mountain-area." When the blossoms are *not* blooming, the country was generally considered a miserable place; but, at this time, there was "a mountain (large number) of onlookers" gazing at the mountain cherries (見る人も山の如くそ山櫻 重供 毛吹草 *miru hito mo yama no gotoku zo yamazakura* shigetomo 1645) Country people were poor, so, *"There are sedans / that sow coins as they go! / mountain cherries"* (銭蒔て通る駕あり山櫻　随吉 新選 *zeni maite tôru kage ari yamazakura* zuikitsu? 1773).

衣笠に牛のあくひや山さくら　野洞 三千花
kinugasa ni ushi no akubi ya yamazakura　yadô 1725
(robe/silk-hats-at cows' yawn:/!/? mountain-cherry/ies)

silken bonnets meet yawning cows mountain cherry	mountain cherry the yawns of oxen and silken bonnets

Cows look like they *should* yawn, but my sister on the farm says that while she has seen her horses do it, and very clearly at that, cows are more liable to burp. We get the idea, nonetheless, and the *ku* is much more interesting then, say, this 7-7: *"The crowing of cocks (or, clucking of chickens?) / can be heard: / mountain cherries"* (雞の声も聞ゆる山櫻　凡兆 猿蓑 *tori no koe mo kikoyuru yamazakura* bonchô 1691). Sometimes, it is harder to tell just what the idea is: *"No matter how / you look at it, a mountain / cherry is a cherry"* (どう見ても櫻也けり山櫻　不角　小弓 1699 *dô mite mo sakura narikeri yamazakura* fukaku 1651-1743). Is this pumping up mountain cherries in the guise of admitting such an elevated being is only a plant/woman, after all, or, deflating them by grudgingly allowing their relatively thin bloom qualifies them for cherry/womanhood? Whether the subject was rightly tree or human, some *ku* were downright nasty. Eg.1: *"Coming to see / my eyes wanted more / mountain cherries"* (来て見れば眼に事かくや山櫻　才丸（才麻呂）句鑑 *kite mireba me ni koto kaku ya yamazakura* saimaro 1655-1738). Eyes (*me*) is homophonic with "female/s." Eg 2: *"Leave 'em behind! / old ghost-houses and / mountain cherries!"* (捨ておけ化物屋敷山櫻　来川　増　補芋環 *sutete oke bakemono-yashiki yamazakura* raisen -1736). Eg 3: *"Though freckled / they still use parasols: / mountain cherries"* (そぼふるや猶傘さして山櫻　不卜　つゝきの原 *sobafuru ya nao kasa sashite yamazakura* futo 1688). Yet, not all references to the cherry and/or women were condescending:

山櫻素顔に無地の小袖よし　八角　蘆別船
yamazakura sugao ni muji no kosode yoshi hakkaku 1694
(mountain-cherry/ies plain-face-with un-patterned small-sleeves fine)

<table>
<tr><td>

mountain cherries
best with a plain *kosode*
and no make-up

</td><td>

the bare faces
with plain *kosode* are fine
mountain cherries

</td></tr>
</table>

The *kosode,* literally "short-sleeve" is an informal robe light enough that it was sometimes worn as an undergarment, with sleeves as long as any other according to the way we define length, but short in the sense that the sleeves are narrow and stay relatively close to the arm rather than hanging down. Wrapped loosely, they showed something Japanese expressed little interest in: cleavage. I feel the *ku* is not only advice for proper mountain blossom-viewing attire but a paean for simplicity.

八重一重見て批難なし山櫻　芳流　俳諧漢和
yae hitoe mite hinan nashi yamazakura hôryû? 18c?
(eight-fold one-fold seeing criticism-none mountain-cherries)

<table>
<tr><td>

i see the single
and the double mountain cher-
ries: no trouble

</td><td>

plenty of room
for single and eight-fold bloom
mountain cherry

</td></tr>
</table>

The single-fold, i.e. single-petal came to be the archetypical mountain cherry, but cherries blossoms in the mountains were, in fact, not always single-fold. This *ku* throws cold water on cherry polemics.

何にすれて端〳〵（隅〳〵）青し山さくら　千代
nani surete hashibashi (sumizumi) aoshi yamazakura chiyo 1701-75
(what missed, edge-edge (nookies) green/pale[?] mountain-cherry/ies)

why off-register
these light green borders?
mountain cherry

With blossoms over bare branches the cherry ideal, the shiny young leaves appearing with the relatively late mountain cherry blossoms were regarded as a minus by many. By alluding to fine art, Chiyo makes the *yamazakura* beautiful by turning its minus – slightly off-register color was a technique of printing and not a fault – into a plus.

折らぬこころ我ははずかし山桜　千代尼　再現
oranu-kokoro ware wa hazukashi yamazakura　chiyo-ni -1775
(break-not heart/mind i-as-for embarrassed/ashamed mountain-cherry/ies)

<table>
<tr><td>

the shyness is mine
i cannot bring myself to take
a mountain cherry

</td><td>

my weak heart
ashamed i cannot break
mountain cherries

</td></tr>
</table>

A metaphorical mountain cherry was shy around strangers. Chiyo, embarrassed not to be up to breaking off a branch to take home and, perhaps, thinking of the next, older *ku,* reverses the trope.

一枝〔折〕は折らぬもわろし山櫻　尚白　猿蓑
hito-eda(ori)wa oranu mo waroshi yamazakura　shôhaku 1649-1722
(one-branch[alt: break]-as-for break-not-also bad[be-would] mountain-cherries)

mountain cherries

not to break
at least one branch off
would be bad

To bring blossoms home for friends to enjoy? Perhaps. But, isn't it more likely he means that even if the wild cherries – or, country girls – are not great beauties compared to the cultivars, they are putting on what charm they have, so a man really should give at least a token response?

我咲て淋し顔也山櫻　支考　類題
ware sakite sabishi kao nari yamazakura　shikô -1731
(i/me/self blooming lonely face become/s mountain-cherry/ies)

they choose to bloom
yet look so damn lonely
mountain cherries

求めたる哀ハなくて山ざくら　素檗
motometaru aware wa nakute yamazakura　sobaku -1821
(seeking-am melancholy/beauty-as-for not mountain-cherry)

<table>
<tr><td>

mountain cherries
they lack the melancholy
we poets seek

</td><td>

mountain cherry
where is the sad beauty
that we desire?

</td></tr>
<tr><td colspan="2" align="center">

mountain cherries
the sad look i sought
was not there

</td></tr>
</table>

Shikô's *ku* is a fine example of facetious displacement. *He* is the lonely one. Does the second *ku* by Sobaku also suggest that melancholy is in – or, *not* in – the mind's eye? Or, was his mountain the problem? If so, could cherry blossoms stand for unwelcome change in the character of mountain girls, once humble but now outgoing if not crass? Note that *aware* meant both sad *and* beautiful. Neither *ku* contradicts my reading of the "not to break a branch" poem by Jôhaku and all three *ku* may have been influenced by a *Kokinshû* (905) *waka* that might be loosely translated thus: *"Flowering cherry / high in the hills beyond / the pale of play / you've no call to be blue / i'll come to sing your charms!"* (山たかみ人もすさめぬさくら花いたくなわびそ我見はやさむ　よみ人しらず *yama takami hito mo susamenu sakura hana itaku na wabi so ware mi-hayasamu* anon (kks#50)). The compound verb *mi-hayasamu*, means to celebrate what one sees and includes an element of humor for ancient Japanese roasted the opposite sex, as such joking was considered proper courtship rather than harassment. No one wished to be left out of the war of the sexes. To be without an enemy was tantamount to being without a lover. This next *ku* may depict what Sobaku expected and did not find in mountain girls.

市知らぬ一人に咲くや山櫻　月尋　伊丹句合
ichi shiranu hitori ni saku ya yamazakura getsujin 1714
(market know-not alone-with bloom:/! mountain-cherry)

blooming alone
no market in her head:
mountain cherry

hillbilly cherry

knowing nothing
of the market, her face
is *our* fortune!

blooming alone
unaware of her worth
mountain cherry

The last reading, plays upon an old English ditty (the pretty maiden tells a suitor she needs no dowry, for "my face is my fortune") in the manner that Japanese haiku build upon their own. Note: change *"hillbilly"* to *"mountain"* if you wish. It is hard to say whether the happy ignorance of the market – where blossoming trees are bought and sold – implies the cherry tree is of a less calculating, hence, better character, or "she" is just lucky not to be sucked into the sad scheme. The *ku* might concern an actual tree.

あれよ／＼といふもの一人山櫻＿＿虚栗
are yo are to iu mono hitori yamazakura lost name 1683
(there/that! there/that! say but [contradictory] alone mountain-cherries)

beauty, beauty, everywhere
(and not a soul to see!)

oh, look! look!
but, here i am alone:
mountain cherry

This poem has a preface: *"Treading Two-rough Mountain"* (二荒の山ふみして). Beauty unshared can make one blue.

山櫻尋ねぬ庭の一木哉　紹巴
yamazakura tazunenu niwa no hitoki kana jôha -1602
(mountain-cherry/ies visiting-not garden/yard's one-tree!/?/'tis)

mountain cherry
one tree in a garden
no one visits

a solitary tree
in a guestless garden
yamazakura

Mountain cherries are aften found singly, tucked in between other trees. I smell a metaphor, but KS imagines a poet visiting a friend and discovering the mountain cherry next door.

名のつかぬところかはゆし山櫻　潮春 花つみ
na no tsukanu tokoro kawayushi yamazakura   koshun -1697
(name-stuck place cute/charming: mountain-cherry/ies)

名にほこる桜ありともやまざくら　素丸
na ni hokoru sakura ari to mo yamazakura   somaru -1795
(name-in/of proud/boast cherry/ies is even/but mt-ch)

namelessness
is part of their charm:
mountain cherries

though some
boast proud names:
hill cherry!

Unlike the cultivars, the archetypical mountain cherry was just "mountain cherry." Is the namefullness of the courtesan (like Sumo wrestlers, *fancy*) contrasted with the namelessness of peasant girls? To better bring out the connotation of the "mountain" in the last *ku*, I made it "hill."

御庭に立はだかって山桜　一茶
on-niwa ni tachihadakatte yamazakura   issa 1822
(honorable-garden-in standing-undaunted mountain-cherry)

standing piss-proud
in an honorable garden
a mountain cherry

standing undaunted
in the honorable garden
pushing her petals

Honorable Garden? Country women, maids, at any rate, allegedly put the polite prefix "*on~*" on everything, for *anything* had a higher status than theirs. Even *horses* were *on*-uma, something *senryû* played upon, with maids talking about "riding the horse" (their periods)! My first reading of this *ku* (without checking the meaning of *hadakatte*) was "Blushing to be / in an honorable garden: / a *yamazakura*." I was wrong. To stand *hadakatte* is to stand in place with legs planted wide, perhaps even blocking something This cherry is no push-over. *She is proud.* Were it not Issa, with his genuine love for plants, I would have seen a proud mountain girl demanding something from her lord.

かんたんの夢かとよいぞ山ざくら　長頭丸
kantan no yume ka to yoi zo yamazakura   teitoku 嵐山集 1651
(kantan's dream?/if then good[+emph]! mountain-cherry/ies)

seen as that dream
of kantan, damn, they're fine!
mountain cherries

mountain cherries
is kantan's dream not good
enough for us!

A poor young Chinese man(邯鄲), Kantan in the Japanese pronunciation, got a wish-fulfilling magical pillow. He took a nap on it and lived a luxurious life for fifty years, waking to find it all happened before his gruel came to boil. The pillow came from a wizard and wizards came from mountains, so the poet may mean these hillbilly trees enjoy and let us share the same magical yet brief flowering.

朝霧にふすべられけり山桜　りん女
asagiri ni fusuberarekeri yamazakura   rinjo 1673-1757
(morning fog-in smoked[emph.] mountain-cherry)

smoked dark
in the morning fog
mountain cherry

It is rare to find this realism in old mountain cherry *ku*. Is this a *just-so* for the larger number of relatively dark pink blossoms in the mountains versus whiter varieties in the cities? Or, does it refer to the darkness of the damp bark, which would set off the white blossoms to fine effect. In another *ku*, Rinjo matter-of-factly observed mountain cherries that were indeed unembellished single-fold (やまざくら取つくろはぬ一重かな　りん女 *yamazakura toritsu kurowanu hitoe kana*　rinjo).

此うへに美人なし山ざくら　素丸 素丸俳句集
kono ue ni oku bijin nashi yamazakura　somaru 1712-95
(this above-at place beauty not: mountain-cherry)

there's no beauty
who can be held over you,
mountain cherry!

Did Somaru, love these wild trees more than the garden varieties with their profuse bloom? Or, did he prefer the darker beauty of country girls to the pale beauties celebrated in the capital? I doubt it, for that would make it *sakura!*, such as *"Mountain cherry / your high laugh is good / cause for a fall"* 山櫻高く笑はゝちりぬべし 不角 *yamazakura takaku warawaba chirinubeshi* fukaku (　)). A mountain showing its spring color is said to "laugh/smile." There are countless *ku*, most, like this facetious morality play, of little value, based on this conceit. *"Cherry blossoms! / When the mountain cracks / its biggest smile"* (櫻哉此時山の大笑ひ　千外　句鑑 *sakura kana kono toki yama no ôwarai*　sengai 18c). *"The backhills / laughing/smiling to/by herself / a blossom-face,"* (奥山や独笑する花の顔　之政　古今句鑑 *okuyama ya hitori emisuru hana no kao*　shisei 1777). Expressing the smile differently to bring out the relatively high location of the cherry on the mountain's "face," we find "Her eyebrows / open wide in delight: / mountain cherry" (よろこひの眉をそ開く山櫻　重頼 犬子 *yorokobi no mayu o hiraku yamazakura*　shigeyori 1633); or, this, the height of absurdity: *"A mountain's laugh / falls all over the trees: / cherry petals!"* (山の笑ひ木に鏤てさくらかな　素丸　素丸発句集 *yama no warai ki ni chiribamete sakura kana*　somaru 1712-95).

折賃に盃とらす山ざくら 桟金 車朧夜集
orichin ni sakazuki torasu yamazakura　sankin? cartman? 1834
(breaking-fee-for *sake*-cup take/taken mountain-cherry)

breaking one off   my sake cup
i pay with my *sake* cup   does for the breaking fee
mountain cherries   mountain cherries

Is the cup actually taken for payment or as a fine? Or is it figuratively taken, i.e., filled with *sake* and drunk, for payment? Is this a guard who looks away, a strong local yokel who helps break the branch for the poet, or a girl at a mountain inn? In the last case, the *break fee* suggests a *weaving fee* (gifts of clothing woman to man). Or, has a mountain gillie (ranger) confiscated the poet's cup to stop him from drinking and breaking off more branches for the hell of it? (専門家のご判断は？)

無理にさす瓶はこけたり山櫻 心圭 芋環
muri ni sasu bin wa koketari yamazakura　shinka? ()
(forced/involun./impractically stuck vase-as-for broke mt ch)

forcing a branch
into a vase, it broke:
mountain cherry

What is the *point* of the *ku*? That large branches are needed because mountain cherry bloom is relatively thin? Because larger branches could be broken off in the hills than in a garden? Because crude behavior matches the wild? Because there is little choice of vases in the mountains?

枝わけて月も折らはや山櫻　昌叱 大発句帳
eda wakete tsuki mo orabaya yamazakura　shôshitsu -1603
(branch/es splitting moon also breaking/stealing would mountin-cherry)

splitting the limbs
i'd break the moon, too,
mountain cherry!

No, it is not so violent as it seems. The poet would pull open the branches the better to see the moon between the "clouds" of bloom. He praises its beauty by admitting he wants to "break," i.e., *take* it.

むし立る饅頭日和や山桜　理曲 失出典
mushitateru manjûbiyori ya yamazakura　rikyoku ()
(steamed-ready/standing dumpling-calm/clear[day/weather]: mountain-cherry)

steam wafts up   a dumpling day
on a dumpling fine day   steam wafting up from
mountain cherries   cherry mountain

cherry bean buns?

haze like steam
rising from a soft mountain
of pink blossoms

When there is no wind, the earth steams. Chinese-style dumplings are soft and sweet, beloved of old people and children (*and* erotic, for Japanese appreciated a plump *mons veneris* more than the vaginacentric West.)

山櫻どこ通ったも覚なし　兎士 類題
yamazakura doko totta mo oboenashi　toshi 1774
(mountain-cherry: where passed-even memory-not)

mountain cherry:
and i can't remember
how i got here!

Lovers in ancient poetry could lose their hearts=minds to the beloved and no longer find their way back. To simply note that falling petals hide trails would be lame.

あと先の道失ふや山さくら　成美 杉柱
ato saki no michi ushinau ya yamazakura　seibi 1816
(after-before-path lose/losing!: mountain-cherry/ies)

poem left by a lost poet   **mountain cherry trail**

yamazakura trail   you lose track
which way did i come from?   of what was before and
which way shall i go?   what comes after

The before-after (*ato-saki*) brings out the nature of getting lost where one ends up going in circles. I imagine Seibi hanging up a poem about being lost on a tree limb and finding it again, oops!

ひめおきし道を教へよ山櫻　紹巴
hime okishi michi o oshieyo yamazakura　jôha
(princess keeping road[obj] teach[me/us]! mt.ch)

奥に入て道はありけり山櫻　紹巴
oku ni haite michi wa arikeri yamazakura　jôha
(deep-in entering road-as-for is mt. cherry/ies) -1602

    mountain cherries,
so, tell me where you
   keep the princess!

    deep in the hills
we find there is a path:
   mountain cherry

The first *ku* refers to the tale of monk Seigen, who abandoned his temple in pursuit of a Cherry Princess (*sakura-hime*), whose retainers killed him, after which his spirit kept living, but I forget what happens. The second *ku* is factual. Where paths like rivulets running up-hill from various sides converge upon pockets of bloom, there can be paths on high where none are visible below!

土取の車に添ふややま櫻　其角 -1707
tsuchitori no kuruma ni sou ya yamazakura　kikaku
(earth[shit]taker's cart-by accompany:/?/! night-cherry/ies)

   mountain cherry
accompanying the cart
  with the night-soil

   me tagging along
with the honey wagon
  mountain cherry

   mountain cherries
just follow the route
 of the honeywagon

I first thought *petals* (Issa has them on nightsoil-laden boats), then blossoms brought by the nightsoil man for customers, but it must be Kikaku himself proud to have out-humbled Bashô to get the inside shit, if it were, on blossom-viewing and put a *haikai* face on those romantic mountain cherries.

朽木たふれ天狗の枝折や山櫻　調鶴　江戸ヘンケイ
kuchigidaore tengu no edaori ya yamazakura　chôkaku 1680
(rotten tree toppled/ing tengu's branch-breaking: mountain-cherry/ies)

  a rotten tree falls
tengu breaking one off?
  mountain cherry

  toppling old trees
do tengu break them so?
  mountain cherry

Remember this long-nosed mountain goblin, a cross between a proboscis monkey, Irish fairy, Tibetan Yeti, Merlin and Batman? One could be tiny as an ant one moment and huge as a giant the next. If we take branches, why couldn't a tengu take a whole tree?

さかさまに枯木倒れて山櫻　超波 古選
sakasama ni karegi taorete yamazakura　chôha 1763
(upside-down-as dry/dead-tree falling mountain-cherry)

   a dead tree
falls upside down:
 mountain cherry

A mere observation of what trees can only do on mountains, but interesting, nonetheless, for in Japanese folklore the Other World is upside-down to ours (and, if you are familiar with the symbolism of *Occidental* mysticism/alchemy, these trees are *human*, for men are depicted as upside-down trees).

山櫻猿も毛並のかはる頃 附専 淡路嶋
yamazakura saru mo kenami no kawaru koro fusen
(mt-cherry/ies monkeys too coat changes time 1698)

狼や人の跡かぐ山櫻 松木 俳諧漢和
ôkami ya hito no ato kagu yamazakura shôboku
(wolf/ves: person's trail sniff mountain cherry)

    mountain cherries
at the same time monkeys
    change their coats

    wolves sniff
the spoor of humans:
    mountain cherry

狼の住むはまことか山櫻 蒼狐 アルス
ôkami no sumu wa makoto ka yamazakura sôko 17-18c
(wolf/ves live-as-for, true? mountain-cherry/ies)

   mountain cherry,
tell me, is it true that
   wolves live here?

   are there really
wolves living up there?
   mountain cherries

Salacious men are not *wolves* in Japan, so there is no B-side, though there may be nominal wit: "mountain-cherry" echoes "mountain-dog" (*yama-inu*), colloquial for *wolf*.

人なれて山あたゝまる櫻かな 失名 葛箒
hito narete yama atatamaru sakura kana lost name 18c
(people used-to mountain warms cherry/ies!/?/'tis)

   these mountains
are warming up to us:
   cherry blossoms

This *ku* is a translator's delight since "becoming used to something" (*narete*) in English *is* "warming up to" (*atatamaru*): the two verbs in the original fuse. For once, the target language is in the black.

谷水や石も歌よむ山櫻 鬼貫
tanimizu ya ishi mo uta yomu yamazakura onitsura -1738
(valley-water!/: rock even song reads/composes mountain-cherry/ies)

   a valley stream!
even stones wax poetic
   mountain cherries

   babbling brooks
the very rocks sing for
   mountain cherry

   snow run-off:
the stones are poets, too
   mountain cherry

   streams in the dale
even stones sing out
   mountain cherry

The foreword to the Kokinshû (905) *waka* collection claims human song/poetry was inspired by frog and birdsong but forgot to mention babbling brooks. Because the *ku's* preface indicates Onitsura received a song (i.e. *waka*) about *haikai* from someone, it may be more a *haikai* effort to bring more nature into art than a naive on-the-spot reverie. "Valley water" (*tanimizu*) means streams swollen with snow melt and spring rain. It is loudest about the time the cherries come into bloom. Are the stones "singing *their* songs" (Blyth, my *italics*), or joining us in a paean *to* the cherry blossoms?

山櫻小川飛びこす女哉　常全 炭俵
yamazakura ogawa tobikosu onna kana　jôzen 1694
(mountain-cherries small-river jumping-cross women!/'tis)

mountain cherry
who jumps over the brook?
it's the women!

i see a woman
jumping over a brook
mountain cherries

A sweet scene. Sweet for a man at any rate. I like this *ku* better than the more general "*Adding color[eros] / the weak-legs [women and children] are out: / mountain cherry*" (色に出る足弱人や山櫻　素外 句鑑 *iro ni deru ashiyowabito ya yamazakura* sogai 1777?); or this: "*Any number / of drunken women: / mountain cherries*" (生酔の女幾人リやまざくら　素丸〜発句集 *namayoi no onna ikutari yamazakura* somaru 1712-95). It would seem that when women dare climb up this far, they tend to become one of the guys.

鼻紙て鹿を叩や山櫻　鳥窓 古選
hanakami de shika o tataku ya yamazakura　chôsô 1763
(nose-paper[tissues]-with deer smacking!/?/: mountain-cherries)

showering deer
with our tissue paper!
mountain cherry

beaning deer
with paper full of snot
mountain cherry

The Japanese had no handkerchiefs; they thought it *filthy* to carry around a snot-filled cloth. Instead, they had tissue paper so popular in some circles [1] it served as currency. I much prefer such a ridiculous observation (I doubt anyone would deliberately throw paper used to blow noses at deer, so we may assume people high up blow their noses a lot because of the chilly air and the tissues they drop float down the slope, presumably to bother deer) to, the usual *sakura!* like "*Mountain cherries: / to the roots of the local / kiddies' hair*" 山櫻里の童の髪に迄　友梅 恒誠 *yamazakura sato no warabe no kami ni made* yûbai ()). The "roots" are mine; the original only observes it is in their hair.

里の名も聞たき花の山の道　存疑芭蕉 〜翁句解
sato no na mo kikitaki hana no yama no michi ?bashô? 1688
(country's/hometown's name even hear-want blossom-mountain-path)

i'd know where
i am with these blossoms
on a mountain path

such fine blossoms
on this mountain path i'd like
to know where i am

さま／＼やけしきあらそふ山櫻　聞至 花七日
samazama ya keshiki arasou yamazakura bunshi 1777
(variety! scenes/views/landscapes battle mountain-cherry[subj])

what variety!
the mountain cherries
contest scenery

1. Tissues. In the Pleasure Quarters, the tissue was particularly visible for it was used to clean up the spendings of love. There was great competition between competing brands. Old prints show sated couples surrounded by what might appear to be pages of paper crumpled up by a novelist unable to finish a decent first page using an old typewriter. (For more on paper and tissues, see *Topsy-turvy 1585*).

We all want to know the name of a place after it impresses us. If the dubious Bashô is not Bashô's *ku* it could be. The *keshiki* in the second *ku* is a scene of the type an artist might paint. In a park, the size of the trunk, shape of the limbs, profusion of bloom and color of the blossoms, i.e. the endowment of the tree itself decides its aesthetic ranking. Background may even be screened out. In the mountains, however, the location of the tree and the view from it mattered as much as the looks of the tree itself.

人々に同じ様なし山桜 言水
hitobito ni onaji sama nashi yamazakura gonsui -1719
(people-people-in/with same style/fashion/way-not mountain-cherries)

each person
a fashion onto himself
mountain cherry

no look-alike
people viewing blossoms
back in the hills

Did people come from farther off, or did they leave their fashionable clothing back home? Regardless, the people echoed the diverse character of the blossoms. (Note: this *ku* is also in the Yoshino chapter)

老は身の宝なりけり山櫻 士朗 -1813
oi wa mi no takara narikeri yamazakura shirô
(age-as-for body's/self's treasure is/becomes[emp])

山里の人美しや遅櫻 継駒 五車反故 -1783
yamazato no hito utsukushi ya osozakura keiku
(mountain-country's people beautiful! late-cherries)

old age is
the treasure of a body
mountain cherries

how beautiful
the mountain folk are
late cherries

Could Shirô have noticed long-lived *Higan*=equinox cherries in the mountains that impressed him as older and more sacred than the younger cultivars in the urban areas? The second *ku* contradicts the all-too-common image of mountain folk as buck-teethed monkeys – where the teeth=leaves (*ha*) appear=stick-out before=beyond the nose=blossom (*hana*) as per Chiyo's print-registration *ku*.

（前書略）草履の尻折て帰らん山櫻 はせを
zôri no shiri otte-kaeran yamazakura bashô 1679
([woven]sandals's butts break/fold-return-let's mt-ch)

after it rained

mountain cherries:
let's bust our sandal butts
and head down

Japanese sandals, like those who wear them, have little butt to begin with, but even that might flick up mud after rain and, going downhill, the less heel the better. Bashô's "sandal-butt-breaking" is a fresh term resembling *shiribashi-ori*, "butt-hem-folding" (tucking up kimonos on the road). Did Bashô play with a popular phrase? Another *ku* about breaking off a spray and returning (一枝は折て帰らん山桜 失名 俳諧江戸蛇之鮓 *hitoeda wa orite-kaeran yama zakura* lost name1679) was published the same year.

さけはちりちるもいく世のやま桜　宗祇　発句帳
sakeba-chiri chiru mo iku yo no yamazakura　sôgi 1420-1502
(bloom-if/when fall/scatter too how-many ages/realms' mountain-cherry)

they blooming, fall
and falling, bloom forever
mountain cherries

My "forever" saves syllables but stretches "how many years!" (*iku yo*) a bit. Does this *ku* reflects an awareness of the wild plant as immortal?

一重づゝちりての後や山櫻　昌叱　大発句帳
hitoe zutsu chirite no ato ya yamazakura　shôshitsu - 1603
(one-layer at-a-time falling-afterward?/: mountain-cherries)

layer by layer
falls away and then
mountain cherry

The mountain cherry blooms relatively late, after the snow melts and men strip off all but one layer of clothing (While Japanese did stuff and unstuff kimono, most temperature control was accomplished by layer upon layer upon layer, rather than sweaters). *Chiru* (*chirite*), the verb I translated as "falls away" (it sounds better than "falls off" here), is the standard one used for falling/scattering/blowing/dropping petals. Had I not wanted to differentiate the mountain cherry from cherry mountain at the outset of the chapter, this season-defining *ku* would have come first. Here is another *ku* that *may* be similar: "The world comes / to an end with this bloom: / mountain cherries" (世の中のあら仕舞也山櫻　蓑虫 小弓 *yononaka no ara shimai nari yamazakura* minomushi? 1699). Does this mean that people stop everything when they see the mountains around their city in bloom, or that the summer doldrums follow?

先さけと都をやまつ山さくら 宗祇
saki sake to miyako o ya matsu yamazakura　sôgi 同
(first bloom[imper]! capital-for [+emph] wait mountain-cherries)

you bloom first!
the mountain cherries wait
for the capital

皆散て隙が明いたか山桜　一茶
mina chirite suki ga aita ka yamazakura　issa 1814
(all/everyone fell/scattered space/leisure is opened? mountain-cherries)

mountain cherries
have all the others blown and
left space for you

are you all free,
now your bloom is blown,
mountain cherries

With Sôgi's *ku,* the faithful country retainers, or mature seniors of the cultured trees in Kyoto, hold off until last. My first reading of Issa's *ku* is least likely. Issa, self-confessed lazy man, probably empathizes with the poor mountain cherries for the work (blooming) they had to do, as per the second reading. There is a *ku* of uncertain parentage in his *Hanami-no-ki* about an old cherry tree to whom blooming was work (古桜花の役とて咲にけり 老女 *furuzakura hana no yaku tote sakinikeri* old lady).

はづかしや見た分ンにする山桜　一茶 浅黄裏
hazukashi ya mita bun ni suru yamazakura issa 1762 -1827
(embarrassing! / saw portion/department-in/as do mountain-cherries)

it's embarrassing
let me just say i *saw*
the *yamazakura*

Judging from young Issa's Journal, he was no brave mountaineer, so I imagine he saw many wild cherries he dared not approach. Or, is he referring to having *seen* behavior that was bad? A somewhat odd *ku* by Suganoya Takamasa (in his sixties in 1702): *"Pity them now / the mountain cherries bloom: / those three monkeys"* (哀れとおもへ三疋の猿山桜　菅野谷高政 伴天連社高政 *awareto omoe sanjô no saru yamazakura*). A Japanese commentator (on the internet) explains: "All the people are high on blossom-viewing (花見に浮かれている) but the *No-see, No-say, No-hear* monkeys cannot do the same. They are something to be pitied." I cannot help but recall that it was specifically *"evil"* that the monkeys (sense-specific egos?) were supposed to avoid. Does that mean we have a fuddy-duddy gentleman too uptight to enjoy the blossom-viewing even up in the hills? Or, is there so much hanky-panky going on up in the hills that he feels sorry for the monkeys having to spend the season covering the holes on their faces? Or, am I thinking too much? The commentator also pointed out that the *ku* played on a *waka* from a book called the Gold Leaf Collection (*Kinyôshû* 1124-6): *"Pity them / the whole damn lot: / mountain cherries // Not a soul but they, / the blossoms know"* (もろともにあはれと思へ山桜花よりほかに知る人もなし 金葉集 *morotomo ni aware to omoe yamazakura hana yori hoka ni shiru hito mo nashi*. What exactly do only the blossoms know? That they bloom? Their beauty?   The heart, i.e., love, of the poets?   Could the *ku*, rather, lament beauty unshared, with the three monkeys little more than a metaphor of the isolated beauty of the mountain cherry? And, Issa's embarrassment? On second thought, maybe he meant he was ashamed *not* to have broken off a two-legged branch. After all, the old *ku* (40-9, 42-46) said it was bad not to break at least one. . .

山桜世にむつかしき接穂〔哉?〕秋の坊
yamazakura yo ni muzukashiki tsugiho[kana?] akinobô - 1718
(mountain-cherry/ies world-in difficult/complexity graft-[!/?/'tis])

mountain cherries:
still alive in this complex
world of graft!

Cultivars were generally grafted. Though many mountain cherries were, shall we say, "feral," they were generally wild and, I think Akinobô celebrates that. This chapter has much about which I was uncertain but I am happy to have been able to hint at the complex symbolism of the *yamazakura*.

オマケ: 鞭もちて遊ぶ子どもを鞭もたぬ子ども見惚るる山ざくら花 （北原白秋・雀の卵 20c）
extra: *muchi mochite asobu kodomo o muchi motanu kodomo mite horeruru yamazakurabana* kitahara hakushû
★*mountain cherries bloom and children without whips are enthralled by children with them*★

Country Blossoms

田舎の花
inaka-no-hana

都へやる返事状に花をつゝみて・君見よや田舎の花の黒き事　鬼貫
miyako e yaru henjijo ni hana o tsutsumite= kimi miyo ya inaka no hana no kuroki kana onitsura 1660-1738
(capital-to send reply-epistle-in blossom bundle // lord/master-look! country blossom's/s' blackness)

◎ *enclosing a blossom with my reply to the capital* ◎

my lord just look
look how black and burnt
this country bloom

Was the *question* whether the poet had found any fair mountain goddesses like the fishing girls discovered by the noble poets of old (in the Manyôshû) on *their* excursions? Onitsura, in line with the new realism of *haikai,* replies, "Are you kidding, the blossoms=women out here are dark as sin!"

山猿と呼ばるゝ里のさくら哉　一茶
yamazaru to yobaruru sato no sakura kana issa 1824
("mountain-cherry" called country/hometown's cherry/ies!)

"mountain monkeys"　　　　　　　　　what cherry bloom
what they call the cherries　　　　　　in a town with folk called
of/in my home town!　　　　　　　　　　"mountain monkeys"

Rural Japanese were called "mountain monkeys." Does Issa mean that cherries from his rurality were not appreciated elsewhere ("of" reading)? Or that country folk, as farmers, put down their own cherry trees as mountain monkeys because, like the crop-raiding macaque they were considered to be a drain on the farm economy and, kept off the flat land, only bloomed on the slopes ("in" reading)? The other reading assumes that the *sato* stood for all the people. Another version has *yado*, or "inn" for *sato*. If it is the local inn that is funny, indeed. If not, the cherry may be a woman from the country. Not funny. Yet another version has *hodo no*, or "that extent." Are they abundant? Are they almost red?

山櫻猿を放して梢かな　其角
yamazakura saru o hanashite kozue kana kikaku -1707
(mountain-cherry/ies monkeys[acc] releasing/ed treetops!/'tis)

mountain cherries
monkeys released pop up
in the tree top

Monkeys were marched about Japan for shows and ritual ceremonies (mostly related to the stable). Since a monkey master would have more than one monkey, I pluralize. The red-faced monkeys and blossoms match. And what a scene it is! Not all country trees were simian:

角田堤・桜木や花の威をかる里の人 一茶 1808
tsunoda zutsumi // sakuragi ya hana no i o karu sato no hito   issa
(cherry-tree/s!/: blossoms' prestige/authority[acc.] borrow country's people)

that's a cherry
the local yokels bask
in its honor

that's a cherry
when it blooms we all wear
borrowed plumes

what a cherry!
the locals borrow
its prestige

This must be a pendulant cherry large enough to have made it into tourism guidebooks. Though bumpkins may not be much into blossom-viewing, once a tree becomes famous . . . . Issa prefaces the *ku* with the location, Tsunoda Bank. The "we" in my second reading is a guess. There was one such tree in Issa's neck of the woods, but, not knowing geography, I do not know if this is it. About the other cherry blossoms in his Kashiwabara back-country, Issa lamented that they were *"gaunt, lacked luster and just plain shabby-looking; compared to the blossoms elsewhere* [the "up-up-countries" (上々国)], *were like mountain sages (ascetics)."* (「痩せ桜」 文政三年春). An awful *ku* claims they *were* blossoms but hardly worthy of the cherry name (花ながらさくらといふが恥しき 同).

あれ畑や人のそしれる桜さく 星布尼
arehata ya hito no soshireru sakura saku   seifu-ni -1814
(ravaged-field!/: peoples' [by] cussed-out cherry/ies bloom/s)

trampled fields
the cherry they cuss-out
is blooming

trampled fields
the cherries people curse
are blooming

Lying in bed, reading a bit of a paperback anthology of the Star-cloth nun's work, damned if I didn't find the *main* reason farmers hated cherry trees (Not my explanation on the previous page). I guess Issa felt he did not need to explain it. Now reconsider Issa's single tree. At first, it might not draw a crowd. But in twenty or thirty years, who knows? Gamblers might even set up a crap table under it. Can you blame the farmers for worrying? More study is needed before I take on country cherries!

◎ ◎ ◎ ◎ ◎ ◎ ◎ ◎

This is a failed chapter. Most cherry *ku* jump from mountain to city with no country in between though some we have seen elsewhere describe the country as the uncouth place crossed on the way to blossom-viewing. The country cherries, themselves, sometimes seem to be mountain (wild) cherries minus respect. And, to add to the confusion, while *sato* means a generally rural hometown, the *sato-zakura*, or, "local/regional cherry" means garden varieties developed in different places and, as such, is opposite to the mountain=wild cherry. Shall we title the below ***"And Where Do All The People Go"***?

十日程花に捨てたる都哉 樗堂 アルス
tôka hodo hana ni sutetaru miyako kana   chodô - 1814
(ten-days about blossoms-for abandoned capital!/'tis)

for ten days
the capital abandoned
for the cherries

Cherry Snappers

桜 鯛
sakura-dai

.魚も木にのぼるためしか桜鯛　宗俊
uo mo ki ni noboru tameshi ka sakuradai sôshun 1633
(fish-even tree-on climb attempt? cherry-snapper)

a fish trying
to climb up a tree?
cherry-snapper

I'm sure you know the little fish with bud-like eyes upon its head that climbs trees, but the connection here is purely nominal. The *sakuradai,* or "cherry snapper," is a red sea bream with an exceptionally long, elegant tail that appears in schools about the time cherries bloom. Another *ku* from the same book: *"Carps climb / waterfalls: blooming up trees / cherry-snapper!"* (鯉は滝木に咲上れ桜鯛　重勝 *koi wa taki ki ni sakinobore sakuradai* shigekatsu 1633). We are talking food here: *"If you want / substance over blossoms, / cherry snapper!"* (花よりも実こそほしけれ桜鯛　兼載 真木柱 *hana yori mo mi koso hoshikere sakuratai* kensai 1697). This puns on the "dumplings over blossoms" saying.

打かけや枯木に花の櫻鯛　宗俊 太夫櫻

uchikake ya karegi ni hana no sakuradai sôshun 1680
(hit-hook! dead/withered-tree-on blossom/s [bloom=]cherry-snapper)

the fishing pole

sudden strike!
and a dead tree blooms:
cherry snapper

This turns the legend of the kind old man who made flowers bloom in mid-winter into a metaphor: *tree-as-fishing pole!* In the original, the first two syllabets in *sakura* first mean "bloom" (*saku*), so we have the phrase: "dead-tree-on blossoms bloom." This pivots into the punch-line, *sakura-dai,* the fish.
.

花はうろこ枝はほねかや桜鯛　ノ身 崑山集

hana wa uroko eda wa hone ka ya sakuradai nomi 1651
(blossom/petals-as-for scales, branches-as-for bones?! cherry-snapper)

petals are scales
and branches are bones!?
cherry snapper

Petal is to scale as branch is to bone. This is translatable, for it relies on similitude rather than pun. Another *ku* based on homophones cannot be properly Englished: "***All The Specs*** // *Protruding eyes=buds, / a nose=blossoms and leaves=teeth: / the cherry-snapper*" (目は出でてはなもはも有るや桜だい　安明　崑山集 *me wa idete hana mo ha mo aru ya sakuradai*　anmei 1651)

水底のむもれ木に花や桜鯛　鈍可 崑山集
suizoku no mumore ki ni hana ya sakuradai junka 1651
(water-botttom's sunken tree-on blossoms! cherry-snapper)

are these blossoms
from a submerged tree?
cherry snappers

優曇花や海中にしも桜鯛　無記名 崑山集
udonge ya watanaka ni shi mo sakuradai anon. 1651
([it's a] udumbara! ocean-inside-even being: cherry snapper)

cherries in the sea:　　　An Udumbara?　　　cherries that grow
is it an *udumbara*?　　Found in the deep blue sea　　in the sea? *sakuradai*
no, a *sakuradai*!　　cherry . . . snappers　　are *udumbara*!

青柳の糸いて釣るかさくら鯛　末得 崑山集
aoyagi no ito nite tsuru ka sakuradai　mitoku 1651
(green/young willow's string-with catch? cherry-snapper)

could we fish
using willow for string?
cherry snapper

Strangely enough, the *sakuradai*, our "cherry snapper" is not in my largest Japanese-English dictionary while the *udonge* or, "udumbara" is: [sanskrit] a plant that flowers, according to legend, once every ten thousand years." The style of the second reading is closest to the Japanese. Respecting the Mitoku's *ku*, recall that the pendulant tree branches are metaphored as "thread/string."

つりあぐる竿や枝折さくら鯛　頼広 夢見草
tsuri-aguru sao ya eda-ori sakuradai　yorihiro 1656
(fish-up pole: branch-break/take/steal cherry-snapper)

a broken branch　　　　　　　　　　　the pole used
the perfect fishing pole:　　　　　　a broken-off limb (of)
cherry-snapper　　　　　　　　　　　cherry . . . snapper

the pole landing
cherry-snapper: snapped off
a blooming branch

Cherry is associated with branches ripped off for aesthetic purposes. Why not get practical? In the original, the branch the broken-branch jumps to the cherry to the fish. I reproduced that in the second reading with the (of) so you can how it does not work in English. The problem is that we must either make it a possessive or stop after the limb. The Japanese *ori* (break) allows either reading.

引網は花に嵐よ櫻鯛　一雪 洗濯物
hikiami wa hana ni arashi yo sakuradai issetsu 1666
(pull/drag-net-as-for blossom's storm! cherry snapper)

the drag-net
is a real bloom-blast!
cherry snapper

A gale spells the end for blossoms; a net dooms the cherry snapper. A large haul of snapper trapped in a closing net would resemble a petal blizzard.

大海も釣りをいとわぬ桜鯛　径重 洗濯物
ôumi mo tsuri o itowanu sakuradai keichô 1666 再現
(big-sea-even fishing hate-not cherry snapper)

to fish the sea
is nothing to hate:
cherry snapper

The Japanese used to call boar "mountain whale" to sanitize the eating of a four-legged creature. Venison was "autumn leaves" (*momiji*) and horse, as noted elsewhere, "cherry" (*sakura*). Fish were a less sinful food to eat, but fishing was still considered a spiritually dirty occupation. Going way out to sea to pursue prey may have been particularly reprehensible and liable to hurt one's next life. But, hey, *this* fish is not *that* bad to catch! Isn't it, at least *nominally* a plant, life defined as insentient in the Sinosphere? (For all the talk about *animism*, in Japanese, at least, "to be" is a different verb for the sentient and insentient.) If it could be caught without the sin of taking (animal) life, it could, by the same convenient logic, be eaten by those to whom meat-eating was not only a sin but illegal:

寺の男鯛喰に出る櫻哉　竹戸 小弓
tera no otoko tai kui ni deru sakura kana chikuko 1699
(temple's men snapper-eating-for go-out cherry!/'tis)

the temple's men
go out to eat snapper
cherry that is!

Men because males hog animal protein? The plant=fish connection is worked in an untranslatable *ku* (釣舟にいけてみよかし桜鯛 親重 犬子集 *tsuribune ni ikete miyokashi sakuradai* chikashige 1633)*,* where the fish is *arranged* (as in flower arrangement) *and* kept alive (as in a fish-well) with one verb, *ikete*.

山海の珍物なれや鷹筑波櫻鯛　長次 鷹つくは
yama-umi no chinmono nare ya sakuradai chôji 1642
(mountain-sea's strange-thing [delicacy/novelty] be! cherry-snapper)

thou art a treat   a novelty made
of both mountain and sea   of mountain and sea, this
o cherry snapper!   cherry snapper!

Delicacies of all types are called "mountain's rare-thing" or "sea's rare-thing" in Japanese. Mountain and sea together sum up the best of the wild world.   This creature is, then, a nominal chimera.

包丁のあたるや嵐櫻鯛　未得 句鑑
hôchô no ataru ya arashi sakuradai mitoku 1777
(knife touches and/!/: gale cherry[blossoms]-snapper)

at the touch
of my knife, a gale
cherry snapper

花吹雪程鱗のちる桜鯛　柳多留 149-16
hanafubuki hodo uroko no chiru sakuradai yanag. 20c
(blossom-blizzard amount falls/scatters cherry-snapper)

scales flying
like a blizzard of petals
cherry snappers

The *ku*, with the knife's moment has more drama than the *senryû* which beats the following *haikai*, unless you love food-fights: *"Cherry snapper / finger-cupped, a blossom / snowball!"* (櫻鯛くつしや花の雪まろけ　近之 洗濯物 *sakuradai kutsushi ya hana no yukimaroge* kinshi 1666).

櫻鯛花にちらばる鱗かな　孤松 (虚子の本に？)
sakuradai hana ni chirabaru uroko kana kôshô (early 20c)
(cherry-snapper blossoms/petals-on/with fall [about] scales!/'tis)

scales scattered
about with petals
cherry snapper

Scaling a fish is torture indoors but fun outdoors where the scales have room to fly and we can catch their rainbow-like gleam. Doing it under a cherry tree would indeed be *trés* poetique, as is this:

あぶるまで火花ちらすや桜鯛　宗継 夢見草
aburu made hibana chirasu ya sakuradai sôkei 1656
(roasted-until sparks fall/scatter!/: cherry-snapper)

let sparks fly
until it is well-roasted
cherry snapper

酒ひてや霞の海の櫻鯛　栄治 鷹つくは
sakabite ya kasumi no umi no sakuradai eiji 1642
(sake-soaked!/: misty ocean's cherry-snapper)

sake-steamed
a sea of mist covers
the cherry snapper

The original of the first *ku* is enhanced by "fire blossoms," a literary term for *sparks*.

桜鯛すゆるはゑびす折敷哉　一正 犬子
sakuradai suyuru wa ebisu oshiki kana issei 1633
(cherry-snapper rots/spoils-as-for, ebisu [a deity] sorry!/'tis)

cherry snapper
when it grows gamey
ebisu is sorry

poor ebisu!
don't let that cherry
snapper spoil!

The proverb says: *"Even if rotten, it is snapper;"* but who wants old fish? I have seen pre-cooked snapper, seemingly shellacked (a different species, common at New Year's) I *assumed* were passed around (presented) until they either petrified or putrified, but a friend swears the decorative fish I had my eye on was probably eaten and replaced. Ebisu, god of prosperity, is generally pictured with what looks like a freshly caught big-eye=*celebratory* (*omedetai*) snapper dangling from a fishing pole. The "sorry" (*oshiki*), may punningly remind readers that he sometimes sat on the fish. Another *ku* places a "cherry" – described by an animal counter, *ippiki*, implying "one fish" because "one tree" would be *ippon* – next to Daikoku, or Big Black, god of wealth, who stands next to Ebisu, on the ship with the 7 gods of good fortune (大黒の側に一匹櫻かな 醉應　*daikoku no soba ni ippiki sakurakana* suiô 1761).

猫の子の初杖負や櫻鯛　遅望
neko no ko no hatsu tsue ou ya sakuradai chibô 17c
(cat's-child's first cane bears!/: cherry-snapper)

the first cane
in a kitten's life:
cherry snapper

The glazed snapper serves duty as food for the eyes before they are eaten. Imagine the torture for a cat: glazed or not, this is a fishy smelling fish. The poor kitten has just been enlightened about who owns fish on land.

孕みても色つばさよしさくら鯛　りん女
haramite mo irotsubasa yoshi sakuradai rinjo 1673-1757
(pregnant/swollen-even color-wings[sexiness] good cherry-snapper)

a swollen belly	fat with child
is still voluptuous	they shine all the more
cherry snapper	cherry snapper

Fish are at their sweetest when plump with roe or milt. In Japan, they are still advertised as "having fat on them" (*abura notte-iru*). The poet, a woman, may be cheering up a gravid friend or bemoaning the difference between herself and a snapper at a time when all people want to look good, blossom-viewing. Rinjo, as mentioned before, is the top shell poet in history (or the only one?).[1] Let's take this opportunity to introduce one that followed on the tail of her gravid snapper: *"Plying the fields / they get bad reputations / cherry-shells"* (野にかよふうき名や立て桜貝 *no ni kayou uki na ya tate sakuragai*). This "kind of carpenter's tellin; *Nitidotelina nitidula*" is tiny, blossom-pink and somewhat translucent. Is Rinjo's *ku* treating cherry petals (= women) blowing in the wind as shells (=women)?, These shells were not eaten nor, as far as I know, sold by venders. People picked them up on the beach as they still do. *"Spume blossoms / petal the seashore / cherry-shells"* (波の花ちりてや磯の櫻貝　竹夜　類題句集？ *nami no hana chirite ya iso no sakuragai* chikuya 1774) They were found together, open or, most commonly half-shell alone. *"Mouth open: / Is that a blossom's smile? / Cherry-shells"* (口あくは花の笑かはさくら貝　弘永　毛吹草 *kuchi aku wa hana no emu ka wa sakuragai* kôei 1645). These two *ku* are normal, which is to say, boring. Rinjo's *ku* is much more interesting. *Did she cross fields going to the beach to collect shells so often that she was suspected of having a secret lover?*

櫻鯛今宵あるしの御料理　重勝
sakuradai koyoi aruji no on/goryôri shigekatsu 1633
(cherry-snapper this-evening host's/master's hon. food/cooking)

tonight's dinner	cherry snapper
for the blossom-viewing host	tonight, the blossom host
cherry snapper	rules the kitchen

---

1 Rinjo's Shells Gravid (?) male shellfish (smooth, whitish grey milt) tend to be more uniformly tasty than females (grainy yellow or orange roe), but Rinjo clearly favors her sex. My favorite concerns the wee shell that makes *miso* soup a true dish (*and* represents a little girl's part) the *shijimi*: *"Corbiculina! / They stand for eons and / countless worlds"* (*chiyo yorozu yo no tatoe niya shijimikai*). Do the countless numbers of *Corbicula japonica* agree with mind-boogling (India-derived) Buddhist visions of world and time? As *shijimi* suggests "*chijimi*=shrunken," could we have a condensed world, a *stupa* of sorts? Would counting such plentitude be "like measuring the ocean with a corbicula?" You will find more shells in *The Mullet in the Maid*, if I ever finish it!

Ryôri is always a problem for translation, for the word can mean food *and* food-preparation, including cooking. Here, I cannot tell if the master is being served or serving. With respect to the latter, let me explain that carving was a prestigious activity in Japan. Perhaps because of the sword-blade connection, it was even a noble occupation – they had masters of the cutting board with ranks, as one might see today in *karate* – and, thanks to *sashimi* and the need to have chopstick-sized morsels even for cooked food, carving could be the greater part of preparing a meal; so, one found something rare in most parts of Europe: men in the kitchen, and not just any man, but the master of the house.

桜鯛や皿にさしみの作り花　定之 嵐山集
sakuradai ya sara ni sashimi no tsukuribana   teishi 1651
(cherry-snapper/s!/: plate-on sashimi-of-artificial-flower)

cherry snapper the paper flowers turn out to be *sashimi*	cherry snapper on my plate the *sashimi* has blossomed

The prettiest raw meat I ever saw was cherry (berry) color and called *sakura-niku*. But, no, it was not fish: it was *horse*. Milder than goat, softer than butter (except for the sinews, which could be cut out), it seems a shame to leave it to dogs, or glue-factories! But, yes, the "raw fish" above is *sashimi*.

骨はいや只みよし野の桜鯛 長頭丸 嵐山集   芳野にてないものを喰ふ櫻鯛 嵐山 雁風呂
hone wa iya tada miyoshino no sakuradai   teitoku 1651   *yoshino nite nai mono o kuu sakuradai*   ranzan 1794
(bones-as-for yuck only miyoshino's cherry-snapper)   (yoshino-at not-thing[acc.] eat cherry-snapper)

bones are yucky give me cherry snapper from yoshino	eating something not found at yoshino cherry snapper

With chopsticks, bones are really not much trouble, but it is heartwarming to find someone in a fish culture who professes to have trouble with them and, I would have all *haikai* scholars who might be reading to note how personal Teitoku is. He cannot be discounted as a poet interested only in nominal puns, though he does, of course, have something up his sleeve here, namely, bean-filled snapper waffles. These are usually called *"taiyaki"* (snapper-roasts) and no mention is made of cherries, but combine them with the most famous blossom-viewing place, Yoshino and Kyôto's well-known sweet-tooth and we can easily imagine what is what. Today, some "fish" are full of custard instead. The second *ku* plays with the idea that Yoshino is tops for anything related to blossom-viewing. The first twelve syllabets subtly suggest something *sakura*-related. I imagine the poet was in Edo, where fresh, seasonally correct fish was an important part of the culture and the *ku* says, you in landlocked Yoshino may boast the *haute* culture of the hills, but we rule the high seas!

日の本や鯛を喰ふて櫻狩　沙月 新選
hinomoto ya tai o kuute sakuragari   sagetsu 1773
(sun's origin [japan]!/: snapper[acc.] eating cherry[blossom] hunting)

the sun's birthplace here we eat red sea bream hunting wild cherry	home of the sun where we sit with cherries eating snapper

The cherry hunt, as mentioned before, included the picnic aspects. This may belong to *Book III* with the nationalistic *sakura,* but boast or not, how better to describe what makes Japan Japan?

45

Scent of the Bloom
花の匂い
hana-no-nioi

月に見ぬ朧は花の匂ひ哉　心敬
tsuki ni minu oboro wa hana no nioi kana shinkei 1405-1475
(moon-by/at see-not haze-as-for, blossom's/s' scent!/tis)

      blossom scent
  the haze we do *not* see
     about the moon

Old poems (*waka*) dwell on the fragrance of the *ume,* or *plum* (Japanese apricot), blossom – a scent I find oppressive, like that of a musty flower-shop – but few mention that of the *sakura*, perhaps because it is subtle to absent in many varieties.[1] The plum blossom scent was thought to be so thick that it percolated up to form a haze around the spring moon, but since that haze was more likely with the lower air pressure and higher temperature of the later cherry spring, and *hana*, since the *Kokinshû* (905) almost always meant cherry, we may say that Shinkei is talking *sakura*. With *"Morning mist / no mountain without / the scent of blossoms"* (朝霞花に匂はぬ山もなし 宗祇 大発句帳*asagasumi hana ni niowanu yama mo nashi* sôgi 1421-1502) and *"A mountain path / the setting sun glazed / by bloom-scent"* (花の香に入日のくもる山路かな　宗長*hana no ka ni iribi no kumoru yamaji kana*　sôchô 1447-1532) the mountains favor cherry while the mist and sun, as New Year themes, favor the plum, yet the era judges for cherry. As silly as this might sound, I would *guess* the inheritance of blossom (*hana*) mantle from the plum helps explain the amount of scent found in cherry blossom *ku*.

とりのねハ花にくはゝるにほひ哉 宗祇
tori no ne wa hana ni kubaruru nioi kana sôgi -1502
(birds' sound-as-for blossoms-to distribute scent!/?/'tis)

the sound of birds:	birds are singing	the sound of birds:
a fragrance distributed	the pink of life is here	does eros spread through
among blossoms	in the blossoms	the new bloom

1. Cherries with Scent The most thorough book on Japanese Flowering Cherries gives only three paragraphs to blossom scent. It starts: "Many Japanese flowering cherries have distinctly scented flowers. Their cumarin-like fragrance is similar to that of crushed almonds, although the scent of 'Ama-no-gawa' [The Milky Way] has been associated also with freesia." (Wybe Kuitert: 1999) As far as I can ascertain, "many" means dozens out of hundreds of varieties. Of these, some were cultivated with the scent in mind, while others are individuals, for cherries like most plants are more individualistic than animals and continually show such variety. In the case of one wild cherry family (Oshima), such individuals are fairly common. It is to be more specific, for it is hard to draw the line for when a blossom can be said to have a scent and, as Kuitert notes, explaining his book's lack of an "odor chart," even blossoms that clearly smell in some meteorological conditions may not be perceptible in others. Ogawa Kazusuke (2000) observes that seemingly wild cherries in the Kinki (old capital) area generally have scent because they were selected for it by the nobility and that we get the impression cherries have no scent today because over ninety persencent of the cherries we encounter are the cloned Somei-yoshino which is, indeed, as scentless as *it* is sterile. Indeed, I was fooled to think of *sakura* as scentless and this has, doubtless, hurt my ability to select and read *ku* on the subject. Perhaps, I will double the size of the chapter some day!

~~~~~~

The idea of birds spreading scent with their singing makes little sense in English where scent is scent, but *in Japanese* scent is not just olfactory. It is *the pink of life*. It is *a luminous splendor*. It is *eros*. These birds bring *that* to the bloom not only by fanning the scent with their wings but by expressing their joy. While blossom-viewing is unabashedly visual, with *hanami* meaning "blossom-see," the other senses occasionally make an appearance. In Sôgi's *ku* we find acoustic, olfactory and, vicariously, in the person of the birds we imagine brushing against the blossoms, tactile elements. A later *ku* by Sôseki describes the sound of the birds *as* the eros/scent (鳥の音も花にさき出るにほひかな).

花の色はかすみにこめて見せずともかをだにぬすめ春の山かぜ　よしみねのむねさだ
hana no iro wa kasumi ni komete misezu to mo ka o dani nusume haru no yamakaze　yoshimune no munesada (kks #91)
(blossom/s' color=sight-as-for mist-by/in hidden show-not even scent at-least steal! spring's mountain-wind　kokinshû (905))

*though you may
not reveal the blossoms
behind that mist*

*mountain winds of spring
at least steal the scent for us!*

Mountains point to wild cherry, and *iro*, or "color," is a sexy word identified more with cherry blossoms than plum, so this is probably about our flower. The pun "at least show [me] your face!"(*kao* v.s. *ka o=scent*(obj)) – is a common request in older poems. This *waka* shows that *haikai* did not invent inanity. Later *haikai* chuckled: *"Rosy round the gills! / "At least steal her scent" / blossom breeze?"* (鼻いきよ香をだにぬすめ花の風　方寸 *hanaiki yo ka o dani nusume hana no kaze* hôsun ())

山は花ありとや匂ふ天つ風　昌休
yama wa hana ari to ya niou amatsukaze shôkyû -1552
(mountain-as-for blossoms are [as-if-said]!/: smells/glows heaven's wind)

| the mountain
has blossoms: how sweet
heaven's wind! | there are blossoms
in the hills: heaven's wind
gains new charm |

The syntax, where one first associates the smell=*niou* (a neutral or good verb in Japanese), with the mountain/s and, *then*, with the wind, does not translate, so I recreated the mood with "new charm" and "sweet" (an attribute only associated with suckers or loose women and not with babies in Japanese).

遠山も風には近き花香哉　利山 洗濯もの
tôyama mo kaze ni wa chikaki hanaka kana risan 1666
(far-mountain/foothills-too, wind-with-as-for close, blossom-scent!/'tis)

| distant peaks
are right in your face
blossom-scent | distant peaks
come close in the wind
blossom-scent |

With scent specified, I thought the wind was unnecessary, hence the first reading of Risan's *ku*.

はなの香をみちのくやまのしほり哉　宗牧
hana no ka o michinoku-yama no shiori kana sôboku - 1545
(blossoms' scent[acc.] landlocked-inner-mountains' trailmark/blaze!/?/'tis)

deep in the hills	bloom-scent
the only paths are blazed by	how trails are marked
blossom scent	in michinoku

As confessed already in a note, I failed to grasp the importance of real scent – as opposed to the figurative scent-as-eros or glowing beauty. The above – a fresh find, squeezed in while proofing – is one of many *ku* I may have overlooked. Michinoku needs to be translated as Appalachia or the Ozarks but, obviously, that won't do. Be that as it may, I am happy to say some poets may have shared my feelings: *"More in the nose / than in the bloom: what / we call "scent"* 花よりも鼻にありける匂ひ哉　守武 *hana yori mo hana ni arikeru nioi kana* moritake -1549. This *ku*, which might be titled "the truth about cherry blossoms" is didactic, for sure, but the homophonic *hana* (nose/blossom) makes it *somewhat* better in the original. Blyth translates *"The sweet smell / Is not so much in the flower / As in the nose."* A good reading, but the *"sweet"* is odd, for the fact there is little scent to speak of *is* the poetry: were the *ku* about the *rose*, it would be mere philosophy. Note, also, that Moritake, head priest of Japan's top Shinto Shrine, is put at the head of many collections of *hokku*. Sôgi, a more prolific poet, usually relegated to the world of *renga* by *haikai* scholars and *saijiki* editors, has what I consider a more sophisticated take on this scent that is and is not:

みるたひにミぬ花さける色香かな　宗祇
miru tabi ni minu hana sakeru iroka kana sôgi 1420-1502
(see time/each-when see-not blossom blooms color-scent!/'tis)

cherry doppelganger

each time i see	each blossom
a blossom unseen blooms:	seen, yet blooms unseen:
sight and scent!	sight *and* scent

The first reading tries to use the "blossom" as a pivot word, but I suspect the reader must say "blossom" twice if the poem is read aloud! The second reading uses a passive to approximate the parallel structure of the original that cannot be Englished because "not see" does not work as an adjective – Japanese verbs in a fully transitive and active state (*as-they-are*) serve as gerunds!

色を姿匂ひを花の心哉　宗祇
iro o sugata nioi o hana no kokoro kana sôgi
(color[acc.] shape, smell/scent[acc.] blossom's/s' heart/mind'tis)

i'd call color
a blossom's appearance,
scent, its soul

As color was generally said to have scent, the two are not as contrary as outer form *vs* heart/mind/soul (*kokoro* is all of these things). Still, scent-as-mind suggests to me it is was subtly perceived, unlike, say, the powerful perfume of the rose. Frois, in the 16c (*Topsy Turvy 1585*) observed that Japanese found the strong scents we favored, in the garden, or the church, fulsome. So subtle scent is fine.

花の香を空にわき出すいづみ哉　宗祇 大原三吟
hana no ka o sora ni wakidasu izumi kana sôgi 1420-1502
(blossom's/s' scent[obj] sky-into gush/boil-exit spring!/?'tis)

    blossom scent   blossom scent
these springs gush up   shoots up into the sky
  through the sky!   tree-as-spring
                          springs of spring
                     spurting bloom-scent
                           into the sky

Invisible springs of fragrance. There is a cherry with fragrant blossoms that has, in the 20c been called "waterfall-scent" (*taki-nioi*) and "incense-waterfall" (*rôkô*) and, by one Japanese botanist, *Prunus serrulata f.* **cataracta**. Kuitert, who complains that the word "cataract" fails to capture "the idea of cascading" explains that the *taki* "refers to the way in which the horizontally feathering branches are held up, producing out of the heart of the tree layer upon layer that make up its cascading crown." Excellent point. Not all cataracts cascade. The fragrance, he continues, is that of "crushed almond" and this "sweet scent . . . surrounds the tree with a waterfall of fragrance" (*Japanese Flowering Cheries*).

見ぬ花の心しらるゝ匂ひ哉　宗牧
minu hana no kokoro shiraruru nioi kana sôboku
(see-not blossom's heart known-is scent!/'tis) -1545

  i know the mind   i know about
of an unseen blossom: the unseen blossoms:
   scent is public   *scent talks*

Mind could as well be *heart*. Here, the scent is surely real. Should I have refrained from turning the last lines into aphorisms.

笑みぬるは香や吹き出す花の口　弘水 毛吹草
emi nuru wa ka ya fukidasu hana no kuchi kôei 1645
(laugh/smiling-as-for?! spurt-out blossom-mouth/s)

   scent bursts out   when they laugh
of litle pink mouths when   sweet scents spill out:
   blossoms laugh   blossom mouths

Mountains or plants sprouting new leaves and/or in bloom are said to smile/laugh. The original is less anthropomorphic, for the connotation of *kuchi* includes far more types of openings than "mouth" does. The central part of a blossom can be a "mouth" without pushing it whatsoever. I added the "little pink" to fill out the poem in the first reading.

秋もいさ青葉に匂ふ花の露　宗牧 東國紀行
aki mo iza aoba ni niou hana no tsuyu sôboku -1545
(fall-too someday, green/new-leaf-in smell blossom-dew)

  autumn will come   the new leaves
soon enough! bloom-dew   fragrant with blossom dew
  paints a new leaf   i think of fall

scent

This "smell" I would guess has nothing to do with real scent. A preface explains that new leaves wet with blossom dew seemed red. Either the dew reflected the dark pink of the opening blossom buds upon the leaves or the leaves themselves were red, as mountain cherry leaves often are, and the dew's glossy finish caught the eye of the poet, who thought about the second time the leaves would color.

花いつく匂ひは袖のみなと哉　宗牧
hana izuku nioi wa sode no minato kana sôboku -1545
(blossom/s whither? scent-as-for sleeve's/s' harbor!/'tis)

whither the bloom	whither they went	blossoms may blow
its fragrance harbours	the blossoms' scent sleeps	but the scent moors within
in these sleeves!	in these sleeves	her sweet sleeve

The fragrance is partly figurative, including the petals left in the sleeve, and partly concrete: imagine the lingering smell of the fires/torches and whatnot of the blossom viewing. Petals falling, or, rather, flying, evoke the departure of Spring. Terminal *harbors* are old trope for departing seasons. .

西行のゑに・花の香や袈裟も衣も腸も　青蘿
hana no ka ya kesa mo koromo mo harawata mo seira -1791
(blossom's/s' scent!/: surplice and robes and bowels too)

on a picture of saigyô

bloom-scent
in his surplice, robe
and bowels

Ka rather than *niou/i* suggests we are talking about scent itself, rather than a general "color" or "eros." The bowels are apocryphal. Saigyô died of old age (a heart attack I guess) and did not cut his belly.   East or West, saints smell good through and through, right? (次の本のために、専門家に訊く：一茶句「廿五の暁植しさくら哉」とは、廿五菩薩の香＝桜＝のことでしょうか？)

日のみかけ花に匂へるあした哉　心敬 新つくは
hi no mikake hana ni nioeru ashita kana shinkei -1475
(sun's looks/appearance blossoms-on smell/glow/ing morning!)

this morning	this morning
how fine the sun looks	how good the sun smells
on the blossoms	on the blossoms

月しづか桜のもとの人薫り 左来 花共養
tsuki shizuka sakura no moto no hito kaori sarai 1795
(moon quiet cherry/ies-below/about's people-scent)

the moon quiet	moon silence
below the cherry trees	under the cherry trees
the scent of men	people scent

> 月 <

46

Soul/heart/mind Blossoms

hana-no-kokoro

世の中にたえてさくらのなかせば春の心はのどけらまし 古今集 #53
yononaka ni taete sakura no nakariseba haru no kokoro wa nodokeramashi narihira kokinshû 905

*were there
no cherry blossoms
in this world
our minds might know
serenity in spring*

Is the pleasure of blossoms worth the pain? This poem by Narihira is the most often cited cherry-blossom *waka* after Saigyo's "When I die" (#36-14) and Norinaga's "If you ask " (#61-5). I once found it *reversed* – no serenity without blossoms – at an English language haiku website. Readers assuming blossoms can only be good for us could not have *dreamed* it was mistranslated!

久方のひかりのどけき春の日にしづ心なく花のちるらむ きのとものり古今集 #84
hisakata no hikari nodokeki haru no hi ni shizugokoro naki hana no chiruramu   kokinshû 905

to think that	*how bright*
on this bright and balmy	*and still, this fine*
day of spring	*spring day!*
blossoms can so lack	*is restlessness why*
peace of mind to fall!	*the petals won't stay?*

This *waka*, well known for being in the popular *Hundred Poet's One Poem* anthology (13c *Hyakuninisshû*), ostensibly concerns blossoms alone, but seems to attribute the dis-ease of men in Spring to the blossoms themselves. One word in these poems, *kokoro* 心 – usually translated "mind" or "heart," but also "feeling," "intent," "answer" (to a riddle), etc. – is, as the reader may have already noticed, ubiquitous in cherry blossom poems. *It is also the most beloved Chinese character in Japan.* I am not kidding. They actually survey such things. What the polls do not say is *why* that is so. Or, rather, when they do, they just say it is because Japanese value feelings (as if other people do not!). Well, it just so happens, I, too, love the character. The reason is that it is literally the least square of all characters. If only a large publisher (which could help with illustrations) would back me, I would do a book of nothing but 心. Now, let's see how the poets played with these natural matters of the heart.

春毎に気をなやまする櫻哉 仙里 四季発[千?]句
harugoto ni ki o nayamasuru sakura kana   senri 1689?
(spring-every-on-spirit[+obj]-troubling-cherry!/'tis)

heart-breaker

upsetting us
every single spring
cherry blossoms!

There is no space for the *word* "heart/mind" (*kokoro*) in this haiku – my title, of course, is an addition – that boils the *waka* down to its essence and, I think, pokes fun at it, though who can say whether the *waka* was serious or not? (I think *not*, but *most* think it is). This *ku*, syntax-wise little more than a modification of cherry blossoms (I hyphenated the gloss to show it), facetiously creates a new "pillow," where "upsetting" evokes the blossom of Narihira's *waka*.

弥生十日過上野にて・櫻見てはや春をしむ心哉　吟江 古き姿
sakura mite haya haru o oshimu kokoro kana   ginkô 1775
(cherry seeing quickly spring[acc.] mourn heart/mind!/?/'tis)

at ueno blossom-viewing grounds on the 10th of the 2nd month

seeing these   viewing *sakura*
cherries in bloom, already   do i already regret
i mourn for spring!   spring's passing?

Day 10 of Month 2 (called the beautiful name *Yayoi* in the preamble) – middle-to-late-March today – is a bit early. As we have seen, the fate of the blossoms was identified with that of Spring herself. But, the relationship of heart/mind to blossoms was not only one of preoccupation for their fate and the all-too short season. Let us see a handful of diverse blossom+heart/mind *waka* by the top *kokoro* poet in Japanese history, before returning to our *haikai/haiku*.

散る花を惜しむ心やとどまりて また来ん春の たねになるべき　西行
chiru hana o oshimu kokoro ya todomarite mata kin?haru no tane ni naru beki   saigyô -1190 山家集 #127
(falling-blossoms laments heart: staying again come-will spring's seed-as become-ought)

and my heart   *does my heart*
that mourns the petals   *lamenting the blossoms*
falling, stays: *fall, stay here*

to seed a new spring   *to seed new flowers*
when she comes back   *when spring returns?*

what to do with
this heart of mine lamenting
the blossoms fall?

let it remain here as seed
for spring will come back!

Hearts as seeds. A line from the preface to the *Kokinshû* says "the *yamato uta*, lit. Japanese songs=poetry (as opposed to Chinese style) has the heart of the people as its seed."

吉野山花の散りにし木の下にとめし心はわれを待つらん　西行　山家集
yoshino yama hana no chiri ni shi konomoto ni tomeshi kokoro wa ware o matsuran saigyô (#1453)

mount yoshino!
there, at the base of
that cherry tree

where blossoms fell,
my heart awaits me

on mt yoshino
beneath a tree where
petals fell, there

it waits for me:
my heart.

Saigyô puts this at the head of a set of ten cherry blossom *waka* which shows us that he is not *leaving* his heart at Yoshino but *coming back*, after a year (or more?), to reclaim it. The separation of heart /mind and body that Saigyô plays with is an expression of infatuation very common in ancient Japanese poetry. Some Japanese critics, perhaps thinking this is not what a monk *should* write, guess he wrote these songs before retiring from active life; but I think them too good to be juvenilia. This next, found much earlier in the book, is honest, but less interesting.

花に染む心のいかで残りけん捨て果ててきと思ふわが身に　西行　山家集 #76
hana ni somu kokoro no ika de nokori ken sutehatete ki to omou waga mi ni saigyô -1190

why in the world
does my blossom-dyed heart
remain with me

when i come here as one
who has abandoned love?

how can a man
who vowed to leave
his self behind

stay so damn attached
to cherry blossoms?

As a Buddhist, Saigyô was not supposed to be so in love with – *i.e.,* attached to – the natural world, which is to say, the body of illusion. Blossoms were preferable to women or boys, but the principle was the same.

吉野山梢の花を見し日より心は身にも添はずなりにき　西行　同 # 66
yoshino yama kozue no hana o mishi hi yori kokoro wa mi ni mo sowazu nariniki saigyô

mount yoshino:
from the day i saw those
blossomed limbs

my heart just would not
stay put in this body

mount yoshino:
from the day i saw bloom
on your limbtips

i have been literally
out of it, out of my mind

Seeing the above three poems one after another, we see a contradiction in the Japanese heart metaphor: love is *attachment* (a heart dyed with, i.e., besotted with blossoms) yet it is also *separation* (heart under a tree, blossoms on top [1]). *Attachment would seem to define itself as separation!* The poem following this (#67) wonders if his heart will come back after the blossoms/petals fall (I think #1453 was the clever answer to this: *No, not until next year!*) Later, Saigyô found a clever new twist:

---

1. **Blossomed Limbs** I first had the usual translation for *kozue,* "treetop." The problem is it means the limb ends and not just what's highest. The *kozue* is where blossoms usually are. Moreover, it is a pretty word often used as a girl's name. At my wit's end for a decent translation, I came up with "blossomed limbs" and "limbtips."

花を見る心はよそに隔たりて 身につきたるは君がおもかげ　西行
hana o miru kokoro wa yoso ni hedatarite mi ni tsukitaru wa kimi ga omokage saigyô #598

> while my heart
> viewing the blossoms
> wanders off
>
> what comes by to stick
> in my mind? your face

> when my heart
> slipped off to view
> the blossoms
>
> your phantom came
> and stole my soul!

> my heart
> out there viewing
> the blossoms
>
> turns about and sees
> you back here with me

I have no idea if the *kimi*, a word meaning gentleman/you or lord is the Emperor or a girlfriend. What interests me is the complexity of the objectified feelings, these things coming and going. Besides the heart/mind *kokoro*, Japanese had more souls, *tama(shii)* than I have been able to figure out.

人も来ず心も散らで山かげは花を見るにもたよりありけり　西行
hito mo kozu kokoro mo chirade yamakage wa hana o miru ni mo tayori arikeri saigyô #1037

> with no people
> coming up here my heart
> doesn't scatter:
>
> mountain retreats are also
> good for viewing blossoms

"My mind / is not distracted" would be more accurate for lines 2 and 3, but the blossom pun would be lost by it. The real wit is in the *tayori* which literally means something that may be *relied upon*. The hermitage can be relied upon not only for the usual spiritual benefits but . . . A later poem (one of ten beginning with sks #1453) reverses this small revelation:

人はみな吉野の山へ入りぬめり都の花にわれはとまらむ　西行
hito wa mina yoshino no yama e iri-numeri miyako no hana ni ware wa tomaran saigyô #1455

> everyone else
> has gone to mt yoshino
> i guess i'll stay
>
> with the blossoms
> here in the capital

> all the world
> is up mount yoshino
> i'll camp out
>
> with the cherry blossoms
> down here in the capital!

The capital (Kyôto) is the blossom capital, but Mount Yoshino, a day or two away, was the top destination for blossom-viewing. If everyone is up on the mountain, monks seeking seclusion might then come down into the capital – the world they abandoned – which had become a ghost-town and enjoy the cherries blooming in it. Saigyô may have already been in the capital. At any rate, the capital is always "up" (East) in Japan. I play with this in my second reading.

惜しまれぬわが身だにも世にはあるものをあなあやにくの花の心や 西行 # 116
oshimarenu mi dani mo yo ni wa aru mono o ana-ayaniku no hana no kokoro ya saigyô -1190

*though plenty
of us, who would be
as happy dead
must stay – how sad that you
blossoms, should go, instead*

*some live on & on
whose passing would draw
not a single tear
what a pity these blossoms
we love have a mind to go*

*though yours
truly would not mind
leaving it all
behind – how cruel of you
blossoms, to actually do so*

The original does not actually say blossoms have a cruel *heart*. *Ayaniku* means something that is terribly unfortunate for going against our hopes or wishes. It has the character for "hate" in it, which my cruel hyperbolizes. The original is subtle, specifying neither the person (first or third) of whoever's passing would not be regretted nor actually saying what the blossoms *do*. Reading 2 catches the 心。

花見ればそのいはれとはなけれども　心のうちぞ　苦しかりける　西行
hana mireba sono iware to wa nakeredomo kokoro no uchi zo kurushikarikeri saigyô (#68)

*when i see
blossoms i do not
know why
my heart begins
to ache like this*

*viewing blossoms
why in particular
i cannot tell
i only know i suffer
deep within my heart*

A Japanese annotation explains that the aching occurs when the heart separates from the body (this, the etymology for *akugare/akogare*=longing) and can't return until the blossoms fall, also something painful to the lover. Personally, I think such suffering is normal for anyone who is a kind person, a lover of the beautiful and alone. It is easy to stay at home and work on a rainy day, but, in the presence of all that beauty, Saigyô must have ached to share it with others. With this, I think we have pretty well covered the world of heart+blossom *waka,* as exemplified by Saigyô. Let me just add that all blossom-loving haiku poets worshipped this man: *"In blossom time / we are not worth Saigyô's / fingernail crud"* (西行の爪糞程や花の時　傘下 *saigyô no tsumeguso hodo ya hana no toki*　sanka c.1700). Note: such "crud" (also in the eyes and nose) in Japanese is literally "shit." Now, let us return to *haikai:*

花に入る山は心のはてもなし 宗祇
hana ni iru yama wa kokoro no hate mo nashi sôgi - 1502
(blossoms into enter/ing mountain-as-for heart/mind's-end too/even not)

*blooming mountains
there is no end to them
or my imagination!*

*within the hills
the blooming hills, mind
goes on and on*

*entering hills
in bloom, my interest
is endless too*

Is this an endless horizon or a three-dimensional maze? Here *kokoro* became *imagination*, *mind* and *interest*, respectively. This bold assertion is qualified by a *ku* suggesting there were things that stopped even Sôgi's indefatigable *kokoro*. Do you recall the idiom of the unattainable, the blossoms-on-the-peak (*takane no hana*) ? Here is a reading of a *ku* that glosses as "*kokoro*-even reaches-not blossoms' high-peak" – "Trees so high / I do not even *dream* / about climbing." (心たに及はぬ花の高根哉　宗祇　*kokoro dani yobanu hana no takane kana*　sôgi 1420-1502). A peak steep enough that the mind may rest. Here, it would seem that *kokoro* means the mind/heart that wants things: "*Blossoms so high / even my desire / fails to rise.*" I must admit to wondering whether an allegory is intended.

見とれては花に花さく心哉　重供 毛吹草
mitorete wa hana ni hana saku kokoro kana shigetomo -1645
(see-infatuated-as-for blossom-to/on blossom bloom heart/mind!/'tis)

fascination is

when the budswhen your mind
in your heart bloommakes even blooming
on the blossomsblossoms bloom

when you too blossom
within the bloom

The poet literally plays with a common idiom for getting excited about something "~ Bloom as a blossom" (*hana ni saku*). Is the extra *hana* the poet enjoying himself or how he sees the blossoms?

哥によむ花は胸よりさく意哉 仁意 夢見草
uta ni yomu hana wa mune yori saku-i kana　jini 1656
(song-as compose/make blossom/s-as-for chest-from bloom-meme!/'tis)

the blossoms you
turn into poetry bloom
from the breast

Saku (phonetically さく) means either "bloom = 咲く" or "compose =作." The character 意 means "idea/intent/heart/ mind." Together with *saku*=作 it means "*motif*" or "creative impulse."

枝葉なし花に向へる人心　梁山 古今鑑
edaha nashi hana ni mukaeru hitogokoro　ryôzan 1777
(branches/twigs-leaves-not/without blossoms-to heads[vb] human-mind/heart/s)

blossom hoh!body and soul
the mind of man brooks nohead straight for the bloom
leafy diversionno leaves, no twigs

If I reverse translated, leaving out the diversion, we get: *Body and soul / head straight for the goal: / cherry blossoms.* The cherry blooms before it fully leaves, so man and tree are of one mind in this.

人の心酒に成にけり花盛　長治 続境海草
hito no kokoro sake ni narinikeri hanazakari　chôji 1670
(people's heart *sake*-into becomes[finality] blossom-acme)

when the bloomthe human willbloom peak
peaks, our humanitydissolves into rice wineminds blossoming
turns into *sake*blossom-viewingin alcohol

Humanity, will, mind. All *kokoro*. The original puns on *sake*'s homophonic double "blooms."

花の乱れさても心の似たる哉　城仄 月夜
hana no midare sate mo kokoro no nitaru kana　jôsoku 1776
(blossom/s' dishevelment/wildness, hmm, heart/mind's resembling!)

a pandemonium
of blossoms and of hearts
which the copy?

the bloom ragged
so, too, we who have
drunken our fill

真盛りの花に入たき心哉　司木 花七日
mazakari no hana ni iritaki kokoro kana　shiboku 1777
(real-acme's blossoms-as enter-want/ing heart/mind!/'tis)

oh, my mind
would join the blossoms
in full bloom

the birds & the bees!
i would dive right into
that rutting bloom

I recall what happened to a professor who was swept up in a spawn-fest of frogs one full-moon night.

目にみちて心も花の盛哉　馬曹 花七日
me ni michite kokoro mo hana no sakari kana　basô 1777
(eyes-in filling, heart/mind, too, blossoms' peak/rut!)

overflowing
the eyes, blossoms riot
in my heart

filling my eyes
the blossom flood pours
into my heart!

the full bloom:
a wild fire leaping from
eye to mind!

If a "riot," "flood" or "fire" is found in any subsequent translation of the *ku*, I'll know where the translator found them, for, as was the case with the "birds and bees" in the last, none are in the original.

一木さく花にはちらぬ心哉　尊氏 つくは
hitoki saku hana ni wa chiranu kokoro kana　sonshi 1356
(one-tree blooms blossom/s-as-for fall/scatter/leave-not heart!/'tis)

~~a tree blooms~~
~~the cherry's heart falls not~~
~~with its petals~~

this heart of mine
will not leave the blossoms
of one pretty tree

~~they won't fall~~
~~for the bloom of one tree~~
~~our hearts~~

~~The first reading credits the poet with a rare achievement, not taking the blossoms for the tree. The second, a single tree will not put us into a bloom-rut, is more likely. The "one-tree" may pun on the homophonic "one-short-period," *i.e.*, a man does not loose his heart over the brief flower of a beauty.~~

ひらけ行心の花は風もなし　紹巴 大発句帳
hirake yuku kokoro no hana wa kaze mo nashi　jôha - 1602
(opening-go heart/mind's blossoms-as-for wind-even/also not/none)

nor can the wind
trouble those blossoms
opening within

no wind, either
for the blossoming of
an open mind

My "nor" is not quite right. The *mo* in the original does not limit what is not to the wind. It provokes thought about *other* advantages, too: no need to fight for viewing space, guard it, worry about rain, etc. Idea-wise, the "open" – a more dynamic but untranslatable "opening-go" in the original – is the only thing saving this *ku*. Before changing the last line of the first reading from "in your heart" to "opening within," I was set to ditch it. For whatever reason, the word "heart" ruined it.

こゝろのミうこきて花にかせもなし 宗碩 大発句帳
kokoro nomi ugokite hana ni kaze mo nashi sôseki - 1533
(heart/mind only moves/ing blossoms-in wind-even not)

even the wind
is absent within the bloom
mind is alone

there's no wind
only our minds still move
among the blossoms

among blossoms
where only mind moves
it is windless

no wind moves
within these blossoms
my mind's alone

What a fine way to describe full bloom on a preternaturally still day! The *mo* here is a bit different than the last poem's and means only "*not even any* ~." The "still" is added to the first reading for rhythm; the second is closer to the original syntax yet only makes sense in the abstract – platonic love is not risky – that, itself, is wrong. The third exercised considerable poetic license.

出入の息や心のはなのかぜ 笑種 崑山集
ide-iri no iki ya kokoro no hana no kaze shôshu 1651
(out/leaving in/entering's breath!/?/: heart/mind's/s' blossom-wind)

cherry blossoms
i feel my breath as wind
visiting the heart

the wind visiting
the blossom of our hearts
it's called breath

are you sighing
the blossom wind visits
blooming hearts

Wind as a blossom-seeking free libido couples with the idea of blossoming within. A pun on nose =blossom (*hana*) justifies the sighing in the last reading. The poet's name Englishes as "laugh-seed."

折えたやなかはこゝろの春のはな 宗祇 発句帳
ori-eda ya nakaba kokoro no haru no hana sôgi - 1502
(broken-branch! half/partly heart's spring's blossom/s)

stolen bloom
spring blossoms in part
a mental thing

breaking one off
half the prize is spirit
spring blossoms

broken limbs
our hearts also bloom
every spring

Since spring (*haru*) is homophonic for *swelling*, I first thought Sôgi meant *"Breaking a spray: / Otherwise the heart swells / with the blossoms."* Logically, it works but, the grammar didn't scan. Thinking of Sôgi's character, I also tried *"Spring blossoms / I've half a mind to / break one off"* &

"I've half a mind / to break off a whole spray / spring blossoms" & *"My heart swells / in spring: I've half a mind / to break one off,"* but these, too, deviate from the original, which, I think, I finally got.

涅槃会や何心なく初櫻　成美 いかに〲

nehan e ya nanigokoronaku hatsuzakura seibi -1816
(nehan meeting/s: what/any-heart/feelings-without: first-cherry)

<table>
<tr><td>enlightenment day
with no mind whatsoever
the first blossoms</td><td>on buddha's day
i happen to bump into
the first blossoms</td></tr>
</table>

At first, I imagined that when Seibi went to a Nehan-e, a get-together to celebrate Buddha's deathday, or translation to Nirvana, he felt either *"Our hearts are /not into buddha day: / first blossoms!"* or, contrarily that on *"Buddha Day: /Why can't we get it up / for first blossoms?"* I liked the idea of a *ku* boldly putting the blossoms and the Buddha at odds rather than trying to explain one as the image or allegory of the other. But, Seibi was wealthy and urbane. His Buddhism would have been Zen. The *kokoro-without* is neither *heartless*, nor *mindless*, but simply being open. The surprisingly late first-blossoms are witnessed without ulterior motive, with no pride for having viewed them first or possessiveness. My second reading is how *I* might have expressed the same thing.

思ひいる心は花のまよひ哉　宗牧 新つくは

omoi-iru kokoro wa hana no mayoi kana sôboku 1495
(considering/brooding mind-as-for blossoms-straying/delusion!/'tis)

<table>
<tr><td>think too much
and you will lose your way
in the blossoms</td><td>it's a mistake
to view blossoms with things
on your mind</td></tr>
</table>

思ふことなきは花見るこゝろかな　紹巴

omou koto naki wa hana miru kokoro kana jôha 1523-1602
(think/love-thing-not-as-for blossom-viewing heart/mind'tis/that's)

the way to view
blossoms is with nothing
on your mind

To appreciate the blossoms as a purely aesthetic experience one should think of nothing else. But one can become attentive to detail usually passed over when suffering from unrequited love – it is a type of grabbing at straws – so I think there is something to be said for less exalted viewings, too.

◎ 夢 ◎ *yume* ◎ 見 ◎ *mi* ◎ 草 ◎ *gusa* ◎

We have overlooked one phenomenon of the mind that *is* and *is not* thought, is *something* yet *nothing*: **dreaming**. 2 *ku* with dream 夢=*yume* are found with *Cherry-hunting*, 1 with *First-blossoms*, 1 with *Inebriation*, 3 with *Zoo* (that butterfly), 1 with *Death*, 1 with *Mountain-cherry*, 1 here in *Heart*, 3 in *Falling*, 1 with *Women*, 1 with *House-cherry*, 2 with *Sex* and 1 between *Books*. That is 18 in total, enough for yet another short chapter that wasn't. Note that one nickname for the cherry tree is *yumemigusa*, or **"dream-viewing-grass."** It first appeared in a *waka* that roughly translates: *"I planted one / and see it as a fable / my **dream-flower** / though my life today / may have no tomorrow."* (〔桜〕うへ置てたとへにやみる夢見草 あすをもしらぬ今日の命を 蔵玉集 *ue oite tatoe niya miru yumemisô asu o mo shiranu kyô no inochi o* 15c? Zôgyokushû). In Japanese, "to dream" is to *dream-see/view* and *kusa* means a *flowering plant* as well as "grass." Hence, the bold discrepancy you see.

世の中のこゝろ絶たる櫻哉　汀躬
yononaka no kokoro taetaru sakura kana　teikyû
(world-among's heart/s run/s-out cherry[blossoms]!/'tis)

                the whole world
              loses its mind when
                 cherries bloom

the vulgar mind   cherries bloom
of the world is blown: and the world we know
cherry blossoms!   loses its mind!

                 this world is
            another world, we are
               in cherry time

worldly things   cherry blossoms!
no longer make sense: business as usual is
cherry blooms!   another world!

                 all the spirit
            in the world has gone
              to the blossoms

見る心しらぬ（ちらぬ）花さく一木哉　宗碩 ~ 発句帳
miru kokoro shiranu (chiranu) hana saku hitoki kana　sôseki -1533
(seeing-heart/mind/feelings know(fall?)-not flowers-blossom one-tree tis/!)

a single tree   *in the mind's eye*   flowers bloom
blooming as if we   *a tree blooms with blossoms*   unknown to our eyes
did not exist!   *that never fall*   there is a tree

The first *ku*, though hyperbolic, seems true. Not really knowing what the poet means, I was tempted to paraverse on and on; The "seeing-heart" (*miru-kokoro*) in the original of the second *ku* means those who see and their desire. My first try, based on the "shiranu" (know-not) rendition found in Shiki's early 20c *Categorical*, *"I watch / a secret tree blooming / in my heart,"* was too far removed from the original. It seems more likely a tree blossoming alone in time or space was seen as unkind to those who seek bloom where and when it is obvious. If this poet had not also written *"I saw them / I did: cherry blossoms / not on limbs"* (見しはミし木すゑにあらぬ花櫻　宗碩 同 *mishi wa mishi kozue ni aranu hanazakura*), I would have guessed it was about a *pine*. The italicized reading in the center is based on the *"chiranu"* (fall/scatter-not) rendition found in the more recent Kotenbunko reproduction of the source, *Hokkuchô*. I cannot tell which is more likely.

見ぬものを見るより嬉しさくら花　千代
minu mono o miru yori ureshi sakurabana　chiyo 1701-75
(see-not thing/s[obj] see-more-than, delighted cherry-blossom/s)

and the unseen   cherry-blossoms!
is more delightful yet: happier for what i don't see
cherry-blossoms!   than for what i do

Vintage Chiyo. For good or bad, many of her *ku* seem made for aphorism. But does she allude to still-to-open buds, trees on other mountains, the blossoms of love or concealing fashion? While she doesn't include the word *kokoro* in the *ku*, the "see-not-thing" suggests it is at the very heart of it.

おもへたゝ心はなれてはなもなし　暁台
omoe tada kokoro hanarete hana mo nashi gyôtai -1792/3
(think! just heart/mind/soul separated blossom even not)

    think but this   why not love
there are no blossoms   there are no blossoms
  outside the mind   outside the heart

                          think about it:
                     without love could there
                         be blossoms?

I would guess this a double-take on the Zen catechism of deliberately mindless (no-heart) viewing, combined with a play on Bashô's famous *ku* saying that people who do not love children cannot experience blossoms (#57-10).

花にそひて身をはなれ行心哉　玄仍
hana ni soite mi o hanareyuku kokoro kana genyô -1607
(blossoms-with accompanying body separating-go heart!/'tis)

                        my body nears
                     the blossoms and my
                      heart goes out

    oh my heart   the closer i get
approaching blossoms   to the bloom, the further
    it departs!   away my heart!

                        as i go into
                   the blossoms, i go out
                       of my mind!

Saigyô's idea of cherry-blossoms-as-the-longed-one-to-whom-one's-heart-goes in a *ku*. How curious that English, for all its talk about sweethearts and sonnets with the poet's heart everywhere but in his/her own body cannot cope with this separation! Our hearts only go out for someone that requires pity, right? That is why many of my translations will not scan outside the protected space of this book.

逍遙鵬鷃之間出入是非之境・花の夢此身を留守に置けるか　蘭雪
hana no yume kono mi o rusu ni okikeru ka ransetsu -1707
(blossoms' dream this body/self[acc.] empty/remain-as placed)

                        what a dream
                 of blossoms! should i leave
                     my body behind?

  blossom dream!   blossoms beautiful
perhaps if i could leave   as a dream: should i leave
   my body here . .   my body for them?

the entrance to paradise

The body cannot help be equated with the person left to guard the house while others go blossom-viewing (ch 25) but Ransetsu wrote this <u>on a mountain peak overlooking a panorama of blooming cherry</u>. Could this describe a moment of giddiness when he thought about jumping off the mountain in a sort of ecstatic union with the unworldly beauty? The strangely deliberate question – about something thought of as pertaining to the unconscious – makes this poem.   The traditional idea of dreaming in Japan had the lover leaving his or her body to visit the dreamer.[1]

咲散るは (も) しらぬは花の心哉　紹巴 富士見道記
saki-chiru wa shiranu wa[mo?] hana no kokoro kana　jôha 1523-1602
(blooming-falling-as-for know-not-as-for[even?] blossom's/s' heart/mind/meaning!/'tis)

the blossom mind:
it has no inkling of when
to bloom or blow

blooming, blowing
who can tell the mind
of the blossoms!

blooming, blowing
never knowing: that's what
blossoms are about!

Do *they* not know? Do *we* not know? Is that just how it is or is this ignorance *bliss?* The third reading uses a meaning of *kokoro* more common later in the Edo era, as *the meaning or answer to a riddle.*

ちるは (や) うきしらぬは花の心哉　政弘 新つくは
chiru wa[ya] uki shiranu wa hana no kokoro kana　masahiro 1495
(falling/scattering-as-for[?] floating know-not-as-for blossom's/s' heart/mind!/'tis)

falling doesn't
make it blue: a blossom's
happy heart

who knows the mind
of a blossom: losing petals
may turn them on

not feeling down
when they fall, that is
the blossom way

We look at the perceived mind-set of falling petals elsewhere, the point here was the use of *kokoro*.

初櫻花の心もけふ成か　佛仙 新選
hatsuzakura hana no kokoro mo kyô naru ka　bussen 1773
(first-cherry[blossoms] blossom's/s' heart/mind too today becomes?)

first blossoms:
so this is the day cherry
bites the apple?

first blossoms:
is today, when cherry gets
a flower's heart?

is this the day
my cherry gains a heart?
first blossoms

If a pre-Bashô, this would allude to a girl's coming of age or, rather, experience; but, this is a century past Bashô and it is more likely to be a celebration for a tree in the poet's garden. Forgive my apple!

---

1. Dream Interpretation in Japan If someone sees another in a dream of love, it would be interpreted to mean the other is thinking of the dreamer. This assigning of responsibility to the party dreamed of rather than the dreamer (which is found in many cultures) creates interesting problems for, as may be imagined, the dreamed of can be wronged. Note, however, it was not the *only* way Japanese understood dreaming, for we also find poems interpreted to mean the poet saw what he or she desired to see, rather than vice-versa.

姿には似さりし花の心哉　紹巴 大発句帳
sugata ni wa nizarishi hana no kokoro kana jôha 1523-1602
(appearance/shape-to-as-for resemble-not blossom's/s' heart/mind!/'tis)

the cherry tree
its bloom looks nothing
like its limbs

and not at all
like she looks, the heart of
a blossom!

blossom-viewing
my heart is a far sight
from my face

The plain limbs of the cherry? A beautiful woman who turns out to have a shallow personality? The poet feeling ugly (Like Bashô's later *ku* wishing he had a suitable singing voice)? My bet is on the latter.

花ハみなこゝろのやとの木すゑ哉　宗祇 大発句帖
hana wa mina kokoro no yado no kozue kana sôgi 1420-1502
(blossoms-as-for all hearts'minds' lodging's branch-tips!/'tis)

cherry trees
all the blossoms are inns
for our minds

blooming cherries
the tip of each branch
holds a heart

吾心うちまかせたる櫻哉　百史 花七日
waga kokoro uchi-makasetaru sakura kana hyakushi 1777
(my heart/mind strike-release[cut-loose]/ing cherry[blossoms]!/'tis)

cherry blossoms!
i let my heart loose
to graze its fill

my old heart
i cut it slack to play
it's cherry time

The compound-verb (*uchi-makasetaru*) used to *release* the heart/mind of the poet in the second *ku* is too good to translate. I have seen pictures of the heart as a horse and used them for my reading.

花にちる心はよもの木末哉　宗祇 大発句帳
hana ni chiru kokoro wa yomo no kozue kana sôgi 1502
(blossoms-on fall heart/mind-as-for night-things tree-ends!/'tis)

our hearts fall
upon the blossoms on
every tree-top

minds scatter
a bit of us on the tip of
each cherry limb

At first I thought our hearts might be left like kittens stuck up the bare boughs after the blossoms fell, but the grammar prefers they fall on the blossom limbs.

風にちる花の行方は知らねども惜しむ心は身にとまりけり　西行
kaze ni chiru hana no yukue wa shiranedomo oshimu kokoro wa mi ni tomarikeri saigyô 1118-90
(wind-in/by fall blossoms' destination/fate-as-for know-not-but grieving-heart-as-for body/self-in/by remain!)

i know not
where all the petals
have gone

but i know my heart
full of grief, remains

Here, the heart does not remain under the tree but with the poet, in his body, as is clearer in the original than in my translation. So Saigyô did not always leave his heart behind. The sad one he kept.

あくがるる心はさても山櫻ちりなむ後や身にかへるべき 西行
akugaruru kokoro wa sate mo yamazakura chirinamu ato ya mi ni kaeru beki saigyô
(longing heart-as-for well-enough, mountain-cherry falls/scatters-should after: body/me return ought!)

longing heart!
after the mountain cherry
loses its petals,

you had better, then
return to me!

In the original, *akugaruru* unites "longing" with "separation" in one verb, used to modify "heart."

山々の落花にちる心哉　蓼太
yama yama no rakka ni chiru kokoro kana ryôta 1707-87
(mountain mountain's falling-blossoms-with fall/scatter heart/s!/?)

on hill after hill
our hearts scatter with
the fallen petals

ちる花や足袋をへだつる足の心 其角 五元集
chiru hana ya tabi o hedatsuru ashi no kokoro kikaku -1707
(falling/scattering blossoms[petals]!/: socks/slippers-from separate feet's heart)

falling blossoms: fallen blossoms
the soles of my two feet   my heart is in my feet and
leave my socks   through my soles

With the first *ku*, interest goes elsewhere. Hearts fly off when petals drop, much as the soul of Homer's boom-brained sailor abandons body as he hits the water. Kikaku's *ku* is trickier. Obviously feet have soles, but hearts (*kokoro*)? Is he so sensitive to those petals, blossoms on cherry limbs a moment before, that he *feels* as if he walks barefoot though wearing *tabi* (sock-like slippers)? There are old *waka* where hopeless love is expressed in terms of being left up in the air, but this seems different. My respondent, recalls a classic *expression,* 隔靴掻痒 *"scratching through the sole of one's shoe,"* i.e. *a sense of frustration,* and wonders if it means Kikaku *feels for the blossoms* and feels helpless to help them. (and Kikaku's *ku* often make me want to scratch through the soles of *my* shoes!)

花をふむ人は少年の心哉　末吉 毛吹草
hana o fumu hito wa shônen no kokoro kana sueyoshi 1645
(blossom[acc.] treads/treading person-as-for youth's heart!/'tis)

whoever treads
on cherry blossoms has
the heart of a youth

Step in mud, become a child again; step on cherry petals, become a youth? The blossoms did their duty. Old viewers may share the youth's lack of concern and know the pure joy of walking on beauty.

花に心かへればかへる山路哉　宗祇
hana ni kokoro kaereba kaeru yamaji kana sôgi -1502
(blossoms-to heart returns-when/if return mountain-road/path 'tis)

<blockquote>

when the blossoms
get my heart back, i head back
the mountain path

when our hearts
return to them, we leave
mountain cherries

</blockquote>

The post-position *ni* with *kaeru,* or "return," is usually "to," but I first convinced myself it was a rare instance of "from" and had the blossoms "*give* my heart back." "Why leave your poor heart behind *ala* Saigyô?" I wrote. "Just stay on the mountain until your heart has roamed enough: *"Knock, knock! I'm back!"* Then, go." But, my respondent was not convinced. Evidently, Sôgi distills rather than contradicts Saigyô. The heart is with the other when we are *not* (専門家の欄外注、求め).

へな／＼とするや小橋もはな心　成美
hena-hena to suru ya kohashi mo hanagokoro seibi -1816
(sagging/squashed? is! small-bridge, too blossom mind/heart/spirit)

<blockquote>

how low it sags!
that small bridge shares
the blossom heart

</blockquote>

Does the bridge, sagging under blossom-viewers, resemble limbs laden with bloom? Japan used to be covered with rivers (now, most rivers are covered) and you can bet bridges broke every year at this time. Or, is Seibi thinking of the beggars and low-class street-walkers who lived under many bridges?

世と共の花の種こそ人心　紹巴　大発句帳
yo to tomo no hana no tane koso hitogokoro jôha 1523-1602
(world-with together's blossom's/s' seed especially people-heart)

<blockquote>

for all of time
blossoms must take root
in human hearts

now as ever
the seed of blossoms
is our heart

a seed for bloom
that never leaves is what
all men want

the one seed
for bloom that's ever new
the human 心

</blockquote>

花を見る心は親も教へぬそ　道彦　アルス
hana o miru kokoro wa oya mo oshienu zo michihiko -1815?/19?
(blossoms[acc.] view heart-as-for parents-even teach-cannot[+emph.])

<blockquote>

the heart is self-taught

your parents
cannot teach you how to
view blossoms!

viewing blossoms
is something your parents
can't teach you

the mind you bring
to the blossoms comes not
from your parents!

</blockquote>

This *ku* is not very poetic, but it does say a lot about the main subject of this book and would make a very good saying. Come to think of it, many haiku would, but they are, unfortunately, never found in quotation dictionaries!

いにしへの人の心のなさけをば老木の花のこずゑにぞ知る　西行 補遺
inishie no hito no kokoro no nasake oba rôki no hana no kozue ni zo shiru saigyô

the kindness
of the ancient heart
is manifest

on the blooming limbs
of this old cherry tree!

the kindness
of the men of old
still blooms

on the branches
of old cherries!

With an old cherry tree, the people who once viewed it may be imagined, and, perhaps even the thoughtful soul who planted and cared for it as well. The untranslatable *kozue* in the original suggests the kindness oozes from the tips of the branches in blossom form. Moreover, Saigyô playfully puts the *sake*=blooming inside of the *nasake* (kindness).

今の我も昔の人も花みてん心の色はかはらじものを　西行 1118-90
ima no ware mo mukashi no hito mo hana miten kokoro no iro wa kawaraji mono o saigyô

i of the now [1]
view blossoms as did
the men of old:

to think that our hearts
haven't changed a wink!

It is not even necessary the tree be old. Cherries in bloom make us feel the passing of time by obliterating it, bringing us face to face with the ghosts of those who used to sit where we do. I say "we" as though I am Japanese imagining my ancestors, which, of course, I am not. But even so, I cannot sit under cherry blossoms without traveling in time. Saigyô, as a Buddhist, seems to lament the fact that no progress has been made toward non-attachment: he, like men of old, still loves cherry blossoms when he should not. But, I cannot help thinking that he was drawn so powerfully to the cherry blossoms because it bonded him to the ancients in a way letters alone could not and secretly was happy with that attachment, anyway.

花ちりて静かになりぬ人心　古友尼
hana chirite shizuka ni narinu hitogokoro koyû-ni *fl.*1770-90
(blossoms fallen, quiet become/s people-heart/mind)

the blossoms have fallen
our minds are now
tranquil

trans. r.h. blyth

This may allude to the *blossoms-make-us-worry* idea found in the famous *waka* at the head of the chapter. I cannot improve on Blyth's translation from his *Haiku* (Spring – my depunct. and centering).

46 56-58

1. *I of the Now?* Or, would you prefer, "this me of now?" If English can verb almost any noun simply by context, Japanese can turn almost anything into a modification. In this case, a possessive article was stuck on *ima*, or "now" to get "now's me," which is to say "i who am alive now." I admit my translation is odd, but to translate "i of the present" when Japanese has Chinese constructs that are equivalent to present, would be changing from a word suited to a children's story to one that was intellectual. [this me of now?]

見て来てハ心にあびる桜かな　素欓
mitekite wa kokoro ni abiru sakura kana　sobaku - 1821
(seeing coming-as-for heart-on shower cherry[blossoms/petals]!/'tis)

| back home after viewing them: when i feel the cherry petals | back home from viewing the blossoms keep filling my heart | my heart awash in cherry blossoms *after* returning home |

This *ku* is a fine contradiction yet complement for Kôyu-ni's *ku*. "Filling" is my metaphor. In the original, Sobaku's *heart/mind* is showered by *sakura* after having viewed them and returned, presumeably home. As we saw in the chapter on *Life Laundry*, Sobaku's countryman and contemporary Issa also used "showered" to describe the effect of cherry blossoms, but it was cathartic and felt during rather than after the viewing. We also finished *that* chapter (30) with this unique observation.

◎ Blossom-heart (*hana-no kokoro*)

1) Said of blossoms having a heart, or referring to that heart/mind/spirit
2) An eulogistic term for another's heart/mind/spirit
3) Thoughts/concern/longing for the blossoms
4) A fickle or cheating heart

This is a rough translation of the gist of the definitions for a sub-category of "blossom," "blossom-heart" in my OJD. As we have seen the heart in most of the *ku* was type 1 and 3 with a bit of 4. I also think I would add:

5) The perspective/attitude brought to a blossom-viewing
6) Trope serving to reify the thoughts/longing/love in 3)
7) Significance of the nature of blossoms or blossom-viewing

We have also seen that some of the best heart/mind *ku* do not specifically mention *kokoro*. Eg.:

(japanese: #22-23) *seibi-tei // toshidoshi ni hana no miyô no kawarikeri* shirô -1813
(seibi's mansion // year-year-with, blossom/s' look-way's changes[+emphatic])

at seibi's garden

| year after year the way we see the blossoms keeps changing | year after year the way the blossoms look has changed |

BOOK III

Falling Petals & other Odds & Ends

☆   ☆

☆

落花風

in english only
a couple low-ku by the author

```
    the cherry tree                              better to shoot
blows kisses to the world                   than fleas, the petal hearts
    flying petals                                 of the cherry
```

The petals look like tiny lips on a face viewed from the side, or like the heart, with a rounded bottom.
Queen Christina of Sweden shot fleas with a miniature cannon (cross-bow) according to Linaeus and others.
Flying cherry petals would do as well and, if one could be pegged to a tree, create a pretty picture.
My personal recommendation for harmless hunting is a pea shooter on soap bubbles.

p o e t i c   p r e f a c e
Dreams End

泣てよむ短冊もあり花は夢 其角
naite-yomu tanzaku mo ari hana wa yume kikaku -1707
(crying read *tanzaku* [paper-strip with a *ku*]-even are: blossom/s-as-for dream)

blossoms are a dream

and there are
short poems that can
make you cry

My short translation puts the blossom/s and dream into the title. I do not know exactly what Kikaku means but I think of the refrain of *Row, row, row your boat*. A *tanzaku* is a strip of paper two or three inches wide and about a foot-long for displaying poems. I have seen pictures of them hanging from blossoming cherry trees. It is hard to imagine Kikaku walking up to such a poem, reading it and crying. But who knows? What if it touched upon someone who passed away without viewing the first blossoms of a tree he planted? Perhaps it doesn't matter.[1] The blossoms are short poems, like haiku, over almost as soon as they begin. And, like dreams, they may be read.

☆ It may not matter, but, since translating the *ku,* I found a three-character preface: 悼湖春 "Mourning Koshun (1644-1697). *Hana* means flourishing as well as cherry blossom and suggests Koshun, the oldest son of Kigin was on the point of flowering in life (quickly advancing in the *bakufu* government's Ministry of Songs(?) 歌所 when he prematurely died. He has one *ku* in this book (#42-53), and his father three. Read his *ku* and you, too, will regret his early death.

f o r e w o r d
Falling for Nature

やどりして春の山辺にねたる夜は夢の内にも花ぞちりける 古今集#117
yadorishite haru no yamabe ni netaru yoru wa yume no uchi ni mo hana zo chirikeru kokinshû 905
(lodging/ed spring's mountain-area-at slept night-as-for dream/s-within-even/ blossoms! fall[+emph.])

*the night i sleep
at a mountain inn
it was spring*

*the blossoms kept on
falling in my dreams*

This is not a particularly good *waka,* and my translation may be worse yet; but what could better show the poet's infatuation for natural beauty than its occupying his dreams, a part of life ancient poetry usually saved for the visits of lovers? We might haiku it thus:

夢の世に散りつづく花山の宿 古今愚
yume no yo ni chiritsuzuku hana yama no yado kokingu

a mountain inn
the petals still falling
in my dreams

We can criticize the safety-first attitude of early modern Japanese that resulted in the extinction of the Japanese wolf and, reinforced in recent times, has forced 80% of Japan's rivers and perhaps 50% of its seashore into cement straight-jackets. But, we must admire the depth of the Japanese attachment to less dangerous seasonal phenomena, the exemplar of which was, and still is, the cherry blossom. Think about it once again. Blossom-viewing (not any religious or national festivals) is *the* main event of spring. Of course, as we have seen, *people*-viewing was part of it. But, still, *hanami* is natural rather than humanistic. It reminds us that, like so much of the artwork in the Sinosphere, leaves, blossoms and shapely branches were once considered more worthy of attention than the human faces and muscles that enthralled and still captivate the Occident and the cultures it influences.

But let me not exaggerate the difference. There is an underlying similarity: hard flesh and soft flowers make equally good symbols for mortality. Only the ends differ. Compare, if you will, the final appearance of well-built men and beautiful women with the graceful fall of the cherry petals!

はかなさをほかにもいはじ櫻花咲きては散りぬあはれ世の中 後徳大寺左大臣新古今集 #141
hakanasa o hoka ni mo iwaji sakurabana sakitewa chirinu aware yononaka shinkokin wakashû (1205)
(ephemeral/vain[obj] other-to-also say-not, cherry-blossom blooming-as-for fall pitiful/sad world)

> *if these blossoms*
> *of the cherry blowing*
> *as they bloom*
>
> *are not a vanity fair*
> *what in the world is!*

In *Book III,* we follow man and plant to the end of the blossoms and the viewing. As the first chapter makes clear, this is by no means depressing. True, the cherry blossom did come to embody the shortness of life about which Japanese and English poets exclaimed, respectively: *aware!* (a three-syllabet word meaning both pitiful *and* beautiful owing to the ephemeral and therefore empty – in the religious sense – nature of the phenomenon) and *alas!* But we will not dwell upon this woeful transience; first, because the above written *aware!* and *alas!* pretty much say all that can be said about it and, second, because haiku pays much less attention to it than one might imagine.

咲く花があわれでなくば何あわれ 敬愚
saku hana ga aware de nakuba nani aware keigu

> *if the cherry*
> *does not bloom in vain*
> *what does?*

This should not be surprising. Haiku ponder, wonder, gasp, wish, complain, waken, smile, purr, chuckle, laugh and sometimes, in my translation, I am afraid that they may howl as well. But, they do precious little sobbing. And, even when they do, they are never fulsome or, worse yet, a bore. That is not because *haijin* are all adepts, but because the haiku form, like the bloom of the cherry and of life itself, is refreshingly short.

So much for my *third* try at a poetic foreword! Let me add that besides the inevitable *Fall of the Blossoms* and the *Return Trip* from the viewing, in this Book, we will play with some of the most entertaining supporting roles. The *Wind,* which we glimpsed in the *Late Cherry* (chapter 12), fills a 20-page chapter, and the idea of *Blossoms as Women,* and the vice-versa, not to mention *Old Men* and *Children* and *Ecology* and *Sex* and *Nationalism* . . . Believe me, it was hard to save this stuff for last . . . It will be easier for me to write and you to read than the ineffable *kokoro* by which we ended Book II.

Good reading.

Flying petals: It's amazing even the roots remain!

散さくら根をうしなハぬばかり也　素檗
chiru sakura ne o ushinawanu bakari nari sobaku -1821
(scatter/drop sakura/petals, roots[obj] lose-not only become/is)

根

47

the Lightness of Falling Petals
散る桜
chiru-sakura   (ω)

(ω)   (ω)

咲をさへおとろくに散初桜　几董
saki o sae odoroku ni chiru[1] *hatsuzakura*   kitô -1789
(blooming even surprised-by fall first-cherry/blossom)

cherry blossoms

the first bloom
was a shock and now
the first fall!

The cherry tree surprises us twice, first with its bloom and second with its bust. This *ku* may concern a specific young cherry tree doing both for the first time. It may *also* allude to a girl growing into womanhood and becoming pregnant.

真先に見し枝ならん (む) ちるさくら　丈草
massaki ni mishi eda naran (-mu) chiru sakura[2] jôsô -1704
(very-first/before seen branch is[it]not? falling cherry[petals])

the first branch   could this be
i noticed: can it be?   the branch i just saw?
the petals fall   falling petals

Changes in unfamiliar branches do not surprise. Familiarity creates expectation which, in turn, shocks us. My respondent favors the first. I suspect an allusion and feel guilty for it.

~~~~~~

1. *Chiru* We have already discussed the difficulty of translating *chiru* many times, but since this chapter is *all about the same*, let us note again that everything blossoms can do to terminate in English = *fall, drop, blow, fly,* or *scatter* and more = is covered in Japanese by that one useful verb. You might say that English verbs lose something by being so specific. *Fall* and *drop* are too heavy and only appropriate for wet petals in still air; *blow* is stilted and reminds us of the rose, *fly* demands a strong wind and *scatter*, though a connotation of *chiru*, is too explicit for suggesting zoomorphic volition rather than natural aerial dispersion. *Flutter down, shower down, trickle through*, and other such more specific expressions are much better, but, unfortunately, often do not fit the *ku* for their length if nothing else.

2. *Sakura* as Petals Likewise for *sakura*. As we have noted already, it means either the tree *or* its blossoms (but not the fruit which is a *sakura-ranbo* or *chieri*), so we must have one or the other as the *chiru*-ing actor. *Sakura* also means the pieces of a blossom that *chiru*, where English prefers "petals." Since "cherry blossom petals" only fit in the middle of the *ku*, which is generally needed for other elements, one is forced to make do with "cherry blossoms," "cherry petals" or "petals" alone, each of which is not quite right for different reasons.

ちるを見に誘ふ花の友も哉　必観 蕉庵再興
chiru o mi ni sasou hana no tomo mogana　shikkan - 1771
(fall/scatter view-to invite blossom /splendid] friend wish-for!)

if only i had
someone to take to see
blossoms fall!

oh, for a friend
who would take me to see
the blossoms fall!

This *ku* fills a big gap. While falling petals are feted as much as the first bloom, people never talk of "going to see the blossoms fall." This is strange to me, at least, because I find it the most beautiful part of the show. I do not mind missing the first bloom, but I sure want to be there for the live show put on by the petals! The first reading seems most likely, as the poet knows *his* taste.

ちり際の又美しき櫻哉　　如壽
chirigiwa no mata utsukushiki sakura kana　joju/nyoju
(falling time/occasion's also/again beautiful cherry/blossoms!/'tis)

cherry blossoms!
b e a u t i f u l
when falling, too

cherry blossoms
falling, once again
beautiful

これは／＼とばかり散るも櫻哉　其角
kore wa kore to bakari chiru mo sakura kana　kikaku -1707
(this-as-for this![wow! wow!] only falls-even cherry!/'tis)

when they fall, too,
all we can say is *wow!*
cherry blossoms

cherry blossoms
they take our voice away
when they fall, too

The very fact this thing needs to be said seems to show the lack of appreciation for falling beauty. I am reminded of what 19c European writers had to say about the Niagara Falls: *very little*. Faced with the sublime (power that awes), what can be said! Kikaku has lifted the first 9 syllabets from a poem by Teishitsu: *"Wow! wow! / what's more to say? / Yoshino cherries!* (#58-1).

遅くとくちるはめでたきさくらかな　錦江女
osoku toku chiru wa medetaki sakura kana　kinkô-jo 18c
(late quickly fall-as-for celebratory/joyful cherry!/'tis)

who's crying?
early or late
to fall is a joy!
cherry blossoms

cherry blossoms

early or late
their fall is something we
should celebrate

celebration

early or late
they fall like confetti
cherry petals

When blossoms fall "without regret," they preach. The *ku* subtly makes the falling itself the subject and only (possibly) speaks for the blossoms. This refreshing affirmation of falling is by a female poet.

falling

声よくばうたはふ (う) ものをさくら散 芭蕉
koe yokuba utawamu mono o sakura chiru   bashô - 1694
(voice good-if sing-would thing-but cherry[blossoms] fall/scatter)

    if my voice   the blossoms fall!
were better, i would sing!   if i had a good voice
  the blossoms fall   i'd sing for them

Bashô was a brilliant and precise man. Such people are often tone-deaf. I would guess that, and not the grain of his voice was the problem. Bashô loved falling petals; he ate them with his fish salad, breathed them as he danced and drank them with the *sake* he scooped up with a fan. Speaking of which:

ちるはなや舞もでべき腰あふぎ 成美
chiru hana ya odori mo debeki koshi-ôgi   seibi -1816
(falling blossoms! dance too appear/burst-into-ought: hip-fan)

                         petals fall!
                     a dance is in order
                       i feel my fan

  falling blossoms   today, they fall
the fan in my belt should   i stick a fan in my belt
  be out dancing!   today, we dance

                   petals are falling,
                   it's time to dance,
                   to draw my fan!

                 ~~~~~~~~

              the petals fall
              time for you
                to draw
              that fan
                 &
               dance

The last five syllabets of the original are "belt-fan" – a fan stuck handle-first into the sash.

<div style="text-align:center">
春雨のふるは涙かさくら花ちるををしまぬ人しなければ 大供くろぬし 古今集#88
harusame no furu wa namida ka sakurabana chiru o oshimanu hito shi nakereba   kokinshû (905)
</div>

    spring rain: *is this shower*
could this be teardrops   *the teardrops of spring*
    once again   *cherry blossoms*

the world (including men)   *even among men none*
mourns the blossoms' end   *but regret your falling*

Ancient Japanese may have believed, or wanted to believe (In the manner of the only real believer, the agnostic: for there is no call to believe if one is *sure* about things, right?) that their wishes influenced the weather. The regret of parting lovers was particularly effective at causing rain because of the natural sympathy of the elements and because both could prevent a lover from leaving. But rain, if anything, would *hasten* the departure of the blossoms. Personally, I would have preferred pluvial tears *in the absence of men* to regret the blossoms falling and fully expect to find such a *waka* someday. Besides the trees, who would have *standing* to cry for their blossoms, the "even" in the second reading (with a phrase lifted from R&H) recalls Sao the Goddess of Spring, and rain as the parent of the bloom we saw earlier.

千本が一時に落花する夜あらん 子規
senpon ga ichiji ni rakka suru yoru aran   shiki -1902
(thousand-poles=trees one-time-at drop-blossoms night be-not=let!)

<table>
<tr><td>

oh, for a night
when a thousand trees
blow at once!

</td><td>

i'll bet tonight
a thousand cherry trees
blow at once!

</td></tr>
</table>

The second reading, where Shiki, lying at home imagines what the wind is doing, is my first guess. By this time, most of the massed cherries were the cloned Yoshino-Somei, so they would be in more or less simultaneous bloom. The only brief way to English *rakka* ("drop-blossom") is "blow," for "fall" would mean the trees themselves did. But does it work without specifying *blossoms*? Do we need to say something like, *"This would be the night / blossoms from a thousand trees / head south!"* instead?

咲いてより散らぬ日もなき櫻哉   吟江 アルス
saite yori chiranu hi mo naki sakura kana   ginkô fl.1780
(blooms-from falls-not-day-even not: cherry/blossoms!/'tis)

cherry blossoms

since blooming
not a day passes when
petals don't fall

An understated epiphany. Petal blizzards do not occur immediately after the first bloom, but *some* petals *do* fall, if nothing else because of the birds. Ginkô really observed what was what.

咲ちるの遅速に花の日数哉 序寂 花七日
saki-chiru no osohaya ni hana no hikazu kana   jojaku 1777
(bloom-fall/scatters' slowly-quickly blossom's day/s-number!/'tis)

<table>
<tr><td>

blooming falling
sooner later a blossom
has its day-count

</td><td>

quick off the block
or not, seven days
is seven days

</td></tr>
</table>

Early or late, cherry blossoms have their allotted life-span. This *ku* was published in a collection called "blossom-seven-days" (*hana nanuka*). Actually, some varieties hang on twice that long.

立ち並ふ中を櫻のちる日哉 蘭更
tachi-narabu naka o sakura no chiru hi kana   rankô 1799
(standing lined-up among cherry's/ies'/blossoms/petals falling-day!/?/'tis)

<table>
<tr><td>

cherries among
cherries, each tree has
its day to fall

</td><td>

standing side by side
the cherry blossoms have
a day all fall

</td><td>

the day when
blossoms fall, they fall
before others

</td></tr>
</table>

The standing in line might refer to the blossom-viewers, but I bet it refers to the cherry trees

人恋し灯ともし頃を桜散る 白雄
hitokoishi hi tomoshi koro o sakura chiru shirao -1792
(people-dear/nostalgic, lamp light time [+contrad.]: cherry/petals fall)

when lamps	now the petals fall
are lit and men are dear	as lamps are lit and hearts
the petals fall	fill with yearning

One Japanese editor-commentator opines this might seem a bit corny today, but I think it a faultless description of what nightfall does to men and blossoms. My "yearning" came from Blyth's *"My heart is full of yearning, / The candles being lit, /Cherry-blossoms falling."* (*Haiku*: Spring). But, note: the *ku* is not about three parallel things. Syntax says two set the scene for the third.

人去れば一ゆるみして散る櫻 梅室
hito sareba hitoyurumi shite chiru sakura baishitsu -1852
(people leave/left-when one-slackness-doing fall/scatter cherry[petals])

people leave	a brief respite
in a moment's slackness	when people leave
falling petals	the petals fall

咲からに見るからに花のちるからに 鬼貫
saku kara ni miru kara ni hana no chiru kara ni onitsura -1738
(bloom/ing-from see/ing-from blossoms' fall/ing from)

because they fall	because they bloom
because we watch them	because we view them
because they bloom	because they fall –

It is hard to explain what makes the first *ku* so good. It just is. Blyth found the answer to Pilate's question to Christ ("What is truth?") in the second *ku* he translates as *"The cherry-blossoms bloom; / We gaze at them; / They fall, and . . ."* Where? you might ask. It is in the "and . . ." which Blyth explains is "the human element in Nature." While it is true this *ku* leaves a lot unsaid, I more humbly would like to point out the fact that the opposite syntax of English and Japanese wreaks havoc on direct translation and that *kara* means both "for/after" *and* "because." My two readings try to treat the order of the verbs and the order of the related parts of the *ku*, respectively. Blyth had to remove all hint of causality to end the poem inconclusively (with the "and . . ."). Onitsura hints at a relationship between the seer and the seen, between people and petals. I do not understand why the *hana-no* (blossoms') is where it is in the poem, unless it is there simply because the syllabet breaks said it should be. I hope to find comments by Japanese scholars for the next edition.

つく／＼と見てをれば散る櫻哉 士朗
tsukuzuku to mite-oreba chiru sakura kana shirô -1823
(intently seeing am/was-when/if fall/scatter cherry!/'tis)

cherry blossoms	i stared
fall when you stare	really hard at a blossom
intently enough	and it fell

cherry blossoms

as i looked
closely at them they
took to flight

Was Shirô testing telepathy? Or is this only an allusion to the shy nature of blossoms. The *~eba* ending allows the poet to *suggest* causality while keeping one foot safe on the unarguable coincidence.

打とけて我にちる也夕ざくら 几董
uchitokete ware ni chirunari yûzakura kitô -1789
(really-melting/releasing me-on/self-by falling-is/are dusk cherries)

in the evening   ~~in the evening~~
when the blossoms release   ~~the blossoms relaxing fall~~
they fall on me   ~~by themselves~~

The double verb *uchi-tokeru* (lit. "break/start-melt") means both "break the ice" and "melt," *i.e.* become relaxed and at ease. This suggests someone's presence; my respondent writes the first reading *for sure*.

さくら／＼散つて佳人の夢に入る 無腸
sakura sakura chitte kajin no yume ni iru muchô -1809
(cherry cherry falling good/beautiful-person's/s' dream/s into enter)

sakura, sakura!
they fall in the dreams
of sleeping beauty

A drowsy noon or languid dusk with petals actually falling on the beauty? Or does the poet imagine she dreams on a night after the blossom-viewing when she sang *sakura sakura* in the bloomshade.

かならすよ人の寝る夜は花のちる   道彦
kanarazu yo hito no neru yo wa hana no chiru michihiko -1819
(definitely/always[+emph.] peoples' sleep/ing night-as-for blossoms fall)

it's always so!   it always happens
when men sleep at night   when others are sleeping
blossoms fall   the blossoms fall

Nature is like that. *Hito* (man/people) has a hint of "others" in it, hence the possibility of the second reading where the poet feels happy as one of the elected, but sad to be alone.

夕風やあひだを置てちる櫻   不中（女）卯辰
yûkaze ya aida o oite chiru sakura fuchû 1691
(dusk-wind!/: interval[acc.] placing falls cherry)

evening breeze
a pause, and, then
the petals fall

falling

My mother and I recently recalled the way coconuts tend to plunk down as it grew dark. She insists they really *do*. I wondered if it might not just be that we *hear* them better when humans, and perhaps the wind, quiets down. We concluded that there was more going on than we could understand. Likewise with this *ku* by a woman with the odd pen name "Not-among.".

風に散り風吹たえて落花哉　蕪村
kaze ni chiri kaze fuki-taete rakka kana buson - 1783
(wind-in/by fall, wind blow-ceases, fallen-blossoms!/?/'tis)

after scattering
in the wind: the wind stops
and all is petals

wind blows
they scatter and it dies
fallen petals

That blossoms scatter in the wind and only settle down when it dies is simple enough, but Buson may be making a linguistic point here: *rakka* is a Chinese-derived term Japanese use for blossoms/petals on the ground, where the process of getting blown around is young and fresh: Japanese. Four years later:

ちるはさくら落るは花のゆふべ哉　蕪村
chiru wa sakura otsuru wa hana no yûbe kan buson - 1783
(scattering-as-for cherry falling-as-for blossoms' evening!/'tis)

call what scatters
sakura! what falls *hana*
in the evening.

dusk blossoms
dancing cherry japanese
lie still chinese

Here, the petals that fly are associated with *sakura,* the native name of the tree and its blossoms, while the stuff that falls to the ground is *hana,* a word which Buson uses in its Japanese pronunciation but, which, in conjunction with the Chinese character used for *otsuru* (fall) suggests *rakka,* the above-mentioned term, used by Chinese poets. Pardon my modernized and *Orientalistic* second reading!

照月にたへかねてちる櫻哉　樗堂　新十家
teru tsuki ni tae-kanete chiru sakura kana chodô -1814
(shining moon-against resist-cannot falls/scatter cherry!/'tis)

petals falling
unable to resist
moon light

This is the last act of the play that began with cherry tree buds unable to resist blooming when wet by the warm rain. While Japanese intellectuals knew about gravity by this time, *this* is not *that*. If I have my religious imagery right, the full moon is the Buddhist Wheel of the Karmic Law and its light the mercy of Buddha. The blossoms have, as an old Hank Williams gospel tune put it, "seen the light."

塗下駄の音やかんじてちる桜　一茶
nurigeta no oto ya kanjite chiru sakura issa
(painted clogs' sound!/: feeling falls cherry[bloss.])

こつ／＼と人行過て花のちる　一茶
kotsukotsu to hito yukisugite hana no chiru issa
(clip-cloppity people go-by blossoms' fall/ing)

feeling the sound
of the painted clogs
blossoms fall

as people *clip-*
-clop by, some cherry
blossoms drop

Painted *clogs/geta* means the shoes of a dancing girl.[1] The reverberations of her dance-steps – or just the brisk clippity-clop of her walk – seem to cause some blossoms to drop petals, and these, perhaps seem to fall more rhythmically than usual. Another of Issa's poems, more boldly claims *"The petals fall / in the direction of / the painted clogs"* (塗下駄の方へと桜ちりにけり 一茶 文政1 *nurigeta no hô e to sakura chirinikeri*) – the reader may substitute "dancing girl" for "painted clogs," for the shoes are filled and Issa would seem to be hinting at some sympathy between the girl and the *sakura*. The clip-clop *ku* is more difficult than the dancing girl, for it is unclear whether or not the relationship is causal or contrastive. I prefer the latter understanding, which is why I write "drop" rather than "let fly."

吉原や烏ないても散る桜　子規
yoshiwara ya karasu naite mo chiru sakura shiki 1896
(yoshiwara:/! crow/s sing/cry-even fall/scatter cherry/ies)

it's yoshiwara!
where blossoms even fall
for crying crows

Too bad that crows can't "cry" in English. There is a saying to the effect that a nubile maiden will strip for a single ant. Does Shiki mean that cherries=women, in this case prostitutes, fall for formally dressed elderly gentlemen who were sometimes metaphorized as crows? Who knows! I suspect there were reports of crows caucusing in the Yoshiwara area that gave Shiki his excuse to be a wise guy.

静かさや散るにすれあふ花の音 樗良 アルス
shizukasa ya chiru ni sure-au hana no oto chora -1780?
(quietness/peace! fall/ing-by/as rub-meet/ing blossoms-sound)

how still it is   this stillness:
the sound of petals   i hear falling petals
sifting down together.   brush together

My first translation borrows from Blyth's *"Stillness: / The sound of the petals / Sifting down together."* (*Haiku* Spring). Hurray for the mimetic verb he found to combine *falling* and *rubbing*. Blyth thinks "the verse is more of the inner mind than of sensation;" but I could swear I have heard it!

ちる花の音聞き出すや朧月 秋瓜 類題
chiru hana no oto kikidasu ya oborozuki shûka 1774
(fall/ing blossoms' sound hear[make-out]: hazy moon)

~ a hazy moon ~
i can make out the sound of
falling blossoms

One might think haziness would blunt rather than sharpen sound, but on deeper thought, the effect might be to insulate the poet from distant sound, heightening his local sensitivity. And, here, unlike the last *ku*, I think we are talking about the sound petals make when they strike the ground.

---

1. Painted Clogs = Dancing Girls A *senryû* puts it snidely: *"Painted clogs: / a higher place than / a painted pillow"* (*nurigeta wa nuri makura yori takai tokoro*). It plays off a refrain "How splendid! How splendid!" (*migoto nari . . .*). That is to say, a dancing girl, as a free agent, beats a prostitute indentured to a pleasure quarter, even if she is cheaper. Since the specialty of the dancing girl was "falling," the cherry petal analogy seems perfect, but the verbs used (*koboru* and *chiru*) are different – Japanese has an embarrassment of verbs for *falling!*

ちる花の顔へつめたし朧月　禹谷 鶉萬立?
chiruhana no kao e tsumetashi oborozuki　ukoku ()
(falling blossoms[petals]' face-to cold hazy moon)

    a hazy moon
the falling petals cold
      to my face

The humidity in the cool night air would make the petals feel especially cold. I felt like naturalizing the English: "*feel* cold *on* my face," but something told me it was necessary.

散桜肌着の汗を吹せけり 一茶 1810　　　袂から下着を脱でさくら哉　葛箒
chiru sakura hadagi no ase o fukasekeri issa　　*tamoto kara shitagi o nuide sakura kana* kuzu..?
(falling cherry[petals] underwear's sweat blows[emph])　　(bossom-from underwear[acc] stripping cherry'tis)

  cherry petals　　　　　　　　　　　　　my underwear
blowing across my　　　　　　　　pulled from my bossom
   sweaty gown　　　　　　　　　　　　blossom-viewing

Did Issa, happy-coat open far enough for petals to glance off his chest, wear the gauzy undershirt/gown, or was it pulled out and hung up to dry? I thought of the latter because of the second, older *ku,* and because I have seen the English comedian Mr. Bean put on a swim-suit without removing his trousers: it took 15 minutes. Removing gown-like underwear from Japanese clothing, with its much greater room to move in, would take a second or two.

ちる花に蝶も重たきけしき哉　葛箒?
chiru hana ni cho mo omotaki keshiki kana　kuzuhoki anth?
(falling blossoms-as butterfly/ies even heavy scenery!/'tis)

   falling petals
a scene where butterflies
    seem heavy

One might imagine such delicacy was patented by the Japanese. But, the finest depiction of falling petals I know is by a black American living in France. Since his only acquaintance with haiku was Blyth's series with its old haiku, I make an exception and include it here:

    a falling petal　　　　　　　　　　　　a falling petal
strikes one floating on a pond　　　　strikes another floating
   and they both sink　　　　　　　　　　and both sink

I cut out an extra foot (right) to shorten Richard Wright's minute observation (left).

準縄にうつくしくちる櫻哉 乙二 アルス
junjô ni utsukushiku chiru sakura kana　otsuni -1823
(prep-twine-on beautifully fall cherry/blossoms!/'tis)

   cherry petals
fall beautifully upon
   a snail-line

Japanese carpenters use inked or powdered lines to make both straight marks and, more incredibly, elegant curves by pinching, lifting and pulling the line up and out to the side where it is released to whack the surface intended to be marked. These lines are always rolled up in a container modeled after a *snail* (the spool being the shell). The line, or the marking made by it, and the petals make an elegant composition.

散花の花より起る嵐哉　青蘿
chiru hana no hana yori okoru arashi kana　seira -1791
(fall/scattering blossoms' blossoms-from arise/ing gale!/?/'tis)

falling petals
of themselves unleashing
a windstorm!

We have seen a number of tranquil falling scenes, but such weather was far from the rule. If we have less windy scenes here, it is because the wind has a chapter of its own (the next).

身をすほめ行や櫻の散木の間　陽子 五車反故
mi o subome yuku ya sakura no chiru ko no ma　yôshi 1783
(body[acc] puckering go!/: cherry/ies fall/scatter trees among)

i squeeze through   petals fly about
a grove of cherry trees   i pass through the cherries
shedding petals   making myself small

Are the blossoms blowing about so strongly the poet hunches up? Or does he only feel small amid the blizzard or in the face of the blossoms' largesse? I am afraid I could not do the *ku* justice.

花ともに蟻の吹かるゝ嵐哉　芝峰 京水
hana tomo ni ari no fukaruru arashi kana　shihô? 1691
(blossoms[petals] together-with ant/s blown gale 'tis)

a spring gale
ants blown away with
the blossoms

This fusion of violent movement with *formic* detail makes it one of the most exciting petal-scattering *ku* of all. These are job-related casualties. The ants are out working the blossoms for the sake of their city. Does young Issa's *"Ant teardrops / upon the scattering / cherry petals"* (散花に蟻の涙のかゝる哉　一茶 *chiru hana ni ari no namida no kakaru kana*) refer to this *ku*? People in the distance were said to look like ants in Japanese as in English. Is Issa thinking of us – or himself – from the perspective of sky-gods? (He does this at times, for one *ku* guesses they are bored in hazy weather.)

ちるは／＼嵐に峰のはなのこゑ　暁台
chiru wa chiru arashi ni mine no hana no koe　gyôtai -1792
([i]fall[emph] [i]fall! gales-to peak's blossoms' voice)

a gale, moan   we fall! fall!
blossoms on the peak   blossom voices from
"i fall! i fall!"   a gale on high

47 38-42

Gyôtai was, on the whole, a subtle poet, but, even in old *haikai,* you would be hard pressed to find something *this* bathetic! There is an erotic overtone: Japanese women typically called out *shinu-wa shinu* (*I'm dying, dying!*) at orgasm. The *blossoms* pun as *nasal,* hence moans or sobs rather than shrieks. The only thing worse I know of is this *ku:* NOW FROM CHERRY-TREES . . . / MILLIONS OF MAIDENS / FLYING / FIERCE WAR-LORD STORM, at least in the Peter Pauper Press translation (*Japanese Haiku* 1955-6). Since the Japanese was not given, at first, I thought the reference might be to Hideyoshi, the womanizing war-lord mentioned in the *Cherry Hunting* chapter, but the poem goes back centuries earlier (see #48-70) and, in the original, mentions no maidens!

風に花ちり／＼ぱっとわかれ哉　無記名
kaze ni hana chirijiri patto wakare kana anon 1651
(wind-in blossoms scatter-x2 suddenly[onamot] leaving!/'tis)

うつりやすき花や美人の仇心　李吟
utsuri yasuki hana ya bijin no adagokoro kigin -1780
(shift/fall-easy flower/s!/?/: beauty's fickle-heart)

the wind blows
blossoms scitter-scatter &
poof! it's over

the fickle heart
of a beauty: blossoms
leave us easily

Taken as mere allusion, a description of desire that spends itself and the other, the first *ku* may be suspect, i.e., concern women-as-blossoms; but I think it still stands better as a haiku, or nature poem than Ginkô's later blossoms-as-women *ku,* though the latter category is generally more acceptable. When the wind blows hard the blossoms do vanish at a fairly rapid pace, a large quantity with each gust until suddenly: *Huh!? Where are they!?* And, without blossoms to incarnate it, the wind might seem to leave at the same time, even if it doesn't die down completely. The *utsuru* in Ginkô's *ku* is a poetic verb for *fading/falling* leaves or blossoms, akin to our "passing away," but also meaning "to shift." Unable to match the connotation, I came up with "leave us." Long before either *ku, Kokinshû* editor Tsurayuki remonstrated, **"People say nothing blows like cherry blossoms, but** // *I don't think / cherry blossoms go / half so fast / as the human heart which / even the wind can't catch!"* (さくらのごとくちる物はなし」と人のいひければよめる・さくら花とくちりぬともおもはえず人の心ぞ風も吹きあへぬ　つらゆき　古今集 # 83 *sakurabana toku chirinu to mo omohoezu hito no kokoro zo kaze mo fuki aenu* 905) and further defended the inconstancy of flowers by selecting a *waka* by Fujiwara no Okikaze, to follow soon after his: *Kokinshû* #101, in Steven D. Carter's translation, *"Of flowers that bloom / in endless variety, / all are inconstant – / yet which of us cherishes / grievances against springtime?"* (さく花は千くさながらにあだなれどたれかははるをうらみたてたる *saku hana wa chigusa nagara ni ada naredo tare ka wa haru o uramihatetaru*). Here, not only are grudges ruled out as artificial, but the paragon, *sakura* is subsumed in a larger world of flowers. After all, not all women were cherries. Be that as it may, complaints about fickleness survive until today. And, to make matters worse, or better, if you, like me, enjoy finding wisdom in the past, we already have a better defense yet in the 8c *Manyôshû (left)*:

sakurabana toki wa suginedo miru hito no
koi no sakari to ima shi chiruramu manyoshû #1855

uchi-?haete?haru wa sa bakari nodokeki o
hana no kokoro ya nani isoguran gosen #92 (951)

it's hardly time
for the cherry trees but
the love of man

for blossoms has peaked
so they would fall right now

spring's here
for good, and calm as
calm can be

so, why *do blossoms*
have to rush like this!

Can you think of a nicer way to just-so the short bloom than that? (桜花時は過ぎねど見る人の恋の盛りと今し散るらむ). A translation in Occidental idiom of the 8c *Manyôshû waka* might go like this: *"It's hardly time / for the cherry blossoms / to lose their petals: / Would they fall when still / apples in the viewer's eye!"* Yet, for all the rationalizing, blossom lovers are sorry to lose their beauty so soon and have every right to lament as per the second, 10c, *waka*, which was eventually seconded by Issa:

桜花何が不足でちりいそぐ 一茶
sakurabana nani ga fuzoku de chiri-isogu issa -1827
(cherry-blossom/s what insufficiency-from scatter-hurry/ies?)

cherry blossoms!	cherry blossoms
what do you lack to be	*why* so unsatisfied
so quick to fall?	you rush to fall?

Issa, in a tone simultaneously lamenting and aggressive questions the blossoms' eagerness to self-destruct. His crisp *ku* is ignored – I've not seen it in any *ku* selection or biographic novels – either because its subjectivity and philosophical content are not considered the mark of a good *ku*, or because of its similarity to the second half of the Gosen #92 *waka*.[1] This is too bad; it deserves mention because Issa did not write it *only* as a paraverse of a *waka* (which he may not have known) but because it represented his heartfelt concern about the rushed urban culture of Edo. In that sense, it is a broader social complaint about something that in the long-run threatens poetry itself. It also deserves to be more widely known in Japan for providing, in retrospect and quite by accident, a thoughtful contradiction to the cherry blossom of the militarist, celebrated for *his* eagerness to shed *his* blossoms (see ch 61). Before we see pure *ku* about falling petals, let us see a sampling of debate between two ideas of what falling is about. In many respects, it resembles that on the *goodness* or *badness* of late-blooming cherries we saw in *Book I*.

こらへぜい (精) つよきが残る花戦 久任 夢見草
koraezei tsuyoki ga nokoru hana-ikusa kyûnin 1656
(forbearing spirit strength remain blossom uprising/army)

late cherries

the heart to endure
only the strong remain:
the blossom war

Hana-ikusa (blossom-uprising/battle). What an expression! Here, like in Issa's blunt *ku*, we contradict the idea that a blossom's bravery consists in falling at the drop of a hat. This idea, once rare, was so firmly set in Japanese metaphor by the 20c that the most famous modern military song (*dôki no sakura* – same-class cherry blossoms) celebrates graduates who fall/scatter, i.e. die, on the battlefield together.

跡に散をかちとやいはん花戦 重純 夢見草
ato ni chiru o kachi to ya iwan hana-ikusa shigezumi 1656
(afterward fall/scatter[obj] win-as! say-let's/not blossom-battle/war/army)

falling later	shall we call
is hardly a victory!	falling later a victory?
the blossom war	blossom battles

My first reading, implying either that there is more honor in falling first (the brave die young) or that such victory in so brief an uprising is Pyrrhic at best, has an ally in this *ku*: "*Are all remaining / after the blossom wars / leaf-second-rate samurai?*" (散る跡は葉武者はかりか花軍 光有 毛吹草 *chiru ato wa habûsha bakari ka hanaikusa* kôyû 1645). But, my respondent thinks the second the correct reading.

1. Gosen #92 and Issa's Influence.
When Santôka wrote *"Something is lacking / leaves fall"* (*nani ka taranai mono ga aru ochiba suru.*) and Shiki lamented a dead friend *"What is the rush? / You who leave us / before spring does?"* (*nani isogu haru yori saki ni yuku kimi wa*) were they following the *Gosen waka* and Issa's *ku?*

~~~~~~

よしやちれちれはこそさく花の春　昌叱 大発句帳
yoshi ya chire chireba koso saku hana no haru　shôshitsu -1603
(ok! fall falling-if/when that's-why bloom blossoms' spring)

go ahead, fall!
what falls, blossoms
in the spring

go on, fall!
that's what you bloom for
that's spring!

it's ok, fall!
because you fall spring
brings flowers

To *lament* scattering blossoms was an age-old conceit. This is a fine turn-about. But the era of early *haikai* was also the tail of the Warring Era (1338-1568). We begin to find increasing martial metaphor in the celebration of falling blossoms: *"To their honor / they announce and fall: / blossom mind/ heart"* (貢なるや名とげてちりし花ごゝろ 盛長 毛吹草 再現 *kô naru ya na togete chirishi hanagokoro* seichô 1645). Unless the metaphor is utter nonsense, the reference is to the way some trees boasted names.

花桜一木／＼のいさほ（を）しや　一茶
hanazakura hitoki hitoki no isaoshi ya　issa -1827
(blossoming-cherry one-tree one-tree's bravery!)

cherries in bloom
one at a time shows off
its bravery

blooming cherry
a tree-by-tree show
of bravery

The "tree by tree" in Issa's *ku* brings out their individuality. Elsewhere Issa uses the *announcing* idea with *young leaves* because *wakaba* sounds like a common name for bold young men, called *waka-*(young) this or that. Be that as it may, winners implies losers. Issa also depicted a blossom past its peak and more than ready to take the dive: *"'I'm here too / so, take me along!' / the fading blossom"*(その連に我もあるぞよすがれ花　一茶　*sono tsure ni ware mo aru zo yo sugarebana*（木母寺の花は大かた青葉にうつりて。。）*Sugare* (fading/wilting) may pun on *sugari*, "clings."

當代も指切事や花こゝろ　元峯 桃も実
tôdai[yo?] mo yubi kiru koto ya hanagokoro　koppô -1694
(this age even finger cut/ting thing! blossom-heart/mind)

even today
fingers are cut off!
cherry petals

In ancient Japan, some retainers committed suicide to accompany their master to the other world. This was rare but not obsolete in the 16c when Jesuits reported it and the more common practice of removing the last joint of the finger. In the Tokugawa era (approx.1600-1850), the amputation and/or presentation of baby-finger-tips came to be associated with romantic pledges and the underworld (where it remains today, with the *yakuza*). The original *ku* ends "blossom *heart*," not "cherry *petals*."

若木など散りもおくれぬ櫻花　紹巴
waka ki nado chiri mo okurenu sakurabana jôha -1602
(young tree/s dropping even delay-not cherry-blossoms)

<table>
<tr><td>with the cherry
even young trees aren't slow
to drop their petals</td><td>even young cherries
do not hold out but let
their petals drop</td></tr>
</table>

This is true. As far as I know the period of bloom is not shorter or longer for young cherry trees.

かゝる身を散て見せたる櫻哉　百芽 新選
kakaru mi o chitte misetaru sakura kana hyakuga 1773
(this [type of] body/ies[obj] fall/scatter-show: cherry/blossom!/'tis)

<table>
<tr><td>blossoms with
all that beauty show us
how to fall</td><td>they show off
the way to fall: blossoms
of slight build</td></tr>
</table>

The *ku* may mean *"The cherry blossoms show the world how to fall with those bodies,"* but *kakaru* has many meanings. "Still *waxing* / it drops petals with élan / the bold cherry" may also be possible.

未練なく散も桜はさくら哉　一茶 1822　　さすが花ちるにみれんはなかりけり 一茶
miren naku chiru mo sakura wa sakura kana issa　　*sasuga hana chiru ni miren wa nakarikeri* issa
(regret-without fall also/even cherry-as-for cherry!/'tis)　　(as-reputed blossoms fall-at regret-as-for not[emph.])

<table>
<tr><td>the blossoms
falling without regret
still blossoms</td><td>blossoms live up
to their reputation: falling
without regret</td></tr>
</table>

This is ever *the* standard line on cherry blossoms, yet saying they fall *without* regret is every bit as ridiculous as saying they fall *with* it. They just fall. Could the undated second *ku* laud Issa's dead wife?

何もかもさらばさらばと散る花か　紫白女 再現
nani mo kamo saraba saraba to chiru hana ka shihakujo -1719
(everything farewell farewell-with fall/ing blossom/s?)

cherry blossoms

<table>
<tr><td>falling petals:
is it all about farewell
to everything?</td><td>farewell to all
to all farewell is that
how they fall</td></tr>
</table>

Saraba, or "farewell" is literally "if so, so be it." Does it also echo the petals whispering?

ちる花は鬼の目にさへ涙かな　一茶 1822
chiru hana wa oni no me ni sae namida kana issa
(falling blossoms-as-for demon's/s' eyes-in even tears!/?)

falling blossoms:
even the eyes of a demon
fill with tears

If running water triggers the urge to urinate, a cataract of cherry blossoms primes the lachrymal glands. Even demons grow morose. This might be because it symbolizes the end of Spring itself. As Buson put it, *"Spring's leaving: / Tears in the eyes of / birds and frogs"* (*yuku haru no tori mo kawazu mo namida kana* -1783). [1] Issa explicitly joins nature's cry-fest: *"Falling blossoms! / the nightingale sings=cries / and i cry"* (ちる花や鶯もなく我もなく 一茶 *chiru hana ya uguisu mo naku ware mo naku* issa 1808). To "sing" and "cry" are homophones, so Issa does not personify the bird as Buson's tears do. Moreover, the bird in question also may refer to singing girl. Issa was 45 and prematurely white-haired with no money, no house, no wife and no followers to speak of. As he put it two years later:

ちる花や已におのれも下り坂　一茶
chiru hana ya sude ni onore mo kudarizaka issa
(falling blossoms!/: already i too downhill)

blossoms fall
and i am already
over the hill

He qualified this by admitting the thoughts were his, not the cherry's: *"More morose / than the falling blossoms / my tears!"* (散がての花よりもろき涙哉　一茶 *chirigate no hana yori moroki namida kana*). In his fifties, Issa beat all odds to get a name, house and wife, but, years later, after Kiku and their last child died, his blossoms turned even sadder than before: *"Even blossoms fall: / Do my wife and child / predict my end?"* (妻や子が我を占ふか花もちる (文化五＝1822 とあるが八月に入っている 翌年のものかと思う) *tsuma ya ko ga ware o uranau ka hana mo chiru* 1823?).

ちるはなの中にたちたる此身かな　成美
chiru hana no naka ni tachitaru kono mi kana seibi -1816
(falling blossoms among standing-is this body/self!/?/'tis)

blossoms fall standing among them by god, it's me!	blossoms falling who stands amid them? *c'est moi*, seibi

among the blossoms
falling, something stands:
it is this poet

Since neither "this body" nor "myself" worked for *kono mi*, we get "this poet" and *c'est moi*, both more affected than the original. Something draws me toward Seibi's *ku*. The "by god" in the first reading sounds right, though it is Occidental (English has a problem: it needs religion to emote).

今そちる我を待けり花盛　宗因
ima zo chiru ware o machikeri hanazakari sôin
(now, hey, fall/ing me/i [obj] wait[+emot.] blossom-acme)

the full bloom do the blossoms wait for one who might fall first?	these blossoms on the verge of falling wait for me?

It is awkward to both modify "I/me" and keep it as the indirect object of "wait." Hence, the boorish "one." I think the ambiguity of the original – we cannot tell if the poet (1604-82) or the blossoms sit on the edge of extinction – makes it more interesting than the Issa *ku* we have just read.

1. **Crying Frogs?** Buson's seemingly ridiculous poem plays on a *ku* by Bashô and mourns the death of his old friend and fellow poet, Shôha (who has sea slugs telling their lament to the moon). See IPOOH-spring)

散る桜ただ悲しさよ嬉しさよ 子規
chiru sakura tada kanashisa yo ureshisa yo shiki 1893
(falling cherry just sadness[+exclam.] happiness[+exclam.]])

falling petals:
just the sadness! and just
the happiness!

petals fall
how sad it is! and
how happy!

This might owe something to an Issa *ku* on the comfort *and* loneliness of sleeping alone, but, regardless, I think it is one of Shiki's best *ku*. As light as cherry petals, it is a perfect sketch of the emotional picture. Compare its style to these next *waka* demonstrating how heavily cherry blossoms fell on those who viewed them from the romantic tradition of longing:

あしひきの山櫻花日並べてかく咲きたらばいと恋ひめやも 赤人万葉集#1425
ashihiki no yamazakurabana kenarabete kaku sakitaraba ito koime yamo manyôshû 8c

legdrag mountain
if your cherry blossoms
just bloomed like this

day after day, my love
might let me be

A loose translation, for "love" in the original "stops," by being fulfilled. But, they don't keep blooming, so longing for what is not will continue. There are many etymologies of the mountain's name, but it brings to *my* mind a Korean song where a woman claims her grief will prevent her lover from leaving by making his legs feel heavier and heavier until he can not go further.

花散らで月は曇らぬよなりせばものを思はぬわが身ならまし 西行
hana chira de tsuki wa kumoranu yo nariseba mono o omowanu wagami naramashi saigyô -1190

were it a world
where blossoms didn't fall
and the full moon

was always free of clouds
longing would let me be

when blossoms
stop falling and the moon
no longer clouds

will the world let me kiss
goodbye to my longing

まてといふにちらでしとまる物ならばなにを桜に思ひまさまし 古今集#70
mate to iu ni chira de shi tomaru mono naraba nani o sakura ni omoimasamashi anon *kokinshû* ()

if saying "stay!"
would stop their
falling, could i hold
these blossoms
more dear?

trans. lewis cook (my decap.)

cherry love

if saying "stay!"
could only stop them
from falling:

but how could we adore
the blossoms any more?

falling

The second poem starts "if only these blossoms, the most beautiful of all plants (and collectively, the most beautiful "installation" in nature) didn't fall so quickly . . .", leading the reader to conclude "they would be perfect;" but ends by doubting whether it matters and, hinting that said imperfection makes them all the more precious. LC adds that a "grammatically less plausible" reading is accepted by some medieval and modern commentators; to wit: "if only the blossoms would stay, per demand, nothing could surpass their beauty." Grammar aside, that would seem unlikely, because, as far as I know, the cherry blossom had no competition. (FYA: a waffling translation by R&H: *"if you would but wait – / lingering on the branches / as we admonish / each spring what could we admire / more oh frail cherry blossoms."* The "you" is fine, but the syllabic padding and parsing is ludicrous.)

散らなくば心はずつとのべの花 敬愚
chiranakuba kokoro wa zutto nobe no hana keigu

if blossoms stayed
my heart would never leave
the fields behind

Keigu has shortened *Kokinshû* poem #96 which has the poet's heart liable to hang out in the fields for a thousand worlds/ages in the event the blossoms fail to fall (いつまでか野辺に心のあくがれむ花しちらずは千世もへぬべし 素性 古今集 kks #96 *itsumade ka nobe ni kokoro no akugaremu hana shi chirazu wa chiyo mo henubeshi* sosei 905). If I am not mistaken, the poet meant, Thank God they fall or we would ever be besotted with love. Compared to this, Saigyô's next seems immature:

勅とかや下す帝のいませかしさらばおそれて花や散らぬと 西行
choku to ka ya kudasu mikado no imasekashi saraba osorete hana ya chiranu to saigyô -1190
(edict or something proclaim emperor being-let / if-so fearing blossoms fall-not)

thou shalt not blow!

*if only we had
a mikado who'd make
a blossom bull*

*in august dread they
wouldn't dare to fall*

The term "Blossom Bull" makes an otherwise uninspired poem sparkle. The cherry blossom clearly inspired metaphysical if not cavalier poetry.

ちるのみを此世のものか春の花 宗祇 老葉
chiru nomi o kono yo no mono ka haru no hana sôgi -1502
(falling only[acc.?] this world's thing? spring-blossoms)

hold your horses!

so, is falling
all this world's about?
spring blossoms

*how about **blooming**?*

so, is falling
the only thing this world
gets credit for?

If my second reading (*including the rhetorical intent of my title*) is correct, Sôgi's *ku* would be infinitely better than the five above *waka* and beat most of the philosophical cherry *haikai* to boot.

つぼむよりちるを心の櫻哉　吟江 古姿
tsubomu yori chiru o kokoro no sakura kana   ginkô 1780
(bud[verb]-from fall[acc.] heart's cherry[blossom]!/?/'tis)

the cherry blossom
in my heart starts to fall
as soon as it buds

cherry	*one-track mind*
from the bud a blossom's mind is set on falling	coming into bud falling is their only aim: cherry blossoms

from bud to blow
the cherry blossoms deep
within my heart

If blossoms are intent on falling, on getting it over with, then –   Sôgi had already answered that question with what must be one of the most pointed early *hokku* ever made:

散らば散れ櫻ばかりの花もなし 宗祇 大発句帳
chiraba chire sakura bakari no hana mo nashi   sôgi -1502
(fall-if fall! cherry only's blossom-even not +裳無し pun?)

if you'd fall
then, fall! cherry is not
the only blossom!

Link-verse *hokku* were not supposed to be about *koi* (love and longing), but can we read the above without recalling the old lyric *"There are more pretty girls than one"*? Cherry does that.

いつはりのある世にちらぬ花も哉 宗祇 老葉
itsuwari no aru yo ni chiranu hana mo gana   sôgi 1420-1502
(falsehood has/is world-in fall-not blossom wish/if-only there were)

in this *maya* i dream of blossoms that don't fall	in this false world why *can't* we have blossoms that do not fall?

Sôgi is careful to contradict himself before anyone else can. In the last *ku*, he pretends to lack concern; in this one, he dreams of guaranteed permanence. I wish I could credit Sôgi with the idea in the second reading, but I am afraid the first reading is more likely. Either way, we have an idea wittier then, say, the King so good the Sun God/dess fulfills his wish for cherry trees that bloom for twenty-one days (三七日) rather than the usual seven (七箇日) found in the *Tales of Heike* (14c). Why do tales always find a broader audience than poetry?

falling

うつし絵をにせてちらざる花も哉　無記名
utsushi e o nisete chirazaru hana mogana   anon. 崑山集 1651
(copy-drawing/picture resembling fall-not blossom/s wish-for)

permanent ink

oh, for flowers that copy their own picture and won't fall!	ah, for bloom that lasts as long as its drawing

This *ku*, like Sôgi's, uses the common ancient expression of wishing, *mogana,* to echo his sentiment in a wittier way. I kept it simple. An *utsushi-e* is a traced copy, a shadow graph or a magical lantern.

ちれはさく花やときは木代々の春　宗祇
chireba saku hana ya tokiwa ki yoyo no haru   sôgi -1502
(fall/scatter-if bloom blossom/s! permanent-tree age-age's spring)

blossoms falling
bloom again, tree-of-ages!
we call it *spring*

Here, Sôgi rises above the seasonal to find solace in the ageless view of life.

なけくなよ残らぬを世の春の花　紹巴
nagekuna yo nokoranu o yo no haru no hana   jôha -1602
(grieve/lament-not! leave[-behind]-not[even if] world's spring-blossoms)

over spilt petals

don't you cry!
it's the way of spring
to leave nothing

This seems a cross between philosophy and nursery rhyme, though the original is a bit more adult, for *nageku* is "lament" rather than "cry." A more ridiculous *ku* by Giun reverses the logic: *"My wish is this / a bloom that doesn't leave / any spring behind"* (いたつらに春をのこさぬ花も哉　義運 新つくは *itazura ni haru o nokosanu hana mo gana*   giun 1495), i.e., it blooms until the very last day of the season.

花の顔もちれは悪女の姿哉　清一 犬子
hana no kao mo chireba akujo no sugata kana   seiichi 1633
(blossom's/s' face/s[emph] fall-when ugly-woman/women's form!/'tis)

after the fall

a cherry tree minus bloom: the face of ugliness	a cherry tree the sweet face fallen leaves ugly limbs

The original says more unkindly "ugly *woman*." Cruel if there is an allusion, the *ku* describes well what is true for many varieties of cherry trees. They are boring of leaf and ugly of limb and bark.

定めなきをさだめて散る櫻哉　青蘿 新五子
sadame naki o sadamete chiru sakura kana seira 1800
(settled-not[acc.]settling fall/s cherry[blossom/s]!/?'tis))

the unsettled
is settled as the cherry
blossoms fall

blossoms fall
settling what cannot
be settled

Is fate *ever* fickle? We are reminded of quantum physics thought-experiments.

散った桜散る桜散らぬ桜哉　子規
chitta sakura chiru sakura chiranu sakura kana shiki 1896
(fallen cherry [blossoms] falling cherry ["] falling-not cherry ["]!/'tis)

blossoms three:
the fallen, the falling and
the yet-to-fall

This is really all that can be said from the objective point of view, isn't it? Still, in English it is a bit off because we cannot use a single word *sakura* for cherry=blossom=petal.

咲ちるやけふも昔にならんず (る)　一茶
saki chiru ya kyo mo mukashi ni naranzu[ru] issa 1806
(blooming falling:/! today also past/long-ago-into become-would)

bloom and fall:
today, too's already
part of the past

bloom and fall:
even today is fast
becoming past

This reminds me of New Year's *ku* where the previous *day* magically becomes the previous *year*, though the vector of thought is contrary. It is closer to Issa's better known *"Evening blossoms / today, too, is now / part of the past"* (# 14-1).

あわたゝし花ちりながら春のくれ　成美 杉柱
awatadashi hana chirinagara haru no kure seibi -1816
(busily blossom/s falling-while spring's dusk/end)

what activity
cherry petals scattering
before summer

how busy
while petals are falling
spring ends

a bustling sight
the last dusk in spring
as petals fall

I like this *ku* a lot. It complements another, where the second month was a busy one for flowering trees going about their business of blooming (ku# 10-8). Here the blossoms' end-of-spring activities echo the year's end for humans in Japan, for it was a time for busy running around taking care of unfinished business called *shiwasu*, literally "teacher-runs" 師走.

◎　◎　◎　◎　◎　◎　◎

Seibi, as most Japanese gentlemen, was a secular poet, but his country bumpkin protégé, Issa, was religious and probably made more clearly Buddhist blossom *ku* (as we saw in Book II) than anyone else. Here is one of the most translated examples, where Issa's language is explicitly Buddhist:

falling

たゝ頼め花は〔も〕はら／＼〔桜ぼた／＼〕あの通り 一茶
tada tanome hana no harahara [sakura botabota] ano tôri　issa -1827
(just trust/ask/request blossom's/s' flutter-flutter[cherry's drip-drop] that way)

> simply trust:
> do not also the petals flutter down,
> just like that
>
> (blyth trans)

simply trust:
like cherry blossoms
trickling down

(lanoue trans¹)

how to let go

just have faith:
how beautiful the petals
fluttering down!

TRUSTING THE WIND

simply have faith: let all attachments go.
do not blossoms scatter, even so?

(stewart trans)

If the Bible says *Look at the Lilly*, this Buddhist says *Look at the cherry blossoms!* One says life is easy if you live on faith, the other says likewise for death.

散るまではその日その日のさくら哉　使帆
chiru made wa sono hi sono hi no sakura kana　shihan 17c
(fall-until-as-for that day that day's cherry/cherry[blossom/s]!/'tis)

until they fall
the *sakura* of that day
that very day!

until they drop
they are cherry blossoms
day after day

This is not popular Buddhism so much as Zen, which is to say the perennial wisdom based on one fact: we all will die. It was hard not to make the blossoms "play" as *day* demands to this rhymester.

ちる桜けふもむちゃくちゃくらしけり 一茶
chiru sakura kyô mo muchakucha kurashikeri　issa 1808
(falling cherry[petals] today too disorderly/a mess living[+emph.])

cherry blossoms
falling, my life, today
a total mess

petals fly
my life as always
pell-mell

scattering petals
today, as always, i sow
my wild oats

Not being religious, I prefer Issa's confession to his catechism. *Muchakucha* is a good word.

~~~~~~

1. *Fluttering and Trickling* The "fluttering" (*hara-hara*) version of Issa's *ku* is more conventional. The "trickling" (*bota-bota*) is problematic; though used to describe the sound of tear-drops, the boppy sound-sense is heavier than ploppy *"pota-pota"* used to describe the plop-down of entire camellia blossoms. Could Issa have intended *hota-hota* which means the same thing as *bota-bota*, but *also* connotes "joy"? The mimesis also brings out the individuality of each petal. I changed David G. Lanoue's "--" to ":" because it works better in a centered form.

散花の桜きげんや小犬ども 一茶
chiru hana no sakura kigen ya koinu domo issa 1815
(falling blossoms' cherry-mood!/?/: small-doggies)

a mood as light
as cherry shedding petals
puppies at play

captured by puppies:
a cherry tree's spirit
when petals fly

how do cherries feel
when their petals let go?
the puppies know

畜生・散花に仏とも法ともしらぬかな 一茶
chiru hana ni butsu to mo hô to mo shiranu kana issa 1812
(falling blossoms-at/with/by buddh- and [+emph] law[-ism] know-not!)

falling blossoms:
hell if they know a thing
about buddhism!

falling petals
knowing not a bit of
budh or *ism*

the beastly

in falling petals
they cannot find a bud
of buddhism?

At first, I thought Issa meant, let's not get mushy about this and credit cherry blossoms with being enlightened for their non-attachment. Reading 1 & 2 follows this idea. Blossoms may demonstrate gracefully letting go in the manner of perfect Buddhists, but they are only what Jonathon Edward's called "shadows of divine things," good for teaching but not real teachers. Or are they? But, this does not explain Issa's preface, 畜生 (chikkushô), the beastly rank of reincarnation. As plants are not beasts, I think the message is that even without knowing Buddha, cherries do right: *how about beastly men?*

寺の花はり合もなく散にけり 一茶
tera no hana hariai mo naku chirinikeri issa 1822
(temples'blossom/s [good]tension/competition-even not fall[fin.])

temple cherries
their blossoms fall
too easily

Neither confession nor catechism, this *ku* is an utterly facetious hyperlogical explanation for a less-than-exciting blossom-viewing at a temple, one which the poet may have arrived to late. The blossoms there, Issa implies, are completely at home with dying and unafraid to let go, do not resist the wind at all. Yet, the phrase "lacking *hari-ai* (stiffness/tension-meet)"– being "psyched up" for something, or feeling especially alive thanks to having a rival is *perfect*. With this *ku*, old Issa finally made his idea sound interesting. The slang wouldn't work in translation, so I made do with "too easily." Or, could the lack of tension be on the part of those viewing?

花ちるや重たき笈のうしろより 蕪村
hana chiru ya omotaki oi no ushiro yori buson 1783
(blossoms fall/scatter:/! heavy altar's [=age's] behind-from)

petals scatter
behind a heavy old
portable altar!

The "altar" was a chest which contained Buddhist items: books, robes, statues, incense, etc which set down on its legs served as a sort of shrine on the spot. In *History of Haiku I*, Blyth writes "the picture here is that of the retreating figure of a weary priest with bent back and the cherry blossoms falling behind him, that is, between him and the viewer." In his older *Haiku*, vol 2 Spring, Blyth mistakenly wrote *"behind me, / old and weak / flowers are scattering."*[1] Wrong or not, I love the gloss he put on it: "This 'behind me' may have the meaning of Marvell's *But, at my back, I always hear / Time's winged chariot hurrying near.*" Why the mistake? The portable altar is homophonic with "old/age."

去年も咲今年もさくや櫻の木　鬼貫
kozo mo saki kotoshi mo saku ya sakura no ki onitsura -1738
(last year too bloomed this year too blooms!/: cherry-tree/s)

why named *sakura*?

blooming last year
blooming this year
bloom-bloom trees

A bad *ku* by the notably subtle poet Onitsura? My guess is that he plays on the name *sakura* as *saku* = *bloom + ra*, the plural suffix. *Blooming this year / blooming that, a saku-ra / plurali-tree!* I could be wrong. He may, in his understated way, only be pointing out that they bloom every year, so why the big deal when the blossoms fall? Actually, that was my first thought and why the *ku* is *here*.

散る時も亦ほめらるゝ櫻哉　文井 坦誠
chiru toki mo mata homeraruru sakura kana bunsei ()
(falling time also again praised-is cherry[tree/s/blossoms]'tis)

when they drop	cherry blossoms	praised even
voices of praise rise again	they gain our praise	when they are litterbugs
cherry blossoms	again, falling	cherry trees

Until reading this *ku*, the negative associations of *chiru*, *i.e.* of *falling/scattering*, escaped my notice. Of course, I knew people regretted the blossoms leaving, but I neglected other connotations of the word such as *messiness* and *loss of interest*, both behavior criticized in a neat and attentive culture.

かかる日にあつはれ花のちる事よ 人左 蕉庵再興
kakaru hi ni appare hana no chiru koto yo jinsa 1771
(this[appropriate] day-on hurray blossoms' falling-thing!)

よい連れのやうに行く春ちるさくら 大江丸 俳諧袋
yoi tsure no yô ni yuku haru chiru sakura ôemaru 1801
(good companions' like-as goes spring falling cherry)

call it confetti

right on the day
hurrah! hurrah! just watch
the blossoms fall!

petals in the air
like a good companion
spring leaves

~~~~~~

@ <u>Blyth Mistranslation</u>   Blyth's editor added a footnote: "For 'Old and weak' read 'Heavy traveling altar.' (Blyth, *History of Haiku....*").   With few exceptions (usually by Japanese translators) books of haiku are full of mistranslation, so reprinted translations in revized editions of the same or different books *should* have many such notes (as David G. Lanoue, to his credit, does for Issa mis/translations on line). I must admit, in this case, the nature of the mistranslation puzzles me because the Chinese character cannot possibly be confused for "old."

散れと吼る鯨や花の波間より 哲阿
chire to hoeru kujira ya hana no namima yori tetsua -1798
("blow!" roars whale!/: blossoms' waves-among-from)

blow ye petals!
spouts the whale amid
blossom waves

The whale *roars* or howls in the original where the verb also means that. Waves of bloom is standard trope but here the phrasing is slightly different and suggests that cherries stand by the sea.

我と花の散は貧報ゆるぎ哉 無記名 崑山集
ware to hana no chiraba (chiru wa?) binbô yurugi kana anon. 1651
(i/self-with blossom/s fall-if/when/as-for poverty-shakes!/?/'tis)

blossoms falling all by themselves i wonder if it's the shakes	under the cherry petals fell and i noticed i had the shakes

The *shakes* in the original is the "poverty-tremble." Japanese are told that jiggling their legs (as we all do occasionally and some do incessantly) is bad luck for it brings poverty. This is the most absurd *ku* in the chapter, if not book. My second reading is very, very unlikely, but it is much better than the almost surely correct first reading.

散る花や木下へ妾の走り込 冬央 小弓俳諧集
chiru hana ya kinoshita e mekake no hashirikomi tôô? 1699
(falling blossoms: tree/s-below-to mistresses' running-within)

the petals fall my mistress runs for the bloomshade	a petal shower the mistresses dive under the trees

I had this *ku* misplaced with the *Sex* chapter. Reading it over I was struck by the image and the idea. People run for shelter when things fall from the sky, but here a woman or women run into the falling stuff, under the tree. As the men are sitting under the trees, the women are walking about and when a bit of breeze sets off a shower of petals they hasten to join their patrons drinking *sake* with a lucky petal in it.

目に見ゆるものの外にも散るさくら 菊地一雄 季題別
me ni miyuru mono no hoka ni mo chiru sakura kikuchi kazuô 1997
(eyes-in see-can-things other than too falling cherry[blossoms])

other things we cannot see falling with the blossoms	cherry petals and something else fall invisibly

This contemporary *ku,* is superb. With millions of cherry blossom *ku* written, there are still room for more. I have come across many good contemporary cherry *ku,* not a few at the haiku bulletin boards where I play. Some day, I might gather them up and translate a bookful of them, but this book just cannot fit more than the handful that for some reason insisted on being included.

falling

わがやどの花見がてらにくる人はちりなむのちぞこひしかるべき　みつね　古今集 67
waga yado no hanamigatera ni kuru hito wa chirinamu nochi zo kohishikarubeki   kokinshû 905

i
to those who visited for the blooming cherries

all you people
who, blossom-viewing
called my home

how i miss your company
now the petals have flown

as for the men
who, blossom-viewing
dare drop in

once they and the petals
go away, i'll miss them

I am more impressed with this picture of one who leaves the world of men for solitude admitting he enjoys human company, sort of, than I am of the following art-*waka* by Saigyo:

花も散り人も来ざらんをりはまたやまのかひにて長閑なるべし　西行
hana mo chiri hito mo kozaran ori wa mata yama no kai nite nodoka naru beshi   saigyô 1190

ii
the quiet after the storm

petals scattered,
people no longer come:
and once again

this mountain world
wins back the peace

these hollars fill . . .
with the sound of silence

Forgive two different endings. It is hard to find, much less keep, the wit of this *waka*. The problem rests on one word, *kai*. Though the most obvious meaning would be the high valleys between the mountains (峡), there are dozens of homophones including *satori* won through austere discipline (果位) and basic character (柄). I have probably overcompensated.

花はちり人はなき世の夕哉　昌叱 1603
hana wa chiri hito wa naki yo no yûbe kana   shôshitsu
(blossoms-the fallen people-the without world's dusk!)

櫻ちる木陰は秋の花野哉　心敬 -1475
sakura chiru kokage wa aki no hanano kana   shinkei
(cherry scatters bloomshade-as-for fall's blossomfield!)

a world of dusk
without man after the blossoms
have scattered

the cherry sheds
and its shade is a flower
field of august

Cherry Wind, Bad Guy?
桜風・花ノ風
sakura-kaze, hana-no-kaze

あらけなや風車売る花の時 薄芝 あらの
arakenaya kazeguruma uru hana no toki hakushi 1689
(loutishness! wind[pin]-wheels selling blossom-time)

of all the gall!
a man selling pin-wheels
in cherry time

This, funniest of the cherry-wind haiku[1] suggests that the pinwheel man bets against the wish for still weather on the part of all who love blossoms. It is as if he is on the side of the wind, the hated wind!

花ちらす風のやどりはたれかしれ我にをしへよ行きてうらみむ そせい法し#76
hana chirasu / kaze-no yadori-wa / tare-ga shiru / ware-ni oshieyo / yukite uramimu kokinshû 905

Terribly Learical

Someone, pray tell me where to find
the dwelling place of Master Wind!
I'll give him a piece of my mind, i will,
that spoiler of flowers, the wind!

Japanese classics scholar Hitaku Kyusojin, in his standard pocketbook edition of the *Kokinshû*, righteously complains that despite the flowers "falling without regret," the poem resorts to anthropomorphism and reeks of artifice. Actually, falling *without* regret is itself an anthromorphism.[2] Moreover, an untimely blow can hurt the blossoms' chance for fertilization and who knows that a tree does *not* want, in its own way, to enjoy a good bloom? Not, that this matters. The poet has a right to be upset with the wind for perfectly human, indeed, selfish reasons, such as wanting to see or show the blossoms to someone (before TV and the movies, such natural entertainment was valued more). As the wind was legendarily tied to wind-caves up mountains, the poet used playful metaphor to express chagrin. People must have chuckled at it.[3] Several less dramatic poems in the older *Manyôshû* collection (#1747*,8, 4395) link the Wind God Tatsudahiko of Mt Tatsuda with cherry blossoms – so they are doubtless the flower in question.

~~~~~~

1. *Funniest or Not?* Another would be as funny if only the puns translated: "The sound of wind: / the loud snoring of blossoms=petals=nose / returned to their root/s=sleep" (*kaze no oto ya ne ni kaeru hana no taka-ibiki* masachoku ( ) 風の音やねにかへる花の高鼾 政直 洗濯もの.) *Sound*, *roots*, and *sleep* are all homophones, *ne*.

2. *Knee-jerk Classicists* Anthropomorphism (*gijin*) and artifice (*gikô*) – supposedly corrupt Chinese influences but, as a matter of fact, common to most indigenous folk songs – are knee-jerk charges by classicists in Japan. What irks me is that the criticism is boldly applied to literature deemed bad taste and virtually ignored in those that are revered.   The *Kokin-* and *Shin-Kokinshû* are trashed while the *Manyôshû* gets off with little criticism and Saigyô, whom we saw (bk 2 *kokoro*) was a champion of these things, is never criticized!

3. Chuckling Translation   Pardon the extreme liberties I took with the translation. To set things straight, here is a more faithful one by the late Helen Craig McCullough: *"Does anyone know / the dwelling place of the wind / scatterer of flowers? / Tell me that I may go there / and deliver a complaint."* *My* only complaint is with the last line. The original *yukite uramimu* is much livelier, like my "give him a piece of my mind." Let me add that when I read the poem, I recall Thoreau mentioning a wind cave on a mountain in Maine and Erasmus Darwin's verses about the *"Immortal Franklin"* seeking the "fiery bed" of Tempest, which shrouds "the seeds of Thunder" in the clouds (this in turn, reminding me of Lucretius, who gives many delightful theories of thunder in his *On The Nature of Things*). According to Erasmus, Franklin's newly invented lightning rod *"besieged with iron points his airy cell, / And pierced the monster slumbering in his shell."*   Finally, note that *the original feels light* because it incorporates so much internal rhyme that slowly singing it would create an end-rhyme-like effect! I have parsed the romanization because I do not think it is by chance. R&H translate "these rough *winds*." "These rough" are mere padding; the plural is significant. Thunder demons are plural, but I imagine only one Wind God per mountain. My Japanese advisors split on this.

風のまへの花は色即是空哉 長頭丸 嵐山集
kaze no mae no hana wa shiki soku zeiku kana   teitoku 1651
(wind-before-blossom-as-for, color-instant/ly-this[is] sky=empty!/'tis)

catechistic translation

a blossom
before the wind: instantly
not there!

This alters an idiom resembling "dew (like our candle) before the wind" and uses the "color/eros" element to fuse it to a phrase of esoteric Buddhism about life's impermanence. Perhaps that is all that can be said about the wind and blossoms without using metaphor.

花の香を盗みてはしる嵐かな 宗鑑 - 1586	出あへ／＼花盗人よ春のかぜ 無記名 嵐山集
hana no ka o nusumite hashiru arashi kana sôkan	*deae deae hananusubito yo haru no kaze* anon 1651
(blossoms' scent[acc.] stealing runs gale!/that's)	(tryst, tryst, blossom-thieves hey! spring-wind/s)
thief with a nose	**he gets around!**
lifting the scent from the blossoms, the gale he runs away	tryst here, tryst there! you flower thief, you! the spring wind

A note about Sôkan's *ku,* from a book of famous *ku:* "Now, this is a worthless poem but, at the time, the anthropomorphic wit was probably felt to be interesting."   IMHO, the problem is not so much a matter of different attitude toward anthropomorphism (*snow-woman*, for one, does well in Japanese haiku circles *today*) as a lack of appreciation for the development of poetic trope, which was once the heart of poetry. To readers accustomed to the wind as a despoiler of blossoms the humor is in the downgrade to a petty thief who runs off with a mere keepsake rather than ravishing the same. Another old *ku* belittles the storm wind even further by having it *"Wipe, wipe the blossoms' faces"* (花の顔をふく／＼春のあらし哉   無記名   嵐山集 *hana no kao o fuku fuku haru no arashi kana* anon. 1651), natural behavior because "wipe" in Japanese is homophonic with "blow" (both are *fuku*). Corny? Yes, but more original than, say: *"It's jealous, too, / of the blossom's pretty face / the spring wind"* (花の顔よきをもそねむ春の風   之也 洗濯物 *hana no kao yoki o mo sonemu haru no kaze*   shiya 1666)!

花さけは都にも聞く嵐哉 宗祇
hana sakeba miyako ni mo kiku arashi kana sôgi -1502
(blossom/s bloom-if/when capital-even-in hear tempest 'tis)

when the cherry's
in bloom, even kyoto
hears the tempest

in blossom time
each gale raises a storm
within the capitol

Farmers, fishermen and those working in the mountains must pay attention to the weather. They are even interested in the storms that miss them. The city folk only care when their recreation is affected. This poem reflects the perspective of Sôgi's humble country origin as well as the fact that the mountains surrounded Kyoto. Note that the character for gale 嵐 puts the wind 風 under a mountain 山. Could local tempests really originate (or seems to originate) in the mountains?

そと (かつ) 吹くも花にあた (さは) るは嵐哉 教清 毛吹草
soto (katsu) fuku mo hana ni ataru (sawaru) wa arashi kana kyôsei 1645
(gently[even] blow even blossom-into hit[touch]-as-for tempest!/?/'tis)

though it blows
ever so soft, on blossoms
it's a storm!

even blowing
like this, touching bloom
it's a tempest!

This *ku* jokes at the overuse of *arashi* (gale/storm) for wind that visits blossoms though it may only stroke them. As we shall see, the *haijin* came to use "spring wind," too. Spring had and still has erotic undertones in Japanese (pornographic prints were called spring-prints, bawdy songs spring-songs, etc.)

花の為や悪事千里の春の風　慶友　犬子、嵐山集
hana no tame ya akuji senri no haru no kaze keiyû 1633, 1651
(blossoms-for!/: bad-things[misdeeds] thousand-leagues' spring-wind/s)

the spring breeze
its evil-doing gets around
thanks to blossoms

it's news

blame the victims?

because of blossoms
the whole world knows
when wind is bad

if not for blossoms
who would think poorly
of the spring wind!

The saying "evil-doings-thousand-leagues"(*murder outs?*) is corny, but the tie-in to wind is well done. There is a parallel to Buddhism blaming woman for male desire. A slightly later *ku* by young Bashô (-1694) plays with this in a different way: *"How blossoms hate it! / The wind's breath is worse / than gossip"* (花にいやよ世間口より風のくち*hana ni iya yo sekenguchi yori kaze no kuchi*). I think this simple later *ku* beats Bashô's *ku*: *"How women / detest the wind that hits / the blossoms"* (女とていかにあなとる花の風　箸？玉藻*onna tote ikani anadoru hananokaze* shin 1774) .[1]

---

1. **Hitting Blossoms** The original says only that women detest "the blossoms' wind," meaning wind at the time the cherries are in bloom. They might also hate it for disheveling their hair (Kimono don't blow up like Occidental dresses, so the antithetical relationship of women and the wind, best described by W.H. Hudson, may not be the problem). Chances are that the poet thought women identified with the plight of the blossoms.

また風のにくみのこりや遅櫻　也有 アルス
mada kaze no nikumi-nokori ya osozakura   yayû 1701-83
(still wind's/s' hate[=love?] remnant?/!/: late-cherry)

something still makes us hate the wind: the late cherries!	something remains to provoke the winds a late cherry

The first reading gives us a first-rate haiku (the first this chapter). Thanks to cherry trees that bloom late, the period during which the wind is disliked expands. However, hating is also said to be the reverse side of strong attraction, hence my alternate. Ah, but *anything* can excite, or, rather, draw the wind:

花笛を吹くや後の山嵐　正貞 太夫櫻
hanabue o fuku ya okure/ushiro no yama-oroshi   seitei 1680
(blossom-flute[acc.] blow after/lag/behind's mountain-tempest)

the mountain gale hums contentedly behind the cherry trees	contented humming under the blossoms – just asking for a mountain gale!	after the blossoms the wind sighs happily up in the hills

The *"nose flute,"* written here with the "nose" replaced by the homophonic character for "blossom" (hence, my *blossoms* and *cherry trees*), means utterly self-absorbed, i.e. contented, humming.[1] My second reading follows the idea found in a 7-7 link by Sôchô (1447-1532): *"All I need say is "cherries" / and the wind storms down the hills"* (*sakura to ieba yamakaze zo fuku* x2 宗長 Yunoyama *renga* sequence). There may also be an "after the deluge" idea here, but I'm betting on another: "happiness comes before disaster."[2] The biggest difficulty is that 後= *behind/after* can describe time or space. Reading One chooses the latter, Reading Two the former. Regardless, the original is probably allusion.

山守も風をはいはぬ櫻かな　兼良 新つくは
yamamori mo kaze o ba iwanu sakura kana   kenryô 1495
(mountain/wilderness-guard-even wind/s [+emph.] say-not cherry!/'tis)

spring taboo

cherry blossoms:
even the gillies dare not
speak of "wind!"

A *yamamori* ("mountain/wilderness-guard") is a "forest ranger," but such a word seems excessively modern. My name being what it is, *gillie* was on the tip of my tongue. Saying *kaze*, or "wind" was taboo, for it was thought that mentioning something feared might draw it to you, or make it angry because it expected to be addressed with a special name. This was particularly true for mountains which tended to be protected by spirits that were not always friendly to outside (lowland) intruders.

---

1. Contented Humming Either Eliza Ruhamah Scidmore or Isabella Bird described what she thought the insufferably self-absorbed humming of the Japanese – or, was it "oriental"? – which I had never noticed. I had never thought humming to be particularly egoistic (as compared to singing or whistling or smug silence), but it is true that the Japanese idiom supports her observation.

2. Too much happiness. Old-fashioned Japanese would understand and like the residents of Garrison Keillor's Lake Wobegon, for they share their tendency to use self-demeaning, much-obliged, wouldn't-want-to-put you-out, humbler-than-thou (rap-opposite?) rhetoric.

山風に雲とみえてや花盛　宗養 大発句帳
yamakaze ni kumo to miete ya hanazakari　sôyô 1538-63
(mountain wind/s-to wind-as-appear!/?/: blossom-acme)

the full bloom:
to the mountain wind
looks like clouds!

mountain winds
see it as so many clouds
the full bloom

Ancient poets were always requesting the wind to blow away clouds to reveal a peak or the moon. If the wind's work was dispelling clouds who can blame it for charging down into the blossoms? I wish this poet lived longer, for I like the way he thinks, or the way I imagine he thinks, anyway.

花ちらす風や目に見ぬ鬼のいき　正網 毛吹草
hana chirasu kaze ya me ni mienu oni no iki　seikô 1645
(blossom-scattering wind: eyes-in/by see-not demon's/s' breath/s)

blossom-scattering
wind: the breath of
an invisible demon

There are no puffy cheeked cherubs on Japanese maps, but artists did draw demons that spread wind=colds and other disease, hanging from the eaves. Is this where the poet got his ridiculous image?

櫻木につなくな馬の鼻嵐　正式 毛吹草
sakuragi ni tsunaguna uma no hana-arashi　seishiki 1645
(cherry-tree-to tie-not! horse's nose-tempest)

wind-machine

don't tie yours up
to a cherry tree! horses
snort out gales!

never tie up
to cherry trees! horses
are too windy!

The original's "nose-tempest" is a homophone of "flower-tempest," a storm that reeks havoc on the blossoms. English cannot do that, but Japanese lacks an equivalent to the English "windy" used to improve the second reading. Ponge who mentions the horse's windiness at both ends would approve.

風入馬蹄軽・木の下か蹄の風や散櫻　蕪村
konoshita ga hizume no kaze ya chiru sakura　buson -1783
(tree-below's hooves wind?/!/: falling cherry[blossom petals])

the lightness of horses

below the trees
the wind from four hooves!
petals scattering

One reason Buson has been less translated than Bashô and Issa is the extraordinary amount of antiquarian detail in many of his poems. Here, the prefatory phrase (in pure Chinese characters: *wind-enter-horse-hooves-light*) is a take on a line in a Chinese poem with the original "four" misread as "horse," – I did not translate it because only Latin beyond my prowess would prevent the repetition of two words already in the *ku*). Then, "below the trees" (*konoshita*), the name of a horse beloved by the son of a hero in the *Tales of Heike*, evokes a young warrior galloping his horse in the place for which he is named, blossoms flying helter-skelter in his path. The *ku* further alludes to a *waka* about living below the trees . . . Because Buson is beloved by scholars, all of his work is annotated, which is the only reason why I caught his allusions. If you ask me, Buson's memory was *too* good and, as a result, he was able to include far more archaic references than we can, or care to follow!

散迄は下馬と書きたき櫻哉　風吟 反故集
chiru made wa geba to kakitaki sakura kana   fûgin 1783?
(scatter until-as-for, "dismount" write-want cherry 'tis)

上野 下馬札や是より花の這入口　一茶 1818
ueno / geba fuda ya kore yori hana no hairiguchi   issa
(dismount sign: this/here-from blossoms' entrance)

whoa

while they bloom
i want to write "dismount!"
for cherry trees

ueno

a sign to dismount
the entrance to the blossoms
begins right here

花にめさば竹馬にても参るべし　かしき 其袋
hana ni mesaba take-uma nite mo mairu beshi   kashiki 1690
(blossom-to-invited-if/when bamboo-horse[stilts]-by-even go-ought)

hanami etiquette

a blossom summons
i'd go mounted though it's on
a bamboo horse

saddle your stilts

if you would pay
a visit to the lord's blossoms
a bamboo mare!

Fugin may be less concerned about damage caused by horses than the principle: one dismounts to give *sakura* the respect they deserve, though we may imagine that not such respect but the large crowds in some of the urban "cherry mountains" such as Ueno were what eventually forced even nobility off their high horses. The last *ku*, which antedates Issa's by about a hundred years, gives us a fantastic solution: horses to lift you into the air without creating it! In Japanese "bamboo-horse" means stilt. They resemble ours except that the feet go *along* rather than across the rungs so one's toe-tips face the stilts. This makes sense when you realize their stirrups also run front-back rather than right-left (See *Topsy-turvy 1585* for more). Kashiki's *ku* plays on at least two famous poems. One is by Saigyô: "*Today, too, I'm ready to go, as I dream of childhood with this bamboo horse serving as my cane!*" (*take-uma o tsue ni mo kyo wa tanomu kana warawa asobi o omoide tsutsu*). The other poem is Bashô's *ku* #57-10, insisting that only people who love children (by implication, a bit childish themselves) really appreciate the blossoms. But horsing around has taken us off-track. Let us return to the wind:

武士も見ながら散す花の風　鬼貫 1738
samurai mo minagara chirasu hana no kaze   onitsura
(samurai also/even viewing-while scatters/trashes blossom-wind)

as the samurai
watch, the wind trashes
the blossoms

samurai watch
as the wind blows away
the blossoms

At first, I translated: "*Petals blowing / in the wind pass before / samurai eyes.*" Petals, I thought, exhibited a character samurai were supposed to have; but a careful reading of the *mo*, "even," and the active verb suggested the wit lay, instead, in the inability of even the warriors to defend the blossoms.

萬人の鼻息に散る櫻かな 子規 1896
向嶋の画に題す *mannin no hana iki ni chiru sakura kana*   shiki
(10,000-men's nose-breath/snorts-by/with scatter cherry!/'tis)

for a picture of mukojima

scattering before
the snorting multitude
cherry blossoms

cherry blossoms
scattering in the breeeze
a million breaths

Mukojima was the prime blossom viewing location for the proles. A "million" is my translation of "ten-thousand/myriad/all." Shiki specifies "nose-breath," connoting people feeling their oats. The English "snort" roughly matches that connotation.

吹風を見よとて花の狂ひかな 来山
fuku kaze o miyo tote hana no kurui kana   raizan -1716
(blowing breeze/wind[acc.] see! [+as-if-to-say] blossom-craziness!/?)

going crazy,
the blossoms would finger
the wind!

Raizan was one of the most clever of Bashô's contemporaries. This is one of the most artificial of all cherry-wind *ku*, yet we must marvel at the imagination that could come up with the idea of the blossoms' motion meaning *"Oh, look! Look what that bad wind is doing to us!"* Compare it to this: *"The blossom faces: / do they fall/scatter/tremble/age out of spite for / the blowhard wind?"* (ふく風をきらひてふるや花の顔　重方 毛吹草 *fuku kaze o kiraitefuru ya hana no kao*   shigekata? 1645). "Face" (*kao*) in Japanese includes more of what English would call "expression" as well as "reputation." Could the poet have genuinely felt the blossoms buffeted by the wind were upset at the treatment they were getting? Does the *ku* allude to women fed up with horny men? If so, it is marginally more interesting than this boring feminism[?]: *"The tempest: / seducing blossoms, it lacks / love for them"* (さそひても花を思はぬ嵐哉 救済 つくは *sasoite mo hana o omowanu arashi kana*   kyûzai 1356).

花に風いや敵にてはなかりけり 百之 太夫櫻
hana ni kaze iya teki nite wa nakarikeri   hyakushi 1680
(blossoms-to/with/and wind no, enemy/ies-as-for not[+emph.])

blossom and wind:
no, you cannot really
call them enemies!

The wind, this poet suggests, loves the blossoms and they are perfectly happy to be ravished by it. Since men and women have traditionally been called each other's "enemy" and the object of one's longing – always a "sweetheart," "honey" and so forth in English – is called "love's enemy" (*koi-no teki*), this poem also hides untranslatable irony.

こち／＼と招く扇や花に風　寸志　太夫櫻
kochi kochi to maneku ôgi ya hana ni kaze sunshi 1680
("here, here" invite fan/s!/?/: blossoms-to/with/and wind)

cherry sirens

beckoning fans
"here!" "over here!"
blossom-wind

wind in the hands
of blossoms: *here! here!*
wave their fans!

A fan can be used to motion a person closer. Is the poet being seduced by women of ill repute? Here, the *hana ni kaze* echoes the standard idea of the wind and blossoms as a set or a relationship, while *also* allowing a new reading, namely that the wind is in the hands of these blossoms=women.

招かるゝ扇の風ぞ花に敵　友知　太夫櫻
manekaruru ôgi no kaze zo hana ni teki yûchi 1680
(inviting fan/s' breeze/wind! blossom/s-to enemy/ies)

beware the wind   fans are inviting
of those inviting fans!   wind, yes, the nemesis
the blossom's foe   within the bloom

"Beware" and "yes" are ways to English the emphatic particle *zo,* following the wind in the original. The *hana ni teki* means either "enemy *of* the blossoms" (fan-size or not, wind is wind), or, "*the* enemy is *by/under/within* the blossoms" (men, watch out for those women (and possibly, your *nose*=blossoms)).

雁がねのかへる羽風やさそふらむ過ぎ行くみねの花も残らぬ　源 重之　新古今集#120
karigane no kaeru hakaze ya sasouramu sugiyuku mine no hana mo nokoranu shinkôkinshû 1205

where did all the flowers go?

*breeze from
the wings of the geese
just departed*

the blossoms on the peak
are also gone

Geese left when flowers came. Issa would later joke that they were stiff-necked (*shibutoi*) for doing so. The fact is recorded in 8c poetry, but this *waka* gives it a new twist. *Did the tailwind pull them along?*

鶯の羽風や花を味かたうち　茂次　鷹つくば
uguisu no hanekaze ya hana o mikata-uchi moji 1642
(nightingale[bush-warbler]'s wing-breeze: blossom[acc.]ally-shot)

blown away   *acceptable casualties*

wind from the wings   blossoms dropped
of the warbler! blossoms   by friendly fire: wind from
felled by friendlies   nightingale's wing

Stop hooting! Of course, "friendly fire" sounds ridiculously modern; but if English has an idiom for "[an] ally's/friend's blows/strikes/attacks" (*mikata-uchi*) I do not know it, this "blow/hit" verb *uchi,* was, in fact, used for guns, and Japan in the early 16c had more firearms than any European country (see Noel Perrine: *Giving Up the Gun*). Seriously, this *ku* belongs in the *hanazakari* chapter, for the full bloom sets the scene. I have seen it so full a bird could not fly in and out without scattering petals.

山たかみ岩根の櫻散る時はあまの羽ごろも撫づるとぞ見る 崇徳院御歌 新古今集 131
yama takami iwane no sakura chiru toki wa ama no hagoromo nazuru to zo miru shûtoku-in skks 1205

when petals fall from the rocky heights of the mountains i see down rubbed off the wings of angels	when petals float down from rocky heights in the mountains i can see it: those wings of angels brushing earth	when petals fall from the rocky heights of the mountains i almost see them brush the wings of angels

What an extraordinary *waka*! Only the middle reading is correct, though the others would be as good of a guess as any *if you did not know*, as I did not know, that "the rub/stroke/brush of heavenly feather-robes" refers to something happening slowly, "longer than the time required to wear down boulders covering 40 square leagues brushed once every 100 years by an angel's wing." Are petals from mountain cherries fluttering down very slowly because of the heat rising from the ground?

闇の花風一口に喰ひけり 峰松 蘆別船
yami no hana kaze hitoguchi ni kuraikeri hôshô 1694
(darkness's blossom-breeze/wind one-mouth-with eat-up!)

dark moon night

yami blossoms
swallowed in a single
gulp by the wind

I use *yami* as is, because English lacks a single word to express a pitch-black night with no moon, the utter darkness identified with the lost soul. Is this venial zoomorphism or powerful poetic imagery?

見ぬ人をうらやむ花の嵐哉 宗祇 老葉
minuhito o urayamu hana no arashi kana sôgi 1420-1502
(view/see-not person/people[acc.] envy blossom-tempest!)

i envy all of you who do *not* see the blossoms in this tempest!	how i envy all who view the blossoms in this storm

Spring carnage. Sôgi certainly covers all the angles but I'm not sure I buy this. Who does not enjoy watching wind ripping through blossoms filling the air with pink petals? Am I a sadist to say so?

花に風呆れ果たる有様也 頼重→重頼? 太夫櫻
hana ni kaze akirehatetaru arisama nari shigeyori 1680
(blossoms-in wind flabbergasting appearance is/becomes)

the wind with the blossoms: it just blows the mind!	the blossoms and their wind: the picture is scandalous!

wind

mister wind and
his blossoms: what horrid
liberties they take!

Akire-hate[ta]ru means one is flabbergasted to see something and either gives up trying to understand or throws up one's hands in disgust. The first reading resorts to slang because "just amazing!" would be too weak, while "flabbergasted," "disgusted" and other standard translations kill the ambiguity. Besides, the "blows" was hard to resist. Is the poet really disgusted, or, turned on to see the blossoms in wild besport, apparently enjoying their fate? Since the collection with the *ku* had many allusions to the relationship of the sexes, post-Bashô or not, I see allegory.

世の中のうさ八番そ花に風 宗因 西翁十百韻
yononaka no usa hachiman zo hana ni kaze sôin 1604-82
(world/men-among gloom/cares[emph.]blossoms-into/and wind)

for spreading gloom,	nothing so good
it's the world's top act:	for making us feel bad as
"Wind & Blossoms!"	wind hitting bloom

At first, I mistook the 八番 = 幡, literally "8th," an abbreviation of the name for the God of War used as an emphatic, for 十八番, literally "18th," meaning the top act, or thing that an actor does best. My first translation is based on that, but it doesn't seem to make much difference.

万句巻頭に・万に一つ花に風なき春も哉 徳元 夢見草
man ni hitotsu hana ni kaze naki haru mogana tokugen 1656
(10,000-to-1 [unlikely] blossoms-on/into wind-not spring wish-for)

ten thousand to one

how nice it would be:
a spring when the blossoms
know no wind!

This *ku* was the first in a ten-thousand volume book of poems – "ten thousand (one *man*) to one" means "highly unlikely," but is often used in a hopeful way: ie, *a long-shot*. But, what if, like Midas, the poet had his will, if everything he were to touch were to remain unmoving for lack of wind?

春風にまかせぬはなのたねもかな 宗祇
harukaze ni makasenu hana no tane mogana sôgi 1420-1502
(spring-wind-to/by lose-not blossom's/s' seed wish-for)

oh, for the seed
of blossoms that can resist
the spring wind!

Does Sôgi allude to women who will not give in to powerful men (excluding poets, of course)? Later poets suggest ways blossoms might defend themselves: *"Oh, for a blossom / that would tell the wind, stop, / don't blow me away!"*(ちらすなと風にものいふ花も哉　つくは*chirasuna to kaze ni mono iu hana mogana* ryôa 1356); "The full bloom – / choke up the wind's throat / with your scent!" (風の口も匂にむせよ花盛　夢見草*kaze no kuchi mo nioi <u>ni</u> museyo hanazakari* anon? 1656). Yeah, *right!*

吹つくせ花さかぬ間の春の風　能阿 大発句集
fuki-tsukuse hana sakanu ma no haru no kaze nôami 1396-1471
(blow-exhaust! blossom bloom-not space's spring-wind/s)

oh, spring winds,
blow yourselves out before
the cherries bloom!

風もまた知らぬ間にさけ春の花　宗祇
kaze mo mada shiranu ma ni sake haru no hana sôgi

(wind/s even still know/s-not-while bloom! spring-blossoms)

さかでまつ嵐をつくせ春の花　宗祇
saka de matsu arashi o tsukuse haru no hana sôgi -1502
(blooming-not wait gale/s[acc] exhaust! spring-blossoms)

spring blossoms,
bloom before the winds
find you out!

until the storms
blow out, spring blossoms,
hold your bloom!

The poor blossoms! Old Sôgi tells them to step on it and bloom before they are blown, then, to wait until the way is clear . . . If he had any daughters, he must have driven them crazy!

一とせの風や今ふく花盛　宗祇 老葉
hitotose no kaze ya ima fuku hanazakari sôgi
(one-year's wind/s!/: now blowing blossom-acme)

見る人を風もまちけり花盛　宗祇 老葉
miru hito o kaze mo machikeri hanazakari sôgi
(viewing people[acc.] wind-too waits[emph] bloom-acme)

wouldn't you know it!

blossom peak
and the storm of the year
is blowing *now*

the full bloom:
the wind, too, waits for
blossom viewers

Speeding up or slowing down is no help when a storm has the blossom's number, and ours . . . . !

時は今花の世なれや風もなし　宗祇 老葉
toki wa ima hana no yo nareya kaze mo nashi sôgi 1420-1502
(time-as-for now blossoms' world becomes/ is wind even not)

now is the time
that flowers own the world
it is windless

the wind is out:
seize the time! it is yours!
blossom world

In real life as in his poems, Sôgi managed to cover all bases. Could he have coined this "time is now!" (*toki wa ima*) which seems to be a cross between vernacular Zen and *carpe diem*?

花さかりこゝろにかかる風もなし　宗祇
hanazakari kokoro ni kakaru kaze mo nashi sôgi - 1502
(blossom-acme heart-on rest/weigh wind even not)

the bloom full
and no wind that weighs
upon the mind

A good day. From other *ku,* we know Sôgi liked just enough breeze to cause some petals to spill over.

wind

ちらしつゝ花をやつさぬ風も哉　心敬 大発
chirashi tsutsu hana o yatsusanu kaze mogana　shinkei
(falling-while blossoms[acc] wear-out-not wind wish-for)

花盛ちらさぬ程の風も哉　宗祇 大発句帳
hanazakari chirasanu hodo no kaze mogana　sôgi
(blossom-acme scatter-not degree of wind wish-for)

<blockquote>
oh, for a wind
that could scatter blossoms
with no harm done!
</blockquote>

<blockquote>
the full bloom:
oh, for just enough wind
not to scatter it!
</blockquote>

Sôgi inherited his wishing for the wind to do just this and not that from Shinkei (Ridiculous requests go back to Japan's first anthology of poetry, the *Manyôshû*. Song #1223 asks the wind to help blow a rowed boat to shore *yet* not raise any waves!). Since all cherry blossoms but some of the eight-fold varieties fall apart before they fall – the petals scatter one at a time – the desire for wind that could leave blossoms whole is a tall order indeed! Shinkei may well be thinking of women, for other worse *ku* of his note how *"The tempest / forgets the blossoms / after they fall"* (ちるを見て花をわするゝ嵐哉　心敬 さゝめこと *chiru o mite hana o wasururu arashi kana*) and *"Falling blossoms / ravished by the tempest / lose their way"* (ちる花や嵐につれて迷ふらん 心敬 自髪 *chiru hana ya arashi ni tsurete mayouran* -1475). ☆ If I misread, and they mean: *"Watching petals fly / the blossoms are forgotten: / mountain storm,"* and *"Scattering petals – / I wish I could get lost / with the wind!"* I must beg monk Shinkei's apology.

見る人に風はおくれよ花盛　宗祇 大発句帳
miru hito ni kaze wa okureyo hanazakari　sôgi 1420-1502
(viewing people-to wind-as-for send! blossom-acme)

<blockquote>
it's full bloom
some wind would be fine
for the viewers
</blockquote>

<blockquote>
send some breeze
to those who are viewing!
the bloom heat
</blockquote>

<blockquote>
blossoms in heat
share some breeze with us
the peeping toms
</blockquote>

It is unclear who is is being addressed, whether the mountain is being asked for some wind or the blossoms and my "peeping toms" is out of line . . . Perhaps we could title it *Pink Suffocation*.

散花の花より起る嵐哉　青蘿 新五子
chiribana no hana yori okiru arashi kana　seira -1791
(fallen blossoms' blossoms-from arise storm!/?/'tis)

<blockquote>
gales arise
from the fallen blossoms
themselves
</blockquote>

<blockquote>
a tempest!
rising from the petals
of the fallen
</blockquote>

One reading assumes the general, and one a specific case. I could not capture both together. The second reading evokes the image of a pink whirlwind, a petal dust devil, which a modern poet saw as the manifestation of a cherry god/dess (I recall reading a translation in the *Japan Times* about ten years ago and liking it. Found it! See *ku* #48-88! Oddly, it does seem male.)

ふけ嵐けさは待みつ花盛　宗祇
fuke arashi kesa wa machimitsu hanazakari　sôgi
(blow, storm! this morn-as-for awaited bloom-acme)

ちるもみん風もうかれよ花盛　宗祇
chiru mo min kaze mo ukareyo hanazakari　sôgi
(falling also see-let's wind-too crazy-get! bloom-acme)

<blockquote>
blow ye, winds!
this morning the full bloom
we've waited for!
</blockquote>

<blockquote>
let's see them fall!
you, too, wind get crazy!
blossoms in heat
</blockquote>

There are about three days when a cherry is in full-bloom (maybe days 4-6 of a blossom's 7). Either Sôgi is of more than one mind as to ideal viewing conditions, or he wants different conditions for different days of the *hanami,* or both.

花に風かろくきてふけ酒の泡　嵐雪
hana ni kaze karoku kite fuke sake no awa ransetsu - 1707
(blossoms-with/to wind lightly come!/ing blow!/ing *sake's* foam)

wind to the blossoms
come and lightly blowing raise
bubbles on my brew!

This, by a protégé of Bashô's, shows more sensitivity to details than the older *ku*. It could be a *haikai* remake of Sôgi's call for a few blossoms to fall in order that the color=eros bubbled, which we saw in the *Bloom-heat* chapter (*ku* #10-25,26). Sorry, I blew it, but the original is also cacophonous.

見尽して後おもしろや風の花　玄化 花七日
mi-tsukushite ato omoshiroya kaze no hana genka 1777
(see-exhausting, afterwards pleasant wind's blossoms)

the jaded blossom-viewer

i've had my fill　　　　　　　　　　　　i've seen it all
so the wind is welcome　　　　　　　now i'd watch the wind
to the flowers　　　　　　　　　　　have his way

花軍や春の血気の夕嵐　厚成 夢見草
hana-ikusa ya haru no kekki no yû-arashi kosei 1656
(blossom-uprising/battle!/?/: spring's blood-spirit's evening-gale)

red sky at night

a blossom riot!　　　　　　　　　　　a dusk storm brings
a storm at dusk spreads　　　　　　the animal spirits of spring:
spring's temper　　　　　　　　　　blossom uprising!

The title was the only way to work in the "blood" found literally but not figuratively in the original. Suffice it to say that this poet would not agree with the static utopia desired by many. He sees the wind as aiding circulation (too bad for the overdone *hana-ikusa,* blossom uprising).

神風をいさなき給へ花盛　康甘 毛吹草
kamikaze o izanaki tamae hanazakari kokan 1645
(god/s-wind/s[obj] invite[+honorific] bloom-acme)

the bloom so full　　　　　　　　　　ancient *kamikaze*
would thou deign to come　　　　　may we invite your honor
mighty godwinds?　　　　　　　　　to this full bloom!

This poet may like petal blizzards and wonder what typhoon-force winds, like those that destroyed the Mongol armada, could do, but the point is the bloom is so full only the *kamikaze* could do it right. Misreading *"o"* as *"mo"* (too), I first translated *"Divine winds, the pink of the bloom is for you, too."*

人は散り花は風ふく夕哉　心敬
hito wa chiri hana wa kaze fuku yûbe kana shinkei -1475
(people-as-for falling/scattering blossoms-as-for wind blows evening!)

<table>
<tr><td>people scatter,
wind wipes up the bloom
this evening</td><td>this is the night
we leave while the wind
takes the bloom</td></tr>
</table>

Is the poet on a hill-top? How beautiful to watch people– and petals scatter! Or, how beautiful it must have been in a time when people wore good colors and cuts of clothing. The conquering of the world – or at least the Far East, including Japan, by ugly Occidental, mostly sport-culture-derived primary color is an aesthetic tragedy. If those in charge of art and design schools had any sense of beauty whatsoever, they would waste little time on so-called fine art and devote themselves to re-creating an environment, that is the landscape, buildings and clothing that surround us! It is hard to say if we are talking bloom in trees or petals on the ground. The pun (we scatter=litter, while the wind blows=wipes-up the bloom) doesn't really English.

ちらはふけ花に恨みん風もなし　宗祇
chiraba fuke hana ni uramin kaze mo nashi　sôgi 1421-1502
(falling-if/when blow! blossom/s-by begrudge-would wind[emph.] not)

when they fall,
blow! no blossom hates
wind for *that!*

There is no *"that"* in the original. My reading is influenced by my memory of Ben Franklin's "Letter to a Young Man," advising him that if he had to do it, he should make an older woman's day rather than ruining a younger woman's name.

朽木にも更に花さく嵐哉　紹巴　大発句帳　　　ふけ嵐木かくれに朽は花もなし 紹巴 大発句帳
kutsuki ni mo sara ni hana saku arashi kana jôha -1602　　*fuke arashi kogakure ni kuchiba hana mo nashi*　jôha
(rotten-tree/s-on even further blossoms bloom gale!)　　(blow! gale tree-covert-in rot-if blossoms even not)

<table>
<tr><td>dead trees, too
once again blossom:
the tempest!</td><td>blow ye winds!
dead rot in the brush
has no bloom</td></tr>
</table>

Wind the equalizer: it spreads bloom around. **Note:** the second *ku* may be a unique environmentally sound justification for the wind: *it lets air and light into thickets thereby making bloom possible.*

吹く風と谷の水としなかりせばみ山がくれの花を見ましや　つらゆき？古今集18
fukukaze to tani no mizu to shinakariseba miyamagakure no hana o mimashiya　kokinshû 905

elemental insight

ah, were it not
for wind and water flowing
through the dale

<table>
<tr><td>could we ever know them:
the blossoms in the ravine?</td><td>who could see the cherries
blooming beyond the pale?</td></tr>
</table>

風うれし目の及ばざる山櫻 登舟 四季発→千? 句
kaze ureshi me no yobazaru yamazakura toshû 1689
(wind delighted eyes-reach-not mountain cherry)

wind's a delight!
mountain cherry blossoms
beyond my sight

this windfall
of petals a joy: what tree
what mountain?

wild cherry

petals from blossoms
i cannot see! the wind is
very good to me!

The original *ku*, as per the first reading, is obscure (unless you know *waka* tradition). In the second reading, I *try* to fill in between the lines. The childish Keigu, who was thrilled to discover that bird doo was not the only thing to drop from the sky, paraverses it like this:

pink present

petals fluttering
down from the blue: wind,
thank you!

If *you* notice the petals, the birds and bees probably do too. As a rule, lighter things travel further and blossoms that fall apart a petal at a time rather than plopping down *en toto*, have an advertising advantage. Petals caught in convections can fly for miles (専門家の御意見は？). Issa beat Keigu by centuries, though he chose to emphasize the divine element of the petals' beauty:

天からでも降たるやうに桜哉 一茶
ten* kara demo futtaru yô ni sakura kana issa 1812
(heaven-from even fall-as/like cherry[blossom petals])

falling down
like they came from heaven
cherry petals

p.s. *Ame* might be a better pronunciation for heaven here, but the official index for Issa's *hokku* lists it as *ten*.

It so happens that the validity or falsity of the oldest mention, or *possible* mention, of the cherry in Japanese – in the *Chronicle of Japan* (720AD) – rests largely upon the nature of wayward petals.

> In the sixth year, eleventh month of the reign of Emperor Richû (402 AD), he and his Empress were out on a pleasure boat in Ichishi Pond when a cherry blossom/petal fell into his sake cup. Surprised by the unseasonable [*toki-naranu*] blossom, the Emperor ordered a courtier to find it, which he did, on Wakigamino mountain.

The flower was bestowed the name "infant cherry" for its precocity – *Month 11* being January by the Gregorian calendar. The name was likewise given to a palace and the courtier, but the more interesting question to *me* is whether the blossom was *whole* or a *petal* (proof of cherry-hood).

ちる花を追かけてふ(ゆ)く嵐哉　失明＝つくば, 定家＝山の井
chiru hana o oikakete fuku (yuku) arashi kana　anon. 1356, sadaie 1648
(falling/scattering blossoms[acc] pursuing-blow/wipe(go) gale!/'tis))

mop-up operation

chasing after	in hot pursuit
the falling blossoms,	of the scattering petals
the tempest	strong winds

With that title, I would not wonder if some readers were to write the authorities to have my poetic license revoked. To tell the truth, I had the poet's name wrong and thought the *ku* a boring paraverse of earlier ones until finding out from Blyth that it was by Fujiwara Sadaie (1162-1241). He uses it (*"The storm / Goes pursuing / The scattering blossoms"*) as one of two examples "of early haiku (continuing to be called *hokku*, wrongly, up to the time of Shiki)." (*History of Haiku*, vol.1)) I agree with Blyth's parenthetical statement. We have *plenty* of 5-7-5 *ku* surely not intended for opening link-verse sessions (the official use of *hokku*) going way back. We have seen many (mostly by Sôgi) in this book.

父を失へる人に・悲しみの風は木のもと花もなし　昌察 三籟
kanashimi no kaze wa konomoto hana mo nashi　shôsatsu 1734
(sadness's wind-as-for tree-below/about blossom/s even not)

to one who lost his father

a sad wind:
not a petal remains
by the tree!

The first part of the *ku* might also be read, "the grieving wind." For once, the poet seems to identify – or have his friend identify – with the wind. But let us not end the chapter on a sad note.

花さそふなごりを雲に吹きとめてしばしはにほへ春の山風　藤原雅經
hana sasou nagori o kumo ni fukitomete shibashi wa nioe haru no yamakaze　shinkokinshû #145 1205

nose-gay in the sky?

*Blow, then, into a cloud keepsakes of your blossom loves,
So the scent remains if but a while, spring mountain wind!*

Absurd? *Perhaps*. But, the idea of a cloud as a bag to store things is based on plentiful evidence of the anecdotal kind. Clouds *have* rained frogs and fish and god knows what! Here, I assume the idea was probably petals; possibly only their scent. I hope the zanny fun of Fujiwara Gakei's old *waka* does not make the next two *ku* by Sôgi seem bland by comparison.

風やミぬこゝろにのこる春のはな　宗祇
kaze yaminu kokoro ni nokoru haru no hana　sôgi -1502
(wind stops　heart-in remain/ing spring's blossoms)

the wind ceases.
spring's blossoms remain
within my heart

風をみて花にわするゝ心哉　宗祇
kaze o mite hana ni wasururu kokoro kana sôgi -1502
(wind[acc.] seeing blossoms-in forget heart/mind!/'tis)

<blockquote>
seeing the wind
i forget myself
in the blossoms
</blockquote>

The inverse side of the last *ku*? Note that the *kokoro=heart/mind/spirit/soul* becomes "myself" here. But, "seeing" the wind? I recall that in the folklore of one of the Carolinas, pigs were said to be able to see the wind. But I am unsure of what it means here. It could mean the way the blossoms scatter, *i.e.,* the flying petals. Or, it could not.

花に風吹治つたり青葉の笛　直方 太夫櫻?
hana ni kaze fuki-naottari aoba no fue naokata 1680
(blossoms-in/to wind blows-)

<blockquote>
blowing afresh
the blossom wind plays
a leaf flute
</blockquote>

saigyô's good cherry wind: eleven *waka*

Bashô's favorite role-model, Saigyô, the 12c nobleman-monk, whose famous *waka* on dying below the blossoms and numerous others on heart/mind (*kokoro*) were introduced in Book II, must have written dozens of poems about the wind and his favorite flower. I started to weave them into the last chapter, but on second thought decided it might be better to keep them together so we might get a better feel for the witty monk whose name is forever linked with the cherry blossom.

憂き世には留め置かじと春風の散らすは花を惜しむなりけり　西行 山家集#117
ukiyo ni wa todome okaji to harukaze no chirasu wa hana o oshimu narikeri saigyô -1190

<blockquote>

for their own good

*not wanting
to leave them in this
world of woe*

*the spring wind blows off
the blossoms out of pity*
</blockquote>

Which is better, slowly shriveling up and turning brown or being blasted through the air? Today, most of us think hanging on is best for humans but not necessarily for blossoms, which gardeners tend to "top." In Saigyô's day, most men would have been ashamed to even *want* to live until they died. In Saigyô's next poem (not given here), he expresses a wish to accompany the petals.   ☆it's a Buddhist sign.

峯に散る花は谷なる木にぞ咲くいたくいとはじ春の山風　西行#155
mine ni chiru hana wa tani naru ki ni zo saku itaku itowaji haru no yamakaze saigyô -1190

every tree a cherry!

the blossoms
that fall from the peaks
blooming below

how can we in the valleys
hate the mountain wind?

the flowers
blow down the peaks
and blossom

in the valley trees: how
can we hate the wind?

Not only does the wind blow for the ultimate benefit of the blossoms, but for all of us. The original spoke of valley trees in which the blossoms – or anglicizing, petals – presumably catch.

立ちまがふ峯の雲をばはらふとも花を散らさぬ嵐なりせば　西行#114
tachimagau mine no kumo oba harau to mo hana o chirasanu arashi nariseba saigyô -1190

discrimination

it would be nice
to have storm winds that
could clean off

clouds from those peaks
yet let the blossoms be!

Waka asking the wind to clear off view-blocking clouds or not to blow off blossoms were commonplace and Saigyô thought to combine them. The next seems to be in the spirit of *haikai*.

花と見ばさすが情をかけましを雲とて風のはらふなるべし　西行#133
hana to miba sasuga nasake o kakemashi o kumo tote kaze no haraunarubeshi saigyô -1190

dutiful blast

seeing blossoms
how could the wind not
want to help?

it is, after all supposed to
clear away clouds, right?

☆ *The foolish wind, thinking blossoms cloud, blows 'em away!*   Saigu (西愚)

山ざくら枝きる風の名残りなく花をさながらわが物にする　西行#140
yamazakura eda kiru kaze no nagori naku hana o sanagara wagamono ni suru saigyô - 1190

while petals lie below **petals face the wind**

the mountain wind
cuts through limbs without
a trace remaining

of the bloom he raped
as if it were nothing!

mountain cherries,
the limb-cutting wind
would carry off

even blossoms already
lying on the ground!

"Raped" in the old sense of carrying off in marriage. The poem's meaning is debatable because the first meaning is more plausible while the original caption (風前落花) favors the second. If I rip the "limb-cutting" adjective from the Wind and drop it down later, a third reading is possible: *"Mountain cherries: / Though the wind takes / every blossom; / I view the bare branches / and call them my own."*

梢ふく風の心はいかがせんしたがふ花のうらめしきかな　西行 #122
kozue fuku kaze no kokoro wa ikaga sen shitagau hana no urameshiki kana saigyô - 1190

male-content, or why we blame them

*the heart and mind
of the wind blowing through
the cherry boughs*

*is fixed: so we blame them,
the blossoms for giving in?*

*for the mind
of the wind nothing
can be done*

*we begrudge blossoms
for letting him have fun*

*lust is given –
what would you do
about the wind?*

*what hurts is to see it –
how blossoms go along!*

After reading many poems that hate the wind for blowing off bloom this is a breath of fresh air; but am I right to make the wind an alpha male and identify us with the powerless? The wind has been let off the hook, but what can you do about things that are l*ike that?* In the maternal words of Tammy Wynette, excusing her man for crawling in the door: "a man is just a man." If the above reading is correct, the *waka* also explains why men, rightly or wrongly, resent women. Yet, look at the next:

心得つただ一筋に今よりは花を惜しまで風をいとはん 西行#131
kokoro etsu tada hitosuji ni ima yori wa hana o oshima de kaze o itowan saigyô - 1190

*i have got it!
from now on i'm taking
a single course:*

*not blaming blossoms
i shall hate the wind!*

Saigyo's *waka* took both sides of practically anything. Selective editing could make him into male chauvinistic pig or the world's foremost feminist.

あながちに庭をさへはく嵐かな さこそ心に花をまかせめ 西行#129
anagachi ni niwa o sae haku arashi kana sakoso kokoro ni hana o makaseme saigyô -1190

*and the gale has
enough strength left over
to sweep the yard!*

*we must, then, give him
his will with the bloom*

*the gale even
insists on sweeping
my garden!*

*how can i not entrust
him with the bloom?*

Is the message that we can't fight the wind's libido, and he does, after all, clean up afterwards?

寄花恋・つれもなき人に見せばや桜花 風にしたがふ心よわさを　西行#597
tsure mo naki hito ni misebaya sakura bana kaze ni shitagau kokoro yowasa o   saigyô -1190

wooing ala blossom

i wish i could
show this person who
won't love me

the heart of a blossom
giving in to the wind!

Poet=wind. He wishes the object of his one-sided love were as pliant as cherry blossoms (The original specifies *sakura*). There are many old Japanese *waka* wishing that the other could only "be in my heart," or, as another of Saigyô's puts it, would *exchange* hearts for a while, i.e. showing one's own heart=love; but wanting the other to see the heart of yet another may be an idea without precedent.

いかでわれ此世の外の思ひ出でに 風をいとはで花をながめん・む 西行#108
ika de ware kono yo no hoka no omoide ni kaze o itowa de hana o nagamen saigyô -1190

how can i keep 　　　　　　　　　　*how can i view*
good thoughts of paradise　　　　*blossoms without hate*
with me viewing　　　　　　　　　*for that wind,*

blossoms and not hate　　　　　*as if i already was there*
that goddamn wind?　　　　　　*on the far side looking in?*

Bad feelings could translate into the spirit world and cause trouble for those who held them and others.

春ふかみ枝もゆるがで散る花は風のとがにはあらぬなるべし 西行#128
haru fukami eda mo yuruga de chiru hana wa kaze no toga ni wa aranu naru beshi saigyô -1190

late in spring
blossoms are falling
from still limbs:

surely the wind cannot
be blamed for this!

Blossoms will fall whether or not the wind blows. This speaks of the nature of *both* parties.

まちてちれ花にかこたん風もなし 宗祇
machite chire hana ni kakotan kaze mo nashi sôgi -1502
(wait! fall! blossoms-to complain-would wind-even-not)

flowers, wait　　　　　　　　　　　*blossoms, wait!*
to fall! how can i rant　　　　　　*who do i blame if you fall*
without the wind?　　　　　　　　*without the wind?*

don't scatter yet
we need a fall-guy, blossoms
wait for the wind

don't fall on me
blossoms! – there's no wind
for us to blame

blossoms, wait
to fall: i've no complaint
without the wind

Stephen D. Carter's translation, read after writing the above: *"Wait to scatter, / blossoms: for now there's no wind / I can complain to"* (*Traditional Japanese Poetry*).

吹け／＼と花に欲なし鯉 千代尼 古今句鑑
fuke fuke to/do hana ni yokunashi koinobori chiyo-ni 1701-75
(blow! blow! blossoms-for desire-not [wind]carp-raising[flying])

blow! blow! where's
your lust for blossoms, now?
windless paper carps

blow, wind, blow!
where is your blossom-lust?
limp paper carps

In Spring, the wind embodied desire. The carps, flown from poles in early summer, represent boys (one fish per boy) in the house beneath them. Could the *ku* indirectly ("now" and "limp" are *mine*) complain that men, in this polygamous society, lost desire for a woman once mating had issue?

散はなのうらみにかはるあらし哉 宗祇
chiru hana [or, *chiribana*] *no urami ni kawaru arashi kana* sôgi -1502
(falling [or, *fallen*] blossom=petals' grudge/hate-to change gale/s!/?/'tis)

the gale renews
this time, with the fury
of falling petals

now female
the fury of the petals
a pink storm

the heart-burne
of fallen blossoms fresh
fuel for the gale

~~~~~~

<div style="text-align: center;">

落花舞ひあがり花神の立つごとし 大野林火
rakka maiagari kashin no tatsu gotoshi ôno rinka 20c

Fallen cherry petals / Whirl suddenly up – / Like the flower god standing.
trans. Kristen Deming + Kôji Suzuki ("Haiku Moments" *Japan Times* 4/11/1996)

</div>

~~~~~~

Sôgi's is extraordinarily *haikai* for a 15c *ku*. Please forgive the olde-english usage "heart-burne" in the second reading and the outlandish third reading. The original does not translate. It has the tempest, acting from male libido when it comes after the blossoms on the tree, *change* into female fury, or to be precise, *urami*, or grudge/enmity, something arising from spurned, deserted, betrayed or unsatisfied love. Such bad spirits were even thought to possess others (as depicted in *The Tale of Genji*). But, why get spooky? It is enough to think of a painting, or rather a set of paintings: the *Before & After* of Rembrant's *Joseph and Potiphar's Wife*. ◎ My respondent votes for the second reading, below ↓

ねるほどは風ふく花の木の間かな 成美
neru hodo wa kaze fuku hana no konoma kana seibi -1816
(sleep-mount/degree-as-for wind blows blossom-trees-among/space!)

the more you sleep
the more the wind blows
through the bloom

a grove of cherry
the wind blows through
like sleeping breath

Cataracts of Petals
花の瀧
hana-no-taki

```
         f
       a l l
    ing  blos
  soms - we  real
 ly  should  call  them
s i l e n t   c a t a r a c t s
```

ちる花は音無の瀧といひつべし 昌意 毛吹草

chiru hana wa oto nashi no taki to iitsu beshi shôi 1645
(falling blossoms-as-for sound-not's waterfall-as say should)

○源はただこの峰や花の瀧 宗春？再現
minamoto wa tada kono mine ya hana no taki sôshun 1734
(source-as-for only this peak!/: blossom-cataract/fall)

the head-water
is on this peak, see it?
blossom cataract

色の水の湧き出る山か花の瀧 昌察 再現
iro no mizu no wakideru yama ka hana no taki shôsai
(colored water's boiling-out mountain? blossom-fall)

a mountain where
pink water bubbles forth?
blossom cataracts

The flows of petals down a mountain were likened to cataracts. Sôshun points out the highest mountain cherry. Shôsai has turned the old metaphor into a riddle. I turned the "color/erotic-water" in the original *pink* for "color" would be too weak (or meaningless), while erotic would be too strong (and inane). . An older *ku* by Sôgi is less interesting for being no more than descriptive metaphor, unless you can really *see it,* in which case it is not bad: *"Waves of blossoms / cascading the boulders / what a gale!"* (瀧なみに花も岩こす嵐哉 宗祇 *taki nami ni hana mo iwa kosu arashi kana* - 1502).

めさましや浴て見上る瀧櫻 旧室 古今句帖
mezamashi ya abite mi-agaru takizakura kyûshitsu -1764
(eye-opener/waker:/! pouring see-up cataract-cherry/ies)

eye-opening!
showered by petals i look up
the cherry fall

alarum clock?
i gaze up the cataract
of white petals

English lacks a general term for things that wake one up, but the idea of a cataract of petals in the face is bracing enough. I added white, for when they fall, even the pink ones are generally white though I often keep them pink for in our minds some of that pink is still there just as it is in the dark.

鶯や水鳥となす花の滝　重頼 犬子
uguisu ya suichô to nasu hana no taki shigeyori 1633
(nightingale [bush-warbler]: waterbird/s-into-become bloom-cataract)

bush warblers
are now water fowl:
blossom cataract

To maximize the hyperlogical wit of the *haikai,* for once, I did not call the *uguisu* a "nightingale."

流れては田毎の花やちる櫻　湖青 未来記　　鯉のぼる瀧の濁りや山櫻　毛納 匂塞
nagarete wa tagoto no hana ya chiruzakura kosei 1765　　*koi noboru taki no nigori ya yamazakura* mogan
(flowing-as-for field-every's blossoms/petals!/: falling-cherry/ies)　　(carp climbs cataract's cloudiness!/?/: mountain cherry)

flowing along　　　　　　　　　the waterfalls
flowers for each field　　　　　the carp climb, clouded!
cherry petals　　　　　　　　　mountain cherry

In the first *ku,* the petals are in water flowing from mountain-side paddy to paddy to paddy, connected by tiny, slightly pink waterfalls. The carp, rather than the salmon, was the symbol of a climbing fish in Japan and the petals, pretty or not, cloud mountain water, identified with pristine clarity.

鯉のぼる戦術も哉花の瀧　定清 暁山
koi noboru senjitsu mogana hana no taki sadakiyo *fl* 1670
(carp/s climbing war-arts wish-for blossom-cataract/s)

i sure could use the martial art
of a carp to climb those
petal cataracts

"Carp climbing" (*koinobori*), actually tubular banners, are raised to celebrate boys and wish them the strength to climb social cataracts and gain success in life. Strangely enough, I have never seen carp demonstrate this ability, for I only see them in ponds. Maybe someone should train them to jump up into a fountain to get food or something.

how i wish
i could climb like a carp
blossom falls

Does the poet mean he would like to climb cataracts full of the petals or a steep mountain with metaphorical cataracts of blossoms? Regardless, my guess is that he fantasizes reaching the tree on high but in reality has knee or hip problems.

髪の花女瀧男瀧のかざし哉　許六 風俗文選
kami no hana metaki otaki no kazashi kana kyôroku -1715
(hairs' blossoms female cataract male cataract's decoration!/'tis)

petals in the hair
decorated female and
male cataracts

The concept of blossom-cataract led the poet to coin a new conceit, *hair as a cataract* – the word is far from felicitous, but "waterfall" is too *explicitly* liquid to work as widely as the Japanese *taki*.

ちる花をあつめて瀧のみかさ哉　蓼太
chiru hana o atsumete <u>taki no mikasa</u> kana　ryôta 1707-87
(falling blossoms/petals[acc] gathering cataract-[honorific] hat!/'tis)

collecting petals
an honorable hat makes
a pink cataract

gathered petals
turn a noble *hanami* hat
into a cataract

Kasa prefixed with *mi* is the *hat* of an honorable personage. I guess that the wit here is in a pun: *takinomi,* or "cataract-drinking." Vulgar chugalugging and spilling pretty petals are conflated.

~~~~~~

花に寝て散りくる花を雪崩とも　石原八束
hana ni nete chirikuru hana o nadare to mo　ishihara yatsuka -1998
(blossoms-by sleeping falling-come blossoms/petals avalanche as even)

napping under blossoms
the tumbling blossoms
seem an avalanche

trans. Kondô and Higginson (*Red Fuji*)

I did not go out looking for 20c cherry blossom haiku, but this one came to me. It happens to depict something I, too, once witnessed on a still day under over-ripe blossoms (Somewhere in the thousands of pages of my notepad I have yet to edit, there is a similar *ku!*), and beats the waterfall analogy. So does this:

わび人の涙に似たる桜かな風身にしめばまづこぼれつつ　西行
wabibito no namida ni nitaru sakura kana kaze mi ni shimeba mazu koboretsutsu　saigyô -1190

*like the tears
of a mountain hermit
cherry petals*

*the cold wind bites
and they start falling*

Saigyô's poem was included in the *nostalgia* section of one of his compilations, which would suggest (to me) his eyes were wet from remembering his days roaming about like the wind having its way with the blossoms. But I prefer to imagine indefinable emotion accompanying tears triggered by the cold wind (the verb *shimeru* suggests it was cold).[1]

~~~~~~

1. *Indefinable Emotion* Teardrops once streamed into my ears while i lay half-asleep at dawn because of the overlapping cries of a dozen or so bell-cricket (called *evening*-cicada by Japanese, they also sing early in the morning). True, I was suffering through a one-sided love-affair (with a married woman who loved someone else who didn't love *her*: can it get more hopeless than *that?*); but I cannot remember *specific* thought coming into it. The sweet rhythmic and tonal crescendo and diminuendo of the polyphonic chorus turned my raw emotion straight into tears. It took me completely by surprise. I think that men and women in a less jaded age than ours would have had such experiences more often (or, we rely on movies?). The *sakura* might well have done it to them *every* year!

50

Where do all the Petals Go?
(and what are they good for?)

落花ノ始末
rakka-no-shimatsu

山桜ちれ／＼腹にたまるほど 一茶
yamazakura chirejire hara ni tamaru hodo issa 1814
(mountain-cherry fall! fall! belly-on/in pile-up/fill amount)

mountain cherries!
drop those petals till they
fill our bellies!

Japanese *belly* idioms could fill a book. An earlier *ku* by Sanpû (1646-1732) locates the full bloom "throughout the big belly" (花盛り大腹中となりけらし 杉風 *hanazakari ôharajû to narikerashi*), whatever that means. Here, Issa means both the belly of the mountain – the part roughly midway between the peak and foot – *and* his own, in the sense of being so satiated he will remain content for some time.

どん欲も連てちれ／＼山桜 一茶
donyoku mo tsurete chirejire yamazakura issa 1810
(deep-greed even take/accompanying scatter! mountain-cherries)

pink ablution	*pink scapegoats*
blow, blow away our avarice! oh, wild cherry petals, go!	scatter, ye wild cherry blossoms, and take my greed with you!

Are these petals performing an ablution or being used as scapegoats, or both?

欲面へ浴せかけたる桜哉 一茶 遺稿
yokuzura e abise-kaketaru sakura kana issa -1827
(greedy-face-to pour-down cherry/blossoms/petals!/'tis)

showering down on faces full of desire cherry blossoms	utterly drenching our greedy maws cherry petals	like cold water splashed on pure lust cherry petals!

On gamblers? On men ringing a stage where petals real and false were used as stage props. On cherry blossom lovers? Probably the best reading is none of the above. Our greed is for *life*.

散桜よしなき口を降埋よ 一茶
chiru sakura yoshinaki kuchi o furi-umeyo issa 1810
(falling cherry[blossoms] foul mouths[acc.] falling-fill!)

      falling petals,   fall petals, fall
fall, and fill that man's   until you bury all of
      filthy mouth!   the foul mouths

"Filthy" and "fowl" is not quite right. This mouth – particular or generic – that is up to no good may be criticizing the cherry blossoms, trying to pick a fight or saying bad things about someone. Who knows! Chronologically speaking, a chapter should not start with Issa, but he wrote so much on petals.

あれ／＼といふ口へちるさくら哉 一茶
are are to iu kuchi e chiru sakura kana issa 1825
(that/huh! that/huh! saying mouth-to fall/ing cherry!)

into a mouth
saying "wow!" "wow!"
cherry petals!

Issa likes to put flying things into mouths. It even happens to his *mosquitoes*. The above may be his best. A ridiculous earlier attempt: *"The open mouth / gets one, plop! / cherry petal"* (先明た口へぼったり桜哉 一茶 *mazu aketa kuchi e bottari sakura kana* issa 1818). *Bottari* is mimesis for something that "plops right in," namely sweet-rice cake called *sakura mochi*, wrapped in a brine-soaked cherry leaf, and the idea would be that one must open one's mouth, or *trust* to receive.

櫻ちる所なりけり膝かしら 嵐外   花ちるやいかにも黒き首筋へ 一茶
sakura chiru tokoro narikeri hizagashira rangai -1845   *hana chiru ya ika ni mo kuroki kubisuji e* issa -1827
(cherry-blooms place-becomes (final) lap-head)   (blossoms fall!/: ever so black neck-nape-on)

   our knee-caps: petals falling
the place where all   on the black nape of
  the petals fall!   a red-neck

The chairless see a lot more of their knees than the chaired. The area is smaller than, say, a lap, but smooth as a bald head (unlike laps, large but wrinkled), it makes a better canvas. There is also humor in things falling down on one's knees rather than vice versa. With Issa, we are talking about a weather-worn "blue-collar" neck contrasted with the delicate beauty of the pale pink petals. Such a neck would certainly show off the petals more than a delicate neck that would provide camouflage.

菅笠に日傘に散しさくら哉 一茶
sugegasa ni higasa ni chirishi sakura kana issa -1827
(sedge-hat/s-on parasol/s-on falling cherry[petals]!/'tis)

cherry petals
falling on hats of sedge
and parasol alike

In Japanese, hat and parasol are called *kasa* (only the characters 笠 & 傘, respectively, differ) and the hat does almost as good a job of shielding one from the sun as the parasols. I cannot tell if the intention is contrast (two different aesthetics) or equality, or if Issa meant to play the saying "a sedge hat and wife are one-<u>year</u>-things (*ichinenmono* are best the first year)" against the *hi*=sun=<u>day</u> in parasol. I assume the main point is that growing heat signals the arrival of summer. As a *senryû* puts it: *How hot it is! / the only sound, the calls / of sedge-hat sellers* (*atsuikoto suge kasa-uri no koe bakari* yanagidaru 9). Of course, these hats might conceal roving lovers, for such activity was a "hot thing."

むまやろや泥も嫌はで落る花　沾徳 1726
muma yaro ya doro mo kirawa de ochiru hana　sentoku
(yummy right? mud even hate-not-with fall/ing blossoms)

feels great, huh!
cherry blossoms gladly
fall into the mud

a pony path
the falling blossoms are
happy with mud

This old *ku* sounds more like Issa than most of Issa's own *ku*! The first five syllabets are probably colloquial: "yummy, right?" but they sound to me like they might be dialect for pony path 馬屋路, too.

大かたは泥にひつゝく桜哉　一茶
ôkata wa doro ni hittsuku sakura kana　issa - 1827
(most-as-for mud-in stick-stay cherry[blossom petals]!/'tis)

most end up
stuck in mud . . .
cherry blossoms

(trans. lanoue)

David Lanoue's translation is sufficient. Note that Issa's *ku*, unlike Sentoku's, just states a fact but is still evocative because of one word which may actually not be true: *most*.

山盛の花の吹雪や犬の椀　一茶
yamamori no hana no fubuki ya inu no wan　issa - 1827
(mountain-heap's blossom-blizzard!/: dog-bowl)

a petal blizzard
buffets a mountain
of dog food!

the petals fly
about a mountain
of dog food

Servings in Japanese are called "mountains." Is the dog eating in a petal blizzard? Gobbling so fast the petals on the food fly about like the down on a bird being mauled by a cat? Have petals that piled up (into a mountain) in an empty bowl flown up upon being hit by a gust of wind? Or, has Issa picked up the dog bowl full of petals and made the blizzard by tossing it into the air? (I should add that dog food in modern times is often *rice*. I have no idea what went into dog bowls, then!)

塵箱にへばり付たる桜哉　一茶 1813
chiribako ni hebaritsuitaru sakura kana　issa
(trash-box/bin-in clinging cherry[blossom-petals]!)

still clinging
to a rubbish bin
cherry petals

田楽のみそにくつゝく桜哉　一茶 1821
dengaku no miso ni kuttsuku sakura kana　issa
(field-happy[food-name]miso-to stick cherry[bl-p]!)

stuck fast
to brown bean paste
cherry petals

where to?

With the first one, I added the "still" to indicate my guess that it is a recently emptied bin, but I could be wrong. I couldn't fit the roasted *tofu* and *konjaku* (devil's tongue) inside the *miso* (bean-paste) coating into the poem, but regret *that* less than the loss of the name for the dish (*dengaku*), which, in Chinese characters, is "field-music/pleasure." Issa's petals on brownish bean-paste mimic his butterflies, who get stuck in this and that *and* provide a stronger zoom-in image than Bashô's petaled fish salad we saw in the *Food* chapter.

飴ン棒にべつたり付し桜哉　一茶
amenbo ni bettari tsukishi sakura kana   issa 1824
(lollipop-to thickly/closely sticking cherry/petals!/'tis)

plastered
to the lollipop
cherry petals

I am no relativist. I prefer this to petals in dog bowls, on dog shit, bean paste (itself identified with shit), garbage or avaricious faces. The *ku*, perhaps old Issa's last word on the subject, adds something the others lack. Cherry petals, to my mind at least, resemble little lips. Need more be said?

百石の小村をうづむさくらかな　許六
hyakuseki no komura o uzumu sakura kana   kyoroku -1715
(hundred-stone[tax=size] small village bury cherry/blossoms!/'tis)

a farming town
covered by a tidal wave:
cherry blossoms

I admit to taking hyperbolic license, but a straight translation was out of the question. We may be speaking more of a deluge of blossom-viewers than a blizzard of petals. The stones of tax are weight-units of the rice in which tax was paid. There was no need to specify this in the translation.

醉死ぬ先から花の埋みけり　丈艸
yoishinanu saki kara hana no uzumikeri   jôsô 1661-1704
(drunk/en-die before[bloom]-from blossoms' bury-for-good)

dead drunk?   before the *sake*
these blossoms will   kills me, i'll be buried
bury me first   by these petals

寝た人にちりかゝる花の吹雪哉　梅父 月夜
neta hito ni chirikakaru hana no fubiki kana   baifu 1776
(slept person-on falling-sets blossoms' blizzard!/'tis)

petal snow
falls on the man who
fell asleep

While Jôsô might have observed someone passed out, the first *ku* works best in the first-person (又、「七草薺」囃子の「渡らぬ先」の借り？). The key to the second *ku* is in the past-tense gerund, the "slept-person." Is this someone who waited a long time to see the petals fall but fell asleep first?

蒲団まく朝の寒さや花の雪　園女-1723
futon maku asa no samusa ya hana no yuki sonojo
(futon/quilt wrap morning's coldness!/: blossom-snow)

出ぎらひの身をふり埋め花の雪　成美
degirai no mi o furi-uzume hananoyuki seibi 1816
(go-out-hater's body[obj] fall-bury! blossom-snow)

a cold morning
even wrapped in a futon
blossom snow

blossom snow
fall and cover for good
this homebody

Blossom-snow usually means blossoms falling *like* snow but can also mean particularly white bloom that looks like snow on the tree. Sonojo, with her *futon,* might have fit better in the *Cold Cherries* (ch. 5). Seibi's *ku* works better in Japanese where a homebody is literally one who *doesn't go out,* for it implies his character won't let him quit the thinning bloomshade.

花吹雪土手に立派な倒れ者　柳多留 71-28
hanafubuki dote ni rippan na taoremono yanagidaru ()
(blossom-blizzard bank/levee-on splendid fallen one/s)

blossom blizzard
grand folk lie passed out
on the embankment

petal blizzard
on the levee the body of
a splendid drunk

This is a *senryû* and *senryû love drunks*. When cherry blossoms bloom, people who normally would not be likely to pass out in public, do. Embankments in Japan almost always serve as streets. Better puked and petaled than tarred and feathered!

散って一度に花見の人を埋めかし　子規
chitte ichido ni hanami no hito o uzumekashi shiki 1896
(falling/en one-time-in blossom-viewing people[acc.] bury!)

all together, *fall!*
and, falling, bury people
blossom viewing!

all together, *fall!*
& turn the blossom viewers
into blossom art!

At first, I thought *burial*; but, on second thought, Shiki's mood might be artistic rather rhan morbid, for the homophone of the emphatic *kashi* is 花姿, "flower-form," *i.e.* "a splendid sight," indeed.

散る花の木陰に残る道も哉　紹巴
chiru hana no kokage ni nokoru michi mogana jôha -1602
(fallen/ing blossoms' tree-shade-in remain path[+wish-for]!)

let's pray the path
can still be found after
the petals scatter!

i'd like to stay
in what was the shade
of the blossoms

Is this a sort of *hana-mayoi,* or blossom-bewilderment poem or something deeper yet? We have seen some hidden trails, but *haikai* do not play with trail-hiding, trail-blocking petals nearly as much as *waka* did, for such trope comes from the poetry of love and of death neither of which are central to *haikai* (though death seems common in recent years, perhaps because the average age of the poet has increased). Be that as it may, the first trail-blocking cherry blossoms/petals, in the premier 10c *waka* anthology are a one-of-a-kind poem borrowing from, but not about either subject:

where to ?

さくら花ちりかひくもれおいらくのこむといふなる道まがふがに　古今集 #349
sakura hana chirikaikumore oiraku no komu to iu naru michi magaugani　arawara-no narihira- (kokinshû 905)

(for the fortieth birthday of chancellor horikawa)

*cherry blossoms
flutter down and cloud
the path they say
old age is bound to come
and make him lose his way*

Year 40 四十 was considered to be the crossroads of life, perhaps because "crossroads" 四つ角 (*yotsukado*) has a 4 四 in it, and 10 十 is a cross (Do you recall the proto-*renga* with the chickadee, the bird with the name that puns as "from forty years old" eg. in the note for *Cherry Song* = ch.26?), after which one heads towards fifty, where "a life," by (Chinese) convention, ended. Personification of the abstract was common in Japanese poetry. In the *Manyôshû* (8c), we have *"If I could only / forget that face! For that / I'd make a fist / and strike Love, but I did / and the jerk didn't flinch"* (*omo-wasure*... #2574); in the *Kokinshû* (10c): *"Because love / he is attacking me / from pillow and foot, / my sole defense is lying / in the middle of the bed!"* (*makura yori ato yori koi no seme kureba semu kata na mi zo tokonaka ni oru* anon #1023). "Love" *means* "longing" or "The Blues," and "lying" here is lying "doubled up."

この里にたびねしぬべしさくら花ちりのまがひにいへぢわすれて 無名 古今集#72
kono sato ni tabineshinubeshi sakurabana no chiri no magai ni ieji wasurete　kokinshû 905

*i seem bound to sleep
in this village tonight:
led astray by falling
blossoms, i've forgotten
my way home*

(trans. LC)

petals, petals, everywhere

*well, i guess
i'll sleeping over here
in your town:

blossom-bewildered, lost
while homeward bound*

Cherry petals swirling through the air can be almost as thick as a blizzard and, because of the contrast with blue-sky and greater visibility of individual petals, more dizzying. Perhaps building on the old trope of cherry=female beauty distracting man from the moral=Buddhist path, this anonymous poet has the blossoms/petals stupify the traveler rather than simply cover-up the path. The original is not "your" town, but "this," as Lewis Cook translates. I like to imagine the poet presenting the poem to the inn-keeper, though I must admit that might be my *haikai* thought; for, with *waka*, it makes more sense to imagine him sending a copy off in a letter to friends waiting in the World, i.e., the capital.

山かぜにさくらふきまきみだれなむ花のまぎれにたちとまるべく 僧正へんぜう 古今集#394
yamakaze ni sakura fukimaki midarenamu hana no magire ni tachitomaru beku　kokinshû 905

< composed under the blossoms while seeing off prince urin-in from a relic ceremony >

*let the mountain wind
sweep the cherry petals
into the air where

dancing wildly they should
keep him here, enthralled*

There was a tradition of poems stopping the coming and going of others. Stopping lovers from leaving was the most common, followed by stopping friends or lords, and more rarely, preventing the dead from traveling to the other world. In the case of the 8c *Manyôshû* #468, the poet says he would have blocked the path for leaving the world had he only known where it was, so I suppose we could say it is not so much bringing back the dead as preventing a death; in the case of the 9c *Kokinshû* #829, however, the poet wishes he had tears enough to flood the Japanese equivalent of the River Styx, in which case she'd have to come back. Since all the tears suggest she was already good and dead, there can be no question that would be a resurrection. Then, there are the poems preventing someone or something from coming, of which the most common is Old Age. I bring this up both because, as we have seen, cherry petals eventually became a major prop in such poems (a comparative study and because it shows how Japanese poetry had lingering elements of what Japanese tend to call word-soul (*kotodama*) and we would call *charm* or *spell* or *prayer* in them.

しひて行く人をとどめむ桜花いづれを道と迷ふまでちれ よみ人しらず 古今集#403
shiite yuku hito o todomemu sakurabana izure o michi to madou made chire anon (kks 10c)

<blockquote>
Cherry blossoms,
stop this man who would
insist on going!

Drop your petals until
he cannot find the road!
</blockquote>

This poem by an anonymous poet is in a section of the *Kokinshû* called "songs of separation." In ancient Japanese poetry, even nobles often had to travel to the boondocks on official work and exile was common as the poetic, if not typical, punishment.[1] So this is not necessarily about a lover, though it brings to mind the many poems asking rain to fall or rivers to rise to impede a lover's departure. But, enough of these classic cherry petals with their limited tricks, asked to do man's bidding, let us return to the more diversified ways they are depicted, which is to say, experienced, in haiku.

散花はきの毒蛇ふむこゝち哉　重信 嵐山集
chiribana wa ki no doku ja fumu kokochi kana shigenobu 1651
(fallen blossoms-as-for piteous/regrettable[=venemous] snake tread feeling!/?/'tis)

<blockquote>
pity the petals!
i feel like i am walking
upon eggshells

feeling regret
i tread cherry petals as
if they were snakes

fallen blossoms
i'd sooner walk on vipers
then on you
</blockquote>

If petals can bury us, we can step on them. The "snake," added to the "poison" at the tail of the idiomatic phrase meaning "piteous," brings out the poet's trepidation. I like to imagine him trying to avoid crushing petals by leaping from bare space (or stone or footprint) to space.

---

1. Exile, the Punishment Fit for Poetry When exile is combined with love, as in the case where the husband gets exiled right after (or before?) marriage, the hopeless desire to prevent his departure rises highest of all, as expressed in this *furious* song # 3724 of the *Manyôshû*: *"How I wish for / fire from the heavens* [i.e., a catastrophe] */ to fold-up / burn and obliterate / the long road you go!"* (*kimi ga yuku michi no nagate o kuri-tatane-yaki-horobosamu ame no hi mogamo*). The "long road" went over the mountains to Echizen, the place of exile and she recognized that rain . . . or cherry blossoms would hardly make a dent in it. See Ella Wheeler Wilcox's *Attraction*.

散る花に踏べからずの札もなし 也有
chiru hana ni fumu bekarazu no fuda mo nashi yayû 1701-83
(falling blossom/petal/s-on step forbidden sign/label[emph] not)

<blockquote>
no sign warns:
it is forbidden to walk
upon the petals
</blockquote>

<blockquote>
no falling petal
bears a sign saying: *don't*
tread on me!
</blockquote>

When I told a Japanese friend I liked Yayû, he noted that he was affluent and could afford to be a sensitive gentleman. In our world, where the wealthy are typically crass and would triumphantly walk upon strewn roses, we could sure use more like Yayû! He may play on this *Kokinshû waka*:

山さとの庭よりほかの道もかな花ちりぬやと人もこそとへ　越前　新古今集#127
yamasato no niwa yori hoka no michi mogana hana chirinu ya to hito mo koso toe shinkokinshû 1205

<blockquote>
is there no other
path to take but this across
my hill retreat?

people, can't you see
the petals on the ground!
</blockquote>

花をふむ人は少年の心哉　末吉 17c
hana o fumu hito wa shonen no kokoro kana sueyoshi
(blossoms[acc.]tread person-as-for youth's heart!/?)

<blockquote>
walking on petals
men feel something
like teenagers
</blockquote>

花をふんでおなじくおしむ日あし哉 正則鷹筑波
hana o funde onajiku oshimu hiashi kana seisoku 1642
(blossoms[acc.]treading similarly regret sun-legs!/?)

<blockquote>
treading blossoms
even sol's rays seem
somewhat reticent
</blockquote>

Only the last *ku* requires comment. In Japanese rain-clouds and the sun both have "legs." In the case of the former, it is the line of rain one may see falling from an individual cloud; in the case of the latter, it is the light, in particular, when we sense rays.

年々や桜を肥やす花の塵 芭蕉
toshidoshi ya sakura o koyasu hana no chiri bashô -1594
(year-year: cherry[tree](obj) fertilize/enrich blossoms' dust)

<blockquote>
year after year
it's own blossoms fatten
the cherry tree
</blockquote>

Why, asks Bashô, get maudlin for the fallen blossoms? Aren't they recycled? I suppose "trees" is more likely and "fertilize" more accurate, but find a single tree sounds better. There may – or may not – be a stronger link between productivity and cherry trees than Bashô's *ku* suggests. As mentioned at the end of Book I, the early 20c maverick scholar Origuchi claimed the ancients saw the spirit of grain in the *sakura* and were very attentive to the state of the bloom as an omen of the size of the harvest.

People felt it was a bad omen for blossoms to fall, so they would have been disturbed with the [modern] idea that the faster the cherry blossoms fell the better. This feeling changed into a desire for the cherry blossoms not to fall. That's why the fall of cherry blossoms was regretted.

In the Heian era (794-1185) when this became reflected in the literature, the understanding was that the falling of blossoms was regretted because they were beautiful. But, the fact is that, as we've seen, this regret once had a solid basis. (Origuchi Nobuo? *"Hana-no Hanashi"* (talk about blossoms) quoted in Shirabata: *Hanami to Sakura*)

The examples Origuchi gives to support his contention, a couple pre-Heian *Manyôshû* poems having nothing to do with agriculture (see *Book II*) that hint at a message in the blossoms, are far from sufficient proof. The most often cited "evidence" I know of is a passage in the *Uji-shui-monogatari* (宇治拾遺物語) where a priest tries to console a little boy (a *chigo*, ostensibly there for schooling, but famously favorite love-toys of the Buddhist priests) who came to the mountain temple from a farm in the country, who was crying as he watched the wind blasting the bloom, by pointing out in his priestly way that mortality was what cherry blossoms were all about. The boy replies, "No,

> it's no big thing if those cherry blossoms blow! What is really sad is when the blossoms are blown off the wheat my father grows and the grain does not come to a head.

If it is no big thing, then why was the boy crying? If it was pure association (seeing cherry blossoms, he thought of wheat), then, this does not prove anything more than a correlation noted by all farm people. But, if the boy means that cherry blossoms blasted on the mountain was an ill *portent,* that is *predictor,* for the farmers below, then Origuchi has something. As noted elsewhere, I have yet to read anything conclusive about the relationship between blossom and crops.

祟りなす杉はふとりてちる桜　一茶
tatari nasu sugi wa futorite chiru sakura　issa 1808
(charmed[protected by deities] cedars-as-for, fattening falling cherry)

trees encircled by a festoon where it is said tengu dance every night

falling, blossoms	sacred cedar
serve to fatten up	growing fat upon
the sacred cedars	cherry petals

The *tengu* are long red-nosed mountain goblins/demons/wizards and the festoons, thick straw rope demarcating space as sacred to keep people from touching them. Sacred nature was protected by the wrath of the local deities and the cedar was *the* tree that surrounded Shinto Shrines found on magical mountains, of which Japan has many. The comma I put between "falling" and "blossoms" in the first reading may be too philosophical, but the subject (blossoms) is correct, unlike the second reading – stylistically better for lack of "falling." This next, too, expands on Bashô:

はら／＼と畠のこやしや桜花　一茶
harahara to hata no koyashi ya sakurabana　issa 1818
(flutter-fluttering field/plots' fertilizer: cherry-blossoms)

garden mulch
comes fluttering down:
cherry petals

山畠やこやしのたしにちる桜 一茶
yamahata ya koyashi no tashi ni chiru sakura issa 1819
(mountain-garden/plot: fertilizer's addition-as/for falls/ing cherry)

    mountain farms   a mountain plot
cherry blossoms fall   the petals help thicken
    for the manure   the fertilizer

a mountain plot
the manure is topped off
by pink petals

While Issa is only stating a fact, the fact that fertilizer was mostly night-soil creates a contrast between the sweet pink petals and what they fall into, or upon (if the field has just been manured [1]).

苗代の水にちりうくさくらかな 許六
nawashiro no mizu ni chiriuku sakura kana kyoroku
(rice-nursery's water-on falling-float sakura/petals 'tis -1715)

さくら散苗代水や星月夜 蕪村
sakura chiru nawashiro mizu ya hoshizukiyo buson
(sakura/petals fall rice-seedlings/nursery: star-moon-night)

    petals fall and   petals falling
float on the water with   on rice nursery water:
    rice seedlings   a clear night

The light pink and green on dark water would be exquisite. By not wasting a word on *floating*, Buson gives us more.

苗代にすくひだされる桜哉 一茶
nawashiro ni sukuhi dasareru sakura kana issa 1820
(rice-nursery-in ladled-out cherry/blossom/petals!/'tis)

the cherry petals
carefully laddled out
a rice nursery

Issa ladles out something new: petals *in the way*. I assume they clog drains in some irrigation channels. Issa also noticed butterflies *in the way*. Such anti-romantic observations are nothing if not haiku.

花散りて木の間の寺となりにけり 蕪村
hana chirite konoma no tera to narinikeri buson -1783
(blossoms falling/fallen, tree-space/gap temple becomes[final])

    blossoms gone,   blossoms scatter
the temple's a temple   giving birth to a temple
  through the trees   of the tree-gaps

A Japanese commentary: "the view has opened up, but it is strangely melancholy, like missing teeth."

---

1. ***Night Soil Reverie.*** The salmon is said to be a superb example of recycling, for after swimming about and eating all sorts of things out in the ocean, it scoots back up the river, which is to say, climbs the mountain that gave it birth, spawns and leaves its body with all its gathered nutrients for the benefit of the other denizens of the mountain. The whale, for its part, gobbles up squid and other creatures deep in the depths of the sea and comes up thousands of feet to the surface to release them as poop. These sort of things – with the cycles elaborated more fully – are found in Shibatani and Tsuchida's book 『エントロピーとエコロジー再考：一生命系の循環回路 』(創樹社 1992). I do not know if the cherry is mentioned, for I have not read the book, but imagine this: People viewing mountain cherries leave their night-soil as fertilizer and the cherry sends its petals down the mountain to help fertilize the fields which produce the food to make more poop to be carried up. I joke, but a dozen pages on the use of human waste for agriculture in Japan and China may be found in *Topsy-turvy 1585.*

花は散りその色となくながむればむなしき空にはるさめぞ降る　式子内親王　新古今集#149
hana wa chiri sono iro to naku nagamureba munashiki sora ni harusame zo furu   shinkokinshû 1205

blossoms gone,
gazing up at a sky
without them

i see the spring rain
falling into emptiness

I had found the "tree-gaps' temple" of Buson's *ku* deliberately philosophical and thought it described a change from a flower temple state to a tree temple one – a sort poetic change of identity – but the kindred spirit of the above *waka* indirectly supports the *Buson Zenshû* commentator's reading. (↑因みに花びらの形を思えば：＜落ちてきた雨を見上げてそのままの形でふいに、唇が欲し＞ ＝ 俵万智)

花散りてよい古びなり一心寺　来山
hana chirite yoi furubi nari isshin-dera raizan -1716
(blossoms/petals falling good patina becoming one-heartemple)

the petals fall
making a nice patina
one-mind temple

The "one-mind," or *heart,* if you prefer, that had been distracted by the blossoms, returns to Buddha alone. It also would be the name of the temple, for my OJD tells me that *one-heart/mind* had several meanings as a Buddhist term. The clever *patina* (old look) brings out the tranquility of the scene which might include a heart-shaped 心 rock-garden..

走りぬけ見るや木の間の散る櫻　成美
hashirinuke miru ya konomano chiru sakura seibi -1816
(run pop-out see/try: trees-among/space's falling cherry[blossoms])

so are they trying
to escape these woods?
the flying petals

I *guess* the "run-clear/escape" refers to the sideways flight of the petals in a steady wind. Petals do not only flutter down like sick butterflies. Sometimes they swoop like swallows and other times skid like skimboards over wet sand. Because a forest used by humans has no underbrush to speak of, even a day with a light breeze may see strong currents such as those that pass between buildings. Living within a bamboo grove, I often marveled at the way neighborhood cherry petals shot the gap (no underbrush because of the shade and the fact most shoots were eaten) and streaked by my window.

where to?

青葉さへ見れば心のとまるかな　散りにし花の名残り思へば　西行
aoba sae mireba kokoro no tomaru kana chirinishi hana no nagori omoeba saigyô - 1190

even green leaves
arrest your eyes and heart
if you hold them

dear as a remembrance
of the fallen blossoms

花ちれは秋の風まつわか葉哉　宗祇　大発句帳
hana chireba aki no kaze matsu wakaba kana sôgi - 1502
(blossoms/petals fall-if autumn-wind a/waits)

blossoms drop,	blossoms drop,
and the winds of fall await	and young leaves wait
the young leaves	for the fall wind

Saigyô's *waka* recommends leaves to get over blossoms, but Sôgi finds they, too, offer little hope for someone seeking permanence. Or does he? Autumn leaves in Japan are, after all, beautiful.

葉櫻の中々ゆかし花の中　几董
hazakura no nakanaka yukashi hana no naka kitô - 1789
(leafed-cherries' very precious/dear blossoms[blooming trees]-among)

something dear	leaf-cherries
about a leafing cherry	among the blooming are
amidst the bloom	such charmers

The leafing or newly leafed cherry usually gets little respect. But, in certain conditions, we all feel their beauty. *Yukashi* has aspects of "precious," "charming," "elegant," "delicate" and "plaintive.".

ふかはふけ櫻に潜て笛の山　哥松
fukaba fuke sakura ni kawatte fue no yama kashô ()
(blow-if blow! cherry-to/with change/ing, flute/s-mountain)

blow, then, blow!	blow if you will!
replace the cherry blossoms	out with the blossoms and in
with flute mountain	with flute mountain

A flute seems right for the new-found shadows growing under the new leaves following the blossoms. Leaf-flutes also come to mind. But the name of the poet, Song-pine (perhaps, made only for this poem, for I find him nowhere else), suggests that the winds which scatter the petals now play pine needles.

行春の尻べた払ふ落花哉　蕪村
yuku haru no shiribeta harau rakka kana buson 1783
(leaving-spring's buttock brushes-off fallen-petals!/'tis)

leaving, spring
brushes off her butt:
cherry petals!

50 44 - 48

There is no shortage of butt dusting in *haikai*. People who sit on chairs do not have to dust off their rear ends very often, but those who sit on the ground do. This is more a "leaving-spring" *ku*, than a cherry one, but how appropriate to find something beautiful even in what the goddess of spring brushes off her rear! A more philosophical Buson *ku* neglects our blossom: *"Spring departs! / Does beauty turn her back / on her self?"* (*yuku haru ya bijin onore ni somuku kana*). Who can say, but, as this next *ku* by Seibi shows, we do not turn our back on Spring:

剪花によせて春を惜むといふこと
kiribana ni yosete haru o oshimu to iu koto

けふの暮落花を粘に集はや 成美
kyô no kure ochibana o nori ni atsumebaya seibi 1816
(today's evening fallen-blossoms/petals[acc.] glue-with gather)

Regretting the Passing of Spring with Cut Blossoms

today at dusk
i would gather the petals
together with glue

Classical metaphor has unraveled blossoms sewn together. Glue seems more *haikai*. As does this:

花ちるや一開帳の集め銭 一茶
hana chiru ya hito kaichô no atsumezeni issa -1827
(blossoms fall/ing: one-open-temple[day's] collected-coins)

petals are falling
on coins collected over
open temple day

ちるも見したえて花なき春も哉 心敬
chiru mo mishi taete hana-naki haru mogana shinkei -1475
(falling also saw ended/ing blossoms-not spring wish-for)

i saw them fall my dream is a spring with no more blossoms	having seen that all blossoms fall: i dream of spring without them!	oh, for a spring without the blossoms for i saw them fall
i saw them fall it would be nice for some spring after the flowers		how i'd love to see them fall and have some spring post-bloom

ちり／＼て花の気違しづまりぬ 大江丸 俳懺悔
chiri-chirite hana no kichigai shizumarinu ôemaru 1790
(falling-falling/fell blossom-craziness quiets-down)

falling, falling
the blossom-craziness
quiets down

Is Shinkei's *ku* a version of the blossoms-make-us-anxious-in-spring lament as per the first three readings? Or, does he wish for an extension of spring, a tranquil spring after the blossoms have fallen, rather than having to move right into the summer? I favor the latter, that is the last two readings, because it seems the more original idea.

庚午の歳家を焼て・焼けにけりされども花は散りすまし 北枝 アルス
kanoe-uma no toshi ie o yakarete // yakenikeri saredomo hana wa chirisumashi hokushi -1718
(horse-year-house burnt // burnt[+finality] however blossoms-as-for fell-finished)

my year of the horse

my hut in ashes:
so what! the cherry blossoms
had all scattered

homeless but happy

burnt down
but my cherry was done
blossoming

This well-known *ku* complements another well-known poem where the thief left the precious thing, the moon, on the window sill. Hokushi's attitude so impressed Bashô that he wrote: *"If the ancients wrote great songs at the cost of their own lives, your exchange of this great poem [for having your house burnt down] should leave your spirit without regret."* Is it not a testament to Japan's best side that a man could gain great respect for loving his tree more than his house? Still, I can't help wondering how many people today would trade their house (or spouse) for a poem, even knowing ahead of time it would be appreciated for centuries. In my case, I *have* chosen. I have no money, no house, no car nor any other possessions excepting a few hundred books and this cheap computer I face alone because not "working" (or loving) was and is still the only way I can make the time to write books such as this one. Hokushi may not have not *chosen* to burn down his house; but, poem or house/spouse is *the* basic choice all artists who are not rich must make. They must choose between sharing their genes and their memes for, lacking money, they have no time for both.

朧庵一周忌・一年の夢眼の前に花散りぬ 蘭更
ichinen no yume me no mae ni hana chirinu rankô 1799
(one-year's dream eyes-before blossoms fall/scatter)

oboro anniversary

a year-long dream
cherry blossoms scattering
before my eyes

Anniversary of the death of Oboro, whose pen-name means the misty or cloudy moon of late spring. Would this *ku* benefit by losing its preface, in which case we could see the fall of the cherry blossoms as a yearly event, namely, the end of the dream of spring? Or, can we do this and still think of Rankô, his eyes wet thinking about his friend?

花散て猶永き日と成にけり 蓼太
hana chitte nao nagaki hi to narinikeri ryôta 1707-87
(blossoms fall/scattered still longer day becomes[fin.+emph])

blossoms fallen
and the days grow longer
longer still!

城を出し落花一片いまもとぶ 山口誓子 20c
shiro o dashi rakka hotohira ima mo tobu yamaguchi seishi
(castle-from leave fallen/falling blossom/s one-petal now even flies)

out of the castle
a single cherry petal
flies even now

Blossom Snow, Snow Blossoms
花ノ雪・雪ノ花
hana-no-yuki, yuki-no-hana

花の雪の庭につもると跡つけじかどなき宿といひちらさせて　西行
hana no yuki no niwa ni tsumoru to ato tsukeji kadonaki yado to ii-chirasasete saigyô -1190

wanting no path
to sully the snowy drift
of petals without
i'd spread this news:
my cottage is gateless

tell the world
this dwelling has no gate
when cherry petals
blanket my yard like snow
i'd have no trace of man

Kadonaki-yado, or "gateless-dwelling," reminds me (can't speak for Saigyô) of the holeless first being of Taoism and the Gateless Gate mysteries of Zen. Visible trails are not so quickly made in blossom snow as the real thing, but, as LC reminded me, trope is trope. Moreover, it indirectly shows Saigyô's affection for even the fallen petals who help hide a hermit.

まことよりますうそなれや花の雪　昌意　毛吹草
makoto yori mazu uso nare ya hana no yuki shôi 1645
(truth more-than first lie become! blossom-snow)

welcome, lie,
before the truth! behold
snow blossoms!

this sight seems
more a lie than a fact:
a snow of petals

Snowfall on yet-to-bloom cherries? Possibly; but it is more interesting to mistake new blossoms for snow, and petals are more probable yet. It is often as hard to tell which is which in poetry as in life! In Japanese, a human blossom, the courtesan may be alluded to, for snow and "going" are both *yuki* and the latter means "coming" in *that* sense. But the lie/s also take me back to an early 12c report 今鏡 about petalfall *so heavy it covered the hooves of oxen*. The writer wondered whether blossoms were not brought from elsewhere and spread on the ground before the cherry blossoms in the temple fell!

さくまでの梢にのこれ雪の花　宗祇　大発句帳
saku made no kozue ni nokore yuki no hana sôgi - 1502
(blooming-until limb-tips-on stay! snow-blossoms)

unmelted snow

until they bloom
stay right on those limbs!
snow blossoms

Note: that is *yuki no hana*, "snow blossom" and not *hana no yuki*, "blossom snow." In other words, this one is *real snow*, included to keep you on your toes. Sôgi is endearing for his bold (or childish?) way of putting all his little wishes, his requests into poems.

いかにせん花をいそけはミねの雪　宗祇
ika ni sen hana o isogeba mine no yuki   sôgi (rôyô) -1502
(what-for do-would? blossoms speed-if/when peak's snow)

unmelted snow

what can we do!
we'd have blossoms hurry
but, look snow!

old winter snow

a hopeless case!
we'd rush the blossoms yet
the peaks are white

If Sôgi appreciated late snow in the last *ku,* here, it would seem to hold back or hurt the bloom.

.冬に似た山のはもあり櫻哉　也蓼　文車
fuyu ni nita yama no ha mo ari sakura kana   yaryô 1772
(winter-like resemble mountain peaks even are cherry!/'tis)

some peaks look
like they did in the winter:
cherry blossoms

This seems to be what Annie Dillard calls "witness" and haiku people call "realism" with respect to the actual landscape. Other *ku* question whether the poet sees blossoms or clouds or snow; but Yaryô has noticed the way some – not all – mountains enjoy a pattern of bloom that matches what was their winter appearance.

雪と見て雪を忘るゝ櫻哉　燕志
yuki to mite yuki o wasurusuru sakura kana   shôshi ()
(snow-as seeing snow[acc.] forget/ting cherry!/'tis)

looking like snow,
they make us forget snow:
cherry blossoms!

i thought it snow
then, i forgot the snow!
cherry blossoms

This is a rare old *ku*. Lacking an allusion, it requires no explanation. I want to believe the poet was actually fooled for a moment as per the second reading.

豊年の雪を又見て花盛　鳥歌　三崎志
hônen no yuki o mata mite hanazakari   chôka 16c
(bountiful year's snow[acc.] again seeing/seen blossom-acme)

we see the snow
of bumper crops again!
cherries in full bloom

According to some, the cherry is, or lodges, the spirit of grain. This is the only *ku* I know of supporting such a connection, but we need to bear in mind the fact that a heavy snow early in the year was, and is a better known omen for a bumper crop. Our metaphorical snow reflects it.

ちる花や雪の稽古を馬の上　来山
chiru hana ya yuki no keiko o uma no ue   raizan -1716
(falling blossoms: snow practice[acc.] horse-upon)

はりまより信濃へ所替して行くゝ仕官のもとへ
(to an official transferring from harima to shinano)

<table>
<tr><td>the blossoms fall!
i'd get on my horse and
do snow practice!</td><td>falling blossoms!
are you now on horseback
practicing for snow?</td></tr>
</table>

Warming up by cooling? I imagine Raizan's friend – devastated at the thought of having to transfer from the temperate coast to the snow country – must have been cheered to receive this *ku*.

信濃・大雪や（山おくの）しなの育も桜哉　一茶
ôyuki ya [yama-oku no]shinano-sodachi mo sakura kana   issa 1819
(big snow[or, mountain-recesses]: shinano-raised even cherries!)

here, in the cold

<table>
<tr><td>a heavy snow
we in shinano, also
enjoy blossoms</td><td>back in the hills
even this shinano man
knows *sakura*</td></tr>
</table>

A response to a ribbing by friends from more cultured parts who thought Shinano was all snow and no bloom, or that Shinanoites' only interest was food? Joking about heavy snow at a time cherries bloomed back in Edo, where he had lived for decades. Or, is he celebrating his good fortune that year? So I thought before noting the *ku* appears in the 11th month of the year, months after his daughter died.

雪國にそも無量壽の櫻かな　梅室
yukiguni ni somo muryôju no sakura kana   baishitsu -1852
(snow-country-in first immeasureable longevity's cherry!/'tis)

in snow country
you might say the blossoms
last forever

My dictionary translates *muryôju* as "immeasurable bliss" though the sutra is "The Book of Constant Life." Does Baishitsu mean the blooming season is sandwiched between long winters so there is no gap between snow and cherry blossoms? Or, is the snow itself the ageless cherry tree?

人声や西もひがしも花吹雪　一茶
hitogoe ya nishi mo higashi mo hanafubuki   issa 1822
(human voice/s!/: west and east[emph] blossom-blizzard)

people's voices
from west and from east
blossom blizzard

Issa has borrowed a device from descriptions of snowfall – the effect on sound has, of course, been recognized – and managed to plop us down in the midst of the heaviest moments of petal-fall.

追善・富士よしのの無言たうとし雪と花 本弘 三千花
fuji yoshino mugon tôtoshi yuki to hana honkyô 1725
(fuji yoshino no-word valuable/noble: snow & blossom)

悼・極楽の山路もさぞな花の雪 此柳 文？夜？星観
gokuraku no yamaji mo sazo na hana no yuki hiryû 1732
(paradise's mountain-road even naturally blossom-snow)

in memoriam

fuji, yoshino:
how precious *sans paroles*
snow and blossoms

in memoriam

so mountain roads
really lead to paradise!
blossom snow

Snow and blossoms, like death, are *sin paroles*, wordless. While it is an oversimplification to call *white* the color of mourning in Japan (See my long inquiry into black & white in *Topsy-turvy 1585*), because of its homophony with "not-knowing," whiteness was a metaphor for the mystery of death, which takes us somewhere none can know, though Japanese had many *possible* locations. The most Chinese of the heavens, the Yellow Spring Paradise was underground, the Buddhist, especially the Pure Land Sect was in the West, and the favorite of the *Manyôshû* poets was up or through the mountains (last stop for the Milky Way?), and there was a way all men trod to get there (*shide-no-michi* = death-exit-path). The second *ku* unites the traditional death-path with the flowers from heaven that met dying saints. Mountain cherry blossom must have fallen shortly after the poet's friend died. Snow being a homophone for "leaving," "blossom snow" is also "a flowery departure."*

花吹雪机をころぶ筆のかさ 柳多留
hanafubuki tsukue o korobu fude no kasa yanagidaru
(blossom-blizzard desk-over rolling brush-cap)

花吹雪生酔ころぶところまで 柳多留
hanafubuki namayoi korobu tokoro made yanagidaru
(blossom-blizzard drunk/s tumble place-until)

blossom blizzard!
rolling about on a desk
the brush's cap

blossom blizzard!
as far as the piss-drunk go
before passing out

These *senryû* (79–11 & 93-5, 131-29, respectively) are two of many playing upon Bashô's famous *ku* saying, in essence: "Let's go out snow-viewing until we fall down!" The verb for fall-down, *korobu*, can also mean "roll-about." My "passing out" is pushing it a bit; but, drunks who fall *do* usually pass out (I once jumped off the platform at a train station to save a drunk who did just that, whacking his head on a rail to boot – it sounded like a coconut falling on a sidewalk.). The brush cap plays upon two Bashô *ku* at once, for he also had a *ku* throwing off his hat, also called a *kasa*. Were parody not intended, it is poetic enough to have been a haiku, speaking of which, here is one:

雪ならで花にころばん檜笠 遊刀
yuki nara de hana ni koroban hinokigasa yûtô (fl 1700)
(snow is-not-so blossoms-on tumble-would sedge-hat)

in memory of bashô

snow won't do,
fall upon these blossoms!
sweet cedar hat!

A cedar frame hat (*hinoki-gasa*) was perfect for blossom-viewing but unsuitable for snow. Bashô had such a signature hat (not so famous as his gnarled cane, but known to many, of which Yûtô was one. Bashô may have laughed at the cold and practiced austerity, but let us hope he tumbles on blossoms as well as wanders the winter fields in the next world.

雪のおる櫻はあたらかさし哉　心敬
yuki no oru sakura wa atara-kazashi kana shinkei -1475
(snow-breaks cherry-as-for regretful [if-not-something] [head]decoration!)

<table>
<tr><td>

what a shame
snow-broken cherry and
no one to wear it

</td><td>

this snowfall
of cherry bloom: a pity
not to wear it!

</td></tr>
</table>

雪も少し若木の櫻や薄化粧　昌友　太夫櫻
yuki mo sukoshi wakaki no sakura ya usugesho shôyû 1680
(snow too a little, young-tree cherry:/as-for, light-makeup)

yes, *some* snow
light make-up looks good
on young cherries

I came within thirty feet of being crushed by a large cherry taken down in the dead of night by the snow with the help of a pack of bamboo who criss-crossed their heavy snow-laden heads upon her crotches; but that story must await another book. The *kazashi* in the first *ku* means sprays of bloom stuck into ones headgear. *Atara* is a fascinating word for it means something good (beautiful, smart, useful) that is a shame to let go, or regretfully cannot be taken advantage of. *Atarasakari* would be about a full-bloom not enjoyed (a beauty sleeping alone). *Atara-kazashi* probably was coined by the poet, all alone in the mountains with his embarrassment of riches. The second *ku* needs no explanation.

窓の雪にさきつく花の光哉　紹巴　大発句帳
mado no yuki ni sakitsugu hana no hikari kana jôha 1523-1602
(window-snow-in blooming-link/continue blossom-light/shine!/'tis)

<table>
<tr><td>

the well-read cherry

what fine light
from blossoms opening to
window snow!

</td><td>

enough to read by

how they glow!
my cherry blossoms succeed
the window snow

</td><td>

a scholar's spring

illuminating
indeed! blossoms born
of window snow

</td></tr>
</table>

The proverbial Chinese scholar studying by moonlight, magnified by snow piled by his window inspired millenia of bookworms. The first reading assumes a budding branch has begun to bloom in a window, which had snow piled up outside to reflect enough sunlight to hatch (?) it. The central reading imagines a tree outside in the moonlight and captures the idea of a succession from snowshine to bloomglow better than the others. *Illuminating / indeed: bloom follows / window snow!* The third reading puts the glow inside the scholar. Buson (-1783) would later exchange the snow for the leading Chinese tree blossom, in Harold Stewart's translation (*A Chime of Windbells*) *"The pear-tree blossoming in the moonlit night, / A lady reads her letter by its light"* (*nashi no hana tsuki ni fumi yomu onna ari.*).

雪を花まなふも窓の光哉　真宗　十?花千句
yuki o hana manabu mo mado no hikari kana shinshû 1516?
(snow-from blossoms study/learn-too window-snow's light!/'tis)

cherry blossoms
that mimic the snow, how
bright my window!

52

Blossom Rafts
花 筏
hana ikada

来たか来い見ずに置てもちる花ぞ 几董
kita ka koi mizu ni oite mo chiru hana zo   kitô -1789
(came[have you]? carps water-in/upon fall/scatter blossoms!)

hey, carps,
you here? the petals fall
in water, too!

I suspect there is some pun about love (*koi*), homophonic with carp, but I'll let it be, for it is enough fun to imagine how the beautiful fish with the voracious appetite copes with the petal pollution.

水鳥のむねに分け行く桜哉 浪花 再現
mizudori no mune ni wake-yuku sakura kana   rôka -1703
(waterbird's/s' breast-with/by/against split-go cherry[blossoms]!/'tis)

<table>
<tr><td>the water-fowl swims
parting with her breast
the cherry petals</td><td>swimming birds
part them with their breasts
cherry blossoms</td></tr>
</table>

(←trans. blyth, my decap/punc.)

If one translated with more natural English, we'd have *"A water-fowl / parting the cherry petals / with her breast;"* but, then, the cherry petals would no longer surprise us at the end. Blyth also makes the right choice with "her." It fits "breast" and a colorful male would be too much.

さゝ波や花に交る古木履 一茶
sazanami ya hana ni majiwaru furu bokuri   issa 1810
(ripples/light-chop: blossoms-with mix/ing old [fancy]clog)

a light chop:
floating with the petals
an old clog

One of Issa's best straight imagist *ku*. The combination of water with a light chop and a *bokuri*, a pretty painted clog (*exchange the "clog" for an old "high-heel" for effect*) worn by a woman, perhaps an entertainer who danced in the bloomshade, is exquisite. We had petals with rice seedlings a couple chapters ago. While a visual treat, I turned them into fertilizer. In this short chapter, we enjoy variety.

池清みちらぬもうかふ櫻哉　宗春 1734
ike kiyomi chiranu mo ukabu sakura kana　sôshun
(pond clears falling-not also float/ing cherry 'tis)

　　　the pond, clear
　those yet to fall still float:
　　　cherry blossoms!

池水の底にも花の盛り哉　紹巴 -1602
ikemizu no soko ni mo hana no sakari kana　jôha
(pond-water's bottom-in-even/too bloom-acme!)

　　　the pink heat
　is found at the bottom
　　of the pond, too!

The "pink heat" in the second *ku* is a creative translation of *sakari* (ch.10). Feel free to substitute *"the full bloom"* if you prefer! The location of that image is a direct translation. For reasons beyond me, Japanese can put reflections at the *bottom* of the water. Logically speaking, it *could be* shadows cast by floating petals or petal "rafts," but I have yet to encounter such an explanation for the odd idiom.

池水を鏡に花の夕化粧　乙由　麦林
ikemizu o kagami ya hana no yûgeshô otsuyû -1739
()

　　with pond water
　for a mirror, the blossoms'
　　evening make-up

The pond reflects sunset colors upon the blossoms, which, in turn, reflect more colorfully in the same.

さくらさきおしろのほりもピンク色　長谷川佳代
sakura saki ushiro no hori mo pinku iro hasegawa kayo (2nd grade)
(cherry/ies bloom/s behind's moat too pink color　福島県城南小二)

　　　cherries bloom
　the moat behind them
　　is also pink!

A pink moat. I like it. This contemporary school-child uses the English word *pinku*. A fine word it is. In K'tut Tantri's classic *Revolt in Paradise*, we learn that Malay, lacking *pink*, calls it "young red."

小盥も水さへあれは散る櫻（櫻散る）其角
kotarai mo mizu sae areba chiru sakura [sakura chiru] kikaku -1707
(small tub even water only is-if fall cherry[petals] [cherry [petals] fall])

cherry blossoms　　　　　　　　　　**maybe, next year**

　if you just have　　　　　　　　　　falling petals!
a small tub and water　　　　　　　if i just had a pail
　petals will fall　　　　　　　　　　and some water

花の中大事にもてよ桶の水　成美
hana no naka daiji ni moteyo oke no mizu seibi -1816
(blossoms-among importantly/carefully carry! tub's/s' water)

　among the blossoms　　　　　　　　cherry blossoms
carry that very carefully!　　　　written on water, take care
　a pail of water　　　　　　　　　　with that pail!

Water is closer to our speed than air. Petals in just the right weather conditions can hang in the air for a long time, but petals on water guarantee we have something to watch. *If you haven't floated petals or blossoms in a while, do!* The second reading is the story of my life. With Seibi's cautionary *ku* we wonder: 1) Was water considered an important part of a blossom-viewing "installation"? 2) Is drinking or washing water running short and in high demand? 3) Would water damage the fine clothing of the blossom viewers? 4) Do the reflection of the blossoms deserve the same respect the moon does (for metaphysical reasons)? 5) Would a spill be a bad omen for the bloom?

水壺にうつるや花の人の出入 丈草
mizutsubo ni utsuru ya hana no hito deiri jôsô -1704
(water-crock-in reflect!/: blossoms' people's exit-entrance)

in the water crock
reflections: people coming
to and fro the bloom

I imagine a large ceramic pot (5-10 gallon, earthenware or not) filled with water, water lilies and perhaps some goldfish or small carp, by the entrance to a temple's blossom-viewing grounds.

落花枝に帰るとかけや水の面 破扇 洗濯物
rakka eda ni kaeru to kake ya mizu no men hasen 1666
(fallen-flower branch-to return pose[as a puzzle]: water-surface)

когда when can the fallen   how can the fallen
blossom return to the branch?   bloom return to the branch?
just ask the water!   look in the water

Like the older *ku* about a blossom that was a butterfly (#16-78), this plays with the saying "a blossom can't return . . ." A pun on "water-surface" may also reveal when it is noticed: "*nomen* = try to drink!"

水の泡の消えかへり行花も哉 紹巴 大発句帳
mizu no awa no kiekaeriyuku hana mo gana jôha -1602
(water-bubbles' vanishing-returning-go/leave blossom/s wish-for)

ah, for blossoms
like water bubbles that
vanishing return!

Blossoms are said to "return to their roots" (*ne-ni kaeru*) and, ideally, fertilize the tree they come from, but bubbles, popping, are instantly one again with water. No illusory reflection can make up for this. Since blossoms die a lot more beautifully than we do, this request only shows that the poet is greedy.

◎ Sorry, no *petal rafts* this book! ◎

There is no specific seasonal word for petals floating on water in the *ku* I gathered. "Blossom raft" (*hana ikada*) is not only a *bona fide* term but beautiful. I have seen about 50 modern *ku* with it, but only a handful of old ones, none of which grabbed me. If I find *ku* I like, there is always another edition. My favorite at present was written to cap a verse of mine (at 浮御堂の 尻取り連句 bbs). I wrote that blossoms falling quickly could be considered a saving grace (as rain beats sun if one does not want to be outdoors), and another poet responded with a verse sending me a cherry petal *life*-raft!

53

Women as Blossom
花ハ女

花はなし人こそ柳櫻なれ　心敬
hana wa nashi hito koso yanagi sakura nare shinkei -1475
(blossoms-as-for not people [+emph.] willow cherry become/are)

there is no bloom
people are the *real* willows
and cherry blossoms

flower tales:
willows and cherries are
really people

A convention of writing where the dots that turn a "ha" (*wa*) into a *"ba"* are not written – left to the reader's good sense – permits my second reading though my reading of other *ku* and *waka* by Shinkei denying reality outside of the heart do not excuse it. Regardless, both readings comment on the nature of Japanese poetry prior to the shift to nature for nature's sake. As we have already seen, there was a long tradition of conflating blossoms and women. One method was by *association. Manyôshû* (8c) poem #3305 starts like this: *"Not thinking of love, just walking along, my eyes wander to the green hills, spotting the azaleas, pretty young maidens, the cherry blossoms / nubile young women . . . (mono omowazu michi yuku yuku mo aoyama o furisake-mireba tsutsujibana nihoe-otome, sakurabana sakae-otome . .).* Another was *allegory. Manyôshû* #1458: *"The bloom of the cherry at our house: Is it buffeted by violent gusts of pine (=waiting/longing) wind, so petals fall to the ground?"* (*yado ni aru sakura no hana wa ima kamo matsukaze hayami tsuchi ni chiruramu*) asks a king to a courtesan, uncertain whether she has taken another lover in his long absence. Her poem (#1459) responds, they were indeed falling, for she couldn't count on *him.* After allegory, there is *name*. The most famous example is Sakurako ("cherry-child"). This eight-year-old (!) charmer was contested by the scions of two mighty families. Afraid their love/desire for her would result in a tragedy (the death of many men more worthy than her), she considerately destroyed the object of contention: she snuck out into the woods and hung herself. This proved she was worthy of their love and, needless to say, the two men cried tears of blood. Still, their respective eulogies (MY#3786 *haru saraba,* 3787 *ima ga na ni*), along the *blossoms-as-women* vector we will review in the next chapter, seem heartlessly upbeat to me:

the spray of cherry
i dreamed would crown
my head this spring?
its blossoms can't be found
they've scattered for good!

when the blossom
of her namesake the cherry
comes into bloom
my longing knows no end
every year, i long again!

These Sakurako poems are cited in Yamada's classic *Sakura Shi* (cherry history: 1941) as examples of the tendency to view the blossoms as women in ancient poetry, as opposed to the early modern idea of them as warriors. Had the ancients been a little less fixated in human romance (like Spanish-language poetry *still* is!), the story itself might have been sung as a just-so-story for the cherry blossom, eg:

そのままと大喧嘩だから散る桜　敬愚
sono mama to ôkenka dakara chiru sakura keigu

short-lived beauty

men will quarrel
if they remain, so cherry
drops her blossoms

Or, "sheds her petals," if you prefer. Keigu's intention was to create an explanatory myth for the brevity of the bloom, but the poem may also read as an allegory for the proverbially short life of the beauty. Speaking of which, there *is* an explanatory myth that *may* be about the cherry blossom in section 37 of the *Kojiki*, or *Record of Ancient Matters*, completed in 712 A.D.. Here is a version of a 1919 translation by Basil Hall Chamberlain. I have shortened it, considerably:

> His Augustness Heaven's-Sun-Height-Prince-Rice-ear-Ruddy-Plenty met a beauty and asked her who she was. "I am a daughter of the Deity-Great-Mountain-Possessor,.. another name by which I am called being Princess-Blossoming-Brilliantly-Like-the-Flowers-of-the-Trees,"[1] said she, at which he charged [sic] her, [saying]: *Ego sum cupidus coiendi tecum. Tibi quomodo videtur?* [I do not know Latin, but let's guess: *I am hot to get it on with you. What do you say?*] She replied that she had to ask her father, who was delighted and sent her and her elder sister Princess Long-as-the-Rocks back to the Prince with a huge dowry. The elder sister being very hideous, the Prince sent her back, keeping only Princess-Blossoming-Brilliantly-Like-the-Flowers-of-the-Trees, whom he wedded for one night. The Deity-Great-Mountain-Possessor was shamed by Princess Long-as-the-Rocks being sent back and sent a message to the Prince saying: "My reason for respectfully presenting both my daughters together was that, by sending Princess-Long-as-the-Rocks, the august offspring of the Heavenly Deity, though the snow fall and the wind blow, might live eternally immovable like unto the enduring rocks, and again that by sending Princess-Blossoming-Brilliantly-Like-the-Flowers-of-the-Trees, [they] might live flourishingly like unto the flowering of the blossoms of the trees. Because of thy behavior, the august offspring of the Heavenly Deity shall be but as frail as the flowers of the trees." It is for this reason that down to the present day the august lives of Their Augustnesses the Heavenly Sovereigns are not long.

There is an Amerindian myth about the choice made by the Ancestor between a sinking stone and floating stick. A short life that could be renewed was chosen over a long life that slowly wore down. The Japanese myth suggests that "we" could have had the long life *and* a measure of beauty but, unable to abide ugliness, apparently preferred to die young. Most Japanese feel the beautiful Tree-blossom-blooming-princess, Konohanasakuyahime, is Sakuya-hime (the first of the 13 etymologies for *sakura* listed in Japan's premier dictionary) the Cherry Goddess. Yet, as remarkable as it might seem, some have argued that this princess could not have been a cherry spirit because the idea of the cherry as a woman was invented in the Edo era and the male tree spirit + mother-earth combination was the global pattern, etc. There may, nevertheless, be more than a kernal of truth here *as it applies to individual cherry mountains.* As poet Takahashi Mutsuo has pointed out in the magazine *Kokubungaku*'s special on the *ecriture* of cherry blossoms (2001/4), some mountains and their cherry trees appear to be male and others female (something coming from both the particular geography and the cultural tradition), while others in poems, such as Norinaga's definition of Yamato (*shikishima no* ~) are ambiguous and were only genderized (read as male in this case) to encourage young men to sacrifice themselves for their country in modern times. Moreover, it bears noting that beauty was once associated with the male sex as well as female. Prince Genji was, like Chinese Princes, a beauty. Yet, for all of that, the poems in the *Manyoshû* that I have introduced here make it clear that for poets, at least, the cherry was obviously female long before the Edo era.

1. **Konohanasakuya-hime.** What fun comparing translations and explanations of the name of the Tree-blossom-blooming-princess! Besides the above, we have: "The goddess who can revive dead flowers" (Masashi Yamaguchi), *"Princesa Florida Brilhantemente como as Flores das Árvores"* (Aliança Cultural Brasil – Japão). Another website comes up with the marvelous phrase "the Numen of the *sakura*" and, perhaps referring to an explanatory myth I have not seen, writes that it is said "the cherry blossom came to Japanese when a Japanese goddess named Konohanasakuyahime planted one atop Mt. Fuji." She does indeed have a relationship with Mount Fuji both because of her father being the deity of the mountain and her fiery volcanic aspect (she gave birth inside a burning hut to prove her children's father was the God, who was suspicious because she became gravid so quickly) but I had not read of her Johnny Appleseed aspect before this!

花毎にふりゆくものは女哉　易難 翁反故
hanagoto ni furiyuku mono wa onna kana　ekinan 1783
(blossoms-each-with aging-go thing-as-for woman!/'tis)

something ages
with each petal that falls:
call it "woman"

This is hopelessly trite and is included only to point out the obvious connection. Still, I prefer such bold generalization to the specific allegories of ancient poetry. A trickier poem:

世の花や五年前の女とは 其角 再現
yo no hana ya gonen mae no onna to wa　kikaku -1707
(world's blossoms: five-years' before's women-as-for)

worldly blossoms: blossoms, yeah, yeah!
and where is the woman   what do you think of your girl
of five years ago?   after five years?

The allegory in the original is stated in an oddly unfinished way: *The world's blossoms: the woman/women of five years ago as for?* It is hard to tell if Kikaku means that a woman who was sexy only five years ago is now an old hag, or whether he has forgotten of her (or vice versa). This *ku* and the previous one play on the old saw (too common to warrant example poems) of the generic man growing old with each new year, or each ever-young Spring.

花にあかぬ浮世男のにくき哉　千子 続虚栗
hana ni akanu ukiyo otoko no nikuki kana　chine -1688
(blossoms-with tire-not floating-world man/men's hateful!)

the beauty blues

how *spiteful* are
men in this world who never
tire of blossoms!

The blossom here is *all woman* and the "men" not generic but clearly *male*. I do not know if Chine means men in the floating-world proper, *i.e.,* those in the water trades, who deal in women and other forms of entertainment, or those in the secular world, who do not retire but continue taking young wives as they age. The word *nikuki* (spiteful/hateful) has a hint of jealousy in it. It seems the *ku* of a middle-aged woman. This is the daughter of a famous poet (Kyorai), but I could not find her birth-date.

woman as

色白にくきやかなりや花の顔　立圃 空礫　　　　　眉くろに薄い化粧や花の顔　無文 太夫櫻
irojiro nikuki ya kanari ya hana no kao ryûho 1594-1669　　*mayuguro ni usui kesshô ya hana no kao* mûmon 1680
(color-white hateful[=attractive]! quite!/: blossom-faces)　　(eyebrow-black-in/with light make-up!/?/: blossom-faces)

<table>
<tr><td>

the whitest ones
are so hateful, quite!
blossom faces

</td><td>

light make-up
and eyebrow mascara
blossom faces

</td></tr>
</table>

Rather than saying "that's wonderful!" Japanese may say *"[I am] jealous!"* or, *"how hateful!"* It is hard to say whether this is honest, or an accident of speech (see *Orientalism & Occidentalism*)? In context, hateful means "adorable," but, because it is rarer than "jealous," we may imagine the blossoms' white skin draws a touch of animosity on the part of the less fortunate. In Japan, a white skin was considered beautiful enough to cover up eight (a multitude) of sins (Perhaps because, as in the West, it reflected more fortunate circumstances (working outside darkens the skin) and was identified with youth). The *ku* maintains a pretence of being about cherry blossoms, but the emotion suggests differently. While the second *ku* is probably about women, it may include men, for men also used make up in Japan. Pretty faces need little make-up and blossom-viewing, as an outdoor event, probably called for the same. A popular ditty, perhaps from the Higo or Tosa area (South-East), provided the opposite (insulting) view: *"Is that make-up (white-powder) / soiling your face? / Girls, you were born / a mountain cherry!"* (顔を汚すは白粉か　生まれながらの山桜　小唄（失出典）*kao o kegasu wa oshiroi ka umarenagara no yamazakura*). The line, from a song of a sort used by baby-sitters to insult one another, plays upon pollen to insult buck-teeth, monkey-eyed, alligator-mouthed girls who even make up would not help.

遠いよりよしや隣家の花を友　百童
tôi yori yoshi ya tonari ie no hana o tomo hyakudô 1775
(far more-than good: neighbor's house's blossoms[acc] friend-as)

<table>
<tr><td>

it beats travel:
making up to the blossom
right next door

</td><td>

better to stay home
and befriend the blossoms
of your neighbor

</td></tr>
</table>

If this *sakura!* refers to a person, let us hope the blossom is the neighbor's *daughter* rather than wife!

小町讃・我恋よ目も鼻もなき花の色　嵐雪
waga koi yo me mo hana mo naki hana no iro ransetsu -1707
(my love! eye and[emph] nose[emph]-not, blossom-color/s))

hymn to komachi

<table>
<tr><td>

here's to my love
no eyes, no nose, the color
of all blossoms!

</td><td>

my love she has
no eyes and no nose she is
blossom color

</td></tr>
</table>

Does Ransetsu refer to an old doll? Japanese dolls often leave all the features to our imagination, for no drawn beauty can approach the ideal. What is "blossom color?" Had the color (*iro*) been modified by *sakura-*(cherry), rather than *hana-* (blossom-), it would be too strong, too specific. As pointed out earlier (where, I forget) *sakura-iro* generally means pregnant nipple-pink-purple. But it also can signify a bright red, for despite the lack of interest in the fruit of the cherry in Japan, the nobility adopted some fabric color names from China. I would guess that *hana-iro* here means the very light pink of a typical cherry blossom, a delicate tint suitable for Japanese love, which was fragile by definition.

Viewer as Lover

John R. Wallace provides a good description of how classic Japanese and Occidental "love" differ in a 1998 (10:3-16) *Japan Review* article, *Anxiety of Erotic Longing and Murasaki Shikibu's Aesthetic Vision*. His larger argument is that the problem of love is common: things don't last; but Western philosophy replaces transience with an eternal object, while Japanese have their beloved vanish to later return in a similar form, as exampled with new women in the *Tale of Genji* and by the death and reappearance of blossoms each spring. A long section titled *"The Image of Sakura"* cites Manyôshû poem #1855 (in this book, #47-46) which he reiterates: "Though it is not time for the cherry blossoms to scatter, no doubt they will scatter for it is just now that people (or I, the author) love them the most. The falling of the blossoms marks a peak experience of supreme beauty. . . to love that which is beautiful is to have that which is beautiful disappear before one's eyes, with the implicit cause being one's own love." (IBID) Wallace's blossoms reify what I would call a doubly tragic (hopeless+guilty) view of romance: where love is equated with longing, consummation is the end of it.

~~~~~~

そとは小町の絵・花の色はうつゝか夢かなれのはて 季吟
hana no iro wa utsusu ka yume ka nare no hate   kigin 1624 - 1705
(blossom's color/eros-as-for real[change/transfer] ? dream? course-end)

a picture of old komachi

blossom color:
is it real or a dream
after it fades?

The *utsusu* hints at a change of color while *meaning* "real." If the attraction of a woman/cherry is a symbol for *the world* – the Buddhist one of false appearances – there may be a genuine question here, but, personally, I think *change changes nothing:* what *was* is *always* what *was*. True, "the trouble with a kitten is *that /* it becomes a cat," (Ogden Nash), but that does not call into question the reality of kittenhood, and a blossomless cherry does not make blooming a dream, unless one is to define reality as those conditions that last the longest time – a sort of crude temporal democracy, where kittens and blossoms don't count. Regardless, without the *color=eros* equation, the *ku* does not fly.

女わかしゆ鼻先高し山桜 友水 東日記
onna-wakashu hanasaki takashi yamazakura   yûsui 1681
(female young-crowd[homosexual/transvestites] nose-tip-high: mountain-cherry)

girls impersonating	young-crowd girls
gay boys look so handsome	in peak form up among
mountain cherries	mountain cherries

In Japan, at least since the Warring Era (1338-1568) prominent noses have been a mark of beauty. Modified as "high," they include the connotation of being *stuck-up*. The "nose = blossom" pun cannot be Englished, but we can notice the common height of nose and mountain. "Young-crowd" (gay) men partially cross-dressed, and female whores with relatively male features –including a large nose – found they attracted more men as "young-crowd" than as women.

花やちるらんて女中をこわがらせ 柳多留 12
hana ya chiruran de jochû o kowagarase　yanagidaru 1777
(blossoms[emph] fall[emph], with[saying] maid/s[acc] frighten)

> blossoms, you know
> end up falling: he says
> scaring the maid

At first glance, this is not woman-as-blossom but blossom-as-woman, but the maid is made to think of the former. This is an exceptionally translatable *senryû*. Many dealing with female blossoms are not. Examples should always be double-petal, but let a single complex one suffice: *"Mister Sakura / how hard for his wife / to be eightfold."* (桜丸女房に八重はきつい事　柳多留 50−12 *sakura maru nyôbo ni yae wa kitsui koto* yanagidaru (19c)). Eightfold, as in *an eightfold (double-blossom)-cherry*, means a courtesan bored because no visitor comes. The idiom derived from an incident where a courtesan with that name lost her patron, Sakura-maru (Cherry-boat or Mr. Cherry). The poet is being facetious. He means, *How ironic* (and unfair) *that the focus of the idiom is on the woman's problem when it was Mr. Cherry who had to suffer the agonizing death of seppuku*, that is, he had to open up his own belly (in order that his family was not also punished for whatever crime he did or was said to have done). In this era, disembowelment in drama was often accompanied by flying cherry petals, so you could say the man, if his name was not posthumously made to fit, had the right name for his role. This next is easier:

年を経て若木の櫻やあはゝはゝ　梅枝 太夫櫻
toshi o hete wakaki no sakura ya ahahahaha　baishi 1680
(year/s elapsing young tree/s cherry-as-for/!/: har!har!har!)

> years pass and   some years later
> my young cherry tree laughs   the shy young cherry tree
> like a hyena   laughs aloud

The allegory is based on a metaphor English lacks: *blooming-as-smile/laugh* and *ahahaha* is a brazen hee-haw (not totally ridiculous because it metaphorically translates as *a bold bloom*). Japanese women typically covered their mouths to hide large smiles and laughter. Today, this practice is slowly dying out, but women are still careful to keep themselves *in*. The metamorphosis from a shy pretty young thing to an in-your-face older woman frightens some men: hence, my "hyena."

Man as blossom?

We see blossom-uprisings insinuating there is a *battle of the blossoms* and the bloom is either valient for falling quickly or for holding on until last in chapter 12, *Late cherry* and we will see the more recent development of *man-as-petal* warriors in chapter 61, *National Cherries*; but what about romantic *man*-as-blossom allegory? Aside from the *Chigozakura*, or *"Boy-cherry"* of chapter 11 there is not much. There may be *one* adult male obliquely referred to in a fascinating *waka* by Princess Shikishi in the *Gyôkuyôshû* #239, as translated by Steven D. Carter (*Traditional Japanese Poetry*): *"Ah, how I have wished / for something besides blossoms / to give me comfort! / So scatter, then – be as aloof / as I will be watching you."* (*hana narade mata nagusamuru kata mogana tsurenaku chiru o tsurenakute min* 1312). Here, men, or one man at least, would seem to be allegorized by, if not equated with, the scattering/vanishing petals? (専門家に頼む：男桜を、どうぞ！)

54

Woman or Blossom
女ヵ桜

ちりちらす奥みえぬ花の心哉　宗祇 大発句帳
chiri chirazu oku mienu hana no kokoro kana　sôgi -1502
(fall, fall-not recesses see-not blossom's/s' heart/mind!/'tis)

to fall or not:
one cannot see far within
a blossom's mind

Is Sôgi attempting to read a cherry tree, or using it to describe woman? It is hard to guess which is metaphor, or if both are meant to metaphor each other! If we are in an anthropomorphic frame of mind, blossom is metaphor, but if we are feeling animistic, woman is metaphor and the cherry tree for real.

何の実と問ふてしりぞく桜かな　千代 草稿
nan no mi to tôte shirizoku sakura kana　chiyo -1775
(what berry/substance[and=saying] asking retreat cherry!/?/'tis)

taken aback   cherry trees
when asked about her fruit   asked about their fruit
the *sakura*   we're at a loss

While the Japanese do not have the expression "by their fruit you shall know them," they do expect flowering trees, as a rule, to bear fruit/nuts/berries (all are the same *mi* in Japanese) so the blossoming cherry was noticeably barren to someone who thought of such things. Chiyo was briefly married but her husband died and she probably never had children, so this may be a self-portrait.

花の顔や咲と散とは二度びくり　光有
hana no kao ya saku to chiru to wa nido bikuri　kôyû 1645?
(blossom's face/s: bloom and fall-as-for two-time surprise)

naive   **new face**

a blossom seems   cherry blossoms
shocked to blossom and   they surprise you twice
shocked to fall!   coming and going

This easy-to-read *ku* is tricky. Does the "face" of the blossom in the original make it human? Is it blossom-as-woman or woman-as-blossom? And, is it the poet or the blossom/woman who is surprised? I often hear that if a *ku* is post-Bashô it is always real, and any metaphor is secondary, an allusion at most. The truth is more complex. If the *ku* is made in a link-verse setting, Bashô or no

Bashô, the *ku* may start with the metaphor even if it is not meant to be taken too seriously and, even when independently created, not a few ku are clearly ambiguous and, I dare say that there were retro poets who did not shy away from metaphor-first *ku*. In many cases, only a broad reading of the poet's work can reveal what is likely, for even in cases where the poet is serious about his Bashôism, such as Issa, we find exceptions (when Issa treats Chrysanthemum, we sometimes are uncertain whether he refers first to a real flower or to his wife, who is named after said flower (Kiku in Japanese).

美人色衰・嵐より雨より花の日数　麦翅　新選
arashi yori ame yori hana no hikazu kana   bakushi -1773
(gale more-than rain more-than blossoms day-number 'tis)

beauty's demise

more than gales
more than rain, blossoms are
a matter of time

the wind and rain
are not to blame: a blossom's
days are numbered

The original title uses *bijin,* "a (human) beauty," who loses *iro,* "color=appeal/sexiness." But we cannot tell whether she was intended as a metaphor for the cherry blossom or vice versa. Gales can be torrid love-affairs (or angry husbands), rain, hardship, etc. There are countless poems complaining about the rain or wind, but no others I can think of addressing time (day-number) as the villain.

見れば目の玉の台ぞ家桜　　時之　夢見草
mireba me no tama no utena zo iezakura   jishi 1656
(look-if/when eye-ball's dais [+emph.] house-cherry)

looking, i found
the apple of my eye
my house cherry!

if you'd look
you'd find her just divine!
your house cherry

The original gives no hint of the person. It seems aphoristic, but I prefer the first-person. Who knows whether the cherry tree is a tree, a woman, or both. There are many old *ku* like this, too confusing to merit full treatment: *"Though a flower / embarrassed to be called / a cherry blossom"* (花ながらさくらといふが恥しき　シンセキ　再現　失典 *hana nagara sakura to iu ga hazukashiki*   shinseki). A woman doesn't mind being seen as something fragrant, beautiful and flourishing, but the cherry blossom tends to stand for a mature woman. Is that the problem? Or, is it the idiomatic meaning of a *sakura,* a draw, or shill? Or, is it the euphemistic meaning and we have a beautiful yet bashful courtesan? Viz this *ku,* obviously courtesan-as-cherry-tree: *"Her redemption / stolen by a monkey, / the cherry tree"* (身の代を猿にとらるゝ櫻哉　一雀 *mi no dai o saru ni toraruru sakura kana*   ichijaku ( )). The "body-fee," money paid to redeem the freedom of a woman sold into prostitution, but, who knows if there is not the minute possibility of a *Golden Bough* reading: to wit, a token left in exchange for a tree, or branch of bloom, is literally stolen by a macaque (Disclaimer: I do not know if Japanese *ever* did this).

我宿の櫻わすれてくらしけり　　蓼太
waga yado no sakura wasurete kurashikeri   ryôta 1707-87
(my lodging's cherry[tree? blossoms?] forgetting live[+emph.])

life at home
my cherry tree blooms
unnoticed!

where i live
we forgot all about
the cherries

at my house
cherries are out of sight
& out of mind

I may have tossed this *ku* in with the house-cherries a little too fast. The *sakura* is ambiguous. We know it means cherry blossoms, but, in retrospect, I feel it means the whole cherry blossom scene, though my first reading is not impossible. Regardless, the final *kurashikeri* is masterful. The verb *kurasu* is the perfect "to live" for the *ku,* as it suggests the monotony of everyday life.

東に住侍し頃・旅の宿都にうゑし花も哉 宗祇 大発句帳
tabi no yado miyako ni ueshi hana mo gana sôgi 1420-1502
(travel-lodge capital-in planted blossom/s wish-for)

while working in the east

the roadside inn
how i miss the cherries
i planted in kyoto

a roadside inn
i wish my kyoto blossoms
would fly here

I cannot tell if Sôgi misses his women (married daughters, perhaps) or the presence of cherries that he planted (for the birth of children, at his home, or as a guest in others gardens) would have been blooming at the time. My second reading incorporates an allusion to a plum tree famous for flying.

花や世人此あだものに迷ひけん 素椿 新虚栗
hana ya yobito kono adamono ni mayoiken sochin 1777
(blossoms!/: world-people this coquettish[pun: vain]-for lost?)

cherry blossoms!
has the whole world been misled
by these charmers?

cherry blossoms!
have we all lost ourselves
in fruitless love?

Better to fall for blossoms than women, for they vanish and that is that. But metaphor can make them equally dangerous. This was in a Bashôite anthology, so it *should be* about the real thing, but . . .

遊女賛・合点して此道迷へ山さくら 二柳 新選
gaten shite kono michi mayoe yamazakura jiryû 1773
(agree-do/got-it this road [get]lost! mountain-cherry/ies)

in praise of harlots

yes, indeed, this
is the road to get lost on
mountain cherries

見せばやの女房つれて桜かな 素丸 ~ 発句集
misebaya no nyôbô tsurete sakura kana somaru 1712-95
(see-would's wife take-along cherry[blossoms]!/?/'tis)

blossom-viewing
with my wife who said
why not show me?

with the wife
who said "show it to me!"
blossom-viewing

the wife who said
why not show me? tags along!
to view *sakura*

The title for the first *ku*, "In Praise of Harlots," prefaces the original. Without it, I would have read the same *ku* to be a risqué praise of mountain cherries, period. The *ku* is good, for mountain paths are notably easy to get lost on. So I include it with *ku* of questionable intent. Somaru's original specifies *sakura*. If it were in a book of *senryû*, it would definitely mean the wife is getting a tour of the pleasure quarters to see top courtesans. As a haiku, by a poet whose work I am familiar with, I think he means a real blossom-viewing; the implication is that she wondered what the men might be up to, so, in her mind at least, there was a question about the identity of the *sakura!* All of this confusion is not only mine, or ours. If I read the following *ku* correctly – which has nothing to do with whether I translate it correctly, for that is easy – Japanese were confused, too: *"I don't see how / they can be the same thing! / blossom-viewing"* (同し事とは思はれぬ花見哉 季遊 onaji koto to wa omowarenu hanami kana kiyû ()). This *ku* must be one of the most subtle *meta-tropical* (as in *trope*) poems ever written. There is no pronoun "they" in the original, but I think we can guess what it refers to.

咲くからに罪作らする桜哉 一茶
saku kara ni tsumi tsukurasuru sakura kana   issa 1810
(blooming-from sin made-is cherry/cherries!/'tis)

cherry trees:
because they bloom
they create sin

Christian "original sin" and its equivalent in Buddhism (the more dynamic concept of *desire-as-bad*) are so broad they mean nothing. Issa saved sin by bringing it down to earth. He found seeds of it *everywhere*, most memorably in the feeding of chickens: it caused fights. Life in this world means that even when we do good, we cannot help doing bad. Issa celebrated beauty *and* its side-effects. This *ku would be* ambiguous were I not familiar with the body of Issa's work; it really *is* about the trees!

人のものをこれ程をしき櫻哉 専跡 其袋
hito no mono o kore hodo oshiki sakura kana senato? 1690
(person's[another's] thing/s[acc.] this amount/degree regretful cherry/ies!)

for example

how we covet
another's things: take
this cherry tree

such regret

to think we feel
this much for blossoms
another owns!

Someone's wife, or, disappointment over not monopolizing the best cherry tree for viewing?

散さくらつらくもまさる見事哉 樗良
chiru sakura tsuraku mo masaru migoto kana chora -1780
(falling cherry painful even exceed magnificent!/?/'tis)

falling blossoms
what hurts is all the more
magnificent!

falling petals
the pain is exceeded by
the splendor

By convention, it is painful to see blossoms fall and spring disappear. But, I cannot help recalling the tortured expressions of women in many Japanese depictions of sex – women, who, like female cats in heat (my female cats rolled about in pleasure *after*), seem masochistic.

花の陰笑上戸の美人あり　蘭更 新五子
hananokage warai jôgo no bijin ari rankô 1625-1798
(bloomshade laughing-heavy-drinker=good-at's beauty is)

the bloom-shade:
there is a beauty with
a bacchant smile

the bloom-shade:
wow, there's a beauty
good at smiling!

the bloom-shade
here you may find a lord
who can smile

English lacks a *jôgo,* i.e., a heavy-drinker, who holds it well, much less its extension to a smile! This is a beauty confident enough to smile. Many do not, for they have too many would-be admirers to know what to do with them. I first imagined a woman in the bloom-shade, then, wondered if she was not the bloom in whose shade the poet basks (unlikely considering the lack of the *femme ideal* in Japanese culture (as noted by Lafcadio Hearn)). The last reading takes an archaic usage of beauty=ruler.

花過てもとの柳にもとりけり　荷翠 真木柱
hana sugite moto no yanagi ni modorikeri kasui 1697
(blossoms passing-even original willow-to return [+emph.])

after the bloom
we go back for good
to the willow

her blossom
days past, she once again
is a willow

The willow greens just before the cherry and still looks fine in early summer. It is also a graceful, slender woman. Could this be about a woman who has graduated from sex without becoming plump? Or, is it, as per my first reading, about fauna only? Because of wisteria and peony, I doubt that.

きのふけふ高根の櫻見えにけり　蕪村
kinô kyô takane no sakura mienikeri buson -1783
(yesterday today high-root=peak's cherry/ies see/n[+fin.+emph.])

yesterday and
today, the cherries on high
were in sight!

yesterday and
today, i *saw* cherries
on the peak

We have seen *taka-ne-no-hana* (high-peak-blossom), an upper-class beauty a mortal cannot hope to mate. My title, cut for space, was "Forbidden Fruit." As a landscape artist, Buson may well have noticed *bona fide* cherry trees blossoming here and there high up the peaks, but I cannot help wondering if this might allude to a two-day parade of top courtesans.

世の花や五年以前の女とは　其角 桃の実
yo no hana ya gonen izen no onna to wa kikaku -1707
(world's blossoms!/?/: five-years before's woman/en-as-for)

flowers you say
what of women you knew
five years ago?

blossoms? big deal!
after five years who thinks
of a girlfriend?

worldly beauty
so where is *your* love
of five years past?

This seemingly addresses blossoms, while being more specific about male-female relationships than any other *ku* we have seen, but not so explicit as the last two readings. Does Kikaku playfully question the ridiculous concern of *waka* poets, inherited by *haikai* poets, for the fate of the cherry blossoms?

55

Blossoms as Women
女ハ花

花の木の持て生たあいそ哉　一茶
hana no ki no motte-umareta aiso kana   issa 1822
(blossom-tree's having-born[natural] amiability!/?/'tis)

blossom-smiles

<table>
<tr><td>

what wonderful
natural amiability!
blossoming trees

</td><td>

oh yes, they are
born to be charmers!
cherry trees

</td></tr>
</table>

花の山鬼の門とはおもわれず　柳多留 十一
hananoyama oni no kado to wa omowarezu   yanagidaru 1776
(blossom-mountain demon-gate-as-for think-cannot)

blossom mountain:
hard to believe it's really
the devil's gate!

The first *ku*, by Issa, is probably a *blossom-as-woman* poem, but who can say it is not the opposite! The blossom mountain in the *senryû* not only suggests a blossom-viewing site modeled after real mountains with hard to reach trees and magical creatures, but *the* mountain = *Mons veneris*. This playful reflection of man's natural love of luscious women is far kinder than the *Shin-Tsukuba ku*, "Once cherries bloom / not a mountain remains / in the mind" (花さきて心にのこる山もなし 後土？門院　新つくは *hana sakite kokoro ni nokoru yama mo nashi* kôshi 1495), which suggests attainment of the goal ends veneration. The devil's gate, or demon-gate, was generally to the North (*down* in the Sinosphere) as was Yoshiwara, the pleasure quarters with respect to Edo.

山の腹一ツや花の種がはり　種次　毛吹草
yama no hara wa hitotsu ya hana no tanegawari   shuji 1645
(mountain's belly-as-for one/singular!/: blossoms seed-change)

a mountain has
a common belly: blossoms
many fathers

The original is better. 1) "Belly" (*hara*) is homophonic with "meadow." 2), It is common to talk of a mountain's *belly*, *back*, or *hip*; in Japanese, mountains share these parts with us rather than borrow them. 3), The term "seed-change," commonly used to describe the reason why one cat can bear so different kittens, sounds natural for plants (unlike my "fathers"); scientific terms are no help for this.

花もさそ待こしはるのあさかすミ 無記名=発句帳
hana mo sazo machi-kojiwaru no asagasumi anon. (pre 17c)
(blossoms [emph. emph.] waiting-poke-split's morning mist)

    blossoms, too
as you might guess, play coy
      morning mist

    with blossoms out
we complain while waiting for
     the mist to clear

     sure enough
blossoms will put you off
    morning mist

In other words, they acted like women were expected to act in Japan and most of the world.

さそひても花をおもはぬあらし哉 無記名=発句帳
sasoite mo hana o omowanu arashi kana anon. (1356=tsukubashû)
(invit/entic/ing even blossom/s[acc. think/care/love-not storm!/'tis)

   it doesn't love
the blossoms it entices
    the wild wind

   this damn wind
stealing blossoms it thinks
    nothing of them

It bids them to come,
but has no real love for blossoms –
this blustery wind.
          – trans. Stephen D. Carter

The way the wind's behavior and mindset are described, the object of his loveless passion, likewise, seems human. *Arashi* is, strictly speaking, a *storm*, but wind personifies well.

三月は実紐とかぬ花もなし 無記名 嵐山集
sangatsu wa geni himo tokanu hana mo nashi anon. 1651
(third-month-as-for really string[under-belt] dissolve-not blossom not)

    the third month
not a blossom doesn't
    undo its garter

Actually, we are not talking about a garter but a piece of string attached to the edges of the wrap-around robes, in this case the inside layer of robes, which is to say, *underwear*. This string was the one that was only untied for, or by a lover, or magically became undone – or rotted away – forecasting his return. I called it a "garter" to create an instantly understandable poem. The reader is free to restore the "string" or "cord."

めつらしき人にけふとけはなのひも 無記名 発句帳
mezurashiki hito ni kyô toke hana no himo anon. (pre 17c)
(rare[honored]-person -for today dissolve! blossoms' string)

  undo your garters
today, blossoms! for
  your rare guest

   a rare guest
comes today: buds feel
   free to bloom!

Is the rare guest (someone treated like a god) the poet? It was a struggle not to write *"blossoms / drop your panties"* to put more life into this ancient conceit explained as follows in my OJD:

as women

◎ *hana-no shita-himo* (blossom's lower string) ◎

"The opening of a bud is likened to the melting (or, untying) of the inner string:

SHINKOKINSHÛ #84 (1205)
fushite omoi okite-nagamuru harusame ni
hana no shitahimo ika ni toku ran anon

SHINCHOKUSEN #52 (1235)
miyoshinono yamai no tsurara musubeba ya
hana no shitahimo osoku tokuran fujiwara kishun

lying, i long,
and, watching, write a song
of spring rain:

how it drops the panties
of the cherry blossoms!

if spring-wells
on beautiful yoshino
are icicle-bound,

blossom panties might
be slow to drop down!

This time, I did it. I replaced the untied below/inner "strings" with dropped "panties" How else could I convey the eroticism? (Other versions of the first: *Lying, I long / and waking i gaze upon / the spring rain // to see how it unties / the belts of all the buds!* Or, *Sleeping, I dream, / waking up i gaze upon / the spring rain // Just how does it manage / to undo the cherry buds?*) The second song may reflect almanac wisdom, the conceit used without real romantic intent, but that "well" *is* suspicious!

花やはらむ大原山の雲の帯　無記名 嵐山集
hana ya haramu ôhara yama no kumo no obi anon. 1651
(blossoms!/: swell/ing big-belly-mountain's cloud-belt)

cloud obi (belt)

what blossoms!
large-belly mountain
is with child

As noted before, an *obi* is the thick belt or sash used with a kimono, that was kept cinched up tight when a woman was pregnant, conversely to the European pregnancy belt that was *looser* than ordinary. In this *ku*, it is not so much the blossom-as-woman as the *entire mountain*-as-woman.

花の顔つは [ぼ?] める内や丸ひたい　貞富 洗濯もの
hana no kao tsuba[bo?]meru uchi ya marubitai teifû -1666
(blossoms-face/s gather-together[bud?] while: round-forehead)

blossom faces:
while still in bud, hoh!
round brows!

The round brow is not what the reader might imagine. It means a brow-line in its natural, yet unshaven state, before adulthood. The bud, really round, plays on the literary meaning.

櫻や色十六七の薄化粧　國友 太夫櫻
sakura ya iro jûroku-shichi no usugeshô kokuyû 1680
(cherry/ies!/: color sixteen, seventeen's light-make-up)

うつくしき顔に化粧や花曇　進歩 蕉尾琴
utsukushiki kao ni keshô ya hanagumori shinpo -1747
(beautiful face/s-on make-up: blossom-overcast)

cherry blossoms:
their color, the light make-up
of a teen-ager

why make-up
on such pretty faces?
blossom haze

Blossom overcast or haze, a standard blossom-term, is usually seen as a light veil, so this is simultaneously new and corny. I like that. In Japanese, "make-up" by itself is white powder.

夜にちるや花も浮名を忍ぶらん 道誉 つくは
yoru[ni] chiru ya hana mo ukina o shinoburan　dôkyô 1356
(night-in falling!/: blossoms too scandals-to averse[+emph])

falling at night!
so blossoms, too, care
for their reputation

見物にちり交りたるさくらかな 許六
kenbutsu ni chiri majiwaritaru sakura kana　kyoroku -1715
(seers-on/in/among falling-mix cherry/blossom/petal!/'tis)

chery petals falling all over the voyeurs	cherry petals falling, mix freely with the audience

The first *ku* is not really blossoms-*as*-women but blossoms facetiously seen as acting *like* women. *Kenbutsu*, in the second *ku*, suggests an *audience* comprising viewers of humans. The first reading imagines Yoshiwara with the cherries' bloom partially hidden, while the second has the cherries putting on a dramatic show. Elsewhere, Kyoroku put the cherry=woman idea into prose:

> The cherry is a *keisei* (castle-toppler: beauty, or top-rank courtesian) at the peak of her popularity. This blossom is absolutely fashionable, so completely *now* that nothing is left for tomorrow.

Perhaps this should have been in the women-as-blossom chapter. As we have noted, courtesans were called *sakura,* and I might add that this poet was ethnographically minded and wrote about various professions; but the above words were part of his sketch of the characteristics of 100 flowers (風俗文選 百花譜 1706) and seem to be about the trees. Regardless, it provides the perfect comeback for the following generalization coming from a sympathetic 19c Occidental, Percival Lowell (SFS:1888) .

> Their [the Japanese] care for tree flowers is not confined to a cultivation, it is a cult. It approaches to a sort of natural nature worship, an adoration in which nothing is personified. For the emotion aroused in the Far Oriental is just as truly an emotion as it was to the Greek; but whereas the Greek personified its object, the Japanese admires that object for what it is. To think of a cherry-tree as a woman, would be to his mind a conception transcending even the limits of the ludicrous.

It is true the Japanese and Chinese did not idealize the human form as the measure for all beauty, nor worship the feminine muse and muscle-bound male in the manner of the West, but, as we shall see in this chapter, it is going too far to claim that the Japanese never personified trees. It would be better to say that the personification is poetic and was not necessary to bring people to view the blossoms.

花の木の持て生たあいそ哉 一茶
hana no ki no motte umareta aisô kana　issa 1822
(blossom-tree's having-born (natural) amiability!/'tis)

born to bloom cherry trees so sweetly natured by nature!	***blossoms*** what charm is born with every cherry tree!

my cherry tree
in bloom: natural
amiability

This is sympathetic rather than pathetic fallacy, and I like the *ku* so much I present it *again* in three more translations. Who knows if Issa is praising trees, reflecting on women or fondly recalling his dead daughter Sato. A couple years later, after his wife, Kiku, dies and he remarries, Issa recycles the *ku* with a small change: *amiability(aisô)* ➔ *good fortune(kahô)*. It is on a card he gave to his new bride's relatives. In Ueda's words, "The tree in the *hokku* must stand for Yuki who the poet thought looked as beautiful as cherry blossoms." The marriage only lasted about as long as a tree blooms. So there is some *woman-as-tree* in Issa. Be that as it may, Lafcadio Hearn, wondering what could make Japanese cherry blossoms so dazzling and luscious, draws out the tree-as-woman metaphor:

> Is it that the trees have been so long domesticated and caressed by man in this land of the gods, that they have acquired souls, and strive to show their gratitude, like women loved, by making themselves more beautiful for man's sake? Assuredly, they have mastered men's hearts by their loveliness, like beautiful slaves. (Glimpses of Unfamiliar Japan: 1894)

As I may have already pointed out elsewhere, cats, not women, make themselves beautiful (by plentiful grooming) *when they are loved;* women do so *when they love*. Hearn's "slave" is not a felicitous metaphor, but, that aside, he does bring out a kernel of truth in Lowell's contrast, for no Japanese writer would lay on *their* anthropomorphizing with such aplomb.

佐保姫や初そめ匂ふ花櫻　肖柏 大発句帳
saohime ya hatsuzome niou hanazakura shôhaku -1527
(saho-princess! first-dyeing[dress] scents/glows bloom-cherry)

it's the princess!
a flowering cherry the scent
of fresh dye

cherry blossoms
glowing from a first dye:
princess sao?

Do you find anything erotic in the smell of newly dyed cloth? It is hard to separate the *blossoms* from the *tree*. We know the former are what was "dyed" but the tree seems central. So long as we are wandering off the path, let us explore another way to link Flora to the cherry blossoms:

さほ姫の染損ひや斑山　一茶
sao-hime no some-sokonai ya madara yama issa -1827
(sao-princess's dyeing-miss/fail! splotchy/spotted mountain)

princess sao
slipped up on her dyeing!
splotchy hills

☆
up
ch rry
mou ta n
pri cess sao
may w ll h ve pis ed
bu the pat hes sho just wh re
s   h   e   m i s s   d !

The first reading shows the *ku*, taken at face-value; but Issa has another about *violets* marking the spots where Princess Sao peed (*sao-hime no bari ya koboshite saku sumire*) – remarkable, when you consider the fact that Ben Franklin, in an aside in his "Letter to the French Academy" on the more pressing problem of farts, observed that piss could be made to smell good, *like violets*, by eating plenty of pine nuts. Issa also tied in colorful leaves to the menses of Tachida Princess of the Fall. *Haikai* once played a lot with body functions and a *ku* about the Princess of Spring's micturation (heavy spring mist is attributed to her peeing while standing and wetting her hem) was particularly well known. I assume the fresh dye in the Shôhaku's *ku* is a purely sartorial metaphor, but with Issa's, who knows! But, let's leave blossom-*by*-woman and return to blossom-*as*-woman:

楊貴妃のさくらや花の雪女 友我 崑山集
yôkihi no sakura ya hana no yuki onna yûga 1651
(yokihi = yang kuei-fei = cherry!/: blossom-snow-woman)

snow-woman
of the blossoms! the cherry
"princess yoki"

Here we have the blossom as a particular woman, the legendary Imperial concubine Yang Kuei-fei (719-756) a Chinese beauty of many talents assassinated by jealous rivals. She is the name of a cherry variety, and since varieties named after particular women were very rare, the poet puts her next to another brilliant fiction, the snow-woman, seen in the icy or snowy adornment of trees and landscape. She was also feared as was, to a lesser degree, the cherry "snow" for its connection with death (bk 2). So we have a double femme-fatal. Still, it is a sorry *ku*, as is this: *"Princess Yôkihi / a cherry that could tip-over / a country!"* (楊貴妃は国も傾く桜哉 宗利 夢見草 *yôkihi wa kuni mo katamuku sakura kana* sôri 1656) Yes, a beauty is formidable. This next I like much better.

くちびるは笛も吹べし貴妃桜 蓼太
kuchibiru wa fue mo fukubeshi kihizakura ryôta -1787
(lips-as-for flute-even blow-should [yô]kihi-cherry)

the talented cherry

her petal lips
should play a flute
yôki-*zakura*

While the number of old haiku on this variety of cherry did not quite warrant a separate chapter, the tree itself is a beauty deserving a word more. Kuitert writes:

> Like Oshokun [another cherry named after a Chinese woman], Yokihi echoes a historical Chinese idea of feminine beauty, and the two cultivars responded to aesthetic ideals associated with China [by the Japanese]. The blushing pink of the blossom of both . . . . and the abundance of the many-petaled flowers set in lush clusters were considered very "Chinese" by the Japanese of the time, resembling for instance, the gorgeous flowers of Chinese tree peonies. (*Japanese Flowering Cherries* 1999)

In other words, Japanese thought of Chinese aesthetics as austere Europeans thought of the Byzantine,

As an objective student of botany, Kuitert continued, "For its botany and horticultural merits, though, 'Yôkihi' resembles 'Edo-zakura' [Edo being about as Japanese as one can get] and 'Ito-kukuri'. It is distinguished from the two by its fewer flowers per cluster . . ." (IBID). So, it/she is not obese, but *embonpoint,* healthy and delightfully plump, like Tinkerbelle, described on the first page of *Peter Pan*. Seriously, the two legendary figures share a trait which Keigu will haiku since no one else has:

puff to petal

a morality play
pride comes before fall
yôki-zakura!

The same for Ôshokun (王昭君 Wang Zhaojun), who is popularly depicted as a beauty too proud of her beauty to bribe a painter to paint her beautifully, which caused her to be sent to the Barbarians (Hsiung-nu tribe) as a tribute because the Chinese Emperor looked at the pictures and sent what he thought was the ugliest woman. In other words, we can use the story of these women as a sort of just-so story for the cherry blossom's falling: *pride comes before fall.* But it is not the only story. The official history books just say she was given because she was beautiful and that "the grass that grew on her grave [she killed herself] the next spring was fresh and green, whereas elsewhere it was yellow and dry" (Kuitert:IBID). Ie, "it is a victim of its own beauty, according to Ingram (1948), who thought it suffering for being beautiful." (IBID) We might sum up that just-so story as *"the beauty tax."*

楊貴妃の玉のありかや花の露　正直　毛吹草
yôkihi no tama no arika ya hana no tsuyu   seichoku   1638/1645
(yôki-princess's drop/gem/soul's/souls' place! blossom's dew)

where do we find   blossom dew:
the soul of princess yôki?   where we find the soul
the blossom's dew   of princess yôki

The correct Chinese characters for a drop (eg of water), a ball/gem and soul are different, but they have been conflated so often in Japanese, where they are homophones, to be traditional. I include the date the publication was edited and published because Kuitert notes that while the Yôkihi-zakura is believed to have originated in Nara, the ancient capital (710-94) founded on the rational Chinese city planning model (a grid), it "is not found in any source earlier than the *Kadan-kômoku* (Flower bed catalog) of 1681." (IBID) We have seen a clear Yôkihi cherry published in 1651 and the apparent one (cherry is not specified but strongly suggested by the "blossom"), above, is even earlier![1]

巫山の神女を・美女の来て我を抱けり花曇　伴水
bijô no kite ware o dakikeri hanagumori   hansui   暁山 1700
(beautiful-woman's coming me[obj] hug[emph.] blossom-overcast)

a beauty comes
and embraces me!
blossom-haze

---

1. *Historical Appeal.* *Haikai* can be a great historical aid (poetic documentation?) – I have just recently written someone who has made the world's largest collection of online *haikai* with the request that there be a listing of search results *by date* (as well as syllabet). This might be already possible at online databases and CD-roms accessible to academia and wealth (not to the likes of me). Scholarship cries for truly PUBLIC patronage.

If Issa's *ku* (#15-17) where blossoms (perhaps glowing in the moon-light) seemed like angels dropped down from heaven (*yozakura ya bijin* . . .) is visual, the almost palpable haze that translates literally as "blossom-cloudiness" in this older *ku* by an obscure poet evokes the sense of touch and is, I think, better. An additional word on Issa's angels I failed to squeeze in the first time around. It will mean more now we know more about the blossoms-as-women-as-blossoms. Issa's vision did not form in a vacuum; he surely had seen pictures of these Goddesses in a book called "Weird Illustrations" (奇妙図絵 = 1803) repeatedly printed in his lifetime together with one of the few *ku* written by Kyôten (山東京伝), better known for his collection of anecdotes about Edo's poets and other cool people: *"What blooms / is a blossom: angels, too / in cloud town"* (さくや花天女も雲の中の町 京伝 *saku ya hana tenjo mo kumo no naka no machi*). Are we are talking about the women of the high-class pleasure quarters, who were out of reach of mere mortals? The book also included a *ku* from Kyôten's earlier *"48 Ways to Buy a Castle-toppler (Pretty Courtesan)"* (傾城買四十八手 = 1790):

西行も末見ぬ花の廓哉　京伝
saigyô mo sue minu hana no chimata kana kyôten -1803
(saigyô even end see-not blossom-town!/'tis)

even saigyô	even saigyô
never saw the blossoms	never knew the blossoms
in this town	of this town

The *sue minu*, or "end view-not" may allude to blossoms falling after the bloom-peak, when Saigyô died (-1190). The Chinese character pronounced *"chimata"* here (accordiing to glosses), usually is pronounced *kuruwa*, meaning "brothel." (参照：「江戸俳諧にしひがし」2002). But, before we pull Issa's night angels down to the ground, let me add that Issa did *not* have harlots on his mind. If he missed the book mentioned in the last paragraph, he may have seen or heard the Zeami (noh) play where a good ruler manages to get the gods to grant a cherry tree the exceptionally long bloom of twenty-one days (泰山府君) in a scene which includes a (female) angel who descends from the full bloom in the moonlight. Issa's angel metaphor probably reflects his deep affection for the trees. Yet Issa did write many *ku* about women of the street, inn and pleasure quarters. My favorites are two summer *ku* he wrote at age 30 outside of what is now Osaka. I translated them in my rhyming days, a decade ago: *"An Okazaki whore / is a good whore / and what's more / it's a cool evening!"* & *"In Newtown tonight / our eyes also enjoy / the cool sight!"* & *"Us poets in Newtown / just lookin' around; / Lord, the whores get hot / when the streets cool down!"* (能い女郎。。、新町や。。). Some are *sakura ku*:

吉原・としよりの目（の）正月ぞさくら花　一茶
toshiyori no me no shôgatsu zo sakurabana   issa 1816
(oldperson's eyes' new-year!!! cherry-blossom/s)

yoshiwara pleasure quarters

this is new year's
one day only for old eyes:
cherry blossoms!

New Year's idiomatically means *once a year*. Is the annual fall tryst of the Herder and Weaver stars reflected in old eyes viewing cherry blossoms and their namesake, the beautifully kimonoed courtesans? These are not women-or-blossoms but a women-as-blossoms *and* blossoms-as-women. As we will see in the *Sexual Blossoms* chapter, there were both real cherry blossoms in Yoshiwara and human ones. We have something we might call a circle, or cycle, of metaphor.

as woman

姥桜小町が果の名なるべし 探吟 珠洲之海
ubazakura komachi ga hate no na narubeshi tangin 18c?
(granny cherry komachi/beauty's end's name be/come-ought)

granny cherry
the right name for what
was komachi

old-witch cherry	babushka cherry
komachi-came-to-this	we should instead call you
should be your name	*komachi's end*

If the first reading is correct, and chances are it is, the next two readings are wrong; though they can be logically justified, the Law of Occam's razor applies in translation, too. As noted in chapter 7, *ubazakura* is a variety of cherry that is leafless=toothless when it blooms and tends to be long-lived. Such is the first definition in any old dictionary, but new ones usually drop the tree entirely for its metaphor, "a faded beauty," or "elderly woman of beauty." For the beautiful, allegedly coy, poetess who never bore fruit (some think she was a hole short), it is a beautiful and kind thought, for her sorry end is usually played upon rather than the beauty of her poetry which like the old tree blooms on.

帽子に花の乳房やお乳の人 虚子
bôshi ni hana no chibusa ya o-chi no hito kyoshi 1901
(hat-on/by blossom-breast/udder: honorable-tit/milk-person [nurse-maid])

tit on tit	*sisters*
a sprig of cherry	her hat touched
blossoms on her hat	by tits of pink blossom:
the nurse-maid	a nurse-maid

Clusters of blossoms may be called *breasts* in Japanese (some dictionaries mislead by claiming it is the *corolla*, which is only the tips of the petals). The original is deliciously ambiguous, evoking the breasts of the woman by animalizing, or rather mammalizing the plant. Japanese claim the tits of pregnant and nursing women turn cherry (blossom) color – purplish pink, though, today, most blossoms are closer to white. The *ku* turns a commonplace into a painting. The second reading is, I think, most likely.

とにかくに胸動く若木櫻かな 北枝 アルス
tonikaku ni mune ugoku wakaki sakura kana hokushi -1718
(at-any-rate breast moves young-tree cherry!/'tis)

at any rate
a young cherry tree
moves the heart

I like Hokushi's "at any rate" because I am reminded of the Socratic dialogue where a discussion on ideal human beauty – after a ridiculous attempt to equate it with the useful and the good – ended with the only conclusion honest men can *ever* reach about that subject: "Well, this we can agree on, a beautiful woman is surely a beauty." (Don't quote me: this is from memory!) But, is there anything special about a young cherry tree? To be sure, a young *willow* is one of them most graceful sights – to me it is pure art – in the vegetable kingdom.[1] But, I don't think a young cherry tree is *that* special compared to an older one. So, I suspect the poet is seeing the cherry-as-woman, or, rather, girl.

ごとならば君とまるべくにほはなむかへすは花のうきにやはあらぬ 幽仙法師 古今集#395
goto naraba kimi tomaru beki nihowanamu kaesu wa hana no uki niya wa aranu kokinshû 905

seeing off prince urin'in under the cherry blossoms

so long as you are
blooming, why not stop him
in his tracks, turn

on your charm lest he leave
your blossom name in doubt

The feminine beauty of the cherry blossoms obliquely alluded to in *Kokinshû* #394 (#50-27), is obvious in this, the second of two poems made at the same occasion (Rodd+Henkenius, trans. ends: *". . . oh, cherries, bloom / your loveliest: hold / him here, for his return might / betray your uncomeliness."*). Both poets were Buddhist priests; it is amusing they should appeal to beauty's power of attachment. One, Henjô, is more famous for his *waka* begging a maiden-flower (*ominaeshi*) not to tell anyone he broke his vows by plucking her only because he loved her *name*. My favorite explanation accompanying the poem has him falling off his horse as he reaches out for "her." *At any rate, cherries are not the only ♀ flowers.*

身をわけて見ぬこずゑなく尽くさばや　よろづの山の花の盛りを　西行
mi o wakete minu kozuenaku tsukusabaya yorozu no yama no hana no sakari o saigyô -1190
(body/self[obj] splitting, see-not tree-tips-not exhaust-would / myriad mountains' blossom-peak[obj])

the cherry lover

i would split
myself up and not miss
a single limb

of any tree blooming
on every mountain

This poem marks Saigyô as the greatest cherry-lover of all time. A Japanese annotator notes that one theory/explanation (*setsu*) is that this concerns the tradition of dividing the Buddha's body (*hotoke-no bunshin-suru*), where the bits and pieces were treasured. Failing to find as much of this religious ghoulishness in Japan as in Europe (saints were torn into "relics" as late as the 17c), I think, instead, of a voluntary Orpheus (*By all means, tear me up!*), and recall the dream of Byron's famous *alter*, Don Juan, *"that Womankind had but one rosy mouth, / To kiss them all at once from North to South."*

榎嶋・花風や天女負はれて歩渡り　其角 五元
hanakaze ya tenjô owarete arukiwatari   kikaku -1707
(blossom-wind!/: heaven-woman carrying walking-cross)

enoki island

blossom wind
i walk across, an angel
on my back

---

1. Young Willow The way just a few shoots come out, or seem to pour out, and sway with the trunk so thin that it sways, too; and the silhouette that such countable limbs create (like the best of the finest Art Deco) must, like the full bloom of the cherry, be seen to be believed. (IPOOH: spring I: willow and, eventually, a spin-off volume!).

56

House Cherries
家桜
ie-zakura

去年折し跡もや今年家桜　正友 _{犬子}
kozo orishi ato mo ya kotoshi iezakura　seiyû 1633
(last year broken mark even!/: this year's house-cherry)

the scars made
last year still marking
my house cherry

the house cherry:
this year you still see
last year's scars

The "house-cherry" (*ie-zakura*) is no more a genuine type of tree than a mountain-cherry. Indeed, it is *less* so, for it can include every type of cherry found, whereas the mountain cherry is supposedly wild and does not properly include cultivars (*sato-zakura*). In one sense, the house-cherry is the contrary of the mountain cherry. By definition, it is domestic; and, growing by a house, the results of ripping off limbs of bloom are seen the following year. Such domestic violence can make some varieties of cherry, by nature plain-limbed unless shaped by strong winds, more attractive in the long run.

枝ふりも主も強かれ家櫻　道二 _{毛吹草}
edaburi mo nushi mo tsuyokare iezakura　dôji 1645
(limb-form and[emph.] owner strong house-cherry)

house-cherries
well-built trees bloom for
strong masters

limbs and master
equally robust: a real
house-cherry

Did it take a strong man to break off enough large limbs to create a powerful-looking plant, or does the *ku* describe a muscular couple? The second definition of a "house-cherry" is a wife.

山陰に咲は隠居か家桜　照盤 _{夢見草}
yamakage ni saku wa [sakeba?] inkyo ka[ga?] iezakura　shôban 1656
(mountain-shade-in bloom-as-for retiree?/retiree's house-cherry)

house cherries
blooming in hidden dales?
hermits have 'em!

house cherries
are those blooming in the hills,
then, hermits?

Does the poet mean house-cherries in the hills are anomalous? Or, does he mean that if the house cherry was a cheerful haus frau, the mountain cherry was a hermit? I prefer the latter reading.

花はよも毛蟲にならじ家櫻　嵐雪 玄峰集
hana wa yo mo kemushi ni naraji iezakura ransetsu -1707
(blossoms-as-for world-even caterpillar-become-not house-cherry)

blossoms today allow no such caterpillars, house cherries!	may our blossoms too, be caterpillar-free house cherries	house cherries may all blossoms remain caterpillar-free

The natural eyebrows of an unmarried woman were called caterpillars, "hair-bugs" in Japanese. My first guess is that Ransetsu's house cherry has been attacked by caterpillars and he is telling it that such a fashion is now out-of-style; but the ambiguity of *yo mo* leaves open other possibilities.

楽や内関白の家ざくら 宗立 夢見草 1656　　入相の後をあるじの花見哉 岨角 蘆分船 1694
tanoshimu ya uchikanpaku no iezakura sôritsu?　　*iriai no ato o aruji no hanami kana* sôkaku
(enjoy: inside-tyrant's house-cherry)　　(vespers after[ ] master's blossom-viewing!)

the happy m[o]use　　　　　　　　**hours of privilege**

i just love it!　　　　　　　　　　after dark: when
me, a lion at home with　　　　　　the owner has his own
my house cherry!　　　　　　　　blossom-viewing

How delightful that "a lion at home and a mouse abroad," i.e., a "house-tyrant" (*uchi-kampaku*) was already recognized hundreds of years ago (by a poet from Ôsaka)! A man who might not cut much of a figure on cherry-mountain can lord it over his private blossom-viewing.

一日は客になりけり家櫻　成美
ichinichi wa kyaku ni narikeri iezakura seibi -1816
(first/one-day-as-for guest-as/into becomes[emph.] house-cherry)

for one day we treat it like a guest! the house cherry	the first day *i* feel like a guest of my house cherry

In Japanese, it is said that "a guest/customer is god" (*okyaku-wa kamisama*), until the magic wears off. But, who is the guest here? The second reading also respects the tree. Usually Seibi, as master of his household and a haikai master with a retinue of disciples, would be the blossom host (*hana no aruji*).

風口に戸障子もがな家櫻 秋月 夢見草 1656　　風のとほる脇道も哉家櫻 作者不知
kazaguchi ni toshôji mogana iezakura shûgetsu　　*kaze no tôru wakimichi mogana iezakura* anon.
(wind's mouth-to door wish-for house-cherry)　　(wind's pass alley wish-for house-cherry)

my house cherry sure could use a paper door to the windward	oh, for an alley the wind can slip through! house cherries!

A paper door to keep out the wind but let in some light? A cherry in the garden can be hurt by the wind, though *as a house cherry* it ought to have at least nominal protection. As "wind" is also a male lover and the house-cherry a wife, the first poet might be alluding to precaution against being cuckolded, while the second, anonymous, of course, wants a way open for swiving.

house-cherry

家櫻風を免許の札も哉 信相 鷹つくは
iezakura kaze o menkyô no fuda mogana shinsô 1642
(house-cherry wind-to license-tablet/pass wish-for)

    house cherries   house cherries
it might be nice to have passes   how i wish the wind, too
      for the wind   needed a pass

People carried passes – wooden tablets presented at gates – to get about in much of Japan, so why not a pass for Mr. Wind? Did the poet think his cherry was short of wind because of walls restricting "his" passage (the bachelor wishing for license identifies with the wind); or, rather, want the access of dangerous elements restricted for his darling tree, (an anti-wind, blossom-master's perspective)? Or do I over-signify a reverie occasioned by a poet enjoying a light breeze with his house-cherry? (39, O.M.)

垣ごしに見るあだ人のいへざくら　花ちるばかり行きておらばや 新古今# 1450
kakigoshi ni miru adabito no iezakura hana chiru bakari ikite orabaya shinkokinshû 1205

   o'er the hedge   *behind the hedge*   *the house-cherries*
i see another man's   *i see the cherry blooming*   *of mine enemy bloom*
  house-cherry!   *by her house*   *behind his hedge*

so long as her petals fall   *While there are petals still*   *petals flying everywhere*
i should go take a spray!   *i'd best go impress my will*   *i'd best get some for me!*

The meaning hedges on the *adabito*. It can mean "another (person)" (他人), "rival"(仇人), "faithless [would-be?] lover" or "stylish person/lover" (徒人) and suggests *adabana*, a flower that bears no fruit, implying the house-cherry is unfulfilled as a woman. In English, tree and woman cannot implicitly co-exist as in the original, where the particle "*no*" links what comes before and after ambiguously, allowing identity (cherry as *adabito*) and/or belonging (cherry of the *adabito*). A few more translations are needed to cover all the possibilities, including a widow with a careless yard. *Behind the hedge* / *a house-cherry belonging* / *to a do-nothing.* / *Petals fall and that is all:* / *better if i do something!*

風有や鼠にしらみ家ざくら　長頭丸 崑山集　　散行は世帯破りか家櫻　　正直 毛吹草 1645
kaze aru ya nezumi ni shirami iezakura teitoku 1651　　*chiriyuku wa shôtaiyaburi ka iezakura* seichoku
  (wind is!/: mice and lice house-cherry/ies)　　 (falling-go house-destroying? house-cherry)

    when there's wind   you fall, you go:
you get mice! you get lice!   is your household ruined,
     house cherries   *ie-zakura?*

Mice, not cats, are the burglars of Japan and lice was typically spread by lovers; so the first *ku* might claim wives cannot be guarded. A nominal association in the second *ku* ridiculously relates petal loss to the end of a lineage. This is totally boring in translation. So is *"If only there were / a home-solidification to keep blossoms from falling: / house-cherries!"* (花の散ぬやがためも哉家ざくら 長頭丸 崑山集 *hana no chiranu yagatame mogana iezakura* teitoku 1651): lacking a *yagatame* ceremony (done for new buildings), the poetry is lost to English. With pure puns it is worse. Everything is lost. Take "house" (*ie*), where it doubles for its homophone "speak!" – *"Buds, when / you open your mouths, / speak=house-cherry!"* (花の口開かは物をいへ櫻　正直 犬子 *hana no kuchi hirakaba mono o iezakura* seichoku 1633) – hopeless, right? To do well in English, we need to *start* with English: *Eg.: "Wishing blossoms / never to leave, we keep them / home cherries."* Or, *"Her first bloom: / How about an open-house for / our home-cherry?"* and so forth.

遠きより近き隣の家桜　頼広 夢見草
tôki yori chikaki tonari no iezakura　yorihiro 1656
(far-away more-than close neighbor's house-cherry)

隣へもたからとなるや家櫻　弘永 毛吹草
tonari e mo takara to naru ya iezakura　kôei 1645
(neighbor-to also treasure becomes!/: house-cherry)

near beats far
enjoy your neighbor's
house cherry

a treasure for
the neighbors, too:
house cherry!

The first plays with proverbs advising us to take advantage of what is to be had nearby and is somewhat risque, while the second, I think, is kind and true.

こちの花咲て隣に酔人哉　也有 アルス？
kochi no hana sakite tonari ni yoibito kana　yayû 1701-83
(this/here's blossom blooming neighbors-at drunken-person'tis)

my cherry blooms
and the guy next door
gets high over it!

our tree blooms
and a neighbor ends up
blossom drunk

Yayû has written a pure haiku about how a fine cherry tree can affect us, but the hint of identification of cherry tree with woman gives the poem an erotic patina it otherwise would not have.

声なふて人やよびこむ家ざくら　無記名 嵐山集
koe noute hito ya yobikomu iezakura　anon. 1651
(voice raising people call-in house-cherry)

she raises her voice
and invites strangers in:
the house cherry!

and i call out
inviting all in to view
my house cherry

Some house cherries were, to use an ugly turn-of-the-century Americanism, clearly *proactive*.

咲を世に知や歌人の家桜　長頭丸 嵐山集
saku o yo ni shiru ya kajin no iezakura　teitoku 1651
(blooming [obj] world-to know: song-person's hse.cherry)

我植て歌よむ人の櫻哉　松葎 小弓俳集 1699
ware uete uta yomu hito no sakura kana　shôritsu?
(i/self planting/ed song compose person's cherry!)

when it blooms
the world knows: a poet's
house-cherry!

lo, this cherry
planted by a man who
makes it a poem

The second *ku* does not use the word "house-cherry," but it is. Both are about *waka* poets. The second one could end: " *~ sings about it.*" In the Occident, we have our poets who immortalized ♀.

見とれゐる程やあらましの家桜　久任
mitoreiru hodo ya aramashi no iezakura　kyûnin 夢見草 1656
(look-transfixed extent! ~~crude~~/be/have[+desire-for-non-existent-state] house-cherry/ies)

~~it's barbarous~~
~~to become besotted with~~
~~a house-cherry!~~

give me a house
cherry with looks enough
to keep me *gaga*!

~~the more you~~
~~look, the rougher *she* looks:~~
~~house cherries~~

~~Japanese men, like Europeans, were not supposed to be uxorious, for marriage was considered a serious business not to be confused with love.~~ *Aramashi* means many things. I changed my mind.

◎ G ◎ A ◎ R ◎ D ◎ E ◎ N

わきむいて咄なからや庭櫻 成美
waki muite hanashinagara ya niwazakura seibi 1816
(side-facing speaking-while: garden-cherry)

talking while i
look over my shoulder:
garden-cherry

散る時は我庭櫻しつかなり 成美 アルス
chiru toki wa waga niwazakura shizuka-nari seibi
(falling time-as-for my garden-cherry quiet becomes)

when it scatters	when its petals
petals, my garden-cherry	fall, my garden-cherry
is very quiet	becomes silent

I first thought a "*garden* cherry" (*niwazakura*) was a precisely located "house-cherry," but later found it was not a true cherry. I leave this cherry-impersonating five-foot shrub (*P. glandulosa*) here, anyway. Is Seibi's garden-cherry his maid, as opposed to the real house-cherry, his wife? Does the second *ku* mean that people notice the cherry-like shrub in bloom but, unlike the case with real cherries, no attention is given to the petals dropping (if the blossoms do drop petal by petal)?

只一木雲のちきれか庭櫻 うすい？
tada hitoki kumo no chigire ka niwazakura usui
(just one tree's cloud's pinch/piece? garden-cherry)

閑かなる雲のとさしや庭櫻 昌察 15c? 18c?
nodoka naru kumo no tozashi ya niwazakura shôsatsu
(tranquil become clouds' locked-up: garden-cherries)

is the whole tree	how peaceful
a mere pinch of cloud?	with the clouds locked up!
my garden cherry	a garden cherry

Usui's *ku* fuses the ideas of blossom clouds and small portions of them brought down from the mountains for those who could not see them *in situ*. The "pinch" (*chigire*=wrested-off piece) emphasizes the small size of the "tree" which, having no trunk to speak of, is pure cloud when in full bloom. Shôsatsu's *ku* is titled *"On the Porch of My City Hermitage"* (隠市軒にて). My reading takes it for a reply to the Chinese conceit of devious, ever-changing wild clouds. An alternate reading, imagines the greater security of the sage retiree in the city, where even the cherry blossom clouds can be protected from the mountain wind: *"The gentle cloud / is locked safely in: / garden cherries."*

門桜ちら（*or* はら）／＼散るが仕事哉 一茶 浅黄空
kadozakura chirajiira (hara-hara) chiru ga shigoto kana issa -1827
(gate-cherry scatter-scatter (flutter-fluttering) falling work!/'tis)

the cherry tree	the cherry tree
in front is scattering	by my gate does its job
petals: its job!	that is *littering*

Contrary to the "garden-cherry," the "gate-cherry" (*kadozakura*) is, like "the united states of America," a description rather than a name, so it *is* a "house-cherry." Issa's *job* talk might seem absurd, but reading his *ku* where mantises kill because it is their job and the old poet naps on a hot day because that is *his* job, etc., we come to realize it is his way of saying *we* – all life – *are one*. But, why a cherry *by the gate?* Perhaps, because that is where Japanese toss salt for charm and water for coolness.

夢心夜を守りけり家ざくら 嘯山 葎亭集
yumegokoro yoru o mamorikeru iezakura shôzan 1717-1801
(dream-heart night[acc] guard[+emph.] house-cherry)

ah, it keeps us dreaming all night long the house cherry	this dream-mind guarding the night hours a house cherry!	house-cherries! our dreams stand guard the whole night

The guarding mentioned in this older poem is a lot harder to comprehend than Issa's simple job! The three phrases (5-8-5) lack explicit causal connection. Is the blossom or the sleeping poet the guard?

咲く花は只白壁そ家櫻 常廣 犬子 1633
saku hana wa tada shiro kabe zo iezakura tsunehiro
(blooming blossom-as-for just white-wall! house-ch.)

花の木にむすびかけたる庵も哉[1] 士郎
hana no ki ni musubi-kaketaru io mogana shirô -1813
(blossom-tree-to tie-fasten house/workshop wish-for)

its blossoms? they're just a white wall! house cherries	oh, for a hut attached to a tree that blooms!

At first reading, this playing with the *house* concept seems 100% inane; but, on second thought, a solid clump of blossoms could be mistaken for a wall in a city, as it could be a cloud on a mountain. Shirô's dream is mine: a hut attached to a fine natural calendar. As cherry trees sometimes drop large branches, it might be wiser to live in a small clearing *among* but not quite *below* the blossoms:

このもしや花の中なるしばの庵 杉風
konomoshi ya hana no naka naru shiba no an sanpû 1646-1732
(delightful/wanted!/: blossoms-among brushwood hut/studio)

how delightful! a hut made of brushwood within the bloom	i want one too a brushwood hut and blossom-hidden	envious, indeed among the blooming trees a brushwood hut

While the poet's desire to be near the blossoms is the same, the hut-among-the-blossoms is contrary to the cherry tree by a house, or within a garden. There is also irony here. It comes from the little-known history – or, should I say, one biography – of the house-cherry given in one of the first chapters of Yamada's classic cherry history (『桜史』1941), *"White Snow in the Garden"* (庭の白雪). Yamada points out that a late Heian garden/landscaping book, the oldest such in Japan, instructed readers to plant blossoms, meaning cherries on the East side and red-leaf=sugar-maples on the West side. The idea was to surround an inner patio-like garden with just the right trees and, to sum up pages, the main reason for this was *kemari*, a type of *football* almost entirely about keeping the ball in the air. The trees had a role as markers and additional significance I cannot make out from the ancient prose (not that a modern translation would help; without illustrations, the terms are cricket to me). A later (1279 弘安二) description has a large number of balls up in the air at the same time, mixed in with petals blowing in the wind. Yamada thinks the popularity of *kemari* helped fill the gardens with cherry trees and notes that the once mixed group of trees marking the space came to be four cherry trees.

1. Oh, For A Hut! Babelfished I tried to English this *ku* with Altavista's Babelfish: "It begins to tie to the wood of the flower, the barrel hermitage kana." The software did not know any archaic grammar, even the simplest like ~*taru* and ~*mogana*, nor recognize a fairly common phrase like *hana no ki!* This irked me (since Japanese word-processors have recognized such words for almost a decade!), so I typed in *chikusho!* which means "damn!" just to see what the Babelfish would spit up. Here it is: *"domesticated fowl and animals raw!"* Babble, indeed!

~~~~~~

酒の科家櫻にて日暮れたり 白雄 アルス
sake no toga iezakura nite higurekeri shirao -1792
(sake's penalty house-cherry-with dusking[emph.])

too much *sake!*
at nightfall, i'm stuck with
the house cherry

Has the poet drunken so much at the daytime viewing that he is out of it and must stay home with his wife? There are worst places to be. Let us hope he appreciated his good fortune to *have* a house-cherry!

家ざくら有明の月と見て立ん 暁台
iezakura ariake no tsuki to mite tatsun gyôtai -1792
(house-cherry dawn-moon-with seeing stand-let's)

the house cherry   house cherries
it may be enjoyed with   stand up and view them with
the dawn moon   the dawn moon

One can camp out with wild cherries and see the moon in the morning, too, but it is not as easy as doing so at home.

折よしと花もほゝゑむ軒端かな 鬼貫
ori yoshi to hana mo hohoemu nokiba kana onitsura 1660-1738
(breaking OK[as if to say] blossom too smiles eave!/'tis)

the blossoms smile   break me, why not?
"break me off" if you wish   the blossoms say smiling
from my veranda   on my veranda

The house-cherry does not appear by name in this *ku,* but we can tell what is what, can't we?

八十賀・八十つゝき猶見ん春や家桜 宗春
yasotsuzuki nao min haru ya iezakura sôshun 1734
(eighty-continue[many-more] still see spring!/: house-cherry)

Celebrating 80

eighty's but a start
for i'd see more spring yet
my house cherry

I cannot tell if this poet is celebrating his 80th and the fact that thanks to having a cherry tree close by he can have a blossom viewing, or if he is also addressing his wife (which would be sweet).

余花あるや是長久の家桜 次郎 夢見草
yoka aru ya kore chôkyû no iezakura   jirô 1656
(leftover-blossoms!/: this longevity-a-while's house-cherry)

> bloom remains!
> doubtless a long life for her
> my house-cherry!

Some blossoms may remain after the main bloom has fallen. A woman who has a baby late in life tends to live for a long time, but my bet is for an eight-fold chrysanthemum cherry (*kikuzakura*), and *chôkyû* (long-life) as a homophone for the 9-9 date of the mum festival. In the Sinosphere, the mum was associated with longevity.

面々の楊貴妃なれや家櫻 政公 毛吹草
tsurazura no yôki-hi nare ya iezakura   seikô 1645
(face-face's yôki-princess/es become/be! house-cherries)

may you all be	face after face	house-cherries
pretty as princess yoki,	a real princess yôki!	may you all be exotic
house-cherries!	house cherries	princess yokis!

The first is very nice but a bit odd, for the famous beauty is Chinese and the cherry is a native tree. My second reading might be too good for it. The third wonders if the poet, high on blossoms, thinks all the married women look sexy! Finally, my favorite house cherry, followed by a surprise.

やまの木のこころで行や庭の花 卓袋
yama no ki no kokoro de yuku ya niwa no hana   takutai 17-18c
(mountain tree/s heart-with go!/: garden's blossoms)

> let's go visit her   out to my garden
> as we would a tree in the hills   i go for my cherry, let's
> my garden's cherry   pretend you're wild

我なくは花こそあるじ見し跡を心のまゝに露も荒らすな　心敬 百首和歌
ware naku wa hana koso aruji mishi ato o kokoro no mama ni tsuyu mo arasuna shinkei - 1475

> when i'm gone
> you, cherry tree, will be
> the blossom host
>
> let nothing change and see
> nary a dewdrop is displaced

In other words, the house-cherry inherits the house with unkempt grass, noted for holding gallons of dew. *Not to worry.* The next *waka* expects a bloomshade bereft of guests other than the moss growing on the cherry's roots. Note that Shinkei follows an older *waka* where the rare open gate seemed to suggest the blossoms of a mountain cherry were hosts who awaited guests (あしびきの山桜戸をまれに開けて花こそあるじ誰を待つらん　定家自撰 拾遺愚草 *ashibiki no yamazakura to o mare ni akete hana koso aruji dare o matsuran* shûigusô 1216-33). Shinkei's twenty blossom poems 花二十首, of which this was one (or two), bring darkness even to the house-cherry. Luckily, *haikai* would see happier times.

57

Children Blossom-viewing
子供ノ花見

大佛を見に行く花の小道哉 子規 x 2
daibutsu o mi ni yuku hana no komichi kana shiki 1896
(big-buddha see-for go blossom-small-road!/'tis)

Great Buddha

going to see
daibutsu on a wee
blossom path

A trail through cherry trees laden with blossoms brings down the clouds and makes us feel like children walking where adults would hit their heads. Shiki may not have thought of that when he wrote the *ku* (which we have already seen in the *Buddhist Blossoms* chapter), but he may have, for the huge statue returns us to the magical world of our childhood: so I put it at the head of the chapter.

子をつれて花くぐる親これ春よ 大江丸? 俳諧袋
ko o tsurete hana kuguru oya kore haru yo ôemaru 1801
(child[acc.] bringing blossoms duck-through parent/s this spring!)

bringing a child
parents duck under blossoms
"this is spring!"

Kuguru means to wind and duck one's way through the low and narrow. Do the parents take a trail particularly pleasing to their child who would not need to duck and enjoy a trail his or her size. The last line is in broken Japanese and would seem to be baby-talk. The next *ku* is not about a child but suggests there is something childish intrinsic to the activity of blossom-viewing, so I include it here:

雛事のつゝきに遊ふ花見哉 李由 韵塞
hinagoto no tsuzuki ni asobu hanami kana riyû -1705
(doll-stuff following play blossom-viewing!/'?/tis)

after we've played   after the dolls
with dolls, is our next such   is this our next plaything?
blossom-viewing?   blossom-viewing

My first reading is a lifetime take, the second has seasonal events recapitulate the same. In that case, the cherries are somewhat late because the doll festival (now *Girls' Day*) is on 3/3.

負ふた子の雲と見てとる櫻哉　呑江 新選
ôta ko no kumo to mite toru sakura kana kôei 1773
(carried child's cloud as seeing takes cherry!/?/'tis)

> a piggyback child
> takes what he thinks a cloud:
> cherry blossoms!

Adults can confuse cherry blossoms for clouds in the distance. Up close, only a bleary eyed baby could make that mistake that is charming for seeming to verify the poetic trope. We wonder if the parent is a poet who has actually spoken the words "clouds of bloom" which the child has overheard.

懐の子が喰たがる桜哉　一茶 1811
futokoro no ko ga kuitagaru sakura kana issa
(bosom's child-the eat-want cherry[blossoms]!)

> at her bosom
> a child wants to eat
> cherry blossoms

稚子は乳をくわへて花見かな　嘯山 葎亭集
osonago wa chichi o kuwaete hanami kana shôzan -1801
(infant-as-for breast[acc.] sucking blossom-viewing!/?)

> a little child
> sucking on a breast:
> blossom-viewing

Is it coincidence that Issa, who comes from a part of Japan where eating was thought to be more desirable than sex? In Japan, the *plum* blossom is identified with motherhood for tits are in the "mother 母" radical included in the character for plum 梅, whereas "cherry color" – strangely enough, the color of the darkest cherry blossoms – is identified with the nipples (or corolla) of a woman who is pregnant or nursing. I must, however, be careful not to see nursing everywhere: a poem of Kikaku's (1807) I translated: *"One blossom: / she pulls a breast out / from her bosom"* (花一つ袂にお乳の手出し哉　其角 *hana hitotsu tamoto ni ochi no tedashi kana*) turned out to mean: *"Placing a spray / her nana helps out with / her sleeve hem."* That is to say, the nurse-maid prevents it from getting wet or otherwise interfering with flower-arranging. I had not known that "honorable-tit" meant nurse-maid!

うしろ手に花盗み行くわらへ哉　青竹 小弓俳諧集
ushirode ni hana nusumiyuku warabe kana seichiku 1699
(behind-hands-in blossoms stealing-go kid/child!/?/'tis)

> hands behind back
> there goes the blossom thief:
> a little child!

Before KS corrected me, I imagined a small child breaking off blossoms, right and left: *"As mama walks / her child, piggyback / steals blossoms."* It is a good image and I *hated* to lose it, but the intended image of a neighborhood child thinking – or deluding himself into believing – that he has managed to hide the branch behind his back is, perhaps, more endearing.

花さくや赤子に慾の親心　渭川 小弓俳
hana saku ya akago ni yoku no oyagokoro isen 1699
(blossoms-bloom: infants-for greedy/ambitious parents' heart)

> cherries bloom
> and parental ambition
> reaches babes

> cherries blossom
> and parents want the world
> for their babies

By the Buddhist book, ambition and desire (*yoku*) breed suffering. The cherry blossom, willing to part with its blossoms, was conventionally not burdened with such worldly attachment. Yet the profuse bloom was *also* a symbol of success, of making it big. Surrounded by this natural magnificence, parents dream of their children's future, *their* bloom. Imagine them holding the infants dressed in beautiful kimonos (though, sometimes, tiny tots were dressed down to avoid the evil eye).

子に飽くと申人には花もなし ばせを
ko ni aku to mosu hito ni wa hana mo nashi bashô -1694
(children-with tire says person-for-as-for blossoms too not)

blossoms are wasted
on anyone who's fed up
with children

there's no bloom
in the life of all who claim
kids bore them

This well-known *ku* by Bashô is atypical of his canon, for being aphoristic if not didactic, yet reflects the natural philosophy of Taoism which would honor the child in all of us.

子をかせと隣からして花見哉 蘭関 末若葉
ko o kase to tonari kara shite hanami kana ranseki? 1697
(child[acc.] lend [says] neighbor-from doing blossom-viewing!)

the neighbors come
and ask to borrow a child:
blossom-viewing

blossom-viewing:
the neighbor pays a visit,
"lend us a child!"

kind neighbors

"we can always use
another child!" they shout:
blossom-viewing trip

The poet's household (or the household he observed) is probably too busy to make a family blossom-viewing expedition and the neighbor, knowing that – for neighbors used to know each other well – kindly invited their child to join his/her family that was going, politely making it seem like having the child along is such a benefit that they would "borrow" him. Before KS kindly explained this for me, I wrote: *I am reminded of Mark Twain, who leased cats from people when he traveled; there is something pushy about that neighbor which makes me suspect that in the days before television even bad people might want children around for their (the adults) own selfish amusement.* Though the readings drastically differ, the first two of the three translations remain the same!

花ひとつたもとにすがる子供哉　立圃？嵐山集
hana hitotsu tamoto ni sugaru warabe kana ryûho 1651
(blossom one sleeve[hanging part]-to cling child/ren!/?/'tis)

one blossom
clinging to her sleeve,
her last child

one blossom
clings to his sleeve
a shy child

A blossom that hangs on a tree after the others have fallen is said to *sugaru,* so one reading makes this a youngest child, but it might be a child clinging to the male poet's sleeve. As pointed out by 19c visitors to Japan, men there were more likely to enjoy the company of children than their European counterparts (this would change in the 20c, after industrialization made Japanese men work 16 hour days in the factories, etc.) .

A *senryû* notes: *"A wife's wisdom / sending a child along / blossom- viewing"* (女房のちえハ花見にこを付る（よいしあんなり／\）柳多留 *nyôbô no chie wa hanami ni ko o tsukeru* yanagidaru 10-30). That is not because the husband will be delighted but to prevent him from doing things he shouldn't.

花を得て人にだかるゝ産子哉 トチ 続虚栗
hana o ete hito ni dakaruru ubuko kana tochi 1687
(blossom[acc.] gaining people-by swarmed newborn!)

the blossom-viewing

gaining a flower
she's swarmed by people:
a newborn babe

All babies old enough to be taken out are cute (as all puppies are cute), but some charm more than others. This child is the flower, the apple in the eye not only of her parents but all who see her.

花の中人の子見れば子もほしき 長翠 あなうれし
hana no naka hito no ko mireba ko mo hoshiki chôsui -1813
(blossoms-among people's child see-when child[+emph.] wanting)

in the bloomshade   seeing children
seeing the children of others   playing under the blossoms
i'd be a father   *i* want one, too

Children, dressed in pretty kimono, running about, playing with petals and the mud or dirt they fall into, reacting with the somewhat drunken (that is friendly) parents are so delightful . . .

花さかり子てあるかるゝ夫婦哉 其角
hanazakari ko de arukaruru fûfu kana kikaku -1707
(blossom-acme child-with walking husband-wife!/'tis)

it's full bloom:
parents are walked about
by their children

The whole world flows out of the cherry cornucopia. .Men and women, even husbands and wives, did not do much walking together in Japan, but with a child, or children along, they can't help it.

親負て子の手を引てさくら哉 一茶 西紀書込
oya outte ko no te o hiite sakura kana issa -1827
(child carrying child's hand[acc] pull/holding cherry'tis)

blossom-viewing: carrying a parent
holding the hand of a child   holding the hand of a child
carrying a parent   cherry blossoms

Let's hope this surreal group quickly finds a good bloom-shade! What an image! You may imagine a man *or* a woman (I have seen an old woman carrying a crippled son larger than she was up the stairs at a train station in Tokyo in the 1990's!) here.

うれしげに這ふ子遊ぶや花筵　江川 翁反古
ureshige ni hau ko asobu ya hanamushiro kôsen 1783
(delightedly crawling child plays!/: blossom-mat)

a blossom mat:
how my child crawls
about in delight!

While a child is happy on the clay and root-top surface under the cherry trees, a straw mat with its comfortable bounds – a home-base with a reassuring feel and smell – is heavenly.

寺子とも墨を落して花見哉　何羨 もゝのみ
tera-kodomo sumi o otoshite hanami kana kasen 1693
(temple[school] children ink clean-off blossom-viewing!/'tis)

temple schoolers	hands and faces
wash off all their ink for	free of ink, temple kids
blossom-viewing!	blossom-viewing

In the Edo era, Japan was the most literate country in the world. Many, if not most children either visited or boarded at temples to get an education. I first imagined children looking about at the blossoms pause too long so ink dripped off their writing brushes, but it is really dropped=washed off, for old prints depict long lines of children all prettied up, following their writing teachers, in neat ducky lines no less, to go cherry viewing and, presumably advertise their schools! The much better known Ransetsu (-1707) describes a group he encountered: *"Forming a ring / around the writing teacher: / flower children!"* (手習の師を車座や花の兒 嵐雪 *tenarai no shi o kurumaza ya hana no chigo* 1707). The "flower" or "blossom" suggests that it is a blossom-viewing, that these might be the most attractive pupils of the school and that they are well-dressed.

花見哉母につれたつめくら兒　其角 -1707　　やつかいや花につれ立座頭か坊　滄洲 花七日
hanami kana haha ni tsuredatsu mekura chigo kikaku　　*yakkai ya hana ni tsuredatsu zatôgabo* soshû 1777
(blossom-viewing!/'tis mother-by brought-out blindchild)　　(troublesome!/: blossoms-to brought-out troupe-head)

blossom-viewing:	their hands full
a mother brings out	a blind-boss is brought out
her blind child	for the blossoms

Kikaku's *ku* brings out the "viewing" part of the blossom-viewing and the non-viewing part. Many of the adult blind in Japan were unionized, which is to say members of a powerful guild of procurers and money-lenders. The most visible rank was the "troupe-head," who managed/pimped a group of musicians and/or massagers? These bosses were stereotypically excellent judges of human character and female flesh, but scary for possessing bad tempers.

ちる花にはにかみとけぬ娘哉　一茶
chiru hana ni hanikami tokenu musume kana issa 1808
(falling blossoms-with/by bashfulness melt daughter/girl 'tis)

falling petals	as petals fall
a little girl overcomes	the shy little girl starts
her bashfulness	to open up

Issa wrote about children such as this one for years before he had a little girl of his own to love and observe in poetry, unfortunately, for a little more than a year. Here is another:

尿をやる子にあれ／\と桜哉　一茶
shito o yaru ko ni are are to sakura kana　issa 1816
(peepee have-do child-to that! that! [saying] cherry 'tis)

a child held up
to pee: looky! looky!
cherry blossoms

KS imagines a veranda facing the garden where a cherry has bloomed. I concur. We cannot tell if it is a little girl dangled in the air or a boy held from behind so he leans out beyond the veranda.

迷ひ子や一膳ひえて櫻花　新真 蕉尾琴 序令 類柑子
mayoiko ya hitozeni hiete sakurabana　shinshin 1701 *or* jorei 1707
(lost child!/: one-meal cooling cherry-blossoms)

cherry-viewing
their meal grows cold
a lost child

The question here is whose meal or meals. I thought it most likely that a lost child suddenly occupied the attention of good-hearted adults whose meal grew cold, but KS thinks it is the meal of the child's mother (and/or other members of the family), and I agree that is more likely.

親ありとこたへてもどる桜哉　一茶	迷子のしつかり掴むさくら哉　一茶 1814
oya ari to kotaete-modoru sakura kana　issa 1797	*mayoiko no shikkari tsukamu sakura kana*　issa
('parent/s have' replying-returns cherry!/'tis)	(lost child's firmly grab-hold cherry!/'tis)
blossom-viewing	the lost child
"i have parents" replies	clings firmly to a branch
the child, leaving	of the cherry

Can't you imagine the voice of the tyke as he or she turns to leave? The unfortunate child in the second *ku* might have a spray of bloom torn off to give to its parents or, more likely, be standing in place, with one hand locked on a low branch of this tree whose blossoms symbolize impermanence.

親と子か一木はなれし花の陰　素外 古今句鑑	親と子がぶん／\に行花見哉　一茶
oya to ko ga ippon hanareshi hananokage　sogai 1707	*oya to ko ga bun bun ni yuku hanami kana*　issa
(parent/s and child/ren one-tree separated bloomshade)	(parents and children-the separately go bl.vwing'tis)
a happy hanami	***separate viewing***
one tree apart	parents and children
parents and children	each making their own way
blossom-viewing	to the blossoms

The same five syllabets/syllables, but *oya to ko* is a lot shorter than "parents and children." For Sogai's *ku*, I was able to stick it into the three-beat middle line and get the right sound-sense. Sogai lived to be 92. I imagine he prospered and filled the bloom-shade of two trees with his descendents!

おじょうさまおとおりなされさくらみち　山元満寿美　大阪府 守口小六
ojôsama otôri nasare sakuramichi　yamamoto masumi (osaka's moriguchi elem. grade 6)
("[honor.+]girl/maiden[+polite] [hon+]pass/take do[+hon]" : cherry-path/lane/road)

my sweet missy
honor us by taking *this*
pink cherry path

little princess
will you deign to take this?
the cherry path

This is by a sixth-grade girl. The imagined honorific+polite language and implicit switch from address to statement (see quotes added to gloss) so easy and natural to Japanese is hell to translate. Were the bloom not mostly in the trees, I might have made "cherry" *petal,* instead. And pardon my Dixie!

スカートのすそひらひらと花の道　池田祥子　島根県 広瀬中
sukatto no suso hirahira to hananomichi　ikeda shoko (shimane pref. hirose mid. school)
(skirt's hem flutter-flutter-with blossom-path/road)

my skirt's hem
flutters as i walk along
the blossom path

Extraordinary! Clothing that flutters in the breeze brings one closer to the blossoms than jeans can.

ふらんどや桜の花をもちながら　一茶　　　　狗をふらんどすなり花の陰　同 1824
burando ya sakuranohana o mochinagara issa　　*inokoro o burando su nari hananokage* issa
([a] swing!/: cherry-blossom/s[obj] holding-while)　(doggy[despite] swing do becomes bloomshade)

s w i n g i n g
i hold fast to a spray
of cherry blossoms

there's a doggy
swinging on a swing
the bloomshade

Why is *this* here with children? Because the party swinging is generally thought to be "... / a child, with cherry blossoms / in her hand" (Ueda), though the original, of unspecified person, could well be a self-portrait of the poet in his dotage clutching at blossoms. While written three years before his death, the location of these *ku* in Issa's notebook suggests they were memories, so child may be right.

懐に寝て帰る子も花見哉　千川　千鳥掛
futokoro ni nete-kaeru ko mo hanami kana　chisen 1712
(bosom-in sleeping-return child-also blossom-viewing!/'tis)

the return trip

a child sleeping
in a bosom: that too
is blossom-viewing

bosom dreams

a child asleep
on the return trip, still
viewing-blossoms

This *ku* is my second favorite of the chapter, perhaps because I remember the return trips of my childhood, dozing off in a humming car, red dashboard lights casting a comfortable glow, or slouched on the sail-bags in the bow of a sharpie ketch with the sound of waves lapping against the flat bottom as I sucked on the salty strap of my life-jacket. This sleepy return trip is as important to a trip as waking is to a dream. How comfortable this child, resting in the bosom of a kimono under, and perhaps sucking, his mother's breasts, themselves the blossoms of life, with cherry petals mixed in!

Sakura Mecca, Mt. Yoshino

吉野・芳野

yoshino! yoshino!

これは／＼とばかり花の吉野山 貞室 笠小文
kore wa kore wa to bakari hana no yoshino yama teishitsu
('this-as-for this-as-for' only, blossoms' yoshino mountain) -1673

4
"oh! oh!"
all one can say
mount yoshino
in flower gay

trans. kenzô wadagaki

1
uttering only
"oh! oh! oh!" i roam over
yoshino's hills ablow.

trans. inazô nitobe

3
cela! cela!
seulement! en fleurs,
le mont yoshino!

trans. michel revon

2
o this! o this!
far beyond words it is!
mountain of cherry bloom, yoshino yama.

trans. curtis hidden page

7
"ah!" i said, "ah!"
it was all that i could say —
the cherry-flowers of mt. yoshino!

trans. blyth

5
"well well!" and "well well!"
is all i can say. – the flowers
on yoshino mountain!

trans. glen shaw

6
the cherry-blossoms of mt. yoshino

"Oh! Oh!"
was all that i could say
on flower-bedecked mount yoshino

trans. miyamori

        8
wow! just, *wow!*
(the bloom of mt yoshino
is mind-blowing)

        child-of-the-sixties

The translations, excluding Blyth and my "child of the sixties," come from Miyamori Asataro's *Haiku Poems Ancient and Modern* (1940). As Miyamori points out, Bashô defended Teishitsu's *ku* from those who put it down because the *"Oh!"* or, *"Ah!"* could be applied to any spectacular view, by pointing out that such "a spontaneous outburst of profound admiration" is itself beautiful. Nitobe's "ablow" may reflect the modern *bushido* bias toward admiring petals bravely letting go, whereas the original thrill was found in the boundless panorama of bloom. Not that the thrill of flying petals had to wait for the militarists. It, too, was natural. Kikaku, playing with Teishitsu's *ku*, later wrote: *"Wow, just, wow! / these scattering petals / also sakura!"* (これは／＼と斗散も櫻哉　其角 *kore wa kore wa to bakari chiru mo sakura kana*). In the original, the first 10 syllabets are identical. Teishitsu's *Wow! Wow!* was not born of a vacuum. The exclamation *kore wa kore wa* was a commonplace in the popular drama (古浄瑠璃) and follows the idea of sublimity beyond words found in the following older *ku*:

    ことのはをうつむや花のよしの山　昌叱
koto no ha o uzumu ya hana no yoshinoyama shôshitsu -1603
(things' leaves[words] +obj bury!/?/: blossoms'/beautiful yoshino mt.)

    our wordleaves
    buried by the blossoms
    of mt yoshino

The wit (if you recall, words in Japanese are "thing-*leave*.") is lost, but the idea translates well enough. After Teishitsu's much more famous *ku,* we find many more of the same in different words. A haiku: *"What you see / can not be put in words: / blooming Yoshino* (見ぬ事はいはれぬ花のよしの山　随尺　淡ちしま *minu koto wa iwarenu hana no yoshinoyama* zuishaku 1698). That puns on a saying that would English as "silence is golden." Should I rewrite, say: *"What we see / at Yoshino reminds us / not to talk"* ? A *senryû*: *"Mount Yoshino: / seventeen syllabets doesn't / suffice for praise"* (よしの山十七文字でほめたらず　柳多留 7-16　*yoshinoyama jûnana moji de hometarazu yanagidaru*). Yoshino worship antedates *haikai's* heyday. Sôgi (-1502) puts it most simply: *"Lovely Yoshino! / Beside you there's no other / blossom mountain!"* (みよしのや外には花の山ももなし 宗祇 老葉 *mi-yoshino ya hoka ni wa hana no yama mo nashi*). Sôin would later provide the perfect envoi, playing with the older idea of there being no need to say "cherry" for "blossom" by itself suggested it:

    花はいはじ所も所吉野山　宗因
hana wa iwaji tokoro mo tokoro yoshino-yama sôin 1604-82
('blossoms=cherry-as-for' say-not, place [is] place yoshino mountain)

    no call to mention
    blossoms: the place says it all
    mount yoshino

No pillow needed. The place did, indeed, "say it all." Depending on the era, the blossoms actually found there varied, for, wild or not, there were extensive plantings supplementing natural life cycles and reflecting the taste of the rulers; but Yoshino was so closely identified with the bloom that even poets who never saw it raved about its beauty. First appreciated as a backdrop for the Imperial reign in Nara, ancient soul of Japan, Yoshino was *the* mountain (actually a hill of many peaks) for cherry blossom-viewing. According to Kuitert, "the hills [of which Yoshino is the exemplar] with their cherries springing up where civilization butted against the manmade edge of wild mountain forests, were seen as an assuring and protective belt around Yamato [ancient Japan before the entire archipelago was conquered]. Names of hills and cherries in poetry carry, therefore, an extended, almost magical meaning that that interprets the landscape as a guardian of the nation." (K:JFC:1999). Stewart credits "a Buddhist priest, En-no-Shôkaku" for planting "its four extensive groves" in the 7c. The favored pronunciation of his name 役小角 is En-no-Ozuno. He was the founder of Shûgendô, a sort of mountaineering asceticism. A Shintô shaman and Buddhist saint, he and generations of his followers are known for their wizardry. How appropriate for the creator of a talismanic bulwark of blossoms! It is one of many legends associated with him and supported by the literally charming name Yoshino (*lucky*-field, or *good*-field), but the poems cited as *evidence* (*Manyôshû* #1047, 1429), like those cited with respect to the relationship of the blossoms to grain, prove little. The most we can say for sure is that the idea of a wall of trees planted to protect civilization is heart-warming when contrasted to the more common "civilized" practice of cutting magical trees down, and, regardless of the deeper significance of the wall, I would be willing to bet that the hills around ancient cities were, for the aristocracy, a grand *installation* in the modern art sense of the term, creating beauty shared by all who had eyes.

もろこしの芳野か花に奥もなし 紹巴 吉野詣記
morokoshi no yoshino ka hana ni okumonashi   jôha
(china's yoshino? blossoms-to recesses not) 1523-1602

<table>
<tr><td>does mt yoshino
reach cathay? the bloom
has no beyond!</td><td>is yoshino
chinese? all the bloom
is patent</td></tr>
</table>

If *oku,* the concept of an inner recess, does not translate, neither does its contrary. But even in Japanese the *ku* is puzzling. The second reading supposes the poet identifies China with pictures, i.e. sees it as two-dimensional! As it happens, the hills of Yoshino are such that one sees more blossoming trees at a glance than on most mountains where the cherries are hidden among other trees.

年をへば見はてん花のよしの山 紹巴
toshi o heba mi-haten hana no yoshinoyama   jôha
(year/s pass-when see-exhaust-would blossoms' yoshino)

<table>
<tr><td>*one man's resolve*
i'd take years
if that's what it takes to
see mt yoshino</td><td>as the years pass on
i wish to see all that mount yoshino
offers of cherry flowers
(trans. earl minor)</td><td>*every cherry tree*
year after year
i'd see all the blossoms
on mt yoshino</td></tr>
</table>

This might be seen as a distillation of Saigyô's waka: *"Mount Yoshino! / Leaving the trail I marked / last spring, / I would know blossoms / I have not yet seen."* (吉野山こぞのしをりの道かへてまだ見ぬかたの花を尋ねむ 西行 *yoshinoyama kozo no shiori no michi kaete mada minukata no hana o tazunemu* (More precisely "I would visit blossoms=cherry-trees in parts I have . . .)). Such is Yoshino. Every year, you see *part* of it. Jôha also put it thus*:* " *As boundless in bloom / as the Musasahi Meadow / Mount Yoshino"* (むさし野もはてあらん花をよしの山 *musashino mo hate-aran hana o yoshinoyama*). Musashi was *the* trope for fields so broad the moon rose from it, rather than the mountains providing the horizon elsewhere, *and* a *sake* cup too big to drain in a gulp. That the extensive bloom was uncommon is proven by poetry such as Kokinshû poem #50, *"Cherry blossoms / blooming on beautiful / Mount Yoshino / you sure had me fooled / i took you for snow!"* (み吉野の山辺に咲ける桜花　雪かとのみぞあやまたれける　紀友則・古今集 *miyoshino no yamabe ni sakeru sakurabana yuki ka to nomi zo ayamatarekeru* kokinshû 905). The large area involved makes Yoshino seem to be a sea of fire in the fall, and in the spring when the cherries bloom, snow – not a cap, but snow-fall covering the entire landscape, like a bridal gown. An anon. *ku* translation by Stewart expresses this well: *"TRAVEL GUIDE // When you can see, whichever way you go / Nothing but blossoms: that's Mount Yoshino."* (*A Chime of Windbells*)

よしの山世界の花は呑くらひ 淡々
yoshinoyama sekai no hana wa nomu kurai tantan 1673-1761
(yoshino mountain, world's blossoms-as-for drink/swallow-amount)

<table>
<tr><td>mount yoshino:
enough to include all
the world's flowers!</td><td>mount yoshino:
do you embody all our
world's blossoms?</td></tr>
</table>

銭買て入るやよしのゝ山櫻　蕪村
zeni katte hairu ya yoshino no yamazakura buson -1783
(change buying enter: yoshino's mountain-cherry/ies)

you buy change
to enter yoshino and see
the wild cherries

Vendors could not handle large denominations so, unless you had plenty of change around the house, money had to be broken before entering the grounds. My "wild" brings some irony to the mountain.

道々の花を一目やよし野山　千代
michi michi no hana o hitome ya yoshino yama chiyo -1775
(road-road's blossoms[obj] one-eyeful/glance yoshino mountain)

<table>
<tr><td>path after path
a glance for each tree
mount yoshino</td><td>mount yoshino
one eyeful at a time
trail after trail</td></tr>
</table>

We are talking about dozens of hills, hundreds of trails, thousands of trees. *Hitome* is usually a single look, or glance, and sometimes an eyeful. It is a word with romantic associations.

みよしのゝちか道寒し山ざくら（又、花一木・初桜）蕪村
miyoshino no chikamichi samushi yamazakura [or, *hana hito-ki/ hatsuzakura*] buson -1783
([hon.]yoshino'shortcut cold mountain-cherry [other versions: blossom-one-tree / first-cherry])

<table>
<tr><td>how chilly this
short-cut to yoshino
first-blossoms</td><td>yoshino short-cut
a wild cherry is blooming
out in the cold</td><td>this short-cut
to mt.yoshino is cold
one tree in bloom!</td></tr>
</table>

Mountain cherry tended to bloom late, but one has jumped the gun. Evidently, Buson, who also wrote *"Wintering in / Mount Yoshino waits / within my heart"* (冬ごもり心の奥のよしの山 *fuyugomori kokoro no oku no yoshi no yama*), a winter *ku* bespeaking his love for Yoshino (though he was, wintering in Kyoto, two or three days away by foot), got an early start on his cherry-hunting.

ふた夜三夜寝て見る花やよし野山　千代
futa yo mi yo netemiru hana ya yoshino yama   chiyo 1701-75
(two nights three nights sleeping-see/try blossom/s!/: yoshino mountain)

    blossoms worth two　　　　　　　　　　　mount yoshino!
or three nights of sleep-and-see　　　　　blossoms not meant for
      yoshino mountain　　　　　　　　　　　a one-night stand

yoshino blossoms

you sleep a night
or two in the foothills, *then*
see the mountain

Chiyo makes it seem the subject is a potential bedmate until she reaches the end of the *ku*. The varied elevation, light and varieties of trees means all parts of the bloom cycle could be found, so a clever hunter/viewer could enjoy a new bloom one day, another tree in full bloom the following day and yet another shedding fast and furious the next. According to Sato Yoshiki (『桜が創った「日本」』 2005), tree varieties at Yoshino included quick-blooming double-petaled Higan and late blooming varieties of cherry that were not limited to the classic single-petal mountain cherry. So, even if some varieties of individual trees finished their performance in a week (most took a bit longer), the total happening took closer to a month. My third reading is a paraverse, probably wrong.

どちらから遊む花の吉の山　千代
dochira kara asobamu hana no yoshino yama   chiyo
(whichever-from play-shall blossoms' yoshino mountain)

     mount yoshino　　　　　　　　　　　　where, oh, where
in bloom: where shall i deign　　　　　to start my day on blooming
   to start my play?　　　　　　　　　　　　mount yoshino!

Did Chiyo use the character for "luck" to write *Yoshino* here because there are lucky directions to start on various days? Who knows. But, if you have only a day, start on a cold dark slope where blossoms are starting to bloom and walk to a bright one where they are dropping; or, do precisely the opposite, following an anti-entropic course to rejuvenate your soul before leaving.

どちみむと花に狂ふやよしの山　千代
dochi min to hana ni kuruu ya yoshino yama   chiyo
(whichever look and blossoms-for rave: yoshino mountain)

wherever you look
the flowers drive you crazy!
mount yoshino

みよし野やころび落ても花の上　千代
miyoshino ya korobi-ochitemo hana no ue   chiyo
([hon.] yoshino!/: tumble-falling even blossoms-upon)

    mount yoshino!　　　　　　　　　　　　mount yoshino!
even if you trip and fall　　　　　though you trip and fall you fall
   it's on blossoms　　　　　　　　　　　　upon blossoms

Chiyo's tripping *ku* is simple and of no deep significance. It is also a fine example of what Bashô called *karumi,* or "lightness" and deserves to be better known.

一本も花は吉野のくずもなし 長頭丸 崑山集
hitomoto mo hana wa yoshino no kuzu mo nashi teitoku 1651
(one-tree-even blossoms-as-for yoshino's trash-even not)

よし野にも花に事かく花もあり 千代尼
yoshino ni mo hana ni koto kaku hana mo ari chiyo 1775
(yoshino-at-even blossom-to thing-lack blossoms also are)

and there is not
a single worthless cherry
on mount yoshino

even on yoshino
there are blossoms that fail
to make the grade

Chiyo, for all her enthusiasm for Yoshino – or, rather because she loved Yoshino enough to look closely? – found cherry trees lacking in some respect or another. This is not to say that Teitoku is wrong, for he may be writing on a different level, contrasting cherries about which nothing bad could possibly be written with the so-called "trash pine/s" identified with worthless *waka* (see #42-14).

只の木もあいそに立やよしの山 一茶
tada no ki mo aiso ni tatsu ya yoshino-yama issa 1824
(plain tree even charm-to/from stand: yoshino mountain)

mount yoshino
even trees with no bloom
add to the charm

on mt yoshino
even the plainest tree
is a charmer!

even trash trees
turn on all their charm
on mt yoshino

If Yoshino were in an English-speaking country, one reading might have begun "Plain jane trees / Unlike the completely artificial urban "cherry mountains," other trees – not just the pine used as a backdrop in some gardens – but nameless trees, are mixed in with the cherries.

枯木にも花は咲くらん吉野山 士朗
kareki ni mo hana wa sakuran yoshino-yama shirô 1813
(withered/dead-tree-on even blossoms bloom[emph] yoshino mountain)

mount yoshino
here even dead trees
bloom away

even dead trees
boast cherry blossoms
mount yoshino

Even dead trees have their day? Shirô was one of Issa's mentors. This *ku* seems a depiction of a floral plentitude, with blossoms dropping or blowing upon all trees; but, I suspect Shirô *means* that he, as an old man, feels like a blooming youth on Mount Yoshino, because the idea of *a dead tree blooming* is associated with a certain legend about an old man who does it (*hana-saki jijii*).

再ひ杖ひけと申けるに・命あらば春あらば花のよしの山 白雄
inochi araba haru araba hana no yoshino yama shirao - 1792
(life is/have-if/when spring is/have-if/when blossoms' yoshino mt)

to someone who said i should, again, take a cane to the blossoms

while i am,
while spring is – look out
mt yoshino!

The parallel structure, "while life *araba*, while spring *araba*" fails in English. Neither "while *there's* life/spring" nor "while *I've* life/spring" sounds good. I played instead with "am" and "is," added "look out!" to catch the determination of the old poet better than nothing would, and made the cane something it is not in the original: *risqué*. Shirao would have sent me a bottle of *sake* for this translation.

目うつりや花にむせたるよしの山 鬼貫 ァルス
meutsuri ya hana ni musetaru yoshinoyama onitsura -1738
(eye-shifting!/: blossoms-by choking yoshino mountain)

人家あれば目が休む也吉野の花 琴風-1726
jinka areba me ga yasumunari yoshino no hana kinpû
(human-house is-if eyes-the rest-become yoshino's bls)

    promiscuous eyes
  choking on the bloom
    of mount yoshino

    a dwelling here
  would mean rest for the eyes
    yoshino blossoms

A solid expanse of bloom, even with *some* variety, can cloy the senses, or bore them, just as the moon without clouds to tease it can become tedious. Onitsura's metaphor of over-indulging or is a fresh one. (「むせたる」後の「よしの」に「よし＝止めよ！」の掛けをかすかに感じるのが私だけか) You might think a house would be an eye*sore*, not a rest, but aside from it being anything but cherry blossoms, I have observed that some buildings (those with thatched or Spanish-tiled roofs or arches) can actually make cherry blossoms look as good as they look in the wild!

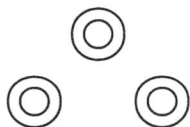

よしの・人々に同じさまなし山櫻　言水
hitobito ni onaji sama nashi yamazakura gonsui 1646-1719
(people-people-with/to same appearance/style not mountain cherries)

yoshino

    people do not
  look like one another
    wild cherries

We have seen another version of the original, without the title =Yoshino and *sama* pronounced *yô* in mountain cherries. At first, I thought it meant that mountain cherries presented a different face to different people, but now I think it means both the viewers and trees were notably diverse.

よしの山変桜（みよしのに変なさくら）もなかりけり 一茶
yoshino-yama kawarizakura (miyoshino ni henna sakura) mo nakarikeri issa 1815
(yoshino mountain changed/novel-cherry[hon. yoshino-at strange-cherry][emp.] not[emph.])

    mount yoshino
  cherry tree novelty
    is not found

    mount yoshino
  where you will not find
    strange cherries

There is variety, but none of the more outlandish cultivars prized by wealthy merchants and put down by tasteful people since the Monk Yoshida Kenko (14c.) were nowhere to be seen here, the noblest of all blossom-viewing sites (In his famous *Tsurezuregusa*, Kenkô compared *bonsai* to deformed humans).

読尽すともよしのや花の砂まひれ 賛柳
yomitsukusu to mo yoshino ya hana no suna-mabire sanryû 1759
(read-exhausting-even yoshino!/: blossoms' sand/dust-covered)

yoshino toasted	countless poems	yoshino toast
by all poets is covered	on yoshino, but count these	of all poets plastered
in blossom dust	grains of pollen	with pollen

Having cut my haiku teeth on Issa, with his horror stories, I first thought the "dust/sand" was proof of hordes of people and/or a drought. Then, I realized my error. We are talking about *pollen*. It is hard to say if the quantity of it counts more or a sense of it being dirty rather than lyrical. Issa's *ku* include one I am unsure of: *"Devoured by men / while they bloom, cherries / on Mt Yoshino"* (人に喰れし桜咲也みよしの山　一茶 *hito ni kuwareshi sakura sakunari miyoshino-yama* issa 1803). I cannot tell if Issa is reacting to the size of the crowds when he visited Yoshino, to the leaves and blossoms of some of the trees being cultivated for consumption, or a miniature Yoshino elsewhere (I can only find reference to the Sumidagawa (low-class) viewing in his Journal this year).

芝の雲上野の櫻咲にけり　一鐡 新道
shiba no kumo ueno no sakura sakinikeri ittetsu ()
(lawn-clouds ueno[=above]'s cherry blooms[+fin])

花見には吉野まさりしや上野山　小山 1680
hanami ni wa yoshino masarishi ya ueno-yama shôzan
(blsm-vwing-as-for yoshino-beating! ueno mt. 太夫桜)

lawn clouds
the cherry trees of ueno
are blooming

as a blossom-bash
it sure beats yoshino!
ueno mountain

Shiba is turf good for gathering on (it is half of the word for theater/drama, *shibai*). The implicit contrast in the first *ku* is with genuine mountains where clouds real or floral typically form. Unlike Yoshino, Ueno was only a blossom-mountain in the idiomatic sense of being a place for blossom-viewing. Note that the second *ku* boasts of the "blossom-viewing" (*hanami*), which is to say the event, rather than the blossoms. Since cherry blossoms may be found in other countries today, while the *bash* is not, Ueno is more Japanese than Yoshino, if Japaneseness is to be measured by difference.

土舟にちれど芳野の桜哉　一茶 1804
tsuchibune ni chiredo yoshino no sakura kana issa
(earth-boat-on falling-though yoshino's cherry!/'tis)

yoshino sakura
though they fall upon
a honey-barge

While some "dirt-boats" carried dirt, most carried *night-soil*. I adapt a word my father used for trucks serving this purpose in Usania, "honey-wagon." I cannot tell whether Issa is serious or satirical here.

三文が桜植けり吉野山　一茶 1804
san mon ga sakura uekeri yoshino yama issa
(three mon [monetary unit] cherry buys[emph.] yoshino mt.)

they've planted
two-bit cherry trees
mount yoshino

just three bits
plants a cherry tree
my yoshino

I would bet on the second reading for if Ueno was meant to be a re-creation of Yoshino, so could anyone's garden. Moreover, Issa has other *ku* where buying a sprig of pine for the same gained him the Immortal Mount Merhu (See *The Fifth Season*). A third reading might be *"For three-bits / I plant my cherry tree / on Mt Yoshino"* meaning that was the cost of admission there or to a tea-shop garden with a supposed Yoshino cherry tree, but this is unlikely, too.

思いひたつよしのゝ人も花見哉 野坂 坂東太郎？
omoitatsu yoshino no hito mo hanami kana nozaka 1679
(resolve/ing yoshino's people too blossom-viewing!/?/'tis)

yoshino people
also view blossoms, when
they resolve to

they strike when
the bloom is hot: yoshino
blossom-viewers

Omoitatsu (resolve) brings to mind Japanese proverbs about there being no lucky and unlucky days when a man really makes up his mind. People living in Yoshino, where there is a whole month of bloom, would have a hard time choosing when to "go" blossom-viewing. It would take a decisive act of will to stop work and do so. Failing to capture this, I created reading two, a paraverse.

おとゝひはあの山こえつ花盛り 去來
ototoi wa ano yama koetsu hanazakari kyorai -1704
(yesterday-as-for that mountain crossing/ed blossom-acme)

two days ago
i crossed *that* mountain
in full bloom

Kyorai said he did not expect anyone to really get this *ku* for a year or two. Since I put it in this chapter, you have an advantage. Do you recall how the chapter-head *ku* was considered to be *about all that could be said about Yoshino?* Well, Kyorai is expressing his appreciation for *that* mountain and *that ku*. And, maybe one more: Kikaku's highly regarded *"There's Venus! / the sunrise clouds help / choose a cherry"* or, *"There's Venus! / I'll settle on that cherry / crowned with the sunrise"* (明星や桜定めぬ山かづら *myôjô ya sakura sadamenu yamakazura*). I may try to explain Kikaku's *ku* with a Japanese natural history of Venus and allusions to legendary contesting mountains, etc. in the next edition.

人はみな吉野の山へ入りぬめり　都の花に　われはとまらん　西行
hito mina yoshino yama e hairinumeri miyako no hana ni ware wa tomaran saigyô

everyone else
is up and about
mount yoshino

i shall remain with
a cherry in the capital

as for me, i'll stay here
with our capital blossoms

I do not know if this is because this blossom-lover also likes solitude or if he has figured out a good way to monopolize a tree/trees . . . or a woman/women.

~~~~~~

☆　オマケ　花の口万句の席をよしの山　孤舟　あやにしき　☆

59

Sexual Blossoms
花ノ艶

ゆめの中に手折し花の枝も哉　紹巴
yume no naka ni taorishi hana no eda mogana jôha 1523-1602
(dream-within hand-breaking blossom-branch wish-for)

oh to have a limb
of the blossom i broke
within my dream

Was Jôha fulfilled in a dream? As much as Japanese love cherry blossoms, I find it hard to believe this dream is about breaking one off; but, what if dreaming just that, he recognized the symbolism? As we have seen with examples from the major collections of Japanese poetry, it was very common to sexualize cherry blossoms so that the rain becomes a seducer, the wind a ravisher and the late-blooming cherry a woman who holds out. The very first song of the *Kanginshû* (閑吟集), a collection of songs – many real, singable songs – compiled in 1518 goes roughly: *"The blossom's belt, that brocade belt below / when it opens up, i can't help myself, whoa! / Who could forget the willow's tangled heart, / that sleep-tangled hair look?* (花の錦の下紐は　解けてなかなかよしなや　柳の糸の乱れ心　いつ忘れうぞ　寝乱れ髪のおもかげ *hana no nishiki no shitahimo wa tokete nakanaka yoshinashi ya // yanagi no ito no midaregokoro, itsu wasurôzo　ne-midaregami no omokage*). Said "brocade" was a Chinese weave that had just begun to feature cherry blossom motif (小川和佑:桜誌).

蝶々や密蔵のはなと口を吸ひ　梢風尼 1668-
chôchô ya mitsuzô no hana to kuchi o suu shôfûni -1758
(butterfly/ies: beloved's/favorite-blossom-with mouth-suck)

!that butterfly!
the blossom has his heart
they're kissing

誰告て床の花さへ吸胡蝶　和風 反故集*
dare tsugete tokonohana sae suu kochô wafû
(someone report! bed-flower even sucks butterfly)

report it, someone!
a butterfly will even suck
a bed blossom!

Haikai was not about romance, but it did *play* with it. Shôfû-ni, the "treetop-wind-nun" is chuckling. Spouses seldom kissed, but people *did* kiss those with whom they were besotted. And Japanese did not kiss in the sense of giving someone a lip-*smack*; when *they* kissed, they *Frenched*. Since they called it "mouth-sucking," (the "*suu*=sucking" is also used for puffing on pipes) it does not sound odd to have butterflies do the same. It both is and is *not* anthropomorphic. As for the second *ku,* there are probably countless old Chinese poems about butterflies landing on painted or needlework flowers – not necessarily cherries – but the expression *"Report it, someone"* must be a new twist! *Report it* to whom? The *Royal Society?* (I plagiarize Auden on Eiseley on spiders' use of street-lamps)　But, could it *also* make fun of men who went down on women?　[*反古衾 1752？翁反古 1783？反古供養 1810？]

口ひるを魚に吸るゝ櫻哉　其角　五元
kuchibiru o uo ni suwaruru sakura kana kikaku -1707
(lips[acc.] fish-by sucked cherry[blossoms]!/'tis)

their little lips
kissed by the sweetfish:
cherry petals

their wee lips
sucked up by the fish
cherry petals

This may have been better in the chapter where we followed the fortune of the petals. The first reading puts them in a mountain stream. The fish could be *koi* rather than *ayu* but, *in English*, I thought *sweetfish* beat *carp*. The second puts them in Bashô's "fish salad" (*namasu*). As Japanese does not specify "petals," both readings could be wrong and Kikaku himself eating a cherry snapper.

抱かれし時よりみたるさくらかな　大江丸？俳諧袋
idakareshi toki yori mitaru sakura kana　ôemaru 1801
(hugged time-from seeing/seen cherry!/?/'tis)

cherry blossoms
we really see them after
we've made love

from the time
of our nursing, we view
cherry blossoms

Before we experience the birds and bees, who appreciates flowers? That was my first reading, but now I favor (with my respondent) the second. Embraced covers lovers and babies cradled by nursemaids.

似たものに似た匂ひなし花盛　鳥醉　鶉立
nita-mono ni nita nioi nashi hanazakari chôsui -1769
(similar thing-with similar smell not blossom-acme)

similar things
do not smell alike!
the bloom-heat

Hanazakari, as "in full bloom," or even "blossom-acme," is too weak when "smell" comes in, so I used my risqué neologism. I do not know if the *ku* concerns the smell of a woman's blossom (or nipples?), the spraying of male cats in heat, or, innocently, the scent of various blossoms!

見る人をかへさぬはなのさかり哉　無名　発句帳 1624-44?
miru hito o kaesanu hana no sakari kana anon. 筑波 1356 ?
(see/viewing person[acc] return-not blossoms' acme/rut!/'tis)

the bloom-peak
it won't let those who
see it go home

blossoms in heat
they won't let those
who see them leave

blossoms in heat
keep those who watch them
from going home

Here, I recall the way tom-cats forget about sleep and food and home when females come into heat. Strangely, we only speak of the females as "in heat," when the males experience an equally strong (or stronger when there are many females in the neighborhood) compulsion to live (or die) for sex alone.

むつかしや毎日花にさそはるゝ 虎國 我庵 1767
mutsukashi ya mainichi hana ni sasowaruru　kokoku
(difficult!/: everyday blossoms-by enticed/invited)

life's so hard!
enticed by the blossoms
day after day

Does this describe a man working in the pleasure quarters? The verb *sasou* (*sasowaruru*) is generally used for sexual temptation, but chances are the poet uses it figuratively and sincerely wants to work (most *haikai* participants had day jobs), but finds cherry-viewing so irresistible or is taking a facetious poke at someone who is in great demand and complains of it.

花の色は乳母にはなれよ櫻町 秋色 玉藻-1725
hana no iro wa uba ni hanareyo sakuramachi　shûshoku
(blossom-color-as for nursemaid-from separate/leave! cherrytown)

blossom color?	real blossoms?
forget about wet-nurses &	leave your nurse and go
see cherry-town!	to cherry-town

I first thought a young man was being advised by his dad that it was time to gain his first experience in the red-light district. Cherry-town (*sakura-machi*) was a pleasure quarter less expensive than the more famous Yoshiwara.. But the *ku* would seem to be by a well-known female poet. Is she suggesting that women go to that part of town to see what is what?

吉原・目の毒としらぬうち（こ）そ桜哉 一茶
me no doku to shiranu uchi koso sakura kana　issa 1813
(eyes' poison-as know-not while especially cherry!/?)

yoshiwara

cherry blossoms!	best before you
best before you know they	know they are addictive
poison the eyes	cherry blossoms!

Beauty, not sex itself, is dangerous. On one level, Issa refers to the courtesans, who were called *sakura*, but since the mid-18c, there were *real* cherry blossoms in this most famous of all pleasure quarters outside of ancient Pompeii. Almost a century after Issa's *ku*, Kyoshi (1875-1959) would write, *"Oh, Yoshiwara! / The peak of the bloom's right / out in the street!"* (吉原や道の間中の花盛 虚子 *yoshiwara ya michi no manaka no hanazakari*). I do not know how cherries were treated in Meiji 27 (1894), but, in Bunka 10 (1813), it is likely that one side of the street was set-off by a temporary fence of green bamboo (it is very green before it passes through a winter) and the cherry trees planted behind them, which is to say, in front of the brothels. The fence was high enough to give privacy to humans within but allow most of the bloom to be visible from the outside. Guests could always be let in to have a seat and view the blossoms up close. 63 year-old Issa wrote a cryptic *ku* that might be read to mean that it is better not to do so: *"Should i leave them / far away and in the night? / Cherry blossoms."* (吉原・夜目戸遠目にておくまいか桜花 一茶 *yometôme nite okumaika sakurabana* 1824). He plays on a proverbial prescription for improving beauty: *distance, darkness and inside a hat/parasol;* he also states a fact known all too well by the poor, who have no choice but to spy from afar, and by the old who were supposed to be thinking of the next world. An earlier *senryû* put it bluntly, *"Night cherries / are not something the elderly / should see"* (夜桜は年寄の見る物でなし 柳多留七 *yozakura wa toshiyori no miru mono de nashi   yanagidaru* 1772). As Martial closed his epigram XLVI, *Summa petas: illic metula vivit annus.* Though Issa saw Yoshiwara through the eyes of an outsider, some *ku*, such as the following three, written when he was 58, suggest he visited, if only for sight-seeing:

提灯ではやし立けり花の雲 一茶
chôchin de hayashi tatekeri hana no kumo issa
(lantern/s-with banter raising[+emph] blossom-clouds)

行灯ではやしたてるや花の雲 一茶
andon de hayashi tateru ya hana no kumo   issa
(portable lantern/s-with banter raise:/! blossom-clouds)

egging them on
with paper lanterns:
cherry blossoms

raising a ruckus
with a folding lantern
cherry clouds

挑灯は花の雲間に入にけり 一茶
chôchin wa hana no kumoma ni irinikeri issa 1820
(lantern-as-for blossoms' cloud-among enter[+fin.])

an old lantern
vanishes within the fold
of blossom clouds

the paper lanterns
vanish within clouds
of cherry blossom

The second version of the first *ku* was prefaced "New Yoshiwara" (it burnt down and was rebuilt), so we may assume all were about the same place. *Hayashi*, as explained elsewhere, has no exact English equivalent. One could as well translate the respective versions of the first *ku*, *"Waving lanterns / we raise a hullabaloo / cherry clouds!"* or *"Who says lanterns / don't make good catcalls / Yoshiwara blossoms!"* Since Issa does not use the Chinese character for the *hayashi*, we could take even greater liberty and translate: *"Lanterns raise / a chorus in the night! / Yoshiwara cherries"* or *"New Yoshiwara / where clouds of blossom / dance to lanterns."* I must confess that when I first read the *ku*, I was under the influence of *senryû*, where (folding-type) lantern was slang for an old man's member, creased and completely telescoped when flaccid. I added the "old" to the last *ku*, just in case. But, in retrospect, I think the *ku* does not need that allusion. I hope I have not killed the *ku* for you by not killing it, but I tell myself that, since Issa read *senryû*, he could not have helped being aware of the possible allusion himself, even if he did not intend it, and, such background is part of reading.

吉原の鳥かご広し夕桜 哲阿 再現 1798
yoshiwara no torikago hiroshi yûzakura tetsua
(yoshiwara's birdcages broad evening-cherries)

傾城は後の世かけて花見哉 蕪村 1783
keisei wa nochinoyo kakete hanami kana buson
(topple-castles-as-for next-world resting-upon bl.vwg)

how spacious
the bird cages of yoshiwara!
night cherries

blossom-viewing
a courtesan dreams of
the next world!

Indentured prostitutes of Yoshiwara were allegorized as birds in cages, gilded perhaps, but not roomy. The "birds" peeked out through slats at the men who passed in the street. At first, I imagined they kept real birds in extra large cages (out of sympathy), but, seeing old prints of Yoshiwara blossom viewing, discovered they were able to join guests within the bamboo fence and curtains which temporarily enlarged their "cage" under the bloom. The "topple-castle" (*keisei*), in Buson's *ku* is a beautiful top-rank courtesan confined to a blossom-viewing in the aforesaid area. I first thought she risked super-natural punishment for enticing men, but, on second thought, realized that her place was already one of punishment for her last life and this "next-world" meant retirement outside of her cage. For her, the blossom-viewing included the possibility of convincing a patron to buy her freedom.

夕暮や鳥とる鳥の花に来る 一茶
yûgure ya tori toru tori no hana ni kuru issa 1803
(evening!/: bird/s-take bird/s' blossom-to come)

it is dusk
when bird-eating birds come
to the blossoms

All commentators agree that Issa's "bird-eating birds" are *yotaka*, or "night-hawks," which is to say the low-class prostitutes or street-walkers we encountered in the daimyô's *ku* (# 3-29). Issa may also have alluded to these hawks in his famous *doka-doka* dropping horse dung poem (# 63-53), for low-class prostitutes were also called "horse-dung." I *thought* a 1725 *ku* by Keikô, *"The spring departs! / dropping down the mountain / horse-dung hawks"* (ゆく春や麓におとす馬糞鷹（再現） 荊口 *yuku haru ya fumoto ni otosu magusodaka*) was about our birds descending from cherry-mountain, but they could be completely genuine hawks (there was a species so named), for I see no evidence of whores called horse-shit until fifty years later. Back to certainty, here's an old *senryû*: *"Night cherries / abandoned for a dumpling / on the levee"* (夜桜を見捨て土手で団子也　一甫 初代川柳 *yozakura o misutete dote de dango nari* 18c), where the "night-cherries" are the expensive courtesans and the "dumpling" is what English may once have called a cheap tart.

遠近やさそへばそちる山櫻 燕 花七日 1777
ochikochi ya sasoeba zo chiru yamazakura tsubame
(far near!/: invite-if/when fall mountain-cherries)

夢山や名ある櫻も目を覚めし 羽黒 月影塚
yumeyama ya na aru sakura mo me o sameshi ukoku ()
(dream-mountain:/! name-has-cherry's/ies' eyes open)

far and near, yes
seduce them and they'll fall
mountain cherries

dream mountain!
cherries with names, too
open their eyes

The first was a hard *ku* to save for this chapter; it could have fit in the *Mountain* or *Blossoms/women-as/or-women/blossoms* chapters. Is it not an example of the city poet confident of having his way with what the bard called "country matters"? The second *ku*, too, *seems* erotic. Dream Mountain probably is something like *yume-sanbô* (夢三宝), where the *sanbô* is the base for a magical New Year's Mountain of Youth and means only "this must be a dream!" though the mountain associates with the cherry blossoms. What type of dream? A dream of the pleasure quarters, I think: but who knows!

花の火や若衆の櫻袖香炉 一雪
hana no hi ya wakashu no sakura sode korô issetsu -1680
(blossoms' fire!/?/: young-crowd[homosexuals]'s cherry sleeve-censers)

real blossom fire
the young crowd burns incense
within their sleeves

If Europeans had their flea-catching vials of liquid hanging under women's clothing, the Japanese had small double skinned devices kept within their sleeves to literally per-*fume* themselves. The lovely homosexual and/or transvestite youth called "young-crowd" (mostly prostitutes) were the blossoms. There is a pun on "fireworks," *blossom-fire* (*hanabi*), and maybe another on "fire-arrows" (*hiya*).

賀剃髪・若衆に目の通ふへし花の山　岡道 小弓
wakashû ni me no toubeshi hananoyama　kôdô 1699
(young-crowd-to-eyes pass-should blossom-mountain)

celebrating a head-shaving

the first thing to do:
look over that young crowd
on cherry mountain

The head-shaving shows that the poet (or third-party) is entering a buddhist order, where *the wide way* (sex with women) was generally frowned upon as likely to foster long-term attachment to this world, whereas *the narrow way* (sex with boys and youth) was permitted as a less addictive practice. Most cultured men (esp. samurai and priests) in Japan, while not homosexual in the Usanian sense of being romantically and physically drawn to ones own sex alone, were *appreciative* of boys and this fondness, in proper circumstances might be physically expressed (see *Topsy Turvy 1585*).

一指より思ふ一枝そ衆道櫻　由平 太夫櫻
hito yubi yori omou hito eda zo shudôzakura　yûhei 1699
(one-finger-more-than think/love one-branch/limb! crowdway-cherry)

a limb gives you
more to long for than a pinkie:
young-crowd cherry

forget the finger
i'm thinking of a twig
wakashu cherry

why take a finger
when you can break a branch
gayboy cherry

Courtesans pledged fidelity or atoned for misdeeds by chopping off the pinky tips (an ancient funereal practice). The original has the poet, or a third-party more attracted to one-limb, i.e. the *wakashu's* third-leg, than to a finger. Does the poet want a to break off a bit o' *wakashu*? Unfortunately, *limb* is too large, *twig* is too small and *branch* sounds wrong as an allusion to you know what.

美をにくむ心の櫻若衆哉　文排 虚栗
bi o nikumu kokoro no sakura wakashu kana　bunpai 1683
(beauty[acc.] hate/hating heart's cherry young-crowd 'tis)

~~blossoms within
minds that hate beauty
the young crowd~~

young crowd
the beauty-hating cherry
in our hearts

~~cherry blossoms
in a beauty-hating mind
the young crowd~~

In Japan, *hate* and *love* were so closely bound that it is hard to tell what is going on here. *Hate* can mean strong attraction. Or, has "beauty" already begun to take on its modern feminine slant, in which case the girly-boys dislike women? Or, did they pioneer an ugly *punk* or *grunge* look? Following Y, who is E, and felt it expresses an adolescent mindset, I have crossed out all but one reading.

花散りて素顔も見よき若衆哉　女水 蘆別船
hana chirite sugao mo mi-yoki wakashu kana　mesui 1694
(blossoms falling plainface-even see-good/pretty youngcrowd!/'tis)

    the blossoms fall　　　　　　　　　　　　when petals blow
  even without make-up　　　　　　　　bare faces look good too
      gays look good　　　　　　　　　　　　　ah, young crowd!

                    after the blossoms
              bare faces are good to see
                    on the young crowd

All men of breeding wore make-up in Japan. "Young crowd" wore a lot, but evidently were still not so heavily made-up as women. Because the expectations were different, plain Janes sometimes passed as young-crowd, especially when/where they were more popular than female prostitutes! Does the poet oddly named "woman-water" (?!) note that after the heavy bloom, for a while, at least, branches bare of blossoms boasting wee leaves are oddly attractive? I have noticed that.

~~~~~~

油凹油

けいせいのきもとは花のあぶら哉　大江丸 ? 俳諧袋
keisei no kimo to wa hana no abura kana　ôemaru 1719-1805
(beauty/courtesan's verve/spirit-as-for blossom-oil!/?/'tis)

   the barm behind　　　　　　　blossom oil　　　　　　　the pluckiness
 a beautiful whore?　　　　the bottom yeast for all　　of a gorgeous whore
    blossom oil　　　　　　　　castle-topplers　　　　　　　blossom oil

The original puns upon the other *hana,* the homophone for "blossom," *nose.* To do big things, one "draws on" something called nose oil (*hana-abura*), said to exude from somewhere between the head of your nose and your small-nose, (the outside of the nostrils?), and excreting it, if I have it right, is the opposite of exuding a cold sweat: it shows confidence. Since the beautiful harlot was, at least in her most prestigious manifestation as a courtesan, called a *sakura* and this cherry was the prototypical blossom, her nose oil – or should we call it grease? – was floral by definition. Of course, you must remember that oil was not only a precious fuel but metaphorically speaking the equivalent of sugar in the Occident. To be oily or fatty was to be delectable. My "yeast," a mistake, came from reading *kimoto* (a rare word for yeast) rather than *kimo to wa*, or "pluckiness/verve-as-for." I kept it anyway.

夜の花恋も思はぬこころから　花賛女
yoru no hana koi mo omowanu kokoro kara　kasanjo 1807-1830
(night-blossom/s love/romance-too/even think/feel-not heart-from)

   night blossoms　　　　　　　born of hearts　　　　　　night blossoms
 born from the loveless　　　that are blind to love　　　love too always comes
    hearts of men　　　　　　　　night blossoms　　　　　　　as a surprise

I cannot tell whether the *mo* here emphasizes the negative or means "too," as per the last reading. If the first two readings are correct, the young female poet, whose name means "flower-praise" is doing something very rare: she is criticizing prostitution.

はなやさく心にかゝる夜着の襟 成美
hana ya saku kokoro ni kakaru yogi no eri seibi 1816
(blossoms[emph] bloom heart-on catch nightclothes' collar)

<blockquote>
the cherries bloom
i notice the collars
of our nightrobes
</blockquote>

I can understand another fine *ku* that I think is by Seibi about becoming conscious of the smell of the burnt fish in one's mouth on a day when the snow settled deep around the house. But I never notice collars so I cannot feel this *ku* as my own. If I *could*, I think I would like the *ku*, perhaps because there is a pleasant sort of sensuality intrinsic to details. There is much of this subtle eros in modern Japanese haiku. We can add a score of them when/if this book is expanded.

雲水の香をせきとめて花の塚 几董
unsui no ko o seki-tomete hana no zuka kitô -1789
(cloud-water's scent[obj.] block-keeping blossom-mound)

<blockquote>
dammed up here
the scent of cloud and water
a blossom mound
</blockquote>

<blockquote>
~~the scent of love~~
~~the birds and bees are here:~~
~~a cherry's grave~~
</blockquote>

This is *not* an erotic *ku*. "Cloud-water" (雲水) is short for a wandering monk or by extension anyone who, like the clouds and water in the mountains, has no fixed abode. I would guess it is meant for the grave of a female poet who spent much time on the road. Why is it in this chapter? Because, I first misread the cloud-*water* as "cloud-*rain*" (雲雨), which is short for *the intercourse of cloud and rain*, and refers to a romantic sexual affair, because of an ancient Chinese tale about a king who was visited by a goddess at the grave of a beloved princess who died before she could marry. The goddess was a dragon of sorts (women who died unfulfilled tended to turn into dragons) and dragons came and went with, or by turning into one of these elements. After coming up with those *birds and bees* to translate the cloud-water into elementary English, I didn't have the heart to do away with it completely.

肌のよき石に眠らん花の山 露通 卯辰
hada no yoki ishi ni nemuran hana no yama rotsû 1691
(skin's good stone-on sleep-would blossom-mountain)

A hill of cherry-blossoms / I will slumber / On a smooth stone. trans. Blyth

<blockquote>
i would lie down
on a smooth-skinned stone
blossom mountain!
</blockquote>

<blockquote>
blooming hills
i will find a smooth stone
and sleep on it
</blockquote>

This famous *ku* is always interpreted as an expression of the ascetic's choice of a boulder over an inn, or even the relatively softer ground. *Maybe*. I feel it may be a warm day and the cool boulder an ideal place to nap. I also wonder whether the combination of smooth skin – literally, beautiful-skin-stone – and blossomy curves was not meant to be *sensual*, to feminize cherry mountain.

うまず女の物やりたがる花見哉 南浦
umazu onna no mono yaritagaru hanami kana nampô
(bear-not woman's thing ~~do~~/give-want blossom-viewing 'tis)

~~how childless~~
~~women want to do it!~~
~~blossom-viewing~~

blossom viewing
childless women want to
give things away

"Barren" fits, for the *sakura* is all flower and no fruit; but I had too much sex on my mind. Luckily, *haiyû* Sky-bug put me straight. *The woman is playing with children.* Memories of childless Aunt B (Beulah: Ant+Bee for us children), who gave us good presents. The *ku* does *not* belong in this chapter!

花びらがさはっても出る涙哉 一茶
hanabira ga sawatte mo deru namida kana issa 1810
(petals-the touching-even come-out tears!/?/'tis)

de lacrimae cerasorum

cherry petals
if you but touch them
flow like tears

tears that drop
at a touch, these cherry
blossom petals

just the touch
of cherry petals and out
come my tears

If this chapter is loose even by my loose standard, it is because, *first*, the ambiguity intrinsic to hypershort poetry is multiplied by that which accompanies sexual innuendo, or, where I am wrong, *imagined* sexual innuendo, and *second*, because it tried to include all from the obvious pleasure quarter to the barely erotic, in the sense of being sensual, as Issa's cherry petals.

凸の凹の凸
Corpus Cavernosum

Either I, or *haikai,* have overlooked one angle on the cherry tree's sexuality. In an article *The Gender of the Cherry, etcetera.* (桜のジェンダー。。。など in 国文学 2001・4), the poet Takahashi Mutsuo mentions the hollow tree (空木) of the Noh play *Saigyô Sakura* from which an old white-haired male spirit emerged and hypothesizes that this hollow stands for motherhood (母性), for the female principle, the womb, *and the blossoms that come out every year represent the male principle, the power that springs from the earth like a mushroom.* Takahashi *also* notes that the powerful demon-scaring bodhisattva Zaôgongen 蔵王権現 whose sculpture was carved from cherry-wood had "angry-swollen" phallic characteristics not found in the Indian and Chinese Buddhist sculptures (This is hard for Occidental readers to imagine, for phallic symbols in the West are long and sleek rather than thick, warty, full of veins and topped by an extremely wide head). If you do not care for that way of putting it, he adds, you can think of it as a manifestation of *fertility*.

◎オマケ：花の山足よわつれがぜつひ出来　雪円　柳多留 9-2　1774（瞽女前級の練りマンか？）◎

Old Men, Old Cherries
老人・老櫻

迷子札爺もさげて花見笠　一茶 1822
maigofuda jijii mo sagete hanamigasa　issa
(lost-child sign geezer also dangling bl.vwing hat)

a "lost-child" sign
dangling from an old man
with his cherry-hat

年寄の腰や花見の迷子札　一茶 1821
toshiyori no koshi ya hanami no maigofuda　issa
(elderly's hip/back!/: blsm.vwing lost-child-sign)

from gramp's waist
a blossom-viewing sign
"this child lost"

花さくや親爺が腰の迷子札　一茶　浅黄空
hana saku ya oyajigakoshi no maigofuda　issa
(blossom bloom: pop's hip/back lost-child sign)

the cherries bloom!
from this old man's waist
a "lost child" sign

夜桜や親爺（が）腰の迷子札　一茶　自筆本
yozakura ya oyajigakoshi no maigofuda　issa
(night-cherry/ies: pop's hip/back lost-child sign)

night blossoms!
from the old man's waist
a "lost child" sign

I do not know if Issa actually saw this, but what an image of the human condition! Blossoms flying about complement being lost. A mother in Zeami's (noh) play *Sakuragawa* (cherry-river) searches desperately for her lost daughter named Sakurako (cherry-child), even going so far as to scoop up cherry petals from the river. But, to my mind, Issa's snapshot beats the famous play. If Kurosawa hasn't started a movie with it, someone should! Issa generally did many versions of his favorite *ku*. The first of these *ku* was his last of them. The "blossom-viewing hat," which I abbreviated to "cherry-hat," makes it clear that the old man knew where he was going when he set out, ...

花の陰一人（我に）おかしき物忘　成美
hana no kage hitori [ware ni] okashiki monowasure　seibi 1816
(bloomshade one-man/alone[self-to] funny thing-forgetting)

in the bloomshade
all alone laughing at my *ab
sentmindedness*

in the bloomshade
laughing at myself: at all
i have forgotten

the bloomshade
my absentmindedness
amuses me *here*

Does Issa's patron Seibi laugh at his forgetfulness during the viewing – *Now where did I put my sake cup? Ouch! How did that branch get there!* – or did he forget to bring something with him?

old 651

見ほれてや花の下なる忘れ杖　龍眠 新選

mihorete ya hananoshita-naru wasurezue ryûmin 1773

(see-loving/gaga!: blossoms-below is forgotten cane)

    head over heels
over the cherry blossoms:
    a forgotten cane

花の山出茶屋に老の忘れ杖　柳多留 145-35

hananoyama dechaya ni rô no wasurezue yanag. 20c

(blossom-mountain temporary-tea-shop-in aged's f.c.)

    in a tea-shop
on cherry mountain, gramp's
    forgotten cane

As far as I know, the Japanese do not have a phrase equivalent to "losing ones marbles," but the falling petals may have something to do with the large amount of forgetfulness and seeming senility in the bloomshade. Canes are big both because many blossom-viewers have done little walking all year (Japanese, like Chinese, were mystified by European visitors' desire to take walks: see *Topsy-turvy 1585*), because hills were usually involved and, in the case of poets, there were an extraordinary number of old ones, which is also why we have this chapter. Yayû wrote *"In cane country / you view and circle about / the full bloom"* (見て回れ杖つく國の花ざかり 也有 *mite-maware tsue tsuku kuni no hanazakari* 1701-83) that seems to say something about this phenomenon. It has an intriguing phrase: "cane-poking/carrying-country/nation." I have not yet discovered whether this is a literary allusion to some old Chinese text or a term for a locality where only the elderly live that is no longer in dictionaries, but I do know that Yayû enjoyed a long life and has a marvelous page in his miscellany *Uzuragoromo* (Quail-Robe) about the charm and benefits of what we might call senile dementia. Next to Lafcadio Hearn's story about "The Man Who Forgot Himself" in *Creole Sketches* (read it and cry for the murdered city/culture of New Orleans!), it is the best there is on this subject. Since Yayû's forgetful man was able to enjoy himself with only a few books – or was it but one? – that he could read over and over again with equal amusement, I suspect one tree would more than do for blossom-viewing, too.

花はたゞ心の老のかざし哉　心敬 新つくは

hana wa tada kokoro no rô no kazashi kana shinkei 1405-1475

(blossoms-as-for only heart's-agedness's head-decoration!/'tis)

cherry blossoms	cherry blossoms	cherry blossoms?
nothing but laurels for	they only grab us when we	nothing but a spray upon
the old at heart	are over-the-hill	spirit's white head

花はいざ年に色そふ心哉　宗祇 老葉

hana-wa iza toshi ni iro sou kokoro kana sôgi (1420-1502)

(blossoms-as-for [emph.] age/years-to color/beauty adds heart!/?/'tis)

~~cherry blossoms?~~	blossoms are	~~cherry blossoms?~~
~~what grow more attractive~~	what bring beauty	~~spirit grown beautiful~~
~~year by year~~	to old age	~~with old age~~

Unfamiliar with Shinkei when I first read his *ku*, I chuckled: *"Blossom viewing? / Something men do once / they lose their edge,"* that is, men enjoy the company of women only after they lose their ability to do real battle. Then, still chuckling, paraversed *"Cherry blossoms? / nothing but the trophy wives / of us old men."* But, after reading his twenty cherry blossom *waka* and finding them *the darkest series of poems I had ever read*, I came to wonder if this might not be something like Issa's *ku* about blossoms in the end-times and viewing blossoms while seated on the roof of Hell. The difference is that Issa lived in times that were not all *that* bad; Shinkei witnessed the destruction of the capital and wholesale massacre. Sôgi, who was Shinkei's successor, also saw some bad times, but he started out poor and came to have much to be thankful for. My readings are tentative, but I am sure of his cheer.

年毎の花には老の心哉 宗春 三籟
toshigoto no hana ni wa rô no kokoro kana sôshun 1734
(year-each's blossom-as-for aged's heart!/?/'tis)

every year
the blossoms have the same
aged hearts

every year
the old give new blossoms
their hearts

年よりも皆丈夫なり櫻狩 荒笑 桃首途
toshiyori mo mina jôbu nari sakuragari kôshô? 1728
(elderly even everyone healthy be/come cherry-hunting)

game indeed!

even the elderly
are fit as a fiddle
hunting cherry!

花に老を忘れ草つむ春野哉 宗祇
hana ni rô o wasure kusa tsumu haruno kana sôgi - 1502
(blossoms-in/with age[acc.] forget-grass pick spring-field!/?/'tis)

after the blossom-viewing

forgetting my age
with cherries i pluck greens
in the spring field

a spring meadow
i pluck greens, my years left
behind with the bloom

櫻さく上野いふらん不老門 蓼太
sakura saku ueno iu-ran furô-mon ryôta -1787
(cherry blooms ueno say/call, yeah, not-age-gate)

ueno with cherry
in full bloom: we enter
an ageless gate

in full bloom
call the entrance to ueno
the gate to agenot

桜へと見へ（え）てじん／＼ばしより哉 一茶
sakura e to miete jinjinbashiyori kana issa 1818
(cherry/ies-to seen-as gramps/geezer/s-edge-fold!/'tis)

his tail uptucked!
anyone can tell gramps
heads for the cherries

off to the cherries
the old man's ass peeks
out from his robe

the blossoms wait
old men, their kimonos
tucked up for speed!

The standard term for tucking a kimono tail into the belt to be cool, take larger strides and keep the hem clean is *shirikarage*. This *jinjinbashori*, or *jijiibashori* only applies to old men (*jijii*, or *jin*). I think this is because old people suffer overheat easily. As Issa often called himself an old man (eg. "And it came to be called / grampa stink-bug's wall" *hehirimushi jiji-ga-kakine to shirarekeri*), this may be a self-portrait. Issa's best-known *ku* on the encounter of age and blossoms are in other chapters. One has him straining to break off a spray of bloom. At that time, I missed an older *ku* by Raizan about yet greater debility: *"Even breaking / a spray is pie in the sky: / I just looked"* (折事も高根の花や見たばかり 来山 いまみや艸 *orukoto mo takane no hana ya mita bakari* -1716).

けふばかり老につもらじ散る櫻　蓼太
kyo bakari rô ni tsumoraji chiru sakura　ryôta
(today only age-to/on pile-not falling cherry -1787)

only today
years do not pile up
falling petals

櫻咲さくら散つゝ我老ぬ　蘭更 -1799
sakura saki sakura chiritsutsu ware oinu　rankô
(cherry blooming cherry [bls] falling-as i age)

cherries bloom
cherry blossoms blow &
i grow *older*

Despite *ku* on canes, senility and the difficulty of breaking bloom, blossom-viewing was generally felt to be a rejuvenating activity. A new year might be considered added burden; but this is not so with cherry blossoms. They bloom, then blow, but, hey, observes Ryôta, who lived to be 80, you feel more alive, not older. Rankô demurs. The moon may wane but it soon waxes anew and the blossoms likewise come back as young as ever, while I, *sob, sob* . . . This complaint is an old one:

春ごとに花のさかりはありなめどあひ見む事はいのちなりけり　よみ人しらず 古今集#97
haru goto ni hana-no sakari wa ari namedo aimimu koto wa inochi narikeri kokinshû 905

every spring	*every spring*	*every spring*
the blossoms do their thing	*blossoms fill the trees*	*the trees explode in bloom*
so much is true	*too bad that we*	*a sweet sight*
but so is this: to view them	*must ante-up one more*	*but only mine to love*
you need a ticket: your life!	*year each time we come!*	*so long as i've a life*

From the variety of wording, even without the verbatim gloss, you could tell I overdid the translations. The next *waka* in the *Kokinshû*, also anonymous, is a different angle on the same complaint: *"If the whole world / were like cherry blossoms / come the spring / we could regain the lost / flower of our own youth!"* (花のごと世のつねならばすぐしてし昔は又もかへりきなまし 古今集#98 *hana no goto yo no tsune naraba sugushite shi mukashi wa mata mo kaeri ki na mashi* anon *kokinshû* 905). In ancient times, and still in Rankô's day, most cherry trees were probably long-lived, and this only changed with the proliferation of the Somei-yoshino, with a life-span as short if not shorter than ours! While an old tree awes us, the short life of the Somei-yoshino does make us feel more sympathy for it (unless we recall that, as a clone, said tree only *appears* to share in our individual sadness, for it is potentially immortal).

年よりの目にさへ桜／＼哉　一茶
toshiyori no me ni sae sakura sakura kana issa 1810
(elderly's eyes-in even cherry [blossoms] cherry [bls]!)

in old eyes, too	*sakura sakura*
they bloom, they bloom	cherry blossoms reflect
sakura! sakura!	in old eyes, too

よるとしや桜のさくも小うるさき 一茶 1810
yoru toshi ya sakura no saku mo ko-urasaki issa
(accruing years: cherry blooms even bothersome)

老ぬれば桜も寒いばかり哉 一茶 1809
oi-nureba sakura mo samui bakari kana issa
(aged-become-when cherry even cold only!)

feeling my age!	getting old
even cherry blossoms can be	the cherry blossoms just
a pain in the ass	seem cold!

The first is the less famous of Issa's two *sakura sakura ku* (the other, sung of an old tree # 28-20). The original is verbless. "Reflect" could as well be "shine," "fill" or "delight." These *ku*, written in Issa's mid-40's, when he was already white-haired and almost toothless, are not maudlin like Rankô's, nor celebratory like Sôgi's and Ryôta's *ku*. Who could guess he would marry a young wife in less than five years! By being personal, Issa breaks fresh ground.

此春は旅にしあれば老が世にあへるはまれの花もかひなし　心敬　花二十首
kono haru wa tabi ni shi areba oi ga yo ni aeru wa mare no hana mo kai nashi　shinkei -1475

*when i travel
this spring, my old world
comes along*

*what blossoms i meet
hold no bloom for me*

*an old man
travels an old world
this spring*

*even the rare bloom
i find is lost on me*

An annotation explains that this was written when Shinkei was still exiled from the capital. Under such circumstances, travel would indeed be *travail*. But, how does age fit in? A Japanese annotator mentions the short time remaining in life. My (fallen?) nature is such that I first thought of pretty women met on the road as little use for an old man, but on second thought, settled upon this: Shinkei means he would be too tired to enjoy an all-night *renga* session below the bloom with his hosts.

物おしむ老に見よとや散る櫻　蓼太
mono oshimu rô ni miyo to ya chiru sakura　ryôta 1787
(things regret old-age-in see! [as if to say] falling cherry [bls])

*we who regret
old age should watch
petals scatter!*

*best watched
in regret-filled old age:
falling petals*

花過て花見の手本習ひけり　集加
hana sugite hanami no tehon naraikeri　shûka 1734
(blossom/s-past blossom-viewing rules learn[+emph])

*my bloom past
i finally learn the way
to view blossoms*

"Fall" is too passive and "scatter" too specific for the more active nuance of the Japanese *chiru* in Ryôta's *ku* that might be called "sympathy." Shûka's *ku* found in 加藤郁也＝市井風流 needs no comment.

七十賀・やよけれと花にわかえん老の春　宗春
yayo keredo hana ni wakaen rô no haru　sôshun 三籟 1734
(hey/hurrah [dialect:wife?] blossom-to rejuvenate-let's old-spring)

hurray for seventy!

*with the blossoms
i'd turn my old spring into
a fountain of youth*

*my old wife
but in this bloom we'll try
to rejuvenate*

Yayokereto may mean "hurray, but/notwithstanding," or, less likely, the "hurray" may be dialect for one's "stupid-wife" (*yayo*). *Wakaen* may refer to the likewise provincial verb for rejuvenating plants through fertilizer and other means. I may well be wrong with both readings. None of my respondents will touch this *ku* with a ten-foot pole. But enough of poets on their own or other human's age. Poems about old *trees* are more pleasant, as concern for others is always more touching than concern for self:

老ぬれど春をやすまぬ櫻哉　嵐外
oinuredo haru o yasumanu sakura kana rangai -1845
(old-be-but spring vacation-take-not cherry/ies!)

this cherry
is old but not about to
take spring off

old, indeed,
but not skipping spring:
this cherry!

Were there not a preface to this *ku* mentioning a 200 year-old tree, one might read it as *"Though I've aged / I sure won't skip the spring: cherry blossoms!"* The verb *yasumu* is the same one used for taking a day off work, so this is a pre-Issa example of a tree doing its *job*.

ことしきり／＼とや古ざくら　一茶
kotoshi kiri kotoshi kiri to ya furuzakura issa - 1814
(this year-only/end, this year-only/end old-cherry)

every year is
the last year, the last time!
an old cherry

The ink-jet glands on the side of a quail's cloaca begin to dry up as it ages, so the pretty patterns on the eggs fades away before it stops laying. How do old cherries show *their* age? When they lose their ability to fight off bugs, they lose limbs and their bloom and foliage suffers. Yet, I have seen an old tree toppled by snow-bamboo, with just one root in the ground keep blooming not one but two or three years after toppling. Evidently, bloom does not stop, but winds down. Issa may identify with the tree, so substitute "our" or "my" for the "the's" if you wish. The wit is in the *"last"* repeated.

わきて見ん老木は花もあはれなり今いくたびか春にあふべき　西行
wakite min oi ki wa hana mo awarenari ima iku tabi ka haru ni aubeki saigyô 1118-90

" Coming across old cherries here and there [1]
ふる木の桜の所々咲きたるを見て

search out old trees
their blossoms possess
a sad beauty:

how many more springs
will we meet?

split the brush
the bloom of an old tree
is touching

how many more springs
may we have together?

---

1. Prefix Politics. *"Coming across old cherries here and there"*. This is a fitting prefix. Happening to encounter old cherry trees, abbot Saigyô came up with the idea of searching them out. Believe it or not, by the time this *waka* was reprinted in 1439 (続新古今集), it had been changed to read *"I read-composed this while* *resting in the bloomshade from my* (religious) *austerities."* This was because of Buddhists attempting to steal the cherry tree from the poets, as mentioned before. (松岡心平：律宗と花下連歌：「国文学」平成 13・4・10

~~~~~~

花にまた契りくちせぬ老木哉　宗祇
hana ni mada chigiri kuchisenu rôki kana sôgi -1502
(blossom-as/to still vow/s rot-not old-tree!/'tis)

it has not allowed
its blossom vows to cloud
the old cherry tree

Heroic, for sure, but should we say the old *prunus* still performs his duties *toward* the blossoms=fair-sex, or, that it is it androgynous, its soul/trunk masculine and its blossoms female?

とふ人に花の春しる老木哉　宗祇
tou hito ni hana no haru shiru rôki kana   sôgi
(calling people-by blossom-spring knows old-tree!)

this grand old tree!
with caring guests enjoys
a flowery spring

思はずの花に又逢ふ老木哉　宗祇
omowazu no hana ni mata au rôki kana sôgi
(think/expect-not's blossom-with again meet oldtree!)

meeting up again
with an unexpected cherry:
this old tree!

The old tree would blossom whether people saw it or not, but feted enjoys a richer spring in its old age. With the second *ku*, it is hard to say whether Sôgi expected to find the tree gone or simply bereft of bloom.! I am delighted to find feelings like this for an individual tree in a haiku-length poem, long before most scholars admit the presence of *bona fide* haiku.

花にわが思ふ色そふ老木哉　宗祇
hana ni waga omou iro sou rôki kana sôgi -1502
(blossom-to/with my thinking/loving color/mood add old-tree'tis))

the old tree
my affection adds a glow
to its bloom

your blossoms
pinker for my thoughts
ah, old tree!

"Color" means so much less in English than in Japanese. How funny we should have "off-color," but no other "color" to speak of, outside of race. *Pink*, however, is full of meaning, so I used it, instead.

手を引て恥かしくなき華見かな 素丸-1795
te o hiite hazukashikunaki hanami kana somaru
(hand[obj] pulling shameful-not blossom-viewing!)

being lead by hand
no cause for embarrassment
blossom-viewing

としよりも嫌ひ給はぬ桜哉　一茶 -1827
toshiyori mo kirai tamawanu sakura kana issa
(elderly also hate are[+honorofic]-not cherry!/'tis)

cherry blossoms:
they don't even dislike
old folk like me!

Does Somaru depict his outing, as an old man? With respect to Issa's *ku*, are blossoms less choosy than real women? *I joke.* Written during Issa's first spring as a married man, the *ku* may express satisfaction with his young wife's attention. The "like me" is not specified by the original.

old

評判の八重山桜あゝ老ぬ 一茶
hyôban no yae yamazakura aa oinu issa 1818
(reputation's/famous eightfold mountain cherry ah,ah aging/aged)

this is the famous	ah, our famous
eight-fold mountain cherry!	eight-fold mountain cherry!
my, we've aged!	you *have* aged!

Specifying "eight-fold" shows mountain cherries were generally not double-petal and proves they sometimes were. At first, I thought Issa contrasted the lush bloom on the tree with his more decrepit state, but a *ku* three years later makes it clear the tree is old and justifies the Royal *We* (and *you*) for the above *ku*: "How decrepit / the enormously famous / cherry tree!" (老いたりな大評判のさくら花 *oitari na ôhyôban no sakurabana*). Actually, it is "aged," not "decrepit," but the nuance is such.

清水寺法楽・たのむ陰あらん限りや花の春 宗因 三籟
kiyomizudera hôgaku// tanomu kage aran kagiri ya hana no haru sôin 1734
(kiyomizu temple[(buddhist) play]// dependable shade be-would extent:/! blossom-spring)

so long as	while there's shade	cherry spring
i've bloom-shade!	below the bloom it is still	i'll enjoy it so long
cherry spring	the cherry spring	as i've shade

This is a *ku* about old age that doesn't mention it. The title "*hôgaku* (a traditional play) at Kiyomizu-dera" doubtless means something, but I can never recall what happened at that temple.

よしや杖頤につかせて花の山 好友 江戸新道
yoshi ya tsue ago ni tsukasete hananoyama kôyû 1678
(well! cane chin-on/against using blossom-mountain)

i've made it again!	up here again!
resting my chin on my cane	chin upon cane, i survey
on cherry mountain	cherry mountain

はつかしの老に気のつく花見哉 鬼貫 1738　　　ちる花に罪も報もしら髪哉 一茶 1814
hazukashi no rô ni ki no tsuku hanami kana onitsura　　*chiru hana ni tsumi mo mukui mo shiraga kana* issa
(embarrassing age-in feeling-note blossom-viewing!)　　(falling blossoms-to sin and reward whitehair!)

suddenly aware	falling blossoms:
of my shameful old age:	my sin and my reward
blossom-viewing!	is this white hair

The *yoshi ya* in the first *ku* is hard to translate. Perhaps it means just *"Phew!"* Paradoxically, age was highly respected as per Confucianism *and* despised because of a warrior die-fighting mindset fused with the Buddhist ideal of letting go. Eight years earlier, Issa lamented a cherry blossoming *"before the house of a worthless survivor"* (長らへて益なき門も桜哉 *nagaraete ekinaki kado mo sakura kana*). His *sin* was not releasing his life when he was ill, and his *reward* was for sticking out the hard path he chose – that of following the butterflies and blossoms, *i.e.*, the *haikai* profession. More such *ku*: "Like me, poor / at letting go of its bloom: / my gate cherry" (我に似てちり下手なるや門の花 *ware ni nite chiri heta naru ya kado no hana*) Or, conversely, "Falling briskly / cherry tree is unsaddled / with shame" (つか／＼とちり恥かゝぬ桜哉 *tsukatsuka to chiri haji kakanu sakura kana*). Such *ku* remind me of Elvis Presley's so-called gospel music, a sickly whine from an otherwise good singer.

御迎ひの雲を待身も桜哉　一茶
omukai no kumo o matsu mi mo sakura kana issa 1805
(hon. pick-up/welcoming clouds[acc.] waits/ing body/self too cherry!)

someone waits for a cloud to swing low: blossom-viewing	like those who wait to leave with a cloud cherry blossoms	someone waiting for his cloud to come is a sakura too

Because the nobility who wrote ancient poems were encrypted in mountain caverns and, later, because of cremation and Buddhist hagiography describing multi-colored clouds carrying off saints, the cloud=soul connection remained strong until modern times. The *o-mukai* is someone or some thing that comes for you. *Escort* did not seem quite right, so I borrowed Christian gospel (song) idiom for the first reading. It is unclear here if Issa refers to himself or to someone else. Because cherry petals are clouds and blow away in clouds, the *ku* is a natural. Indeed, it is so natural that I am afraid my allegory may be backwards and Issa may only be praising cherry blossoms as per the last reading.

よるとしや桜のさくも小うるさき　一茶 1810
yoru toshi ya sakura no saku mo ko-urusaki issa
(approach years: cherry's blooming too annoying)

how we age!
even cherries blooming
a nuissance

花見るも役目也けり老にけり　一茶 1814
hana miru mo yakume narikeri oinikeri issa
(blssms vwng also duty become[emph.] age[+fin.])

you grow old,
viewing cherry blossoms
becomes a duty

While these are probably self-referential, there is an off-chance Issa, still in his late forties and early fifties, describes an old friend, hence the inclusive "we" and generic "you." If Buson had a way with classical allusion and nostalgic landscape, Issa had a way with simple words. His "small-bothersome" (*ko-urusaki*) and "duty/role" (*yakume*) are perfect. Speaking of age, the first *ku* is #60-19. *Mea culpa.*

おとろへや見た分にする花の山　一茶 1816
otoroe ya mita bun ni suru hana no yama   issa
(weakening! seen amount-as do blossom-mountain)

i'm over the hill!
"blossom viewing" now includes
bloom spied afar

四十から花に追はるゝ寝覚哉　花明 1771
shijû kara hana ni owaruru nesame kana   kamei
(40-from blossoms-by chased waking up!) 芭蕉庵再興集

from forty
the blossoms hound you:
waking up

In respect to Issa's *ku,* I think he refers to some of the problems he had with his legs. He had to let his eyes do the walking. On the face of it, age makes it harder for the poet to get up; but something about the way Kamei claims to be hounded makes one wonder if his real complaint is about getting *it* up!

花は雲人はけぶりと成にけり　一茶 1822
hana wa kumo hito wa keburi to narinikeri issa
(blossoms-as-for cloud people-as-for smoke become[fin])

blossoms turn
into clouds and people
turn to smoke

花さくや今廿年前ならば　一茶 1822
hana saku ya ima nijûnen mae naraba issa
(cherries bloom!/: now twenty-years-before was-if)

flowers bloom
if this day were only
twenty years ago!

old

ことしきりなどゝいふ也花見笠　一茶

kotoshi kiri nado to iu nari hanamigasa　issa 1822
(this-year end/finish etc. say-is/be blossom-viewing-hat)

saying *"this is it,*	its very last year!"
my last year!" and so forth	i say, putting on my old
a blossom-viewing hat	blossom-viewing hat

Issa and his wife were not in good health. The second *ku* expresses the agony of one finally becoming well-known and capable of taking care of a family when his "quality time" is over. I agonize with Issa, for it is my situation, or hopefully will be, as I *still* have not made it. But I will be game, as Issa was: *"I'll blossom-view! / i'll do it! [though] my stay in this world / will be brief"* (花見せん娑婆の逗留の其の中は　一茶　*hanami sen shaba no tôryu no sono uchi wa* 1822). Who knows if Issa's *kotoshi kiri* poem concerns himself, his hat or both.

老の浪の立よる嶋や花の陰　土方竪　八仙専

rô no nami no tachiyoru shima ya hananokage　dôhôken ()
(age's waves' standing-approach island!/?/: bloomshade)

an island where	this oasis for
old ripples=wrinkles meet?	men past the pink of life!
the bloom-shade	the bloom-shade

The idea of waves/ripples as wrinkles may derive from the way waves were painted in the Far East. Waves are also appropriate here because the Japanese commonly speak of blossom *tides* rising up mountains, then receding. The idea of the bloomshade as an oasis for the old, rather than the usual fountain of youth, is beautiful. The final *ku* is by a brilliant nun I assume goes blossom-viewing.

いにしへに我も追つく花の杖　智月尼

inishie ni ware mo oitsuku hana no tsukue　chigetsu-ni 17c
(past/longago-to i too catch[+pun on age]-up blossom-desk)

my blossom cane
i, too, will catch up
to long ago

~~~~~~

<div style="text-align:center">
watakushi no hone to sakura ga mankai ni　ônishi yasuyo (20c)
(my bones and cherry [tree/s/blossoms]-the full-bloom-in/as)
</div>

my bones	my bones
and cherry blossoms	and the cherry trees
in full bloom	in full bloom

The first translation, by Fay Aogi, from her column in the *Frogpond* (Haiku Society of America: Winter 2005) is left-margin in the original. My translation guesses (*I could be wrong! This is a last minute addition*) the poet, old and thin, is all dressed up blossom-viewing. It could be a house cherry, in which case "my cherry tree" would be a suitable translation. The *ku* intrigues us for being so alike yet unlike the famous skeleton bedecked *ku* by Onitsura, here, I feel the companionship of the trees is heartwarming.

Nativist, Then Nationalist Cherry

にほん、否
ニッポンのさくら

日本の人鼻高し山櫻　竹苞　四季発(千?)句
hinomoto no hito hana takashi yamazakura　chikuhô 1689?
(suns' origin's people nose high mountain-cherry/ies)

heads held high
in the land of the rising sun:
mountain cherries!

born of the sun
we're stuck up for a reason
mountain cherries

When it comes to the plum, China had Japan beat, but Japan was blessed with wild cherry blossoms, many of which were found in lofty places (though originally they too may have come from China and gone feral). The original of the above *ku* is not without wit: "high-nose" (meaning "pride") is a homophone for "high blossoms," but boasting *ku* (or *waka*, as we shall see) could be both juvenile and witless: *"In full bloom / nothing like it in China! / Mount Yoshino"* (花盛唐にもあらし吉野山　作者不知　毛吹草 *hanazakari kara ni mo araji yoshino yama* anon. 1645). For that matter, as we have seen, there is nothing like Mount Yoshino elsewhere in Japan, either!

けさそ匂ひ櫻にうつす日の始　昌察　三籟
kesa zo nioi sakura ni utsusu hi no hajime　shôsatsu 1734
(this-morning[emph.]scent/glow cherry-to spread sun=day's start)

this morning is magic
the first sun moves
upon the cherry

on this morning
the light of the first sun-rise
fills the cherry

"Sun's beginning" suggests a New Year's *ku*, but no cherry blooms at that time. Should we feel sunlight quickening the bare tree or see it gravid with the bloom to come and glowing as only a pregnant woman does? Probably not. I think we have a passing of the baton from the rising sun of the New Year to the blossoming cherry. Because the New Year in Japan celebrates nationhood, the cherry has been conscripted. The *nioi* (scent/glow) will reappear in later clearly nationalistic cherry blossoms. But first, a word about an older *ku* (1688), by Bashô: *"This fragrance! / from the blossoms of what / tree i know not"* 伊勢山田・何の木の花とは知らず匂い哉　芭蕉 *nan no ki no hana to wa shirazu nioi kana*). The syntax of the *ku* is closer to "from which tree's bloom / it comes, I do not know – / this fragrance," (Ueda) except that "comes" is implicit in the original. Some interpreters cited by Ueda think the tree was imaginary and only served "to describe how Bashô felt as he kneeled at the shrine." Others felt the scent was real, from blossoms or wood. No one guesses at the blossoms, but cherry is likely, for the *ku* was composed in the second month. We know Bashô is deeply moved, for he draws upon, or commemorates, a *waka* by Saigyô, also composed in Ise, that says, in a word: "I know not what it (this presence) is; but overcome, my tears run." And Saigyô is synonymous with cherry blossoms. Because Ise was the spiritual capital of Shinto, or should we say the soul of ancient Japan, Bashô's *ku,* to me at least, is not just personal but a quiet affirmation of the national polity.

敷島の大和心を人とはば朝日に匂う山桜花　本居宣長 1790
shikishima no yamatogokoro o hito towaba asahi ni nihofu yamazakurabana　motoori norinaga

yamato-gokoro

*if you would know
the soul of this our isle,
there is but one:*

*mountain cherry blossoms
glowing in the rising sun!*

This openly didactic *waka* is generally seen as the turning point in the metaphorical fortunes of the cherry blossom. Before Norinaga, cherry blossoms were almost exclusively female and had no martial associations other than the *ikusa* – spontaneous rebellion/riot/uprising – metaphor sometimes used to describe the explosion of petals and an occasional hint of nationalism, for the cherry's rival, the plum was, after all, an import. Norinaga's *waka,* written at age 61 upon a self-portrait as a symbolic summary of his philosophy does not, in itself, seem nationalistic. It is certainly not as *in your face* as the anonymous "nothing like that in China" *ku*. The *shiki* prefixing the isle – sometimes translated as "august" because the term itself is an ancient convention – means "spread-out" (as one spreads a picnic cloth or bedding), *yamato* which I moved to the title is what Japanese called themselves and translates as "big-harmony." A nationalistic (or, nativist) reading is only possible when the poem is combined with Norinaga's history and ideas, which celebrate Japan, the Japanese and their language as superior to other nations, generally meaning the Chinese [1] and two less subtle poems:

桜なきこまもろこしの国人は春とて何に心やるらむ 宣長 鈴屋歌集一の巻
sakura naki koma morokoshi no kunibito wa haru tote nani kokoro yaruramu　norinaga 1730-1801

*spring is spring:
but what do the korean
and chinese folk*

*give their heart and soul to,
wanting cherries as they do?*

さくらなき仏の国はなにかせむ七重のなみ木花はさくとも 宣長 本居宣長全集 15
sakura naki hotoke no kuni wa nanika semu nanae no namiki hana wa saku to mo　norinaga 1730-1801

*and what do all
those buddhist countries
without cherries do*

*though magic flowers bloom
seven-fold on other trees?*

*what good is
the land of the dead
without cherries*

*though rows of trees
bloom with treasure?*

Actually, the more common varieties of mountain cherries were found *throughout* East Asia; but when Norinaga brings the next world into argument, he is pretty safe from contradiction! The seven-fold tree found in the Western Paradise was generally called *nanae no uegi* (七重の植樹) and bloomed with seven Buddhist treasures. What would Norinaga have aliens do? Cry because they are not lucky enough to have been born in the land of the cherry blossom? If I seem a bit harsh on Norinaga, it is because I *detest* his ethnocentric blathering that puts down other languages as beastly or dead.[1] Indeed, considering his prose, I felt tempted to translate the "Buddhist" above "as-good-as-dead" (the other meaning of *hotoke* being a corpse)! Norinaga's best known *"If you would know"* waka (#61-5) might also be considered a fusion of two *waka* by his teacher, the nativist Kamo Mabuchi:

うら／\ とのどけき春の心よりにほひ出でたる山櫻ばな　加茂真淵
uraura to nodokeki haru no kokoro yori nioi idetaru yamazakurabana kamo mabuchi -1769

high on the mountain

*from the soul
of the spring, luminous in
its serenity*

*this beauty comes forth:
wild cherry blossoms!*

The usual problem of scent=beauty=erotic-essence is exacerbated by the *ura-ura* (like *uraraka*) an adverb that may apply to either the Spring or the cherry and suggests a serenely splendid beauty.[2]

もろこしの人に見せばや三吉野のよしのゝやまのの山ざくらばな　加茂真淵
morokoshi no hito ni misebaya miyoshino no yoshino no yama no yamazakurabana mabuchi

*i'd love to show them
to the people of china:
beautiful yoshino's fine
mountain cherry blossoms*

Nationalisms such as *Nihon* or *Yamato* are not used, but cherry blossoms born of the *kokoro* (heart/mind/essence/soul/spirit) have become symbolic of something Japanese worth showing off to the world.

櫻咲これぞ和國の姿 (景色) 哉　蘭更 新五子・半化坊発句集
sakura saku kore zo wakoku no sugata (keshiki) kana rankô 1725-1798
(cherries bloom/ing this[emph.] peace/savage [3]-country's form/landscape!)

the cherries bloom: the cherries bloom:
yes, this is the likeness   lo, the very incarnation
of the peace country!   of peace country!

~~~~~~

1. Motoori Norinaga While I dislike Norinaga's pride and prejudice, the Japanese have good reason to revere him for rediscovering, translating and explaining ancient literature, including the long-neglected *Manyôshû*. He did so in a prose style as good for Japanese literature as his influence on politics was bad. At least, *his* image is not found on *Japanese* money, as the man responsible for putting the Cherokees on the Trail of Tears ("the Supreme Court made their decision, now let them enforce it!") and massacre of Seminoles + fugitive slaves in Florida, Andrew Jackson is – *for shame! for shame!* – on ours!

2. Types of Beauty If we made a sequence, say "cute →

pretty →beautiful → _____." *uraraka* would fill in the blank. "Gorgeous" won't do; it is ostentatious, whereas *uraraka*, a serenely glorious, almost magical, full beauty that comes from within lacks such negative connotation.

3 *Peace or Savage* Two Chinese characters for *wa* were in common use. One means "savage," one "peace."

The question is what exactly makes Kamo Mabuchi and his disciple Norinaga's cherry blossoms so special and why they stand for the Japanese spirit. Here, the greatest of the cherry historians, Yamada Takeo, writing in 1941, begged to differ with the stereotypical understanding of his day, namely that the blossoms fell like courageous warriors and illustrated the particular sensitivity of a poetic people to the ephemeral nature of life. If it were a matter of the way they *fell*, more older poems would celebrate rather than regret their falling, and the serene scene of blossoms meeting the morning sun would hardly be representative of that moment. If we want to look at warrior-like willingness to die in an instant, what about the poppy that blows in a day? Or the camellia whose blossoms decapitate themselves at any time without warning? *Dying*, Yamada wrote, is *not* what cherry blossoms are all about, and those who play with such a metaphor are captivated by rationalistic Chinese thinking, precisely what Norinaga preached against. As for Japanese being a particularly sensitive people who identified with the ephemeral, he found such sentimentalism equally Chinese and the result of intellectualizing. To rub in the depth of this sin, he quoted a *precious* paragraph by a Western woman – for the West, he wrote, was even more addicted to rationality than the Chinese. No, Yamada continued, the blossoms blooming in mass, resembling phenomena like the mist and clouds, are simply *uraraka*, or *urawashii*, beautiful in the deepest sense of the word and that is all that can be said. If it is explained, the experience is falsified and that, *pace* Norinaga, goes for the Japanese spirit, too.

花盛世に理屈なき匂哉　瓜涼　花七日
hanazakari yo ni rikutsu-naki nioi kana karyo 1777
(blossom-acme world-in rationalizing-not smell/scent!/'tis)

the bloom peak
there's no logic or reason
just beauty!

the full bloom
there is illumination
beyond thought

pure scent
a world beyond words
bloompeak

Yamada neglected *haikai* in his otherwise thorough book.[1] Otherwise, he might have found and introduced this *ku* which predates Norinaga's famous work, but marvelously sums up his antithetical worldview, artificial, logic-corrupted Chinese *vs* natural, straight-from-the-heart Japanese. I hate translating *nioi/niou*. In Norinaga's poem, I used "glow," in Mabuchi's I used "scent" and, here, finding neither right, used "eros," itself too harsh on the ears to properly convey the magic. I felt tempted to end the poem "simply eros!" for the term *hanazakari* is sensual for sharing something with animals coming into heat and one *almost* feels there is a smell.

---

1. *Haikai of Quick to Fall Flowers* Here alone, Yamada quotes *ku* to make his point, respectively, with camellia and poppy: *"Falling within / the light of "lightning," / camellias!"* (*inazuma no tsuma ni ochitaru tsubaki kana*); *"When it falls / the camellia never / looks back"* (*ochigiwa ni nokoru nen naki tsubaki kana*); *"Until one falls / the picture is not of falling / the camellia"* (*chiru made mo chiranu keshiki o tsubaki kana*). *"When poppies fall / the other flowers are / full of shame"* (*keshi chiru ya hoka no hana ni wa haji ôshi* zongi (存義); *"I see it / then it's on its leaves / the poppy flower"* (*mireba haya ha ni koborekeri keshinohana*). Yamada knew his readers knew that the camellia falls so suddenly it makes you start, not a petal at a time, but the whole head – in fact, samurai saw it as an unlucky omen, rather than identifying with it! – and the poppy, with its tenuous hold on flowerhood agreeing with its homophone "erase," also meant a young boy sold into apprenticeship or sent to a Buddhist temple where the death rate was high enough to merit the name – again, hardly something people would want to emulate.

二日酔朝日や匂ふ山桜　才麿？丸？坂東太郎・江戸蛇之鮓
futsukayoi asahi ya [zo] niou yamazakura saimaro? teitoku? 1679
(hangover morning sun!/: smells/glows mountain-cherry/ies)

what a *hangover*
the rising sun stinks
mountain cherry

mountain cherries
glow in the morning sunlight
i'm hungover

This *ku*, refreshing when placed within a patriotic context, actually predates all but the first two *ku* at the head of this chapter. It is typical early *haikai* irreverence, playing, perhaps with this old *waka*:

朝日影にほへる山のさくらはなつれなくきえぬ雪かとそ見る　藤原有家　新古今集
asahikage nioeru yama no sakura hana tsurenaku kienu yuki ka to zo mieru fujiwara arike skks 1205

illuminated by
morning sunshine, mountain
cherry bloom

i'd swear it spring snow,
mercilessly melting away

While there are countless poems about melting snow and falling blossoms, this is, as far as I know, the only poem to have the sun thawing out, as it were, blossoms, that would quickly melt to nothing. The less original first part of the *waka* may, ultimately, have inspired all the other poems in this chapter, though the total effect is one of sad melancholy rather than a celebration of Japaneseness!

日の本の山のかひある桜哉　一茶　　　　桜木や花の威をかる里の人　一茶 -1827
hinomoto no yama no kai aru sakura kana issa   *sakuragi ya hana no i o karu sato no hito* issa
(sun's base/source's mountains' value is/have cherry!)   (cherry-tree's/s'[emph] prestige[acc.] borrow local folk)

japan's mountains
are really worth something:
cherry blossoms!

cherry blossoms!
and borrowing their prestige
the local folk

This seemingly boastful poem probably reflects an inferiority complex with respect to the dinky reality of Japanese mountains (excluding Fuji) compared to those of mainland Asia. It may play off an older *ku* "That blossom-viewing crowd / the mountains have something of worth: / cherry blossoms" (花見衆山のかひある桜哉　一正　毛吹草 *hanamishû yama no kai aru sakura kana* issei 1645), which is identical for the last 12 syllabets but different in spirit for suggesting all mountains are generally sorry places; but, considering Issa's interest in the writings of Norinaga – possibly turning critical a few years before he died 一茶云、儒道、仏道ニゴリテ神道ノ一人スムモフシギ也 (it is hard to guess the direction of Issa's rhetoric so i do not translate) – contrast with China was probably most on his mind.

花おの／＼日本だましひいさましや　一茶
hana ono-ono nihondamashii isamashi ya   issa 1807
(blossoms each-each nihon[japanese] soul valiant!)

what courage!
each and every blossom
the spirit of nippon

how valiant!
each and every blossom
a japanese soul

Instead of Buddhist blossoms falling without regret in unattached enlightenment, here we have dauntless warriors. Did Issa recall the *hokku* by a fellow Katsusa resident, with which he opened his first poem notebook (寛政句帖) in 1791? *"The cherries / all bloom with / Japanese soul!"* (さくらみな日本魂もて咲ぬ 西湖 *sakura mina yamato-damashii mote sakinu* seiko). Viewing the body of Issa's work, he seems almost as much the patriot as the Buddhist. He constantly lauds his *kimigayo,* or lord's-era (the current reign), with scores of *ku* finding good in everything from the wind settling down so the mountain can sleep to pine branches adorning even the grave of an unknown person. Yet, he also has no small number of *ku,* some of which we have seen, describing his times as the end of the world! We can read most of his laudatory and lamenting *ku* without groaning because they tend toward witty reporting of the times rather than pedagogy. The one's starting with "Gods' country" are often downright hilarious (see *The Fifth Season*). I would also like to point out that not a few of the *ku* included under *kimigayo=current reign* eulogies in the one book I know to treat this subject (青木美智男『一茶の時代』) are probably neutral ("In these times / even the women are / out hoeing" – from the date, I'd guess it is Issa's new wife!) or even poking fun at his own country: *"In these times / even dark blue curtains / boast* sakura*"*(君が代は紺のうれんも桜哉 文政二 *kimigayo wa kon no nôren mo sakura kana*). The "curtains" are the short type (*noren*) hung from entrances (commonly stores) to block sun or keep in the warmth. Often, indigo they are navy blue when new. Eggplant motif, being a rebus for "becoming" (*nasu*) is appropriate. Cherry blossoms are wrong, not only from a color standpoint but from a metaphysical one, as neither households nor merchants want a flash of glory followed by bare branches. In other words, the popularity of the blossom took it places it did not belong. Be that as it may, Issa was indeed both nationalistic and Buddhist in a fundamentalist (rather than Zen) manner and these positions on the world, as we see with respect to cherry blossoms, were what I call culturally bipolar (a concept I introduce in *Orientalism & Occidentalism* with Tanizaki and Mishima representing the serial and parallel versions). Thank goodness, he did not take himself too seriously.

桜さく大日本ぞ／＼　一茶 1814
sakura saku dai-nippon zo nippon zo　issa
(cherry bloom big-nippon [emph. for nihon] x2!)

nippon, hurrah!
big nippon with the cherry
blooming away!

花さくやあれが大和の小口哉　一茶 1798
hana saku ya are ga yamato no koguchi kana　issa
(blossoms bloom: that is big-peace[japan]'s small-mouth!)

cherries bloom
this is the magic mallet
of our big peace

The first *ku* is a *haikai*-fication of the far older *Manyôshû* tradition of elegy (*banka*). The *nippon* makes cherry trees pop open like bottles of champagne. The emphatic particle "*zo*" is hard to English, for our emphatics are tied to a specific culture (Judeo-Christianity) [*"Nippon, by god / you are a big Nippon / when cherries bloom!"* or *"Big Nippon! / When cherries bloom, you're / damn big Nippon!"*] The second *ku* plays with the "small-mouth (of the magic mallet)" which, wherever it strikes, pours forth a cornucopia, purely aesthetic in the case of Japan, country of the "Big-Harmony" or *peace*.

日本はばくちの銭もさくら哉　一茶 #27-42
nihon wa bakuchi no zeni mo sakura kana　issa 1816

in our japan
even gambling chips are
cherry blossoms

If this is a facetious boast, we may wonder if the bombastic "Big Japan" (*dai-nippon*) was serious or if Issa, knowing Japan was but a leaf floating in a sea of nations, as pointed out by Norinaga's antagonist, the playwright Ueda Akinari, might not have been poking fun at his pompous nationalism?

花よりあくる/みよしのの/春の曙/みせたらば/からくに人もこまびとも/やまとごころに/なりぬべし
hana yori akuru miyoshino no haru no akebono misetaraba karakunihito mo komabito mo yamatogokoro ni narinubeshi nikawa? 二川相近＝松蔭　(-1836)?　誤伝＝頼山陽　(『桜史』306-8頁)

Could we but show them! / Mi-yoshino dawning in the light / of the cherry blossoms –
All the Chinese and the Koreans / would become Japanese at heart!

Yamada, who introduces this *Imayo* song (later popularized as another man's) in his *Sakura-shi*, treats it as an extension of Norinaga's *waka*. I find it heart-warming for the way it *includes*, rather than denies the common humanity of foreigners. At the same time, I realize it may be read as a precursor of Japan's assimilative colonialism, based on the ethnocentric assumption that the other Asians would willingly give up their inferior culture for Japan's, proven superior by success in fighting off the West. For the cherry tree, however, pride would come before fall *and after:*

國のためといわれて山のはな折りぬ　敬愚   國のためと花化粧無き山の顔　敬愚
kuni no tame to iwarete yama no hana orinu keigu   *kuni no tame to hanagesho naki yama no kao*

for country's sake   for country's sake
the mountain's nose=bloom   no fancy=blossom make-up on
is broken=taken   the mountain's face

國のためとハナ欠く顔で笑ふやま　敬愚
kuni no tame to hana kaku kao de warau yama

for country's sake
the mountain boasts
a blossom=nose-less smile!

Keigu's post facto *ku* describe what comes next. Norinaga and his cherry blossoms eventually – long after his death – found supporters, the most famous being Sakuma Shôzan (1811-64), who capped his prodigious studies of Japanese classics with Dutch-learning, which is to say Western science, for the sake of keeping the foreigners at bay and restoring the nation to greatness. His group, the Cherry-Brigade (櫻賊) had a strong influence in key provinces and, together with others, helped to restore the power of the Emperor and reinvent what might be called a sacred state. But, in the zeal to out-West the West, economic logic dictated that *only trees useful to the material state* – that is to say, quick-growing lumber or food for silk-worms serving fabric export, etc. – were allowed to occupy the limited and therefore precious land. Ironically, cherry-born nationalism ended up cutting down the cherry trees! Yamada, who, in 1941, courageously pointed out that the initial comparison of the Japanese spirit with the cherry was due to love for the beauty of the blossoms and that it was wrong for moralists and philosophers to *use* the *sakura* in order to define the "true Japanese spirit," worked with a group, the Sakura Kai, or "Cherry [Blossom] Association," that successfully helped the cherry tree make a comeback.   But let us go back and tell it again.

花散るや腹を切るより仏かな　敬愚
hana chiru ya hara o kiru yori hotoke kana keigu

petals falling
it's more like the buddha
than *harakiri*

This is how Keigu might have *protested* had he seen the *kabuki* play Chûshingura, put on by Takeda Izumo *et. alia* in 1748. As the heroic 47 cut their bellies to atone for disobeying the new laws against vendettas taken without permission, the cherry petals (Not knowing the date, I suspect they were cut from paper) started flying, and the line that would echo for centuries was uttered:

> *The cherry tree is the blossom of blossoms and the samurai the man of men!*

If many phrases from Elizabethan drama made it into our common vocabulary, the same was true, perhaps even more so with *kabuki*. This and subsequent plays were, according to literary scholar Ogawa Kazusuke (桜と日本人:1993) the main reason the earlier image of the blossoming cherry as a sort of holy tree, then, a young woman overflowing with life, changed into that of *a warrior* ready to die and, in one novella, a ghoulish tree of preternatural beauty owing to the corpse upon which it grew. Drama probably does not deserve all the credit/blame for the change which occurred over the last two or three centuries. The cherry trees themselves changed. Varieties bred to bloom brighter and faster came to comprise the vast majority of cherries in Japan over this period. No sooner do the Somei-yoshino open their blossoms and *bang!* the white petals explode. And they manage to do this on all their limbs simultaneously and at the same time as all the neighboring trees for they are, as clones, literally the same tree. Thus, they do indeed seem magnificently and perversely *born to die! These* are the cherries that inspired the most famous of all World War II songs, 同期の桜 *"Cherry Blossoms of the Same Class"* (Off we go to gloriously scatter together for the Emperor . . .).[1] Before that, they helped shape the character of the composers of such blossom songs. A Meiji 43 (1910) book about the reciprocal effect of the environment and the Japanese character on one another argued that the explosively active character of the Japanese was formed by the very blossoms they helped create over the ages. This character, also tied into earthquakes and typhoons, was, I think, the *alter* to the supposedly indolent people of mainland Asia and Taiwan whom Japan was beginning to exercise (to use a Usanian term) their *manifest destiny* upon. Not surprisingly, the cherry trees were exported to Japanese colonial possessions in order to help instill them with Japanese character, though, as Sato Toshiki notes, *that* argument was not used to justify sending trees to Washington DC.

> The cherry blossom is not solitary but collective. The cherry is not the only collective flower, but compared to the lotus or the rose, the difference is plain to see. A single lotus blossom in a vase is clearly worthy of appreciation. A single rose is likewise sufficient to adorn the lapel of a suit. They are both suitable expressions of individuality. The cherry blossom alone is very different. A single blossom is so inconsequential that it is unworthy of being viewed. The cherry blossoms merit is in its collectivity. A branch of blossoms as a collectivity is superior to the individual blossoms, a tree of blossoms as a collectivity is superior to a branch of blossoms and a mountain of blossoms as a collectivity is superior to a tree of blossoms. In the same way, it ought to be said that the strong point of we Japanese as a people is expressed in group activity, not individualism. (井上哲次郎 「桜花」 in 国定教科書『高等小学読本』大正二年 in 佐藤俊樹『桜が創った「日本」』2005).

---

1. Marching Songs "Cherries of the Same Class" (*dôki-no sakura*) is a rousing song. I have enthusiastically sung along on many occasions (drunk, are we not *all* ready to fall?). Before you think that makes me a Japanese militarist, let me add that I enjoy Christmas Caroling more than any Christian who believes in that stuff. The words include: "You and I are *sakura* of the same season/class blooming in the same aircraft-carrier garden; As blossoms, we know we will fall, and we will fall beautifully, for the sake of the country!" and, "You and I are *sakura* of the same season/class; Though we may fall far apart from one another / At the Yasukuni Shrine, capital of the blossoms / blooming on the boughs of Spring, let us meet again!" It wasn't just songs either. In *"Kamikaze, Cherry Blossoms, and Nationalisms: The Militarization of Aesthetics in Japanese History,"* (2002) Emiko Ohnuki-Tierney notes that girls would line the runway and wave branches of blossoms as the cherry-blossom division pilots, headgear adorned with the blossoms, took off in their "cherry-blossom planes/gliders" carrying "cherry-blossom bombs." Vice-versa to her sub-title, the militarist ideology was beautified through the symbolism of the cherry blossom. My summary is based on reviews. As I have not yet seen O-T's book, I cannot comment on her history of the rise of the cherry blossom "as a dominant and evocative trope for *pro rege et patria mori.*"

This paragraph from a 1913 school reader shows how the establishment *used* the blossoms to teach their idea of good citizenship. As Sato Toshiki notes, the author of the above paragraph (Inoue Tetsujirô) celebrated both the bloom and the fall of the blossoms in his essay celebrating the cherry blossom as the perfect symbol of the Japanese spirit. Sato does not comment on the lotus, which I find significant for it indirectly reminds us of the tea master Rikkyu (1522-91) and the existence of fiercely independent minds among the Japanese, but goes on to example the manner in which the gallantly blowing=dying side of the blossoms that were the incarnation of the soul of the people, who were conversely themselves manifesting the *sakura* god/s came to be played up more than the bloom as the global situation became more desperate (参考：「桜の花神、化して、日本国民となれるか。日本国民の魂出でて、桜の花となれるか」＝大町桂月『筆艸』「日本国民と桜」in 佐藤 同). Then, in the 1970's, Japanese intellectuals began to regain the confidence they lost with the War, they turned with a vengeance upon their representative cherry blossom; Sato quotes botanist Koshimizu Takuji:

> The variety of cherry called Somei-yoshino has no class whatsoever and after it sheds its blossoms is an ugly sight. . . . No matter where it is planted, it is as good as dead to its surroundings, and changes its expression not a whit. In other words, it needs no environmental background. . . . Moreover, this cherry's native place has nothing to do with Yoshino and probably came from Chejudo (a Korean island). (小清水卓二『万葉の草・木・花』1970 in 佐藤俊樹 同)

Koshimizu went on to explain how classy cherries exhibit themselves in suitable sites. This charming idea reminds me of John Muir describing the aesthetic import of boulders dropped by the foot of cliffs by earthquakes. But, as Sato Toshiki points out, the mountain cherry championed by this writer and others is found throughout Asia, while the maligned Somei-yoshino is truly Japanese. Another such:

> But this view of cherry blossoms [the bravado of males ready to die at the drop of a hat] is really a pseudo-tradition manufactured after the Meiji Era (1868 - 1912). . . . The cherry behind the *yakuza*=mobster-like petal-scattering/falling tradition is the *yakuza*=mobster-like Somei-yoshino . . . the blossoms are low quality and pale. . . The cherry that Japanese were once tuned in with were not "scattering/falling cherry [petals]" (*chiru sakura*) but "*not* falling cherry [blossoms]" (*chiranai sakura*) . . . After Meiji, [the concept of] *sakura* came to be dominated by the Somei-yoshino, a vulgar artificial tree compared to the character shown by mountain cherries growing in the wild. . . . I want to be counted on the side of the cherry [blossoms] that do *not* fall. (Yamada Munemutsu? 山田宗睦　花の文化史 1977　佐藤俊樹：『桜が創った「日本」』より)

As Satô points out, the Somei-yoshino is unfairly scapegoated when the dichotomy with mountain cherries is overblown. Yet it is interesting to find the warrior and the gangster conflated, or, rather *equated* in order to make what most once considered admirable something deplorable and it is nice to find no contrast with the Occident (the *alter* being a cop-out). Here is one I found *before* reading Satô's book (though, sure enough, Satô found it, too!):

> No, don't get me wrong. I like all cherries; I love a Somei-yoshino blossom-viewing. It is just that that the impetus of the beauty behind white blossoms alone in full bloom is, I think, Occidental. Wasn't the pursuit of Western taste the reason they spread? Somewhere in the reverence for blossoms in full bloom with the leaves perfectly excluded we find something analytical, paternal logic, even monotheistic. On the other hand, in the case of the Yoshino mountain cherry, red leaves and green leaves and the verdure from other plants are all jumbled together, creating something polytheistic and maternal . . . [here, on the mountain] Finally, I felt the image of cherry I had since grade-school of the Somei-yoshino fade and the mountain cherry begin to take root in my heart. (Akasegawa Genpei 赤瀬川源平『仙人の桜、俗人の桜』1993/2000 also in 佐藤俊樹)

Considering the fact the cherry variety that came to be called Somei-yoshino dates back to the 18c, the spread in the late 19c was due to the clever use of the name Yoshino (though the plant had nothing to due with the mountain) – linked with Japanese nationalism – and the combination of rapid growth and profuse flowering made it a natural for planting in the burgeoning cities, Akasegawa Genpei's dualistic argument is far-fetched, though it makes perfect sense in the context of *nihonjinron*, or pop-Japanology which had come to put Koreans on the Japanese side and contrast Japanese and Occidentals (see my *Orientalism & Occidentalism*). Countless Japanese have claimed the big bright pink petals of certain eight-fold cherries (see next chapter) are just what foreigners, with their lack of delicacy, appreciate, but, as far as I know, Akasegawa is the first to connect what is now the standard cherry blossom with the West. He also admits that the Japanese tendency to go for novelties and be overly cleanly or fastidious may have *something* to do with it, but his main thesis is that it was no accident that the Somei-yoshino took-off in the Meiji era, when Japanese, like Occidentals, experienced the pride of humans set upon the conquering of nature. I feel he misses something important, that Satô Toshiki pegged, to my delight (because he's right) and chagrin (I wanted to be the first to point it out). After introducing a passage about how a child draws cherry trees as solid blossom, he introduces two haiku antedating the Somei-yoshino. One is Bashô's famous *ku* mentioning clouds of flowers (13-7). The other is one similar to many we have seen in Book I:

咲きみちて花より外の色もなし 足利義政
sakimichite hana yori hoka no iro mo nashi   yoshimasa ()
(blooming-overflowing blossom-other-than color even not)

bloom overflows
and there is no beauty
but the blossoms

bloom overflows
no eros is not consumed
by the blossoms

Beauty or "color/eros." Satô goes on to write the words that delight/upset me because they are *exactly* what I found to be the case and wished to be the first to point out:

> Yoshimasa and Bashô's . . . *ku* teach us another important fact: any number of people read=wrote poems that describe the appearance/landscape of Somei-yoshino cherry blossoms *before* the Somei-yoshino cherry even appeared. The scene created once this cherry blossom was realized *already existed in the imagination.* This idea of the ideal beauty of the cherry existed from the beginning. (佐藤俊樹：『桜が創った「日本」』)

The only thing I – or, rather, my *alter* – would add concerns the city which gave birth to the ideal cherry tree:

染井吉野花火名所の江戸育ち 敬愚
somei-yoshino hanabi meisho no edosodachi   keigu
(somei-yoshino fireworks-famous-place-edo-bred)

the cherry bomb

somei-yoshino
from the city known
for fireworks!

In other words, there was not only a tendency to idealize a tree of blossoms, but a city, the *de facto* capital of modern Japan, which boasted a culture widely known to be explosive (do you recall fighting in the bloom *ku*?) behind the *sakura* revolution. To me, the Somei-yoshino is an Edokko, or child of Edo. Keigu wrote a *ku* about the rapid spread of this cherry from what was the world's largest nursery zone (not surprising since greater Edo was also the world's largest city in the last half of the 19c) :

散らばるもはやい全国染井吉野　敬愚
chirabaru mo hayai zenkoku somei yoshino　keigu

fast to scatter
about the country, too
somei-yoshino

In other words, infection by an alien cultural virus is not a necessary hypothesis, for no Western people can hold a candle to the brisk, clean-cut (sometimes refreshing and sometimes terrifying) decisiveness found in the Edoite. No, the only help from the West was its threat to Japan's sovereignty. When the majority of cherry trees near major roads were butchered for "development" in early Meiji, Somei-yoshino cherries happened to be waiting in the wings to replace them. If it is true that this plant has the power to knock people off their feet, to make them feel the emptiness of life and lose their fear of losing their own, then, I suppose they bear *some* responsibility for the war. But I am glad that McArthur and the shy marine biologist we knew as Hirohito spared them. Since they have short life-spans (50 or 60 years), as might be expected from overdoing it, most of the individual trees responsible, like the Shôwa Emperor (Hirohito's posthumous name), are no longer with us today.

従軍の時・行かばわれ筆の花散る処まで　子規
ikaba ware fude no hana chiru tokoro made　shiki 1895
(go-if i brush's [pen's] blossom falls place-until)

accompanying the army

if i go, i go –
'til the blossom of my pen
falls, until then

二大隊花見の中を通りけり　子規　　　　　この國の男に生れ櫻かな　子規 1896
ni daitai hanami no naka o tôrikeri　shiki 1896　　*kono kuni no otoko ni umare sakura kana*　shiki
(two divisions blossom-viewing's middle pass[emph])　(this country's man/men-as born cherry[blossom/s]!/?)

two divisions　　　　　　　　　　　　　　born as men
march through the middle　　　　　　　of this country, are we
of the blossom-viewers　　　　　　　　　cherry blossoms?

The first *ku* plays on a snow-viewing *ku* by Bashô and various *haiku* and *senryû*. The third is ambiguous. It could be reflective, as per my reading, celebratory (*We are _!*), or lamenting (*Born a man*). The war with Russia was popular, but if Shiki has already become ill, he may be staring at death.

小坊主の太刀はきたがる桜哉　子規
ko-bôzu no taikô wa kitagaru sakura kana　shiki 1896
(small monk[boy]'s big-sword wear-want/ing cherry[blossom-time]!)

a little monk
wants to wear a real sword
cherry blossoms

A "little monk" probably means *a kid* or *tiny tyke;* but the expression suggests how boom and bloom come together for even the innocent! Note that little boys already wore little swords.

62

the "Unjapanese" Eight-fold
八重桜
yae-zakura

金の間の庭一はいや八重櫻 李由 韻塞
kinnoma no niwa ippai ya yaezakura riyû -1705
(gold-room's garden full!/: eight-fold cherry/ies)

the garden for
the golden room is full!
eightfold cherry

The gold-room is that occupied by the most honored guest. The cherry, too, would be the best. My dictionary calls the "eight-fold cherry" one with "double cherry blossoms;" but *double* does not do justice to the difference between "eight-fold" and "single-fold" cherries. The blossom does not have only ten petals to a "single-fold's" five. It may have *dozens* (25-50), and such blossoms tend to cluster, creating luscious *pompoms of bloom!* An eight-fold cherry in full bloom is to the eyes what a banana-split is, or was (I have not seen one in a while), to the mouth. There is yet another type called chrysanthemum-cherry (*kiku-zakura*) with twice again more petals, but it was too rare to make it into haiku and we shall skip it. The maximum is 180 petals. At any rate, "eight" means *profuse* in Japanese.

庭に咲く程や遠山八重櫻 周桂 大発句帳
niwa ni saku hodo ya tôyama yaezakura shûkei -1544
(garden-in bloom extent!/: far-mountain eightfold cherry/ies)

seemingly abloom
in my garden! the distant
eightfold cherry

A laudatory *ku*. So luxuriant a bloom destroyed the very laws of perspective! The "distant *mountain*" (*tôyama*) would not fit in the translation. *No loss:* where *else* could a tree, seen afar, be?

俳諧は幕なしひとへ櫻哉 素雪 三千花
haikai wa makunashi hitoezakura sosetsu 1725
(haikai-as-for scene/curtain-not one-fold-cherry)

single act

our *haikai* is   an undivided
a single-petal cherry   single-petal cherry:
with no curtain   that's *haikai*

62 1-3

This "curtain" plays upon the curtain that the elite hung about trees for privacy or to monopolize space for themselves, but, here, it also means *an act*. *Haikai* of various number – 50, 100, 1000 – were composed in single sessions without breaks, where the most popular entertainment of the day, *kabuki* – the finery of which does remind us of the posh eight-fold cherry – had many curtains=acts. There may also be an allusive meaning: while early *haikai* was marked by eight-fold punning (partly because punning was a fine way to compress information and partly because of the proponents open pursuit of wit in the face of the old-school fuddy-duddies) the same shortness of form *also* encouraged the appreciation of simplicity and subtlety, what we might call bare bone poetry. Needless to say, this favors *The Way of the Single-fold* wild cherry, which had been pointedly preferred to the artificial monster, the eight-fold cherry, by that doyen of good taste, monk Kenkô (-1352).[1]

山桜九重で咲も一重かな　兼吉 崑山集
yamazakura kokonoe de saku mo hitoe kana kenkichi 1651
(mountain-cherry nine-fold-at blooming still one-fold!/?/'tis)

mountain cherries
even within ninefold clouds
single blossoms!

Nine-fold means Imperial property, one cloud-bank higher than the eight-fold, or myriad clouds. Call it *Cloud Nine* if you wish. Judging from the *ku*, the mountain cherry came to be identified with simple five-petal "single-layer" blossoms. This was not always true. Where *haikai* first bloomed, in the West (Kyoto, Osaka, Nara), it was, but in the East, the provinces surrounding what came to be Edo, then Tokyo (meaning Eastern capital), semi-double wild varieties (most notably Edo *higan*) were quite common and even double, i.e. genuine eight-fold freaks were occasionally found. But, even in the West, the modest wild vs. plush garden model was imperfect, if for no other reason than the fact that copies of beloved trees were kept in nurseries outside of the cities – cities, including Imperial palaces, were constantly burning down and this usually killed the trees who, could not jump on the ox carts and flee with the people. Since many of these "garden" cherries were long-lived (up to 500 years) and tended to outlive their owners and nearby architecture, they were not uncommonly found in the wild. Hence, "mountain cherries" in *waka* generally meant only cherry trees encountered in the mountains.

九重にみたらぬものや八重櫻　諸光 毛吹草
kokonoe ni mitaranu mono ya yaezakura shokô 1645
(nine/th-fold/layer-in see-suffice-not thing!/: eightfold-cherries)

in the ninefold   eightfold cherry
they can't get enough of   the gods on cloud nine
eightfold cherry   never tire of it

1. **Kenkô's Taste** In respect to the *yaezakura*, Kenkô wrote "As for cherry blossoms, the single-petaled variety is preferable. . . . The double-petaled cherry is an oddity, most exaggerated and perverse." (Donald Keene trans passage 139) This should be understood together with his story of a man who threw away his *bonsai* after seeing a crowd of deformed men and realizing it was the normal not the oddity that was worth preserving (passage 154 – I think the analogy is wrong, but will save that argument for a *bonsai* magazine) and his most well-known remarks on the value of seeing the moon *not* full and blossoms *before* or *after* full-bloom, or better yet, *not seeing them at all but just thinking about them* without stirring from the house! (passage 137). It is instructive to compare him with stay-at-home aesthetes in the West who celebrated artificial nature (The apogee was reached by a character in a Huysman novel) In short, Kenkô did not really like what was *normal* – love of full moons, full bloom and some, but not all, odd things – but what was *subdued*. The most prolific writer on the history and literature of the Japanese flowering cherry, Ogawa Kazusuke, goes so far as to say that Kenkô's opinion is the solitary monk's perverse reaction (*amanojaku no kokoro*) to the popularity of the garden variety (日本の桜、歴史の桜).

Various garden varieties of the eight-fold had been popular for centuries before Kenkô and other aesthetes decided they were unnatural for being cultivars, late-bloomers and drawing too many bugs. A generation or two later, they were once again appreciated as much as ever. The *shôgun* of the Muramachi era (also, the Warring Era: 1338-1568) were famous lovers of luxury and not about to pass up blooming beauty. But, with the establishment of the Tokugawa state (1603-1867), Zen, Confucian and Samurai values favored austere minimalism. Shokô's *ku* may mean that only the Imperial clan (as opposed to civil rulers) still loved the plush blooms. Or, he may be *ku*-ing the historical attachment of the same with cultivars as demonstrated by a famous limb-stealing incident involving one of the editors of the third most famous Imperial anthology of poetry, the *Shinkonkinshû* (1205). Forced out of the palace by politics, Fujiwara Teika took solace in cultivating cherry trees, which is to say transplanting and grafting them. There was a certain tree back in the Imperial villa that he coveted, so he disguised himself and snuck into the garden where he had his servant remove a limb which he then slipped inside his capacious clothing. Someone noticed and told the retired Emperor, Ô-mikado, who brushed a poem for the thief: *"It would not do / to blame Anonymous: / an eightfold cherry / has moved to a home / that is hardly hidden"* (なき名ぞと後にとがむな八重桜うつさんやどはかくれしもせず *naki na zo to nochi ni togamuna yaezakura utsusan yado wa kakureshi mo seji*), to which Teika replied, *"Day and night / out of your shade, missing / the nine-fold / and cherry blooming eightfold / in the service of my lord"* (くるとあく君につかふる九重のやへさく花のかげおしぞ思ふ *kuru to aku kimi ni tsukauru kokonoe no yae saku hana no kage oshizo omou*). The Emperor's poem is witty for including a "six-seven-eight" (*mu-na-ya*) and Teika's for equating his desire for the cherry with missing the Emperor. This was in Kyôto. The previous capital of Nara is more often identified with the eight-fold, partly due to the following poem supposedly made in the spur of a moment to accompany a gift of a Nara Eight-fold to the new Court in Kyôto, the "kyô" subtly punned by the homophonic "today."

いにしへの奈良の都のやへざくらけふここのへににほひぬるかな 伊勢 大輔
inishie no nara no miyako no yaezakura kyo kokonoe nioinuru kana ise-no-ôsuke 10c

*This eight-fold cherry of our ancient capital Nara –
It blossoms anew, today, in nine-layered splendor!*

Someone in Nara cultured a good tree and, with poetry, it became forever attached to the place and to nostalgia for a capital that was. The *waka* was well enough known to spawn parody: *"When it blows, our sleeves reek of spring: Ancient Nara-fart's eight-fold-fart cherry."* (そよと春辺に匂ひぬる袖 古への御ならの京の八重桜 一滴（一茶の七番日記 9-11) *soyo to harube ni nioi-nuru sode inishie-no onara no miyako-no yae[he]zakura* itteki 18c? 19c?) The most common words for "fart" in Japanese are *"onara"* and *"he."* An honorific "o" before the city of Nara makes it break wind politely, while the silent "h" in the "e" in "yae," written in the old-style "*he*," may be vocalized to mispronounce it as eight=multiple farts.[1] The single-fold cherry has never suffered this indignity.

奥はけふ雛の都や八重櫻 山只 三千花
oku wa kyo hina no miyako ya yaezakura sanshi 1725
(depths[inner court] today dolls' capital! eight-fold cherry)

today our court
is the capital of dolls!
eightfold cherry

Thank goodness the eight-fold cherry was appreciated by some! The *oku* is the innermost part of a nobleman's mansion, a large garden. This one was evidently planted with eight-fold cherry trees. The late-blooming eight-fold coincided with the Festival of the (well-dressed) Dolls. It fits.

1. **Farting in Japan**   The term *onara* is now plain Japanese, but it was once euphemism and my OJD gives two derivations: 1) an honorific pegged onto a word that might best translate as "release" (nara, from narasu: release/sound/trumpet); 2)from the capital city's name – just as the parody does, because the *nioi-nuru* (reeks of) in the original *waka* ties in with *Nara*. For more on farts – bigger in Japanese poetry than English – see IPOOH: Fall 2, *fart bug* and IPOOH: Winter 1, *wintering in* when/if they are published (*poverty cannot plan*).

たもとより低き花あり八重桜 草兵衛 改造社
tamoto yori hikuki hana ari yaezakura   sôbei c 1900
(sleeve-bag-more-than low blossoms are eight-fold-cherry/ies)

there's a blossom
lower than your sleeves
eightfold cherry!

An old *ku* claims that "The trees look good / from all=eight sides / the *yaezakura*." (木のふりは八方よしそ八重櫻 一正 毛吹草 *ki no furi wa happô yoshi zo yaezakura* issei 1645). I cannot claim to know all eight-fold cherries, but the limbs of those on the path I used to walk through three days a week on my route to work were thick, tediously straight and stuck far out from the tree. When it rained and the blossoms turned into sponges, the limbs came down close to the ground. Another poet *ku* jokes, "The *yaezakura* / viewing it your legs / make an 八= eight" (八重桜見る足もとや八文字 由当 崑山集 *yaezakura miru ashimoto ya hachi-moji* yûtô 1651). In other words, to view the cherry on your feet, you must do what a giraffe does to drink from a water-hole. An adult looks down on much of the bloom. Walking through a grove, you must duck and weave. I have seen parties of children sitting on blankets or on little chairs by little tables and wished I was them, in the way one wishes to be small again when discovering a low-ceiling path through the woods, or any attractive cavity.[1] Your only solace is to turn the bloom into clouds and imagine yourself flying as a bird or a pilot. Such a magical place might indeed be described just as the nobleman's courtyard was: *a capital of dolls*.

雛抱てたかかれて八重の姿哉 春来 アルス
hina daite dakarete yae no sugata kana   shunrai c1763
(dolls/chicks hugging/hugged eight-fold's shape!/'tis)

~~like a doll hugged~~   ~~eight-fold cherry:~~   both gathering
~~and mobbed with admirers,~~   ~~like nest upon nest~~   and swarmed by its chicks
~~eight-fold cherries~~   ~~full of chicks!~~   eightfold cherry

My first reading is probably wrong, for K concludes the *hina* here means baby *birds*, not dolls. Regardless, it is a friendly description of the profuse and warm bloom of the eight-fold cherry. It warmly gathers its brood together and is over-run by the same. Call it the *yae*-as-mother image.

1. **Eightfold Cherry Way.**   I was amazed to find a Japanese writer describe the same thing I experienced, though at a different location. Here is Akasegawa Genpei describing some of the cherry blossoms he viewed on the grounds of the National Mint at Osaka:

> For a famous row of trees, the cherry tunnel was not nearly as tall and imposing as I had imagined it would be. No, not at all. The blossomy limbs of the eight-fold cherries swayed about the chests and heads of the strolling people and made you feel like you were threading your way through a herd of gentle animals. (1993/2000)

These may have been particularly small trees (or just broad like those I knew), but there is something of that dumb but sweet beast-like quality in the limbs of the larger eight-fold cherry trees also. One doesn't find the dramatic sharp angles of the standard Japanese cherry.

eight-fold

八重桜地上に書く大伽藍　鬼城　改造社
yaezakura chijô ni egaku ôgaran　kijô　1864-1938
(eight-fold cherry/ies earth-on depict *samgharama*)

eightfold cherry like a huge cathedral drawn on earth	eightfold cherry it paints a *samgharama* here on earth

A *garan* is a large and cool Buddhist temple. In Japan, they are generally of plain wood exterior belied by gilt within. For some reason, the word conjures up memories of colorful Korean temples for me. But, why *egaku* (depict) – is the *drawn* or *painted* more *fantastic* than what might actually be built or grow? Specifying "on earth" oddly implies the metaphor and tree are heavenly indeed!

金色の千手観音八重桜　辻井五十生
konjiki no senju-kannon yaezakura　tsujii isô　季題別 1997
(gold-colored thousand-hand kannon[god/dess of mercy] eightfold-cherry)

a gold colored
thousand-hand kannon
eightfold cherry

What an elegy for the *yaezakura*! The mellow atmosphere of the eight-fold in bloom (in the golden glow of late afternoon sunlight?) evokes Kannon, god/dess of mercy. If standard cherry blossoms are beautiful angels from heaven, the eight-fold has a thousand (usually forty-two) hands.

楽さへやいざ皆見さい八重櫻　光重
raku sae ya iza mina misai yaezakura　mitsushige
(easy even! byallmeans all see[courtesan argot] eightfold cherry)

it's easy as pie / all can peek, all can sigh / eightfold cherry

Suffice it to say that *raku* means easy. Viewing this cherry is a piece of cake, but a palindrome is hard to make! (You will only find it in the Japanese – remember, it is syllabic). The eight-fold blooms late, after Winter's back is broken for good, when it is comfortably warm. With ample time for the spring rain to dye the blossoms, *"The color and scent (appeal) run deep: / eightfold cherry"* (浅からぬ色香も深し八重櫻　周桂　大発句帳 *asakaranu iroka mo fukashi yaezakura*　shûkei 1544). And, it was mild out, for the wind had spent his fury: *"Blooming again / in ninefold splendor / eightfold cherries / serenely ignorant / of the spring wind"* (九重に久しく匂へ八重桜のどけき春の風と知らずや　実行　金葉 *kokonoe ni hisashiku nioe yaezakura nodokeki haru no kaze to shirazu ya*　fujiwara saneyuki? 1124~7). This song probably celebrates new splendor and peace felt in the Imperial residence after a hiatus.

春風や世は七ころひ八重櫻　吟江　心花 1776 *harukaze ya yo wa shichikorobi yaezakura*　ginkô (spring wind!/: world-as-for seven tumbles eightfold ch)	奈良七重七堂伽藍八重櫻　はせを 1594 *nara nanae shichidôgaran yaezakura*　bashô (nara seven-fold 7-pavillion/hall temple 8-fold ch.)
Get up! Aren't you a Little Priest?	**Ancient Blossoms**
the spring wind! seven falls and up anew eightfold cherry!	seven-fold nara seven hall temples and eightfold cherry!

I have not yet cracked Ginkô's preface, *"Get up! Aren't you a little priest?"* (起やれ小法師といへるものに), but there is an old Chinese saying *"seven falls eighth rise,"* or *"seven down eight up,"* if you prefer. The Spring wind has blown down one group of flowers after another but, at long last, the eight-fold cherry finishes the spring, triumphant. Bashô works-in the same number idea more subtly with the temple=*garan,* almost mimesis for a sharp drop (*gara to*), and by reminding us that the ancient capital of Nara, identified with the eight-fold blossom, was the seventh reign in Japanese history! A seven-hall (or -pavilion) is a large, top-class temple, the plentitude of which parallels the eight-fold cherry, symbol of the once flourishing Nara. Ironically, the rulers decided to build their new Chinese style grid-streeted capital elsewhere, in Kyôto, to escape the plethora of temples in Nara.

一里はみな花守の子孫かや 芭蕉
hitosato wa mina hanamori no shison ka ya bashô -1694
(one/whole locality-as-for all blossom-guard's descendents?/!)

eightfold, indeed

the whole county
everyone claims descent from
that blossom guard

Why *eightfold?* Basho prefaced his poem with a brief mention of a local priest, who lead a protest by the whole populace to prevent the beloved eight-fold cherry named Kyôfukuji (Incite-Prosperity-Temple) from being dug up and sent to Nara as a tribute. Rather than becoming angry, the Empress, Fujiwara no Shôshi (中宮彰子 988-1074) was so impressed with his unyielding atitude that she let the tree remain, gave him the name of "Flower-fence = protector (*hanagaki*) Shô" (「花垣の庄」と名づけ), a glebe (寺領) and, best of all – if you love wit in high places – renamed the tree "My Cherry" (*waga-sakura*). I like to think "our" Elizabeth I would have done the same!

酔てから咄も八重の桜哉 一茶 1789
yotte kara hanashi mo yae no sakura kana issa
(drunken-from talk also eightfold cherry!/?/'tis)

lush indeed   **leaves or blossoms?**

after drinking   our talk blooms
our talk also blossoms   drunk, all are as lush as
eightfold cherry!   eightfold cherries

While Edoites can get quarrelsome drinking at the cherry bash, this is different. Here, the drunken poets – the original says "drunken-from" and I imagine pink faces, too – are waxing nostalgic, for the passing of spring, for the days of old. I say this not because the *ku* does, but because of the weight of tradition suggests it. To wit, some older *ku:*

いにしへも奈良酒て見ん八重櫻 政公
inishie mo nara shû de min yaezakura seiko 毛吹草 1645
(ancient times even nara *sake*-with see-let's eightfold-cherry)

let's view them
with auld *nara-zake!*
eightfold cherries

Shû is another way to say 酒=*sake*. Nara's was famous and, naturally what the children of the gods, *i.e.,* the imperial family, drank. It was and still is sweet and mellow, the mark of good *human* aging.

八重櫻京にも移る奈良茶哉 沾圃 続猿蓑
yaezakura kyô ni mo utsuru naracha kana senpo 1698
(eightfold-cherry capital-to-even spread/ing nara tea!)

奈良漬の根本問はん八重櫻 浪花
narazuke no konpon towan yaezakura rôka -1703
(nara-pickles' fundament ask-would 8fold cherry)

eightfold cherry
transplanted to the capital
this nara tea!

ask me where
narazuke comes from!
eightfold cherry

The "capital" *kyô* means Kyôto. Senpo may play on the old transplanted tree idea to give or accept a gift of Nara tea. With more women and children at an eight-fold viewing, tea would be more fitting than *sake*. A *ku* by Issa's fellow countryman Sobaku (-1821) notes *"The reflection / of an eightfold cherry / in one penny tea"* (一銭の茶にうつりけり八重櫻 素檗 *hito zeni no cha ni utsurikeri yaezakura*). A reflection on the fortunes of this blossom? The second *ku* is a masterpiece if you savor *narazuke,* a dark golden-russet *daikon* "nara-pickle," with its rich, strangely ancient taste (the "pickle" equivalent of a fine sherry), even if you are not certain what it means. The *narazuke* stands in sharp contrast to the bright yellow, in-your-face tartness of the Kantô (Tokyo) area pickle, the *takuwan*.

八重櫻けふ九重の晒哉 有文 三千花
yaezakura kyô kokonoe no sarashi kana yûmon 1725
(eight-fold-cherry today[pun=capital] nine-fold's sunning!)

the glory of nara

eightfold cherries
today, the ninefold past
basks in the sun

The nine-fold, as noted before, means the Imperial court; here, it means specifically that of Nara, including the regent Shotoku, beloved for his compassion for others based upon a philosophy of relativism recognizing one's right might be another's wrong. The verb *sarasu* (the *sarashi* above) today means to weather, or bake in the sun, but it originally meant things lined up beautifully in the sunlight (Perhaps because *drying out* was once ritual). My "basks" is semantically wrong but feels right.

九重を落武者須磨の八重櫻 休花 太夫櫻
kokonoe o ochi busha suma no yaezakura kyûka 1680
(ninefold-to fallen/fled warriors suma's eightfold ch.)

木の下に古き瓦や八重櫻 泰里 新選
kinoshita ni furuki kawara ya yaezakura tairi 1773
(tree-below-at old [roof] tiles: eightfold-cherry)

from nine to eight

like warriors
fallen from grace: suma
eightfold cherries

while touring yamato

under the tree
i find old roof tiles!
eightfold cherry

To the extent the eight-fold is identified with eclipsed glory, it is melancholic. Ever since the Shining Prince Genji was exiled to Suma – or even before that, for why would Shikibu Murasaki have chosen it? – Suma is known as a place of banishment, a place where life barely hangs on. It is no accident that Buson's bepissed *futon* and Issa's vaguely viewed sea cucumbers are Suma *ku*. While Yamato may be synonymous with Japan, in the second *ku,* above, it means in the vicinity of Nara.

古庭に一重ばかりの桜かな 子規
furuniwa ni hitoe bakari no sakura kana   shiki 1895
(old garden one-fold only's cherry/cherries'tis))

       the old garden
   its cherries are one and
        all singlefold

Japanese history has so many layers of history, so many masks each with another beneath it, that one cannot speak of the past without irony, intended or not. When Shiki wrote, Japanese were well aware of the ornate taste of the *fin de siecle* Occident which made theirs, by contrast, subdued if not austere. While the Somei-Yoshino clone was making headway at the time, the patriotic ideal was the mountain cherry, which was single-fold. So, we have single-fold as the good-conservative old-fashioned blossom and the eight-fold that only yesterday stood for ancient Japanese culture once again despised for its artificiality (ala Kenkô), and becoming foreign, to boot. Shiki doesn't go that far in his *ku,* but the writing is on the wall.

八景もこれにはいかで八重櫻　重貞
yakkei mo kore ni wa ika de yaezakura   shigesada ()
(eight-sights[emph.] me-to-as-for go/do-won't-so 8-fold-ch)

        as i can't see
    the eight sights, i see
       eightfold cherry

  if i can't afford   the eight sights
the eight sights, i can buy   beyond me: i'll make do
 an eightfold cherry   eightfold cherry!

The "eight sights" are the best sight-seeing spots in the whole land, province or city, etc.. They fill the tourism literature of old Edo. Getting around consumed time and money beyond many. Making do with *yaezakura,* the poet praises the bloom for the lavishness Kenkô would belittle it for. But praise or criticism, *yaezakura* deserves more close attention than it got. Here is the only really fine old observation I know of:

こほれても花や朝露八重櫻　肖柏 大発句帳
koboretemo hana ya asa tsuyu yaezakura   shôhaku -1527
(spilling/dropping even blossoms!/for, morning-dew eightfold-ch)

      though it may drip
   i love an eightfold cherry
       with morning dew

  though they drip   though they drip
for dew on blossoms at dawn   dewy blossoms are the best
  eightfold cherry   eightfold cherry

      ~~even fallen~~
~~they are blossoms: dawn dew~~
     ~~on *yaezakura*~~

eight-fold

Eight-fold blossoms of the *kikuzakura* type, at least, fall whole. At first, I imagined the blossoms in this *ku* on the ground, i.e., dew on blossoms that, still whole, are as good as dead. It would be a nice new tooth on the ephemeral dew on ephemeral blossom conceit, but is just too far from convention (and *koboretemo* is a bit off). The blossoms are in the tree and heavy with dew. Because of my familiarity with eight-fold blossoms and the lack of observant *ku*, I will make an exception for this chapter and introduce many *ku* by keigu and other contemporaries to round out the picture.

一二重開けてやミモノ八重桜　敬愚
hito-futa-e akete ya mimono yaezakura　keigu

八重桜初花ばかモ七日哉　敬愚
yaezakura hatsubana baka mo nanuka kana

worth viewing
with one or two folds open:
eight-fold cherry

eight-fold cherry
its first blossoms alone
a one-fold's life

The limbs may be plain and the tightly stitched clumps of eight-fold blossoms in full bloom lack the quivering delicacy of the individually more obvious petals of the simple standard. Yet, there are ways in which the eight-fold is a treat. When the blossoms are just starting to open – it takes as long for all of the blossoms to open as it does for a standard cherry to complete its whole show, a week or two – the combination of some random early blossoms with neat stem clusters of large buds is in itself aesthetically interesting. It is like viewing fireworks in slow motion. True, that is not so exhilarating as feeling like *you* are in slow motion – something that happens in a blizzard of cherry petals – but it is a fine art form of its own.

the heavy bloom
cool if shade, hot if clothes
eightfold cherry

eightfold cherry
the shadow dappling a good
part of the bloom

after all the rain
street-walkers past their prime
eightfold cherry

The dapple shadow and sheer bulk of the bloom, pink insulation between you and the sky impress, but after a long rain, the blossoms, for most remain, are a sorry sight. At least, this holds for the chrysanthemum eight-fold I knew. A long stretch of good weather, on the other hand, turns the entire grove into a flower shop of dried flowers – nose-gays or cherry mummies, as you please. Once, a late blizzard hit this "capital of dolls." The blossoms held so much snow some of those huge limbs broke:

雪折やそれこそ武士の八重桜　敬愚
yuki-ori ya sorekoso bushi no yaezakura　keigu

snow-broken:
who says the eightfold
is no warrior!

In the 20c, the eight-fold cherry was popularly put down for cowardly retaining its petals unlike the real ones that "fall without regret." Once, looking for *yaezakura*, when I was too late for the other cherries, a public park employee in Yokohama responded scornfully, "We Japanese don't like *yaezakura!*" I had been told the same thing by someone at work (I worked for a Japanese publisher) when I suggested a couple of the other editors walk home a different way to see the blossoms. I could not resist countering that the tenaciousness of the eight-fold cherry blossoms reflected the grin-and-bear-it *ganbaru*-ism of the Japanese far better than the quick-drop cherries everyone praised!

八重桜夜は己の重さかな　角谷 添子 季題別
yaezakura yoru wa onore no omoki kana kakutani tomoko 1997
(eight-fold cherry night-as-for own/self's heaviness!/?/'tis)

eightfold cherry
at night it must feel
its heaviness

八重桜身もだえに似て枝ごと揺れ　田鎖雷峰 同
yaezakura mimodae ni nite eda goto yure tagusari raihô? 1997
(eightfold-cherry body-convulsing-to resemble branch-each shaking/swaying)

the eightfold cherry
a body convulsing, each limb
swaying by itself

Precisely. These contemporary *ku* describe just the trees I knew. I'll bet that the limbs *do* drop ever so slightly at night, and such movement does indeed mark an umbrellate (wide-branched) tree.

花個々の小煩きとも八重桜　敬愚   個々越えて咲くる心や一重桜　敬愚
hana koko no ko-urusaki to mo yaezakura keigu   *ko ko koete sakurugokoro ya hitoezakura* keigu

each blossom   hearts bloom
catching the eye loses us!   without clear objects: a cherry
eightfold cherry   of single petal

These last two are less keigu than a poetic take on Yamada's argument. In the appendix (附録) to his history of *sakura*, he dared to reconsider the matter of what exactly made the single-fold mountain-cherry Mabuchi and Norinaga's choice for Japan. After making his main point that it was *clouds* of cherry blossoms, great masses of them *in bloom* – not falling warriors! – *illuminated by the morning sun* that they praised, Yamada contrasted the single=no-fold cherries favorably to the eight-fold, for a reason that, as far as I know, he was the first to put into words. It was *not* because there was anything unnatural or foreign about the latter, but that the individual blossoms were too powerful a presence (as a rose would be). If we risk losing the forest for being infatuated with a lovely tree, the eightfold's blossoms catch our attention, causing us to lose sight of the bloom as a whole.[1] I am not sure the blossoms that made the ancient poets proud were *never* appreciated as individuals but only in the mass; and I must admit Yamada added some gratuitous comments about analytical Western cognition, which would get hung up on individual blossoms and take decades to appreciate one scene at Yoshino, claimed "national emotion" (*kokumin-teki kanjô*) favored "blossom clouds" and "blossom mist" because it embodied collectivism, i.e., "sink-self-return-one" (没我帰一 submerging the ego in a greater identity), and concluded *this* was the natural form (*sugata*) of the Japanese, who also had exceptional appreciation for the collective beauty of the bush-clover and a number of other plants with so-and-so blossoms more notable in the mass. *This was, after all, January, 1941;* Yamada probably feared his criticism of the militarization of the cherry put him on dangerous ground and thought he had to make his interpretation *more-patriotic-than-thou* in another way to compensate. Yet, there is, I think, something to his contrast, perhaps the first pure cherry blossom criticism since that of Sei Shonagon.[2]

---

1. Panoramic Japanese? I was tempted to counter Yamada's argument with Hasegawa Nyozekan, who less than ten years later would claim the Japanese tendency "not to see the wood for the trees" was to blame for the lack of natural landscape parks in their cities and that "the failure of the present day Japanese to appreciate nature means that modern Japanese culture cannot be truly creative." (in John Bester trans. *The Japanese Character*: Kodansha). Neglecting haiku, Hasegawa went a bit too far when he put down the nature found in ancient Japanese poetry as lyrical rather than "direct appreciation" as found in Western literature.

2. *Sei Shônagon on Cherry Blossoms* This diva of taste, who included cherry blossoms with her list of *"things which look worse when depicted,"* wrote she liked "large petals with dark red leaves on slender branches" She clearly does not mean eight-fold, for they tend to have thick limbs and small petals. Yamada thought her up-close opinion suggested she hadn't climbed a mountain to see wild cherries in mass bloom at their best. I would go further and say her mention of large petals proves she appreciated just that, individual petals, which, with their tiny lip-like indentation are delicately beautiful in their own right which, as we have seen with Kikaku's kissing fish and other *ku*, some too pun-filled to translate was noticed by *haikai*. Keigu, too, cannot help adding one: *"Drop me off / here!" say blossom lips / to the wind"* (そこ迄と花のくちびる、風下し 敬愚 *soko made to hana no kuchibiru kaze oroshi*). The fact is that the individual petals of the standard cherry blossom are attractive in their delicacy. When one floats down from the blue, it does so like a feather. Whole blossoms just fall down, *plop*. Though I appreciate the eight-fold cherries in their own right, I do not feel those blossoms that do not disintegrate are as precious as the one-fold's for this reason.

~~~~~~

ちる時ぞ人間の苦も八重櫻　重頼 犬子 1633
chiru toki zo ningen no kû mo yaezakura　shigeyori 1601-1680
(falling time[emph.] human's troubles also eight-fold cherry.ies)

<div style="text-align:center">

when they fall
our troubles multiply
eight-fold cherries

</div>

This may be about the *kikuzakura*. I don't mind seeing blossoms rotting on the ground, but to the fastidious, they are a plague. As far as I know, the clean-up problem was not picked up by later haiku poets. Neither was the problem which underlies this chapter: why was the single-fold thought more Japanese than the eight-fold, which, artificial or not, was, after all, the product of native nurseries?

八重に咲く花や蛛手の絲桜 無記名 嵐山集
yae ni saku hana ya kumode no itozakura anon. 1651
(eight-fold bloom blossom!/: spider-hands' thread-cherry)

<div style="text-align:center">

thread cherry
blooming eight-fold
a pink spider

</div>

八重桜二重で四季に咲も哉　正幸 失典
yaezakura futae de shiki ni saku mogana　seikô ()
(eightfold cherry two-fold-with four-seasons-in bloom wish-for)

eight-fold cherry　　　　　　　　　　　　eight-fold cherry
i wish for two-fold petals　　　　　　　　why not bloom double
over four seasons!　　　　　　　　　　　in each season?

八重桜まぶた重たき共暮らし　時実新子
yaezakura mabuta omotaki tomogurashi tokizane shinko (20c)
(eightfold-cherry [blossoms] eyelid/s heavy co-living)

<div style="text-align:center">

eight-fold cherry
how heavy the eyelids
of cohabitation

</div>

63

Conserving Cherry
困った桜

山桜人をば鬼と思ふべし 一茶
yamazakura hito oba oni to omoubeshi issa 1810
(mountain cherry/ies people [emph.] devils think-must)

mountain cherries:
they surely must think
men are devils!

Issa used the devil (or demon) to good effect to describe humans from the point of view of birds or, toward the end of his life, Japanese from the Ainu point of view. While a parent bird warning its child of human devils seems more natural, and the cultural relativism of introducing the Ainu perspective more revolutionary, these thinking trees are the most delightfully animistic of these empathetic *ku*. Issa was not the first to note the way men mistreated cherry trees, just the best. An earlier poet:

むれて問ふ人にはかすめ山さくら 心敬 再現
murete tou hito ni wa kasume yamazakura shinkei -1475
(herding call/inquire person/people-from-as-for haze-over! mt. cherries)

hide yourself in haze
from people who come in droves
mountain cherries!

trans. steven d. carter TJP

The year Schumaker's celebrated *Small Is Beautiful* came out, his teacher Ezra J. Mishan published a more important book: *The Costs of Economic Growth*. Professor Mishan noted that with a limited number of natural "wonders of the world" and masterpieces, the increased tourism bound to come with increased wealth would trample the precious island into the sea and make us line up for miles for a glimpse of Mona's smile.[1] I like encountering the apprehension of multitudes in 15c Japan.

---

1. Coping With Multitudes As an economist, Mishan's main contribution was to the shadow-pricing of hidden costs such as those to the environment we share; as a thinker, his suggestion to limit travel by air to many locations so that only those willing to take the time to go by ship – energy-wise, more efficient, too – deserves kudos, for today, even environmentalists tend to take flying for granted, even flying in to islands to protest the building of airports there! We should have to pay *more* not less for each mile we travel, each flight we take. Frequent Flier programs, considered perfectly moral by our short-sighted culture, reward waste and will, in the future, be evidence of our *criminal behavior*. We have no excuse. This has been obvious as sin since 1956.

conservation

折てからは跡は野となれ山桜 俳諧江戸通り町
orite kara wa ato wa no to nare yamazakura maiboku 1678
(breaking-from-as-for aftermath field become! mountain-cherry)

mountain cherry:
you get your limb and
leave a wasteland

limbs ripped off
what if they look like hell?
mountain cherries

Bishop Shinkei did not say exactly *how* people bother cherry trees. This does. To say something "turns into fields and mountains" is to say that the farm plots of civilization are over-run and it goes wild, to hell, so to speak. The poet cleverly dovetails the "mountain" of the idiom with the wild cherry. The mood of *nare* (become) suggests an uncaring attitude as with our "after the deluge."

見苦しや折残されし山櫻 琴風 アルス
migurushi ya orinokosareshi yamazakura kinpû -1726
(see-painful: broken-left mountain-cherries)

此女折べからずと山櫻 来仲? 米恩? 18c?
kono onna ori bekarazu to yamazakura raichû
(this woman break-ought-not: mountain-ch)

an ugly sight
broken and abandoned
mountain cherries

this is a woman
who should not be ruined:
mountain cherry

With some of these *ku*, we are back to our woman or blossom problem. It is hard to tell what stands for what. Are men admonished for knocking up (leaving pregnant) country girls (sometimes called "mountain cherries") or knocking down trees? One connotation of "breaking" is "knowing" in the Biblic sense. But, it did not ordinarily "ruin" a young woman in Japan (see the *Woman* chapter of *Topsy-turvy 1585*) and, as post-Bashô *ku*, the standard assumption is that we are talking trees. Yet, another poet of the same age wrote: *"A ghost-house / and mountain cherries are / best abandoned!"* (捨てゝ置け化物屋敷 移竹 *sutete-oke bakemono-yashiki yamazakura* ichiku -1760). Unless the poet means that it is not wise to try to dig up a mountain cherry and carry it home (an unlikely reading), this is dastardly mysogyny. So, one never knows. Here is clearly wholesome *pre-Bashô* fare:

折る枝を言の葉なれや山櫻 宗祇 大発句帳
oru-eda o kotonoha nare ya yamazakura sôgi 1420-1502
(breaking limb[acc/lament?.] words become? mountain-cherry)

may your limb lost
gain thee a new tongue,
mountain cherry!

the limb i break
will become small talk
mountain cherry

can we break limb
missing, provide a story
mountain cherry!

Mountain cherries, unlike some cultivated cherries, were known to have a bit of leaf appear with the blossoms. "Language" in Japanese is "word-leaves." The first wit of what came to be called haiku has come up with a fine rationalization for taking limbs, though he had mixed feelings about the practice:

折らで只心にかざせ山櫻 宗祇 大発句帳
ora de tada kokoro ni kazase yamazakura sôgi -1502
(break-not-with just heart-in wear/adorn mt. cherry)

人のもる花は心のかさし哉 心敬 -1475
hito no moru hana wa kokoro no kazashi kana shinkei
(people's/s' guard blossom-as-for heart's adorn.!)

without breaking
let it adorn your heart:
mountain cherry

the blossoms
that we guard decorate
our hearts

Removing limbs is not necessarily bad. With plums, it must be done or the tree turns into a Slovenly Peter. But that is *before* the buds open. With mountain cherries, it seems people would rip off branches in bloom, decorate themselves with smaller parts, carry them to other scenic locations or home to the city to keep a while or give to a lover. We gave a whole chapter to these practices. Here, we'll dwell on the harm done by it and worse practices!

伐口を人のをしむや山櫻 徐宇 滑稽伝・均塞
kirikuchi o hito no oshimu ya yamazakura jou ()
(cut-mouth[scar] [acc.] person regrets: mountain-cherry)

    their raw scars   how men regret
 fill others with regret   the sight of their stumps
   mountain cherries   mountain cherries

We have a word, "kerf," for a notch cut out of a tree, but nothing for the scar left when a limb is amputated. Stumps is a bit off, but I wanted a word with equivalent punch. Still, this cutting down or ripping off of nature's art gallery is nothing compared to what people would do to make money:

何ものが皮剥だやら山ざくら 蝶羽
nanimono ga kawa haida yara yamazakura chôu -1741
(what-thing/personage bark[obj] peeled?/!/: mountain-cherry)

     who in the world   mountain cherries:
 stripped off your bark,   what creature peeled off
    mountain cherry?   all their bark!

山桜皮を剥れて咲きにけり 一茶
yamazakura kawa o hagarete sakinikeri issa -1814
(mountain-cherry bark[acc.] stripping bloom/ed[finality]))

strip-mining

   mountain cherries   mountain cherries
 stripped of their bark   with their bark peeled off
     have bloomed!   still blooming!

咲かけて桜は皮を剥れけり 一茶
sakikakete sakura wa kawa o hagarekeri issa -1814
(blooming-underway cherry/ies-as-for bark[acc.] strip[emph.])

   mountain cherries   cherry trees
their bark stripped even   in full bloom stripped
    as they bloom!   of their bark!

While dyers after material for rare colors are notorious for overhunting, weavers who made use of cherry bark usually tread lightly. Today, cherry bark is stripped for handicrafts, but my first guess here was an herb collector. The bark treated hives and belly aches. A *senryû* about the practice of eating fresh (but *high*) bonito: *"If he [the fish-monger] comes / tomorrow, slug him!" / [he says, while] sucking on cherry bark"* (あす来たらぶてと櫻の皮をなめ 柳多留 5—25 *asu kitara bute to sakura-no kawa-o name* yanagidaru 1770). People everywhere have always been willing to kill *anything* to cure themselves. But chances are that humans did not strip the bark here. *Haikai* experts credit the damage to boars or deer.

conservation

咲からになでへらさるゝ桜哉 一茶
saku kara ni nadeherasaruru sakura kana   issa -1811
(bloom-from stroke-wear-down cherry/ies!/'tis)

<blockquote>
since it blooms
the cherry is worn down
by kind strokes
</blockquote>

<blockquote>
since it blooms
people rub it away
the cherry tree
</blockquote>

According to saying, certain things could or could not be lent, depending upon whether they wore away or not. One might lend a wife, but not a mortar or a pestle. A cherry might be a woman, but a famous tree drawing thousands of viewers had it rough. Or that is how I read the *ku*.

帳に詣、おく山にて・咲からに縄を張れし桜哉 一茶
saku kara ni nawa o harareshi sakura kana   issa 1804
(bloom-from rope[acc] stretch/ed cherry!/'tis)

open temple day in the mountains

<blockquote>
after it starts
to bloom the cherry gains
a straw festoon
</blockquote>

<blockquote>
once it blooms
that's when they rope it off
the cherry tree
</blockquote>

If the last *ku* presented a problem, this provides a solution. The festoon of braided straw rope is a mark of the sacrosanct. It protects the tree from damage by making it out of bounds. Such ropes permanently encircle the largest cedars, while cherries were evidently guarded only at special times.

風をなくより棒も哉花の番 一雪 洗濯物
kaze o naku yori bô mogana hana no ban   isseki 1666
(wind-for cry rather-than cudgel wish-for blossom's guard)

<blockquote>
rather than crying
over the wind, this bloom guard
wants a cudgel!
</blockquote>

<blockquote>
rather than crying
over wind, give me a rod
i'll guard the bloom
</blockquote>

花掘し跡をおぼへて風の吹く 一茶 真蹟
hana horishi ato o oboete kaze no fuku   issa -1827
(blossom [ch. tree] dug-spot[acc] remembering wind blows)

<blockquote>
a lonely hole

the wind blows!
it remembers where
the cherry was
</blockquote>

<blockquote>
over the place
where blossoms were dug up
blows the wind

trans. steven d. carter
</blockquote>

Issa might not put it like me but, I cannot help but recall how the wind in classical poetry staked out his cherries as surely as Tom Cat did his pussies. *What pathos in the combination hole and wind!* Not only limb, not only bark; sometimes the whole tree was carried off. *Where to?* In this case, we know. Issa wrote that the tree, dug up that morning, was sold by nurseryman Iheibei (Issa and Seibi traversed his nursery) to the Yoshiwara pleasure district for its coming High-Snake Festival. *What irony!* It sold, as country girls were sold, to Yoshiwara, for a festival occurring on the day we now know as Girl's Day.

花咲と直に掘らるゝ桜哉　一茶 真蹟
hana saku to sugu ni horaruru sakura kana   issa -1827
(blossom blooms and immediately dug-up cherry!/'tis)

a cherry blooms
and immediately
is dug up!

Was this a tree dug up to take to town, possibly Yoshiwara? Or, is it one dug up following its "performance," sold for wood, carried back to the nursery, or planted in a private garden? Whatever be the case, trees, like cats, dislike moving (except for air-plants such as those that happily accompanied me in a golf-cart bought because I could not afford treatment for an injured knee). Issa's explanation sighs, *"Even plants suffer in this world."* About ten years later, he *ku's*: *"Planted/potted cherries: / flowers, too, must suffer / in this world"* (植桜花も苦界はのがれざる　一茶 *uezakura hana mo kûkai o nogarezaru* 1820). He finishes morosely, *"This is the sort of time when blossoms shed tears. Yes, how sad the plant/s must be!"* He may allude to the Chinese poet Du Fu's terse "feeling-time-blossom-secretes-tears." (Some of my phrasing and the Englishing of the Chinese poet's name are from Carter: TJP) Should the fact that the plants are grown at a nursery rather than kidnapped in the wild lessen our concern for them? We can feel Issa's familiarity with the nursery business and love for plants in *ku* such as the above and this: *"That sad sack? / A three hundred mon / cherry tree."* (いまだ時ならざる満花を植木屋おこしたるに別世界に入心ちして・あのくたら三百文の桜哉　一茶　*ano kutara san-byaku mon no sakura kana* 1812). Issa prefaces the *ku* with the remark that he felt like he was in another world before the full bloom of a cherry at a nursery. If I am not mistaken, we are being treated to the way nurserymen talked.

市に出て二日ほさるゝ桜哉　一茶 1812　　　　　　年々に櫻すくなき故郷かな　素檗 1821
ichi ni dete futsuka hosaruru sakura kana　issa　　*toshidoshi ni sakura sukunaki furusato kana* sobaku
(market-in appears second day thinning cherry/ies!)　　(year-year-by cherry/ies few hometown/county 'tis)

in the market　　　　　　　　　　　year by year
thinner on day two　　　　　　　less cherry trees
a cherry tree　　　　　　　　　　　my hometown

The tree out in a market is exposed to the hot air of the street and the withering glances of the passerby. The blossoms don't hold up so long as cherry trees in a grove, and, to a tree-lover, they look pitiful, like dogs hoping to be adopted at a pound. Sobaku, Issa's better-known contemporary and compatriot helps us to understand why Issa was so attentive to the troubles of the cherry. Evidently, these were not happy times for the plant in the fiefdom of Shinano.

売ものゝ札を張られし桜哉　一茶
urimono no fuda o harareshi sakura kana issa 1811
(sell-thing[on-sale] tag/sign[acc.] attached cherry/ies!/'tis)

cherry trees
with "for sale" tags among
their blossoms

Though just beginning in the West, the use of tags with fixed prices was already common in Japan. Considering the deep feeling poets had for the cherry, this must have seemed somewhat sacriligious or, worse yet, smacked of slavery. I imagine some buds already in bloom.

conservation

大桜さらに買人はなかりけり 一茶
ôsakura sara ni kaite wa nakarikeri issa 1811
(big-cherry[tree] furthermore buyer-as-for not[+emph])

    the big cherry
chances are it won't
      find a buyer

    the big cherry:
after that no other
    buyer came

Did someone make an offer the nurseryman balked at and regretted later, when the large tree remained unsold and would require hauling back to the nursery to be replanted for sale the following year. The next *ku,* perhaps by Big Ant (大蟻), expresses well the affection Japanese had for blossoming trees.

古寺や誰が植捨し花一木 存儀芭蕉 翁反古
furudera ya daga uesuteshi hana hito-ki ?bashô? 1783
(old temple: who planted-abandoned blossom one-tree)

an old temple
who planted and abandoned it?
one cherry tree

~~~~~~

A Human World

山桜世はむつかしき接木哉 猿水
yamazakura yo wa muzukashiki tsugiki kana   ensui
(mountain-cherries world-as-for difficult grafting!/'tis 1655-1739)

    in our world
so bedeviled by graft!
    wild cherries

    wild cherries
in this world, look-out
    for grafters!

Grafting cherry trees was a noble sport (I borrow the term from Charles Darwin's day, when breeds were called *sports*)[1] going back at least as far as the twelfth century (#62-7) when monk Kenkô reacted with his anti-artificiality, minimalist aesthetics. With the spread of Zen and the tea ceremony in the 16 and 17c, many people philosophically opposed the tradition of art-cherry blossoms and we see what became a cult of the mountain-as-wild=pure=honest=plain=single-fold(petaled) blossom. My first reading assumes the poet is of that school. Because young mountain=wild cherries were indeed commonly used for root-stock to graft cultivars, the second reading is also possible.

今の代 (世) や行儀に並ぶ山ざくら 一茶
ima no yo ya gyôgi ni narabu yamazakura issa 1817
(now's world: [good]manners-in line-up mountain-cherries)

    modern times!
the mountain cherries
    stand in a line!

    brave new world
well-mannered wild cherry
    stand in a row

    the world today
how politely they line up:
    mountain cherries!

☆ I promise a gloss in a future edition for anyone who selects, edits and translates a page (or, as many pages as can be read with interest) from Fujiwara Teika's copious diary jottings on cherry cultivation.

窮屈に並られけり山桜　一茶
kyûkutsu ni naraberarekeri yamazakura issa
(crampedly lined-up[emph.] mountain-cherry)

> made to line up
> in a cramped manner
> mountain cherries

At first, I wondered whether Issa's attention was caught by tasteless planting or docile crowds. The middle line of the third reading was "politely lining up *for*." But, respondent KS strongly favored the plants, and the passive verb in Issa's second *ku* strongly seconded him. Moreover, I later found a more subtle complaint about rows of trees (not in the hills, however) was made over 300 years earlier!

ならふやと一木つれなき花もかな　宗祇
narabu ya to hitoki tsurenaki hana mogana sôgi 1420-1502
([they are?] lined up!/: one-tree accompaniment-not blossom wish!)

> all in a row   all lined up?
> how i'd like a blooming   give me just one tree
> tree by itself!   a lonely flower

To be without a companion (*tsurenaki*) also means to be out of luck, but Sôgi turns the bad into the good, or rather the desired in the last part of the *ku*. Sôgi does not want his blooming beauties in a chorus line. And, there are other advantages to single trees. A fifth-grade student recently put it like this: *"In the forest, / like this big light! / a blooming cherry"* (森の中あかりのような桜花　宮本みどり *mori no naka akari no yô na sakurabana* Miyamoto Midori (Hokkaido, Kurokawa Elementary).

立上る埃の中の花見哉　蕉桐 淡ちしま 1698   人足のほこりを浴るさくら哉　一茶 1810
tachiagaru hokori no naka no hanami kana shôtô   *hitoashi no hokori o abiru sakura kana* issa
(rising dust-among's blossom-viewing!/?)   (people-feet' dust showers cherry/ies!/'tis)

> we sit within   cherries bloom
> a cloud of dust: is this   bathed in dust raised
> blossom-viewing?   by human feet

むまやろや泥も嫌はで落ちる花　沾徳 1726
muma yaro ya doro mo kirawa de ochiru hana sentoku
(luscious-right? mud even hate-not-from falling-blossoms)

> luscious, is it?
> blossoms falling don't
> mind the mud

Forgive the Japanese expression in the first *ku*. If the cherry trees in the next were known to be white elephants (see ch.39), they might find the dust bath comforting. With enormous crowds of people, a dry year meant dust, a wet one mud. Sentoku's *ku* with its positive attitude toward mud-bathing is remarkably similar to Issa's style hundreds of years later and I like it so much I repeat it here.

conservation 689

花ふゝき泥わらんじで通りけり 一茶
hanafubuki doro waranji de tôrikeri issa 1821
(blossom-blizzard mud-sandals-in pass[+emph.])

muddy *waraji*
pass right through
a petal blizzard

a petal blizzard
muddy *waraji* pass
right through

The *waraji* (Issa uses a colloquial *waranji*) is a crude straw throw-away sandal used by travelers. That sounds cheap. And, they were. But, as explained in *The Fifth Season,* material crudity in Japan could evoke the celebratory spirit. Doubtless, the sandals carried off some petals stuck to the mud.

短冊や泥よりなりて花の山 廣千立 雑中
tanzaku ya tei yori narite hananoyama kôsenryû ()
(short-bind: mud-from becoming blossom-mountain)

cherry mountain
for our *tanzaku* we use
this muddy clay

A *tanzaku* is a strip of paper a couple inches wide and about a foot-long, which was used to write poems on. I changed "mud" to "clay," for using mud too muddy would be like writing on water.

一すぢに芝ふみからす櫻哉 全峯 続虚栗
hitosuji ni shiba fumi-karasu sakura kana zenpô 1687
(one-line-in lawn/grass tread-wither cherry/ies!/ 'tis)

tread till dead
a single line in the turf:
it's the cherry!

a single path
of tread to death turf
for the cherry

We saw muddy trails in Book I, but *this* must happen every year, whatever the weather. I see people heading straight for the celebrated feature and paying little attention to nature's side-shows. Even so, people trails are never as narrow as those made by cows. We just don't walk one foot after another.

たいらなる山や花見の足たまり 沽徳
taira naru yama ya hanami no ashidamari sentoku -1726
(level be/come mountain!/: blossom-viewing base[for])

mountains flattened
base-camps for blossom
viewing campaigns

flat mountains
where blossom-viewers
catch their breath

flattened hills
respite between blossom
battlefields

The "base" metaphor describes military, not political, campaigns. The second and third readings are less likely, but imagining hills flattened by generations of viewers (based on a rare usage of *ashidamari*) is fun.

63 33-36

身を捨る山陰もなき櫻哉　蘭更 アルス
yo[mi] o suteru yamakage mo naki sakura kana   rankô -1799
(body[acc.] abandon mountain-shade-even not, cherry[trees/blossoms]!/'tis)

up in the mountains

no dark glens
to lose oneself for good
the cherry blooms

世をいかに捨どころなき山桜　存擬芭蕉
yo o ika ni sutedokoronaki yamazakura   ?bashô? 17c
(world/society[obj] how abandon/leave place-not mountain-cherry)

even in the hills   no place to leave
there's no place for retreat: the world of man remains
cherry blossoms   mountain cherries

Who can tell if Rankô is really complaining or expressing the popularity of blossom-viewing! Hermits had mixed feelings about blossom viewers. Some enjoyed showing off "their" trees, but most, who lived on little mountains on the edge of town and, like Thoreau at Walden, had visitors enough, couldn't wait for tranquility to be restored. Or, could he be describing a practice that has continued to modern time of going into the wilderness to die?   The second *ku* is attributed to Bashô, but dubious.

人くさし鬼なき世なり花の山　宗雅 雑中
hitogusashi oni naki yo nari hananoyama   sôga - 1790
(people-stinking demon-not world becomes blossom-mt.)

the demons gone
how it stinks of man!
cherry mountain

鬼すむと聞くは昔よ花の山　素陽 拍挙千句   鬼の住むさたもなくなる桜哉　一茶
oni sumu to kiku wa mukashi yo hananoyama   soyô -1563   *oni no sumu sata mo nakunaru sakura kana   issa*
(demon/s live hear-as-for long-ago! blossom-mt.)   (demon/s live news even gone cherry!/'tis)

long ago demons   not only demons
were said to live here: but all news of them gone:
cherry mountain   cherry blossom

Mountains were guarded by their spirits, tutelary deity or demon, so man had to take care not to do anything that might incur a *tatari,* supernatural retribution. Fear of *tatari* is usually explained in the context of the rice-growing valley people coming to Japan from the Asian mainland and feeling uncomfortable with the wilderness and the native peoples inhabiting it. It is hard to tell whether these *ku* celebrate the progress of the civilization-bearing Yamato culture – for cherries accompanied their expansion – or lament the heavy footprint of the growing population of blossom viewers!

花見にと群れつつ人の来るのみぞあたら桜のとがにはありける　西行
hanami ni to muretsutsu hito no kuru nomi zo atarazakura no toga ni wa arikeru   saigyô

しづかならんと思ひける頃、花見に人々まうで来たりければ

when i feel like being alone and people come blossom-viewing

*people just keep
coming and coming to
view blossoms*

*and it's all the fault of
those damn cherry trees!*

Blaming the cherries for the crowds is like blaming women for men losing their senses over them. Indeed, we feel that *is* the metaphor. Like *haikai* poets centuries later, Saigyô had fun. Obviously, this is the hermit guarding his solitude and not an environmental statement. Be that as it may, I include it in this chapter to show that some saw the mountains as overcrowded before they really were.

あしおもや爪あかりなる花の山　嵐雪
ashio mo ya tsume agarinaru hana no yama　ransetsu - 1707
(leg-heavy? hawk-footstrap?! nails/talons rising-are/become blossom-mountain)

cherry mountain
like tethered hawks
we try to rise

cherry mountain
even tatami knights
standing tiptoe

even house-poets!
pushing toe-nails into dirt:
cherry mountain

This yet unsolved *ku* may be about crowding. The last two readings, based on the guess that Ransetsu coined *ashiomo* (leg-heavy), as an antonym for "lightlegs," (*ashigaru*) or "foot-soldier," are almost surely wrong. *Ashio*, the leather leg-strap for a hunting hawk, is more likely. Hawking and cherry-time were one. The equivalence of *talon* and *toe-nail* in Japanese allows metaphor in the original.

Piss & Poop

山里やかりの後架も（後架といふも）花の陰　一茶
yamasato ya kari no koka mo hananokage　issa 1814
(mountain-locality: temporary/borrowed toilet even bloomshade)

a mountain town
our temporary toilets:
the bloom-shade

a mountain town
even our rest rooms
in bloom-shade

Were privies set under cherry trees or people just doing their business in the bloomshade? The former is likely because of the value of human "waste." Yet supply could overwhelm the facilities:

花咲くやそこらは野糞野小便　一茶
hana saku ya sokora wa noguso noshôben　issa 1823
(blossoms bloom: here-and-there-as-for field-shit field-piss)

cherries bloom:
here and there open-air
shitting, pissing!

the cherry blooms:
here and there, alas, i see
my doo, my pee!

Japanese has an expression for doing it *al fresco*, *"no-guso,"* or "field-shit." Buson used it a couple times, Issa more. As is often true for problematic *ku*, my temptation is to paraverse: *"Blossom-viewing / so many people doing their / business outside;" "Petals falling / far and wide / we answer nature's call / outside;"* etc.. *Ku* written the previous month, and others about piss-stinking grass – not to mention pee-hole-ridden snow – suggest Issa did not always husband his wastes, and this tendency to chuckle at what he did to his surroundings might have been exacerbated by the recent death of his wife, his palsy and heavy drinking, so we may have a local one-cherry-hill rather than a large bash.

小便に花を咲かせる俳諧師 柳多留 23-31
shôben ni hana o sakaseru haikaishi yanagidaru 1822
(pissing-by blossom[obj] bloom-make haikai masters)

making flowers blossom with piss: the haiku master!	the haiku-master who turned pissing into poetry

小便に花が咲たで名句也 柳多留 60-24
shôben ni hana ga saita de meiku nari yan. mid-19c
(piss-in blossom bloomed-from famous ku becomes)

花の山と書て小便よみがへり 柳多留 52-11
hananoyama to kaite shôben yomigaeri ya. mid-19c
(blossom-mountain writing piss [urge?] restoring)

piss making cherries bloom made it a famous poem	writing the words "cherry mountain," again he wants to pee

The first *senryû* seems to suggest strange techniques of horticulture, but probably refers to the way *haikai* masters got a lot of mileage out of pissing, most notably with the Goddess of Spring whom we have noted already, somewhere. It and the second *ku* do not specify the cherry, but use *blossom* in the sense of flourishing. Still, taken together, the three *senryû* suggest some link between our blossom and pissing. *But what?* Could it refer to a *ku* about a WC curtain for answering the call of nature under the bloom I once read in a book of well-known haiku (and, strangely enough, have not been able to find it again)? We will leave the riddle unanswered – one more incentive for an expanded edition of this book to come – and join the savior of modern haiku, Shiki, with one of his most delightful *ku* not included in Kyoshi's anthology of his poetry:

うれしげに小便するや花の山　子規
ureshige ni shôben suru ya hananoyama shiki 1896
(joyously peeing/urination do!/: blossom-mountain)

how delightful to take a piss upon cherry mountain!	what a delight to pee! looking upon cherry mountain

Shiki could be describing a boy, but it is more likely he has captured his child within. He follows this *ku* with one I put with the *Patriotic Cherries*: *"Being born / a man of this country: / cherry blossoms!"* (#61-27). Was he thinking of the ease with which a man can piss compared to a woman? Unlike most *ku* in this chapter, this is joyful and reminds me of what I would call a blue-sky *senryû*: *"What fine weather! / You hunt for a ladder / to piss from!"* (小便にはしごをさがすいゝ天気　柳多留 23-30 *shôben ni hashigo o sagasu ii tenki* yanagidaru 1822) – the original starts with the piss and ends with the weather. That great friend of New Orleans and Japan, Lafcadio Hearn, who once peed from a steeple, would have appreciated both *haiku* and *senryû*. Another contemporary wrote less enthusiastically:

吉野厠借りて谷恐しや花の山　大春　ホトトギス
kawaya karite tani osoroshi ya hana no yama　ôshun　c 1900
(privy borrowing valley frightful!/: blossoms' mountain)

using a privy
how dreadful the valley!
cherry mountain

how dreadful
the valley from a privy
on mt cherry!

Were there no caption specifying "Yoshino" and I not read *a certain essay*, I would have thought this referred to the pit inside a public restroom at an urban blossom-viewing park. The essay is Tanizaki Junichiro's *Outhouse Miscellany* (厠のいろ／＼ 1935). It starts with his most memorable experience, which took place when he went to a restaurant of *udon* (a thick noodle) in Yamato and suddenly had to answer nature. The backhouse jutted out over the plain of the Yoshino River, and, as Tanizaki squatted, he saw through the hole his excrement dropped from, the farm plots with blooming rape, butterflies and, yes, people walking far below! *He loved it;* I guess the poet was terrified by the same.

それそこは（が）犬の雪隠ぞ山桜　一茶　　　　　　大猫が尿かくす也花の雪　一茶
sore soko wa inu no setchin zo yamazakura　issa　　*ôneko ga shito kakusunari hananoyuki*　issa
(that there-as-for dog's snow-hide[shit]! mt-cherry)　(big-cat[the] urination hide-is blossom-snow)

hey, watch it!
that's dog shit over there,
mountain cherry

a petal snow
settles over the piss
of the big cat

Unless the mountains were overrun with dogs, the *cave (merdem) canem* in the first *ku* is not so much for fellow blossom-viewers, as for the trees or, rather, blossoms, advising them to look out as they fall. Pollution by men and their pets is not at issue. The dog-shit is a vehicle to convey old Issa's sympathy for the blossoms. At first, I translated the second *ku* "*This big cat covers up its urine with / a petal blizzard;*" but cats are more vigorous at covering up shit than piss and big cats generally advertise rather than hide the latter. I wanted to have the cat kick up a blizzard, but settled on the above. A third reading might have the cat covering its scat *and* the petal snow falling.

どか／＼と花の上なる馬ふん哉　一茶
dokadoka to hana no ue naru bafun kana　issa 1812
(thud-thud-with blossoms-upon be/come horse-shit!/?/'tis)

thudding down
on the cherry petals:
horse shit!

Most translations of this, most famous of all shit/dung/turd/poop *ku*, mention *flowers*. I first pictured the heavy brown balls smashing white periwinkles, for *I have seen it* (in Florida). But, to people familiar with haiku, the use of the plain *hana* (flower/blossom) in Japanese suggests cherry petals or, perhaps, fallen plum blossoms.[1] The plum as a symbol of purity would bring a whiff of iconoclasm to the *ku*, but Japanese plum (*ume*) groves are too cramped for horses and Issa also wrote: "*Falling petals / covering up a mound / of horse shit*" (散花の降りつもりけり馬糞塚　一茶 1824 *chiru hana no furitsumorikeri magusozuka*); and he had a tendency to balance the scale. For example: his flies pray not to be swatted in one *ku* and he, or someone, swats them and says *amen* in another (see **Fly-ku!**); a horse farts from fear of a firefly and, years later, another horse *threatens* a firefly with a powerful fart! So, if Issa had *petals on horse-shit, horse-shit on petals* would be no surprise.

1. Plum Blossoms and Horse Shit Plum blossoms and *bird* shit are the more usual combination. Buson chuckled: *"Red plum blossoms! / i thought the horse dung / was smoldering"* (*kôbai no rakka moyuramu uma no kuso*) – that is my reading, different from Blyth's (see IPOOH: spring I), but this combination is far less common.

~~~~~~

日／＼の糞だらけ也花の山　一茶
nichinichi no kuso darake nari hananoyama issa 1815
(day-day's shit-plastered become blossom-mountain)

day by day
cherry mountain grows
full of shit

All of the call-of-nature haiku until this last one were non-judgmental. Here, Issa describes not just *the* truth but the *sorry* truth of any large event. The word I translated as "full of" (*darake*) is always used in a bad sense, as *"plastered with* [make-up]" *"bedeviled with* [ants]." It is "lot's of" with a negative slant. Issa has more shitty *ku* than any poet I know of (excluding horse-shit, where Shiki is world champion), and one of them is the most positive shit I have ever encountered. While it has nothing to do with our cherry blossoms, it does belong to the same season, and, I think, deserves a special airing:

なぐさみ (に) 野屎をたれる日永哉　一茶
nagusami ni noguso o tareru hinaga kana issa -1827
(relief/consolation-for, field-shit-hang day-long/lengthening!/'tis)

days lengthen	& out i go	a long, long day!
for diversion i poop	to shit away this	i find my consolation
al fresco	spring ennui	shitting outside

Since Japanese squat in the field exactly as they always squat (and read books, etc. as we do on our porcelain thrones), they do not find *al fresco* the least trying. To them, it is pure refreshment.

Cherry Lice

のさ／＼とさし出て花見虱かな　一茶
nosanosa to sashidete hanami-jirami kana issa 1822
(vigorously sallying-forth blossom-viewing lice!/?/'tis)

bold *en masse*
the blossom-viewing lice
sally forth today

Masses in the mountains (usually urban parks with cherry trees) spread more than excrement. Some lice awoke at the dawn of Spring in time for plum blossoms (see IPOOH spring I), but the bulk awaited warmer weather. The psychological mimesis *nosa-nosa* qualifies a verb of movement with quantity and confidence. Needless to say, English has no such adverb, so I had to improvise. The fancy compound verb I Englished as "sally forth" puns on the stab (*sashi*) of the louse. The "today" was added for sound style. Another of Issa's lice *ku* points out that *"We, ourselves / are blossom-viewing lice, / parasites!"* (おのれらも花見虱〔に、の?〕候よ *onorera mo hanami-jirami[ni?no?] sôrô yo*). "Parasite" is my word; but this, like Issa's "we are the devils" *ku*, is welcome humility coming from our species. Was Issa the first to make the identification, i.e., make *us* parasites? Be that as it may, there are many earlier blossom-viewing lice poems. Even Bashô wrote a beauty:

手のひらに蚤這はする花のかげ 芭蕉
tenohira ni shirami hawasuru hananokage bashô -1694
(hand's palm-in/on louse/lice crawl/s blossom's/s' shade)

under cherry flowers	in the bloomshade
he watches as new spring lice	watching new spring lice
crawl upon his palm	crawl on his hand
trans. miner	miner+me

Oddly, this is not in Iwanami's standard collection of Bashô's *ku*. Perhaps the editor didn't feel it should stand alone, for it completed an opening 7-7 *"while his lord is out / and the hall stands vacant,"* part of the verse-jam Ichinaka ("Throughout the Town" translated by Miner *Japanese Linked Poetry*). Kyorai's 7-7 verse following Bashô's lice is worth a look:

*the spring haze hangs motionless
at the drowsy midday hours*

Miner's translation is long but I cannot beat it.[1] And Kyorai's second (*tsuke-ku*) can not be beat. It provides a perfect frame for the hand with those wee lice. Miner notes that the Spring session for the *kasen* (the proper term for a *renku* verse-jam) – which ended on this *ku* was exceptionally short. I'd say Bashô's image was so good and Kyorai's fix so perfect, who would want to continue? While the context of the verse-jam makes us English Bashô's *ku* in the third-person, had I not seen the context, I would have assumed Bashô spoke for himself. Maybe he *did*. If so, it is remarkably lenient to the damn bugs. Only Issa can get friendlier yet: *"Skinny lice / you have lived to meet / a world of bloom!"* (痩虱花の御代にぞ逢にけり *yasejirami hana no miyo ni zo ainikeri*).

梟の虱落すな花の陰 北枝 -1718
fukurô no shirami otosuna hananokage hokushi
(owl's lice drop not! bloomshade)

花見虱かゝには告よさつま櫛 安明 江戸新道
hanamijirami kaka ni wa tsuge yo satsumakushi anmei 1678
(blm-viewing lice mother-to tell! satsuma comb)

hey, owl, stop!	blossom-viewing lice!
stop dropping your lice, here	you'd better tell mom!
in the bloom-shade!	*the satsuma comb*

Hokushi's *ku* is *odd*. Lice was supposed to crawl out of seams of clothing and up into the hair in warm weather. The Satsuma comb is like a flea comb, fine-toothed to catch lice. Does it go without saying in English, too, that the *ku* means *"Tell her to bring it!"*?

---

1. ***Miner: Japanese Linked Poetry*** Miner knows good English idiom, but follows the mistaken convention of counting syllables rather than beat, so his translations tend to be long. In the above case, however, syllable padding allows additional information that improves the *ku* for the reader happily unfamiliar with the life-cycle of the parasite in question. Lice come to life and are even endeared with "new spring" and the creative "watches!"

うつるとも花見虱ぞよしの山 一茶
utsuru to mo hanamijirami zo yoshinoyama   issa -1827
(catching even blossom-viewing lice [+emph.] yoshino mt)

itchy but content

<table>
<tr><td>though you get 'em
they are blossom-viewing lice
yoshino, no less!</td><td>whose complaining?
these are mount yoshino
blossom-viewing lice!</td></tr>
</table>

Issa had a fine eye for status because he was not lucky enough to have it. He once was *honored* to donate blood to *uptown* mosquitoes.

ちる時はつふりかく花見しらみ哉 鷺舟 洗濯物
chiru toki wa tsuburi kaku hanami jirami kana   roshû 1666
(when they fall head/s scratch blossom-viewing lice!/'tis)

when they fall
we scratch our heads:
hanami lice

The verb *chiru* (fall/scatter) is so suggestive of what the blossoms do that "they" seems to mean *the petals* and the scratching only our apprehension for the blossoms . . . until we get to the lice.

Cherry Colds

this mini-chapter is dedicated to ogden nash

Lice was not the only thing caught blossom-viewing, as a *ku* by young Issa put it, lamely, *"In the bloom-heat / winds=colds are always / pandemic,"* or *"The full bloom: / This is when influenza / is indeed in"* (花盛必風（邪）のはやりけり 一茶 *hanazakari kanarazu kaze hayarikeri* 1808) . A few years later, he explains *"After blooming / the cherries' wind=cold is / passed on [to us]"* (咲からに桜の風（邪）をうつしけり 一茶 *saku kara ni sakura no kaze o utsushikeri* 1812). Years later, he wrote *"When the cold=wind / epidemic is over / so, too, the blossoms"* (風はやり仕廻へば花も仕舞哉 *kaze hayarishimaeba hana mo shimai kana* 1821) and less causally: *"Cherries bloom / then, people too / catch [the] wind=colds"* (花は咲也人も風（邪）引ぬ *hana wa sakunari hito mo kaze hikinu* 1821) and more punfully, *"Mountain cherry / we catch [the] wind=cold / from the blossoms=[the]nose"* (山桜花から風をうつり（し）けり *yamazakura hana kara kaze o utsurikeri* 1820). With said disease called a "wind" rather than a "cold" and no blossom=nose homophone, the metaphors are shot to hell in translation. "Influenza" with its fluid movement is close, but a bit too heavy and Latin roots go by most English-speaking readers. One *ku*, resembling the Yoshino lice we just met, but better if you prefer affection for a plant to affection for a place, works, so long as the reader remembers that *a cold* is *a wind*:

うつるとも桜の風（邪）ぞ花の陰　一茶
utsuru to mo sakura no kaze zo hananokage issa 1820
(spreading even cherry's/ies' wind=cold[+emph.] blossomshade)

this cold of mine?
a cherry cold, caught in
the bloom-shade!

don't care if
i do catch it, by god!
it's a cherry cold

The "cherry makes it something to boast about" idea is found centuries earlier, in this *ku*: *"I'd pull a switch / the same white hair's fine / as snow on blossoms"* (すりかへんおなじしらがも花の雪 長頭丸 嵐山集 *surikaen onaji shiraga mo hananoyuki* teitoku 1651). A *possibly* more direct scoop *ku* by Hyakuri I first took to mean: *There's something / classy about cutting wind / under the blossoms"* could well mean *"It has class / that wind=cold that blows=spreads / under the bloom;"* (手柄あり花の下ふく人の風　百里　あやにしき *tegara ari hananoshita fuku hito no kaze* hyakuri 1732). In other words, it is a cool cold to catch; or to "wipe," for *fuku* (blows/spreads) can *also* mean that, for "under the bloom=*nose*." Then, again, the "people-wind" could be metaphor alluding to the time when an ancient poet got many people to come to *his* party under the bloom rather than a rival's. . . A clear example of the "cold with a pedigree" from the late-19c: *"Sleeping on a train / I catch a Suma wind=cold: / night chills"* (汽車に寝て須磨の風（邪）ひく夜寒 子規 *kisha ni nete suma no kaze hiku yosamu* 1898). A Suma cold would be melancholy and romantic for historical reasons.

花にうき風を散する医者も哉 長頭丸 嵐山集
hana ni uki kaze o chirasuru isha mogana teitoku 1651
(blssms-for blue/awful wind=cold[acc] dispell doctor wish-for)

blue in the bloom:
oh, for a doctor to dispel
the wind / my cold

The wit in the original (untranslatable *as a poem*) is in a role reversal, for "dispel" is *chirasu,* or "scatter," exactly what the wind does to the blossoms. Issa was a Johnny-come-lately with his cherry cold *ku*, for there are dozens of old ones like the above. Eg.: *"Spring's third act / the epidemic is here / cherry-wind=nose-cold"* (三春のやく病かうき花のかぜ　好永 嵐山集 *sanshun no yakubyô ga uki hananokaze* yoshinaga 1651); *"The blossom-scattering / wind=flu-feeling [as when coming down with a sickness] is a purely / human disease"* (花ちらす風気は人の病哉　季治　夢見草 *hana chirasu kazake wa hito no yamai kana* kiji 1656). This last switches mid-sentence from trees to people and, in doing so, facetiously puts the onus on people for the wind, making it come from *their* minds if it were. Perhaps, pollinosis plays a role, too, for one old *ku* using an untranslatable pun on nose=blossom states, *"More apparent / in my nose than outside: / the cherry blossoms"* (花よりも鼻にあらはるゝ櫻哉　光有　毛吹草 *hana yori mo hana ni arawaruru sakura kana* kôyû 1645). It is *possible,* however, the *ku* describes a situation where the bloom is not so much visible to the eye as sensible to the nose of the poet. Let me add a qualification about these colds=winds I do not have space to example in this edition. The earliest *blossom=nose+cold* poems in Japanese are not about cherry blossoms but *plum*. The *ume* is particularly suitable, for it blooms two months earlier, when there are more runny noses, and it boasts an obvious nasal property: more visible blossom=nose hairs. Also, if prestigious colds are an invention of *haikai,* the cherry-cold idea, like so many things, goes back to *waka.*

山桜霞のころもあつく着てこの春だにも風つつまなん　西行 1190
yamazakura kasumi no koromo atsuku kite kono haru dani mo kaze tsutsumanan　saigyô

> *mountain cherries*
> *put on a thick robe*
> *of warm mist*
>
> *take care not to catch*
> *a cold this spring*

Saigyô. He really did care for his cherries. Of course, the *cold* is "a wind." As the cold-factor is vastly increased by the wind, the thick robe, which is not specifically "warm" in the original, would help. I suspect this *ku* was meant as a allegorical greeting for a friend, but the use of only the "wind" character by itself makes it probable that he really is addressing the trees, alone.

> 花寒し犬ものがれぬ嚔哉　一茶 1821
> *hana samushi inu mo nogarenu kusame kana* issa
> (blossoms cold dog even avoid-not sneeze!/'tis)

> cold blossoms
> even the dog cannot
> help sneezing!

Sickness is hard on poor people who cannot take advantage of it to spoil themselves like the wealthy. Issa, a poor man, may have so many *ku* about cherry colds because he wrote to keep his spirit up. Be that as it may, his range was wider than his predecessors. "Blossom-cold" (*hana samushi* – my "cold blossoms") is a rare phrase and probably intended to suggest "*nose*-cold." Dogs generally have cold noses (unlike cats who should have warm ones), so one wouldn't think *they* would sneeze here.

> さくら迄風（邪）引けりなかぢけ花　一茶
> *sakura made kaze hikikerina kajikebana* issa 1821
> (cherry until/even cold catching[emph.] runt-blossoms)

~~runt blossoms~~	even cherries	~~my cherry tree~~
~~don't even you cherry trees~~	catch cold, just look at these	~~don't you too catch cold!~~
~~catch a cold~~	runt blossoms	~~runt blossoms~~

If English have a word for deformed, or somewhat shriveled small blossoms I do not know it. My respondent felt my favorite reading was wrong. Still, Issa's warm feelings for the cherry tree translates well enough. Only Sôgi, centuries earlier, managed a warmer cold *ku* yet. To translate it, I'll change the "cold" to a kindred disease with a name more suggestive of the bad old wind, or *malas air:*

> たかいへはかせはよきけんをそ桜　宗祇
> *tagai e wa kaze wa yokiken osozakura* sôgi - 1502
> (mutual-to wind/cold-as-for, avoid-let's late-cherry/ies)

> late-blooming cherry
> let us both avoid
> influenza

A different translation of this *ku* appears in the *Late-Cherry* chapter. I do not mind more than one introduction of it, for I think haiku-lovers should know that someone with such a mindset was already around in the 15c. And, there is a *ku* by Shôha meaning either *"You can always / tell our day for blossom-viewing: / we all have colds,"* or, because "wind" also means "style/tradition," *"At our house / we have a fixed date / for blossom-viewing"* (定リの花見の日あり家の風　召波　春泥集 *sadamari no hanami no hi ari ie no kaze/fû* -1771). In the former case, it belongs here, in the latter, it does not, as it depicts a weird family that must search far and wide to find blossoms to fit their annual schedule.

垂れこめて春のゆくへも知らぬまに待ちし桜もうつろひにけり 藤原因香　古今集#80
tarekomete haru no yukue mo shiranu ma ni machishi sakura mo utsuroinikeri　kokinshû 905

under the weather

knowing nothing
of spring's fate, within
my bamboo curtain

a cherry branch tells me
i've missed the blossoms

knowing nothing
of spring's fate, within
my bamboo curtain

even the cherry blossoms
i longed for are no longer

Knowing not
where goes the spring, i hid
from the wind

in my room, with one branch
of bloom – we missed it all!

Strictly speaking, this poem may not belong here; the poet explained in a preface that he was holed up to *avoid* catching a cold – lit. to avoid the *wind* – because he was feeling under the weather (from what other ailment he does not specify, but I would suspect he had intestinal problems, for poor absorption from within leaves one helpless to germs from without), and his broken branch was starting to drop its petals. The second is closest to the original. In the first reading, I incorporated the branch into the poem, where it should have been all along, and that left no space for the "even" or the "longed for" (awaited), though my "missed" vaguely implies such. The last creates a sympathy between the poet and the branch.

~~~~~~

◎　御霊 An expl の sive spirit 吹き荒れ?　◎

"If people saw life revived in a blooming cherry, they also saw in the scattering petals, the explosive spirit of those who died before their time. Because of this, people thought scattering petals spread epidemics or caused natural disasters." I would add to these words of Ono Sawako (1992), the fact that cherries bloomed in flu season may have something to do with this. She adds there are temples that hold spirit-placating festivals/rites when the blossoms scatter to help send off the god/s of epidemic (I thought they were always hiding in the eaves!) and pray that the flowers on the rice plants do not follow suit and blow too quickly to bear well (早苗の花が桜の如く早く散らないという、お寺の祈りの実例教えて頂ければ、再版に加えます). "According to [anthropologist] Yamaguchi Masao, who draws on the opinion of 筑土鈴寛, "blossom" means "edge" [homophonic etymology is involved here] and blossoms "from old, bear, for Japanese, a dual image of death and rebirth, the double representation of divine sacrifice and revival. The blossoms' energizing power comes from its/our direct confrontation with death." (Ibid) Then, Ono goes on to recall flowers and funerals. *Remember Onitsura's skeletons in silk and Issa's terror?* If we associate blossoms with death, could we not, sitting *six-feet under* a cherry tree in full bloom, feel we are in our graves or coffins?

Return from the Viewing
花戻り
hana-modori

さむしろに銭置花の別れ哉　几董 アルス
samushiro ni zeni oku hana no wakare kana   kitô -1789
(mat-on coins/change place blossoms' departure/splitting!/'tis)

leaving change
on the mat, i depart
the blossoms

placing change
on her rush mat, i leave
my blossom

A rented mat? Small change for the poor or to banish bad spirits? A gambler who lost his last bet? Money for friends who gave him more *sake* than he gave them? Payment for someone's company? Or, is he mystically leaving it in thanks to the tree? In the last case, he also leaves his mat . . .

瓢竹庵より芳野へ旅立とて・此程を花に禮いふ別れ哉　はせを
kono hodo o hana ni rei iu wakare kana   bashô 1544 - 94
(this degree[obj] blossoms-to thanks say parting!/'tis)

for this stay
i thank the blossoms
as we leave!

A Bashô book (今栄蔵注) "translates" this poem (into modern Japanese) as follows: "For these past twenty days you have been of so much assistance, facing the flowers [I] bow my head and offer thanks, making this my greeting of departure." If you ask me, Bashô traveled too much and that made most of his poems *hellos* and *goodbyes*, that I, at least, could do without. The idea of thanking blossoms is clever because his preamble says he leaves his friend's "gourd-bamboo-hut" for Yoshino of cherry-blossom fame. While, Bashô and his friend doubtless enjoyed blossom-viewing, I suspect Bashô is thanking the women of the household for their work, though the annotators do not mention it.

なまなかにかへる家ありはなざかり 成美
namanaka ni kaeru ie ari hanazakari   seibi 1816
(incompletely returning-house-having bloom-acme)

leaving the full bloom

having a house
to return to, i am
afraid we do

blossoms yet
to fall but i've a home
to go back to

return

leaving in the peak
of the bloom, a house can be
a mixed blessing

Did Seibi know Issa's *ku* about having no home to return to and think to turn his own blessing into a lament? The "blossoms yet to fall" idea may be off. It could be the night-experience Seibi misses. The original only specifies that it was the acme of the bloom and he returns *namanaka-ni,* an adverb meaning *to do something without properly finishing it,* or *half-assedly.* The last is the best reading.

花のもと去かねて人に呼れけり 雅郊 拍掌十句
hananomoto sarikanete hito ni yobarekeri gakô 1777
(blossoms-about leave-cannot people-by called[emph.])

don't go-ers!

people calling me:
no easy matter leaving
the blossoms!

This *ku* is unique for treating the initial decision to leave the blossoms rather than the trip back. There is, however, an older *waka* –

けふのみと春をおもはぬ時だにも立つことやすき花のかげかは みつね 古今集#134
kyo nomi *to* haru o omowanu *toki* dani mo *tatsu koto* yasuki hana no kage ka wa   kokinshû 905

even on days	*even knowing*
before we must lament	*this is not the last*
spring's end	*day of spring*
is it any easier to leave	*leaving the bloomshade*
the shade of the bloom?	*is no easy thing*

This is clever, juxtaposing the end of spring and the end of a blossom-viewing. The approach is philosophical, while the previous *haikai* was on-the-spot realism. It is a representative difference.

だしぬくは誰が足跡ぞ花の陰 如湖 蘆別船
dashinuku wa daga ashiato zo hananokage joko 1694
(pull-out-as-for whose footprints?[+emph.] bloomshade)

who pulled out	whose footprints
before us? those footprints	in the bloomshade? who got
in the bloomshade	the jump on us?

Is this about someone returning from a viewing? *Perhaps.* Shiki's *Categorical* puts it right after this:

入相の踵に花を見せしよな 常矩 雑中
iriai no kubisu ni hana o miseshiyona [*miseshi yona?*] tsunenori ()
(vespers' heel/s to blossom/s[acc.] show do let's [or, shown night-work?])

the vesper peals	on the heels
so let's show the blossoms	of the vesper, new bloom:
to our heels	night-workers

This has me and my respondents stumped. Imagine the sun setting and the glow, perhaps reflected, lighting-up the blossoms one last time while the vesper chases out the viewers. But why show the blossoms *"to"* our heels? Or, could *yona* be short for *yonabe,* or "night-work? (専門家、ご意見は？)

夕暮はもとの旅也花の山　一茶 1810
yûgure wa moto no tabi nari hananoyama   issa
(evening-as-for original trip becomes blossom-mountain)

cherry mountain:	at nightfall	cherry mountain
at dusk we find ourselves	it's the same trip down	at dusk, again, i'm back
where we began	mount cherry	on the same road

Neither sadder nor wiser, but happily exhausted, the poet leaves "blossom-mountain," which, as one might expect from a park, has but one way in and out. Maybe that last point is Issa's point. I felt like writing "the same *damn* trip" for the second reading, but, who knows, maybe Issa enjoyed the familiar.

僧寺に帰る月夜の櫻哉　正巴
sô tera ni kaeru tsukiyo no sakura kana shôha ()
(priest/s temple/s-to return/s moon[lit]night's cherry!/'tis)

monks return	a full moon
to their temple, the moon	on the blossoms, monks
full on the cherry	heading back

If it were fall, monks on such a night would definitely view the Light of the Law, the moon. But, we wonder (and I include Japanese who might not know in the "we") if that is so on this Spring night.

帰るさの夕日櫻や胸に杖　巴人＝宋阿 俳諧古選
kaerusa no yuhizakura ya mune ni tsue   hajin = soa -1742
(returning's evening-sun's-cherry/ies!/: chest-on/to cane/staff)

going home

a last gaze
at the sunset blossoms
cane to chest

Japanese canes tend to be more like staffs. When old men are tired, they rest their chins against them or their breasts and become tripods. I imagine Hajin as an old-fashioned still-camera. A caption to the poem in one collection suggests the poet was returning from a temple rather than a blossom-viewing but, then again, blossom-viewing may have been his reason for visiting the temple. There may be a light pun on the pink-petaled fire-cherry (*hizakura*), for fire burned in the breast.

帰路・花の事いひ／\もとる山路哉　士朗
hana no koto ii ii modoru yamaji kana   shirô - 1813
(blossom-things saying saying return mountain path 'tis)

talking blossoms	a mountain trail
as we head back down	blossom talk, talk, talk,
the mountain path	as we walk home

花の嵐立ち返る我か後吹く 欄更 アルス
hana no arashi tachikaeru waga ushiro fuku   rankô 1726-99
(blossom-gale returning my back/behind[me] blows)

a gale of petals
rises up behind me
as i turn to leave

heading back
petals blowing up a storm
behind me

At first I imagined petals chasing down after the poet but, on second thought, I recalled the nature of a mountain, a place where a storm can rage a hundred yards further up, as if it were another world.

見かへればうしろを覆ふ櫻かな 樗良
mi-kaereba ushiro o ôu sakura kana   chora -1780
(looking back behind covering[pun=*chase*] cherry!)

looking over my shoulder
all behind was covered
in cherry blossoms

trans. blyth

pink behind

looking back
a world plastered with
cherry petals

looking back
cherry petals cover up
my trail back

Blyth's comment: "The poet had a feeling of exultation [exhilaration?], of luxuriousness, as though bathing in cherry-flowers. Like the Jabberwocky, "He chortled in his glee." (*Haiku* v2 spring).

うかれけり花の追風裾につく 成美　　　　　後から吹来る櫻／\哉 一茶 1805
ukarekeri hana no oikaze suso ni tsuku seibi 1816   *ushiro kara fukikuru sakura sakura kana* issa
(giddy[emph.]blossoms-tailwind hem-to stick)   (behind-from blowing-come cherry cherry!)

still high, we
descend with blossom wind
on our skirts

sakura! sakura!
the cherry petals blowing
up from behind

I was happy to leave the concept of *ukare* or *floated*, i.e. being *high* or in *heat*, that is so hard to translate, behind with the chapters on the *Full Bloom* and *Inebriation*. Issa's *ku* doesn't specify that the poet is returning from blossom-viewing. It could also be *"High as kites / a tail-wind from the blossoms / on our skirts"* and mean the party is proceeding from one stand of blooming cherry trees to another. But simplicity favors the return. The second *ku* is one of several by Issa repeating *sakura, sakura* like a cherry song or songs that eventually metamorphosed into Japan's best known song.

ふり帰り／\けり山櫻 吟江 心の花
furikaerikeri kaerikeri yamazakura ginkô 1780
(turning=looking back[emph.] returning[emph] mt. ch.)

looking back
on the road back from
mountain cherries

The original seamlessly flows from looking back (repeatedly) to going back. Still, it is less interesting than a *ku* about looking back at the *moon* on the way from moon-viewing (another book).

身にそはぬ心は花のかへさ哉　宗春 三籟
mi ni sowanu kokoro wa hana no kaesa kana sôshun
(body-to accompany-not heart-as-for blossom-return!/)

花に気のとろけて戻る夕日哉　杉風
hana ni ki no torokete modoru yûhi kana sanpû
(blossoms-to spirit melted return evening sun!/)

    returning from
the blossoms my heart
      lags my body

    the sun setting
i return, mind melted
     into blossoms

The first *ku* (1734) and is a haiku-length Saigyô-like concept. The blend of melted *chi* and "evening sun" in the second *ku* (-1732) is masterful. One thinks of the way sunlight diffuses as the sun sinks. As detailed in ch. 30, *Catharsis*, blossom-viewing takes the edge off the viewer.

酒浴て帰る山路や花吹雪　士髪　新選
sake abite kaeru yamaji ya hanafubuki shiyu? 1773
(*sake* showered return mt-path!/: cherry blizzard)

両の手に花と酔人や山戻り 也有 -1783
ryô no te ni hana to yoibito ya yamamodori yayû
(both hands-in blossom/s & drunk!/: mt. return)

    sloshed with wine
coming down the mountain road:
     a blossom blizzard

    down the mountain
a blossom in each hand
     one happy drunk

Yayû may be drunk with sprigs of cherry blossom in each hand, but "blossoms in both hands" is idiomatic for a man who is in male heaven with a beauty on each arm, so we might better imagine a drunk man fortunate enough to have two women helping him get home, or a woman + bloom-spray.

花を見て帰るうしろや朧月　熊二 花櫻帖
hana o mite kaeru ushiro ya oborozuki yuji ()
(blossoms[obj] viewing return behind: hazymoon)

帰るさに松風きゝぬ花の山　集兆
kaerusa ni matsukaze kikinu hananoyama shûchô ()
(returntrip-on pinewind hear blossom-mountain)

    there, behind us!
as we leave the blossoms,
      the hazy moon

    on the way back
i hear the wind in the pine
     cherry mountain

The hazy moon is the perfect symbol for a hangover, not just the poet's but that of Spring, itself. With the second *ku*, I was tempted to write *"pine-wind"* to echo the original or *"I hear the moaning pine"* to reflect the hint of the possible allusion (spring is ending and before long fall will come), though awareness of the evergreen may, rather, prove the poet has, for better or worse, regained his sobriety.

鰒の夜に似たる花見の戻り哉　蝶羽
fugu no yo ni nitaru hanami no modori kana chôu -1741
(blowfish-night-to resemble blossom-viewing return!/'tis)

   the trip back from
blossom-viewing: like night
    after blowfish?

   like the night after
eating puffer, returning
    from a *hanami*

Eating blowfish (swellfish, globefish, puffer) carries the risk of death. Metaphysically speaking, so does blossom-viewing. On the trip back the poet is besides himself. Or, does the poet allude to the warmth gained from eating blowfish which was prescribed for snowy weather, resembling a petal blizzard?

return

寝たままでもどりかけはや山桜 失名 (御免!)
neta mama de modorigakebaya yamazakura (lost name)
(slept/sleeping-justlikethat return-would mountain-cherry)

    i'd like to sleep   fast asleep   i'd like to make
  through the trip back   all the way back   the trip back sleeping
    mountain cherry   mountain cherry   mountain cherry

Unless the poet is a somnambulist, he'd return in a sedan box or a cheaper net hung from a pole shouldered by two men. I once fell off a cliff after downing a litter of vodka in a half-hour while bondancing after finding I had no chance with someone I had a crush on for a decade and didn't come to until the next morning, in a hospital, minus some skin but otherwise fine. I recall blinking my eyes and thinking "I could have *died* and not even noticed it!" That is why I put the sleep *ku* after the blowfish.

さつとちるはなを拍子やもどりあし 成美
satto chiru hana o byôshi ya modoriashi seibi - 1816
(pouring[mimesis] falling-blsms beat!/?/: returning-feet [prob. this ↓ one])

    a stream of petals   to the rhythm
  syncopated by the beat   of petals falling our feet
    of returning feet   take us home

すさましや花見戻りの橋の音　子規
susamashi ya hanami modori no hashi no oto shiki
(terrifying!/: blossom-viewing return's bridge's sound)

    thunderous noise!
  the bridge back from
    blossom-viewing

Remember the thunder of people pouring down the ramps of a stadium after a game? Add to that the greater exhaustion of the body and senses of someone who has spent a day or more partying outside, ie. blossom-viewing, and the echo of those feet changes into something I will not try to describe.

櫻狩かへさは野への菫哉 宗祇 老葉   砂道となるや花見の戻足 寄任 夢見草
sakuragari kaesa wa nobe no sumire kana sôgi   *sunamichi to naru ya hanami no modoriashi* kinin
(cherry-hunting return-as-for meadow violet/s!/?)   (sandpath becomes: blssm-vwng return-feet 1656)

    cherry hunting: the road back
  & on our return trip,   from blossom-viewing
    meadow violets!   is pure sand!

Most blossom-viewing was in the foothills. Serious mountain cherry lovers, like serious hunters might go further back in the hills. The return trip was long enough to warrant diversion. The idea of noticing a small flower close to the ground after viewing clouds of blossoms is good. I cannot help wondering what Bashô, who noticed the same violets by a mountain road, thought of this *ku*. With respect to the second *ku*, I imagine the green grass sprouts of spring were trampled down on the way up and the pink cherry petals ground into dust on the way down. But, I may be missing something. A sandy road could have been *chosen* for how it amplifies a small amount of moon and starlight. Or, it may even be a clever way to speak of going whoring, for beaches with clams were called sand-paths.

花に暮れて我が家遠き野道哉 蕪村
hana ni kurete waga ie tôki nomichi kana buson
(blossoms-with dusked, my home far field-road!/'tis)

after blossom-viewing

viewing 'til dusk
this path through a field
far from home

staying 'til dark
my home is far away
a rural path

with the bloom
until dark now i walk
a grassy path

Buson could not resist staying long enough to enjoy the changing shades of the bloom as the sun set. So now, his pupils open wide, he walks or rides a rural road, alone. Who can not remember a similar experience, generally in childhood? That uncanny eye for nostalgia, not the much ballyhooed fact that Buson, "as a painter," could create a pretty picture, marks many if not most of his best *ku*. Not all of his *ku* have it: *"Blossom dusk / now it's back to my home / the capital!"* (花にくれぬ我住む京に帰去来 *hana ni kurenu waga sumu kyô ni kaerinan* (1715-83)). Be that as it may, both translations suffer from Englishes inability to "dusk with" or "by" the blossoms in English. We can *drink* with them or *sit* with them but we cannot *dusk* with them.

花そなきかさして春や帰るらん 心敬
hana zo naki kazashite haru ya kaeruran shinkei -1475
(blossoms [+exclam] not/none! adorned spring! returns [+excl])

重箱に入てもどるや山ざくら 梢風尼
jûbako ni irete modoru ya yamazakura shôfû-ni -1758
(multi-layer-box-in putting return!/: mountain-cherry/ies)

the blossoms!
spring has gone home
wearing them

putting them into
the lunch-boxes we return
mountain cherries

Shinkei was generally very dark. But this makes us smile. Blossom don't die. Spring *wears* them and stores them for next year. Why let Spring leave with them? I write cherries for the *sakura* in nun Shôfû's *ku* above because I *like* to imagine seedlings, but it is probably some twigs with blossoms or handfuls of petals. Feel free to change the last line to "mountain cherry *petals*."

花戻り鞍に見えたる嵐哉 正川 鞭随筆
hanamodori kura ni mietaru arashi kana shôsen 1759
(blossom-return saddle-in visible gale!/'tis)

pink traces

just back from
the blossoms, his saddle
shows the gale

Here and there in the nooks and crannies of the saddle, petals carried down from the mountain tell about the cherry blossom "gale."

花の戸に脱ぎもそろはぬ草履かな 多代女
hana no to ni nugi mo sorowanu zôri kana tayojo
(blossom-gate-at removing[emph] match-not sandals)

花衣ぬぐやまつはる紐いろ／＼ 久女
hanagoromo nugu ya matsuwaru himo iroiro hisajo
(blossom-clothing strip: encircling strings variety)

removing sandals
at a blossom lodge, i see
they do not match

undressing after
blossom-viewing, so many
strings about me

Japanese are usually good at neatly arranging shoes by the door. Usually, this is something the host, host's wife or servant does. They are sometimes put into stands or drawers as we might do for hats or coats or umbrellas, but it is more common for them to be turned around and placed to the side of the entrance. If I am not mistaken, one or both of the sandals Tayojo (1775-1865) wore home was not hers. This could happen because people under a large tree would be sitting (and dancing) on a mat with their sandals set outside the mat on the ground. Her *ku* is a retrospective of a wild blossom-viewing. I found the second *ku* by Hisajo (-1946) in an anthology of 350 excellent *ku* on "play" (遊). Were it in hand earlier, I would have given it a half-dozen translations and a paragraph. When one is exhausted, it is no easy thing to undo the knots on the various (probably variously colored) strings related to belts/sashes on formal kimono. A bra-strap or getting unzipped is nothing compared to what Japanese women faced. *Back from blossom-viewing, belt after belt after belt, string after string . . .*

花戻り隣に風呂の有夜哉 春洲 花櫻帖
hanamodori tonari ni furo no aru yo kana shunshû ()
(blossom-returning neighbors-too bath's have night 'tis)

back from bloom
my neighbor has a bath
boiling tonight

blossom return
on a night my neighbor
takes a bath

Is the poet allowed to share the bath? Do the splashes of the pails of water on the bathers (they wash and rinse outside the tubs before climbing in) echo with memories of petal showers? Or are the neighbors bathing outside (it could be out in front in plain view) with great abandon after having come back from blossom-viewing themselves? I took license with this translation. There is no "boiling" and no "on" in the original.

居風呂に後夜聞く花の戻り哉 蕪村
sueburo ni goya kiku hana no modori kana buson -1783
(be/stay/sitting-bath-in after-[mid]night's return 'tis)

after the blossoms
i sit in a bath and hear
the wee-hour bells

in my bath tub
hearing wee-hour bells
after the bloom

Have we seen the following *ku* by Buson? *"Coming to the blossoms / I end up taking a nap: / talk about leisure!"* (花に来て花にいねぶるいとまかな *hana ni kite hana ni ineburu itoma kana*). Does that practice and the long trip back (#64-29/30) help explain why Buson bathes to the bells marking the start of the last third of the night? The bath, like the time, is more specific in the original. A *sueburo* is a bottom-burner, a primitive, or should I say, direct arrangement where the stoking hole is right below the tub. I once used one like that. If you have long arms, you can reach out of the tub and shove in wood or paper as you please. Doing so adds to the enjoyment of the bath. We cannot pull ourselves up by our bootstraps, but, with proper engineering, we can warm our own asses.

65

Sundry Cherries
雑桜

This irregular chapter will hold some some themes that were too small to warrant chapters and some haiku I failed to fit into other chapters which I just couldn't toss away, perhaps never to be Englished.

Cherry in Sack-Cloth
墨染櫻
sumizome-zakura

筆にこそ墨染櫻かばさくら 徳元
fude ni koso sumizomezakura kabazakura   tokugen 1558-1647
(brush-for espec. sumi[ink]-dyed-cherry, birch-cherry)

right for painting!
ink-dyed-cherries and
birch-cherries

As noted before, Taigi (-1772) once opined: "All these names! / if you ask me *sakura* / is good enough" (# 0-7), but in early *haikai*, there were never enough names to play with. While *sumi*-dyed material was a grey shade and identified with mourning and/or otherworldly bonzes (the English "sack-cloth" comes to mind) here, the name evokes the black *sumi* ink, as the birch-cherry (See Kuitert. We will not even try to identify it; suffice it to say the current one is different) does paper, and Tokugen quips that with those two at hand a writer or artist – the same ink was used to write and to paint – was ready to go.

硯箱絵も墨染の櫻哉 光家 犬子
suzuribako e mo sumizome no sakura kana   kôka 1633
(inkstone box-in/on too ink-dyed-cherry!/?/'tis)

and the picture
on my ink-stone box?
sumi-dyed cherry

The ink-stone (*suzuri*) is a piece of stone with the hollow for water/ink and a slope for rubbing the ink-stick against. The play on the name, as with Tokugen's poem, is shallow if not ridiculous when we learn where this blossom's name comes from:

ふかくさののべの桜し心あらばことし許はすみぞめにさけ　かむつけのみねを　古今集832
fukakusa no nobe no sakura shi kokoro araba kotoshi bakari wa sumizome ni sake kokinshû (9c)

the year chancellor horikawa died

if you can feel,
then, cherries of the field
of fukakusa,

this year, this spring alone,
may thy bloom be ash-grey

Japanese nobility had a long tradition of making poetic demands upon nature. The elements (clouds, wind, etc) received most of these demands, but occasionally members of the biosphere were addressed. The *Kokinshû* poem before this one asks the Fukakusa mountain to vent some smoke for the recently interned chancellor (also called Fujiwara no Mototsune). Two poems back, a lamentation for a different member of the Fujiwara clan buried near Shirakawa, literally "white-river," has an old Chinese saw, the poet's bloody tears, turning the river red, and suggests that its name will no longer do. Cross these two poems and funereal grey blossoms seem very logical. Kuitert, who loosely translates, *"Oh, cherries of Fukakusa's fields / You must lament his death / Your blossom will be gloomy gray this spring,"* writes "the poetical artifice lies in the connection of the gloominess of the place ["deserted and shaggy" fields] to the sharply contrasting bright beauty of cherries in flower." I wonder. He continues, "the poet is not suggesting that the cherries should change color, nor that they are black; rather it was his wish that their bloom would be felt by all people as a gloomy reminder of the uncertainty of life." (*Japanese Flowering Cherries*). Though the color in this poem is usually mistranslated as "black" – two of two I've seen so far by literary scholars who should know better! – Kuitert does not do it, so it is strange that *black* remains in his explanation. Knowing the way places and things that were poeticized could move people for generations – Japanese landscape shares something with that of the Navajo in that respect – the poet may indeed have hoped to turn the cherries of Fukakusa into a long-lasting *memento mori*, but I hate to see his subtlety defined in terms of "not" this or that, or "rather" this or that. Kuitert is more helpful in showing what the real blossom *is*. I had imagined greyish petals, but he points out that most of the alleged Sumizome cherry trees are not that for "appealing names were sometimes applied more than one time to unrelated cherries" and that only ones going by that name today have blossoms with very dark pink hearts.

ちる事を知て墨染櫻哉　雁立 新選
chiru koto o shitte sumizome sakura kana garyû 1773
(falling-thing[acc] knowing ink-dyed cherry/ies!/?/'tis)

knowing they'll fall,
they dye themselves ash-grey:
sumizome cherry

sumizome blossoms
do they so dye themselves
knowing they'll die?

Here, like the two *ku* heading this section, the name is taken, but it is not taken in vain. This is clever for shifting the desired concern of the blossoms for the death of a human in the classical conceit – which, popularized in *kabuki* was well known – to a more natural (?) concern for the self. Since Shinto/shamanism is more likely to espouse white robes to die in, I think of this cherry as Buddhist.

捨る身也墨染櫻花もうし 治好 太夫櫻?
suteru mi nari sumizomezakura hana mo ushi jikô 1680?
(abandon self becoming ink-dyed cherries: blossoms too depressing)

***sumizome* cherry blossoms**

the gray of one
who leaves this world: imagine
a sad flower!

"Leaves" *means* "abandons" (the count demanded it). Does this evoke the women of a defeated clan, forced to become nuns, or a specific incident? Since the ancient poem only asked for the cherries to bloom grey for *one* Spring, the reader might wonder where such *ku*, ostensibly about real plants, come from. Are the poets pretending the name of the cherry – for the tree's descendents are said to live – is reflected in the reality? I have seen an honest-to-goodness grey-looking blossom on the internet . . .

Fire Cherry

火櫻のごよじ／＼や花の風　近之 洗濯物
hizakura no goyoji goyoji ya hana no kaze　kinshi 1666
(fire-cherry's 'caution!' 'caution!'/: blossom-wind)

danger! danger!　　　fire-cherries bloom　　　*danger! danger!*
the fire-cherry spreads!　exercise caution, caution!　a blossom wind fans
a blossom wind　　　　a blossom wind　　　　the fire-cherries

The fire-cherry is all or part of the name for varieties with bright pink cherry blossoms and/or red leaves. While the *hi* in 13 of 14 *hizakura* in Shiki's *Categorical* is written as "fire = 火," and the *ku* rely heavily upon pyrrhic puns, and the oldest example in my OJD, a *waka,* uses "fire-cherry" (火さくら) and chuckles at the lack of smoke where there is fire, dictionaries and books about flowering cherries today only admit the other *hi* = 緋, meaning "scarlet." This discrepancy is odd but welcome.

ぱっと散はそのまゝ花火桜哉 信安 嵐山集
patto chiru wa sonomama hana-bi/hi-zakura kana shinan 1651
(suddenly fall-as-for that-like-just blossoming/<u>fire</u>works-<u>cherry</u> 'tis/!/?)

! kabloom !

exploding petals　　　　　　　　　blowing bloom
call it a "cherry bomb"　　　　　the fireworks of nature
igni-cerasus　　　　　　　　　a fire-cherry

Because "-works" must come *after* the *fire,* we cannot pun from the explosive display to the cherry, as in Japanese. The Japanese, on the other hand, cannot speak of a "cherry bomb." As true with many translations in this book, we have lost one and gained one. I hope you will forgive me for both.

いなづまのやどり木なりし櫻哉　其角
inazuma no yadorigi narishi sakura kana　kikaku
(ricewife=lightning's lodge/roost is, cherry! -1707)

<blockquote>
the cherry tree
this is the real home
of lightning
</blockquote>

<blockquote>
it is a tree
which puts up lightning
the cherry
</blockquote>

<blockquote>
the rice-wife
lightning resides within
a cherry tree
</blockquote>

<blockquote>
cherry trees
the spirit of lightning
dwells here
</blockquote>

This is *not* specifically a fire-cherry *ku* (unless there is a caption saying so that I have not seen). We have already met Sakuyahime, the goddess of the mountain, cherry and fire. We have also mentioned the assertion that the spirit of the grain dwells in the cherry. Kikaku would seem to fuse these concepts, for *lightning* is literally "rice-mate/wife" (*ina-zuma*). And, speaking of lightning –

花の陰よい雷といふも有り　一茶
hana no kage yoi kaminari to iu mo ari　issa 1807
(bloom-shade: good?/evening? thunder says also/even are)

<blockquote>
in the bloomshade
i hear someone speak
of "good thunder"
</blockquote>

<blockquote>
in the bloomshade
i hear someone predict
evening thunder
</blockquote>

I first thought this meant the gentle thunder accompanying heat-lightning, but have been told such was out of season. Could the *yoi*-as-evening allude to blossom guards yelling at people to go home at night?

散る花を又吹上る舞台哉　淵水　小弓俳諧集
chiru hana o mata fukiagaru butai kana　ensui 1699
(falling blossoms[obj] again blow-raise stage!/'tis)

<blockquote>
fallen blossoms
on the dance-stage once
again blown up
</blockquote>

There are many types of cherries I missed, as there are many good *ku* I missed. I hope to catch them if/when *Cherry Blossom Epiphany* is expanded into three separate books. At that time, I would also expand the natural history to include things the botanist might overlook, such as the taste of cherry blossoms and leaves, the distance petals fly under various conditions, etc.. Please send me glosses (poetry or science). If I use yours, you will get credit and, if you wish, a mention of *your* work. Good illustrations (+rights) would be a godsend. I am particularly eager to find pictures of wild *hanami*.

花みんとうへけん人もなき宿の桜は去年の春そさかまし

大江喜言　新古今集　七六三

Postscript

i

The Higher Mind's outgrowing the Barbarian,	I dread this like the dentist, rather more so:
It's hardly thought hygienic now to kiss;	To me Art's subject is the human clay,
The world is surely turning vegetarian;	And landscape but a background to a torso;
And as it grows too sensitive for this.	All Cézanne's apples I would give away
It won't be long before we find there is	For one small Goya or a Daumier.
A Society of Everybody's Aunts	I'll never grant a more than minor beauty
For the Prevention of Cruelty to Plants.	To pudge or pilewort, petty-chap or pooty.

In a stanza buried deep within his *"Letter To Lord Byron,"* Auden, who " . . . at the age of twenty-nine / Just read *Don Juan* and . . . found it fine," wrote something we might call the Classic position on poetry. It is on the right above, and immediately follows the stanza on the left, which itself follows others expressing his distaste for *"This interest in waterfalls and daisies, / Excessive love for the non-human faces"* that he connects with the popularity of Einstein, Jeans and Eddington. *Heaven forbid*, Auden laments: *"The humblest is acquiring with facility / A Universal-Complex sensibility."* One wonders if he read Lowell's *Soul of the East* and, if he did, what glosses he may have scribbled on the margins of the paragraphs about blossom-lovers quoted at length in the *Foreword* of Book 2.

Auden was no fool. The verse preceding the above two contains a warning for the environmental movement, ecological consciousness, or whatever your preferred term is, that still holds true: *"For now we've learnt we mustn't be so bumptious / We find the stars are one big family, / And send out invitations for a scrumptious / Simple, old-fashioned, jolly romp with tea / To any natural objects we can see. / We can't, of course, invite a Jew or Red / But birds and nebulae will do instead."*

Auden was right. Who were bigger naturists than the Nazis? We must not allow love for the non-human to replace concern for our fellow species. But he got the larger picture wrong. Unless one can prove that focusing on human beauty and romance translates into a more progressive, which is to say, *kind*, society, it is ridiculous to blame the nature-loving "Higher Mind" alone for prejudice/cowardice.

I hate to criticize one who writes so well and, admittedly, "simplified the facts to be emphatic." But, I think *I know* what is happening: in Auden's day, English schoolboys had to read more Wordsworth than they cared for. Like Bashô, he is just too calm, too subtle for the young (and, not a little of the Nature poetry filling school readers on both sides of the Atlantic at the turn of the century was so lame that Wordsworth seems thrilling). Bright children naturally soured on nature. And Auden, at the time he wrote the poem, was "twenty-nine," an age when many of us are drawn to *human* beauty (faces and bodies) and bored by everything else. Perhaps, the higher mean level of testosterone in whites (and blacks) makes this *more* true for the Occident than for the Sinosphere, but we must remember that early Japanese poetry was *also* overwhelmingly romantic (or, as was true in the Classic world, *erotic*), so it might be argued that "our" way is not the one needing explanation.

The standard explanation for what seems to the heirs of Rome a puzzling if not unnatural love for nature is that China was so advanced a civilization that sensitive souls were forced to escape from the overwhelmingly human world by heading to the hills and, because these men were literati, they created a tradition of nature poetry unknown to the Barbarians (Occidentals) whose socio-economic system was backward and could only support a low population density. Well, we finally caught up in the eighteenth and nineteenth centuries and Auden, self-proclaimed barbarian *and* humanist, did not approve.

Once, the Mediterranean had a high population density and a fair amount of nature poetry (at least, an appreciation for singing insects), but it failed to keep pace with the cult of the body, the Classic Nude that to this day marks our civilization as indelibly as the cross of Christianity, that, itself often boasts . . . a naked male! Could the degradation of the habitat (the bare hills once covered with trees) have made escape to Nature unattractive, while the limited resources in that increasingly barren land favored war-making and the muscle-worship that accompanies it (How remarkable that Islam came to be so militant yet never worshipped muscle!). But I am no more convinced by an environmental explanation than I am by the testosterone. I just offer them as hypotheses to emphasize how strange we *all* are. My pet hypothesis is that the difference comes from *the tools by which we write.* Using a brush of the type used in the Sinosphere, rather than a stiff stylus or pen changes the sensitivity of the student so that the love for nature generally not felt by Occidentals until they reach their fifties is felt at an age young enough to influence one's poetic and pictorial sense. More precisely, it comes from the union of the pleasure felt repeating a motor-function learned with difficulty (what Konrad Lorenz's teacher called *funktionlust*) with the abstract yet material beauty of the characters both in form and grain. The pleasure of such brushwork can be as intense as that of love-making or musical improvisation. One must actually practice writing with a brush for a long time to fully experience that joy, but, my argument is that *the fruit of that joy may be eaten by partying under the flowering cherry.*

ii

Fixing the format of this book was easy. Poverty decided for me. Without the money to pay for offset printing or time to waste searching for an agent able to reach a decent publisher (assuming they still exist), I had to settle on one large un-illustrated tome of 740 pgs., the limit for my POD printer, which, I might add, miraculously requires no money upfront. I would have liked not one, but *three* well-illustrated volumes, but even if said printer could handle color (at present only possible for the cover: they just changed and can do it, but it is too late for me!), pursuing copyrights, preparing pictures and whatnot without an assistant – in this cruel economy, no one works for free – would have left me with no time to write, much less edit myself. Illustrated books require wealth.

I tell myself that avoiding color illustrations is good, for it creates less pollution, and that I perform a service by sticking to print alone in a world buried in pictures,. Yet, pictures *do* enrich the reading experience and what you see on the internet will add nothing to global warming unless you insist on printing everything out. So, search *cherry blossoms*, *blossom-viewing*, *sakura* or *hanami* – romanized Japanese is fine – on the Image-search pages of Google *et alia* and you will find scores of thumbnails. You will be *astounded* by the huge trees supported by veritable groves of crutches. There are whole books with nothing but beloved old cherry trees in Japanese, and this is reflected in such photos. The crowds of viewers on blue tarps or red cloth (all too rare now) should also catch your eye. However, if you want a thorough overview of the types of cherry trees, you really need to see Kuitert's book, without which I would not have found the *Shirotae*, a relatively small white-blossomed cherry tree with more horizontal spread than I have ever seen in a tree that is not a parasite reaching out for a host, and its opposite, the *Amanogawa*, or Milky Way, with branches that seem to cascade *up* into the sky.

Thanks to Kuitert, I also learned that there were more flowering cherries in the world, especially in Europe than I imagined, though I had already happened upon hundreds in Edinburgh, a delightful town of hills and dancing shadows where no rain ever falls (it always *flies* sideways) and people disciplined enough not to trouble others yet free enough to respond to wit coming from a stranger with the same. But, even in this paradise, I found a number of impediments to proper blossom-viewing. First, there were flowers planted below most of the trees where people should have been sitting! Second, trees with or without these multi-colored flowers clashing with the cherry blossoms, were often surrounded by an even more people-unfriendly device, a fence! Third, the otherwise sensible Scots insisted upon drinking in smoke-filled bars rather than out in the clean air. Now, if this be the case in a country which features a distillery on one of its paper bills, imagine the situation in drier countries! In parts of Usania, where individualism and personal responsibility is always preached but seldom practiced or allowed, one risks arrest merely for being tipsy in public! An organization might encourage the Japanese Ambassador to prime the pump by taking advantage of his or her diplomatic immunity to spread out a mat and sit and drink openly in the bloomshade. It could instruct mimes to carry water-filled bottles of booze and pretend they are drunk in parks. It could find brave politicians to introduce bills (or add-ons to bills) making the space below a cherry tree in bloom a sanctuary of the spirit, where all laws against drinking in public are null and void. Perhaps, this might be achieved most rapidly by linking up with the Society of a certain dead but immortal poet. But why stop with Scotland? Couldn't the world's largest drink manufacturer, Suntory, start an international blossom-viewing organization to help establish the conditions for real *hanami* outside of Japan?

I have mixed feelings, however, about creating *hanami* almanacs one might consult to go blossom-viewing, for I feel we *already* gallivant about far too much. Better to find your cherry blossoms – or apple or pear – nearby. And, when you go there, remember the advice I gave earlier: *Do not just walk. Sit under the blossoms and drink. If possible, do it on a clear blue sky-day, before lunch.* If you have not yet experienced the same love for the natural world you have surely felt for a human of whatever sex attracts you, doing this will help take you there. If you have, all the better: this will be your second consummation. If the blossoms are not within walking distance and you reside in an underdeveloped country (such as most of Usania) without drinker-friendly public transportation, be sure to go more than one day so you and your friend/s can take turns driving. Over thirty years ago, while a student at Georgetown (BS International Politics) in Washington DC, I saw the cherries blooming by the Reflecting Pool and thought they were pretty and all, but, in retrospect, *it was not enough*. So long as we remain on our feet we never meet the blossoms. They insist we *sit down, drink up and stay put.*

iii

Someday, I would like to follow the Northing cherry blossoms in Japan, or, if it turns out there are enough around, in Usania or Europe. I would carry with me colored "sand" of different sizes and make pictures on the ground, sit by them and play a 1-3-stringed instrument of my invention. After making the pictures, the best of which might be photographed, I would re-sort the sand using my sieves – or, perhaps, one adjustable sieve – and move on. Ideally, I will have a wife and child by then. Though, I would not need the money, I would collect it for my music and my pictures, together with the cherry petals, using a hat or, better yet, a tin cup that goes "pling!" with each coin.

> Then the petals fall. What was a nuptial veil becomes a winding-sheet, covering the sod as with winter's winding-sheet of snow, destined itself to disappear, and the tree is nothing but a common cherry-tree once more. Percival Lowell **The Soul of the Far East** (1888)

Waking-up, i see ◎ *my one-man blossom-viewing left* ◎ *writing on the wall* – Chisen (misc.)

朝起や独花見の壁訴訟　千川

雑

The "writing on the wall" is literally a *direct appeal*, or suit, for *what* no one knows, and the *ku* could also mean:
< *i wake to write / graffitti: my one-man / blosssom-viewing* > – . . . whatever *that* means.

Bibliographilia

よい物の果もさくらの紅葉かな　塵生
yoi mono no hate mo sakura no momiji kana jinsei ()
(good thing's end even cherry's red[autumnal]-leaves!/?/'tis)

                blossom-viewing
           and now the cherry trees'
                 colored leaves!

beauty ends   sometimes beauty
like this, too: a cherry's   comes to a good end, fall
leaves in fall   cherry leaves

               after such beauty
          an encore? the cherry tree's
                 autumn colors

I have gotten almost as much enjoyment from the leaves of cherry trees as the bloom. The colors are not so bright as sugar maple, but their combination is more interesting by far. Unlike blossoms, *this* beauty is not found in the mass but the individual leaf. The poet probably knew this, but the *ku* does not give such detail. It is classic *haikai*: the *yoi* means *good=beautiful* and the *mo* or "also/even" alludes to the stereotypical end of beauty, which, we have seen already: Komachi's skull with a leaf of sawgrass growing through an orbit. Yet, it *also* has a plain fact many have missed.

Debts & Public Access.

I *first* found about 50% of the *ku* in this book in Shiki's twelve volume *Categorical* (see below), but owing to the great number of *ku* in it, *eventually* found about 70-80% of all the *ku* in it. My other main sources are given in the descending order of my debt (the guestimated number of *ku* found in them), however, number does not tell the whole story. I owe a special debt to the late Kato Ikuya for his book *Kokkei Haiku Daizen* because it gives *the date of publication* of hundreds of old haikai books. Most of the moderate success I had dating *ku* by poets *not* found in the *Haikujinmei-jiten* Kikuchi Shinichi was kind enough to give me, I owe to Kato's index. I owe an equal debt to Takazawa Yoshikazu for putting hundreds of thousands of *haikai* and *haiku* online = making them searchable. While I had already found most of the *haikai* in his online collection in Shiki's *Categorical*, I had not yet typed in the Japanese, so I was able to copy and paste them, saving dozens, possibly hundreds of hours of time (otherwise lost searching and typing). In English, as far as I know, only R.H. Blyth and David G. Lanoue have translated a substantial number of *ku* on cherry blossoms. I cite Blyth more than Lanoue because all of Lanoue's are by Issa (see his fine, searchable site) who, as it happens, is my *forte* (I own all his works and have 2,000 unpublished pages of writing on him). ⓒMost help with interpreting *ku* came from Prof. Kikuchi a few years ago, from contributors to my more recent online *Haiku Mondôjô* set up by Tenki and, at the last moment but far from least, from Masako, who deserves to be the *first* mentioned. ~~~~~~~~~~ I would have loved to have read articles in J-STOR to cite more scholars and rummage the enormous collection of British Poetry for comparison-sake, but the Miami Dade Public Library system had neither. Likewise, for the large data-banks of Japanese literature that require University ID's and the insanely expensive CD's publishers sell to wealthy libraries. *No access.* I have encountered helpful librarians, but have yet to find a data base kind enough to make an exception for the poor unaffiliated scholar, no matter how deserving he might be. I did manage to borrow a few books from World-cat, but it was time-consuming with the ridiculous paperwork required for the antiquated public library system. In the case of cherry blossom *ku*, I console myself by speculating that this lack of access may have been beneficial: I cannot fit what I already have in the book. But, I cannot pretend not to be what I am, angry: *There is far too much copyright protection and far too little public access.*~~~~~~~~~~~ Let me be specific. Take *ku* #55-6. I found it in *Hokkuchô*, so I knew it was pre-17c. The style suggested it was older. Finding it again in Carter's *Trad. Jap. Poetry*, I learned it was in the *Tsukubashû* (1356). Perhaps that was the case for other anon. *ku* in *Hokkuchô*. Had I either the money to buy many books or access to a good db, it would be easy to check such things, or, for that matter, the pronunciation of poets' names. The *noms de plume* of early *haikai* poets generally allow for *at least* two different pronunciations that can only be settled by checking the appropriate book or db. As it was, I had to trouble friends. Their guesses (Special thanks to Tenki and Masako, & *sorry!*) improved mine, but *a guess is still a guess!* For us (I speak for all poor and unaffiliated scholars) to serve *you*, the reader, we must have fair access to more resources hogged by the establishment.

biblio

B*ooks in* E*nglish* (or worth mention in English for those who cannot read Japanese)

I am most indebted to the following:

◎Wybe Kuitert with Arie Peterse: ***Japanese Flowering Cherries*** (Timber Press 1999). All tree blossom-lovers owe the authors a debt for this 400 page bk sorting out and indexing the complex variety of these cherries (including their names and some horticultural detail!), throwing in a good dose of history and many superb color photographs.

◎The **OJD**. My shorthand for **The Only Japanese Dictionary** = what I call the **Nihon Kokugo Daijiten**, or Japanese National Language Large Dictionary, a ten (small-print) or twenty (large-print) volume dictionary that includes many poems, from the classy *waka* to obscene *senryû*, as examples. In Japanese only. *It is more fun than Samuel Johnson . .*

◎***Shiki's Categorical*** is my shorthand for The **Bunrui-betsu Haiku Zenshû**, a 12-volume set of haiku, seasonally and phenomenologically arranged by Shiki, and published in the early 20c. In an ideal world, it would be improved, enlarged and put up on the web, but the establishment in Japan, like that in the English-speaking world, does not share.

To a lesser degree:

◎***Manyôshû***. The 8c collection of Japanese poetry. I depend on annotated Japanese pocketbooks.
◎**Kokinshû**. The 905 collection of Japanese poetry. I depend on annotated Japanese pocketbooks.
◎ ***Saigyo***, great lover of cherry blossoms. **Sankashû.** The 1190 collection of Japanese poetry. My Japanese pocketbook has no annotation, so I had to wing it alone.
◎***Shinkokinshû.*** The 1205 collection of Japanese poetry. My Japanese pocketbook has no annotation.
◎***Yanagidaru***. The series of books most of the *senryû* come from. I have the pocketbooks which end in the early 19c. Later ones mostly came from the OJD, above, and a quick perusal of a larger compilation I could not afford to buy.

I cite Blyth often, and must confess I was half-sad to find he found so many of the best ku before me!

◎R.H. Blyth: **Haiku**, vol.2, *Spring* (Hokuseido Press. 1950/1981). Many of the best *ku* on cherry blossoms are in this volume. Blyth is always fun. You can find something to agree with and disagree with on every lively page.

I occasionally dig into:

◎**Steven D. Carter** ***Traditional Japanese Poetry*** (Stanford university Press: 1991) The best anthology of Japanese poetry (not just *haiku*) I have read. Carter not only gives the classics but has a good nose for interesting metaphor. Though he doggedly clings to the English syllabet, he usually keeps the beat count low enough that it is not a problem.

◎**Laurel Rasplica Rodd & Mary Catherine Henkenius** *Kokinshû* Cheng & Tsui Company (1984/96). I got the book used, and cheap for all 1,111 poems of this second of the major ancient anthologies. Some of the translations deserve praise for bold choices and coming up with the right hard-found word, but the enjambment after articles (imagine a line ending in "the!"), weird spaces within lines and padding for the sake of strict syllable-ism is unfortunate.

◎**Makoto Ueda:** ***Bashô and His Interpreters*** Stanford Univ. press 1992. Quoted only a few times, I mention it here as it is the *only* book about Japanese haiku in English that I am completely satisfied with! Because the text is almost entirely translated selections of commentary/interpretation of Bashô's *ku* – as opposed to the critical analysis or pre-digested pabulum which are the only templates recognized by Usanian reviews of the scholarly and popular ilk, respectively – it has received far too little attention. (My only wish is for an enlarged edition!) I also checked some *ku* and quoted a few lines from Ueda's ***Dew On the Grass*** (Brill: 2004), a book about Issa's life and poetry.

And, I cite my own books, mostly:

◎**Robin D. Gill:** **Topsy-turvy 1585** (Paraverse Press 2004). This 740 pg. translation+explication of the 611 ways Europeans and Japanese were contrary, according to Luis Frois SJ in 1585, covers so much ground I cannot help citing it whenever I think the reader might want to "see" this or that about Japanese culture. Note: you may search within the book *for free* at Amazon. A 500 page "short" version is also on sale for readers afraid of being crushed by the weight! *Ah, I also mention the soon-to-be published* The Fifth Season. It has more concerning Shiki's *Categorical*.

There are more, but I will refrain from listing them, as I give enough information *when they are cited* – how I *despise* the practice of segregating the notes from the text and placing them at chapter or book's end! – that all may be easily found on the web, and, because I am afraid I would be tempted to add more criticism, which would only make me enemies! If you want more in English on my sources, especially with respect to haiku, I have more information on both English and Japanese sources in Rise, Ye Sea Slugs! (2003). Here, I will give more information on Japanese sources *in Japanese alone,* for it only matters to those who read it, and because I would like people who do not read Japanese to cite *me* instead of something they never read or could read! Of course, this will not prevent Japanese-reading scholars from pretending I do not exist, but that cannot be helped. The independent is used to being invisible.

Books in Japanese　　　　　　　　　　　　　　　日本語の文献

桜・花見の本

◎山田孝雄『櫻史』（櫻書房　昭和十六）。開戦まもなくの出版ながら、女性美としての桜を強く支持、その武士化、つまり散る事に懲る軍国主義の姿勢を見事に批判もしたが、個の花にではなく、はっきりと分けられない多くの花に魅力あるところをもって、自分なりの国民性論も加えてしまった。とは言え、桜の古典に値するすばらしいエッセイ流歴史である。その散文が小生にとっては、やや難し過ぎる。でなければ、もっと引用した。

◎小野佐和子『江戸の花見』（築地書館 1992）。これほどうまく花見だけでなく、その前後と周りを描写する本は、多分ない。花見支度も桜狩に近いかたちの遊山、野遊び、花見へ途中の田舎道、農業と風邪などと桜の関係。ごくわかりやすい文体で外人の私も簡単に読める良書。出典のはっきりしなかった幾つかの川柳をこの本から借りた。

◎白幡洋三郎『花見と桜』（PHP 2000）。日本的なるもの、とりわけ和風の花見が外国のそれとどこが異なるという点に絞る。花のみならず、大衆で、しかも大酒飲みというところですね。そうした日本の花見の系譜、それを発見するまでの外国人の日本の花見観、外国における木と接しあう、花見。

◎佐藤俊樹『桜が創った「日本」』（岩波新書 2005）。染井吉野桜の出現にまつわるさまざまの主張を公平に裁く。その出現の前にも、そのような圧倒的な花量を誇る桜が夢で、詠まれたこともある（小生も前から古句でそれが判った）との指摘。読本からのごく適切な引用で戦前の国民教育のために利用された桜の系譜を紹介すれば、戦後の反・染井吉野考えの馬鹿げた過剰も紹介してくれるバランスよき、文体も高質な秀書。

◎小川和佑『日本の桜、歴史の桜』（NHK 出版 2000）。氏の桜本を、他にも三冊読んだが、現代文学の桜を加えた以外には、山田著『櫻史』の内容に加えたことをあまり感じなかった。が、本書は違う。その突っ込み、たとえば西の山桜と東の染井吉野、桜と文明の関係、あるいは編集の良さが一段と高い。それが、やっと歴史と自然科学の知識が文学分析とうまく合わせるようになったためか、よく知らないが、これでやっと『桜史』の跡継ぎ（？）となる総合紹介書ができた、と思う。

◎水上勉　『在所の桜』（立風書房　1991・1998）特定の桜の木の状況を伺う、ゆったりあるエッセイーと素晴らしい写真。本書に言及あるかどうか覚えていないが、一、二章でも英訳したくなるいい本ですよ。

◎梶美知子『季語の低力』（日本放送出版協会 2003）。十七、八頁が桜に。適切な紹介＋私的な情の絶妙なコンビ。

◎　赤瀬川原平　『仙人の桜俗人の桜』（平凡社 1993・2000）。随筆っぽいルポ集で一部だけは桜が、腹を割ったような体験談の戦争、敵、出陣＝桜狩り比喩の超男ぶりが面白かった。

◎　国文学　2001・4 号「桜：桜花のエクチュール」。幾つかの面において、いい記事・随筆あります。

歌・句の出典

◇歌　〇『万葉集』は岩波の中西注。〇『古今』は講談社学術文庫の久方注。〇『新古今』も『山家』も岩波の古い文庫で、注など皆無。高松注「新古今」あるが全歌もない、注が短い。〇「拾遺集」は web で。〇「閑吟集」は、小学館の『日本古典文学全集』　心敬「花二十首」がその「百首和歌」に、それが『和歌文学大系 66』（明治書院）。愛国主義っぽい歌、その他のマイナーものが web。Yahoo で捜索すれば。

◇句　〇別な方で見つけた句も含めて、本書の句の大半までも掲載する子規の『分類別全俳句』（アルス）への借りが最も大きいが、各句の出典の年付けが殆ど加藤郁乎『近世滑稽俳句大全』（読売新聞社 1993）の引用書目のお陰でわかった。〇『一茶全集』（信濃毎日新聞＝全巻）では、一茶句だけではなく、△「素丸句集」と△「花供養」も掲載。〇戦前に出た『俳諧歳時記』（改造社）と今井著『俳句大全』）、アルス子規全集の 11、12 巻にある『俳家別全集』も大いに利用。〇宗祇ら二万句も季別『大発句帳』古典文庫版。「発句」の多くが只句と思うが！〇岩波体系の DB 捜索三回も断れた（涙）〇「犬子」と「談林十百韻」などの『初期俳諧集』（岩波）が手元にある。〇集英社の「俳書体系」も数冊、十年前に読み、句をコピーしたりしたが、間違いないように確認することができない。

〇芭蕉は、岩波文庫の他、山本兼吉の解説本もある。〇『加賀の千代全集』1955 は＝尚美さん、有難う。〇尾形他注『蕪村全集』（講談社 1992）〇素檗の句が殆ど矢羽編『俳人藤森。。』から。〇柳多留も初期川柳も岩波文庫（三万円の奴も欲しイ！）が中心。〇子規の句は何年か前全集を読んだときのノットから。岩波の子規句集の句数が少な過ぎるが全句も読んだ。虚子句は 1902 年まで全句読んだ。〇少しだけ載せた子供の句は金子兜太ら編『子どもの俳句歳時記』（蝸牛社 1997）、現在大人は『季題別現代俳句遍集』俳人協会編（平成九）。〇上記通り、小野佐和子『江戸の花見』に川柳があった。〇『類別』で句を再び見つけるのが大変で、高沢良一の膨大な俳諧 DB が大きいな助けになった。部分的に捜索できる、俳家ごとにも見られた。しかも、りん女、紫白女、花贊女などの句がほとんどその DB のおかげで見つけたが、万人から情報を隠したがる、お金持ちばかりに文学を配る著作権の問題のためか、只今 Net から Site のアクセスが難しくなった）。☆敬愚の句とは、拙句。『Rise, Ye Sea Slugs!』の場合と違って、初句索引などに入れなかった。

◇歌＋句＋川柳　〇『日本国語大辞典』小学館。例句、歌などのみならず、無数の事を教えてくれた。そのおかげでマイアミにおりながらこのような本でも書ける。

☆「再現」とある所？ わが PC が日本語できなかった頃からのローマ字句を再び見つけなかった場合、再現しました。同じ句のつづり方が日本語の出典変れば、全然違うから、よくないとおもいながらも、許せる範囲かと思いました。

ACなしの寝屋＋事務所では、扇風機二台、守宮数匹。その名付けは夢蔵とか蝶次郎とか。夏は下着一枚也

← 両手うしろに縛れて

いうまでもなく、なるべく多くの俳家を同定し、その俳号の発音と没年をつき留めたかった。季題とその複題の一番古い句、あるいはある発想、比喩などの発明?の系譜を手にとるように、文学の瀧を鯉登る如く遡りたかった。　◎　が、である。それを上手く果たすためには、適当な図書あるいは pc で捜索できる db が不可欠。後者の申し込みは、すでに三回も断れ、それ以上に断れてはあんまりにも惨めな思いで、今年は、日本古典文学大系の使用申し込みをせんともしなかったが、その岩波の文学大系も、集英社の俳書のそれ、そのほかも cd として売れているかという噂だけ届きました。若しも、小生はなにもしないで労働者の一年分の賃金を一日の朝食前に「稼ぐ」ceo であったら、何十万円（!）もする cd 等を、よろこんで買うが、十年も休まず、毎日一生懸命に研究・執筆し、ペイジ番号と表紙までの校正も自分でやってきた、その苦労あっても、お金とまったく縁がない貧乏神に富む小生だから、買うわけない! 大学所属もなければ、その db も cd も、日本研究の宝蔵である J-STOR も、オンライン・アクセスできない。物を探そうと、門なき壁にぶつかる。それが、だれか決めた番号の 403 あるいは、次の無情なる二語

△　ACCESS DENIED　△

左記の自画像はその心を示す。アクセス拒否、即ち両手背後に縛られていながらも、めげずＰＣに向い、執筆を続く哀れたる貧乏学者の姿。英語では「手が背後に」という慣用語は、ハンディと意味する。競馬やらゴルフやら、結構だろうが、研究にハンディさせられるのが、やはり好ましくない。すくなくとも、私みたいに、テニヲハすら完璧に習得していない、タイプ打つ指が鈍い弱才弱技者にとっては、ハンディどころか、オマケが要るんですよ、と言いたくなる!　〇　誰か。俳諧の季題中心研究＋英訳を大切に思う研究所あるいは大学を通して、いろいろな db アクセスを敬愚に開けてくれませんか? あるいは、私の代わりに、本書と『浮け海鼠』など拙著を手持ち、国研へ行って、無断直訴でもやってみませんか?

状況説明文、感謝文、俳句問答場へのご紹介など

◎　難句あるいは、私にとっての難句を解くための help、常に求めております。句によっては、日本人で直感の効く者なら、誰でもいい場合もあれば、江戸歴史、あるいは生活様式の研究家、初期連歌以前の語彙＋文法に自信ある古語学者、特定の俳諧家の専門家でなければ、解決できない場合も少なくない。本書にある数百句（全句の一割弱）の問いを bbs に投稿してみたが、その内、約半分に対して、何らかの答を頂きました。嬉しかったが、専門家の参加が乏しかったため、「これ、絶対!」と納得もできた答えが、又その半分ほどでしかなかった。〔一段飛んで続く〕

☆　感謝します。☆四、五年前になるが、数十桜句の解読援助を下さった本物の日本文学の研究家菊池真一へ。☆校正中、百、二百問題句についてご意見を下さった、俳句門外ではあるが、直観も翻訳の才能が世界一の OM さんへ。☆多忙ながら bbs を作ってくださった天気さんへ。☆その Bbs で協力をして下さった答っ子の皆様へ。☆幾つかの和歌に関する間に答えた連歌研究家の LC へ☆和文を少し見ていただいた HP さんへ。☆虚子句の問に何回も答えてくれた、虚子記念文学館。☆執筆に不可欠なった数ヶ月分の家賃ほどの大金を送って下さった一度ともお会っていない M さんへ。☆古本の取り付けに大気配り屋の苔花堂の広子さんへ。Thank you, again!

◎〔続く〕というわけで、あてずっぽで英訳せざるをえなかった句の数も、それだけ多かった。本書にある英訳句数（三千句）が、一冊の本として、おそらく世界一多い。同時に、その誤訳の数も世界一多いかもしれない!　ただし、原文もあるし、一句に複数の翻訳もあるから、その誤訳が致命傷にならないはずです。もともと、再版もあるから、本書を＜工事中＞と考えて欲しい。☆在日の身なら、俳諧研究の雑誌の編集部や、大学の教授などに、無断電話を入れたりした。俳句問答場へ招いた。又、逆に、雑誌で俳句問答場の連載でも書かせてくれ、と頼んだ。きっと、もっと協力を得たかと思います（E-mail では、なかなか始まらないみたい）。拙著のせんとする事に好感を持つ、在日の皆さんに頼みます! わが俳諧研究の外交者、いや仲人となって下さい!

ロビン・D・ギル著の英訳俳諧書の好評抜粋

Rise, Ye Sea Slugs!（海鼠千句）について。五大学 (Amherst, Smith 等) の Literary Translation 誌、Metamorphoses 2005 春号評者＝スミスカレッジ日本語学、日本文学教授トーマス・H・ローリック

（前略）ギルの手によるその翻訳は簡潔で的をえており、しばしば優雅な味わいがある。これほど翻訳を詳細に説明してある俳句の英訳書は、私の知る限り他に類を見ない。すでに熟練した翻訳家であり、俳人でもある（本書中百句以上が敬愚というペンネームをもつ著者の作である）著者は、芸術としての翻訳の強力な擁護者でもある。どの句にも彼の翻訳のあとに続いて、それぞれ微妙に異なる解釈のあいだを日本文学、歴史、現代の文化についての余談、さまざまな色合いの逸話、ときには暴言までが自由に往来する。（中略）文学についても日常生活についても必ず信頼でき、しばしば愉快でもある彼の日本文化観に私は舌を巻くほかなかった。なにしろ徹頭徹尾ナマコが句題の俳句を集めた本と聞けば当然期待される（事実そのとおりの）風変わりな点はともかく、著者はくろうとの俳人であり、文化と文化間の違いを機敏に理解しながらものを読むことのできる優れた才能に恵まれた魅力ある評論家である。興味津々の本書は、広く俳句愛好家、日本文学と海洋生物の研究者、プロ，アマをとわず翻訳家のすべてに喜ばれるにちがいない。

Rise, Ye Sea Slugs!（海鼠千句）について。Modern Haiku 現代俳句（2004 年冬春 35．1 号）Haiku World:1996 の著者、ウィリアム J. ヒギンソン の 5 ページにわたる書評より

（前略）一人の翻訳者として、わたしはギルの俳句翻訳に対する姿勢は刺激的で挑戦的であると思う。彼は「翻訳者の原作に対する責任」（「対応する力」＝ ロバート ダンカン）という点で、果たすべき水準をきわめて高いところまで引き上げてきているのだ。（中略）この単一季語の大著は、日本の俳句文化の迷宮への、今までで一番優れた英語の窓口であろう。（中略）もし、ヤスダやブライスや、ヘンダーソンやウエダやシラネ＊［注：過去半世紀の俳句英訳名家］を読んだことがあるなら、ギルもお読みなさい。あなたの意識を深く広く拡大させてくれるから。そして、先の方々の著作を読んだことがないのなら、やっぱり先にギルをお読みなさい。彼のほうがずっとおもしろいから。

科学者の評 ＝「凄い！惚れてしまった。小柄な我が友を何年も研究してきたが、悪態をつかれるか、さもなければ忘れられた存在でしかない、と思っていた。ナマコ文学をめぐる日欧の差！悲しいかな、互いに隔てられた科学と文学には、理論においてはむろんのこと、用語上ですら、とてつもないギャップが隋所にみられる。両者を深いところで見事に融合した本で、科学者も納得させる。恐れ入りました。」Alexander Kerr 博士 ＝ Web of Life プロジェクトの海鼠科担当、独語の海鼠研究（古典）の英訳、環境進化論の研究に従事する気鋭の生物学者。James Cook 大学属。

『*Fly-ku！*（蝿句）』について。オンライン句誌『Simply Haiku』創立者かつ編集者ロバート・D・ウイルソンの書評より

（前略）それだけにアメリカの詩人で学者のロビン・D・ギルの著書に出くわしたときの私の驚きは大きかった。書きぶりはジャック・ケルアック流即興を思わせ、ものの考え方はヘルマン・ヘッセ、小林一茶、ルイス・キャロル、このすべてを丸めて一つにしたような本なのだ。。。

全文は、http://www.paraverse.org でどうぞ。

Critical Acclaim of Previous Haiku-related books by robin d. gill

Re: **Rise, Ye Sea Slugs!** (Close to 1,000 *ku* about sea cucumbers translated from Japanese).

"I wondered, can one really devote 480 pages to haiku on sea slugs? The answer is emphatically 'yes.' Although difficult to read from beginning to end, this book contains great learning and insight, and deserves a wide reading among specialists and non-specialists alike."

"For many of the haiku, Gill gives multiple translations as a way of showing possible interpretations. I know of no other book of English translations of haiku that goes to such lengths to explain translations, which in Gill's hands are accurate, economical, and often elegant. In addition to being an accomplished translator and poet (over 100 of the poems are by the author, under the nom de plume keigu), Gill is an articulate defender of the art of translation."

"Gill is also a master of the discursive footnote, and at times I found myself reading along the bottoms of the pages, jumping among footnotes, and marveling at his often amusing and always reliable views of Japanese culture, both literary and everyday. For all the eccentricities one might expect (and does find) in a book devoted entirely to Japanese haiku on the sea slug, the author is an accomplished haiku writer, a very talented and engaging critic, capable of reading with an acute understanding of culture and cultural differences. Haiku enthusiasts, scholars of Japanese literature and marine biology, and professional and amateur translators alike will certainly welcome this interesting book."

–Thomas H. Rohlich, Professor of Japanese Language and Literature at Smith College, from *Metamorphoses*: the journal of the five college faculty seminar on literary translation (Spring 2005 (Vol. 13.1)).

"Some of the most engaging commentary on haiku (and *senryû* and the occasional *tanka* or *kyôka*) ever to see print. . . ."

"Reading it, we see the deep affection of the Japanese for the phenomena of their own environment and culture. At the same time, we encounter one of the most original minds to take up the related subjects of haiku and cross-cultural communication. . . ."

"This single-topic tome may be our best English-language window yet into the labyrinth of Japanese haikai culture. If you have read Yasuda, Blyth, Henderson, Ueda, and Shirane, then read Gill. He will expand your mind. If you have not read those guys yet, then read Gill first. He's more fun."

– William J. Higginson, author, in *Modern Haiku* (volume 35.1 winter-spring 2004). From a five-page review.

Re: **Fly-ku!** (Translations of fly & fly-swatting *ku*, with an in-depth study of Issa's famous fly-ku, *"Don't swat!"*)

"An American scholar and poet who writes in an extemporaneous style akin to that of Jack Kerouac; thinks like Herman Hesse, Koyabashi Issa, and Lewis Carroll, all rolled into one."

– Robert D. Wilson, publisher+editor of the on-line magazine *Simply Haiku* (2005-summer)

"For those with the patience, the unfolding of 600 variations on a theme, with elegant discourse, is a treat, and, at times, when the author delves into the lively back-and-forth on the internet, the past and present of haiku, or the root and uses of various Japanese words, it becomes quite jolly."

"Gill strikes us as no less than amazing. Why isn't he teaching at Yale, or the University of California, or Tokyo University? His references include no end of obscure Japanese lore, plus quotes and notes from such artists as Clare, Lovelace, Steinbeck, Dumont, Verdi, Satie, Blyth, Shakespeare, Emily Dickinson."

– Carlos Amantea, author of *The Blob That Ate Oaxaca* in R.A.L.P.H. (Review of Art, Literature, Philosophy & History)

☆   ☆   ☆   ☆   ☆

for more of these reviews, visit the respective websites or http://www.paraverse.org

ペコペコAppealペコペコ
Patrons of Paraverse Press

With books of translated haiku, one typically gets about 10 haiku per dollar: 10 cents/*ku*.
Paraverse gives you about 100 per dollar: the *ku* in our books cost only a penny each!
Moreover, each *ku* has, on average, two translations, you get far more explanation,
(with notes on the same page), and something all too rare, the original Japanese!

*The price of the books is right for me, too. Almost a third of the retail price goes to the press,
in this case, the author. That is fine recompense, or would be, if only more books sold.
Unless my readers are odd birds indeed, so many of the few who have read my books
found them fun and informative that there* must *be a large market for them.*

Yet, sales are so bad (more pages than readers!) that I must consider a new career,
doubling the prices of the books (for price seems to make no difference), or both.
If you would like me to continue, please make an effort to publicize the books
however you see fit and/or become Patrons of Paraverse Press.

*I am afraid Patrons of the Paraverse will get no tax deductions.
Despite the org. on our web address, at present, Paraverse press is only a dba.
I (there is no* we *yet) cannot afford the money=time to become nonprofit. If you wish,
however, you can be acknowledged &/or repaid in the eventuality of success.*

Blyth's famous books carry a *Thank You* page for the Governor of the Bank of Japan.
Though it sounds horribly commercial, direct patronage is actually more personal and less
onerous than our institutional grants that make ridiculous demands on the applicant,
favoring those amenable to writing applications over those driven to create.

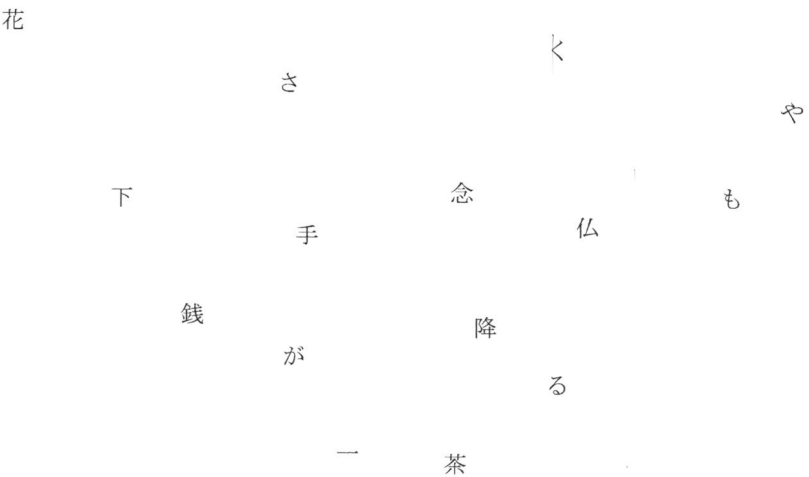

I would be happy to follow R.H. Blyth
giving patrons a *Thank You* page and/or mention
at my website, signed books, artwork, etc.
I am not embarrassed to beg your assistance,
for I have wasted little money or time in my life,
and am poor only because I have concentrated
on study and preparing the many books
I am now ready to finish,
with your help!

POET index: Only the *nome de plume*, or *haigo* is given here. Because many poets used more than one *haigo*, their number is overstated. Some names were ad-hoc affairs made to fit the content of the *ku*. A hyphen+ single date means year of death, while a hyphen-less single date means the work in which the *ku* appears. *Ku* and poet could be older! It is often impossible to tell what pronunciation of a name was intended. Lacking sufficient references, my respondents and I often had to settle on an educated guess. Please check the Errata at paraverse.org before quoting. Saigyô, Norinaga, etc. excepted, *waka* poet names are generally not given. Neither are *senryû* poets (usually anon. anyway). Instead, the names of the *waka* anthologies are. 注：発音未定の場合、原則として音読みにするが、古き俳号には訓読みも多いし、紹巴はjôhaであり、shôhaでなく、乙州がotokuniとよむべきなどと専門書にある。気が付かなかった変読も多いはず。再版の前に専門家のご協力を乞う。歌人名は西行と宣長以外にないが、和歌実体がPOEM素引にある。和歌集の名だけ、ここにある。

Akinobô 秋之坊 (-1718) 4-96? 42-99
allegedly issa 28-42
anetsu 安悦() 7-17
anmei 安明(1651) 14-7, 44-6, 63-60
anon 1-3/11, anon 2-2/8/13, anon 3-44, anon (1633), 6-16, anon (1633) 7-11 , anon. 10-23, anon? 12-36,13-17,26-33, 42-78, 56-9 ◦嵐山集(1651) 6-9, 7-7/9/22/30, 37-4, 38-4, 40-32, 44-8, 47-43/79/99, 48-6/7, 55-7/11, 56-19, 62-37, ささめ 6-18 毛吹草(1645) 16-66/70/71, 37-3,61-2◦ 発句帳() 12-116 , 55-8, 59-9◦筑波(1356) 29-9,55-5/6, ◦犬子(1633) 17-14, 29-19◦犬筑波 2-9LR 壁草 12-89, 夢見草 48-43, 鷹筑波(1652) 14-8,白髪集 6-4, うやむや() 3-11
antô 安当() 11-1
arimichi 蟻道(-1711) 28-35

Baida 梅雫() 33-19
baie 楳江() 9-69, ◎baifu 梅父() 50-19
baika 梅霞() 9-45, 16-67
baikan 梅軒(1694) 3-26
baiô 梅翁 →**sôin**

baisei 梅盛(1613-1702) 16-65
baishi 梅枝 13-29 /31, 53-18
baishi (梅志) 17-76
BAISHITSU 梅室(1768-1852) 4-84, 6-32, 8-53, 8-72,-35,12-57,13-12,14-15,15-46,17-41,17-55,22-15,21-8, 28-13, 24-36,36-8, 38-32,40-26, 40-36, 40-44,40-45 , 47-17, 51-10
baishû 梅舟(1680) 11-9
baiu (梅雨) 16-16; ◎baiu 梅塢(1795) 22-8
baizetsu 梅舌() 8-42
bakushi 麦翅 1773: 54-4
bakô 馬光(1751: 13-32, 17-2, 38-20
bansui 伴水(1700) 55-24
banzan 伴山() 8-82
basen 馬泉() 32-52
BASHÔ 芭蕉 1654-94 1-19, 1-23, 2-1, 3-36, 4-37,4-43,4-51, 7-21, 8-18, 9-68, 13-7/13, 15-23, 15-33,**16**-30/64/88/90, **17**-11/32, BK II-3, 22-26, **24**-37/38, 26-38, 28-11b/19, **33**-1, **32**-7/9/14, 17-33,**40**-1/51 **42**-24/88, 47-9, 48-12, 50-33, 57-10, 61-4, **62**-21/22, 63-57, 64-2 [& see below]
?bashô = dubious bashô 存擬芭蕉 8-58b, 28-10b, 40-63b, 42-83b, 63-24b/38
basô 馬曹() 46-24
beichû 米仲 16-23 ◎bikoku 尾谷() 8-32
望一 bô→môichi ◎bokushi 牧子·() 7-35
bonchô 凡兆-1714 42-37
bôshi or hoshi? 畝司 38-35
bunpai 文排() 59-28
bunsei 文性 1633: 2-22; ◎ 文丼 47-95
bunshi 文士 1795: 13-10◎聞至 1777 42-84
bunson 汶村(-1713?) 1-24
BUSON 蕪村 1715-83 0-5, 1-39, **3**-45/60, 5-8,**12**-62/-73/85/86/87,**15**-32/47/49,**17**-36/59/60, 18-2, 22-30, 28-30, 29-8, 34-7, 40-65, 42-14, **47**-24/25/93b, 48-21, **50**-38/40/48, 54-19, **58**-12/14/15, 59-20, **64**-29/30/36/37
bussen 佛仙() 46-41

Chibô 遅望(17c) 44-24
CHIGETSU-NI 智月尼 1622-1703/06) 1632-1708? 4-39,10-19,36-20,38-15,60-53
chikamatsu (-1724)17-31
chikashige 親重(-1669) 2-18,44-14
chikubô 竹房() 40-31
chikuhô 竹苞() 61-1
chikuko 竹戸() 44-13
chikuô 竹翁糸巻() 3-25
chikutei 竹亭() 19-3
chikuya 竹也(竪並) 15-21
chikuya 竹夜() 44-27
chine 千子[〜女](-1688) 53-9
chinji 陳次 9-31, 18-17
chinshû 珍舟？三重() 11-3
chira 智蘿(1470) 15-15
chiri 知里(1647-1716) 33-21
chisen 千川 (ba 1) 4-22, 24-39, 57-34
chishi (or) tomoyuki? 知之 **12-46**
chiun 智蘊() 17-64
CHIYO-NI 千代 （尼） (1701-75)3-55,**4**-28/29/49/62/66/67/68/69/70/71/72/73/78/79, **8**-62, 13-21, **16**-69/74, 17-46, **23**-23/24/24b, 30-1, 34-5, 36-21, **42**-44/45, 46-35, 48-86, 54-2, **58**-13/16/17/18/19/21
CHODÔ 樗堂 (1748-1814) 3-48/58,4-61,10-42/43, 12-1/115, 43-7, 47-26
chôei (調栄() 12-63 ◎chôfu 長父() 4-83

chôha 超波 42-74; □chôhô→shigekata
chôji 重次 1633 () 29-10,
chôji 長次 44-15 ◦chôji長治( ) 46-21
chôka 鳥歌 (三崎志 16c) 51-7
chôkaku 調鶴() 42-73
chôkichi 長吉 1633 7-4, 39-4
chôkô 長虹(fl1650-1700) 4-32,12-44 26-37
choku-→nao- 直知,~ 行,~ 方,~ 治
chokunen or naotoshi 直年 or kikyô 桔梗?
kzs 9-18
chôkyû 長久 欅炭 23-28
chômu 蝶夢(1731-1795) 3-19
CHORA 樗良 (-1780?) 1-17, 4-26/58, 9-43,15-29, 31-9, 47-31, 53-13, 54-16,64-13
chôsei 長正(skg) 2-12
chôseki 鳥跡 17-68
chôseki 朝隻 1701: 4-17
chôsenshi (調泉子) 24-44
chôshô 長(or kasanaru?) 昌(1645) 24-28
chôsui 鳥 酔 (-1769?) 9-55, 36-47, 59-8
chôsui 長翠(-1813) 57-15
chôsô 鳥窓(1763) 42-83
chôto 鳥兎 14-12
chôtô 彫棠(1694) 41-6
chôu 蝶羽(-1741)16-7,36-54, 63-11, 64-23
chôwa or nagakazu 長和() 6-40;
chûkô or nakayoshi 中好 12-13/14

Daifu 倅布() 15-53
daishun 大春 63-50
dansui 談水() 12-64
dôboku 洞木(18c) 10-30
dohôken 土方竪(八仙専)60-52
dôin 道院(1759) 14-20
dôji 道二() 56-2
dôyo 道誉(1356) 55-15
dôyû 道悠(恒誠) 40-73

Eihô 永峰 3-53, ◎eiji 永次 1645 15-22
eiji 永治(1633)6-10, 12-99, 44-21
eikô 栄行 1680 28-33
ekinan 易難(1783) 53-7
enga 沾峨() 16-14
enkarô 煙霞郎() 12-7
enshi (艶士) 33-17
ensui 猿水(1655-1739) 63-25
ensui 淵水() 65-10
ensui 猿推(1639-1704) 16-79
etsujin 越人-1702?1739 8-75, 17-63, 36-39

Fuan 不案 1633: 2-25
fuboku フト (d 1691?) 9-61, 42-41
fûchiku 諷竹(1698) 5-15, 15-53c
fuchû 不中 (女 1691) 47-23
fugetsu 府月() 17-48
fûgin 風吟(翁？反故集 1783) 48-22
fui 吹衣(p1698) 32-10
fujiwaranomitsutsune? 藤原光経集() 40-14
fujiwara saneyuki? 実行 金葉(d) 62-19
fujiwara teika62-7
fukaku 不角(1651-1743)3-6, 42-21/38/60
fukan 不干(1734) 24-55
fukufû or fukutomi (?)福富 12-17
fukuhô? 福富 misc. 25-8
fûon 風音() 28-14
fûritsu 風律(1685 or 1773) 42-18
fûsei 風生 29-28 ◎ fusen 附専 42-75

fûshiki 楓色 1795（秋田女）29-6
fushû 布風( ) 12-8
fûsô 風草() 41-8 ◎fuson 不存 1651 16-28
fusui 富水 1773: 42-7 ◎fûsui 風睡() 26-11
futo 珧卜 19-10

Gain 雅因(-1818?) 1-15, 23-19
gakei 雅計 33-14
gakô 雅郊(1777) 6-26, 64-4
ganryû 雁立 65-4◎gansen 丸川 36-48
ganseki 丸夕 12-41◎ganshaku 丸 29-14
ganshi? 岩芝 41-5
gekkyo 月居(1745-1824) 12-20
genchô 元重 3-34
genju? 玄＋木偏に需にしんにゅう 7-16
genka 玄化() 48-60, genpô→koppô 元峯
genshi 玄馴 1731 9-51; 玄茂 42-6
genshin 元辰(1651) 38-19
genshû or motonari 元就(春霞) 1-8, 4-59, 42-32
genyô・genjô 玄仍(-1607) 4-2, 46-37
getsujin 月尋 1714 42-50
蟻道 gidô → arimichi
GINKÔ 吟江 1780 0-8, 6-26/31, 12-107/113, 15-37, 16-77, 17-56, **18**-5/59, 28-21, 35-3, 38-12, 46-4, **47**-13/76, 62-20, 64-16
giteki 義的(1642) 12-23
gitoku   祇徳 BK II-pref.2
giun 義運( ) 47-82
gochiku 呉竹 (1777) 40-20
gochô 五潮() 8-36
GOCHÛ 吾仲(-1733) 4-3/97, 5-4, 8-39, 10-3,27-18
goin? 午飲(1820) 13-30
gojin or agato 吾人() 32-8
GONSUI 言水(1646-1719) 1-40, 9-26,13-19, 32-19/47, 42-85, 58-27
goryû 五立(1795) 22-18
gosen harushita (anthol 951) #92 47-47
gukô 愚候? or gukyô if~侠> ( ) 16-76
gusai tsukuba-shû (anthol) 1356 15-11
gyodô 魚道() 34-11,38-14
gyôji 行次 (1680) 28-32
gyôjo?行助(1624/44) 12-84, 17-35
gyôkuô? 玉（革＋央）( ) 7-10
gyokuho 玉圃() 15-24
gyokuryû 玉柳() 9-57
gyokuyôshû waka anthol. 1312 53-19
gyôro 行露(1701) 3-29
GYÔTAI (also kyôtai/gyôdai) 暁 台 (1731-92) (1732-93) 4-31, 12-102, 36-22, 37-8, 40-5, 46-36, 47-42,56-33

Hafû 1698 巴風 29-23
hajin 巴人(1672-1742) 3-59, 8-83, 16-34, 64-10 = sôa 宋阿
hajô 巴静(1680-1744) 9-20
hakkaku? 八角 42-42
hakusetsu 白雪(1694) 9-50, 22-11
hakushi 薄芝(1689) 48-1
hakushi 白支(1712) 9-11
haryû 破笠 or yaburegasa (1687) 24-34
hasegawa kayo 長谷川佳代 52-7
hasen 破扇(1666) 52-11
hatsui shizue 初井しず枝 14-25
hideyoshi ( ) 3-42
hihan 此藩( )6-29
hinba 1777 (濱馬) 18-12

hironao/kôchoku? 廣直 16-87b
hiryû 此柳( ) 51-13
hisajo 久女 64-34b
hôchô 峯鳥( ) 17-69
hôgetsu? i 抱月(1699) 32-11
hôjû 芳重() 28-2
hôkichi (保吉)16-44
HOKUSHI 北枝(-1718) 40-4, 42-31, 55-30, 50-53, 63-59
hokyô 浦京(1777) 35-13
honkô 本弘() 51-12
honpô 本包?() 5-1
hôrô mushu??? 32-36
hôryû 芳流(俳諧漢和) 42-43
hôsa 包抄(1694) 9-54
hôsun 方寸() 45-6; hôshô (峰松) 48-36
hoyû 保友(1651) 36-49
hyakuchi 百池(1748?57-1835?6?) 16-26
hyakudô 百童(1775) 17-49, 53-12
hyakuga 百芽( ). 47-58
hyakuman 百萬() 40-48b
hyakuri 百里() 63-69
hyakushi 百史() 46-44 ◎百之( ) 48-30

Ichibu 一武( ) 7-29
ichigin 一吟 1680 32-4
ichigu 一具(-1853) 26-42
ichijaku 一雀 54-7
ichiji or kazuharu 一治(1651) 21-14
ichiku 移竹(d.1759?60?) 27-48, 63-6
ichimi 一味() 10-29
ichirôyû? 一郎友(?) 12-119
ichiyo [dai/kuro?] 一代／黒 () ( ) 12-91
ichiyôshi 一葉子 1642 6-13
ichiyû 一祐 (1680) 11-10
ichû 惟中 13-34
ihoku 渭北 1702 kk 16-8
ikeda shoko 池田祥子() 57-31
ikkei 一敬(kuwanasogorokichi in kzs) 7-28
ikkyô 一橋 1689 40-8
ippyô (1840) oops! *Between* 10-6b
ise-no-ôsuke 伊勢 大輔(10c) 62-8
isen 渭川() 57-9
ishihara yatsuka (contemp.) 49-12
ishikawa chiharu 石川千晴(cont.) 14-22
ISSA (1762-1827) 0-2/4/14 , **1**-14/35, **3**-2/3/8/54/56, **4**-30/40/41/46/80/87/94/95, **5**-2/10, **6**-25/35/37/45/47/48/49/52/55, **7**-13, **8**-6/13/30/43/45/46/47/48/65/66/67/68/70/71/73/74/78/84/85/87/88/89/90/92, **9**-15/24/42,10-6/ 18/22/36,12-19/28/29/30/ 67,13-9/11,14-1/10/16/21/24, **15**-6/17/18/ 19/45/48/50/51/52/56/57/58-4/6/9/10/17/ 18/19/20/21/22/32/33/38/40/42/43/56/61/80,**17**-24/28/29/43/47/50/51/52/53/74/80,18-13, BK II-4/6,21-1/15,**22**-7/27/32/38/39/40,**23**-1/10/12/13/14/15/16/18,**24**-4/5/14/15/16/17/21/24, **26**-31/32/40,**27**-5/7/8/15/16/   20/21/24/25/29/30/31/33/34/35/36/37/38/39/42,**28**-37/41/43/44 **28**-12/16/18/20/26/27/36,**29**-29, **30**-5/12/13/14/15/20/22/23/24/25/26/30,**31**10/11/12/13/14/15/16/17/18/21/22/   23/13/14/15/19/21/22/23/33/34/35/37/38/39/40/43/44/49/53,**33**-4/5/7/8/9/18,**34**-4/20,**35**-10/11/12/14, **35**-6/13/29/36/30/31/32/33/34/34b/35/36/51/53**38**-7/8/9/10/17/21/22/23/24/25/29/26/38/31/43/2/43/47/52/56/57,**40**-24/46/47/49/64/70/71/75/76,**42**-20/55/94/96,**43**-2/5,45-17,**47**-27/ 28/29/34/40/41/44/48/54/55/57/59/60/62/63/64/65/66/86/88/90/91/92/93,**48**-23/69,**50**-1/3/4/5/6/7/9/10/12/13/15/16/34/35/36/39/50, **51**-9/11, **52**-3, **54**-14, **55**-1/17/19/27, **56**-27, **57**-5/17/23/24/26/27/29/30/31/32/33,**58**-22/28/30/33/34;**59**-12/14/16/17/18/21/36;**60**-1/2/3/4/13b18/19/20/26/33/34/35/38/39/40/42/43/44/45/49/50/50b,51,**61**-14/15/17/19/20/21/22,**62**-2363-1/12/13/15/15b/17/18/19/20/21/23/24/26/27/31/33/41/44/45/51/52/53/54/54/b/55/56/58/61/63/64/65/66/67/75/76;**64**-8/15, **65**-9

ISSEI 一正 (1633) 34-6, 38-6,39-3, 44-22,61-16,62-12
issei 一井 (1651) 30-11, 40-28
ISSETSU 一雪(-1680) 16-37,26-44, 44-11, 59-25,63-16
isshô 一笑(-1688) 6-36,24-48
isshô 一松 6-14
issô 一草(1742-1830)皮草片／龍摺 4-10
issoku 一束( ) 6-24; ittei   一貞 27-43
itteki 一笛 1699 24-45
itteki 一滴 (一茶の七番日記 9-11) 62-9
ittetsu 一鐵(鉄= f.1675?) 58-31
ittoku 一徳 鷹筑波 11-6
izen 惟然(-1710?11?) 10-49,28-10

Jakushi 寂芝(17-18c) 8-93
jichiku 二逐 恒誠 42-6b
jichikuriki? 自逐力 () 26-12
jigento 次广都 29-30
jikô 治好(?)65-5 , jini 仁意() 46-19
jinsa 人左(1759) 8-14,47-96
jinsei? 塵生 biblio!
jirô 次郎 osaka () 56-36
jiryû 二柳() 54-11
jishi? 時之(1656) 41-3,54-5
jishô 二松(1698) 24-18
jisui 次推() 21-13
jittei 実定(btt 俳諧坂東太郎) 24-43
jôboku 常牧() 4-77
JÔHA 紹 巴(1523-1602) **4**-4/5, 8-25,**15**-12/13, 12-24,14-17,15-10,17-37,**19**-1/4/8, 23-2, 24-3, **35**-5/14, 40-6/37/38/39/40/79/80, **42**-52/70/71,**46**-26/31/39/42/54,**47**-57/81,48-65/66, 50-24,51-19,**52**-5/12,**58**-8/9,59-1
jojaku 序寂( ) 47-14
joju or nyoju 如壽 ( ) 47-6
joko 如湖() 15-59, 64-6
jokô 如行(1699) 3-37
jôku? tsunenori?常矩 1774:2-3, 26-41 64-7
jôkyû 常久(1645) 11-4
jonen 助然() 3-24
joritsu 鋤立 16-47
JÔSÔ 丈草,丈艸(-1704) 5-3,16-48, 25-5,10, 30-17,36-38, 47-4, 50-18, 52-10
jôsoku 城仄(1776) 46-22
josui (女水) 59-29 ◎josui 如翠() 6-6
jou 徐宇(滑稽伝・均塞) 63-10
jôzen 常全() 42-80
jû allstarting 重 might be SHIGE
jûbutsu 十佛(1356) 5-17; jûho[?LJ] ( ) 1-32
jûji 重似(?) 26-45
jûkyô 十境() 35-9
junka 鈍児(1651) 44-7
jûttei 述貞 (1666) 15-9
jûwa/shigekazu? 重和() 11-5

Kabun 荷分 108 sk12 36-46
kaen 花渕(1731) 42-3
kaifû 快風() 17-17 ◎kaikaku (海角)17-20
kakei 荷分 (-1716) (1689) 15-34
kakutani tomoko 角谷添子 (1997) 62-34
kakyû 可休(42-19 ◎kamei 花明()60-46
kameyama 亀山殿百韻(1324?) 17-25
kanera 兼良 141-1481 48-17
kangen-hôshi 完元法師( ) 6-20
kanginshû (anthol. 1518) 40-82, 59-2
kangyoku 寒玉( ) 26-18
kankan (1763) 閑々 12-33
kankyo 官橋 26-39 ◎kanpo 漢甫 40-53b
kanro 寒露　増補をた巻 33-20
karai 何来 (1782) 9-33
kasanjo 花賛女(1807-1830) 10-4, 32-48, 36-12, 59-31
kaseki 可石(1777) 6-39
kasen 何羨 1693 () 57-19
kasetsu 可雪( ) 11-7
kashiku (18c) 3-12 ◎kashô 哥松()50-47
kasotsu? 荷卒(1774) 34-9
kasui1697 荷翠 19-5, 54-18
katsû 可通 1680 11-11
katsushige? 勝重(1651) 7-31
katsuzo 葛三(1751-1818) 8-15
kazen 可全 33-6
kazunaga 和長 (月影塚) 3-46
keibô? 桂坊() 9-1
keichô 径重 1666 44-12
keiei 敬英 16-3
keigu 敬愚 1-36, 53-6 and a score more I wrote that you'll have to find in context.
keiku 継駒? 1783 42-87
keishi (桂史?) 26-20
keiyû 慶友 1651 29-3, 48-11
kenkichi 兼吉 (1651) 62-4
kensai 兼載(d.1510) 19-2, 35-1, 44-3
kenshi 賢之(1651) 17-71
kibun 亀文() 9-63
kichiku 洪竹( ) 8-33
kidô 亀洞(fl 1690~) (c1700) 17-58, 26-30, 28-24, 33-12
kien 寄園　(春遊 1767) 17-30
kifu 箕夫(1777) 27-19
kigin 季吟 (1624-1705) 24-47, 47-44, 53-15
kiin 希因 (-1748) 3-15
kiji 季治 1656 63-72
kijô (1864-1938) 62-15
kika[?酒を妻妻を妾の花見かな?] 24-22
KIKAKU 其角(-1707)3-7, 4-21/23, 8-79, 9-59, 10-15,12-10, 13-3, 16-12/25/59, 19-7, BKI-end-1, 24-42/49, 26-16/27, 27-2/32, 31-7, 32-29, 38-33/49/53, 40-3/27/29/43/48, 42-72,43-3/4, 46-50, BKIII-1, 47-7, 52-8, 53-8, 54-20,55-33, 57-7/16/21, 58-2/37, 59-6, 65-8
kikuchi kazuô 菊地一雄 1997 47-101
kikujo きく女 24-37b 加藤郁平 市井風流 (is she 菊舎尼 kikusha-ni? -1812?)
kimô (亀毛) 9-66
kinba 琴馬 (月影塚) 30-16
kinin 寄任 64-28
kinkô-jo 錦江女(18c) 47-8
kinkôkyû 近江朽( ) 40-60
kinpû 琴風-1726 12-50, BK-2, 58-26, 63-4

kinshi 琴詩( ) 9-4; kinsui 錦水(18c) 13-6
kinshi 近之 1666 28-7, 33-22, 44-18, 65-6
kinyôshû 金葉集 1124-6　42-98
kisa or sokusa? 塞佐(1697) 36-16
kisaki morio 10-47 ◎kisei 亀世 36-6
kiseki 綺石(1820) 14-2
kishu 鬼守(1765) 8-26
kishû 紀州(1795) 枕石? 16-91
kissei or kichimasa 吉政(1645) 8-28, 29-11
kisui 其水 17-67
kisui 器水(1699) 6-34,12-70
kitahara hakushû 42-100
kitai ( ) 其袋 48-24
kitsu/kichihei 橘平　月影塚( ) 4-45
KITÔ 几董(1740-89) 6-21/54, 9-34, 12-92/109, 14-20, 22-6, 24-20, 40-66 , 42-13, 47-1,20, 50-46, 52-1, 59-33, 64-1
kiya 奇哉 (1795) 13-17
kiyû 亀友　(1777) 8-35 ○季遊 54-13
kizen 亀全( ) (入＋王)　18-1
kizoku 葵足 36-55
kôfun 黄吻?(1678) 江戸広小路? 9-67
kochû 壺中 (c1700) 27-3
kôdô (岡道)59-26
KÔEI 弘永(1645) 7-32, 11-20, 16-75, 17-15, 36-23,38-54, 40-55, 44-28, 56-17
kôei 呑江(1773) 57-4
koen 乎焉( ) 15-15
kôgyô 光暁(1795) 22-13
koito 小いと( ) 24-8
kojû 湖十(d.1738? 46? 80? 89?*) 36-41
kôka 弘嘉 (1795) 19-11, kôka 光家()65-2
kokan 康甘( ) 48-62;
KOKINSHÛ(waka anthology) (905) 4-7/8, 12-52,17-18, 36-17, 36-25/50, 40-11/15/15b, 42-49, 45-5, 46-1/2, Bk III forewd 1, 47-11/45/72/73/102, 48-2/67, 50-25/26/27/28, 55-31, 58-10, 60-16/17, 63-79, 64-5,65-3
kokoku 虎國 1767 59-10
kokuyu 國友( ) 55-13
kônei 広寧(1656) 7-23, 32-3
konpu 混夫( ) 36-56
koppô 兀峰(1633-94) 6-59, 24-52, 47-56
koryû 胡柳 (15-36; kôsa 幸佐(芋環) 24-19
kôsaishi 江斎子-(1699) 25-1
kosei 厚成 1656　48-61　○湖青( ) 49-7
koseki 湖石 (月影塚) 17-70
kôsen 江川(1783) 57-18
kôsenryû? 廣千立()63-34
kôshi 後士( ) 55-3,
kôshô 高翔　(1712) 4-92
koshô 孤松(early 20c) 44-19
koshô 荒笑() 60-11
koshû 孤舟 58-37
koshun 潮?. → 湖春(-1697) 42-53
kôsui 弘水 (毛吹草) 45-13(→?-kôei?)
kôsui 孝水() 6-7
kôtei/mitsusada?'s 光貞妻 wife?( ) 29-20
kotobana wakashû 詞花和歌集 38-13
kotô 枯藤(1694) 17-42
kotô 狐桐(1773) 3-38
kôtoku 幸徳( ) 8-9
kôyû 好友 60-37◎kôyû 口遊独活 3-51
kôyû 光有 1645 47-51, 54-3, 63-73
koyû-ni 古友尼( ) 46-58
kûga? 1699 空牙 26-19

kuga1795 空我 24-40
kukû 句空(1646-1714) 8-40, 16-81, 32-46
kûzon 空存() 21-6
kuzu hôki? 葛箒 anthol? 47-36
kyôden 京伝(1803) 55-25/26
kyôei → kôei
kyôfû 狂風( ) 40-19
kyohaku 挙白 ? (-1696?) 18-6, 42-24b
kyôhei 鏡平()16-86
kyôichi 許一( ) 15-54
kyokô 虚吼(-1935) 16-24
kyokugen 曲言(1678) 26-29
kyôma 京馬() 1-28
KYORAI 去来(-1704) 1-13, 16-15, 17-81, 23-3/5, 31-5, 34-15, 38-1
KYOROKU (sometimes kyoriku, too) 許六(-1715) 36-13, 49-10, 50-17/37, 55-16
kyosei 巨井 1772 4-74
kyôsei (教清) 48-10
KYOSHI 虚子(-1959) 1-22, 6-57, 8-44, 9-47, 24-27, 28-31, 55-29, 59-13, 61-25
kyôshi* ( ) 9-48
kyôson 杏村(1763) 28-23
kyûan 休安( ) 6-11,7-25, 28-4
kyûga 求我　(安中)　22-14
kyûka 休花 62-29,
kyûnin 久任(1656) 47-49, 56-22
kyûsai 救済 (1356) 48-29
kyûshitsu 旧室 (-1764) 49-5

Lost Name 失名 1-11, 32-27/38-48/42-51/89, 葛箒/47-35/36; 61-12, 64-24
Lost Ref.失出典 2-16 LR 3-47 LR ( ) 6-19

Mabuchi 真淵(d.1769) 61-8/9
maiboku 埋木 (1678) 63-3
makkon 末昆 12-48 ◎manka 満家() 21-7
manô 萬翁[?] 9-3, 15-1
manpei 万平　(1699) 27-17
manshi 万子() 15-35
MANYÔSHÛ 8c 1-30/31, 12-2/37, 23-21/22/29, 40-41/42/72, 47-46/70, 53-2/3/4/5
masaakira 正章(-1673) 8-29, 10-16
masahide 正秀 21-11
masahiro 政弘(1495) 46-40
masanao 政直( ) 48-3
masanori or masanobu 政宣 1651: 16-31
masatomo→seiyû
masatora　正虎() 39-6
masayuki 正行(1651) 16-29
matsuyû 末祐( ) 12-97
mayuzumi madoka 黛まどか(contem)36-26
meimô 明網 1680 28-34
menbaku 面白(1680) 11-13
MICHIHIKO　道彦((1755-1815)d.1819) 4-64, 12-120, 40-35,46-55, 47-22
migaku 未学 28-8
mikaku 美角(1724-93) 15-38
mine 小女　みね 古撰( ) 6-56
minomushi (蓑虫) 42-92
minshi 眠獅() 17-5
mitoku 末得(1651) 44-9/16
mitsushige 光重( ) 62-17
miyamoto midori 63-29
mogan 毛紈　勾藻 49-8
môichi (-1643) 望一( ) 6-12/68
moji 茂次(1642) 48-34

mokudô 木導 (-1723) 18-11
monjûriki? 文十力(1694) 9-44
moritake (-1549) 9-49, 16-78, 38-2, 45-9
moroshige or shochoku 諸重(1651) 2-15
môtan 盲探( ) 34-10
muchô 無腸(d.1809) 47-21
mukan 無關( ) 16-82
mûmon or mubun 無文(1680) 53-11

Nambutsu 南佛 17-72
namka 南化 9-29
namshô 南昌(1793) 3-61
nanpo 南浦 59-35
naoharu 直治( ) 11-19
naokata 直方(1648-28/75
naotomo 直知(1651) 10-12
naoyuki 1666 直行 29-16
nari 那李 1731 22-21
nikawa? 誤后=頼山陽 （『桜史』）二川 相近=松蔭(-1836)? 61-23
nikyû 似一休(1734) 24-54
ninkô 任口(1605-86) 26-1
niryû 二柳( ) 42-22
nôa(mi) 能阿(1396-1471) 48-44
nogiku 野菊 (1784) 4-13
noma 野馬 24-9
nomi ノ身(1651) 44-5
yaotsu 野乙(1772-80) 27-27b
norinaga 宣長 1730-1801 61-5/6/7
nyodaku? 如濁( ) 9-7
nyogen 如元（ ） 12-118
nyotei 如貞(1651) 39-1
ÔEMARU 大江丸(1719-1805) 俳懺悔 4-1, 4-24/25, 5-13?, 10-7, 12-9/34/98, 16-50,26-25, 47-97?, 50-52,57-2?, 59-7/3?
ôkaku (櫻角) 34-19
ô-mikado 62-6
ônishi yasuyo 60-54
ONITSURA 鬼貫 1660-1738 0-1,4-47/48, 8-69,11-2,12-26,16-5,17-6,36-1,36-24,38-5, 40-59,42-79,43-1,47-18/94,48-25,**56**-34,58-25,60-41
onoe 尾上(1734) 36-12b
ôno rinka 20c 大野林火 48-88;
otokuni 乙州(-1720) 19-6
OTSUNI (also **otsuji**) -1823 乙二 3-62,5-12, 14-9, 15-42, 21-9/10,36-57,47-37
otsuyû 乙由(1670-1739) 4-82,29-22,52-6

Raichû 来仲? 米恩 ( ) 63-5
raigi 来儀( ) 21-5
raiô 来鴎 1767 春遊 42-8/29
RAIZAN 来山 (-1716) 0-6 , 36-58, 40-12? 42-48-27, 50-42, 51-8, 60-13c
raisen 来川(-1736) 42-40
rajin 羅人 4-98
rakka 1701（落霞) 34-16
rangai (-1845) 27-28, 50-8, 60-25
rankan 蘭関(1697) 57-11
RANKÔ 蘭更(1726-99) 3-4/35, 4-27, 6-42/43, 9-9/36/58, 13-33, 15-25, 22-17, 24-7, 30-28, 34-2, 36-28/40, 47-15, 50-54, 54-17, 60-15, 61-10, 63-37, 64-12
ranran 嵐蘭 (-1689) 32-13
RANSETSU (-1707) 嵐雪 9-62, 33-2, 40-16, 46-38, 48-59, 53-14, 56-4, 57-20, 63-43
ransha 蘭杜(1777) 5-14
ranshû 蘭秀( ) 9-60

ranzan 嵐山( ) 44-32
reikan 鈴竿(18c?) 16-73
renshi 蓮之(1732) 25-11
richû 李仲(1725) 18-15
rida 狸唾(1699) 18-8
rigyû 利牛(17-18c) 3-57
rihan 理帆 ）40-25
riji? 利次( ) 42-33
rijû 理重 (1656) 30-19
rikô 蜊口 17-4
rikyoku 理曲() 42-67
rikyû 利休 古選 ( ) 6-38
rimon 李門 恒誠( ) 4-9
RINJO りん女 (1673-1757) 3-32/39, 4-11/81/88/89/ 90, 6-44, 24-35/51/53/56, 29-5, 42-57/58, 44-25/26
risan 利山 1666 45-8
rishô 利勝(1642) 12-21
rissha 立些() 42-17
RIYÛ 李由(-1705) 9-21, 18-9, 26-6, 42-4, 57-3, 62-1;李友 41-7
rocho/tei 魯丁翁反故 3-21
rochô 露蝶安永 4 ( ) 42-25
rogen 露言( ) 19-13
rôi (朧意) 9-22
rôjo 老女(old lady) 42-95
RÔKA 浪花 (1669-1703) 1-27, 16-49, 32-15, 35-7, 52-2, 62-26
rokei 路景(花櫻帖) 42-27
rokujô-naidaijin 六條内大臣(1356)40-50
rokusô（六窓）36-59
rosen 露沾(1654-1733) 5-6
rosen 露川(1660-1743) 16-1
rosetsu 露節( ) 40-74
roshû 鷲舟(1666) 63-62
rotei 露汀( ) 42-95
rotsû 路通(d.1738) 10-40 40-61 59-34
ryôa 良阿(-)48-42
ryômô ア毛＝了毛[ls] 4-52
ryôzan（梁山）46-20
ryôsen 良栓? 良詮 ? or kyôsui ( ) 24-52b
RYÔTA 蓼太(1707-87) 1-16, 4-53, 6-30, 8-80, 10-9, 15-43/60,16-45/57, 17-7/77, 36-27/43, 38-11, 40-57/78, 46-49,49-11, 50-55,54-8, 55-22, 60-13/14/22,
ryôto 凉斗( ) 6-41
ryôtoku 良徳 1633 2-23, 37-6/9
ryûdô 柳童（鹿嶋立) 18-16
ryûhi 柳眉 19-9
RYÛHO 立圃(1594-1669) 3-20 +?, 9-6? 17-21/73, 22-1, 42-30, 53-10, 57-12
ryûjin 柳儿(鹿嶋立) 17-34
ryûki 柳儿（鹿嶋）3-1, 32-20,39-9
ryûmin 龍眠( ) 60-6
ryûshi (柳士 c.1700) 28-25
ryûshi -1681 高井立志 28-38
ryûsho 龍昇 拍挙千句 33-3
ryûsui 龍水( ) 6-22
ryûzan 竜山(1795) 22-20

Sadaie → teika
sadakiyo 定清(fl 1670) 49-9
sadanari or teisei 貞成? 22-6
sagetsu 沙月( ) 44-33
SAIGYÔ (1118-90) 西行 0-3, 1-1, 4-63/75/76, **7**-15, 12-5,**15**-5/8,**17**-1/8/9/12,36-

14,**46**-5/6/7/8/9/10/11/12/13/47/48/56/57, **47**-71/74/103,**48**-76/76b,77/78/79/79b/80/ 81/82/83/84,**49**-13, 50-44, 51-1, 55-32, 58-38, 60-27, **63**-42/74
saikaku 犀角(-1693) 13-35, 17-65, 26-7
saimaro (1655-1738) 42-39
saji (左次) 12-25
sakô 左江( ) 16-27
sakô さかふ(1773) 6-28
sanshi 山只 (1725)62-10
sanka c.1700 傘下 17-10, 24-30, 33-25,46-14
sankin, a cart-man? 桟金 車( ) 42-64
sankô.三光(1736) 13-18, 13-22
SANPÛ 杉風(1646-1732) 30-31,32-51,50-2,56-31,64-18
sanryû 賛柳( ) 58-29
sansen 山川( ) 12-42
santôka (-1940) 23-25, 23-27
sarai 左来( ) 45-15
saren 左簾(d.1779) 27-1
satô shigeru 佐藤 滋 4th grade 32-35
seia 青亜(?) 16-89; seian 成安-1664 4-54
SEIBI 成美(1748-1816) **1**-12/25, **3**-22, 4-19, **8**-34/49,**13**-2, **14**-3/5,**16**-54,22-31/37, **23**-11, **24**-11, 32-26, 36-11,38-31,40-68/69,42-69,**46**-29b/53,**47**-10/67/87,**48**-89, **50**-21/43/49, **52**-9, **56**-7/23/24, 59-32, 60-5, **64**-3/14/25
seichiku 青竹() 57-8; seichô 盛澄() 12-93
seichô or morinaga 盛長( ) 47-53;
seichô or masashige 正重 1651 12-68
seichô or masatomo 正朝(1651) 39-5
seichoku 正直(1633) 6-15,55-23, 56-13/15
seichû 正忠(1667) 8-91
seifu-ni (星布尼 1732-1814) 36-42, 43-6
seiichi 清一() 47-83
seijin 青人(1687) 26-13
seiju 静壽 37-2; seijun 性遵( ) 42-1
seiko 西湖 18c 61-18
seikô or masahiro?政公 5-11, 56-37, 62-24
seikô 正幸() 62-38
seima 西馬(1848) 36-18
seimô 正網 if not 綱＝kô/masatsuna 48-19
seira 青蘿(1791) 45-16, 47-38/84, 48-56
seirin 正隣 17-62
seiryô 正良 1638 28-6
seiryû 青流(1707) 28-15
seishi 清之 1651 13-8
seishiki 正式 12-114, 48-20
seishin or masatatsu? 政辰(yms?) 12-100
seishin or kiyochika 清親(1633) 12-38
seishô→masaakira
seisoku 正則( ) 50-32
seitei? 正貞(1680) 48-15
seiwa? 西和(btt) 2-11
seiyû 正友(-1676) 7-12, 56-1
seizan (晴山) 22-16
sekifu 石斧() 8-77
sekkyo 雪居( ) 15-28
sekijo せき女( ) 15-39
senei 沾永(1736) 8-81
senga 沾峨(1776)16-46,18-14/26-14/38-51
sengai 千外 42-61
sengin (專吟) 26-36
senjô 千条（1773) 26-8
senjô 仙丈（1795) 22-12

senka 沽荷( ) 4-57; senkaku 扇角 3-40
senpo 沽圃(-1730) 33-24, 62-25
senri 仙里( ) omake 13-1, 46-3
senryô 沽涼(1679-1747) 9-30
SENRYÛ 2-4, 3-62b,6-46/60/61/62/63,**8**-38/76/94/95/96/97/98, 9-28/37/38/39/40/41/64, **10**-14/21/30/33/35, 13-27,16-41, 17-61, **24**-41/46/57, **25**-3/4/6/9, 26-34/35, 27-9/10/11/12, 28-40, 30-18, 31-6/8, **32**-2/5/6/34/37b/41/42,**33**-11,36-60,**40**-23/30, **44**-17, 50-22, **51**-14/15,53-15,55-22,57-13, **58**-5, 59-15/22, **60**-7,62-3,**63**-14/46/47/48
senryû 川柳(1682, so not karai s.) 12-47
senryû (a haiku poet) 潜柳 1725: 9-8
senseki 專跡 54-15; senseki 川石 16-60
sensô (仙鼠) 鹿島立 17-26
sentoku -1726 沽德 13-15, 50-11, 63-32, 63-36
senzaishû (w.anth)千載集(1188) 33-15
senzen? (仙舟) 26-10
setsutsu? 1645? 摂津守 12-4
setsue? 淅江 26-22
shadô 捨童( ) 36-9
shagetsu 沙月 (or, zamei d 1727?) 23-7
shakujû 尺樹( ) 32-1
shamo 車莫(1795) 14-18
shamyô or samei? 沙明 (1795) 13-28
shara 舍蘿(late 17c) 10-5
sashû 茶州(1773) 15-31
shiboku? 司木( ) 46-23
shida? 柴雫(1774) 12-11
shidô 紫道(17-18c) 3-30, 12-45
shige = 重 - see jû for 18c & later
shigehiro 重弘(1642, 51) 2-21, 37-10
shigekata 重方 1645 1-32,8-86, 28-3, 39-7
shigekatsu 重勝 (1633) 44-2/29
shigemasa? 重雅(1642) 41-4
shigenobu 重信(1651) 56-29
shigenori 重徳 (1690) 30-29
shigesada 重貞( ) 12-71, 62-32
shigetomo 重友(1651) 2-14
SHIGETOMO? 重供 (1645) 16-72, 17-13,30-10, 42-34,46-18
SHIGEYORI 重頼(1601-1680) 2-5/19, 3-28, 6-8 , 7-8/14, 12-96, 13-16, 40-10, 41-1, 42-62b, 48-38? or 頼 重 ?,49-6, 62-2 (&many anon. (崑山集 1651) may be his,
shigezumi 重純 (1656) 47-50
shihakujo 4-16
shihakujo 紫白女(-1719)4-15, 28-17, 47-61
shihan 使帆 (鼠)(17c) 47-89
shihatsu 士髪( ) 64-19
shiho 史邦 fumikuni? (1695) 18-3
shihô 芝峰( ) 47-40 ◎之方 1676: 30-6
shijû 氏重(1633) 7-26,16-62,39-8
SHIKI 1867-1902 子規 9-14/16/19/25/46/48/65,**10**-39/48, **12**-3/40/81/101/110, **13**-20, 15-40/55, 17-39, **19**-14, **22**-8/29, **23**-20, **24**-10/23/24/25,**25**-12/13, **26**-5,27-40/45/46/47, **28**-22/29/39, **29**-27, **30**-21, 33-16, **36**-44, **38**-30/34, **42**-2, 47-10/12/69/85, 48-26, **50**-23, **57**-1, 61-25~8, **62**-1, **63**-49/70, **64**-26
shikkan 必観 1771 47-5
shikô 士巧(花櫻帖) 36-52
shikô 支考 (-1731) 6-51,10-8,16-11,42-47
shimei 史明 12-105
shin 簪? (1774) 48-13

shinan 信安 (1642,1651) 9-52, 65-7
shinchokusen w 新勅選 1235 55-10
shingi 心祇(fl 1760) 4-56
shinjiki or nobunao? 信直() 9-2
shinjin or chikanobu 親信 ( ) 11-18
shinka 辰下(1774) 8-1
shinkei 心圭 42-65
SHINKEI 心 敬 (-1475) 4-6, 10-24, **22**-30b/33/34,23-9,25-2,38-45/46,45-1/18,47-105, 48-51/ 53 /54/63, 50-51, 51-17,53-1,56-39, 60-8b/21, 63-2/9,64-31
shinkei 心計洗濯物(1666) 12-12
shinki (信規) 月影塚 22-43
shinkô 申候 34-3
SHINKOKINSHÛ (waka anthol 1205)
13-14, 23-29, 34-3, Bk III foreword 2, **48**-33/35/72, 50-30b, 41,55-9, 56-11, 61-13
shinpo 進歩(-1747) 55-14
shinseki?: lost japanese 54-6
shinsenzai wakashû 新千載集 1359 40-13
shinshin 新真 or jorei 序令 57-25
shinshô 信照 (筑波?) 10-45
shinshû 真宗(花千句) 51-20
shinsô 信相 鷹つ (1651) 12-22, 56-10
shintoku 信徳(1632-1698) 12-106
shintô 申桃( ) 13-5
shinzei nobumasa? 信政 26-24
shion 思温 1783 42-11
SHIRAO=通称 or hakuyû 白雄(-1792) 3-13,36-19,47-16, 56-32, 58-24,
SHIRÔ 士 朗 (1742-1813) 1-43,3-17,5-9,16-85,**22**-23/24/36/41, 34-17,38-37,40-54, 42-86, 46-60,47-19, 56-30, 58-23, 64-11
shiryû 史流(1765) 16-52
shisan 子珊 (d. 1699) 32-16
shisei (枝静 1777) 41-9 shisei (之政) 42-62
shisen 姿仙 24-12 ◎shisû 之数 9-53
shishi 嗜之(18c?) in 市井風流 8-7
shisô 1700 是相 29-24
shiteijo 紫貞女(-1751) 32-12,33-23
shitsumei (失明),
shiya or koreya 之也 48-8
shiyû 之由 1725 18-4◎shiyû 之友 7-19
shôban (照盤) 56-3
shôbi 松琵(1671-1760) 9-10
shôboku 松木 俳諧漢和 42-76
shôchô 正朝 (kzs) 10-28
shôfû-ni 梢風尼(1668-1758) 59-3, 64-32
shôha 召波(-1771)12-88b, 23-6, 63-78
shôha 松波 40-21 ◎shôha? 正巴 64-9
△紹巴see jôha!
SHÔHAKU 尚白(-1722?) 15-26, 27-14, **32**-21/30, 40-9, 42-5/46,
SHÔHAKU 肖 柏 (1527) 4-12, 8-5,12-94,55-18, 62-33
shôhaku? 尚白( )
shôhei 正平 1642 12-16, 29-17
shôhei 趙平 1773 10-17
shôi (akinori? other?) 昌意 49-1, 51-2
shôji ? 紹二() 7-1, shôichi?紹一 1642: 2-6
shôka-ni 4-91 ◎shôkin 松琴() 9-12
shôkitsu 勝吉 1651 37-11
shokô 諸光()62-5
shôkoku 蕉 (点の下にヨ右左) 國( ) 3-52
shôkoku 蕉國(花桜帖) 30-8
shôkyû 昌休 (d.1552) 4-55, 8-4, 45-7

shômei 正名 14-13 ◎shoo 松鶯 27-50
shôritsu 松藲 56-21
SHÔSATSU 昌察 1734 or 1481 老葉ならば 1-6, 8-27, 38-55, 48-71,49-3,56-26,61-3
shôsei 松井 15-27
shôsei 松星 32-25 ◎shôsen 正川()64-33
shôshi? 燕志( ) 51-6
shôshi or katsuyuki 勝之( ) 10-46
shôshin 松二 1690 夵逐 42-23
SHÔSHITSU 昌叱(-1603),8-2,10-11, 17-54,35-2,40-7/81,42-66/91,47-52/104, 58-3,
shôshu 笑種(1651) 46-28
shôsui 松水() 15-58 ◎shôtô 正冬() 29-32
shôtô 蕉桐 1698 63-30
shôyû 正友 1732 13-24
shôyû 昌友 1680 51-18
SHÔZAN(1717-1801) 8-37, 9-27, 12-49/76, 16-13, 22-35, 23-4, 24-33, 26-23, 28-41, 32-24, 34-1, 56-28, 57-6
shôzan? 小山 58-32 ◎shûchô 集兆()64-22
shuei 種栄 1651 37-7b
shûgetsu 秋月 ( ) 56-8
shûgyo 秀魚 (1783) 12-69
shûgyô 秀暁 (1759)10-37
shûigusô anthol? 拾遺愚草(13c)56-40
shuji 種次 55-4 ◎shûka 集加() 60-23
shûka 秋瓜(1774) 47-32
shunka 桜可(1642) 7-2,7-34
SHÛKEI -1544 周桂 4-44,35-16,17,62-2/18
shunji 俊次(1651) 7-27
shunpo 春峰 ( ) 24-6
shunrai 春来(1763) 32-32 ,62-14
shunshû 春舟 26-9
shunshû 春洲()64-35 ◎shunsui 春水() 14-6
shunya or shunoku 俊屋 2-20
shusei or tanemasa 種政 2-24
shusetsu 朱拙(1655-1733) 4-33
shûsen 習先(1773) 8-16
shûshoku 秋色(-1725) 9-32,13-4, 59-11
skks→ shinkokinshû
soa 素阿(14c) 1-38 soa 宋阿or see hajin
SOBAKU 素 檗 (1758-1821) 1-21, 4-50/60/99 **15**-4, **22**-25, **29**-31, **30**-7/31b, 36-37, **42**-48, 46-59, Bk III foreword end, 62-27, **63**-22
sôbei 草兵衛()62-11
SÔBOKU 宗牧(-1545) 3-23, 12-32, 14-11, 45-12/14/15, 46-30
sôbô 宗房→ bashô ○
sochin 素椿(1777) 54-10
SÔCHÔ 宗長(1447-1532) 3-33, 6-17, 8-22, 10-2, 15-16, 45-3, 48-16
sôdan 鼠弾( ) 32-45
sôdô 宗勳(1778?) 12-43
sodô 素堂(1641-1716) 4-20, 16-58
sôga 宗雅(d.1790) 63-39
sogai 素外(-1809) 42-81, 57-28 ;
素丸→そまる
sogetsu 組月(1712) 24-13;
SÔGI 1420-1502 宗祇 1-2/4/5/34/37, 3-9/10, **5**-16, **6**-27/33/58,**8**-3/8/17/19/20/23/24, **10**-1/25/26/32/44,**12**-53/54/56/59/75/81b/90/112/117, **15**-2/3, 16-35/36, 17-19, 19-12, 22-19,29-1/2, 35-18, 36-2,40-2/18, **42**-15/16/90/93,**45**-2/4/9b/10/11, **46**-16/17/29/43/46/52,**47**-75/77/78/80, **48**-9/37/41/45/46/47/48/

49/50/52/55/57/58/64/73/74/85/87,**49-4**, **50-45**,**51**-3/4,**54**-1/9, **58-**6, **60-**9/12/28/29/30/31, **63**-7/8/28/77, **64**-27
sôha 宗波(fl c 1700?) 16-55
sôi 宗伊 (-1485) 40-33,
SÔIN 宗因(1604-82) 4-18, 6-1, 7-6, 8-12, **12-**6/35/39/83/111, **22-**5/22, 24-1, 29-12, 31-1/2/3/4, 35-6, 37-7, **40-**56/58, 40-62, 42-28, 47-68, 48-39, 58-7, 60-36
sôji 宗治( ) 21-3
sôjun 宗純 1680 11-15
sôkaku 岨角( ) 56-6
sôkan 宗鑑(1465-1553) 48-5
sôkei 宗継( ) 44-20
sokô 礎江 1692 36-45
sôko 蒼狐 1777 9-23, 42-77
sôkyo 宗居(1767) 1-26
sogyoku 素玉(1782) 8-31
SOMARU 素丸(1712-95) 1-20, 4-35, **9-**5,56, 10-27,41,12-27,14-23, 15-61, **22-**2/3/9, 27-27, **42-**54/59/63/82,54-12, 60-32
sôjin 宗仁(1633) 2-7
sôritsu 宗立( ) 56-5
SONOJO 園女/庭女(d.1723?26?) 1-18, 3-41, 5-18, 26-28, 28-28,40-52/53, 50-20
sonshi? 尊氏(1356) 46-25
soran 素覽 8-41
sôri 宗利( ) 55-21
SÔSEKI 宗碩(1474-1533) 1-7,10-34, **46-**27/33/34
sosen 素洗(1692) 3-18
sosetsu 素雪( )62-3
sôshin or sôtatsu 宗辰(kzs) 2-10
soshû? 滄洲(1777) 57-22
sôshun 宗俊( ) 44-4
SÔSHUN 宗春(1734) 3-49, **4-**85/93, **12-**77/95, 14-19, 17-22, 24-2, 49-2, 52-4, 56-35, **60-**10/24, 64-17
sôshun 宗俊 1633 犬子 44-1
sotachi or sotatsu 素達 拍掌十句 4-34
sôtei or munesada 宗貞) 3-50, 10-13
sôya 宋屋(1773) 21-2 ◎sôya 草也 6-50
soyô 素陽( ) 63-40
SÔYÔ 宗養 (1538-63) 8-21, 13-23,17-16/38, 35-4, 48-18
sôzei 宗砌(-1455) 1-29, 3-43, 12-74
sueyoshi 末吉(17c) 46-51,50-31
suigin1680 水吟 11-14
suihaku? 吹白(1651) 17-45
suiô 醉應(1761)宝暦1 1 44-23
suiun (睡雲) 17-66
sunshi 寸志   (1680) 48-31
sûtô 巣？桃 15-41

Tadan? 田旦( ) 38-50
tadatoshi 忠利( ) 35-8
tagusari raihô 田鎖雷峰 (1997) 62-35
TAIGI (1709-72) 0-7 4-38, 10-20, **12-**103/104, 16-83, 26-4, 27-23, 40-34
taikei 泰渓 22-10
tairi 泰里( ) 4-86, 62-30
tairo 大魯(-1778) 22-30c
taisui 岱水 early 18c) 17-79
tajo? 田女(1789) 13-26
takenomon (竹の門) 27-44
takutai 卓袋(17-18c) 3-31,56-38
tangin 探吟(珠洲之海) 55-28

tanri 旦理(1699) 15-7
TANTAN 淡々(1673-1761)   1-42, 3-14, BK II -1,10-38,16-39, 26-21, 29-7, 58-11
tatsu たつ( ) 30-9
TAYOJO (1775-1865) Page 1!, 4-14, 6-53, 9-17,12-79, 12-80,15-30,18-7, 27-22, 64-34
teichô or sadashige 定重(1651) 37-1
teifû 貞富 (d.1712) 55-12
teiji? 定時(1645) 29-18
teiji? 定次() 29-26 teiji 定時(1645) 6-23
teijun 貞順(1642), 7-3 teikei?
teika (sadaie) 藤原の定家 (-1241) 48-70
teikei or sadatsugu 貞継() 12-82, 28-5
teikô or sadayoshi 貞好(1651) 40-17
teikyû 汀躬 46-32
teiseki 汀石 27-13
teishi or sadayuki 定之 1651 44-30
teishitsu 貞室(1609-73) 1-10, 58-1
teisui 亭水( ) 17-57
TEITOKU 1570-1653 貞徳 1-33, 2-8/17, 3-5, 6-5, 7-5/18/20, **11-**8/16, **12-**31/51, 16-87, 26-43, 32-28, 37-5, 38-3, 39-2, 41-2, 42-56, 44-31, 48-4, **56-**12/14/20 58-20, 63-68,70b
tekijin or ogito 荻人 (18c) 1-41
tenryô 沾涼(1679-1747) 38-16
tenzan 沾山(1669-1739) 17-40
TETSUA (哲亜(彌) 哲阿-1798) 17-3/78, 21-12, 34-14, 47-98, 59-19
tetsusha (轍車) 16-2
tochi トチ( ) 57-14
togetsu 吐月 (-1780) 9-13
togyoku 菟玉 ( ) 16-63
tojaku (-1729) 杜若 22-42
tojô 兎丈 15-53-b
tokizane shinko 時実新子-(20c) 62-39
tôko 棟戸(1742) 15-14 江戸俳諧にしひがし
tokô 斗孝( ) 34-12, ◎tokô (吐江) 24-29
TOKUGEN 徳 元 (1558-1647) 12-15/66/72?, 29-15, 48-40, 65-1
tomoyuki or chishi? 知之 12-46
tônyu 斗入 26-3; tôô 冬央() 47-100
tôon 稲音(1773) 23-8
torajo (虎女) 24-31
tôrin 桃隣(-1719, or -1806) 16-51
tôsen 桃先(1701) 29-4;
tôshin 當信 21-4 ◎tôshô 冬松 1689 38-1
tôshu 桃種(1771) 24-50
toshû 登舟( ) 48-68 ◎tosui 斗醉 12-108
tôu 桃雨   c1900 31-22
tôyôbô 東鴦坊( ) 30-2
tsubame 燕( ) 59-23
tsuji-enshi 辻猿子(1651) **29-**20/22
tsujii isosei 辻井五十生(1997) 62-16
tsukiji masako 築地正子 14-4/26
tsunehiro 常廣 56-29
tsurayuki → kokinshû anthol.
tsurusuke 1777 鶴介 33-10

Uchû 宇中 (d 1725) 12-18
ukoku or haguro 羽黒( )59-24
ukoku 雨谷 42-12
ukoku 禹谷鶉萬立? 47-33
unkin 雲巾() 30-3, ◎unshi 雲子 1777 42-9
uoji 魚兒(1687) 9-41

uryû 羽笠 1642-1726 27-6
usei (雨青) 17-23
ushichi (-1727?) 卯七 4-96
usui 雨水(1768) 12-58,56-25
Wafû 和風(1866-)7-33,59-4
waka 菅野谷高政 42-97
wakaku 和角( ) 16-84
wakyû 和久(-1692) 4-42
wasen? (和賎) 27-49
wasui 和推(1736) 17-44
watsujin 日人(1758-1836) 8-10
wright, richard 4-36
Yadô 野洞( ) 42-36
yahan or nosaka 野坂(？) 58-35
yamaguchi seishi 山口誓子 20c 50-56
yamamoto masumi   山元満寿美 57-30
yanagidaru → senryû
yaryô 也蓼(1772) 51-5
yasen (mid 18c) 野泉 8-11
yasetsu 夜雪 ( ) 14-14
yasui 野水(1657-1743) 40-63
yatô 野刀(1728) 5-7
YAYÛ 也有(1701-83) 4-65, **12-**55/78, 17-75, 18-10, 25-7, 26-17, 28-11, 30-27, 34-8, 38-27/28, **40-**22/67/77, 48-14, 50-30, 56-18, 60-8, 64-20
yorihiro 頼広 (1656) 44-10, 56-16
yorizane 頼実( ) 11-17
yôsen 鷹仙 12-60◎yôshi 1783 陽子 47-39
yoshimasa 足利義政 DATE 28-9, 61-24
yoshinaga 好永 1651 63-71
yoshitaka 吉隆 29-13
yôsui? (揚水) 34-13
yûchi 友知( ) 48-32
yûga 友我(1651) 55-20
yûhaku 祐博? 6-3
yûhei 由平(-1704) 12-61, 59-27
yûho (祐甫) 24-32 ; yûin 幽印( ) 26-15
yuji 熊二( )
yûkan? 幽閑 新道 22-4
yûkei 遊系 or yûshi 遊糸 1759 7-24;
yûbun 有文( ) 62-28
yûô 夕翁(1651) 27-4
yûryû 遊流 12-65, 29-25
yûsa 有佐 (1736) 27-26
yûsei 悠川( ) 64-21
yûsei 友清(1680) 3-27
yûshô 友勝(1642) 11-12
yûsui 友水( ) 53-16
yûshi 由之(1687) 10-10
yuteijo 有貞女(1774)16-64
yûshô 友尚(1774) 28-1
yûtô 由当 1651 62-13
yûtô 遊刀(fl 1700) 51-16
yûzan 雄山(-1706) 1-9,13-25
zaia 在亜 36-10
Zaikan 在貫   (1772-80) 33-13
zegan (是岩) 15-44
zekei 是計(新選) 10-31
zenpô 全峯 ( )63-35
zenshû 前舟(1688) 3-16
zôgyokushû anthol. 蔵玉集 c15c? 46-31b
zuikitsu 随吉 1773 42-35
zuishaku 随尺(1698) 58-4

POEM index: Because words are not islands in Japanese (there is no space around them as in English) and tend to clump together (as with German), it is hard to say when we have one word or many. The alphabetic order of this index ignores spaces & hyphens.

日本人の読者にとってABC順は不便でしょうが、この程度はナシよりマシ。。。作者別素引の方に比べてこの方の出来がいい。けれど、完成する寸前、引越しなどあって、疲れてしまいました。誤謬など、お許し下さい。

Abu mo 28-23, aburu made 44-20
ada nari to 40-3, aeba mazu 4-18
akagami 27-20, akebono 13-5,
ake no hana 15-53, akenuredo 4-68
aki mo iza 45-14, ~ saku 41-3
akufû mo 37-11 akugaruru 46-48
amari miba 22-6; amazake 9-22
ame harete hana 6-33,~sakura 6-20
ame kaze 4-58
ame mo [zo] 6-4, ~ naranu 14-17
amenbo ni 50-16
ame ni hana 6-17, ~ ni katsu 6-18
    ~ ni sakanu 6-16, ~ ni sou 11-12
    ~ ni yuki 6-9, ~ no hi o 6-45
    ~ no hi ya 6-39, ame sopo- 6-43
    ~ wa oya 6-8,
ametsuyu 6-32 anagachi ni 48-81
anaichi no 27-34 andon de 59-17
ano kutara 63-20 aoba sae 50-44
aokusaki 27-15 aoyagi no 44-9
aoyagi wa 29-4, arake naya 48-1
arashi yori 54-4 are are to iu 50-6
are kore 12-25, are misai 22-1
are yo are 42-51 arehata ya 43-6
arehateshi 22-43 arehodo ni 9-45
ari-awase o 32-12
arigataiya 29-32, arikiri no 27-9
ari yô wa sake 9-48, ari yô wa ware 32-37, aru ga naka 22-12
asa asa ni 4-96, asa hitori 22-20
asa o min 1-42, asagasumi hana 45-2
asagasumi komeba 8-22
asagiri ni 42-57
asahan o 13-2 asahikage 61-13
asakaranu 62-18, ashi yori mo 3-32
ashiato wa daga 4-73, ~ otoko 4-72
ashibiki no yamazakura to 56-40
ashihiki no yamazakurabana 47-70
ashio mo 63-43, ashiyowa no 12-62
asobe to 10-41, asobi yô 23-19
assari 31-18, asu kitara 63-14
asu mo hana 24-48, ~ no bun 3-54
asu wa tata 4-61 ato ni chiru 47-50
ato-oi (oware?)shi 40-20
ato saki no 42-69
atomodorishite 13-12 atsurae 18-3

aware to omoe 42-97
awatadashi hana 47-87, ~ kyo 4-19
ayu koayu 16-58

Baba ga 32-33 babadono mo 12-67
baketaru ka 7-27, bashi ni 40-44
benkei wa 30-29 bentô ga 32-4
bentô mo 32-3, bi o nikumu 59-28
bijô no kite 55-24
bin ni sake 26-39 binbô ga 8-49
binbônin 8-90 bosatsu koso17-73
bosatsu 17-74 bôshi ni 55-29
botsu botsu 12-102
bôtsuki ga 34-4, ~ mo 33-18
bôtsuki ni 26-4 bukkai-16-88
bun yarasu 17-77 burabura 30-30
burando 57-32 buttasha 12-61

Cha ni 33-12 ~ sake 33-13
chawan 33-17
chayamura no hitoyo 33-5
    ~ no shutsugen 33-4
chi e [chie] 39-5
chigozakura11-16
chikamichi 10-30 chikazuki 21-11
chi ni 38-31
chiraba chire 47-77 ~ fuke 48-64
chiranu nobe 8-17 chirashi 48-51
chirasuna 48-42 chire to 47-98
chireba 47-80
chiri hijite 17-78 ~ chirite 50-52
chiribako 50-14, chiribana 50-29;
chiri chirazu 54-1, chiri-gate 47-65
chirigiwa 47-6 chiri-kakaru 9-36
chiriyuku 56-13 chirizuka 16-81
chiru ato 47-51 ~ hana mo 27-41
    hana ni ari 47-41, ~butsu 47-92
    ~ cho 47-36, ~fumu 50-30
    ~ hachi 8-48, ~ hanikami 57-23
    ~ kenka 31-12, ~mukaeba 5-14
    ~ sugata 16-77, ~ tsukete 38-10
    ~ tsumi 60-38
chiru hana no furi-63-54
chiru hana no hana yori okiru 48-56
    ~ okoru 47-38
chiru hana no kao 47-33,
    ~ kokage 50-24, ~ moto 36-42,
    ~naka ni 47-67, ~ naka ya 12-7,
    ~oto 47-32, ~ sakura 47-91,
    ~urami 48-87, ~ waraji 15-50
chiru hana o atsumete 49-11
    ~he 22-40, ~ katsugi 16-55
    ~ mata 65-10, ~ namu 38-2
    ~oikakete 48-70, ~ oshimu 46-5
    ~ shian 16-53, ~ zabuzabu 16-42
chiru hana wa
    ~ oni 47-62, ~ oto nashi 49-1
chiru hana ya arashi 48-54
    ~ ato 36-45, ~ ima 24-21
    ~ konoshita 47-100, ~ odori 47-10
    ~ sude ni 47-64, tabi 46-50
    ~ uguisu mo 47-63, ~yuki 51-8
chiru hito 6-26, ~ kaze 5-15,
    ~ koto o hana 38-12, ~ shitte 65-4
chiru made wa geba 48-22
    ~ sono hi 47-89, uka-uka 30-18
chiru mo min 48-58, ~mishi 50-51
chiru mono 10-33; ~ nado 4-38
    ~ nomi 47-75;
chiru o mi ni 47-5, ~ mite 48-53

~ oto 22-19
chiru sakura hadagi 47-34
    ~ fukuchû 30-13
    ~ kokoro no oni mo idete 30-12
    ~ kokoro no oni mo tsuno 30-15
    ~ kyo 47-90, mite-inagara 1-20
    ~ ne o Bk III foreword-end,
    ~ tada 47-69, ~ tsuraku 54-16,
    ~ waga 9-58, ~yoshinaki 50-5
chiru toki mo 47-95, ~ ni 24-50
chiru toki wa otokoge 42-17
    ~ tsuburi 63-62, ~ waga 56-24
chiru toki zo 62-36
chiru wa chiru 47-42
chiru wa sakura 47-25
chiru wa[ya] uki 46-40
chisu 11-18, chitta sakura 47-85
chitta to 1-18, chitte hiru 12-95
chitte ichido 50-23,
chôchin de 59-16
    ~ no 15-41, chôchin wa 59-18
chôcho ya hananusubito 40-22
    ~ mitsuzô 59-3
chô ichiwa 40-21,
choku to 47-74
chô tori mo mina 16-85
chô tori[chô?]mo junnomai16-62

Daga irite 4-77, ~ haha 24-32
dai ichi 21-1, dai no 30-20
daibutsu hiza 38-33, ~ o 38-34, 57-1
    ~ ushiro 10-40
daikuro 44-23, daimyô 8-30
dakikome 33-21, dakitsuite 9-41
damasarete 4-66
dango 33-7, dare ga 9-53
dare tote 8-86, ~ tsugete 59-4
dashi ire 17-66, dashinuku 64-6
deae deae 48-6, degirai 50-21
degitte 8-67, dengaku 50-15
deru hito 8-32, detemireba18-12
doburoku 26-10,
dochi mimu[min] 58-18
dochira 58-17 dokadoka 63-53
doko no hana 36-57, ~ soko 40-76
~ zo 24-35, dokosoko 28-12
dô mite 42-38; domori 12-100,
donyoku 50-3; dorobô 27-32,
dôraku 22-41,

Ebigoshi 37-5
edaburi 56-2, eda eda 10-37,
edaha nashi 46-20
eda kitte 11-6, ~ nari 22-15,
    ~wa momo 7-31, ~ tsue 7-4,
eda wakete 42-66
edo o mi 27-29, ~ motte 31-4
edogoe ya atari 31-16, ~ hanami 31-15
edoshû 31-17, edozakura 31-21
eiri shinu 50-18; other ei→yoi
emi nuru 45-13, endôki 12-70
enma-ô 27-25, etadera 8-87

Fude ni 65-1, fue no 28-34
fugenzô chirite 39-6
    ~ no hana 39-3, ~ no kage 39-4
fugu no yo/yoru 36-54, 64-23
fuji wa 35-6, fukaba 50-47
fukakusa no nobe 65-3

fuke arashi hana 10-23, ~ kesa 48-57
   ~ kogakure 48-66
fuke fuke 48-86, fuki-tsukuse 48-44
fukiburi 13-9, fukidashita 27-18
fukinoha 32-49,
fuku kaze mo 40-14, ~ o kirai 48-28
   ~ o miyo 48-27, ~ to tani 48-67
fukurô no shirami 63-59
fumi wa 40-43, fumidai 28-10
funbetsu 9-21, fundoshi 30-21
fune de 31-22, ~ yosete 40-34
fura koko 23-4, furikaeri 64-16
furu ame ni 6-48, ~ mo 6-25
furudera ya 63-24b
furuki hi 22-27, furumai 16-86
furuniwa 62-31, furuzakura 42-95
fushite 55-9, futa yo 58-16
futokoro ni 57-34, ~ no 57-5
   ~ o kaze 4-81, ~ wa 4-82
futon 50-20, futsuka-ei mono 9-68
futsukayoi asahi 61-12
fuyu ni nita 51-5, ~ saki[ku?]12-15
   fuyugomori 58-15, fûryû 42-31

G
aikotsu 0-1, 36-1, gakumon 11-8
gaten shite 54-11, geba fuda 48-23
ge ge no 8-75, gekkô nishi 15-32
geko hana 9-26, ~ nagara 9-29
   ~ no mi 9-12, ~ wa 9-13
   ~ren wa 15-24, ~shû wa 9-24
gohyaku 11-13, goku tsubushi 8-92
gokuraku e 36-55, ~ no 51-13
gorogoro 18-9, goto naraba 55-31

H
ada 59-34, haekakaru 4-34
hagoromo 29-5, haha 24-33
haikai no 28-42 (see *kaiwai*)
haikai wa 62-3, haji 27-3
hakanasa Book III intro 2
hakkiri to 15-34, 36-46
hakuchô 9-62,
haku hito 40-67, haku kumo 17-61

HANA araba 25-7, ~ arite 2-3
~ bana ni 14-7, ~ no ki? 12-72,
   ~ tsubomi 38-4
   ~ bira ga 59-36, ~ no 6-49
   ~ bue o 48-15, ~ bukuro 7-16
   ~ busa o 16-68, ~ dorobo 40-23
   ~ chira de 47-71
   ~ chirasu kazake 63-72
      ~ kaze no 48-2, ~ kaze ya 48-19
      ~ kotori 29-21
   ~ chireba 50-45
   ~ chirite konoma 50-40
      ~ shizuka 46-58, ~ sugao 59-29
   ~ yoi 50-42,
hana chiru ya higasa 26-32
   ~ hito 50-50, ika 50-9,
   ~ omotaki 47-93b
hana chitte dotto 38-56, ~ nao 50-55
hanafubuki doro 30-22, doro 63-33
   ~ dote 50-22, ~ hodo 44-17
   ~ namayoi 51-15, ~ tsukue 51-14
hana funda ko 30-27, ~ waraji 15-52
hana ga ha 23-27, ~ hitoki 35-5
hanagasa 24-31, hanagirai 9-31
hanagoromo nugu 64-34b, ~yog 1-14
hanagoto 53-7
hanagumori makoto 18-14, ~ oboro 18-2

hanaguruma 12-66
hana hitotsu sato 35-12,
   ~ tamoto ni ochi 57-7, ~ sugaru 57-12
   ~ yosogokoronaki 16-66
hana horishi 63-17, ~ iki yo 45-6
   ~ ikusa 48-61, ~ ippon 15-15
   ~ izuku 45-15, ~ kage mo 8-64
   ~ kami de 42-83, ~ kami ni 4-83
   ~ kaze ya 55-33, ~ kui 16-57
hanami kana 57-21; hana min 8-63,
hanami ni mo 16-15, ~ ni to iwanu 3-9,
   ~ muretsutsu 63-42
hanami niya (nya) 24-54
hana mireba sono 46-13, ~ tada 38-48
hana miru mo yakume 60-44, ~zeni 8-53
hanami ni wa ashigaru 8-29
   ~ maegiri 17-21, rôjaku 8-12
   ~ yoshino 58-32
hanami sa 24-41, ~ sen 60-51
   ~ tote 26-26, ~ shû 29-25
   ~ jirami 63-60, ~ kago 3-27
hanamishû 61-16, ~ zake 26-23
   ~ zake hajime 26-42, ~ noma 9-2
   ~ tare ka 12-65

hana MO chiri 47-103,
hanamodori kura 64-33, ~ tonari 64-35
hana mogana 12-59
hana mo haru no 12-46, ~ haru yuku
   12-84, ~ hi 38-14 ~ hito 13-27,
   ~ iku 12-90, ~ sazo 55-5, ~ yo 10-1
   ~ nagara 54-6, ~ naki 17-22,
   ~ nakuba 3-25
hanamori ga 34-8, ~ ni eraruru 34-16
   ~ ni ga 34-6, ~ no mi 34-7
   ~ to narite 34-2, ~ to naru 34-14
   ~ wa 34-12, ~ ya mukashi 34-1
   ~ ya hana aru 34-10,
   ~ ya hana no kokage 34-9
   ~ ya hito no arashi 34-5
   ~ ya shiroki 23-5/34-15, ~ yoru 34-20
hana nara de itsu 42-1, ~ mata 53-19
hana nara hana 24-57

hana NI akanu nageki 28 11-b,
   ~ ukiyo 53-9
hana ni ame 6-13
   ~ chiru 46-46, ~ chô no 37-9
   ~ chô nemuru 16-70
   ~ dete 16-18, ~ eeri 24-37, ~ ha 2-7
   ~ haru 12-84, ~ hi 16-26,
   ~ iru 46-16, ~ iya 48-12
   ~ kane 31-7, ~ kaze akire 48-38
hana ni kaze fukiattari 48-75
   ~ iya 48-30, ~ karoku 48-59,
   ~ yowaru 12-53,
hana ni ki . . . yûbe 30-31
hana ni ki . . . yûhi 64-18
hana ni kite hana naki 17-54
   ~ hana 15-47, 64-37, ~ haya 8-72
   ~ musubu 32-20, ~ oru 40-38
   ~ shibaraku 3-62, ~ tsuide 38-20
   ~ utsukushiku 30-9, yuki 5-17
hana ni kokimazeshi 12-6
   ~ kokoro 46-52, ~ koso 6-44
   ~ kurenu 64-30, ~ kurete 64-29,
   ~ kyo 6-42
   ~ mada 60-28, ~ mau16-84,
   ~ mawa de 28-30, ~ me no 9-35
   ~ mesaba 48-24, ~ naru 17-2,

~ nenu 16-30
   ~ nete chirikuru 49-12, ~ ikanaru 16-1
   ~ tsuki 15-28
   ~ rô 60-12, ~ sake musashi 26-9,
   ~ sake ya 26-15, ~ se o 32-37b
   ~ shin 36-19,~ soite 46-37,~ somu 46-7
   ~ togete/toide? 3-7, ~ tori 28-32
   ~ tsuki 15-30, ~ tsuku 13-33
   ~ ukare 13-17, ~ ukikaze 63-70b,
   ~ ukiyo 32-7
   ~ umarete 36-39, ~ waga 60-31,
   ~ yeite (youte?) 3-20, ~ yo o 26-25,
   ~ yoru 16-82, ~ yôte 9-19, you ten 9-7,
   ~ yuku kokoro 36-2, ~ ware 3-58,

hana NO ame hito 6-41
~ nezu 6-60, ~ ôgi 6-37, yomo 6-40
hana no arashi 64-12, ~ aru 40-73
   ~ ato 16-47, ~ chiranu 56-14
   ~ chiri 38-55, ~ eda motte 9-37
   ~ eda o 40-39, hana no en 15-22
   ~ goto 60-17, ~ haru 0-5,~ hi ya 59-25
   ~ himo mo 38-6,~ himo shinjitsu 38-19
   ~ iro mo 14-11, ~ ni 40-80, no 7-7
   ~ wa kasumi 45-5, ~ uba 59-11
   ~ utsusu 53-15

hananokage aka 8-6, ~ chirashi 33-22,
~ da ga 8-70, ~ hima 27-33
   ~ hitori/ware 60-5, ~ kane mo 13-28,
   ~ katana 24-37b, ~ kono 36-51,
   ~ kuchi 24-11, nemaji 15-19 / 36-36
   ~ nete 14-5, ~ ni 8-28, oboro 24-29,
   ~ warai 54-17, ~ ware 16-9,
   ~ yoi 65-9, ~ suzuri 28-10b
hana no ka ni 45-3, ~ o michi- 45- 8b
   ~ o nusumite 48-5, ~ o sora 45-11,
   ~ ya 45-16
hana no kao mo 47-83, ~ ni 15-23
   ~ o 48-7, ~ tsubomeru 55-12, ~ ya 54-3
   ~ yoki 48-8, hana no katami 28-33
hananoki mo 4-8, ~ ni musubi 56-30
   ~ ni niwatori 16-32, ~ no motte 55-1/17
   ~ no narabu 28-9, o sugi 19-14,
   ~ o ushiro 31-20
hana no ko/ka14-9
hana no koro taiko 27-50, ~ tare10-13
hana no koto 64-11,
   ~ kuchi hirakaba 56-15, ~ man 58-37
hana no kumo achira 17-23,
   ~ kane wa bashô ()13-7/17-32/17-33
   ~ no ue 17-52
   ~ hana no ma 13-6, ~ midare 46-22
hananomoto ni mi 15-20, ~ kozorite
27-4
hananomoto sarikanete 64-4, ~ zehi 8-60
hana no nai 27-13
hana no naka daiji 52-9, ~ haya 27-22
   ~ hito 57-15, ~ keiba 27-44
hana no nami chirasu 13-8, ~hitai 7-10
hana no nishiki 59-2, ~ rusu muko 25-6
   ~ rusu yatsu 25-4, ~ saku ki 10-8,
   ~ saku koro 24-18, ~ tame 48-11,
   ~ to ni 64-34, ~ toki 31-1,
   ~ tomo 23-10, ~ tsuyu 16-67
   ~ ue ni fuku 19-4, ~ ue ni umi 37-8
hananoyama cha 32-42
   ~ dango 32-41, ~ dechaya 60-7,
   ~ dobachi 33-24, ~ dochira 10-31
   ~ donata 36-60/6-46, ~ hinaka 22-8
   ~ hotoke 27-24, ~ inochi 30-5,

~ makoto 9-1, ~ maku 8-97,
~ mata 17-67, ~ oni 55-2,
~ shôben 33-11, ~ to kaite 63-48,
~ tomo 8-15, ~ tsune 40-28,
~ tsuyu 14-20, ~ ukiyoe 24-25,
~ uta 28-1, ~ ya 17-49
hana no yo ni ana16-10, ~ nishi 38-39
hana no yoi fune 32-6, ~ kaku 26-20
~ shosho 6-63
hana no yokuba 2-15, ~ yo o 36-34b,
~ yube? 13-20, ~ yuki 51-1,
hana no yume kiki 16-73, ~ kono 46-38
hana O ame 6-12, ~ ete 57-14
~ fumishi 15-49, ~ fumu 46-51/50-31
~ fun de 16-37, ~ funde hebi 16-50
~ funde onajiku 50-32, ~ tatara 13-25
~ isogu 6-1, ~ kyô 8-25/40-79
~ matsu hikazu 1-13, ~ kokoro 1-6
~ mireba/miba? 6-27
~ miru hito 27-48,
  ~ kokoro wa oya 46-55, ~ yoso 46-9
~ mite kaeru 64-21, ~ waga 16-89
~ nonde 17-60, ~ oru byôshi 40-70
~ oru kokoro 40-69, ~ kyokusha 40-26
~ terashi 15-29, ~ towaba 1-9
hana ono-ono 61-17
hana orite hito 40-29, ~ hachi 40-19
hana saichû 9-69,
hana saite ahô 27-5, ~ hon 10-18
~ imo 32-50, ~ ki wa 7-28
~ mejiro 1-27, ~ nanuka 1-23
~ omoidasu 23-20, ~ shaba 38-47
~ shinitomunai 36-58, ~ soshi 32-44
hana sakaba tsugemu 33-25
~ ushi 12-68,
hana sakanu saki 5-1, ~ wakaki 7-30
hana sakeba bôzu 3-59
~ miyako 48-9, ~ waga 8-27
hana sake to [or, do] uchinuru 6-11
~ saisoku 6-3
hana sakinu asoko 38-30,
~ suzume 16- 41
hana sakishi nochi 1-38
hana sakite 55-3 [see saite for others]
hana SAKU to 63-18
hana saku ya akago 57-9, ~ are 61-21
~ ashi 8-52,~ enoki 27-8
~ goshaku 4-39, ~ hatachi 13-11,
~ heta 8-46, ~ higana 8-68,
~ ima 60-50 ~ inaka 28-26
~ me 16-33, ~ oi 7-22, ~ oyaji 60-3
~ sakura 27-36, ~ shamisen 28-36
~ sokora 0-4/63-45, tabibito 8-45
~ ushi 23-13
hana samushi 63-75, hana sasou 48-72
hana sugite hanami 60-23,
~ moto 19-5/54-18
hana ta-oru 40-66, hana to miba 48-78
hana tomo 47-40,
hana tori mo 3-43, ~ no 9-20
hana WA chiri hito 47-104,
~ chiri sono iro 50-41
hana wa iwaji 58-7, ~ iza 60-9
~ kumo 60-49, ~ mina 46-43,
~ miyako27-2, ~ nashi 53-1,
~ ne ni dejaya 33-14
~ kaeru 29-26, ~ osatogaeri 11-5

~ tori wa 33-15
~ sakase 30-11, ~ sakunari 63-65
~ sakura 17-46, ~ tada 60-8b,
~ uroko 44-5, ~ yo 56-4
hana ya haramu 17-13/55-11
~ saku 59-32, ~ yobito 54-10
hana yori akuru 61-23,
~ mo hana ni arawaruru 63-73
~ mo hana ni arikeru 45-9
~ mo mi 44-3, ~ mo yoshi 32-27
hanazakari aji 27-14/32-21
~ chirasanu 48-52, ~ chiru 10-42
~ dare ga 10-2, ~ fukube10-15
~ iwaba 9-49, ~ kami 10-6/7
~ kanarazu 63-63
~ kara 61-2, ~ ko de 57-16
~ koko de 36-9, ~ kokoro 48-50
~ kumo ni 17-37, ~ kumo yori 17-38
~ kumoi 8-23, ~ nanuka 1-23
~ nioi 8-24, ~ ôharajû 50-2
~ tenka 9-56, ~ ware 10-17,~ yo 61-11
hanazakura hitoki 47-54, kore-ni 22-7
hana zo hitoe 7-9, ~ naki 64-31
haori kite 24-36/40-45
harahara no 32-17, harahara to 50-35
haramite 44-25,
HARU fukami 48-84,
haru goto ni hana 60-16, ~ ki 46-3
haru ikuyo 19-12, ~ kaere 12-34
~kaze ni 48-41, ~ kaze ya 62-20
~ mo mata 5-11, ~ mo minu 12-116
~ ni naru sakura 1-1,
haru no hana ima 40-72,
~ hana to iite 12-114, ~ hi 15-14
~ kusa 21-8, ~ no no 35-13
haru o omou 12-81b, ~ waka 15-2
harusame ni 12-2, ~ no furu 47-11
~ no niwa 6-58, ~ wa 6-50, ~ ya 1-10
haru saraba 53-4, ~ shibashi12-91
~ shinaba 36-13, ~ to iu 17-4
haru wa hana 8-91, ~ mina 1-3
~ nao 12-83, ~ tada 8-20
haru yogite 12-112, hashiri- 50-43
hataberi 26-31, hatanaka 35-15
hata-tose 24-20
HATSUhana ni
~ atonomatsuri 4-87
~ chiru 4-6, ~ dare 4-32
~ hito 16-86, ~ inochi 4-43
~ kokoro 4-93, ~ onna 4-80
~ ukaruru 4-10
hatsuhana no 4-64, ~ tengu 4-21
hatsuhana wa chira 4-59, ~ dare 4-29
hatsuhana ya fukumen 4-33, hito 4-17
~ kasanegasane 4-92,
~ omoitogetaru 4-14
~ suso 4-31, hatsuzakura amata 4-55
hatsuzakura bentô 32-1,
~ hana no kokoro 46-41,
~ hana no yononaka 4-62
~ hana to 8-84, ~ haya 4-94
~ hisoka 4-13, ~ inaka 4-24
~ ni 28-40,~no 50-46, ~ waga 4-74,
~ ya 28-41, ~ yae 4-42
ha wa nai 2-6
hayaku sake nani 12-12, ~zendai 12-13
hazukashi no 60-41, ~ya mita 42-96,
~ ya tatami 36-18

hebi idete 26-40, ~ nakuba 16-51
~to 26-17
hedataru 28-8, hena-hena 46-53,
heta 22-11
HIno kami 4-1, hi no mikake 45-18
~ tomosaba 2-14
hibari 18-15, hidarusa 15-6,
higan nite 41-6, ~ tote 41-1, hige 16-25
higurashi 31-14, hikiami 44-11
hikikaete 15-5, hikikunde 9-43
hima 31-10, hime 42-70
hina dakite 62-14, ~ no 12-118
~goto 57-3
hinomoto no hito 61-1, ~ no yama 61-14
~ ya 44-33
hiradaru 26-7, hirake 46-26, hiraki 28-6
hirari 10-14, hiroitaru 32-11, hiru 12-9
hisakata 46-2, hishihishi 21-9
HITOashi ni 8-59, ~ no 63-31
hitobito ni 42-85/58-27
hitobito[ya] kasa 17-43
hito-eda wa oranu 40-9, 42-46
~ orite 42-89
hito-erami 23-16, hitoe zutsu 42-91
hitogao 4-95, hitogoe ni 14-21
hitogoe no 42-8/42-29, ~ ya 51-11
hitogokoro hyôtan10-16,
~ mazushiki 8-31
hito goto ni 1-30, ~ no 8-8
hitogui 2-17
hitohana ni 19-1, ~ ya 4-2
hitokakae 28-17
hito ki hito ki 22-16,
~ saku hana ni 46-25, ~ ya 35-4
hitokoishi 47-16,
hito kureba 23-15, ~ kusashi 63-39
~maru 29-18, ~ mo kozu 46-10,
~moto 58-20, ~ mo ware 32-46
~nami 6-52, ~ narete 42-78,
hito no chiru 14-15, ~ kokoro 46-21
~ me 42-10, ~ mono54-15,
~ moru 63-9, ~ tame 4-79, ~yuku 3-48
~ ni hana 0-2, 36-7,
~ ni kuchi 16-60, ~ ni kuwareshi 58-30
~ o min 9-46
hito oto ni 42-9,
~ya inu 16-14, ~ kuma 16-2
hito oute 16-83
hitori ato 12-51,~yukite 30-8,~zutsu 3-22
hito sake 9-54,
hito saki 23-24b
hito sareba 47-17
hito sarite sakura 15-60, ~ kureru 22-18
hitosato 62-22, hito satte 8-80,
hito shizuku 6-35, ~ suji 63-35
~ tabi 7-33, ~ ten 17-58
~ tose no kaze 48-47 [& ichinen],
~ tsukami 40-78
hitotsu nugu 18-7
hito wa chiri 48-63, ~ hana 1-11
~ mina 46-11/ 58-38
~ saite?sakite 10-38
hitoyasa 32-48
hito yubi 59-27, ~zato 28-44
~ zeni 62-27, -ashi 32-12
hiya tsuku 1-21 / 4-99 / 36-37
hiyajiru 32-15, hizakari 22-9
hizakura 65-6, hizamoto 6-42

hôchô 44-16,
hoka hoka 6-34, ~ naranu 22-25
~ no ki 42-12, hoka no mimi 28-15
~ no tame 24-12
hokorobi 8-96, honburi 14-24
honchô 18-11, hônen 51-7,
hone wa 44-31,
horagai BK II -1, hosogoe 16-54
hôsô no 24-30, hotoke 38-49,
hototogisu 12-4
hyakuseki 50-17, hyôban 60-34

Icchi 3-62b
ichi ban 38-9, ~ boku 24-47,
~ nichi no 16-39 ~ nichi wa 4-27,
~ ni dete 63-21 ~ hana 3-28
ichinen no (hitotose?) yume 50-54
ichinichi mo 22-17, ~ wa chaya 12-64
~ wa kome 32-8, ~ wa kyaku 56-7
ichi ri 8-58b, ~ shiranu 42-50
idakareshi 59-7
ide-iri 46-28, idetachi 4-22
idobata 9-32, iejû 32-10
ietsuto 17-76
iezakura ariake 56-33, ~ kaze 56-10
~ mabore 2-20,
ii hiyori 25-3, ikaba 61-25,
ikadashi 9-34
ika de 48-83, ~ ni 5-16/51-4
ike kiyomi 52-4, ~ mizu no 52-5
~ mizu o 52-6, ~ noha? 12-110,
~ o nomu 16-12
ikite au 23-1, ~ iru BK II-4, ikizue 18-8
ikken shite 16-11, ~ wa 33-20
iku yo 4-44,
ima ga 53-5, ~ no ware 46-57
~ no yo ya gyôgi 63-26,
~ hanamigatera 27-31, ~ neko 8-13
~sara 7-15, ~ zo chiru 47-68,
~ zo ueno 24-43
inazuma appendix to bk I, 65-8
inishie mo 62-24, ~ ni ware 60-53
~ no hito 46-56, ~ no nara 62-8
inochi araba 58-24
inokoro o 57-33
inudomo ya 16-20, ~koro ga 16-17
inuzakura kaze 2-5, ~ mite 2-23
ippai ni 9-14, ippen no 17-62
ippon mo yamaji 35-16, 35-17
~ ni katamaru 12-78, ~ no naru 35-14
~ no eda 22-42, ~ hana 22-34
~ hikazu 35-3
~ o 35-7, ~ wa (or no) 35-10
iranu hana 40-75
iriai ni 13-29, ~ no ato 56-6
~ kane 13-24, ~ no kubisu 64-7
~ no kuromi 13-19, ~ o hiru 13-22
~ o matsu 8-77, ~ nikumi 13-26
~ oshimu 8-76, ~ sora ni 13-21
~ ya sakura 13-30
iro iro na 0-7, ~ no hana 21-6
~ no hito 24-8
iro ni deru 42-81,
~ ni ka 12-38, ~ no mizu 49-3,
~ o sugata 45-10, ~ yo ka 12-39
irojiro 53-10, isamashiku 13-1
ise-zakura 37-7b, ishibotoke 5-10,
isogashiki 24-6, issen 33-8
itozakura mireba 29-2, ~ ni 47-82

~ no hana 29-9, ~ shita 29-27
~ sunawachi 29-7
itsu to naku 4-84, 17-55, ~ sakura 23-25
itsumade 47-73, itsuwari 47-78
iu koto no 15-4, ~ o 9-41
iya iyan 12-97, i-yukiai 23-22
iza orite 40-12, ~ sakura 36-17
~ saraba 36-32, ~ tomo 9-60

Janosuke 26-41, jiji-inu 16-22
jinka 58-26, jiutai 19-7
jôgowa 31-13,
jômon de 8-94, ~ no 14-25
jûbako ni irete 64-32, ~ tai 32-26
jûnana 32-5,
jûniha 16-49, jûnin 6-55,
ju ni san 26-3, junjô ni 47-37

Kabin 40-17,
kadoguchi 17-36, kadozakura 56-27
kaerusa ni 64-22, ~ no 64-10
kage ni BK-2
kago kaku 16-3, ~ kaki 24-26, ~ orite 42-6b
kaichô no niwa 38-27, ~ hi 4-65,
~ meate 38-22
kaiwai no kuchisugi 28-43
kakaru hi 47-96, ~ mi 47-58
kakigoshi 56-11, kama de 40-74
kamakura no ana 8-83
kami hige 27-21, ~ katachi 32-24
~ no hana 49-10, ~ zo kami 37-2
~ginu 40-1, ~goto 38-11, ~kaze 48-62,
~kuzu 12-11, ~shimo 9-42
kanarazu 47-22, kanashimi 48-71
kane kakete 13-3, ~ kiete 13-13
~ no koe 13-23, ~ tsuki no 13-32
~ tsukite 41-8
kanete 10-32, kankodori 12-120
kannon 21-15, kantan 42-56
ka o kakeba 2-25,
kao ni 4-37, kao o 53-11b
karasu 16-44, kareki 58-23
karigane 48-33, karikurete 36-28
kasa de 7-39, kasamochi 27-38
kashikokumo 6-54, kashinoki 17-11
kasumu 17-17, katakoto 24-53
katakage 3-16, katawaki 8-61
katsu 10-34, kawarame 8-4
kazabukuro 29-20, kazadoko 35-11
kazagoe 12-86, kazaguchi 56-8

KAZE aru 56-12, ~ fukanu 1-37
~ fukeba hanazono 8-21
~ fukeba obosônaruya 2-1
~ mo mada 48-45, ~ mo miyo 12-54
~ ni chiri 47-24, ~ ni chiru 46-47
~ ni hana chirijiri 47-43, ~ ya 29-16
~ ni ugoku 29-15, ~ no kuchi 48-43
~ no mae 41-17, ~ no oto 48-3
~ no tôru 56-9, ~ o mite 48-74
~ o naku 63-16, ~ tsukite 9-17
~ ureshi 48-68, ~ yaminu 48-73
kazukazu 30-7, kedamono 39-1
keiba 31-8
keisei no hana 24-40, ~ kimo 59-30
keisei wa hone 29-31, ~nochinoyo 59-20
kenbutsu ni chiri 55-16, ~ yama 10-28
kenkakai 31-11, kesa zo 61-3

KI hitotsu 0-6, ~ ni itta 3-56
~ no furi 62-12, ~ furui 27-1
~ rakusa 30-19, ~ tsukishi 21-7
~ wa futatsu 3-40, kigi 40-62
kikori 12-79, kimi miyo 43-1
kimigayo no higasa 8-1,
~ no ôhan 32-23, ~ wa 61-19
kin/kane no hako/fun 8-88, 24-4
kinô auta 23-8, ~ kara 4-9
~ kyô hana 8-35, ~ kyô takane 54-19
kinomata 15-42. kinô mishi 4-53
kin no ma 62-1,
kinoshita or kinomoto or konomoto
kinoshita ni furuki ~ 62-30,
~shakushi 32-32,
kinsatsu 3-12, kinugasa 42-36
kinu-uri 33-23,
kiori 12-16, kirei 24-24, kirikuchi 63-10
kisaragi 36-41, kisen 26-44
kisha 63-70, kita inu 16-13
kita ka 52-1, kite mireba 42-39
kitsutsuki 16-48,

KÔban 9-16, koboretemo 62-33
ko-bôzu no 61-28, ~ ya 38-29
kochi fukeba 36-48, ~ kochi to 48-31,
~ no hana 56-18
kochô mo 16-75, kodorobô 27-30
koe notte 56-19,
~ yokuba utaô/utawamu 28-19, 47-9
~goe ni 27-35
kogoto 23-14, kô ikite-iru II-636-4
koi noboru senjitsu 49-9, ~ taki 49-8
kô iru 10-49, koi wa taki 44-2
kojiki mo 8-43, ~ no 8-44, ~ to 8-39
koki-mazeru 19-6,
kokonoe ni hisashiku 62-19,
~ ni mitaranu 62-5, ~ o ochi 62-29
kokoro aru 12-111, ~ dani 46-17
~ etsu 48-80, ~ kara 36-6,
~ nokoru 13-31
~ nomi 46-27, ~ yukite 26-24
komebukuro 8-50, 32-31
komushiro 16-80, konjiki 62-16
konnyaku 32-52, ko ni aku 57-10
konogoro no mori 12-107, ~ uta 34-19
konogoro ya atosaki 16-79, ~ neko 10-7
kono hana ga 12-3,
~ no hitoyo no uchi ni 40-41, ~ wa 40-42
kono haru 60-21, ~hodo 64-2,
~kuni 61-27
konomoshi 56-31
konomoto o 38-13,
~ wa(ni) shiru 32-14
kono nemuri 36-27, ~ omoi 15-53b,
~ onna 63-5, ~ sato 50-26,
ko no shita ga 48-21
kono sora 18-4, ~ ue 42-59, ~ yô 38-43
konu made 23-29
ko o kase 57-11, ~ o tsurete 57-2
koraebukuro 12-22, koraezei 47-49
kôraibito yo 2-16
kore de 36-20, ~ kara 42-7,
~ made mo 30-1, ~ made no 4-15,
~ o miyo 2-12,
~ wa kore . . . chiru 47-7, 58-2
~ hana 58-1
koronde 10-3, ko-samuki 5-12,
kosegare 10-22, ~tarai 52-8, ~tatami 5-3

koto no ha mo 24-5, ~ o uzumu 58-3
koto o 16-8,
kotoshi kiri kotoshi 60-26,
　　~ nado 60-50b
kotoshi mata 23-6, ~ yori 4-7
kotsukotsu 47-28
kozo mo 47-94, ~ ni 4-4,
　　~ orishi 56-1, ~ kitari 4-20,
kozue 48-79b

KUbi 22-4, kuchi aku 44-28
kuchibiru o 16-59, 59-6
　　~ wa 55-22, kuchigidaore 42-73
kufû 15-40, kui/e-domo 32-22
kuimono ni 32-13, ~ o 26-6,
kumagai 11-10
kumo bakari 17-41, ~ e iru 17-40
　　~ harau 17-70, ~ mo kakare 17-8
　　~ no naka 17-48, ~ no ue 40-6
　　~ o fumu 6-21, ~ hana 41-4,
　　~ nonde 17-59
kumori 8-14, kumoru hi wa ichi 18-6
kumoru hi wa kumoru 18-5
kumo to mishi 17-64, ~ saku 17-69
kuniguni 38-16, ku no shaba 38-44
kure-oshimu 15-36, kurete 14-14
kureyuku 4-98, kururu hi 14-6
kururu iro 10-11, kuru to 62-7
kusaki 39-8, kusatte 12-49,
kutabirete 40-65
kutsuki 48-65, kutsutabi 4-23
kyô bakari 60-14, ~ e 12-103
　　~ koso 27-57, ~ kozuba 4-71,
　　~ jû 12-104, ~ made no 30-1, ~ wa 3-8
　　~ mo mata hana 34-11, ~ sakura 1-35
　　~ no hi 10-43, no kure 50-49,
　　~ no tame 12-37, ~ nomi 64-5,
　　~ onna 24-27, ~ to 12-36
kyôsoku 40-48,
kyô wa hana mimaji 36-35, ~
　　　　sakujitsu 4-54
　　~ wa kyû 8-18, ~ wa yo 3-49
kyû suete 4-3, 4-97, kyûkutsu 63-27

Machi machishi 23-12, ~oshimu 1-5
machidô 12-43, machite 48-85
mada kaze 12-55, 48-14, mado 51-19
magau 17-12, mago ya 7-34,
maigofuda 60-1
makkuro na 27-11, makkuro ni 10-39
makoto 51-2, mamorarete 24-28
manekaruru 48-32,
maneku ogi kaze mo 11-14
maneku ogi kaze nya 11-15
manjû de 32-29, ~ wa 32-28
mankai 10-47, mannichi 12-10
man ni hitotsu 48-40, mannin no 48-26
manten 17-3
masao 29-28, massaki 47-4, masse 38-42
mata hito no 4-30, ~ hitotsu 36-24
　　~ kaze 48-14, ~reshi 40-40
　　~ shite 8-57, ~ tagui 22-13, ~ to 23-9
mataru tote 1-7, mate to 36-25, 47-72
matsuba hiroi 19-13
matsubara ya hana 26-13, ~ tenjin 24-44
matsu hana 1-15, ~ hito ni 12-117
　　~ hito mo 40-15b, ~ no 42-16,
　　~ hodo ohana 1-8, ~ wakokoro 1-4
~kaze 19-8, ~ kitta 42-13
　　~ koro 6-2, ~ ni 12-48

mayoi-ko no 57-27, ~ ya 57-25
mayu hirake 29-1, mayuguro 53-11
mazakari no 46-23
mazu aketa 50-7, ~ yado 9-50
meguri-au 23-2, ~ meguri 7-2,
mekura sennin 8-38
me ni michite 46-24, ~ miyuru 47-101
me no denu 2-18, ~ doku 59-12
me o tojite 28-2, me wa idete 44-6
meutsuri 58-25, mezamashi 49-5
mezurashiki 55-8

MI-agureba 22-3, ~ akanu 37-6
michi ari 3-14,
　　~ michi no 58-13,~ ya 3-11,
　　~bata no 16-7, ~bata wa 29-10
　　~gusa ni chô 16-74, ~ hatenu 24-56
migurushi 63-4, mihorete 60-6
mihotoke 38-24, mijikayo12-30
mi-kaereba 64-13, mikka hodo 1-25
miko no mai 37-10, mimi yori 30-3
mimizuku 16-43
mina chirite 42-94, ~bito 8-33
minagara　First page of the book!
minamoto 49-2, minaosu 24-13
mine 48-76b
mi ni shimite 6-30, ~ sowanu 64-17
　　~ tome 22-14, ~ yuku 2-13
mi no 54-7, ~ o subome47-39
　　~ o wakete 55-32
minu hana mo 17-19, ~ hana no 45-12
　　~ hito no12-69, ~hito o 48-37
　　~ koi 17-20, ~ koto 58-4,
　　~ mono 3-55,46-35, ~ oku 42-11
mireba 54-5, miren 47-59

MIRU hana ya 21-4
miru hito mo hana 7-19, horuru 7-18
　　~ kikyôranshû 9-18, ~ naki 12-52,
　　~ sosôna 4-67, ~ yama 42-34
miru hito ni kaze 48-55, ~ kumo 17-44
　　~ warai 21-13,
miru hito no hana 23-28, ~ tama 16-76
miru hito o kaesanu 10-45, 59-9
　　~ kaze 48-48, ~ ketsukutsunagu 2-2
　　~ miru ya 24-3,
miru hito wa 29-11, ~ ya 29-19
miru kokoro 46-33,
　　~tabi-ni kusuri 21-2, ~ minu 45-9b
　　~ uchi ni aranu 22-30b, ~ saku 6-28,
　　~ samurai 24-55; ~ uchi ya 7-17,
　　~ wakashu 24-19, ~ ya 42-28,
　　~ yori 28-5
misebaya 54-12, mishi wa 46-34
mishirarete 34-18, mishiraruru 8-9
mite ireba 22-2, ~kite 30-31b,46-59
　　~ maware 60-8, ~modoru 4-69
　　~ nomi 40-11, ~ru17-16,
mitoreiru 56-22, mitorete 46-18
mi-tsukushite 48-60,
mi-tsurete 27-23, miwayama 17-18
miyabito 8-89, miyage 26-21
miyama 12-29
miyoshino no chikamichi 58-14
　　~ yamabe 58-10 yamai 55-10
miyoshino ya hoka 58-6
　　~ korobi 58-19, ~ ne-oki 17-51
　　~ yamato 28-4
mizuchaya 33-10, ~ dori 52-2
　　~ no awa 52-52, ~ tsubo 52-10

MOchi de 9-30, ~ samete 32-36
mochite (motte?) okuru 17-75
modokashi 24-52b, momiji 30-16
mono iu 2-37, ~ iwanu 16-31
　　~ iwazu 42-21, ~ omowazu 53-2
　　~ oshimu 60-22, ~gatari 37-7
　　~ hoshi 17-79,
mori 63-29, morobito 4-86
morokoshi no hito 61-9, yoshino 58-8
moshi furaba amatsu 18-13, ~ shibai 32-2
môsumai 26-18, motometaru 42-48,
motte-okuru 40-77, muchi 42-100
muhitsu 28-11,
mukashi kana ran [?] 3-34
　　~ to wa　14-4, 14-26
muma 50-11, 63-32, mume wa koso 4-5
muramura 17-10
murasaki 8-95, murete 63-2
muri koki 4-91, ~ ni sasu 42-65
mushitateru 42-67, musôji 38-28,
musume 27-10
mutsukashi ya hana 22-35,
　　~ mainichi 59-10
myaku 21-10, myôjô 15-61

Nabe 18-17, nagaishite 15-53c,
nagajike 1-40, nagaki 12-109,
nagametsutsu 22-33
nagamu 22-5, nagaraete 60-39
nagarete 49-7, nagekazu 38-45
nagekuna 47-81, nagusami 42-18
nai sode 8-54, naite-yomu BKIII-1
nakashimo 8-41, naki na 62-6
naki ni 22-30, namakeru 28-18
namanaka ni hana 38-32, ~ kaeru 64-3
namayoi mo 10-35, ~ ni 9-33
namayoi no munen12-17
　　~ onna 42-82, ~ tsuki-ataru 9-38
namayoi o 40-30, naminaranu12-24,
nami no 44-27, namu namu36-34,
nan no ki 61-4, ~ no mi 54-2
nani hitotsu 4-50, na ni hokoru 42-54
nani kure 8-69, ~ mo kamo 47-61
　　~ mono 8-65, ~ nite 9-57,
　　~ sakura zakura 8-56, ka 8-55
　　~ surete 42-44,
nanibito no 32-47, ~ goto mo 22-32
　　~goto ni 10-10, ~goto zo 31-5
nanimokamo 30-2, nanimono 63-11
na no 42-53, nantonaku 8-36
nao iku 10-44, nao mitashi BK II-3
na ore 40-56, ~ o shira 23-7,
　　~ o yobeba 11-20
narabu 63-28, nara nanae 62-21
narazuke no 62-26, ~ o maru 32-43
narete 38-46, naru 47-53
nawashiro ni 50-39, ~ no 50-37

NE-nokotte 15-26, ne-oshimi 15-46
neburasete 6-5, nedaruma 38-54
negawakuba hananomoto de 36-16
　　~ nite 36-14
negoki 26-43, negokoro 15-56
nehan 46-29b
neko ni 25-1, ~ no 44-24
nekoronde 8-81, nemuki 1-12
nenarande 24-15
neru hima 15-45, ~ hodo 48-89
　　~ koto 9-23

neta hito 50-19, ~ mama 64-24
netaru ma 36-23
nete hana 6-7, ~itte 29-24, ~kikeba 27-45
  ~ machishi 16-71, ~miredo15-58
  ~okite 15-48, ~matsu 8-66,
  ~ shiranu 6-31
neyo 8-79

NI-awashi 3-36
nichi-nichi 63-54b
ni daitai 61-26, ~do to wa 9-28
nigiyaka14-22, nihon wa 27-42, 61-22
nijûgo 45-17,
ni ki bakari 12-77, ~ ni saku 41-2,
nikui hôdo 8-85, nikui yatsu 23-11,
nikumarenu 17-34
ninaichaya 33-6, ninozen 32-16
nioi koso 3-51, nippon 37-4
nishi higashi 9-9, nishiyama 36-52
nita kao 8-40, nita-mono 59-8
niwa ni 62-2, ~ no 9-27, niwatori16-34

NOdoka naru 56-26
nodokesa no18-1, ~ wa 10-9
  ~ ya dechaya 33-16, ~ ya hana 15-31
nokorinaku 4-60, nomi-akete 40-51
nomu 15-35
no ni 44-26, no o 8-93
norimono 40-46, nosanosa 63-55

NUkegara 25-9
nurigeta no hô 47-29, ~ oto 47-27
nuru chô 2-21, nusumarete 40-60
nyôbo no ku 10-21, ~ no chie 57-13

Obi 17-15, obotsukana 4-63
ôburi 6-47, ochikochi mo 15-12, ~ya 59-23
ochitsuki 3-57
ôdera 13-10, odoroku 15-27
odosareta 16-21, ôgi 26-38;
ôhara 17-14 ohyakudo 38-36
oi wa 42-86, ~nureba 60-20, ~nuredo 60-25
  ~tari 60-35, ojôsama 57-30
ôkami no 42-77, ~ ya 42-76, ~ôkata 50-12
okikotatsu 5-18, okoto koso 7-6
oku ni haite 42-71, ~ ni nao 12-5
okurareshi 17-80, okureru 1-43
oku wa 62-10, okuyama mo 37-3
okuyama wa 37-1, ~ ya 42-62
omoe 46-36, omohitsutsu 3-50
omoi-iru 46-30, ~komete 22-22
  ~ne 4-85, ~tatsu 58-35, ~yare 35-18
omoshiro 17-63, omou koto hana 22-31
omou koto naki 46-31, omowanu 15-11
omowazu 60-30, omukai 60-42

ON-niwa 42-55, onaigi 9-66
onaji hito24-10, ~ koto54-13, ~ku 15-8
ôneko 63-52,
oni no sumu 63-41, ~ tsuno 30-14,
  ~ sumu 63-40
onnadomo 30-25, ~ tote 48-13
  ~wakashu 53-16
ono no 42-25, onorera 63-56
onshaku no akararu 5-6, ~ hada 5-7
onyama 27-7, oraba waga 2-10,
oraba ore 40-5,
ora de kaeru 40-53b, ~ tada 63-8
oranda 1-19, oranu 42-45, orazunba 40-10
ore nusume 40-68, ~ ore to 40-57,
  ~ wa 24-46

orichin 42-64, ~eda o 29-30, ~ ya 46-29
  ~ kaeru 40-37, ~ kuru 11-4,
  ~ okose 40-52
orinokosu eda 40-7, ~ kosue 40-81
orite 63-3, ~toraba 40-15, ~toru 40-55
oritotemo 40-27, ~ yoshi 40-59, 56-34
oru-eda 63-7
oru hito no sune2-9, ~ te 2-8
oru hito ni 40-18, ~ o 40-32
orukoto 60-13c, ôsakura 63-24
osanagao 7-29, oshimanu 1-2
oshimarenu 46-12, oshinabete 1-26,
osoi 12-18,
osoki hana 6-14, ~ mono 12-42
osoku saku 7-14, ~ toki 12-75
  ~ toku 47-8, osonago 57-6
osozakura ari 12-106, ~ hito12-76
  ~ mi 12-81, ~ na o 12-74, ~ nashi 12-8
  ~ onoga 12-20, ~ osoki 12-40
  ~ shizuka 12-101, ~tsukuzuku 12-115
  ~ zen 12-50
ôta (outa) ko 57-4, ôte (oute) 11-3
otokodate 31-9
otoroe ya hana 40-71, ~ mita 60-45
ototoi 58-36
ôuma 16-4, ôumi 44-12,
oya ari 57-26, ~ ki 11-11
  ~ nakuba 15-1, ~ ôte/outte ko 57-17
  ~ to ko ga bun 57-29,57-31
  ~ to ko ga ippon 57-28
ôyuki 51-9, ôzakura 10-48
ôzei 9-11, ô-zô mo 29-29,
ozô(ôsô?) no 11-7, ôzora 9-4

Patto 65-7

Rainen 10-6, 36-3
rakka eda ni kaeru to kake 52-11
  ~ mireba 16-78
rakka maiagari 48-88, rakkasame 6-24,
raku sae 62-17, rakugaki 28-16
rinki 12-47, ro fusaide 5-5
ro o fusagu 5-4
ryô no te 64-20, rô no nami 60-52,
rôsai 12-21, rôsoku 15-38

Sabishikare 22-24,
sabishiki 33-19
sadamari 63-78, sadame 47-84
sahohime → saohime, saifu 32-18
saigyô-ki 36-47, ~ mo 55-26, ~ ni 42-19
  ~ no 46-14
saisen 38-23, saite 47-13, saka de 48-46
sakabite 44-21, sakagura 9-61
sakanu ma no1-33, ~ o 1-34, ~ ya 30-6
sakari ja 24-38, ~ naru 38-5
  ~ ni wa 27-43, ~sugi 7-12
sakasama 42-74,
sakazuki mo 9-10, ~ no 26-14, ~ o 26-19
sake abite 24-12
sakeba-chiri 42-90, sakeburi 4-88
sake kau 26-8, ~kusaki 14-18, ~ nakute
  mireba 26-34, ~ nakute nan 26-33
  ~ no toga 56-32, ~ no toku 26-1
  ~ nome 16-23
  ~ o tsuma tsuma o mekake 24-22
                                ~ sake 9-47
  ~ sake to hana 6-6, ~ negau 9-52
  ~ to nanoru 27-26, ~ tôshi 26-45
  ~ ukete 26-37, ~ uranu 26-36 ~ yori 7-8

SAKI chiru 47-86, ~ ni yuku 3-39,
  ~ o sae 47-1,
  ~ sakazu 8-5, ~ sake to 42-93
saki-chiru no 47-14, ~ wa 46-39
sakikakete 63-13, ~kanete 12-44
  ~komete 10-24, ~michite hana 61-24
  ~michite hitoki 35-9, ~midasu 4-51

SAKU fuji 12-94,
  ~ hana ni keburi 27-16
saku hana ni subete 38-40
  ~ ni ukiyo 38-18, ~ no kumo 17-50
  ~ no naka 38-41, ~ wa tada 56-29
  ~ ya matsu 1-32, ~ ya toshi 12-26
sakujitsu 6-19
saku kara ni miru 47-18,
  ~nadeherasaruru 63-15,
  ~nawa 63-15b, ~ sakura 63-64
  ~ tsumi tsukurasuru 8-73, 54-14
saku made 51-3, ~ mae 4-36,
  ~ mo 42-24b, ~ o 56-20
sakurabana chirikai 50-25,
  ~ dotchi 15-57, ~ nani 47-48,
  ~ saki 23-18, ~ toki 47-46, toku 47-45
sakura chiru kokage 47-105
  ~ nawashiro 50-38, ~ tokoro 50-8
sakuradai hana 44-19, ~ koyoi 44-29
  ~ kutsushi 44-18, ~ su 44-22, ~ya 44-30
sakura e 60-13b, sakuragai 10-12
sakuragari bijin 3-45, hotoke 3-2
  ~ kaesa 64-27, ~ sake 3-19, ~ ya 3-53
  ~ yodaka 3-29, ~ yoki 3-4
sakuragi ni 48-20, ~ ya hana 43-5, 61-15
  ~ ya onaji 10-36
sakura hitoki 12-73, ~ hodo 14-2,
  ~ iro 8-19, ~ kana 42-61
  ~ kara dehairu 0-8, kara sakura 9-39
  ~ konnyaku 32-51, ~ made 63-76
  ~ maru 53-17, ~ mi ni 3-61,
  ~ mina 61-18, ~ mite aruku 22-38,
  ~ mite haya 46-4, ~ iki- 8-42,
  ~ kagami 24-45
  ~ mochi minna 32-34, ~ pakutto 32-35
  ~ mo muga 26-35, ~ moru 9-64
  ~ naki hotoke 61-7, ~ naki koma 61-6
  ~ ni mo 24-7, 30-28; ~ saite 40-63b
  ~ saki sakura 60-15, ~ saki ushiro 52-7
sakura saku dai 61-20, ~ haru ni 14-23
  ~ haru wa ironaki 19-2, ~ yado 25-2
sakura saku kana 5-2, ~ kore 61-10
  ~ koro 16-5, ~ tôyama 19-9, ~ueno 60-13
sakura sakura chitte 47-21, ~ kaeri 28-29
  ~ koyoi 36-26, ~ to utawareshi 28-20
sakura to ieba 48-16, ~ ya 55-13
saku ya hana 55-25

SAMazama no hito 24-9,
  ~ no koto 22-26, ~ ya 42-84
samisen (see shamisen) de oya 28-27
samukaranu 15-21
samurai ga 31-6, ~ mo 48-25
samushiro ni 64-1, ~ ya 15-51
san mon 58-34, ~ shaku 4-40, ~ gatsu
  ni 5-13, ~gatsu wa 55-7, ~gen 28-28
sanshun no yaku ya 12-96, ~byô 63-71
santôgawa 7-20
saohime(saobime/sahohime) no aya 29-6,
  ~ no some 55-19, ~ ya hatsu 55-18
sareba koso 40-76b
saru mo 2-24, ~ no 26-27, ~ shina-

no12-33
sashitaru 28-21, sasoite mo kyûzai () 48-29, anon 55-6
sasuga 47-60, sato no 42-83b
satori 21-14, satto 64-25
sawagashiki 12-28, sayu-uri 33-9
sazanami 52-3
seibutsu 36-43, seijin 38-38, seishi 36-56
semi 27-28, sen mo 35-8, senkin 13-34
senpon ga ichiji 47-12, ~ no hana 30-10
senri o 8-2, 35-2,
shami hiku 28-31, ~ taiko 28-39
shamisen ya chaya 3-37, ~ kari-au 28-25
SHIan 12-99, shibagari 22-21, shiba no 58-31, shibaraku 15-33
shibarareru 40-31, shigonichi 42-33
shiite ya 40-82, ~ yuku 50-28
shijû 60-46, shikararete 9-65
shikararuru 3-18, shikishima 61-5
shima 16-91, shimofushi 29-23
shimojimo ni 8-74, ~ wa 8-11
shinabaya 36-11, shinanoji 12-63
shinareginu 3-23, shinda 25-10
shinhatsui 40-16, shinibana 38-9b
shinibeta no 36-30, ~ to 36-29
shinijitaku 36-33, shinisôna BK II-5
shinitashi 36-10,
shinobiji 4-49
shiodara 32-45, shiraga 7-3
shiragumo ni nori 39-2
shiragumo no hana 17-56, ~ kaze 17-57
 ~ne 17-5,~ sakura 17-47, ~ tsuchi 17-30
shiragumo o 17-45, ~ to 17-42,
 ~ wa 17-6, ~ ya 17-31
shiranu 26-5, shirigataki 12-1
shiro o 13
shirokeredo 21-5, shirotae 40-4,
shiru hito 23-4
shiru shirazu hana 8-16, ~ yamaji 3-10
shirôto 38-8, shito 57-24, shizukesa 47-31
SHOkuji 32-25, shujô 41-5,
shukkeshû 7-5
shôben ni hana ga 63-47, ~ o 63-46
shôben ya onoga 2-11
sobafuru 42-41, sodetake 4-41
sôji senu 16-87b
soko tataku 12-92, sokosoko 38-35
somo ware 13-4,
sono hana 26-16, ~ hito 26-22,
 ~ mama ni 36-44, ~ mama to 53-6
sono tsure 47-55
sora ni 4-12, ~ o neme 6-61
 ~ o yowase[?] 9-5, ~-iro 17-29
sore de 36-20,~ hana 28-14,~ soko 63-51
sori-sutete 38-50, sorya 6-62, sô tera 64-9, soto 48-10; soyo 62-9,
sueburo 64-36
sugata 46-42, sugegasa 50-10,
sugimura 12-108, sugiyukeba 53-13
suitsukete 27-12, suizoku 44-7
sukasuka 42-23, sukatto 57-31
sukite-miru 29-13,
sukoshi chire iro naki 10-25, ~ waku 10-26
sukosuko 12-119, suma ni 28-35
sumigama 42-27, ~uri 40-63
sumiyaki no inu 16-16, ~ kokoro 42-26
sumizumi 15-39, sunamichi 64-28

sunao 4-16, surikaen 63-68
susamashi 64-26, susoguro 3-24
suteru 65-5, sutete 42-40, 63-6
suzuribako 65-2, ~ ishi 28-38

Tabibito 5-8, ~ kago 36-8,
 ~ no yado 54-9
tachiagaru 63-30, ~domari 3-31
 ~ magau 48-77, ~narabu 47-15
tada hitoki 56-25, ~ hitori 25-12
 ~ kaeru/modoru 4-70, ~ no ki 58-22
 ~ tanome hana 47-88, ~ sakura 36-31
tade kuu 22-30c
tagai e 12-56, 63-77, taga tama 3-44
tagui 0-3, taguruma 8-37, taira 63-36
takai no 17-28, takara 36-21
takayama 38-21, takenoko 12-80
taki nami 49-4, ~ ni 17-71
tamashii 15-59
tamoto kara 47-35, ~ yori 62-11
tanabata 4-47, 4-48, tane-imo 33-1
tanimizu 42-79, tanomarete 1-39
tanomoshiki 7-35, tanomu 60-36
tanoshimi 16-64, tanoshimu 56-5
tanzaku mo 28-13, ~ ya 63-34
ta-oranu 40-2, ta-orose 40-48b, ta-ori mote 40-58, taorite mo 40-25, taorite wa 40-50, taori tote 40-13,
tarachine 25-13, tare ga 27-19
tarekomete 63-79, taru 26-29
tatari 50-34, tazuneiru 4-75
tazunemiba 12-32,
TEki-mikata 11-19
te no hira 16-90, ~ todoku 40-8
te o 60-32, tegara 63-69
tenjin 16-63, ~ ka/ga 11-1
ten kara 48-69
ten mo 9-6, te-narai 57-20
tenjô 42-4, tenohira 63-57
tera-bôshi/hôshi 38-3, ~ furite 41-9,
 ~ no hana 47-93, ~ no otoko 44-13
 ~ dera o 3-13, ~dera ya 28-37
 ~kodomo 57-19
teru tsuki 47-26,
TObu 16-65, tôdai 24-52, 47-56
toga 6-15, tôge 3-47, toitaki 40-54
tôi yori 53-12, tôka 43-7
toki osoki 6-10, ~ wa 48-49,
tôki yori 56-16, tokkuri-kyojin 9-59,
tokugawa no sakura meiji 27-47
 ~ nokorite 27-46
toku saku 11-17, tometemiru 4-89
tomo+niku[i] [?] 6-56
tô-mori 9-15, tomo to 8-7,
tonari e 56-17, tonari kara 12-19
tonaridonari 17-39, tonikaku 55-30
tono 33-2, to o 38-15
tori no koe 42-37, ~ ne mo 16-36
 ~ ne wa 45-4, ~ su 16-40
tori to 16-38, tôsato 12-57
toshidoshi ni hana 22-23, 46-60,
 ~ ni sakura 63-22, ~ no 4-46,
toshidoshi ya hanamoru 34-17,
 ~ mada 22-10, ~ sakura 50-33
toshigoto no hana 60-10, ~ hito 24-1
toshi makari 32-38, 32-39
 ~ no 11-9, ~ o heba 58-9,
toshi o hete mata 36-49, ~ wakaki 53-17

toshiyori mo kirai 60-33, ~ mo mina 60-11, ~ ni hana 7-24, ~ no koshi 60-2
toshiyori no me ni 60-18, ~ no 24-17, 55-27,
toshiyori no mi 32-40, toshizuki 3-42
totemo 12-14, toto kuuta 38-17
tou hito ni hana 60-29, ~ kyo 12-35
tôyama mo 45-8, tôyama no hana 38-57
 ~ no matsu 19-11, no oku 12-31
 ~ to mishi 17-27, tôyama ya 17-24
tsubomi kara 4-11, 4-90, tsubomu 47-76
tsuchi ni naru 36-59, ~ ni umete 11-2
~bune 58-33, ~tori 42-72,
tsuetsuki 7-1, tsui kokete 13-15
tsuizen 51-12, tsukatsuka 60-40
tsuki matou 10-20, ~ mo 15-54, ~ ni 45-1
 ~ no yo 16-69, ~ shizuka 45-19
 ~ yo yoshi 15-30b, 17-35, ~ai 23-18,
 ~hana 6-51
tsukuzuku to ame 6-29, ~ hana 9-63
 ~ kawazu 16-56, ~mite-oreba 47-19
tsuma ni 24-34, ~ tsurete 24-23,
 ~ ya 47-66
tsune 4-45,
tsuno ireshi 30-17, ~ pishi 26-28
tsura ya 6-59, ~zura 56-37,
tsure 48-82, tsuri-aguru 44-10
tsuribari 16-61, ~ bune 44-14, ~gane 38-1
tsuru 1-24, tsuyu 14-19

Ubasuteshi 7-13, ~zakura hana 7-26
Ubazakura komachi 55-28, ~ saku 7-21
uchi-haete 47-47, ~kake 44-4,
 ~tokete 47-20
udonge 44-8, uekata 3-26, ue mo 36-22
ue-oite 46-31b
ueshi 15-16, uezakura 63-19
uguisu mo 6-38, ~ no hanekaze 48-34
 ~ no ne 12-60, ~ no take 9-8
 ~ ya nodo 28-24, ~ ya suichô 49-6
ukarekarasu 16-46, ~keri 64-14,
 ~tatsu 12-27, ~ yoru 24-39
uka-uka to kite 25-5, ~mugi 3-30, ~ta 8-26
ukigumo 17-72, ~ wa 16-35
 ~yo ni 48-76, ~yo to 9-25
uma ni 3-35, ~kata 28-22, ~ orite 3-60
umazu onna 59-35
ume chireba 1-28, ~ kobore 19-3
 ~ ni oru 21-12, ~ ni uguisu 9-40
 ~ no 1-31, ~ sakura hana 1-29
 ~ sakura mokuren 1-36, ~ wa koso 4-5
umi 17-81, unsui 59-33, uo 44-1
ura ni 16-24, ura-ura 61-8
urayamashi 42-24,
ureshige ni hau 57-18, ~ shôben 63-49
ureshii ka hana 16-45, ~ sakura 16-52
ureshisa 4-56, urimono 63-23
uru 30-26, ushi no 16-6,
ushirode 57-8
ushiro kara fukikuru 64-15
 ~ inu 16-19
uso makoto 14-12, ~ tsukanu 3-52
usuiro 4-52, utagawazu 41-7
uta ishû 17-7, ~ kuzu 42-14
 ~nenbutsu 3-6, ~ ni 46-19, ~ no 28-3
utatane 1-22, utazuka 28-7
utsuketaru 27-6,
utsukushiki kao 55-14, ~ tsure 3-38
utsu mono 3-1, utsuri 47-44

utsuru to mo hanami 63-61,
~ sakura 63-67
utsushi 47-79, uzumu 36-40

W
abibito 49-13
waga kage 14-8, ~ kao 7-11
~ koi 53-14, ~ kokoro awabi 12-71
~ kokoro uchi 46-44, ~ me 39-9
~ niwa ni 6-22, ~ ya 4-57
~ toshi 10-19
~ yado no hanami 47-102, ~ sakura 54-8
~ yakko 24-49, ~mama 40-61
waka-busha 10-46, ~ ki nado 47-57
~ ki ni 12-41, ~ishi ni 8-71,
~shû ni 59-26, ~yaku 40-49
wakeireba 3-15, ~ irite 3-21
~ noboru 3-46, ~raruru 31-2
waki muite 56-23, ~michi 4-78
wakite min 60-27
wakizashi e 36-12b, ~ wa 10-4, 36-12
waranji no guai ku 30-24, ~warosa 30-23
wara no hi 27-17
ware mo 12-23,~ naku 56-39,~ ni 60-39b
~ nomi 6-53, ~ sakite 42-47,
~ra 24-14, ~ to hana 47-99,
~ uete 56-21, ~ware 24-16
ware yande hana 22-29, ~ sakura 22-28
wasurenuru 18-16, wayakuya 15-7
watakushi 60-54

Y
aa 13-16
yabumichi 33-3
yado karan 15-13, ~ ni 53-3,
~ rishite Book III intro 1
yae hitoe 42-43, ~ ni saku 29-17,
62-37
yaezakura chijô 62-15, ~ futae 62-38
~ kyô kokonoe 62-28, ~ kyô ni 62-25
~ mabuta 62-39, ~ mimodae 62-35
~ miru 62-13, ~ yoru 62-34
yakatabune 24-42, yakenikeri 50-53
yakimeshi 32-19, yakkai 57-22,
yakkei 62-32,

YAMA
bime 12-93,
~ bukashi kane 12-58
~bukashi konome 12-105, ~dera no 6-57
~dera ya 5-9, ~ eiri 10-29, ~gai 23-21
~hata 50-36, ~hiko 23-24,
~hime→bime, ~hito 40-53
~ hitotsu 27-27,
yamakage ni saku 56-3, ~yase 2-2
yamakawa 29-14,
~kaze ni kumo 48-18, ~ sakura 50-27
yamamatsuri 3-3, ~mori mo 48-17
~mori no 50-13, ~ mo umi 16-29
yamanba 12-85
yama no hana makoto 17-65
~ hana shita 42-2, ~ hara 55-4
~ ki 56-38, ~ na 42-3, ~ tera 17-53,
~ tsuki 40-24, ~ warai 4-35, 42-63
yamasato 50-30b
yama takami hito 42-49, ~ iwane 48-35
yama tôshi 29-12, ~ umi 44-15
~ wa hana 45-7, ~ wa mina 8-3,
~ ya hana 26-30,
yamayama no fûryû 42-30, ~ rakka 46-49,
~ o meguritemiru 15-9
yamazakura chirejire 50-1, ~ doko 42-68
~ eda 48-79, ~ hana kara 63-66

~ hana no 40-64, ~ hiru 26-11,
~ hito ni 42-20, ~ hito oba 63-1
~ hitori 23-23, ~ kagami 38-53
~ kaminaki 38-52, ~ kasumi 63-74
~ kawa 63-12, ~ kinô 31-19
~ kokonoe 62-4, ~ mitsutsu 42-6
~ ogawa 42-80, ~ sakari 10-27,
~ sakinu 4-76, ~ saru mo 42-75
~ saru o 43-3, ~ sugao 42-42,
~ takaku 42-60, ~ tazunenu 42-52,
~ toritsu 42-58~ yo ni 42-99,
~ yo wa 63-25, ~ zeni 42-5
yamazaru 43-2
yamazato ni sakeru 42-15,
~ ni tabemono 32-30
~ no hana 42-32, ~ no haru 13-14
~ no hito 42-87, ~ ya kari 63-44
yama sô 34-3, yami 48-36, yanagi 29-3,
yasejirami 63-58, yasekokeru 10-5,
yaso tsuzuki 56-35,
yayoi 16-27, ya yo 60-24

YO
-arashi 3-41
yoi kara 1-41,~ koto 9-55,~ mono
~ samete okireba 15-25 ~ dote 40-36
~ tsure 47-97, ~ shinanu saki 36-38
yôki-hi mo12-45, ~ no sakura 55-20
~ no tama 55-23, ~ wa 55-21
yo ni hitoki 35-1
yo no hana . . . izen/mae 53-8, 54-20
yo no katachi 24-2
yononaka ni 46-1
yononaka no ara 42-92,
~ no kiki 8-34, 14-3
~ no kokoro 46-32, ~ no usa 48-39
~ o kinoshita 8-10, ~ wa jigoku 36-5
~ wa mikka 1-16
yo no usagi 16-28, ~ o ika ni 63-38
~ o sute 38-37, ~ to tomo 46-54
~ wa hanami 25-8, ~ wa sake 26-12
yo[mi] o suteru 63-37
yoka aru ya kore 56-36, ~ rô 7-25,
yoka wa 7-23
yoki hito 8-62, ~ hodo 3-17
~ inu ya 34-13, ~ koto 22-36
yoku-aka 38-26
yokuzume e abise/otose 38-25, 50-4
yometôme 59-14, yomitsukusu 58-29
yomoyama 3-5, yori-akite 23-17
yorokobi no namida 6-23,
~ mayu 42-62b
yoru mo 15-3
~ no hana iyashiki 8-82, ~ koi 59-31
~ toshi 60-19, 60-43, ~ [ni]chiru 55-15
yoshi mine 21-3
yoshino ni mo 58-21, ~ nite 44-32
yoshino yama hana 46-6
yoshino yama hito 17-1
~ jûnana 58-5, ~ kawari 58-28
~ kozue 46-8, ~ sakura 17-9
~ sekai 58-11, ~ ta 4-28
yoshiwara no 59-19, ~ ya ame 27-40
~ ya karasu 47-30, ~ michi 59-13
yoshi ya chire 47-52, ~ hana 6-36,
~ tsue 60-37
yotsu goki no 32-9, ~ashi no 2-19
yotta sora? kyo 9-3
yotte-asobu 9-51,~ kara 62-23, ~ nao 26-2
yowai inu 2-4
yozakura ni fukurô 15-44

~ ni kokoro 9-44, ~ o hitori 15-37
~ o misutete 59-22, ~ wa 59-15
~ ya ama 15-18, 36-53, ~ bijin 15-17
~ hitoshizumarite 15-55
~ oyajigakoshi 60-4
~ shamisen 15-43,
~ shibaraku 19-10
~ yo 25-11
yôrô no taki 7-32, yôyô 27-49

YU
bi kande 42-22, ~ sashita 17-26
~ kiri 24-51
yudan shite hana 1-17, 4-26
~ nibanzakura 4-25,
yûgure wa 64-8, ~ ya hana 14-13
~ ya heta 38-7, ~ ya kumo 17-68
~ ya tori 59-21
yûkaze ya aida 47-23, ~ onoga 29-22
yukibotoke 39-7, ~guni 51-10
~ kurete 29-8,~ mo 51-18,~ nara 51-16
~ no 51-17, ~ o 51-20, ~ to 51-6
yuku haru no atonigiwashi 12-82
~ mo 12-88, ~no shikoro 12-98,
~ no shiribeta 50-48, ~ no shunjun 12-87,
~ no todomaru 12-88b, ~ no yado 12-89,
~ ya imada 12-113
yuku kokoro 40-33, ~ sue no 17-25
~sue o 15-10
yume no naka 59-1, ~gokoro 56-28
~ no 16-72, ~yama 59-24
yumi 3-33, yusayusa 40-35, yû sugi 22-39
yûzakura ari 8-78, ~ ie aru 14-16
~ kyo 14-1, ~ oni 14-10,
yûzuki 40-47

Z
eni fure 8-47,~ katte 58-12,
~ maite 42-35
~ motanu 8-53, ~ nashi 8-51
zo chiru 13-35, zôri 42-88,
zukin 38-51, zûtsû 18-10

www.ingramcontent.com/pod-product-compliance
Lightning Source LLC
Chambersburg PA
CBHW081412230426
43668CB00016B/2209